Prentice Hall

Physical Science

Concepts in Action

With Earth and Space Science

PEARSON

Prentice Hall

Needham, Massachusetts
Upper Saddle River, New Jersey

ISBN 0-13-115310-2
   3 4 5 6 7 8 9 10   07 06 05

How to Use Your Easy Planner

Planning is as easy as 1-2-3

The *Easy Planner* provides you with all the information needed for grading and organizing classroom activities for *Physical Science: Concepts in Action*. It's your guidebook for daily lesson planning, resources to use, and when to use them. With this all-in-one planner, ❶ preview the **Chapter Planning Guides**, ❷ follow the detailed **Lesson Plans**, and ❸ review the **reduced ancillary pages** of the program resources.

❶ Chapter Planning Guides

Save time and improve classroom instruction. The Chapter Planning Guide provides a complete overview of the chapter, including Section Objectives, Standards, Activities and Labs, Program Resources, Section Assessment, and Technology Resources.

Plan labs and activities with ease when materials are organized for you.

Customize lesson plans by various learning abilities

Find all technology resources organized in one convenient location

Locate all assessment materials for the program in one spot.

❷ Lesson Plans

Lesson Plans for each section save
you planning time with instructional
strategies to meet individual student
needs. In addition, targeted resources
support standards mastery.

Name_____

Class_____ Date_____ M T W T F

LESSON PLAN 5.1

Organizing the Elements

Section Objectives

Time
2 periods
1 block

- Describe how Mendeleev arranged the elements in his table.
- Explain how the predictions Mendeleev made and the discovery of new elements demonstrated the usefulness of his periodic table.

Local Standards

Vocabulary periodic table

1 FOCUS

Build Vocabulary: Related Word Forms
Use the word *periodical* to help students understand the meaning of *periodic*. Explain that a periodical is published at regular intervals. L2

Targeted Resources
- ☐ Transparency: Chapter 5 Pretest
- ☐ Transparency: Interest Grabber 5.1
- ☐ Transparency: Reading Strategy 5.1

2 INSTRUCT

Build Reading Literacy: Sequence
Have students create a flowchart showing the sequence in which elements were organized into groups. L1

Integrate Social Studies
Have students research and compare discovery dates for elements with the dates those elements were first isolated. L2

Quick Lab: Making a Model of a Periodic Table
Students organize items in an array based on properties. Students predict where an additional item would fit in an incomplete array. L2

Address Misconceptions
Have students research the contributions of different scientists on one scientific advance. L2

Targeted Resources
- ☐ Transparency: Figure 3: Mendeleev's Table of Elements (1872)
- ☐ GRSW Section 5.1
- ☐ *PHSchool.com* Periodic table

3 ASSESS

Reteach
Use Figure 3 to review Mendeleev's strategy for arranging the elements into rows and columns to form a periodic table.

Evaluate Understanding
Have each student write a review question related to the content of one of the four pages in Section 5.1. L2

Targeted Resources
- ☐ *PHSchool.com* Online Section 5.1 Assessment
- ☐ iText Section 5.1

Physical Science Chapter 5 • Lesson Plan

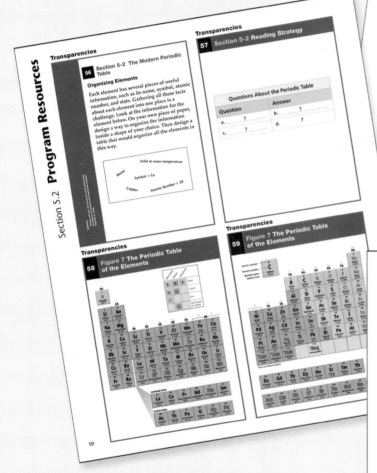

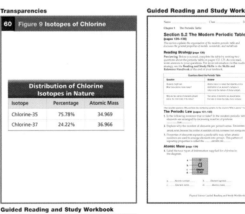

❸ Reduced Ancillary Pages

Includes Transparencies, Guided Reading
and Study Workbook, Teacher's Edition
of the Laboratory Manual, and Chapter
and Unit Tests.

Chemistry

Physics

Earth and Space Science

Chapter 1 Science Skills

CHAPTER 1

Planning Guide

SECTION OBJECTIVES	STANDARDS NATIONAL (See p. T18.)	STATE	ACTIVITIES and LABS
1.1 What Is Science? pp. 2–6 🕐 1 block or 2 periods **1.1.1 Explain** how science and technology are related. **1.1.2 List** the major branches of natural science and **describe** how they overlap. **1.1.3 Describe** the main ideas of physical science.	A-1, A-2, B-1, B-2, B-4, B-5, D-4, E-2, G-1, G-2, G-3		**SE** Inquiry Activity: How Do Scientists Use Their Observations? p. 1　L2 **TE** Teacher Demo: The Compass, p. 3　L2
1.2 Using a Scientific Approach, pp. 7–11 🕐 1 block or 2 periods **1.2.1 Describe** the steps in a scientific method. **1.2.2 Compare** and **contrast** facts, scientific theories, and scientific laws. **1.2.3 Explain** the importance of models in science. **1.2.4 Explain** the importance of safety	in science. A-1, A-2, E-2, F-1, G-2		**TE** Build Science Skills: Observing, p. 8　L2 **TE** Teacher Demo: Flaps on an Airplane, p. 10　L2
1.3 Measurement, pp. 14–20 🕐 1 block or 2 periods **1.3.1 Perform** calculations involving scientific notation and conversion factors. **1.3.2 Identify** the metric and SI units used in science and **convert** between common metric prefixes. **1.3.3 Compare** and **contrast** accuracy and precision. **1.3.4 Relate** the Celsius, Kelvin, and Fahrenheit temperature scales.	A-1, A-2, G-2		**SE** Quick Lab: Comparing Precision, p. 18　L2 **SE** Application Lab: Determining the Thickness of Aluminum Foil, pp. 26–27　L2 **TE** Teacher Demo: Conversion Factor, p. 18　L2 **LM** Investigation 1A: Evaluating Precision　L2 **LM** Investigation 1B: Measuring Volume and Temperature　L1
1.4 Presenting Scientific Data, pp. 22–25 🕐 1 block or 2 periods **1.4.1 Organize** and **analyze** data using tables and graphs. **1.4.2 Identify** the relationship between a manipulated variable and a responding variable. **1.4.3 Explain** the importance of communicating data. **1.4.4 Discuss** the process of peer review.	A-1, A-2, E-2, G-1		

Ability Levels

L1 For students who need additional help
L2 For all students
L3 For students who need to be challenged

Components

SE	Student Edition	**GRSW**	Guided Reading
TE	Teacher's Edition		& Study Workbook
LM	Laboratory Manual		With Math Support
PLM	Probeware Lab	**CUT**	Chapter and Unit
	Manual		Tests

CTB	Computer Test Bank	**T**	Transparencies
TP	Test Prep Resources	**P**	Presentation Pro
iT	iText		CD-ROM
DC	Discovery Channel	**GO**	Internet Resources
	Videotapes		

RESOURCES PRINT and TECHNOLOGY		SECTION ASSESSMENT
GRSW Section 1.1	L1	**SE** Section 1.1
T Chapter 1 Pretest	L2	Assessment, p. 6
Section 1.1	L2	iText **iT** Section 1.1
P Chapter 1 Pretest	L2	
Section 1.1	L2	
SCiLINKS **GO** Motion	L2	
GRSW Section 1.2	L1	**SE** Section 1.2
DC Cracking the Case	L2	Assessment, p. 11
T Section 1.2	L2	iText **iT** Section 1.2
P Section 1.2	L2	
SCIENCE NEWS **GO** Nature of science	L2	
GRSW Section 1.3	L1	**SE** Section 1.3
GRSW Math Skill	L2	Assessment, p. 20
T Section 1.3	L2	iText **iT** Section 1.3
P Section 1.3	L2	
PLANETDIARY **GO** Universal measurements	L2	
PHSchool.com **GO** Data sharing	L2	
GRSW Section 1.4	L1	**SE** Section 1.4
T Section 1.4	L2	Assessment, p. 25
P Section 1.4	L2	iText **iT** Section 1.4
SCiLINKS **GO** Graphing	L2	

Go Online

Go online for these Internet resources.

PHSchool.com
Web Code: ccd-0010
Web Code: cca-0015

SCIENCE NEWS
Web Code: cce-0011

NSTA *SCiLINKS*
Web Code: ccn-0011
Web Code: ccn-0014

PLANETDIARY
Web Code: ccc-0013

Materials for Activities and Labs

Quantities for each group

STUDENT EDITION

Inquiry Activity, p. 1
25 mL of copper(II) chloride
solution in a 50-mL beaker,
scissors, metric ruler, aluminum
foil, glass stirring rod

Quick Lab, p. 18
3 plastic bottles of different
sizes, beaker, graduated cylinder

Application Lab, p. 26
metric ruler, aluminum foil,
scissors, balance, graph paper

TEACHER'S EDITION

Teacher Demo, p. 3
compass, magnet, chalk

Build Science Skills, p. 8
low-wattage incandescent bulb,
power source for the bulb

Teacher Demo, p. 10
sheet of paper

Build Science Skills, p. 12
modeling clay, at least
5 different toy cars with
similar-sized tires that have
different tread, cooking oil,
magnifying glass

Teacher Demo, p. 18
1-lb object, 0.25-lb object,
balance

Chapter Assessment

CHAPTER ASSESSMENT

SE Chapter Assessment,
pp. 29–30
CUT Chapter 1 Test A, B
CTB Chapter 1
iT Chapter 1
PHSchool.com GO
Web Code: cca-0015

STANDARDIZED TEST PREP

SE Chapter 1, p. 31
TP Diagnose and Prescribe

iText—interactive textbook with
assessment at PHSchool.com

Name_____ Class_____ Date_____ M T W T F

LESSON PLAN 1.1

What Is Science?

Time
2 periods
1 block

Section Objectives

- **1.1.1 Explain** how science and technology are related.
- **1.1.2 List** the major branches of natural science and **describe** how they overlap.
- **1.1.3 Describe** the main ideas of physical science.

Vocabulary science • technology • chemistry • physics • geology • astronomy • biology

Local Standards

1 FOCUS

Build Vocabulary: Word-Part Analysis
Explain that the root of a word is the key to its meaning. Ask students to identify the roots in the vocabulary words and to name other words with the same root. For example, students may suggest *sci-, conscience; tech-, technique; or phys-, physical.* **L2**

Targeted Resources
❏ Transparency: Chapter 1 Pretest
❏ Transparency: Interest Grabber 1.1
❏ Transparency: Reading Strategy 1.1

2 INSTRUCT

Use Visuals: Figure 2
Point out Figure 2 and have students list the differences between the phones. **L1**

Build Reading Literacy: Outline
Have students outline the information on page 5. Tell students to write the subheads, leaving room between each one. As students read, they can list details under each subhead. **L1**

Build Science Skills: Predicting
Have students observe a lit candle in an open jar. Have students predict what will happen if the jar is covered. Cover the jar. Ask students what substances are present in the experiment. **L2**

Teacher Demo: The Compass
Use a magnet and a compass to show students that a magnet will deflect the compass needle from north toward the east or west. **L2**

Integrate Biology
Have students pick an area of biophysics and make a poster that shows how physics and biology contribute to understanding in that area. **L2**

Targeted Resources
❏ Transparency: Figure 3: Branches of Science
❏ GRSW Section 1.1
❏ **NSTA** *sci*$_{LINKS}$ Motion

3 ASSESS

Reteach
Use Figure 2 to emphasize that over time advances in technology can lead to the use of new materials and the addition of new features to machines like the telephone. **L1**

Evaluate Understanding
Have students name and describe a branch of science. They may describe a main branch or an area shown in Figure 3, or another area. **L2**

Targeted Resources
❏ **PHSchool.com** Online Section 1.1 Assessment
❏ iText Section 1.1

Transparencies

1 **Chapter 1 Pretest**

1. True or False: Science and technology are not related.

2. Which of the following are areas of science?
   a. biology and chemistry
   b. astronomy and geology
   c. zoology and botany
   d. all of the above

3. Why do scientists document their observations and experiments?

4. Which number is largest?
   a. 1.13×10^9
   b. 3.51×10^3
   c. 5.88×10^5
   d. 7.92×10^2

3. Sample answer: to remember them correctly or analyze them at a later time
4. a

ANSWERS
1. False
2. d

Transparencies

2 **Chapter 1 Pretest** *(continued)*

5. Which unit can be used to measure volume?
   a. m
   b. m^2
   c. m^3

6. Which of the following units is the longest?
   a. meter
   b. centimeter
   c. kilometer
   d. millimeter

7. What is the slope of a line?

8. What types of graphs have you seen before?

8. Sample answers: line, bar, and circle graphs

ANSWERS
5. c
6. c
7. The ratio of a vertical change to the corresponding horizontal change.

Transparencies

3 **Section 1.1 Interest Grabber**

Science Improves Our Quality of Life

Advances in science have led to devices that make our lives easier and more pleasant. For example, the microwave oven makes it possible to prepare meals and snacks in minutes rather than hours.

1. Name five household devices that make your life easier or more pleasant.

2. Go through your list and describe how each device's function was accomplished before its invention.

2. Student answers will vary. Before the invention of the hair dryer, hair was air dried. Before the invention of the electric curling iron, hair was rolled onto brush or plastic rollers. Before the electric steam iron, metal irons were heated on the surface of wood cooking stoves.

ANSWERS
1. Student answers will vary. Sample answers include an electric hair dryer, electric curling iron, electric razor, electric steam iron, compact disc player, home computer, or television.

Transparencies

4 **Section 1.1 Reading Strategy**

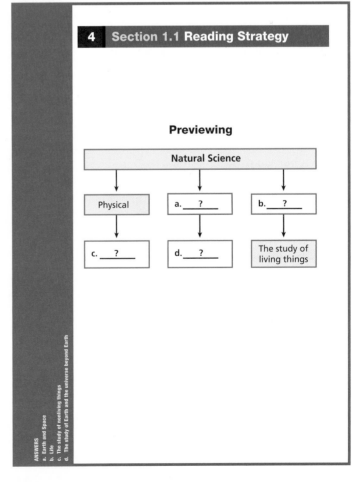

Previewing

Natural Science

Physical | a. ___?___ | b. ___?___

c. ___?___ | d. ___?___ | The study of living things

ANSWERS
a. Earth and Space
b. Life
c. The study of nonliving things
d. The study of Earth and the universe beyond Earth

Transparencies

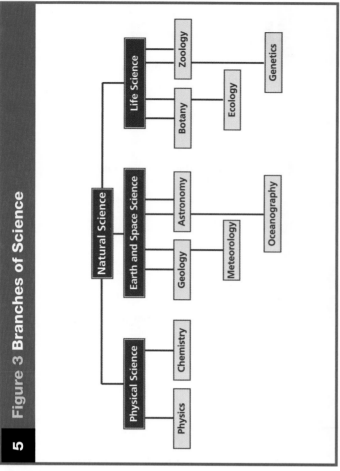

Guided Reading and Study Workbook

Name _____ Class _____ Date _____

Chapter 1   Science Skills

Section 1.1 What Is Science?
(pages 2–6)

This section describes the characteristics of science and technology. It also discusses the big ideas of physical science.

Reading Strategy (page 2)

Previewing Skim the section to find out what the main branches of natural science are. Complete the concept map based on what you have learned. For more information on this Reading Strategy, see the **Reading and Study Skills** in the **Skills and Reference Handbook** at the end of your textbook.

Natural Science		
Physical	Earth and space	Life
The study of nonliving things	The study of Earth and the universe beyond Earth	The study of living things

Science From Curiosity (pages 2–3)

1. Define science. <u>Science is a system of knowledge and methods you use to find knowledge.</u>

2. The questions that lead to scientific discovery are provided by <u>curiosity</u>.

3. Is the following sentence true or false? The results of every scientific experiment are quantitative. <u>false</u>

Science and Technology (page 3)

4. Is the following sentence true or false? The use of knowledge to solve practical problems is known as curiosity. <u>false</u>

5. How are science and technology related? <u>They are interdependent. Advances in science lead to advances in technology and vice versa.</u>

Branches of Science (page 4)

6. Name the two general categories that the study of science can be divided into.
   a. <u>Social science</u>   b. <u>Natural science</u>

7. Circle the letters of each branch of natural science.
   (a.) physical science   (b.) Earth and space science
   c. social science   (d.) life science

Guided Reading and Study Workbook

Name _____ Class _____ Date _____

Chapter 1   Science Skills

8. Circle the letter of each sentence that is true about the field of chemistry.
   (a.) Chemists study reactions involving matter.
   (b.) Chemists study the composition of matter.
   (c.) Chemists study the structure of matter.
   (d.) Chemists study the properties of matter.

9. The study of matter, energy, and the interactions between the two through forces and motion is known as <u>physics</u>.

10. Identify the topics that are included in the science of geology.
    <u>The science of geology includes the origin, history, and structure of the Earth.</u>

11. Is the following sentence true or false? The foundation of space science is astronomy. <u>true</u>

12. Scientists who study the origin and behavior of living things are called biologists, and the study of living things is known as <u>biology</u>.

The Big Ideas of Physical Science (pages 5–6)

13. Is the following sentence true or false? All of the important rules of nature have already been discovered. <u>false</u>

14. Circle the letter of each sentence that is true about the diameter of the observable universe.
    a. It is one hundred million meters.
    b. It is seven hundred billion meters.
    c. It is seven hundred million billion meters.
    (d.) It is seven hundred million billion billion meters.

15. Name the two characteristics of matter.
    a. <u>Mass</u>
    b. <u>Volume</u>

16. The basic building blocks of matter are called <u>atoms</u>.

17. Is the following sentence true or false? A force causes a change in time. <u>false</u>

18. Describe kinetic energy. <u>Kinetic energy is the energy of motion.</u>

19. Two general types of energy are kinetic energy and <u>potential</u> energy.

Science and Your Perspective (page 6)

20. Is the following sentence true or false? The scientific facts of today will not change in the future. <u>false</u>

LESSON PLAN 1.2

Using a Scientific Approach

Time
2 periods
1 block

Section Objectives

- **1.2.1 Describe** the steps in a scientific method.
- **1.2.2 Compare** and **contrast** facts, scientific theories, and scientific laws.
- **1.2.3 Explain** the importance of models in science.
- **1.2.4 Explain** the importance of safety in science.

Vocabulary scientific method • observation • hypothesis • manipulated variable • responding variable • controlled experiment • scientific theory • scientific law • model

Local Standards

---

1 FOCUS

Build Vocabulary: Paraphrase
As students read, have them write the definitions of each vocabulary term in their own words. **L2**

Targeted Resources
❑ Transparency: Interest Grabber 1.2
❑ Transparency: Reading Strategy 1.2

---

2 INSTRUCT

Use Visuals: Figure 10
Ask students why the scientists in Figure 10 are wearing goggles. **L1**

Build Science Skills: Observing
Students will observe that the bulb radiates light in all directions and that as distance from the bulb increases, the bulb's brightness decreases. **L2**

Build Science Skills: Inferring
Have students discuss how scientific laws are affected by new scientific theories. Ask students if scientific laws apply in countries other than where they are developed. **L2**

Address Misconceptions
Help students understand the basic definitions of *hypothesis, theory,* and *law.* **L2**

Teacher Demo: Flaps on an Airplane
Use a paper airplane to demonstrate how wing flaps can affect an airplane's flight. Students observe that the paper airplane is an appropriate model for a real airplane. **L2**

Targeted Resources
❑ Transparency: Figure 7: A Scientific Method
❑ GRSW Section 1.2

---

3 ASSESS

Reteach
Use Figure 7 to review the scientific method. Point out that when scientists learn new information, they may go back to an earlier step in the method. **L1**

Evaluate Understanding
Ask students to name scientific laws. If they name a theory instead of a law, help them understand why what they chose is a theory and not a law. **L2**

Targeted Resources
❑ **PHSchool.com** Online Section 1.2 Assessment
❑ iText Section 1.2

Transparencies

6 Section 1.2 Interest Grabber

Design Your Own Experiment

Suppose that you want to conduct a test to see which brand of cleanser produces the best results when cleaning a kitchen floor. Think about how you would conduct this test.

1. What materials would you need?

2. What procedure would you follow?

3. How would you determine which cleanser produces the best results?

ANSWERS
1. Sample answers may include two or more brands of cleansers; sponge or rag; stopwatch; and different materials to produce stains.
2. Sample procedures might test the effect of various cleansers on one type of stain, or on several types of stains. Students might try to control certain variables in the experiments, such as the amount of cleanser used or the time spent scrubbing.
3. The quality of each cleanser could be described in terms of how fast it cleans, how many types of stains it cleans, or how much is needed to clean a stain.

Transparencies

7 Section 1.2 Reading Strategy

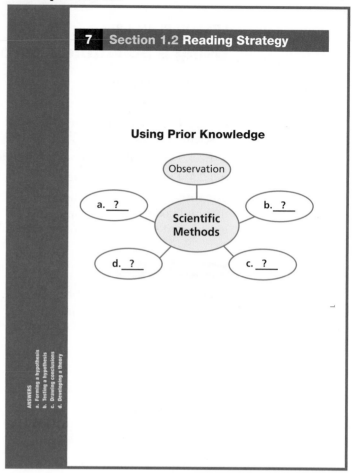

Using Prior Knowledge

Observation

a. ?

Scientific Methods

b. ?

d. ?

c. ?

ANSWERS
a. Forming a hypothesis
b. Testing a hypothesis
c. Drawing conclusions
d. Developing a theory

Transparencies

8 Figure 7 A Scientific Method

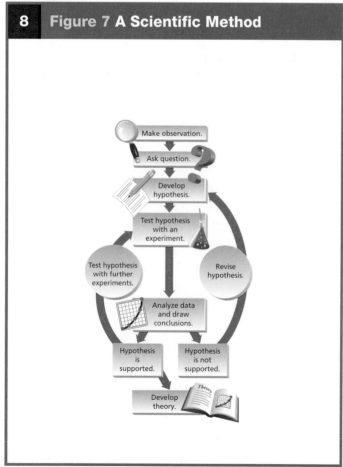

Name _____ Class _____ Date _____

Chapter 1   Science Skills

Section 1.2 Using a Scientific Approach
(pages 7–11)

This section describes scientific methods and how they are used to understand the world around you.

Reading Strategy (page 7)

Using Prior Knowledge Before you read, add to the web diagram what you already know about scientific methods. After you read the section, revise the diagram based on what you have learned. For more information on this Reading Strategy, see the **Reading and Study Skills** in the **Skills and Reference Handbook** at the end of your textbook.

```
              Observation
Forming a                    Testing a
hypothesis     Scientific    hypothesis
                Methods
        Drawing        Developing
       conclusions      a theory
```

Scientific Methods (pages 7–9)

1. Identify the goal of any scientific method. The goal of any scientific method is to solve a problem or better understand an observed event.

2. Name three types of variables in an experiment.
   a. Manipulated variable   b. Responding variable   c. Controlled variable

3. Is the following sentence true or false? If the data from an experiment do not support your hypothesis, you can revise the hypothesis or propose a new one. true

4. How does a scientific theory differ from a hypothesis? A hypothesis is an untested explanation for an observation while a theory is a well-tested explanation for a set of observations.

Match the following vocabulary terms to the correct definition.

	Definition	Vocabulary Terms
c	**5.** Information that you obtain through your senses	a. theory
a	**6.** A well-tested explanation for a set of observations	b. hypothesis
b	**7.** A proposed answer to a question	c. observation

Name _____ Class _____ Date _____

Chapter 1   Science Skills

8. Complete the model of a scientific method by filling in the missing steps.
   a. Analyze data and draw conclusions   b. Revise hypothesis
   c. Test hypothesis with further experiments   d. Develop theory

Scientific Laws (page 9)

9. Is the following sentence true or false? A scientific law attempts to explain an observed pattern in nature. false

10. All scientists may accept a given scientific law, but different scientists may have different scientific theories to explain it.

Scientific Models (page 10)

11. Why do scientists use scientific models? Scientists use scientific models to make it easier to understand things that might be too difficult to observe directly.

12. Circle the letters that correctly state what scientists do if data show that a model is wrong.
    a. Change the model.   b. Replace the model.
    c. Ignore the data.   d. Revise the data.

Working Safely in Science (page 11)

13. Circle the letters of safety precautions to follow whenever you work in a science laboratory.
    a. Study safety rules.   b. Never ask questions.
    c. Read all procedural steps.   d. Understand the procedure.

14. Why should you wash your hands after every experiment? You should wash your hands after experiments to remove chemicals that you may have touched.

Name_____ Class_____ Date_____ M T W T F

LESSON PLAN 1.3
Measurement

Section Objectives

■ **1.3.1 Perform** calculations involving scientific notation and conversion factors.

■ **1.3.2 Identify** the metric and SI units used in science and **convert** between common metric prefixes.

■ **1.3.3 Compare** and **contrast** accuracy and precision.

■ **1.3.4 Relate** the Celsius, Kelvin, and Fahrenheit temperature scales.

Vocabulary scientific notation • length • mass • volume • density • conversion factor • precision • significant figures • accuracy • thermometer

Local Standards

---

1 FOCUS

Build Vocabulary: LINCS
Use LINCS (List, Imagine, Note, Connect and Self-test) to help students learn and review section vocabulary. **L2**

Targeted Resources
❑ Transparency: Interest Grabber 1.3
❑ Transparency: Reading Strategy 1.3

---

2 INSTRUCT

Use Visuals: Figure 19
Have students study Figure 19. Ask students if any one of the three scales is more accurate than the others. Ask students why they think scientists use degrees Celsius for measuring temperature. **L1**

Build Science Skills: Inferring
Using Figure 15, ask students what factor the metric prefixes are based on and how that makes it convenient for converting between units. **L2**

Teacher Demo: Conversion Factor
Give students the calculation for converting pounds to grams, and ask them to use the conversion factor to calculate the mass of a 0.25-lb object in grams. Students see how conversion factors convert between units of different measure. **L2**

Quick Lab: Comparing Precision
Students estimate the volumes of plastic bottles, and then determine the volume by pouring water from the bottles into beakers and graduated cylinders. Students describe and distinguish accuracy and precision, and compare the precision of measuring devices. **L2**

Targeted Resources
❑ Transparency: Figure 13: SI Base Units
❑ Transparency: Math Skills: Using Scientific Notation
❑ GRSW Section 1.3

---

3 ASSESS

Reteach
Help students understand how prefixes modify units of measurement. Give students examples such as kilogram, milliliter, and microsecond and ask them to name units that are larger or smaller. **L1**

Evaluate Understanding
Ask students to write three conversion problems (with solutions) based on the prefixes used in the metric system. **L2**

Targeted Resources
❑ **PHSchool.com** Online Section 1.3 Assessment
❑ iText Section 1.3

Transparencies

9 **Section 1.3 Interest Grabber**

Measuring Length by the Handful

The English units that we use in the United States developed over a long period of time. For example, the hand was devised in ancient times as a unit of length. It was defined as the length of a person's hand from the little finger to the thumb. Today the height of horses is still measured in hands, but the definition of a *hand* is standardized at 4 inches or 10.16 centimeters.

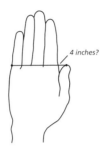

4 inches?

1. Why did the hand produce unreliable measurements before it was standardized?

2. Measure the height of your desk in hands. Compare your results with other classmates. How do the results vary?

Transparencies

10 **Section 1.3 Reading Strategy**

Previewing

Measurement
Why is scientific notation useful?
a. _____?_____
b. _____?_____

Transparencies

11 **Figure 13 SI Base Units**

SI Base Units		
Quantity	Unit	Symbol
Length	meter	m
Mass	kilogram	kg
Temperature	kelvin	K
Time	second	s
Amount of substance	mole	mol
Electric current	ampere	A
Luminous intensity	candela	cd

Transparencies

12 **Math Skills Using Scientific Notation**

Math Skills

Using Scientific Notation

A rectangular parking lot has a length of 1.1×10^3 meters and a width of 2.4×10^3 meters. What is the area of the parking lot?

1 **Read and Understand**
What information are you given?

Length $(l) = 1.1 \times 10^3$ m

Width $(w) = 2.4 \times 10^3$ m

2 **Plan and Solve**
What unknown are you trying to calculate?

Area $(A) = ?$

What formula contains the given quantities and the unknown?

$A = l \times w$

Replace each variable with its known value.

$A = l \times w = (1.1 \times 10^3 \text{ m})(2.4 \times 10^3 \text{ m})$
$= (1.1 \times 2.4)(10^{3+3})(\text{m} \times \text{m})$
$= 2.6 \times 10^6 \text{ m}^2$

3 **Look Back and Check**
Is your answer reasonable?

Yes, the number calculated is the product of the numbers given, and the units (m^2) indicate area.

Guided Reading and Study Workbook

Name _____ Class _____ Date _____

Chapter 1   Science Skills

Section 1.3 Measurement
(pages 14–20)

This section discusses units of measurement, making and evaluating measurements, and calculations with measurements.

Reading Strategy (page 14)

Previewing Before you read the section, rewrite the green and blue topic headings in this section as questions in the table below. As you read, write answers to the questions. For more information on this Reading Strategy, see the **Reading and Study Skills** in the **Skills and Reference Handbook** at the end of your textbook.

Measurement
Why is scientific notation useful? It makes very large or very small numbers easier to work with.
What is SI? SI is a set of metric measuring units used by scientists.
What are base units? Base units are the fundamental units of SI. There are seven SI base units, including the meter, the kilogram, the kelvin, and the second.

Using Scientific Notation (pages 14–15)

1. Scientific notation expresses a value as the product of a number between 1 and 10 and ____a power of ten____.

2. Circle the letter of the value that is expressed as 3×10^8.

   a. 300   b. 300,000

   c. 30,000,000   (d.) 300,000,000

3. Why is scientific notation useful? It makes very large or very small numbers easier to work with.

SI Units of Measurement (pages 16–18)

4. Circle the letters of elements that are required for a measurement to make sense.

   a. scientific notation   (b.) numbers

   c. exponents   (d.) units

5. Is the following sentence true or false? Units in the SI system include feet, pounds, and degrees Fahrenheit. _____false_____

Match the SI base unit with the quantity that is used to measure.

	SI Base Unit	Quantity
c	6. meter	a. Mass
a	7. kilogram	b. Time
d	8. kelvin	c. Length
b	9. second	d. Temperature

Guided Reading and Study Workbook

Name _____ Class _____ Date _____

Chapter 1   Science Skills

SI Prefixes			
Prefix	Symbol	Meaning	Multiply Unit By
giga-	G	billion (10^9)	1,000,000,000
mega-	M	million (10^6)	1,000,000
kilo-	k	thousand (10^3)	1000
deci-	d	tenth (10^{-1})	0.1
centi-	c	hundredth (10^{-2})	0.01
milli-	m	thousandth (10^{-3})	0.001
micro-	µ	millionth (10^{-6})	0.000001
nano-	n	billionth (10^{-9})	0.000000001

10. Complete the table of SI prefixes by filling in the missing information.

11. A ratio of equivalent measurements that is used to convert a quantity expressed in one unit to another unit is called a(n) ____conversion factor____.

Limits of Measurement (page 19)

12. Circle the letter of each expression that has four significant figures.

   a. 1.25×10^4 (b.) 12.51

   c. 0.0125   (d.) 0.1255

13. Is the following sentence true or false? The precision of a calculated answer is limited by the least precise measurement used in the calculation. _____true_____

14. Calculate the density if the mass of a solid material is measured as 15.00 grams and its volume is measured as 5.0 cm^3? Round off your answer to the proper number of significant figures.
   Density = 15.00 g/5.0 cm^3 = 3.3 g/cm^3

15. Describe the difference between precision and accuracy. Precision refers to how exact a measurement is (the more significant figures, the more precise the measurement is), while accuracy refers to how close the measurement is to the actual value.

Measuring Temperature (page 20)

16. Circle the letter of the base unit of temperature in SI.

   a. degree Fahrenheit (°F)   b. degree Celsius (°C)

   c. candela (cd)   (d.) kelvin (K)

17. Write the formula used to convert degrees Celsius to kelvins.
   K = °C + 273

LESSON PLAN 1.4

Presenting Scientific Data

Time
2 periods
1 block

Section Objectives   Local Standards

- **1.4.1 Organize** and **analyze** data using tables and graphs.
- **1.4.2 Identify** the relationship between a manipulated variable and a responding variable.
- **1.4.3 Explain** the importance of communicating data.
- **1.4.4 Discuss** the process of peer review.

Vocabulary slope • direct proportion • inverse proportion

1 FOCUS

Build Vocabulary: Paraphrase
As students read, have them write the definitions of each vocabulary term in their own words and a formula that illustrates the term. **L2**

Targeted Resources
❏ Transparency: Interest Grabber 1.4
❏ Transparency: Reading Strategy 1.4

2 INSTRUCT

Use Visuals: Figure 23
Have students study the bar graph in Figure 23 and ask which pairs of cities have similar annual precipitation. **L1**

Build Science Skills: Using Graphs and Tables
Use Figure 21 to help students review how to read line graphs. Point out the labels on the horizontal and vertical axes. **L2**

Address Misconceptions
Point out to students that graphs are merely a method of presenting data, not validating data. Tell students that one way to validate data is to make multiple measurements. **L2**

Integrate Language Arts
Have students pick an area of biophysics and make a poster that shows how physics and biology contribute to understanding in that area. **L2**

Targeted Resources
❏ Transparency: Figure 21: Mass vs. Volume of Water
❏ GRSW Section 1.4
❏ **NSTA** sc*LINKS* Graphing

3 ASSESS

Reteach
Use Figures 21 and 22 to compare the meanings of *direct proportion* and *inverse proportion*. **L1**

Evaluate Understanding
Show students a graph or chart from a newspaper or similar source. Ask students to create a data table that represents the data on the graph or chart. **L2**

Targeted Resources
❏ **PHSchool.com** Online Section 1.4 Assessment
❏ iText Section 1.4

Transparencies

13 **Section 1.4 Interest Grabber**

Creating and Interpreting Graphs

Many people have pets. One survey of pet owners showed the following breakdown of the type of pets owned: 35% dogs; 35% cats; 10% birds; 5% hamsters, gerbils, mice, rats; 5% reptile; and 10% other.

1. Copy the incomplete circle graph below on your paper. Complete the graph using the survey data. Estimate the angle of each section of your completed circle graph . Give your graph a title and label what each section of the graph represents.

2. Explain how viewing the graph conveys information to the reader more quickly than reading the list of data.

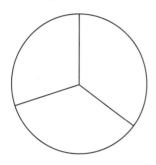

ANSWERS
1. The students should complete the circle graph using the given data. Each section should be labeled. Students should not be assessed on the accuracy of their angles.

2. Using the graph, the reader can quickly see relationships and comparisons of the data. For example, the reader can see from the graph that dogs and cats represent the largest groups of pets. This information is more readily apparent in graphical form than in list form.

Transparencies

14 **Section 1.4 Reading Strategy**

Comparing and Contrasting

Type of Graph	Description	Used For
Line	a. ___?___	b. ___?___
Bar	c. ___?___	d. ___?___
Circle	e. ___?___	f. ___?___

ANSWERS
a. Variable y is plotted VS. variable x.
b. Showing how a variable responds to changes in another
c. Scaled bars are used to represent various measurements.
d. Comparing a set of similar data
e. A divided circle, with each "slice" representing a proportional fraction
f. Showing how a part relates to the whole

Transparencies

15 **Figure 21 Mass vs. Volume of Water**

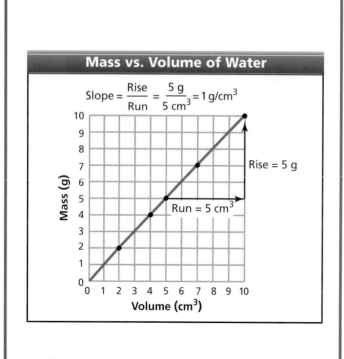

Mass vs. Volume of Water

$$\text{Slope} = \frac{\text{Rise}}{\text{Run}} = \frac{5 \text{ g}}{5 \text{ cm}^3} = 1 \text{ g/cm}^3$$

Rise = 5 g

Run = 5 cm³

Mass (g) / Volume (cm³)

Guided Reading and Study Workbook

Name _____ Class _____ Date _____

Chapter 1   Science Skills

Section 1.4 Presenting Scientific Data
(pages 22–25)

This section describes how scientists organize and communicate data.

Reading Strategy (page 22)

Comparing and Contrasting After you read this section, compare the types of graphs by completing the table. For more information on this Reading Strategy, see the **Reading and Study Skills** in the **Skills and Reference Handbook** at the end of your textbook.

Type of Graph	Description	Used For
Line graph	A graph in which a line is plotted to describe changes that occur in related variables	Showing how a variable responds to changes in another
Bar graph	A graph that uses scaled bars to represent various measurements	Comparing sets of measurements or changes
Circle graph	A graph consisting of a divided circle, with each "slice" representing a proportional fraction	Showing how a part or share of something relates to the whole

Organizing Data (pages 22–24)

1. Circle the letters of tools that scientists use to organize their data.
   a. the Internet   b. newspapers
   c. tables   d. graphs

2. The simplest way to organize data is to present them in a(n) _data table_.

3. Circle the letter of the place on a line graph where the manipulated variable is generally plotted.
   a. the *y*-axis   b. the rise
   c. the *x*-axis   d. the run

4. On a line graph, the ratio of the change in the *y*-variable to the corresponding change in the *x*-variable is called the line's _slope_.

5. Circle the letters of the relationships that are direct proportions.
   a. distance traveled versus time at a constant speed
   b. the mass of a substance versus its volume
   c. the time to travel a given distance versus average speed
   d. the number of fingers in your classroom versus the number of people

Name _____ Class _____ Date _____

Chapter 1 Science Skills

6. Is the following sentence true or false? An inverse proportion is one in which the product of the two variables is constant. _____true_____

7. Identify each data organizing tool shown below.

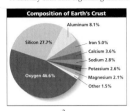

a.

City	Average Annual Precipitation (cm)
Buffalo, N.Y.	98.0
Chicago, Ill.	91.0
Colorado Springs, Colo.	41.2
Houston, Tex.	117.0
San Diego, Calif.	25.1
Tallahassee, Fla.	166.9
Tucson, Ariz.	30.5

b.

c.

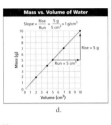

d.

a. ___Circle graph___   b. ___Data table___
c. ___Bar graph___   d. ___Line graph___

Communicating Data (page 25)

8. Name two ways that scientists can report results of their experiments.
   a. ___By writing in scientific journals___   b. ___By speaking at scientific conferences___

9. Is the following statement true or false? Scientists always interpret a given set of data the same way. ___false___

10. Why is peer review an important part of scientific research? ___It encourages feedback from other scientists and helps researchers to reevaluate their data.___

Name _____ Class _____ Date _____

Chapter 1 Science Skills

WordWise

Answer the questions by writing the correct vocabulary term in the blanks. Use the circled letter in each term to find the hidden vocabulary word. Then write a definition for the hidden word.

Clues	Vocabulary Terms
The study of matter, energy, and their interactions	p (h) y s i c s
The closeness of a measurement to the actual value of what is being measured	a c c u r a c (y)
A gauge of how exact a measurement is	(p) r e c i s i o n
The ratio of a vertical change to the corresponding horizontal change in a line	s l (o) p e
An instrument used to measure temperature	t h e r m o m e (t) e r
The use of knowledge to solve practical problems	t e c (h) n o l o g y
A representation of an object or event	m o d (e) l
A system of knowledge and the methods used to find that knowledge	(s) c i e n c e
A statement that summarizes a pattern found in nature	s c i e n t (i) f i c l a w
Information that you obtain through your senses	o b (s) e r v a t i o n

Hidden word: ___h y p o t h e s i s___

Definition: ___A proposed answer to a question___

Name _____ Class _____ Date _____

Chapter 1 Science Skills

Using Scientific Notation

Light travels through space at a speed of 3.00×10^8 meters per second. How long does it take for light to travel from the sun to Earth, which is a distance of 1.50×10^{11} meters?

Math Skill: Scientific Notation

You may want to read more about this Math Skill in the Skills and Reference Handbook at the end of your textbook.

1. Read and Understand

What information are you given?

Speed = 3.00×10^8 m/s

Total distance = 1.50×10^{11} m

2. Plan and Solve

What unknown are you trying to calculate?

Time = ?

What formula contains the given quantities and the unknown?

$$\text{Time} = \frac{\text{Total distance}}{\text{Average speed}}$$

Replace each variable with its known variable and known value.

$$\text{Time} = \frac{1.50 \times 10^{11} \text{ m}}{3.00 \times 10^8 \text{ m/s}}$$

$$= \frac{1.50}{3.00} \times (10^{11-8})(\text{m}/(\text{m/s}))$$

$$= 0.50 \times 10^3 \text{ s} = 5.00 \times 10^2 \text{ s}$$

3. Look back and check

Is your answer reasonable?

Yes, the number calculated is the quotient of distance and speed, and the units (s) indicate time.

Math Practice

On a separate sheet of paper, solve the following problems.

1. The flow of water in a stream is 210,000 liters per hour. Use scientific notation to calculate the amount of water that flows in a week (168 hours).

   2.1×10^5 L/hr $\times (1.68 \times 10^2$ hrs) = 3.5×10^7 L

2. The density of a liquid is 8.03×10^{-1} kilogram per liter. What is the mass (in kg) of liquid in a full 100,000 liter tank?

   $\frac{8.03 \times 10^{-1} \text{ kg}}{\text{L}} \times (1 \times 10^5$ L) = 8.03×10^4 kg

3. How many balloons, each containing 6.02×10^{23} particles of helium gas, can be filled from a tank that contains 1.204×10^{25} helium particles?

   $\frac{1.204 \times 10^{25} \text{ particles}}{6.02 \times 10^{23} \text{ particles/balloon}} = \left(\frac{1.204}{6.02}\right)(10^{25-23})$ balloons = 0.2×10^2 balloons = 20 balloons

---

Name _____ Class _____ Date _____

Chapter 1 Science Skills   **Consumer Lab**

Determining the Thickness of Aluminum Foil

Many products such as aluminum foil are too thin to measure easily. However, it is important for manufacturers to know how thick these products are. They wouldn't be useful if they were made too thick or too thin. In this lab, you will use the same method that manufacturers use to determine the thickness of aluminum foil.

See pages 26 and 27 in the Teacher's Edition for more information.

Problem How can you determine the thickness of aluminum foil?

Materials
- metric ruler
- aluminum foil
- scissors
- balance
- graph paper

Skills Measuring, Calculating, Using Graphs

Procedure

1. Cut out three squares of aluminum foil with sides of the following lengths: 50 mm, 100 mm, and 200 mm.

2. To determine the area of the 50-mm foil square, measure the length of one of its sides and then square it. Record the length and area in the data table.

DATA TABLE

Length (mm)	Area (mm²)	Mass (g)	Volume (mm³)	Thickness (mm)
50.0	2500	0.10	36.9	0.015
100.0	10,000	0.40	148	0.015
200.0	40,000	1.60	590	0.0148

Density of aluminum = ___0.00271___ g/mm³

Student Edition Lab Worksheet

Name _____ Class _____ Date _____

3. Place the foil square on the balance to determine the mass of the foil. Record the mass of the foil square in the data table.

4. You will need the density of aluminum foil to calculate the volume of the foil square from its mass. The density of aluminum foil is 2.71 g/cm³. Convert cm³ to mm³ and record the density of aluminum foil (in g/mm³) on the line provided at the bottom of the data table.

5. To determine the volume of the foil square, divide its mass by its density in g/mm³. Record the volume in the data table.

6. To determine the thickness of the foil square, divide its volume by its area. Record this thickness in the data table.

7. Repeat Steps 2 through 6, using the 100-mm foil square.

8. Repeat Steps 2 through 6, using the 200-mm foil square.

9. Construct a graph of your data on a separate sheet of graph paper. Plot length on the horizontal axis and thickness on the vertical axis. Draw a straight line connecting all three points.

Analyze and Conclude

1. **Measuring** How many significant figures were there in your measurement of the length of each square of aluminum foil?

There were three significant figures for the 50-mm square and four for the 100-mm and

200-mm squares.

2. **Using Graphs** What effect, if any, did the length of the square have on your estimate of the thickness of the foil?

The length of the square had no effect on the estimated thickness of the foil.

3. **Comparing** Which estimate of thickness was most precise? Explain your answer.

The thickness calculated for the 200-mm square is most precise because it has the most significant

figures (three). The precision of a calculated answer is limited by the least precise measurement used

in the calculation. For the 200-mm square, the least precise measurement (mass) has three significant

figures. For the 50-mm and 100-mm squares, the least precise measurement (mass) has only two

significant figures.

4. **Controlling Variables** What factors limited the precision of your measurements?

Precision was limited by the spacing of the smallest markings on the ruler and the balance.

Lab Manual

Name _____ Class _____ Date _____

Chapter 1   Science Skills   **Investigation 1A**

Evaluating Precision

Refer students to pages 14–20 in their textbooks for a discussion of measurement, precision, and accuracy.

SKILLS FOCUS: Measuring, Evaluating   **CLASS TIME:** 30 minutes

Background Information

When an object is measured more than once, the measurements may vary. The closeness of a set of measured values to each other is called **precision.** Many people confuse precision with accuracy. **Accuracy** is a measure of how close the values are to the actual value. A set of values can be in close agreement, or precise, without being accurate.

For example, suppose you repeatedly measure the mass of a 4.00-g object by using a balance that reads too low by 3.00 g every time. You might get nearly identical readings—for example, 1.00 g, 1.01 g, and 0.99 g. These readings are quite precise because they are close together. However, they differ from the actual value by a large amount. Therefore, the measurements are very inaccurate.

In this investigation, you will make several measurements of length, temperature, and volume. Then, you will evaluate the precision of your measurements by comparing them to measurements made by your classmates.

Problem

How can you determine the precision and accuracy of measurements?

Pre-Lab Discussion

Read the entire investigation. Then, work with a partner to answer the following questions.

1. **Applying Concepts** Use the example of a series of repeated length measurements to explain the meaning of precision.

The precision of a series of repeated measurements describes how closely the individual

measurements agree. For example, if a meter stick is used to measure the length of a desk three

times, the measurements 75 cm, 74 cm, and 76 cm are more precise than measurements of 70 cm,

75 cm, and 80 cm.

2. **Inferring** What information would you need to determine the accuracy of a measurement?

You would need a reliable measurement to which you could compare your measurement.

Lab Manual

Name _____ Class _____ Date _____

3. **Drawing Conclusions** In this investigation, you will compare measurements that you make to measurements that your classmates make. Will you do this to determine the accuracy or the precision of your measurements?

Comparing measurements made by different students can determine precision, but not accuracy.

4. **Designing Experiments** Identify the manipulated, responding, and controlled variables in this investigation.

   a. Manipulated variable

   Teams making the measurements

   b. Responding variable

   Precision of measurements

   c. Controlled variables

   Devices for measuring length, temperature, and volume; the objects whose properties are

   being measured

5. **Analyzing Data** Two students measure the mass of a wooden disk, using the same balance. The first student repeats the weighing three times and obtains mass readings of 47 g, 52 g, and 51 g. The second student obtains mass readings of 45 g, 55 g, and 50 g. Explain which set of measurements is more precise. Can you tell if the measurements are accurate? Why or why not?

The first student's measurements are more precise because the values are closer together. Although

both sets of measurements suggest that the disk has a mass of nearly 50 g, this may not be true.

The balance may not be properly calibrated, and so it could be providing consistently inaccurate

measurements.

Lab Manual

Name _____ Class _____ Date _____

Materials *(per group)*

meter stick

Celsius thermometer   Provide only non-mercury thermometers.

500-mL beaker filled with room-temperature water   Fill a 500-mL beaker with water and allow it to sit at room temperature for at least 1 hour before class.

10 pennies

50-mL graduated cylinder

Safety 🥽🧤🔺🧪

Put on safety goggles and a lab apron. Be careful to avoid breakage when working with glassware. Note all safety alert symbols next to the steps in the Procedure and review the meaning of each symbol by referring to the Safety Symbols on page xiii.

You may wish to start with one lab group measuring length, a second group measuring temperature, and a third group measuring volume, and then rotate the groups to minimize waiting time between measurements.

Procedure

1. You and your partner make up a team. Your team and two other teams will make up a group of six. Your teacher will tell you and your partner whether you are Team A, B, or C of your group. The three teams in your group will measure the same objects separately. You will not share your measurements with the other teams in your group until you complete the procedure.

   In any case, make sure all students within a group use the same measuring devices.

🧤 2. Working with your partner, use the meter stick to measure the length of a desk indicated by your teacher. Measure as carefully as possible, to the nearest millimeter. Record the length of the desk in the data table. (*Hint:* Do not reveal the measurements you make to the other teams in your group. They must make the same measurements and must not be influenced by your results.)

🔺 3. Use the thermometer to measure the temperature of the beaker of room-temperature water. **CAUTION:** *Do not let the thermometer hit the beaker.* Record this measurement in the data table.

4. Place 25 mL of tap water in the graduated cylinder. Measure the volume of the water. Record this volume in the data table to the nearest 0.1 mL. (*Hint:* Remember to read the volume at the bottom of the meniscus.)

   You may need to show students how to read a liquid volume at the bottom of the meniscus.

5. Add the 10 pennies to the graduated cylinder. Read the volume of the water and pennies. Record this volume in the data table to the nearest 0.1 mL.

6. Subtract the volume of the water from the volume of the water and pennies. The result is a measurement of the volume of the pennies. Record this value in the data table.

7. After all three teams in your group have finished measuring the same objects for length, temperature, and volume, share your results with the other two teams. Record their measurements in the data table.

Name _____ Class _____ Date _____

Observations Sample data are shown.

DATA TABLE

Measurement	Team A	Team B	Team C
Length of desk (mm)			
Temperature of water (°C)	18.0–21.0		
Volume of water (mL)	24.5–25.5		
Volume of water and pennies (mL)	27.5–29.0		
Volume of pennies (mL)	3.0–3.5		

Analysis and Conclusions

1. **Calculating** Average the three length measurements you compared by adding them together and dividing the result by 3. Find the range of values by calculating the difference between the largest and smallest values. Record the results of your calculations in the space below.

Calculations should be correctly carried out. Actual results will depend on student data.

a. Average of length measurements (mm)

_____

b. Range of length measurements (mm)

_____

Name _____ Class _____ Date _____

2. **Making Generalizations** Would it be correct to use the range of values you calculated in Question 1 to describe the precision of the measurements? The accuracy of the measurements? Explain your answer.

The range of values can be used to describe the precision of the measurements. The narrower the range is, the more precise the measurements are. The range cannot be used to describe the accuracy of the measurements, which depends on the difference between the measurements and the actual value.

3. **Analyzing Data** Which of the three sets of measurements had the least spread among the measurements? Suggest reasons for the precision of these measurements.

Answers may vary for each group. Reasons for good precision in a set of measurements depend on the smaller units with which the measuring instrument can be read, consistency of technique in making and reading measurements, and the care that the conditions under which the measurements are made are kept the same.

4. **Applying Concepts** Figure 1 shows the results of three people's attempts to shoot as many bull's-eyes as possible. Below Figure 1, label each of the results as *accurate* or *not accurate*, and as *precise* or *not precise*.

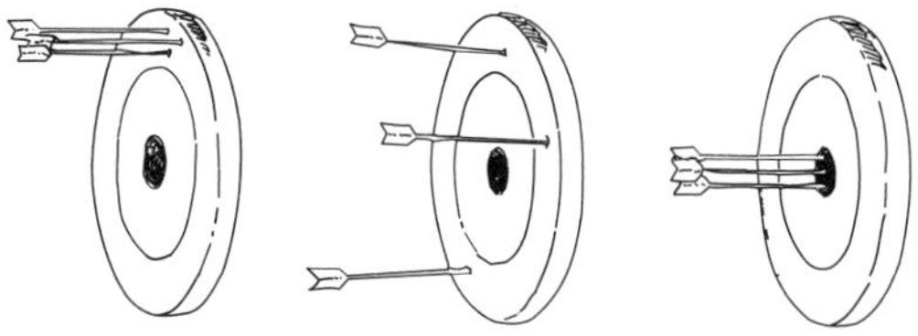

Figure 1

Precise _____ Not Accurate _____ Accurate _____

Not Accurate _____ Not Precise _____ Precise _____

Name _____ Class _____ Date _____

5. **Evaluating and Revising** Discuss the reasons for the differences among the teams' measurements with the members of your group. Describe these reasons and explain how the measurements could be made more precise.

Students may cite skill and care of measurement and the limited precision of the measuring instruments as factors that limited the precision of the measurements. Students may suggest having one person make all the measurements or using more precise instruments.

Go Further

Design an experiment to compare the precision of two or more measuring instruments. Is the precision of each instrument the same throughout its range of measurements? Write a procedure you would follow to answer these questions. After your teacher approves your procedure, carry out the experiment and report your results.

Measuring instruments differ in precision. For example, a micrometer is more precise than a ruler. The precision of a well-made measuring instrument is nearly the same throughout its range of measurements except for a decline in precision for values near zero. At very low values, the precision declines as the size of the measurement approaches the sensitivity of the instrument, which is the smallest nonzero value it can measure.

Name _____ Class _____ Date _____

Chapter 1 Science Skills   Investigation 1B

Measuring Volume and Temperature

Refer students to pages 14–20 in their textbooks for a discussion of

Background Information measurement. **SKILLS FOCUS:** Measuring **CLASS TIME:** 40 minutes

The amount of space an object takes up is called its volume. A commonly used unit of volume is the liter (L). Smaller volumes can be measured in milliliters (mL). One milliliter is equal to 1/1000 of a liter. In the laboratory, the graduated cylinder is often used to measure the volume of liquids.

Temperature is measured with a thermometer. The unit of measurement for temperature is the degree Celsius (°C).

In this investigation, you will practice making measurements of the volume and temperature of a liquid.

Problem

How can you accurately measure the volume and temperature of a liquid?

Pre-Lab Discussion

Read the entire investigation. Then, work with a partner to answer the following questions.

1. **Measuring** How many significant figures are there in the measurement shown in Figure 1?

Three significant figures

2. **Inferring** Why is it important to read the volume of water in a graduated cylinder by using the bottom of the meniscus?

Because water curves upward at the edges of the cylinder wall, the bottom of the meniscus is nearer to being the true top of the water column. By using this same point each time a measurement is made, the measurement is less likely to be in error.

3. **Designing Experiments** Why should you leave the thermometer in beaker B when you add ice?

Removing the thermometer from the water would expose the thermometer bulb to the air. The resulting change in the thermometer reading would be because of a temperature change other than that caused by the ice melting in the water.

4. **Measuring** If each mark on a thermometer represents 1°C, which part of a temperature measurement will be the estimated digit?

Tenths of a degree

Lab Manual

Name _____ Class _____ Date _____

Materials *(per group)*
2 150-mL beakers Provide beakers with volume graduations.
100-mL graduated cylinder
glass-marking pencil

2 Celsius thermometers Provide only non-mercury thermometers.
watch or clock
ice cube

Safety 🥽 🧤 ⚡

Put on safety goggles and a lab apron. Be careful to avoid breakage when working with glassware. Note all safety alert symbols next to the steps in the Procedure and review the meaning of each symbol by referring to the Safety Symbols on page xiii.

Procedure

Part A: Measuring the Volume of a Liquid

⚡ 1. Fill a beaker halfway with water.

2. Pour the water in the beaker into the graduated cylinder.

3. Measure the amount of water in the graduated cylinder. To accurately measure the volume, your eye must be at the same level as the bottom of the meniscus, as shown in Figure 1. The meniscus is the curved surface of the water.

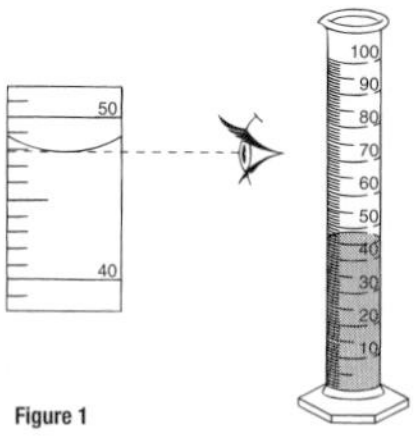

Figure 1

4. Estimate the volume of water to the nearest 0.1 mL. Record this volume in Data Table 1.

5. Repeat Steps 1 through 4, but this time fill the beaker only one-fourth full of water.

Part B: Measuring the Temperature of a Liquid

6. Use the glass-marking pencil to label the beakers *A* and *B*.

7. Use the graduated cylinder to put 50 mL of water in each beaker.

8. Place a thermometer in each beaker. In Data Table 2, record the temperature of the water in each beaker.

Tell students not to stir the water with the thermometer.

9. Carefully add one ice cube to the water in beaker B. Note and record the time.

10. After 1 minute, observe the temperature of the water in each beaker. Record these temperatures in Data Table 2.

11. After 5 minutes, observe the temperature of the water in each beaker. Record these temperatures in Data Table 2.

12. After the ice in beaker B has melted, use the graduated cylinder to find the volume of water in each beaker. Record these volumes in Data Table 3.

Lab Manual

Name _____ Class _____ Date _____

Observations Sample data are shown.

DATA TABLE 1

Measurement	Volume of Water (mL)
Half-filled beaker	47.0–53.0
One-fourth filled beaker	22.0–28.0

DATA TABLE 2

Beaker	Temperature at Beginning	(°C) Temperature After 1 Minute (°C)	Temperature After 5 Minutes (°C)
A	18.0–20.0	18.0–20.0	18.0–20.0
B	18.0–20.0	15.0–17.0	8.0–14.0

DATA TABLE 3

Beaker	Volume of Water at Beginning (mL)	Volume of Water at End (mL)
A	50.0	50.0
B	50.0	58.0–68.0

Lab Manual

Name _____ Class _____ Date _____

Analysis and Conclusions

1. **Observing** What is the largest volume of a liquid that the graduated cylinder is able to measure? What is the smallest volume that the graduated cylinder is able to measure?

100 mL; 1 mL

2. **Analyzing Data** Describe how the temperature of the water in beakers A and B changed during the investigation.

The temperature of the water in beaker A did not change. The temperature of the water in beaker B decreased after the ice cube was added.

3. **Analyzing Data** How did the volume of water in beakers A and B change during the investigation? What do you think caused this change?

The volume of water in beaker A did not change. The volume of water in beaker B increased because the melted ice added to the total amount of liquid water.

4. **Applying Concepts** Would you use a 100-mL graduated cylinder, a 25-mL graduated cylinder, or 10-mL graduated cylinder to measure 8 mL of a liquid? Explain your answer.

To measure 8 mL of liquid, it is best to use a 10-mL graduated cylinder because it has the finest graduations and provides the most precise measurement.

Go Further

Some liquids do not form a meniscus in a graduated cylinder as water does. Use a 10-mL graduated cylinder to measure 8.0 mL each of water, isopropyl (rubbing) alcohol, and vegetable oil. Observe and draw the meniscus of each liquid. Label your drawings to show how you think the volume of each liquid should be measured. Explain why you think that the volumes should be measured in this way.

Vegetable oil and alcohol form a convex meniscus in a clean glass container. The volumes of these liquids are read at the top of the meniscus because most of the surface of these liquids is near the top of the meniscus (unlike water, whose surface is mostly near the bottom of the meniscus).

Chapter Test A

Name _____ Class _____ Date _____

Chapter 1 Science Skills

Chapter Test A

Multiple Choice

Write the letter that best answers the question or completes the statement on the line provided.

_____ 1. How are science and technology related?
a. Technology is a branch of natural science.
b. Science is a branch of technology.
c. Advances in science may lead to advances in technology and vice versa.
d. Science and technology are not related.

_____ 2. How does Earth science overlap with life science?
a. Earth science involves the study of Earth's rocks.
b. Earth science involves the study of systems that may include living organisms.
c. Earth science involves the study of the composition of matter.
d. Earth science does not overlap with life science.

_____ 3. What are the building blocks of all matter?
a. forces
b. atoms
c. magnetic fields
d. kinetic and potential energy

_____ 4. What happens when the data in an investigation do not support the original hypothesis?
a. The scientist gives up and starts an investigation on a new topic.
b. The data must be incorrect and are thrown out.
c. The hypothesis will be revised.
d. The data are altered so that they support the original hypothesis.

_____ 5. Which of the following statements is true about scientific theories?
a. Scientific theories become scientific laws.
b. Scientific theories are never proven.
c. Scientific theories become hypotheses.
d. Scientific theories summarize patterns found in nature.

_____ 6. Why are scientific models important?
a. They prove scientific theories.
b. They help visualize things that are very complex, very large, or very small.
c. They make it harder to understand things.
d. They never change.

Chapter Test A

_____ 7. Which of the following is an example of a safe laboratory procedure?
   a. tying back long hair and loose clothing
   b. eating or drinking from laboratory glassware
   c. touching hot objects with your bare hands
   d. testing an odor by directly inhaling the vapor

_____ 8. Which of the following conversion factors would you use to change 18 kilometers to meters?
   a. 1000 m/1 km   b. 1 km/1000 m
   c. 100 m/1 km   d. 1 km/100 m

_____ 9. There are 1660 megawatts of wind-generated electricity produced globally every year. This amount is equivalent to
   a. 1,660,000 watts   b. 1,660,000 kilowatts
   c. 16,600,000 watts   d. 166,000 kilowatts

_____ 10. Which of the following clocks offers the most precision?
   a. a clock that measures time to the nearest hour
   b. a clock that measures time to the nearest minute
   c. a clock that measures time to the nearest second
   d. a clock that measures time to the nearest tenth of a second

_____ 11. Approximately how many kelvins are equal to 60°F?
   a. 439   b. 212   c. 902   d. 289

_____ 12. The type of graph used to show how a part of something relates to the whole is a
   a. circle graph   b. bar graph
   c. line graph   d. direct proportion

_____ 13. How do scientists who speak different languages make their data understandable to one another?
   a. They all use different systems of measurement.
   b. They all use SI.
   c. They communicate through a universal translator.
   d. They all must speak French.

_____ 14. Why are peer reviews important?
   a. Scientists receive questions and criticism from their peers.
   b. Data are checked for accuracy.
   c. Scientists receive comments and suggestions from other scientists.
   d. all of the above

_____ 15. If the relationship between the manipulated variable and the responding variable is a direct proportion, what will a line graph of this relationship look like?
   a. a straight line   b. a curved line
   c. a jagged line   d. none of the above

Chapter Test A

Completion

Complete each statement on the line provided.

1. A measurement must include both a number and a(an) _____.

2. An experiment in which only one variable, the manipulated variable, is changed at a time is called a(an) _____.

3. The two main areas of physical science are physics and _____

4. In an experiment, if doubling the manipulated variable results in a doubling of the responding variable, the relationship between the variables is a(an) _____.

5. The three values—10.714 m, 12.821 m, and 13.646 m—have the same number of _____.

Short Answer

In complete sentences, write the answers to the questions on the lines provided.

1. Explain how technology and science are related.

   _____
   _____
   _____

2. What type of graph would be the best to use to compare the levels of lead contamination in six water wells?

   _____
   _____

3. What is the relationship between two variables if the product of the variables is constant?

   _____
   _____

4. What happens to the number in a measurement that is converted from kilometers to meters?

   _____
   _____

5. Describe a main idea of physical science that deals with space and time.

   _____
   _____
   _____
   _____

Chapter Test A

Using Science Skills

Use the diagram to answer each question. Write the answers on a separate sheet of paper.

1. **Analyzing Data** What is the slope of the line shown in Figure 1-1?
2. **Controlling Variables** In Figure 1-1, what is the responding variable?
3. **Analyzing Data** In Figure 1-1, what is the relationship between mass and volume?
4. **Using Graphs** In Figure 1-1, what quantity does the slope represent?
5. **Analyzing Data** In Figure 1-1, what metric units are represented by points on the plotted line?

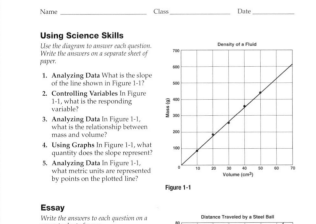

Figure 1-1

Essay

Write the answers to each question on a separate sheet of paper.

1. Use Figure 1-2 to describe how the steel ball moved during the experiment. Average speed is calculated by dividing total distance by time. Did the steel ball speed up, slow down, or remain at the same speed throughout the experiment?
2. What is the difference between a scientific law and a scientific theory?
3. Describe some of the main ideas of physical science.
4. Describe a possible order of steps of a scientific method used in an investigation.
5. Explain how peer reviews are important in either supporting a hypothesis or revising a hypothesis.

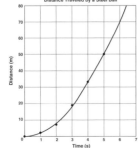

Figure 1-2

Chapter Test B

Multiple Choice

Write the letter that best answers the question or completes the statement on the line provided.

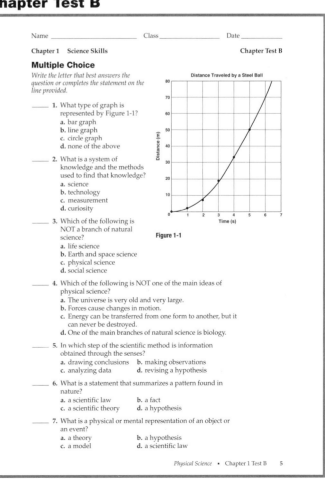

Figure 1-1

_____ 1. What type of graph is represented by Figure 1-1?
   a. bar graph
   b. line graph
   c. circle graph
   d. none of the above

_____ 2. What is a system of knowledge and the methods used to find that knowledge?
   a. science
   b. technology
   c. measurement
   d. curiosity

_____ 3. Which of the following is NOT a branch of natural science?
   a. life science
   b. Earth and space science
   c. physical science
   d. social science

_____ 4. Which of the following is NOT one of the main ideas of physical science?
   a. The universe is very old and very large.
   b. Forces cause changes in motion.
   c. Energy can be transferred from one form to another, but it can never be destroyed.
   d. One of the main branches of natural science is biology.

_____ 5. In which step of the scientific method is information obtained through the senses?
   a. drawing conclusions   b. making observations
   c. analyzing data   d. revising a hypothesis

_____ 6. What is a statement that summarizes a pattern found in nature?
   a. a scientific law   b. a fact
   c. a scientific theory   d. a hypothesis

_____ 7. What is a physical or mental representation of an object or an event?
   a. a theory   b. a hypothesis
   c. a model   d. a scientific law

Chapter Test B

Name _____ Class _____ Date _____

_____ 8. What is the most important safety rule?
  a. Never work with chemicals.
  b. Always use unbreakable glassware.
  c. Always follow your teacher's instructions and textbook directions exactly.
  d. Never do experiments that involve flames or hot objects.

_____ 9. How is 0.00025 written in scientific notation?
  a. 25×10^{-5} b. 2.5×10^{4}
  c. 0.25×10^{-3} d. 2.5×10^{-4}

_____ 10. Which of the following is equal to 1 centimeter?
  a. 100 meters
  b. 1/10 of a millimeter
  c. 10 millimeters
  d. 100 millimeters

_____ 11. Timers at a swim meet used four different clocks to time an event. Which recorded time is the most precise?
  a. 55 s   b. 55.0 s
  c. 55.2 s   d. 55.25 s

_____ 12. On the Celsius scale, at what temperature does water boil?
  a. 0°   b. 212°
  c. 100°   d. 32°

_____ 13. What is the relationship in which the ratio of the manipulated variable and the responding variable is constant?
  a. inverse proportion
  b. direct proportion
  c. slope
  d. interdependent

_____ 14. How do scientists communicate the results of investigations?
  a. by publishing articles in scientific journals
  b. by giving talks at scientific conferences
  c. by exchanging e-mails
  d. all of the above

_____ 15. What is a peer review?
  a. a process in which only close friends of a scientist review the scientist's work
  b. a process in which scientists examine other scientists' work
  c. a process in which scientists copy other scientists' work
  d. a process in which scientists keep their work secret

Chapter Test B

Chapter Test B

Name _____ Class _____ Date _____

Completion
Complete each statement on the line provided.

1. The SI base unit of mass is the _____.
2. An organized plan for gathering, organizing, and communicating information is called a(an) _____.
3. A(An) _____ is a way of plotting data to show changes that occur in related variables.
4. Computers are an example of _____ that helps people solve problems.
5. Natural science is divided into life science, Earth and space science, and _____.
6. The _____ is the variable that changes in response to the manipulated variable.
7. A(An) _____ is a statement that summarizes a pattern found in nature.
8. A(An) _____ makes it easier to understand things that are too small, too large, or too hard to observe directly.
9. The measurement 0.014 seconds equals _____ milliseconds.
10. _____ is the closeness of a measurement to the actual value being measured.

Short Answer
In complete sentences, write the answers to the questions on the lines provided.

1. What is the single most important laboratory safety rule?
   _____
   _____

2. Why do scientists speak at conferences and write articles in scientific journals?
   _____
   _____
   _____

3. What is a peer review?
   _____
   _____
   _____

Chapter Test B

Chapter Test B

Name _____ Class _____ Date _____

4. How many significant figures will the answer to the calculation 65.25×37.4 have?
   _____

5. What is the temperature at which water freezes, expressed in Fahrenheit, Celsius, and kelvins?
   _____
   _____
   _____

Using Science Skills
Use the diagram to answer each question. Write the answers on a separate sheet of paper.

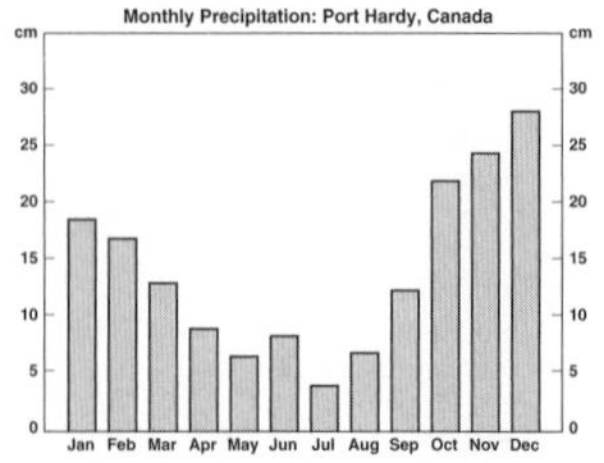

Figure 1-2

1. **Using Graphs** What measurements are compared in Figure 1-2?
2. **Analyzing Data** In Figure 1-2, which month had the highest amount of precipitation?
3. **Inferring** Why might the data in Figure 1-2 be important to share with a scientist studying agriculture trends in Port Hardy?
4. **Using Graphs** Use Figure 1-2 to determine the approximate total annual precipitation.
5. **Calculating** In Figure 1-2, how many meters of precipitation were recorded during January?

Chapter 1 Test A Answers

Multiple Choice

1. c **2.** b **3.** b **4.** c **5.** b **6.** b
7. a **8.** a **9.** b **10.** d **11.** d **12.** a
13. b **14.** d **15.** a

Completion

1. unit **2.** controlled experiment **3.** chemistry
4. direct proportion **5.** significant figures

Short Answer

1. Science is a system of knowledge, while technology is the practical application of that knowledge to the solving of problems.
2. a bar graph **3.** an inverse proportion **4.** It gets larger. **5.** The universe is very large (7.0×10^{26} meters in diameter) and very old (about 13.7 billion years old).

Using Science Skills

1. 8.8 g/cm^3 **2.** mass **3.** a direct proportion **4.** the density of the fluid **5.** g/cm^3

Essay

1. The steel ball started out slowly. Then it continued to speed up throughout the experiment.
2. A scientific law is a statement that summarizes a pattern found in nature, without attempting to explain it. A scientific theory explains the pattern.
3. Possible answers: The universe is very large and very old. A small amount of the universe is matter. Matter on Earth usually is either a solid, liquid, or gas. All matter is made of atoms. Forces cause changes in motion. Energy can be transferred from one form or object to another, but it can never be destroyed.
4. Possible answer: 1) make observations, 2) ask questions, 3) develop a hypothesis, 4) test the hypothesis, 5) analyze data, 6) draw conclusions, 7) revise hypothesis.
5. In peer reviews, scientists review and question other scientists' data. Scientists also help determine if the data is accurately reported. If the review finds errors in the data, in the conclusions, or in the experimental procedures, the hypothesis may need to be revised.

Chapter 1 Test B Answers

Multiple Choice

1. b **2.** a **3.** d **4.** d **5.** b **6.** a
7. c **8.** c **9.** d **10.** c **11.** d **12.** c
13. b **14.** d **15.** b

Completion

1. kilogram (kg) **2.** scientific method **3.** line graph
4. technology **5.** physical science **6.** responding variable
7. scientific law **8.** scientific model; model
9. 14 **10.** Accuracy

Short Answer

1. Always follow your teachers instructions and textbook directions exactly. **2.** to communicate with other scientists about the results of their investigations **3.** a process in which scientists examine other scientists' work **4.** three **5.** 32°F, 0°C, and 273 K

Using Science Skills

1. monthly precipitation in centimeters **2.** December
3. The precipitation data might provide insight into agricultural growth trends. **4.** approximately 165 cm
5. 0.18 meters ·

Chapter 2 Properties of Matter

CHAPTER

2

Planning Guide

SECTION OBJECTIVES	STANDARDS		ACTIVITIES and LABS
	NATIONAL (See p. T18.)	STATE	
2.1 Classifying Matter, pp. 38–44 ⏱ 1 block or 2 periods **2.1.1 Classify** pure substances as elements or compounds. **2.1.2 Describe** the characteristics of an element and the symbols used to identify elements. **2.1.3 Describe** the characteristics of a compound. **2.1.4 Distinguish** pure substances from mixtures. **2.1.5 Classify** mixtures as heterogeneous or homogeneous. **2.1.6 Classify** mixtures as solutions, suspensions, or colloids.	A-1, A-2, G-1, G-2, G-3		**SE** Inquiry Activity: What Properties Could You Use to Describe Materials? p. 37 **L2** **TE** Teacher Demo: Transmission Versus Scattering, p. 43 **L2**
2.2 Physical Properties, pp. 45–51 ⏱ 1 block or 2 periods **2.2.1 Describe** physical properties of matter. **2.2.2 Identify** substances based on their physical properties. **2.2.3 Describe** how properties are used to choose materials. **2.2.4 Describe** methods used to separate mixtures. **2.2.5 Describe** evidence that indicates a physical change is taking place.	A-1, A-2, B-2, E-2, F-1		**SE** Quick Lab: Comparing Heat Conductors, p. 46 **L2** **TE** Teacher Demo: Comparing Melting Points, p. 48 **L2** **TE** Build Science Skills: Applying Concepts, p. 50 **L2** **LM** Investigation 2B: Determining the Densities of Liquids **L1**
2.3 Chemical Properties, pp. 54–58 ⏱ 1 block or 2 periods **2.3.1 Describe** chemical properties of matter. **2.3.2 Describe** clues that indicate that a chemical change is taking place. **2.3.3 Distinguish** chemical changes from physical changes.	A-1, A-2, B-3		**SE** Quick Lab: Identifying a Chemical Change, p. 56 **L2** **SE** Forensics Lab: Using Properties to Identify Materials, pp. 60–61 **L2** **TE** Teacher Demo: Oxygen Is Needed, p. 55 **L2** **LM** Investigation 2A: Recognizing Chemical and Physical Changes **L2**

Ability Levels

L1 For students who need additional help
L2 For all students
L3 For students who need to be challenged

Components

SE Student Edition	**GRSW** Guided Reading & Study Workbook With Math Support	**CTB** Computer Test Bank	**T** Transparencies
TE Teacher's Edition		**TP** Test Prep Resources	**P** Presentation Pro CD-ROM
LM Laboratory Manual	**CUT** Chapter and Unit Tests	**iT** iText	**GO** Internet Resources
PLM Probeware Lab Manual		**DC** Discovery Channel Videotapes	

RESOURCES — PRINT and TECHNOLOGY / SECTION ASSESSMENT

GRSW Section 2.1 — L1
T Chapter 2 Pretest — L2
Section 2.1 — L2
P Chapter 2 Pretest — L2
Section 2.1 — L2
sci LINKS **GO** Mixtures — L2

SE Section 2.1 Assessment, p. 44
iText iT Section 2.1

GRSW Section 2.2 — L1
GRSW Math Skill — L2
DC Fresh-Squeezed Water — L2
T Section 2.2 — L2
P Section 2.2 — L2
SCIENCE NEWS **GO** Properties of matter — L2

SE Section 2.2 Assessment, p. 51
iText iT Section 2.2

GRSW Section 2.3 — L1
T Section 2.3 — L2
P Section 2.3 — L2
sci LINKS **GO** Chemical and physical changes — L2

SE Section 2.3 Assessment, p. 58
iText iT Section 2.3

Go Online

Go online for these Internet resources.

PHSchool.com
Web Code: cca-1020
Web Code: cch-1020

NSTA SCi LINKS
Web Code: ccn-1021
Web Code: ccn-1023

SCIENCE NEWS
Web Code: cce-1022

Materials for Activities and Labs

Quantities for each group

STUDENT EDITION

Inquiry Activity, p. 37
rubber band, copper wire, steel paper clip, wooden toothpick, graphite pencil filler

Quick Lab, p. 46
2 plastic foam cups, scissors, metric ruler, metal rod, wooden rod, 2 liquid crystal thermometers, hot water, clock or watch with second hand

Quick Lab, p. 56
3 test tubes; test-tube rack; glass-marking pencil; 3 10-mL graduated cylinders; solutions of copper sulfate, calcium chloride, and sodium chloride

Forensics Lab, pp. 60–61
2 spot plates, glass-marking pencil, 5 laboratory spatulas, cornstarch, baking soda, baking powder, wash bottle of water, vinegar, iodine solution, sample from crime scene, sample from suspect's shoe

TEACHER'S EDITION

Teacher Demo, p. 43
2 beakers, water, iodine solution, table salt, stirring rods, milk, fish tank, flashlight, white paper

Teacher Demo, p. 48
water, ethanol, foam cups, freezer, large beaker, thermometer

Build Science Skills, p. 50
a mixture of salt, sand, and iron filings; beaker; magnet; plastic bag; water; funnel; filter paper

Build Science Skills, p. 52
tap water, bottled water, distilled water

Teacher Demo, p. 55
2 small candles, matches, large beaker

Chapter Assessment

CHAPTER ASSESSMENT
SE Chapter Assessment, pp. 63–64
CUT Chapter 2 Test A, B
CTB Chapter 2
iT Chapter 2
PHSchool.com GO
Web Code: cca-1020

STANDARDIZED TEST PREP
SE Chapter 2, p. 65
TP Diagnose and Prescribe

iText—interactive textbook with assessment at PHSchool.com

Name_____ Class_____ Date_____ M T W T F

LESSON PLAN 2.1

Classifying Matter

Time
2 periods
1 block

Section Objectives

Local Standards

- **2.1.1 Classify** pure substances as elements or compounds.
- **2.1.2 Describe** the characteristics of an element and the symbols used to identify elements.
- **2.1.3 Describe** the characteristics of a compound.
- **2.1.4 Distinguish** pure substances from mixtures.
- **2.1.5 Classify** mixtures as heterogeneous or homogeneous.
- **2.1.6 Classify** mixtures as solutions, suspensions, or colloids.

Vocabulary pure substances • element • atom • compound • heterogeneous mixture • homogeneous mixture • solution • suspension • colloid

1 FOCUS

Build Vocabulary: Paraphrasing

Help students understand the definitions of vocabulary terms by replacing less familiar words in a definition with more familiar words or phrases **L2**

Targeted Resources

❏ Transparency: Chapter 2 Pretest
❏ Transparency: Interest Grabber 2.1
❏ Transparency: Reading Strategy 2.1

2 INSTRUCT

Build Reading Literacy: Compare and Contrast

Have students gather information on different classifications of mixtures. Then, have students create a chart that compares and contrasts each type of mixture. **L1**

Build Science Skills: Observing

Ask students to list some characteristics of the elements in Figure 2. Have students hypothesize about why the iodine sample is in a closed container. **L2**

Integrate Language Arts

Have students research and explain the origin of element symbols that are not abbreviations for element names in English. **L2**

Teacher Demo: Transmission Versus Scattering

Use a beaker of water and iodine solution and a beaker of water and table salt to help students observe light passing through different mixtures. **L2**

Build Science Skills: Classifying

Have students research categories of colloids. Have students identify household examples of each type. **L3**

Targeted Resources

❏ GRSW Section 2.1
❏ **NSTA** *sci*_{INKS} Mixtures

3 ASSESS

Reteach

Use Figure 6 as a visual aid to summarize the key differences among different types of mixtures. **L1**

Evaluate Understanding

Have students make a game of concentration using the terms in the chapter and their definitions **L2**

Targeted Resources

❏ **PHSchool.com** Online Section 2.1 Assessment
❏ iText Section 2.1

Transparencies

16 **Chapter 2 Pretest**

1. What instrument would you use to measure temperature?

2. Which of the following is a unit of volume?

   a. gram

   b. atmosphere

   c. meter

   d. liter

3. What characteristic of matter can you measure using a graduated cylinder?

4. The sides of a cube are 2 cm by 2 cm. What is the volume of the cube?

ANSWERS
1. a thermometer
2. d
3. volume
4. 8 cm³

Transparencies

17 **Chapter 2 Pretest** *(continued)*

5. What additional quantity would you need to calculate the density of the cube described in Question 4?

6. Which of the following is not studied in chemistry?

   a. composition of matter

   b. reactions of substances

   c. properties of materials

   d. motion of large objects

ANSWERS
5. the cube's mass
6. d

Transparencies

18 **Section 2.1 Interest Grabber**

Classifying Items

People classify objects for different reasons. Classifying foods into groups, such as grains, vegetables, and fruits helps people plan meals that maintain a healthy diet. Biologists classify organisms into groups that have similar characteristics, which makes the relationships among organisms easier to see.

1. Devise a classification system for the following items: orange, lime, plum, apple, pear, rose, violet, daisy, gold, and silver.

2. Explain what criteria you used to place items into each category of your classification system.

ANSWERS
Student answers may vary. Sample answer: Fruit-orange,
lime, plum, apple, pear; Flower-rose, violet, daisy; and
Element-gold, silver. Students could also classify the list
based on whether or not the item is a color name.

Transparencies

19 **Section 2.1 Reading Strategy**

Summarizing

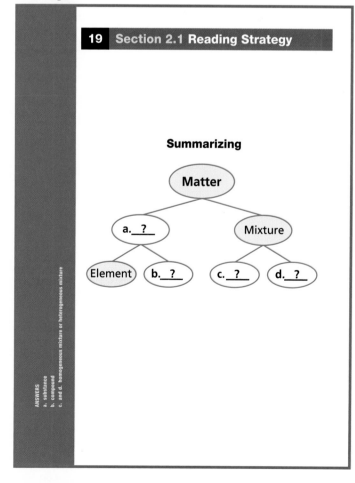

ANSWERS
a. substance
b. compound
c. and d. homogeneous mixture or heterogeneous mixture

Name _____ Class _____ Date _____

Chapter 2   Properties of Matter

Section 2.1 Classifying Matter
(pages 38–44)

This section explains how materials are classified as pure substances or mixtures. It discusses types of pure substances and mixtures.

Reading Strategy (page 38)

Summarizing As you read, complete the classification of matter in the diagram below. For more information on this Reading Strategy, see the **Reading and Study Skills** in the **Skills and Reference Handbook** at the end of your textbook.

```
                    Matter
            ┌──────────┴──────────┐
        Substance             Mixture
        ┌────┴────┐         ┌─────┴──────┐
    Element   Compound  Homogeneous  Heterogeneous
                          mixture       mixture
```

Pure Substances (page 39)

1. Is the following sentence true or false? Every sample of a pure substance has exactly the same composition and the same properties. _____true_____

2. What are the two categories of pure substances?
   a. _____Elements_____   b. _____Compounds_____

Elements (pages 39–40)

3. What is an element? An element is a substance that cannot be broken down into simpler substances.

4. Is the following sentence true or false? The smallest particle of an element is an atom. _____true_____

5. Why does an element have a fixed, uniform composition? An element has a fixed composition because it contains only one type of atom.

6. Circle the letter before each element that is a gas at room temperature.
   a. carbon   (b.)oxygen
   c. mercury   (d.)nitrogen

Match each element to its correct symbol.

	Element	Symbol
_b_	7. aluminum	a. C
_c_	8. gold	b. Al
_a_	9. carbon	c. Au

Name _____ Class _____ Date _____

Chapter 2   Properties of Matter

Compounds (page 40)

10. What is a compound? A compound is a substance that is made from two or more simpler substances and can be broken down into those simpler substances.

11. Circle the letter of each sentence that is true about compounds.
    (a.)A compound always contains at least two elements.
    (b.)The substances that make up a compound are always joined in a fixed proportion.
    c. A compound has the same properties as the elements from which it is formed.
    (d.)A compound can be broken down into simpler substances.

Mixtures (pages 41–42)

12. Why do the properties of a mixture vary? The properties of a mixture can vary because the composition of a mixture is not fixed.

13. A(n) _____heterogeneous_____ mixture is a mixture whose parts are noticeably different from one another.

14. Is the following sentence true or false? A homogeneous mixture is a mixture in which it is difficult to distinguish the substances from one another. _____true_____

Solutions, Suspensions, and Colloids (pages 42–44)

15. A mixture can be classified as a solution, a suspension, or a colloid based on the size of its _____largest_____ particles.

16. Circle the letter of the term that identifies the homogeneous mixture that forms when sugar is dissolved in a glass of hot water.
    (a.) solution   b. suspension
    c. colloid   d. substance

17. Complete the table about solutions, suspensions, and colloids.

Solutions, Suspensions, and Colloids			
Type of Mixture	**Relative Size of Largest Particles**	**Homogeneous or Heterogeneous?**	**Do Particles Scatter Light?**
Solution	Small	Homogeneous	No
Colloid	Intermediate	Homogeneous	Yes
Suspension	Large	Heterogeneous	Yes

18. Circle the letter before each example of a colloid.
    a. windshield wiper fluid   (b.)fog
    (c.)homogenized milk   d. muddy water

19. Is the following sentence true or false? If salt water is poured through a filter, the salt will be trapped on the filter. _____false_____

LESSON PLAN 2.2

Physical Properties

Section Objectives

- **2.2.1 Describe** physical properties of matter.
- **2.2.2 Identify** substances based on their physical properties.
- **2.2.3 Describe** how properties are used to choose materials.
- **2.2.4 Describe** methods used to separate mixtures.
- **2.2.5 Describe** evidence that indicates a physical change is taking place.

Vocabulary physical property • viscosity • conductivity • malleability • melting point • boiling point • filtration • distillation • physical change

Local Standards

---

1 FOCUS

Build Vocabulary: LINCS
Have students use the LINCS strategy to learn and review the terms *viscosity*, *conductivity*, and *malleability*. **L2**

Targeted Resources
❑ Transparency: Interest Grabber 2.2
❑ Transparency: Reading Strategy 2.2

---

2 INSTRUCT

Use Visuals: Figure 10
Ask students what properties of gold they can identify from Figure 10. Ask students what other property gold could exhibit given the age of the jewelry. **L1**

Build Reading Literacy: Outline
Have students read pp. 48–50 and gather information on identifying, choosing, and separating substances based on their physical properties. Then, have students use the headings as major divisions in an outline. **L1**

Quick Lab: Comparing Heat Conductors
Students will record the temperature of a metal rod and a wooden rod in hot water, in order to distinguish a material that is a good conductor of heat from a material that is a poor conductor of heat. **L2**

Teacher Demo: Comparing Melting Points
Place a foam cup filled with water and a second foam cup filled with ethanol in the freezer overnight so that students can observe the differences in melting points of two substances. **L2**

Build Science Skills: Applying Concepts
Students use properties to separate the components of a mixture **L2**

For Enrichment
Have students find out about sand molds and use them to make candles or plaster casts of their footprints or handprints. **L3**

Targeted Resources
❑ Transparency: Figure 12: Melting and Boiling Points of Some Substances
❑ GRSW Section 2.2

---

3 ASSESS

Reteach
Use the How it Works feature on p. 49 to review with students the importance of examining physical properties when choosing a material **L1**

Evaluate Understanding
Ask students how a cook might remove the layer of fat that rises to the top in a pot of chicken soup. **L2**

Targeted Resources
❑ **PHSchool.com** Online Section 2.2 Assessment
❑ iText Section 2.2

Transparencies

20 **Section 2.2 Interest Grabber**

Distinguishing Features

Physical characteristics can be used to describe and distinguish a person from other people. An accurate physical description can often be used to identify a person in a crowd. Practice identifying physical characteristics with the animals listed below. Your teacher will supply you with pictures of each animal.

lion	cheetah
ocelot	leopard
tiger	bobcat

1. What characteristics make these animals similar?

2. What characteristics make them different?

ANSWERS
1. Student answers will vary. All the animals have four legs, fur, sharp teeth, and a tail.
2. Student answers will vary. There are differences in color, size, and shape of face and body.

Transparencies

21 **Section 2.2 Reading Strategy**

Building Vocabulary

Physical Property	Definition
Viscosity	a._____?_____
Malleability	b._____?_____
Melting point	c._____?_____

ANSWERS
a. The tendency of a liquid to resist flowing
b. The ability of a solid to be hammered without shattering
c. The temperature at which a substance changes from a solid to liquid.

Transparencies

22 **Figure 12 Melting and Boiling Points of Some Substances**

Melting and Boiling Points of Some Substances		
Substance	Melting Point	Boiling Point
Hydrogen	−259.3°C	−252.9°C
Nitrogen	−210.0°C	−195.8°C
Ammonia	−77.7°C	−33.3°C
Octane (found in gasoline)	−56.8°C	125.6°C
Water	0.0°C	100.0°C
Acetic acid (found in vinegar)	16.6°C	117.9°C
Table salt	800.7°C	1465°C
Gold	1064.2°C	2856°C

Name _____ Class _____ Date _____

Chapter 2   Properties of Matter

Section 2.2 Physical Properties
(pages 45–51)

This section discusses physical properties and physical changes. It also explains how physical properties can be used to identify materials, select materials, and separate mixtures.

Reading Strategy (page 45)

Building Vocabulary As you read, write a definition for each term in the table below. For more information on this Reading Strategy, see the **Reading and Study Skills** in the **Skills and Reference Handbook** at the end of your textbook.

Defining Physical Properties	
Physical Property	**Definition**
Viscosity	The tendency of a liquid to resist flowing
Malleability	The ability of a solid to be hammered without shattering
Melting Point	The temperature at which a solid changes to a liquid

Examples of Physical Properties (pages 45–47)

1. A physical property is any characteristic of a material that can be observed or measured without changing the ____composition____ of the substances in the material.

2. Explain why a wooden spoon is a better choice than a metal spoon for stirring a boiling pot of soup. The handle of a wooden spoon will stay cool because wood is not a good conductor of heat.

3. Is the following sentence true or false? A liquid with a high viscosity flows more slowly than a liquid with a low viscosity at the same temperature. ____true____

4. Is the following sentence true or false? Discovering which of two materials can scratch the other is a way to compare the hardness of the materials. ____true____

Match each term to its definition.

	Term	Definition
c	5. viscosity	a. The ability of a solid to be hammered without shattering
d	6. conductivity	
a	7. malleability	b. The temperature at which a substance changes from a liquid to a gas
f	8. melting point	c. The resistance of a liquid to flowing
b	9. boiling point	d. The ability to allow heat to flow
e	10. density	e. The ratio of the mass of a substance to its volume
		f. The temperature at which a substance changes from a solid to a liquid

Physical Science Guided Reading and Study Workbook • Chapter 2   **13**

Name _____ Class _____ Date _____

Chapter 2   Properties of Matter

11. Which of the substances in the table below are gases at room temperature?
   a. ____Hydrogen____ b. ____Nitrogen____ c. ____Ammonia____

Melting and Boiling Points of Some Substances		
Substance	**Melting Point**	**Boiling Point**
Hydrogen	−259.3°C	−252.9°C
Nitrogen	−210.0°C	−195.8°C
Ammonia	−77.7°C	−33.3°C
Octane (found in gasoline)	−56.8°C	125.6°C
Water	0.0°C	100.0°C
Acetic acid (found in vinegar)	16.6°C	117.9°C

Using Physical Properties (page 48)

12. Describe three steps that can be used to identify a material. First, decide which properties to test. Second, do a test on a sample of the unknown. Third, compare the results with data reported for known materials.

13. Is the following sentence true or false? Usually, people consider only one property when choosing a material. ____false____

Using Properties to Separate Mixtures (page 50)

14. Two processes that are commonly used to separate mixtures are ____filtration____ and ____distillation____.

15. Explain how filtration separates materials based on the size of their particles. Particles that are small enough to pass through the filter are separated from larger particles, which are trapped on the filter.

16. Explain why distillation works for converting seawater into fresh water. Water has a much lower boiling point than the compounds dissolved in seawater. Water can be boiled and collected in a separate container. The dissolved compounds are left behind in the original container.

Recognizing Physical Changes (page 51)

17. Is the following sentence true or false? In a physical change, some of the substances in a material change, but the properties of the material stay the same. ____false____

18. Explain why the boiling of water is a physical change. When water changes from a liquid to a gas, it remains the same substance.

19. Circle the letter for each process that is a reversible physical change.
   a. wrinkling a shirt   b. freezing water
   c. cutting hair   d. peeling an orange

14 *Physical Science* Guided Reading and Study Workbook • Chapter 2

Name_____ Class_____ Date_____ M T W T F

LESSON PLAN 2.3

Chemical Properties

Time
2 periods
1 block

Section Objectives

- **2.3.1 Describe** chemical properties of matter.
- **2.3.2 Describe** clues that indicate that a chemical change is taking place.
- **2.3.3 Distinguish** chemical changes from physical changes.

Vocabulary chemical property • flammability • reactivity • chemical change • precipitate

Local Standards

---

1 FOCUS

Build Vocabulary: Word-Part Analysis
After looking up the words *flammable*, *inflammable*, and *nonflammable*, have students find two meanings of the prefix *in-* to explain why the terms are confusing. **L2**

Targeted Resources
❏ Transparency: Interest Grabber 2.3
❏ Transparency: Reading Strategy 2.3

---

2 INSTRUCT

Build Reading Literacy: Preview
Have students skim this section's headings, visuals, and boldfaced material to preview how the text is organized. **L1**

Use Visuals: Figure 20
Have students describe baking soda and vinegar before they are mixed. Ask what clue indicates that a chemical change is taking place. **L1**

Teacher Demo: Oxygen Is Needed
Light two candles and place a large beaker over one of the candles so that students can observe that air is needed for a candle to burn. **L2**

Build Science Skills: Designing Experiments
Challenge students to describe a material that they could test for flammability without changing its composition. **L2**

Quick Lab: Identifying a Chemical Change
Combine solutions in test tubes so that students will recognize evidence of a chemical change. **L2**

Address Misconceptions
Explain that the composition of *some* substances must change during a chemical change, but the composition of *all* substances must remain the same during a physical change. **L2**

Targeted Resources
❏ GRSW Section 2.3

❏ **NSTA** *sci*_{LINKS} Chemical and physical changes

---

3 ASSESS

Reteach
Use Figures 18, 19, and 20 to review the clues that indicate that a chemical change is taking place. **L1**

Evaluate Understanding
Have students list three clues that indicate that a chemical change is taking place and give an example of each. Then, have them exchange their work with a partner and discuss examples of physical changes that also exhibit these clues. **L2**

Targeted Resources
❏ **PHSchool.com** Online Section 2.3 Assessment
❏ iText Section 2.3

Transparencies

23 | **Section 2.3 Interest Grabber**

Safety Symbols

It is important to pay attention to warning labels when working with chemicals. Look at the safety symbols below.

Write a brief statement for each symbol explaining what actions you need to take to avoid a possible danger.

 A.

 B.

 C.

 D.

(vertical text, left margin:)
C. Avoid getting corrosive chemicals on skin or clothing, or in the eyes.
D. Tie back long hair and loose clothing, and put on safety goggles before using a burner.

ANSWERS
A. No flames, sparks, or exposed sources of heat should be present during an experiment.
B. When working with poisonous or irritating vapors, work in a well-ventilated area. Avoid inhaling a vapor directly.

Transparencies

24 | **Section 2.3 Reading Strategy**

Relating Text and Visuals

Clue	Example
Change in color	a.____?____
Production of gas	b.____?____
Formation of precipitate	c.____?____

(vertical text, left margin:)
c. Formation of cottage cheese curds when acid is added to milk.

ANSWERS
a. Copper roof changing color from red to green when exposed to moist air
b. Formation of carbon dioxide gas when vinegar is added to baking soda

---

Guided Reading and Study Workbook

Name _____ Class _____ Date _____

Chapter 2   Properties of Matter

Section 2.3 Chemical Properties
(pages 54–58)

This section discusses chemical properties and describes clues that may show that a chemical change has taken place.

Reading Strategy (page 54)

Relating Text and Visuals As you read, complete the table by finding examples of the clues for recognizing chemical changes in Figures 19 and 20. For more information on this Reading Strategy, see the **Reading and Study Skills** in the **Skills and Reference Handbook** at the end of your textbook.

Recognizing Chemical Changes	
Clue	**Example**
Change in color	Copper roof changing color from red to green when exposed to moist air
Production of gas	Formation of carbon dioxide gas when vinegar is added to baking soda
Formation of precipitate	Formation of cottage cheese curds when acid is added to milk.

Observing Chemical Properties (pages 54–55)

1. Is the following sentence true or false? The substances in paraffin do not change when a candle burns. _____false_____
2. Circle the letters of the compounds formed when a candle burns.
   a. paraffin
   b. hydrogen
   c. water
   d. carbon
3. What is a chemical property? A chemical property is any property that produces a change in the composition of matter.

4. Is the following sentence true or false? Flammability is a material's ability to burn in the presence of carbon dioxide. _____false_____
5. The property that describes how readily a substance combines chemically with other substances is _____reactivity_____.
6. Circle the letter of each property that is a chemical property.
   a. hardness
   b. density
   c. flammability
   d. reactivity
7. Is the following sentence true or false? Nitrogen is a more reactive element than oxygen. _____false_____

Physical Science Guided Reading and Study Workbook • Chapter 2   **15**

Guided Reading and Study Workbook

Name _____ Class _____ Date _____

Chapter 2   Properties of Matter

8. Why isn't iron used to make coins? Iron is highly reactive in the presence of oxygen and water.
9. What is the benefit of pumping nitrogen gas into seawater that is stored in steel tanks? The nitrogen displaces dissolved oxygen from the seawater, reducing the amount of rust that forms inside the tanks.

Recognizing Chemical Changes (pages 56–57)

10. A(n) _____chemical_____ change occurs when a substance reacts and forms one or more new substances.
11. What are three examples of chemical changes?
    a. _____A cake baking_____   b. _____Leaves on trees changing color_____
    c. _____Food being digested_____
12. Circle the letters of examples of evidence for a chemical change.
    a. a change in color
    b. a filter trapping particles
    c. the production of a gas
    d. the formation of a solid precipitate

Match each example to evidence of a chemical change.

Example	Chemical Change
__b__ 13. Lemon juice is added to milk.	a. the production of a gas
	b. the formation of a precipitate
__c__ 14. A silver bracelet darkens when exposed to air.	c. a change in color
__a__ 15. Vinegar is mixed with baking soda.	

Is a Change Chemical or Physical? (page 58)

16. Is the following sentence true or false? When iron is heated until it turns red, the color change shows that a chemical change has taken place. _____false_____
17. When matter undergoes a chemical change, the composition of the matter _____changes_____.
18. When matter undergoes a chemical change, the composition of the matter _____stays the same_____.
19. Complete the following table about chemical changes.

Chemical Changes		
Type of Change	**Are New Substances Formed?**	**Example**
Chemical	Yes	Iron rusting
Physical	No	Sugar dissolving in water

16   *Physical Science* Guided Reading and Study Workbook • Chapter 2

Guided Reading and Study Workbook

Name _____ Class _____ Date _____

Chapter 2   Properties of Matter

WordWise

Answer the questions by writing the correct vocabulary term in the blanks.
Use the circled letter in each term to find the hidden vocabulary word. Then,
write a definition for the hidden word.

Clues	Vocabulary Terms
A mixture that results when substances dissolve to form a homogeneous mixture	Ⓢ o l u t i o n
A substance that can be broken down into two or more simpler substances	c o m p o Ⓤ n d
A change in which the composition of matter stays the same	p h y Ⓢ i c a l c h a n g e
A solid that forms and separates from a liquid mixture	p r e c i Ⓟ i t a t e
A substance that cannot be broken down into simpler substances	Ⓔ l e m e n t
The ability of a material to allow heat to flow	c o Ⓝ d u c t i v i t y
A classification for matter that always has the same composition	p u r e Ⓢ u b s t a n c e
The ability of a material to burn	f l a m m a b i l Ⓘ t y
A homogeneous mixture containing particles that scatter light	c Ⓞ l l o i d
The temperature at which a substance changes from a liquid to gas	b o i l i n g p o i Ⓝ t

Hidden Term: s u s p e n s i o n

Definition: A heterogeneous mixture that separates into layers over time

Guided Reading and Study Workbook

Name _____ Class _____ Date _____

Chapter 2   Properties of Matter

Melting and Boiling Points

Math Skill:
Data Tables

You may want to read more about this **Math Skill** in the **Skills and Reference Handbook** at the end of your textbook.

Melting and Boiling Points of Some Substances

Substance	Melting Point	Boiling Point
Hydrogen	−259.3°C	−252.9°C
Nitrogen	−210.0°C	−195.8°C
Water	0.0°C	100.0°C
Acetic acid (found in vinegar)	16.6°C	117.9°C
Table salt	800.7°C	1465°C

Which of the substances in the table above are solids at a temperature of −40°C?

1. **Read and Understand**

   What information are you given?
   Temperature = −40°C

   The melting and boiling points of five substances are listed in the table.

2. **Plan and Solve**

   What unknown are you trying to find?
   Which of the five substances are solids at −40°C?

   What guideline can you use?
   Any substance that is a solid at −40°C must have a melting point greater than −40°C.

   Check the melting point of each substance in the table to find out whether it satisfies the guideline.
   Water, acetic acid, and table salt are solids at −40°C.

3. **Look Back and Check**

   Is your answer reasonable?
   Because water, acetic acid, and table salt have melting points equal to or greater than 0°C, they will all be solids at a temperature well below 0°C.

Math Practice

On a separate sheet of paper, solve the following problems.

1. Which substance in the table is a liquid at 105°C? _____ acetic acid _____
2. Which substance in the table has a melting point closest to room temperature (20°C)? _____ acetic acid _____
3. Which substance in the table boils at the lowest temperature? _____ hydrogen _____
4. Which substance has the smallest temperature range as a liquid, hydrogen or nitrogen? _____ hydrogen _____

Student Edition Lab Worksheet

Name _____ Class _____ Date _____

Chapter 2   Properties of Matter   Forensics Lab

Using Properties to Identify Materials

See pages 60 and 61 in the Teacher's Edition for more information.

Forensic chemists test the physical and chemical properties of materials found at a crime scene. They also do similar tests on the materials found on a suspect's skin or clothing. These materials are often complex mixtures, such as soil, which contain many substances. In this lab, you will compare the properties of three known materials with two samples of "evidence." These samples represent evidence from a crime scene and evidence from a suspect's shoe. Although your materials and equipment are less complex than those used by forensic chemists, your overall method will be similar to the methods they use.

Problem Can the properties of materials that appear similar be used to tell them apart?

Materials
- 2 spot plates
- glass-marking pencil
- 5 laboratory spatulas
- cornstarch
- baking soda
- baking powder
- wash bottle of water
- vinegar
- iodine solution
- sample from crime scene
- sample from suspect's shoe

Skills Observing, Inferring, Predicting

Procedure

Part A: Properties of Known Substances

1. Use a glass-marking pencil to label 15 wells A through O on the spot plates. Make a mark next to each well, not in the well.
2. Use a spatula to place a small amount of cornstarch in wells A, B, and C. In the data table, record any physical properties of the cornstarch that you observe.

DATA TABLE

Sample	Description	Result of Adding Water	Result of Adding Vinegar	Result of Adding Iodine
Cornstarch	White powder	No change	No change	Blue-black
Baking soda	White powder	Dissolves	Bubbles	No change
Baking powder	White powder	Partly dissolves bubbles	Bubbles	Bubbles
Crime scene sample	White powder	Partly dissolves bubbles	Bubbles	Bubbles
Sample from suspect's shoe	White powder	Dissolves	Bubbles	Bubbles

3. Use a clean spatula to place a small amount of baking soda in wells D, E, and F. Record any physical properties of baking soda that you observe.
4. Using a clean spatula, place a small amount of baking powder in wells G, H, and I. Record any physical properties of baking powder that you observe.

Student Edition Lab Worksheet

Name _____ Class _____ Date _____

5. Fill wells A, D, and G with water. Record any observed changes.
6. Fill wells, B, E, and H with vinegar. Record any observed changes.
7. Add one drop of iodine solution to wells C, F, and I. Record any changes that you observe. **CAUTION:** *Iodine solution is corrosive and poisonous. It can stain skin and clothing. Rinse any iodine spills with water.*

Part B: Properties of Unknown Substances

8. **Predicting** Look at the sample from the crime scene and the sample from the suspect's shoe. Based on your observations, predict whether testing will show that the samples are identical.

   _____

   _____

9. Use a clean spatula to place a small amount of the sample from the crime scene in wells J, K, and L. In the data table, record any physical properties of the sample that you observe.
10. Use a clean laboratory spatula to place a small amount of the sample from the suspect's shoe in wells M, N, and O. In the data table, record any physical properties of the sample that you observe.
11. Fill wells J and M with water. In the data table, record your observations.
12. Fill wells K and N with vinegar. In the data table, record your observations.
13. Add 1 drop of iodine solution to wells L and O. In the data table, record your observations.
14. Rinse all materials off the spot plates and flush them down the drain with at least ten times as much water. Dispose of your plastic gloves as directed by your teacher. **CAUTION:** *Wash your hands thoroughly with soap or detergent before leaving the laboratory.*

Analyze and Conclude

1. **Analyzing Data** Were you able to use the ability to dissolve in water to distinguish all three materials? Explain your answer.

   The ability to dissolve in water distinguished only cornstarch from baking soda and baking powder,

   but not baking soda from baking powder.

2. **Drawing Conclusions** Are the samples from the suspect's shoe and from the crime scene identical?

   The results did not indicate that the sample from the suspect's shoe (baking soda) has the same

   properties as the sample from the crime scene (baking powder).

3. **Evaluating and Revising** Did the data you collected support your prediction? Explain your answer.

   Yes or no (depending on the prediction made). Students should use evidence from the water and

   iodine solution tests to support their answers.

Lab Manual

Name _____ Class _____ Date _____

Chapter 2   Properties of Matter   Investigation 2A

Recognizing Chemical and Physical Changes

Refer students to pages 51 and 56–58 in their textbooks for a discussion of physical and chemical changes. **SKILLS FOCUS:** Observing, Classifying **CLASS TIME:** 40 minutes

Background Information

Some chemical and physical changes are easy to recognize. Other changes may be easy to observe, but difficult to classify as a chemical or a physical change just by observation. Many events that occur in nature, such as volcanic eruptions, include both chemical and physical changes. When you observe a complicated event, you may need more information before you can identify the chemical and physical changes that have occurred.

In this investigation, you will observe several events and identify the chemical and physical changes involved in each.

Problem

How can you identify chemical and physical changes?

Pre-Lab Discussion

Read the entire investigation. Then, work with a partner to answer the following questions.

1. **Observing** What evidence of chemical changes will you look for in this investigation?

   Evidence of chemical changes includes formation of a precipitate, production of a gas,

   and changes in color.

2. **Inferring** What are some examples of physical changes that you might observe in this investigation?

   Changes in shape, melting

3. **Predicting** In which step of this investigation is a physical change most likely to occur? Explain your answer.

   Step 8, because the paraffin is likely to melt when it is heated

4. **Predicting** In which step of this investigation is a chemical change most likely to occur? Explain your answer.

   Step 8, because chemical changes occur during burning

Lab Manual

Name _____ Class _____ Date _____

Materials *(per group)*

4 test tubes
glass-marking pencil
test-tube rack
magnesium chloride solution
sodium carbonate solution
copper sulfate solution
white vinegar (acetic acid solution)
aluminum foil
calcium carbonate chip
paraffin candle
matches
clock or watch

Prepare 0.1 M solutions of magnesium chloride, sodium carbonate, and copper(II) sulfate by dissolving 20.3 g $MgCl_2 \cdot 6H_2O$, 10.6 g Na_2CO_3 and 25.0 g $CuSO_4 \cdot 5H_2O$, respectively, in 1 L of water.

Place candles in holders or melt the non-wick ends and attach them to sturdy, nonflammable bases.

Review with students the safety information in the MSDS for each chemical before performing this investigation. Used solutions may be flushed down the drain with at least 10 volumes of water. If your school is served by a septic system, do not dispose of chemical waste in this way. Instead, allow the used solutions to evaporate and dispose of them as dry chemical waste.

Safety

Put on safety goggles and a lab apron. Be careful to avoid breakage when working with glassware. Always use caution when working with laboratory chemicals, as they may irritate the skin or stain skin or clothing. Never touch or taste any chemical unless instructed to do so. Be careful when using matches. Tie back loose hair and clothing when working with flames. Do not reach over an open flame. Wash your hands thoroughly after carrying out this investigation. Note all safety alert symbols next to the steps in the Procedure and review the meaning of each symbol by referring to the Safety Symbols on page xiii.

Procedure

1. Use the glass-marking pencil to label the test tubes *1* to *4*. Place the test tubes in a test-tube rack.

2. Fill each test tube one-third full with the solution indicated in Data Table 1.

3. Observe each of the solutions and record your observations in Data Table 1.

4. Observe the appearance of the aluminum foil, the calcium carbonate chip, and the paraffin candle. Record your observations in Data Table 1.

5. Pour the sodium carbonate solution from test tube 2 into the magnesium chloride solution in test tube 1. Observe what happens and record your observations in Data Table 2.

6. Crumple up the aluminum foil and drop it into the copper sulfate solution in test tube 3. Observe test tube 3 every 2 minutes for 10 minutes. Record your observations in Data Table 2.

   Students can continue to work on the following steps as they observe test tube 3.

7. Carefully drop the calcium carbonate chip into the vinegar (acetic acid solution) in test tube 4. Record your observations in Data Table 2.

Lab Manual

Name _____ Class _____ Date _____

8. Use a match to light the paraffin candle. Observe what happens to the candle for 5 minutes. In Data Table 3, record what happens to the candle. **CAUTION:** *Be careful not to burn yourself or others.*

9. Complete Data Tables 2 and 3, identifying each change you observed as chemical or physical.

10. Follow your teacher's instructions for disposing of the used chemicals. Wash your hands thoroughly with warm water and soap or detergent before leaving the laboratory.

Observations   Sample data are shown.

DATA TABLE 1

Material	Observations
Test tube 1: magnesium chloride solution	Clear solution
Test tube 2: sodium carbonate solution	Clear solution
Test tube 3: copper sulfate solution	Blue solution
Test tube 4: vinegar (acetic acid solution)	Clear or slightly yellow solution
Aluminum foil	Flexible, shiny, silvery solid
Calcium carbonate	Hard, brittle, white solid
Paraffin candle	Soft, white solid

Lab Manual

Name _____ Class _____ Date _____

DATA TABLE 2

Materials	Observations	Type of Change (chemical or physical)
Magnesium chloride and sodium carbonate solutions	White precipitate forms.	Chemical
Copper sulfate solution and aluminum foil	Aluminum turns reddish, and eventually darkens until it is black. Solution turns reddish brown. Bubbles form.	Chemical Chemical Chemical
Calcium carbonate and vinegar	Bubbles form.	Chemical

DATA TABLE 3

Observation	Type of Change (chemical or physical)
Flame	Chemical
Smoke produced.	Chemical
Wick chars.	Chemical
Wax melts.	Physical

Lab Manual

Name _____ Class _____ Date _____

Analysis and Conclusions

1. Inferring What type of change occurred when you mixed the magnesium chloride solution with the sodium carbonate solution? Explain your answer.

After the solutions were mixed, a white precipitate formed. Formation of a precipitate is often

evidence of a chemical change.

2. Inferring What type of change occurred in the copper sulfate solution when you placed the aluminum foil in it? Explain your answer.

The copper sulfate solution was initially a clear blue liquid, which turned reddish brown when the

aluminum foil was added. A color change is often evidence of a chemical change.

3. Inferring What type of change occurred in the acetic acid solution when you placed the calcium carbonate chip in it? Explain your answer.

Gas bubbles formed. Formation of a gas is often evidence of a chemical change.

4. Evaluating What evidence was there that new substances formed as the candle burned?

Evidence included the formation of solid black particles and the presence of a flame.

5. Evaluating What evidence of a physical change did you observe as the candle burned?

Melting of the candle was evidence of a physical change.

Lab Manual

Name _____ Class _____ Date _____

6. Drawing Conclusions What signs of chemical changes did you observe in this investigation?

The formation of a precipitate, color changes, and formation of gas

7. Evaluating and Revising Formation of a solid, formation of a gas, and a color change can also occur during some physical changes. Give examples of physical changes that could produce these clues. What evidence suggests that the changes you observed in test tubes 1–3 were, in fact, chemical changes?

Sample answer: A solid may form when a liquid is cooled. A gas may form when a liquid is heated.

A solid may change color when it is heated. During the procedure, the test tubes were not heated or

cooled. In test tube 1, the change occurred after two liquids were mixed. In test tubes 2 and 3,

changes occurred after solids were added to liquids.

Go Further

Many activities that people do at home on a regular basis can involve both physical and chemical changes. Examples include cooking or gardening. Pick an activity that you participate in at home and make a list of tasks for that activity. Divide the list into tasks during which a physical change occurs and tasks during which a chemical change occurs. Give reasons for your classifications.

Sample answers: For cooking, physical changes occur when food is sliced, ingredients are mixed, or ingredients melt or freeze; chemical changes usually occur when the color or texture of the food changes. For gardening, physical changes occur when a lawn is mowed, shrubs are pruned, or soil is tilled; chemical changes occur when fertilizer is added to soil, when fruit ripens, or materials are composted.

Lab Manual

Name _____ Class _____ Date _____

Chapter 2 Properties of Matter 🔍 Investigation 2B

Determining the Densities of Liquids
Refer students to page 47 in their textbooks for a discussion of density. **SKILLS FOCUS:** Measuring, Calculating **CLASS TIME:** 40 minutes

Background Information

Mass and volume are properties of all matter. **Density** is the ratio of an object's mass to its volume. The density of a specific kind of matter helps to identify it and distinguish it from other kinds of matter. It is possible to determine the densities of liquids in grams per milliliter (g/mL).

In this investigation, you will determine the densities of several liquids by measuring their masses and volumes.

Problem

How can you determine the densities of liquids?

Pre-Lab Discussion

Read the entire investigation. Then, work with a partner to answer the following questions.

1. Formulating Hypotheses For identical volumes, what will the relationship be between the mass and the density of a sample?

For identical volumes, as mass increases, the density will increase.

2. Controlling Variables What are the manipulated and responding variables in this investigation?

The type of liquid used is the manipulated variable, and the mass of the liquid is the responding

variable.

3. Controlling Variables What is the controlled variable in this investigation?

Volume

4. Calculating Why is it necessary to know the mass of the graduated cylinder in order to find the mass of the liquid?

The mass of the cylinder must be subtracted from the mass of the cylinder and liquid to determine

the mass of the liquid.

Lab Manual

Name _____ Class _____ Date _____

5. Predicting Predict which liquid will be the most dense and which will be the least dense.

Salt water will be the most dense, and ethanol will be the least dense.

Materials *(per group)*

2 100-mL graduated cylinders
triple-beam balance
50 mL denatured ethanol (ethyl alcohol)
50 mL salt water
paper towels

To prepare this solution, add 100 g of NaCl to enough water to make 1 L of solution.

Safety 🥽🧤🔥🧪🧯

Put on safety goggles and a lab apron. Be careful to avoid breakage when working with glassware. Always use caution when working with laboratory chemicals, as they may irritate the skin or stain skin or clothing. Never touch or taste any chemical unless instructed to do so. Keep alcohol away from any open flame. Wash your hands thoroughly after carrying out this investigation. Note all safety alert symbols next to the steps in the Procedure and review the meaning of each symbol by referring to the Safety Symbols on page xiii.

Review with students the safety information in the MSDS for denatured ethyl alcohol before performing this investigation.

Procedure

🥽🧤🧪 **1.** Place a clean graduated cylinder on the laboratory balance. In the data table, record the mass of the graduated cylinder.

2. Place about 50 mL of water in the graduated cylinder. Record the exact volume to the nearest tenth of a milliliter. Use a paper towel to wipe any water from the outside of the cylinder. Find the mass of the graduated cylinder and the water. Record this mass in the data table. **CAUTION:** *Wipe up any spilled liquids immediately to avoid slips and falls.*

3. Calculate the mass of the water by subtracting the mass of the graduated cylinder from the mass of the graduated cylinder and water. Record your answer in the data table.

4. Calculate the density of water, using the following equation. Record the density of water in the data table.

$$\text{Density} = \frac{\text{Mass}}{\text{Volume}}$$

🔥🧪 **5.** Repeat Steps 1 through 4. This time, use a clean graduated cylinder and denatured ethanol instead of water. **CAUTION:** *Denatured ethanol is poisonous and flammable. Do not drink it. Do not use denatured ethanol near an open flame.*

6. Empty the graduated cylinder containing water and dry it thoroughly with a paper towel. Repeat Steps 1 through 4, using this graduated cylinder and the sample of salt water.

Lab Manual

Name _____ Class _____ Date _____

Observations Sample data are shown.

DATA TABLE

Liquid	Mass of Graduated Cylinder (g)	Mass of Graduated Cylinder and Liquid (g)	Mass of Liquid (g)	Volume of Liquid (mL)	Density of Liquid (g/mL)
Water			49.5–50.5	49.5–50.5	0.98–1.02
Ethanol			40.0–41.0	49.5–50.5	0.79–0.83
Salt water			54.0–55.0	49.5–50.5	1.07–1.11

Analysis and Conclusions

1. **Analyzing Data** List the three liquids you studied in order of increasing density.

   Denatured ethanol, water, salt water

2. **Comparing and Contrasting** Which has the greater mass—1 L of water or 1 L of denatured ethanol? Explain your answer.

   1 L of water because water is denser than ethanol. A given volume of ethanol would have less

   mass than an equal volume of water.

3. **Comparing and Contrasting** Which has a greater volume—1000 g of water or 1000 g of denatured ethanol? Explain your answer.

   1000 g of denatured ethanol because ethanol is less dense than water. A given mass of

   denatured ethanol would have a greater volume than an equal mass of water.

Lab Manual

Name _____ Class _____ Date _____

4. **Inferring** Which is more dense—1 mL of water or 50 L of water? Explain your answer.

   They have equal density because the density of a substance is a property that does not

   change, regardless of the quantity of the sample.

5. **Predicting** Predict what would happen to the density of the salt solution if more salt was dissolved in a given volume of solution. Explain your answer.

   The mass of the solution would increase. Therefore, the density of the solution would increase.

Go Further

Use your data to predict the position of a small wooden dowel (or small pencil) placed in samples of the liquids used in this investigation. Would more or less of the dowel be visible above the surface of the liquid in each case? Plan a new investigation to test your predictions. Show your plan to your teacher. If your teacher approves your plan, carry out your experiment and report your results.

Students should carefully place a small wooden dowel or small pencil (about 10 cm in length) in a graduated cylinder of water, noting how high the rod or pencil floats. Students could remove the rod, dry it completely, and repeat the procedure with salt water and then with denatured ethanol. The higher the density of the liquids, the higher the rod or pencil should float.

Chapter Test A

Name _____ Class _____ Date _____

Chapter 2   Properties of Matter   Chapter Test A

Multiple Choice

Write the letter that best answers the question or completes the statement on the line provided.

_____ 1. Which of the following is NOT a pure substance?
   a. milk
   b. oxygen
   c. water
   d. carbon dioxide

_____ 2. If an unknown substance CANNOT be broken down into simpler substances, it is
   a. a compound.
   b. an element.
   c. made of one kind of atom.
   d. both b and c

_____ 3. The symbol for gold is
   a. Au.   b. Al.   c. Gl.   d. Go.

_____ 4. Water is a compound because it
   a. can be broken down into hydrogen and oxygen.
   b. has a fixed composition.
   c. is made of water atoms joined together.
   d. both a and b

_____ 5. Which of the following is a characteristic of a mixture?
   a. can have varying properties
   b. has a fixed composition
   c. contains no pure substances
   d. both a and d

_____ 6. Which of the following is a heterogeneous mixture?
   a. water in a swimming pool
   b. sugar water
   c. a jar of mixed nuts
   d. stainless steel

_____ 7. You are about to open a container of soy milk but notice that there are instructions to "shake well before serving." The soy milk is most likely a
   a. solution.
   b. pure substance.
   c. colloid.
   d. suspension.

_____ 8. Which of the following has the highest viscosity?
   a. corn syrup
   b. milk
   c. water
   d. orange juice

_____ 9. A material that is malleable and conducts electricity is most likely
   a. wood.
   b. ice.
   c. a metal.
   d. motor oil.

Chapter Test A

Name _____ Class _____ Date _____

_____ 10. Which of the following materials is useful for making molds because it has a low melting point?
   a. wood   b. metal   c. clay   d. wax

_____ 11. What method can be used to separate parts of a liquid mixture when the entire mixture can pass through a filter?
   a. filtration   b. distillation   c. straining   d. screening

_____ 12. Which of the following is a physical change?
   a. sawing a piece of wood in half
   b. burning a piece of wood
   c. rust forming on an iron fence
   d. a copper roof changing color from red to green

_____ 13. A substance that has high reactivity
   a. easily combines chemically with other substances.
   b. burns in the presence of water.
   c. displaces dissolved oxygen.
   d. has a high boiling point.

_____ 14. During which of the following chemical changes does a precipitate form?
   a. Vinegar is added to baking powder.
   b. Lemon juice is added to milk.
   c. Lemon juice is added to water.
   d. A banana ripens.

_____ 15. Which of the following is evidence of a chemical change?
   a. Iron changes color when heated.
   b. Gas bubbles form in boiling water.
   c. Balls of wax form when melted wax is poured into ice water.
   d. A gas forms when vinegar and baking soda are mixed.

Completion

Complete each statement on the line provided.

1. Pure substances are either _____ or _____

2. The symbols for elements have either _____ or _____ letters.

3. A compound can be made from two or more elements or other _____ joined together in a fixed composition.

4. Rust forms because iron and oxygen are highly _____ elements.

5. When a metal changes color because it has been heated, a(an) _____ change occurred. When a metal changes color because it has reacted with another substance, a(an) _____ change occurred.

Chapter Test A

Name _____ Class _____ Date _____

Short Answer
Use complete sentences to write the answers to the questions on the lines provided.

1. How can you change the properties of a mixture?

_____

_____

_____

_____

Melting and Boiling Points of Some Substances		
Substance	Melting Point	Boiling Point
Hydrogen	−259.3°C	−252.9°C
Nitrogen	−210.0°C	−195.8°C
Acetic acid	16.6°C	117.9°C
Gold	1064.2°C	2856°C

Figure 2-1

2. Based on the information in Figure 2-1, which substances would be solids at 10.0°C?

_____

_____

3. How do changes in temperature usually affect the viscosity of a liquid?

_____

_____

_____

4. Give an example of a physical change that can be reversed and an example of a physical change that cannot be reversed.

_____

_____

_____

5. What kind of change is taking place if you see white mold growing on a strawberry?

_____

_____

Chapter Test A

Name _____ Class _____ Date _____

Using Science Skills
Use the table to answer each question. Write the answers on a separate sheet of paper.

Properties of Three Mixtures			
	Scatters Light	Separates into Layers	Can Be Separated by Filtration
Mixture A	Yes	No	No
Mixture B	No	No	No
Mixture C	Yes	Yes	Yes

Figure 2-2

1. **Classifying** Based on the data in Figure 2-2, is Mixture C a homogeneous or heterogeneous mixture? Explain your answer.
2. **Analyzing Data** Which of the mixtures in Figure 2-2 is a solution? Explain how you know.
3. **Analyzing Data** Which of the mixtures in Figure 2-2 is a colloid? Explain how you know.
4. **Classifying** Rank the mixtures in Figure 2-2 in order of the size of their largest particles, starting with the mixture with the smallest particles.
5. **Predicting** Why can't Mixture B in Figure 2-2 be separated by filtration? What method might be used to separate the substances in Mixture B?

Essay
Write the answer to each question on a separate sheet of paper.

1. Compare the properties of water to the properties of the elements it contains.
2. Explain how you could use a physical property to test the purity of a silver coin without damaging the coin.
3. Suppose you want to separate the leaves, acorns, and twigs from a pile of soil. Filtration and distillation are two processes of separating mixtures. Explain which process you would use and why.
4. Explain why rust forms in steel tanks that hold seawater in ships. How can nitrogen be used to reduce rust in these tanks?
5. Suppose you heat a liquid and then gas bubbles are produced. With no other evidence, can you tell if a physical change or chemical change is occurring? Explain your answer.

Chapter Test B

Name _____ Class _____ Date _____

Chapter 2   Properties of Matter   **Chapter Test B**

Multiple Choice
Write the letter that best answers the question or completes the statement on the line provided.

_____ 1. Which of the following are pure substances?
   a. solutions
   b. compounds
   c. homogeneous mixtures
   d. colloids

_____ 2. A substance that is made up of only one kind of atom is a(an)
   a. compound.   b. homogeneous mixture.
   c. element.   d. solution.

_____ 3. What is the symbol for aluminum?
   a. AL   b. Al   c. Au   d. A

_____ 4. If a material contains three elements joined in a fixed proportion, it is a(an)
   a. mixture.   b. solution.
   c. atom.   d. compound.

_____ 5. Which of the following is a mixture?
   a. carbon dioxide   b. silicon
   c. silicon dioxide   d. sand

_____ 6. A mixture that appears to contain only one substance is a(an)
   a. homogeneous mixture.
   b. heterogeneous mixture.
   c. compound.
   d. element.

_____ 7. A mixture can be classified as a solution, suspension, or colloid based on the
   a. number of particles it contains.
   b. size of its largest particles.
   c. color of its particles.
   d. size of its smallest particles.

_____ 8. Which of the following is malleable?
   a. glass   b. pottery
   c. ice   d. gold

_____ 9. A substance has a melting point of 0°C and a boiling point of 100°C. The substance is most likely
   a. water.   b. hydrogen.
   c. gold.   d. table salt.

Chapter Test B

Name _____ Class _____ Date _____

_____ 10. What physical properties of nylon and leather make them good materials to use for shoelaces?
   a. high density and low conductivity
   b. durability and flexibility
   c. hardness and durability
   d. low viscosity and flexibility

_____ 11. Filtration can be used to separate mixtures based on
   a. their boiling points.
   b. their densities.
   c. their melting points.
   d. the size of their particles.

_____ 12. When a physical change occurs in a sample of matter which of the following does NOT change?
   a. shape   b. mass
   c. volume   d. composition

_____ 13. Flammability is a material's ability to burn in the presence of
   a. hydrogen.   b. nitrogen.
   c. oxygen.   d. carbon dioxide.

_____ 14. Which of the following is NOT a clue that a chemical change has occurred?
   a. change in color
   b. production of a gas
   c. formation of a precipitate
   d. change in shape

_____ 15. Which of the following is a chemical change?
   a. ice melting
   b. ice being carved
   c. water boiling
   d. water breaking down into hydrogen and oxygen

Completion
Complete each statement on the line provided.

1. Matter that always has exactly the same composition is classified as a(an) _____.
2. An element has a fixed composition because it contains only one type of _____.
3. The substances in a(an) _____ mixture are evenly distributed throughout the mixture.
4. If a spoon gets hot quickly when it is used to stir a pot of soup, it is probably made of _____.

Name _____ Class _____ Date _____

Melting and Boiling Points of Some Substances		
Substance	Melting Point	Boiling Point
Hydrogen	−259.3°C	−252.9°C
Nitrogen	−210.0°C	−195.8°C
Acetic Acid	16.6°C	117.9°C
Gold	1064.2°C	2856°C

Figure 2-1

5. Based on the information in Figure 2-1, the _____ point of nitrogen is −210.0°C and the _____ point of nitrogen is −195.8°C.

6. _____ is a process that could be used to separated dissolved particles from the liquid in a solution.

7. A(An) _____ change occurs when a material changes shape or size but composition does not change.

8. _____ properties can be observed only when the substances in a sample of matter are changing into different substances.

9. A solid that forms and separates from a liquid mixture is a(an) _____.

10. A cake rises as it bakes because a chemical change causes _____ to be produced.

Short Answer

In complete sentences, write the answers to the questions on the lines provided.

1. How do the properties of a compound compare to the properties of the elements it contains?

2. How is the composition of a substance different from the composition of a mixture?

3. If you looked at a glass containing a solution and a glass containing a suspension, how could you tell which glass contained the suspension?

Name _____ Class _____ Date _____

4. What are three common clues that a chemical change has occurred?

5. How is a chemical change different from a physical change?

Using Science Skills

Use the table to answer each question. Write the answers on a separate sheet of paper.

Physical Properties of Four Materials Used to Make Sculptures			
	Malleability	Hardness	Melting Point
Wax	Soft enough to be carved and molded	Soft but keeps its shape at room temperature	Low melting point
Unbaked clay	Can be molded	Soft	Very high melting point
Baked clay	Brittle after being baked at a high temperature	Hard	Very high melting point
Metal (a mixture of copper, zinc, and lead)	Can be hammered without shattering	Hard	High melting point

Figure 2-2

1. **Comparing and Contrasting** Use Figure 2-2 to compare the physical properties of clay before and after it is baked at a high temperature.

2. **Using Tables and Graphs** Which of the materials in Figure 2-2 are malleable?

3. **Comparing and Contrasting** Based on the information in Figure 2-2, compare the properties of a sculpture made from metal and a sculpture made from baked clay.

4. **Inferring** An object made from a material listed in Figure 2-2 changes shape when you leave it in a sunny window. Which material is the object made from? How do you know?

5. **Inferring** Which of the materials described in Figure 2-2 would be least likely to be recycled? Explain your choice.

Chapter 2 Test A Answers

Multiple Choice

1. a **2.** d **3.** a **4.** d **5.** a **6.** c
7. d **8.** a **9.** c **10.** d **11.** b **12.** a
13. a **14.** b **15.** d

Completion

1. elements, compounds **2.** one, two **3.** compounds
4. reactive **5.** physical, chemical

Short Answer

1. Accept any of the following: by adding more of a substance in the mixture; by adding a new substance; by removing a substance from the mixture. **2.** acetic acid, and gold **3.** The viscosity of a liquid usually decreases as the liquid is heated and increases as the liquid cools. **4.** For a physical change that can be reversed, accept any of the following: freezing water, melting ice, braiding hair, wrinkling clothes. For a physical change that cannot be reversed, accept any of the following: cutting hair, slicing a tomato, peeling an orange. **5.** a chemical change

Using Science Skills

1. A heterogeneous mixture; the mixture scatters light, separates into layers, and can be separated by filtration.
2. Mixture B; it does not scatter light, does not separate into layers, and cannot be separated by filtration.
3. Mixture A; it scatters light, does not separate into layers, and cannot be separated by filtration.
4. Mixture B, Mixture A, Mixture C
5. Possible answer: Mixture B is a solution and all the particles would pass through a filter. Distillation might be used to separate the substances in Mixture B.

Essay

1. Water is a liquid at room temperature, does not burn, and can be used to put out fires. Oxygen and hydrogen are the elements that make up water. Both elements are gases at room temperature. Hydrogen can fuel a fire, and oxygen can keep a fire burning.
2. Silver has a known density at room temperature (10.5 g/cm^3). You can measure the density of the coin and compare it to the density of silver. If the densities of the coin and silver are the same, the coin is pure silver. If the densities of the coin and silver are different, the coin contains at least one other substance in addition to silver. **3.** Filtration would be used because it is the process of separating mixtures based on the size of their particles (or pieces). A screen could be used to separate the mixture. The holes in the screen would need to be large enough to allow the soil to pass through but not the leaves, acorn, or twigs. **4.** Rust forms in the tanks because oxygen dissolved in the water reacts with iron in the steel. Nitrogen gas can be pumped into the tanks. The nitrogen displaces some of the dissolved oxygen. Because nitrogen is less reactive than oxygen, less rust forms. **5.** With no other evidence, the gas could be the result of either a physical or chemical change. A liquid could be changing to a gas, which is a physical change. A reaction that produces a gas could be occurring as the liquid is heated. Without testing the composition of the liquid before and after heating, there is no way to tell.

Chapter 2 Test B Answers

Multiple Choice

1. b **2.** c **3.** b **4.** d **5.** d **6.** a
7. b **8.** d **9.** a **10.** b **11.** d **12.** d
13. c **14.** d **15.** d

Completion

1. pure substance; substance **2.** atom **3.** homogeneous
4. metal **5.** melting, boiling **6.** Distillation **7.** physical **8.** Chemical
9. precipitate **10.** a gas; carbon dioxide

Short Answer

1. They are different. **2.** The composition of a substance is fixed, while the composition of a mixture can vary. **3.** Accept any of the following: the suspension would appear cloudy, while the solution would be clear; the particles in the suspension would settle to the bottom, while the particles in the solution would not settle.
4. a change in color, the production of a gas, and the formation of a precipitate **5.** A chemical change involves a change in the composition of matter. During a physical change, the composition of matter does not change.

Using Science Skills

1. Before clay is baked, it is soft and can be molded. After clay is baked, it is hard and brittle. **2.** wax, unbaked clay, and metal
3. Both sculptures would be hard and would only melt at very high temperatures. The metal sculpture might be dented if it was hammered, but if the sculpture made from baked clay was hammered, it would shatter. **4.** The object would have been made from wax because wax has a low melting point. It is the only material listed that would soften enough in a sunny window to change shape. **5.** Baked clay; it is brittle and shatters.

Chapter 3 States of Matter

Planning Guide

Use these planning tools
Easy Planner
Resource Pro
Online Lesson Planner

SECTION OBJECTIVES	STANDARDS		ACTIVITIES and LABS
	NATIONAL (See p. T18.)	STATE	
3.1 Solids, Liquids, and Gases, pp. 68–74 🕐 1 block or 2 periods **3.1.1 Describe** the five states of matter. **3.1.2 Classify** materials as solids, liquids, or gases. **3.1.3 Explain** the behavior of gases, liquids, and solids, using kinetic theory.	A-1, B-2, B-5, F-5, G-1, G-2, G-3		**SE** Inquiry Activity: How Easy Is It to Compress Air and Water? p. 67 **L2** **TE** Teacher Demo: Comparing Liquid Volume, p. 69 **L2** **TE** Teacher Demo: Detecting the Motion of a Gas, p. 72 **L2** **LM** Investigation 3B: Measuring Spaces Between Particles of Matter **L1**
3.2 The Gas Laws, pp. 75–81 🕐 1 block or 2 periods **3.2.1 Define** pressure and gas pressure. **3.2.2 Identify** factors that affect gas pressure. **3.2.3 Predict** changes in gas pressure due to changes in temperature, volume, and number of particles. **3.2.4 Explain** Charles's law, Boyle's law, and the combined gas law. **3.2.5 Apply** gas laws to solve problems involving gases.	A-1, A-2, B-2, B-4, B-5, G-1, G-2, G-3		**SE** Quick Lab: Observing the Effect of Temperature on Gas Pressure, p. 79 **L2** **TE** Build Science Skills: Observing, p. 75 **L2** **TE** Teacher Demo: Changing Volume of a Balloon, p. 76 **L2**
3.3 Phase Changes, pp. 84–91 🕐 1 block or 2 periods **3.3.1 Describe** phase changes. **3.3.2 Explain** how temperature can be used to recognize a phase change. **3.3.3 Explain** what happens to the motion, arrangement, and average kinetic energy of water molecules during phase changes. **3.3.4 Describe** each of the six phase changes. **3.3.5 Identify** phase changes as endothermic or exothermic.	A-1, A-2, B-2, B-5		**SE** Quick Lab: Observing Phase Changes, p. 90 **L2** **SE** Exploration Lab: Investigating Changes in Temperature During Heating of Solids, pp. 92–93 **L2** **TE** Teacher Demo: Energy Transfer, p. 86 **L2** **LM** Investigation 3A: Performing a Fractional Distillation **L2**

Ability Levels

L1 For students who need additional help
L2 For all students
L3 For students who need to be challenged

Components

SE	Student Edition	**GRSW**	Guided Reading & Study Workbook With Math Support	**CTB**	Computer Test Bank	**T**	Transparencies
TE	Teacher's Edition			**TP**	Test Prep Resources	**P**	Presentation Pro CD-ROM
LM	Laboratory Manual			**iT**	iText		
PLM	Probeware Lab Manual	**CUT**	Chapter and Unit Tests	**DC**	Discovery Channel Videotapes	**GO**	Internet Resources

RESOURCES PRINT and TECHNOLOGY		SECTION ASSESSMENT	
GRSW Section 3.1	L1	**SE** Section 3.1 Assessment, p. 74	
T Chapter 3 Pretest	L2	**iT** Section 3.1	
Section 3.1	L2		
P Chapter 3 Pretest	L2		
Section 3.1	L2		
SCILINKS **GO** Kinetic theory	L2		
GRSW Section 3.2	L1	**SE** Section 3.2 Assessment, p. 81	
GRSW Math Skill	L2	**iT** Section 3.2	
DC Up, Up, and Away	L2		
T Section 3.2	L2		
P Section 3.2	L2		
SCIENCE NEWS GO Properties of matter	L2		
PLM Lab 1: Investigating Changes in Temperature During Heating of Solids	L2	**SE** Section 3.3 Assessment, p. 91	
GRSW Section 3.3	L1	**iT** Section 3.3	
T Section 3.3	L2		
P Section 3.3	L2		
SCILINKS **GO** Phases of matter	L2		
PHSchool.com GO Data sharing	L2		

Go Online

Go online for these Internet resources.

PHSchool.com
Web Code: ccd-1030
Web Code: cca-1030

SCIENCE NEWS
Web Code: cce-1032

NSTA **SCI**LINKS
Web Code: ccn-1031
Web Code: ccn-1033

Materials for Activities and Labs

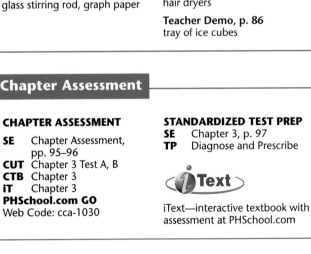

Quantities for each group

STUDENT EDITION

Inquiry Activity, p. 67
syringe (sealed at narrow end), water

Quick Lab, p. 79
pan, metric ruler, empty beverage can, masking tape, hot plate, clock, tongs

Quick Lab, p. 90
250-mL Erlenmeyer flask, graduated cylinder, thermometer, dry ice

Exploration Lab, pp. 92–93
500-mL beaker, crushed ice, thermometer, hot plate, clock with second hand, test tube of lauric acid with thermometer, glass stirring rod, graph paper

TEACHER'S EDITION

Teacher Demo, p. 69
3 glass jars or bottles with lids, each having a noticeably different diameter but about the same volume; graduated cylinder; water

Teacher Demo, p. 72
spray can of air freshener, 3 stopwatches

Build Science Skills, p. 75
clay, CD case, textbook

Teacher Demo, p. 76
inflated balloons, refrigerator, warm place

Build Science Skills, p. 82
plastic bag (dry cleaner or thin garbage bag), string, hair dryers

Teacher Demo, p. 86
tray of ice cubes

Chapter Assessment

CHAPTER ASSESSMENT

SE Chapter Assessment, pp. 95–96
CUT Chapter 3 Test A, B
CTB Chapter 3
iT Chapter 3
PHSchool.com GO
Web Code: cca-1030

STANDARDIZED TEST PREP

SE Chapter 3, p. 97
TP Diagnose and Prescribe

iText

iText—interactive textbook with assessment at PHSchool.com

LESSON PLAN 3.1

Solids, Liquids, and Gases

Time
2 periods
1 block

Section Objectives

- **3.1.1 Describe** the five states of matter.
- **3.1.2 Classify** materials as solids, liquids, or gases.
- **3.1.3 Explain** the behavior of gases, liquids, and solids, using kinetic theory

Vocabulary solid • liquid • gas • kinetic energy

Local Standards

1 FOCUS

Build Vocabulary: Word Origins
Explain that the origin of the word *gas* is the Greek word *khaos*. Point out that the English word *chaos* refers to a disordered state. Relate this definition to the relative disorder of gases. **L2**

Targeted Resources
❑ Transparency: Chapter 3 Pretest
❑ Transparency: Interest Grabber 3.1
❑ Transparency: Reading Strategy 3.1

2 INSTRUCT

Build Reading Literacy: Relate Text and Visuals
Have students compare the drawings of a solid and a liquid in Figures 2 and 3 to the definitions for these states of matter. **L1**

Use Visuals: Figure 6 and 7
Have students compare the models of collisions shown in Figures 6 and 7. Ask how the paths of the billiard balls and helium atoms are the same. Ask how the motion of the billiard balls is different from the motion of the helium atoms. **L1**

Teacher Demo: Comparing Liquid Volume
Using three jars of roughly the same volume, but each having different diameters, have students predict which container has the largest volume. Students observe that it is difficult to compare the volume of liquids in different containers because liquids take the shape of their containers. **L2**

Teacher Demo: Detecting the Motion of a Gas
Spray air freshener at a distant corner of the room, and have students located in various parts of the room time how long it takes before they smell the gas. Students infer that particles in gases are in constant motion. **L2**

Build Science Skills: Using Analogies
Have students think of analogies for the motion of particles in a liquid other than the analogy shown in Figure 8. **L2**

Build Science Skills: Using Models
Gently move a clear plastic box of marbles back and forth. Ask students what state of matter the model represents and how the particles in a solid are like the marbles in the model. **L2**

Targeted Resources
❑ GRSW Section 3.1
❑ **NSTA** *sci*INKS Kinetic theory

3 ASSESS

Reteach
Use Figure 1 to encourage students to think of practical applications in which the state of matter is important. **L1**

Evaluate Understanding
Have each student write a paragraph explaining how kinetic theory can be used to explain the general characteristics of solids, liquids, and gases. **L2**

Targeted Resources
❑ **PHSchool.com** Online Section 3.1 Assessment
❑ iText Section 3.1

Transparencies

25 **Chapter 3 Pretest**

1. What is the density of a sample whose mass is 12.02 g and whose volume is 6.01 mL?

2. Which of the following is an element?
   a. sand
   b. water
   c. gold
   d. sugar

3. Differentiate heterogeneous from homogenous mixtures.

4. Which of the following is not a step in a valid scientific method?
   a. developing a procedure to test your hypothesis
   b. drawing a conclusion without any supporting evidence
   c. forming a testable hypothesis
   d. making observations

ANSWERS
1. 2.00 g/mL
2. c
3. heterogeneous mixture: parts are noticeably different; homogeneous mixture: parts are difficult to distinguish
4. b

Transparencies

26 **Chapter 3 Pretest** *(continued)*

5. Identify the tools needed to measure temperature and length.

6. True or False: All of the following units are SI units: meter, pound, and kelvin.

7. Density, mass, and volume are related by the equation density = mass/volume. What equation would you use to find volume if you knew the density and mass?

8. Bromine boils at a temperature of 58.63°C. What is this temperature in kelvins?

ANSWERS
5. thermometer and ruler
6. False
7. volume = mass/density
8. 331.78 K

Transparencies

27 **Section 3.1 Interest Grabber**

States of Matter

Imagine that you have a baseball and a small packet of ketchup.

1. If you squeeze the ketchup packet, how would it change?

2. If you squeeze the baseball, how would it change?

3. What would these results tell you about the properties of solids and liquids?

ANSWERS
1. The shape of the packet would change.
2. The baseball would not change shape in any noticeable way.
3. Students may say that solids have a shape that doesn't change under ordinary circumstances but that a liquid can change shape (flow) as the shape of its container changes.

Transparencies

28 **Section 3.1 Reading Strategy**

Comparing and Contrasting

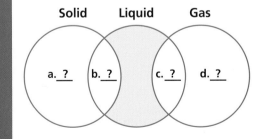

Solid   Liquid   Gas

a. ?   b. ?   c. ?   d. ?

ANSWERS
a. definite shape
b. definite volume
c. variable shape
d. variable volume

Name _____ Class _____ Date _____

Chapter 3   States of Matter

Section 3.1 Solids, Liquids, and Gases
(pages 68–73)

This section explains how materials are classified as solids, liquids, or gases. It also describes the behavior of these three states of matter.

Reading Strategy (page 68)

Comparing and Contrasting As you read about the states of matter, replace each letter in the diagram below with one of these phrases: *definite volume, definite shape, variable volume,* or *variable shape.* For more information on this Reading Strategy, see the **Reading and Study Skills** in the **Skills and Reference Handbook** at the end of your textbook.

Solid   Liquid   Gas

Definite shape   Definite volume   Variable shape   Variable volume

Describing the States of Matter (pages 68–70)

1. What are three common states of matter?
   a. _____Solids_____   b. _____Liquids_____   c. _____Gases_____

2. Is the following sentence true or false? The fact that a copper wire can be bent shows that some solids do not have a definite shape. _____false_____

3. Circle the letter of each phrase that describes how particles at the atomic level are arranged within most solids.
   a. randomly arranged   (b.) packed close together
   (c.) arranged in a regular pattern   d. spaced far apart

4. Is the following sentence true or false? A liquid takes the shape of its container. _____true_____

5. What is the state of matter in which a material has neither a definite shape nor a definite volume? _____gas_____

6. Compare and contrast the arrangement of particles at the atomic level for a liquid and a solid. _Particles in a solid are packed close together in an orderly arrangement. The arrangement of particles in a liquid is more random._

7. What determines the shape and volume of a gas? _A gas takes the shape and volume of its container._

8. On the sun, where temperatures are extremely high, matter exists in a state known as _____plasma_____.

Name _____ Class _____ Date _____

Chapter 3   States of Matter

9. The state of matter that can exist at extremely _____low_____ temperatures is called a Bose-Einstein condensate.

10. Complete the table about states of matter.

States of Matter		
State	**Shape**	**Volume**
Solid	Definite	Definite
Liquid	Not definite	Definite
Gas	Not definite	Not definite

Kinetic Theory (page 71)

11. Describe kinetic energy. _Kinetic energy is the energy an object has due to its motion._

12. Circle the letter of the phrase that describes all particles of matter in the kinetic theory of matter.
   a. randomly arranged   b. constant temperature
   (c.) in constant motion   d. orderly arrangement

Explaining the Behavior of Gases (pages 72–73)

13. Is the following sentence true or false? There are forces of attraction among the particles in all matter. _____true_____

14. Why can scientists ignore the forces of attraction among particles in a gas under ordinary conditions? _The particles in a gas are apart and moving fast, so the forces of attraction are too weak to have a noticeable effect._

15. Is the following sentence true or false? Because of the constant motion of the particles in a gas, the gas has a definite shape and volume. _____false_____

Explaining the Behavior of Liquids (page 73)

16. Do forces of attraction have a stronger effect on the behavior of the particles in a gas or in a liquid? _____a liquid_____

17. Circle the letter of each factor that affects the behavior of liquids.
   a. fixed location of particles
   (b.) constant motion of particles
   c. orderly arrangement of particles
   (d.) forces of attraction among particles

Explaining the Behavior of Solids (page 74)

18. Solids have a(n) _____definite_____ volume and shape because particles in a solid vibrate in _____fixed_____ locations.

LESSON PLAN 3.2

The Gas Laws

Time
2 periods
1 block

Section Objectives

- **3.2.1 Define** pressure and gas pressure.
- **3.2.2 Identify** factors that affect gas pressure.
- **3.2.3 Predict** changes in gas pressure due to changes in temperature, volume, and number of particles.
- **3.2.4 Explain** Charles's law, Boyle's law, and the combined gas law.
- **3.2.5 Apply** gas laws to solve problems involving gases.

Vocabulary pressure • absolute zero • Charles's law • Boyle's law

Local Standards

1 FOCUS

Build Vocabulary: Paraphrase
Replace less familiar words in a definition with more familiar words or phrases. **L2**

Targeted Resources
❑ Transparency: Interest Grabber 3.2
❑ Transparency: Reading Strategy 3.2

2 INSTRUCT

Build Reading Literacy: Predict
Have students predict how increasing or decreasing volume, temperature, and number of particles will affect gas pressure in a closed container. **L1**

Use Visuals: Figure 14
Ask students what variables change as the balloon in Figure 14 rises. Ask students how the variables change. Ask students how each change affects the volume of the balloon. **L1**

Build Science Skills: Observing
Students use clay to learn the effect of area on pressure. **L2**

Teacher Demo: Changing Volume of a Balloon
Place balloons that have been refrigerated overnight in a warm place so that students can observe the effect of temperature on the volume of a balloon. **L2**

Quick Lab: Observing the Effect of Temperature on Gas Pressure
Students heat a can and place it upside down in a pan of cold water, in order to predict the effect of temperature on the pressure of a gas. **L2**

Integrate Math
Have students show how the combined gas law can be used to derive Boyle's law and Charles's law. **L2**

Targeted Resources
❑ Transparency: Figure 13A: Charles's Law
❑ Transparency: Figure 13B: Boyle's Law
❑ Transparency: Math Skills: The Combined Gas Law
❑ GRSW Section 3.2

3 ASSESS

Reteach
Write Charles's law and Boyle's law on the board. Have students quiz each other about the behavior of the responding variable when another variable increases or decreases. **L1**

Evaluate Understanding
Have students look at the mathematical presentations of Charles's law on p. 78 and Boyle's law on p. 79 and describe the relationships in their own words. **L2**

Targeted Resources
❑ **PHSchool.com** Online Section 3.2 Assessment
❑ iText Section 3.2

Transparencies

29 Section 3.2 Interest Grabber

Inside a Helium Balloon

A tank of compressed helium gas is often used to fill party balloons.

1. What is happening to the helium atoms inside the balloon?

2. What might happen if more helium were added to the balloon? How could adding more helium cause this result?

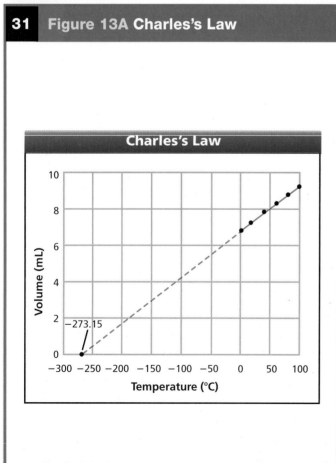

ANSWERS
1. The atoms are constantly moving. They move in a straight line until they collide with other atoms or the inner surface of the balloon.
2. If enough helium is added to the balloon, it will burst. Accept any logical explanation.

Transparencies

30 Section 3.2 Reading Strategy

Identifying Cause and Effect

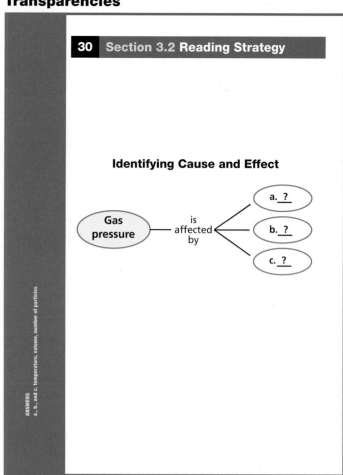

ANSWERS
a., b., and c. temperature, volume, number of particles

Transparencies

31 Figure 13A Charles's Law

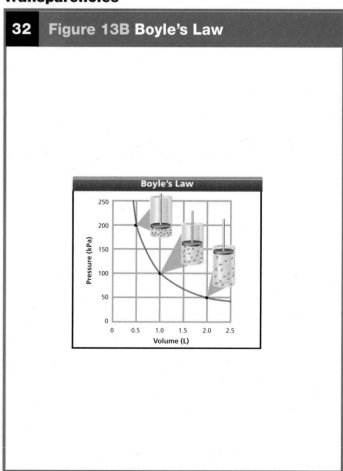

Transparencies

32 Figure 13B Boyle's Law

| 33 | **Math Skills The Combined Gas Law** |

The Combined Gas Law

A cylinder that contains air at a pressure of 100 kPa has a volume of 0.75 L. The pressure is increased to 300 kPa. The temperature does not change. Find the new volume of air.

1 Read and Understand

What information are you given?

$$P_1 = 100 \text{ kPa} \qquad P_2 = 300 \text{ kPa} \qquad V_1 = 0.75 \text{ L}$$

2 Plan and Solve

What unknown are you trying to calculate?

$$V_2$$

What expression can you use?

$$\frac{P_1 V_1}{T_1} = \frac{P_2 V_2}{T_2}$$

Cancel out the variable that does not change and rearrange the expression to solve for V_2.

$$P_1 V_1 = P_2 V_2 \qquad V_2 = \frac{P_1 V_1}{P_2}$$

| 34 | **Math Skills The Combined Gas Law** *(continued)* |

Replace each variable with its known value.

$$V_2 = 100 \text{ kPa} \times \frac{0.75 \text{ L}}{300 \text{ kPa}} = 0.25 \text{ L}$$

3 Look Back and Check

Is your answer reasonable?

Volume should decrease as pressure increases. The pressure tripled from 100 kPa to 300 kPa. The answer, 0.25 L, is one third the original volume, 0.75 L.

Guided Reading and Study Workbook

Name _____ Class _____ Date _____

Chapter 3   States of Matter

Section 3.2 The Gas Laws
(pages 75–81)

This section discusses gas pressure and the factors that affect it. It also explains the relationships between the temperature, volume, and pressure of a gas.

Reading Strategy (page 75)

Identifying Cause and Effect As you read, identify the variables that affect gas pressure, and write them in the diagram below. For more information on this Reading Strategy, see the **Reading and Study Skills** in the **Skills and Reference Handbook** at the end of your textbook.

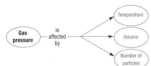

Pressure (pages 75–76)

1. What is pressure? Pressure is a result of a force distributed over an area.

2. Circle the letter of each unit used to express amounts of pressure.
   a. newton
   b. joule
   (c.) pascal
   (d.) kilopascal

3. What causes the pressure in a closed container of gas? Collisions between particles of gas and the walls of the container cause the pressure.

Factors that Affect Gas Pressure (pages 76–77)

4. Name the factors that affect the pressure of an enclosed gas.
   a. ___Its temperature___   b. ___Its volume___   c. ___The number of its particles___

5. Is the following sentence true or false? In a closed container, increasing the temperature of a gas will decrease the force with which particles hit the walls of the container. ___false___

6. What effect does raising the temperature of a gas have on its pressure, if the volume of the gas and the number of its particles are kept constant? The pressure of the gas will increase.

7. How does reducing the volume of a gas affect its pressure if the temperature of the gas and the number of particles are constant?
Reducing the volume of a gas increases its pressure if the temperature and volume are constant.

8. Increasing the number of particles of a gas will ___increase___ its pressure if the temperature and the volume are constant.

Guided Reading and Study Workbook

Name _____ Class _____ Date _____

Chapter 3   States of Matter

Charles's Law (page 78)

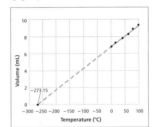

9. Jacques Charles recorded the behavior of gases on a graph like the one above. The data shows that the volume of a gas increases at the same rate as the ___temperature___ of the gas.

10. A temperature equal to 0 K on the Kelvin temperature scale is known as ___absolute zero___.

11. What does Charles's law state? The volume of a gas is directly proportional to its temperature in kelvins if the pressure and the number of particles of the gas are constant.

Boyle's Law (page 79)

12. If the temperature and number of particles of gas in a cylinder do not change, and the volume of the cylinder is reduced by half, the pressure of the gas will be ___twice as much___ as the original pressure.

13. Boyle's law states that there is an inverse relationship between the pressure and volume of a gas. Circle the letter of the correct expression of this relationship.
   (a.) $P_1 V_1 = P_2 V_2$
   b. $P_1 V_2 = P_2 V_1$
   c. $\dfrac{P_1}{V_1} = \dfrac{P_2}{V_2}$
   d. $P_1 P_2 = V_1 V_2$

The Combined Gas Law (pages 80–81)

14. Circle the letters of the factors that are included in the expression of the combined gas law.
   (a.) temperature
   b. number of particles
   (c.) volume
   (d.) pressure

Name_____ Class_____ Date_____ M T W T F

Phase Changes

Time
2 periods
1 block

Section Objectives

Local Standards

- **3.3.1 Describe** phase changes.

- **3.3.2 Explain** how temperature can be used to recognize a phase change.

- **3.3.3 Explain** what happens to the motion, arrangement, and average kinetic energy of water molecules during phase changes.

- **3.3.4 Describe** each of the six phase changes.

- **3.3.5 Identify** phase changes as endothermic or exothermic.

Vocabulary phase change • endothermic • heat of fusion • exothermic • vaporization • heat of vaporization • evaporation • vapor pressure • condensation • sublimation • deposition

1 FOCUS

Build Vocabulary: Word-Part Analysis
List on the board the following word parts and meanings: *-ion*, "the act of" or "the result of an action"; *-ic*, "related to or characterized by"; *endo-*, "inside"; *exo-*, "outside"; *therm*, "heat"; *-ize*, "to become." Have students identify these word parts in the vocabulary terms. **L2**

Targeted Resources
❏ Transparency: Interest Grabber 3.3
❏ Transparency: Reading Strategy 3.3

2 INSTRUCT

Use Visuals: Figure 15
Ask students which two phases of water are visible in Figure 15. Ask them where the third phase would most likely be located. **L1**

Teacher Demo: Energy Transfer
Place a tray of ice cubes on a counter at the beginning of class so that it begins to melt during the course of the class. Students observe that the phase change from ice to water is endothermic. **L2**

For Enrichment
Challenge students to propose a way to have solid, liquid, and gaseous water together in the same test tube. **L3**

Targeted Resources
❏ Transparency: Figure 16: Phase Changes
❏ Transparency: Figure 17: Heating Curve for Naphthalene
❏ GRSW Section 3.2
❏ **NSTA** *scilINKS* Phases of matter

3 ASSESS

Reteach
Use Figure 16 to review the six phase changes described in this section. Ask what the phase changes with red arrows have in common. Ask what the phase changes with blue arrows have in common. **L1**

Evaluate Understanding
Have students write the six terms that describe phase changes. Next to each term, students should describe the type of change. **L2**

Targeted Resources
❏ **PHSchool.com** Online Section 3.3 Assessment
❏ iText Section 3.3

Transparencies

35 Section 3.3 Interest Grabber

Three States of Water

Water is an abundant substance on Earth. It can be found as a solid, a liquid, and as a gas called water vapor.

1. How many words can you think of to describe solid water?

2. Where is most of the liquid water on Earth found? Where is most of the water vapor found?

3. Describe a natural event you have observed when water changed from a liquid to a solid? When water changed from a liquid to a vapor?

ANSWERS
1. Student answers may include forms such as ice, sleet, snow, or hail or formations such as glaciers, icebergs, and ice caps.
2. Most liquid water is found in oceans (which cover 71% of Earth's surface). Water vapor is found in Earth's atmosphere.
3. Student answers may include a pond freezing over or water evaporating from a puddle.

Transparencies

36 Section 3.3 Reading Strategy

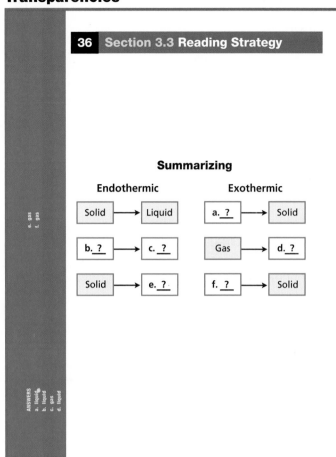

Summarizing

Endothermic   Exothermic

e. gas
f. gas

ANSWERS
a. liquid
b. liquid
c. gas
d. liquid

Transparencies

37 Figure 16 **Phase Changes**

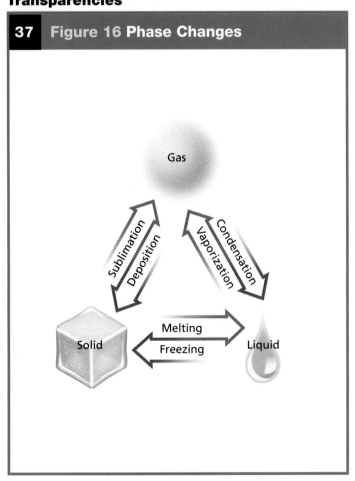

Transparencies

38 Figure 17 Heating Curve for Naphthalene

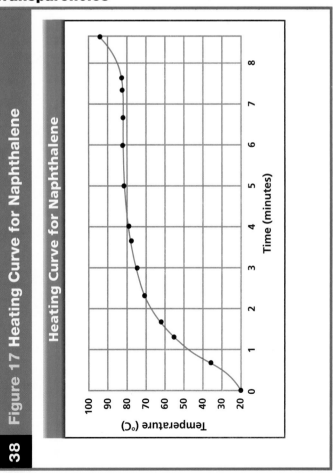

Heating Curve for Naphthalene

Guided Reading and Study Workbook

Name _____ Class _____ Date _____

Chapter 3   States of Matter

Section 3.3 Phase Changes
(pages 84–91)

This section explains what happens when a substance changes from one state of matter to another and describes six phase changes.

Reading Strategy (page 84)

Summarizing As you read, complete the description of energy flow during phase changes in the diagram below. For more information on this Reading Strategy, see the **Reading and Study Skills** in the **Skills and Reference Handbook** at the end of your textbook.

Endothermic

Solid → Liquid

Liquid → Gas

Solid → Gas

Exothermic

Liquid → Solid

Gas → Liquid

Gas → Solid

Characteristics of Phase Changes (pages 84–86)

1. What is a phase change? <u>A phase change is the reversible physical change that takes place</u>
   <u>when a substance changes from one state of matter to another.</u>

Match each term with the letter of the phase-change description that best describes it.

Term	Phase-Change
<u>d</u> 2. freezing	a. Solid to gas
<u>a</u> 3. sublimation	b. Liquid to gas
<u>e</u> 4. condensation	c. Gas to solid
<u>f</u> 5. melting	d. Liquid to solid
<u>c</u> 6. deposition	e. Gas to liquid
<u>b</u> 7. vaporization	f. Solid to liquid

8. What happens to the temperature of a substance during a phase change? <u>The temperature of a substance remains constant during a phase change.</u>

9. Is the following sentence true or false? The temperature at which a substance freezes is lower than the temperature at which it melts. _____false_____

10. Circle the letter that describes the behavior of a substance during a phase change.
    a. neither absorbs nor releases energy   b. always absorbs energy
    c. always releases energy   (d.) either absorbs or releases energy

---

Guided Reading and Study Workbook

Name _____ Class _____ Date _____

Chapter 3   States of Matter

11. A substance absorbs energy from its surroundings during a(n) ___endothermic___ change.

12. The energy absorbed by one gram of ice as it melts is known as the _____heat of fusion_____ for water.

13. As water freezes, it releases heat to its surroundings. Freezing is an example of a(n) ___exothermic___ change.

Melting and Freezing (page 88)

14. Is the following sentence true or false? Water molecules have a more orderly arrangement in ice than in liquid water. _____true_____

15. When liquid water freezes, the average kinetic energy of its molecules _____decreases_____, and the arrangement of the molecules becomes more orderly.

Vaporization and Condensation (page 88–90)

16. Vaporization is the phase change in which a substance changes from a(n) ___liquid___ into a(n) ___gas___.

17. The energy absorbed by one gram of water as it changes from its liquid phase into water vapor is known as the _____heat of vaporization_____ for water.

18. Is the following sentence true or false? When water vapor collects above the liquid in a closed container, the pressure caused by the collisions of this vapor and the walls of the container is called vapor pressure. _____true_____

19. The phase change in which a substance changes from a gas into a liquid is called _____condensation_____.

20. Compare and contrast the processes of evaporation and boiling by completing the table below.

Evaporation and Boiling			
Process	**Phase Change**	**Where It Occurs**	**Temperature**
Evaporation	Vaporization	At the surface of a liquid	Below the boiling point of the liquid
Boiling	Vaporization	Throughout a liquid	At the boiling point of the liquid

21. Is the following sentence true or false? A gas absorbs energy as it changes into a liquid. _____false_____

Sublimation and Deposition (page 91)

22. Dry ice can change directly from a solid to a gas without forming a liquid first. This process is an example of ___sublimation___.

23. What is deposition? <u>Deposition is the phase change in which a substance changes directly</u>
    <u>from a gas to a solid without changing to a liquid first.</u>

Guided Reading and Study Workbook

Name _____ Class _____ Date _____

Chapter 3   States of Matter

WordWise

Answer the questions by writing the correct vocabulary term in the blanks. Use the circled letter in each term to find the hidden vocabulary word. Then, write a definition for the hidden word.

Clues	Vocabulary Terms
What is the process that changes a substance from a liquid to a gas below the substance's boiling point?	e v a ⓟ o r a t i o n
Which gas law states that the volume of a gas is directly proportional to its temperature?	C h a ⓡ l e s's L a w
What is the phase change in which a substance changes directly from a gas to a solid?	d ⓔ p o s i t i o n
In what state does matter have both a definite shape and a definite volume?	ⓢ o l i d
What is the phase change in which a substance changes from a gas to a liquid?	c o n d e n ⓢ a t i o n
What is the phase change in which a substance changes directly from a solid to a gas?	s ⓤ b l i m a t i o n
During what type of phase change does a substance release energy to its surroundings?	e x o t h e ⓡ m i c
During what type of phase change does a substance absorb energy from its surroundings?	ⓔ n d o t h e r m i c

Hidden Term: <u>p r e s s u r e</u>

Definition: <u>The property of matter that is the result of a force distributed over an area.</u>

Guided Reading and Study Workbook

Name _____ Class _____ Date _____

Chapter 3   States of Matter

The Combined Gas Law

A gas in a cylinder has a pressure of 235 kPa at a volume of 5.00 L. The volume is reduced to 1.25 L. The temperature does not change. Find the new pressure of the gas.

Math Skill: Calculating with Significant Figures

You may want to read more about this **Math Skill** in the **Skills and Reference Handbook** at the end of your textbook.

1. Read and Understand

What information are you given?

$V_1 = 5.00$ L $V_2 = 1.25$ L $P_1 = 235$ kPa

2. Plan and Solve

What unknown are you trying to calculate? P_2

What expression can you use?

$$\frac{P_1 V_1}{T_1} = \frac{P_2 V_2}{T_2}$$

Cancel out the variable that does not change and rearrange the expression to solve for P_2.

$$P_1 V_1 = P_2 V_2 \qquad P_2 = \frac{P_1 V_1}{V_2}$$

Replace each variable with its known value.

$$P_2 = 235 \text{ kPa} \times \frac{5.00 \text{ L}}{1.25 \text{ L}} = 940 \text{ kPa}$$

3. Look Back and Check

Is your answer reasonable?

The volume of a gas is inversely proportional to its pressure if the temperature and number of particles are constant. The volume decreased by a factor of four, from 5.00 L to 1.25 L. The answer, 940 kPa, is four times the original pressure, 235 kPa.

Math Practice

On a separate sheet of paper, solve the following problems. The number of particles remains constant for all problems.

1. A gas has a pressure of 340 kPa at a volume of 3.20 L. What happens to the pressure when the volume is increased to 5.44 L? The temperature does not change. $P_2 = 340 \text{ kPa} \times \dfrac{3.20 \text{ L}}{5.44 \text{ L}} = 200 \text{ kPa}$

2. A gas has a pressure of 180 kPa at a temperature of 300 K. At what temperature will the gas have a pressure of 276 kPa? The volume does not change. $T_2 = 276 \text{ kPa} \times \dfrac{300 \text{ K}}{180 \text{ kPa}} = 460 \text{ K}$

3. At 47°C, a gas has a pressure of 140 kPa. The gas is cooled until the pressure decreases to 105 kPa. If the volume remains constant, what will the final temperature be in Kelvins? In degrees Celsius?

   $K = 273 \text{ K} + 47°C = 320 \text{ K}$ $T_2 = \dfrac{105 \text{ kPa}}{140 \text{ kPa}} \times 320 \text{ K} = 240 \text{ K}$
   $240 \text{ K} - 273 = -33°C$

Name _____ Class _____ Date _____

Chapter 3   States of Matter   Exploration Lab

Investigating Changes in Temperature During Heating of Solids

See pages 92 and 93 in the Teacher's Edition for more information.

Lauric acid is a solid that is found in coconuts and processed foods that are made with coconut oil. Lauric acid is also used to make some soaps and cosmetics. In this lab, you will measure the temperature of ice and of lauric acid as these solids are heated and melt. You will graph the data you collect and compare the heating curves for ice and lauric acid.

Problem What happens to the temperature of a substance during a phase change?

Materials
- 500-mL beaker
- crushed ice
- thermometer
- hot plate
- clock or watch with second hand
- test tube of lauric acid with thermometer
- glass stirring rod
- graph paper

Skills Measuring, Using Graphs

Procedure 🖾 🖽 🗓 🖾 🖾

Part A: Heating Ice

1. Fill a 500-mL beaker halfway with crushed ice. **CAUTION:** *Use care when handling glassware to avoid breakage. Wipe up any spilled ice immediately to avoid slips and falls.*

2. Place the beaker on a hot plate. Don't turn the hot plate on yet. Insert a thermometer into the ice. It takes several seconds for the thermometer to adjust to the temperature of its surroundings. Wait 20 seconds and then measure the temperature of the ice. Record this temperature next to the 0 minutes entry in the data table.

DATA TABLE

Time (minutes)	Temperature of Water (°C)	Temperature of Lauric Acid (°C)
0		
1		

3. Turn the hot plate to a low setting. **CAUTION:** *Be careful not to touch the hot plate because contact with the hot plate could cause a burn.*

4. Observe and record the temperature at one-minute intervals until all the ice has changed to liquid water. Circle the temperature at which you first observe liquid water and the temperature at which all the ice has changed to liquid water.

5. After all the ice has melted, make five more measurements of the temperature at one-minute intervals. Turn off the hot plate.

6. On a separate sheet of graph paper, graph your data with time on the horizontal axis and temperature on the vertical axis.

Part B: Heating Lauric Acid

7. Empty the water from the beaker into the sink. Fill the beaker halfway with cool tap water.

8. Place a test tube containing lauric acid and a thermometer into the beaker. If necessary, add or remove water from the beaker so that the surface of the water is above the surface of the lauric acid but below the opening of the test tube.

9. Place the beaker on the hot plate. After 20 seconds, measure the temperature of the lauric acid. Record this temperature next to the 0 minutes entry in the data table.

10. Repeat Steps 3 through 6, using the lauric acid instead of the ice. To keep the temperature the same throughout the water bath, use the glass stirring rod to stir the water after you take each temperature measurement.

Analyze and Conclude

1. **Using Graphs** Describe the shape of your graph for ice.

   The graph rises quickly to 0°C and remains horizontal at that temperature for a number of

   minutes. Then, it begins to rise again.

2. **Analyzing Data** What happened to the temperature of the ice-water mixture during the phase change?

   The temperature remained constant until the phase change was completed.

3. **Drawing Conclusions** What happened to the energy that was transferred from the hot plate to the ice during the phase change?

   At first, the energy absorbed by the ice was used to overcome the forces of attraction holding

   water molecules in fixed positions. After all of the ice had melted, the energy absorbed increased

   the kinetic energy of the molecules in the liquid water.

4. **Comparing and Contrasting** Compare the shapes of the ice and lauric acid graphs. Compare the melting points of ice and lauric acid.

   The two graphs had similar shapes. However, ice melted at 0°C and lauric acid melted at

   about 43°C.

Lab Manual

Lab Manual

Name _____ Class _____ Date _____

Chapter 3   States of Matter   Investigation 3A

Desalinization by Distillation

Refer students to pages 84–91 in their textbooks for a discussion of phase changes. **SKILLS FOCUS:** Observing, Designing Experiments **CLASS TIME:** Part A, 30 minutes; Part B, 20 minutes setup, 1–2 weeks for completion

Background Information

"Water, water everywhere, but not a drop to drink." This quotation is from *The Rime of the Ancient Mariner* by Samuel Coleridge, a poem that describes the fate of sailors in a boat that is stranded in the middle of the Pacific Ocean. The sailors are surrounded by water that they cannot drink. Both fresh water and seawater contain dissolved salts. But the amount of dissolved salts in a liter of seawater is much larger. Drinking seawater causes water to flow out of cells in the body, which increases dehydration. This effect is the exact opposite of the desired effect of drinking water.

In regions where the supply of fresh water is limited, seawater can be treated to make it safe to drink. The general name for processes that remove salts from seawater is desalinization. One method for separating dissolved salts from water is called distillation. During a distillation process, a liquid undergoes phase changes—vaporization followed by condensation.

Temperature and pressure affect the rate of vaporization. At atmospheric pressure, the rate of vaporization will be most rapid when a liquid is at a temperature equal to its boiling point. The container in which the hot vapor is collected must be chilled so that the vapor will rapidly condense. Distilling a liquid at its boiling point requires heat-resistant containers and a source of energy to heat the liquid, such as a gas burner. Sunlight can be used as the source of energy for distillation, but the process will take more time.

In Part A of this investigation, you will distill salt water by heating and boiling the salt water. In Part B of this investigation, you will use sunlight to vaporize the water.

Problem

How is the desalinization of salt water accomplished by distillation?

Pre-Lab Discussion

Read the entire investigation. Then, work with a partner to answer the following questions.

1. **Predicting** In Part A, how will the contents of the cooled flask differ from the contents of the heated flask?

   The liquid in the heated flask contains dissolved salts. The liquid in the cooled flask will not contain

   dissolved salts.

2. **Measuring** In Part A, are you measuring the temperature of the liquid in the flask or the vapor? Explain your answer.

   Because the bulb of the thermometer is located in the space above the liquid, the thermometer

   records the temperature of the vapor.

Name _____ Class _____ Date _____

3. **Designing Experiments** In Part B, why is it important to keep the clear bottle away from direct sunlight?

   The temperature of the clear bottle must be kept low enough so that the water

   vapor will condense.

4. **Formulating Hypotheses** In Part B, why is the bottle containing the salt water placed on a board? (*Hint:* Assume that some water vapor condenses in the plastic tubing.)

   If the bottles were at the same height, the tube would be level and any condensed water vapor

   could flow back into the black-painted bottle, which would defeat the goal of the distillation.

5. **Inferring** Differences in what physical property are used to separate the table salt from the water in the salt-water mixture?

   Differences in boiling point are used to separate the dissolved table salt from water.

Materials *(per group)*

2 250-mL flasks	ring stand and ring	Wrap the tubing in a thick towel for your protection when gently inserting it in the stopper. Use a lubricant such as glycerol. **CAUTION:** Inserting glass through a stopper can cause the glass to break. Then, gently insert the thermometer until the thermometer bulb is 2 to 4 cm below the bottom of the stopper. To reduce the risk of breakage, you may wish to attach the plastic tubing to the right-angle glass tubing in advance. Prepare the mixture by dissolving 50 g of salt for each liter of tap water. Paint half of the plastic bottles black under a fume hood or outside.
100-mL graduated cylinder	wire gauze	
500-mL beaker	salt water	
Lab burner	crushed ice	
2-hole rubber stopper with glass tubing and non-mercury thermometer inserted	2 2-L plastic bottles	
	electrical or masking tape	
	wooden board, at least 3 cm thick	
2 40-cm pieces of clear plastic tubing	glass marking pencil	
	graph paper	

Safety 🖾 🖽 🗓 🗓 🖾 🖾 🖾 🖾

Put on safety goggles and a lab apron. Be careful to avoid breakage when working with glassware. Never touch or taste any chemical unless instructed to do so. Use extreme care when working with heated equipment or materials to avoid burns. Observe proper laboratory procedures when using electrical equipment. Tie back loose hair and clothing when working with flames. Be careful when using matches. Do not reach over an open flame. Note all safety alert symbols next to the steps in the Procedure and review the meaning of each symbol by referring to the Safety Symbols on page xiii.

Lab Manual

Name _____ Class _____ Date _____

Procedure
Part A: Distillation of Salt Water By Boiling

1. Set up the apparatus, as shown in Figure 1. **CAUTION:** *Be sure that all glassware used in this investigation is heat-resistant.*

2. Place 100 mL of the salt-water solution in the flask to be heated.

3. Gently push one end of the rubber tubing onto the right-angle glass tubing. Place the stopper containing the right-angle glass tubing and thermometer firmly on the flask of salt water. The bulb of the thermometer should be near the top of the flask and not in the liquid. If necessary, ask your teacher to adjust the position of the thermometer.

4. Fill the beaker with crushed ice and set it away from the burner. Place the second flask in the crushed ice. Insert the open end of the plastic tubing in the middle of the flask, making sure that the tubing does not touch the bottom of the flask.

If you are using a hot plate instead of a Bunsen burner, use a flat-bottomed (Erlenmeyer) flask for the salt-water solution. Have students begin with the hot plate set to a high setting, and reset to a lower setting once the liquid begins to boil.

Figure 1

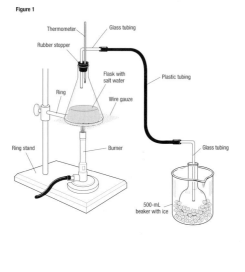

Thermometer
Glass tubing
Rubber stopper
Flask with salt water
Plastic tubing
Ring
Wire gauze
Ring stand
Burner
Glass tubing
500-mL beaker with ice

Lab Manual

Name _____ Class _____ Date _____

5. Observe the temperature in the flask containing salt water. Record this temperature in the data table. Turn on the burner. Note and record the temperature at 2-minute intervals as you complete Steps 6 and 7. Attach a separate sheet of paper if you need more space to record the temperature.

6. When the temperature stops rising, you should notice a liquid beginning to collect in the flask in the beaker of crushed ice. Circle the temperature at this time in the data table. **CAUTION:** *Do not allow the plastic tubing to touch the liquid being collected.*

7. Continue collecting liquid in the cooled flask until about three-fourths of the liquid in the heated flask has been vaporized. Turn off the burner.

8. Observe the appearance of the contents of the cooled flask and the heated flask.

9. Allow the heated flask to cool. **CAUTION:** *Be careful in handling equipment that has been heated. Hot glass looks like cold glass. Do not touch the heated flask or burner.*

10. When the flask has cooled enough to handle, pour both of the solutions down the drain. *Instead of disposing of the distillate and the concentrated salt solutions, you may want to collect them in marked containers and use them for the Go Further activity.*

If the tubing is below the liquid, the condensed liquid may be drawn back into the tubing. If this occurs, help students to shake the liquid back out of the tubing into the cooled flask. If the liquid spills back into the heated flask, students will need to repeat the distillation.

Observations

DATA TABLE Sample data are shown.

Time (minutes)	Temperature (°C)
0	22
2	26
4	40
6	60
8	80
10	100
12	100
14	100
16	100

Lab Manual

Name _____ Class _____ Date _____

Part B: Distillation of Salt Water by Evaporation

11. Set up the apparatus, as shown in Figure 2. Wrap the electrical or masking tape around both ends of the plastic tube so that the tube will fit tightly into the necks of the plastic bottles.

12. Place 100 mL of tap water in the clear bottle. Use a glass marking pencil to mark the height of the water. Pour the water down the drain.

13. Place 100 mL of the salt-water solution in the black bottle.

14. Insert one end of the plastic tubing into the neck of the black bottle, and the other end into the neck of the clear bottle.

15. Set both bottles on a window sill that has exposure to sunlight during at least half of the day. Set the black bottle on the wooden board so that it is at a higher position than the clear bottle. Arrange the bottles so that the black bottle receives sunlight as much as possible, while the clear bottle is kept out of the sun as much as possible.

16. Check the bottles daily until at least 75 percent of the liquid has been transferred to the clear bottle.

17. Pour the liquid from the black bottle clear container into a graduated cylinder and record the volume.

18. Observe the appearance of the two liquids. Then pour the liquids down the drain. *Depending on the location* *and configuration of your classroom, students may have to work in larger groups while doing Part B or you may need to do Part B as a demonstration. Depending on the height of your window ledges and tables, you may be able to place the clear bottles on the floor. With such a setup, you will not need to elevate the black bottles. If your classroom has a northern exposure, you could use incandescent lights to heat the black bottles.*

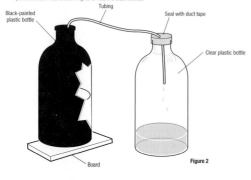

Tubing
Black-painted plastic bottle
Seal with duct tape
Clear plastic bottle
Board
Figure 2

Lab Manual

Name _____ Class _____ Date _____

Analysis and Conclusions

1. **Using Tables and Graphs** Draw a graph of your data from Part A. Plot time along the horizontal axis and temperature along the vertical axis. Label the point on your graph that corresponds to the time when you started to collect distilled liquid in the cooled flask.

Student graphs should show a rising curve with a plateau close to 100°C.

2. **Observing** Did you observe any evidence that the liquids in the heated and cooled flasks had different compositions?

Students may say that the salt solution appeared cloudy as it became more concentrated or that

some salt crystals formed. They may also say that there was no observable difference.

3. **Designing Experiments** Suggest at least one procedure that you could use to demonstrate that the liquids in the heated and cooled flasks have different compositions.

Students may suggest heating both liquids in open containers until all the water evaporated. There

would be a solid residue with the salt solution upon evaporation, but no residue with the distilled

water. Students may also suggest measuring and comparing the densities of the liquids. The salt

solution would have a greater density. If students suggest tasting the liquids, remind them that they

should not taste any material in the laboratory.

4. **Applying Concepts** How do you know that distillation is a physical change rather than a chemical one?

Distillation is a physical change because no new substances are formed during the distillation.

A mixture of existing substances is separated.

5. **Designing Experiments** What is the major difference between the experiments in Part A and Part B? What effect does this difference have on the experiments?

The major difference between the experiments is the heat source—a gas burner (or hot plate) in

Part A and sunlight in Part B. This difference affects the rate at which the distillation occurs.

Lab Manual

Name _____ Class _____ Date _____

6. **Comparing and Contrasting** List the advantages of each method used in this investigation for distilling water.

Part A advantages: change occurs faster, not dependent on availability of sunlight;

Part B advantages: requires simpler equipment, conserves non-renewable energy sources,

can be more easily imitated in a non-laboratory environment

_____

_____

7. **Classifying** During vaporization, a liquid changes to a gas or a vapor. Explain how the temperature at which vaporization takes place determines whether the process is described as evaporation or boiling. (*Hint:* These terms occur in the titles for Parts A and B of this investigation.)

If vaporization occurs at a temperature below the boiling point of a liquid, the process is described

as evaporation. When vaporization occurs at the boiling point, the process is classified as boiling.

_____

_____

Go Further

Distilled water can be distinguished from salt water based on a difference in density. You can use a fresh, raw egg to demonstrate this difference. Predict what you will observe when you place the egg in the liquids. Have your teacher supervise your experiment. Wash your hands thoroughly with soap or detergent after you complete the experiment.

The egg should float easily in salt water if the concentration is at least 5 mL of table salt in 200 mL of water. A fresh egg should not float in distilled water. Students may also want to test tap water. In some regions tap water will contain enough dissolved salts so that the egg will rise slightly in the water. The size of the egg can also affect the results.

Lab Manual

Name _____ Class _____ Date _____

Chapter 3 States of Matter   Investigation 3B

Investigating Space Between Particles in Matter

Refer students to pages 68 and 69 in their textbooks for a discussion of the arrangement of particles in solids and liquids.
SKILLS FOCUS: Measuring, Calculating, Drawing Conclusions
CLASS TIME: 30 minutes

Background Information

If you have ever seen water drain through beach sand, you know that there are spaces between the grains of sand. Because the grains of sand are relatively small and separate, you can pour sand almost as if it was a liquid. There are also spaces between the tiny particles that make up all matter.

In this investigation, you will first measure the volume of the space between grains of sand by filling a container with sand and water. Then, you will measure the volume of the space between the particles in a liquid by mixing two liquids together.

Problem

How much space is there between grains of sand or between particles in liquids?

Pre-Lab Discussion

Read the entire investigation. Then, work with a partner to answer the following questions.

1. **Using Analogies** Why is there space between marbles in a bowl? What factors might determine how much space there is between particles in a solid or liquid?

Because the marbles are round, there will be spaces between them when they are

packed in a container. Students may say that the size and shape of particles in a

solid or liquid will affect how closely they can be packed together. (They may also

mention the forces of attraction between particles.)

2. **Predicting** What do you expect to happen to the height of the material in the beaker when you begin to add water to the sand? Explain your answer.

The height will not change because water can occupy the spaces between the grains of sand.

_____

_____

_____

_____

Lab Manual

Name _____ Class _____ Date _____

3. **Predicting** In the investigation, you will mix 100 mL of water with 100 mL of isopropyl alcohol. Predict whether the volume of this mixture will be less than, equal to, or more than 200 mL. Explain your answer.

Students may choose "less than" if they may assume that the alcohol and water molecules can be

more closely packed in the mixture than they are in either the alcohol or the water. Some may

choose "equal to" if they assume that the volume of the space between the particles does not

change when the liquids are mixed.

_____

Materials *(per group)*

2 250-mL graduated cylinders   Adjust quantities of sand, water, and alcohol
100-mL graduated cylinder   used to match available graduated cylinders.
isopropyl alcohol Provide 95% isopropyl alcohol.
sand
glass stirring rod

Safety 🥽 🧤 🔥 ⚗️ ☠️ 🧪

Put on safety goggles and a lab apron. Be careful to avoid breakage when working with glassware. Always use caution when working with laboratory chemicals, as they may irritate the skin or stain skin or clothing. Never taste any chemicals unless instructed to do so. Keep alcohol away from any open flame. Wash your hands thoroughly after carrying out this investigation. Note all safety alert symbols next to the steps in the Procedure and review the meaning of each symbol by referring to the Safety Symbols on page xiii.

Review with students the safety information in the MSDS for isopropyl alcohol before performing this investigation.

Procedure

1. Fill a 250-mL graduated cylinder to its 200-mL mark with sand.
2. Fill the 100-mL graduated cylinder to the 100-mL mark with water. Slowly pour a little water into the graduated cylinder containing the sand. Continue pouring until the level of the water in the sand reaches the 200-mL line. Observe the volume of water remaining in the 100-mL graduated cylinder. Record this volume in Data Table 1.
3. Calculate the volume of water added to the sand by subtracting the volume of water remaining in the graduated cylinder from the total volume of water. Record your result in Data Table 1.
4. Pour 100 mL of isopropyl alcohol into the 250-mL graduated cylinder. **CAUTION:** *Isopropyl alcohol is poisonous and flammable.*
5. Fill the 100-mL graduated cylinder to the 100-mL mark with water. Slowly pour the water into the graduated cylinder containing the isopropyl alcohol. Use the glass stirring rod to mix the two liquids. Observe the volume of the mixture. Record this volume in Data Table 2.

Lab Manual

Name _____ Class _____ Date _____

6. Subtract the volume of the alcohol-water mixture from the total volume of alcohol and water. Record this difference in Data Table 2. Wash your hands thoroughly after completing the investigation.

Observations   Sample data are shown.

DATA TABLE 1

Material	Volume (mL)
Total water	100
Remaining water	52
Water added = total water − remaining water	48

DATA TABLE 2

Material	Volume (mL)
Alcohol	100
Water	100
Mixture	190
Volume change = mixture − (alcohol + water)	10

Lab Manual

Name _____ Class _____ Date _____

Analysis and Conclusions

1. **Analyzing Data** What was the total volume of the space between the grains of sand?

   The space between the grains of sand was equal to the water added to the sand, which was 48 mL.

   _____

   _____

2. **Drawing Conclusions** Based on this investigation, how do you know that there is space between the particles in alcohol or water?

   There must be space between the particles because the total volume of the mixture is less than

   the sum of the measured volumes of alcohol and water.

   _____

   _____

   _____

   _____

3. **Formulating Hypotheses** Why did the total volume of water and alcohol decrease when the liquids were mixed together?

   Students may say that the shapes and sizes of the particles (molecules) of alcohol

   and water allowed them to be more closely packed when the liquids were mixed.

   (Some students may say that forces of attractions between alcohol and water draw

   the particles closer together in the mixture.)

   _____

   _____

   _____

Go Further

If the distances between the particles of a material change, will the volume of the material change? Design an experiment to determine the percentage change in volume that occurs when materials such as water, paraffin, or shortening change from solid to liquid or from liquid to solid. When your teacher has approved your experiment, perform it under your teacher's supervision, using all necessary safety procedures. Report your observations and conclusions.

Water has the unusual property of expanding upon freezing. Encourage students to compare this behavior to that of other more typical materials such as paraffin. Examine student plans for safety and review with students the MSDS safety information for any materials that they will use before approving student experiments. Supervise all student laboratory work.

Chapter Test A

Name _____ Class _____ Date _____

Chapter 3   States of Matter   **Chapter Test A**

Multiple Choice

Write the letter that best answers the question or completes the statement on the line provided.

_____ **1.** Ninety-nine percent of all the matter that can be observed in the universe exists as
   a. gases.   b. plasmas.
   c. liquids.   d. solids.

_____ **2.** If you move a substance from one container to another and its volume changes, the substance is a
   a. solid.   b. liquid.
   c. gas.   d. solution.

_____ **3.** Forces of attraction limit the motion of particles most in
   a. a solid.   b. a liquid.
   c. a gas.   d. both b and c

_____ **4.** Collisions of helium atoms and the walls of a closed container cause
   a. condensation.   b. gas pressure.
   c. a decrease in volume. d. an overall loss of energy.

_____ **5.** Raising the temperature of a gas will increase its pressure IF the volume of the gas
   a. and the number of particles are increased.
   b. is increased, but the number of particles is constant.
   c. and the number of particles are constant.
   d. is constant, but the number of particles is increased.

_____ **6.** Which of the following will cause a decrease in gas pressure in a closed container?
   a. lowering the temperature
   b. reducing the volume
   c. adding more gas
   d. both a and b

_____ **7.** Boyle's law states that the volume of a gas is inversely proportional to its pressure if the
   a. temperature and number of particles are constant.
   b. temperature reaches absolute zero.
   c. number of particles decreases.
   d. temperature and number of particles are doubled.

_____ **8.** At a temperature of 274 K, the gas in a cylinder has a volume of 4.0 liters. If the volume of the gas is decreased to 2.0 liters, what must the temperature be for the gas pressure to remain constant?
   a. 137 K   b. 273 K
   c. 378 K   d. 556 K

Chapter Test A

Name _____ Class _____ Date _____

_____ **9.** The phase change that is the reverse of condensation is
   a. freezing.   b. sublimation.
   c. vaporization.   d. melting.

_____ **10.** During a phase change, the temperature of a substance
   a. increases.   b. decreases.
   c. does not change.   d. increases or decreases.

_____ **11.** If a solid piece of naphthalene is heated and remains at 80°C until it is completely melted, you know that 80°C is the
   a. freezing point of naphthalene.
   b. melting point of naphthalene.
   c. boiling point of naphthalene.
   d. both a and b

_____ **12.** The heat of fusion for water is the amount of energy needed for water to
   a. freeze.   b. boil.
   c. melt.   d. evaporate.

_____ **13.** Which of the following statements about ice melting is true?
   a. Energy flows from the ice to its surroundings.
   b. Water molecules move from their fixed position.
   c. Water molecules lose energy.
   d. The temperature of the ice increases as it melts.

_____ **14.** The phase change in which a substance changes from a solid to a gas or vapor without changing to a liquid first is
   a. sublimation.   b. deposition.
   c. vaporization.   d. melting.

_____ **15.** The phase change in which a substance changes from a gas directly to a solid is
   a. condensation.   b. vaporization.
   c. deposition.   d. sublimation.

_____ **16.** Which of the following phase changes is an exothermic change?
   a. sublimation.   b. deposition
   c. vaporization.   d. melting

Completion

Complete each statement on the line provided.

1. The state of matter that exists only at extremely low temperatures is called a Bose-Einstein _____.

2. The motion of one particle of a gas is unaffected by the motion of other particles of the gas unless the particles _____.

Chapter Test A

Name _____ Class _____ Date _____

3. The pascal is the SI unit for _____.

4. During vaporization, a substance changes from a(an) _____ to a(an) _____.

5. Evaporation is the process that changes a substance from a liquid to a gas at temperatures below the substance's _____ point.

Short Answer

Use complete sentences to write the answers to the questions on the lines provided.

1. Solid, liquid, and gas are three states of matter. What are two other states of matter, and under what conditions do they exist?

   _____

   _____

   _____

   Substance A   Substance B   Substance C

Figure 3-1

2. What substance in Figure 3-1 is a solid? Explain how you know.

   _____

   _____

3. If a gas in a sealed container has a pressure of 50 kPa at 300 K, what will the pressure be if the temperature rises to 360 K?

   _____

4. Describe what happens to the arrangement of water molecules as ice melts.

   _____

   _____

   _____

Chapter Test A

Name _____ Class _____ Date _____

5. How could you determine if a phase change is endothermic?

_____

_____

_____

Using Science Skills

Use the graph to answer each question. Write the answers on a separate sheet of paper.

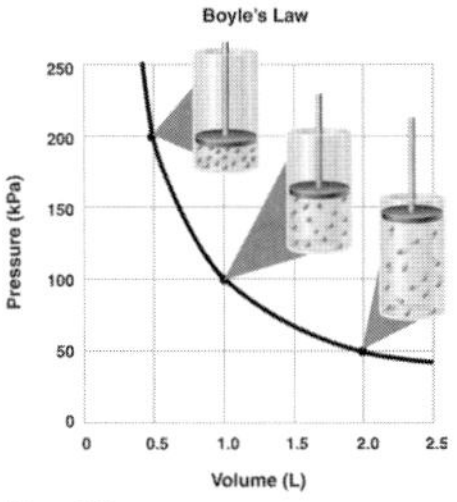

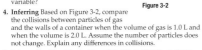
Boyle's Law
Figure 3-2

1. **Interpreting Graphics** In Figure 3-2, what is the unit used for pressure? What is the pressure when the volume is 0.5 L? What is the pressure when the volume is 1.0 L?

2. **Interpreting Graphics** In Figure 3-2, what is the manipulated variable, and what is the responding variable?

3. **Predicting** How would the graph in Figure 3-2 change if the volume of the cylinder remained constant and temperature was the manipulated variable?

4. **Inferring** Based on Figure 3-2, compare the collisions between particles of gas and the walls of a container when the volume of gas is 1.0 L and when the volume is 2.0 L. Assume the number of particles does not change. Explain any differences in collisions.

5. **Interpreting Graphics** In Figure 3-2, if P_1 is 200 kPa and P_2 is 50 kPa, what are V_1 and V_2?

Essay

Write the answer to each question on a separate sheet of paper.

1. Use billiard balls to describe the motion of particles in a gas. Use students in a crowded hallway to describe the motion of particles in a liquid. Use an audience in a movie theater to describe the motion of particles in a solid.

2. Use breathing as an example to explain the relationship between volume and air pressure.

3. What factors affect the volume of a weather balloon as it rises through the atmosphere?

4. Why does pasta take longer to cook in boiling water at elevations above sea level?

5. Describe how water can change from a liquid to a vapor at temperatures lower than its boiling point.

Chapter Test B

Name _____ Class _____ Date _____

Chapter 3   States of Matter   Chapter Test B

Multiple Choice

Write the letter that best answers the question or completes the statement on the line provided.

_____ 1. A gas has
a. a definite volume but no definite shape.
b. a definite shape but no definite volume.
c. no definite shape or definite volume.
d. a definite volume and definite shape.

_____ 2. Matter that has a definite volume but no definite shape is a
a. liquid.   b. solid.
c. gas.   d. plasma.

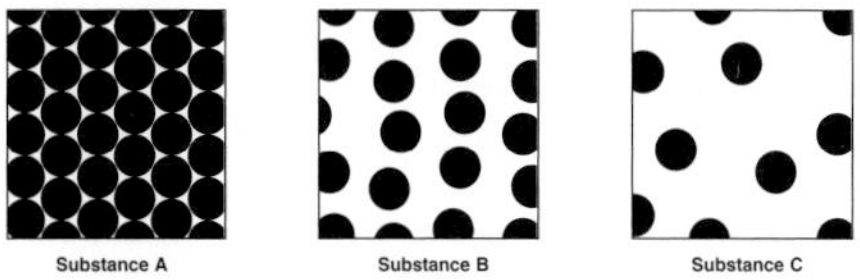

Substance A   Substance B   Substance C
Figure 3-1

_____ 3. In which of the substances in Figure 3-1 are the forces of attraction among the particles so weak that they can be ignored under ordinary conditions?
a. Substance A   b. Substance B
c. Substance C   d. all of the above

_____ 4. What is the result of a force distributed over an area?
a. temperature   b. volume
c. pressure   d. mass

_____ 5. Which of the following factors affect the pressure of an enclosed gas?
a. temperature   b. volume
c. number of particles d. all of the above

_____ 6. The temperature and volume in a closed container of gas remain constant. If the number of particles of gas is increased, the gas pressure will
a. increase.
b. decrease.
c. remain constant.
d. cause a decrease in the average kinetic energy of the particles.

Chapter Test B

Name _____ Class _____ Date _____

_____ 7. The law that states that the volume of a gas is directly proportional to its temperature in kelvins if the pressure and the number of particles is constant is
a. Boyle's law.
b. Bose's law.
c. Einstein's law.
d. Charles's law.

_____ 8. If the volume of a cylinder is reduced from 4.0 liters to 2.0 liters, the pressure of the gas in the cylinder will change from 100 kilopascals to
a. 50 kilopascals.
b. 150 kilopascals.
c. 200 kilopascals.
d. 400 kilopascals.

_____ 9. What type of change occurs when water changes from a solid to a liquid?
a. a phase change
b. a physical change
c. an irreversible change
d. both a and b

_____ 10. During a phase change, the temperature of a substance
a. increases.
b. decreases.
c. stays the same.
d. either increases or decreases, depending on the change.

_____ 11. During what phase change does the arrangement of water molecules become more orderly?
a. melting   b. freezing
c. boiling   d. condensing

_____ 12. The phase change in which a substance changes from a liquid to a gas is
a. deposition.   b. sublimation.
c. condensation.   d. vaporization.

_____ 13. The phase change in which a substance changes from a solid to a liquid is
a. freezing.   b. melting.
c. sublimation.   d. condensation.

_____ 14. Which of the following phase changes is an endothermic change?
a. condensation   b. vaporization
c. deposition   d. freezing

Chapter Test B

Name _____ Class _____ Date _____

Completion

Complete each statement on the line provided.

1. A(an) _____ has a definite volume and a definite shape.

2. Materials can be classified as solids, liquids, or gases based on whether their shapes and _____ are definite or variable.

3. The shape of a material remains constant when it is moved from one container to another. This material is a(an) _____.

4. The _____ theory of matter states that all particles of matter are in constant motion.

5. _____ between the particles of a gas and the walls of the container cause pressure in a closed container of gas.

6. Reducing the volume of a gas _____ its pressure if the _____ of the gas and the number of particles are constant.

7. A graph representing Charles's law shows that the _____ of a gas increases at the same rate as the _____ of the gas.

8. If you are using Charles's law to find the volume of a gas at a certain temperature, the temperature must be expressed in _____.

9. Water boils when its vapor pressure becomes equal to _____ pressure.

10. During a(an) _____ change, the system releases energy to its surroundings.

Short Answer

Use complete sentences to write the answers to the questions on the lines provided.

1. Compare the shape and volume of solids, liquids, and gases.

_____

_____

_____

2. Why is the volume of a liquid constant?

_____

_____

_____

Chapter Test B

Name _____   Class _____   Date _____

3. Why does the air pressure in a car's tires increase after a long drive?

_____

_____

_____

_____

4. Describe what happens to the average kinetic energy of water molecules as water freezes.

_____

_____

_____

_____

5. Name and describe the phase change that occurs when dry ice is placed in an open container at room temperature.

_____

_____

_____

_____

_____

Using Science Skills

Use the diagram to answer each question. Write the answers on a separate sheet of paper.

1. **Interpreting Graphics** Identify the phase changes in Figure 3-2 that are labeled a, b, and c.

2. **Interpreting Graphics** Explain why the phase changes in Figure 3-2 are shown in pairs.

3. **Comparing and Contrasting** Use the terms in Figure 3-2 to compare the phase changes that occur when water vapor changes to dew or frost.

4. **Interpreting Graphics** Describe the two phase changes represented in Figure 3-2 that can happen to a liquid.

5. **Applying Concepts** What three phase changes in Figure 3-2 are endothermic?

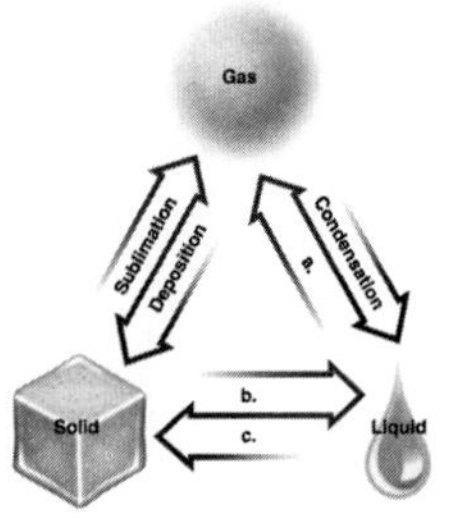

Gas

Sublimation
Deposition

Condensation

a.

Solid

b.

c.

Liquid

Figure 3-2

Chapter 3 Test A Answers

Multiple Choice

1. b **2.** c **3.** a **4.** b **5.** c **6.** a
7. a **8.** a **9.** c **10.** c **11.** d **12.** c
13. b **14.** a **15.** c **16.** b

Completion

1. condensate **2.** collide **3.** pressure **4.** liquid, gas **5.** boiling

Short Answer

1. Plasma exists at extremely high temperatures, and a Bose-Einstein condensate can exist at extremely low temperatures.
2. Substance A; its particles are packed close together and arranged in a regular pattern. **3.** The new pressure would be 60 kPa. **4.** At the melting point of water, some molecules gain enough energy to move from their fixed positions. **5.** Take temperature measurements of the surroundings during the phase change. If the temperature decreases, the phase change is endothermic; a system absorbs energy from its surroundings during an endothermic phase change.

Using Science Skills

1. the kilopascal; 200 kPa; 100 kPa **2.** Volume is the manipulated variable. Pressure is the responding variable. **3.** The pressure would increase, so the graph would be a straight line. **4.** The number of collisions will increase when the volume is reduced from 2.0 L to 1.0 L because particles occupy a smaller space and will collide more often with the walls of the container. **5.** V_1 is 0.5 L, and V_2 is 2.0 L.

Essay

1. Like a particle in a gas, a billiard ball moves in a straight line until it collides with another object. During a collision, kinetic energy can be transferred between billiard balls or particles in a gas. Students in a crowded hallway are closely packed like the particles in a liquid. The motion of the students is restricted by interactions with other students. The motion of particles in a liquid is limited by forces of attraction. The fixed positions of the audience in a movie theater are like the fixed locations of particles in solids. However, both the audience and the particles can move within or around their locations. **2.** The volume of the chest cavity increases as the diaphragm contracts and the rib cage is lifted. This increase in volume allows the particles in air to spread out, which lowers the air pressure in the lungs. Air rushes into the lungs because the air pressure outside the body is greater than the air pressure in the lungs. As the diaphragm relaxes and the rib cage moves down and in, the volume of the chest cavity decreases. This decrease in volume increases the air pressure, and air is forced out of the lungs. **3.** Temperature and air pressure affect the volume of a weather balloon. As the balloon rises, the temperature decreases, which should cause the volume of the balloon to decrease. However, pressure in the atmosphere also decreases, which should cause the volume of the balloon to increase. **4.** Water boils when its vapor pressure equals atmospheric pressure. Atmospheric pressure is lower at higher elevations. Therefore, the vapor pressure of water will equal atmospheric pressure at temperatures below 100°C. Pasta takes longer to cook at lower temperatures. **5.** Water can evaporate at temperatures lower than its boiling point. Evaporation can take place at the surface of water because some water molecules are moving fast enough to escape the liquid and vaporize. The higher the temperature is, the faster the water molecules move, on average, and the faster evaporation takes place.

Chapter 3 Test B Answers

Multiple Choice

1. c **2.** a **3.** c **4.** c **5.** d **6.** a **7.** d
8. c **9.** d **10.** c **11.** b **12.** d **13.** b **14.** b

Completion

1. solid **2.** volumes **3.** solid **4.** kinetic **5.** Collisions **6.** increases, temperature **7.** volume, temperature **8.** kelvins **9.** atmospheric **10.** exothermic

Short Answer

1. Solids have a definite shape and definite volume, liquids have a definite volume but not a definite shape, and gases do not have a definite volume or a definite shape. **2.** The volume of a liquid is constant because forces of attraction keep the particles close together. **3.** The constant motion of the tires on the road causes the tires and the air in the tires to warm up. The increase in temperature increases the average kinetic energy of the air in the tires. The frequency and force of collisions between particles increases, which increases the air pressure. **4.** As water freezes, it releases energy to its surroundings, and the average kinetic energy of the water molecules decreases. **5.** At room temperature, dry ice changes from solid carbon dioxide to carbon dioxide gas, which is an example of sublimation.

Using Science Skills

1. a. vaporization; b. melting; c. freezing **2.** Each pair represents the opposing endothermic and exothermic changes that occur between the same two states of matter. **3.** Water vapor is a gas. The phase change from water to liquid dew is called condensation. The phase change from water vapor to solid frost is called deposition. **4.** Vaporization is the phase change in which a liquid changes to a gas. Freezing is the phase change in which a liquid changes to a solid. **5.** melting, vaporization, and sublimation

Chapter 4 Atomic Structure

CHAPTER

Planning Guide

Use these planning tools
Easy Planner
Resource Pro
Online Lesson Planner

SECTION OBJECTIVES	STANDARDS		ACTIVITIES and LABS
	NATIONAL (See p. T18.)	STATE	
4.1 Studying Atoms, pp. 100–105 ⏱ 1 block or 2 periods **4.1.1 Describe** ancient Greek models of matter. **4.1.2 List** the main points of Dalton's atomic theory and **describe** his evidence for the existence of atoms. **4.1.3 Explain** how Thomson and Rutherford used data from experiments to produce their atomic models.	A-1, A-2, B-1, B-2, B-6, E-2, G-1, G-2, G-3		**SE** Inquiry Activity: How Can You Study Objects That Are Not Visible? p. 99 **L2** **SE** Quick Lab: Investigating Charged Objects, p. 102 **L2** **TE** Teacher Demo: Comparing Atomic Models, p. 104 **L2**
4.2 The Structure of an Atom, pp. 108–112 ⏱ 1 block or 2 periods **4.2.1 Identify** three subatomic particles and **compare** their properties. **4.2.2 Distinguish** the atomic number of an element from the mass number of an isotope, and use these numbers to **describe** the structure of atoms.	A-1, B-1, B-2, E-1, G-1, G-2, G-3		**TE** Teacher Demo: Particles and Numbers, p. 110 **L2**
4.3 Modern Atomic Theory, pp. 113–118 ⏱ 1 block or 2 periods **4.3.1 Describe** Bohr's model of the atom and the evidence for energy levels. **4.3.2 Explain** how the electron cloud model represents the behavior and locations of electrons in atoms. **4.3.3 Distinguish** the ground state from excited states of an atom based on electron configurations.	A-1, A-2, B-1, B-2, G-1, G-2, G-3		**SE** Quick Lab: Comparing Excited States, p. 117 **L2** **SE** Forensics Lab: Using Flame Tests, p. 119 **L2** **TE** Teacher Demo: Electron Cloud Model, p. 116 **L2** **LM** Investigation 4A: Constructing a Model of an Atom **L2** **LM** Investigation 4B: Modeling an Electron Cloud **L1**

Ability Levels

L1	For students who need additional help
L2	For all students
L3	For students who need to be challenged

Components

SE	Student Edition	**GRSW**	Guided Reading & Study Workbook With Math Support	**CTB**	Computer Test Bank
TE	Teacher's Edition			**TP**	Test Prep Resources
LM	Laboratory Manual			**iT**	iText
PLM	Probeware Lab Manual	**CUT**	Chapter and Unit Tests	**DC**	Discovery Channel Videotapes
T	Transparencies				
P	Presentation Pro CD-ROM				
GO	Internet Resources				

RESOURCES

PRINT and TECHNOLOGY / SECTION ASSESSMENT

GRSW Section 4.1 **L1**

DC Go For Gold **L2**

T Chapter 4 Pretest **L2**
Section 4.1 **L2**

P Chapter 4 Pretest **L2**
Section 4.1 **L2**

SciLINKS **GO** Atomic theory **L2**

SE Section 4.1
Assessment, p. 105

iT Section 4.1

GRSW Section 4.2 **L1**

GRSW Math Skill **L2**

T Section 4.2 **L2**

P Section 4.2 **L2**

SCIENCE NEWS **GO** Atomic chemistry **L2**

SE Section 4.2
Assessment, p. 112

iT Section 4.2

GRSW Section 4.3 **L1**

T Section 4.3 **L2**

P Section 4.3 **L2**

SciLINKS **GO** Energy levels **L2**

SE Section 4.3
Assessment, p. 118

iT Section 4.3

Go Online

Go online for these Internet resources.

PHSchool.com
Web Code: cca-1040

 *SciLINKS*
Web Code: ccn-1041
Web Code: ccn-1043

SCIENCE NEWS
Web Code: cce-1042

Materials for Activities and Labs

Quantities for each group

STUDENT EDITION

Inquiry Activity, p. 99
2 sealed, brown paper bags

Quick Lab, p. 102
transparent tape, metric ruler, scissors

Quick Lab, p. 117
fluorescent ("neon") markers, glow-in-the-dark toy, ultraviolet (UV) lamp

Forensics Lab, p. 119
solutions of calcium chloride, boric acid, potassium chloride, copper(II) sulfate, sodium chloride, and an unknown; Bunsen burner; nichrome wire loop; dilute solution of hydrochloric acid; wash bottle with distilled water

TEACHER'S EDITION

Teacher Demo, p. 104
3 clear, round bowls; flavored gelatin mix; canned blueberries; maraschino cherries

Build Science Skills, p. 106
modeling clay, plastic knives

Teacher Demo, p. 110
overhead projector, red and green gummy candies

Teacher Demo, p. 116
small, round balloon; large, round balloon; 10 beads with 4-mm diameter; 5 beads with 2-mm diameter

Chapter Assessment

CHAPTER ASSESSMENT

SE Chapter Assessment, pp. 121–122
CUT Chapter 4 Test A, B
CTB Chapter 4
iT Chapter 4
PHSchool.com GO
Web Code: cca-1040

STANDARDIZED TEST PREP

SE Chapter 4, p. 123
TP Diagnose and Prescribe

iText—interactive textbook with assessment at PHSchool.com

Name_____ Class_____ Date_____ M T W T F

Studying Atoms

Time
2 periods
1 block

Section Objectives

Local Standards

- **4.1.1 Describe** ancient Greek models of matter.

- **4.1.2 List** the main points of Dalton's atomic theory and **describe** his evidence for the existence of atoms.

- **4.1.3 Explain** how Thomson and Rutherford used data from experiments to produce their atomic models.

Vocabulary nucleus

1 FOCUS

Build Vocabulary: Latin Plural Forms
Explain that the word *nucleus* comes from the Latin word meaning "kernel." Ask students to discuss how the definition of the term *nucleus* relates to its Latin origin. **L2**

Targeted Resources
❏ Transparency: Chapter 4 Pretest
❏ Transparency: Interest Grabber 4.1
❏ Transparency: Reading Strategy 4.1

2 INSTRUCT

Use Visuals: Figure 3
Have students examine Figure 3 and ask them why they think there are holes in Dalton's wooden spheres. **L1**

Build Reading Literacy: Compare and Contrast
Have students read about the different atomic models described in Section 4.1. Then, have students create a chart that compares and contrasts each model. **L1**

Build Science Skills: Evaluating
As students read Chapter 4, have them evaluate what portions of Dalton's model were accurate and what portions needed to be revised. **L2**

Quick Lab: Investigating Charged Objects
Students will use two pieces of tape to explain that like charges repel and unlike charges attract. **L2**

Teacher Demo: Comparing Atomic Models
Using blueberries, cherries, and bowls of gelatin mix, create three different atomic models for students to compare. **L2**

Build Science Skills: Using Models
Have students model the gold foil experiment by shooting marbles across the floor at an arrangement of widely spaced, smaller objects and recording the angle of the marbles that are deflected. **L2**

Targeted Resources
❏ Transparency: Figure 5: Thomson's Experiments
❏ Transparency: Figure 7: The Gold Foil Experiment
❏ GRSW Section 4.1
❏ **NSTA** *sci*$_{LINKS}$ Atomic theory

3 ASSESS

Reteach
Use the Science and History time line on p. 114 to present and discuss a summary of the three models. **L1**

Evaluate Understanding
Ask groups of students to summarize Dalton's, Thomson's, and Rutherford's atomic theories. Have them come up with simple word phrases or mnemonic devices to help them easily distinguish among the three theories. **L2**

Targeted Resources
❏ **PHSchool.com** Online Section 4.1 Assessment
❏ iText Section 4.1

Transparencies

39 **Chapter 4 Pretest**

1. True or False: Compounds have fixed compositions.

2. What is an atom?

3. Which of the following units is a unit of mass?
   a. mL
   b. °C
   c. g
   d. cm

4. Volume is
   a. the straight-line distance between two points.
   b. the quantity of matter in an object.
   c. the amount of space taken up by an object.
   d. a representation of an object or event.

Transparencies

40 **Chapter 4 Pretest** (continued)

5. What is density?

6. Which two of the following events can take place when a liquid absorbs energy?
   a. The average kinetic energy of the particles in the liquid increases.
   b. The temperature decreases.
   c. The liquid freezes.
   d. The liquid changes to a gas.

Transparencies

41 **Section 4.1 Interest Grabber**

Using Analogies

The network of blood vessels in your body is like the network of streets and highways in a large city. How are the two networks similar? Both networks are used to transport objects from one location to another. The comparison is an example of an analogy. An analogy uses a similarity to compare two objects or systems. A familiar object is often used to help explain a less familiar object.

1. Atoms in compounds are like bricks in a wall. Explain this analogy.

2. Think of another analogy for atoms in compounds.

Transparencies

42 **Section 4.1 Reading Strategy**

Summarizing

Scientist	Evidence	Model
a. ___?___	Ratio of masses in compounds	b. ___?___
c. ___?___	Deflected beam	d. ___?___
Rutherford	e. ___?___	Positive, dense nucleus

Transparencies

43 Figure 5 Thomson's Experiments

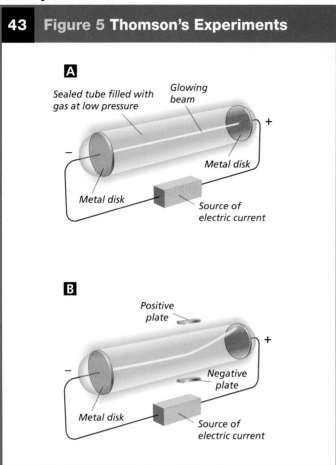

Transparencies

44 Figure 7 The Gold Foil Experiment

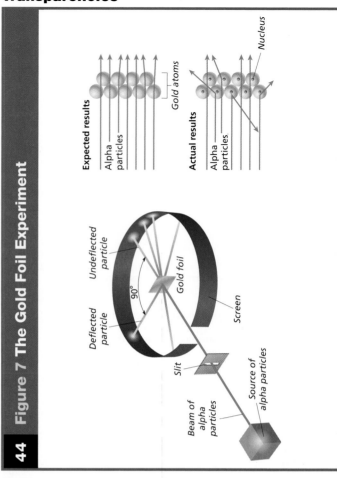

Guided Reading and Study Workbook

Name _____ Class _____ Date _____

Chapter 4   Atomic Structure

Section 4.1 Studying Atoms
(pages 100–105)

This section discusses the development of atomic models.

Reading Strategy (page 100)

Summarizing As you read, complete the table about atomic models. For more information on this Reading Strategy, see the **Reading and Study Skills** in the **Skills and Reference Handbook** at the end of your textbook.

Atomic Models		
Scientist	**Evidence**	**Model**
Dalton	Ratio of masses in compounds	Indivisible, solid spheres
Thomson	Deflected beam	Negative charges evenly scattered through positively charged mass of matter (plum pudding model)
Rutherford	Deflection of alpha particles passing through gold foil	Positive, dense nucleus

Ancient Greek Models of Atoms (page 100)

1. Democritus named the smallest particles of matter ____atoms____ because they could not be divided.
2. List the four elements that Aristotle included in his model of matter.
   a. ____Earth____   b. ____Air____
   c. ____Fire____   d. ____Water____

Dalton's Atomic Theory (page 101)

3. Is the following sentence true or false? John Dalton gathered evidence for the existence of atoms by measuring the masses of elements that reacted to form compounds. ____true____
4. What theory did Dalton propose to explain why the elements in a compound always join in the same way? He proposed that all matter is made up of individual particles called atoms, which cannot be divided.
5. Circle the letters of the sentences that represent the main points of Dalton's theory of atoms.
   (a.) All elements are composed of atoms.
   (b.) In a particular compound, atoms of different elements always combine the same way.
   c. All atoms have the same mass.
   (d.) Compounds contain atoms of more than one element.

Physical Science Guided Reading and Study Workbook • Chapter 4 **27**

Guided Reading and Study Workbook

Name _____ Class _____ Date _____

Chapter 4   Atomic Structure

Thomson's Model of the Atom (pages 102–103)

6. Objects with like electric charges ____repel____, and objects with opposite electric charges ____attract____.
7. What happened to the beam when Thomson placed a pair of charged metal plates on either side of the glass tube? The beam was attracted by the positively charged plate and repelled by the negatively charged plate.
8. Thomson concluded that the particles in the glowing beam had a(n) ____negative____ charge because they were attracted to a positive plate.
9. Is the following sentence true or false? Thomson's experiments provided the first evidence for the existence of subatomic particles. ____true____
10. Describe Thomson's model. Negative charges are evenly scattered throughout an atom filled with positively charged mass of matter.

Rutherford's Atomic Theory (pages 104–105)

11. What is an alpha particle? An alpha particle is a fast-moving particle that carries a positive charge.
12. Fill in the table to show what Rutherford hypothesized would happen to the paths of alpha particles as they passed through a thin sheet of gold.

Rutherford's Hypothesis	
Most particles would travel in a straight path from their source to a screen that lit up when struck.	Particles that did not pass straight through would be deflected only slightly.

13. Circle the letters of the sentences that describe what happened when Marsden directed a beam of particles at a piece of gold foil.
   a. Fewer alpha particles were deflected than expected.
   (b.) More alpha particles were deflected than expected.
   c. None of the alpha particles were deflected.
   (d.) Some alpha particles bounced back toward the source.
14. Circle the letter of the sentence that states what Rutherford concluded from the gold foil experiment.
   a. An atom's negative charge is concentrated in its nucleus.
   b. Thomson's model of the atom was correct.
   (c.) An atom's positive charge is concentrated in its nucleus.
   d. An atom's positive charge is spread evenly throughout the atom.

28 *Physical Science* Guided Reading and Study Workbook • Chapter 4

LESSON PLAN 4.2

The Structure of an Atom

Time
2 periods
1 block

Section Objectives

Local Standards

- **4.2.1 Identify** three subatomic particles and **compare** their properties.
- **4.2.2 Distinguish** the atomic number of an element from the mass number of an isotope, and use these numbers to **describe** the structure of atoms.

Vocabulary proton • electron • neutron • atomic number • mass number • isotopes

1 FOCUS

Build Vocabulary: Word-Part Analysis
Have students look up the term *isotope* in a dictionary that provides word prefixes. Have them use the prefix *iso-* to help them understand the term. **L2**

Targeted Resources
❑ Transparency: Interest Grabber 4.2
❑ Transparency: Reading Strategy 4.2

2 INSTRUCT

Build Reading Literacy: Identify Main Idea/Details
Have students read Atomic Number and Mass Number on p. 110. Ask them to identify the main idea of each paragraph. **L1**

Build Science Skills: Calculating
Have students confirm the relative masses given in Figure 10 by dividing the mass given for an electron by the mass given for a neutron. **L2**

Problem Solving Activity: Designing an Atomic Exhibit
Students will design an exhibit that compares the size of a lithium atom to the size of its nucleus. **L2**

Teacher Demo: Particles and Numbers
Using red and green candies, create models of a lithium-7 nucleus, an oxygen-16 nucleus, and a boron-11 nucleus. Students will observe the relationship between number of protons, number of neutrons, atomic number, and mass number. **L2**

Build Science Skills: Calculating
Uranium-238 has a mass number of 238 with 146 neutrons in the nucleus. Uranium-235 has 143 neutrons in the nucleus. Ask students what the atomic number of uranium is. **L2**

For Enrichment
Encourage students to explore the use of scanning tunneling microscopes in research on surface textures, crystal structure, or molecular shape. Have them present their findings to the class in the form of a poster. **L3**

Targeted Resources
❑ Transparency: Figure 10: Properties of Subatomic Particles
❑ GRSW Section 4.2

3 ASSESS

Reteach
Revisit Figure 10 to review the differences among protons, neutrons, and electrons. **L1**

Evaluate Understanding
Have students write three review questions for this section. Students should then break into groups of three or four and ask each other their questions. **L2**

Targeted Resources
❑ **PHSchool.com** Online Section 4.2 Assessment
❑ iText Section 4.2

45 Section 4.2 Interest Grabber

The "Rutherford" Atom

In Section 4.1 you were told that if the Houston Astrodome were a model for an atom, then a marble could represent its nucleus.

1. Think of another physical analogy for a "Rutherford" atom other than the astrodome.

2. Identify what represents the atom and what represents the nucleus in your analogy.

3. How good a match is your analogy for an actual atom? In what ways is it misleading?

ANSWERS
1. and 2. Sample answers: a fruit with a seed representing the nucleus; a small object embedded in the center of a transparent glass or plastic sphere; a chocolate-covered cherry out; the smallest object in a set of nested objects of increasing size.

3. The main flaws in most physical analogies are the relative sizes of the "nucleus" and "atom," and the lack of unfilled space surrounding the nucleus.

46 Section 4.2 Reading Strategy

Monitoring Your Understanding

What I Know About Atoms	What I Would Like to Learn	What I Have Learned

ANSWERS
Most students will know that atoms are the "building blocks" of matter and some may know that atoms contain subatomic particles. Based on the title of the section, students may say that they want to learn more about the structure of atoms.

47 Figure 10 Properties of Subatomic Particles

Properties of Subatomic Particles

Particle	Symbol	Relative Charge	Relative Mass (proton = 1)	Actual Mass (g)	Model
Electron	e^-	$1-$	$\frac{1}{1836}$	9.11×10^{-28}	
Proton	p^+	$1+$	1	1.674×10^{-24}	
Neutron	n	0	1	1.675×10^{-24}	

Name _____ Class _____ Date _____

Section 4.2 The Structure of an Atom
(pages 108–112)

This section compares the properties of three subatomic particles. It also discusses atomic numbers, mass numbers, and isotopes.

Reading Strategy (page 108)

Monitoring Your Understanding Before you read, list in the table shown what you know about atoms and what you would like to learn. After you read, list what you have learned. For more information on this Reading Strategy, see the **Reading and Study Skills** in the **Skills and Reference Handbook** at the end of your textbook.

What I Know About Atoms	What I Would Like to Learn	What I Have Learned
Most students will know that atoms are the "building blocks" of matter, and some may know that atoms contain subatomic particles.	Based on the title of the section, students may say that they want to learn more about the structure of atoms.	

Properties of Subatomic Particles (pages 108–109)

1. What are three subatomic particles?
   a. _____Protons_____   b. _____Electrons_____   c. _____Neutrons_____

2. Circle the letter that identifies a subatomic particle with a positive charge.
   a. nucleus   (b.) proton
   c. neutron   d. electron

3. Why did Chadwick conclude that the particles produced by his experiment were neutral in charge? _A charged object did not deflect the paths of the particles._

Comparing Subatomic Particles (pages 109–110)

4. Circle the letters of properties that vary among subatomic particles.
   a. color   (b.) mass
   (c.) charge   (d.) location in the atom

5. Circle the letter of the expression that accurately compares the masses of neutrons and protons.
   (a.) mass of 1 neutron = mass of 1 proton
   b. mass of 2000 neutrons = mass of 1 proton
   c. mass of 1 electron = mass of 1 proton
   d. mass of 1 neutron = mass of 1 electron

Name _____ Class _____ Date _____

Atomic Number and Mass Number (page 110)

6. Is the following sentence true or false? Two atoms of the same element can have different numbers of protons. _____false_____

7. What is an atomic number? _The atomic number of an element equals the number of protons in an atom of that element._

8. Circle the letters that identify quantities that are always equal to an element's atomic number.
   a. number of nuclei
   (b.) number of protons
   c. number of neutrons
   (d.) number of electrons

9. Is the following sentence true or false? Two different elements can have the same atomic number. _____false_____

10. What is the mass number of an atom? _The mass number of an atom is the sum of the protons and neutrons in the nucleus of that atom._

11. Complete the equation in the table below.

Number of neutrons =	Mass number	–	Atomic number

Isotopes (page 112)

12. Every atom of a given element has the same number of _____protons_____ and _____electrons_____.

13. Every atom of a given element does not have the same number of _____neutrons_____.

14. What are isotopes? _Isotopes are atoms of the same element that have different numbers of neutrons and different mass numbers._

15. All oxygen atoms have 8 protons. Circle the letter of the number of neutrons in an atom of oxygen-18.
    a. 8   b. 9
    (c.) 10   d. 18

16. Is the following sentence true or false? Isotopes of oxygen have different chemical properties. _____false_____

17. Water that contains hydrogen-2 atoms instead of hydrogen-1 atoms is called _____heavy water_____.

Name_____ Class_____ Date_____ M T W T F

Modern Atomic Theory

Time
2 periods
1 block

Section Objectives

Local Standards

- **4.3.1 Describe** Bohr's model of the atom and the evidence for energy levels.

- **4.3.2 Explain** how the electron cloud model represents the behavior and locations of electrons in atoms.

- **4.3.3 Distinguish** the ground state from excited states of an atom based on electron configurations.

Vocabulary energy levels • electron cloud • orbital • electron configuration • ground state

1 FOCUS

Build Vocabulary: LINCS
Have students use the LINCS strategy to learn the terms *energy levels, electron cloud, orbital, electron configuration,* and *ground state.* **L2**

Targeted Resources
❏ Transparency: Interest Grabber 4.3
❏ Transparency: Reading Strategy 4.3

2 INSTRUCT

Build Reading Literacy: Relate Text and Visuals
Have students read Bohr's Model of the Atom on pp. 113–116. Then, have students examine the diagram of Bohr's model in the time line on p. 115. Ask students what the circles around the nucleus represent. **L1**

Integrate Space Science
Have students research when Pluto will next be closer to the sun than Neptune. **L2**

Science and History
Have groups of students build or draw models that represent the changes over time in scientists' understanding of atomic structure. **L2**

Build Science Skills: Using Models
Have students examine the propeller in Figure 14, and ask how the moving propeller is similar to an electron cloud. Ask for other examples that could model the concept of an electron cloud. **L2**

Teacher Demo: Electron Cloud Model
Use balloons and beads to create a model of the nucleus of a boron atom. Students will use this model to describe the probable position of electrons. **L2**

Quick Lab: Comparing Excited States
Have students use fluorescent markers to draw a picture. Then, have them observe their drawings under a UV lamp. Students will explain how UV light causes objects to glow, and they will be able to use the persistence of light to compare excited states. **L2**

Targeted Resources
❏ Transparency: Figure 15: Number of Orbitals and Electrons in Energy Levels
❏ GRSW Section 4.3
❏ **NSTA** *scLINKS* Energy levels

3 ASSESS

Reteach
Use the diagrams on p. 115 in the Science and History feature to review Bohr's model, energy levels, and electron clouds. **L1**

Evaluate Understanding
Have students draw and label a diagram that represents Bohr's model of an atom. Then, have students explain how the electron cloud model differs from Bohr's model. **L2**

Targeted Resources
❏ **PHSchool.com** Online Section 4.3 Assessment
❏ iText Section 4.3

Transparencies

48 **Section 4.3 Interest Grabber**

Probability

Scientists use probability to describe how electrons behave in atoms. Try the following activity to learn more about probability.

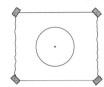

Tape a large piece of paper to the wall. Draw a circle 1-foot in diameter in the center of the paper. Mark the exact center of the circle. Leave plenty of room on all sides of the circle. Blindfold a partner. Place your partner two arm lengths away from the wall facing the wall. Give your partner a small sticker. Have your partner walk forward and try to place the sticker at the center of the circle. Repeat this process five times.

1. Describe the pattern of the stickers.

2. Was the probability of placing a sticker in the center of the circle high or low?

3. What could increase the probability of placing a sticker inside the circle?

Transparencies

49 **Section 4.3 Reading Strategy**

Sequencing

Electrons and Energy Levels

a. ___?___ → Excited state → b. ___?___ → Emits energy

Transparencies

50 **Figure 15 Number of Orbitals and Electrons in Energy Levels**

Energy Levels, Orbitals, and Electrons		
Energy Level	Number of Orbitals	Maximum Number of Electrons
1	1	2
2	4	8
3	9	18
4	16	32

Guided Reading and Study Workbook

Name _____ Class _____ Date _____

Chapter 4   Atomic Structure

Section 4.3 Modern Atomic Theory
(pages 113–118)

This section focuses on the arrangement and behavior of electrons in atoms.

Reading Strategy (page 113)

Sequencing After you read, complete the description in the flow chart below of how the gain or loss of energy affects electrons in atoms. For more information on this Reading Strategy, see the **Reading and Study Skills** in the **Skills and Reference Handbook** at the end of your textbook.

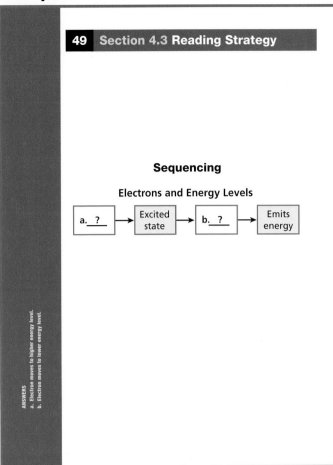

Electron moves to higher energy level → Excited State → Electron moves to lower energy level → Emits energy

Bohr's Model of the Atom (pages 113–116)

1. Circle the letter of the sentence that tells how Bohr's model of the atom differed from Rutherford's model.
   a. Bohr's model focused on the nucleus.
   b. Bohr's model focused on the protons.
   c. Bohr's model focused on the neutrons.
   d. Bohr's model focused on the electrons.

2. Is the following sentence true or false? In Bohr's model of the atom, electrons have a constant speed and move in fixed orbits around the nucleus. _____true_____

3. What can happen to an electron in an atom when the atom gains or loses energy? The electron can move from one energy level to another.

4. What evidence do scientists have that electrons can move from one energy level to another? Scientists can measure the energy gained or lost by electrons.

5. Is the following sentence true or false? When electrons release energy, some of the energy may be released as visible light. _____true_____

Electron Cloud Model (page 116)

6. Is the following sentence true or false? Bohr's model was correct in assigning energy levels to electrons. _____true_____

7. When trying to predict the locations and motions of electrons in atoms, scientists must work with _____probability_____.

8. What is an electron cloud? An electron cloud is a visual model of the most likely locations for the electrons in an atom.

Guided Reading and Study Workbook

Name _____ Class _____ Date _____

Chapter 4   Atomic Structure

9. Is the following sentence true or false? Scientists use the electron cloud model to describe the exact location of electrons around the nucleus. _false_

Atomic Orbitals (page 117)

10. Is the following sentence true or false? An orbital is a region of space around the nucleus where an electron is likely to be found. _true_

11. An electron model is a good approximation of _how electrons behave in their orbitals_.

Use this table to answer questions 12 and 13.

Energy Level	Number of Orbitals	Maximum Number of Electrons
1	1	2
2	4	8
3	9	18
4	16	32

12. Higher energy levels have ____more____ orbitals than lower energy levels do.

13. What is the relationship between the number of orbitals and the maximum number of electrons in an energy level? _The maximum number of electrons in an energy level is twice the number of orbitals._

Electron Configurations (page 118)

14. What is an electron configuration? _An electron configuration is the arrangement of electrons in the orbitals of an atom._

15. Circle the letter of the number of energy levels needed for a lithium atom's three electrons when the atom is in its ground state.
a. zero   (b.) one
c. two   d. three

16. Is the following sentence true or false? An excited state is less stable than a ground state. _true_

17. Circle the letters of each sentence that is true when all of the electrons in an atom are in orbitals with the lowest possible energies.
(a.) The electrons are in the most stable configuration.
b. The electrons are in an unstable configuration.
c. The atom is in an excited state.
(d.) The atom is in its ground state.

Guided Reading and Study Workbook

Name _____ Class _____ Date _____

Chapter 4   Atomic Structure

WordWise

Solve the clues to determine which vocabulary terms from Chapter 4 are hidden in the puzzle. Then find and circle the terms in the puzzle. The terms may occur vertically, horizontally, or diagonally.

Clues	Hidden Words
Dense, positively charged mass in the center of an atom	nucleus
Positively charged subatomic particle found in the nucleus	proton
Neutral subatomic particle found in the nucleus	neutron
Number of protons in an atom of an element	atomic number
Sum of the protons and neutrons in the nucleus of an atom	mass number
Atoms of the same element having different numbers of neutrons	isotopes
Possible energies that electrons in an atom can have	energy levels
Visual model of the most likely locations for electrons in an atom	electron cloud
Region of space where an electron is likely to be found	orbital
Term for an atom whose electrons have the lowest possible energies	ground state

---

Guided Reading and Study Workbook

Name _____ Class _____ Date _____

Chapter 4   Atomic Structure

Electrons and Orbitals

Use the table on page 117 of your textbook to find the ratio of the maximum number of electrons to the number of orbitals for each of four energy levels.

Math Skill: Ratios and Proportions

You may want to read more about this **Math Skill** in the **Skills and Reference Handbook** at the end of your textbook.

1. Read and Understand

What information are you given?
The number of orbitals and the maximum number of electrons per energy level

2. Plan and Solve

What unknown are you trying to calculate?
The ratio of the maximum number of electrons to the number of orbitals in energy levels 1 through 4

What mathematical expression can you use to calculate the unknown?

$$\frac{\text{maximum number of electrons}}{\text{number of orbitals}}$$

Level 1: $\frac{2}{1} = \frac{2}{1}$ Level 3: $\frac{18}{9} = \frac{2}{1}$

Level 2: $\frac{4}{2} = \frac{2}{1}$ Level 4: $\frac{32}{16} = \frac{2}{1}$

3. Look Back and Check

Is your answer reasonable?
The ratio is the same for all four energy levels. Also, each orbital can contain only two electrons.

Math Practice

On a separate sheet of paper, solve the following problems.

1. Calculate the maximum number of electrons for energy levels 5 and 6. Energy level 5 contains 25 orbitals; energy level 6 contains 36 orbitals. Each orbital can contain two electrons at most. For energy level 5, $2 \times 25 = 50$, so the maximum number is 50 electrons. For energy level 6, $2 \times 36 = 72$, so the maximum number is 72 electrons.

2. Energy level 7 can contain a maximum of 98 electrons. How many orbitals are there in energy level 7? Each orbital can contain two electrons at most, so 98 electrons divided by 2 electrons per orbital equals 49 orbitals.

3. A sodium atom has 11 electrons. How many orbitals in a sodium atom contain electrons? Each orbital can contain up to 2 electrons, so 11 electrons divided by 2 is 5 with a remainder of 1. There are 6 occupied orbitals.

Student Edition Lab Worksheet

Name _____ Class _____ Date _____

Chapter 4   Atomic Structure   **Forensics Lab**

Using Flame Tests

See page 119 in the Teacher's Edition for more information.

Forensic scientists use various approaches to distinguish substances. In this lab, you will observe the flame colors of several substances and use the data to determine the identity of an unknown substance.

Problem How can the color of a flame be used to distinguish substances?

Materials
• solutions of calcium chloride, boric acid, potassium chloride, copper(II) sulfate, sodium chloride, and an unknown
• Bunsen burner
• nichrome wire loop
• dilute solution of hydrochloric acid
• wash bottle with distilled water

Skills Observing, Predicting, Using Data Tables

Procedure 🥽 🧤 🔥 ✖ 🧥
Part A: Observing Flame Colors

1. Light the Bunsen burner. **CAUTION:** *Put on safety goggles and a lab apron. Tie back loose hair and clothing before working with a flame.*

2. Dip the wire loop into the calcium chloride solution and then place the loop in the flame. Observe and record the color of the flame in the data table.

DATA TABLE

Solution	Flame Color
Calcium chloride	Orange
Potassium chloride	Violet
Boric acid	Light green
Copper(II) sulfate	Green
Sodium chloride	Yellow-orange
Unknown	
Identity of unknown	

Student Edition Lab Worksheet

Name _____ Class _____ Date _____

3. Clean the loop by dipping it into hydrochloric acid. Then, while holding the loop over a sink, rinse away the acid with distilled water. **CAUTION:** *Keep hydrochloric acid away from your skin and clothing. Do not breathe in its vapor.*

4. Repeat Steps 2 and 3 with each of the other solutions. Be careful not to transfer any solution from one container to another. **CAUTION:** *These chemicals are poisonous. Do not let them get on your skin.*

Part B: Examining an Unknown Solution

5. Obtain the unknown solution from your teacher.

6. Repeat Steps 2 and 3, using the unknown solution. Compare your observations with the other data that you recorded to identify the unknown. **CAUTION:** *Wash your hands thoroughly before leaving the laboratory.*

Analyze and Conclude

1. **Comparing and Contrasting** Is there a relationship between the color of the flame and the color of the solution?

There is no relationship between flame color and solution color.

2. **Formulating Hypotheses** How do these substances produce light of different colors?

When the compounds are placed in the flame, atoms absorb energy and electrons move to

higher energy levels. As these electrons move back to lower energy levels, they release energy

as visible light. The color of light produced depends on the difference in energy between two

specific energy levels in an atom.

3. **Drawing Conclusions** A forensic scientist does a flame test on a substance that was found at a crime scene. What might the scientist conclude if the flame turns green?

The green flame indicates that the substance may contain copper, barium, or boron.

Lab Manual

Name _____ Class _____ Date _____

Chapter 4   Atomic Structure   Investigation 4A

Constructing Models of Atoms

Background Information Refer students to pages 108–118 in their textbooks for a discussion of atomic structure. **SKILLS FOCUS:** Using Models **CLASS TIME:** 45 minutes

With an electron microscope, scientists can observe the arrangement of atoms on the surface of a material. But they cannot observe the arrangement of subatomic particles within an atom. Scientists use models to describe the structure of atoms.

Atomic models are revised as scientists learn more about atoms. Thomson revised Dalton's model of atoms as solid spheres when he discovered that atoms contained subatomic particles. To explain why most alpha particles could pass through a thin metal foil without being deflected, Rutherford proposed an atomic model with a dense, positively charged nucleus. The nucleus contains protons and neutrons. In the Bohr model of the atom, electrons move in fixed orbits around the nucleus, like planets around a sun. The currently accepted model of the atom assumes that the movement of electrons is less predictable. In the current model, an electron cloud is used to describe the likely locations for electrons in atoms.

Isotopes are atoms of a given element that contain different numbers of neutrons. Isotopes have the same atomic number, but different mass numbers. In this investigation, you will construct a model of an isotope. Then, you will evaluate your model and identify ways in which it can be improved.

Problem

How might the structure of an atom be modeled?

Pre-Lab Discussion

Read the entire investigation. Then, work with a partner to answer the following questions.

1. **Classifying** How do isotopes of the same element differ?

The isotopes of an element have different numbers of neutrons.

2. **Using Tables and Graphs** How can you use the information in Figure 1 to determine the number of protons, neutrons, and electrons in an isotope?

The number of electrons and protons is equal to the atomic number. The number of neutrons

can be calculated by subtracting the atomic number from the mass number, which is included

in the name of the isotope.

Lab Manual

Name _____ Class _____ Date _____

3. **Using Models** What will you use the following items to represent: red pushpins, green pushpins, beads, pipe cleaners?

Red pushpins represent protons, green pushpins represent neutrons, beads represent electrons, and

pipe cleaners represent energy levels.

4. **Using Models** How will you model different isotopes of the same element?

Isotopes are modeled by varying the number of green pushpins, which represent neutrons

that are attached to the plastic-foam ball.

5. **Drawing Conclusions** Which model of the atom does the model you will construct most resemble? Explain your answer.

The model resembles the Bohr model of an atom because the electrons have paths that resemble

the orbits of planets.

Materials *(per group)*
2 plastic-foam balls
pipe cleaners
red pushpins
green pushpins
beads Provide beads that are smaller than the pushpins but large enough to thread onto the pipe cleaners.
2 coat hangers
fishing line Provide about 2 m for each model that students construct.
scissors

Safety ⚠️ ✂️

Put on safety goggles. Be careful when handling sharp instruments. Note all safety alert symbols next to the steps in the Procedure and review the meaning of each symbol by referring to the Safety Symbols on page xiii.

Lab Manual

Name _____ Class _____ Date _____

Procedure

1. Construct a model of one of the isotopes assigned by your teacher. Use the information in Figure 1 to predict the number of protons, neutrons, and electrons in the isotope. In the data table, record this information and the name of the isotope.

Figure 1

Element	Atomic Number	Stable Isotopes
Hydrogen	1	hydrogen-1, hydrogen 2
Helium	2	helium-3, helium-4
Lithium	3	lithium-6, lithium-7
Boron	5	boron-10, boron-11
Carbon	6	carbon-12, carbon-13
Nitrogen	7	nitrogen-14, nitrogen-15
Oxygen	8	oxygen-16, oxygen-17, oxygen-18
Neon	10	neon-20, neon-21, neon-22
Magnesium	12	magnesium-24, magnesium-25, magnesium-26
Silicon	14	silicon-28, silicon-29, silicon-30
Sulfur	16	sulfur-32, sulfur-33, sulfur-34, sulfur-36
Chlorine	17	chlorine-35, chlorine-37
Argon	18	argon-36, argon-38, argon-40

Assign two isotopes of a single element to each group. Groups with more than two students can be assigned elements with more than two stable isotopes.

2. In your model, red pushpins will represent protons, green pushpins will represent neutrons, and beads will represent electrons. Collect the appropriate number of each item for your model.

3. The plastic-foam ball will represent the nucleus. Insert the appropriate number of red and green pushpins into the ball to represent the correct number of protons and neutrons.

4. Recall that the first energy level can hold 2 electrons, the second energy level can hold 8 electrons, and the third energy level can hold 18 electrons. Calculate the number of energy levels occupied by electrons when atoms of your isotope are in the ground state. Record this number in the data table.

Lab Manual

Name _____ Class _____ Date _____

5. Use pipe cleaners to construct the appropriate number of energy levels for your isotope, as shown in Figure 2. Twist the ends of several pipe cleaners together to make the energy levels long enough to circle the nucleus, but do not close up the pipe-cleaner circles.

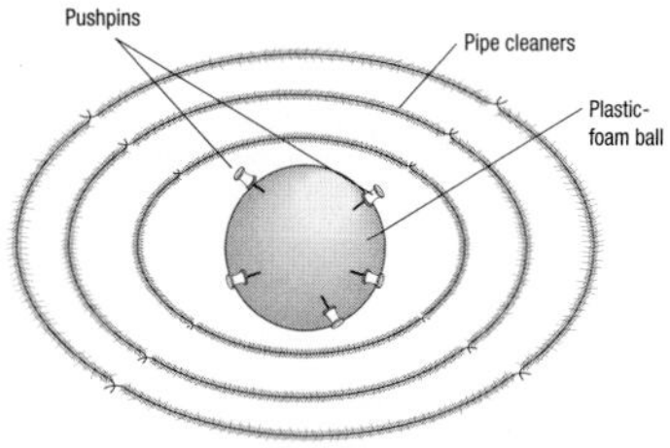

Figure 2
Pushpins
Pipe cleaners
Plastic-foam ball

6. Place the appropriate number of beads on each pipe-cleaner circle to represent the electrons in each energy level. In the data table, record the number of electrons in each energy level.
7. Place the energy levels around the nucleus. If there is more than one occupied energy level, place the levels in the correct order.
8. Use fishing line to attach the nucleus and energy levels to a coat hanger, as shown in Figure 3. Your model is now complete.
9. Repeat Steps 1–8 to model the second isotope of your element.

The easiest way to attach the fishing line to the ball is to wrap and tie the fishing line around one or more of the pushpins.

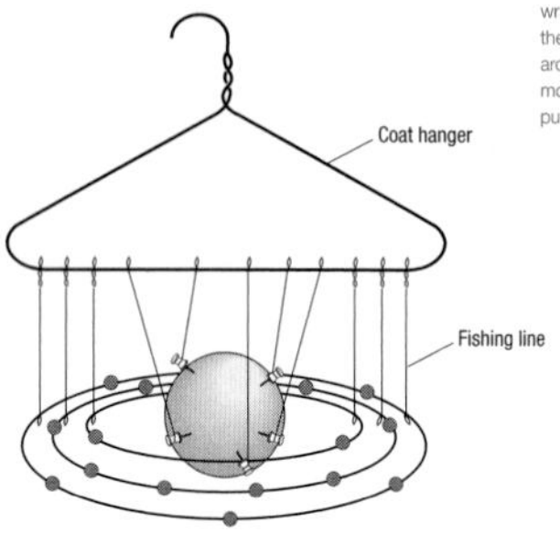

Figure 3
Coat hanger
Fishing line

Lab Manual

Name _____ Class _____ Date _____

Observations

DATA TABLE Sample data are shown.

Isotope	Chlorine-35	Chlorine-37
Atomic number	17	17
Mass number	35	37
Number of protons	17	17
Number of neutrons	18	20
Number of electrons	17	17
Number of energy levels occupied by electrons	3	3
Number of electrons in first energy level	2	2
Number of electrons in second energy level	8	8
Number of electrons in third energy level	7	7

Analysis and Conclusions

1. **Using Models** Why were pushpins with the same mass used to represent protons and neutrons in your model?

   Protons and neutrons have nearly the same mass.
   _____
   _____
   _____

2. **Using Models** Why were the objects used to represent electrons smaller than the objects used to represent protons and neutrons?

   An electron has a much smaller mass than a proton or a neutron (about 1/2000 as massive).
   _____
   _____
   _____

3. **Comparing and Contrasting** How were the two models that you constructed similar? How were they different?

   The models had the same number of red pushpins and beads because isotopes have the same

   number of protons and electrons. The models had a different number of green pushpins because

   isotopes have different numbers of neutrons.

Lab Manual

Name _____ Class _____ Date _____

4. **Applying Concepts** Explain why a model of an atom must always contain the same number of protons and electrons.

   Because atoms are neutral (zero net charge), they always have the same number of positively

   charged protons and negatively charged electrons.
   _____
   _____

5. **Evaluating** What are some inaccuracies in the way your models represent the nucleus?

   The models represent the nucleus as too large compared to the overall volume of an atom.

   The models represent the protons and neutrons as attached to the nucleus. In fact, the collection

   of protons and neutrons is the nucleus.
   _____
   _____

6. **Evaluating and Revising** In what two ways does your model fail to accurately depict the electrons in an atom?

   Electrons in atoms are in constant motion. Electrons do not travel in fixed paths around

   the nucleus.
   _____
   _____
   _____

Go Further

Describe a physical model that could more closely represent the currently accepted model of an atom. Focus on how the model could best represent the behavior of electrons.

Models will vary, but should reflect the fact that electrons are in constant motion and that the locations of the electrons are unpredictable. One approach would be to use a fan to blow the objects representing electrons around within a container. Students might suggest using the appropriate number of small flying insects within a closed container to represent the motion of electrons. Students may propose a general approach, using a computer program to randomly assign "electrons" to given locations around a nucleus. Those locations would be constantly changing.

Lab Manual

Name _____ Class _____ Date _____

Chapter 4   Atomic Structure   Investigation 4B

Modeling the Location of an Electron in an Atom

Refer students to pages 108–118 in their textbooks for a discussion of atomic structure. **SKILLS FOCUS:** Inferring, Using Models **CLASS TIME:** 25 minutes

Background Information

In the atomic models of the early twentieth century, electrons were said to move around the nucleus along specific paths, much as the planets move around the sun. However, experimental evidence has indicated that the precise position of an electron in an atom cannot be known or predicted. Scientists can speak only of the probability of finding electrons at various locations, not of their exact positions.

Probability is a measure of how often a certain event will occur out of a total number of events. For example, there are two ways a coin can land—with its head facing up or its tail facing up. Each side has a 50 percent (or one out of two) probability of landing face up for any toss.

An **electron cloud** provides a visual model for the probable behavior of an electron in an atom. The electron cloud shows the likelihood that an electron will be found in a given part of the atom around the nucleus. If the electron is not likely to be found at a particular position, the cloud appears less dense. If the electron is more likely to be found at a particular position, the cloud has a denser appearance, as shown in Figure 1.

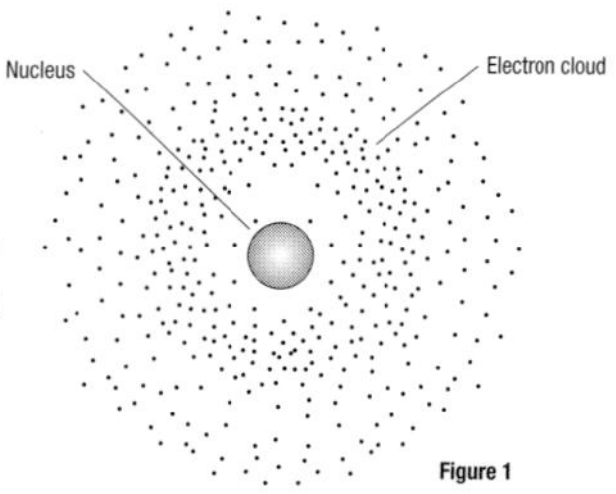

In this investigation, you will use probability to describe the location of an electron in an atom.

Nucleus
Electron cloud
Figure 1

Problem

How can the location of an electron in an atom be described?

Pre-Lab Discussion

Read the entire investigation. Then, work with a partner to answer the following questions.

1. **Applying Concepts** Scientists use probability to predict the behavior of electrons in an atom. What is probability?

   Probability is the likelihood of an event occurring. Probability is equal to the number of times a

   particular event occurs divided by the total number of events.

Lab Manual

Name _____ Class _____ Date _____

2. Applying Concepts According to the way you will mark your die at the beginning of this investigation, what is the probability of the electron being found in the zone closest to the "nucleus" (0–4 cm)? In the second closest zone (4–6 cm)? In the third closest zone (6–8 cm)?

1/6; 4/6 = 2/3; 1/6

3. Predicting Describe the results you expect to observe.

Most colored-in squares will be between 4 cm and 6 cm from the center, while fewer

colored-in squares will be between 0 cm and 4 cm, and between 6 cm and 8 cm.

4. Inferring What can you infer about the probable locations of an electron in an atom from the above prediction?

The electron is not likely to be found at the closest possible distances to the nucleus, nor is it likely

to be very far away. The most probable location of the electron is within a band on either side of

a given radius from the nucleus.

5. Comparing and Contrasting Do you expect your results to be identical to those of other students, or similar to those of other students, or completely different from those of other students? Explain your answer.

Students should expect similar, but not identical results because not all students will fill in exactly

the same squares, nor will they obtain exactly the same results when they roll the die. On the average,

however, their results should not differ greatly.

Materials (per group)
game die
masking tape
graph paper   Provide graph paper with about 2 squares per centimeter.
pencil
red pencil
metric ruler

Procedure

1. Cover all six sides of the die with masking tape. Mark one of the sides with one dot, four of the sides with two dots each, and the remaining side with three dots.
2. Select a square near the center of the graph paper and use a red pencil to color it red. This red square will represent the nucleus of a hydrogen atom with one electron.

Lab Manual

Name _____ Class _____ Date _____

3. Toss the die. Use a regular pencil to color in a square according to the following rules:

If the number 1 appears face up on the die, color in any square that is between 0 cm and 4 cm from the "nucleus."

If the number 2 appears face up on the die, color in any square that is between 4 cm and 6 cm from the "nucleus."

If the number 3 appears face up on the die, color in any square that is between 6 cm and 8 cm from the "nucleus."

4. Repeat Step 3, tossing the die and marking the graph for a total of 50 tosses. Record your results in the data table.

Observations   Sample data are shown.

DATA TABLE

Distance from "Nucleus"	Number of Colored-in Squares
0–4 cm	6–10
4–6 cm	30–38
6–8 cm	6–10

Analysis and Conclusions

1. Observing In which zone are most of the colored-in squares on your diagram?

The second zone, which is between 4 cm and 6 cm from the "nucleus"

2. Using Models What does each colored-in square on your diagram represent?

Each square represents a chance of finding the electron in a particular location around the nucleus.

3. Inferring Based on your data, where would you be most likely to find an electron? Explain your answer.

The electron would be most likely found in the region with the most colored-in squares,

which is between 4 cm and 6 cm from the "nucleus."

Lab Manual

Name _____ Class _____ Date _____

4. Comparing and Contrasting Compare your diagram to a classmate's. Are they identical? In what ways are they alike or different?

The average concentration of colored-in squares at the various distances is similar.

The actual positions of the colored-in squares are different in each diagram.

5. Drawing Conclusions Can the exact position of an electron in an atom be determined? What can you know about an electron's location?

The exact position of an electron cannot be determined. The probability that an electron is located

at a certain distance from the nucleus can be known.

6. Predicting Suppose you had tossed the die 100 times. How do you think your results would have compared with the results you obtained by tossing the die 50 times?

The probabilities should remain about the same, although the number of darkened squares in each

area would approximately double.

Go Further

Redesign the procedure in this investigation to model the behavior of the two electrons in a helium atom. Can the electrons be in the same location at the same time? Can they be in the same location at different times? Describe the modified procedure and the results you might expect.

Students might suggest using a second die to represent the second electron and tossing both dies each time. They could use different colored pencils to represent the probable locations of each electron. To adjust for the possibility of the electrons occupying the same location at different times, students might fill in only half a square at a time. They could complete the square for the other electron on a later toss. The overall distribution would not change. More filled squares would be in the zone between 4–6 cm than in the zones between 0–4 cm or 6–8 cm.

Chapter Test A

Name _____ Class _____ Date _____

Chapter 4   Atomic Structure   Chapter Test A

Multiple Choice

Write the letter that best answers the question or completes the statement on the line provided.

_____ **1.** Democritus thought that matter was made of tiny particles
   a. of earth, air, fire, and water.
   b. that could not be divided.
   c. that could be divided.
   d. that were all round and smooth.

_____ **2.** If 2 grams of element X combine with 4 grams of element Y to form compound XY, how many grams of element Y would combine with 12 grams of X to form the same compound?
   a. 6 grams   **b.** 12 grams
   c. 18 grams   **d.** 24 grams

_____ **3.** Which of the following most accurately represents John Dalton's model of the atom?
   a. a tiny, solid sphere with an unpredictable mass for a given element
   b. a hollow sphere with a dense nucleus
   c. a tiny, solid sphere with a predictable mass for a given element
   d. a sphere that is hollow throughout

_____ **4.** J.J. Thomson's experiments provided evidence that an atom
   a. is the smallest particle of matter.
   b. contains negatively charged particles.
   c. has a negative charge.
   d. has a positive charge.

_____ **5.** Rutherford's gold foil experiment provided evidence for which of the following statements?
   a. Negative and positive charges are spread evenly throughout an atom.
   b. Alpha particles have a positive charge.
   c. Gold is not as dense as previously thought.
   d. There is a dense, positively charged mass in the center of an atom.

_____ **6.** Which statement best describes Rutherford's model of the atom?
   a. It is like an avocado with the pit representing the nucleus.
   b. It is like an aquarium with swimming fish representing positive charges.
   c. It is like a fried egg with the yolk representing the nucleus.
   d. It is like a huge stadium with a positively charged marble at the center.

Chapter Test A

Name _____ Class _____ Date _____

_____ 7. Which statement about subatomic particles is true?
  a. Protons, neutrons, and electrons all have about the same mass.
  b. Unlike protons or neutrons, electrons have no mass.
  c. Neutrons have no charge and no mass.
  d. An electron has far less mass than either a proton or neutron.

_____ 8. Which of the following is unique for any given element?
  a. the number of neutrons
  b. the charge on the electrons
  c. the number of protons
  d. the mass of a neutron

_____ 9. Suppose an atom has a mass number of 35. Which statement is true beyond any doubt?
  a. The atom has an odd number of neutrons.
  b. The atomic number is less than 17.
  c. The atom is not an isotope.
  d. The number of protons in the nucleus does not equal the number of neutrons.

_____ 10. Which statement is true about oxygen-17 and oxygen-18?
  a. They do not have the same number of protons.
  b. Their atoms have an identical mass.
  c. They are isotopes of oxygen.
  d. The have the same mass number.

_____ 11. How was Bohr's atomic model similar to Rutherford's model?
  a. It assigned energy levels to electrons.
  b. It described electron position in terms of the electron cloud model.
  c. It described how electrons gain or lose energy.
  d. It described a nucleus surrounded by a large volume of space.

_____ 12. Which statement accurately represents the arrangement of electrons in Bohr's atomic model?
  a. Electrons vibrate in fixed locations around the nucleus.
  b. Electrons travel around the nucleus in fixed energy levels with energies that vary from level to level.
  c. Electrons travel around the nucleus in fixed energy levels with equal amounts of energy.
  d. Electrons travel randomly in the relatively large space outside the nucleus.

_____ 13. What do scientists use to predict the locations of electrons in atoms?
  a. probability   **b.** algebra
  c. geometry   **d.** ratios and proportions

Chapter Test A

Name _____ Class _____ Date _____

_____ 14. Which statement about electrons and atomic orbitals is NOT true?
  a. An electron has the same amount of energy in all orbitals.
  b. An orbital can contain a maximum of two electrons.
  c. An electron cloud represents all the orbitals in an atom.
  d. An atom's lowest energy level has only one orbital.

_____ 15. The glowing of a neon light is caused by electrons emitting energy as they
  a. move from lower to higher energy levels.
  b. collide with other electrons.
  c. move from higher to lower energy levels.
  d. collide with the nucleus.

Completion
Complete each statement on the line provided.

1. Unlike Democritus, Aristotle did not believe that matter was composed of tiny, indivisible _____.

2. John Dalton observed that elements always combine in the same ratio to form a particular _____.

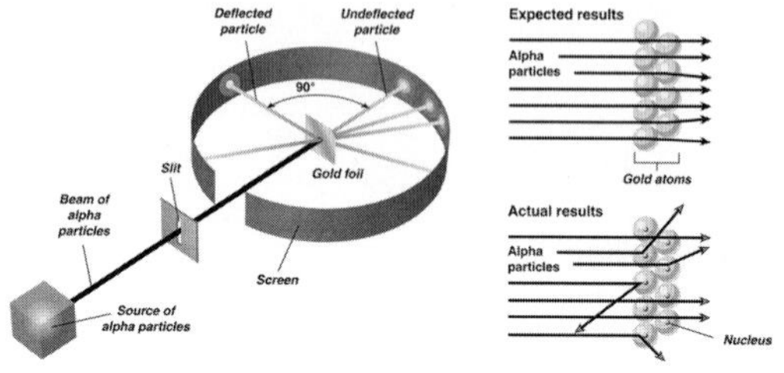

Figure 4-1

3. In Rutherford's gold foil experiment, shown in Figure 4-1, alpha particles that bounce straight back from the foil have struck _____ in the gold atoms.

4. The region in which an electron is most likely to be found is called a(an) _____.

5. An atom in which an electron has moved to a higher energy level is in a(an) _____ state.

Chapter Test A

Name _____ Class _____ Date _____

Short Answer
Use complete sentences to write the answers to the questions on the lines provided.

1. What scientific word comes from a Greek word meaning "uncut"? Which Greek philosopher first used the word to describe matter?

2. If an atom of an element has a mass number of 31 and 16 neutrons in its nucleus, what is the atomic number of the element?

3. If an atom of germanium has a mass number of 70 and an atomic number of 32, how many neutrons are in its nucleus?

4. What did Bohr's model of the atom do that Rutherford's model did not?

5. How does the electron cloud model of the atom represent the locations of electrons in atoms?

Chapter Test A

Name _____ Class _____ Date _____

Using Science Skills
Use the diagram to answer each question. Write the answers on a separate sheet of paper.

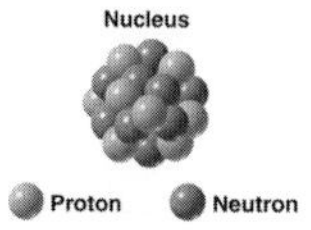

Figure 4-2

1. **Analyzing Data** What subatomic particles are represented in Figure 4-2? Assuming all the particles in the nucleus are visible, what are the atomic and mass numbers of the atom shown?
2. **Inferring** Would Dalton have recognized the model of a nucleus shown in Figure 4-2? Explain your answer.
3. **Inferring** Would Rutherford have recognized the model of a nucleus in Figure 4-2? Explain your answer.
4. **Inferring** Why do you think the proton was discovered before the neutron? (*Hint:* Consider the properties of protons and neutrons.)
5. **Evaluating** Is Figure 4-2 a useful model of an atom? Explain your answer.

Essay
Write the answer to each question on a separate sheet of paper.

1. Why did Rutherford propose a new model of the atom after seeing the results of the gold foil experiment?
2. A sample of calcium contains calcium-40, calcium-44, calcium-42, calcium-48, calcium-43, and calcium-46 atoms. Explain why these atoms can have different mass numbers, but they must have the same atomic number.
3. Why is Bohr's model of the atom often called the planetary model?
4. What is the difference between an orbital and the electron cloud?
5. Explain what the colors in a fireworks display reveal about the movement of electrons in atoms.

Name _____ Class _____ Date _____

Chapter 4 Atomic Structure   Chapter Test B

Multiple Choice

Write the letter that best answers the question or completes the statement on the line provided.

_____ 1. The Greek philosopher Democritus coined what word for a tiny piece of matter that cannot be divided?
a. element   b. atom
c. electron   d. molecule

_____ 2. According to John Dalton's observations, when elements combine in a compound,
a. the ratio of their masses is always the same.
b. each element contributes an equal number of atoms.
c. their volumes are always equal.
d. their masses are always equal.

_____ 3. Which of the following is NOT part of John Dalton's atomic theory?
a. All elements are composed of atoms.
b. All atoms of the same element have the same mass.
c. Atoms contain subatomic particles.
d. A compound contains atoms of more than one element.

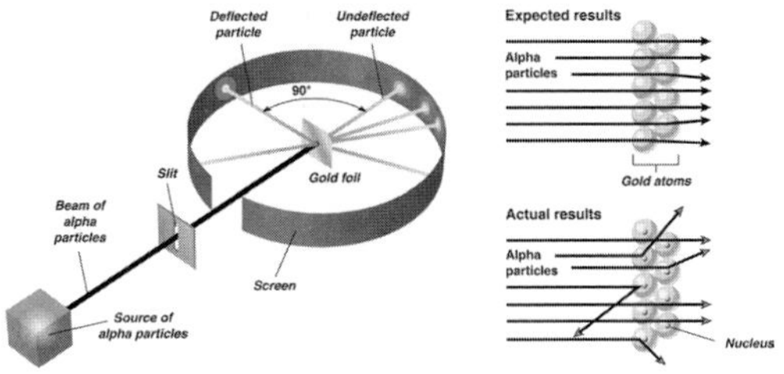

Figure 4-1

_____ 4. The diagram in Figure 4-1 shows the results of Rutherford's gold foil experiment. What caused some of the alpha particles to bounce straight back from the gold foil?
a. electrons in the gold atoms
b. negative charges in the gold atoms
c. other alpha particles
d. nuclei in the gold atoms

Name _____ Class _____ Date _____

_____ 5. Who provided evidence for the existence of a nucleus in an atom?
a. John Dalton
b. J.J. Thomson
c. Democritus
d. Ernest Rutherford

_____ 6. In an atomic model that includes a nucleus, positive charge is
a. concentrated in the center of an atom.
b. spread evenly throughout an atom.
c. concentrated at multiple sites in an atom.
d. located in the space outside the nucleus.

_____ 7. Which subatomic particle has a negative charge?
a. electron   b. alpha particle
c. neutron   d. proton

_____ 8. Which statement about subatomic particles is NOT true?
a. Protons and neutrons have almost the same mass.
b. Protons and electrons have opposite charges.
c. Unlike protons and electrons, neutrons have no charge.
d. Protons and neutrons have the same charge.

_____ 9. The number of protons in one atom of an element is that element's
a. mass number.   b. balanced charge.
c. atomic number.   d. isotope.

_____10. To find the number of neutrons in an atom, you would subtract
a. mass number from atomic number.
b. atomic number from mass number.
c. atomic number from electron number.
d. isotope number from atomic number.

_____11. In Niels Bohr's model of the atom, electrons move
a. like balls rolling down a hill.
b. like planets orbiting the sun.
c. like popcorn in a popcorn popper.
d. like beach balls on water waves.

_____12. What can you assume has happened if an electron moves to a higher energy level?
a. The atom has become more stable.
b. The electron has lost energy.
c. The electron has gained energy.
d. The atom has lost an electron.

Name _____ Class _____ Date _____

_____13. What does the electron cloud model describe?
a. the most likely locations of electrons in atoms
b. the precise locations of electrons in atoms
c. the number of electrons in an atom
d. the mass of the electrons in an atom

_____14. Which of the following provides the best analogy for an electron in an atomic orbital?
a. a bee moving from flower to flower in a garden
b. a bird resting on a tree branch
c. an ant crawling on the surface of a leaf
d. a bee trying to escape from a closed jar

_____15. What is the difference between an atom in the ground state and an atom in an excited state?
a. The atom in the ground state has less energy and is less stable than the atom in an excited state.
b. The atom in an excited state has one fewer electron than the atom in the ground state.
c. The atom in an excited state has more energy and is less stable than the atom in the ground state.
d. The atom in an excited state has one more electron than the atom in the ground state.

Completion

Complete each statement on the line provided.

1. According to _____, all matter was made up of four elements—earth, air, fire, and water.
2. John Dalton concluded that all the atoms of a single _____ have the same mass.
3. The subatomic particle that J.J. Thomson discovered has a(an) _____ charge.
4. In Rutherford's gold foil experiment, some of the _____ aimed at gold atoms bounced back, suggesting that a solid mass was at the center of the atom.
5. Protons and _____ are found in the nucleus of an atom.
6. If element Q has 11 protons, its atomic _____ is 11.
7. The nuclei of isotopes contain different numbers of _____.
8. In Bohr's model of the atom, _____ move in fixed orbits around the nucleus.
9. The moving blades of an airplane propeller provide an analogy for the electron _____ model.

Name _____ Class _____ Date _____

10. When all the electrons in an atom are in orbitals with the lowest possible energy, the atom is in its _____ state.

Short Answer

Use complete sentences to write the answers to the questions on the lines provided.

1. What did Democritus believe about matter?
_____
_____
_____

2. How did the results of J.J. Thomson's experiments change how scientists thought about atoms?
_____
_____
_____
_____

3. What did Rutherford conclude about the location of positive charge in an atom?
_____
_____
_____
_____

4. What is the maximum number of electrons that an atomic orbital can contain?
_____
_____
_____

5. How does the state of atoms in a neon light change when light is emitted?
_____
_____
_____
_____

Chapter Test B

Name _____ Class _____ Date _____

Using Science Skills

Use the diagram to answer each question. Write the answers on a separate sheet of paper.

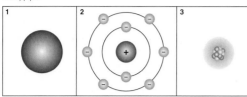

Figure 4-2

1. **Comparing and Contrasting** In Figure 4-2, what is the main difference between the atomic model in panel 1 and the model in panel 2?

2. **Comparing and Contrasting** In Figure 4-2, what is the main difference between the atomic model in panel 2 and the model in panel 3?

3. **Interpreting Graphics** Are the atomic models in Figure 4-2 arranged in the order that they were developed? Explain your answer.

4. **Using Analogies** Read the following analogy and explain how it applies to panels 1 and 2 in Figure 4-2: The atomic model in panel 1 is to the model in panel 2 as a drawing of the outside of a house is to a blueprint of the inside.

5. **Evaluating** In Figure 4-2, how is the atomic model in panel 2 helpful to your understanding of the atom? In what ways is it not helpful?

Chapter 4 Test A Answers

Multiple Choice

1. b **2.** a **3.** c **4.** b **5.** d **6.** d
7. d **8.** c **9.** d **10.** c **11.** d **12.** b
13. a **14.** a **15.** c

Completion

1. atoms **2.** compound **3.** nuclei **4.** orbital **5.** excited

Short Answer

1. atom; Democritus **2.** 15 **3.** 38 **4.** Bohr's model focused on electrons. **5.** It provides a visual model of the most likely locations of electrons in an atom.

Using Science Skills

1. The particles are protons and neutrons. This atom has an atomic number of 8 and a mass number of 17. **2.** Dalton probably would not have recognized this model because he thought of the atom as a solid indivisible ball and had no knowledge of subatomic particles. **3.** Yes; Rutherford demonstrated the existence of a nucleus, named subatomic particles with a positive charge protons, and predicted the existence of neutrons. **4.** The proton has a positive charge, but the neutron has no charge. It was easier to detect the existence of a charged particle because its path could be deflected by a charged plate. **5.** Students may answer yes because the model shows the composition of the nucleus of an atom. Students may answer no because the model does not include any electrons or show the position of the nucleus in the atom.

Essay

1. Thomson's model no longer explained all the available evidence. In Thomson's model, for example, positive charge was spread evenly throughout the atom. Rutherford had concluded that the positive charge of an atom was concentrated in the center of the atom. **2.** All the atoms of an element have the same atomic number because the atomic number equals the number of protons in an atom. If one of the atoms had a different number of protons, the atom would not be a calcium atom. The mass number can vary because it is the sum of the protons and neutrons and because isotopes of an element can have different numbers of neutrons. **3.** Bohr's atomic model represents electrons as moving in fixed orbits around the nucleus like planets moving in orbits around a sun. **4.** An orbital is a region of space around the nucleus where an electron is likely to be found. The electron cloud is a visual model that represents all the orbitals in an atom. **5.** When fireworks explode, the heat produced by the explosions causes some electrons in atoms to move to higher energy levels. When the electrons return to lower energy levels, some of the energy is released as visible light. The colors vary because each element has a different set of energy levels.

Chapter 4 Test B Answers

Multiple Choice

1. b **2.** a **3.** c **4.** d **5.** d **6.** a
7. a **8.** d **9.** c **10.** b **11.** b **12.** c
13. a **14.** d **15.** c

Completion

1. Aristotle **2.** element **3.** negative **4.** alpha particles **5.** neutrons
6. number **7.** neutrons **8.** electrons **9.** cloud **10.** ground

Short Answer

1. Democritus believed all matter consisted of tiny particles that could not be divided into smaller particles. **2.** Scientists realized that atoms contained smaller subatomic particles. **3.** Rutherford concluded that positive charge was concentrated in the nucleus of an atom. **4.** two **5.** The atoms return from an excited state to the ground state.

Using Science Skills

1. Panel 1 depicts an atom as a solid sphere without any subatomic particles. Panel 2 shows an atom that has a subatomic structure. **2.** The main difference is the way in which electron motion is depicted. In panel 2, the movement of electrons is represented by fixed circular orbits. In panel 3, the probable locations of the moving electrons are represented by a cloud. **3.** Yes; they go from the simplest (the solid sphere in 1) to the most complex (the electron cloud model in panel 3). Students may specifically cite John Dalton in connection with panel 1 and Niels Bohr in connection with panel 2 to support their answers. **4.** The solid ball in panel 1 is like the drawing of the exterior of a house. It provides no details about the internal structure of an atom. The model in panel 2 shows the locations of different parts of the atom within the atom and their relative sizes. It is like a blueprint that shows the size and location of rooms in a house. **5.** It is helpful because it shows the general locations of the subatomic particles in an atom. It is not helpful because it implies that electrons travel in fixed paths around the nucleus.

Chapter 5 The Periodic Table

Planning Guide

Use these planning tools
Easy Planner
Resource Pro
Online Lesson Planner

SECTION OBJECTIVES	STANDARDS		ACTIVITIES and LABS
	NATIONAL (See p. T18.)	STATE	
5.1 Organizing the Elements, pp. 126–129 🕐 1 block or 2 periods **5.1.1 Describe** how Mendeleev arranged the elements in his table. **5.1.2 Explain** how the predictions Mendeleev made and the discovery of new elements demonstrated the usefulness of his periodic table.	A-1, A-2, B-2, G-1, G-2, G-3		**SE** Inquiry Activity: How Much Data Do You Need to Identify a Pattern? p. 125 **L2** **SE** Quick Lab: Making a Model of a Periodic Table, p. 128 **L2**
5.2 Modern Periodic Table, pp. 130–138 🕐 1 block or 2 periods **5.2.1 Describe** the arrangement of elements in the modern periodic table. **5.2.2 Explain** how the atomic mass of an element is determined and how atomic mass units are defined. **5.2.3 Identify** general properties of metals, nonmetals, and metalloids. **5.2.4 Describe** how properties of elements change across a period in the periodic table.	A-1, A-2, B-1, B-2		**SE** Quick Lab: Defining a Metal, p. 135 **L2** **SE** Exploration Lab: Predicting the Density of an Element, pp. 150–151 **L2** **TE** Teacher Demo: Period 3 Properties, p. 138 **L2** **LM** Investigation 5A: Analyzing Patterns in the Periodic Table **L2**
5.3 Representative Groups, pp. 139–145 🕐 1 block or 2 periods **5.3.1 Relate** the number of valence electrons to groups in the periodic table and to properties of elements in those groups. **5.3.2 Predict** the reactivity of some elements based on their locations within a group. **5.3.3 Identify** some properties of common A group elements.	B-1, B-2, B-3, C-1, C-5, F-1, F-3, F-5		**TE** Teacher Demo: Comparing Alkaline Earth Metals, p. 141 **L2** **LM** Investigation 5B: Comparing Chemical Properties **L1**

Ability Levels

- **L1** For students who need additional help
- **L2** For all students
- **L3** For students who need to be challenged

Components

SE Student Edition	**GRSW** Guided Reading	**CTB** Computer Test Bank	**T** Transparencies
TE Teacher's Edition	& Study Workbook	**TP** Test Prep Resources	**P** Presentation Pro
LM Laboratory Manual	With Math Support	**iT** iText	CD-ROM
PLM Probeware Lab	**CUT** Chapter and Unit	**DC** Discovery Channel	**GO** Internet Resources
Manual	Tests	Videotapes	

RESOURCES PRINT and TECHNOLOGY

GRSW Section 5.1 — L1

T Chapter 5 Pretest — L2
Section 5.1 — L2

P Chapter 5 Pretest — L2
Section 5.1 — L2

NSTA SC*LINKS* **GO** Periodic table — L2

PLM Lab 2: Predicting the
Density of an Element — L2

GRSW Section 5.2 — L1

GRSW Math Skill — L2

T Section 5.2 — L2

P Section 5.2 — L2

NSTA SC*LINKS* **GO** Periodic law — L2

GRSW Section 5.3 — L1

Discovery SCHOOL DC You Are What
You Eat — L2

T Section 5.3 — L2

P Section 5.3 — L2

SCIENCE NEWS **GO** Elements — L2

SECTION ASSESSMENT

SE Section 5.1
Assessment, p. 129

iText iT Section 5.1

SE Section 5.2
Assessment, p. 138

iText iT Section 5.2

SE Section 5.3
Assessment, p. 145

iText iT Section 5.3

Go Online

Go online for these Internet resources.

PHSchool.com
Web Code: cca-1050

NSTA SC*LINKS*
Web Code: ccn-1051
Web Code: ccn-1052

SCIENCE NEWS
Web Code: cce-1053

Materials for Activities and Labs

Quantities for each group

STUDENT EDITION

Inquiry Activity, p. 125
stapled stack of paper with
familiar phrases (some letters
replaced with squares)

Quick Lab, p. 128
resealable plastic sandwich
bag, different colored paint
chip strips

Quick Lab, p. 135
forceps; magnesium; test
tubes; test-tube rack; graduated
cylinder; 20 mL 2 M HCl; small
pieces of sulfur, aluminum, and
silicon

Exploration Lab, pp. 150–151
unlined white paper, scissors,
metric ruler, balance, forceps,
silicon, tin, lead shot, 50-mL
graduated cylinder, graph
paper, periodic table

TEACHER'S EDITION

Teacher Demo, p. 138
6-volt battery, flashlight bulb
with holder, 3 pieces of
insulated wire with the ends
stripped, 2.5-cm aluminum
strip, small silicon chip,
2.5-cm piece of sulfur

Teacher Demo, p. 141
small samples of beryllium,
magnesium, and calcium;
cold and hot water; 5 500-mL
beakers

Build Science Skills, p. 147
empty containers of fortified
food products such as milk,
juice, salt, and bread

Chapter Assessment

CHAPTER ASSESSMENT

SE Chapter Assessment,
pp. 153–154
CUT Chapter 5 Test A, B
CTB Chapter 5
iT Chapter 5
PHSchool.com GO
Web Code: cca-1050

STANDARDIZED TEST PREP

SE Chapter 5, p. 155
TP Diagnose and Prescribe

iText—interactive textbook with
assessment at PHSchool.com

The Periodic Table   **124B**

Name_____ Class_____ Date_____ M T W T F

LESSON PLAN 5.1

Organizing the Elements

Time
2 periods
1 block

Section Objectives

■ **5.1.1. Describe** how Mendeleev arranged the elements in his table.

■ **5.1.2 Explain** how the predictions Mendeleev made and the discovery of new elements demonstrated the usefulness of his periodic table.

Vocabulary periodic table

Local Standards

1 FOCUS

Build Vocabulary: Related Word Forms
Use the word *periodical* to help students understand the meaning of *periodic*. Explain that a periodical is published at regular intervals. **L2**

Targeted Resources
❏ Transparency: Chapter 5 Pretest
❏ Transparency: Interest Grabber 5.1
❏ Transparency: Reading Strategy 5.1

2 INSTRUCT

Build Reading Literacy: Sequence
Have students create a flowchart showing the sequence in which elements were organized into groups. **L1**

Integrate Social Studies
Have students research and compare discovery dates for elements with the dates those elements were first isolated. **L2**

Quick Lab: Making a Model of a Periodic Table
Students use color chips to organize items in an array based on properties. Students predict where an additional item would fit in an incomplete array. **L2**

Address Misconceptions
Have students research the contributions of different scientists on one scientific advance. **L2**

Targeted Resources
❏ Transparency: Figure 3: Mendeleev's Table of Elements (1872)
❏ GRSW Section 5.1
❏ **NSTA** *sci*$_{LINKS}$ Periodic table

3 ASSESS

Reteach
Use Figure 3 to review Mendeleev's strategy for arranging the elements into rows and columns to form a periodic table. **L1**

Evaluate Understanding
Have each student write a review question related to the content of one of the four pages in Section 5.1. **L2**

Targeted Resources
❏ **PHSchool.com** Online Section 5.1 Assessment
❏ iText Section 5.1

51 **Chapter 5 Pretest**

1. Which of the following is a symbol for an element?

   a. Aluminum

   b. Al

   c. al

   d. AL

2. Is flammability a physical property or a chemical property?

3. What happens to the composition of matter during a physical change?

4. What does the atomic number of an element represent?

52 **Chapter 5 Pretest** (continued)

5. Different isotopes of an element have different numbers of

   a. neutrons.

   b. electrons.

   c. protons.

   d. nuclei.

6. True or False: Electrons in atoms occupy orbitals in energy levels.

7. Which element is more reactive, oxygen or nitrogen?

53 **Section 5.1 Interest Grabber**

A Logical Organization

The ability to organize information in a logical way is a valuable skill. Have you ever noticed the way shoeboxes are arranged in a shoe store? Sometimes the shoeboxes are separated into a series of vertical stacks (or columns) by style. Within each stack, the shoes are arranged by size.

1. How is this system of organizing shoes useful?

2. Explain how a calendar organizes time.

3. Think of another example of how information is organized.

54 **Section 5.1 Reading Strategy**

Identifying Main Ideas

Topic	Main Idea
Mendeleev's proposal	a._____?_____
Mendeleev's prediction	b._____?_____
Evidence supporting Mendeleev's table	c._____?_____

Transparencies

55 Figure 3 Mendeleev's Table of Elements (1872)

Group I	Group II	Group III	Group IV	Group V	Group VI	Group VII	Group VIII
H = 1							
Li = 7	Be = 9.4	B = 11	C = 12	N = 14	O = 16	F = 19	
Na = 23	Mg = 24	Al = 27.3	Si = 28	P = 31	S = 32	Cl = 35.5	Fe = 56, Co = 59,
K = 39	Ca = 40	— = 44	Ti = 48	V = 51	Cr = 52	Mn = 55	Ni = 59, Cu = 63.
(Cu = 63)	Zn = 65	— = 68	— = 72	As = 75	Se = 78	Br = 80	Ru = 104, Rh = 104,
Rb = 85	Sr = 87	Yt = 88	Zr = 90	Nb = 94	Mo = 96	— = 100	Pd = 106, Ag = 108.
(Ag = 108)	Cd = 112	In = 113	Sn = 118	Sb = 122	Te = 125	I = 127	
Cs = 133	Ba = 137	Di = 138	Ce = 140				
(—)	—	Er = 178	La = 180	Ta = 182	W = 184	—	Os = 195, Ir = 197,
							Pt = 198, Au = 199.
(Au = 199)	Hg = 200	Tl = 204	Pb = 207	Bi = 208		—	
			Th = 231		U = 240		

Guided Reading and Study Workbook

Section 5.1 Organizing the Elements
(pages 126–129)

This section explains how Mendeleev organized elements into a periodic table. It also discusses the predictions he made about undiscovered elements and how the discovery of those elements supported his version of the table of the table.

Reading Strategy (page 126)

Identifying Main Ideas As you read, complete the table by identifying the main idea for each topic. For more information on this reading strategy, see the **Reading and Study Skills** in the **Skills and Reference Handbook** at the end of your textbook.

Topic	Main Idea
Mendeleev's proposal	Mendeleev arranged the elements into rows in order of increasing mass so that elements with similar properties were in the same column.
Mendeleev's prediction	Mendeleev used the properties of existing elements to predict properties of undiscovered elements.
Evidence supporting Mendeleev's table	The close match between Mendeleev's predictions and the actual properties of new elements showed how useful his periodic table could be.

The Search for Order (page 126)

1. Is the following sentence true or false? The first elements to be identified were mainly gases. _____false_____
2. As the number of known elements grew, so did the need to organize them into groups based on their ____properties____.
3. Circle the letter of each category that the French chemist Antoine Lavoisier used to classify elements.
   (a.) gases   (b.) metals
   c. liquids   (d.) nonmetals

Mendeleev's Periodic Table (pages 127–129)

4. Is the following sentence true or false? Mendeleev needed to organize information about 63 elements. _____true_____
5. Mendeleev's strategy for classifying elements was modeled on a(n) ____card game or solitaire____.
6. Circle the letter of each type of information Mendeleev knew about each element.
   (a.) name
   b. number of protons
   (c.) relative mass
   (d.) properties

Guided Reading and Study Workbook

7. Mendeleev arranged the elements into rows in order of ____increasing mass____ so that elements with similar properties were in the same column.
8. Is the following sentence true or false? A periodic table is an arrangement of elements in columns, based on a set of properties that repeat from row to row. _____true_____

Group I	Group II	Group III	Group IV	Group V	Group VI	Group VII	Group VIII
H = 1							
Li = 7	Be = 9.4	B = 11	C = 12	N = 14	O = 16	F = 19	
Na = 23	Mg = 24	Al = 27.3	Si = 28	P = 31	S = 32	Cl = 35.5	Fe = 56, Co = 59,
K = 39	Ca = 40	— = 44	Ti = 48	V = 51	Cr = 52	Mn = 55	Ni = 59, Cu = 63.
(Cu = 63)	Zn = 65	— = 68	— = 72	As = 75	Se = 78	Br = 80	Ru = 104, Rh = 104,
Rb = 85	Sr = 87	Yt = 88	Zr = 90	Nb = 94	Mo = 96	— = 100	Pd = 106, Ag = 108.
(Ag = 108)	Cd = 112	In = 113	Sn = 118	Sb = 122	Te = 125	I = 127	
Cs = 133	Ba = 137	Di = 138	Ce = 140				
(—)	—	Er = 178	La = 180	Ta = 182	W = 184	—	Os = 195, Ir = 197,
							Pt = 198, Au = 199.
(Au = 199)	Hg = 200	Tl = 204	Pb = 207	Bi = 208		—	
			Th = 231		U = 240		

9. Mendeleev published the table above in 1872. Why did Mendeleev leave some locations in his periodic table blank? He left room for undiscovered elements.
   _____

10. Circle the letters of two elements that have similar properties.
    a. zinc (Zn)   (b.) chlorine (Cl)
    c. nitrogen (N)   (d.) bromine (Br)
11. How did Mendeleev decide where to place arsenic (As) and selenium (Se)? He placed them where they fit best based on their properties.
    _____

12. Is the following sentence true or false? Mendeleev was the first scientist to arrange elements in a periodic table. _____false_____
13. Describe a test for the correctness of a scientific model. One test is whether the model can be used to make accurate predictions.
14. Mendeleev used the ____properties of elements____ located near the spaces in his table to predict properties for undiscovered elements.
15. The close match between Mendeleev's predictions and the actual properties of new elements showed ____how useful his periodic table could be____.
16. Circle the letter of each element that was discovered after Mendeleev published his periodic table that supported Mendeleev's predictions and provided evidence validating the table.
    (a.) gallium   (b.) scandium
    (c.) germanium   d. aluminum

LESSON PLAN 5.2

The Modern Periodic Table

Section Objectives

- **5.2.1 Describe** the arrangement of elements in the modern periodic table.
- **5.2.2 Explain** how the atomic mass of an element is determined and how atomic mass units are defined.
- **5.2.3 Identify** general properties of metals, nonmetals, and metalloids.
- **5.2.4 Describe** how properties of elements change across a period in the periodic table.

Vocabulary period • group • periodic law • atomic mass unit (amu) • metals • transition metals • nonmetals

Local Standards

1 FOCUS

Build Vocabulary: Vocabulary Knowledge Rating
Have students keep track of their vocabulary knowledge before and after reading the section.
L2

Targeted Resources
❑ Transparency: Interest Grabber 5.2
❑ Transparency: Reading Strategy 5.2

2 INSTRUCT

Build Reading Literacy: Preview
Have students preview the section, focusing on headings, visuals, and boldfaced material. **L1**

Integrate Language Arts
Have students identify strategies used to name elements. **L2**

Build Science Skills: Comparing and Contrasting
Have students compare and contrast an up-to-date periodic table with a periodic table that is a few years old. **L2**

Address Misconceptions
Explain to students that all atoms of an element are isotopes. **L2**

Quick Lab: Defining a Metal
Students add hydrocholoric acid to magnesium, sulfur, aluminum, and silicon. Students will use a chemical property to distinguish metals. **L2**

Teacher Demo: Variation Across a Period
Touch the free ends of an open circuit to samples of aluminum, silicon, and sulfur. Students observe differences in electrical conductivity among three elements. **L2**

For Enrichment
Students research the techniques of glassblowers for shaping glass with the molding process described on page 137. **L3**

Targeted Resources
❑ Transparency: Figure 7: The Periodic Table of Elements
❑ Transparency: Figure 9: Isotopes of Chlorine
❑ GRSW Section 5.2
❑ **NSTA** sc*L*INKS Periodic law

3 ASSESS

Reteach
Use Figure 13 to illustrate how the properties of elements change from left to right across a period. **L1**

Evaluate Understanding
Ask students to identify the general properties of metals, nonmetals, and metalloids. **L2**

Targeted Resources
❑ **PHSchool.com** Online Section 5.2 Assessment
❑ iText Section 5.2

Transparencies

56 | **Section 5.2 Interest Grabber**

Displaying Information About Elements

For each element there are many useful pieces of information, such as its name, symbol, atomic number, and state at room temperature. Look at the information for the element copper. There are different ways to display this information. On a piece of paper, design a way to organize the information inside a small square. You can use devices such as color to help fit the information in the square. Think about how this square will fit in a table that includes all the elements.

Copper
Symbol = Cu
Metal
Atomic Number = 29
Solid at room temperature

Transparencies

57 | **Section 5.2 Reading Strategy**

Previewing

Questions About the Periodic Table	
Question	Answer
a._____?_____	b._____?_____
c._____?_____	d._____?_____

Transparencies

58 | **Figure 7 Periodic Table of the Elements**

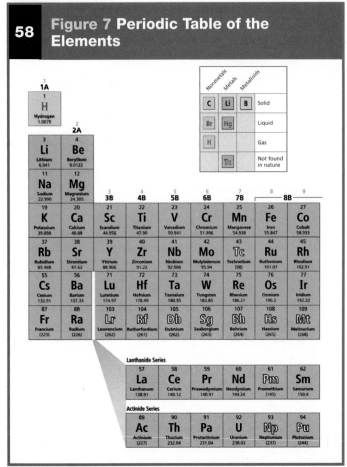

Transparencies

59 | **Figure 7 Periodic Table of the Elements** (*continued*)

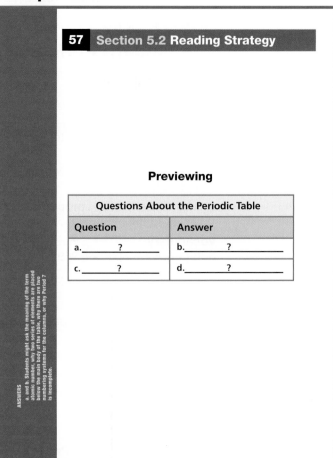

Transparencies

60 Figure 9 Isotopes of Chlorine

Distribution of Chlorine Isotopes in Nature

Isotope	Percentage	Atomic Mass
Chlorine-35	75.78%	34.969
Chlorine-37	24.22%	36.966

Guided Reading and Study Workbook

Name _____ Class _____ Date _____

Chapter 5   The Periodic Table

Section 5.2 The Modern Periodic Table
(pages 130–138)

This section explains the organization of the modern periodic table and discusses the general properties of metals, nonmetals, and metalloids.

Reading Strategy (page 130)

Previewing Before you read, complete the table by writing two questions about the periodic table on pages 132–133. As you read, write answers to your questions. For more information on this reading strategy, see the **Reading and Study Skills** in the **Skills and Reference Handbook** at the end of your textbook.

Questions About the Periodic Table	
Question	**Answer**
Students might ask: What does atomic mass mean?	Atomic mass is a value that depends on the distribution of an element's isotopes in nature and the masses of those isotopes.
Why are two series of elements placed below the main body of the table?	Two series of elements are placed below the table to make the table more compact.

Other possible questions: Why are there two numbering systems for the columns? Why is period 7 incomplete?

The Periodic Law (pages 131–133)

1. Is the following sentence true or false? In the modern periodic table, elements are arranged by increasing number of protons. _____ true

2. Explain why the number of elements per period varies. The number of elements per period varies because the number of available orbitals increases from energy level to energy level.

3. Properties of elements repeat in a predictable way when atomic numbers are used to arrange elements into groups. This pattern of repeating properties is called the _____ periodic law.

Atomic Mass (page 134)

4. Label the four types of information supplied for chlorine in the diagram.

   a. ___ 17
   b. ___ Cl
   c. ___ Chlorine
   d. ___ 35.453

a. ___ Atomic number   b. ___ Element symbol
c. ___ Element name   d. ___ Atomic mass

Guided Reading and Study Workbook

Name _____ Class _____ Date _____

Chapter 5   The Periodic Table

5. Define atomic mass. Atomic mass is a value that depends on the distribution of an element's isotopes in nature and the masses of those isotopes

6. Circle the letter of each sentence that is true about a carbon-12 atom.
   (a.) It has 6 protons and 6 neutrons.
   b. Scientists assigned a mass of 6 atomic mass units to the carbon-12 atom.
   (c.) It is used as a standard for comparing the masses of atoms.
   (d.) An atomic mass unit is defined as one twelfth the mass of a carbon-12 atom.

7. Is the following sentence true or false? Most elements exist as a mixture of two or more isotopes. _____ true

8. The mass of an atom of chlorine-37 is _____ greater _____ than the mass of an atom of chlorine-35.

9. Is the following sentence true or false? All values are equally important in a weighted average. _____ false

Classes of Elements (pages 135–136)

10. Name the three categories into which elements are classified based on their general properties.
   a. _____ Metals
   b. _____ Metalloids
   c. _____ Nonmetals

11. Is the following sentence true or false? All metals react with oxygen in the same way. _____ false

12. An important property of transition elements is their ability to form compounds with distinctive colors

13. Circle the letter of each sentence that is true about nonmetals.
   (a.) Nonmetals are poor conductors of heat and electric current.
   (b.) Many nonmetals are gases at room temperature.
   (c.) Some nonmetals are extremely reactive and others hardly react at all.
   d. Nonmetals that are solids tend to be malleable.

Variation Across a Period (page 138)

14. Across a period from left to right, the elements become _____ less _____ metallic and _____ more _____ nonmetallic in their properties.

15. Circle the letter of each Period 3 element that is highly reactive.
   (a.) sodium   b. silicon
   (c.) chlorine   d. argon

Name_____ Class_____ Date_____ M T W T F

LESSON PLAN 5.3

Representative Groups

Time
2 periods
1 block

Section Objectives
Local Standards

- ■ **5.3.1 Relate** the number of valence electrons to groups in the periodic table and to properties of elements in those groups.
- ■ **5.3.2 Predict** the reactivity of some elements based on their locations within a group.
- ■ **5.3.3 Identify** some properties of common A group elements.

Vocabulary valence electron • alkali metals • alkaline earth metals • halogens • noble gases

1 FOCUS

Build Vocabulary: Concept Map
Have students construct a concept map with eight branches titled Groups in the Periodic Table. **L2**

Targeted Resources
❏ Transparency: Interest Grabber 5.3
❏ Transparency: Reading Strategy 5.3

2 INSTRUCT

Build Reading Literacy: Identify Main Idea/Details
Have students apply the reading strategy to look for main idea and supporting details on page 143. **L1**

Integrate Space Science
Have students research and write a comparison and contrast of the cores of Jupiter and Earth. **L2**

Build Science Skills: Relating Cause and Effect
Have students research the origin of the terms *cesium* and *rubidium*. **L2**

Teacher Demo: Comparing Alkaline Earth Metals
Demonstrate reactions of beryllium, magnesium, and calcium when mixed with water of different temperatures. Students use observations to distinguish three alkaline earth metals. **L2**

Integrate Math
Have students create a circle graph showing eight elements that make up 98.5% of Earth's crust. **L2**

Build Science Skills: Inferring
Explain that a light bulb with tungsten filament contains small amounts of gases that do not react easily. **L2**

Address Misconceptions
Remind students that the air they breathe is a mixture of gases—not only oxygen. **L2**

Targeted Resources
❏ GRSW Section 5.3
❏ **NSTA** *sci*$_{LINKS}$ Elements

3 ASSESS

Reteach
Use segments of the periodic table shown throughout section 5.3 to review each A group. **L1**

Evaluate Understanding
Have students write information about A group elements on separate index cards. **L2**

Targeted Resources
❏ **PHSchool.com** Online Section 5.3 Assessment
❏ iText Section 5.3

Transparencies

61 Section 5.3 Interest Grabber

Other Periodic Tables

Most periodic tables of the elements have the same general organization as the one in your textbook. However, there are some periodic tables that look quite different. Look at Theodor Benfey's version of a periodic table, which he made in 1960.

1. How is it similar to the periodic table in your book?

2. How is it different from the periodic table in your book?

3. Is there any advantage to Benfey's arrangement of the elements?

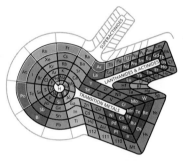

Theodore Benfey's version of the Periodic Table

SAMPLE ANSWERS
1. Both tables have the elements arranged in order of increasing atomic number and in groups with similar properties.
2. In Benfey's table the elements are arranged in a spiral instead of columns and rows. Benfey's table contains no data except the symbols of the elements.
3. The lanthanides and actinides are more closely connected to the other elements and it is clearer that hydrogen has the atomic number 1. (The most significant advantage is that the spiral format shows the connection between periods and atomic structure.)

Transparencies

62 Section 5.3 Reading Strategy

Monitoring Your Understanding

Element	Important Fact
Magnesium	a._____?
Aluminum	b._____?
Chlorine	c._____?

ANSWERS
Possible answers:
a. Magnesium plays a key role in the production of sugar in plants. Mixtures of magnesium and other metals can be as strong as steel, but much lighter.
b. Aluminum is the most abundant metal in Earth's crust. Much less energy is needed to purify recycled aluminum than to extract aluminum from bauxite.
c. Chlorine is a highly reactive, nonmetal gas that is used to kill bacteria in water.

Guided Reading and Study Workbook

Name _____ Class _____ Date _____

Chapter 5 The Periodic Table

Section 5.3 Representative Groups
(pages 139–145)

This section discusses how the number of valence electrons affects the properties of elements. It also describes properties of elements in Groups 1A through 8A.

Reading Strategy (page 139)

Monitoring Your Understanding As you read, record an important fact about each element listed in the table. For more information on this reading strategy, see the **Reading and Study Skills** in the **Skills and Reference Handbook** at the end of your textbook.

Element	Important Fact
Magnesium	Possible answers: Magnesium plays a key role in the process that uses sunlight to produce sugar in plants. Mixtures of magnesium and other metals are used in transportation because they can be as strong as steel, but much lighter.
Aluminum	Aluminum is the most abundant metal in Earth's crust. It is strong, lightweight, malleable, and a good conductor of electric current. Much less energy is needed to purify recycled aluminum than to extract aluminum from bauxite.
Chlorine	Chlorine is a highly reactive, nonmetal gas. Chlorine is used to kill bacteria in drinking water and swimming pools.

Valence Electrons (page 139)

1. An electron that is in the highest occupied energy level of an atom is a(n) ____valence____ electron.

2. Elements within a group have the ____same____ number of valence electrons.

The Alkali Metals (page 140)

3. The reactivity of alkali metals ____increases____ from the top of Group 1A to the bottom.

4. Sodium is stored under oil because it ____reacts with water vapor in air____.

The Alkaline Earth Metals (page 141)

5. Differences in reactivity among alkaline earth metals are shown by the way they react with ____water____.

Find and match two properties to each element listed.

	Alkaline Earth Metal	Property
b, c	6. magnesium	a. Helps build strong teeth and bones
a, d	7. calcium	b. Helps plants produce sugar
		c. Is used to make lightweight bicycle frames
		d. Is the main ingredient in limestone

Guided Reading and Study Workbook

Name _____ Class _____ Date _____

Chapter 5 The Periodic Table

The Boron Family (page 142)

8. List the four metals in Group 3A.

   a. ____Aluminum____ b. ____Gallium____

   c. ____Indium____ d. ____Thallium____

9. Circle the letter of each sentence that is true about aluminum.

   a. It is the most abundant metal in Earth's crust.

   b. It is often found combined with oxygen in bauxite.

   c. It is more reactive than sodium and magnesium.

   d. It is a good conductor of electric current.

The Carbon Family (page 142)

10. List the two metalloids in Group 4A.

   a. ____Silicon____ b. ____Germanium____

11. Except for water, most of the compounds in your body contain ____carbon____

The Nitrogen Family (page 143)

12. List the nonmetals in Group 5A.

   a. ____Nitrogen____ b. ____Phosphorus____

13. Name two elements in the nitrogen family that are contained in fertilizer.

   a. ____Nitrogen____ b. ____Phosphorus____

The Oxygen Family (page 143)

14. List the nonmetals in Group 6A.

   a. ____Oxygen____ b. ____Sulfur____ c. ____Selenium____

15. Name the most abundant element in Earth's crust.
   ____Oxygen____

The Halogens (page 144)

16. List the four nonmetals in Group 7A.

   a. ____Fluorine____ b. ____Chlorine____

   c. ____Bromine____ d. ____Iodine____

17. Halogens have similar ____chemical____ properties but different ____physical____ properties.

The Noble Gases (page 145)

18. Name three characteristics of noble gases.

   a. ____Colorless____ b. ____Odorless____ c. ____Extremely unreactive____

19. How can an element that does not react easily with other elements be useful? ____It can be used to prevent reactions with such highly reactive elements as oxygen.____

Guided Reading and Study Workbook

Name _____ Class _____ Date _____

Chapter 5   The Periodic Table

WordWise

Match each definition with the correct term by writing the definition's number in the grid. When you have filled in all the boxes, add up the numbers in each column, row, and the two diagonals. Hint: The sum should be 15 in each case.

Definitions

1. An arrangement of elements in columns based on a set of properties that repeat from row to row
2. A pattern of repeating properties that occurs when atomic numbers are used to arrange elements into groups
3. One twelfth the mass of a carbon-12 atom
4. Elements that are good conductors of heat and electric current
5. Elements that form a bridge between the elements on the left and right sides of the periodic table
6. Elements that are poor conductors of heat and electric current
7. Elements with properties that fall between those of metals and nonmetals
8. An electron that is in the highest occupied energy level of an atom
9. Colorless, odorless, and extremely unreactive gases

			diagonal = ___ 15
nonmetals 6	periodic table 1	valence electron 8	= ___ 15
metalloids 7	transition metals 5	atomic mass unit 3	= ___ 15
periodic law 2	noble gas 9	metals 4	= ___ 15
= ___ 15	= ___ 15	= ___ 15	diagonal = ___ 15

Guided Reading and Study Workbook

Name _____ Class _____ Date _____

Chapter 5   The Periodic Table

Calculating Average Atomic Mass

Carbon has two stable isotopes. Carbon-12 has an assigned atomic mass of 12.0000 and a percentage in nature of 98.93%. The atomic mass of carbon-13 is 13.0034 and its percentage in nature is 1.070%. What is the average atomic mass for carbon?

Math Skill: Percents and Decimals

You may want to read more about this **Math Skill** in the **Skills and Reference Handbook** at the end of your textbook.

1. Read and Understand

What information are you given?

carbon-12: atomic mass = 12.0000, % in nature = 98.93
carbon-13: atomic mass = 13.0034, % in nature = 1.070

2. Plan and Solve

What unknown are you trying to calculate?

Average atomic mass for carbon = ?

What equation can you use?

(atomic mass C-12) (% C-12) + (atomic mass C-13) (% C-13) = average atomic mass of C

Convert the percentages to decimals and multiply the atomic mass of each isotope by the decimal representing its percentage in nature.

(12.0000) (0.9893) = 11.8716 rounded to 11.87
(13.0034) (0.01070) = 0.1391364 rounded to 0.1391

Add the products of the two multiplications to find the average atomic mass for carbon.

11.87 + 0.1391 = 12.0091 rounded to 12.01

3. Look Back and Check

Is your answer reasonable?

Because almost all the carbon atoms in nature are carbon-12 atoms, the average atomic mass of carbon (12.01) is close to the atomic mass of carbon-12 (12.0000).

Math Practice

On a separate sheet of paper, solve the following problems.

1. The element boron has two stable isotopes. Boron-10 has an atomic mass of 10.0129 and a percentage in nature of 19.78% The atomic mass of boron-11 is 11.0093 and its percentage in nature is 80.22% What is the average atomic mass for boron?

$$\frac{(1.978 \times 10.0129) + (0.8022 \times 11.0093)}{2} = \frac{1.980 + 8.831}{2} = 10.81$$

2. Nitrogen has two stable isotopes, nitrogen-14 and nitrogen-15. Nitrogen-14 has an atomic mass of 14.0031. Its percentage in nature is 99.63%. What is the percentage in nature of nitrogen-15?

$100.00\% - 99.63\% = 0.37\%$

Student Edition Lab Worksheet

Name _____ Class _____ Date _____

Chapter 5   The Periodic Table   **Exploration Lab**

Predicting the Density of an Element
See pages 150 and 151 in the Teacher's Edition for more information.

Density is a useful property for identifying and classifying elements. In this exploration, you will determine the densities of three elements in Group 4A—silicon, tin, and lead. Then, you will use your data to predict the density of another element in Group 4A—germanium.

Problem Can the densities of elements within a group be used to help predict the density of another element in the group?

Materials
• unlined white paper
• scissors
• metric ruler
• balance
• forceps
• silicon
• tin
• lead shot
• 50-mL graduated cylinder
• graph paper
• periodic table

Skills Measuring, Observing, Using Graphs, Calculating

Procedure 🖾 🖾 🖾 🖾 🖾
Part A: Measuring Mass

DATA TABLE

Element	Mass of Paper (g)	Mass of Paper and Element (g)	Mass of Element (g)	Volume of Water (cm³)	Volume of Water and Element (cm³)	Volume of Element (cm³)	Density of Element (g/cm³)
Silicon							
Tin							
Lead							

Student Edition Lab Worksheet

Name _____ Class _____ Date _____

1. Cut out three 10-cm × 10-cm pieces of paper from a sheet of unlined white paper. Label one piece of paper Silicon, the second Tin, and the third Lead. Find the mass of each piece of paper and record it in the data table.

2. Using forceps, place the silicon onto the paper labeled Silicon. Find the mass of the silicon and the paper. Record this mass in the data table. Then, subtract the mass of the paper from the mass of the silicon and paper. Record the mass of silicon in the data table. Set the paper containing the silicon aside for now.

3. Repeat Step 2 to find the masses of tin and lead.

Part B: Measuring Volume

4. Place 25 mL of water in the graduated cylinder. Measure the volume of the water to the nearest 0.1 mL. Record the volume (in cm³) in the data table. (*Hint:* 1 mL = 1 cm³)

5. Tilt the graduated cylinder and carefully pour the silicon from the paper into the graduated cylinder. Make sure that the silicon is completely covered by the water. Measure and record the volume of the water and silicon in the data table. Then, subtract the volume of water from the volume of the water and silicon. Record the result in the data table.

6. Repeat Steps 4 and 5 to find the volumes of tin and lead.

Part C: Calculating Density

7. To calculate the density of silicon, divide its mass by its volume.

$$\text{Density} = \frac{\text{Mass}}{\text{Volume}}$$

Record the density of silicon in the data table.

8. Repeat Step 7 to find the densities of tin and lead.

9. Make a line graph that shows the relationship between the densities of silicon, tin, and lead and the periods in which they are located in the periodic table. Place the number of the period (from 1 to 7) on the horizontal axis and the density (in g/cm³) on the vertical axis. Draw a straight line that comes as close as possible to all three points.

10. Germanium is in Period 4. To estimate the density of germanium, draw a dotted vertical line from the 4 on the horizontal axis to the solid line. Then, draw a dotted horizontal line from the solid line to the vertical axis. Read and record the density of germanium.

_____

11. Wash your hands with warm water and soap before you leave the laboratory.

Student Edition Lab Worksheet

Name _____ Class _____ Date _____

Analyze and Conclude

1. Classifying List lead, silicon, and tin in order of increasing density.

Silicon, tin, and lead

2. Comparing and Contrasting How does your estimate of the density of germanium compare with the actual density of germanium, which is 5.5 g/cm³?

A typical student estimate for the density of germanium is 4.6 g/cm³, which is a rough

approximation of the actual value of 5.5 g/cm³.

3. Calculating Use the formula for percent error (PE) to calculate a percent error for your estimate of the density of germanium.

$$PE = \frac{\text{Estimated value} - \text{Accepted value}}{\text{Accepted value}} \times 100$$

Student estimates are likely to be approximately 16% lower than the actual value.

4. Drawing Conclusions How does the density of the elements change from silicon to lead in Group 4A?

From silicon to lead, the density of the element increases.

Physical Science Lab Manual • Chapter 5 Exploration Lab **291**

Lab Manual

Name _____ Class _____ Date _____

Chapter 5   The Periodic Table   Investigation 5A

Using Clues to Identify Elements

Refer students to pages 130–145 in their textbooks for a discussion of the periodic table, classes of elements, and representative groups. **SKILLS FOCUS:** Analyzing Data, Classifying, Drawing Conclusions **CLASS TIME:** 45 minutes

Background Information

Chemical elements can be classified according to their properties as metals, nonmetals, and metalloids. **Metals** are good conductors of heat and electricity. Many metals are malleable and ductile. **Nonmetals** are poor conductors of heat and electricity, and solid nonmetals tend to be brittle. **Metalloids** have properties between those of metals and nonmetals.

Elements in the same group on the periodic table have the same number of **valence electrons,** which are electrons in the highest occupied energy level of an atom. The number of an A group matches the number of valence electrons in atoms of each element in the group. For example, the Group 4A elements each have four valence electrons per atom. The exception to this pattern is the element helium, which is in Group 8A but has two valence electrons.

Because elements in a group have the same number of valence electrons, they tend to have similar properties. The most reactive metals are the **alkali metals** in Group 1A on the far left side of the periodic table. The Group 2A elements are the **alkaline earth metals,** which are somewhat less reactive than the alkali metals. Groups of elements become less metallic in their properties from left to right across the periodic table. The most reactive nonmetals are the **halogens** in Group 7A. Group 8A contains the **noble gases,** which are colorless and odorless, and rarely react with other elements.

In this investigation, you will use a list of clues to identify 34 elements and place them in their correct locations in the periodic table.

Problem

Where do the elements described in the clues fit in the periodic table?

Pre-Lab Discussion

Read the entire investigation. Then, work with a partner to answer the following questions.

1. Analyzing Data How will the index cards be useful when you are reading the clues to the elements?

Each clue can be summarized on an index card. Index cards that contain clues about the same

element can be easily compared. An index card can be set aside when all the elements referred

to in the clue are identified.

Physical Science Lab Manual • Investigation 5A **47**

Lab Manual

Name _____ Class _____ Date _____

2. Inferring Do you have to know a specific, identifying property for each element in order to place all 34 elements in the partial periodic table? Explain your answer.

No, many of the elements will be identified by a process of elimination. For example, if all the

elements in a group have been identified and only one empty box remains in that group, then the

remaining element belongs in that box.

3. Classifying Are elements with similar properties in the same row or the same column of the periodic table?

Elements with similar properties are in the same column or group.

4. Analyzing Data Explain how information about an element's physical state at room temperature will help you fill in the partial periodic table.

As shown in the periodic table in the textbook, elements that are gases at room temperature

are nonmetals, which are located on the right of the periodic table (except for hydrogen).

5. Classifying How would information about number of valence electrons be useful for placing elements in the periodic table?

When the number of valence electrons is known, the representative group to which the element

belongs is known.

6. Analyzing Data Why is it important to review the clues after you have read all of the clues once?

The elements cannot all be identified and located after a single reading of the individual clues.

Information from multiple clues must be combined. Once some of the boxes are filled, some

clues will become more useful.

48 *Physical Science* Lab Manual • Investigation 5A

Lab Manual

Name _____ Class _____ Date _____

Materials *(per group)*
25 index cards
copy of the periodic table from the textbook for reference

Procedure

1. Work in pairs. Examine the partial periodic table that follows the list of clues. Note that it contains spaces for the 34 elements in Periods 1 through 5 and Groups 1A through 8A. The locations of the metalloids are shaded.

2. For this investigation, these 34 elements have been randomly assigned a number from 1 to 34. (*Hint:* This number has no relation to the atomic number or mass of the element.) By using the list of clues, you will identify where each element belongs in the partial periodic table.

3. Read the clues in order. You will probably find it useful to summarize the information in each clue by using index cards, to which you can refer later as needed. Fill in the partial periodic table by placing each element's assigned number in the appropriate box. Use a pencil so that you can correct any mistakes.

4. Sometimes a single clue will enable you to identify an element and place its number in the correct box. In most cases, however, you will need to combine information from different clues in order to identify the element.

5. Reread the clues as many times as necessary. When you are certain that you have correctly identified all the elements referred to in a clue, set that index card aside.

List of Clues

1. Elements 2, 5, 18, 29, and 33 are colorless, odorless, unreactive gases. Of these gases, element 29 has the largest atomic mass.
2. Elements 13, 19, 23, and 34 have six valence electrons, and element 13 is a metalloid.
3. Elements 9, 14, 16, and 21 are highly reactive metals in the same group. Of these metals, element 16 is the least reactive.
4. Elements 1, 8, 11, 13, 14, 17, 24, and 29 are in the same period.
5. Elements 11, 26, 27, and 28 have three valence electrons.
6. Elements 1, 4, 6, and 30 are found in the same group. Element 6 is in chlorophyll molecules.
7. Elements 10, 22, 24, and 32 are in the same group. Element 22 is a liquid at room temperature.
8. Elements 2, 10, 15, and 34 are nonmetals in the same period.
9. Elements 7, 15, 17, and 25 are in the same group. Of these, only element 7 is a gas at room temperature.
10. Elements 12, 20, and 26 are metalloids. Elements 20 and 12 are in the same group.

Physical Science Lab Manual • Investigation 5A **49**

Program Resources Chapter 5

Lab Manual

Name _____ Class _____ Date _____

11. Element 30 is important to maintain strong bones and teeth.
12. An atom of element 21 has one more proton than an atom of element 2.
13. Elements 3 is a nonmetal with one valence electron.
14. Element 27 is the most abundant metal in Earth's crust.
15. Element 31 is a solid at room temperature. Most of the compounds in your body contain this element.
16. Element 18 has two electrons.
17. Element 33 has a smaller atomic mass than element 5.
18. Element 32 is the most reactive nonmetal.
19. Element 20 and element 19 are combined in a compound found in glass.
20. Glass that contains element 26 does not shatter easily.
21. Element 19 is the most abundant element in Earth's crust.

Observations

Partial Periodic Table

Answers are shown.

	1A			3A	4A	5A	6A	7A	8A
1	3								18
		2A							
2	16	4		26	31	7	19	32	33
3	9	6		27	20	15	34	10	2
4	21	30		28	12	25	23	22	5
5	14	1		11	8	17	13	24	29

Lab Manual

Name _____ Class _____ Date _____

Analysis and Conclusions

1. **Drawing Conclusions** Identify each element in the list of clues by matching its assigned number to the correct name of the element.

1 strontium, 2 argon, 3 hydrogen, 4 beryllium, 5 krypton, 6 magnesium, 7 nitrogen, 8 tin, 9 sodium, 10 chlorine, 11 indium, 12 germanium, 13 tellurium, 14 rubidium, 15 phosphorus, 16 lithium, 17 antimony, 18 helium, 19 oxygen, 20 silicon, 21 potassium, 22 bromine, 23 selenium, 24 iodine, 25 arsenic, 26 boron, 27 aluminum, 28 gallium, 29 xenon, 30 calcium, 31 carbon, 32 fluorine, 33 neon, 34 sulfur

2. **Analyzing Data** Were you able to place some elements in the partial periodic table with just a single clue? Use examples to explain.

Yes, examples include tellurium (metalloid with six valence electrons), magnesium (metal found in chlorophyll), bromine (liquid at room temperature), aluminum (most abundant metal in Earth's crust), carbon (contained in most compounds in the human body), and fluorine (most reactive nonmetal).

3. **Analyzing Data** Provide at least two examples of when you needed to use more than one clue to identify an element.

Helium (element 18) is a colorless, odorless, unreactive gas (clue 1) with two electrons (clue 16). Indium (element 11) has three valence electrons (clue 5) and is in the same period as tellurium, element 13 (clues 2 and 4).

Lab Manual

Name _____ Class _____ Date _____

4. **Applying Concepts** Why were you able to use clues about atomic mass to place elements, even though the periodic table is organized by atomic number?

The atomic mass of elements within a group increases from top to bottom in the group.

5. **Comparing and Contrasting** Which elements are not included in the partial periodic table? Compare the number of elements in the partial periodic table to the number of known elements.

The partial periodic table does not include transition metals or elements in Periods 6 and 7.

Of the 113 known elements, only 34 are in the partial periodic table.

Go Further

Now that you have identified the elements from the list of clues, write at least five additional clues based on information from Chapter 5.
Student answers will vary. Examples of acceptable responses: Element 24 (iodine) is required by the thyroid gland. Elements 7 and 15 (nitrogen and phosphorus) are important components of fertilizers.

Lab Manual

Name _____ Class _____ Date _____

Chapter 5 The Periodic Table   Investigation 5B

Comparing Chemical Properties Within a Group

Refer students to pages 131–138 in their textbooks for a discussion of the periodic table, page 139 for a discussion of valence electrons, and page 141 for a description of the alkaline earth elements. **SKILLS FOCUS:** Observing, Comparing **CLASS TIME:** 45 minutes

Background Information

The properties of elements repeat in a regular pattern across the periods in the periodic table. From left to right across each period, elements tend to be less metallic and more nonmetallic. Elements in the same group in the table have similar properties because they have the same number of valence electrons. A valence electron is an electron that is in the highest occupied energy level of an atom. These electrons play a key role in chemical reactions. The properties of elements within a group are not identical because the valence electrons are in different energy levels.

The elements in Group 2A in the periodic table are known as alkaline earth metals. Many properties of alkaline earth metals change in a predictable way from top to bottom within the group. One of those properties is reactivity, or the tendency to combine chemically with other substances. The reactivity of an element can be demonstrated by how the element reacts or how its compounds react with other substances.

The formation of a precipitate in a solution is one clue that a chemical change has occurred. A precipitate is a solid that forms and separates from a liquid mixture. In this investigation, you will mix solutions of similar alkaline earth compounds with a set of test solutions and observe whether or not precipitates form. You will use the results to predict how the reactivity of the alkaline earth metals changes from top to bottom within Group 2A.

Problem

How does reactivity vary among the alkaline earth metals?

Pre-Lab Discussion

Read the entire investigation. Then, work with a partner to answer the following questions.

1. **Controlling Variables** Why is it important not to mix the test solution in one well with the solution in another well on your spot plate?

If the test solutions were mixed, it would not be possible to tell which combinations of solutions produced precipitates.

2. **Designing Experiments** Why is the order of the rows in the well plate the same as the order of elements in the periodic table?

With the compounds tested in order of the placement within Group 2A, it is easier to see the pattern of the results.

Lab Manual

Name _____ Class _____ Date _____

3. Controlling Variables What are the manipulated, responding, and controlled variables in this investigation?

Manipulated: the alkaline earth metal in the nitrate compound; responding: formation of a

precipitate (reactivity); controlled: the solutions used to test reactivity

4. Predicting Write a prediction of how the reactivity of the alkaline earth metals will change from the top of Group 2A to the bottom.

Reactivity will increase from the top of group 2A to the bottom.

Materials (per group)

spot plate
sheet of notebook paper
dropper bottles containing solutions
of the following compounds:
  magnesium nitrate
  barium nitrate
  calcium nitrate
  potassium carbonate
  potassium chromate
  potassium sulfate
  strontium nitrate

To prepare the aqueous solutions:
0.2 M $Mg(NO_3)_2$ 29.7 g in 1 L
0.1 M $Ca(NO_3)_2$ 16.4 g in 1 L
0.1 M $Sr(NO_3)_2$ 21.2 g in 1 L
0.1 M $Ba(NO_3)_2$ 26.1 g in 1 L
0.2 M K_2CO_3 27.6 g in 1 L
0.2 M K_2SO_4 34.9 g in 1 L
0.2 M K_2CrO_4 38.8 g in 1 L

Safety

Put on safety goggles and a lab apron. Be careful to avoid breakage when working with glassware. Some chemicals used in this investigation are toxic. Always use special caution when working with laboratory chemicals, as they may irritate the skin or stain skin or clothing. Never touch or taste any chemical unless instructed to do so. Follow your teacher's instructions for disposing of used chemicals. Wash your hands thoroughly after carrying out this investigation. Note all safety alert symbols next to the steps in the Procedure and review the meaning of each symbol by referring to the Safety Symbols on page xiii.

Review with students the safety information in the MSDS for each chemical before performing the investigation. Supervise students closely to be sure that they follow all recommended safety procedures and do not get the solutions on their skin or in their eyes or mouths.

Procedure

1. Place the spot plate in the center of a sheet of notebook paper, as shown in Figure 1. There should be four wells per column and three wells per row.

2. Along the side of the notebook paper next to each of the four rows of wells, write the names of the four alkaline earth metals that are present in each nitrate compound you are using. Write the names in the order shown in Figure 1. This is the order of these four elements in Group 2A.

3. Label the paper above each of the three columns of wells, as shown in Figure 1.

Lab Manual

Name _____ Class _____ Date _____

4. Place 3 drops of potassium carbonate in each of the four wells under the label Potassium Carbonate. Place 3 drops of potassium sulfate in each of the four wells under the label Potassium Sulfate. Place 3 drops of potassium chromate in each of the four wells under the label Potassium Chromate. Make sure that each solution is placed in the wells of only column one. **CAUTION:** *Some chemicals used in this investigation are toxic. Be careful not to get the solutions on your skin.*

Figure 1

5. Place 3 drops of magnesium nitrate in each of the three wells in the row labeled Magnesium. Observe whether or not a precipitate forms in each well and record the results in the data table.

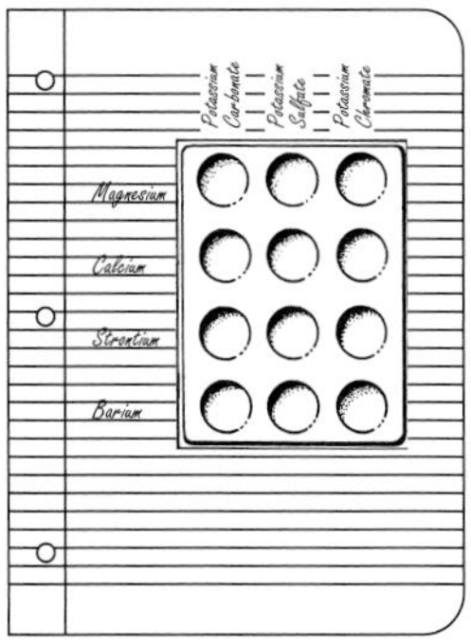

6. Place 3 drops of calcium nitrate in each of the three wells in the row labeled Calcium. Observe whether or not a precipitate forms in each well and record the results in the data table.

7. Place 3 drops of strontium nitrate in each of the three wells in the row labeled Strontium. Observe whether or not a precipitate forms in each well and record the results in the data table.

8. Place 3 drops of barium nitrate in each of the three wells in the row labeled Barium. Observe whether or not a precipitate forms in each well and record the results in the data table.

9. Follow your teacher's instructions for disposing of the chemicals on the spot plate. Wash the spot plate and your hands thoroughly with soap or detergent and warm water. Have students drain their spot plates into a designated chemical waste container.

Observations   Sample data are shown.

DATA TABLE

Alkaline Earth Metal	Carbonate	Sulfate	Chromate
Magnesium	White precipitate	No precipitate	No precipitate
Calcium	White precipitate	Small amount of white precipitate	No precipitate
Strontium	White precipitate	White precipitate	No precipitate
Barium	White precipitate	White precipitate	Yellow precipitate

---

Lab Manual

Name _____ Class _____ Date _____

Analysis and Conclusions

1. **Observing** What evidence did you observe of a chemical change occurring in any of the wells?

A white or yellow precipitate formed.

2. **Analyzing Data** Which alkaline earth metal formed the smallest number of precipitates?

Magnesium

3. **Analyzing Data** Which alkaline earth metal formed the most precipitates?

Barium

4. **Drawing Conclusions** Based on your data, list the alkaline earth metals in order of their reactivity, from most reactive to least reactive. What is the relationship between reactivity and the location of each alkaline earth metal in the periodic table?

Barium, strontium, calcium, magnesium; The more reactive alkaline earth elements are nearer the

bottom of the group.

5. **Evaluating and Revising** Did your data support or contradict your prediction?

The data supported the prediction that reactivity increases from top to bottom within the group.

6. **Predicting** Group 1A in the periodic table contains alkali metals. Based on your investigation of the Group 2A elements, which element in Group 1A, other than francium, would you predict to be most reactive? Least reactive?

Cesium; lithium

7. **Predicting** Can the results for reactivity in this investigation be applied to the elements in Group 7A? Explain your prediction.

No, because Group 7A elements are nonmetals and reactivity for nonmetals increases from bottom

to top within the group.

Go Further

If you had a solution containing a mixture of magnesium nitrate, strontium nitrate, and barium nitrate, how could you separate the mixture? (*Hint:* Review the information in the data table.)

Add potassium chromate so that barium forms a precipitate. Pour off the liquid and add potassium sulfate to it so that strontium forms a precipitate. Pour off the remaining liquid in which the magnesium nitrate is dissolved.

Chapter Test A

Name _____ Class _____ Date _____

Chapter 5   The Periodic Table   Chapter Test A

Multiple Choice

Write the letter that best answers the question or completes the statement on the line provided.

_____ 1. Mendeleev arranged the known chemical elements in a table according to increasing
a. atomic number.   b. number of electrons.
c. number of protons.   d. mass.

_____ 2. Mendeleev gave the name *eka-aluminum* to a(an)
a. compound containing aluminum.
b. mixture of aluminum and an unknown element.
c. unknown element he predicted would have properties similar to those of aluminum.
d. rare isotope of aluminum.

_____ 3. Moving from left to right across a row of the periodic table, which of the following values increases by exactly one from element to element?
a. isotope number   b. atomic number
c. atomic mass unit   d. mass number

_____ 4. The standard on which the atomic mass unit is based is the mass of a
a. proton.   b. neutron.
c. chlorine-35 atom.   d. carbon-12 atom.

_____ 5. The atomic mass of an element is
a. the sum of the protons and neutrons in one atom of the element.
b. twice the number of protons in one atom of the element.
c. a ratio based on the mass of a carbon-12 atom.
d. a weighted average of the masses of the element's isotopes

_____ 6. At room temperature, none of the metals are
a. soft.   b. liquids.
c. malleable.   d. gases.

_____ 7. Which general statement does NOT apply to metals?
a. Most metals are ductile.
b. Most metals are malleable.
c. Most metals are brittle.
d. Most metals are good conductors of electric current.

_____ 8. Two highly reactive elements in Period 4 are the metal potassium and the
a. metalloid arsenic.   b. nonmetal selenium.
c. nonmetal bromine.   d. nonmetal krypton.

Chapter Test A

Name _____ Class _____ Date _____

_____ 9. Atoms of the most reactive elements tend to have
  a one or seven valence electrons.
  b. eight valence electrons.
  c. four or five valence electrons.
  d. no valence electrons.

_____ 10. An alkali metal has one valence electron, while an alkaline earth metal has
  a. none.   b. two.
  c. four.   d. three.

_____ 11. Which statement is NOT true about the elements fluorine, chlorine, and iodine?
  a. They are all halogens.
  b. They react easily with metals.
  c. They are similar to noble gases.
  d. They are all nonmetals.

_____ 12. Among the alkali metals, the tendency to react with other substances
  a. does not vary among the members of the group.
  b. increases from top to bottom within the group.
  c. varies in an unpredictable way within the group.
  d. decreases from top to bottom within the group.

_____ 13. Which halogen is most likely to react?
  a. Br (bromine)   b. F (fluorine)
  c. I (iodine)   d. Cl (chlorine)

_____ 14. To keep them from reacting, some highly reactive elements are stored in
  a. water.   b. pure oxygen.
  c. liquid mercury.   d. argon.

_____ 15. Which element is found in nature only in compounds?
  a. sodium   b. helium
  c. oxygen   d. nitrogen

Completion

Complete each statement on the line provided.

1. When Mendeleev organized elements in his periodic table in order of increasing mass, elements with similar properties were in the same _____.

2. Mendeleev predicted that the undiscovered element he called *eka-aluminum* would have a(an) _____ melting point.

3. The pattern of repeating properties of elements revealed in the periodic table is known as the _____.

Chapter Test A

Name _____ Class _____ Date _____

4. Fertilizers usually contain two elements from Group 5A, which are _____ and phosphorus.

5. One way to demonstrate reactivity among the alkaline earth metals, Group 2A, is to observe what happens when they are placed in _____.

Short Answer

Use complete sentences to write the answers to the questions on the lines provided.

1. Why did Mendeleev want to make a periodic table of the elements?

   _____

   _____

2. What do the whole numbers on the periodic table represent?

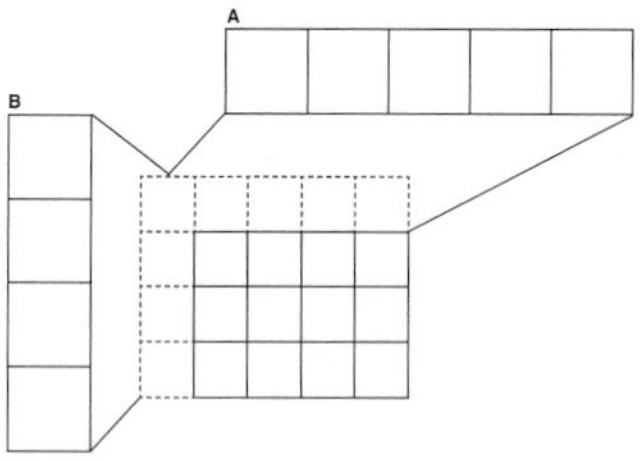

   _____

   _____

Figure 5-1

3. In which segment of Figure 5-1, A or B, will properties of the elements vary the most?

   _____

   _____

4. Selenium has six valence electrons, while rubidium has one valence electron. Identify each element as a metal or a nonmetal.

   _____

   _____

Chapter Test A

Name _____ Class _____ Date _____

5. Silicon (atomic number 14) and chlorine (atomic number 17) are both in Period 3. Which is the more reactive element?

   _____

   _____

6. Sulfur is often found in nature as an element, not combined with other elements in a compound. What does this fact tell you about the reactivity of sulfur?

   _____

   _____

Using Science Skills

Use the chart to answer each question. Write the answers on a separate sheet of paper.

1. **Classifying** Classify the elements in Figure 5-2 as metals, metalloids, or nonmetals. Explain your answer.

2. **Inferring** Identify the most reactive element shown in Figure 5-2. Explain your answer.

3. **Predicting** Explain why knowing the properties of K, Ca, Sc, and Ti would allow you to predict the properties of Rb, Sr, Y, and Zr.

4. **Using Tables and Graphs** What do the numbers in the boxes in Figure 5-2 represent? What is the importance of these numbers?

5. **Comparing and Contrasting** Describe ways in which the elements in Group 1A are similar. Then describe ways in which Group 2A elements differ from elements in Group 1A.

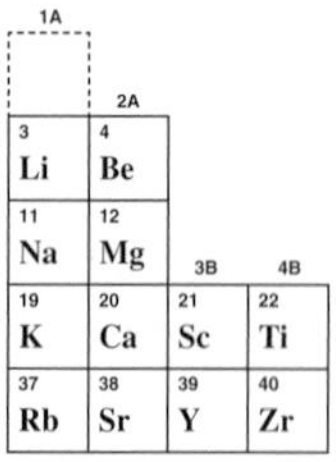

Figure 5-2

Essay

Write the answer to each question on a separate sheet of paper.

1. In a laboratory procedure, you form a highly reactive compound. How could you store the compound so that it will not react?

2. In science lab, your teacher gives you two small pieces of matter and tells you that one piece is a metal and one is a nonmetal. Without changing the size or shape of the pieces, how could you test them to determine which is the metal?

3. How are the octaves on a keyboard an analogy for the periods in a periodic table?

4. Although lithium and neon are both in Period 2 of the periodic table, they have very different properties. Explain how this is possible.

Chapter Test B

Name _____ Class _____ Date _____

Chapter 5   The Periodic Table   Chapter Test B

Multiple Choice

Write the letter that best answers the question or completes the statement on the line provided.

_____ 1. In a periodic table, a set of properties repeats from
  a. element to element.   b. group to group.
  c. column to column.   d. row to row.

_____ 2. The usefulness of Mendeleev's periodic table was confirmed by
  a. the discovery of subatomic particles.
  b. its immediate acceptance by other scientists.
  c. the discovery of elements with predicted properties.
  d. the discovery of the nucleus.

_____ 3. Figure 5-1 shows a portion of a blank periodic table. Identify the segments labeled A and B.
  a. A and B are both periods.
  b. A is a period and B is a group.
  c. A and B are both groups.
  d. A is a group and B is a period.

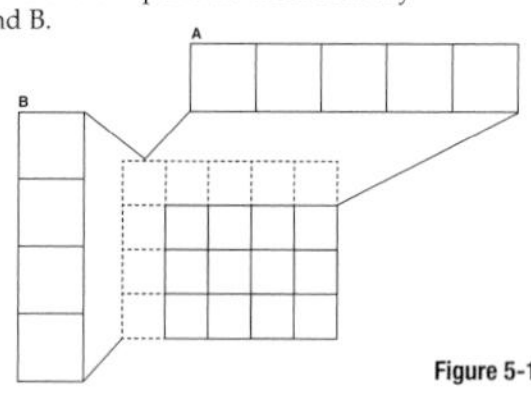

Figure 5-1

_____ 4. One-twelfth the mass of a carbon-12 atom is used to define a(an)
  a. atomic number.   b. atomic mass.
  c. mass number.   d. atomic mass unit.

_____ 5. How is the atomic mass of an element determined?
  a. Average the atomic masses of all its isotopes.
  b. Use the atomic mass of the most abundant isotope.
  c. Take a weighted average of the masses of the isotopes present in nature.
  d. Count the number of protons and neutrons in an atom of the element.

_____ 6. Which list of elements contains only metals?
  a. helium, carbon, gold
  b. sodium, chromium, copper
  c. iodine, iron, nickel
  d. phosphorus, nitrogen, oxygen

Chapter Test B

Name _____ Class _____ Date _____

_____ 7. Which statement is true about the metalloid silicon?
   a. Silicon is a better conductor of an electric current than silver is.
   b. Silicon does not conduct electric current under any conditions.
   c. Silicon's ability to conduct an electric current does not vary with temperature.
   d. Silicon is a better conductor of an electric current than sulfur is.

_____ 8. The column on the far left of the periodic table contains the
   a. most reactive metals.   b. most reactive nonmetals.
   c. least reactive nonmetals.   d. least reactive metals.

_____ 9. As you move from left to right across a period, the number of valence electrons
   a. increases.
   b. stays the same.
   c. increases and then decreases.
   d. decreases.

_____ 10. Compared with Group 1A elements, Group 7A elements have
   a. more atoms in ground state.
   b. more valence electrons.
   c. more isotopes.
   d. fewer valence electrons.

_____ 11. The tendency of an element to react chemically is closely related to
   a. its atomic mass.
   b. attractions between its atoms.
   c. the number of valence electrons in atoms of the element.
   d. the ratio of protons to neutrons in atoms of the element.

_____ 12. Which of these Group 1A elements is the most reactive?
   a. Cs (cesium)   b. Li (lithium)
   c. K (potassium)   d. Na (sodium)

_____ 13. Which of these Group 7A elements is the most reactive?
   a. Cl (chlorine)   b. I (iodine)
   c. F (fluorine)   d. Br (bromine)

_____ 14. Which of the following gases emit colors when an electric current is applied?
   a. hydrogen and helium   b. helium and neon
   c. fluorine and chlorine   d. oxygen and nitrogen

_____ 15. Which element is found in most of the compounds in your body except for water?
   a. iodine   b. potassium   c. iron   d. carbon

Chapter Test B

Name _____ Class _____ Date _____

Completion

Complete each statement on the line provided.

1. Mendeleev organized elements in his periodic table in order of increasing _____.

2. Mendeleev's periodic table was useful because it enabled scientists to predict properties of unknown _____.

3. Phosphorus is one block to the left of sulfur in the periodic table. The atomic number of sulfur is 16. The atomic number of phosphorus is _____.

4. The atomic mass unit (amu) is defined as one-twelfth the mass of a(an) _____-12 atom.

5. Elements can be classified as metals, nonmetals, and _____.

6. From left to right across a period in the periodic table, elements become less _____ and more _____ in their properties.

7. Element 3, lithium, has one valence electron, and element 4, beryllium, has two valence electrons. Element 5, boron, has _____ valence electrons.

8. In general, a(an) _____ metal will be more reactive than an alkaline earth metal in the same period.

9. Although they are called _____ lights, they can contain any noble gas.

10. Reactive elements, such as alkali metals and halogens, are found in nature only as _____.

Short Answer

Use complete sentences to write the answers to the questions on the lines provided.

1. Suppose you are looking at elements in the periodic table in this order: element 23, element 24, element 25, element 26, and so on. Are you looking across a period or down a group? Explain your answer.

   _____

2. What determines an element's chemical properties?

3. On the periodic table, there are two numbers in the block for the element krypton (Kr): 36 and 83.80. What are each of these numbers, and what do they represent?

   _____

Chapter Test B

Name _____ Class _____ Date _____

4. Sodium chloride is a compound of sodium and chlorine. Which of these elements is the alkali metal, and which is the halogen?

   _____

5. Why is argon gas used instead of air in light bulbs that contain a filament that is heated to glowing?

   _____

Using Science Skills

Use the chart to answer each question. Write the answers on a separate sheet of paper.

* Atomic number = 11

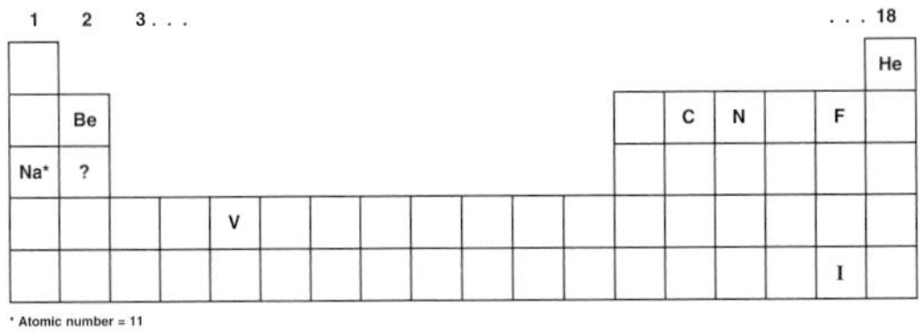

Figure 5-2

1. **Using Tables and Graphs** Which of the elements shown in Figure 5-2 are in the same period?
2. **Classifying** Which element in Figure 5-2 is a transition metal? Which is a noble gas?
3. **Using Tables and Graphs** Which elements in Figure 5-2 have the same number of valence electrons? How do you know?
4. **Comparing and Contrasting** Based on what you know about elements and the periodic table, compare and contrast the elements beryllium (Be) and iodine (I).
5. **Inferring** Find the block labeled ? in Figure 5-2. Predict the properties of this element. What is its atomic number? How many valence electrons does it have? Which of the elements shown in Figure 5-2 will it most resemble?

Essay

Write the answer to the question on a separate sheet of paper.

1. Why were the elements gallium (Ga), scandium (Sc), and germanium (Ge) important to Mendeleev?

Chapter 5 Test A Answers

Multiple Choice

1. d **2.** c **3.** b **4.** d **5.** d **6.** d
7. c **8.** c **9.** a **10.** b **11.** c **12.** b
13. b **14.** d **15.** a

Completion

1. column **2.** low **3.** periodic law **4.** nitrogen **5.** water

Short Answer

1. He wanted to organize information about the elements for a textbook he was writing. **2.** atomic number, number of protons in each element **3.** Properties will vary the most in segment A, which is a period. **4.** Selenium is a nonmetal. Rubidium is a metal. **5.** chlorine **6.** Sulfur is not a highly reactive element under ordinary conditions.

Using Science Skills

1. These elements are all metals. The elements in Groups 1A and 2A are the alkali metals and alkaline earth metals, respectively. The elements in Groups 3B and 4B are transition metals. **2.** Rb is the most reactive element shown. Group 1A alkali metals are the most reactive metals, and the reactivity of elements in Group 1A increases from top to bottom. **3.** When elements are arranged in a periodic table in order of increasing atomic number, the properties of elements repeat from period to period so that elements in the same group have similar properties. **4.** The numbers shown are atomic numbers. An atomic number is the number of protons and the number of electrons in an atom. The periodic table is organized in order by increasing atomic number. No two elements have the same atomic number. **5.** The elements in Group 1A, the alkali metals, are soft and extremely reactive. Atoms of these elements have a single valence electron. Atoms of elements in Group 2A have two valence electrons. The alkaline earth metals are harder, less reactive, and have higher melting points than the alkali metals in the same period.

Essay

1. You could store the compound in a jar filled with a noble gas such as argon. Students may also recall that reactive elements are stored under oil. **2.** You could see which piece conducts an electric current or which piece is a better conductor of heat. **3.** Answers should include a discussion of properties that repeat at regular intervals. **4.** Lithium is an alkali metal in Group 1A. Alkali metals are the most reactive metals. Neon is a noble gas in Group 8A. Noble gases are highly unreactive nonmetals.

Chapter 5 Test B Answers

Multiple Choice

1. d **2.** c **3.** b **4.** d **5.** c **6.** b
7. d **8.** a **9.** a **10.** b **11.** c **12.** a
13. c **14.** b **15.** d

Completion

1. mass **2.** elements **3.** 15 **4.** carbon **5.** metalloids
6. metallic, nonmetallic **7.** three **8.** alkali **9.** neon
10. compounds

Short Answer

1. across a period because the atomic number is increasing by one each time **2.** the number of valence electrons **3.** The integer, 36, is the atomic number, or number of protons in an atom of krypton. The decimal number, 83.80, is the atomic mass, which is the weighted average of the atomic masses of krypton isotopes found in nature. **4.** Sodium is the alkali metal, and chlorine is the halogen. **5.** The heated filament will react with the oxygen in air but not with argon, which is a noble gas and hardly ever reacts.

Using Science Skills

1. Be, C, N, and F **2.** V is a transition metal, and He is a noble gas. **3.** F and I have the same number of valence electrons because they are in the same group in the periodic table. **4.** Beryllium is a reactive metal with two valence electrons. Iodine is a highly reactive nonmetal with seven valence electrons. **5.** The element has an atomic number of 12 and has two valence electrons. It will most resemble beryllium.

Essay

1. Mendeleev predicted the properties of these undiscovered elements from data in his periodic table. When the elements were discovered, their actual properties were found to be a close match to those Mendeleev had predicted. Their discovery provided evidence of the usefulness of Mendeleev's periodic table.

Chapter 6 Chemical Bonds

Planning Guide

Use these planning tools

Easy Planner
Resource Pro
Online Lesson Planner

SECTION OBJECTIVES	STANDARDS		ACTIVITIES and LABS
	NATIONAL (See p. T18.)	STATE	
6.1 Ionic Bonding, pp. 158–164 ⏱ 1 block or 2 periods **6.1.1 Recognize** stable electron configurations. **6.1.2 Predict** an element's chemical properties using number of valence electrons and electron dot diagrams. **6.1.3 Describe** how an ionic bond forms and how ionization energy affects the process. **6.1.4 Predict** the composition of an ionic compound from its chemical formula. **6.1.5 Relate** the properties of ionic compounds to the structure of crystal lattices.	A-1, B-1, B-2, G-1		**SE** Inquiry Activity: What Can the Shape of a Material Tell You About the Material? p. 157 L2
6.2 Covalent Bonding, pp. 165–169 ⏱ 1 block or 2 periods **6.2.1 Describe** how covalent bonds form and the attractions that keep atoms together in molecules. **6.2.2 Compare** polar and nonpolar bonds, and **demonstrate** how polar bonds affect the polarity of a molecule. **6.2.3 Compare** the attractions between polar and nonpolar molecules.	A-1, A-2, B-2		**SE** Quick Lab: Analyzing Inks, p. 167 L2 **SE** Consumer Lab: Improving the Dyeing of Nonpolar Fabrics, pp. 184–185 L2 **TE** Teacher Demo: Modeling Overall Polarity, p. 168 L2 **TE** Teacher Demo: Surface Tension, p. 169 L2 **LM** Investigation 6B: Comparing Ionic and Covalent Compounds L1
6.3 Naming Compounds and Writing Formulas, pp. 170–175 ⏱ 1 block or 2 periods **6.3.1 Recognize** and **describe** binary ionic compounds, metals with multiple ions, and polyatomic ions. **6.3.2 Name** and **determine** chemical formulas for ionic and molecular compounds.	A-1, A-2, B-2, G-2		**SE** Quick Lab: Modeling Molecules, p. 173 L2 **LM** Investigation 6A: Playing the Ionic Compounds Card Game L2
6.4 The Structure of Metals, pp. 176–181 ⏱ 1 block or 2 periods **6.4.1 Describe** the structure and strength of bonds in metals. **6.4.2 Relate** the properties of metals to their structure. **6.4.3 Define** an alloy and **demonstrate** how the composition of an alloy affects its properties.	A-1, A-2, B-2, B-6, E-2, G-1, G-2, G-3		**TE** Teacher Demo: Comparing Bond Types, p. 177 L2 **TE** Teacher Demo: Bronze and Brass Tones, p. 180 L2

Ability Levels

L1 For students who need additional help
L2 For all students
L3 For students who need to be challenged

Components

SE	Student Edition	**GRSW**	Guided Reading & Study Workbook With Math Support	**CTB**	Computer Test Bank
TE	Teacher's Edition			**TP**	Test Prep Resources
LM	Laboratory Manual			**iT**	iText
PLM	Probeware Lab Manual	**CUT**	Chapter and Unit Tests	**DC**	Discovery Channel Videotapes
				T	Transparencies
				P	Presentation Pro CD-ROM
				GO	Internet Resources

RESOURCES PRINT and TECHNOLOGY / SECTION ASSESSMENT

RESOURCES PRINT and TECHNOLOGY		SECTION ASSESSMENT
GRSW Section 6.1	L1	**SE** Section 6.1 Assessment, p. 164
T Chapter 6 Pretest Section 6.1	L2 / L2	**iText iT** Section 6.1
P Chapter 6 Pretest Section 6.1	L2 / L2	
SC_LINKS_ **GO** Ionic bonds	L2	
GRSW Section 6.2	L1	**SE** Section 6.2 Assessment, p. 169
T Section 6.2	L2	**iText iT** Section 6.2
P Section 6.2	L2	
SC_LINKS_ **GO** Covalent bonding	L2	
GRSW Section 6.3 **GRSW** Math Skill	L1 / L2	**SE** Section 6.3 Assessment, p. 175
T Section 6.3	L2	**iText iT** Section 6.3
P Section 6.3	L2	
SC_LINKS_ **GO** Chemical formulas	L2	
GRSW Section 6.4	L1	**SE** Section 6.4 Assessment, p. 181
DISCOVERY SCHOOL DC Good Conduct	L2	**iText iT** Section 6.4
T Section 6.4	L2	
P Section 6.4	L2	
SCIENCE NEWS GO Metals	L2	

Go Online

Go online for these Internet resources.

PHSchool.com
Web Code: cca-1060

SCIENCE NEWS
Web Code: cce-1064

NSTA SC_LINKS_
Web Code: ccn-1061
Web Code: ccn-1062
Web Code: ccn-1063

Materials for Activities and Labs

Quantities for each group

STUDENT EDITION

Inquiry Activity, p. 157
4 wood splints or small lab spatulas, sodium chloride, black construction paper, hand lens, alum, Epsom salts, sucrose

Quick Lab, p. 167
test paper, metric ruler, felt-tip markers, stapler, beaker, alcohol-water mixture, Petri dish

Quick Lab, p. 173
blue plastic-foam ball, black plastic-foam ball, 7 white gumdrops, toothpicks

Consumer Lab, pp. 184–185
tongs, 2 fabric test strips, hot dye bath containing methyl orange, clock or watch, paper towels, scissors, soap, hot iron(II) sulfate solution

TEACHER'S EDITION

Teacher Demo, p. 168
molecular model kit, 4 12-inch pieces of string or yarn, tape, overhead projector

Teacher Demo, p. 169
200-mL beaker, water, sewing needle, tweezers, dropper pipet

Teacher Demo, p. 177
salt lick (or rock salt), copper wire, hammer, goggles

Teacher Demo, p. 180
brass bell, bronze bell

Build Science Skills, p. 182
access to a library or the Internet, notepad for data collection

Chapter Assessment

CHAPTER ASSESSMENT

SE	Chapter Assessment, pp. 187–188
CUT	Chapter 6 Test A, B
CTB	Chapter 6
iT	Chapter 6
PHSchool.com GO Web Code: cca-1060	

STANDARDIZED TEST PREP

SE	Chapter 6, p. 189
TP	Diagnose and Prescribe

iText

iText—interactive textbook with assessment at PHSchool.com

LESSON PLAN 6.1

Ionic Bonding

Time
2 periods
1 block

Section Objectives

Local Standards

- **6.1.1 Recognize** stable electron configurations.

- **6.1.2 Predict** an element's chemical properties using number of valence electrons and electron dot diagrams.

- **6.1.3 Describe** how an ionic bond forms and how ionization energy affects the process.

- **6.1.4 Predict** the composition of an ionic compound from its chemical formula.

- **6.1.5 Relate** the properties of ionic compounds to the structure of crystal lattices.

Vocabulary electron dot diagram • ion • anion • cation • chemical bond • ionic bond • chemical formula • crystals

1 FOCUS

Build Vocabulary: Word Forms
Have students think of word forms related to *crystals* such as *crystalline* and *crystallize*. **L2**

Targeted Resources
❏ Transparency: Chapter 6 Pretest
❏ Transparency: Interest Grabber 6.1
❏ Transparency: Reading Strategy 6.1

2 INSTRUCT

Use Visuals: Figure 7
Ask students what happens to the positions of the ions when the hammer hits the crystal in Figure 7. Ask how objects with the same charge behave. **L1**

Build Science Skills: Predicting
Have students look at Figure 2 and ask them to predict the electron dot diagrams for rubidium, strontium, indium, tin, antimony, tellurium, iodine, and xenon. **L2**

Build Reading Literacy: KWL
Have students construct a KWL chart before they read Ionic Compounds. Have them fill out the final column after they read. **L1**

Integrate Earth Science
Ask students to use the library or Internet to find photographs of minerals that have cubic crystals or hexagonal crystals. **L2**

Build Science Skills: Applying Concepts
Encourage students to think of three-dimensional analogies for lattices, such as scaffolding on a building. **L2**

For Enrichment
Have students make a poster presentation explaining other methods for synthesizing gemstones. **L3**

Targeted Resources
❏ Transparency: Figure 2: Electron Dot Diagrams for Some Group A Elements
❏ GRSW Section 6.1
❏ **NSTA** *sci*$_{LINKS}$ Ionic bonds

3 ASSESS

Reteach
Use the diagram at the bottom of p. 161 to review the formation of cations, anions, and ionic bonds. **L1**

Evaluate Understanding
Have students describe the formation of anions, cations, and ionic bonds. **L2**

Targeted Resources
❏ **PHSchool.com** Online Section 6.1 Assessment
❏ iText Section 6.1

63 Chapter 6 Pretest

1. Describe the structure of atoms.

2. True or False: Objects with opposite charges attract one another.

3. What are valence electrons?

4. Which group in the periodic table contains elements that hardly react at all?

5. Where on the periodic table are nonmetals generally found?

6. How do the compositions of mixtures differ from those of substances?

ANSWERS
1. An atom consists of a dense, positively charged nucleus containing protons and neutrons, surrounded by space in which negatively charged electrons move.
2. True
3. electrons in the highest occupied energy level of an atom
4. the noble gases
5. the right side
6. The composition of a mixture can vary. The composition of a substance is fixed.

64 Chapter 6 Pretest *(continued)*

7. What property is being described when someone says that a solid is easily hammered into sheets?

a. conductivity

b. malleability

c. melting point

d. density

ANSWERS
7. b

65 Section 6.1 Interest Grabber

Observing Charged Objects

Record your observations as your teacher does the following demonstration. Cut two pieces of string about 3 feet in length (or long enough to extend from your teacher's head to the ceiling). Tie the ends of the strings together and use a thumbtack to hang them from the ceiling. Tie a balloon to the end of each string. Stand under and between the balloons and rub both them on your hair. Let go of the balloons and walk away from the balloons.

1. What happens to the balloons?

2. Offer an explanation for the behavior of the balloons.

3. Predict which subatomic particle is most likely to be transferred during the rubbing. Give a reason for your choice.

ANSWERS
1. The balloons move apart, or repel each other.
2. Rubbing caused the balloons to gain a similar charge.
3. Electrons are most likely to be transferred based on their location in atoms and their motion.

66 Section 6.1 Reading Strategy

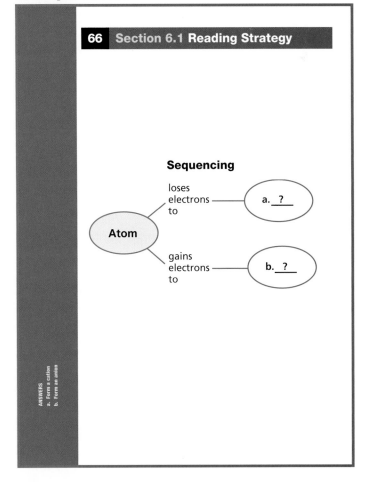

Sequencing

Atom
— loses electrons to — a. __?__
— gains electrons to — b. __?__

ANSWERS
a. Form a cation
b. Form an anion

Transparencies

67 **Figure 2 Electron Dot Diagrams for Some Group A Elements**

Electron Dot Diagrams for Some Group A Elements

			Group				
1A	2A	3A	4A	5A	6A	7A	8A
H·							He:
Li·	·Be·	·B·	·C·	·N·	·O·	:F·	:Ne:
Na·	·Mg·	·Al·	·Si·	·P·	:S·	:Cl·	:Ar:
K·	·Ca·	·Ga·	·Ge·	·As·	:Se·	:Br·	:Kr:

Guided Reading and Study Workbook

Name _____ Class _____ Date _____

Chapter 6   Chemical Bonds

Section 6.1 Ionic Bonding

(pages 158–164)

This section describes the formation of ionic bonds and the properties of ionic compounds.

Reading Strategy (page 158)

Sequencing As you read, complete the concept map to show what happens to atoms during ionic bonding. For more information on this Reading Strategy, see the **Reading and Study Skills** in the **Skills and Reference Handbook** at the end of your textbook.

Stable Electron Configurations (page 158)

1. Describe the type of electron configuration that makes an atom stable and not likely to react. When the highest occupied energy level of an atom is filled with electrons, the atom is stable and not likely to react.

2. Describe an electron dot diagram. An electron dot diagram is a model of an atom in which each dot represents a valence electron.

Ionic Bonds (pages 159–161)

3. Some elements achieve stable electron configurations through the transfer of _____electrons_____ between atoms.

4. By losing one valence electron, a sodium atom achieves the same electron arrangement as an atom of _____neon_____.

5. Circle the letter that states the result of a sodium atom transferring an electron to a chlorine atom.
  (a.) Each atom ends up with a more stable electron arrangement.
  b. The sodium atom becomes more stable, but the chlorine atom becomes less stable.
  c. The chlorine atom becomes more stable, but the sodium atom becomes less stable.
  d. Each atom ends up with a less stable electron arrangement.

6. Is the following sentence true or false? An ion is an atom that has a net positive or negative electric charge. _____true_____

7. An ion with a negative charge is called a(n) _____anion_____.

Guided Reading and Study Workbook

Name _____ Class _____ Date _____

Chapter 6   Chemical Bonds

8. An ionic bond forms when _____electrons_____ are transferred from one atom to another.

9. Is the following sentence true or false? The lower the ionization energy, the easier it is to remove an electron from an atom. _____true_____

Ionic Compounds (pages 161–164)

10. Circle the letter of each piece of information provided by the chemical formula of an ionic compound.
  (a.) which elements the compound contains
  b. the charge on each ion in the compound
  c. how the ions are arranged in the compound
  (d.) the ratio of ions in the compound

11. Circle the letter of the correct answer. The formula for magnesium chloride is $MgCl_2$. The charge on the magnesium ion is 2+. What is the charge on each chloride ion?
  a. 2−   (b.) 1−
  c. 0   d. 1+

Na⁺   Cl⁻

12. Look at the arrangement of ions in a sodium chloride crystal. How many sodium ions surround each chloride ion in this three-dimensional structure?
  a. 3   b. 4
  (c.) 6   d. 8

13. The shape of an ionic crystal depends on ___the arrangement of ions in its lattice___

14. Identify two factors that determine the arrangement of ions in an ionic crystal.
  a. ___The ratio of ions___ b. ___The relative sizes of the ions___

15. Is the following sentence true or false? The attractions among ions within a crystal lattice are weak. _____false_____

LESSON PLAN 6.2

Covalent Bonding

Time
2 periods
1 block

Section Objectives

Local Standards

- **6.2.1 Describe** how covalent bonds form and the attractions that keep atoms together in molecules.
- **6.2.2 Compare** polar and nonpolar bonds, and **demonstrate** how polar bonds affect the polarity of a molecule.
- **6.2.3 Compare** the attractions between polar and nonpolar molecules.

Vocabulary covalent bonding • molecule • polar covalent bond

1 FOCUS

Build Vocabulary: Concept Map
Have students construct a concept map using the terms *atoms, molecules, ions, covalent bonds, ionic bonds, polar, nonpolar,* and *electrons.* **L2**

Targeted Resources
❑ Transparency: Interest Grabber 6.2
❑ Transparency: Reading Strategy 6.2

2 INSTRUCT

Use Visuals: Figure 10
Have students examine Figure 10, and ask why the atoms in the models of diatomic molecules are not complete spheres. Ask why the spheres in the models of fluorine, chlorine, and bromine are different sizes. **L1**

Build Reading Literacy: Visualize
Have students draw diagrams that demonstrate the differences between three types of bonding: nonpolar covalent, polar covalent, and ionic. **L1**

Address Misconceptions
Ask students to make drawings that represent an atom, a molecule, and an ion. **L2**

Teacher Demo: Modeling Overall Polarity
Use ball-and-stick models of carbon dioxide and water molecules to demonstrate molecular polarity for students. **L2**

Build Science Skills: Using Models
Ask students to predict whether an ammonia molecule is polar or nonpolar and to give a reason for their choice. Ask the same question about a sulfur trioxide molecule. **L2**

Teacher Demo: Surface Tension
Use a needle and a beaker of water to help students observe how surface tension can support a needle. **L2**

Targeted Resources
❑ Transparency: Figure 9: Molecular Models of Hydrogen
❑ GRSW Section 6.2
❑ **NSTA** *scLINKS* Covalent bonding

3 ASSESS

Reteach
Use Figures 11, 12, and 13 as visual aids while reviewing polar covalent bonds, nonpolar and polar molecules, and attractions between molecules. **L1**

Evaluate Understanding
Have students make a chart that compares and contrasts polar covalent bonds and nonpolar covalent bonds. **L2**

Targeted Resources
❑ **PHSchool.com** Online Section 6.2 Assessment
❑ iText Section 6.2

Transparencies

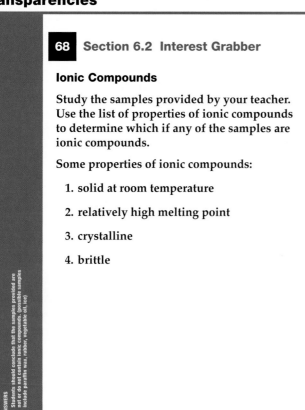

68 Section 6.2 Interest Grabber

Ionic Compounds

Study the samples provided by your teacher. Use the list of properties of ionic compounds to determine which if any of the samples are ionic compounds.

Some properties of ionic compounds:

1. solid at room temperature
2. relatively high melting point
3. crystalline
4. brittle

ANSWERS
Students should conclude that the samples provided are not or do not contain ionic compounds. (possible samples include paraffin wax, rubber, vegetable oil, ice)

Transparencies

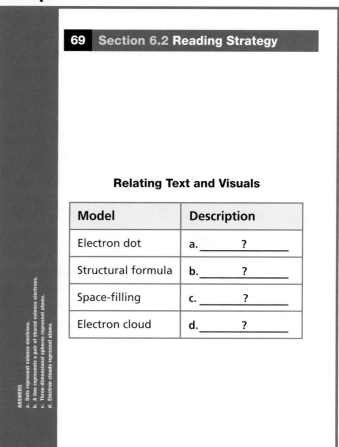

69 Section 6.2 Reading Strategy

Relating Text and Visuals

Model	Description
Electron dot	a. _____?_____
Structural formula	b. _____?_____
Space-filling	c. _____?_____
Electron cloud	d. _____?_____

ANSWERS
a. Dots represent valence electrons.
b. A line represents a pair of shared valence electrons.
c. Three-dimensional spheres represent atoms.
d. Electron clouds represent atoms.

Transparencies

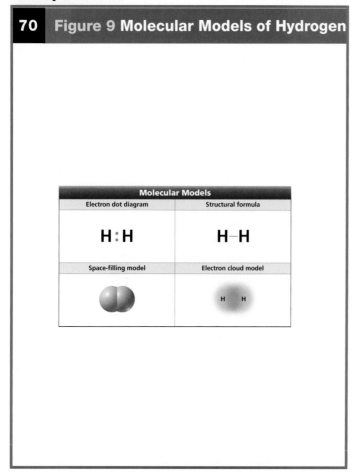

70 Figure 9 Molecular Models of Hydrogen

Molecular Models	
Electron dot diagram	Structural formula
H:H	H–H
Space-filling model	Electron cloud model

Name _____ Class _____ Date _____

Section 6.2 Covalent Bonding
(pages 165–169)

This section discusses the formation of covalent bonds and the factors that determine whether a molecule is polar or nonpolar. It also discusses attractions between molecules.

Reading Strategy (page 165)

Relating Text and Visuals As you read the section, look closely at Figure 9. Complete the table by describing each type of model shown. For more information on this Reading Strategy, see the **Reading and Study Skills** in the **Skills and Reference Handbook** at the end of your textbook.

Molecular Models	
Model	**Description**
Electron dot	Dots represent valence electrons.
Structural formula	A line represents a pair of shared valence electrons.
Space-filling	Three-dimensional spheres represent atoms.
Electron cloud	Electron clouds represent atoms.

Covalent Bonds (pages 165–167)

1. Describe a covalent bond. A covalent bond is a chemical bond in which two atoms share a pair of valence electrons.

2. Circle the letters of molecular models that show orbitals of atoms overlapping when a covalent bond forms.
   a. electron dot   b. structural formula
   c. space-filling   d. electron cloud

3. Describe a molecule. A molecule is a neutral group of atoms that are joined together by one or more covalent bonds.

4. Is the following sentence true or false? In a covalent bond, the atoms are held together by the attractions between the shared electrons and the protons in each nucleus. _____true_____

5. Circle the correct answer. Nitrogen has five valence electrons. How many pairs of electrons must two nitrogen atoms share in order for each atom to have eight valence electrons?
   a. zero   b. one
   c. two   d. three

Name _____ Class _____ Date _____

Unequal Sharing of Electrons (pages 167–168)

6. In general, elements at the _____top_____ of a group have a greater attraction for electrons than elements at the _____bottom_____ of a group have.

7. In a hydrogen chloride molecule, the shared electrons spend more time near the _____chlorine_____ atom than near the _____hydrogen_____ atom.

8. Describe a polar covalent bond. A polar covalent bond is a covalent bond in which electrons are not shared equally.

9. When atoms form a polar covalent bond, the atom with the greater attraction for electrons has a partial _____negative_____ charge.

10. Is the following sentence true or false? In a molecule of a compound, electrons are always shared equally by both atoms. _____false_____

11. Circle the letter of each factor that determines whether a molecule is polar or nonpolar.
    a. the number of atoms in the molecule
    b. the type of atoms in the molecule
    c. the number of bonds in the molecule
    d. the shape of the molecule

CO_2 H_2O

12. Compare the shapes of carbon dioxide and water molecules. Circle the letter of the polar molecule.
    a. carbon dioxide   b. water

13. Is the following sentence true or false? In a water molecule, the hydrogen side of the molecule has a partial positive charge, and the oxygen side has a partial negative charge. _____true_____

Attraction Between Molecules (page 169)

14. Water has a higher boiling point than carbon dioxide because attractions between polar molecules are _____stronger_____ than attractions between nonpolar molecules.

15. Is the following sentence true or false? Attractions among nonpolar molecules explain why nitrogen can be stored as a liquid at low temperatures and high pressures. _____true_____

Section 6.3 Lesson Plan

Naming Compounds and Writing Formulas

Time
2 periods
1 block

Section Objectives

Local Standards

- **6.3.1 Recognize** and **describe** binary ionic compounds, metals with multiple ions, and polyatomic ions.
- **6.3.2 Name** and **determine** chemical formulas for ionic and molecular compounds.

Vocabulary polyatomic ion

1 FOCUS

Build Vocabulary: Word-Part Analysis
Ask students what words they know that have the prefix *poly-*. Define the prefix and have students predict the meaning of the term *polyatomic ion*. **L2**

Targeted Resources
❑ Transparency: Interest Grabber 6.3
❑ Transparency: Reading Strategy 6.3

2 INSTRUCT

Build Reading Literacy: Outline
Have students use the headings from pages 171–175 to create an outline. **L1**

Use Visuals: Figure 18
Have students compare the two models of an ammonium ion. Have them discuss the advantages of each model. Ask students the charge of the ion, the number of covalent bonds, and the number of valance electrons involved in the bonds. **L1**

Build Math Skills: Positive and Negative Numbers
Ask students how many atoms of a halogen would combine with one atom of an alkaline earth metal and why. **L1**

Integrate Language Arts
Explain the history of lime and have students research the origin of the phrase "in the limelight." **L2**

Quick Lab: Modeling Molecules
Students will make models of ammonia and methane molecules and compare their shapes. **L2**

Integrate Language Arts
Have students think of words they know that contain the Greek prefixes listed in Figure 20. **L2**

Targeted Resources
❑ Transparency: Figure 16: Common Anions
❑ Transparency: Figure 17: Some Metal Cations
❑ Transparency: Figure 19: Some Polyatomic Ions
❑ Transparency: Math Skills: Writing Formulas for Ionic Compounds
❑ GRSW Section 6.3
❑ **NSTA** sc*i*$_{LINKS}$ Chemical formulas

3 ASSESS

Reteach
Review naming and writing formulas for ionic compounds and molecular compounds. **L1**

Evaluate Understanding
Have students write chemical formulas for three substances and chemical names for another three substances. Then, have students work in pairs to check each other's work. **L2**

Targeted Resources
❑ **PHSchool.com** Online Section 6.3 Assessment
❑ iText Section 6.3

Transparencies

71 **Section 6.3 Interest Grabber**

Writing Formulas

The names of some compounds contain clues about their chemical formulas. Look at the names of the compounds below. Try to write a formula for each compound based on what you can derive from its name and what you know about the elements the compound contains. Explain how you determined each formula.

1. sulfur trioxide

2. magnesium bromide

3. iron(II) chloride

Transparencies

72 **Section 6.3 Reading Strategy**

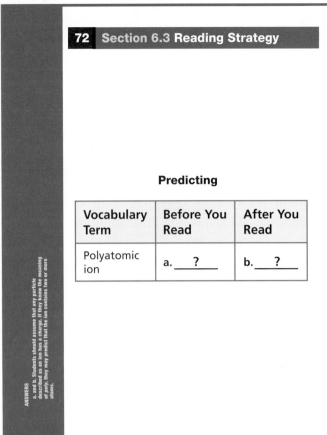

Predicting

Vocabulary Term	Before You Read	After You Read
Polyatomic ion	a. _____?_____	b. _____?_____

Transparencies

73 **Figure 16 Common Anions**

Common Anions			
Element Name	Ion Name	Ion Symbol	Ion Charge
Fluorine	Fluoride	F^-	1−
Chlorine	Chloride	Cl^-	1−
Bromine	Bromide	Br^-	1−
Iodine	Iodide	I^-	1−
Oxygen	Oxide	O^{2-}	2−
Sulfur	Sulfide	S^{2-}	2−
Nitrogen	Nitride	N^{3-}	3−
Phosphorus	Phosphide	P^{3-}	3−

Transparencies

74 **Figure 17 Some Metal Cations**

Some Metal Cations			
Ion Name	Ion Symbol	Ion Name	Ion Symbol
Copper(I)	Cu^+	Chromium(II)	Cr^{2+}
Copper(II)	Cu^{2+}	Chromium(III)	Cr^{3+}
Iron(II)	Fe^{2+}	Titanium(II)	Ti^{2+}
Iron(III)	Fe^{3+}	Titanium(III)	Ti^{3+}
Lead(II)	Pb^{2+}	Titanium(IV)	Ti^{4+}
Lead(IV)	Pb^{4+}	Mercury(II)	Hg^{2+}

75 **Figure 19 Some Polyatomic Ions**

Some Polyatomic Ions			
Name	**Formula**	**Name**	**Formula**
Ammonium	NH_4^+	Acetate	$C_2H_3O_2^-$
Hydroxide	OH^-	Peroxide	O_2^{2-}
Nitrate	NO_3^-	Permanganate	MnO_4^-
Sulfate	SO_4^{2-}	Hydrogen sulfate	HSO_4^-
Carbonate	CO_3^{2-}	Hydrogen carbonate	HCO_3^-
Phosphate	PO_4^{3-}	Hydrogen phosphate	HPO_4^{2-}
Chromate	CrO_4^{2-}	Dichromate	$Cr_2O_7^{2-}$
Silicate	SiO_3^{2-}	Hypochlorite	OCl^-

76 **Math Skills Writing Formulas for Ionic Compounds**

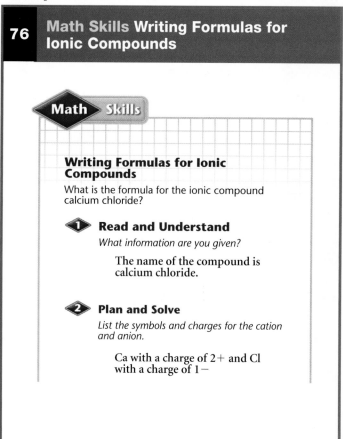

Math Skills

Writing Formulas for Ionic Compounds

What is the formula for the ionic compound calcium chloride?

1 Read and Understand

What information are you given?

> The name of the compound is calcium chloride.

2 Plan and Solve

List the symbols and charges for the cation and anion.

> Ca with a charge of 2+ and Cl with a charge of 1−

77 **Math Skills Writing Formulas for Ionic Compounds** *(continued)*

Determine the ratio of ions in the compound.

> It takes two 1− charges to balance the 2+ charge. There will be two chloride ions for each calcium ion.

Write the formula for calcium chloride.

> $CaCl_2$

3 Look Back and Check

Is your answer reasonable?

Each calcium atom loses two electrons and each chlorine atom gains one electron. So there should be a 1-to-2 ratio of calcium ions to chloride ions.

Name _____ Class _____ Date _____

Chapter 6   Chemical Bonds

Section 6.3 Naming Compounds and Writing Formulas
(pages 170–175)

This section explains how to name and write formulas for ionic and molecular compounds.

Reading Strategy (page 170)

Predicting Before you read, predict the meaning of the term *polyatomic ion*, and write your prediction in the table. After you read, if your prediction was incorrect, revise your definition. For more information on this Reading Strategy, see the **Reading and Study Skills** in the **Skills and Reference Handbook** at the end of your textbook.

Vocabulary Term	Before You Read	After You Read
Polyatomic ion	Students should assume that any particle described as an ion has a charge. If they know the meaning of *poly*, they may predict that the ion contains two or more atoms.	A covalently bonded group of atoms that has a positive or negative charge and acts as a unit.

Describing Ionic Compounds (pages 171–173)

1. Is the following sentence true or false? The name of an ionic compound must distinguish the compound from other ionic compounds containing the same elements. __true__

2. What information is provided by the formula for an ionic compound? The formula for an ionic compound describes the ratio of the ions in the compound. The formula indicates which elements the compound contains.

3. Circle the letter of the word that describes a compound made from only two elements.
a. ionic
(b) binary
c. diatomic
d. polar

4. Is the following sentence true or false? Names of anions are formed by placing the suffix *-ide* after part of the name of the nonmetal. __true__

5. When a metal forms more than one ion, the name of the ion contains a Roman numeral to indicate the __charge__ on the ion.

6. What is a polyatomic ion? A polyatomic ion is a covalently bonded group of atoms that has a positive or negative charge and acts as a unit.

7. Is the following sentence true or false? Because all compounds are neutral, the total charges on the cations and anions in the formula of an ionic compound must add up to zero. __true__

Name _____ Class _____ Date _____

Chapter 6   Chemical Bonds

8. Circle the letter of the correct answer. The formula for sodium sulfide is Na_2S. The sodium ion has a charge of 1+. What must the charge on the sulfide ion be?
a. 1+
b. 0
c. 1−
(d) 2−

Some Polyatomic Ions			
Name	**Formula**	**Name**	**Formula**
Ammonium	NH_4^+	Acetate	$C_2H_3O_2^-$
Hydroxide	OH^-	Peroxide	O_2^{2-}
Nitrate	NO_3^-	Permanganate	MnO_4^-
Sulfate	SO_4^{2-}	Hydrogen sulfate	HSO_4^-
Carbonate	CO_3^{2-}	Hydrogen carbonate	HCO_3^-
Phosphate	PO_4^{3-}	Hydrogen phosphate	HPO_4^{2-}

9. Circle the letter that identifies the number of ammonium ions needed to form a compound with one phosphate ion.
a. one
b. two
(c) three
d. four

Describing Molecular Compounds (pages 174–175)

10. What information is provided by the name and formula of a molecular compound? The name and formula of a molecular compound describe the type and number of atoms in a molecule of the compound.

11. Describe the general rule for naming molecular compounds. The most metallic element appears first in the name.

12. Is the following sentence true or false? The formula for a molecular compound is written with the symbols for the elements in the same order as the elements appear in the name of the compound. __true__

13. Circle the letter that identifies the method of naming the number of atoms in molecular compounds.
(a) prefix
b. suffix
c. number
d. symbol

14. In the formula of a molecular compound, the number of atoms of an element in the molecule is represented by a(n) __subscript__ .

Name_____ Class_____ Date_____ M T W T F

The Structure of Metals

Time
2 periods
1 block

Section Objectives

Local Standards

- **6.4.1 Describe** the structure and strength of bonds in metals.
- **6.4.2 Relate** the properties of metals to their structure.
- **6.4.3 Define** an alloy and **demonstrate** how the composition of an alloy affects its properties.

Vocabulary metallic bond • alloy

1 FOCUS

Build Vocabulary: Vocabulary Knowledge Rating Chart

Have students construct a chart with four columns labeled Term, Can Define It/Use It, Heard It/Seen It, and Don't Know. Have them place the terms *metallic bond*, *metal lattice*, *alloy*, and *metallurgy* in the first column and then rate their term knowledge in the other columns. **L2**

Targeted Resources

❑ Transparency: Interest Grabber 6.4

❑ Transparency: Reading Strategy 6.4

2 INSTRUCT

Build Reading Literacy: Compare and Contrast

Have students read the passage on copper alloys. Have students construct a chart that identifies two copper alloys described in the text, lists the properties the alloys have in common, and lists the properties that differ between the alloys. **L1**

Integrate Social Studies

Have students research the search for an effective filament. Students can present their findings in a poster or other visual display. **L2**

Teacher Demo: Comparing Bond Types

Safely pound rock salt and copper with a hammer and let students observe the differences in the properties of substances with ionic bonds and metallic bonds. **L2**

Address Misconceptions

Ask students to describe the motion of cations in a metal when the metal is not being struck by a hammer. **L2**

Teacher Demo: Bronze and Brass Tones

Ring a brass bell and a bronze bell. Have students observe the difference in tone between the two bells. **L2**

Integrate Materials Science

List the properties of an alloy that are determined by its composition and ask students what properties of steel make it useful for the cables and towers of the Golden Gate Bridge. **L2**

Targeted Resources

❑ Transparency: Figure 22: Bonding and Malleability of a Metal

❑ GRSW Section 6.4

3 ASSESS

Reteach

Use Figure 22 to review how the structure within a metal affects the properties of a metal. **L1**

Evaluate Understanding

Have students write the names of the following elements on index cards: copper, gold, silver, nickel, zinc, tin, iron, carbon, and aluminum. On the opposite side of the cards, have students write common uses for these elements. **L2**

Targeted Resources

❑ **PHSchool.com** Online Section 6.4 Assessment

❑ iText Section 6.4

Transparencies

78 **Section 6.4 Interest Grabber**

Comparing Melting Points

The table below compares the melting points of some metal elements, nonmetal elements, and ionic compounds. Study the table and answer the question.

	Name	Melting Point
Metals	Chromium (Cr)	1907°C
	Titanium (Ti)	1668°C
Nonmetals	Sulfur (S₈)	115°C
	Iodine (I₂)	114°C
Ionic Compounds	Calcite (CaCO₃)	1330°C
	Magnesium Oxide (MgO)	2825°C

Is bonding in metals more like bonding between nonmetals or bonding in ionic compounds? Give a reason for your answer.

ANSWERS
Bonding in metals is more like the bonding in ionic compounds because the melting points of metals and ionic compounds are higher than those of nonmetals.

Transparencies

79 **Section 6.4 Reading Strategy**

Relating Cause and Effect

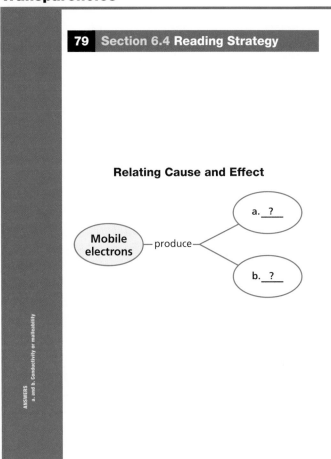

ANSWERS
a. and b. Conductivity or malleability

Transparencies

80 **Figure 22 Bonding and Malleability of a Metal**

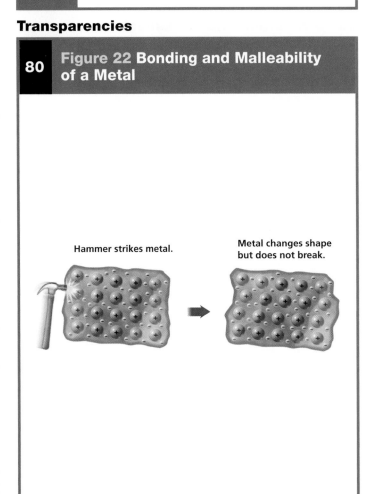

Hammer strikes metal.

Metal changes shape but does not break.

Guided Reading and Study Workbook

Name _____ Class _____ Date _____

Chapter 6   Chemical Bonds

Section 6.4 The Structure of Metals
(pages 176–181)

This section discusses metallic bonds and the properties of metals. It also explains how the properties of an alloy are controlled.

Reading Strategy (page 176)

Relating Cause and Effect As you read, complete the concept map to relate the structure of metals to their properties. For more information on this Reading Strategy, see the **Reading and Study Skills** in the **Skills and Reference Handbook** at the end of your textbook.

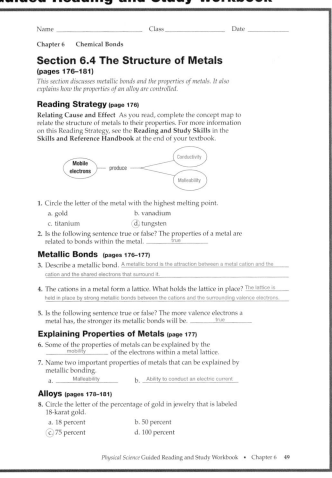

1. Circle the letter of the metal with the highest melting point.
   a. gold   b. vanadium
   c. titanium   d. tungsten

2. Is the following sentence true or false? The properties of a metal are related to bonds within the metal. _____true_____

Metallic Bonds (pages 176–177)

3. Describe a metallic bond. A metallic bond is the attraction between a metal cation and the cation and the shared electrons that surround it.

4. The cations in a metal form a lattice. What holds the lattice in place? The lattice is held in place by strong metallic bonds between the cations and the surrounding valence electrons.

5. Is the following sentence true or false? The more valence electrons a metal has, the stronger its metallic bonds will be. _____true_____

Explaining Properties of Metals (page 177)

6. Some of the properties of metals can be explained by the _____mobility_____ of the electrons within a metal lattice.

7. Name two important properties of metals that can be explained by metallic bonding.
   a. _____Malleability_____   b. _____Ability to conduct an electric current_____

Alloys (pages 178–181)

8. Circle the letter of the percentage of gold in jewelry that is labeled 18-karat gold.
   a. 18 percent   b. 50 percent
   c. 75 percent   d. 100 percent

Guided Reading and Study Workbook

Name _____   Class _____   Date _____

Chapter 6   Chemical Bonds

9. Is the following sentence true or false? When a metal such as copper is mixed with gold, the gold becomes softer.
   false

10. Describe an alloy. An alloy is a mixture of two or more elements, at least one of which is a metal.

11. How do the hardness and strength of bronze compare to the hardness and strength of copper alone and tin alone? Bronze is harder and stronger than either copper or tin alone.

12. Name two factors that scientists can vary to design alloys with specific properties.
   a. The types of elements in the alloy
   b. The amounts of elements in the alloy

13. Complete the following table.

Comparing Bronze and Brass			
Alloy	Component Metals	Comparative Hardness of Bronze and Brass	Comparative Speed of Weathering
Bronze	Copper, tin	Harder	Weathers more slowly
Brass	Copper, zinc	Softer	Weathers more quickly

14. When carbon is added to iron, the lattice becomes harder and stronger than a lattice that contains only iron.

15. Circle the letters of the elements that all types of steel contain.
   (a.) carbon   b. chromium
   (c.) iron   d. manganese

16. Circle the letters of each correct description of stainless steel.
   a. Stainless steel contains more carbon than chromium.
   (b.) Chromium forms an oxide that protects stainless steel from rusting.
   (c.) Stainless steel is more brittle than steels that contain more carbon.
   d. Stainless steel contains more than 3 percent carbon by mass.

17. Explain why pure aluminum is not the best material for the body of a plane.
   Although aluminum is lighter than most metals, it bends and dents too easily.

18. What type of alloy is used to make airplane parts that need to be extremely lightweight? an aluminum-magnesium alloy

---

Guided Reading and Study Workbook

Name _____   Class _____   Date _____

Chapter 6   Chemical Bonds

WordWise

Unscramble the terms from the following list to fit each of the clues given below.

claimlet   ecumelol   levoctan
lorpa   loyal   marfulo
mooctyliap   nocii   nonia
odbn   starscly   tonica

Clues	Vocabulary Terms
A type of bond that holds cations and anions together	ionic
A type of bond in which two atoms share a pair of valence electrons	covalent
A neutral group of atoms that are joined together by one or more covalent bonds	molecule
A term describing a covalent bond in which electrons are not shared equally	polar
An ion that contains a covalently bonded group of atoms	polyatomic
An ion with a negative charge	anion
An ion with a positive charge	cation
A notation that shows what elements a compound contains and the ratio of the atoms or ions of these elements in the compound	formula
Solids whose particles are arranged in a lattice structure	crystals
A mixture of two or more elements, at least one of which is a metal	alloy
A type of bond that exists between a metal cation and the shared electrons that surround it	metallic
The force that holds atoms or ions together	bond

Guided Reading and Study Workbook

Name _____   Class _____   Date _____

Chapter 6   Chemical Bonds

Writing Formulas for Ionic Compounds

Math Skill: Ratios and Proportions

You may want to read more about this **Math Skill** *in the* **Skills and Reference Handbook** *at the end of your textbook.*

What is the ratio of the ions in magnesium iodide?
What is the formula for magnesium iodide?

1. Read and Understand
   What information are you given?
   The name of the compound is magnesium iodide.

2. Plan and Solve
   List the symbols and charges for the cation and anion.
   Mg ion has a charge of 2+ and I ion has a charge of 1−.

   Determine the ratio of ions in the compound.
   Mg with a 2+ charge needs two I ions, each with a charge of 1+.
   The ratio of the ions in the compound is 1 to 2.

   Write the formula for magnesium iodide.
   MgI_2

3. Look Back and Check
   Is your answer reasonable?
   Each magnesium atom loses two electrons and each iodine atom gains one electron. So there should be a 1-to-2 ratio of magnesium ions to iodide ions.

Math Practice

On a separate sheet of paper, solve the following problems. Refer to Figures 16, 17, and 19 to help you solve the problems.

1. What is the formula for magnesium fluoride?
   Mg ion has a charge of 2+ and F ion has a charge of 1−. The ratio is 1 to 2, so the formula is MgF_2

2. What is the formula for iron(III) chloride?
   Fe(III) ion has a charge of 3+ and Cl ion has a charge of 1−. The ratio is 1 to 3, so the formula is $FeCl_3$

3. What is the formula for mercury(II) sulfide?
   Hg ion has a charge of 2+ and S ion has a charge of 2−. The ratio is 1 to 1, so the formula is HgS.

4. What is the formula for potassium dichromate0?
   K ion has a charge of 1+ and CrO_7 ion has a charge of 2−. The ratio is 2 to 1, so the formula is $K_2Cr_2O_7$.

5. What is the formula for barium nitrate?
   Ba is in the same group as Mg, so its ion has a charge of 2+. Nitrate (NO_3) ion has a charge of 1−, so the ratio is 1 to 2. The formula is $Ba(NO_3)_2$.

Student Edition Lab Worksheet

Name _____   Class _____   Date _____

Chapter 6   Chemical Bonds   **Consumer Lab**

Improving the Dyeing of Nonpolar Fabrics   See pages 184 and 185 in the Teacher's Edition for more information.

Most natural fibers, such as cotton and wool, consist of large molecules that have regions with a partial positive or partial negative charge. These polar molecules have a strong attraction for dyes that contain either polar molecules or ions.

The molecules in some manufactured fibers, such as nylon, are nonpolar molecules. These synthetic fibers are difficult to dye. Molecules of other synthetic fibers, such as polyester and rayon, have only a few polar regions. As you might suspect, polyester and rayon have intermediate attractions for dyes. In this lab, you will investigate a process for improving a fiber's ability to absorb and retain dye.

Problem How can you increase the dye-holding capacity of nonpolar fibers?

Materials
• tongs   • paper towels
• 2 fabric test strips   • scissors
• hot dye bath containing methyl orange   • soap
• clock or watch   • hot iron(II) sulfate solution

Skills Observing, Drawing Conclusions

Procedure
Part A: Dyeing Without Treatment

1. Use the tongs to immerse a fabric test strip in the methyl orange dye bath. **CAUTION:** *The dye bath is hot. Do not touch the glass. The dye will stain skin and clothing.*

2. After 7 minutes, remove the strip from the dye bath. Allow as much of the dye solution as possible to drip back into the bath. Rinse off the excess dye with water in the sink.

3. Place the strip on a paper towel to dry. Be careful to avoid splashes when transferring the strip between the dye bath and paper towel. Record your observations in the data table.

DATA TABLE

Dye Treatment	Dyeing of Fibers	Colorfastness of Fibers
Methyl orange	Intensity of color varies; wool is strongest, synthetics weakest	Wool and cotton are colorfast;synthetic fibers are not.
Iron sulfate and methyl orange	Intensity of color varies, but increase in intensity is strongest in synthetics.	All fibers are colorfast.

Student Edition Lab Worksheet

Name _____ Class _____ Date _____

4. After the fabric strip is dry, test it for colorfastness, or the ability to hold dye. Cut the strip in half lengthwise and wash one half of the strip in the sink with soap and water.

5. Allow the washed half-strip to dry and then compare the washed half to the unwashed half. Record your observations in the data table. Staple the half-strips to a sheet of paper and label each half-strip to indicate how you treated it.

Part B: Dyeing With Treatment

6. Use the tongs to place the second fabric strip in the iron(II) sulfate solution for 25 minutes. Then, use the tongs to lift the strip and allow it to drain into the iron(II) sulfate solution. Wring the strip as dry as possible over the solution. **CAUTION:** *The strip will be hot. Allow it to cool before touching it. Wear plastic gloves.*

7. Repeat Steps 1 through 3, using the strip that you treated with iron(II) sulfate.

8. To test the strip for colorfastness, repeat Steps 4 and 5.

9. Clean up your work area and wash your hands thoroughly with warm water and soap before leaving the laboratory.

Analyze and Conclude

1. **Comparing and Contrasting** How did the color of the untreated strip compare with the color of the treated strip?

   Treatment increased the intensity of the colors for synthetic fibers.

2. **Comparing and Contrasting** How did the colorfastness of the untreated strip compare to the colorfastness of the treated strip?

   In general, treatment improved colorfastness, especially in synthetic fabrics.

3. **Applying Concepts** Silk blouses and shirts can be purchased in many intense colors. Why do you think silk is able to hold a variety of intense dyes?

   Silk is a natural fiber. Like most natural fibers, it has many polar regions that allow the dye to

   attach to the fibers.

4. **Drawing Conclusions** How does iron(II) sulfate affect the ability of a fabric to absorb dyes? (*Hint:* What kind of compound is iron(II) sulfate?)

   Iron(II) sulfate is an ionic compound. Treatment with this compound adds ionic sites to the fabric,

   increasing its ability to bind dyes.

5. **Predicting** A care label might read *Wash in cold water only.* What might happen to the color of a piece of clothing with this label if you washed the clothing in hot water?

   The hot water would remove more dye than would cold water, and the colors would run.

Lab Manual

Name _____ Class _____ Date _____

Playing the Ionic Compounds Card Game

Refer students to pages 170–175 in their textbooks for a discussion of naming compounds and writing formulas.
SKILLS FOCUS: Calculating, Observing, Applying Concepts, Relating Cause and Effect **CLASS TIME:** 45 minutes

Background Information

Ionic compounds are composed of charged particles called **ions.** Positively charged ions are called **cations,** and negatively charged ions are called **anions.** Although ionic compounds are composed of ions, they are electrically neutral. The sum of the positive charges of the cations and the negative charges of the anions is zero. The formula of an ionic compound can be determined from the ratio of cations and anions needed to produce a total charge equal to zero. The symbol for the cation always appears first in the formula.

The names of ionic compounds are based on the names of their ions. For most cations, the name of the cation is the same name as the element name. However, many transition metals form more than one ion. For these ions, a Roman numeral is used to show the charge. For example, Fe^{2+} is iron(II) and Fe^{3+} is iron(III). Anions are named by combining part of the name of the element and the ending *–ide.* For example, the name for O^{2-} is oxide. A covalently bonded group of atoms that has a positive or negative charge is called a **polyatomic ion.** These ions have names that reflect their composition.

In this investigation, you will practice naming ionic compounds and writing their formulas by playing a card game.

Problem

How are the names and formulas of ionic compounds determined?

Pre-Lab Discussion

Read the entire investigation. Then, work with a partner to answer the following questions.

1. **Inferring** What is the object of the game?

   The object of the game is to make as many matches as possible. A match consists of a

   set of cation and anion cards that match the formula for the compound represented by a

   player's cation and anion name cards. Players receive one point for each ion in the formula.

2. **Classifying** How many cation symbol cards, cation name cards, anion symbol cards, and anion name cards are required for this card game?

   Forty cation symbol cards, 10 cation name cards, 40 anion symbol cards, and 10 anion

   name cards are required.

Lab Manual

Name _____ Class _____ Date _____

3. **Inferring** How many cards of each type does each player receive at the beginning of a round?

   Each player receives three cation symbol cards, three anion symbol cards, one cation

   name card, and one anion name card.

4. **Inferring** What happens after a player makes a correct match?

   The player draws new ion symbol cards and name cards to replace the ones shown in the

   match. The used name cards are set aside and are out of play. The used ion symbol cards

   are placed in the appropriate discard piles.

5. **Making Judgments** When does the game end?

   The game ends when either the cation or anion name cards are used up.

Materials *(per group)*
100 unlined index cards

Procedure

1. Work in groups of four. Use the index cards to prepare four decks of playing cards. Examples of cards are shown in Figure 1.

   a. Cation symbol cards. Prepare four cation symbol cards for each of the following cations. Write the symbol for each cation on the front of an index card. On the back of each card, write "Cation Symbol."

   Na^+ K^+ Mg^{2+} Ca^{2+} Al^{3+} Fe^{2+} Fe^{3+} Cu^+ Cu^{2+} Zn^{2+}

   b. Cation name cards. Prepare one cation name card for each of the following cations. Write the name of each cation on the front of an index card. On the back of each card, write "Cation Name."

   sodium potassium magnesium calcium aluminum
   iron(II) iron(III) copper(I) copper(II) zinc

   c. Anion symbol cards. Prepare four anion symbol cards for each of the following anions. Write the symbol for each anion on the front of an index card. On the back of each card, write "Anion Symbol."

   F^- Cl^- O^{2-} S^{2-} PO_4^{3-} CO_3^{2-} NO_3^- N^{3-} Br^- OH^-

   d. Anion name cards. Prepare one anion name card for each of the following anions. Write the name for each anion on the front of an index card. On the back of each card, write "Anion Name."

   fluoride chloride oxide sulfide phosphate
   carbonate nitrate nitride bromide hydroxide

Lab Manual

Name _____ Class _____ Date _____

Figure 1

2. After you finish preparing the cards, shuffle each deck of cards separately and place the decks facedown on the table.

3. To determine who goes first, have each player draw a cation symbol card. The player who draws the ion with the highest charge goes first. If players draw the same charge, they should draw another card. Replace the cards and shuffle the cation symbol deck. Play continues clockwise.

4. To start the game, each player draws three cation symbol cards, three anion symbol cards, one cation name card, and one anion name card. Then, turn over one card from each deck of symbol cards to start a discard pile, as shown in Figure 2.

   Figure 2

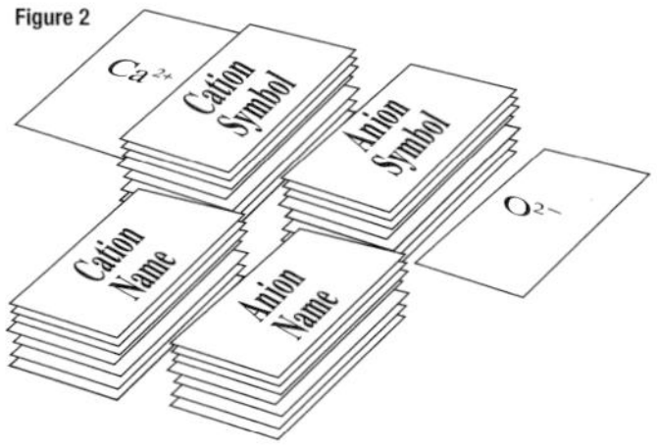

5. The object of the game is to gather the correct number and type of symbol cards to match the formula of the compound represented by the selected cation and anion name cards. As soon as you think you have a match, declare it and show your cards. If you are correct, you will receive one point for each ion in the compound. For example, you would receive three points for the ions in $MgCl_2$.

6. When you show your cards, any other player can challenge your match by providing the correct formula. If your formula is incorrect (the charges do not add up to zero) or if your formula does not match your name cards, the challenger gets the points.

7. During a player's turn, the player may do one of the following:

   a. Draw a card from either the cation symbol deck or discard pile, or from the anion symbol deck or discard pile, and discard a cation or anion symbol card to the appropriate discard pile; or

   b. Draw a new cation name card, anion name card, or both, and place the old name cards at the bottom of the appropriate decks.

   If you can make a match after drawing a card, you must declare it before discarding any cards. Once cards are discarded, the turn is over, and play continues.

Lab Manual

Name _____ Class _____ Date _____

8. If there is no challenge after you declare a match, record the formula, the name, and the number of points in the data table. If there is a challenge, the group must determine who is correct and who gets the points. If you challenge another player and receive the points, record "Challenge" in the data table instead of the name of the compound.

9. After you declare a match and the group determines who gets the points, draw new ion symbol cards and ion name cards to replace the ones you showed to make a match. Put the used ion symbol cards in the appropriate discard pile. Set the used name cards aside and out of play. At that point, your turn is over, and play continues.

10. If either the cation symbol cards or the anion symbol cards are all used, mix the appropriate discard pile, turn it over, and continue play. When either the cation name cards or the anion name cards are all used, the game is over. The winner is the player with the most points.

Observations

DATA TABLE   Sample data are shown.

Match	Compound Name	Compound Formula	Points
1	Calcium nitrate	$Ca(NO_3)_2$	3
2	Iron(III) carbonate	$Fe_2(CO_3)_3$	5
3	Sodium chloride	$NaCl$	2
4	Aluminum bromide	$AlBr_3$	4
5	Challenge	$Zn(OH)_2$	3
6	Copper(I) oxide	Cu_2O	3
7			
8			
9			
10			
		Total	20

Lab Manual

Name _____ Class _____ Date _____

Analysis and Conclusions

1. **Calculating** Describe how to determine the correct ratio of ions in a compound.

   Use the ratio of cations to anions that produces a net charge of zero.
   _____
   _____

2. **Inferring** Explain why it is not possible to write a formula for a compound of sodium and calcium.

   Because both elements form only cations, the sum of the charges on their ions can never equal
   zero. When an ionic compound forms, one element must lose electrons and one element must
   gain electrons during the transfer of electrons.
   _____
   _____
   _____
   _____

3. **Applying Concepts** Each of the chemical names below contains an error. Describe the nature of the error in each name.
   a. Potassium sulfur

   The correct name for an anion of sulfur is sulfide.
   _____
   _____

   b. Oxide potassium

   The ions are in the wrong order. The name of the cation comes before the name of the anion in
   the name of an ionic compound. The correct name is potassium oxide.
   _____
   _____

   c. Copper oxide

   Copper can form two different cations—copper(I) and copper(II). The name should indicate which
   ion is present.
   _____
   _____

Lab Manual

Name _____ Class _____ Date _____

4. **Relating Cause and Effect** How many anions are required to balance one aluminum ion? Explain your answer.

   Three anions are required because an aluminum ion has a charge of 3+.
   _____
   _____

5. **Drawing Conclusions** How are the name and formula of an ionic compound determined?

   In the name of an ionic compound, the name of the cation is followed by the name of the anion.
   The formula of an ionic compound can be determined from the ratio of cations and anions needed
   to produce a total charge equal to zero. The symbol for the cation always comes first in the formula.
   _____
   _____
   _____
   _____

Go Further

In this investigation, you used the charges on ions to determine the formulas of compounds. How could you change this game so you could play it with covalent compounds? Design a card game that you could use to practice writing formulas and naming covalent compounds containing two elements.
Students may need to review pages 174 and 175 in their textbooks.

Lab Manual

Name _____ Class _____ Date _____

Chapter 6   Chemical Bonds   Investigation 6B

Comparing Ionic and Molecular Compounds

Refer students to pages 158–169 in their textbooks for a discussion of ionic and covalent bonds. **SKILLS FOCUS:** Observing, Comparing and Contrasting, Predicting, Inferring, Drawing Conclusions, Evaluating and Revising
CLASS TIME: 45 minutes

Background Information

Ions in an ionic compound and molecules in a molecular compound are held together by forces of attraction called **chemical bonds.** An **ionic bond** is the force that holds positively charged cations and negatively charged anions together in a crystal lattice. Each cation is attracted to all the neighboring anions in the lattice. Each anion is attracted to all the neighboring cations in the lattice.

In molecules, atoms are held together by covalent bonds. In a **covalent bond,** two atoms share a pair of valence electrons. The atoms are held together by the attractions between the protons in each nucleus and the shared electrons. If one atom in a covalent bond has a greater attraction for electrons than the other atom does, the electrons are not shared equally between the atoms. The atom with the greater attraction has a partial negative charge, while the other atom has a partial positive charge. This type of covalent bond is called a **polar covalent bond.** When the electrons are shared equally between the atoms, the bond is called a **nonpolar covalent bond.** Whether a molecule is polar or nonpolar depends on the type of covalent bonds and the shape of the molecule.

In this investigation, you will use ease of melting to compare the strength of the ionic bonds in sodium chloride to the strength of intermolecular attractions in paraffin. Paraffin is a mixture of hydrocarbons, which are molecular compounds that contain only hydrogen and carbon. Then, you will compare the ability of the molecules in sugar and the molecules in paraffin to dissolve in water.

Problem

How do different forces of attraction affect the behavior of ionic compounds and molecular compounds?

Pre-Lab Discussion

Read the entire investigation. Then, work with a partner to answer the following questions.

1. **Inferring** How would you expect the strength of the forces that hold a solid together to affect the melting point of the solid?

   The stronger the forces, the higher the melting point would be.
   _____
   _____

Lab Manual

2. Predicting A solid can dissolve in water if the particles in the solid are attracted to water molecules. Would you expect an ionic compound to dissolve easily in water? A compound with polar molecules? A compound with nonpolar molecules? Explain your answers. (*Hint:* Water molecules are strongly polar.)

The ends of polar molecules such as water have partial positive and negative charges. Therefore,

water molecules are attracted to ions and other polar molecules. Water molecules are not

attracted to nonpolar molecules. Therefore, ionic compounds and polar molecules dissolve

in water much more easily than nonpolar molecules do.

3. Controlling Variables Identify the manipulated and responding variables in this investigation.

The manipulated variable is the type of compound, and the responding variables are the ease of

melting and the ease of dissolving in water.

4. Formulating Hypotheses Record your hypothesis of whether the bonds that hold ions together in a crystal are stronger than the intermolecular attractions that hold molecules together in a solid.

The bonds that hold ions together are stronger.

5. Evaluating What results in this investigation would support your hypothesis?

The hypothesis that the bonds that hold ions together in a crystal are stronger than the

intermolecular attractions that hold molecules together in a solid would be supported if the

paraffin melts more easily than the sodium chloride does.

Materials *(per group)*

sodium chloride	clay triangle	sugar
paraffin	Bunsen burner	test-tube rack
3 spatulas	tongs	clock or watch
2 crucibles	2 test tubes with stoppers	Provide laboratory grade sodium chloride, not table salt, which may contain other substances.
ring stand with iron ring	glass-marking pencil	

Safety 🥽 👐 🔥 🔺 🔥

Put on safety goggles and a lab apron. Be careful to avoid breakage when working with glassware. Tie back loose hair and clothing when working with flames. Do not reach over an open flame. Use extreme care when working with heated equipment or materials to avoid burns. Note all safety alert symbols next to the steps in the Procedure and review the meaning of each symbol by referring to the Safety Symbols on page xiii.

Lab Manual

Procedure

🔥 👐 **1.** Use a spatula to place a pea-sized quantity of sodium chloride in a crucible. Use a second spatula to place a pea-sized quantity of paraffin in a second crucible.

2. Use the ring stand, iron ring, and clay triangle to support the crucible of sodium chloride above a burner.

🔺 🔥 **3.** Light the burner and observe the contents of the crucible for 1 minute. Keep the flame away from the contents of the crucible. Record your observations in the data table. **CAUTION:** *Be careful when working with flames. Tie back loose hair and clothing.*

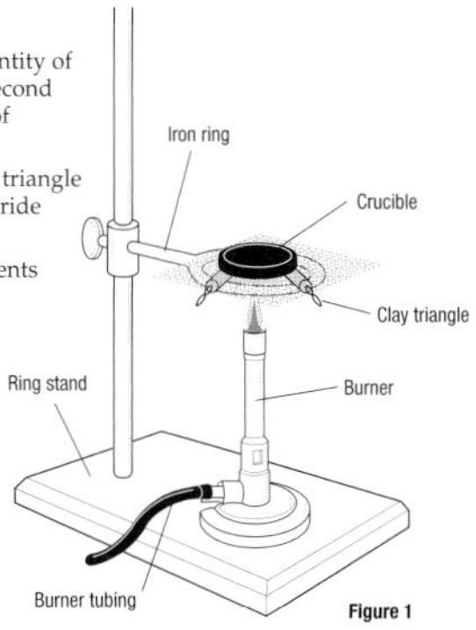

Iron ring
Crucible
Clay triangle
Burner
Ring stand
Burner tubing
Figure 1

4. Use tongs to carefully remove the crucible from the flame. Gently place the crucible in a safe place on the lab table where you will not accidentally touch it as it cools. **CAUTION:** *Use extreme care when working with heated equipment or materials to avoid burns. Do not touch objects after they have been heated. Allow them to cool completely first.*

5. Repeat Steps 2 through 4 with the crucible of paraffin. Turn off the gas supply to the burner when you are done.

6. Label two test tubes *1* and *2* with the glass-marking pencil. Fill the test tubes halfway with water.

7. Use a new spatula to place a pea-sized quantity of sugar in test tube 1. Use the spatula that you used for paraffin in Step 1 to place a pea-sized quantity of paraffin in test tube 2.

8. Stopper the test tubes. Holding the stoppers firmly in place, shake each test tube to speed up the dissolving of the salt and paraffin.

9. Observe the contents of the test tubes and record your observations.

Observations

DATA TABLE Sample data are shown.

Solid Material	Melting	Dissolving in Water
Sodium chloride	Did not melt	_____
Paraffin	Melted	Does not dissolve
Sugar	_____	Does not dissolve

Lab Manual

Analysis and Conclusions

1. Inferring Based on your data on melting, which forces are stronger—the ionic bonds in sodium chloride or the attractions between molecules in paraffin? Explain your answer.

The ionic bonds in sodium chloride are stronger than the intermolecular attractions in paraffin

because the paraffin melted, but the sodium chloride did not melt.

2. Inferring Based on your data on dissolving in water, which material is more likely to contain polar molecules—sugar or paraffin? Explain your answer.

Sugar is more likely to contain polar molecules because it dissolved in water, and the paraffin

did not dissolve in water.

3. Evaluating and Revising Did your data support or contradict your hypothesis?

The data support the hypothesis that ionic bonds are stronger than molecular attractions.

4. Predicting Which type of compound—ionic or molecular—would you expect to have a higher boiling point? Explain your answer.

An ionic compound would have a higher boiling point because more energy is needed to separate

the particles of the ionic compound.

Go Further

Suppose you had a sample of sodium chloride and paraffin mixed together. How could you separate the sodium chloride from the paraffin?

One simple method would be to mix the sample with water and separate the solution of sodium chloride from the undissolved paraffin. Then, evaporate the water to retrieve the sodium chloride. Students may suggest additional methods.

Chapter Test A

Name _____ Class _____ Date _____

Multiple Choice

Write the letter that best answers the question or completes the statement on the line provided.

_____ 1. Which of the following groups contain three elements with stable electron configurations?
   a. lithium, krypton, argon   b. argon, neon, barium
   c. xenon, neon, boron   d. helium, xenon, neon

_____ 2. Ionization energies tend to
   a. decrease from left to right across a period.
   b. increase from the top of a group to the bottom.
   c. increase from left to right across a period.
   d. decrease from the bottom of a group to the top.

_____ 3. The formation of an ionic bond involves the
   a. transfer of electrons.   b. transfer of neutrons.
   c. transfer of protons.   d. sharing of electrons.

_____ 4. Which of the following statements correctly describes the substance with the formula KI?
   a. Molecules of potassium iodide contain one atom of potassium and one atom of iodine.
   b. There is a one-to-one ratio of potassium ions to iodide ions.
   c. Potassium iodide is a molecular compound.
   d. Potassium iodide is a polyatomic ion.

_____ 5. Which statement best describes the properties of sodium chloride?
   a. Sodium chloride is a malleable solid.
   b. Solid sodium chloride is a good conductor of electric current.
   c. Sodium chloride has a low melting point.
   d. Liquid sodium chloride is a good conductor of electric current.

_____ 6. When two atoms of the same nonmetal react, they often form a(an)
   a. ionic bond.   b. polyatomic ion.
   c. diatomic molecule.   d. polar molecule.

_____ 7. Which of the following formulas represents a compound whose molecules contain a triple bond?
   a. N≡N   b. O=O=O   c. O_3 d. SO_3

_____ 8. In a polar covalent bond,
   a. electrons are shared equally between atoms.
   b. a cation is bonded to an anion.
   c. electrons are transferred between atoms.
   d. electrons are not shared equally between atoms.

Chapter Test A

Name _____ Class _____ Date _____

_____ 9. Because water molecules are polar and carbon dioxide molecules are nonpolar,
   a. water has a lower boiling point than carbon dioxide does.
   b. attractions between water molecules are weaker than attractions between carbon dioxide molecules.
   c. carbon dioxide cannot exist as a solid.
   d. water has a higher boiling point than carbon dioxide does.

_____ 10. Fluorine, F, forms a binary ionic compound with lithium, Li. What is the name of this compound?
   a. fluorine lithide   b. lithium fluoride
   c. lithium fluorine   d. fluorine lithium

_____ 11. If *copper(II)* appears in the name of a compound, it indicates that the compound contains
   a. copper ions with a 11+ charge.
   b. copper ions with a 2+ charge.
   c. copper ions with a negative charge.
   d. two types of copper ions.

_____ 12. Beryllium, Be, and chlorine, Cl, form a binary ionic compound with a one-to-two ratio of beryllium ions to chloride ions. The formula for the compound is
   a. Be_2Cl.   b. 2BeCl.
   c. $BeCl_2$.   d. Be_2Cl_2.

_____ 13. Metallic bonding is similar to ionic bonding because
   a. electrons are transferred between atoms.
   b. electrons are shared between atoms.
   c. the lattice that forms contains anions and cations.
   d. there is an attraction between positively charged and negatively charged particles.

_____ 14. Many metals can be drawn into thin wires without breaking because
   a. cations are still surrounded by electrons when they shift their positions in the lattice.
   b. metals generally have low melting points.
   c. when a metal is struck with a hammer, the positions of the anions do not change.
   d. electrons have fixed positions in a metallic lattice.

_____ 15. How does increasing the amount of carbon in steel affect its properties?
   a. Carbon makes the lattice harder and stronger.
   b. Carbon forms an oxide that protects the steel from rusting.
   c. Carbon makes the steel light enough to use for airplane parts.
   d. Carbon makes the steel softer and easier to cut.

Chapter Test A

Name _____ Class _____ Date _____

Completion

Complete each statement on the line provided.

1. In the binary ionic compound potassium bromide, KBr, the element that forms cations is _____.
2. KBr is the formula for an ionic compound. The fact that neither symbol is followed by a subscript means that there is a(an) _____ ratio of ions in the compound.
3. You are given the melting points of three unknown substances and asked to predict which is an ionic compound. You would select the compound with the _____ melting point.
4. Among the elements potassium, lithium, and iron, the metallic bonds are likely to be strongest in _____.
5. To produce stainless steel, steelmakers add _____ to iron.

Short Answer

Use complete sentences to write the answers to the questions on the lines provided.

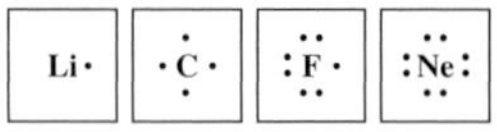

Li·   ·C·   :F: :Ne:

Figure 6-1

1. Study the electron dot diagrams in Figure 6-1. Which of the elements are most likely to react and form a compound? What type of compound are they likely to form?

_____
_____

2. In the binary ionic compound lithium iodide, LiI, which element forms anions?

_____
_____

3. The molecules in compound AB are strongly polar, while the molecules in compound XY are nonpolar. Which substance probably has the higher boiling point?

_____
_____

4. In potassium bromide, KBr, which element forms anions?

_____

5. Why are metals good conductors of electric current?

_____
_____
_____

Chapter Test A

Name _____ Class _____ Date _____

Using Science Skills

Use the table to answer each question. Write the answers on a separate sheet of paper.

	Substances	Compound	Remarks
A	potassium, K, and iodine, I	KI	Iodine is a member of the halogen group; potassium is an alkali metal.
B	carbon, C, and oxygen, O	CO_2	Carbon and oxygen are both nonmetals.
C	Al, O, and H	$Al(OH)_3$	OH^- (hydroxide) is a polyatomic ion.

Figure 6-2

1. **Applying Concepts** How does the saying "Opposites attract" apply to the bonding in the compound shown in row A of Figure 6-2?
2. **Comparing and Contrasting** What kind of bond forms between the elements in row B of Figure -2? How is this type of bond different from the type of bond that forms between the elements in row A?
3. **Comparing and Contrasting** How are the compounds in rows A and C of Figure 6-2 similar? How are they different?
4. **Inferring** A hydroxide ion has a charge of 1–. What is the charge on the aluminum ion? Explain your answer. Use Figure 6-2 to answer this question.
5. **Predicting** Suppose you could substitute sulfur, S, for iodine in row A in Figure 6-2. What would the formula for the resulting compound be? Explain your answer.

Essay

Write the answer to each question on a separate sheet of paper.

1. Fluorine is the most reactive nonmetal. To fluorine's immediate right in the periodic table is neon, a noble gas that does not form chemical bonds. Explain this contrast in reactivity in terms of atomic structure.
2. How is an electron dot diagram a useful model for focusing on the chemical properties of an element?
3. Water droplets tend to have a spherical, round shape. Explain this fact in terms of the polar nature of water molecules.
4. Compare and contrast the lattice in an ionic compound, such as sodium chloride, with the lattice in a metal, such as tungsten. How do any differences affect the malleability of these solids?
5. How does the ability of metals such as copper and alloys such as steel to be drawn into wires affect the possible uses of these materials?

Chapter Test B

Name _____ Class _____ Date _____

Chapter 6   Chemical Bonds   **Chapter Test B**

Multiple Choice

Write the letter that best answers the question or completes the statement on the line provided.

_____ 1. Typically, atoms gain or lose electrons to achieve
   a. an exchange of energy.
   b. ionization.
   c. a stable electron configuration.
   d. vaporization.

_____ 2. In an electron dot diagram, the symbol for an element is used to represent
   a. the nucleus.
   b. the nucleus and all electrons.
   c. the nucleus and valence electrons.
   d. the nucleus and all nonvalence electrons.

_____ 3. Study the electron dot diagrams for lithium, carbon, fluorine, and neon in Figure 6-1. Choose the statement that correctly identifies the most stable of the elements.

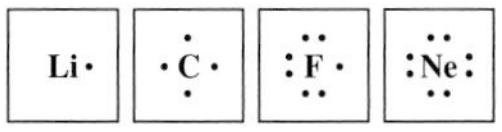

Li ·   · C ·   : F ·   : Ne :

Figure 6-1

   a. Lithium is the most stable element because it has to lose only one electron to achieve a stable configuration.
   b. Carbon is the most stable element because it can form four bonds.
   c. Fluorine is the most stable element because it has to gain only one electron to achieve a stable configuration.
   d. Neon is the most stable element because its highest occupied energy level is filled.

_____ 4. In the compound $MgCl_2$, the subscript 2 indicates that
   a. there are two magnesium ions for each ion of chlorine.
   b. the chloride ion is twice the size of the magnesium ion.
   c. magnesium and chlorine form a double covalent bond.
   d. there are two chloride ions for each magnesium ion.

_____ 5. Which of the following is a typical property of an ionic compound?
   a. low melting point
   b. poor conductor of electric current when melted
   c. tendency to shatter when struck
   d. all of the above

_____ 6. Which of the following compounds does NOT contain molecules?
   a. H_2 b. NaCl
   c. CO_2 d. H_2O

Chapter Test B

Name _____ Class _____ Date _____

_____ 7. You see a structural formula in which the symbols for elements are connected by a long dash. You can assume that the chemical bonds in the compound are
   a. ionic.   b. covalent.
   c. metallic.   d. unstable.

_____ 8. The water molecule H_2O is polar because it contains two polar single bonds and
   a. its molecule has a linear shape.
   b. molecules that contain polar bonds are always polar.
   c. its molecule has a bent shape.
   d. the attractions between water molecules are strong.

_____ 9. Water has a higher boiling point than expected because
   a. there is so much water vapor in the atmosphere.
   b. water molecules are not very massive.
   c. hydrogen and oxygen form single covalent bonds.
   d. of the strong attractions between polar water molecules.

_____ 10. The elements most likely to form more than one type of ion are the
   a. transition metals.   b. alkali metals.
   c. halogens.   d. alkaline earth metals.

_____ 11. Which of the following statements about ions is true?
   a. All metals form more than one type of ion.
   b. Many transition metals can form more than one type of ion.
   c. Halogens form more than one type of ion.
   d. Alkali metals form more than one type of ion.

_____ 12. In the name *carbon dioxide*, the prefix of the second word indicates that a molecule of carbon dioxide contains
   a. two carbon atoms.   b. two oxygen atoms.
   c. a polyatomic ion.   d. an ionic bond.

_____ 13. Which phrase *best* describes a metallic bond?
   a. a bond that is formed by a metal
   b. the attraction between a metal anion and a shared pool of electrons
   c. a bond that forms between a metal and a nonmetal
   d. the attraction between a metal cation and a shared pool of electrons

_____ 14. Which statement about metals is true?
   a. A metal lattice is extremely rigid.
   b. The bonds within a metal lattice are weak.
   c. Electrons in a metal lattice are free to move.
   d. Generally, metals have a low melting point.

Chapter Test B

Name _____ Class _____ Date _____

_____ 15. An alloy that contains mainly copper and tin is
   a. sterling silver.   b. stainless steel.
   c. brass.   d. bronze.

Completion

Complete each statement on the line provided.

1. In an electron dot diagram, each dot represents a(an) _____.

2. In an ionic compound, the attractions between cations and _____ hold the compound together.

3. The chemical formula for calcium chloride, $CaCl_2$, shows that the compound contains two _____ ions for every _____ ion.

4. The ions in solid sodium chloride are arranged in a structure called a(an) _____ lattice.

5. A polar covalent bond forms when _____ are not shared equally between atoms.

6. A(An) _____ ion is a covalently bonded group of atoms that has a positive or negative charge.

7. In ionic compounds, the sum of the charges of all the cations and anions must be _____.

8. The metallic bonds in a transition metal, such as tungsten, are stronger than the metallic bonds in a(an) _____ metal, such as sodium.

9. In a metal lattice, _____ are surrounded by a pool of shared electrons.

10. In its simplest form, the alloy brass consists of zinc and _____.

Short Answer

Use complete sentences to write the answers to the questions on the lines provided.

1. In a periodic table that included electron dot diagrams, in which column would the diagrams contain more dots—Group 2A (the alkaline metals) or Group 7A (the halogens)?

2. In an electron dot diagram of rubidium, there is one dot. In an electron dot diagram of silicon, there are four dots. Which element would you expect to be more reactive?

Chapter Test B

Name _____ Class _____ Date _____

3. Potassium, an alkali metal, and bromine, a halogen, are both in Period 4 of the periodic table. Which element has a higher ionization energy? Explain your answer.

_____

_____

_____

4. Which material is most likely to shatter if you strike it with a hammer—sodium chloride or bronze?

_____

_____

5. Mixing magnesium and aluminum together produces an excellent lightweight material from which to make airplane parts. What is this type of mixture called?

_____

_____

Using Science Skills

Use the table to answer each question. Write the answers on a separate sheet of paper.

Chemical Formula	Name	Type of Bond	Description of Bond
NaCl	(1)	ionic	(2)
CO_2	carbon dioxide	(3)	Atoms share pairs of valence electrons.
W	tungsten	(4)	Metal cations are attracted to the shared electrons that surround them.

Figure 6-2

1. **Using Tables and Graphs** Write a description to place in box (2) in Figure 6-2.
2. **Using Tables and Graphs** What compound name belongs in box (1) in Figure 6-2?
3. **Classifying** What type of bond belongs in box (3) in Figure 6-2?
4. **Classifying** What type of bond belongs in box (4) in Figure 6-2?
5. **Comparing and Contrasting** How are metallic bonds and ionic bonds similar? How are they different? Use Figure 6-2 to answer these questions.

Chapter 6 Test A Answers

Multiple Choice

1. d **2.** c **3.** a **4.** b **5.** d **6.** c
7. a **8.** d **9.** d **10.** b **11.** b **12.** c
13. d **14.** a **15.** a

Completion

1. potassium **2.** one-to-one **3.** highest **4.** iron **5.** chromium

Short Answer

1. lithium, Li, and fluorine, F; an ionic compound **2.** iodine,
3. substance AB **4.** bromine, Br **5.** Metals contain a shared pool
of electrons that are free to move.

Using Science Skills

1. Potassium is a highly reactive metal with one valence electron.
Iodine is a highly reactive nonmetal with seven valence electrons.
When electrons are transferred from potassium atoms to iodine
atoms, there is an attraction between the oppositely charged ions
that form. Thus, opposites do attract in an ionic bond.
2. Covalent bonds form between the nonmetals carbon and
oxygen. In a covalent bond, atoms share electrons. When
potassium and iodine react, electrons are transferred from
potassium atoms to iodine atoms. Ionic bonds form between
potassium cations and iodide anions. There is no sharing of
electrons in an ionic bond. **3.** The compounds in rows A and C are
both ionic compounds. However, KI is a binary ionic compound,
which forms between a metal and a nonmetal. The compound in
row C contains a polyatomic hydroxide ion (OH^-). The atoms in a
polyatomic ion are joined by covalent bonds. **4.** The charge on the
aluminum ion is 3+. The formula $Al(OH)_3$ indicates that there are
three hydroxide ions for each aluminum ion in aluminum
hydroxide. Since each hydroxide ion has a 1– charge, each
aluminum ion must have a charge of 3+ for the overall charge on
the compound to be zero. **5.** K_2S; because sulfur has six valence
electrons, its atoms gain two electrons when they form ionic
compounds. Potassium atoms donate one valence electron when
they form ionic compounds. It takes two potassium atoms to
donate two electrons to one sulfur atom.

Essay

1. The electron configuration of an element determines its
reactivity. Fluorine, with seven valence electrons, tends to gain one
electron to fill its highest occupied energy level. Neon, with eight
valence electrons, has a stable electron configuration. Neon's
highest occupied energy level holds the maximum possible
number of electrons. **2.** An electron dot diagram shows the
number of valence electrons. The chemical properties of an
element depend on the number of valence electrons in its atoms.
3. Because water molecules are polar, there are strong attractions
between water molecules. The molecules on the surface of water
droplets are pulled toward the center by their attractions to water
molecules below the surface. **4.** In both lattices, positively charged
cations are attracted to negatively charged particles. In an ionic
lattice, the negative particles are anions. In a metal lattice, the
negative particles are electrons. Because the electrons are mobile,
electrons still separate cations when the shape of the metal
changes. When an ionic lattice is struck, ions with similar charges
are pushed near one another. Repulsions between these ions
cause the crystal to shatter. **5.** Possible answer: Metal wires are
used to carry electric current. The cables on suspension bridges
are made from thin strands of steel.

Chapter 6 Test B Answers

Multiple Choice

1. c **2.** d **3.** d **4.** d **5.** c **6.** b
7. b **8.** c **9.** d **10.** a **11.** b **12.** b
13. d **14.** c **15.** d

Completion

1. valence electron **2.** anions **3.** chloride, calcium
4. crystal **5.** electrons; valence electrons **6.** polyatomic **7.** zero
8. alkali **9.** cations **10.** copper

Short Answer

1. Group 7A, the halogens **2.** rubidium **3.** Bromine; it gains
electrons rather than losing them. **4.** sodium chloride **5.** an alloy

Using Science Skills

1. The atoms of a metal lose one or more valence electrons and
form cations. The atoms of a nonmetal gain one or more electrons
and form anions. There is an attraction between the oppositely
charged ions. **2.** sodium chloride **3.** covalent **4.** metallic
5. In both metallic and ionic bonds, there are attractions between
particles with positive and negative charges—cations and
electrons in a metallic bond, and cations and anions in an ionic
bond. Ionic bonds are found in compounds. Metallic bonds are
found in a single metal or in alloys.

Chapter 7 Chemical Reactions

Planning Guide

Use these planning tools
Easy Planner
Resource Pro
Online Lesson Planner

SECTION OBJECTIVES	STANDARDS		ACTIVITIES and LABS
	NATIONAL (See p. T18.)	**STATE**	
7.1 Describing Reactions, pp. 192–198 🕐 1 block or 2 periods **7.1.1 Interpret** chemical equations in terms of reactants, products, and conservation of mass. **7.1.2 Balance** chemical equations by manipulating coefficients. **7.1.3 Convert** between moles and mass of a substance using molar mass. **7.1.4 Calculate** amounts of reactants or products by using molar mass, mole ratios, and balanced chemical equations.	A-1, A-2, B-2, B-3		SE Inquiry Activity: How Is Mass Conserved in a Chemical Change? p. 191 L2 SE Quick Lab: Modeling a Mole, p. 196 L2 TE Teacher Demo: Counting Particles, p. 195 L2 TE Build Science Skills: Measuring and Calculating, p. 197 L2
7.2 Types of Reactions, pp. 199–205 🕐 1 block or 2 periods **7.2.1 Classify** chemical reactions as synthesis, decomposition, single-replacement, double-replacement, or combustion reactions. **7.2.2 Describe** oxidation-reduction reactions, and **relate** them to other classifications of chemical reactions.	A-1, A-2, B-1, B-2, B-3, F-1		SE Quick Lab: Identifying a Type of Reaction, p. 203 L2 TE Teacher Demo: Exothermic Reaction, p. 200 L2 LM Investigation 7A: Using Single-Replacement Reactions to Compare Reactivities L2 LM Investigation 7B: Recognizing a Synthesis Reaction L1
7.3 Energy Changes in Reactions, pp. 206–209 🕐 1 block or 2 periods **7.3.1 Describe** the energy changes that take place during chemical reactions. **7.3.2 Classify** chemical reactions as exothermic or endothermic. **7.3.3 Explain** how energy is conserved during chemical reactions.	B-2, B-3, B-5, F-1, F-5		TE Build Science Skills: Observing, p. 208 L2
7.4 Reaction Rates, pp. 212–215 🕐 1 block or 2 periods **7.4.1 Explain** what a reaction rate is. **7.4.2 Describe** the factors affecting chemical reaction rates.	A-1, A-2, B-3, C-1		SE Quick Lab: Observing the Action of Catalysts, p. 214 L2 TE Build Science Skills: Calculating, p. 213 L2 TE Teacher Demo: Temperature and Rate, p. 213 L2
7.5 Equilibrium, pp. 216–219 🕐 1 block or 2 periods **7.5.1 Identify** and **describe** physical and chemical equilibria. **7.5.2 Describe** the factors affecting chemical equilibrium.	A-1, A-2, B-2, B-3, C-1, E-1, G-1, G-3		SE Design Your Own Lab: Manipulating Chemical Equilibrium, pp. 220–221 L2 TE Build Science Skills: Using Models, p. 216 L2

Ability Levels

L1 For students who need additional help
L2 For all students
L3 For students who need to be challenged

Components

SE	Student Edition
TE	Teacher's Edition
LM	Laboratory Manual
PLM	Probeware Lab Manual
GRSW	Guided Reading & Study Workbook With Math Support
CUT	Chapter and Unit Tests
CTB	Computer Test Bank
TP	Test Prep Resources
iT	iText
DC	Discovery Channel Videotapes
T	Transparencies
P	Presentation Pro CD-ROM
GO	Internet Resources

RESOURCES
PRINT and TECHNOLOGY

GRSW Section 7.1 **L1**

GRSW Math Skill **L2**

🖳 **T** Chapter 7 Pretest Section 7.1 **L2** **L2**

💿 **P** Chapter 7 Pretest Section 7.1 **L2** **L2**

SCI LINKS GO Conservation of mass **L2**

SCIENCE NEWS GO Chemical reactions **L2**

GRSW Section 7.2 **L1**

🖳 **T** Section 7.2 **L2**

💿 **P** Section 7.2 **L2**

SCI LINKS GO Chemical reactions, Oxidation and reduction **L2**

GRSW Section 7.3 **L1**

Discovery SCHOOL DC Taming the Flames **L2**

🖳 **T** Section 7.3 **L2**

💿 **P** Section 7.3 **L2**

GRSW Section 7.4 **L1**

🖳 **T** Section 7.4 **L2**

💿 **P** Section 7.4 **L2**

SCI LINKS GO Factors affecting reaction rate **L2**

GRSW Section 7.5 **L1**

🖳 **T** Section 7.5 **L2**

💿 **P** Section 7.5 **L2**

SCI LINKS GO Factors affecting equilibrium **L2**

SECTION ASSESSMENT

SE Section 7.1 Assessment, p. 198

iText iT Section 7.1

SE Section 7.2 Assessment, p. 205

iText iT Section 7.2

SE Section 7.3 Assessment, p. 209

iText iT Section 7.3

SE Section 7.4 Assessment, p. 215

iText iT Section 7.4

SE Section 7.5 Assessment, p. 219

iText iT Section 7.5

Go Online

Go online for these Internet resources.

PHSchool.com
Web Code: cca-1070

SCIENCE NEWS
Web Code: cce-1071

NSTA SCI LINKS
Web Code: ccn-1071
Web Code: ccn-1072
Web Code: ccn-1074
Web Code: ccn-1075
Web Code: ccn-1076

Materials for Activities and Labs

Quantities for each group

STUDENT EDITION

Inquiry Activity, p. 191
100-mL graduated cylinder, resealable quart-sized plastic bag, 10-cm × 10-cm piece of paper, effervescent antacid tablet, triple-beam balance

Quick Lab, p. 196
bolt, 2 nuts, 2 washers, balance

Quick Lab, p. 203
piece of zinc, copper(II) sulfate solution, 250-mL beaker, tongs, paper towel

Quick Lab, p. 214
5 test tubes, test-tube rack, marking pencil, dropper pipet, wood splint, platinum wire, 0.1 g manganese dioxide, 5 drops of copper(II) chloride solution, 0.1 g raw potato, graduated cylinder, 25 mL hydrogen peroxide

Design Your Own Lab, pp. 220–221
iodine-starch solution, 150-mL beaker, 4 dropper pipets, spot plate, ascorbic acid solution, chlorine bleach solution

TEACHER'S EDITION

Teacher Demo, p. 195
14 g graphite powder, small beaker, spatula, balance, a bag of rice, stack of paper plates

Build Science Skills, p. 197
copper wire, aluminum foil, water, sodium chloride, hydrogen peroxide, wire snips, metal spatulas, beakers, balances

Teacher Demo, p. 200
balance, evaporating dish, copper powder, ring stand, wire gauze, Bunsen burner, tongs

Build Science Skills, p. 208
beaker, water, thermometer, 1 tsp baking soda, 1 tsp calcium chloride

Build Science Skills, p. 210
fire extinguishers, fire extinguisher ratings

Build Science Skills, p. 213
clay, rulers, plastic knives

Teacher Demo, p. 213
2 chemical light sticks, 2 large beakers, hot water, ice water

Build Science Skills, p. 216
playing cards, watch

Chapter Assessment

CHAPTER ASSESSMENT
SE	Chapter Assessment, pp. 223–224
CUT	Chapter 7 Test A, B
CTB	Chapter 7
iT	Chapter 7

PHSchool.com GO
Web Code: cca-1070

STANDARDIZED TEST PREP
SE	Chapter 7, p. 225
TP	Diagnose and Prescribe

iText—interactive textbook with assessment at PHSchool.com

Chemical Reactions   190B

LESSON PLAN 7.1

Describing Reactions

Time
2 periods
1 block

Section Objectives   Local Standards

- **7.1.1 Interpret** chemical equations in terms of reactants, products, and conservation of mass.
- **7.1.2 Balance** chemical equations by manipulating coefficients.
- **7.1.3 Convert** between moles and mass of a substance using molar mass.
- **7.1.4 Calculate** amounts of reactants or products by using molar mass, mole ratios, and balanced chemical equations.

Vocabulary reactants • products • chemical equation • coefficients • mole • molar mass

1 FOCUS

Build Vocabulary: Concept Map
Have students construct a concept map of the terms *reactant*, *products*, *chemical equations*, *coefficients*, and *moles*. **L2**

Targeted Resources
- ❑ Transparency: Chapter 7 Pretest
- ❑ Transparency: Interest Grabber 7.1
- ❑ Transparency: Reading Strategy 7.1

2 INSTRUCT

Build Reading Literacy: Summarize
Have students summarize the steps required to determine the number of grams of oxygen needed to make 144 grams of water. **L1**

Teacher Demo: Counting Particles
Compare using molar mass to counting out particles so that students see the efficiency of using molar mass. **L2**

Build Science Skills: Measuring and Calculating
Have students calculate and measure out molar quantities of various samples. **L2**

For Enrichment
Have students assemble a variety of new molecules with the same number of atoms but with different-sized pieces. Have students determine whether the mass of the molecule changes and whether it is possible to assemble molecules that are different in structure but have the same mass. **L3**

Targeted Resources
- ❑ Transparency: Figure 2: Burning of Carbon
- ❑ Transparency: Math Skills: Balancing Chemical Equations
- ❑ Transparency: Figure 8: Calculations With Chemical Equations
- ❑ GRSW Section 7.1
- ❑ **NSTA** *scLINKS* Conservation of mass

3 ASSESS

Reteach
Use Figure 2 to summarize the key concepts in this section. Have students determine the mole ratio of carbon to carbon dioxide in the balanced equation. **L1**

Evaluate Understanding
Give students a chemical equation to analyze. Ask them to determine whether the equation is balanced, and to explain how conservation of mass applies. **L2**

Targeted Resources
- ❑ **PHSchool.com** Online Section 7.1 Assessment
- ❑ iText Section 7.1

Transparencies

81 Chapter 7 Pretest

1. Which of the following is an example of a physical change?

   a. Wood burns and becomes ash.

   b. A steel nail rusts over time.

   c. Ice melts and becomes water.

   d. Milk curdles when acid is added to it.

2. Which of the following characteristics can you determine about a substance based on its chemical formula?

   a. the number and types of atoms that make up the substance

   b. the mass of an unknown sample of the substance

   c. the melting point of the substance

   d. the density and state of the substance at room temperature

3. How do you find the atomic mass of an element?

Transparencies

82 Chapter 7 Pretest *(continued)*

4. Which conversion factor would you multiply 0.020 m by in order to express the quantity in centimeters?

   a. 1000 m/1 km

   b. 1 km/1000 m

   c. 1 m/100 cm

   d. 100 cm/1 m

5. Which is the correct chemical formula for potassium hydroxide?

   a. POH

   b. KOH

   c. P_5OH

   d. K_2OH

Transparencies

83 Section 7.1 Interest Grabber

Equation Analogy

Imagine that you work at a skateboard shop and you are in charge of assembling the skateboards. Every skateboard requires one deck (the board), two trucks (the mounted axels), and four wheels.

1. Your boss asks you to make five skateboards. How many trucks do you need?

2. The following diagram shows the "recipe" for one skateboard. What do you notice about the relative amounts of each part on either side of the arrow?

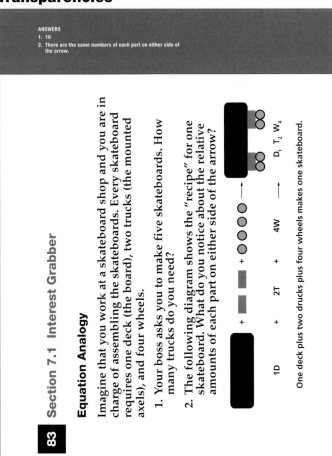

$1D \quad + \quad 2T \quad + \quad 4W \quad \longrightarrow \quad D_1 \ T_2 \ W_4$

One deck plus two drucks plus four wheels makes one skateboard.

Transparencies

84 Section 7.1 Reading Strategy

Monitoring Your Understanding

What I Expect to Learn	What I Learned
a. _____?_____	b. _____?_____
c. _____?_____	d. _____?_____

Transparencies

85 Figure 2 Burning of Carbon

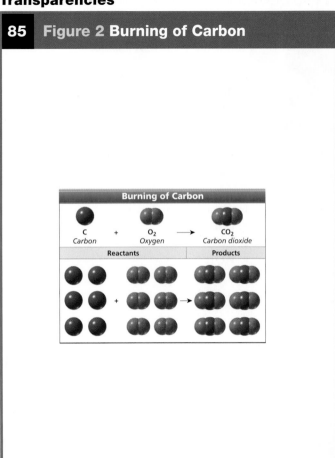

Transparencies

86 Math Skills Balancing Chemical Equations

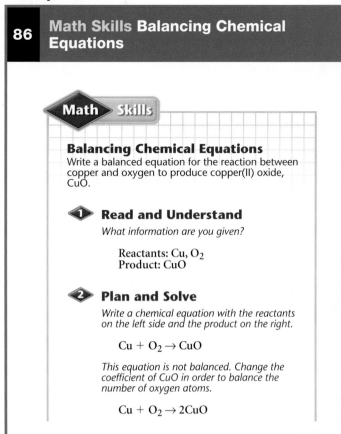

Math Skills

Balancing Chemical Equations
Write a balanced equation for the reaction between copper and oxygen to produce copper(II) oxide, CuO.

1 Read and Understand
What information are you given?

Reactants: Cu, O_2
Product: CuO

2 Plan and Solve
Write a chemical equation with the reactants on the left side and the product on the right.

$$Cu + O_2 \rightarrow CuO$$

This equation is not balanced. Change the coefficient of CuO in order to balance the number of oxygen atoms.

$$Cu + O_2 \rightarrow 2CuO$$

Transparencies

87 Math Skills Balancing Chemical Equations *(continued)*

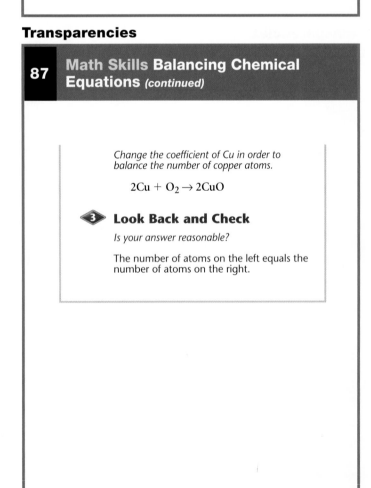

Change the coefficient of Cu in order to balance the number of copper atoms.

$$2Cu + O_2 \rightarrow 2CuO$$

3 Look Back and Check
Is your answer reasonable?

The number of atoms on the left equals the number of atoms on the right.

Transparencies

88 Figure 8 Calculations With Chemical Equations

Formation of Water				
Equation	$2H_2$	$+$ O_2	$\rightarrow$	$2H_2O$
Amount	2 mol	1 mol		2 mol
Molar Mass	2.0 g/mol	32.0 g/mol		18.0 g/mol
Mass (Moles × Molar Mass)	4.0 g	$+$ 32.0 g	$\rightarrow$	36.0 g

Name _____ Class _____ Date _____

Chapter 7   Chemical Reactions

Section 7.1 Describing Reactions
(pages 192–198)

This section discusses the use of chemical equations and how to balance them. It also demonstrates the use of calculations in chemistry.

Reading Strategy (page 192)

Monitoring Your Understanding Preview the Key Concepts, topic headings, vocabulary, and figures in this section. List two things you expect to learn. After reading, state what you learned about each item you listed. For more information on this Reading Strategy, see the **Reading and Study Skills** in the **Skills and Reference Handbook** at the end of your textbook.

What I Expect to Learn	What I Learned
Answers may vary. Possible answers: How to balance chemical equations	Answers may vary. Possible answers: An unbalanced equation can be balanced by changing the coefficients.
How to convert from mass to moles	The mass of a substance can be converted to moles by using the molar mass as a conversion factor.

Chemical Equations (pages 192–193)

1. Is the following sentence true or false? The new substances formed as a result of a chemical reaction are called products. ____true____

2. Circle the letter of each sentence that is a correct interpretation of the chemical equation $C + O_2 \longrightarrow CO_2$.
   a. Carbon and oxygen react and form carbon monoxide.
   b. Carbon and oxygen react and form carbon dioxide.
   c. Carbon dioxide yields carbon and oxygen.
   d. The reaction of carbon and oxygen yields carbon dioxide.

3. Is the following sentence true or false? The law of conservation of mass states that mass is neither created nor destroyed in a chemical reaction. ____true____

4. Circle the letter of the correct answer. According to the equation $C + O_2 \longrightarrow CO_2$, how many carbon atoms react with 14 molecules of oxygen to form 14 molecules of carbon dioxide?
   a. 1   b. 7
   c. 14   d. 28

5. In the reaction represented by the equation $C + O_2 \longrightarrow CO_2$, the mass of carbon dioxide produced equals the total mass of carbon and oxygen that reacted _____.

Name _____ Class _____ Date _____

Chapter 7   Chemical Reactions

Balancing Equations (pages 194–195)

6. Is the following sentence true or false? A chemical equation must be balanced in order to show that mass is conserved during a reaction. ____true____

7. Circle the letter of the name given to the numbers that appear before the formulas in a chemical equation.
   a. subscripts   b. mass numbers
   c. atomic numbers   d. coefficients

8. Is the following sentence true or false? Because the equation $N_2H_4 + O_2 \longrightarrow N_2 + H_2O$ has two nitrogen atoms on each side, the equation is balanced. ____false____

Counting With Moles (pages 195–196)

9. Chemists use a counting unit called a(n) ____mole____ to measure amounts of a substance because chemical reactions often involve large numbers of small particles.

10. Circle the letter of the correct answer. If one carbon atom has an atomic mass of 12.0 amu and one oxygen atom has an atomic mass of 16.0 amu, what is the molar mass of carbon dioxide?
    a. 28.0 amu   b. 44.0 amu
    c. 28.0 g   d. 44.0 g

11. Circle the letter of the correct answer. To convert grams of carbon dioxide to moles of carbon dioxide, you must multiply by which conversion factor?
    a. $\dfrac{44.0 \text{ g CO}_2}{1 \text{ mol CO}_2}$ b. $\dfrac{1 \text{ mol CO}_2}{44.0 \text{ g CO}_2}$
    c. $\dfrac{28.0 \text{ g CO}_2}{1 \text{ mol CO}_2}$ d. $\dfrac{1 \text{ mol CO}_2}{28.0 \text{ g CO}_2}$

Chemical Calculations (pages 197–198)

12. Complete the table.

Formation of Water			
Equation	$2H_2$ +	O_2 $\longrightarrow$	$2H_2O$
Amount	2 mol	1 mol	2 mol
Molar Mass	2.0 g/mol	32.0 g/mol	18.0 g/mol
Mass (Moles × Molar Mass)	4.0 g	32.0 g	36.0 g

13. Circle the letter of the correct answer. One mole of oxygen has a mass of 32 grams. What is the mass of four moles of oxygen?
    a. 128 g   b. 144 g
    c. 128 amu   d. 144 amu

Name_____ Class_____ Date_____ M T W T F

LESSON PLAN 7.2

Types of Reactions

Time
2 periods
1 block

Section Objectives

■ **7.2.1 Classify** chemical reactions as synthesis, decomposition, single-replacement, double-replacement, or combustion reactions.

■ **7.2.2 Describe** oxidation-reduction reactions, and **relate** them to other classifications of chemical reactions.

Vocabulary synthesis reaction • decomposition reaction • single-replacement reaction • double-replacement reaction • combustion reaction • oxidation-reduction reaction

Local Standards

1 FOCUS

Build Vocabulary: Word Forms
Ask students to write simple definitions of the words *synthesize*, *decompose*, and *replace*. Then, have students explain how these simple definitions relate to the terms *synthesis reaction*, *decomposition reaction*, *single-replacement reaction*, and *double-replacement reaction*. **L2**

Targeted Resources
❏ Transparency: Interest Grabber 7.2
❏ Transparency: Reading Strategy 7.2

2 INSTRUCT

Use Visuals: Figure 11
Ask students what evidence of a chemical change there is in Figure 11. Ask students where water would be placed in the chemical equation, if they were to include it. **L1**

Teacher Demo: Exothermic Reaction
Heat copper powder in an evaporating dish to demonstrate a synthesis reaction for students. **L1**

Integrate Earth Science
Have students research cave formations. Ask them what the difference is between stalactites and stalagmites. **L2**

Quick Lab: Identifying a Type of Reaction
Students will determine whether a chemical reaction has occurred between the zinc and copper sulfate solution and identify a single-replacement reaction. **L2**

Build Science Skills: Classifying
Have students search the section and identify redox reactions, which have a product or a reactant that is an element. **L2**

For Enrichment
Have students research the benefits and drawbacks of including airbags in automobiles. **L3**

Targeted Resources
❏ GRSW Section 7.2
❏ **NSTA** *sci*$_{INKS}$ Chemical reactions

3 ASSESS

Reteach
Make a chart of the number of reactants and products each reaction has. **L1**

Evaluate Understanding
Have students draw and label illustrations of different reactions on index cards. Have them exchange the cards and practice identifying each type of reaction. **L2**

Targeted Resources
❏ **PHSchool.com** Online Section 7.2 Assessment
❏ iText Section 7.2

Transparencies

89 **Section 7.2 Interest Grabber**

Models of Reactions

The following drawings represent reactants and products of three different chemical reactions.

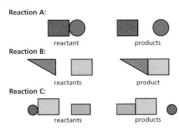

Reaction A:
reactant   products

Reaction B:
reactants   product

Reaction C:
reactants   products

1. Synthesis means "putting something together." Which drawing represents a synthesis reaction? Explain your answer.

2. Decomposition means "taking something apart." Which drawing represents a decomposition reaction? Explain your answer.

3. Replacement means "something taking the place of the other." Which drawing represents a replacement reaction? Explain your answer.

(left margin)
ANSWERS
1. Reaction B is synthesis, because the two reactants come together to make one product.
2. Reaction A is decomposition, because the reactant is taken apart to make two products.
3. Reaction C is replacement, because one reactant takes the place of part of another.

Transparencies

90 **Section 7.2 Reading Strategy**

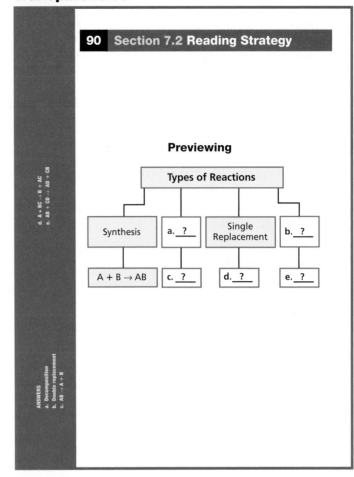

Previewing

Types of Reactions

Synthesis | a. ? | Single Replacement | b. ?

A + B → AB | c. ? | d. ? | e. ?

(left margin)
d. A + BC → B + AC
e. AB + CD → AD + CB

ANSWERS
a. Decomposition
b. Double replacement
c. AB → A + B

Guided Reading and Study Workbook

Name _____ Class _____ Date _____

Chapter 7   Chemical Reactions

Section 7.2 Types of Reactions
(pages 199–205)

This section discusses how chemical reactions are classified into different types.

Reading Strategy (page 199)

Previewing Skim the section and begin a concept map like the one below that identifies types of reactions with a general form. As you read, add the general form of each type of reaction. For more information on this Reading Strategy, see the **Reading and Study Skills** in the **Skills and Reference Handbook** at the end of your textbook.

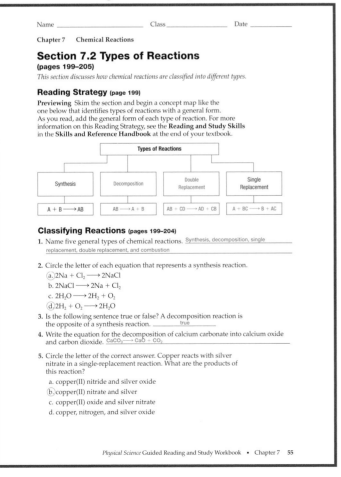

Types of Reactions

Synthesis | Decomposition | Double Replacement | Single Replacement

A + B → AB | AB → A + B | AB + CD → AD + CB | A + BC → B + AC

Classifying Reactions (pages 199–204)

1. Name five general types of chemical reactions. Synthesis, decomposition, single replacement, double replacement, and combustion

2. Circle the letter of each equation that represents a synthesis reaction.
   a. $2Na + Cl_2 \longrightarrow 2NaCl$
   b. $2NaCl \longrightarrow 2Na + Cl_2$
   c. $2H_2O \longrightarrow 2H_2 + O_2$
   d. $2H_2 + O_2 \longrightarrow 2H_2O$

3. Is the following sentence true or false? A decomposition reaction is the opposite of a synthesis reaction. _____ true _____

4. Write the equation for the decomposition of calcium carbonate into calcium oxide and carbon dioxide. $CaCO_3 \longrightarrow CaO + CO_2$

5. Circle the letter of the correct answer. Copper reacts with silver nitrate in a single-replacement reaction. What are the products of this reaction?
   a. copper(II) nitride and silver oxide
   b. copper(II) nitrate and silver
   c. copper(II) oxide and silver nitrate
   d. copper, nitrogen, and silver oxide

Physical Science Guided Reading and Study Workbook • Chapter 7 **55**

Guided Reading and Study Workbook

Name _____ Class _____ Date _____

Chapter 7   Chemical Reactions

6. What is a double-replacement reaction? A double-replacement reaction is a reaction in which two different compounds exchange positive ions and form two new compounds.

7. Complete the chart by filling in the general forms of the reactions shown.

General Forms	
Single-Replacement Reaction	Double-Replacement Reaction
$A + BC \longrightarrow B + AC$	$AB + CD \longrightarrow AD + CB$

8. Lead(II) nitrate reacts with potassium iodide to form lead(II) iodide and potassium nitrate. Write the balanced equation for this double-replacement reaction. $Pb(NO_3)_2 + 2KI \longrightarrow PbI_2 + 2KNO_3$

9. Circle the letter of the correct answer. Calcium carbonate, $CaCO_3$, reacts with hydrochloric acid, HCl, in a double-replacement reaction. What are the products of this reaction?
   a. calcium chloride, $CaCl_2$, and carbonic acid, H_2CO_3
   b. calcium hydride, CaH_2, chlorine, Cl_2, and carbon dioxide, CO_2
   c. calcium hydrogen carbonate, $Ca(HCO_3)_2$, and chlorine, Cl_2
   d. calcium perchlorate, $Ca(ClO_4)_2$, and methane, CH_4

10. Is the following sentence true or false? A combustion reaction is a reaction in which a substance reacts with carbon dioxide, often producing heat and light. _____ false _____

11. Methane, CH_4, burns in oxygen to form carbon dioxide and water. Write the balanced equation for this reaction. $CH_4 + 2O_2 \longrightarrow CO_2 + 2H_2O$

12. Is the following sentence true or false? The reaction that forms water can be classified as either a synthesis reaction or a combustion reaction. _____ true _____

Reactions as Electron Transfers (pages 204–205)

13. What is an oxidation-reduction reaction? An oxidation-reduction reaction is a reaction in which electrons are transferred from one reactant to another.

14. Calcium reacts with oxygen to form calcium oxide. Which reactant is oxidized in this reaction? _____ calcium _____

15. Is the following sentence true or false? When calcium reacts with oxygen, each calcium atom gains two electrons and becomes a calcium ion with a charge of 2–. _____ false _____

16. Is the following sentence true or false? Oxygen must be present in order for an oxidation-reduction reaction to take place. _____ false _____

17. The process in which an element gains electrons during a chemical reaction is called _____ reduction _____.

56 *Physical Science* Guided Reading and Study Workbook • Chapter 7

Section 7.3 Lesson Plan

LESSON PLAN 7.3

Energy Changes in Reactions

Time
2 periods
1 block

Section Objectives

- **7.3.1 Describe** the energy changes that take place during chemical reactions.
- **7.3.2 Classify** chemical reactions as exothermic or endothermic.
- **7.3.3 Explain** how energy is conserved during chemical reactions.

Vocabulary chemical energy • exothermic reaction • endothermic reaction

Local Standards

---

1 FOCUS

Build Vocabulary: Word-Part Analysis
Define the prefixes *exo-* and *endo-* for students. Have them predict the meaning of the terms *exothermic reaction* and *endothermic reaction* given that the word root *thermo* means heat. **L2**

Targeted Resources
❏ Transparency: Interest Grabber 7.3
❏ Transparency: Reading Strategy 7.3

---

2 INSTRUCT

Build Reading Literacy: Relate Text and Visuals
After reading pages 206 and 207, have students use Figures 16 and 17 to describe the path of energy that takes place in the barbecue scene. **L1**

Build Science Skills: Using Models
Have students use molecular model kits to make ball-and-stick models for propane. Have students count the number of bonds that will break in the combustion of a propane molecule. **L2**

Address Misconceptions
Explain that while combustion reactions are highly exothermic, they are not always accompanied by a blast. **L2**

Build Science Skills: Observing
Have students observe an endothermic reaction between baking soda and calcium chloride. **L2**

Address Misconceptions
Chemical equations do not clearly show conservation of energy. Have students refer to the energy diagrams in Figure 18 for a visual representation of the energy of the reactants and the products. **L2**

Targeted Resources
❏ Transparency: Figure 17: Combustion of Propane
❏ Transparency: Figure 18A: Reaction Energy Diagram for an Exothermic Reaction
❏ Transparency: Figure 18B: Reaction Energy Diagram for an Endothermic Reaction
❏ GRSW Section 7.3

---

3 ASSESS

Reteach
Compare and contrast the ways energy is notated in the equation on p. 206, in Figure 17, in Figure 18, and in the equation on p. 208. **L1**

Evaluate Understanding
Have students sketch and label energy diagrams for exothermic and endothermic reactions. **L2**

Targeted Resources
❏ **PHSchool.com** Online Section 7.3 Assessment
❏ iText Section 7.3

Transparencies

91 Section 7.3 Interest Grabber

Exothermic and Endothermic Processes

Energy is either absorbed or released during chemical and physical changes. During an **endothermic** change, energy is absorbed from the surroundings. During an **exothermic** change, energy is released to the surroundings. Two different physical changes are described below. Read each description and decide if the change is exothermic or endothermic.

1. A plastic bottle of water is placed in a freezer. After several hours, the water has frozen solid.

2. A chef places a stick of solid butter in a saucepan, and heats the saucepan over low heat on a stove. After several minutes, the stick of butter has melted.

Transparencies

92 Section 7.3 Reading Strategy

Comparing and Contrasting

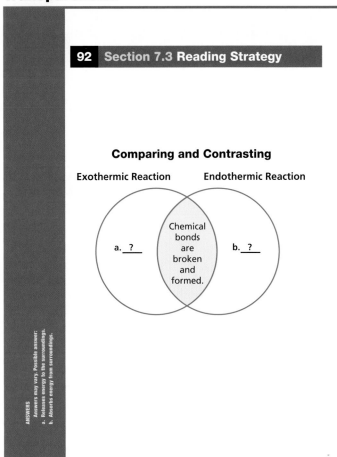

Exothermic Reaction   Endothermic Reaction

a. __?__   Chemical bonds are broken and formed.   b. __?__

Transparencies

93 Figure 17 Combustion of Propane

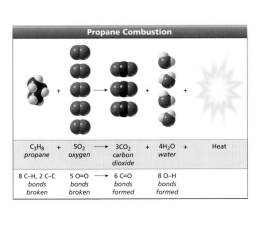

Propane Combustion

| C_3H_8 propane | + | $5O_2$ oxygen | → | $3CO_2$ carbon dioxide | + | $4H_2O$ water | + | Heat |

| 8 C–H, 2 C–C bonds broken | 5 O=O bonds broken | → | 6 C=O bonds formed | 8 O–H bonds formed |

Transparencies

94 Figure 18A Reaction Energy Diagram for an Exothermic Reaction

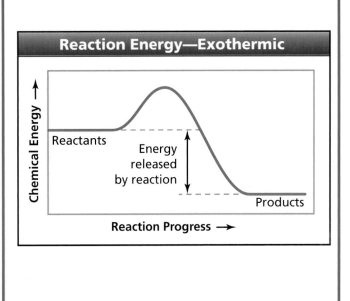

Reaction Energy—Exothermic

Chemical Energy →

Reactants

Energy released by reaction

Products

Reaction Progress →

Transparencies

95 **Figure 18B** Reaction Energy Diagram for an Endothermic Reaction

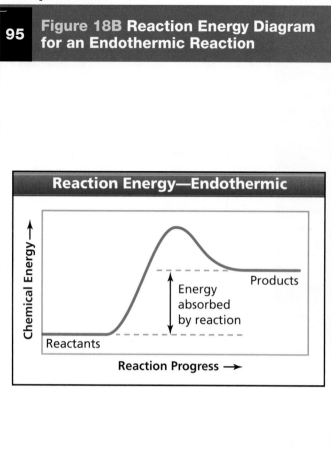

Reaction Energy—Endothermic

Chemical Energy →

Products

Energy absorbed by reaction

Reactants

Reaction Progress →

Guided Reading and Study Workbook

Name _____ Class _____ Date _____

Chapter 7   Chemical Reactions

Section 7.3 Energy Changes in Reactions
(pages 206–209)

This section discusses how chemical bonds and energy relate to chemical reactions.

Reading Strategy (page 206)

Comparing and Contrasting As you read, complete the Venn diagram below to show the differences between exothermic and endothermic reactions. For more information on this Reading Strategy, see the **Reading and Study Skills** in the **Skills and Reference Handbook** at the end of your textbook.

Exothermic Reaction   **Endothermic Reaction**

Releases energy to the surroundings

Chemical bonds are broken and formed.

Absorbs energy from surroundings

Chemical Bonds and Energy (pages 206–207)

1. What is chemical energy? Chemical energy is the energy stored in the chemical bonds of a substance.

2. Chemical reactions involve the breaking of chemical bonds in the reactants and the formation of chemical bonds in the _____products_____.

3. Is the following sentence true or false? The formation of chemical bonds absorbs energy. _____false_____

4. What role does the spark from the igniter play in the reaction that takes place when propane is burned in a gas grill? The spark provides enough energy to break the bonds of reacting molecules and get the reaction started.

5. Is the following sentence true or false? The heat and light given off by a propane stove result from the formation of new chemical bonds. _____true_____

6. The combustion of one molecule of propane (C_3H_8) results in the formation of _____6_____ C=O double bonds and _____8_____ O–H single bonds.

Guided Reading and Study Workbook

Name _____ Class _____ Date _____

Chapter 7   Chemical Reactions

Exothermic and Endothermic Reactions (pages 208–209)

7. During a chemical reaction, energy is either released or _____absorbed_____.

8. Is the following sentence true or false? Physical and chemical changes can be either exothermic or endothermic changes. _____true_____

9. What is an exothermic reaction? An exothermic reaction is a chemical reaction that releases energy to its surroundings.

10. Is the following sentence true or false? In exothermic reactions, the energy required to break the bonds in the reactants is greater than the energy released as the products form. _____false_____

Reaction Energy—Exothermic

Chemical Energy →

Reactants

Energy released by reaction

Products

Reaction Progress →

11. Circle the letter of each sentence that is correct for the graph above.
   a. The energy required to break the bonds in the reactants is greater than the energy released as the products form.
   b. The energy released as the products form is greater than the energy required to break the bonds in the reactants.
   c. The chemical energy of the reactants is greater than the chemical energy of the products.
   d. The chemical energy of the products is greater than the chemical energy of the reactants.

12. In an exothermic reaction, the difference between the chemical energy of the reactants and the chemical energy of the products equals the amount of heat released by the reaction

13. Where does the energy term appear in the equation for an endothermic reaction? The energy term appears on the left side.

Conservation of Energy (page 209)

14. In an endothermic reaction, heat from the surroundings plus the chemical energy of the reactants is converted into the chemical energy of the products

LESSON PLAN 7.4

Reaction Rates

Time
2 periods
1 block

Section Objectives   Local Standards

- **7.4.1 Explain** what a reaction is.
- **7.4.2 Describe** the factors affecting chemical reaction rates.

Vocabulary reaction rate • catalyst

1 FOCUS

Build Vocabulary: LINCS
Have students use the LINCS strategy to learn and review the terms *reaction rate*, *surface area*, *concentration*, and *catalyst*. **L2**

Targeted Resources
❑ Transparency: Interest Grabber 7.4
❑ Transparency: Reading Strategy 7.4

2 INSTRUCT

Build Math Skills: Ratios and Proportions
To help students understand reaction rates, review other rates that students might be familiar with, such as speed as the ratio of distance traveled over time. **L1**

Build Reading Literacy: Outline
After reading the section, have students use the headings as major divisions in an outline. **L1**

Build Science Skills: Calculating
Have students measure the surface area of a clay cube and then cut it in half and measure again. Students learn how to increase surface area. **L2**

Teacher Demo: Temperature and Rate
Students observe the effect of temperature on reaction rate when two chemical light sticks are placed in water with different temperatures. **L2**

Quick Lab: Observing the Action of Catalysts
Students will describe how a catalyst is able to promote a chemical reaction. **L2**

Targeted Resources
❑ Transparency: Figure 23: Reaction Energy Diagram for a Catalyzed and an Uncatalyzed Reaction
❑ GRSW Section 7.4
❑ **NSTA** *sci*$_{LINKS}$ Factors affecting reaction rate

3 ASSESS

Reteach
As a class, list five factors that affect reaction rate. Then, have students give an example of each and explain why the factor affects reaction rate. **L1**

Evaluate Understanding
Have students make flashcards that list the ways they could increase the rate of a reaction, with examples on the back of how each factor affects reaction rates. **L2**

Targeted Resources
❑ **PHSchool.com** Online Section 7.4 Assessment
❑ iText Section 7.4

Transparencies

96 Section 7.4 Interest Grabber

Changing Reaction Rate

1. Place one effervescent antacid tablet into a plastic cup filled with hot tap water and a second tablet into a plastic cup filled with cold water at the same time. In which cup did the fizzing last longer?

2. On a small piece of paper, crush a third tablet into a powder using a plastic spoon. Place the crushed tablet into a cup of cold water and a fourth (whole) tablet into another cup of cold water at the same time. In which cup did the fizzing last longer?

3. How does temperature affect the rate of fizzing?

4. How does crushing the reactant into a powder affect the rate of fizzing?

Transparencies

97 Section 7.4 Reading Strategy

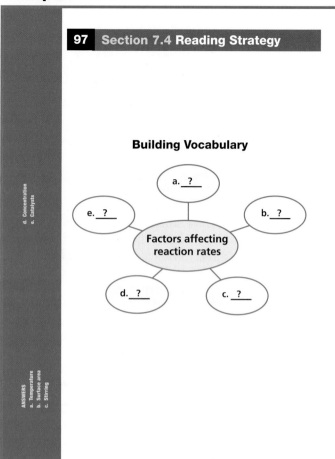

Building Vocabulary

Transparencies

98 Figure 23 Reaction Energy Diagram for a Catalyzed and an Uncatalyzed Reaction

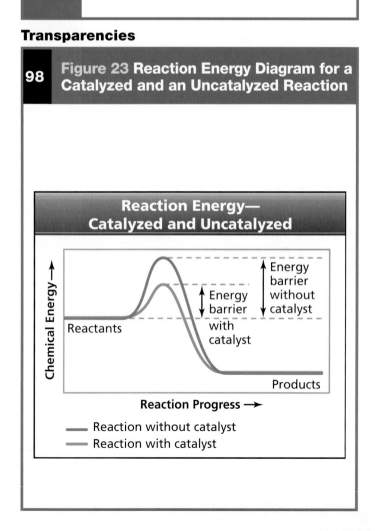

Name _____ Class _____ Date _____

Chapter 7   Chemical Reactions

Section 7.4 Reaction Rates
(pages 212–215)

This section discusses the factors that affect reaction rates.

Reading Strategy (page 212)

Building Vocabulary As you read, complete the web diagram below with key terms from this section. For more information on this Reading Strategy, see the **Reading and Study Skills** in the **Skills and Reference Handbook** at the end of your textbook.

Reactions Over Time (page 212)

1. Any change that happens over time can be expressed as a(n) _____rate_____.

2. What is a reaction rate? A reaction rate is the rate at which reactants change into products over time.

Factors Affecting Reaction Rates (pages 213–215)

3. Is the following sentence true or false? One way to observe the rate of a reaction is to observe how fast products are being formed. _____true_____

4. Is the following sentence true or false? The rate of any reaction is a constant that does not change when the reaction conditions change. _____false_____

5. Generally, an increase in temperature will _____increase_____ the reaction rate.

6. Is the following sentence true or false? Storing milk in a refrigerator stops the reactions that would cause the milk to spoil. _____false_____

7. How does an increase in surface area affect the exposure of reactants to one another? An increase in surface area increases the exposure of reactants to one another.

Name _____ Class _____ Date _____

Chapter 7   Chemical Reactions

8. Why does increasing the surface area of a reactant tend to increase the reaction rate? The increase in exposure of reactants to one another results in more collisions involving reactant particles. With more collisions, more particles will react.

9. Stirring the reactants in a reaction mixture will generally _____increase_____ the reaction rate.

10. Is the following sentence true or false? Increasing the concentration of the reactants will generally slow down a chemical reaction. _____false_____

11. Is the following sentence true or false? A piece of material dipped in a concentrated dye solution will change color more quickly than in a dilute dye solution. _____true_____

12. Why does an increase in pressure speed up the rate of a reaction involving gases? Concentration of a gas increases with pressure, and an increase in concentration results in a faster reaction rate due to more frequent collisions between reacting particles.

13. What is a catalyst? A catalyst is a substance that affects the rate of a reaction without being used up in the reaction.

14. Circle the letters of the sentences that correctly identify why chemists use catalysts.
   (a.) to speed up a reaction
    b. to enable a reaction to occur at a higher temperature
    c. to slow down a reaction
   (d.) to enable a reaction to occur at a lower temperature

15. Is the following sentence true or false? Because a catalyst is quickly consumed in a reaction, it must be added to the reaction mixture over and over again to keep the reaction going. _____false_____

16. Identify where the catalyst V_2O_5 should go in the formula shown and write it in the correct location.

$$2SO_2 + O_2 \xrightarrow{V_2O_5} 2SO_3$$

17. Circle the letter of the correct answer. In the reaction represented by the equation $2H_2O_2 \xrightarrow{Pt} 2H_2O + O_2$, which substance acts as a catalyst?
    a. H_2O_2 (b.) Pt
    c. H_2O d. O_2

18. One way that a catalyst can lower the energy barrier of a reaction is by providing a surface on which the _____reacting particles_____ can come together.

LESSON PLAN 7.5

Equilibrium

Time
2 periods
1 block

Section Objectives   Local Standards

- **7.5.1 Identify** and **describe** physical and chemical equilibria.
- **7.5.2 Describe t**he factors affecting chemical equilibrium.

Vocabulary equilibrium • reversible reaction

1 FOCUS

Build Vocabulary: Paraphrase
To help students understand the vocabulary terms, paraphrase their definitions using words and phrases students are more familiar with. **L2**

Targeted Resources
❑ Transparency: Interest Grabber 7.5
❑ Transparency: Reading Strategy 7.5

2 INSTRUCT

Build Reading Literacy: Reciprocal Teaching
Have students read the section with a partner, alternating between paragraphs. After one partner reads aloud, the other partner summarizes the paragraph's contents and explains the main concepts. **L1**

Build Science Skills: Using Models
Students model dynamic equilibrium using playing cards. **L2**

Address Misconceptions
Give students the following example. A beaker at 0°C contains 2 g of ice and 8 g of water. The rate of melting equals the rate of freezing. Ask students if the system is at equilibrium. **L2**

Integrate Industry
Ask students what factors are used to shift equilibrium in the industrial synthesis of ammonia. **L2**

Targeted Resources
❑ Transparency: Figure 25: Physical Equilibrium
❑ GRSW Section 7.5
❑ **NSTA** *sci*$_{LINKS}$ Factors affecting equilibrium

3 ASSESS

Reteach
Compare the symbols used to show the movement of the water molecules with the double-arrow symbol used in a chemical equation that represents a reversible reaction. Ask students to discuss how these symbols are appropriate for describing equilibrium. **L1**

Evaluate Understanding
Have students work in groups to perform a brief play that models a system in chemical or physical equilibrium. **L2**

Targeted Resources
❑ **PHSchool.com** Online Section 7.5 Assessment
❑ iText Section 7.5

Section 7.5 **Lesson Plan**

Transparencies

99 Section 7.5 Interest Grabber

Opposing Changes

Imagine that you are emptying a swimming pool using a pump that removes 5 gallons of water each minute. Meanwhile, your friend turns on a hose that adds 5 gallons of water to the pool each minute.

1. What happens to the water level of the swimming pool?

2. What would happen to the water level of the swimming pool if you increased the rate that the pump removed water to 7 gallons of water each minute?

ANSWERS
1. The water level stays the same.
2. The water level would go down.

Transparencies

100 Section 7.5 Reading Strategy

Outlining

I. Equilibrium
  A. Types of Equilibria
    1. _____
    2. _____
  B. _____
    1. Temperature
    2. Pressure
    3. _____

ANSWERS
1. Physical equilibrium
2. Chemical equilibrium
B. Factors affecting chemical equilibrium
3. Concentration

Transparencies

101 Figure 25 Physical Equilibrium

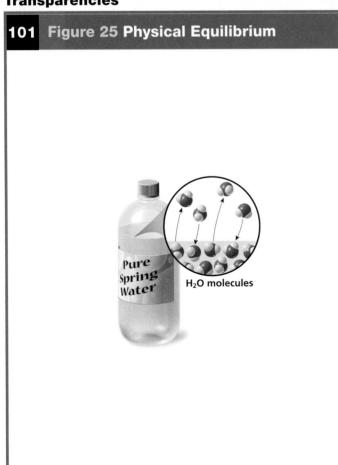

Pure Spring Water

H₂O molecules

Guided Reading and Study Workbook

Name _____ Class _____ Date _____

Chapter 7   Chemical Reactions

Section 7.5 Equilibrium
(pages 216–219)

This section explains physical and chemical equilibria, and describes the factors that affect chemical equilibrium.

Reading Strategy (page 216)

Outlining As you read, make an outline of the most important ideas from this section. For more information on this Reading Strategy, see the **Reading and Study Skills** in the **Skills and Reference Handbook** at the end of your textbook.

I. Equilibrium
  A. Types of Equilibria
    1. Physical equilibrium
    2. Chemical equilibrium
  B. Factors affecting chemical equilibrium
    1. Temperature
    2. Pressure
    3. Concentration

Types of Equilibria (pages 216–217)

1. What is equilibrium? Equilibrium is a state in which the forward and reverse paths of a change take place at the same rate.

2. Circle the letter of the correct answer. In the system described by the equation $H_2O(l) \rightleftharpoons H_2O(g)$, at room temperature, which of the following two physical changes are in equilibrium?
   a. sublimation and condensation
   b. evaporation and melting
   c. sublimation and deposition
   (d.) evaporation and condensation

3. What happens when a physical change does not go to completion?
   A physical equilibrium is established between the forward and reverse changes.

4. What does the single arrow imply about the reaction described in the following equation?
   $$CH_4(g) + 2O_2(g) \longrightarrow CO_2(g) + 2H_2O(g)$$
   The single arrow implies that the forward reaction goes to completion.

Guided Reading and Study Workbook

Name _____ Class _____ Date _____

Chapter 7   Chemical Reactions

5. Circle the letter of the correct answer. In the system described by the equation $2SO_2(g) + O_2(g) \rightleftharpoons 2SO_3(g)$, what two reaction types are in equilibrium?

(a.) synthesis and decomposition   b. single replacement and decomposition

c. synthesis and combustion   d. synthesis and double replacement

6. What happens when a chemical change does not go to completion?
A chemical equilibrium is established between the forward and reverse reactions.

Factors Affecting Chemical Equilibrium (pages 218–219)

7. Is the following sentence true or false? A change in reaction conditions does not affect a chemical equilibrium. ___false___

8. Circle the letter of each correct answer. The synthesis of ammonia is described by the equation $N_2(g) + 3H_2(g) \rightleftharpoons 2NH_3(g) + heat$. Which reaction is favored when the temperature is lowered?

(a.) the forward reaction

b. the reverse reaction

c. the reaction that removes heat from the system

(d.) the reaction that adds heat to the system

9. Circle the letter of each correct answer. During the synthesis of ammonia, which reaction is favored when hydrogen is added to the system?

(a.) the forward reaction

b. the reverse reaction

(c.) the reaction that removes hydrogen from the system

d. the reaction that adds hydrogen to the system

10. According to Le Châtelier's principle, how does lowering the concentration of a reaction product affect a chemical equilibrium? Lowering the concentration of a reaction
product causes the equilibrium to shift in the direction that forms more of the product.

11. Use the equation $C(s) + H_2O(g) + heat \rightleftharpoons CO(g) + H_2(g)$ to complete the table below.

An Example of Le Châtelier's Principle		
An increase in	**Shifts the equilibrium so as to**	**Favoring the**
Temperature, concentration of C, or concentration of H_2O	Remove heat	Forward reaction
Pressure	Produce fewer gas molecules	Reverse reaction
Concentration of H_2	Remove H_2, produce fewer gas molecules, or add heat	Reverse reaction

Guided Reading and Study Workbook

Name _____ Class _____ Date _____

Chapter 7   Chemical Reactions

WordWise

Answer the questions by writing the correct vocabulary term in the blanks. Use the circled letter in each term to find the hidden vocabulary word. Then, write a definition for the hidden word.

Clues	Vocabulary Terms
Describes a reaction that releases energy to its surroundings	e x o t h e (r) m i c
A state in which the forward and reverse paths of a change take place at the same rate	(e) q u i l i b r i u m
A substance that affects the reaction rate without being used up in the reaction	c (a) t a l y s t
A reaction in which a compound breaks down into two or more simpler substances	d e (c) o m p o s i t i o n
A reaction in which two or more substances react to form a single substance	s y n (t) h e s i s
The mass of one mole of a substance	m o l (a) r m a s s
A number that appears before a formula in a chemical equation	c o e f f i c i e (n) t
A reaction in which a substance reacts rapidly with oxygen, often producing heat and light	c o m b u s (t) i o n
The substances formed as the result of a chemical change	p r o d u c t (s)

Hidden Term: _r_ _e_ _a_ _c_ _t_ _a_ _n_ _t_ _s_

Definition: The substances that undergo change in a chemical reaction

Guided Reading and Study Workbook

Name _____ Class _____ Date _____

Chapter 7   Chemical Reactions

Balancing Chemical Equations

Write a balanced equation for the reaction between potassium and water to produce hydrogen and potassium hydroxide, KOH.

1. Read and Understand

What information are you given?

Reactants: K, H_2O

Products: H_2, KOH

2. Plan and Solve

Write a chemical equation with the reactants on the left side and the products on the right.

$K + H_2O \longrightarrow H_2 + KOH$

This equation is not balanced. The number of hydrogen atoms on the left does not equal the number of hydrogen atoms on the right. Change the coefficients of H_2O and KOH in order to balance the number of hydrogen atoms.

$K + 2H_2O \longrightarrow H_2 + 2KOH$

Change the coefficient of K in order to balance the number of potassium atoms.

$2K + 2H_2O \longrightarrow H_2 + 2KOH$

3. Look Back and Check

Is your answer reasonable?

The number of atoms on the left equals the number of atoms on the right.

Math Practice

On a separate sheet of paper, solve the following problems.

1. Magnesium burns in the presence of oxygen to form magnesium oxide, MgO. Write a balanced equation for this reaction.
$2Mg + O_2 \longrightarrow 2MgO$

2. Hydrogen peroxide, H_2O_2, decomposes to form water and oxygen. Write a balanced equation for this reaction.
$2H_2O_2 \longrightarrow 2H_2O + O_2$

3. Barium hydroxide, $Ba(OH)_2$, reacts with nitric acid, HNO_3, to form barium nitrate and water. Write a balanced equation for this reaction.
$Ba(OH)_2 + 2HNO_3 \longrightarrow Ba(NO_3)_2 + 2H_2O$

Math Skill: Formulas and Equations

You may want to read more about this **Math Skill** in the **Skills and Reference Handbook** at the end of your textbook.

Student Edition Lab Worksheet

Name _____ Class _____ Date _____

Chapter 7   Chemical Reactions   **Design Your Own Lab**

Manipulating Chemical Equilibrium

See pages 220 and 221 in the Teacher's Edition for more information.

Chemical reactions tend to go to equilibrium. It is possible to shift the equilibrium by changing the conditions under which the reaction occurs. Factors that can affect chemical equilibrium include the concentration of reactants and products, temperature, and pressure. In this lab, you will observe a chemical reaction and use your observations to predict how one factor will shift the equilibrium of the reaction. Then, you will perform an experiment to test your prediction.

Problem How can you change the equilibrium of a chemical reaction?

Materials

• iodine-starch solution
• 150-mL beaker
• 4 dropper pipets
• spot plate
• ascorbic acid (vitamin C) solution
• chlorine bleach (sodium hypochlorite, NaOCl) solution

Skills Formulating Hypotheses, Designing Experiments, Observing

Procedure 🔲🔲🔲🔲🔲

Part A: Observing a Reversible Reaction

1. Pour 50 mL of iodine-starch solution into the 150-mL beaker. The dark color of this solution is caused by the presence of iodine molecules (I_2) within the grains of starch. **CAUTION:** *Handle iodine solutions with care. Iodine is toxic.*

2. Use a dropper pipet to transfer 3 drops of iodine-starch solution from the beaker to one well on the spot plate.

3. Use another clean dropper pipet to add 1 drop of ascorbic acid solution to the iodine-starch solution on the spot plate. Continue to add ascorbic acid solution to the mixture on the spot plate, 1 drop at a time, until the mixture becomes clear. When an iodine molecule reacts with ascorbic acid, the iodine molecule is reduced and breaks down into two colorless iodide ions ($2I^-$).

4. Use the third clean dropper pipet to transfer one drop of colorless iodide solution to a second well on the spot plate.

5. Use the last clean dropper pipet to add bleach solution to the drop of colorless iodide solution, one drop at a time. Continue until the dark color of the iodine-starch solution reappears. **CAUTION:** *Bleach can damage skin and clothing.* The chlorine bleach (NaOCl) oxidizes iodide ions (I^-), converting them to iodine molecules (I_2).

Student Edition Lab Worksheet

Name _____ Class _____ Date _____

6. Write a chemical equation showing the equilibrium between iodine molecules and iodide ions. This equation does not need to be balanced. Label the two sides of your equation to indicate which substance appears dark and which appears colorless.

$$I_2 \rightleftharpoons 2I^-$$
dark   colorless

Part B: Design Your Experiment

7. **Predicting** Select one of the solutions used earlier that affects the equilibrium between iodine molecules and iodide ions. Record your prediction of the change you will observe in an iodine-starch solution as you add the solution that you selected.

Students may select either ascorbic acid solution or chlorine bleach solution. Students may predict

that adding ascorbic acid to a dark iodine-starch solution will produce a clear solution or that

adding chlorine bleach to a clear iodine-starch solution will produce a dark solution.

8. **Designing Experiments** Design an experiment to test your prediction. Your experimental plan should describe in detail how you will perform your experiment.

In their experimental designs, students should understand that the color of the resulting mixture is

the responding variable and that the type of solution added (ascorbic acid solution or chlorine

bleach solution) is the manipulated variable.

9. Construct a data table like the sample data table shown in which to record your observations. (*Hint:* Your data table may not be exactly like the sample data table.)

SAMPLE DATA TABLE

Initial Solution	Solution Added	Quantity Added	Color of Resulting Mixture
Dark iodine-starch solution	Ascorbic acid solution	27 drops	Clear
Clear iodine-starch solution	Chlorine bleach solution	70 drops	Dark

Student Edition Lab Worksheet

Name _____ Class _____ Date _____

10. Perform your experiment only after your teacher has approved your plan. Record your observations in your data table.
    CAUTION: *Wash your hands with soap or detergent before leaving the laboratory.*

Analyze and Conclude

1. **Analyzing Data** What factor did you investigate? How did it affect the equilibrium between iodine molecules and iodide ions?

   Students should observe that increasing the quantity of chlorine bleach shifts the equilibrium

   toward iodine molecules, and increasing the quantity of ascorbic acid shifts the equilibrium toward

   iodide ions.

2. **Predicting** How would you expect the equilibrium to change if you added more iodide ions to the mixture? Explain your answer.

   Adding iodide ions would shift the equilibrium toward the formation of more iodine.

3. **Calculating** When chlorine bleach (sodium hypochlorite, NAOCl) oxidizes iodide ions to iodine molecules, sodium hypochlorite is reduced to sodium chloride (NaCl) and water (H_2O). Write a balanced chemical equation for this reaction, beginning with the reactants sodium hypochlorite, iodide ions, and hydrogen ions (H^+).

   $NaOCl + 2I^- + 2H^+ \rightarrow I_2 + NaCl + H_2O$

4. **Drawing Conclusions** How does the addition of more product affect the chemical equilibrium of a reaction?

   Adding more product shifts the equilibrium toward the reactants in a reaction.

Lab Manual

Name _____ Class _____ Date _____

Chapter 7   **Chemical Reactions**   🔍 **Investigation 7A**

Using Single-Replacement Reactions to Compare Reactivities

Refer students to page 202 in their textbooks for a discussion of single-replacement reactions. **SKILLS FOCUS:** Observing, Inferring, Applying Concepts, Evaluating and Revising, Drawing Conclusions **CLASS TIME:** 30 minutes

Background Information

In nature, elements can occur either free (uncombined with other elements) or chemically combined in a compound. The tendency of an element to combine with other substances is called the reactivity of that element. The more reactive an element is, the more likely it is to combine with other substances. In a **single-replacement reaction,** one element takes the place of another element in a compound. In general, more reactive elements replace less reactive elements. As a result of the reaction, the less reactive element is freed from the compound. Consider the following reaction.

$$Zn + CuSO_4 \rightarrow Cu + ZnSO_4$$

The more reactive zinc replaces copper and combines with the sulfate ion. The less reactive copper is released from the compound and becomes a free element.

When a metal is placed in hydrochloric acid (HCl), a single-replacement reaction can occur. If the metal is more reactive than the hydrogen in the acid, the metal will replace the hydrogen, and bubbles of hydrogen gas (H_2) will be produced. The more reactive a metal is, the more vigorously it will react with hydrochloric acid.

The alkali metals and alkaline earth metals have only one or two electrons in their highest energy level. By losing those electrons, these elements can easily acquire a stable electron configuration with a completely filled highest energy level. As a result, the alkali metals and alkaline earth metals tend to be highly reactive.

In this investigation, you will determine whether various metals undergo single-replacement reactions when placed in hydrochloric acid. Based on your observations of these reactions, you will then rank the metals by reactivity.

Problem
Which metals are most reactive?

Pre-Lab Discussion

Read the entire investigation. Then, work with a partner to answer the following questions.

1. **Predicting** If any of the metals react with hydrochloric acid, what kind of compound will be formed?

   Reaction of a metal with HCl will form a metal chloride (such as magnesium chloride or aluminum

   chloride) and hydrogen gas.

Lab Manual

Name _____ Class _____ Date _____

2. **Inferring** How will your observations help you determine which metals are the most reactive? Explain your answer.

   The more reactive metals will react quickly with the HCl, rapidly releasing hydrogen gas. The metals

   that are the most reactive will produce the most bubbles and show the most evidence of chemical

   change, such as a change in color or dissolving in the acid.

3. **Controlling Variables** Identify the manipulated, responding, and controlled variables in this investigation.
   a. Manipulated variable

   Type of metal

   b. Responding variable

   Visible signs of a chemical reaction, such as bubbling, change of color or temperature, or

   dissolving of the metal

   c. Controlled variables

   Volume and concentration of HCl

4. **Formulating Hypotheses** State a hypothesis about which metals are the most reactive.

   The alkali metals and alkaline earth metals are the most reactive.

5. **Predicting** Based on your hypothesis, predict which metal will react most vigorously with hydrochloric acid. Explain the reason for your prediction.

   Magnesium, an alkaline earth metal, will react most vigorously with HCl. The other metals used

   are neither alkali metals nor alkaline earth metals.

Lab Manual

Name _____ Class _____ Date _____

Materials (per group)
glass-marking pencil
5 test tubes
test-tube rack
10-mL graduated cylinder — Add 170 mL of 6 M HCl to enough water to form 1 L of solution. Wear safety goggles, a lab apron, and neoprene gloves while doing this. Always add acid to water, never water to acid.
1 M hydrochloric acid
zinc (Zn) Provide mossy zinc.
copper (Cu) Cut up uninsulated copper wire or pieces of copper sheeting into 1-cm lengths.
aluminum (Al) Provide aluminum shot or turnings.
iron (Fe) Provide small iron nails or pellets.
magnesium (Mg) Provide magnesium ribbon cut into 1 cm lengths.
Polish each metal sample with steel wool to remove surface oxide that can interfere with the reaction with HCl.

Safety 🥽🧤🔬💧⚠️🧪🗑️🔥
Put on safety goggles and a lab apron. Be careful to avoid breakage when working with glassware. Wear plastic disposable gloves when handling chemicals, as they may irritate the skin or stain skin or clothing. Never touch or taste any chemical unless instructed to do so. Follow your teacher's instructions for disposing of the used hydrochloric acid. Wash your hands with warm water and soap or detergent before leaving the laboratory. Note all safety alert symbols next to the steps in the Procedure and review the meaning of each symbol by referring to the Safety Symbols on page xiii. Review the MSDS for hydrochloric acid with students before performing this investigation.

Procedure
1. Use the glass-marking pencil to label each test tube with the symbol for each metal listed in Materials. Place the test tubes in a test-tube rack.

2. One at a time, place the appropriate metal in each test tube. Carefully pour 5 mL of hydrochloric acid into each of the five test tubes, using the graduated cylinder. **CAUTION:** *Put on gloves when working with hydrochloric acid. Handle hydrochloric acid with care. It is corrosive. If it spills on your skin, rinse it off with plenty of cold water and notify your teacher immediately.*

3. Observe what happens to the metal in each test tube and feel each test tube as the reaction proceeds. Record your observations in the data table.

4. When you have completed the investigation, follow your teacher's instructions for disposing of the used acid. Rinse the pieces of metal several times with water and put them into a container provided by your teacher. Do not put any metal in the sink.
Provide a container in which students can deposit the used, rinsed metals. Used acid may be rinsed down the drain with 10 volumes of cold water. If your school is served by a septic system, dispose of the used acid as chemical waste.

Lab Manual

Name _____ Class _____ Date _____

Observations Sample data are shown.

DATA TABLE

Metal	Observations
Magnesium (Mg)	Rapid bubbling; magnesium disappears; test tube warm
Aluminum (Al)	Rapid but less active bubbling than magnesium; test tube warm
Iron (Fe)	Very slow bubbling
Copper (Cu)	No reaction
Zinc (Zn)	Slow bubbling

Analysis and Conclusions

1. **Analyzing Data** Which of the metals that you tested in this investigation are more reactive than hydrogen? Explain your answer.

   Magnesium, aluminum, iron, and zinc. These metals all showed evidence of reaction with HCl.
   _____
   _____
   _____

2. **Analyzing Data** Which of the metals that you tested in this investigation are less reactive than hydrogen? Explain your answer.

   Copper; copper did not react visibly with HCl.
   _____
   _____
   _____

Lab Manual

Name _____ Class _____ Date _____

3. **Drawing Conclusions** The rate at which hydrogen gas is produced as a result of these single-replacement reactions is an indication of the relative reactivity of the metals. List the metals in order of their reactivity from the most reactive to the least reactive.

   Magnesium, aluminum, zinc, iron, copper
   _____
   _____
   _____

4. **Inferring** Were these reactions endothermic or exothermic? Explain your answer.

   Exothermic. The test tubes in which the reactions occurred most vigorously felt warm to the touch.
   _____
   _____
   _____

5. **Evaluating and Revising** Did the results of the lab support or contradict your hypothesis?

   The results should support the hypothesis that alkaline earth metals are among the more reactive metals.
   _____
   _____

6. **Calculating** Write a balanced chemical equation for the single-replacement reaction, if any, that occurred between the acid and each metal. Refer to Figure 1 for the charges of the ions involved.

   a. Magnesium
   $Mg + 2HCl \rightarrow H_2 + MgCl_2$

   b. Aluminum
   $2Al + 6HCl \rightarrow 3H_2 + 2AlCl_3$

   c. Iron
   $2Fe + 6HCl \rightarrow 3H_2 + 2FeCl_3$

   d. Copper
   No reaction

   e. Zinc
   $Zn + 2HCl \rightarrow H_2 + ZnCl_2$

Element	Charge of Ion
H	1+
Cl	1−
Mg	2+
Al	3+
Fe	3+
Cu	2+
Zn	2+

Figure 1

Lab Manual

Name _____ Class _____ Date _____

7. **Inferring** What could you do to determine whether the gas produced as a result of these reactions is hydrogen?

   Collect the gas in an inverted or partly closed test tube. Then, insert a flaming splint into the test tube.
   A pop is heard as the hydrogen burns.
   _____
   _____

8. **Applying Concepts** Nonmetals can also be involved in single-replacement reactions. If chlorine is more reactive than bromine, write a balanced chemical equation for the reaction between chlorine gas (Cl_2) and potassium bromide (KBr).

   $Cl_2 + 2KBr \rightarrow Br_2 + 2KCl$

Go Further

Balance each of the following chemical equations. Then, classify each reaction as a synthesis, decomposition, or single-replacement reaction.

1. $Cu + AgNO_3 \rightarrow Ag + Cu(NO_3)_2$
   $Cu + 2AgNO_3 \rightarrow 2Ag + Cu(NO_3)_2$
   single-replacement

2. $H_2 + O_2 \rightarrow H_2O$
   $2H_2 + O_2 \rightarrow 2H_2O$
   synthesis

3. $Al + ZnCl_2 \rightarrow Zn + AlCl_3$
   $2Al + 3ZnCl_2 \rightarrow 3Zn + 2AlCl_3$
   single-replacement

4. $Al(OH)_3 \rightarrow Al_2O_3 + H_2O$
   $2Al(OH)_3 \rightarrow Al_2O_3 + 3H_2O$
   decomposition

Lab Manual

Chapter 7   Chemical Reactions   Investigation 7B

Recognizing a Synthesis Reaction
Refer students to page 200 and pages 208 and 209, respectively, in their textbooks for a discussion of synthesis reactions and energy changes during chemical reactions.

Background Information
SKILLS FOCUS: Observing, Calculating, Inferring, Classifying, Analyzing

In a **synthesis reaction,** two or more substances combine to form a single substance. The substances that combine can be elements, compounds, or both. The general equation for a synthesis reaction is

Data **CLASS TIME:** 40 minutes

$$A + B \rightarrow AB$$

The symbols A and B represent two elements or compounds that combine to form the compound AB. For example, when a metal combines with oxygen from the air, a synthesis reaction occurs. A compound called a metal oxide is produced. The reaction can be described by the following word equation:

$$\text{Metal} + \text{Oxygen} \rightarrow \text{Metal oxide}$$

In this investigation, you will heat copper metal in air. Then, you will examine the product to determine whether a synthesis reaction has occurred.

Problem
How can you know when a synthesis reaction has occurred?

Pre-Lab Discussion
Read the entire investigation. Then, work with a partner to answer the following questions.

1. **Calculating** If the balance indicated that the evaporating dish has a mass of 44.8 g and you want to have exactly 5.0 g of copper, what should the balance read with the copper in the evaporating dish?

   The total mass of the copper and the evaporating dish should be 44.8 g + 5.0 g = 49.8 g.

2. **Inferring** Why is it necessary to spread the copper powder out in a thin layer in Step 5? (*Hint:* What substance do you expect to react with the copper?)

   The copper powder must be spread out so that as much of its surface area as possible will be exposed to the air.

3. **Predicting** What evidence of a chemical change might you observe in this investigation?

   A change in color and mass may be observed. Students may also predict that a flame, smoke, or odor will be produced.

4. **Predicting** What would be evidence of a synthesis reaction? Explain your answer.

   An increase in mass would be evidence of a synthesis reaction. It would indicate that something in the air has combined with the copper.

Lab Manual

Materials *(per group)*

ring stand	evaporating dish	copper powder
iron ring	triple-beam balance	clock or watch
wire gauze	scoop	tongs
Bunsen burner		

Safety 🥽🧤🔥🧪⚠️🔥
Review the MSDS safety information for copper powder with students before performing this investigation.

Put on safety goggles, plastic gloves, and a lab apron. Be careful when using matches. Use caution when handling breakable equipment. Tie back loose hair and clothing when working with flames. Do not reach over an open flame. Use extreme care when working with heated equipment and materials to avoid burns. Note all safety alert symbols next to the steps in the Procedure and review the meaning of each symbol by referring to the Safety Symbols on page xiii.

Procedure

🥽🧤 1. Set up the ring stand, iron ring, and wire gauze as shown in Figure 1.

2. Place the Bunsen burner on the base of the ring stand. Do not light the burner yet. Adjust the position of the iron ring so that its center is directly over the burner and about 5 cm above the top of the burner.

🧪 3. Place the evaporating dish on the balance and find its mass to the nearest 0.1 g. Record this mass in the data table.

4. To measure 5.0 g of copper powder, add 5.0 g to the mass of the evaporating dish and move the riders on the balance to this number.

🧤 5. Using the scoop, slowly add copper powder to the evaporating dish until the pointer of the balance is centered. In the data table, record the mass of the copper powder and evaporating dish.

🔥 6. Place the evaporating dish containing the copper powder on the wire gauze. Use the scoop to spread out the copper powder in a thin layer in the bottom of the dish.

🔥 7. Light the Bunsen burner and heat the evaporating dish for 5 to 10 minutes until you observe a change in the color of the copper powder. **CAUTION:** *Tie back loose hair and clothing before working with flames. Do not reach over an open flame.*

8. Turn off the Bunsen burner and allow the evaporating dish to cool for 10 minutes. Use tongs to place the evaporating dish on the balance and find its mass. **CAUTION:** *The evaporating*

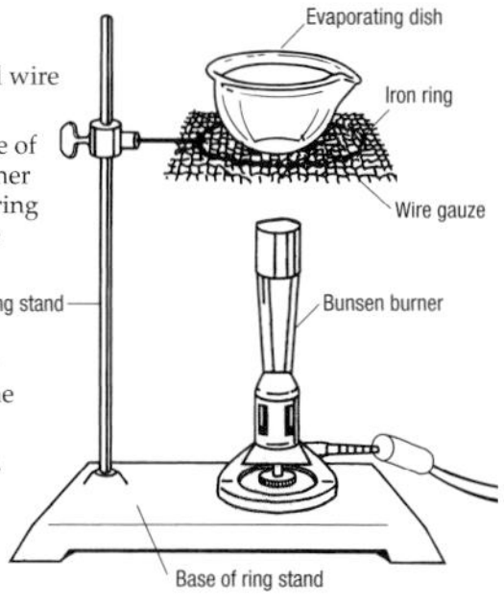

Figure 1

(Labels: Evaporating dish, Iron ring, Wire gauze, Ring stand, Bunsen burner, Base of ring stand)

Lab Manual

dish and its contents may still be hot. Handle the evaporating dish only with tongs. In the data table, record the mass of the evaporating dish and its contents.

Have students complete the calculations in the data table or work on another short assignment while waiting for the evaporating dish to cool.

9. Use the scoop to examine the product of the reaction. Observe its color or colors. Record your observations below the data table.

Observations   *Sample data are shown.*

DATA TABLE

Measurement	Mass (g)
Mass of evaporating dish	
Mass of evaporating dish and copper powder	
Mass of copper powder	5.0
Mass of evaporating dish and product after heating	
Mass of product	5.4–6.2

Observations of Product

Part or all of the copper powder has changed into a mixture of black and dark red granules.

Analysis and Conclusions

1. **Observing** What did you observe as a result of heating the copper powder that might indicate that a chemical reaction took place?

   The contents of the evaporating dish changed in color, mass, and texture.

2. **Inferring** Explain why there was a change in mass as a result of heating the copper powder in the evaporating dish.

   Oxygen from the air combined with the copper powder and added to its mass.

3. **Classifying** What type of chemical reaction occurred?

   Synthesis (The reaction can also be classified as oxidation-reduction.)

4. **Inferring** Was this reaction endothermic or exothermic? Explain your answer.

   The reaction was endothermic. Energy had to be absorbed for the reaction to occur.

5. **Calculating** Calculate the percent change in mass by using the following formula.

   $$\text{Percent change in mass} = \frac{\text{Change in mass}}{\text{Mass of product}} \times 100\%$$

   The mass is likely to change by 8–24 percent.

6. **Drawing Conclusions** There are actually two different oxides of copper produced as a result of this reaction. They are copper(I) oxide and copper(II) oxide. If all the copper changed to copper(I)

Lab Manual

oxide, the mass would change by 12 percent. If all the copper changed to copper(II) oxide, the mass would change by 25 percent. Based on the percent change in mass, what must have been produced as a result of the reaction?

Probably a mixture of copper(I) and copper(II) oxide

7. **Calculating** Write a balanced chemical equation for the synthesis reactions that took place.

   $$2Cu + O_2 \rightarrow 2CuO$$

   $$4Cu + O_2 \rightarrow 2Cu_2O$$

8. **Evaluating** Compare the percent change in mass that you calculated with those calculated by your classmates. What variables could account for differences between your results and those of your classmates?

   Answers may include the temperature of the burner flame, the length of time the copper was heated, the accuracy of mass measurements, or how well the copper powder was distributed in the evaporating dish.

9. **Controlling Variables** How could these variables be controlled so that the results obtained are more precise?

   Make sure that all burner flames are the same. Heat all samples for exactly the same length of time. Measure masses. Distribute the copper powder evenly.

10. **Observing** Copper(II) oxide is black and copper(I) oxide is red. Do your observations support your answer to Question 7? Explain your answer.

    Yes, there will be both black and red particles in the evaporating dish.

Go Further

Caulking compound is used to make a watertight seal around bathtubs, sinks, and pipes. A synthesis reaction occurs when caulking compound is placed on a surface and exposed to the air. This reaction leads to hardening of the soft caulking compound. To investigate the role of water in this reaction, place a small amount of caulking compound on two small pieces of wood or cardboard. Place one of the pieces in a beaker and cover it with water. Leave the other piece exposed to the air. After 5 minutes, use a glass stirring rod to probe each sample of caulking compound and compare the firmness of the two samples. Record your observations. Repeat this observation every 5 minutes for 30 minutes or until one of the samples becomes firm and rubbery. Report your conclusions about the role of water in this synthesis reaction.

Water is a reactant in the chemical reaction that leads to hardening of the caulking compound. Students should find that submerging the caulking compound in water accelerates this process.

Chapter Test A

Name _____ Class _____ Date _____

Chapter 7   Chemical Reactions   Chapter Test A

Multiple Choice

Write the letter that best answers the question or completes the statement on the line provided.

_____ 1. Hydrochloric acid, HCl, is added to solid NaOH. After the reaction is complete, NaCl dissolved in water remains. What are the products of this chemical reaction?
    a. NaOH and HCl   b. NaOH and H_2O
    c. HCl and NaCl   d. NaCl and H2O

_____ 2. Which of the following does NOT show the law of conservation of mass?
    a. 24 g of Mg burn in 32 g O_2 to produce 56 g of MgO.
    b. 24 mL of Mg burn in 32 mL O_2 to produce 56 mL of MgO.
    c. 2 atoms of Mg react with 1 molecule of O_2 to produce 2 units of MgO.
    d. 1 atom of Mg reacts with 1 atom of O to produce a unit of MgO that contains 2 atoms.

_____ 3. Which of the following is a chemical equation that accurately represents what happens when sulfur and oxygen react to form sulfur trioxide?
    a. Sulfur and oxygen react to form sulfur trioxide.
    b. S and O_2 produce SO_3.
    c. $S + O_2 \rightarrow SO_3$
    d. $S + 3O_2 \rightarrow 2SO_3$

_____ 4. Methane, CH_4, burns in oxygen gas to form water and carbon dioxide. What is the correct balanced chemical equation for this reaction?
    a. $CH_4 + O \rightarrow H_2O + CO_2$
    b. $CH_4 + 4O \rightarrow 2H_2O + CO_2$
    c. $CH_4 + O_2 \rightarrow H_2O + CO_2$
    d. $CH_4 + 2O_2 \rightarrow 2H_2O + CO_2$

_____ 5. How many grams of HNO_3 are in 2.6 mol of the compound?
    a. 24.2 g   b. 63.0 g
    c. 93.0 g   d. 163.8 g

_____ 6. An industrial process makes calcium oxide by decomposing calcium carbonate. Which of the following is NOT needed to calculate the mass of calcium oxide that can be produced from 4.7 kg of calcium carbonate?
    a. the balanced chemical equation
    b. molar masses of the reactants
    c. molar masses of the product
    d. the volume of the unknown mass

Chapter Test A

Name _____ Class _____ Date _____

_____ 7. When magnesium carbonate, $MgCO_3$, reacts with nitric acid, HNO_3, magnesium nitrate and carbonic acid form. Carbonic acid then breaks down into water and carbon dioxide. What two types of reactions take place in this process?
    a. synthesis and decomposition
    b. single-replacement and combustion
    c. double-replacement and decomposition
    d. double-replacement and combustion

_____ 8. In a chemical reaction, an iron atom became the ion Fe^{2+}. What happened to the iron atom?
    a. It lost electrons and was oxidized.
    b. It lost electrons and was reduced.
    c. It gained electrons and was oxidized.
    d. It gained electrons and was reduced.

_____ 9. Which of the following statements is true about what happens during a chemical reaction?
    a. Bonds of the reactants are broken, and bonds of the products are formed.
    b. Bonds of the reactants are formed, and bonds of the products are broken.
    c. The bonds of both the reactants and the products are broken.
    d. The bonds of both the reactants and the products are formed.

_____ 10. For the chemical reaction $C_2H_6 + 137$ kJ $\rightarrow C_2H_4 + H_2$, the chemical energy of the
    a. reactant is greater than the chemical energy of the products.
    b. products is greater than the chemical energy of the reactant.
    c. reactant and the chemical energy of the products are equal.
    d. reaction is conserved.

_____ 11. For the chemical reaction $H_2 + CO_2 \rightarrow H_2O + CO$, the energy contained in the reactants is 352 kJ, and the energy contained in the products is 394 kJ, assuming 1 mol of each substance is present. Which of the following statements is true?
    a. 42 kJ is released, and the reaction is exothermic.
    b. 42 kJ is released, and the reaction is endothermic.
    c. 42 kJ is absorbed, and the reaction is exothermic.
    d. 42 kJ is absorbed, and the reaction is endothermic.

Chapter Test A

Name _____ Class _____ Date _____

_____ 12. Reaction rates do NOT tell you how fast
    a. reactants are being consumed.
    b. products are being formed.
    c. substances are changing state.
    d. energy is being absorbed or released.

_____ 13. What happens to the reaction $2NO_2 \rightleftharpoons N_2O_4 + 57.2$ kJ when the temperature of the reaction is increased?
    a. More reactant is formed.
    b. More product is formed.
    c. No change occurs in the amounts of reactant and product present.
    d. The effect depends on whether or not a catalyst is present.

_____ 14. The reaction $H_2CO_3 + H_2O \rightleftharpoons H_3O^+ + HCO_3^-$ takes place in water. What happens to the equilibrium when the pressure is increased?
    a. It favors formation of reactants.
    b. It favors formation of products.
    c. It does not change.
    d. It is conserved.

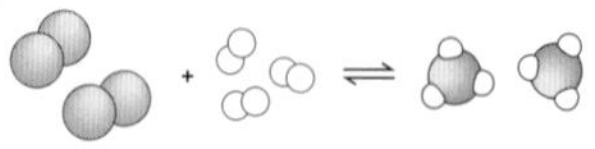

$2N_2$ + $3H_2$ $\rightleftharpoons$ $2NH_3$ + energy

Figure 7-1

_____ 15. The reaction in Figure 7-1 shows the formation of ammonia from nitrogen and hydrogen in the Haber process. What will be the effect on the equilibrium if the temperature is increased and some of the ammonia is removed from the system?
    a. More ammonia will definitely form.
    b. More reactants will definitely form.
    c. The changes definitely will have no overall effect on the reaction.
    d. Any effect will depend on the amount of change of temperature and concentration.

Completion

Complete each statement on the line provided.

1. In an experiment, 44 g of propane were burned, producing 132 g of carbon dioxide and 72 g of water. The mass of oxygen that was needed for the reaction was _____.

Chapter Test A

Name _____ Class _____ Date _____

2. A sample of HBr contains 186 g of the compound. The sample contains _____ moles of HBr.

3. An iron fence is left unpainted, and it reacts with the oxygen in the air, forming rust. The formation of rust is an oxidation-reduction reaction, but it is also an example of a(an) _____ reaction.

4. A catalyst is used in a catalytic converter in vehicles to help control pollution. For example, the catalytic converter _____ the rate at which carbon monoxide is oxidized to carbon dioxide. ($2CO + O_2 \rightarrow 2CO_2$)

5. Many manufacturing processes involve chemical reactions that reach equilibrium. One way to increase the amount of product formed is to decrease the _____ of the product in the system.

Short Answer

Use complete sentences to write the answers to the questions on the lines provided.

1. A student balanced the chemical equation $Mg + O_2 \rightarrow MgO$ by writing $Mg + O_2 \rightarrow MgO_2$. Was the equation balanced correctly? Explain your answer. If the equation was not balanced correctly, write the correctly balanced equation.

_____

_____

_____

_____

2. How many moles of nitrogen are contained in 1.61×10^{24} atoms of nitrogen?

_____

3. In a decomposition reaction, a compound is broken down into two or more simpler substances. Explain why the term *compound* is used to refer to the reactant and the term *substances* is used to refer to the products.

_____

_____

_____

_____

_____

Chapter Test A

Name _____ Class _____ Date _____

4. When most fuels burn, water and carbon dioxide are the two main products. Why can't you say that water and carbon dioxide are products of all combustion reactions?

_____

_____

_____

_____

_____

5. Explain why batteries and film will stay fresh longer if they are kept in a refrigerator or freezer.

_____

_____

_____

_____

_____

Using Science Skills

Use the diagram to answer each question. Write the answers on a separate sheet of paper.

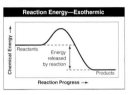
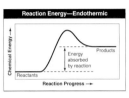

Figure 7-2

1. **Applying Concepts** In an exothermic reaction as seen in Figure 7-2, do the reactants or the products contain more chemical energy?

2. **Inferring** Cooking an egg white involves an endothermic reaction. Which has more chemical energy in its chemical bonds—an uncooked egg white or a cooked egg white? Use Figure 7-2 to explain your answer.

Chapter Test A

Name _____ Class _____ Date _____

3. **Problem Solving** If the bonds in the reactants of Figure 7-2 contained 432 kJ of chemical energy and the bonds in the products contained 478 kJ of chemical energy, what would be the amount of energy change during the reaction? Would this energy be absorbed or released?

4. **Using Tables and Graphs** What do the peaks on the graphs in Figure 7-2 represent?

5. **Interpreting Graphics** Although the amount of energy involved is small enough that it is not noticed, iron rusts according to the following word equation:

$$iron + oxygen \rightarrow rust + energy$$

Which of the energy diagrams in Figure 7-2 could be applied to the formation of rust? Explain your answer.

Problem

Write the answers to each question on a separate sheet of paper.

1. Balance the following chemical equation.
$$Cu + HNO_3 \rightarrow Cu(NO_3)_2 + NO_2 + H_2O$$

2. When iron metal reacts with oxygen, the reaction can form Fe_2O_3. Write a balanced chemical equation for this reaction, and find the number of moles of oxygen that are needed to form 6 mol of Fe_2O_3.

3. Sodium reacts with chlorine gas to form sodium chloride. Write a balanced chemical equation for the reaction, and find the mass of chlorine gas that will react with 96.6 g of sodium.

Essay

Write the answers to each question on a separate sheet of paper.

1. Which two types of reactions are also always redox reactions? Explain your answer.

2. Explain the difference between a physical equilibrium and a chemical equilibrium.

Chapter Test B

Name _____ Class _____ Date _____

Chapter 7   Chemical Reactions   Chapter Test B

Multiple Choice

Write the letter that best answers the question or completes the statement on the line provided.

_____ 1. The substances that are present before a chemical reaction takes place are called
a. reactants.   b. products.
c. coefficients.   d. elements.

_____ 2. Which of the following does NOT state what the arrow means in a chemical equation?
a. forms   b. produces
c. conserves   d. yields

_____ 3. Which of the following is a balanced chemical equation for the synthesis of NaBr from Na and Br_2?
a. $Na + Br_2 \rightarrow NaBr$
b. $2Na + Br_2 \rightarrow NaBr$
c. $Na + Br_2 \rightarrow 2NaBr$
d. $2Na + Br_2 \rightarrow 2NaBr$

_____ 4. How many atoms are present in 2 moles of chromium?
a. 6.02×10^{23} atoms   b. 1.20×10^{23} atoms
c. 1.20×10^{24} atoms   d. 52.0 atoms

_____ 5. How many moles of Cr are in 156 g of the element?
a. 1.0 mol   b. 3.0 mol
c. 6.5 mol   d. 156 mol

_____ 6. The coefficients in a balanced chemical equation always can express the ratio of
a. moles of reactants and products.
b. volume of reactants and products.
c. atoms of reactants and products.
d. mass of reactants and products.

_____ 7. Which of the following is NOT always true about a synthesis reaction?
a. One product is formed.
b. There is only one reactant.
c. The general formula is $A + B \rightarrow C$.
d. A reactant might be a compound, or it might be an element.

_____ 8. Which of the following takes place during a redox reaction?
a. Electrons are gained only.
b. Electrons are lost only.
c. Electrons are both gained and lost.
d. Electrons are neither gained nor lost.

Chapter Test B

Name _____ Class _____ Date _____

_____ 9. In a compound, chemical energy is contained in the
a. nuclei of the atoms.
b. unbonded electrons.
c. bonds.
d. movement of the electrons.

_____ 10. In terms of energy, how would you classify the following chemical reaction? $2Cu + O_2 \rightarrow 2CuO + 315$ kJ
a. endothermic
b. exothermic
c. both endothermic and exothermic
d. neither endothermic nor exothermic

_____ 11. The total amount of energy before and after a chemical reaction is the same. Thus, energy is
a. created.   b. destroyed.
c. conserved.   d. the same as mass.

_____ 12. In general, if the temperature of a chemical reaction is increased, reaction rate
a. increases.   b. decreases.
c. remains the same.   d. cannot be predicted.

_____ 13. A log is burning in a fireplace. If the amount of oxygen reaching the log is decreased, which of the following statements is true?
a. The reaction rate increases.
b. The reaction rate decreases.
c. The reaction rate remains the same.
d. The reaction rate depends only on the temperature.

_____ 14. When the forward and reverse paths of a change occur at the same rate,
a. the system is conserved.
b. the system is in equilibrium.
c. he change must be physical.
d. the change must be chemical.

_____ 15. The equation $2NO_2 \rightleftharpoons N_2O_4$ shows a system
a. in chemical equilibrium.
b. in physical equilibrium.
c. that does not reach equilibrium.
d. that does not change.

Completion

Complete each statement on the line provided.

1. The statement that in chemical reactions, the total mass of the reactants equals the total mass of the products is the law of _____.

Chapter Test B

Name _____ Class _____ Date _____

2. A(An) _____ is the number that appears before a formula in a chemical equation.

3. The molar mass of chlorine is _____.

4. Butane burns as shown in the balanced chemical equation $2C_4H_{10} + 13O_2 \rightarrow 10H_2O + 8CO_2$. If 6 mol of butane burn, _____ mol of carbon dioxide are produced.

5. The element _____ is always present in a combustion reaction.

6. In a double-replacement reaction, there are two reactants and _____ product(s).

7. When fluorine reacts with a metal, it forms an F^- ion. The fluorine atom has gained an electron and undergone _____.

8. In terms of energy, the general chemical equation AB + CD + energy $\rightarrow$ AD + CB represents a(an) _____ reaction.

9. Measuring how quickly a reactant disappears is one way to measure the _____ of the reaction.

10. The statement that when a change is introduced to a system in equilibrium, the equilibrium shifts in the direction that relieves the stress on the system is known as _____.

Short Answer

Use complete sentences to write the answers to the questions on the lines provided.

1. How does the law of conservation of mass explain why only a bit of ash is left after burning a large sheet of paper?

_____
_____
_____

2. What is the purpose of balancing a chemical equation?

_____
_____
_____

3. How many grams of Mn are in 4.0 mol of the element?

_____

4. Explain why ice in liquid water at 0°C is an example of physical equilibrium.

_____
_____
_____

Name _____ Class _____ Date _____

5. In Figure 7-1, both the reactants and the product of the reaction are gases. In this equilibrium, the reaction that produces fewer gas molecules is favored. Explain why increasing the pressure on the reaction favors the formation of ammonia rather than the formation of the reactants.

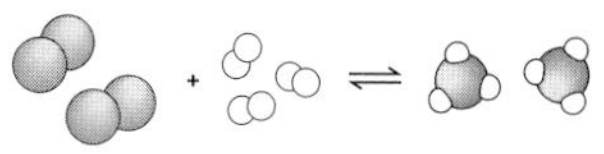

$2N_2$ + $3H_2$ $\rightleftharpoons$ $2NH_3$ + energy

Figure 7-1

_____
_____
_____
_____
_____
_____

Using Science Skills

Use the diagram to answer each question. Write the answers on a separate sheet of paper.

Unbalanced equation:

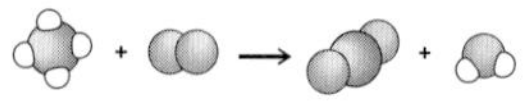

CH_4 + O_2 $\rightarrow$ CO_2 + H_2O

Figure 7-2

1. **Interpreting Graphics** How many of each type of atom are present on each side of the equation in Figure 7-2?

2. **Inferring** If the total number of atoms on the left side of the equation in Figure 7-2 equaled the total number of atoms on the right side of the equation, would this necessarily mean that the equation was balanced? Explain your answer.

3. **Drawing Conclusions** If there are 4 hydrogen atoms on the left side of equation in Figure 7-2, how many hydrogen atoms must there be on the right side in order to balance this reaction?

4. **Problem Solving** How do you balance the number of hydrogen atoms in the equation in Figure 7-2?

5. **Communicating Results** What is the balanced chemical equation for the reaction represented in Figure 7-2?

Chapter 7 Test A Answers

Multiple Choice

1. d **2.** b **3.** d **4.** d **5.** d **6.** d
7. c **8.** a **9.** a **10.** b **11.** d **12.** c
13. a **14.** c **15.** d

Completion

1. 160 g **2.** 2.3 **3.** synthesis **4.** speeds up **5.** concentration

Short Answer

1. The equation was not balanced correctly because it was balanced by changing a subscript instead of changing coefficients. The correctly balanced equation is $2Mg + O_2 \rightarrow 2MgO$.
2. 2.67 mol **3.** The reactant must be a compound because it is being broken down; an element cannot be broken down in a chemical reaction. The products can be either compounds or elements, and substances include both compounds and elements.
4. Some other substances, such as hydrogen, also burn. When the fuel does not contain carbon, carbon dioxide does not form.
5. Lowering the temperature lowers the rate of reaction, so the reactants in the film and batteries are less likely to react before they are used.

Using Science Skills

1. the reactants **2.** The cooked egg white has more chemical energy in its chemical bonds because energy was absorbed during the reaction. **3.** 46 kJ would be absorbed during the reaction. **4.** the amount of energy required to break the chemical bonds of the reactants **5.** The diagram on the left; rusting is an exothermic reaction because it releases energy. This diagram represents the energy changes in an exothermic reaction.

Problem

1. $Cu + 4HNO_3 \rightarrow Cu(NO_3)_2 + 2NO_2 + 2H_2O$
2. $4Fe + 3O_2 \rightarrow 2Fe_2O_3$; 9 mol O_2
3. $2Na + Cl_2 \rightarrow 2NaCl$; 149 g Cl_2

Essay

1. Single-replacement reactions are redox reactions because one element in the compound is reduced, and the free element is oxidized. Combustion is a redox reaction because oxygen is always reduced, and another element is oxidized. **2.** In a physical equilibrium, there is a difference in the form of the substance, but its chemical composition remains the same. In a chemical equilibrium, chemical changes occur, and the reactants are different substances than the products.

Chapter 7 Test B Answers

Multiple Choice

1. a **2.** c **3.** d **4.** c **5.** b **6.** a
7. b **8.** c **9.** c **10.** b **11.** c **12.** a
13. b **14.** b **15.** a

Completion

1. conservation of mass **2.** coefficient **3.** 35.5 g/mol
4. 24 **5.** oxygen **6.** two **7.** reduction **8.** endothermic
9. rate **10.** LeChâtelier's principle

Short Answer

1. In addition to the ash, gases are formed. The total mass of the paper and oxygen equals the total mass of the ash and the gases formed. **2.** A balanced chemical equation shows that mass is conserved. The number of each type of atom in the reactants must equal the number of each type of atom in the products.
3. The molar mass of Mn is 55 g/mol, so 4.0 mol of Mn have a mass of 220 g. **4.** Equilibrium exists because liquid water is freezing and ice is melting at the same rate. The equilibrium is physical because no new substances form. **5.** There are more gas molecules on the reactant side. Increased pressure will thus cause the system to shift in the direction that decreases the pressure of the system (that is, produces fewer gas molecules) and the reaction will shift to form more product.

Using Science Skills

1. On the left side, there are 1 carbon atom, 4 hydrogen atoms, and 2 oxygen atoms. On the right side, there are 1 carbon atom, 3 oxygen atoms, and 2 hydrogen atoms. **2.** No; the total number of atoms can be the same without the number of each type of atoms on both sides being the same. **3.** 4 hydrogen atoms
4. Place a coefficient of 2 in front of water on the right side. There will then be 4 hydrogen atoms on both sides of the equation.
5. $CH_4 + 2O_2 \rightarrow CO_2 + H_2O$

Chapter 8 Solutions, Acids, and Bases

CHAPTER 8
Planning Guide

Use these planning tools
Easy Planner
Resource Pro
Online Lesson Planner

SECTION OBJECTIVES	STANDARDS		ACTIVITIES and LABS
	NATIONAL (See p. T18.)	STATE	
8.1 Formation of Solutions, pp. 228–234 ⏱ 1 block or 2 periods **8.1.1 Describe** how a substance can dissolve in water by dissociation, dispersion, or ionization. **8.1.2 Describe** how the physical properties of a solution can differ from those of its solute and solvent. **8.1.3 Identify** energy changes that occur during the formation of a solution. **8.1.4 Describe** factors affecting the rate at which a solute dissolves in a solvent.	A-1, A-2, B-2, B-3, B-6, F-1		**SE** Inquiry Activity: How Do Shaking and Heating Affect a Carbonated Beverage? p. 227 **L2** **SE** Quick Lab: Comparing Heats of Solution, p. 232 **L2** **TE** Teacher Demo: Freezing Points of Solutions, p. 231 **L2**
8.2 Solubility and Concentration, pp. 235–239 ⏱ 1 block or 2 periods **8.2.1 Define** solubility and **describe** factors affecting solubility. **8.2.2 Classify** solutions as unsaturated, saturated, or supersaturated. **8.2.3 Calculate** and **compare** and **contrast** solution concentrations expressed as percent by volume, percent by mass, and molarity.	B-2, E-1		**TE** Teacher Demo: Crystallization, p. 236 **L2** **TE** Build Science Skills: Measuring, p. 237 **L2** **LM** Investigation 8B: Comparing Solubilities and Rates of Dissolving **L1**
8.3 Properties of Acids and Bases, pp. 240–245 ⏱ 1 block or 2 periods **8.3.1 Define** acid and **describe** some of the general properties of an acid. **8.3.2 Define** base and **describe** some of the general properties of a base. **8.3.3 Identify** a neutralization reaction, and **describe** the reactants and products of neutralization. **8.3.4 Explain** how acids and bases can be defined as proton donors and proton acceptors.	A-1, A-2, B-2, B-3, F-1		**SE** Quick Lab: Using an Indicator, p. 243 **L2** **SE** Exploration Lab: Preparing a Salt by Neutralization, pp. 254–255 **L2** **TE** Teacher Demo: Neutralization Reaction, p. 244 **L2** **LM** Investigation 8A: Comparing Antacids **L2**
8.4 Strength of Acids and Bases, pp. 246–249 ⏱ 1 block or 2 periods **8.4.1 Define** pH, and **relate** pH to hydronium ion concentration in a solution. **8.4.2 Distinguish** between strong acids and weak acids, and between strong bases and weak bases. **8.4.3 Define** buffer, and **describe** how a buffer can be prepared. **8.4.4 Explain** how electrolytes can be classified.	A-1, A-2, B-2, B-3, C-1, F-1, G-1, G-2, G-3		**SE** Quick Lab: Making a Battery, p. 248 **L2**

Ability Levels

L1	For students who need additional help
L2	For all students
L3	For students who need to be challenged

Components

SE	Student Edition	**GRSW**	Guided Reading & Study Workbook With Math Support	**CTB**	Computer Test Bank
TE	Teacher's Edition			**TP**	Test Prep Resources
LM	Laboratory Manual			**iT**	iText
PLM	Probeware Lab Manual	**CUT**	Chapter and Unit Tests	**DC**	Discovery Channel Videotapes
				T	Transparencies
				P	Presentation Pro CD-ROM
				GO	Internet Resources

RESOURCES
PRINT and TECHNOLOGY

GRSW Section 8.1	L1
T Chapter 8 Pretest	L2
Section 8.1	L2
P Chapter 8 Pretest	L2
Section 8.1	L2
SCiLINKS **GO** Solutions	L2

GRSW Section 8.2	L1
GRSW Math Skill	L2
T Section 8.2	L2
P Section 8.2	L2

PLM Lab 3: Preparing a Salt by Neutralization	L2
GRSW Section 8.3	L1
T Section 8.3	L2
P Section 8.3	L2
SCiLINKS **GO** Bases	L2

GRSW Section 8.4	L1
DC Suspended in Blood	L2
T Section 8.4	L2
P Section 8.4	L2
SCiLINKS **GO** pH	L2

SECTION ASSESSMENT

SE Section 8.1 Assessment, p. 234

iText **iT** Section 8.1

SE Section 8.2 Assessment, p. 239

iText **iT** Section 8.2

SE Section 8.3 Assessment, p. 245

iText **iT** Section 8.3

SE Section 8.4 Assessment, p. 249

iText **iT** Section 8.4

Go Online

Go online for these Internet resources.
PHSchool.com
Web Code: cca-1080

NSTA SCiLINKS
Web Code: ccn-1081
Web Code: ccn-1083
Web Code: ccn-1084

Materials for Activities and Labs

Quantities for each group

STUDENT EDITION

Inquiry Activity, p. 227
plastic bottle of carbonated beverage, small balloon, bucket, hot water

Quick Lab, p. 232
2 large test tubes, 10-mL graduated cylinder, distilled water, thermometer, 1 g KCl, 5 mL 95% isopropyl alcohol solution, stirring rod

Quick Lab, p. 243
1/4 cup frozen blueberries, foam cup, spoon, 4 small plastic cups, 2 dropper pipets, lemon juice, white vinegar, window cleaner, baking soda

Quick Lab, p. 248
1 large fresh lemon, plastic knife, zinc strip, 2 copper strips, multimeter

Exploration Lab, pp. 254–255
3 dropper pipets, labels, 10-mL graduated cylinder, test tube rack, 2 10-mL test tubes, distilled water, hydrochloric acid, sodium hydroxide solution, 3 stirring

rods, phenolphthalein solution, 2 25-mL beakers, pH paper, large watch glass, 100-mL beaker, hot plate

TEACHER'S EDITION

Teacher Demo, p. 231
2 trays, ice, rock salt, water, 2 small plastic containers (clear), thermometer

Teacher Demo, p. 236
beakers, 200 g sodium acetate trihydrate, distilled water, spatula, hot plate

Build Science Skills, p. 237
2 400-mL beakers, water, ice, hot plate, 2 70-mL test tubes, salt, scoop, 2 stirring rods, thermometer, weigh paper, balance, test tube tongs

Teacher Demo, p. 244
2 lemons, beaker, 0.1-M solution of NaOH, phenolphthalein solution (indicator), syringe, knife

Build Science Skills, p. 251
calcium hydroxide (pickling lime); 2 large, sealable jars; clear plastic cups; straws; stopwatches; jump ropes

Chapter Assessment

CHAPTER ASSESSMENT

SE Chapter Assessment, pp. 257–258
CUT Chapter 8 Test A, B
CTB Chapter 8
iT Chapter 8
PHSchool.com GO Web Code: cca-1080

STANDARDIZED TEST PREP

SE Chapter 8, p. 259
TP Diagnose and Prescribe

iText—interactive textbook with assessment at PHSchool.com

Solutions, Acids, and Bases **226B**

Name_____ Class_____ Date_____ M T W T F

LESSON PLAN 8.1

Formation of Solutions

Time
2 periods
1 block

Section Objectives

Local Standards

- **8.1.1 Describe** how a substance can dissolve in water by dissociation, dispersion, or ionization.

- **8.1.2 Describe** how the physical properties of a solution can differ from those of its solute and solvent.

- **8.1.3 Identify** energy changes that occur during the formation of a solution.

- **8.1.4 Describe** factors affecting the rate at which a solute dissolves in a solvent.

Vocabulary solute • solvent • dissociation • dispersion • ionization

1 FOCUS

Build Vocabulary: Word Forms
Ask students to name the verb forms for the three types of dissolving: *dissociation, dispersion,* and *ionization.* **L2**

Targeted Resources
❏ Transparency: Chapter 8 Pretest
❏ Transparency: Interest Grabber 8.1
❏ Transparency: Reading Strategy 8.1

2 INSTRUCT

Build Reading Literacy: Relate Text and Visuals
Have students read pages 229 and 230. In groups of three, have each student explain one type of dissolving and what happens on a particle level when substances dissolve. **L1**

Teacher Demo: Freezing Points of Solutions
Use ice water and saltwater solution to show students the lower freezing point of saltwater solution. **L2**

Quick Lab: Comparing Heats of Solution
Students will add potassium chloride to distilled water and add an alcohol solution to distilled water, in order to determine whether a solution process is exothermic or endothermic. **L2**

For Enrichment
Have students design a method for testing the effectiveness of different brands of hot or cold packs. **L3**

Targeted Resources
❏ Transparency: Figure 4: Dispersion of Sugar in Water
❏ Transparency: Figure 7: Factors Affecting Rates of Dissolving
❏ GRSW Section 8.1
❏ **NSTA** sc*i_{INKS}* Solutions

3 ASSESS

Reteach
Use Figures 3, 4, and 6 to summarize key concepts about solutions, including dissociation, dispersion, and freezing point depression. **L1**

Evaluate Understanding
Have students draw illustrations that represent the terms *solvent, solute, dissociation, dispersion,* and *ionization.* Then, have students shuffle the cards and exchange them with a partner. The partner tries to identify what each illustration represents. **L2**

Targeted Resources
❏ **PHSchool.com** Online Section 8.1 Assessment
❏ iText Section 8.1

Transparencies

102 **Chapter 8 Pretest**

1. Describe the charge and location within an atom of the following subatomic particles: protons, electrons, and neutrons.

2. Which of the following is true of molecular compounds but not of ionic compounds?
   a. consist of two or more elements
   b. are found in nature
   c. contain ionic bonds
   d. contain covalent bonds

3. Conductivity, freezing point, and boiling point are all
   a. related to volume.
   b. chemical properties.
   c. physical properties.
   d. mass.

ANSWERS
1. Protons are positive and located in the nucleus. Electrons are negative and surround the nucleus in an electron cloud. Neutrons are neutral and are located in the nucleus.
2. d
3. c

Transparencies

103 **Chapter 8 Pretest** (continued)

4. True or False: Endothermic processes release energy.

5. Which of the following is always true of a polar covalent bond?
   a. One atom in the bond has a partial negative charge.
   b. One atom in the bond is an ion.
   c. Both atoms in the bond are of the same element.
   d. Both atoms in the bond have partial positive charges.

6. A sample of O_2 gas has a mass of 64.0 grams. How many moles of O_2 gas does the sample contain?

7. True or False: Double-replacement reactions involve ionic compounds.

8. Describe chemical equilibrium in terms of reaction rates.

ANSWERS
4. False
5. a
6. 2.00 moles
7. True
8. Chemical equilibrium is a state in which the forward and reverse reactions are taking place at the same rate.

Transparencies

104 **Section 8.1 Interest Grabber**

Observing Dissolving

1. Fill a clear plastic cup with water. Describe the physical properties of the water.

2. Your teacher will give you a sugar cube. Describe the physical properties of the sugar.

3. Place the sugar cube into the water. Examine it closely. Describe your observations.

4. Stir the water and sugar until you observe no more changes in the mixture. Describe the physical properties of the mixture.

ANSWERS
1. Water is a clear, colorless liquid at room temperature.
2. The sugar has white, solid crystals that have been pressed into a cubical shape.
3. The sugar mixes with the water making clear trails in the water. The cube breaks up and gets smaller over time.
4. The sugar is no longer visible. The mixture appears to have the same properties as the pure water. It is a clear, colorless liquid.

Transparencies

105 **Section 8.1 Reading Strategy**

Comparing and Contrasting

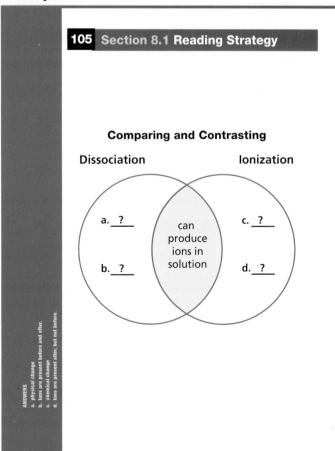

Dissociation   Ionization

a. __?__   can produce ions in solution   c. __?__

b. __?__   d. __?__

ANSWERS
a. physical change
b. ions are present before and after.
c. chemical change
d. ions are present after, but not before.

106 | Figure 4 Dispersion of Sugar in Water

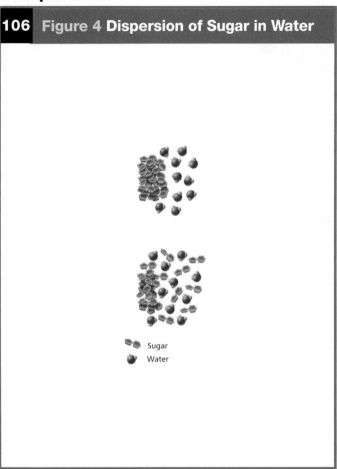

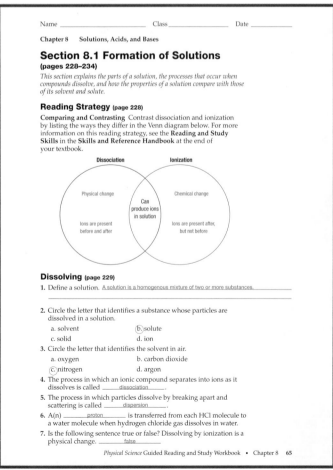

Sugar

Water

107 | Figure 7 Factors Affecting Rates of Dissolving

Crushed solid

Stirring

Heat

Guided Reading and Study Workbook

Name _____ Class _____ Date _____

Chapter 8   Solutions, Acids, and Bases

Section 8.1 Formation of Solutions
(pages 228–234)

This section explains the parts of a solution, the processes that occur when compounds dissolve, and how the properties of a solution compare with those of its solvent and solute.

Reading Strategy (page 228)

Comparing and Contrasting Contrast dissociation and ionization by listing the ways they differ in the Venn diagram below. For more information on this reading strategy, see the **Reading and Study Skills** in the **Skills and Reference Handbook** at the end of your textbook.

Dissociation   **Ionization**

Physical change   Chemical change

Can produce ions in solution

Ions are present before and after

Ions are present after, but not before

Dissolving (page 229)

1. Define a solution. A solution is a homogenous mixture of two or more substances.

2. Circle the letter that identifies a substance whose particles are dissolved in a solution.
  a. solvent   (b.) solute
  c. solid   d. ion

3. Circle the letter that identifies the solvent in air.
  a. oxygen   b. carbon dioxide
  (c.) nitrogen   d. argon

4. The process in which an ionic compound separates into ions as it dissolves is called ____dissociation____.

5. The process in which particles dissolve by breaking apart and scattering is called ____dispersion____.

6. A(n) ____proton____ is transferred from each HCl molecule to a water molecule when hydrogen chloride gas dissolves in water.

7. Is the following sentence true or false? Dissolving by ionization is a physical change. ____false____

Guided Reading and Study Workbook

Name _____ Class _____ Date _____

Chapter 8   Solutions, Acids, and Bases

Properties of Liquid Solutions (page 231)

8. What physical properties of a solution can differ from those of its solute and solvent?
  a. ____Conductivity____
  b. ____Freezing point____
  c. ____Boiling point____

9. Compare the conductivities of solid sodium chloride and saltwater. Solid sodium chloride is a poor conductor of electric current. However, when you dissolve sodium chloride in water, it becomes a good conductor of electric current.

10. Circle the letters that identify what happens to water as it freezes.
  (a.) The water molecules become more organized.
  b. The water molecules become more disorganized.
  c. The water molecules ionize.
  (d.) The water molecules arrange themselves in a hexagonal pattern.

Heat of Solution (page 232)

11. Dissolving sodium hydroxide in water is a(n) ____exothermic____ process, as it releases heat.

12. Dissolving ammonium nitrate in water is a(n) ____endothermic____ process, as it absorbs heat.

13. Is the following sentence true or false? Breaking the attractions among solute particles and the attractions among solvent particles releases energy. ____false____

14. Describe heat of solution. The heat of solution is the difference between the energy required to break the attractions among solute particles and the attractions among solvent particles, and the energy released as attractions form between solute and solvent particles.

Factors Affecting Rates of Dissolving (page 234)

15. How are rates of dissolving similar to rates of chemical reactions? Like reaction rates, dissolving rates vary with the conditions under which the change occurs.

16. Why does powdered sugar dissolve in water faster than granulated sugar? Powdered sugar has more surface area per unit mass than granulated sugar, so collisions between solute and solvent particles can occur at a greater rate.

17. Heating a solvent ____increases____ the energy of its particles, making them move faster on average, and ____increases____ the rate at which a solid solute can dissolve in the solvent.

18. Explain how stirring or shaking a mixture of powdered detergent and water can affect the rate of dissolving. Stirring or shaking a solution that contains a solid solute moves dissolved particles away from the surface of the solid. It also causes more frequent collisions between the solute and solvent particles.

Name_____ Class_____ Date_____ M T W T F

LESSON PLAN 8.2

Solubility and Concentration

Time
2 periods
1 block

Section Objectives

- **8.2.1 Define** solubility and **describe** factors affecting solubility.
- **8.2.2 Classify** solutions as unsaturated, saturated, or supersaturated.
- **8.2.3 Calculate** and **compare** and **contrast** solution concentrations expressed as percent by volume, percent by mass, and molarity.

Vocabulary solubility • saturated solution • unsaturated solution • supersaturated solution • concentration • molarity

Local Standards

1 FOCUS

Build Vocabulary: Word-Part Analysis
Ask students what words they know that have the prefix *super-*. Define the word part. Have students predict the meaning of *supersaturated*, given that saturated means "unable to hold more." **L2**

Targeted Resources
❏ Transparency: Interest Grabber 8.2
❏ Transparency: Reading Strategy 8.2

2 INSTRUCT

Build Reading Literacy: Outline
Have students read the section and use the headings as major divisions in an outline. **L1**

Teacher Demo: Crystallization
Prepare a supersaturated solution and add a crystal of sodium acetate to show students crystallization of a solute from a supersaturated solution. **L2**

Build Science Skills: Measuring
Have students approximate the solubility of sodium chloride at two different temperatures. **L2**

Build Science Skills: Interpreting Diagrams
Have students examine the label in Figure 12. Then, have students calculate the volume of real cranberry juice in 300 mL of Smith's Cranberry Juice. **L2**

Targeted Resources
❏ Transparency: Figure 8: Solubility of Some Common Substances
❏ GRSW Section 8.2

3 ASSESS

Reteach
Use the table on p. 235 to review solubility. Have students describe how much solute would be in an unsaturated, saturated, and supersaturated solution of each type of solute given in the table. **L1**

Evaluate Understanding
Have students write three math problems (with solutions) bases on the equations given for percent by volume, percent by mass, and molarity. Students can take turns analyzing and solving the problems in class. **L2**

Targeted Resources
❏ **PHSchool.com** Online Section 8.2 Assessment
❏ iText Section 8.2

Transparencies

108 **Section 8.2 Interest Grabber**

Solute Concentration

Your teacher will provide you with five clear plastic cups, colored drink mix, measuring spoons, and water. Copy the table below onto a piece of paper. Label the plastic cups 1–5. In each of the cups, dissolve the given amounts of solute into the corresponding amounts of solvent according to the table.

Cup	Solute Amount	Solvent Amount	Color Intensity Rating
1	$\frac{1}{2}$ teaspoon	250 mL	
2	1 teaspoon	250 mL	
3	2 teaspoon	250 mL	
4	4 teaspoon	250 mL	
5	1 teaspoon	125 mL	

1. Rate each solution with a number 1–4 that corresponds to the intensity of its color (1 = least intense, 4 = most intense). In the table, fill in the color intensity rating for each solution.

2. Describe the relationship between the amount of solute contained in the solution and the color intensity of the solution.

3. Are there any exceptions to the relationship you observed? Explain.

ANSWERS
1. Cup 1 = 1, cup 2 = 2, cup 3 = 3, cup 4 = 4, cup 5 = 3
2. In general, as the amount of solute added increases, so does the color intensity of the solution.
3. Yes. In cup 5, the amount of solute is the same as the amount in cup 2, but the color intensity rating of cup 5 is same as that of cup 3. This difference can be explained by the fact that half the usual amount of solvent was used for the solution in cup 5. For a given volume, as the amount of solute increases, so does the color intensity of the solution.

Transparencies

109 **Section 8.2 Reading Strategy**

Previewing

Question	Answer
What is solubility?	a._____?_____
b._____?_____	Solvent, temperature, and pressure
c._____?_____	d._____?_____

ANSWERS
a. the maximum amount of solute that dissolves in a given amount of solvent at a given temperature
b. What factors affect solubility?
c. How is the concentration of a solution expressed?
d. percent by volume, percent by mass, molarity

Transparencies

110 **Figure 8 Solubility of Some Common Substances**

Solubility in 100 g of Water at 20°C	
Compound	**Solubility (g)**
Table salt (NaCl)	36.0
Baking soda (NaHCO$_3$)	9.6
Table sugar (C$_{12}$H$_{22}$O$_{11}$)	203.9

Chapter 8   Solutions, Acids, and Bases

Section 8.2 Solubility and Concentration
(pages 235–239)

This section explains solubility, the factors affecting solubility, and different ways of expressing the concentration of a solution.

Reading Strategy (page 235)

Previewing Before you read the section, rewrite the topic headings as *how*, *why*, and *what* questions. As you read, write an answer to each question. For more information on this reading strategy, see the **Reading and Study Skills** in the **Skills and Reference Handbook** at the end of your textbook.

Question	Answer
What is solubility?	Solubility is the maximum amount of solute that dissolves in a given amount of solvent at a given temperature.
How can the concentration of solutions be expressed?	Solvent, temperature, and pressure
What factors affect solubility?	Percent by volume, percent by mass, molarity

Solubility (pages 235–237)

1. Define solubility. Solubility is the maximum amount of a solute that dissolves in a given amount of solvent at a constant temperature.

2. List the following solutes in order from most soluble to least soluble in water: table salt, baking soda, table sugar.
   a. _____Table sugar_____
   b. _____Salt_____
   c. _____Baking soda_____

3. Circle the letters that identify how solutions can be classified based on solubility.
   (a.) unsaturated   b. desaturated
   (c.) saturated   (d.) supersaturated

4. Describe a saturated solution. A saturated solution is one that contains as much solute as the solvent can hold at a given temperature.

5. A solution that has less than the maximum amount of solute that can be dissolved is called a(n) _____unsaturated solution_____.

6. Is the following sentence true or false? It is impossible for a solution to contain more solute than the solvent can hold at a given temperature. _____false_____

Chapter 8   Solutions, Acids, and Bases

Factors Affecting Solubility (page 237)

7. Circle the letters of factors that affect the solubility of a solute.
   (a.) polarity of the solvent
   b. amount of solvent
   (c.) pressure
   (d.) temperature

8. What is a common guideline for predicting solubility? like dissolves like

9. Describe how soap cleans grease off your hands. The polar end of a soap molecule attracts water molecules, and the nonpolar end of the soap molecule attracts grease. The soap molecule breaks up the grease into small droplets that are soluble in water.

10. Is the following statement true or false? In general, the solubility of solids increases as the solvent temperature increases. _____true_____

11. In general, the solubility of gases decreases as the solvent temperature _____increases_____.

12. In general, the solubility of a gas increases as pressure _____increases_____.

Concentration of Solutions (pages 238–239)

13. What does the concentration of a solution refer to? The concentration of a solution is the amount of a solute dissolved in a given amount of solution.

14. Circle the letters that identify ways to express the concentration of a solution.
   a. density
   (b.) percent by volume
   (c.) percent by mass
   (d.) molarity

15. Complete the equation.
   $$\text{Percent by volume} = \frac{\text{Volume of solute}}{\text{Volume of solution}} \times 100\%$$

16. Write the equation used to calculate percent by mass.
   $$\text{Percent by mass} = \frac{\text{Mass of solute}}{\text{Mass of solution}} \times 100\%$$

17. Is this sentence true or false? Molarity is the number of moles of a solvent per liter of solution. _____false_____

18. How many grams of NaCl are needed to make 1.00 liter of a 3.00 M NaCl solution? _____176 g_____

Section 8.3 Lesson Plan

LESSON PLAN 8.3

Properties of Acids and Bases

Time
2 periods
1 block

Section Objectives

- **8.3.1 Define** acid and **describe** some of the general properties of an acid.
- **8.3.2 Define** base and **describe** some of the general properties of a base.
- **8.3.3 Identify** a neutralization reaction, and **describe** the reactants and products of neutralization.
- **8.3.4 Explain** how acids and bases can be defined as proton donors and proton acceptors.

Vocabulary acid • indicator • base • neutralization • salt

Local Standards

---

1 FOCUS

Build Vocabulary: Concept Map

Have students construct a concept map of the vocabulary terms used in this section with the main concept (Properties of Acids and Bases) at the top or the center. **L2**

Targeted Resources

❑ Transparency: Interest Grabber 8.3
❑ Transparency: Reading Strategy 8.3

---

2 INSTRUCT

Build Reading Literacy: Compare and Contrast

As students read the section, have them create lists of how acids and bases are similar and different. **L1**

Quick Lab: Using an Indicator

Students will extract an indicator from blueberries and use it to classify substances as acids or bases. **L2**

Teacher Demo: Neutralization Reaction

Use lemons, the indicator phenolphthalein, and NaOH to show students a neutralization reaction. **L2**

For Enrichment

Have students use their blueberry indicator on other substances. Ask them if they can conclude that a substance, such as water, is acidic if it does not turn the indicator green. **L3**

Targeted Resources

❑ Transparency: Figure 15: Common Acids and Their Uses
❑ Transparency: Figure 17: Common Bases and Their Uses
❑ Transparency: Figure 19: Common Salts and Their Uses
❑ GRSW Section 8.3
❑ **NSTA** *sci*$_{INKS}$ Bases

---

3 ASSESS

Reteach

Use Figure 20 to summarize the key features of acids, bases, and neutralization reactions. **L1**

Evaluate Understanding

Have students write the equation for a neutralization reaction and label each reactant or product as an acid, base, salt, proton donor, or proton acceptor. Then, have them indicate the color each reactant and product would turn red and blue litmus paper. **L2**

Targeted Resources

❑ **PHSchool.com** Online Section 8.3 Assessment
❑ iText Section 8.3

Transparencies

111 **Section 8.3 Interest Grabber**

Acidic, Basic, or Neutral

1. Place three strips of universal indicator paper on a paper towel. Dip a clean stirring rod into a solution of saltwater. Touch a drop of saltwater onto one strip of indicator paper. Rinse the stirring rod in deionized water. Record your observations.

2. Dip the clean stirring rod into the ammonia cleaning solution. Touch a drop of the ammonia solution onto the second strip of indicator paper. Rinse the stirring rod in deionized water. Record your observations.

3. Dip the clean stirring rod into the vinegar. Touch a drop of the vinegar onto the third strip of indicator paper. Record your observations.

4. Refer to the color chart provided with the indicator paper. Your teacher will explain which colors indicate an acid, which colors indicate a base, and which color indicates a neutral solution. Classify each solution as acidic, basic, or neutral.

Transparencies

112 **Section 8.3 Reading Strategy**

Using Prior Knowledge

Term	Your Definition	Scientific Definition
Acid	a. ?	b. ?
Base	c. ?	d. ?
Salt	e. ?	f. ?

Transparencies

113 **Figure 15 Common Acids and Their Uses**

Common Acids		
Name	**Formula**	**Use**
Acetic acid	CH_3COOH	Vinegar
Carbonic acid	H_2CO_3	Carbonated beverages
Hydrochloric acid	HCl	Digestive juices in stomach
Nitric acid	HNO_3	Fertilizer production
Phosphoric acid	H_3PO_4	Fertilizer production
Sulfuric acid	H_2SO_4	Car batteries

Transparencies

114 **Figure 17 Common Bases and Their Uses**

Common Bases		
Name	**Formula**	**Uses**
Aluminum hydroxide	$Al(OH)_3$	Deodorant, antacid
Calcium hydroxide	$Ca(OH)_2$	Concrete, plaster
Magnesium hydroxide	$Mg(OH)_2$	Antacid, laxative
Sodium hydroxide	$NaOH$	Drain cleaner, soap production

Transparencies

115 **Figure 19 Common Salts and Their Uses**

Common Salts		
Name	**Formula**	**Uses**
Sodium chloride	NaCl	Food flavoring, preservative
Sodium carbonate	Na_2CO_3	Used to make glass
Potassium chloride	KCl	Used as a salt substitute to reduce dietary intake of sodium
Potassium iodide	KI	Added to table salt to prevent iodine deficiency
Magnesium chloride	$MgCl_2$	De-icer for roads
Calcium carbonate	$CaCO_3$	Chalk, marble floors, and tables
Ammonium nitrate	NH_4NO_3	Fertilizer, cold packs

Guided Reading and Study Workbook

Name _____ Class _____ Date _____

Chapter 8   Solutions, Acids, and Bases

Section 8.3 Properties of Acids and Bases
(pages 240–245)

This section describes the general properties of acids and bases.

Reading Strategy (page 240)

Using Prior Knowledge Before you read, write your definition of each vocabulary term in the table below. After you read, write the scientific definition of each term and compare it with your original definition. For more information on this reading strategy, see the **Reading and Study Skills** in the **Skills and Reference Handbook** at the end of your textbook.

Term	Your Definition	Scientific Definition
Acid	Answers will vary.	A compound that produces hydronium ions (H_3O^+) when dissolved in water.
Base	Answers will vary.	A compound that produces hydroxide ions (OH^-) when dissolved in water.
Salt	Answers will vary.	A compound produced when the negative ions in an acid combine with the positive ions in a base during neutralization.

Identifying Acids (pages 240–241)

1. Define an acid. An acid is a compound that produces hydronium ions (H_3O^+) when dissolved in water.

Match these common acids to their uses.

	Acids	Uses
c	**2.** acetic acid	a. Fertilizer production
d	**3.** sulfuric acid	b. Carbonated beverages
e	**4.** hydrochloric acid	c. Vinegar
b	**5.** carbonic acid	d. Car batteries
a	**6.** nitric acid	e. Digestive juices in stomach

7. Describe some general properties of acids. Acids have sour taste, react with metals, and turn blue litmus paper red.

8. Place the following substances in the correct column in the table: lemons, vinegar, grapefruit, sour milk, tomatoes.

Foods Containing Acetic Acid	Foods Containing Citric Acid	Foods Containing Butyric Acid
Vinegar	Lemons, grapefruit, tomatoes	Sour milk

Physical Science Guided Reading and Study Workbook • Chapter 8   **69**

Guided Reading and Study Workbook

Name _____ Class _____ Date _____

Chapter 8   Solutions, Acids, and Bases

9. The reaction between an acid and a metal can be classified as a(n) single-replacement reaction.

10. Explain why an indicator is useful. It allows you to classify a solution as an acid or a base.

Identifying Bases (pages 242–243)

11. Define a base. A base is a compound that produces hydroxide ions (OH^-) when dissolved in water.

12. Use the following compounds to complete the chart: aluminum hydroxide, calcium hydroxide, magnesium hydroxide, and sodium hydroxide.

Common Bases		
Name	**Formula**	**Uses**
Sodium hydroxide	NaOH	Drain cleaner, soap production
Magnesium hydroxide	$Mg(OH)_2$	Antacid, laxative
Calcium hydroxide	$Ca(OH)_2$	Concrete, plaster
Aluminum hydroxide	$Al(OH)_3$	Deodorant, antacid

13. What can a gardener add to the soil to change the flowers of a hydrangea from pink to blue? acid

14. Circle the letter that describes how basic solutions generally taste.
   a. sweet   b. sour
   c. bitter   d. salty

15. Is the following sentence true or false? Bases turn red litmus paper blue. true

Neutralization and Salts (page 244)

16. The reaction between an acid and a base is called neutralization.

17. Describe how a salt can be produced by a chemical reaction. During neutralization, the negative ions from the acid combine with the positive ions from the base to produce a salt.

18. Write a chemical equation describing the neutralization reaction between calcium hydroxide and hydrochloric acid. $Ca(OH)_2 + 2HCl \longrightarrow CaCl_2 + 2H_2O$

Proton Donors and Acceptors (page 245)

19. Acids can be described as proton donors; bases can be described as proton acceptors.

20. When hydrogen chloride ionizes in water, which reactant is the proton donor? Which reactant is the proton acceptor? HCl is the proton donor. H_2O is the proton acceptor.

70   *Physical Science* Guided Reading and Study Workbook • Chapter 8

Name_____ Class_____ Date_____ M T W T F

LESSON PLAN 8.4

Strength of Acids and Bases

Time
2 periods
1 block

Section Objectives

- **8.4.1** **Define** pH, and **relate** pH to hydronium ion concentration in a solution.
- **8.4.2** **Distinguish** between strong acids and weak acids, and between strong bases and weak bases.
- **8.4.3** **Define** buffer, and **describe** how a buffer can be prepared.
- **8.4.4** **Explain** how electrolytes can be classified.

Vocabulary pH • buffer • electrolyte

Local Standards

---

1 FOCUS

Build Vocabulary: Word Meanings

Ask students to brainstorm examples of product advertising that contain the terms *pH*, *electrolyte*, or *buffer*. Have students look up the definition of each term and speculate what is meant by the advertisers' claims. **L2**

Targeted Resources

❏ Transparency: Interest Grabber 8.4

❏ Transparency: Reading Strategy 8.4

---

2 INSTRUCT

Build Reading Literacy: Identify Main Idea/Details

Have students read the section and make a list of the main headings on each page. Under each heading, have them identify the main idea of the passage. **L1**

Build Math Skills: Exponents

Be sure that students understand that a value with a large negative exponent is significantly smaller than a value with a small negative exponent. **L1**

Integrate Biology

Have students find out how hydrochloric acid in the stomach aids in digestion. Have them make a poster illustrating the stomach's role in digestion and explain how food is digested by stomach acid. **L2**

Quick Lab: Making a Battery

Students will make a battery using a lemon as a source for electrolytes. **L2**

For Enrichment

Have students perform the Quick Lab activity with metals to determine which pairs of metals produce the greatest voltages. Then, refer them to a chemistry text to read about electronegativity. **L3**

Targeted Resources

❏ Transparency: Figure 22: The pH Scale

❏ GRSW Section 8.4

❏ **NSTA** *SCILINKS* pH

---

3 ASSESS

Reteach

As a class, make a chart that lists what strong acids, strong bases, and strong electrolytes have in common. Do the same for weak acids, weak bases, and weak electrolytes. **L1**

Evaluate Understanding

Have students make note cards for each of the Key Concepts questions listed on p. 246 and for each of the answers. **L2**

Targeted Resources

❏ **PHSchool.com** Online Section 8.4 Assessment

❏ iText Section 8.4

Transparencies

116 **Section 8.4 Interest Grabber**

Concentration

Bottled fruit juice often contains pure fruit juice, sugar, and other ingredients dissolved in water. The concentration of pure fruit juice can vary with the brand. Look at five different samples of juice made from the same fruit. The label of each bottle or carton should tell you the concentration (percent by volume) of pure fruit juice in the beverage.

1. List the concentrations of all five juice samples.

2. Pour a small sample of the juice with the highest concentration and the juice with the lowest concentration. Taste each juice. What can you conclude about the relationship between the concentration of pure juice and the taste of the juice?

ANSWERS
1. Concentrations will vary.
2. Students may come to the conclusion that juices with high concentrations of pure juice taste more like the fruit they come from. They may also notice that juices with low concentrations taste watery or sugary.

Transparencies

117 **Section 8.4 Reading Strategy**

Comparing and Contrasting

Strong acid   Strong base

a. _?_   b. _?_   c. _?_

ANSWERS
a. ionizes almost completely when dissolved in water
b. is a strong electrolyte
c. dissociates almost completely when dissolved in water.

Transparencies

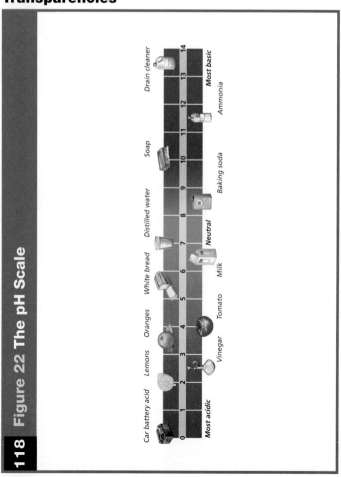

118 **Figure 22 The pH Scale**

Guided Reading and Study Workbook

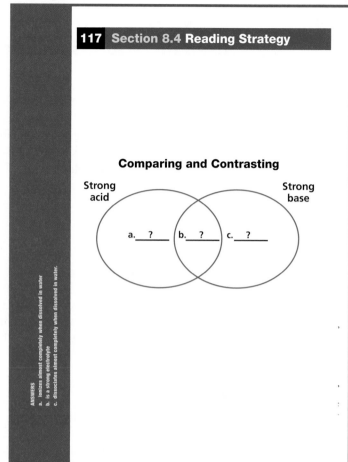

Name _____ Class _____ Date _____

Chapter 8   Solutions, Acids, and Bases

Section 8.4 Strength of Acids and Bases
(pages 246–249)

This section explains how to describe acids and bases in terms of both concentration and strength.

Reading Strategy (page 246)

Comparing and Contrasting As you read, complete the diagram by comparing and contrasting acids and bases. For more information on this reading strategy, see the **Reading and Study Skills** in the **Skills and Reference Handbook** at the end of your textbook.

Strong acid   Strong base

Ionizes almost completely when dissolved in water   Is a strong electrolyte   Dissociates almost completely in water

The pH Scale (page 247)

1. What is the name of the number scale chemists use to describe the concentration of hydronium ions in a solution? __the pH scale__

2. The pH scale ranges from ___0___ to ___14___.

3. Circle the letter that indicates the pH of a neutral solution.
   a. 0
   b. 3
   (c.) 7
   d. 12

4. Water is neutral because it contains small but equal concentrations of __hydronium ions__ and __hydroxide ions__.

5. Is the following sentence true or false? The higher the pH value of a solution, the greater the H_3O^+ ion concentration is. __false__

6. If you add acid to pure water, the concentration of H_3O^+ __increases__ and the concentration of OH __decreases__.

Physical Science Guided Reading and Study Workbook • Chapter 8 **71**

160

Guided Reading and Study Workbook

Name _____ Class _____ Date _____

Chapter 8   Solutions, Acids, and Bases

Strong Acids and Bases (pages 247–248)

7. What happens when strong acids and bases dissolve in water? The compounds ionize or dissociate almost completely.

8. Is the following sentence true or false? A strong acid always has a lower pH than a weak acid. _____ false

9. Circle the letters that identify a strong acid.
   (a) HCl   b. Ca(OH)₂
   c. H₂O   (d) HNO₃

10. When dissolved in water, sodium hydroxide almost completely dissociates into ___sodium (Na⁺)___ and ___hydroxide (OH⁻)___ ions.

11. Circle the sentences that are true.
    a. Strong bases have a higher concentration of hydronium ions than pure water.
    (b) Strong bases dissociate almost completely in water.
    c. Strong bases have a pH below 7.
    (d) Examples of strong bases include sodium hydroxide and calcium hydroxide.

Weak Acids and Bases (page 248)

12. What happens when weak acids and bases dissolve in water? The compounds ionize or dissociate only slightly.

13. Is the following sentence true or false? A weak acid has a higher pH than a strong acid of the same concentration. _____ true

14. Describe the difference between concentration and strength. Concentration is the amount of solute dissolved in a given amount of solution. Strength refers to the solute's tendency to form ions in water.

15. Describe a buffer. A buffer is a solution that is resistant to large changes in pH.

Electrolytes (page 249)

16. An electrolyte is a substance that ionizes or dissociates into ions when it is dissolved in water

17. Is the following sentence true or false? Strong acids and bases are weak electrolytes because they dissociate or ionize almost completely in water. _____ false

18. Is acetic acid an example of a weak electrolyte? Explain. Yes. Acetic acid only partially ionizes.

Guided Reading and Study Workbook

Name _____ Class _____ Date _____

Chapter 8   Solutions, Acids, and Bases

WordWise

Use the clues below to identify some of the vocabulary terms from Chapter 8. Write the words on the line, putting one letter in each blank. When you finish, the words enclosed in the circle will reveal an important term.

Clues

1. A(n) _____ solution is one in which you can dissolve more solute.
2. A substance in which other materials dissolve is called a(n) _____.
3. A(n) _____ is a substance that forms ions when dissolved in water.
4. A(n) _____ is a solution containing either a weak acid and its salt or a weak base and its salt.
5. A(n) _____ is a compound that produces hydroxide ions when dissolved in water.
6. The process in which a substance breaks up into smaller particles as it dissolves is called _____.
7. The reaction between an acid and a base is called _____.
8. A(n) _____ is a compound that produces hydronium ions when dissolved in water.
9. When neutral molecules gain or lose electrons, the process is known as _____.
10. The number of moles of solute that is dissolved in 1 liter of solution is _____.

Vocabulary Terms

1. u n s a t u r a t e d
2. s o l v e n t
3. e l e c t r o l y t e
4. b u f f e r
5. b a s e
6. d i s p e r s i o n
7. n e u t r a l i z a t i o n
8. a c i d
9. i o n i z a t i o n
10. m o l a r i t y

Hidden Word: s o l u b i l i t y
Definition: The maximum amount of solute that normally dissolves in a given amount of solvent at a certain temperature.

Guided Reading and Study Workbook

Name _____ Class _____ Date _____

Chapter 8   Solutions, Acids, and Bases

Calculating the Molarity of a Solution

Suppose you dissolve 58.5 grams of sodium chloride into enough water to make exactly 1.00 liter of solution. What is the molarity of the solution?

Math Skill: Calculating with Significant Figures

You may want to read more about this **Math Skill** in the **Skills and Reference Handbook** at the end of your textbook.

1. Read and Understand

What information are you given?
   Mass of solute = 58.5 g NaCl
   Volume of solution = 1.00 L

2. Plan and Solve

What unknown are you trying to solve?
   Molarity = ?

What equation can you use?

$$\text{Molarity} = \frac{\text{moles of solute}}{\text{liters of solution}}$$

Convert the mass of the solute into moles.

$$\text{Moles of solute} = \frac{\text{Mass of NaCl}}{\text{Molar mass of NaCl}}$$

$$= \frac{58.5 \text{ g NaCl}}{58.5 \text{ g NaCl/mol NaCl}} = 1.00 \text{ mol NaCl}$$

Solve the equation for molarity.

$$\text{Molarity} = \frac{1.00 \text{ mol NaCl}}{1.00 \text{ L}} = 1.00 \text{ M NaCl}$$

3. Look Back and Check

Is your answer reasonable?
   A 1.00 M NaCl solution contains 1.00 mole of NaCl per liter of solution. The answer is reasonable.

Math Practice

On a separate sheet of paper, solve the following problems.

1. Suppose you had 4.0 moles of solute dissolved into 2.0 liters of solution. What is the molarity?
   $\text{Molarity} = \frac{\text{moles of solute}}{\text{liters of solution}} = \frac{4.0 \text{ moles}}{2.0 \text{ liters}} = 2.0 \text{ M}$

2. A saltwater solution containing 43.9 grams of NaCl has a total volume of 1.5 liters. What is the molarity?
   $\text{Molarity} = \frac{43.9 \text{ g NaCl} \times (1 \text{ mol NaCl/58.5 g NaCl})}{1.5 \text{ L}} = 0.50 \text{ M}$

3. Table sugar has a molar mass of 342 grams. How many grams of table sugar are needed to make 2.00 liters of a 0.500 M solution?
   2.00 L × 0.500 mol/L × 342 g/mol = 342 g

Student Edition Lab Worksheet

Name _____ Class _____ Date _____

Chapter 8   Solutions, Acids, and Bases   **Exploration Lab**

See pages 254 and 255 in the Teacher's Edition for more information.

Preparing a Salt by Neutralization

In this lab, you will prepare table salt by reacting hydrochloric acid (HCl) with sodium hydroxide (NaOH). To be sure that all of the acid and base have reacted, you will use phenolphthalein. You will first have to test the colors of this indicator with a known acid and base. After the acid and base have reacted, you will measure the pH of the solution with pH paper. Finally, you will evaporate the water and collect the sodium chloride.

Problem How can you produce a salt by neutralization?

Materials
- 3 dropper pipets
- labels
- 10-mL graduated cylinder
- test tube rack
- 2 10-mL test tubes
- distilled water
- hydrochloric acid
- sodium hydroxide solution
- 3 stirring rods
- phenolphthalein solution
- 2 25-mL beaker
- pH paper
- large watch glass
- 100-mL beaker
- hot plate

Skills Observing, Measuring, Analyzing Data

Procedure
Part A: Preparing for the Experiment

1. Place about 10 mL of distilled water in a 25-mL beaker. Set the graduated cylinder on the table and add distilled water to the 5-mL mark. Be sure that the *bottom* of the meniscus is on the 5-mL line.

2. To determine the number of drops in 1 mL, use a clean dropper pipet to add 1 mL of water to the graduated cylinder. Hold the dropper pipet straight up and down with the tip of the dropper pipet just inside the mouth of the cylinder. As your partner watches the liquid level in the cylinder, add drops of water one at a time while counting the drops. Continue adding drops until the liquid level reaches 6 mL. In the data table, record the number of drops in 1 mL.

3. Label one clean dropper pipet *Hydrochloric acid (HCl)* and the other *Sodium hydroxide (NaOH)*.

4. Using the HCl dropper pipet, add 3 mL of hydrochloric acid to a clean test tube. **CAUTION:** *Hydrochloric acid is corrosive. In case of spills, clean thoroughly with water.* Add 2 to 3 drops of phenolphthalein to the test tube. Use a clean stirring rod to mix the hydrochloric acid and indicator. Record your observations.

DATA TABLE

Material(s)	Observation	
1 mL	22	drops
HCl + phenolphthalein	Clear	(color)
NaOH + phenolphthalein	Pink	(color)
Drops of HCl used	88	drops
mL of HCl used	4	mL
Drops of NaOH used	88	drops
mL of NaOH used	4	mL
pH of final solution	7	

Student Edition Lab Worksheet

Name _____ Class _____ Date _____

5. Using the dropper pipet labeled NaOH, add 3 mL of sodium hydroxide solution to a clean test tube. **CAUTION:** *Sodium hydroxide is corrosive. In case of spills, clean thoroughly with water.* Add 2 to 3 drops of phenolphthalein to the test tube. Use a clean stirring rod to mix the sodium hydroxide solution and indicator. Record your observations.

Part B: Making the Salt

6. Using the HCl dropper pipet, add 4 mL of hydrochloric acid to a clean 25-mL beaker. Record the number of drops you used. Add 2 to 3 drops of phenolphthalein to the beaker.

7. Use the NaOH dropper pipet to add sodium hydroxide drop by drop to the beaker of hydrochloric acid and phenolphthalein, stirring constantly. Count the drops as you add them. As a pink color remains longer, add the drops more slowly.

8. Continue to add and count the drops of sodium hydroxide until a light pink color remains for at least 30 seconds. (*Hint:* If you add too much sodium hydroxide, add a few more drops of hydrochloric acid until the color disappears.) Record any additional drops of hydrochloric acid that you added. Then, carefully add sodium hydroxide until 1 drop produces a lasting pink color. Record the total number of drops of sodium hydroxide used.

9. Use a piece of pH paper to determine the pH of the final solution. Record the pH. If the pH is higher than 7.0, add hydrochloric acid drop by drop, testing the pH with pH paper after each drop, until the pH is equal to 7.0. Record the pH and the total number of drops of HCl you added.

10. Use the solution in the beaker to fill the watch glass halfway.

11. Fill the 100-mL beaker about half full of water. Place the beaker on top of the hot plate.

12. Set the watch glass on top of the beaker.

13. Turn on the hot plate to a low setting. Adjust the heat as the water in the beaker warms. The water should simmer, but not boil. **CAUTION:** *Do not touch the hot plate or the beaker.* Heat until a solid is visible at the edges of the water in the watch glass and the water is nearly evaporated. Turn off the heat.

14. Allow the remaining water to evaporate. Observe the contents of the watch glass. Record your observations.

   A white solid deposits on the watch glass.

15. When the watch glass has cooled, dispose of the contents as directed by your teacher. Clean up your equipment. Wash your hands with soap and water.

Student Edition Lab Worksheet

Name _____ Class _____ Date _____

Analyze and Conclude

1. **Comparing and Contrasting** What was the total amount of hydrochloric acid used to make the neutral solution? What was the total amount of sodium hydroxide? How do the amounts compare?

   See the data table. Students should recognize that they used the same volume of base as the volume

   of acid they began with (assuming the concentrations of the acid and the base are the same).

2. **Drawing Conclusions** What do you conclude about the concentrations of hydrochloric acid and sodium hydroxide in the solutions?

   The concentrations are the same.

3. **Predicting** If the acid had been twice as concentrated as the base, how would your data have changed?

   It would have taken twice as much base to reach the color change.

Lab Manual

Name _____ Class _____ Date _____

Chapter 8   Solutions, Acids, and Bases   **Investigation 8A**

Comparing Antacids

Refer students to pages 240–249 in their textbooks for a discussion of acid-base chemistry. **SKILLS FOCUS:** Observing, Measuring, Inferring, Analyzing Data, Designing Experiments, Drawing Conclusions, Evaluating and Revising **CLASS TIME:** 45 minutes

Background Information

Acids are substances that produce hydronium ions (H_3O^+) when dissolved in water. **Bases** are substances that produce hydroxide ions (OH^-) when dissolved in water. The reaction between an acid and a base is called **neutralization.** Antacids are basic substances that are taken to neutralize excess stomach acid. Different brands of antacids may differ in a number of ways, including their chemical composition, the quantity of acid neutralized per dose, and the speed with which neutralization occurs.

An **indicator** is a substance that changes color in the presence of acids and bases. Indicators are used to show whether a solution is acidic or basic and to show when a neutralization reaction is complete.

In this investigation, you will use an indicator to compare the quantity of acid that several antacids neutralize. The amount of indicator that you will use is very small and will not affect the reaction that you are studying.

Problem

Which brand of antacid neutralizes the most acid per dose?

Pre-Lab Discussion

Read the entire investigation. Then, work with a partner to answer the following questions.

1. **Predicting** In Part A of this investigation, which sodium hydroxide solution do you predict will neutralize more acid? Explain your answer.

   The 0.5 M NaOH solution will neutralize more acid because it is more concentrated.

2. **Designing Experiments** In Part A of this investigation, how will you determine which sodium hydroxide solution neutralized more acid?

   The sodium hydroxide solution that neutralized more acid will leave less acid remaining in the

   solution. As a result, less NaOH solution will be needed to neutralize the remaining acid.

Lab Manual

Name _____ Class _____ Date _____

3. **Formulating Hypotheses** State a hypothesis that you could test in Part B of this investigation.

   Student hypotheses should be specific and subject to testing by an experiment that students

   could perform. Examples of acceptable answers are the hypotheses that all the antacids are

   equal in neutralizing power or that brand A has more neutralizing power than brands B and C have.

4. **Designing Experiments** Describe an experiment you could perform to test your hypothesis.

   Students should describe a modification of the procedure in Part A of the investigation to compare

   the neutralizing power of the antacids.

5. **Controlling Variables** What are the manipulated, responding, and controlled variables in the experiment that you described in your answer to Question 4?

   Answers will depend on student experimental designs, but may include type of antacid as a

   manipulated variable, final pH or quantity of acid neutralized as a responding variable, and

   quantity of indicator and concentration of base as controlled variables.

Suggested Materials *(per group)*

glass-marking pencil
2 250-mL beakers
10-mL graduated cylinder
50-mL graduated cylinder
0.1 *M* hydrochloric acid (HCl) solution
dropper bottle of bromthymol blue solution
3 glass stirring rods
0.1 *M* sodium hydroxide (NaOH) solution
0.5 *M* NaOH solution
buret of 0.1 *M* NaOH solution on ring stand
3 different brands of antacid tablets
3 spoons
2 dropper pipets
Ask your teacher for any additional materials that you will need to carry out Part B of this investigation.

Prepare all solutions with distilled or deionized water. Use neoprene gloves, safety goggles, and a lab apron when preparing the HCl and NaOH solutions. Working in a fume hood, prepare 0.1 M HCl by adding 44 mL of concentrated HCl to enough water to make 1 L of solution. To prepare 0.5 M NaOH, dissolve 20 g NaOH in enough water to make 1 L of solution. Dilute part of this solution with 4 volumes of water to prepare 0.1 M NaOH. Set up burets of 0.1 M NaOH solution in advance for students. You will need to refill the burets as students perform this investigation.

Name _____ Class _____ Date _____

Safety

Put on safety goggles, plastic gloves, and a lab apron. Be careful to avoid breakage when working with glassware. Never touch or taste any chemical unless instructed to do so. Always use caution when working with laboratory chemicals, as they may irritate the skin or stain skin or clothing. Wash your hands thoroughly after carrying out this investigation. Note all safety alert symbols next to the steps in the Procedure and review the meaning of each symbol by referring to the Safety Symbols on page xiii.

Design Your Experiment
Part A: Comparing the Neutralizing Power of Basic Solutions

1. Use a glass-marking pencil to label two 250-mL beakers 0.1 M NaOH and 0.5 M NaOH.

2. Use the 50-mL graduated cylinder to place 50 mL of 0.1 M HCl solution into each beaker.

3. Add 1 drop of the bromthymol blue solution to the beaker labeled 0.1 M NaOH and stir with a glass stirring rod. Count each drop as you continue to add bromthymol blue solution 1 drop at a time, until the solution becomes yellow. Add the same number of drops of bromthymol blue solution to the beaker labeled 0.5 M NaOH and stir with the same glass stirring rod.

4. Use the 10-mL graduated cylinder to add 5 mL of 0.1 M NaOH solution into the beaker labeled 0.1 M NaOH. Stir the solution with a clean glass stirring rod.

5. In the sink, rinse the 10-mL graduated cylinder thoroughly with water. Then, use the graduated cylinder to add 5 mL of 0.5 M NaOH solution into the beaker labeled 0.5 M NaOH. Stir the solution with a clean glass stirring rod. **CAUTION:** *Handle the 0.5 M NaOH solution with care. It is poisonous and can burn skin and clothing.*

6. To compare the quantity of HCl remaining in each beaker, place the beaker labeled 0.5 M NaOH under the buret. Record the initial volume of the 0.1 M NaOH solution that is in the buret in Data Table 1. Show students how to read and operate the burets.

7. In the sink, rinse all three glass stirring rods thoroughly with water. Stir the contents of the beaker labeled 0.5 M NaOH with a clean glass stirring rod as you slowly add 0.1 M NaOH solution from the buret to the beaker. Stop adding NaOH solution to the beaker as soon as the color of the solution in the beaker changes to blue. Observe the volume of solution remaining in the buret. Record this volume in Data Table 1.

8. Subtract the volume of NaOH solution remaining in the buret from the initial volume of the NaOH solution to determine the volume of NaOH solution that you added to the beaker. Record this volume in Data Table 1.

Before performing this investigation, check the eyewash and shower in the laboratory to make sure that they are operational, and demonstrate their location and use to students. Share the safety information in the MSDS for each chemical with students and demonstrate safe, accurate use of the buret before students begin the investigation.

Name _____ Class _____ Date _____

9. Ask your teacher to refill your buret with 0.1 M NaOH solution. Repeat Steps 6 through 8 with the beaker labeled 0.1 M NaOH.

Part B: Using Indicators to Determine Antacid Strength

10. Design an experiment to compare the neutralizing power of three different brands of antacid tablets. Record the hypothesis that you will test.

    Possible answer: One tablet of antacid brand A neutralizes more acid than one tablet of

    brands B and C.

    _____

    _____

    _____

11. Write a detailed plan of how you will carry out your experiment. You may choose to base your experiment on the method of comparing the neutralizing power of solutions that you used in Part A of this investigation. Construct Data Table 2 in which to record your observations in the space provided on page 82. If you need more space, attach additional sheets of paper.

    Using Part A as a guide, students should design a controlled experiment to compare the

    strengths of three different antacid tablets by measuring how much acid each tablet can

    neutralize. In their experiments, students may choose to measure the neutralizing powder of

    each antacid brand on a per-tablet or per-gram basis. Students should explain all the steps

    involved, specify what data is to be collected, and provide a complete materials list.

    _____

    _____

    _____

    _____

    _____

    _____

    _____

    _____

    _____

    _____

    _____

    _____

    _____

Name _____ Class _____ Date _____

12. What are the manipulated, responding, and controlled variables in your experiment?

    a. Manipulated variable

    Typical experimental designs will include the brand of antacid as the manipulated variable.

    _____

    b. Responding variable

    Typical experimental designs will include pH or the volume of NaOH solution added to

    neutralize the remaining acid as the responding variable.

    c. Controlled variables

    Controlled variables may include the volume or concentration of HCl and NaOH solutions,

    temperature, and the indicator used.

13. What safety precautions will you need to take in your experiment?

    Students need to wear safety goggles, lab aprons, and plastic gloves when working with

    solutions of acids or bases.

    _____

    _____

14. List the possible results of your experiment and whether each possible result would support or contradict your hypothesis.

    Results of the experiment may indicate that one brand of antacid neutralizes more acid

    per tablet (or per gram) than the others or that two or all three brands neutralize equal quantities

    of acid per tablet (or per gram).

    _____

    _____

    _____

    _____

15. Show your written experimental plan to your teacher. When your teacher approves your plan, carry out your experiment and record your observations in your data table.

Name _____ Class _____ Date _____

Observations Sample data are shown.

DATA TABLE 1

Beaker	Initial Volume of NaOH Solution in Buret (mL)	Final Volume of NaOH Solution in Buret (mL)	Volume of NaOH Solution Used (mL)
0.1 M NaOH	100	55	45
0.5 M NaOH	100	75	25

DATA TABLE 2
If you need more space, attach an additional sheet of paper.

Antacid Brand	Initial Volume of NaOH Solution in Buret (mL)	Final Volume of NaOH Solution in Buret (mL)	Volume of NaOH Solution Used (mL)
Tum-Eze	100	54	46
Speedy Relief	100	77	23
Alkasimple	100	62	38

Lab Manual

Name _____ Class _____ Date _____

Analysis and Conclusions

1. Inferring What can you infer from the volume of NaOH solution that you added to each beaker in Steps 7 through 9?

The volume of NaOH solution added indicated the quantity of hydrochloric acid remaining in

each beaker.

2. Analyzing Data Based on the results of Part A of this investigation, which NaOH solution neutralized more acid in Steps 4 and 5 of Part A? Explain your answer.

The 0.5 M NaOH solution neutralized more acid. The data showed that less acid remained in the

0.5-M beaker than in the 0.1-M beaker.

3. Analyzing Data Which antacid tablet neutralized the most acid? Which tablet neutralized the least acid? Explain your answers.

Answers should reference the data from Part B. The sample data indicate that the Speedy Relief

brand neutralized the most acid per tablet.

4. Evaluating and Revising Did your data support or contradict your hypothesis? Explain your answer.

Answers will depend on student hypotheses. In their explanations, students should

reference their data from Part B.

Lab Manual

Name _____ Class _____ Date _____

5. Observing How did the antacid tablets differ from the NaOH solutions you used in Part A of this investigation? How did these differences affect the way you tested the tablets?

The tablets were solid and had different volumes and masses, unlike the NaOH solutions that

were liquids and had no particular volumes or masses. Therefore, students had to crush or

dissolve the tablets before testing them. Students may have chosen to determine the masses of

the tablets. Students also had to decide whether to compare equal masses or equal doses

(number of tablets) of the antacids.

6. Drawing Conclusions What chemical properties other than the quantity of acid that it neutralized might make one brand of antacid tablet better than another?

Answers may include the rate of dissolving or neutralization, whether the reaction

produces bubbles of a gas, and whether the tablets contain substances that affect taste

or health.

Go Further

Safety officers at chemical factories must plan for the possibility that a large quantity of a dangerous acid might be spilled in a work area. Use resources in the library or on the Internet to research what methods and materials are used to safely clean up acid spills. Use your knowledge of neutralization reactions to explain how these emergency procedures work

Handbooks and Web sites that deal with industrial safety and hazardous materials cleanup can provide the necessary information. Basic solutions and highly absorbent materials are often used to neutralize or remove spilled acids.

Lab Manual

Name _____ Class _____ Date _____

Chapter 8 Solutions, Acids, and Bases   Investigation 8B

Comparing Solubilities and Rates of Dissolving

Refer students to pages 228 and 239 in their textbooks for a discussion of solutions, solubility, and factors that affect rates of dissolving. **SKILLS FOCUS:** Inferring, Predicting, Measuring, Using Tables and Graphs, Applying Concepts, Drawing Conclusions **CLASS TIME:** Part A, 30 minutes; Part B, 45 minutes

Background Information

When one substance dissolves in another, the mixture is called a solution. The substance that dissolves is the **solute**. A substance that dissolves other substances is called a **solvent**. The rate at which a solid solute dissolves depends on several factors including temperature, stirring, and the surface area of the solute. **Solubility** is the maximum amount of a solute that can dissolve in a given amount of a solvent at a certain temperature. The solubility of different substances varies, but it is always the same for a given substance at a given temperature.

In this investigation, you will determine the effect of surface area on the rate at which table salt (sodium chloride, NaCl) dissolves in water. You will also investigate how temperature affects the solubility of ammonium chloride (NH_4Cl) in water.

Problem

How do surface area and temperature affect the rate of dissolving and solubility?

Pre-Lab Discussion

Read the entire investigation. Then, work with a partner to answer the following questions.

1. Controlling Variables In Part A, what is the manipulated variable that you will use to investigate the rate of dissolving?

Particle size (or surface area) of the solute

2. Predicting In Part A, what do you predict will be the effect of the manipulated variable on the rate of dissolving?

Smaller particles with more surface area will dissolve more quickly.

3. Predicting In Part B, what do you predict will be the effect of the manipulated variable on solubility?

More solid will dissolve at higher temperatures.

Materials *(per group)*

rock salt (sodium chloride, NaCl)
table salt (sodium chloride, NaCl)
paper towel
hand lens
3 150-mL beakers
triple-beam balance
2 scoops
100-mL graduated cylinder

clock or watch
3 glass stirring rods
thermometer
ammonium chloride (NH_4Cl)
small spoon
hot plate
graph paper

Sodium chloride (NaCl) can be substituted for ammonium chloride, but the solubility increase with temperature is much less dramatic than for NH_4Cl. To save time and to simplify the massing procedure for students, you may wish to dispense 5-g to 10-g samples of sodium chloride for students to mass.

Lab Manual

Name _____ Class _____ Date _____

Safety 🥽🧤🧥🔥⚗️🧪🔥

Review with students the safety information in the MSDS for ammonium chloride before performing this investigation. Provide only non-mercury thermometers.

Put on safety goggles, plastic gloves, and a lab apron. Be careful to avoid breakage when working with glassware. Use extreme care when working with heated materials to avoid burns. Never touch or taste any chemical unless instructed to do so. Wash your hands thoroughly after carrying out this investigation. Note all safety alert symbols next to the steps in the Procedure and review the meaning of each symbol by referring to the Safety Symbols on page xiii.

Procedure

Part A: The Effect of Surface Area on Rate of Dissolving

1. Place a few grains of rock salt and a few grains of table salt on a paper towel. Observe the rock salt and table salt. Then, use a hand lens to compare the particles of rock salt and the particles of table salt. Record which salt has the smaller particles in Data Table 1.

2. Place a beaker on the balance. Measure and record the mass of the beaker.

3. Use the scoop to place a sample of rock salt in the beaker. Measure the mass of the beaker and salt. Add or remove rock salt from the beaker if necessary until the mass of the beaker and salt is 5 to 10 grams more than the mass of the beaker alone. Record the mass of the beaker and salt.

4. Repeat Steps 2 and 3 with a second beaker and a sample of table salt. Be sure that the mass of table salt in the beaker does not differ from the mass of the rock salt by more than 0.1 g.

5. Use a graduated cylinder to add 75 mL of room-temperature water to each beaker. Note the time. Observe the solutions for 2 minutes. After 2 minutes, look for any signs of dissolving. Record your observations.

6. Place a glass stirring rod in each beaker. Note the time. Working with a partner, stir the water gently in each beaker. Be sure to stir both samples at the same time and at the same slow rate. Note the time when each sample completely dissolves. Record the time it took for each salt sample to dissolve completely.

Part B: The Effect of Temperature on Solubility

7. To investigate solubility, put 50 mL of room-temperature water into a clean beaker. Use a thermometer to measure the temperature of the water. Record this temperature in Data Table 2. Remove the thermometer from the beaker.

8. Add one spoonful of ammonium chloride to the water in the beaker. Stir vigorously with a clean glass stirring rod until no more of the solid will dissolve. Make sure that you allow enough time for the solid to dissolve. **CAUTION:** *Be careful handling ammonium chloride and its solutions, which are poisonous.*

Name _____ Class _____ Date _____

9. Repeat Step 8 until no more ammonium chloride will dissolve. Note the number of spoonfuls of ammonium chloride that you added. Be sure to allow enough time for each spoonful of ammonium chloride to dissolve before adding more. Record the number of spoonfuls that dissolved in Data Table 2.

🔥 10. Place the beaker of ammonium chloride solution on a hot plate. Place the thermometer in the beaker. Turn the hot plate to the medium-low setting and warm the solution to 40°C. **CAUTION:** *Be careful handling the hot plate and hot solutions. They can cause burns.*

11. Remove the thermometer from the beaker. Add more spoonfuls of ammonium chloride to the beaker. Stir the solution and use the thermometer to check the temperature of the solution after you add each spoonful. Note the total number of spoonfuls of ammonium chloride that you added. Be sure to allow enough time for each spoonful of ammonium chloride to dissolve before adding more. Use the heat setting of the hot plate to keep the temperature constant as you add ammonium chloride to the beaker.

12. Record the total number of spoonfuls that have dissolved.

13. Turn up the hot plate to warm the solution to 60°C. Then, repeat Steps 11 and 12 with the solution at this temperature.

14. Turn up the hot plate to warm the solution to 80°C. Then, repeat Steps 11 and 12 with the solution at this temperature.

🔥 15. When you have recorded all of your data, turn off the hot plate and allow the solution to cool. Follow your teacher's instructions for disposing of the used chemicals. Wash your hands thoroughly with warm water and soap or detergent before leaving the laboratory.

16. On a sheet of graph paper, make a graph of the solubility of ammonium chloride versus temperature. Plot temperature on the horizontal axis and solubility (in spoonfuls per 50 mL water) on the vertical axis.

Used solutions may be flushed down the drain with at least 10 volumes of water. If your school is served by a septic system, do not dispose of chemical waste in this way. Instead, allow the used solutions to evaporate and dispose of them as dry chemical waste.

Observations *Sample data are shown.*

DATA TABLE 1

Type of Sodium Chloride	Particle Size	Mass of Beaker (g)	Mass of Beaker and Salt (g)	Mass of Salt (g)	Appearance of Mixture After 2 Minutes Without Stirring	Time to Dissolve (seconds)
Rock salt	Larger			7.0 g	Most salt is undissolved.	Longer
Table salt	Smaller			7.0 g	Most salt is undissolved.	Shorter

Name _____ Class _____ Date _____

DATA TABLE 2

Temperature (°C)	Number of Spoonfuls of Ammonium Chloride Dissolved
18–20	Data will depend on the size of the spoons supplied. The solubility of ammonium chloride in 50 mL of water is approximately 18 g at 20°C, 22 g at 40°C, 28 g at 60°C, and 32 g at 80°C.
40	
60	
80	

Analysis and Conclusions

1. **Inferring** How did stirring affect the rate at which the salt dissolved? Explain how you think stirring caused this effect.

The rate of dissolving was greater in stirred water because stirring moved the more concentrated part of the solution away from the solid salt and moved the less concentrated part of the solution closer to the solid salt, allowing more particles of salt to move into solution.

2. **Inferring** Why do you think the different types of salt dissolved at different rates?

Dissolving takes place at the surfaces of solids. The more finely divided a solid is, the greater its surface area and rate of dissolving will be. Therefore, the smaller particles of table salt dissolved more quickly than the larger particles of rock salt.

3. **Predicting** Predict what effect, if any, you think the size of salt grains would have on their solubility. Explain your answer.

The solubility is the same for all sizes of salt grains because the same substance is involved.

4. **Using Graphs** Based on your graph and your observations in Part B, what do you think the solubility of ammonium chloride (in spoonfuls per 50 mL water) would be at 10°C? At 70°C? At 100°C?

Graphs should show an upward curve, indicating an increase in solubility with increasing temperature. Exact values will depend on spoon size. The actual solubility in grams NH_4Cl per 50 mL water is approximately 16 at 10°C, 30 at 70°C, and 38 at 100°C.

Go Further

Design an experiment to determine the effect of temperature on the rate of dissolving of a different solid in water. Write a detailed plan of your experiment. Your plan should state a hypothesis, identify variables, and describe the procedures and safety precautions that you will use. Show your plan to your teacher. When your teacher approves your plan, carry out your experiment and report your results and conclusions.
Examine student plans for sound experimental design and safety. Most solid substances dissolve more quickly at higher temperatures.

Chapter Test A

Name _____ Class _____ Date _____

Chapter 8 Solutions, Acids, and Bases   **Chapter Test A**

Multiple Choice

Write the letter that best answers the question or completes the statement on the line provided.

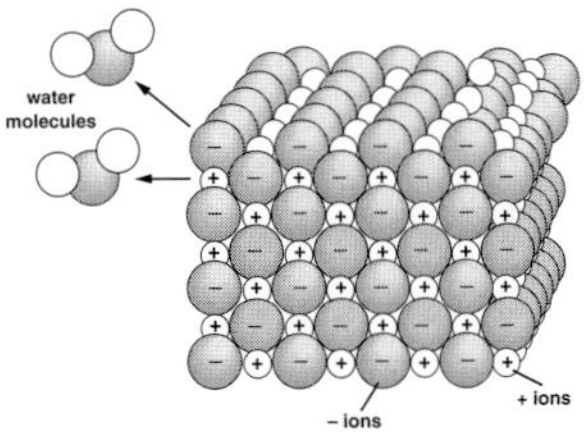

water molecules

Figure 8-1

– ions
+ ions

_____ 1. Study Figure 8-1. When the ionic compound KI is dissolved in water, the I⁻ ions are pulled into solution by the attraction between
  a. the K^+ and I^- ions.
  b. the K^+ ion and the negative end of a water molecule.
  c. the I^- ion and the negative end of a water molecule.
  d. the I^- ion and the positive end of a water molecule.

_____ 2. The more particles a solute forms in solution, the greater is its effect on the freezing point of the solution. Which of the following will lower the freezing point the most if 1 mol of it is added to 1 L of water?
  a. the molecular compound propanol, C_2H_5OH
  b. the ionic compound NaCl
  c. the ionic compound $MgCl_2$
  d. the ionic compound $AlCl_3$

_____ 3. The amount of energy required to break the attractions among the solute particles and among the solvent particles is
  a. greater than the energy released as attractions form between solute and solvent particles.
  b. less than the energy released as attractions form between solute and solvent particles.
  c. equal to the energy released as attractions form between solute and solvent particles.
  d. equal to the heat of solution.

_____ 4. All materials that are considered to be insoluble will dissolve in a solvent to a very small extent. The rate of dissolving of a rock in a streambed would be increased by all of the following EXCEPT
  a. breaking the rock into smaller pieces.
  b. moving the rock to a faster-moving current.
  c. moving the rock to warmer water.
  d. reducing the exposure of the rock to the water.

Chapter Test A

Name _____ Class _____ Date _____

_____ 5. The solubility of carbon dioxide gas in water can be increased by
  a. increasing the temperature.
  b. agitating the mixture.
  c. increasing the pressure.
  d. using more solvent.

_____ 6. One way to determine the degree of saturation of a solid-liquid solution is to drop a crystal of the solute into the solution. If the crystal sits at the bottom of the container, the solution is
  a. saturated.   b. unsaturated.
  c. supersaturated.   d. concentrated.

_____ 7. A 25-g sample of sugar was dissolved in 50 g of water. The concentration of the solution is
  a. 50 percent by mass.
  b. 33 percent by mass.
  c. 0.5 M.
  d. 50 percent by volume.

_____ 8. A girl tasted each of the following foods. Which of the following would NOT taste acidic to her?
  a. lime   b. tomato
  c. orange   d. celery

_____ 9. Which of the following is NOT a common property of bases?
  a. feels slippery
  b. tastes bitter c. reacts with metals
  d. changes colors of indicators

_____ 10. The products of the neutralization reaction between hydrochloric acid and magnesium hydroxide are
  a. $MgCl$ and H_2O.   b. $MgCl_2$ and H_2O.
  c. HCl and $MgOH$.   d. HCl and $Mg(OH)_2$.

_____ 11. Ammonia, NH_3, can be classified as a base because in a chemical reaction with an acid, ammonia will
  a. produce hydroxide ions in solution.
  b. produce hydronium ions in solution.
  c. donate a proton and become NH_2^-.
  d. accept a proton and become NH_4^+.

_____ 12. Tomatoes have a hydronium ion concentration of 1×10^{-4} M. What is the pH of a tomato?
  a. 4   b. –4   c. 10   d. 1×10^{-4}

Chapter Test A

_____ 13. The hydroxide ion concentration in pure water at 25°C is NOT equal to
a. the hydronium ion concentration.
b. 1×10^{-7} M.
c. the hydroxide concentration in a solution with a pH of 7.
d. 1×10^{7} M.

_____ 14. A compound has a pH of 1 in solution, where it has completely ionized. The compound is a
a. strong base.   b. weak base.
c. strong acid.   d. weak acid.

_____ 15. Calcium hydroxide forms very few hydroxide ions in solution, but it is still considered a strong base because
a. calcium hydroxide is insoluble.
b. all the calcium hydroxide in solution ionizes.
c. all the calcium hydroxide in solution dissociates.
d. very little of the calcium hydroxide in solution ionizes.

_____ 16. Which of the following would NOT form a buffer solution?
a. $NH_3 + NH_4Cl$ b. $HC_2H_3O_2 + NaC_2H_3O_2$
c. $HCl + NaCl$ d. $H_2CO_3 + NaHCO_3$

_____ 17. Which of the following are examples of strong electrolytes?
a. strong and weak bases
b. strong acids and strong bases
c. weak acids and weak bases
d. pure water and buffers

Completion

Complete each statement on the line provided.

1. A substance dissolves in water by breaking up into smaller pieces. These pieces of the same substance spread throughout the water. This process is known as _____ .

2. Antifreeze is added to a radiator because it _____ the boiling point and _____ the freezing point of the solution contained in the radiator.

3. Stirring increases the rate of solution of a solid in a liquid because solute particles in solution are moved _____ the surface of the solute.

4. Many foods are acidic. These foods do not hurt you when you eat them because they contain _____ acids.

5. Acetic acid is considered a weak _____ because it only partially ionizes.

Chapter Test A

Short Answer

In complete sentences, write the answers to the questions on the lines provided.

1. Both ionization and dissociation produce ions of the solute in solution. How do the two processes differ?

2. Compare and contrast an exothermic chemical reaction and an exothermic solution formation by dissociation.

3. A solid solute is added to a liquid solvent. The solution is stirred, but it is also cooled. Can you predict whether the solution process will speed up or not? Explain your answer.

4. You place a drop of a solution on red litmus paper, and no color change occurs. Can you conclude that the solution is neutral because no color change occurred? Explain your answer.

5. Explain how water can act as either a proton donor or a proton acceptor, depending on the other reactant. Use examples.

Chapter Test A

Using Science Skills

Use the diagram to answer each question. Write the answers on a separate sheet of paper.

Substance	Solubility (g/100 g H_2O, 20°C)	Substance	Solubility (g/100 g H_2O, 20°C)
Barium hydroxide	3.89	Potassium chloride	34.2
Barium nitrate	9.02	Sodium chloride	35.9
Calcium hydroxide	0.173	Sucrose (table sugar)	203.9

Figure 8-2

1. **Classifying** A 71.8-g sample of NaCl was added to 200.0 g of water at 20°C. Is the solution saturated, unsaturated, or supersaturated? Use Figure 8-2 to answer this question.

2. **Calculating** Potassium chloride was added to 40 g of water at 20°C until the solution was saturated. How much potassium chloride was used? Use Figure 8-2 to answer this question.

3. **Applying Concepts** A boy wanted to make candy from crystalized sugar. He dissolved 300.0 g of sucrose in 75 g of water at 100°C. To the nearest gram, how much sugar crystalized out of the saturated solution when it cooled to 20°C? Use Figure 8-2 to answer this question.

4. **Calculating** A sample of calcium hydroxide is placed into a jar containing water. The mass of the calcium hydroxide sample is 1.34 g. Assume the water is at 20°C and that the resulting calcium hydroxide solution is saturated. What mass of water was present in the jar? Use Figure 8-2 to answer this question.

5. **Using Tables and Graphs** A student was given a sample of either barium hydroxide or barium nitrate. How could she use the solubility information from Figure 8-2 to determine which compound she was given?

Problem

Write the answers to each question on a separate sheet of paper.

1. A sample of 54.7 g of HCl gas is dissolved to make 1 L of solution. What is the molarity of the solution?

2. Rubbing alcohol is often a 70 percent solution by volume of alcohol and water. If a bottle of rubbing alcohol contains 0.50 L, what volume of alcohol does it contain?

3. The buffer system in the blood contains HCO_3^- ions and H_2CO_3. Write a balanced chemical equation that shows what happens when a small amount of acid is added to blood and another equation that shows what happens when a small amount of base is added.

Chapter Test A

Essay

Write the answers to each question on a separate sheet of paper.

1. Compare and contrast the factors that affect rate of solution and those that affect solubility.

2. Describe how you would prepare 2.00 L of a 1.20-M solution of potassium chloride, KCl, in water.

Chapter Test B

Name _____ Class _____ Date _____

Chapter 8 Solutions, Acids, and Bases   Chapter Test B

Multiple Choice

Write the letter that best answers the question or completes the statement on the line provided.

_____ 1. In order for a solution to form,
    a. one substance must dissolve in another.
    b. a solid must dissolve in a liquid.
    c. the solvent must be water.
    d. a gas must dissolve in a liquid.

_____ 2. A salt is dissolved in water, which has a boiling point of 100°C. The boiling point of the solution will be
    a. greater than 100°C.
    b. less than 100°C.
    c. exactly equal to 100°C.
    d. exactly equal to 0°C.

_____ 3. During the formation of a solution, energy is
    a. either released or absorbed.
    b. neither released nor absorbed.
    c. released only.
    d. absorbed only.

_____ 4. A student dissolved equal amounts of salt in equal amounts of warm water, room-temperature water, and ice water. Which of the following is true?
    a. The salt dissolved most quickly in the warm water.
    b. The salt dissolved most quickly in the room-temperature water.
    c. The salt dissolved most quickly in the ice water.
    d. none of the above

_____ 5. The maximum amount of a solute that will dissolve in a certain amount of solvent at a given temperature is that solute's
    a. solubility.   **b.** concentration.
    c. degree of saturation.   **d.** rate of solution.

_____ 6. A solution that contains more solute than it would normally hold at that temperature is said to be
    a. saturated.   **b.** unsaturated.
    c. supersaturated.   **d.** concentrated.

_____ 7. To calculate the molarity of a solution, you need to know the moles of solute and the
    a. volume of the solvent.
    b. volume of the solution.
    c. mass of the solution.
    d. volume of the solute.

Chapter Test B

Name _____ Class _____ Date _____

_____ 8. Which of the following is NOT a property of an acid?
    a. tastes sour
    b. usually reacts with a metal
    c. changes the color of an indicator
    d. feels slippery

_____ 9. A base is defined as a compound that produces
    a. hydroxide ions in solution.
    b. hydrogen ions in solution.
    c. hydronium ions in solution.
    d. sodium ions in solution.

_____ 10. The salt that is formed during the reaction between potassium hydroxide and hydrochloric acid is
    a. NaCl. **b.** H_2O. **c.** KCl. **d.** K_2Cl.

_____ 11. An acid can be defined as
    a. a proton acceptor.
    b. a proton donor.
    c. neither a proton donor nor a proton acceptor.
    d. both a proton donor and a proton acceptor.

_____ 12. A small amount of acid is added to a buffer solution. The pH of the solution will
    a. increase.   **b.** decrease.
    c. stay about the same.   **d.** become neutral.

_____ 13. A substance that ionizes or dissociates into ions when placed in water is always a(an)
    a. conductor.   **b.** electrolyte.
    c. strong acid.   **d.** strong base.

Completion

Complete each statement on the line provided.

1. When sugar dissolves in water, water is the _____ and sugar is the _____

2. Study Figure 8-1. When KBr dissolves in water, the K⁺ and Br⁻ ions are pulled into solution in a process known as _____

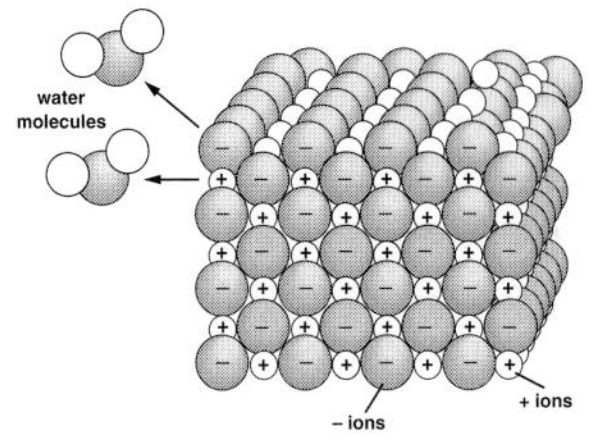

Figure 8-1

Chapter Test B

Name _____ Class _____ Date _____

3. The physical properties of a solution that differ from those of its solute and solvent include freezing point, boiling point, and _____.

4. A food packet taken on a camping trip has a warming packet. This packet contains water and a solute that releases heat when it is dissolved. The dissolving process for this solute and solvent can be described as _____.

5. The rate that a solid solute dissolves in a liquid solvent depends on the frequency and energy of the _____ between the particles of the solute and solvent.

6. Table salt is _____ soluble in cold water than it is in hot water.

7. If a saturated solution of sugar water is heated, the solution will become _____.

8. An acid produces _____ when it is dissolved in water.

9. When a substance donates a proton during a chemical reaction, that substance can be classified as a(an) _____.

10. Acids that contain carbon are weak acids, which means that they _____ only to a small extent in solution.

Short Answer

In complete sentences, write the answers to the questions on the lines provided.

1. If a liquid dissolves in a gas, in what state will the solution be? Explain your answer.
_____
_____
_____
_____

2. Which will freeze at a higher temperature—a freshwater marsh or a saltwater marsh? Explain your answer.
_____
_____
_____

3. What is the difference between a saturated solution and an unsaturated solution?
_____
_____
_____

Chapter Test B

Name _____ Class _____ Date _____

4. What is a buffer solution?
_____
_____
_____

5. What type of electrolyte is a weak acid?
_____
_____
_____

Using Science Skills

Use the diagram to answer each question. Write the answers on a separate sheet of paper.

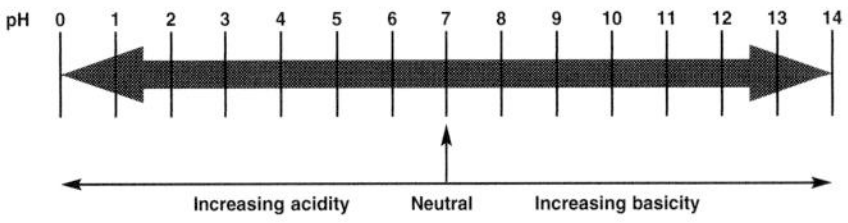

Figure 8-2

1. **Interpreting Graphics** Detergent has a pH of about 10. Is detergent acidic or basic? Use Figure 8-2 to answer this question.

2. **Drawing Conclusions** Oven cleaner has a pH of 14, and household ammonia has a pH of about 11.2. What generalization might you make about whether most cleaners contain acids or bases? Use Figure 8-2 to answer this question.

3. **Applying Concepts** Unpolluted rain has a pH of about 6. Is this rain acidic, basic, or neutral? Why is the term *acid rain* used to refer to rain that has been polluted with oxides of nitrogen and sulfur? This rain frequently has a pH between 4 and 5 and has been found to have a pH as low as 1.8. Use Figure 8-2 to answer these questions.

4. **Problem Solving** Stomach acid has a pH of about 2. What conclusion can you reach about the pH of an antacid solution that is used to neutralize excess stomach acid? Use Figure 8-2 to answer this question.

5. **Inferring** Sea water has a pH of about 8, and pure water has a pH of 7. Would sea water change the color of red litmus paper? Explain your answer. Use Figure 8-2 to answer this question.

Chapter 8 Test A Answers

Multiple Choice

1. d	**2.** d	**3.** a	**4.** d	**5.** c	**6.** a
7. b	**8.** d	**9.** c	**10.** b	**11.** d	**12.** a
13. d	**14.** c	**15.** c	**16.** c	**17.** b	

Completion

1. dispersion **2.** raises, lowers; increases, decreases
3. away from **4.** weak **5.** eletrolyte

Short Answer

1. Dissociation is a physical change involving solutes that are ionic compounds. Ionization is a chemical change involving molecular compounds. **2.** In an exothermic chemical reaction, chemical changes occur, and the reactants and the products are not the same substances. In an exothermic solution formation by dissociation, the solute undergoes a physical change and does not change identity. Energy is released in both processes.
3. No; stirring favors an increased rate, and cooling favors a slower rate. **4.** No; both a neutral and an acidic solution would result in the litmus paper remaining red. **5.** Water can accept a proton to become a hydronium ion or donate a proton to become a hydroxide ion. Examples: $HCl + H_2O \rightarrow Cl^- + H_3O^+$;
$NH_3 + H_2O \rightarrow NH_4^+ + OH^-$

Using Science Skills

1. saturated **2.** 13.7 g KCl **3.** 147 g sucrose **4.** 775 g of water
5. She could measure a mass that is between the two solubilities, such as 5 g. If all of the compound dissolves in 100 g of water at 20°C, it is barium nitrate. If the compound forms a saturated solution with some undissolved solute, the compound is barium hydroxide.

Problem

1. 1.50 M **2.** 0.35 L
3. $HCO_3^- + H^+ \rightarrow H_2CO_3$; $H_2CO_3 + OH^- \rightarrow HCO_3^- + H_2O$

Essay

1. Both are affected by temperature. Rate of solution is also affected by surface area and stirring because both of these factors affect the number of collisions between solute and solvent particles. Solubility is also affected by polarity of the solute and solvent and, if a gas is involved, pressure. The number of collisions does not affect solubility unless a gas is involved.
2. One liter of the solution would contain 1.20 mol KCl, so 2.00 L would contain 2.40 mol KCl. The molar mass of KCl is 74.55 g/mol, so you would use 179 g of KCl. Add the KCl to enough distilled water to dissolve it, then add additional water to make 2.00 L of solution.

Chapter 8 Test B Answers

Multiple Choice

1. a	**2.** a	**3.** a	**4.** a	**5.** a	**6.** c
7. b	**8.** d	**9.** a	**10.** c	**11.** b	**12.** c
13. b					

Completion

1. solvent, solute **2.** dissociation **3.** conductivity
4. exothermic **5.** collisions **6.** less **7.** unsaturated
8. hydronium ions **9.** acid **10.** ionize; form ions

Short Answer

1. A gas; the state of the solvent determines the state of the solution. **2.** A freshwater marsh; in a saltwater marsh, the dissolved salt lowers the freezing point of the water. **3.** A saturated solution contains all the solute it can hold at that temperature. More solute will dissolve at that temperature in an unsaturated solution. **4.** a solution that resists change in its pH when small amounts of acid or base are added to it **5.** a weak electrolyte

Using Science Skills

1. basic **2.** Most cleaners contain bases. **3.** Slightly acidic; other acids also form in rain when oxides of nitrogen and sulfur dissolve in water. **4.** The antacid solution must be basic, so its pH is greater than 7. **5.** Yes; since sea water has a pH greater than 7, it is a base. Red litmus paper turns blue when it comes into contact with a base.

Chapter 9 Carbon Chemistry

CHAPTER 9

Planning Guide

Use these planning tools
Easy Planner
Resource Pro
Online Lesson Planner

SECTION OBJECTIVES	STANDARDS		ACTIVITIES and LABS
	NATIONAL (See p. T18.)	STATE	
9.1 Carbon Compounds, pp. 262–269 ⏱ 1 block or 2 periods **9.1.1 Relate** the structures of three forms of carbon to their properties. **9.1.2 Explain** why there are millions of different organic compounds. **9.1.3 Relate** the number and arrangement of carbon atoms in hydrocarbons to their properties. **9.1.4 Distinguish** unsaturated from saturated hydrocarbons. **9.1.5 Classify** hydrocarbons using structural formulas and names. **9.1.6 Describe** the formation, composition, and uses of three types of fossil fuels. **9.1.7 Distinguish** complete combustion from incomplete combustion of fossil fuels. **9.1.8 Describe** the effects of some products of the combustion of fossil fuels.	A-1, A-2, B-3, C-5, D-2, F-1, F-2, F-3, F-4, F-5, G-1, G-2, G-3		**SE** Inquiry Activity: Do All Carbon Compounds Have Similar Properties? p. 261 **L2** **SE** Quick Lab: Comparing Isomers, p. 265 **L2** **TE** Teacher Demo: Comparing Models of Molecules, p. 264 **L2** **TE** Teacher Demo: Fractional Distillation, p. 267 **L2**
9.2 Substituted Hydrocarbons, pp. 272–274 ⏱ 1 block or 2 periods **9.2.1 Classify** substituted hydrocarbons based on their functional groups. **9.2.2 Describe** some properties and reactions of five types of substituted hydrocarbons.	A-1, B-2, F-1, F-3, F-4, F-5		**TE** Teacher Demo: Modeling Functional Groups, p. 272 **L2**
9.3 Polymers, pp. 275–280 ⏱ 1 block or 2 periods **9.3.1 Distinguish** a monomer from a polymer. **9.3.2 Compare** three examples of synthetic polymers. **9.3.3 Describe** the structures and functions of four types of natural polymers.	B-2, C-1, C-2, C-5, G-1, G-3		**SE** Quick Lab: Distinguishing Sugars from Starches, p. 278 **L2** **LM** Investigation 9A: Testing for Nutrients in Foods **L2** **LM** Investigation 9B: Comparing Cross-Linked Polymers **L1**
9.4 Reactions in Cells, pp. 282–284 ⏱ 1 block or 2 periods **9.4.1 Compare** photosynthesis and cellular respiration. **9.4.2 Explain** how enzymes and vitamins help reactions take place in cells.	A-1, A-2, B-3, C-1, C-5, F-1		**SE** Consumer Lab: Comparing Vitamin C in Fruit Juices, p. 285 **L2** **TE** Teacher Demo: Photosynthesis and Cellular Respiration, p. 283 **L2** **TE** Teacher Demo: Denaturing an Enzyme, p. 284 **L2**

Ability Levels

L1 For students who need additional help
L2 For all students
L3 For students who need to be challenged

Components

SE	Student Edition	**GRSW**	Guided Reading & Study Workbook With Math Support	**CTB**	Computer Test Bank
TE	Teacher's Edition			**TP**	Test Prep Resources
LM	Laboratory Manual			**iT**	iText
PLM	Probeware Lab Manual	**CUT**	Chapter and Unit Tests	**DC**	Discovery Channel Videotapes

T	Transparencies
P	Presentation Pro CD-ROM
GO	Internet Resources

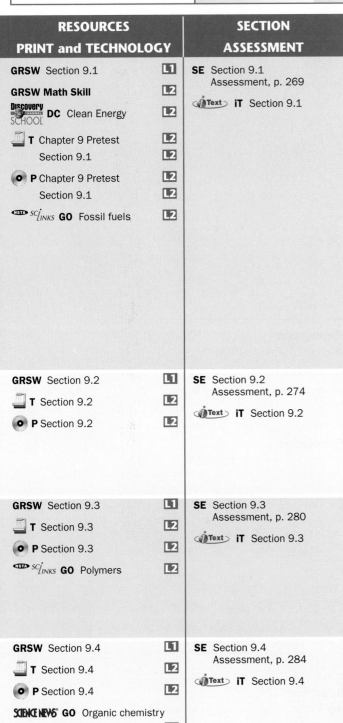

RESOURCES PRINT and TECHNOLOGY

GRSW Section 9.1 **L1**

GRSW Math Skill **L2**

DC Clean Energy **L2**

T Chapter 9 Pretest **L2**
     Section 9.1 **L2**

P Chapter 9 Pretest **L2**
     Section 9.1 **L2**

SCILINKS GO Fossil fuels **L2**

GRSW Section 9.2 **L1**

T Section 9.2 **L2**

P Section 9.2 **L2**

GRSW Section 9.3 **L1**

T Section 9.3 **L2**

P Section 9.3 **L2**

SCILINKS GO Polymers **L2**

GRSW Section 9.4 **L1**

T Section 9.4 **L2**

P Section 9.4 **L2**

SCIENCE NEWS GO Organic chemistry and biochemistry **L2**

SECTION ASSESSMENT

SE Section 9.1 Assessment, p. 269

iT Section 9.1

SE Section 9.2 Assessment, p. 274

iT Section 9.2

SE Section 9.3 Assessment, p. 280

iT Section 9.3

SE Section 9.4 Assessment, p. 284

iT Section 9.4

Go Online

Go online for these Internet resources.

PHSchool.com
Web Code: cca-1090
Web Code: cch-1090

NSTA SCILINKS
Web Code: ccn-1091
Web Code: ccn-1093

SCIENCE NEWS
Web Code: cce-1094

Materials for Activities and Labs

Quantities for each group

STUDENT EDITION

Inquiry Activity, p. 261
sucrose (table sugar), cellulose (paper), isopropyl alcohol, polystyrene (foam cup), polypropylene (food storage container)

Quick Lab, p. 265
30 marshmallows, 70 raisins, 50 toothpicks

Quick Lab, p. 278
1 slice each of potato, ripe apple, and bread; 15 mL cornstarch; 15 mL table sugar; iodine in dropper bottle; 6 small paper plates

Consumer Lab, p. 285
apple juice, variety of other fruit juices, test tubes and rack, 10-mL graduated cylinder, methylene blue indicator, dropper pipet, stirring rods

TEACHER'S EDITION

Teacher Demo, p. 264
molecular model kit

Teacher Demo, p. 267
distillation apparatus with stand, 50 mL water, 50 mL ethanol, 60 mL mineral oil, hot plate, 60-mL beakers (6), concave glass beaker covers (3), shield, dropper pipets (5)

Build Science Skills, p. 270
100-mL beaker containing 1:1 mixture of sulfur powder and coal dust, plastic pipet, 100-mL graduated cylinder, stirring rod, distilled water, 100-mL beaker

Teacher Demo, p. 272
any appliance that has attachments with different functions

Teacher Demo, p. 283
methylene blue, water, 500-mL beaker, *elodea* sprig, straw

Teacher Demo, p. 284
potato, sharp knife, cutting surface, 3% hydrogen peroxide solution, water, 500-mL beakers (2), hot plate

Chapter Assessment

CHAPTER ASSESSMENT

SE Chapter Assessment, pp. 287–288
CUT Chapter 9 Test A, B
CTB Chapter 9
iT Chapter 9
PHSchool.com GO
Web Code: cca-1090

STANDARDIZED TEST PREP

SE Chapter 9, p. 289
TP Diagnose and Prescribe

iText—interactive textbook with assessment at PHSchool.com

Carbon Chemistry **260B**

Name_____ Class_____ Date_____ M T W T F

LESSON PLAN 9.1

Carbon Compounds

Section Objectives

Local Standards

- **9.1.1 Relate** the structures of three forms of carbon to their properties.

- **9.1.2 Explain** why there are millions of different organic compounds.

- **9.1.3 Relate** the number and arrangement of carbon atoms in hydrocarbons to their properties.

- **9.1.4 Distinguish** unsaturated from saturated hydrocarbons.

- **9.1.5 Classify** hydrocarbons using structural formulas and names.

- **9.1.6 Describe** the formation, composition, and uses of three types of fossil fuels.

- **9.1.7 Distinguish** complete combustion from incomplete combustion of fossil fuels.

- **9.1.8 Describe** the effects of some products of the combustion of fossil fuels.

Vocabulary organic compound • network solid • hydrocarbon • saturated hydrocarbon • isomers • unsaturated hydrocarbon • aromatic hydrocarbons • fossil fuels

1 FOCUS

Build Vocabulary: Word-Part Analysis
Have students make a concept map with the word *hydrocarbons* as the starting point. **L2**

Targeted Resources
❑ Transparency: Chapter 9 Pretest
❑ Transparency: Interest Grabber 9.1
❑ Transparency: Reading Strategy 9.1

2 INSTRUCT

Build Reading Literacy: Relate Cause and Effect
Have students read page 262 and ask them what caused scientists to change the definition of an organic compound. **L1**

Quick Lab: Comparing Isomers
Students will use structural formulas and models to describe the isomers of hexane. **L2**

Teacher Demo: Fractional Distillation
Using ethanol, show students fractional distillation of a mixture of organic compounds. **L2**

Targeted Resources
❑ Transparency: Figure 2: Forms of Elemental Carbon
❑ Transparency: Figures 4 and 5: Types of Alkanes
❑ GRSW Section 9.1
❑ **NSTA** *sci*$_{LINKS}$ Fossil fuels

3 ASSESS

Reteach
Use the structural formulas in the text on pages 265 and 266 to review each type of hydrocarbon. **L1**

Evaluate Understanding
Have students make flashcards for the key concepts and vocabulary in this section. **L2**

Targeted Resources
❑ **PHSchool.com** Online Section 9.1 Assessment
❑ iText Section 9.1

Transparencies

119 **Chapter 9 Pretest**

1. What kind of bonds are found in molecules?

2. How many electrons are shared in a double bond?

3. How many bonds can a carbon atom form?

4. Tell which of the following are formulas for a molecular compound.

   a. H_2

   b. CO_2

   c. CH_4

   d. NaCl

5. In the following chemical equation, how many hydrogen atoms are in a molecule of the product?
   $$2H_2 + O_2 \longrightarrow 2H_2O$$

ANSWERS
1. covalent bonds
2. 4
3. 4
4. b and c
5. 2

Transparencies

120 **Chapter 9 Pretest** *(continued)*

6. Which of these properties can be used to separate substances in a mixture?

   a. boiling point

   b. hardness

   c. malleability

   d. flammability

7. True or False: Attractions between molecules are stronger than covalent bonds.

8. True or False: An exothermic reaction releases energy.

9. How does a catalyst affect the progress of a chemical reaction?

ANSWERS
6. a
7. False
8. True
9. It lowers the energy barrier, which increases the reaction rate.

Transparencies

121 **Section 9.1 Interest Grabber**

Classifying Carbon Compounds

Use the structural formulas below to answer the questions.

1. How many bonds does each carbon atom form in each of the compounds shown?

2. What is the chemical formula for each compound? Use the format C_XH_Y.

3. Classify the compounds into two groups. Explain the classification system.

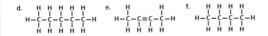

ANSWERS
1–4
2. a. C_4H_{10} b. C_5H_{10} c. C_5H_{12} d. C_5H_{12} e. C_5H_{10} f. C_5H_{12}
3. Sample answers include: a, b, and e have four carbons, c and d have 5 carbons; a, c, d and f contain only single bonds, b and e contain a double bond; in b, d, e and f, all the carbons are in a straight chain but in a and c there is a branch.

Transparencies

122 **Section 9.1 Reading Strategy**

Previewing

Forms of Carbon Compounds	
Diamond	a. ?
Graphite	b. ?
Buckminsterfullerene	c. ?

ANSWERS
a. rigid three-dimensional network
b. widely spaced layers
c. hollow spheres with a surface of carbon atoms arranged in alternating hexagons and pentagons

Transparencies

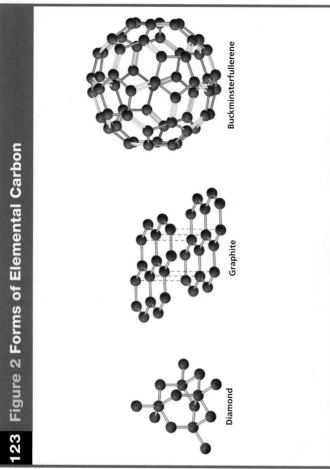

123 Figure 2 Forms of Elemental Carbon

Buckminsterfullerene

Graphite

Diamond

Transparencies

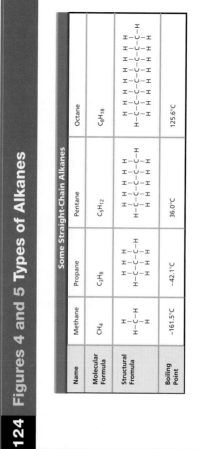

124 Figures 4 and 5 Types of Alkanes

Some Straight-Chain Alkanes

Name	Methane	Propane	Pentane	Octane
Molecular Formula	CH_4	C_3H_8	C_5H_{12}	C_8H_{18}
Structural Fromula				
Boiling Point	−161.5°C	−42.1°C	36.0°C	125.6°C

Cyclobutane C_4H_8

Isobutane C_4H_{10}

Butane C_4H_{10}

Guided Reading and Study Workbook

Name _____ Class _____ Date _____

Chapter 9   Carbon Chemistry

Section 9.1 Carbon Compounds
(pages 262–269)

This section describes different forms of carbon that exist in nature. It also discusses saturated and unsaturated hydrocarbons. It explains the formation of fossil fuels and describes the products of their combustion.

Reading Strategy (page 262)

Previewing Before you read, use the models in Figure 2 to describe the arrangement of carbon atoms in each form of carbon. For more information on this Reading Strategy, see the **Reading and Study Skills** in the **Skills and Reference Handbook** at the end of your textbook.

Forms of Carbon	
Diamond	Rigid, three-dimensional network
Graphite	Widely spaced layers
Buckminsterfullerene	Hollow spheres with a surface of carbon atoms arranged in alternating hexagons and pentagons

1. The two elements that all organic compounds contain are _____ carbon and hydrogen _____.

2. Circle the letter of the approximate percentage of all known compounds that are organic compounds.
   a. 10 percent   b. 30 percent
   c. 60 percent   **d.** 90 percent

Forms of Carbon (page 263)

3. Circle the letter of each form of carbon.
   a. soot   **b.** diamond
   c. fullerenes   **d.** graphite

4. Describe a network solid. A network solid is a solid in which all the atoms are linked by covalent bonds.

5. Circle the letter of each property of graphite.
   a. soft   b. rigid
   c. compact   **d.** slippery

Saturated Hydrocarbons (pages 264–265)

6. Is the following sentence true or false? A hydrocarbon is an organic compound that contains carbon, hydrogen, and oxygen. ___ false ___

7. Is the following sentence true or false? A saturated hydrocarbon contains only single bonds. ___ true ___

Physical Science Guided Reading and Study Workbook • Chapter 9   **75**

Guided Reading and Study Workbook

Name _____ Class _____ Date _____

Chapter 9   Carbon Chemistry

8. Name the factors that determine the properties of a hydrocarbon.
   a. The number of carbon atoms   b. How the atoms are arranged

9. Name the three ways that carbon atoms can be arranged in hydrocarbon molecules.
   a. A straight chain   b. A branched chain   c. A ring

10. Circle the letter of the correct answer. What does a structural formula show that a molecular formula does not?
    a. the type of atoms in the compound
    b. the number of atoms in a molecule of the compound
    c. the arrangement of atoms in the compound
    d. the state of the compound at room temperature

11. Describe isomers. Isomers are compounds that have the same molecular formula but different structural formulas.

Unsaturated Hydrocarbons (page 266)

12. Circle the letter of each type of unsaturated hydrocarbon.
    a. alkene   b. alkane
    c. alkyne   **d.** aromatic hydrocarbon

13. Circle the letter of the most reactive type of hydrocarbon.
    a. alkanes   b. alkenes
    c. alkynes   d. aromatic hydrocarbons

Fossil Fuels (page 267–268)

14. Define fossil fuels. Fossil fuels are mixtures of hydrocarbons that formed from the remains of plants or animals.

15. Circle the letter of each fossil fuel.
    a. coal   **b.** natural gas
    c. ferns   **d.** petroleum

16. Is the following sentence true or false? In a distillation tower, compounds with lower boiling points condense first. ___ false ___

Combustion of Fossil Fuels (pages 268–269)

17. Circle the letter of each primary product of the complete combustion of fossil fuels.
    a. carbon dioxide   b. carbon monoxide
    c. sulfur dioxide   **d.** water

18. When an insufficient amount of oxygen is available for complete combustion of a fossil fuel, one product of the combustion reaction is the deadly gas ___ carbon monoxide ___.

19. Why is rain always slightly acidic? Carbon dioxide dissolves in water droplets and forms carbonic acid.

76   *Physical Science* Guided Reading and Study Workbook • Chapter 9

LESSON PLAN 9.2

Substituted Hydrocarbons

Time
2 periods
1 block

Section Objectives

- **9.2.1 Classify** substituted hydrocarbons based on their functional groups.
- **9.2.2 Describe** some properties and reactions of five types of substituted hydrocarbons.

Vocabulary substituted hydrocarbon • functional group

Local Standards

1 FOCUS

Build Vocabulary: Word Forms

Have students look up the words *substitute* and *functional*. Have them write a prediction for the meanings of the vocabulary words for this section. After students study the section, have them discuss whether their predictions were correct or not. **L2**

Targeted Resources

❏ Transparency: Interest Grabber 9.2
❏ Transparency: Reading Strategy 9.2

2 INSTRUCT

Build Reading Literacy: Compare and Contrast

Have students read pages 273 and 274 and ask them how organic acids and bases differ. Ask how organic acids and bases are similar. **L1**

Teacher Demo: Modeling Functional Groups

Demonstrate any appliance and the functions of its attachments. Students should see the analogy between the appliance's attachments and functional groups. **L2**

Address Misconceptions

Have students smell some fragrant objects, such as fruit or flowers. Explain that some of the compounds responsible for the odors are esters. **L2**

Use Community Resources

Have a pharmacist speak to the class about how functional groups determine the effect of a medicine. **L2**

Targeted Resources

❏ GRSW Section 9.2

3 ASSESS

Reteach

Use short phrases to summarize the characteristics of functional groups. **L1**

Evaluate Understanding

Have students design and play a matching game that uses cards that identify the formulas and characteristics of each functional group described in the section. **L2**

Targeted Resources

❏ **PHSchool.com** Online Section 9.2 Assessment
❏ iText Section 9.2

Transparencies

125 **Section 9.2 Interest Grabber**

Comparing Models

Your teacher has made ball-and-stick models of compounds with the formulas CH_4 and CH_3Cl.

1. How are the two compounds similar?

2. How are the two compounds different?

3. What is the name of the compound with the formula CH_4?

ANSWERS
1. In both compounds a carbon atom is bonded to four other atoms.
2. In the compound with the formula CH₃Cl, a hydrogen atom has been replaced with a chlorine atom.
3. The compound with the formula CH₄ is methane.

Transparencies

126 **Section 9.2 Reading Strategy**

Monitoring Your Understanding

Functional Group	Type of Compound
–OH	a. ?
–COOH	b. ?
–NH₂	c. ?

ANSWERS
a. alcohol
b. organic acid
c. organic base

Guided Reading and Study Workbook

Name _____ Class _____ Date _____

Chapter 9   Carbon Chemistry

Section 9.2 Substituted Hydrocarbons
(pages 272–274)

This section discusses organic compounds that contain atoms of elements other than carbon and hydrogen. It also explains the relationship between the properties of organic compounds and functional groups.

Reading Strategy (page 272)

Monitoring Your Understanding As you read, complete the table by connecting each functional group with the type of compound that contains the functional group. For more information on this Reading Strategy, see the **Reading and Study Skills** in the **Skills and Reference Handbook** at the end of your textbook.

Connecting Functional Groups to Types of Compounds	
Functional Group	**Type of Compound**
–OH	Alcohol
–COOH	Organic acid
–NH₂	Organic base

1. Name the two main products when methane and chlorine react.
   a. ___Hydrogen chloride___
   b. ___Chloromethane___

2. To which environmental problem have researchers connected halocarbons containing chlorine and fluorine? Halocarbons containing chlorine and fluorine are connected to the depletion of Earth's protective ozone layer.

3. Describe a substituted hydrocarbon. A substituted hydrocarbon is a hydrocarbon in which one or more hydrogen atoms have been replaced by an atom or group of atoms.

4. Is the following sentence true or false? The functional group in a substituted hydrocarbon determines the properties of the compound. ___true___

Alcohols (page 273)

5. Methanol and ethanol are two examples of a class of organic compounds called ___alcohols___.

6. The functional group in an alcohol is represented as –OH and is called a(n) ___hydroxyl___ group.

7. Identify two ways a halocarbon can be produced.
   a. ___A halocarbon reacts with a base___
   b. ___An alkene reacts with water___

Guided Reading and Study Workbook

Name _____ Class _____ Date _____

Chapter 9   Carbon Chemistry

Organic Acids and Bases (pages 273–274)

8. What two physical properties do organic acids tend to have?
   a. ___A sharp taste___
   b. ___A strong odor___

9. Is the following sentence true or false? Amines are organic bases. ___true___

10. Name three products where amines can be found.
    a. ___Paints___
    b. ___Dyes___
    c. ___Disinfectants___

11. Complete the following table.

Substituted Hydrocarbons		
Type of Compound	**Name of Functional Group**	**Formula of Functional Group**
Alcohol	Hydroxyl	–OH
Organic acid	Carboxyl	–COOH
Organic base	Amino	–NH₂

Esters (page 274)

12. What type of compound gives many flowers a pleasant odor? ___Esters___

13. Which two types of compounds can react and form esters?
    a. ___Organic acid___
    b. ___Alcohol___

14. Circle the letter of the other product of the reaction that forms an ester.
    a. an alcohol
    b. carbon dioxide
    c. a salt
    (d) water

15. Is the following sentence true or false? Esters are used to make various fruit flavors in processed foods. ___true___

LESSON PLAN 9.3

Polymers

Time
2 periods
1 block

Section Objectives

- **9.3.1** **Distinguish** a monomer from a polymer.
- **9.3.2** **Compare** three examples of synthetic polymers.
- **9.3.3** **Describe** the structures and functions of four types of natural polymers.

Vocabulary polymer • monomers • carbohydrates • nucleic acids • amino acid • protein

Local Standards

---

1 FOCUS

Build Vocabulary: Word-Part Analysis
Have students break the vocabulary terms *polymer*, *monomer*, and *carbohydrate* into roots, prefixes, or suffixes. Students may need to use a dictionary to find the meanings of some parts. **L2**

Targeted Resources
❏ Transparency: Interest Grabber 9.3
❏ Transparency: Reading Strategy 9.3

---

2 INSTRUCT

Build Reading Literacy: Use Prior Knowledge
Before students read, ask them to list different fibers used to make fabrics. Have them discuss which fibers they think are natural and identify their sources. **L1**

Integrate Social Studies
Have students research current efforts to recycle plastics, including codes used on plastic products. Have students use posters or computer graphics to prepare a report on their research. **L2**

Quick Lab: Distinguishing Sugars From Starches
Students will use iodine to test for the presence of starch in foods. **L2**

Build Science Skills: Comparing and Contrasting
Have students compare and contrast proteins and nucleic acids. Ask them what these two types of polymers have in common and how they differ. **L2**

Integrate Health
Have students research and prepare posters showing foods that provide the complete set of essential amino acids. **L2**

For Enrichment
Have students work in pairs and devise an experiment to compare two types of commercially-available adhesives. **L3**

Targeted Resources
❏ GRSW Section 9.3
❏ **NSTA** *sci*$_{INKS}$ Polymers

---

3 ASSESS

Reteach
Use the equation in the text on pages 276 and 278 to compare a synthetic and a natural polymer. **L1**

Evaluate Understanding
Have students write down the following list of polymers: polyethylene, starch, cellulose, nucleic acid, and proteins. Then, have students identify the monomers for each polymer. **L2**

Targeted Resources
❏ **PHSchool.com** Online Section 9.3 Assessment
❏ iText Section 9.3

Transparencies

127 **Section 9.3 Interest Grabber**

Making Large Structures From Small Units

Work with a partner. Use five pieces of construction paper of different colors. Cut each piece of paper into narrow strips. Mix all the strips together in a pile. Have your partner start making a chain of paper links using random strips of paper from the pile. Then choose one color for yourself and make a chain of paper links using only that color.

1. How are the two paper-link chains similar?

2. How are the two paper-link chains different?

3. *Mono-* means "one" and *poly-* means many. To which structure in the activity could *mono* apply? To which structure could *poly* apply?

Transparencies

128 **Section 9.3 Reading Strategy**

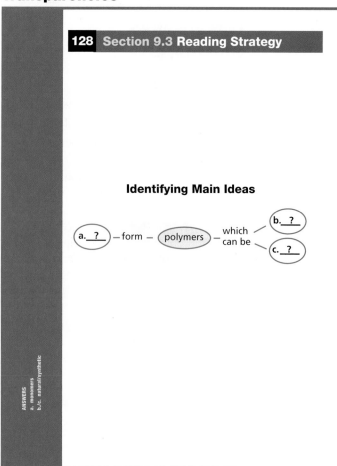

Identifying Main Ideas

a. ___?___ — form — polymers — which can be — b. ___?___ / c. ___?___

Guided Reading and Study Workbook

Name _____ Class _____ Date _____

Chapter 9   Carbon Chemistry

Section 9.3 Polymers
(pages 275–280)

This section explains how polymers form. It also discusses examples of synthetic and natural polymers.

Reading Strategy (page 275)

Identifying Main Ideas As you read, complete the concept map to summarize two main ideas about polymers. For more information on this Reading Strategy, see the **Reading and Study Skills** in the **Skills and Reference Handbook** at the end of your textbook.

Monomers — form — polymers — which can be — natural / synthetic

1. Describe a polymer. A polymer is a large molecule that forms when many smaller molecules are linked together by covalent bonds.

2. The smaller molecules that join together to form a polymer are called _____monomers_____.

3. Is the following sentence true or false? More than one type of monomer can be present in some polymers. ____true____

4. Name the two general classifications of polymers.
   a. ____Natural____ b. ____Synthetic____

Synthetic Polymers (page 276)

5. Name three polymers that can be synthesized.
   a. ___Polyethylene___ b. ___Nylon___ c. ___Rubber___

6. Is the following sentence true or false? The more carbon atoms there are in a polyethylene chain, the harder the polymer is. ____true____

Natural Polymers (pages 278–280)

7. Name four types of polymers that are produced in plant and animal cells.
   a. ___Starches___ b. ___Nucleic acids___
   c. ___Cellulose___ d. ___Proteins___

8. Circle the letter of the molecular formula of a simple sugar.
   a. CH_2O b. $C_6H_{12}O_6$
   c. $C_{12}H_{22}O_{11}$ d. $C_{12}H_{24}O_{12}$

Guided Reading and Study Workbook

Name _____ Class _____ Date _____

Chapter 9   Carbon Chemistry

9. Circle the letter of the simple sugar glucose and fructose can react to form.
   a. glucose b. fructose
   c. cellulose d. sucrose

10. How are starches used in plants? Plants store starches for food and to build stems, seeds, and roots.

11. Simple sugars, slightly more complex sugars, and polymers built from sugar monomers are classified as ___carbohydrates___.

12. Circle the letter of the main component of cotton and wood.
    a. cellulose b. glucose
    c. protein d. starch

13. Define nucleic acids. Nucleic acids are large nitrogen-containing polymers found mainly in the nuclei of cells.

14. Name the two types of nucleic acid.
    a. ___Deoxyribonucleic acid (DNA)___ b. ___Ribonucleic acid (RNA)___

15. Name the three parts of a nucleotide in DNA.
    a. ___Phosphate group___ b. ___Deoxyribose sugar___ c. ___Organic base___

16. Circle the letter of the term that best describes the structure of DNA.
    a. helix b. double helix
    c. ring d. chain

17. How does DNA store information? The order of the base pairs in a strand is a code that is used to produce proteins.

18. Is the following sentence true or false? The human body can manufacture all of the essential amino acids. ____false____

19. Amino acids are the monomers that cells use to build the polymers known as ___proteins___.

20. Complete the following concept map about amino acids.

Amino Acids
— contain —
Carboxyl / Amino
functional groups, which form the bonds in
Proteins

LESSON PLAN 9.4

Reactions in Cells

Time
2 periods
1 block

Section Objectives

- **9.4.1 Compare** photosynthesis and cellular respiration.
- **9.4.2 Explain** how enzymes and vitamins help reactions take place in cells.

Vocabulary photosynthesis • enzymes • vitamins

Local Standards

1 FOCUS

Build Vocabulary: Web Diagram
Have students create a web diagram relating the terms *photosynthesis, cellular respiration, glucose, energy, carbohydrates, digestion,* and *polymers.* **L2**

Targeted Resources
❏ Transparency: Interest Grabber 9.4
❏ Transparency: Reading Strategy 9.4

2 INSTRUCT

Build Reading Literacy: Sequence
Have students create a flowchart that follows a carbon atom through photosynthesis and cellular respiration. Have students mark where oxygen, water, and energy enter and exit the overall process. **L1**

Integrate Biology
Have interested students research chlorophyll's structure. **L2**

Address Misconceptions
Students may confuse cellular respiration, respiration, and breathing. Explain the difference between the three processes. **L2**

Teacher Demo: Photosynthesis and Cellular Respiration
Use methylene blue and an *elodea* sprig to help students learn about the products of photosynthesis and cellular respiration. **L2**

Teacher Demo: Denaturing an Enzyme
Use a potato to show students how enzyme activity is affected by temperature. **L2**

Targeted Resources
❏ Transparency: Figure 19: Photosynthesis and Cellular Respiration
❏ GRSW Section 9.4

3 ASSESS

Reteach
Have students use Figure 19 to review the relationships between photosynthesis and cellular respiration. **L1**

Evaluate Understanding
Have groups of students write four review questions with answers. **L2**

Targeted Resources
❏ **PHSchool.com** Online Section 9.4 Assessment
❏ iText Section 9.4

Transparencies

129 Section 9.4 Interest Grabber

Examining a Cellular Process

The equation below summarizes the process of photosynthesis, which takes place in plants.

water + carbon dioxide + light ⟶
carbohydrates + oxygen

1. Identify the reactants.

2. Identify the products.

3. Is the reaction exothermic or endothermic?

ANSWERS
1. The reactants are water and carbon dioxide.
2. The products are carbohydrates and oxygen.
3. The reaction is endothermic.

Transparencies

130 Section 9.4 Reading Strategy

Summarizing

Heading	Main Idea
Photosynthesis	a. ?
Cellular Respiration	b. ?
Enzymes and Vitamins	c. ?

c. Enzymes and vitamins are compounds that help cells function efficiently at normal body temperature.

ANSWERS
a. During photosynthesis, energy from sunlight is converted into chemical energy.
b. During cellular respiration, the energy stored in products of photosynthesis is released.

Transparencies

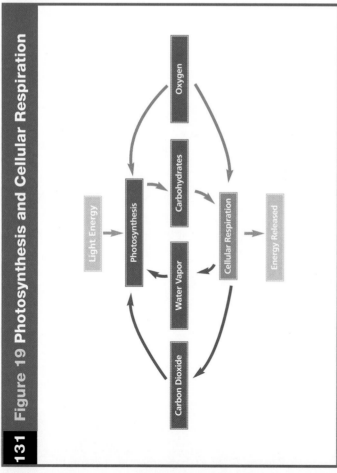

131 Figure 19 Photosynthesis and Cellular Respiration

Guided Reading and Study Workbook

Name _____ Class _____ Date _____

Chapter 9   Carbon Chemistry

Section 9.4 Reactions in Cells
(pages 282–284)

This section describes and compares photosynthesis and cellular respiration. It also discusses the roles of enzymes and vitamins.

Reading Strategy (page 282)

Summarizing As you read, complete the table by recording a main idea for each heading. For more information on this Reading Strategy, see the **Reading and Study Skills** in the **Skills and Reference Handbook** at the end of your textbook.

Heading	Main Idea
Photosynthesis	During photosynthesis, energy from sunlight is converted into chemical energy.
Cellular Respiration	During cellular respiration, the energy stored in the products of photosynthesis is released.
Enzymes and Vitamins	Enzymes and vitamins are compounds that help cells function efficiently at normal body temperature.

1. Two processes that allow organisms to meet their energy needs are __photosynthesis__ and __cellular respiration__.

Photosynthesis (page 282)

2. Describe what happens during photosynthesis. During photosynthesis, plants chemically combine carbon dioxide and water into carbohydrates.

3. Circle the letter of each requirement for photosynthesis to occur.
   (a.) chlorophyll   b. oxygen
   c. carbohydrates   (d.) light

4. Identify the energy conversion that takes place during photosynthesis. Energy from sunlight is converted into chemical energy.

5. Circle the letter of each product of photosynthesis.
   a. carbon dioxide   (b.) carbohydrates
   (c.) oxygen   d. water

6. Is the following sentence true or false? When all the reactions in photosynthesis are complete, energy from sunlight has been stored in the covalent bonds of molecules. __true__

Cellular Respiration (page 283)

7. During cellular respiration, the __energy__ stored in the products of photosynthesis is released.

Name _____ Class _____ Date _____

Chapter 9   Carbon Chemistry

8. How is cellular respiration related to photosynthesis? Each process produces
the reactants for the other process.

9. Is the following sentence true or false? Carbohydrates produce more energy per
gram than fats do. _____ false

10. Complete the diagram relating photosynthesis to cellular respiration.
   a. _____ Water vapor   b. _____ Oxygen   c. _____ Energy released

Enzymes and Vitamins (page 284)

11. Describe what enzymes and vitamins have in common. Enzymes and vitamins
help cells function efficiently at normal body temperature.

12. Define enzymes. Enzymes are proteins that act as catalysts for reactions in cells.

13. Is the following sentence true or false? Enzymes require high
temperatures in order to function. _____ false

14. Is the following sentence true or false? Some enzymes require a
co-enzyme in order to function. _____ true

15. Define vitamins. Vitamins are organic compounds that organisms need in small amounts,
but cannot produce.

16. Is the following sentence true or false? All vitamins dissolve in
water and must be replaced daily. _____ false

17. Identify the property of vitamin A that allows it to build up in
body tissues over time. _____ Vitamin A dissolves in fats.

Name _____ Class _____ Date _____

Chapter 9   Carbon Chemistry

WordWise

Complete the following crossword puzzle, using the clues provided below.

Clues across:

1. A hydrocarbon in which all of the
   bonds are single bonds
2. A compound containing carbon and
   hydrogen, often combined with other
   elements such as oxygen and nitrogen
3. A small molecule that joins with other
   small molecules to form a polymer
4. _____ acid: a large nitrogen-containing
   polymer found mainly in the nuclei
   of cells
5. Organic compounds that contain only
   carbon and hydrogen

Clues down:

6. An organic compound that organisms
   need in small amounts, but cannot
   produce
7. Organic compounds that contain both
   carboxyl and amino functional
   groups
8. Compounds with the same molecular
   formula but different structural
   formulas
9. A polymer in which at least 100
   amino acid monomers are linked
   through bonds between an amino
   group and a carboxyl group
10. _____ solid: a type of solid in which
    all of the atoms are linked by covalent
    bonds

Name _____ Class _____ Date _____

Chapter 9   Carbon Chemistry

Balancing Equations for Organic Reactions

Math Skill:
Ratios and
Proportions

When propane, C_3H_8, combines with oxygen, the products are
carbon dioxide and water. Write a balanced equation for the
complete combustion of propane.

You may want to read
more about this **Math**
Skill *in the* **Skills and**
Reference Handbook
at the end of your
textbook.

1. Read and Understand

What information are you given?

   Reactants = propane (C_3H_8) and oxygen (O_2)

   Products = carbon dioxide (CO_2) and water (H_2O)

2. Plan and Solve

What unknowns are you trying to determine?

   The coefficients for the equation

What equation contains the given information?

   $C_3H_8 + O_2 \longrightarrow CO_2 + H_2O$ (unbalanced equation)

First, balance the equation for carbon. Because there are 3 carbon atoms in
C_3H_8, you need to place the coefficient 3 in front of CO_2.

   $C_3H_8 + O_2 \longrightarrow 3CO_2 + H_2O$

Next, balance the equation for hydrogen. Because there are 8 hydrogen
atoms in C_3H_8 and only 2 hydrogen atoms in H_2O, you need to place the
coefficient 4 in front of H_2O.

   $C_3H_8 + O_2 \longrightarrow 3CO_2 + 4H_2O$

Finally, balance the equation for oxygen. Because there are 6 oxygen atoms
in 3 molecules of CO_2 and 4 oxygen atoms in 4 molecules of H_2O for a
total of 10 oxygen atoms, you need to place the coefficient 5 in front of O_2.

   $C_3H_8 + 5O_2 \longrightarrow 3CO_2 + 4H_2O$

3. Look Back and Check

Is your answer reasonable?

   Each side of the equation has 3 carbon atoms, 8 hydrogen atoms,
   and 10 oxygen atoms. The equation is balanced.

Math Practice

On a separate sheet of paper, solve the following problems.

1. Balance the equation for the reaction of benzene and hydrogen to
form cyclohexane.

   $C_6H_6 + \underline{\ 3\ } H_2 \xrightarrow{Pt} C_6H_{12}$

2. Write a balanced equation for the complete combustion of
methane, CH_4. $CH_4 + 2O_2 \longrightarrow CO_2 + 2H_2O$

3. Write a balanced equation for the combustion of glucose, $C_6H_{12}O_6$.
   $C_6H_{12}O_6 + 6O_2 \longrightarrow 6CO_2 + 6H_2O$

Name _____ Class _____ Date _____

Chapter 9   Carbon Chemistry   Consumer Lab

Comparing Vitamin C in Fruit Juices

See page 285 in the Teacher's Edition
for more information.

Various brands of juices often claim to be good sources of vitamin C, but
which juices are the best sources? Vitamin C is an organic acid called
ascorbic acid. Like other organic acids, vitamin C reacts with indicators to
produce a color change. This reaction can be used to determine the amount of
vitamin C present in foods, such as fruit juices. In this lab, you will add an
indicator to a sample of apple juice. The indicator will change color when all
the vitamin C has reacted. Then, you will test and compare the vitamin C
content in other juices with the results for apple juice.

Problem Which juice provides the most vitamin C?

Materials
• apple juice
• a variety of other fruit juices
• test tubes and rack
• 10-mL graduated cylinder
• methylene blue indicator
• dropper pipet
• stirring rods
• graph paper

Skills Observing, Measuring, Analyzing Data

Procedure 🔲 🔦 ✅ 🔧
Part A: Measuring Vitamin C in Apple Juice

1. Use a graduated cylinder to measure 10 mL of apple juice. Pour the
juice into a test tube.

2. Add a drop of methylene blue indicator to the test tube. Stir until
the color of the indicator disappears.

3. Add more indicator, one drop at a time, stirring after each addition.
Count the drops that you add. Stop adding the indicator when the
last drop of indicator does not change color. Record the number of
drops that you used in the data table.

DATA TABLE

Type of Juice	Number of Drops
Apple	

Student Edition Lab Worksheet

Name _____ Class _____ Date _____

Part B: Measuring Vitamin C in Other Juices

4. Formulate and record a hypothesis about which juice will have the greatest amount of vitamin C. You will need to decide which variables must be kept the same, as well as how to account for bits of solid in some juices.

_____

_____

5. List the steps in your procedure and write the names of each of the juices to be tested in the left column of the data table.

_____

_____

_____

_____

_____

_____

6. Have your teacher check your procedure before you begin your experiment.

Analyze and Conclude

1. Using Graphs Make a bar graph of your data. Which juice required the most drops of indicator? Which required the least?

The graph and answers will vary depending on the samples tested.

_____

_____

2. Drawing Conclusions Based on your data, which juice contained the most vitamin C? How did you reach this conclusion?

The juice that required the most drops of methylene blue indicator is the one that contained the

most vitamin C.

3. Evaluating and Revising What unexpected problems did you encounter? Explain how you could revise your procedure to avoid these problems.

Acceptable answers include that juices with large amounts of pulp were a problem. Students

may suggest filtering those samples, but removing the pulp removes some of the vitamin C.

(Students could process the samples in a blender instead.) Students may also state that dark juices,

such as prune juice or grape juice, obscure the color change. Students might suggest diluting all

samples with the same amount of distilled water.

Lab Manual

Name _____ Class _____ Date _____

Chapter 9   Carbon Chemistry   **Investigation 9A**

Testing for Nutrients in Foods

Background Information

Nutrients are those substances in food that are necessary for health. There are three main classes of organic nutrients. The first class, **carbohydrates,** consists of sugars and starches, which are polymers of the sugar glucose. The second class, lipids, includes fats and oils. The third class consists of **proteins,** which are polymers of amino acids. Because the compounds in each class of nutrients contain different functional groups, a different chemical test can be used to detect each type of nutrient.

For carbohydrates, there are two tests, one to detect sugars and one to detect starches. A mixture called Benedict's solution changes color when it is heated with many types of sugars, and a solution of iodine changes color in the presence of starch. A solution of copper sulfate, called biuret reagent, changes color when it reacts with proteins. A bright red dye called Sudan IV dissolves in lipids, but not in water. If a material has the ability to dissolve Sudan IV dye, this is a sign that the material contains lipids.

In this investigation, you will observe the reaction of each of these test materials with samples of glucose (a sugar), starch, vegetable oil, and powdered gelatin (protein). Then, you will design an experiment using each of the test materials to determine which classes of organic nutrients are present in several foods.

Problem

Which foods contain sugars, starches, lipids, and proteins?

Pre-Lab Discussion

Read the entire investigation. Then, work with a partner to answer the following questions.

1. Controlling Variables Why is a test tube of water included in the Procedure for Part A of this investigation? Explain your answer.

The test tube is a control. Tests on the water will be negative, allowing easy comparison to positive

tests for other materials.

2. Predicting In Part A of this investigation, which food substance(s) do you expect to react with each test material?

a. Benedict's solution

Glucose

b. Iodine solution

Cornstarch

Refer students to pages 278, 280, and 283 in their textbooks for a discussion of carbohydrates, proteins, and digestion. **SKILLS FOCUS:** Observing, Analyzing Data, Comparing and Contrasting, Designing Experiments **CLASS TIME:** Part A, 35 Minutes; Part B, 45 minutes

---

Lab Manual

Name _____ Class _____ Date _____

c. Sudan IV dye

Vegetable oil

d. Biuret reagent

Gelatin

3. Controlling Variables Identify the manipulated, responding, and controlled variables in Part A of this investigation.

a. Manipulated variables

Food substances

b. Responding variables

Reactions between test materials and food substances

c. Controlled variables

Chemical test procedures

4. Predicting Which nutrients do you think are present in each food that you will test in Part B of this investigation?

a. Orange juice

Sugar

b. Potato

Starch (Some potatoes contain enough sugar to detect with Benedict's solution.)

c. Whole milk

Proteins, lipids, sugar

d. Skim milk

Proteins, sugar

e. Margarine

Lipids

f. Egg yolk

Lipids, proteins

g. Egg white

Proteins

Lab Manual

Name _____ Class _____ Date _____

5. Designing Experiments Describe a set of procedures you could use in Part B to test your predictions.

Students should describe a modification of the procedures in Part A to test each

food for the presence of sugar, starch, lipids, and proteins.

_____

_____

_____

_____

_____

_____

_____

_____

_____

_____

_____

_____

_____

Materials *(per group)*

500-mL beaker	tongs	Benedict's solution and biuret reagent can be purchased. They can also be prepared. To prepare Benedict's solution, dissolve 173 g sodium citrate ($Na_3C_6H_5O_7 \cdot 2H_2O$) and 200 g sodium carbonate (Na_2CO_3) in 800 mL of distilled water. Do not use sodium bicarbonate. Separately, dissolve 17.3 g of copper sulfate ($CuSO_4$) in 100 mL of distilled water. Mix the two solutions slowly and add distilled water to bring the volume to 1 liter.
hot plate	clock or watch	
paper towel	iodine solution	
glass-marking pencil	Sudan IV dye	
5 test tubes	5 stoppers for test tubes	
test-tube rack	biuret reagent	
4 spatulas	orange juice	
glucose	minced potato	
cornstarch	whole milk	
powdered gelatin	skim milk	To prepare biuret reagent, make a 0.1 *M* solution of sodium hydroxide by dissolving 4 g NaOH in 1 L of water. Add 2.2 g $CuSO_4 \cdot 5H_2O$. Prepare fresh biuret reagent no more than one day in advance and store it away from light.
2 dropper pipets	margarine	
vegetable oil	egg yolk	
3 10-mL graduated cylinders	egg white	
Benedict's solution		Because of the quantity of materials required for this investigation, you may want students to work in groups of three or four.

Lab Manual

Name _____ Class _____ Date _____

Safety 🥽🧤🔬🧪🔥🧹🧫🌡️⚠️

Put on safety goggles and a lab apron. Wear plastic disposable gloves when handling chemicals, as they may irritate the skin or stain skin or clothing. Be careful to avoid breakage when working with glassware. Use extreme care when working with heated equipment or materials to avoid burns. Keep Sudan IV dye away from any open flame. Observe proper laboratory procedures when using electrical equipment. Never touch or taste any chemical unless instructed to do so. Wash your hands thoroughly after carrying out this investigation. Note all safety alert symbols next to the steps in the Procedure and review the meaning of each symbol by referring to the Safety Symbols on page xiii.

You may wish to boil the eggs in advance to reduce the hazard of Salmonella contamination. If you do, remind students that they will need to find a way to test the insoluble cooked egg white and yolk.

Design Your Experiment
Part A: Observing Chemical Tests for Nutrients

1. Fill a 500-mL beaker about one-fourth of the way with water. Place the beaker on the hot plate. Turn the hot plate to a high setting and bring the water to a boil. **CAUTION:** *Be careful using the hot plate and handling boiling water and hot glassware.*

2. On a sheet of paper towel, write *glucose, cornstarch, gelatin,* and *vegetable oil* near different corners of the towel.

3. Use a glass-marking pencil to label five test tubes 1 through 5 and place them in the test-tube rack. Using a separate clean spatula for each substance and just enough of each substance to cover the end of the spatula, place glucose in test tube 1, cornstarch in test tube 2, and gelatin in test tube 3. Use a dropper pipet to place 4 drops of vegetable oil in test tube 4. Store the spatulas and pipet in the appropriate places on the paper towel when they are not in use.

4. Use a graduated cylinder to add 3 mL of water to each test tube, including test tube 5.

5. Fill each of the test tubes halfway with Benedict's solution.

6. Use tongs to place the test tubes into the beaker of boiling water. Leave the test tubes in the boiling water for 5 minutes.

7. After 5 minutes have passed, use tongs to return each test tube to the test-tube rack. Observe any changes in the appearance of the contents of each test tube. Record your observations in Data Table 1.

8. Thoroughly wash the five test tubes and discard the contents in the sink. Carefully dry the test tubes and place them back in the test-tube rack.

9. Repeat Steps 3 and 4.

10. Use a dropper pipet to add 1 or 2 drops of iodine solution to each test tube. Note whether the iodine remains brown or if it changes to another color. Record your observations in Data Table 1.

11. Again, wash and dry the test tubes, and repeat Steps 3 and 4.

12. Use a clean spatula to add a few grains of Sudan IV dye to each test tube. **CAUTION:** *Do not get any on your skin or clothing. Keep the dye away from any open flames.*

Lab Manual

Name _____ Class _____ Date _____

13. Place a stopper firmly into each test tube and shake the test tubes gently. Observe whether the dye has been absorbed by any material in the test tube. Record your observations in Data Table 1. **CAUTION:** *Make sure that the test tubes are securely closed to avoid spilling.*

14. Wash and dry the test tubes, and repeat Steps 3 and 4. Use a clean dropper pipet to add 3 drops of biuret reagent to each test tube. Observe any changes in the appearance of the contents of each test tube. Record your observations in Data Table 1. **CAUTION:** *Biuret reagent is poisonous and can burn and stain skin and clothing.*

Part B: Using Chemical Tests to Identify Nutrients

15. Design an experiment to test the predictions you made in Pre-Lab Discussion Question 4. Write a detailed plan of how you will carry out your experiment. Use your knowledge of chemical tests for organic nutrients from Part A of this investigation to help you plan your procedures. Construct Data Table 2 in which to record your observations in the space provided on page 94.

    Experimental designs should be based on the tests used in Part A.

    _____
    _____
    _____
    _____

16. What are the manipulated, responding, and controlled variables in your experiment?
    a. Manipulated variables
    Typical experimental designs will list the foods as manipulated variables.

    b. Responding variables
    Typical experimental designs will list the reactions between the test materials and foods as the responding variable.

    c. Controlled variables
    Controlled variables may include the volume or mass of each food tested, the volume of water added to each sample, and the procedure for performing each test.

17. What safety precautions will you need to take?
    Check students' plans for appropriate safety precautions. Students should wear safety goggles, lab aprons, and plastic gloves when working with the test chemicals. Monitor students closely when they work with hazardous chemicals or hot equipment.

18. Show your written experimental plan to your teacher. When your teacher approves your plan, carry out your experiment and record your observations.

Lab Manual

Name _____ Class _____ Date _____

Observations Sample data are shown.

DATA TABLE 1

Test Tube	Food	Benedict's Solution	Iodine Solution	Sudan IV Dye	Biuret Reagent
1	Sugar	Red-yellow	No change	No change	No change
2	Cornstarch	No change	Blue-black	No change	No change
3	Gelatin	No change	No change	No change	Pink-violet
4	Vegetable oil	No change	No change	Red-orange	No change
5	Water	No change	No change	No change	No change

DATA TABLE 2
If you need more space, attach additional sheets of paper.

Food	Benedict's Solution	Iodine Solution	Sudan IV Dye	Biuret Reagent
Orange juice	Red-yellow	No change	No change	No change
Potato	Red-yellow	Blue-black	No change	No change
Whole milk	Red-yellow	No change	Red-orange	Pink-violet
Skim milk	Red-yellow	No change	No change	Pink-violet
Margarine	No change	No change	Red-orange	No change
Egg yolk	No change	No change	Red-orange	Pink-violet
Egg white	No change	No change	No change	Pink-violet
Water	No change	No change	No change	No change

Lab Manual

Name _____ Class _____ Date _____

Analysis and Conclusions

1. **Observing** Which food(s) reacted with Benedict's solution in Part B?
   Orange juice, potato, whole milk, and skim milk reacted.

2. **Observing** Which food(s) reacted with iodine solution?
   The potato reacted.

3. **Analyzing Data** What change did you observe in the Sudan IV dye test? Which foods caused this change?
   A red-orange color from the dissolving dye spread through the whole milk, margarine, and egg yolk.

4. **Analyzing Data** What color change did you observe for the biuret solution test? Which foods caused this change?
   A pink-to-violet color appeared for the whole milk, skim milk, egg yolk, and egg white.

5. **Comparing and Contrasting** Based on your data from Part B, what is the major difference between whole milk and skim milk?
   Based on the results of the Sudan IV test, whole milk contains lipids but there is no noticeable amount of lipids in skim milk.

6. **Comparing and Contrasting** Which nutrient did you find in the egg yolk that you did not find in the egg white?
   The egg yolk contains lipids.

Lab Manual

Name _____ Class _____ Date _____

7. **Evaluating and Revising** Which of your predictions did your data support?

Answers should be consistent with student predictions and data.

_____
_____
_____
_____
_____
_____

8. **Drawing Conclusions** On a diet consisting almost entirely of milk, human babies grow rapidly and maintain good health. Use your data to explain how this is possible.

Milk contains substances from all three groups of organic nutrients—carbohydrates (in the form

of sugar), lipids, and proteins.

_____
_____
_____

Go Further

Benedict's solution does not react with all sugars. Design an experiment to compare the reactions of Benedict's solution with various sugars. After your teacher approves your experimental plan, obtain samples of several sugars and perform your experiment. Then, use a biology or chemistry textbook to determine the molecular structures of the sugars you used in your experiment. Compare your data to these structures. Formulate a hypothesis about the relationship between the molecular structure of a sugar and its ability to react with Benedict's solution.

Benedict's solution reacts with sugars that have a carbonyl group (a double bond between a
carbon atom and an oxygen atom). These sugars are called reducing sugars. They include all
monosaccharides, such as glucose and fructose, and most disaccharides, such as lactose.
The major exception is sucrose. (When glucose and fructose join to form sucrose, the bond
forms between carbon atoms in the carbonyl group.)

Lab Manual

Name _____ Class _____ Date _____

Cross-Linked Polymers

Refer students to pages 275–280 in their textbooks for a discussion of polymers. **SKILLS FOCUS:** Observing, Inferring, Comparing and Contrasting **CLASS TIME:** 30 minutes over 2 days (Day 1, 15 minutes; Day 2, 15 minutes)

Background Information

A **polymer** is a large molecule that forms when smaller molecules called monomers are linked together through covalent bonds. In some polymers, all of the monomer molecules are identical. Other polymers contain more than one type of monomer. Under certain conditions, two polymer molecules can be joined at different locations along the molecule by covalent bonds called cross-links. These links can also form between two sections of a single polymer molecule. The existence of cross-links can make the polymer more elastic (able to return to its original shape after being pushed or pulled) and stronger (harder to tear apart).

Some cross-linked polymers form a type of colloid called a gel when they are dispersed in a liquid such as water. Gels have a loose, irregular structure, which prevents the liquid from flowing. In a water-based gel, the amount of water also affects the physical properties of the gel. Adding water to a gel makes it more like a liquid in its properties. Reducing the amount of water makes the gel more like a solid.

In this investigation, you will observe the properties of cross-linked protein polymers in gelatin.

Figure 1

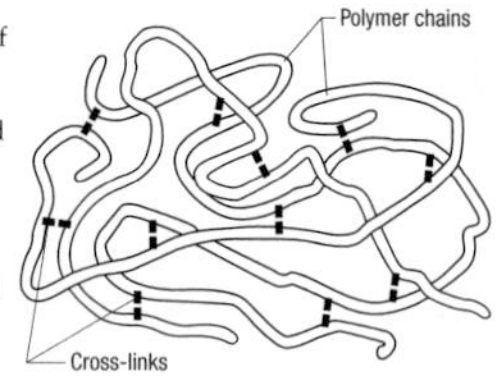

Polymer chains
Cross-links

Problem

How does cross-linking affect the physical properties of polymers?

Pre-Lab Discussion

Read the entire investigation. Then, work with a partner to answer the following questions.

1. **Formulating Hypotheses** State a hypothesis about how increasing the amount of gelatin added to a given volume of water will affect the amount of cross-linking in the resulting polymer.

As more gelatin is added to a given volume of water, more cross-linking occurs, and the strength

and flexibility of the polymer increases.

2. **Observing** How can you test the gelatin to determine the extent of cross-linking that has occurred?

The gelatin with more cross-links cannot be as easily torn apart when it is twisted and stretched.

It will return to its original shape more quickly.

Lab Manual

Name _____ Class _____ Date _____

3. **Controlling Variables** Identify the manipulated, responding, and controlled variables.
   a. Manipulated variable

   The amount of gelatin in a given volume of water

   b. Responding variable

   The elasticity and strength of the resulting polymer

   c. Controlled variables

   Water temperature and time

4. **Inferring** Wood glue, like gelatin, consists of proteins extracted from the bones and tissues of animals, which are mixed with water. As the water evaporates, the glue hardens. Explain what causes the glue to harden.

   Answers may vary, but should indicate that more cross-links form as the water evaporates,

   making the glue more solid and stronger.

Materials *(per group)*

250-mL beaker
measuring spoons (in SI units of volume)
hot plate
3 paper cups
20 mL (4 teaspoons) sugar-free gelatin mix
3 wooden splints

If SI measuring spoons are not available, use spoons that measure in units of tablespoons and teaspoons, using the conversion factor of 15 mL to 1 tablespoon and 4.9 mL to 1 teaspoon.

Safety 🥽🧤🔥⚡🧪🔬

Put on safety goggles and a lab apron. Be careful to avoid breakage when working with glassware. Never touch or taste any chemical unless instructed to do so. Use extreme care when working with heated equipment or materials to avoid burns. Observe proper laboratory procedures when using electrical equipment. Note all safety alert symbols next to the steps in the Procedure and review the meaning of each symbol by referring to the Safety Symbols on page xiii.

Procedure

Day 1

1. Label the three paper cups with your name.
2. Place 100 mL of water in the beaker. Place the beaker on a hot plate and turn the hot plate to a high setting. **CAUTION:** *The hot plate and beaker will get very hot. Be careful not to burn yourself.*
3. When the water boils, reduce the setting to low. Using the measuring spoons, carefully remove 30 mL (2 tablespoons) of hot water and place it in one of the paper cups. **CAUTION:** *Use heat-resistant gloves when removing hot water from the beaker.*

Lab Manual

Name _____ Class _____ Date _____

4. Add 2.4 mL (0.5 teaspoon) of gelatin to the paper cup. Stir the gelatin with one of the wooden splints until the gelatin is mixed completely in the water. **CAUTION:** *Do not taste the gelatin.*

5. Repeat Steps 2 and 3, placing 4.9 mL (1.0 teaspoon) of gelatin in the second cup and 9.8 mL (2.0 teaspoons) of gelatin in the third cup. Turn off the hot plate and set the paper cups aside to cool.

6. Observe the gelatin. Record your observations in the data table. Leave the gelatin exposed to air in an area where it will remain undisturbed overnight.

Day 2

7. Tear the paper cup away from the 2.4-mL gelatin sample.

8. Observe the gelatin disk. To investigate its elasticity and strength, try to twist it, squash it, and pull it apart. Try to change the polymer's shape slowly, and then rapidly. Record your observations in the data table.

9. Repeat Steps 7 and 8 with the other two gelatin samples. The polymer gels may be disposed of in a dry waste container.

Observations Sample data are shown.

DATA TABLE

Gelatin Volume (in 30 mL water)	Sample Properties: Day 1	Sample Properties: Day 2
2.4 mL (0.5 teaspoon)	Liquid slightly thicker than water	Resembles gelatin dessert; good elasticity: returns to shape quickly after twisting and squashing; poor strength: easily pulls apart
4.9 mL (1.0 teaspoon)	Thick liquid	More rubbery than first sample; very elastic: returns to shape quickly after twisting and squashing; limited strength: pulls apart easily, but not as easily as first sample
9.8 mL (2.0 teaspoons)	Very thick liquid	Most rubbery solid; highly elastic: returns to shape after twisting and squashing; good strength: does not pull apart very easily

Lab Manual

Name _____ Class _____ Date _____

Analysis and Conclusions

1. Observing How did the polymer gels change when you left them out overnight?

The liquids became more solid and elastic.

2. Inferring Which gelatin sample do you think contained more cross-links? Explain your answer.

The sample with the most gelatin added to the water had the most cross-links because

it was strongest and most elastic.

3. Evaluating and Revising Did the results of this investigation support or contradict your hypothesis? Explain your answer.

The results support the hypothesis that when more gelatin is added to a quantity of water, more

cross-links form. An increase in the number of cross-links increases the strength and elasticity

of the polymer.

Go Further

Flour made from grains such as wheat contains proteins called gliadin and glutelin. When dough (water mixed with the flour) is kneaded, these protein molecules are stretched, and cross-linked bonds form between them. Use resources in the library or on the Internet to find out how this cross-linking in bread dough takes place. Then, use the information you find to design an experiment to test how too little or too much kneading affects the dough. Show your teacher a written plan for your experiment. When your teacher approves your plan, carry out your experiment and report the results.

Stretching and cross-linking of gliadin and glutelin molecules during kneading forms a gel called gluten. The cross-links in gluten increase the elasticity of the dough so that bubbles of carbon dioxide gas (from yeast, baking soda, or baking powder) can be contained by the dough. Expansion of these gas bubbles during baking gives bread its light, porous texture. While kneading is essential to form gluten, too much kneading can cause the cross-links to break, which produces a dough that is strong but inelastic.

Review student experimental plans for safety, practicality, and design. Well-designed experimental plans should identify the materials and variables involved and should include a detailed description of the procedure. The procedure should test a prediction that follows from a clearly stated hypothesis.

Chapter Test A

Name _____ Class _____ Date _____

Chapter 9   Carbon Chemistry   Chapter Test A

Multiple Choice

Write the letter that best answers the question or completes the statement on the line provided.

_____ **1.** In buckminsterfullerene, carbon atoms are
  a. bonded in a network solid.
  b. bonded to three other carbon atoms in a widely spaced layer.
  c. bonded in alternating hexagons and pentagons on the surface of a hollow sphere.
  d. not bonded to each other.

_____ **2.** Which of the following statements is true?
  a. Organic compounds always contain carbon and hydrogen.
  b. Organic compounds contain only carbon and hydrogen.
  c. Organic compounds are produced only in organisms.
  d. About 10 percent of all known compounds are organic compounds.

_____ **3.** Butane has the formula C_4H_{10}. Which of the following is the formula of cyclobutane?
  a. C_4H_4 **b.** C_4H_6 **c.** C_4H_8 **d.** C_4H_{10}

_____ **4.** Which of the following is a saturated hydrocarbon?
  a. isopropane
  b. butene
  c. pentyne
  d. benzene

_____ **5.** The prefix *dec-* means "ten." Which of the following best describes the structure of decene?
  a. It contains ten carbon atoms and only single bonds.
  b. It contains ten carbon atoms and at least one double bond.
  c. It contains ten carbon atoms and at least one triple bond.
  d. It contains a total of ten atoms.

_____ **6.** Burning coal usually produces more soot than burning natural gas or petroleum products because coal
  a. formed in ancient swamps.
  b. is formed from the remains of marine organisms.
  c. contains aromatic hydrocarbons with high molar masses.
  d. contains a mixture of hydrocarbons.

Chapter Test A

Name _____ Class _____ Date _____

_____ **7.** One of the gases released after gasoline burns in a car's engine is carbon monoxide. Which of the following statements explains why there is carbon monoxide in this mixture of gases?
  a. Not enough oxygen is present when gasoline is burned in the engine.
  b. Gasoline contains carbon monoxide.
  c. The combustion of gasoline in the engine is complete.
  d. Carbon monoxide is produced during the complete combustion of a fossil fuel.

_____ **8.** Which of the following statements explains why inhaling carbon monoxide is dangerous?
  a. Carbon monoxide reacts with oxygen to produce carbon dioxide.
  b. Carbon monoxide keeps hemoglobin in the blood from carrying oxygen to cells.
  c. Carbon monoxide is a colorless, odorless gas.
  d. all of the above

_____ **9.** The functional group in butanoic acid, which is an organic acid, is the
  a. amino group.   **b.** hydroxyl group.
  c. carboxyl group.   **d.** butane group.

_____ **10.** Propanoic acid and ethyl alcohol can react. The products of this reaction are water and an
  a. organic base.   **b.** ester.
  c. organic acid.   **d.** amine.

_____ **11.** In a polymer, monomers are linked by
  a. ionic bonds.
  b. covalent bonds.
  c. metallic bonds.
  d. polyatomic ions.

_____ **12.** Which of the following statements about natural rubber and synthetic rubber is true?
  a. Natural and synthetic rubber contain different monomers.
  b. There is an unlimited supply of both types of rubber.
  c. Both types of rubber are made from petroleum products.
  d. Natural and synthetic rubber have exactly the same properties.

_____ **13.** The monomers from which proteins are made are
  a. sugars.   **b.** amino acids.
  c. nucleic acids.   **d.** starches.

Chapter Test A

Name _____ Class _____ Date _____

_____ 14. Which of the following statements is true?
   a. Photosynthesis occurs only in plants, and cellular respiration occurs only in animals.
   b. Photosynthesis occurs only in animals, and cellular respiration occurs only in plants.
   c. Both photosynthesis and cellular respiration occur in plants.
   d. Both photosynthesis and cellular respiration occur in animals.

_____ 15. Proteins that act as catalysts for chemical reactions that occur in cells are
   a. vitamins.
   b. enzymes.
   c. carbohydrates.
   d. amino acids.

_____ 16. Which of the following statements is true about enzymes?
   a. Enzymes allow a reaction to occur that would never occur without the enzymes.
   b. Enzymes allow reactions to proceed at temperatures near 37°C.
   c. Enzymes cannot be produced within cells.
   d. One enzyme can control all the reactions in a cell.

Completion

Complete each statement on the line provided.

1. More than 90 percent of all known compounds are organic compounds, mainly because carbon contains _____ valence electrons and can form multiple carbon-to-carbon bonds.

2. Straight-chain hydrocarbons that contain one to three carbon atoms are likely to be _____ at room temperature.

3. Suppose a saturated and unsaturated hydrocarbon both contain the same number of carbon atoms. The saturated hydrocarbon contains more of the element _____ than the unsaturated hydrocarbon does.

4. During photosynthesis, _____ energy is converted to _____ energy in the bonds of the products.

5. Some enzymes require a(an) _____ which is often a metal ion or a water-soluble _____ to function.

Chapter Test A

Name _____ Class _____ Date _____

Short Answer

Use complete sentences to write the answers to the questions on the lines provided.

1. Based on the structure of graphite shown in Figure 9-1, explain why graphite is a good lubricant.
   _____
   _____
   _____
   _____
   _____
   _____

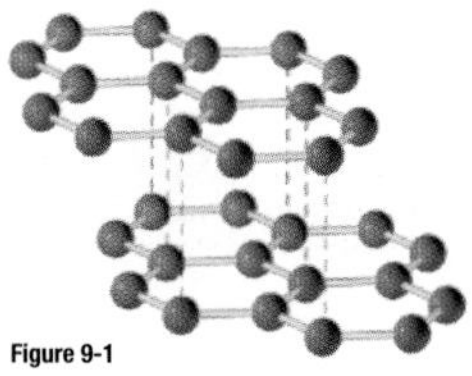

Figure 9-1

2. How can butane and isobutane both have the formula C_4H_{10}?
   _____
   _____
   _____
   _____
   _____

3. Compare the bonding in alkenes and alkynes.
   _____
   _____
   _____
   _____

4. What two products are formed from the reaction of a halocarbon and a base?
   _____
   _____

Chapter Test A

Name _____ Class _____ Date _____

5. One important difference between DNA and RNA is that RNA contains the base uracil instead of thymine. What base will pair with uracil in RNA—adenine, guanine, or cytosine?
   _____
   _____

Using Science Skills

Use the structural formulas to answer each question. Write the answers on a separate sheet of paper.

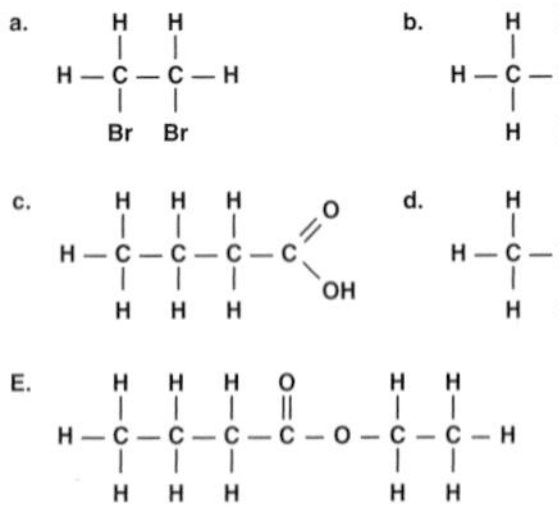

Figure 9-2

1. **Inferring** The ester ethyl butanoate provides the taste and smell to pineapple. Identify the structural formula in Figure 9-2 for ethyl butanoate.

2. **Interpreting Graphics** Amines are formed during the breakdown of proteins in animal cells. Identify the structural formula in Figure 9-2 for an amine, and name the functional group.

3. **Interpreting Graphics** Which of the structures in Figure 9-2 is the formula for propanol? What is the functional group in this compound?

4. **Applying Concepts** Which diagram in Figure 9-2 shows the structural formula of a halocarbon? Why is the prefix *halo-* used?

5. **Using Models** Butanoic acid is found in rancid butter. Which of the structural formulas in Figure 9-2 is butanoic acid? What is the functional group in an organic acid?

Chapter Test A

Name _____ Class _____ Date _____

Problem

Write the answer to each question on a separate sheet of paper.

1. Write a balanced chemical equation for the complete combustion of methane, CH_4, and one for the incomplete combustion of methane.

2. Write a balanced chemical equation for the formation of carbonic acid from carbon dioxide and water.

Essay

Write the answer to each question on a separate sheet of paper.

1. In terms of their structures, explain why diamond is so much harder than graphite.

2. Suppose a gas furnace is producing a large amount of carbon monoxide. What process is causing carbon monoxide to be produced, and how can the amount that is produced be reduced?

3. Describe the structure of the nucleotides in DNA, and explain how two strands join to form the double helix.

Name _____ Class _____ Date _____

Chapter 9   Carbon Chemistry   Chapter Test B

Multiple Choice

Write the letter that best answers the question or completes the statement on the line provided.

_____ 1. Figure 9-1 is a model of graphite. Which of the following statements is true about graphite?
   a. Within each layer, the atoms form alternating single and double bonds.
   b. Graphite is an example of a network solid.
   c. Each carbon atom in graphite is bonded to four other carbon atoms.
   d. The bonds between graphite layers are weaker than the bonds within graphite layers.

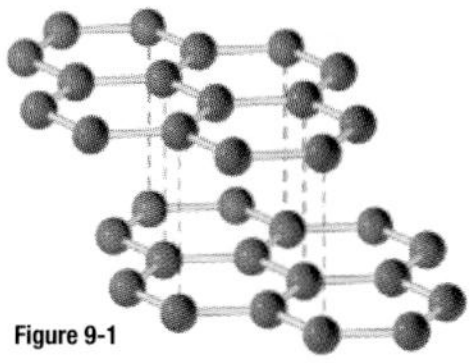

Figure 9-1

_____ 2. Which of the following statements helps explain why there are millions of carbon compounds?
   a. Carbon has four valence electrons.
   b. Carbon atoms form bonds with other carbon atoms.
   c. Carbon atoms can form single, double, and triple bonds.
   d. all of the above

_____ 3. The carbon atoms in a hydrocarbon CANNOT be arranged in
   a. straight chains.   b. branched chains
   c. rings.   d. a network solid.

_____ 4. Which of the following is another name for a saturated hydrocarbon?
   a. alkane   b. alkene
   c. alkyne   d. alkali

_____ 5. Which of the following compounds is most reactive?
   a. ethane
   b. ethene
   c. ethyne
   d. They are all equally reactive.

_____ 6. Which of the following is NOT an example of a fossil fuel?
   a. coal   b. petroleum
   c. natural gas   d. methanol

Name _____ Class _____ Date _____

_____ 7. What are the main products of the incomplete combustion of fossil fuels?
   a. water and carbon dioxide
   b. oxygen and hydrocarbons
   c. water and carbon monoxide
   d. carbon dioxide and hydrocarbons

_____ 8. Which of the following is NOT a result of the complete combustion of fossil fuels?
   a. The amount of carbon dioxide in the atmosphere increases.
   b. The amount of carbon monoxide in the atmosphere increases.
   c. Nitrogen oxides are released into the atmosphere.
   d. Sulfur dioxide is released into the atmosphere.

_____ 9. In the compound CH_3F, the fluorine atom is a(an)
   a. functional group.   b. substituted hydrocarbon.
   c. hydroxyl group.   d. amino group.

_____ 10. The smell of rotten fish is caused by the presence of an
   a. amine.   b. alcohol.   c. ester.   d. organic acid.

_____ 11. When monomers link together, they usually form
   a. a polymer.   b. another monomer.
   c. ionic bonds.   d. a network solid.

_____ 12. Which of the following exists as both a natural and a synthetic polymer?
   a. cellulose   b. nylon   c. polyethylene   d. rubber

_____ 13. Natural polymers are produced
   a. only in plant cells.
   b. only in animal cells.
   c. in both plant and animal cells.
   d. in neither plant nor animal cells.

_____ 14. Plants convert energy from sunlight into chemical energy during
   a. cellular respiration.   b. photosynthesis.
   c. vaporization.   d. depolymerization.

Completion

Complete each statement on the line provided.

1. Diamond is an example of a(an) _____ in which all the carbon atoms are linked by covalent bonds.
2. Compounds with the same molecular formula but different structural formulas are _____.

Name _____ Class _____ Date _____

3. In a saturated hydrocarbon, all the bonds are _____ bonds.
4. The primary products of the complete combustion of fossil fuels are _____ and _____.
5. Some products of the combustion of fossil fuels cause the _____ of rain to increase.
6. The manufacture of chlorofluorocarbons has been restricted because they deplete Earth's _____ layer.
7. Glucose is the monomer in the natural polymers _____ and _____.
8. The strands of DNA are held together in the double helix by _____ between hydrogen atoms on one strand and nitrogen or oxygen atoms on the other strand.
9. The energy that your body needs is released by the process of _____.
10. Vitamins B and C are examples of vitamins that can dissolve in _____.

Short Answer

Use complete sentences to write the answers to the questions on the lines provided.

1. What elements do organic compounds always contain?
   _____

2. Classify the compounds ethyne, heptane, and benzene.
   _____
   _____
   _____

3. What fossil fuel formed from the remains of buried plants in ancient swamps?
   _____

4. Why can't people survive without plants?
   _____
   _____

5. Why might it be harmful for a person to take large quantities of many vitamins each day?
   _____
   _____

Name _____ Class _____ Date _____

Using Science Skills

Use the diagram to answer each question. Write the answers on a separate sheet of paper.

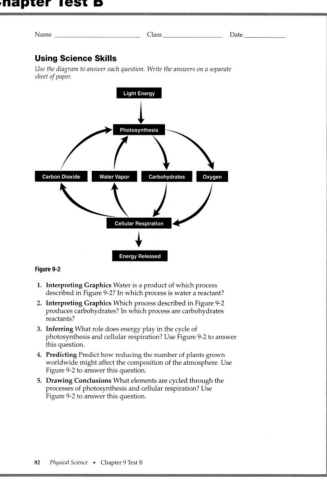

Figure 9-2

1. **Interpreting Graphics** Water is a product of which process described in Figure 9-2? In which process is water a reactant?
2. **Interpreting Graphics** Which process described in Figure 9-2 produces carbohydrates? In which process are carbohydrates reactants?
3. **Inferring** What role does energy play in the cycle of photosynthesis and cellular respiration? Use Figure 9-2 to answer this question.
4. **Predicting** Predict how reducing the number of plants grown worldwide might affect the composition of the atmosphere. Use Figure 9-2 to answer this question.
5. **Drawing Conclusions** What elements are cycled through the processes of photosynthesis and cellular respiration? Use Figure 9-2 to answer this question.

Chapter 9 Test A Answers

Multiple Choice
1. c   **2.** a   **3.** c   **4.** a   **5.** b   **6.** c
7. a   **8.** b   **9.** c   **10.** b   **11.** b   **12.** a
13. b   **14.** c   **15.** b   **16.** b

Completion
1. four **2.** gases **3.** hydrogen **4.** light, chemical
5. co-enzyme, vitamin

Short Answer
1. Each carbon atom in graphite forms strong covalent bonds to three other atoms within a layer. However, the bonds between the graphite layers are weak, allowing the layers to slide easily past one another. **2.** The compounds are isomers. Butane is a straight-chain alkane. Isobutane is a branched-chain alkane.
3. Alkenes are hydrocarbons that contain at least one carbon-carbon double bond. Alkynes are hydrocarbons that contain at least one carbon-carbon triple bond. **4.** an alcohol and a salt
5. adenine

Using Science Skills
1. E **2.** D; the amino group, $-NH_2$ **3.** B; the hydroxyl group, $-OH$
4. A; the functional group is a halogen.
5. C; the carboxyl group, $-COOH$

Problem
1. Complete combustion: $CH_4 + 2O_2 \rightarrow CO_2 + 2H_2O$
Incomplete combustion: $2CH_4 + 3O_2 \rightarrow 2CO + 4H_2O$
2. $CO_2 + H_2O \rightarrow H_2CO_3$

Essay
1. Diamond is a network solid in which all the atoms are linked by covalent bonds. The structure is rigid, compact, and strong. In graphite, carbon atoms are arranged in widely spaced layers. Because the attractions between layers are weak, the layers can slide easily past one another. Therefore, graphite is soft and slippery. **2.** Carbon monoxide is produced during incomplete combustion of a fossil fuel. The amount of oxygen available for combustion needs to be increased. **3.** A nucleotide in DNA contains a phosphate group, a sugar (deoxyribose), and one of four organic bases. When the strands line up, pairs of bases (adenine and thymine, cytosine and guanine) are arranged like rungs on a ladder. Strong intermolecular attractions hold the strands together as they twist around one another.

Chapter 9 Test B Answers

Multiple Choice
1. d   **2.** d   **3.** d   **4.** a   **5.** c   **6.** d
7. c   **8.** b   **9.** a   **10.** a   **11.** a   **12.** d
13. c   **14.** b

Completion
1. network solid **2.** isomers **3.** single **4.** carbon dioxide, water
5. acidity **6.** ozone **7.** starch, cellulose **8.** intermolecular attractions; attractions **9.** cellular respiration **10.** water

Short Answer
1. carbon and hydrogen **2.** Ethyne is an alkyne, heptane is an alkane, and benzene is an aromatic hydrocarbon. **3.** coal
4. People need the energy stored in plants and the oxygen produced during photosynthesis. **5.** Vitamins that are soluble in fat can build up in body tissues over time.

Using Science Skills
1. cellular respiration; photosynthesis **2.** photosynthesis; cellular respiration **3.** Light energy is absorbed during photosynthesis. This energy is stored as chemical energy in the covalent bonds of molecules. During cellular respiration, this energy stored in the products of photosynthesis is released as heat. **4.** The amount of carbon dioxide removed from the atmosphere and the amount of oxygen released into the atmosphere would be reduced.
5. carbon, hydrogen, and oxygen

Chapter 10 Nuclear Chemistry

Planning Guide

Use these planning tools
Easy Planner
Resource Pro
Online Lesson Planner

SECTION OBJECTIVES	STANDARDS		ACTIVITIES and LABS
	NATIONAL (See p. T18.)	STATE	
10.1 Radioactivity, pp. 292–297 ⏱ 1 block or 2 periods **10.1.1 Describe** the process of nuclear decay. **10.1.2 Classify** nuclear radiation as alpha particles, beta particles, or gamma rays. **10.1.3 Balance** nuclear equations. **10.1.4 Identify** sources of nuclear radiation, and **describe** how nuclear radiation affects matter. **10.1.5 Describe** methods of detecting nuclear radiation.	A-1, B-1, B-6, D-1, F-1, F-5, G-1, G-2, G-3		**SE** Inquiry Activity: What Happens When an Atom Decays? p. 291 **L2** **TE** Teacher Demo: Stopping Radiation, p. 294 **L2** **LM** Investigation 10B: Detecting Radiation **L1**
10.2 Rates of Nuclear Decay, pp. 298–301 ⏱ 1 block or 2 periods **10.2.1 Define** half-life, and **relate** half-life to the age of a radioactive sample. **10.2.2 Compare** and **contrast** nuclear reaction rates with chemical reaction rates. **10.2.3 Describe** how radioisotopes are used to estimate the age of materials.	A-1, A-2, B-1, B-3		**SE** Quick Lab: Modeling Half-Life, p. 300 **L2** **TE** Teacher Demo: Predicting Decay, p. 299 **L2** **LM** Investigation 10A: Modeling Radioactive Decay **L2**
10.3 Artificial Transmutation, pp. 303–305 ⏱ 1 block or 2 periods **10.3.1 Describe** and **identify** examples of transmutation. **10.3.2 Describe** how transuranium elements are synthesized. **10.3.3 Explain** how particle accelerators have been used in scientific research.	A-1, A-2, B-1, B-6, E-2, F-1, F-5, G-1, G-2, G-3		**SE** Quick Lab: Modeling Transmutation, p. 304 **L2**
10.4 Fission and Fusion, pp. 308–315 ⏱ 1 block or 2 periods **10.4.1 Compare** and **contrast** nuclear forces. **10.4.2 Describe** the process of nuclear fission. **10.4.3 Explain** how nuclear reactors are used to produce energy. **10.4.4 Describe** the process of nuclear fusion.	A-1, A-2, B-1, E-2, F-1, F-2, F-4, F-5, G-1, G-2, G-3		**SE** Exploration Lab: Modeling a Chain Reaction, pp. 316–317 **L2** **TE** Teacher Demo: Nuclear Processes, p. 311 **L2**

Ability Levels

L1	For students who need additional help
L2	For all students
L3	For students who need to be challenged

Components

SE	Student Edition	**GRSW**	Guided Reading	**CTB**	Computer Test Bank
TE	Teacher's Edition		& Study Workbook	**TP**	Test Prep Resources
LM	Laboratory Manual		With Math Support	**iT**	iText
PLM	Probeware Lab	**CUT**	Chapter and Unit	**DC**	Discovery Channel
	Manual		Tests		Videotapes

T	Transparencies
P	Presentation Pro
	CD-ROM
GO	Internet Resources

RESOURCES PRINT and TECHNOLOGY		SECTION ASSESSMENT
GRSW Section 10.1	L1	**SE** Section 10.1 Assessment, p. 297
GRSW Math Skill	L2	
T Chapter 10 Pretest	L2	**iT** Section 10.1
Section 10.1	L2	
P Chapter 10 Pretest	L2	
Section 10.1	L2	
PLANETDIARY **GO** Radioactivity activity	L2	
GRSW Section 10.2	L1	**SE** Section 10.2 Assessment, p. 301
T Section 10.2	L2	
P Section 10.2	L2	**iT** Section 10.2
SCi_LINKS **GO** Half-Life	L2	
GRSW Section 10.3	L1	**SE** Section 10.3 Assessment, p. 305
Discovery SCHOOL **DC** Nuclear Medicine	L2	
T Section 10.3	L2	**iT** Section 10.3
P Section 10.3	L2	
GRSW Section 10.4	L1	**SE** Section 10.4 Assessment, p. 315
T Section 10.4	L2	
P Section 10.4	L2	**iT** Section 10.4
SCi_LINKS **GO** Fission	L2	

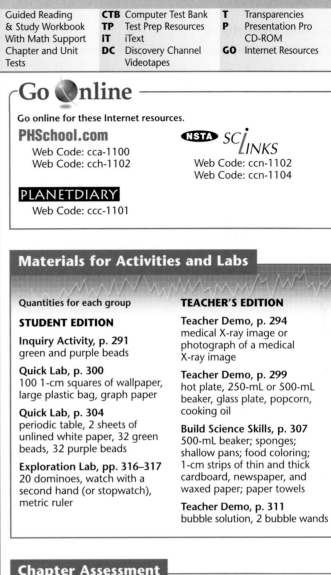

Go Online

Go online for these Internet resources.

PHSchool.com
Web Code: cca-1100
Web Code: cch-1102

NSTA SC_LINKS
Web Code: ccn-1102
Web Code: ccn-1104

PLANETDIARY
Web Code: ccc-1101

Materials for Activities and Labs

Quantities for each group

STUDENT EDITION

Inquiry Activity, p. 291
green and purple beads

Quick Lab, p. 300
100 1-cm squares of wallpaper, large plastic bag, graph paper

Quick Lab, p. 304
periodic table, 2 sheets of unlined white paper, 32 green beads, 32 purple beads

Exploration Lab, pp. 316–317
20 dominoes, watch with a second hand (or stopwatch), metric ruler

TEACHER'S EDITION

Teacher Demo, p. 294
medical X-ray image or photograph of a medical X-ray image

Teacher Demo, p. 299
hot plate, 250-mL or 500-mL beaker, glass plate, popcorn, cooking oil

Build Science Skills, p. 307
500-mL beaker; sponges; shallow pans; food coloring; 1-cm strips of thin and thick cardboard, newspaper, and waxed paper; paper towels

Teacher Demo, p. 311
bubble solution, 2 bubble wands

Chapter Assessment

CHAPTER ASSESSMENT

SE	Chapter Assessment, pp. 319–320
CUT	Chapter 10 Test A, B
CTB	Chapter 10
iT	Chapter 10
PHSchool.com GO	
Web Code: cca-1100	

STANDARDIZED TEST PREP

SE Chapter 10, p. 321
TP Diagnose and Prescribe

iText—interactive textbook with assessment at PHSchool.com

Nuclear Chemistry   290B

LESSON PLAN 10.1

Radioactivity

Time
**2 periods
1 block**

Section Objectives

- **10.1.1 Describe** the process of nuclear decay.
- **10.1.2 Classify** nuclear radiation as alpha particles, beta particles, or gamma rays.
- **10.1.3 Balance** nuclear equations.
- **10.1.4 Identify** sources of nuclear radiation, and **describe** how nuclear radiation affects matter.
- **10.1.5 Describe** methods of detecting nuclear radiation.

Vocabulary radioactivity • radioisotope • nuclear radiation • alpha particle • beta particle • gamma ray • background radiation

Local Standards

---

1 FOCUS

Build Vocabulary: Word-Part Analysis
Point out the two vocabulary terms that contain the word *radiation*. Explain that the word comes from a Latin word meaning "to spread out from a point." **L2**

Targeted Resources
❑ Transparency: Chapter 10 Pretest
❑ Transparency: Interest Grabber 10.1
❑ Transparency: Reading Strategy 10.1

---

2 INSTRUCT

Build Reading Literacy: Compare and Contrast
Ask students to construct a compare/contrast table. Have them skim the sections on alpha decay, beta decay, and gamma decay. Then, ask students to describe similarities and differences of the decay types in their table. **L1**

Build Science Skills: Inferring
Have students look at Figure 3 and ask which type of radioactive decay causes the largest change in the atomic number of a nucleus. **L2**

Teacher Demo: Stopping Radiation
Use a medical X-ray to show students that radiation can be blocked to varying degrees by different materials. **L2**

Integrate Earth Science
Encourage students to work in small groups to research the concentrations of uranium in their community. They may use library resources, such as the Internet, to assist them in their research. **L2**

Targeted Resources
❑ Transparency: Figure 4: Penetrating Powers of Nuclear Radiation
❑ Transparency: Math Skills: Balancing Nuclear Equations
❑ Transparency: Figure 6: How Radon Gas Enters a Building
❑ GRSW Section 10.1

---

3 ASSESS

Reteach
Use Figure 4 to summarize the three different types if nuclear decay and how each type affects matter. **L1**

Evaluate Understanding
Randomly ask students to name the symbol or charge for each type of nuclear decay. **L2**

Targeted Resources
❑ **PHSchool.com** Online Section 10.1 Assessment
❑ iText Section 10.1

Transparencies

132 **Chapter 10 Pretest**

1. According to the law of conservation of mass, if element X has a molar mass of 3 g/mol, and element Y has a molar mass of 5 g/mol, what must be the total mass of products formed when one mole of the compound X_2Y decomposes?

2. True or False: A reaction rate is the rate at which reactants change into products over time.

3. If you tossed 128 coins in the air, about how many could you expect to land heads up?

4. Suppose you were to remove any coins that landed heads up, and then toss the remaining coins in the air. How many times could you expect to repeat this process until you had removed all of the coins?

ANSWERS
1. 11 g
2. True
3. about 64 coins
4. about 7 times

Transparencies

133 **Chapter 10 Pretest** *(continued)*

5. The element uranium belongs to
   a. Group 7A (halogens)
   b. Group 8A (noble gases)
   c. the lanthanide series
   d. the actinide series

6. Which subatomic particles are found in the nucleus of an atom?

ANSWERS
5. d
6. protons and neutrons

Transparencies

134 **Section 10.1 Interest Grabber**

Modeling Beta Decay

Cut out a strip of blue paper and a strip of red paper. Cut each strip of paper into 10 squares. Use the red squares to represent protons, and the blue squares to represent neutrons.

1. Arrange the correct number of each type of square on your desk in order to model a carbon-14 nucleus. How many of each type of square did you use in your model?

2. Switch out one blue square in your nuclear model with one red square so that the nucleus contains the same total number of subatomic particles. What isotope does your model now represent?

3. When a carbon-14 nucleus undergoes the change you have modeled, an electron is emitted. What is the nuclear charge of carbon-14? How does this compare to the sum of the charge of an electron and the nuclear charge of the new isotope formed?

ANSWERS
1. 6 red squares (protons), 8 blue squares (neutrons)
2. nitrogen-14
3. The nuclear charge of carbon-14 is 6+, which is equal to the sum of the charge of an electron (1−), and the nuclear charge of nitrogen-14 (7+).

Transparencies

135 **Section 10.1 Reading Strategy**

Previewing

Question	Answer
What is nuclear decay?	a. ____?____
b. ____?____	Alpha, beta, gamma
c. ____?____	d. ____?____
e. ____?____	f. ____?____

ANSWERS
a. Nuclear decay is the spontaneous change of one isotope into another.
b. What are the types of nuclear radiation?
c. What are the effects of nuclear radiation?
d. One effect of nuclear radiation is the ionization of matter.
e. How can nuclear radiation be detected?
f. Nuclear radiation can be detected by a Geiger counter or film badge.

193

Transparencies

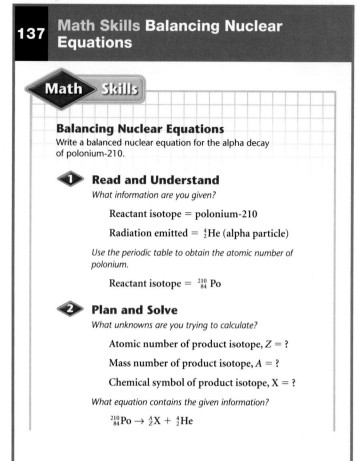

Transparencies

137 Math Skills Balancing Nuclear Equations

Math **Skills**

Balancing Nuclear Equations

Write a balanced nuclear equation for the alpha decay of polonium-210.

1 Read and Understand

What information are you given?

Reactant isotope = polonium-210

Radiation emitted = $^4_2$He (alpha particle)

Use the periodic table to obtain the atomic number of polonium.

Reactant isotope = $^{210}_{84}$Po

2 Plan and Solve

What unknowns are you trying to calculate?

Atomic number of product isotope, Z = ?

Mass number of product isotope, A = ?

Chemical symbol of product isotope, X = ?

What equation contains the given information?

$$^{210}_{84}\text{Po} \rightarrow {}^A_Z\text{X} + {}^4_2\text{He}$$

Transparencies

138 Math Skills Balancing Nuclear Equations *(continued)*

Write and solve equations for atomic mass and atomic number.

$$210 = A + 4 \qquad 84 = Z + 2$$
$$210 - 4 = A \qquad 84 - 2 = Z$$
$$206 = A \qquad 82 = Z$$

According to the periodic table, the element with an atomic number of 82 is lead, Pb. So, X is Pb. The balanced nuclear equation is shown below.

$$^{210}_{84}\text{Po} \rightarrow {}^{206}_{82}\text{Pb} + {}^4_2\text{He}$$

3 Look Back and Check

Is your answer reasonable?

The mass number on the left equals the sum of the mass numbers on the right. The atomic number on the left equals the sum of the atomic numbers on the right. The equation is balanced.

Transparencies

139 Figure 6 How Radon Gas Enters a Building

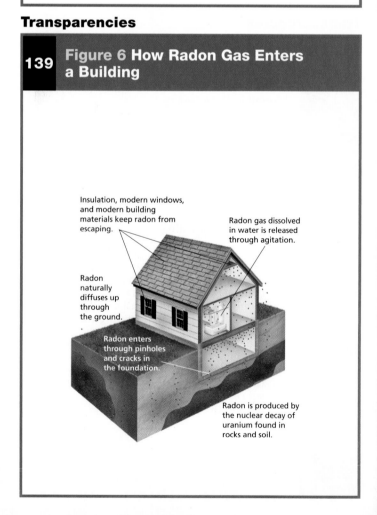

Insulation, modern windows, and modern building materials keep radon from escaping.

Radon gas dissolved in water is released through agitation.

Radon naturally diffuses up through the ground.

Radon enters through pinholes and cracks in the foundation.

Radon is produced by the nuclear decay of uranium found in rocks and soil.

Name _____ Class _____ Date _____

Chapter 10 Nuclear Chemistry

Section 10.1 Radioactivity
(pages 292–297)

This section discusses the different types of nuclear radiation and how they affect matter.

Reading Strategy (page 292)

Previewing Before you read the section, rewrite the topic headings in the table as *how, why,* and *what* questions. As you read, write an answer to each question. For more information on this Reading Strategy, see the **Reading and Study Skills** in the **Skills and Reference Handbook** at the end of your textbook.

Exploring Radioactivity	
Question	**Answer** Student answers may include:
What is nuclear decay?	Nuclear decay is the process in which a radioisotope spontaneously decays into another isotope.
What are types of nuclear radiation?	Alpha, beta, gamma
What are the effects of nuclear radiation?	Nuclear radiation can ionize atoms, molecules may change, and cellular function may break down.
How can nuclear radiation be detected?	Nuclear radiation can be detected with devices such as Geiger counters and film badges.

Nuclear Decay (pages 292–293)

1. Describe radioactivity. Radioactivity is the process in which an unstable atomic nucleus emits charged particles and energy.

2. A radioisotope is any atom that contains an unstable _____nucleus_____.

3. Describe what happens to radioisotopes during nuclear decay. Over time, radioisotopes spontaneously change into other isotopes, including isotopes of other elements.

Types of Nuclear Radiation (pages 293–296)

4. Nuclear radiation is charged particles and energy that are emitted from the _____nuclei_____ of radioisotopes.

5. Circle the letters that identify each common type of nuclear radiation.
   a. X-rays
   (b.) alpha particles
   (c.) beta particles
   (d.) gamma rays

6. Circle the letters that identify which groups of particles make up an alpha particle.
   a. two electrons
   (b.) two protons
   (c.) two neutrons
   d. four neutrons

Name _____ Class _____ Date _____

Chapter 10 Nuclear Chemistry

7. How is the product isotope different from the reactant isotope in alpha decay? The product isotope has two fewer protons and two fewer neutrons than the reactant isotope.

8. Circle the letters that identify each event that takes place during beta decay.
   a. A proton decomposes into a neutron and an electron.
   (b.) A neutron decomposes into a proton and an electron.
   (c.) An electron is emitted from the nucleus.
   d. A neutron is emitted from the nucleus.

9. Why are beta particles more penetrating than alpha particles? Beta particles have a smaller mass and a faster speed.

10. Is the following sentence true or false? All nuclear radiation consists of charged particles. _____false_____

11. What is a gamma ray? A gamma ray is a penetrating ray of energy emitted by an unstable nucleus.

12. How fast do gamma rays travel through space? Gamma rays travel through space at the speed of light.

13. Complete the following table about nuclear radiation.

Characteristics of Nuclear Radiation			
Radiation Type	**Charge**	**Mass (amu)**	**Usually Stopped By**
Alpha particle	−1	4	Paper or clothing
Beta particle	1−	$\frac{1}{1836}$	Aluminum sheet
Gamma ray	0	0	Several meters of concrete

Effects of Nuclear Radiation (pages 296–297)

14. How does nuclear radiation affect atoms? Nuclear radiation can ionize atoms.

15. Is the following sentence true or false? One potential danger of radon gas is that prolonged exposure to it can lead to lung cancer. _____true_____

Detecting Nuclear Radiation (page 297)

16. Name two devices that are used to detect nuclear radiation.
   a. ____Geiger counters____   b. ____Film badges____

Name_____ Class_____ Date_____ M T W T F

LESSON PLAN 10.2

Rates of Nuclear Decay

Time
2 periods
1 block

Section Objectives

■ **10.2.1 Define** half-life, and **relate** half-life to the age of a radioactive sample.

■ **10.2.2 Compare** and **contrast** nuclear reaction rates with chemical reaction rates.

■ **10.2.3 Describe** how radioisotopes are used to estimate the age of materials.

Vocabulary half-life

Local Standards

1 FOCUS

Build Vocabulary: Paraphrase
Have students write a definition of *half-life* in their own words. After students read the section, ask them to draw a diagram that illustrates the definition. **L2**

Targeted Resources
❑ Transparency: Interest Grabber 10.2
❑ Transparency: Reading Strategy 10.2

2 INSTRUCT

Build Science Skills: Drawing Conclusions
After examining Figure 8, ask students if the tools shown are made of stone. Ask if the stone tools contain carbon-14. Ask students how the age of the tools was determined if the stones do not contain carbon-14. **L2**

Teacher Demo: Predicting Decay
Use the analogy of popping popcorn to show students that it is not possible to predict which atom decays in a radioactive sample. **L2**

Quick Lab: Modeling Half-Life
Using squares of wallpaper, students will analyze data to calculate the "half-life" of a model radioactive element. **L2**

Build Science Skills: Measuring
Ask students to choose a radioactive isotope for dating a hypothetical fossil. Tell students that archaeologists hypothesize that the fossil is about 20,000 years old. Ask students which isotope they would recommend that scientists try first and why. **L2**

Targeted Resources
❑ Transparency: Figure 9: Nuclear Decay of Iodine-131
❑ GRSW Section 10.2
❑ **NSTA** *sciLINKS* Half-life

3 ASSESS

Reteach
Use Figure 10 to review how different radioisotopes may be used to date objects of different ages. **L1**

Evaluate Understanding
Randomly ask students to determine the number of particles present after one, two, or three half-lives have passed from a specified initial number of particles. **L2**

Targeted Resources
❑ **PHSchool.com** Online Section 10.2 Assessment
❑ iText Section 10.2

Transparencies

140 Section 10.2 Interest Grabber

Analogy for Half-Life

The diagrams below represent the charge level of a battery in a robotic dog at different times during the day. You charged the battery so that it was at its highest level at 9:00 AM Examine the diagrams, and then answer the questions that follow.

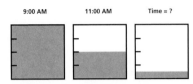

9:00 AM   11:00 AM   Time = ?

1. The dog uses half of any remaining charge every 2 hours. So, if the battery is fully charged at 9:00 AM, then the charge level will be $\frac{1}{2}$ at 11:00AM, two hours later. If it uses half of the remaining charge another two hours later, what will the energy level be at 1:00 PM?

2. Given the same trend, what time is it when the battery's charge is at the level shown in the last diagram?

3. The battery must be recharged when its charge level reaches $\frac{1}{16}$. What time will the battery need to be recharged?

ANSWERS
1. 1/4
2. 3:00 PM
3. 5:00 PM

Transparencies

141 Section 10.2 Reading Strategy

Identifying Details

Radiocarbon dating

uses the radioisotope

a. ?

can be used to date objects as old as

b. ? years

ANSWERS
a. carbon-14
b. 50,000

Transparencies

142 Figure 9 Nuclear Decay of Iodine-131

Nuclear Decay

Radioisotope Remaining (%)

100
50
25
12.5
0

● Iodine-131
● Xenon-131

1 half-life   2 half-lives   3 half-lives
Time

Section 10.2 Program Resources

Name _____ Class _____ Date _____

Chapter 10   Nuclear Chemistry

Section 10.2 Rates of Nuclear Decay
(pages 298–301)

This section discusses half-lives and explains how nuclear decay can be used to estimate the age of objects.

Reading Strategy (page 298)

Identifying Details As you read, complete the concept map below to identify details about radiocarbon dating. For more information on this Reading Strategy, see the **Reading and Study Skills** in the **Skills and Reference Handbook** at the end of your textbook.

```
              Radiocarbon
                dating

   uses the radioisotope        can be used to date
                                objects as old as

      Carbon-14                  50,000  years
```

Half-life (pages 299–300)

1. A nuclear decay rate describes _how fast nuclear changes take place in a radioactive substance_

2. Is the following sentence true or false? All radioisotopes decay at the same rate. _____false_____

3. Describe a half-life. _A half-life is the time required for one half of a sample of a radioisotope_ _to decay._

4. Circle the letter that describes a sample of a radioisotope after two half-lives.
   a. One eighth of the original sample is unchanged.
   (b.) One quarter of the original sample is unchanged.
   c. Half of the original sample is unchanged.
   d. Three quarters of the original sample is unchanged.

5. Circle the letter of the correct answer. Iodine-131 has a half-life of 8.07 days. What fraction of a sample of iodine-131 is left unchanged after 16.14 days?
   a. $\frac{1}{2}$ (b.) $\frac{1}{4}$
   c. $\frac{1}{8}$ d. $\frac{1}{16}$

6. Is the following sentence true or false? Like chemical reaction rates, nuclear decay rates vary with the conditions of reaction. _____false_____

Name _____ Class _____ Date _____

Chapter 10   Nuclear Chemistry

Use the following table to answer questions 7 and 8.

Half-Lives of Selected Radioisotopes	
Isotope	**Half-life**
Radon-222	3.82 days
Iodine-131	8.07 days
Thorium-234	24.1 days
Radium-226	1620 years
Carbon-14	5730 years

7. Circle the letter that identifies which sample would be the most unchanged after 100 years.
   a. iodine-131   (b.) radium-226
   c. radon-222   d. thorium-234

8. Circle the letter of the correct answer. How much of a 1.00 gram sample of radium-226 is left unchanged after 4860 years?
   a. 0.500 g   b. 0.250 g
   (c.) 0.125 g   d. 0.050 g

Radioactive Dating (pages 300–301)

9. How is carbon-14 formed in the upper atmosphere? _Carbon-14 is formed in the upper_ _atmosphere when neutrons produced by cosmic rays collide with nitrogen-14 atoms._

10. Circle the letter that identifies the correct equation for the beta decay of carbon–14.
   (a.) $^{14}_{6}C \longrightarrow ^{14}_{7}N + ^{0}_{-1}e$ b. $^{14}_{6}C \longrightarrow ^{13}_{5}B + ^{1}_{1}p$
   c. $^{14}_{6}C \longrightarrow ^{14}_{5}B + ^{0}_{-1}e$ d. $^{14}_{6}C \longrightarrow ^{10}_{4}Be + ^{4}_{2}He$

11. Is the following sentence true or false? Plants and animals continue to absorb carbon from the atmosphere after they die. _____false_____

12. How is the age of an object determined in radiocarbon dating? _The age of an object_ _is determined by comparing its carbon-14 levels with carbon-14 levels in the atmosphere._

13. Circle the letter of each characteristic of radiocarbon dating.
   (a.) Carbon-14 levels in the atmosphere can change over time.
   b. Carbon-14 levels in the atmosphere stay constant.
   (c.) Scientists often use objects of known age in radiocarbon dating.
   d. Objects of known age are not useful in radiocarbon dating.

14. Is the following sentence true or false? Radiocarbon dating is highly accurate in dating objects that are more than 50,000 years old. _____false_____

LESSON PLAN 10.3

Artificial Transmutation

Section Objectives

Local Standards

- **10.3.1 Describe** and **identify** examples of transmutation.
- **10.3.2 Describe** how transuranium elements are synthesized.
- **10.3.3 Explain** how particle accelerators have been used in scientific research.

Vocabulary transmutation • transuranium elements • quark

1 FOCUS

Build Vocabulary: Paraphrase
Ask students to write the vocabulary words on a sheet of paper. Instruct the students to write a definition, in their own words, for each term as they encounter the term while reading the section. **L2**

Targeted Resources
❑ Transparency: Interest Grabber 10.3
❑ Transparency: Reading Strategy 10.3

2 INSTRUCT

Build Reading Literacy: Visualize
Have students close their books and listen to you read aloud the paragraph about synthesizing neptunium. Ask students to describe how they visualize what happens in the transmutation. **L1**

Address Misconceptions
Challenge students to find out why scientists do not manufacture gold for profit using transmutation. **L2**

Quick Lab: Modeling Transmutation
Using beads to represent protons and neutrons, students will balance equations that describe simple nuclear reactions. **L2**

Build Science Skills: Inferring
After reading Particle Accelerators, ask students what evidence supports the claim that most transuranium elements can exist only when atoms are bombarded with particles at very high speeds. **L2**

Targeted Resources
❑ GRSW Section 10.3

3 ASSESS

Reteach
Have students look at the transmutation equations in the section and ask them to explain how transmutation differs from nuclear decay. **L1**

Evaluate Understanding
Ask students to write three completed equations for transmutations. Have students take turns giving the reactants for the equation while another student determines the product. **L2**

Targeted Resources
❑ **PHSchool.com** Online Section 10.3 Assessment
❑ iText Section 10.3

Transparencies

143 **Section 10.3 Interest Grabber**

Introduction to Transmutation

Examine the diagram below that represents the nuclei of isotopes in a nuclear reaction, and answer the questions that follow. In the diagram, the light circles represent protons, and the dark circles represent neutrons.

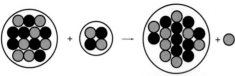

1. What isotopes are represented by the starting nuclei?

2. What isotope is represented by the larger nucleus that is produced in the nuclear reaction?

3. What other particle is produced?

Transparencies

144 **Section 10.3 Reading Strategy**

Monitoring Your Understanding

What I Expect to Learn	What I Learned
a. _____?_____	b. _____?_____
c. _____?_____	d. _____?_____

Guided Reading and Study Workbook

Name _____ Class _____ Date _____

Chapter 10   Nuclear Chemistry

Section 10.3 Artificial Transmutation
(pages 303–305)

This section discusses transmutations, transuranium elements, and particle accelerators.

Reading Strategy (page 303)

Monitoring Your Understanding Preview the Key Concepts, topic headings, vocabulary, and figures in this section. List two things you expect to learn. After reading, state what you learned about each item you listed. For more information on this Reading Strategy, see the **Reading and Study Skills** in the **Skills and Reference Handbook** at the end of your textbook.

Understanding Artificial Transmutation	
What I Expect to Learn Student answers may include:	**What I Learned**
Examples of artificial transmutation	Rutherford's transmutation of nitrogen-14 into oxygen-17; the synthesis of neptunium-239
Uses of transuranium elements	Smoke detectors (americium-241); space probes (plutonium-238)

Nuclear Reactions in the Laboratory (page 303)

1. Define transmutation. Transmutation is the conversion of atoms of one element to atoms of another element.

2. An example of a transmutation that occurs naturally is ___nuclear decay___.

3. How do scientists perform artificial transmutations? Scientists can perform artificial transmutations by bombarding atomic nuclei with high-energy particles such as protons, neutrons, or alpha particles.

4. Circle the letter that identifies the scientist who performed the first artificial transmutation.
   a. Ernest Rutherford   b. Niels Bohr
   c. Enrico Fermi   d. Lise Meitner

5. The experiment that produced the first artificial transmutation also provided evidence that the nucleus contains ___protons___.

Transuranium Elements (page 304)

6. Describe a transuranium element. A transuranium element is an element with an atomic number greater than that of uranium (92).

7. Is the following sentence true or false? All transuranium elements are radioactive. ___true___

Guided Reading and Study Workbook

Name _____ Class _____ Date _____

Chapter 10   Nuclear Chemistry

8. Scientists can synthesize a transuranium element by the artificial transmutation of a(n) ___lighter___ element.

9. Circle the letter of the first transuranium element to be synthesized.
   a. plutonium   b. americium
   c. technetium   d. neptunium

10. Circle the letter of the element that is used as a source of radiation in smoke detectors.
    a. uranium   b. americium
    c. technetium   d. plutonium

Particle Accelerators (page 305)

11. Why are particle accelerators needed for some transmutations? Some transmutations will occur only if the bombarding particles are moving at extremely high speeds.

12. Is the following sentence true or false? A particle accelerator can accelerate charged particles to speeds very close to the speed of light. ___true___

13. Describe a quark. A quark is a subatomic particle theorized to be among the basic units of matter.

14. Circle the letter that identifies the number of quarks in each proton or neutron.
    a. zero   b. two
    c. three   d. six

15. Complete the following concept map about alpha particles.

Alpha Particles

consist of

2 protons   2 neutrons

which are electrically   each of which is made up of   which are electrically

Positive   3 quarks   Neutral

LESSON PLAN 10.4

Fission and Fusion

Time
2 periods
1 block

Section Objectives

- **10.4.1 Compare** and **contrast** nuclear forces.

- **10.4.2 Describe** the process of nuclear fission.

- **10.4.3 Explain** how nuclear reactors are used to produce energy.

- **10.4.4 Describe** the process of nuclear fusion.

Vocabulary strong nuclear force • fission • chain reaction • critical mass • fusion • plasma

Local Standards

---

1 FOCUS

Build Vocabulary: Word-Part Analysis
Point out the words *fission* and *fusion*. Tell students that *-ion* means "the act of" or "the result of an act." Explain that *fiss-* comes from a Latin word meaning "split" and the *fus-* comes from another Latin word meaning "melted." **L2**

Targeted Resources
❑ Transparency: Interest Grabber 10.4
❑ Transparency: Reading Strategy 10.4

---

2 INSTRUCT

Build Math Skills: Formulas and Equations
Ask students to examine the mass-energy equation and determine the units of measurement that *E* is equivalent to. **L1**

Integrate Language Arts
Have students write a brief biography of one of the scientists who contributed to the understanding of nuclear fission. **L2**

Teacher Demo: Nuclear Processes
Use bubbles to show students a model of nuclear fission and fusion. **L2**

Build Science Skills: Observing
Tell students that the sun produces energy by nuclear fusion. Explain that fusion releases very large amounts of energy. Ask how we know that the sun produces large amounts of energy. **L2**

For Enrichment
Ask students to research how nuclear reactors in ships differ from those in nuclear power stations. **L3**

Targeted Resources
❑ Transparency: Figure 15: Comparing Strong Nuclear Forces and Electrical Forces

❑ Transparency: Figure 16: Effect of Nuclear Size on Nuclear and Electrical Forces

❑ Transparency: Figure 18: Nuclear Fission of Uranium-235

❑ Transparency: Figure 19: Chain Reaction of Uranium-235

❑ GRSW Section 10.4

❑ **NSTA** *sci*$_{INKS}$ Fission

---

3 ASSESS

Reteach
Use Figures 18 and 19 to summarize controlled and uncontrolled fission reactions. **L1**

Evaluate Understanding
Have students write down three characteristics of nuclear fission and fusion. Have students take turns giving a characteristic while the other students identify whether it is typical of fission or fusion. **L2**

Targeted Resources
❑ **PHSchool.com** Online Section 10.4 Assessment
❑ iText Section 10.4

Transparencies

145 Section 10.4 Interest Grabber

Observing Attractive and Repulsive Forces

1. Arrange two bar magnets so that they stick together. Reverse the orientation of one of the magnets. Record your observations.

2. With a pencil, make 20 marks on an index card, each 1 mm apart. Place the magnets on the index card and orient them so that they repel one another. Gently tap them closer together until they will not move closer due to the repelling force. Using the pencil marks, record the distance between the two magnets.

3. Place the magnets on the index card and orient them so that they attract one another. Gently tap them closer together until they snap together on their own. Using the pencil marks, record the distance between the two magnets at the point just before they snap together.

Transparencies

146 Section 10.4 Reading Strategy

Comparing and Contrasting

Fission   Fusion

a. ___?___   releases large amounts of energy   c. ___?___

b. ___?___   d. ___?___

Transparencies

147 Figure 15 **Comparing Strong Nuclear Forces and Electrical Forces**

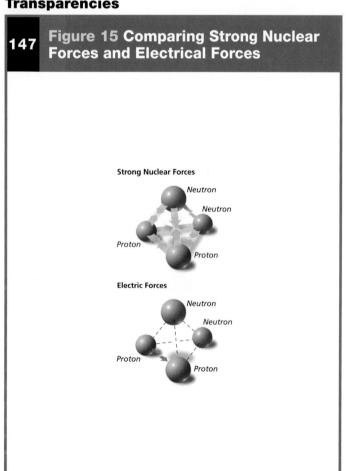

Strong Nuclear Forces

Neutron
Neutron
Proton
Proton

Electric Forces

Neutron
Neutron
Proton
Proton

Transparencies

148 Figure 16 **Effect of Nuclear Size on Nuclear and Electrical Forces**

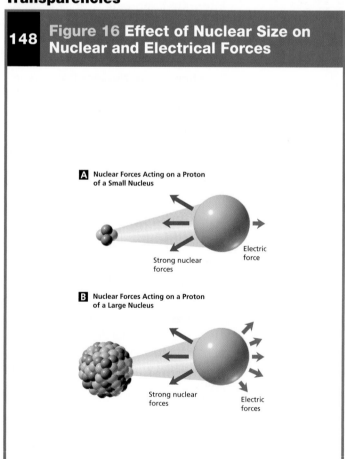

A Nuclear Forces Acting on a Proton of a Small Nucleus

Strong nuclear forces

Electric force

B Nuclear Forces Acting on a Proton of a Large Nucleus

Strong nuclear forces

Electric forces

Transparencies

149 Figure 18 **Nuclear Fission of Uranium-235**

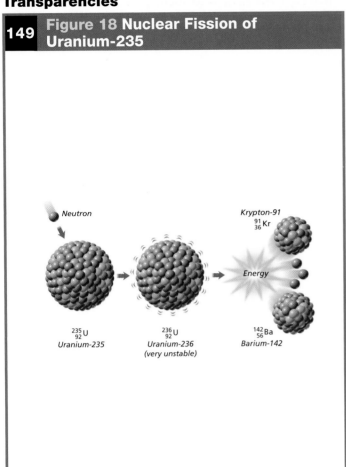

Transparencies

150 Figure 19 **Chain Reaction of Uranium-235**

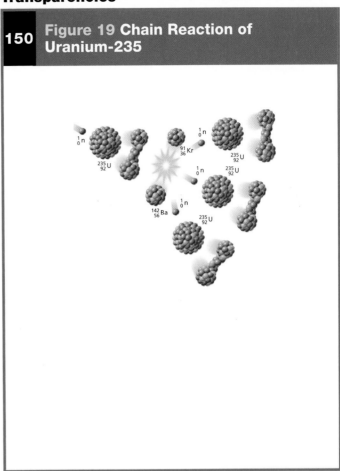

Transparencies

151 Figure 19 **Chain Reaction of Uranium-235** *(continued)*

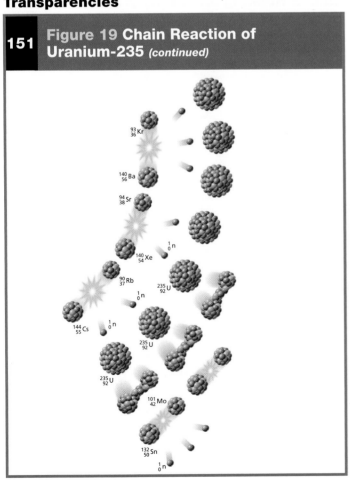

203

Guided Reading and Study Workbook

Name _____ Class _____ Date _____

Chapter 10 Nuclear Chemistry

Section 10.4 Fission and Fusion
(pages 308–315)

This section discusses nuclear forces and the conversion of mass into energy. It also describes the nuclear processes of fission and fusion.

Reading Strategy (page 308)

Comparing and Contrasting As you read, contrast fission and fusion in the Venn diagram below by listing the ways they differ. For more information on this Reading Strategy, see the **Reading and Study Skills** in the **Skills and Reference Handbook** at the end of your textbook.

Contrasting Fission and Fusion

Fission — Involves the splitting of a large nucleus into two smaller fragments; Is widely used as an alternate energy source

Releases large amounts of energy

Fusion — Involves the fusing of two small nuclei into one larger nucleus; Is still being researched and developed as an alternate energy source

Nuclear Forces (pages 308–309)

1. Describe the strong nuclear force. The strong nuclear force is the attractive force that binds protons and neutrons together in the nucleus.

2. Is the following sentence true or false? Over very short distances, the strong nuclear force is much greater than the electric forces among protons. true

3. Electric forces in atomic nuclei depend on the number of protons.

4. Is the following sentence true or false? The strong nuclear force on a proton or neutron is much greater in a large nucleus than in a small nucleus. false

5. All nuclei with 83 or more protons are radioactive.

Fission (pages 309–313)

6. Describe fission. Fission is the splitting of an atomic nucleus into two smaller parts.

7. Fission can produce very large amounts of energy from very small amounts of mass.

Guided Reading and Study Workbook

Name _____ Class _____ Date _____

Chapter 10 Nuclear Chemistry

8. Circle the letter that identifies what *c* represents in Einstein's mass-energy equation, $E = mc^2$.
   a. the charge on a proton
   (b.) the speed of light
   c. the charge on an electron
   d. the specific heat of the material

9. Is the following sentence true or false? During nuclear reactions mass is not conserved, but energy is conserved. false

10. Describe what can happen to a uranium-235 nucleus that absorbs a neutron. The nucleus can undergo fission, splitting into two smaller nuclei and releasing energy and more neutrons.

11. Complete the following table.

Chain Reactions		
Type of Chain Reaction	**Description**	**Example of An Application**
Uncontrolled	All neutrons released during fission are free to cause other fissions.	Nuclear weapons
Controlled	Some of the neutrons released during fission are absorbed by nonfissionable materials.	Nuclear power plants

12. Describe a critical mass. A critical mass is the smallest possible mass of a fissionable material that can sustain a chain reaction.

13. Is the following sentence true or false? Unlike power plants that burn fossil fuels, nuclear power plants do not emit air pollutants such as oxides of sulfur and nitrogen. true

14. Describe what happens during a meltdown. During a meltdown, the core of the reactor melts and radioactive material may be released.

Fusion (page 315)

15. The state of matter in which atoms have been stripped of their electrons is plasma.

16. Circle the letter of each main problem that scientists must face in designing a fusion reactor.
   (a.) Extremely high temperatures are necessary for a fusion reaction to start.
   (b.) The plasma that results from the reaction conditions must be contained.
   c. The hydrogen needed as a starting material is extremely scarce.
   d. Fusion reactions produce large quantities of radioactive waste.

Guided Reading and Study Workbook

Name _____ Class _____ Date _____

Chapter 10 Nuclear Chemistry

WordWise

Write the answer to each definition using one of the scrambled words below.

abte petalric   dorataivyicit   fonius
gnostr rauncel crefo licticar sams   lunarce tiadorian
magma yar   onisifs   pahal claptrie
pieatodorsoi   ruqak   samlap

Definition	Term
A subatomic particle theorized to be among the basic units of matter	quark
Charged particles and energy that are emitted from the nuclei of radioisotopes	nuclear radiation
A positively charged particle made up of two protons and two neutrons	alpha particle
A state of matter in which atoms have been stripped of their electrons	plasma
The process in which an unstable atomic nucleus emits charged particles and energy	radioactivity
A penetrating ray of energy emitted by an unstable nucleus	gamma ray
The attractive force that binds protons and neutrons together in the nucleus	strong nuclear force
The splitting of an atomic nucleus into two smaller parts	fission
An electron emitted by an unstable nucleus	beta particle
The smallest possible mass of a fissionable material that can sustain a chain reaction	critical mass
A process in which the nuclei of two atoms combine to form a larger nucleus	fusion
Any atom containing an unstable nucleus	radioisotope

Guided Reading and Study Workbook

Name _____ Class _____ Date _____

Chapter 10 Nuclear Chemistry

Nuclear Equations for Alpha Decay

Write a balanced nuclear equation for the alpha decay of polonium-218.

Math Skill: Formulas and Equations

You may want to read more about this **Math Skill** in the **Skills and Reference Handbook** at the end of your textbook.

1. **Read and Understand**

   What information are you given?

   Reactant isotope = polonium-218

   Radiation emitted = $^4_2$He (alpha particle)

   Use the periodic table to obtain the atomic number of polonium.

   Reactant isotope = $^{218}_{84}$Po

2. **Plan and Solve**

   What unknowns are you trying to calculate?

   Atomic number of product isotope, Z = ?

   Mass number of product isotope, A = ?

   Chemical symbol of product isotope, X = ?

   What equation contains the given information?

   $$^{218}_{84}\text{Po} \longrightarrow ^A_Z X + ^4_2\text{He}$$

   Write and solve equations for atomic mass and atomic number.

   $218 = A + 4$ $84 = Z + 2$
   $218 - 4 = A$ $84 - 2 = Z$
   $214 = A$ $82 = Z$

   On the periodic table, lead, Pb, has an atomic number of 82. So, X is Pb. The balanced nuclear equation is shown below.

   $$^{218}_{84}\text{Po} \longrightarrow ^{214}_{82}\text{Pb} + ^4_2\text{He}$$

3. **Look Back and Check**

   Is your answer reasonable?

   The mass number on the left equals the sum of the mass numbers on the right. The atomic number on the left equals the sum of the atomic numbers on the right. The equation is balanced.

Math Practice

On separate sheet of paper, solve the following problems.

1. Write a balanced nuclear equation for the alpha decay of uranium-238.

   $$^{238}_{92}\text{U} \longrightarrow ^{234}_{90}\text{Th} + ^4_2\text{He}$$

2. Write a balanced nuclear equation for the alpha decay of thorium-230.

   $$^{230}_{90}\text{Th} \longrightarrow ^{226}_{88}\text{Ra} + ^4_2\text{He}$$

Student Edition Lab Worksheet

Name _____ Class _____ Date _____

Chapter 10 Nuclear Chemistry   **Exploration Lab**

Modeling a Chain Reaction
See pages 316 and 317 in the Teacher's Edition for more information.

In a nuclear fission chain reaction, a nucleus is struck by a neutron, which causes the nucleus to split into two smaller nuclei and to release other neutrons. If these neutrons strike other nuclei, a chain reaction can occur. In this lab, you will model a nuclear fission chain reaction, using dominoes.

Problem How can you make a model of a nuclear fission chain reaction?

Materials
- 20 dominoes
- watch with a second hand, or stopwatch
- metric ruler

Skills Observing, Using Models

Procedure
1. Stand 15 dominoes in a single straight row in such a way that the distance between them is about one-half of their height. Knock over the first domino. Measure and record the time it takes for all the dominoes to fall.

2. Repeat Step 1 two more times. Then, average the three time measurements to get a more accurate time.

   0.7–0.9s

3. Arrange 15 dominoes, as shown below, so that each domino will knock over two others. Observe what happens when you knock over the first domino. Measure and record how long it takes for the whole set of dominoes to fall over.

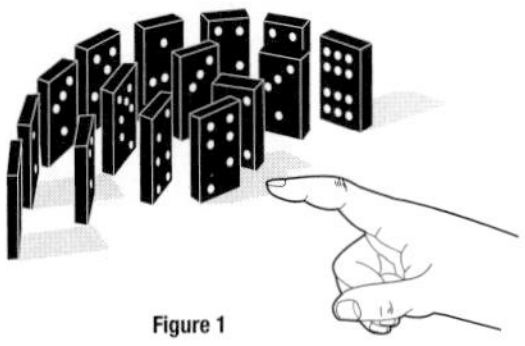

Figure 1

Student Edition Lab Worksheet

Name _____ Class _____ Date _____

4. Repeat Step 3 two more times. Average the three time measurements to get a more accurate time.

   0.5–0.7s

5. Set up 15 dominoes again as you did in Step 3. This time, however, hold a metric ruler on end, in the middle of the arrangement of dominoes. Knock over the first domino. Observe what happens.

   The ruler prevents some of the dominoes from falling.

6. Set up 15 dominoes as you did in Step 3, but this time, place 5 additional dominoes behind and at right angles to 5 randomly chosen dominoes for support, as shown below. The 5 supported dominoes represent atoms of a different isotope that must be struck with more energy to undergo fission.

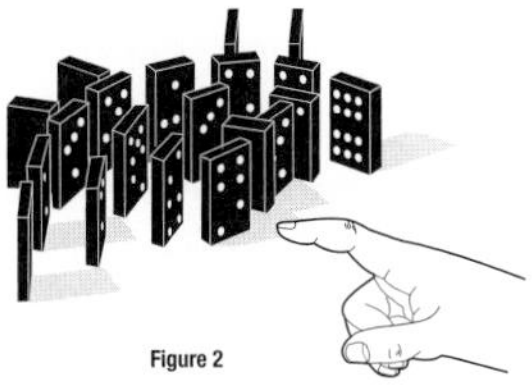

Figure 2

7. Knock over the first domino. Measure and record the time it takes for the dominoes to fall and how many dominoes fall.

   7–10 dominoes fall

8. Repeat Steps 6 and 7 two more times. Then, average the three time measurements to get a more accurate time.

   0.4–0.5s

Student Edition Lab Worksheet

Name _____ Class _____ Date _____

9. Repeat Steps 6 through 8, but this time, place supporting dominoes behind only 3 dominoes.

   10–12 dominoes fall; 0.3–0.4s

10. Repeat Steps 6 through 8, but this time, place a supporting domino behind only 1 domino.

    12–14 dominoes fall; 0.3–0.4s

Analyze and Conclude
1. **Calculating** What was the average fall time for the arrangement of dominoes in Steps 1 and 2? In Steps 3 and 4?

   The time should be shorter in Steps 3 and 4.

2. **Applying Concepts** What type of reaction was modeled in Steps 3 and 4?

   A nuclear fission chain reaction was modeled in Steps 3 and 4.

3. **Using Models** In your falling-dominoes model of nuclear fission chain reactions, what did a standing domino represent? What did the fall of a domino represent?

   A standing domino represented the nucleus of an atom. The fall of a domino represented

   the fission of the nucleus and the release of neutrons.

4. **Using Models** In your falling-dominoes model of nuclear fission chain reactions, what did the striking of one domino by another represent? What did the metric ruler represent?

   The striking of one domino by another represented the striking of a nucleus of a nearby atom

   by a neutron. The ruler represented a control rod.

Student Edition Lab Worksheet

Name _____ Class _____ Date _____

5. **Analyzing Data** Before a sample of an easily fissionable isotope is used, it is refined by removing less fissionable isotopes of the same element. On the basis of your observations in Steps 6 through 10, explain why this refinement is necessary.

   Atoms of the less-easily fissionable isotopes can absorb some of the energy released during

   the fission of other atoms, which can interfere with development of a chain reaction.

6. **Inferring** What factors do you think would affect the rate of a nuclear fission chain reaction?

   The number of neutrons released when a nucleus undergoes fission and the number of other

   atoms that are nearby and available for the released neutrons to strike affect the rate of the

   reaction.

7. **Drawing Conclusions** What do you think would happen to the nuclear fission chain reaction if control rods were not present?

   The reaction would go out of control, perhaps leading to a meltdown or an explosion.

8. **Evaluating and Revising** What are some of the limitations of using falling dominoes to model a nuclear fission chain reaction? Suggest how you might revise this model to make it more representative of a chain reaction.

   One limitation of the model in Step 3 is that it treats each fission reaction as the same. In reality,

   the fission of a nucleus does not always release exactly two neutrons. The model could be revised

   by using dominoes of varying sizes and/or colors to represent differing numbers of neutrons

   released during fission.

Lab Manual

Name _____ Class _____ Date _____

Modeling Radioactive Decay

Refer students to pages 292–301 in their textbooks for a general discussion of radioactivity and half-life.

Background Information

SKILLS FOCUS: Using Models, Measuring, Using Tables and Graphs, Comparing and Contrasting, Analyzing Data, Calculating

CLASS TIME: 45 minutes

Radioactive material decays by emitting **alpha particles, beta particles,** or **gamma rays.** During the process of nuclear decay, a radioisotope spontaneously changes into a different element. The time it takes for one-half of a sample of a radioisotope to decay into another element is called **half-life.** The half-lives of various radioisotopes vary from less than a second to billions of years.

A capacitor is a device that can store a large quantity of electric charge and then slowly release that charge. The process of releasing charge is called discharging. The ability of a capacitor to store charge can be measured in units called microfarads. Like a radioisotope, a discharging capacitor has a half-life. Unlike radioactive materials, capacitors do not give off nuclear radiation. As a result, a discharging capacitor can be used as a safe model of radioactive decay.

In this investigation, you will determine the half-lives of two capacitors. Then, you will use your observations to explain the difference between the decay of two radioactive elements.

Problem

How can a model help describe the decay of radioactive isotopes?

Pre-Lab Discussion

Read the entire investigation. Then, work with a partner to answer the following questions.

1. **Using Analogies** What property of a capacitor makes it useful for modeling the decay of a radioactive isotope?

   Like the decay of a radioactive isotope, the discharge of a capacitor has a half-life.

   _____

   _____

   _____

2. **Designing Experiments** How will you observe the discharge of the capacitors?

   The discharge of the capacitors will be observed by measuring the difference in voltage between

   the two sides of the capacitor.

   _____

   _____

   _____

Lab Manual

Name _____ Class _____ Date _____

3. **Predicting** The rating of each capacitor (4600 or 6000 microfarads) indicates its ability to store charge. Which capacitor do you expect to have the longer half-life?

   The capacitor with the higher rating (6000 microfarads) will have the longer half-life.

   _____

   _____

4. **Designing Experiments** You will use the power source to charge the capacitors. Why do you think you will need to disconnect the power source from each capacitor before you discharge the capacitor?

   The power source keeps the capacitor charged as long as the power source and capacitor

   are connected.

   _____

5. **Controlling Variables** Identify the manipulated, responding, and controlled variables in this investigation.

   a. Manipulated variable

   Rating of capacitor

   _____

   b. Responding variable

   Voltage across the capacitor

   _____

   c. Controlled variables

   Power source, voltmeter

   _____

Materials *(per group)*

4 alligator clips
5 insulated wires
2 capacitors (4600 and 6000 microfarads)
DC voltmeter
DC power source
switch
clock or watch with second hand
graph paper
metric ruler

The voltage range of the voltmeter should be equal to or slightly greater than the power source. For example, if you use a 0–10V voltmeter, use a 9-V power source.
Be sure that the positive terminal of the capacitor is connected to the positive terminal of the power source, or the capacitor might be damaged.
Use wire-cutting pliers to cut 15-cm lengths of wire and to remove 2 cm of insulation from each end of the wires.
Actual numbers of alligator clips and wires used may vary, depending on the type of switch and on the external leads of the capacitors and voltmeter used. Provide fresh batteries or an electronic DC power source. Other capacitors rated between 2000 and 6000 microfarads may be substituted if necessary.

Lab Manual

Name _____ Class _____ Date _____

Safety 🥽🧤

Put on safety goggles. Observe proper laboratory procedures when using electrical equipment. Keep all electrical equipment away from water. Do not apply more voltage to the capacitors than their safe operating voltage. Note all safety alert symbols next to the steps in the Procedure and review the meaning of each symbol by referring to the Safety Symbols on page xiii. Inform students of the rated voltage of the capacitors. Remind students not to exceed this voltage. Excessive voltage can cause the capacitors to burn or explode.

Procedure

🧤🥽 1. Work in groups of three. Use alligator clips and insulated wires to connect the 4600-microfarad capacitor, voltmeter, power source, and switch as shown in Figure 1. To avoid damaging the capacitor, make sure that the positive terminal of the capacitor is connected to the positive terminal of the power source and that the negative terminal of the capacitor is connected to the negative terminal of the power source. **CAUTION:** *Be very careful when using electricity. Do not close the switch yet. Before continuing with Step 2, have your teacher check your setup.*

Check student setups before allowing students to continue with Step 2. Make sure that all components are connected correctly.

2. Carefully examine the scale on the voltmeter. Because you will have to read the voltage very quickly, determine what each division on the voltmeter scale represents.

3. Close the switch and read the voltage. Do not start timing yet. Record this voltage in the data table next to 0 seconds.

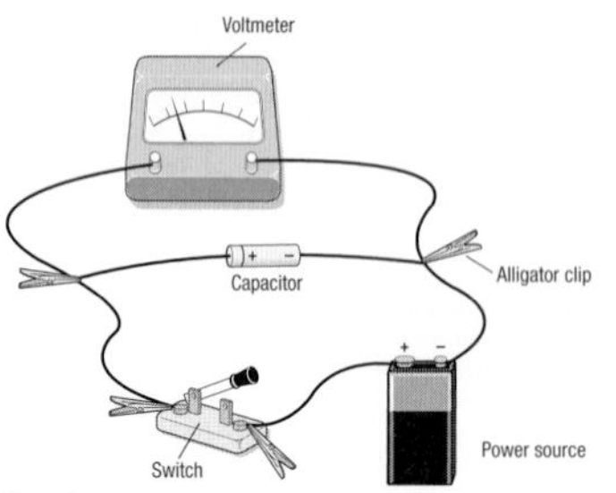

Voltmeter

Capacitor

Alligator clip

Switch

Power source

Figure 1

4. One member of your group will be the timer. This person will watch the clock and alert the others in the group to each 10-second interval. A second group member, the reader, will watch and read the voltmeter and call out the voltage when the timer announces each 10-second interval. A third group member will be the recorder. This person will record the voltages in the data table.

5. Start timing the 10-second intervals as you open the switch. After 10 seconds, the timer should call out "10 seconds," while the reader tells what the voltage is. **Note:** *The reader should try to anticipate each 10-second interval. Otherwise, it may take more than 10 seconds to decide what the reading is.*

Lab Manual

Name _____ Class _____ Date _____

6. Continue to record the voltage for 230 seconds. If the voltage becomes too small to measure before that time, you may stop at that point. If necessary, you may continue the data table on another sheet of paper.

7. Replace the 4600-microfarad capacitor with the 6000-microfarad capacitor.

8. Repeat Steps 1 through 6 with the 6000-microfarad capacitor.

Observations   Sample data are shown.

DATA TABLE

Time (seconds)	Voltage (volts) 4600-Microfarad Capacitor	Voltage (volts) 6000-Microfarad Capacitor	Time (seconds)	Voltage (volts) 4600-Microfarad Capacitor	Voltage (volts) 6000-Microfarad Capacitor
0	9.8	9.9	120	2.8	4.2
10	8.5	9.2	130	2.5	3.9
20	7.5	8.8	140	2.3	3.6
30	6.9	8.2	150	2.0	3.4
40	6.1	7.7	160	1.8	3.2
50	5.6	7.1	170	1.6	3.0
60	5.0	6.7	180	1.4	2.8
70	4.7	6.2	190	1.3	2.7
80	4.2	5.7	200	1.2	2.5
90	3.8	5.4	210	1.1	2.4
100	3.4	4.9	220	1.0	2.3
110	3.1	4.5	230	0.9	2.2

Analysis and Conclusions

1. **Using Graphs** On a sheet of graph paper, construct a graph of your data. Plot time on the horizontal axis and voltage on the vertical axis. Draw a smooth curve that comes as close as possible to each of your data points for the 4600-microfarad capacitor. Draw a second smooth curve for the data points for the 6000-microfarad capacitor. Label each curve with the rating of the capacitor it represents.

Student graphs should show two exponential decay curves. The 4600-microfarad capacitor will discharge faster than the 6000-microfarad capacitor.

Name _____ Class _____ Date _____

2. **Analyzing Data** Use your graph to find the half-life of the 4600-microfarad capacitor. To do this, calculate half of the voltage across this capacitor at 0 seconds. For example, if the voltage at 0 seconds was 10 volts, half of the voltage is 5 volts. Then, locate this voltage on the vertical axis. Use the metric ruler to draw a horizontal line from this voltage to the curve for the 4600-microfarad capacitor. Mark the point where this line intersects the curve. Then, draw a vertical line from this point down to the horizontal axis. The half-life is the time at which the vertical line intersects the horizontal axis. Record the half-life of the 4600-microfarad capacitor below.

Half-life of 4600-microfarad capacitor: _____60_____ seconds

3. **Analyzing Data** Use the procedure you used to answer Question 2 to determine the half-life of the 6000-microfarad capacitor.

Half-life of 6000 microfarad capacitor: _____100_____ seconds

4. **Evaluating** Did your data support or contradict your prediction?

The data support the prediction that the 6000-microfarad capacitor has the longer half-life.

5. **Analyzing Data** How long did the 4600-microfarad capacitor take to reach one-fourth of its original voltage?

120 seconds (2 half-lives)

6. **Calculating** If the voltage across the 4600-microfarad capacitor was 9.0 volts at 0 seconds, how many half-lives would be needed for the voltage to fall to 0.1 volts? How many seconds would that take?

A typical result is 7 half-lives or 420 seconds.

7. **Calculating** If the voltage across the 6000-microfarad capacitor was 9.0 volts at 0 seconds, how many half-lives would be needed for the voltage to fall to 0.1 volts? How many seconds would that take?

A typical result is 7 half-lives or 700 seconds.

8. **Comparing and Contrasting** Which capacitor would take longer to fall to a voltage that is too low for the voltmeter to measure? Explain your answer.

The 6000-microfarad capacitor would take longer because it has a longer half-life.

Name _____ Class _____ Date _____

9. **Using Models** Carbon-14 has a half-life of 5730 years. Uranium-238 has a half-life of 4.47×10^9 years. A radioisotope can be used to date an object only if enough of the radioisotope remains in the object to measure. Use your observations of the two capacitors to explain why carbon-14 can be used to date objects as old as 50,000 years, but uranium-238 can be used to date the objects that ar millions of years old.

The 6000-microfarad capacitor has a longer half-life than the 4600-microfarad capacitor has. As a result, the 6000-microfarad capacitor retains a measurable voltage longer than the 4600-microfarad capacitor. Similarly, because uranium-238 has a much longer half-life than carbon-14, traces of uranium-238 in an object can still be detected long after the amount of carbon-14 remaining in the object has become too small to measure.

Go Further

Use resources in the library or on the Internet to research how a technique called fission-track dating can be used to estimate the age of an object.

Fission tracks in rocks and other materials are created when uranium-238 undergoes spontaneous fission. During fission, the uranium-238 nucleus splits into two fragments. These fragments are driven apart by the energy of the nuclear reaction, resulting in a trail of damage in the host material. In fission-track dating, samples of mica or glass (natural or synthetic) are treated with a solution, such as an acid, to make the tracks more visible. The tracks are then viewed under a microscope and counted. The age of the sample can be estimated from the number of tracks per square centimeter of sample and the concentration of uranium in the sample.

Name _____ Class _____ Date _____

Chapter 10   Nuclear Chemistry   🔍 **Investigation 10B**

Detecting Nuclear Radiation

Refer students to pages 292–297 in their textbooks for a general discussion of radioactivity. **SKILLS FOCUS:** Observing, Comparing and Contrasting, Making Judgments, Evaluating and Revising **CLASS TIME:** 45 minutes

Background Information

A cloud chamber is a device that can be used to observe **radioactivity.** In the chamber, vapor of a substance such as alcohol is cooled to a low temperature. A particle of high energy passing through the chamber ionizes the molecules that the particle strikes in its path. Alcohol vapor condenses around the ions, producing a thin white trail. Each white trail reveals the path of a radioactive particle.

There are many sources of nuclear radiation. Cosmic rays, or high-energy particles from space, are one common source of nuclear radiation. Many rocks and building materials also produce small amounts of nuclear radiation. You can use a cloud chamber to determine whether background sources or radioactive samples produce measurable levels of radiation in your environment.

In this investigation, you will build a cloud chamber and use it to determine whether you are usually exposed to nuclear radiation.

Problem

Are you exposed to nuclear radiation in your daily life?

Pre-Lab Discussion

Read the entire investigation. Then, work with a partner to answer the following questions.

1. **Formulating Hypotheses** State a hypothesis about whether you are usually exposed to nuclear radiation.

People are generally exposed to low levels of background radiation.

2. **Controlling Variables** Identify the manipulated, responding, and controlled variables in this investigation.

   a. Manipulated variable

   Source of nuclear radiation

   b. Responding variable

   Number of white trails observed (or number of radioactive particles detected)

   c. Controlled variables

   Temperature, time, cloud chamber used

3. **Predicting** Based on your hypothesis, predict what you will observe in Step 7.

   A small number of white trails will be observed.

Name _____ Class _____ Date _____

4. **Predicting** Predict how your observations will differ in Steps 7 and 10. Explain the reasons for your prediction.

More white trails will be observed in Step 10 because the alpha source produces more nuclear radiation than the surrounding sources of background radiation.

5. **Inferring** Why is dry ice used in this lab?

Dry ice lowers the temperature, making the alcohol vapor more likely to condense.

Materials *(per group)*

black felt	dropper pipet	clock or watch
scissors	isopropyl alcohol	sealed alpha-radiation source
large glass jar with screw-on lid	dry ice	powerful flashlight
thick blotting paper	plastic tray	small wooden block
fast-drying glue	Wear heavy, insulated gloves when handling dry ice.	

Safety 🥽🧤🧪🔥✂️❄️⚠️

Put on safety goggles and a lab apron. Be careful to avoid breakage when working with glassware. Wear plastic disposable gloves when handling chemicals, as they may irritate the skin or stain skin or clothing. Never touch or taste any chemical unless instructed to do so. Keep alcohol away from any open flame. Be careful when handling sharp instruments. Be careful using dry ice. Never allow dry ice to touch your skin. Be careful with the alpha-radiation source. Alpha particles cannot pass through skin, but the source of the particles can be dangerous if swallowed or inhaled. Wash your hands thoroughly after carrying out this investigation. Note all safety alert symbols next to the steps in the Procedure and review the meaning of each symbol by referring to the Safety Symbols on page xiii.

Procedure

1. To construct a cloud chamber, use scissors to cut a circle of black felt slightly smaller than the inside diameter of the glass jar. **CAUTION:** *Be careful when using scissors.*

2. Place the felt circle in the bottom of the jar, as shown in Figure 1.

3. Cut a circle of thick blotting paper slightly smaller than the inside of the lid of the jar. Use fast-drying glue to stick the blotting paper to the bottom of the lid.

4. Use the dropper pipet to apply isopropyl alcohol to the blotting paper until it is saturated, but not so wet that alcohol drips from it. Let any excess alcohol drain into the sink. **CAUTION:** *Be careful handling isopropyl alcohol. It is poisonous.*

5. Screw the lid onto the jar.

Review the MSDS safety information for isopropyl alcohol, dry ice, and the alpha-radiation source with students before they perform this investigation. Sealed alpha-radiation sources appropriate for school laboratories are available from scientific supply companies. Keep the sources in a locked, labeled cabinet when students are not using them. Note how many are used and make sure that all are returned. Supervise students especially closely in this investigation. Before class, open the sources for use as directed by the manufacturer, but then tape a small square of aluminum foil over each of them. Use a needle to pierce a small, narrow hole through the foil for the radiation. Be careful not to allow the needle to touch the dangerous material inside the container.

Lab Manual

Name _____ Class _____ Date _____

6. Place the jar onto a large piece of dry ice that your teacher has placed into the tray. **CAUTION:** *Do not touch the dry ice. It can damage your skin.*

7. Working in a room that is partially darkened, direct the beam of the flashlight through the side of the jar. Observe the cloud chamber for the next 5 minutes. Count the number of white trails you observe. Record your observations in the data table. Partially darken the laboratory.

8. Unscrew the lid of the jar, leaving the jar in place on the dry ice. Put the wooden block on the felt at the bottom of the jar. If the blotting paper in the lid has begun to dry out, use the dropper pipet to place a few more drops of alcohol onto it. Obtain an alpha-radiation source from your teacher. Place the radiation source on top of the block. **CAUTION:** *Do not touch the radioactive material inside the alpha source.*

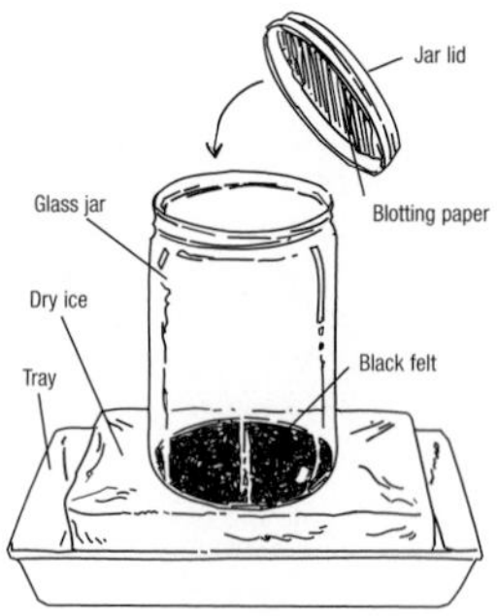

9. Screw on the lid of the jar again.

10. Direct the flashlight beam into the jar and watch what happens for the next 5 minutes. If possible, count the number of white trails you observe. Record your observations in the data table.

11. Return the radiation source to your teacher. Wash your hands thoroughly with warm water and soap or detergent before leaving the laboratory.

Jar lid
Glass jar
Blotting paper
Dry ice
Black felt
Tray

Figure 1

Observations Sample data are shown.

DATA TABLE

Source of Nuclear Radiation	Number of White Trails
Background	5–30
Background plus alpha source	More than 100

Lab Manual

Name _____ Class _____ Date _____

Analysis and Conclusions

1. **Evaluating and Revising** From your observations, what can you conclude about your predictions?

   The observations should support the prediction that the background radiation present will produce fewer white trails than the alpha source will.

2. **Comparing and Contrasting** Compare the amount of nuclear radiation usually reaching you with the amount you would receive when near a radioactive sample.

   Much more radiation would be received near a radiation sample.

3. **Evaluating and Revising** From your observations, what can you conclude about your hypothesis?

   The observations should support the hypothesis that people are usually exposed to small amounts of nuclear radiation.

4. **Making Judgments** Based on your observations, how would you advise someone who wanted to protect people's health by completely eliminating exposure to nuclear radiation?

   Completely eliminating exposure to nuclear radiation is not a realistic goal. It is also not necessary for protecting people's health. Small quantities of nuclear radiation are present at all times.

Go Further

Suppose that you had a source of both alpha and beta radiation in a cloud chamber. What could you do to make the paths of the two kinds of particles different so that you could tell them apart? Explain your answer. (*Hint:* Recall that alpha and beta particles are oppositely charged.)
Placing a strong magnet or a device that produces an electric field near the cloud chamber would produce a magnetic field or an electric field. The opposite charges of the alpha and beta particles would cause their paths to curve in opposite directions.

Chapter Test A

Name _____ Class _____ Date _____

Chapter 10 Nuclear Chemistry   **Chapter Test A**

Multiple Choice

Write the letter that best answers the question or completes the statement on the line provided.

_____ 1. Uranium-238 undergoes nuclear decay. Therefore, uranium-238 will
   a. remain stable.
   b. change into a different element altogether.
   c. emit neutral particles and no energy.
   d. none of the above

_____ 2. When radium-226 decays to form radon-222, the radium nucleus emits a(an)
   a. alpha particle.   b. beta particle.
   c. gamma ray.   d. electron.

_____ 3. Carbon-14 forms nitrogen-14 by
   a. alpha decay.   b. beta decay.
   c. gamma decay.   d. none of the above

_____ 4. Alpha-emitting substances, such as radon gas, can be a serious health hazard only if
   a. they are inhaled or eaten.
   b. their radiation strikes the skin.
   c. exposure to them is external.
   d. none of the above

_____ 5. Which of the following is NOT a step in the operation of a Geiger counter?
   a. Nuclear radiation ionizes gas in a tube.
   b. Ionized gas produces an electric current.
   c. Magnets cause the ions to conduct electricity.
   d. The electric current is detected and measured.

_____ 6. The half-life of tritium, or hydrogen-3, is 12.32 years. After about 37 years, how much of a sample of tritium will be left?
   a. ⅛   b. ¼   c. ⅓   d. ½

_____ 7. In a water solution, HCl and NaOH react to form H_2O and NaCl. Radium-226 undergoes alpha decay to form radon-222. The temperature of both of these reactions is increased. Which of the following statements is true?
   a. The rate of the chemical reaction will increase, but the rate of the nuclear reaction remains the same.
   b. The rate of the nuclear reaction will increase, but the rate of the chemical reaction remains the same.
   c. The rates of both reactions will increase.
   d. The rates of both reactions will remain the same.

Chapter Test A

Name _____ Class _____ Date _____

_____ 8. Carbon-14 has a half-life of 5730 years. If the age of an object older than 50,000 years cannot be determined by radiocarbon dating, then
   a. carbon-14 levels in a sample are undetectable after approximately ten half-lives.
   b. carbon-14 levels in a sample are undetectable after approximately nine half-lives.
   c. the half-life of carbon-14 is too long to accurately date the object.
   d. a radioisotope with a shorter half-life should be used to date the object.

_____ 9. Which of the following is NOT an example of a transmutation?
   a. Uranium-238 emits an alpha particle and forms thorium-234.
   b. Uranium-238 is bombarded with a neutron to produce uranium-239.
   c. Potassium-38 emits a beta particle and forms argon-38.
   d. Plutonium-239 is bombarded with two neutrons to produce americium-241 and a beta particle.

_____10. When curium-242 is bombarded with an alpha particle, two products are formed, one of which is a neutron. What is the other product?
   a. californium-246   b. californium-245
   c. californium-247   d. plutonium-239

_____11. The main purpose of a particle accelerator is to
   a. magnetize small particles.
   b. speed up small particles.
   c. slow down reaction products.
   d. reproduce reaction conditions found in nature.

_____12. In general, the nucleus of a small atom is stable. Therefore, over very short distances, such as those in a small nucleus,
   a. the strong nuclear force is much greater than the electric force.
   b. the electric force is much greater than the strong nuclear force.
   c. the strong nuclear force equals the electric force.
   d. the strong nuclear force and the electric force are both attractive.

_____13. Suppose three neutrons are released when an atom in a sample of fissionable nuclei undergoes fission. Each of these neutrons has enough energy to cause another fission reaction in another nucleus of the material. If the reaction is not controlled, how many atoms will have undergone fission after a series of five additional nuclear fissions?
   a. 15   b. 18   c. 243   d. 729

Name _____ Class _____ Date _____

_____ 14. Which of the following is NOT a way that water is used in a nuclear power station?
  a. Water cools the steam in the turbine chamber.
  b. Water is changed to steam by heat released by the reactor core.
  c. Steam makes the turbines rotate.
  d. Running water cools the rotating turbines.

_____ 15. Which of the following is NOT an advantage of using a fusion reaction instead of a fission reaction to produce energy?
  a. Workers are not in as much danger from radiation.
  b. Hydrogen is used, and hydrogen is easily obtained from water.
  c. No harmful waste products are produced.
  d. Fusion reactors require less energy than fission reactors do.

Completion
Complete each statement on the line provided.

1. Francium has 36 isotopes, but only francium-223 occurs in nature. Francium-223 spontaneously emits particles and energy, so francium-223 is a(an) _____ of francium.

2. You want to be shielded from all three types of nuclear radiation. If you find shielding that blocks _____ radiation, then it will most likely also block the other two types.

3. A less common type of radioactive particle emitted is the positron. If potassium-38 forms argon-38 by positron emission, the mass number of a positron is _____ and the charge is _____.

4. The fission reaction within a nuclear reactor is kept under control by the use of _____ that absorb extra _____.

5. Although the fusion of hydrogen to produce helium is the most common fusion reaction occurring in the sun, several other fusion reactions occur. In one of these, two helium-4 nuclei fuse to form one unstable _____ nucleus.

Short Answer
In complete sentences, write the answers to the questions on the lines provided.

1. How is an electron in a stable atom similar to a beta particle?

Name _____ Class _____ Date _____

2. Radiation treatments are commonly used to treat cancerous tumors. Explain why the radiation for these treatments comes in many different beams from many different directions toward the body instead of just one beam aimed toward the tumor.

3. Americium-241 is used in smoke detectors. What two particles are used to bombard an atom of plutonium-239 to create an atom of americium-241 if a beta particle is also produced?
$$^{239}_{94}\text{Pu} + 2 \ \ ? \rightarrow \ ^{241}_{95}\text{Am} + \ ^{0}_{-1}\text{e}$$

4. In terms of electrical attraction, why is it necessary to accelerate an alpha particle in order for it to effectively bombard a nucleus of a large atom?

5. Use the equation $E = mc^2$ to explain why large amounts of energy are produced by very small amounts of mass during nuclear fission.

Name _____ Class _____ Date _____

Using Science Skills
Use the diagram to answer each question. Write the answers on a separate sheet of paper.

1. **Applying Concepts** What product isotope is formed by the decay of radon-222? Use Figure 10-1 to answer this question.

2. **Calculating** Assume you have a 100-g sample of iodine-131. What product isotope is formed by the decay of this radioisotope? How much iodine-131 will remain unchanged after 24.21 days? Use Figure 10-1 to answer these questions.

3. **Calculating** Study Figure 10-1. How much nitrogen-14 will be produced from a 200-g sample of carbon-14 after 17,190 years?

4. **Applying Concepts** A rock sample contains one-fourth as much radium-226 as the relatively newly formed rock around it contains. How old is the rock sample? Use Figure 10-1 to answer this question.

5. **Using Tables and Graphs** What product isotope is produced by the decay of thorium-234? If an initial sample contains 48 g of thorium-234, how much of this product isotope will be present after 72.3 days? Use Figure 10-1 to answer these questions.

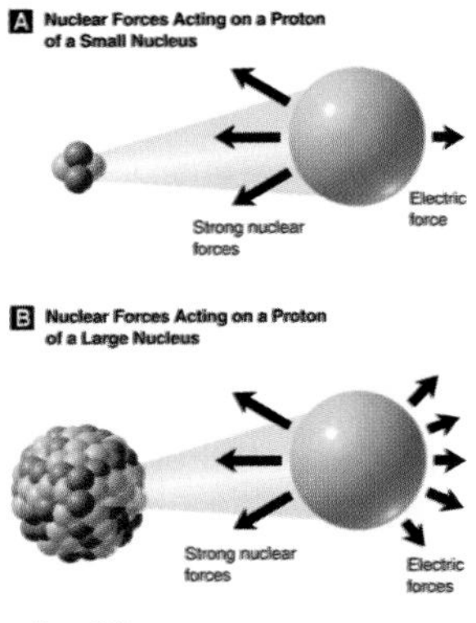

A Nuclear Forces Acting on a Proton of a Small Nucleus

Strong nuclear forces
Electric force

B Nuclear Forces Acting on a Proton of a Large Nucleus

Strong nuclear forces
Electric forces

Figure 10-1

Problem
Write the answers to each question on a separate sheet of paper.

1. Astatine-218 has a half-life of 1.6 s. Suppose you have a 1.2-g sample of astatine-218. How much of the sample remains unchanged after 6.4 seconds?

2. A sample of phosphorus-32 has a half-life of 14.28 days. If 25 g of this radioisotope remain unchanged after approximately 57 days, what was the mass of the original sample?

3. After 15 minutes, 30 g of a sample of polonium-218 remain unchanged. If the original sample had a mass of 960 g, what is the half-life of polonium-218?

Name _____ Class _____ Date _____

Essay
Write the answers to each question on a separate sheet of paper.

1. Compare and contrast the processes of fission and fusion.
2. Explain the path followed by carbon-14 atoms from when they form in the atmosphere until they are found in compounds in the human body.

Chapter Test B

Name _____   Class _____   Date _____

Chapter 10   Nuclear Chemistry   **Chapter Test B**

Multiple Choice

Write the letter that best answers the question or completes the statement on the line provided.

_____ 1. What is the process in which an unstable atomic nucleus emits charged particles or energy or both?
   a. radioactivity   b. oxidation
   c. decomposition   d. none of the above

_____ 2. What type of nuclear decay produces energy instead of a particle?
   a. alpha decay   b. beta decay
   c. gamma decay   d. electron decay

_____ 3. What type of radiation is emitted when polonium-212 forms lead-208?
   a. an alpha particle   b. a beta particle
   c. gamma radiation   d. all of the above

_____ 4. Which of the following statements is NOT true?
   a. You are exposed to nuclear radiation every day.
   b. Most of the nuclear radiation you are exposed to occurs naturally in the environment.
   c. Naturally occurring nuclear radiation is called background radiation.
   d. All natural radiation is at a level low enough to be safe.

_____ 5. Many people work near a source of nuclear radiation. To detect the amount of exposure they have to radiation, they most likely will use a
   a. Geiger counter.   b. film badge.
   c. radon kit.   d. lead shield.

_____ 6. The half-life of a radioisotope is the amount of time it takes for
   a. half the sample to decay.
   b. all the sample to decay.
   c. the age of an artifact to be calculated.
   d. detectable radiation to be absorbed by a sample.

_____ 7. Which of the following statements is true?
   a. Chemical reaction rates vary with the conditions of the change, but nuclear decay rates do not.
   b. Nuclear decay rates vary with the conditions of the change, but chemical reaction rates do not.
   c. Both chemical reaction rates and nuclear decay rates vary with the conditions of the change.
   d. Neither chemical reaction rates nor nuclear decay rates vary with the conditions of the change.

Chapter Test B

Name _____   Class _____   Date _____

_____ 8. Which of the following is a radioisotope used to date rock formations?
   a. carbon-14   b. potassium-40   c. cobalt-60   d. carbon-12

_____ 9. Transmutation involves
   a. nuclear change.   b. chemical change.
   c. both a nuclear change and a chemical change.
   d. neither a nuclear nor chemical change.

_____ 10. Which of the following is an example of a transuranium element?
   a. samarium, Sm   b. uranium, U
   c. curium, Cm   d. thorium, Th

_____ 11. Which of the following particles is smaller than the rest?
   a. electron   b. proton   c. neutron   d. quark

_____ 12. Study Figure 10-1. The strong nuclear force felt by a single proton in a large nucleus
   a. is much greater than that felt by a single proton in a small nucleus.
   b. is much less than that felt by a single proton in a small nucleus.
   c. is about the same as that felt by a single proton in a small nucleus.
   d. is about the same as the electric force felt by a single proton in a small nucleus.

Nuclear Radiation			
Radiation Type	Symbol	Charge	Mass (amu)
Alpha particle	α, $^4_2$He	2+	4
Beta particle	β, $^0_{-1}$e	1−	$\frac{1}{1836}$
Gamma ray	γ	0	0

Figure 10-1

_____ 13. During nuclear fission, great amounts of energy are produced from
   a. very small amounts of mass.   b. tremendous amounts of mass.
   c. a series of chemical reactions.   d. particle accelerators.

_____ 14. Which of the following is an advantage of using nuclear power plants to produce electricity?
   a. Nuclear power plants do not pollute the air.
   b. Nuclear power plants produce wastes that are easy to dispose.
   c. Nuclear power plants produce more stable wastes compared to fossil fuel combustion.
   d. all of the above

_____ 15. In what state must matter exist for fusion reactions to take place?
   a. solid   b. liquid   c. gas   d. plasma

Chapter Test B

Name _____   Class _____   Date _____

Completion

Complete each statement on the line provided.

1. An alpha particle is the same as a(an) _____ nucleus.

2. In the symbol $^4_2$He, the superscript *4* is the _____ for helium, and the subscript 2 is the _____ for helium.

3. When a human body is exposed to external nuclear radiation, the amount of tissue damage depends on the _____ power of the radiation.

4. A sample of a radioisotope had a mass of 100.0 g. After exactly 24 days, 6.25 g of the sample remained. The half-life of the isotope is _____ days.

5. In radiocarbon dating, the carbon-14 levels in the object being dated is compared to the carbon-14 levels in the _____.

6. Scientists can synthesize a transuranium element by the artificial _____ of a lighter element.

7. The particle that makes up protons and neutrons and is thought to be a basic unit of matter is a(an) _____.

8. One purpose of collision experiments is to study _____ structure.

9. In nuclear reactions, _____ is converted into energy.

10. In a(an) _____, neutrons released during a fission reaction cause a series of other fission reactions.

Short Answer

In complete sentences, write the answers to the questions on the lines provided.

1. How did the physicist Becquerel first observe the effects of nuclear decay?

_____
_____
_____
_____
_____

2. What particle will balance the following nuclear equation?
$$^{234}_{91}Pa \rightarrow U + ?$$
_____

Chapter Test B

Name _____   Class _____   Date _____

3. What is one common source of background radiation?

_____
_____
_____

4. What radioisotope is used as the fuel for a nuclear reactor?

_____

5. What two problems must be overcome before fusion can be used to produce energy?

_____
_____

Using Science Skills

Use the diagram to answer each question. Write the answers on a separate sheet of paper.

1. **Drawing Conclusions** A beta particle does have mass, so why is zero the mass number for a beta particle? Use Figure 10-2 to answer this question.

2. **Calculating** Study Figure 10-2. What type of nuclear radiation completes the following decay equation?
$$^{218}_{84}Po \rightarrow ^{214}_{82}Pb + ?$$

3. **Calculating** Study Figure 10-2. What type of nuclear radiation completes the following decay equation?
$$^{210}_{83}Bi \rightarrow ^{204}_{84}Po + ?$$

4. **Using Tables and Graphs** Why doesn't emission of gamma radiation change either the mass number or the atomic number of the nucleus? Use Figure 10-2 to answer this question.

5. **Drawing Conclusions** Study Figure 10-2. Explain how the mass and atomic numbers of an alpha particle can be used to determine the number of neutrons in the particle.

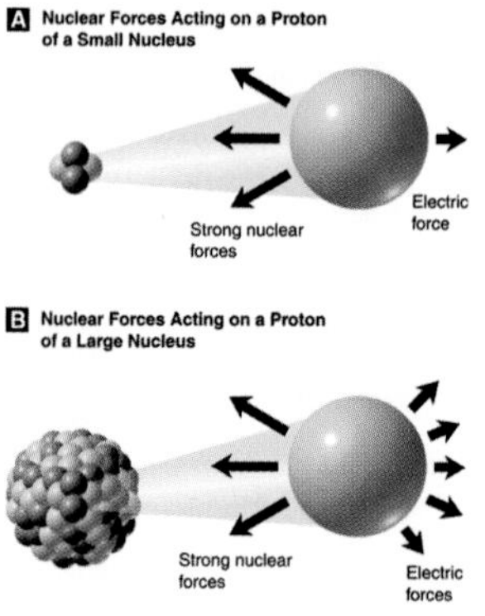

A Nuclear Forces Acting on a Proton of a Small Nucleus

Strong nuclear forces

Electric force

B Nuclear Forces Acting on a Proton of a Large Nucleus

Strong nuclear forces

Electric forces

Figure 10-2

Chapter 10 Test A Answers

Multiple Choice

1. b   **2.** a   **3.** b   **4.** a   **5.** c   **6.** a
7. a   **8.** b   **9.** b   **10.** b   **11.** b   **12.** a
13. c   **14.** d   **15.** d

Completion

1. radioisotope   **2.** gamma   **3.** 0, +1   **4.** control rods, neutrons
5. beryllium-8

Short Answer

1. Both particles are identical in mass and charge.
2. Focusing the beam from many different directions keeps healthy tissue from being exposed to too much radiation. The only tissue that receives a large amount of radiation is the tumor. **3.** neutrons
4. Both the nucleus and the alpha particle are positively charged. The alpha particles must be accelerated enough to overcome the repulsion of two positively charged particles. **5.** The amount of energy produced equals the amount of mass times the speed of light squared. Because the speed of light is such a large number, a very small amount of mass multiplied by this large number produces a large amount of energy.

Using Science Skills

1. polonium-218   **2.** xenon-131; 12.5 g   **3.** 175 g
4. 3240 years old   **5.** protactinium-234; 42 g

Problem

1. 0.075 g   **2.** 400 g   **3.** 3 min

Essay

1. Possible answer: During fission, a larger nucleus is broken down into two smaller nuclei. During fusion, a larger nucleus is formed from smaller nuclei. Fission produces potentially harmful products, but fusion does not. Fission is currently used as a power source, but fusion requires too much energy and is too difficult to contain.
2. Carbon-14 is produced in the atmosphere when neutrons produced by cosmic rays collide with nitrogen-14 atoms. Carbon-14 reacts with oxygen in the atmosphere, forming carbon dioxide. Plants take in the carbon dioxide during photosynthesis. When humans eat plants, the carbon-14 atoms in the plants are incorporated into compounds in the human body.

Chapter 10 Test B Answers

Multiple Choice

1. a   **2.** c   **3.** a   **4.** d   **5.** b   **6.** a
7. a   **8.** b   **9.** a   **10.** c   **11.** d   **12.** c
13. a   **14.** a   **15.** d

Completion

1. helium   **2.** mass number, atomic number
3. penetrating   **4.** 6   **5.** atmosphere   **6.** transmutation
7. quark   **8.** atomic   **9.** mass   **10.** chain reaction

Short Answer

1. Uranium salts wrapped in paper left a pattern on unexposed photographic film. He concluded that the salts emitted rays that exposed the film. **2.** a beta particle **3.** Accept any of the following: collisions between cosmic rays and particles in the atmosphere; radioisotopes in air, water, rocks, plants, and animals.
4. uranium-235 **5.** containment of the plasma and attainment of extremely high temperatures

Using Science Skills

1. The mass of the beta particle is so small ($\frac{1}{1836}$ amu) that it is not significant compared to the mass of a proton or neutron (1 amu).
2. an alpha particle **3.** a beta particle **4.** Gamma radiation is not a particle. It is a ray of energy that has neither charge nor mass. **5.** The atomic number tells the number of protons. The mass number tells the total number of protons and neutrons. The mass number (4) minus the atomic number (2) tells you that there are 2 neutrons in an alpha particle.

Unit 1 Test A

Name _____ Class _____ Date _____

Unit 1   Chemistry   Unit Test A

Multiple Choice

Write the letter that best answers the question or completes the statement on the line provided.

_____ 1. How are science and technology related?
   a. Technology is a branch of natural science.
   b. Science is a branch of technology.
   c. Advances in science may lead to advances in technology and vice versa.
   d. Science and technology are not related.

_____ 2. Why are scientific models important?
   a. They prove scientific theories.
   b. They help visualize things that are very complex, very large, or very small.
   c. They make it harder to understand things.
   d. They never change.

_____ 3. The type of graph used to show how a part of something relates to the whole is a
   a. circle graph   b. bar graph
   c. line graph   d. direct proportion

_____ 4. Which of the following is a characteristic of a mixture?
   a. has varying properties
   b. has a fixed composition
   c. contains only pure substances
   d. both a and b

_____ 5. Which of the following has the highest viscosity?
   a. corn syrup   b. milk
   c. water   d. orange juice

_____ 6. A substance that has high reactivity
   a. easily combines chemically with other substances.
   b. burns in the presence of water.
   c. displaces dissolved oxygen.
   d. has a high boiling point.

_____ 7. Forces of attraction limit the motion of particles most in
   a. a solid.   b. a liquid.
   c. a gas.   d. both b and c

_____ 8. The phase change that is the reverse of condensation is
   a. freezing.   b. sublimation.
   c. vaporization.   d. melting.

_____ 9. The phase change in which a substance changes from a solid to a gas or vapor without changing to a liquid first is
   a. sublimation.   b. deposition.
   c. evaporation.   d. melting.

Unit 1 Test A

Name _____ Class _____ Date _____

_____ 10. Which of the following most accurately represents John Dalton's model of the atom?
   a. a tiny, solid sphere with an unpredictable mass for a given element
   b. a hollow sphere with a dense nucleus
   c. a tiny, solid sphere with predictable mass for a given element
   d. a sphere that is hollow throughout

_____ 11. Which statement about subatomic particles is true?
   a. Protons, neutrons, and electrons all have about the same mass.
   b. Unlike protons or neutrons, electrons have no mass.
   c. Neutrons have no charge and no mass.
   d. An electron has far less mass than either a proton or neutron.

_____ 12. What do scientists use to predict the locations of electrons in atoms?
   a. probability   b. algebra
   c. geometry   d. ratios and proportions

_____ 13. The standard on which the atomic mass unit is based is the mass of a
   a. proton.   b. neutron.
   c. chlorine-35 atom.   d. carbon-12 atom.

_____ 14. Atoms of the most reactive elements tend to have
   a. one or seven valence electrons.
   b. eight valence electrons.
   c. four or five valence electrons.
   d. no valence electrons.

_____ 15. Which element is found in nature only in compounds?
   a. sodium   b. helium
   c. oxygen   d. nitrogen

_____ 16. Which of the following groups contain three elements with stable electron configurations?
   a. lithium, krypton, argon
   b. argon, neon, barium
   c. xenon, neon, boron
   d. helium, xenon, neon

_____ 17. Ionization energies tend to
   a. decrease from left to right across a period.
   b. increase from the top of a group to the bottom.
   c. increase from left to right across a period.
   d. decrease from the top of a group to the bottom.

Unit 1 Test A

Name _____ Class _____ Date _____

_____ 18. The name *copper(II)* indicates that a compound contains
   a. copper ions with a 11+ charge.
   b. copper ions with a 2+ charge.
   c. copper ions with a negative charge.
   d. two types of copper ions.

_____ 19. An industrial process makes calcium oxide by decomposing calcium carbonate. Which of the following is NOT needed to calculate the mass of calcium oxide that can be produced from 4.7 kg of calcium carbonate?
   a. the balanced chemical equation
   b. molar masses of the reactants
   c. molar masses of the product
   d. the volume of the unknown mass

_____ 20. For the chemical reaction $C_2H_6 + 137$ kJ $\rightarrow C_2H_4 + H_2$, the chemical energy of the
   a. reactant is greater than the chemical energy of the products.
   b. products is greater than the chemical energy of the reactant.
   c. reactant and the chemical energy of the products are equal.
   d. reaction is conserved.

_____ 21. The reaction $H_2CO_3 + H_2O \rightleftharpoons H_3O^+ + HCO_3^-$ takes place in water. What happens to the equilibrium when the pressure is increased?
   a. It favors formation of reactants.
   b. It favors formation of products.
   c. It does not change.
   d. It is conserved.

_____ 22. The solubility of carbon dioxide gas in water can be increased by
   a. increasing the temperature.
   b. agitating the mixture.
   c. increasing the pressure.
   d. using more solvent.

_____ 23. Which of the following is NOT a common property of bases?
   a. feels slippery   b. tastes bitter
   c. reacts with metals   d. changes colors of indicators

_____ 24. The products of the neutralization reaction between hydrochloric acid and magnesium hydroxide are
   a. $MgCl$ and H_2O.   b. $MgCl_2$ and H_2O.
   c. HCl and $MgOH$.   d. HCl and $Mg(OH)_2$.

Unit 1 Test A

Name _____ Class _____ Date _____

_____ 25. Butane has the formula C_4H_{10}. Which of the following is the formula of cyclobutane?
   a. C_4H_4 b. C_4H_6 c. $4H_8$ d. C_4H_{10}

_____ 26. Which of the following statements explains why inhaling carbon monoxide is dangerous?
   a. Carbon monoxide reacts with oxygen to produce carbon dioxide.
   b. Carbon monoxide keeps hemoglobin in the blood from carrying oxygen to cells.
   c. Carbon monoxide is a colorless, odorless gas.
   d. all of the above

_____ 27. Proteins that act as catalysts for chemical reactions that occur in cells are
   a. vitamins.   b. enzymes.
   c. carbohydrates.   d. amino acids.

_____ 28. Uranium-238 undergoes nuclear decay. Therefore, uranium-238 will
   a. remain stable.
   b. change into a different element altogether.
   c. emit neutral particles and no energy.
   d. none of the above

_____ 29. In a water solution, HCl and NaOH react to form H_2O and NaCl. Radium-226 undergoes alpha decay to form radon-222. The temperature of both of these reactions is increased. Which of the following statements is true?
   a. The rate of the chemical reaction will increase, but the rate of the nuclear reaction remains the same.
   b. The rate of the nuclear reaction will increase, but the rate of the chemical reaction remains the same.
   c. The rates of both reactions will increase.
   d. The rates of both reactions will remain the same.

_____ 30. Suppose three neutrons are released when an atom in a sample of fissionable nuclei undergoes fission. Each of these neutrons has enough energy to cause another fission reaction in another nucleus of the material. If the reaction is not controlled, how many atoms will have undergone fission after a series of five additional nuclear fissions?
   a. 15   b. 18   c. 243   d. 729

Completion

Complete each statement on the line provided.

1. An experiment in which only one variable, the manipulated variable, is changed at a time is called a(an) _____.

Name _____ Class _____ Date _____

2. In scientific notation, $(8.2 \times 10^4 \text{ m}) \times (3.7 \times 10^2 \text{ m})$ equals
_____.

3. In a(an) _____ mixture, the parts of the mixture are noticeably different from one another.

4. Rust forms because iron and oxygen are highly _____ elements.

5. If you know the volume and pressure of a gas and the pressure changes, you can find the new volume by multiplying P_1 by V_1 and _____ this number by P_2.

6. During vaporization, a substance changes from a(an) _____ to a(an) _____.

7. The difference between a sample of heavy water and regular water is that a hydrogen atom in heavy water has an extra _____.

8. An atom in which an electron has moved to a higher energy level is in a(an) _____ state.

9. The pattern of repeating properties of elements revealed in the periodic table is known as the _____.

10. Fertilizers usually contain two elements from Group 5A, which are _____ and phosphorus.

11. When cesium and fluorine react, they form an ionic compound called cesium _____.

12. The compound whose formula is SO_3 is called sulfur _____.

13. For a certain chemical reaction, the reactants contain 362 kJ of chemical energy, and the products contain 342 kJ of chemical energy. In order for energy to be conserved, 20 kJ of energy must be _____.

14. A sample of HBr contains 186 g of the compound. The sample contains _____ moles of HBr.

15. Antifreeze is added to a radiator because it _____ the boiling point and _____ the freezing point of the solution contained in the radiator.

16. The pH of a solution is 11. The concentration of hydronium ions in the solution is _____.

17. Suppose a saturated and unsaturated hydrocarbon both contain the same number of carbon atoms. The saturated hydrocarbon contains more of the element _____ than the unsaturated hydrocarbon does.

18. High-density polyethylene (HDPE) is much harder than low-density polyethylene (LDPE). You can conclude that there are more carbon atoms in a chain of _____.

Name _____ Class _____ Date _____

19. A less common type of radioactive particle emitted is the positron. If potassium-38 forms argon-38 by positron emission, the mass number of a positron is _____ and the charge is _____.

20. Although the fusion of hydrogen to produce helium is the most common fusion reaction occurring in the sun, several other fusion reactions occur. In one of these, two helium-4 nuclei fuse to form one unstable _____ nucleus.

Short Answer

In complete sentences, write the answers to the questions on the lines provided.

1. The study of an organism that lived 10 million years ago would most likely fall under which two branches of natural science?

_____
_____

2. How do changes in temperature usually affect the viscosity of a liquid? Explain how the viscosity of motor oil makes it a good choice for protecting an automobile engine in both hot and cold weather.

_____
_____
_____
_____

3. How could you determine if a phase change is endothermic?

_____
_____
_____
_____

4. How does the electron cloud model of the atom represent the locations of electrons in atoms?

_____
_____
_____

5. The elements silicon (atomic number 14) and chlorine (atomic number 17) are both in Period 3. Which is the more reactive element?

Name _____ Class _____ Date _____

6. In potassium bromide, KBr, which element forms anions?

_____

7. A student balanced the chemical equation $Mg + O_2 \rightarrow MgO$ by writing $Mg + O_2 \rightarrow MgO_2$. Was the equation balanced correctly? Explain your answer. If the equation was not balanced correctly, write the correctly balanced equation.

_____
_____
_____
_____

8. Compare and contrast an exothermic chemical reaction and an exothermic solution formation by dissociation.

_____
_____
_____
_____

9. What two products are formed from the reaction of a halocarbon and a base?

_____
_____

10. In terms of electrical attraction, why is it necessary to accelerate an alpha particle in order for it to effectively bombard a nucleus of a large atom?

_____
_____
_____
_____
_____
_____

Using Science Skills

Use the diagram to answer each question. Write the answers on a separate sheet of paper.

1. **Using Tables and Graphs** In Figure 1-1, what quantity does the slope represent?

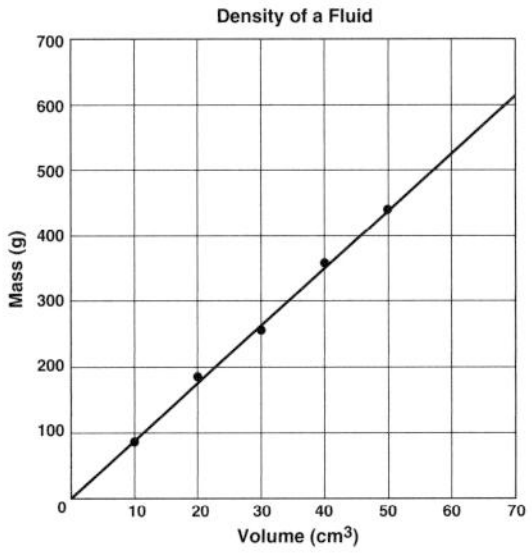

Density of a Fluid
Figure 1-1

Name _____ Class _____ Date _____

Properties of Three Mixtures			
	Scatters Light	Separates into Layers	Can Be Separated by Filtration
Mixture A	Yes	No	No
Mixture B	No	No	No
Mixture C	Yes	Yes	Yes

Figure 1-2

2. **Analyzing Data** Which of the mixtures in Figure 1-2 is a colloid? Explain how you know.

3. **Interpreting Graphics** In Figure 1-3, what is the unit used for pressure? What is the pressure when the volume is 0.5 L? What is the pressure when the volume is 1.0 L?

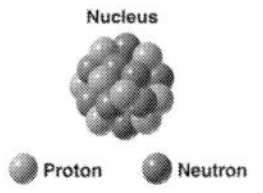

Nucleus
● Proton   ● Neutron   **Figure 1-4**

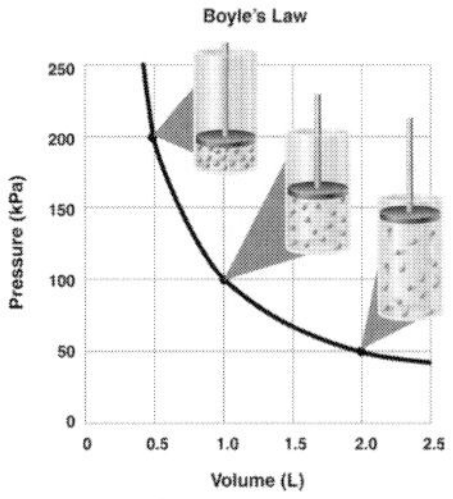

Boyle's Law
Figure 1-3

4. **Evaluating** Is Figure 1-4 a useful model of an atom? Explain your answer.

5. **Inferring** Identify the most reactive element shown in Figure 1-5. Explain your answer.

6. **Comparing and Contrasting** In Figure 1-6, how are the compounds in rows A and C similar? How are they different?

Figure 1-5

Figure 1-6

	Substances	Compound	Remarks
A	potassium, K, and iodine, I	KI	Iodine is a member of the halogen group; potassium is an alkali metal.
B	carbon, C, and oxygen, O	CO_2	Carbon and oxygen are both nonmetals.
C	Al, O, and H	$Al(OH)_3$	OH^- (hydroxide) is a polyatomic ion.

Unit 1 Test A

Name _____ Class _____ Date _____

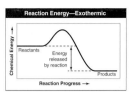 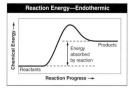

Figure 1-7

7. Using Tables and Graphs What do the peaks on the graphs in Figure 1-7 represent?

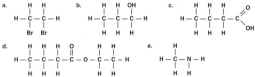

Substance	Solubility (g/100 g H_2O, 20°C)	Substance	Solubility (g/100 g H_2O, 20°C)
Barium hydroxide	3.89	Potassium chloride	34.2
Barium nitrate	9.02	Sodium chloride	35.9
Calcium hydroxide	0.173	Sucrose (table sugar)	203.9

Figure 1-8

8. Applying Concepts A boy wanted to make candy from crystallized sugar. He dissolved 300.0 g of sucrose in 75 g of water at 100°C. To the nearest gram, how much sugar crystallized out of the saturated solution when it cooled to 20°C? Use Figure 1-8 to answer this question.

a. H H
H—C—C—H
Br Br

b. H H OH
H—C—C—C—H
H H H

c. H H H O
H—C—C—C—C
H H H OH

d. H H H O H H
H—C—C—C—C—O—C—C—H
H H H H H

e. H
H—C—N—H
H H

Figure 1-9

9. Inferring The ester ethyl butanoate provides the taste and smell to pineapple. Identify the structural formula in Figure 1-9 for ethyl butanoate.

Unit 1 Test A

Unit 1 Test A

Name _____ Class _____ Date _____

10. Using Tables and Graphs What product isotope is produced by the decay of thorium-234? If an initial sample contains 48 g of thorium-234, how much of this product isotope will be present after 72.3 days? Use Figure 1-10 to answer these questions.

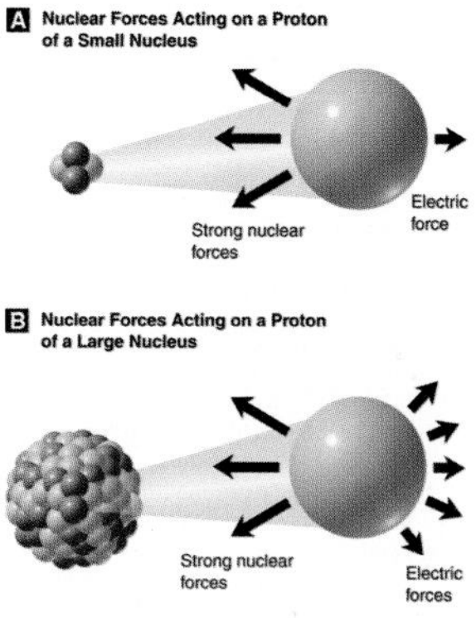

A Nuclear Forces Acting on a Proton of a Small Nucleus

Strong nuclear forces

Electric force

B Nuclear Forces Acting on a Proton of a Large Nucleus

Strong nuclear forces

Electric forces

Figure 1-10

Problem

Write the answers to each question on a separate sheet of paper.

1. When iron metal reacts with oxygen, the reaction can form Fe_2O_3. Write a balanced chemical equation for this reaction, and find the number of moles of oxygen that are needed to form 6 mol of Fe_2O_3.
2. Write a balanced chemical equation for the formation of carbonic acid from carbon dioxide and water.

Essay

Write the answers to each question on a separate sheet of paper.

1. Explain how peer reviews are important in either supporting a hypothesis or revising a hypothesis.
2. Suppose you want to separate the leaves, acorns, and twigs from a pile of soil. Filtration and distillation are two processes of separating mixtures. Explain which process you would use and why.
3. Use breathing as an example to explain the relationship between volume and air pressure.

Unit 1 Test B

Name _____ Class _____ Date _____

Unit 1 Chemistry   Unit Test B

Multiple Choice

Write the letter that best answers the question or completes the statement on the line provided.

_____ 1. Which of the following is NOT one of the main ideas of physical science?
a. The universe is very old and very large.
b. Forces cause changes in motion.
c. Energy can be transferred from one form to another, but it can never be destroyed.
d. One of the main branches of natural science is biology.

_____ 2. What is the most important safety rule?
a. Never work with chemicals.
b. Always use unbreakable glassware.
c. Always follow your teacher's instructions and textbook directions exactly.
d. Never do experiments that involve flames or hot objects.

_____ 3. How do scientists communicate the results of investigations?
a. by publishing articles in scientific journals
b. by giving talks at scientific conferences
c. by exchanging e-mails
d. all of the above

_____ 4. A substance that is made up of only one kind of atom is a(an)
a. compound.
b. homogeneous mixture.
c. element.
d. solution.

_____ 5. A mixture can be classified as a solution, suspension, or colloid based on the
a. number of particles it contains.
b. size of its largest particles.
c. color of its particles.
d. size of its smallest particles.

_____ 6. Which of the following is a chemical change?
a. ice melting
b. ice being carved
c. water boiling
d. water breaking down into hydrogen and oxygen

_____ 7. A gas has
a. a definite volume but no definite shape.
b. a definite shape but no definite volume.
c. no definite shape or definite volume.
d. a definite volume and definite shape.

Unit 1 Test B

Unit 1 Test B

Name _____ Class _____ Date _____

_____ 8. The temperature and volume in a closed container of gas remain constant. If the number of particles of gas is increased, the gas pressure will
a. increase.
b. decrease.
c. remain constant.
d. cause a decrease in the average kinetic energy of the particles.

_____ 9. During what phase change does the arrangement of water molecules become more orderly?
a. melting
b. freezing
c. boiling
d. condensing

_____ 10. Which of the following is NOT part of John Dalton's atomic theory?
a. All elements are composed of atoms.
b. All atoms of the same element have the same mass.
c. Atoms contain subatomic particles.
d. A compound contains atoms of more than one element.

_____ 11. Which subatomic particle has a negative charge?
a. electron
b. alpha particle
c. neutron
d. proton

_____ 12. What does the electron cloud analogy suggest?
a. An electron cannot be precisely located at any one moment in time.
b. Protons move occasionally.
c. Protons and neutrons spin around each other.
d. Atoms do not stay still long enough to be observed.

_____ 13. One-twelfth the mass of a carbon-12 atom is used to define a(an)
a. atomic number.
b. atomic mass.
c. mass number.
d. atomic mass unit.

_____ 14. The column on the far left of the periodic table contains the
a. most reactive metals.
b. most reactive nonmetals.
c. least reactive nonmetals.
d. least reactive metals.

_____ 15. As you move from left to right across a period, the number of valence electrons
a. increases.
b. stays the same.
c. increases and then decreases.
d. decreases.

_____ 16. Typically, atoms gain or lose electrons to achieve
a. an exchange of energy.
b. ionization.
c. a stable electron configuration.
d. vaporization.

_____17. Which of the following compounds does NOT contain molecules?
   a. H_2 b. NaCl   c. CO_2 d. H_2O

_____18. Which statement about metals is true?
   a. A metal lattice is extremely rigid.
   b. A metal lattice has weak bonds within a metal.
   c. Electrons in a metal lattice are free to move.
   d. Generally, metals have a low melting point.

_____19. Which of the following is a balanced chemical equation for the synthesis of NaBr from Na and Br2?
   a. $Na + Br_2 \rightarrow NaBr$ b. $2Na + Br_2 \rightarrow NaBr$
   c. $Na + Br_2 \rightarrow 2NaBr$ d. $2Na + Br_2 \rightarrow 2NaBr$

_____20. Which of the following takes place during a redox reaction?
   a. Electrons are gained only.
   b. Electrons are lost only.
   c. Electrons are both gained and lost.
   d. Electrons are neither gained nor lost.

_____21. When the forward and reverse paths of a change occur at the same rate,
   a. the system is conserved.
   b. the system is in equilibrium.
   c. the change must be physical.
   d. the change must be chemical.

_____22. A salt is dissolved in water, which has a boiling point of 100°C. The boiling point of the solution will be
   a. greater than 100°C.   b. less than 100°C.
   c. exactly equal to 100°C.   d. exactly equal to 0°C.

_____23. A base is defined as a compound that produces
   a. hydroxide ions in solution.
   b. hydrogen ions in solution.
   c. hydronium ions in solution.
   d. sodium ions in solution.

_____24. A substance that ionizes or dissociates into ions when placed in water is always a(an)
   a. conductor.   b. electrolyte.
   c. strong acid.   d. strong base.

_____25. Which of the following statements helps explain why there are millions of carbon compounds?
   a. Carbon has four valence electrons.
   b. Carbon atoms form bonds with other carbon atoms.
   c. Carbon atoms can form single, double, and triple bonds.
   d. all of the above

_____26. Which of the following is NOT an example of a fossil fuel?
   a. coal   b. petroleum
   c. natural gas   d. methanol

_____27. Natural polymers are produced
   a. only in plant cells.
   b. only in animal cells.
   c. in both plant and animal cells.
   d. in neither plant nor animal cells.

_____28. What type of nuclear decay produces energy instead of a particle?
   a. alpha decay   b. beta decay
   c. gamma decay   d. electron decay

_____29. Which of the following statements is true?
   a. Chemical reaction rates vary with the conditions of the change, but nuclear decay rates do not.
   b. Nuclear decay rates vary with the conditions of the change, but chemical reaction rates do not.
   c. Both chemical reaction rates and nuclear decay rates vary with the conditions of the change.
   d. Neither chemical reaction rates nor nuclear decay rates vary with the conditions of the change.

_____30. In what state must matter exist for fusion reactions to take place?
   a. solid   b. liquid   c. gas   d. plasma

Completion

Complete each statement on the line provided.

1. A(An) _____ is a way of organizing data that is used to show changes that occur in related variables.

2. _____ is a process that could be used to separated dissolved particles from the liquid in a solution.

3. A(An) _____ change occurs when a material changes shape or size but the composition of the material does not change.

4. Reducing the volume of a gas _____ its pressure if the _____ of the gas and the number of particles are constant.

5. According to _____ all matter was made up of four elements: earth, air, fire, and water.

6. In Bohr's model of the atom, _____ move in fixed orbits around the nucleus.

7. In general, a(an) _____ metal will be more reactive than an alkaline earth metal in the same period.

---

8. A(An) _____ ion is a covalently bonded group of atoms that has a positive or negative charge.

9. The statement that in chemical reactions, the total mass of the reactants equals the total mass of the products is the law of _____.

10. A food packet taken on a camping trip has a warming packet. This packet contains water and a solute that releases heat when it is dissolved. The dissolving process for this solute and solvent can be described as _____.

11. The rate that a solid solute dissolves in a liquid solvent depends on the frequency and energy of the _____ between the particles of the solute and solvent.

12. The primary products of the complete combustion of fossil fuels are _____ and _____.

13. The energy that your body needs is released by the process of _____.

14. A sample of a radioisotope had a mass of 100.0 g. After exactly 24 days, 6.25 g of the sample remained. The half-life of the isotope is _____ days.

15. In a(an) _____, neutrons released during a fission reaction cause a series of other fission reactions.

Short Answer

In complete sentences, write the answers to the questions on the lines provided.

1. What is the temperature at which water freezes, expressed in Fahrenheit, Celsius, and kelvins?

2. If you looked at a glass containing a solution and a glass containing a suspension, how could you tell which glass contained the suspension?

3. What are three common clues that a chemical change has occurred?

---

4. Why is the volume of a liquid constant?

5. What did Democritus believe about matter?

6. How did the results of J.J. Thomson's experiments change how scientists thought about atoms?

7. Sodium chloride is a compound of sodium and chlorine. Which of these elements is the alkali metal, and which is the halogen?

8. Potassium, an alkali metal, and bromine, a halogen, are both in Period 4 of the periodic table. Which element has a higher ionization energy? Explain your answer.

9. Explain why ice in liquid water at 0°C is an example of physical equilibrium.

10. Which will freeze at a higher temperature—a freshwater marsh or a saltwater marsh? Explain your answer.

Unit 1 Test B

Name _____ Class _____ Date _____

11. What is the difference between a saturated solution and an unsaturated solution?

_____

_____

_____

12. What elements do organic compounds always contain?

_____

_____

13. Classify the compounds ethyne, heptane, and benzene.

_____

_____

14. How did the physicist Becquerel first observe the effects of nuclear decay?

_____

_____

_____

15. What two problems must be overcome before fusion can be used to produce energy?

_____

_____

Using Science Skills

Use the diagram to answer each question. Write the answers on a separate sheet of paper.

1. Using Tables and Graphs Use Figure 1-1 to determine the approximate total annual precipitation.

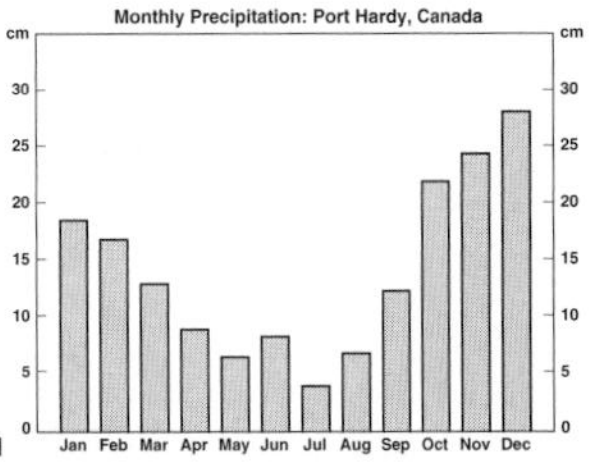

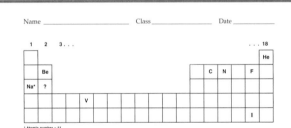

Figure 1-1

Unit 1 Test B

Name _____ Class _____ Date _____

Physical Properties of Four Materials Used to Make Sculptures			
	Malleability	**Hardness**	**Melting Point**
Wax	Soft enough to be carved and molded	Soft but keeps its shape at room temperature	Low melting point
Unbaked clay	Can be molded	Soft	Very high melting point
Baked clay	Brittle after being baked at a high temperature	Hard	Very high melting point
Metal (a mixture of copper, zinc, and lead)	Can be hammered without shattering	Hard	High melting point

Figure 1-2

2. Comparing and Contrasting Use Figure 1-2 to compare the physical properties of clay before and after it is baked at a high temperature.

3. Interpreting Graphics Identify the phase changes in Figure 1-3 that are labeled a, b, and c.

4. Using Analogies Read the following analogy and explain how it applies to panels 1 and 2 in Figure 1-4: The atomic model in panel 1 is to the model in panel 2 as a drawing of the outside of a house is to a blueprint of the inside.

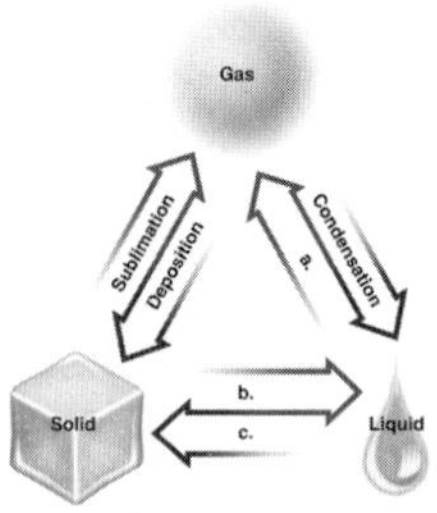

Figure 1-3

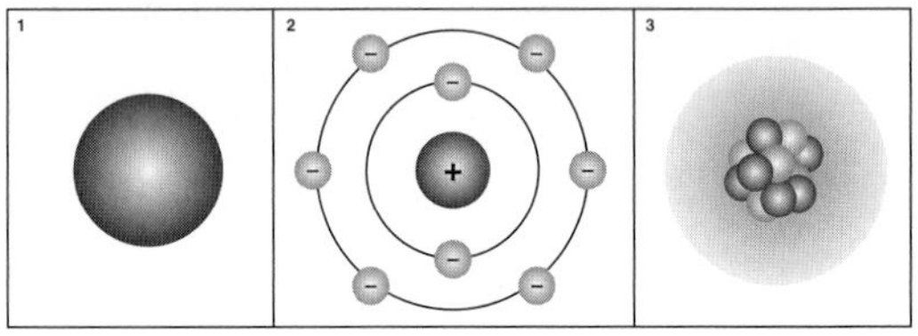

Figure 1-4

Unit 1 Test B

Name _____ Class _____ Date _____

Figure 1-5

* Atomic number = 11

5. Classifying Which element in Figure 1-5 is a transition metal? Which is a noble gas?

Chemical Formula	Name	Type of Bond	Description of Bond
NaCl	(1)	ionic	(2)
CO_2	carbon dioxide	(3)	Atoms share pairs of valence electrons.
W	tungsten	(4)	Metal cations are attracted to the shared electrons that surround them.

Figure 1-6

6. Using Tables and Graphs Write a description to place in box (2) in Figure 1-6.

7. Interpreting Graphics How many of each type of atom are present on each side of the equation in Figure 1-7?

Unbalanced equation:

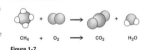

$$CH_4 + O_2 \longrightarrow CO_2 + H_2O$$

Figure 1-7

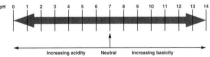

Figure 1-8

8. Drawing Conclusions Oven cleaner has a pH of 14, and household ammonia has a pH of about 11.2. What generalization might you make about whether most cleaners contain acids or bases? Use Figure 1-8 to answer this question.

Unit 1 Test B

Name _____ Class _____ Date _____

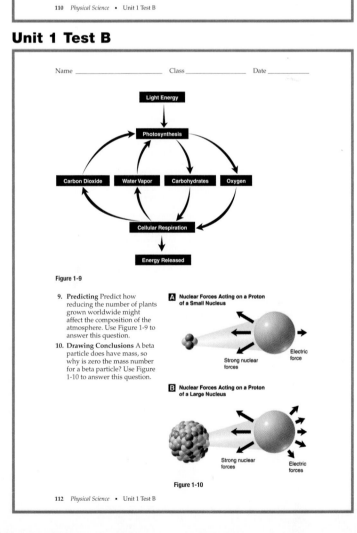

Figure 1-9

9. Predicting Predict how reducing the number of plants grown worldwide might affect the composition of the atmosphere. Use Figure 1-9 to answer this question.

10. Drawing Conclusions A beta particle does have mass, so why is zero the mass number for a beta particle? Use Figure 1-10 to answer this question.

Figure 1-10

Unit 1 Test A Answers

Multiple Choice

1. c	**2.** b	**3.** a	**4.** a	**5.** a	**6.** a
7. a	**8.** c	**9.** a	**10.** c	**11.** d	**12.** b
13. d	**14.** a	**15.** a	**16.** d	**17.** c	**18.** b
19. d	**20.** b	**21.** c	**22.** c	**23.** c	**24.** b
25. c	**26.** b	**27.** b	**28.** b	**29.** a	**30.** c

Completion

1. controlled experiment **2.** 3.0×10^7 **3.** heterogeneous
4. reactive **5.** dividing **6.** liquid, gas **7.** neutron **8.** excited
9. periodic law **10.** nitrogen **11.** fluoride **12.** trioxide **13.** released
14. 2.3 **15.** raises, lowers; increases, decreases **16.** 1×10^{-11} M
17. hydrogen **18.** high-density polyethylene; HDPE **19.** 0, +1
20. beryllium-8

Short Answer

1. life science and Earth and space science **2.** The viscosity of a liquid usually decreases as the liquid is heated and increases as the liquid cools. Motor oil does not get too thin in hot weather or too thick in cold weather. **3.** Take the temperature measurements of the surroundings during the phase change. If the temperature decreases, the phase change is endothermic; a system absorbs energy from its surroundings during an endothermic phase change. **4.** It provides a visual model of the most likely locations of electrons in an atom. **5.** chlorine **6.** bromine, Br **7.** The equation was not balanced correctly because it was balanced by changing a subscript instead of changing coefficients. The correctly balanced equation is $2Mg + O_2 \rightarrow 2MgO$. **8.** In an exothermic chemical reaction, chemical changes occur, and the reactants and the products are not the same substances. In an exothermic solution formation by dissociation, the solute undergoes a physical change and does not change identity. Energy is released in both processes. **9.** an alcohol and a salt **10.** Both the nucleus and the alpha particle are positively charged. The alpha particles must be accelerated enough to overcome the repulsion of two positively charged particles.

Using Science Skills

1. the density of the fluid **2.** Mixture A; it scatters light, does not separate into layers, and cannot be separated by filtration.
3. the kilopascal; 200 kPa; 100 kPa **4.** Students may answer yes because the model shows the composition of the nucleus of an atom. Students may answer no because the model does not include any electrons or show the position of the nucleus in the atom. **5.** Rubidium is the most reactive element shown. Group 1A alkali metals are the most reactive metals, and the reactivity of elements in Group 1A increases from top to bottom. **6.** The compounds in rows A and C are both ionic compounds. However, KI is a binary ionic compound, which forms between a metal and a nonmetal. The compound in row C contains a polyatomic hydroxide ion (OH^-). The atoms in a polyatomic ion are joined by covalent bonds.

7. the amount of energy required to break the chemical bonds of the reactants **8.** 147 g sucrose **9.** D **10.** protactinium-234; 42 g

Problem

1. $4Fe + 3O_2 \rightarrow 2Fe_2O_3$; 9 mol O_2
2. $CO_2 + H_2O \rightarrow H_2CO_3$

Essay

1. In peer reviews, scientists review and question other scientists' data. Scientists also help determine if the data is accurately reported. If the review finds errors in the data, in the conclusions, or in the experimental procedures, the hypothesis may need to be revised.
2. Filtration would be used because it is the process of separating mixtures based on the size of their particles (or pieces). A screen could be used to separate the mixture. The holes in the screen would need to be large enough to allow the soil to pass through but not the leaves, acorn, or twigs. **3.** The volume of the chest cavity increases as the diaphragm contracts and the rib cage is lifted. This increase in volume allows the particles in air to spread out, which lowers the air pressure in the lungs. Air rushes into the lungs because the air pressure outside the body is greater than the air pressure in the lungs. As the diaphragm relaxes and the rib cage moves down and in, the volume of the chest cavity decreases. This decrease in volume increases the air pressure, and air is forced out of the lungs.

Unit 1 Test B Answers

Multiple Choice

1. d	**2.** c	**3.** d	**4.** c	**5.** b	**6.** d
7. c	**8.** a	**9.** d	**10.** c	**11.** a	**12.** a
13. d	**14.** a	**15.** a	**16.** c	**17.** b	**18.** c
19. d	**20.** c	**21.** b	**22.** a	**23.** a	**24.** b
25. d	**26.** d	**27.** c	**28.** c	**29.** a	**30.** d

Completion

1. line graph **2.** Distillation **3.** physical **4.** increases, temperature
5. Aristotle **6.** electrons **7.** alkali **8.** polyatomic **9.** conservation of
mass **10.** exothermic **11.** collisions **12.** carbon dioxide, water
13. cellular respiration **14.** 6 **15.** chain reaction

Short Answer

1. 32°F, 0°C, and 273 K **2.** Accept any of the following: the
suspension would appear cloudy, while the solution would be
clear; the particles in the suspension would settle to the bottom,
while the particles in the solution would not settle. **3.** a change in
color, the production of a gas, and the formation of a precipitate
4. The volume of a liquid is constant because forces of attraction
keep the particles close together. **5.** Democritus believed all
matter consisted of tiny particles that could not be divided into
smaller particles. **6.** Scientists realized that atoms contained
smaller subatomic particles. **7.** Sodium is the alkali metal, and
chlorine is the halogen. **8.** Bromine; it gains electrons rather than
losing them. **9.** Equilibrium exists because liquid water is freezing
and ice is melting at the same rate. The equilibrium is physical
because no new substances form. **10.** A freshwater marsh; in a
saltwater marsh, the dissolved salt lowers the freezing point of the
water. **11.** A saturated solution contains all the solute it can hold at
that temperature. More solute will dissolve at that temperature in
an unsaturated solution. **12.** carbon and hydrogen **13.** Ethyne is
an alkyne, heptane is an alkane, and benzene is an aromatic
hydrocarbon.**14.** Uranium salts wrapped in paper left a pattern on
unexposed photographic film. He concluded that the salts emitted
rays that exposed the film. **15.** The atomic number tells the
number of protons. The mass number tells the total number of
protons and neutrons. The mass number (4) minus the atomic
number (2) tells you that there are 2 neutrons in an alpha particle.

Using Science Skills

1. approximately 165 cm **2.** Before clay is baked, it is soft
and can be molded. After clay is baked, it is hard and brittle.
3. a. vaporization; b. melting; c. freezing **4.** The solid ball in panel 1
is like the drawing of the exterior of a house. It provides no details
about the internal structure of an atom. The model in panel 2
shows the locations of different parts of the atom within the atom
and their relative sizes. It is like a blueprint that shows the size and
location of rooms in a house. **5.** V is a transition metal, and He is a
noble gas. **6.** The atoms of a metal lose one or more valence
electrons and form cations. The atoms of a nonmetal gain one or
more electrons and form anions. There is an attraction between
the oppositely charged ions. **7.** On the left side, there are 1 carbon
atom, 4 hydrogen atoms, and 2 oxygen atoms. On the right side,
there are 1 carbon atom, 3 oxygen atoms, and 2 hydrogen atoms.
8. Most cleaners contain bases. **9.** People need the energy stored
in plants and the oxygen produced during photosynthesis.
10.1. The mass of the beta particle is so small ($\frac{1}{1836}$ amu) that it is
not significant

Chapter 11 Motion

Planning Guide

Use these planning tools
Easy Planner
Resource Pro
Online Lesson Planner

SECTION OBJECTIVES	STANDARDS		ACTIVITIES and LABS
	NATIONAL (See p. T18.)	STATE	
11.1 Distance and Displacement, pp. 328–331 1 block or 2 periods **11.1.1 Identify** frames of reference and **describe** how they are used to measure motion. **11.1.2 Identify** appropriate SI units for measuring distances. **11.1.3 Distinguish** between distance and displacement. **11.1.4 Calculate** displacement using vector addition.	A-1, A-2, B-4		**SE** Inquiry Activity: How Does a Ramp Affect a Rolling Marble? p. 327 **L2** **SE** Quick Lab: Comparing Distance and Displacement, p. 330 **L2** **TE** Teacher Demo: Frames of Reference, p. 329 **L2** **LM** Investigation 11A: Measuring Distance and Displacement **L2**
11.2 Speed and Velocity, pp. 332–337 1 block or 2 periods **11.2.1 Identify** appropriate SI units for measuring speed. **11.2.2 Compare** and **contrast** average speed and instantaneous speed. **11.2.3 Interpret** distance-time graphs. **11.2.4 Calculate** the speed of an object using slopes. **11.2.5 Describe** how velocities combine.	A-1, B-4, E-2, F-1, G-1, G-3		**SE** Exploration Lab: Investigating the Velocity of a Sinking Marble, p. 349 **L2** **TE** Teacher Demo: Ticker Tape Car, p. 334 **L2** **LM** Investigation 11B: Investigating Free Fall **L1**
11.3 Acceleration, pp. 342–348 1 block or 2 periods **11.3.1 Identify** changes in motion that produce acceleration. **11.3.2 Describe** examples of constant acceleration. **11.3.3 Calculate** the acceleration of an object. **11.3.4 Interpret** speed-time and distance-time graphs. **11.3.5 Classify** acceleration as positive or negative. **11.3.6 Describe** instantaneous acceleration.	A-1, A-2, B-4, D-1		**TE** Teacher Demo: Pendulum Accelerometer, p. 344 **L2**

Ability Levels

L1 For students who need additional help
L2 For all students
L3 For students who need to be challenged

Components

SE	Student Edition	**GRSW**	Guided Reading	**CTB**	Computer Test Bank
TE	Teacher's Edition		& Study Workbook	**TP**	Test Prep Resources
LM	Laboratory Manual		With Math Support	**iT**	iText
PLM	Probeware Lab	**CUT**	Chapter and Unit	**DC**	Discovery Channel
	Manual		Tests		Videotapes

T	Transparencies
P	Presentation Pro
	CD-ROM
GO	Internet Resources

RESOURCES PRINT and TECHNOLOGY	SECTION ASSESSMENT
GRSW Section 11.1 **L1**	**SE** Section 11.1 Assessment, p. 331
T Chapter 11 Pretest **L2**	
Section 11.1 **L2**	**iT** Section 11.1
P Chapter 11 Pretest **L2**	
Section 11.1 **L2**	
SCᶤLINKS GO Comparing frames of reference **L2**	
GRSW Section 11.2 **L1**	**SE** Section 11.2 Assessment, p. 337
GRSW Math Skill **L2**	
DC Charting New Ground **L2**	**iT** Section 11.2
T Section 11.2 **L2**	
P Section 11.2 **L2**	
SCᶤLINKS GO Motion **L2**	
PHSchool.com GO Data sharing **L2**	
GRSW Section 11.3 **L1**	**SE** Section 11.3 Assessment, p. 348
T Section 11.3 **L2**	
P Section 11.3 **L2**	**iT** Section 11.3
SCᶤLINKS GO Acceleration **L2**	

Go Online

Go online for these Internet resources.

PHSchool.com
Web Code: ccd-2110
Web Code: cca-2110

NSTA SCᶤLINKS
Web Code: ccn-2111
Web Code: ccn-2112
Web Code: ccn-2113

Materials for Activities and Labs

Quantities for each group

STUDENT EDITION

Inquiry Activity, p. 327
1-m long wooden board at least 10 cm wide, 6 identical textbooks, stopwatch, marble

Quick Lab, p. 330
graph paper, metric ruler

Exploration Lab, p. 349
clear shampoo, 100-mL graduated cylinder, 2 small marbles, stopwatch, forceps, masking tape, metric ruler, 10-mL graduated cylinder, long glass stirring rod, dropper pipet, graph paper

TEACHER'S EDITION

Teacher Demo, p. 329
tennis ball

Teacher Demo, p. 334
toy car, ticker tape, ticker timer (acceleration timer), masking tape

Build Science Skills, p. 340
handheld GPS receivers, 1 per group

Teacher Demo, p. 344
short pendulum (25 cm), turntable, lab stand, tape

Chapter Assessment

CHAPTER ASSESSMENT

SE Chapter Assessment, pp. 351–352
CUT Chapter 11 Test A, B
CTB Chapter 11
iT Chapter 11
PHSchool.com GO
Web Code: cca-2110

STANDARDIZED TEST PREP

SE Chapter 11, p. 353
TP Diagnose and Prescribe

iText—interactive textbook with assessment at PHSchool.com

Name_____ Class_____ Date_____ M T W T F

LESSON PLAN 11.1

Distance and Displacement

Time
2 periods
1 block

Section Objectives

Local Standards

- **11.1.1 Identify** frames of reference and **describe** how they are used to measure motion.
- **11.1.2 Identify** appropriate SI units for measuring distances.
- **11.1.3 Distinguish** between distance and displacement.
- **11.1.4 Calculate** displacement using vector addition.

Vocabulary frame of reference • relative motion • distance • vector • resultant vector

---

1 FOCUS

Build Vocabulary: Vocabulary Knowledge Rating Chart
Before reading the section, have students make and fill out a chart with four columns using the following headings: Term, Can Define or Use It, Have Heard or Seen It, and Don't Know. **L2**

Targeted Resources
❑ Transparency: Chapter 11 Pretest
❑ Transparency: Interest Grabber 11.1
❑ Transparency: Reading Strategy 11.1

---

2 INSTRUCT

Use Visuals: Figure 1
Ask students to describe the motion of the girl in the butterfly's frame of reference. Ask them to describe the motion of the butterfly in the butterfly's frame of reference. Ask which one is "really" moving, the butterfly or the girl. **L1**

Build Reading Literacy: Monitor Your Understanding
After students read page 329, have them write down the main ideas in the passage. Ask them if they had any trouble reading the passage and why. Then, have students come up with strategies to improve their understanding. **L1**

Teacher Demo: Frames of Reference
Toss a tennis ball in different positions to show students how motion can appear differently in different frames of reference. **L2**

Quick Lab: Comparing Distance and Displacement
Students will draw a path on graph paper and use a ruler to distinguish between distance and displacement. **L2**

Build Science Skills: Measuring
Have students use a map of the city or area to measure the distance from their homes to the school. Then, using the odometer, have them determine the distance between home and school as they travel in a car. Have students compare the straight-line distance on the map to the distance traveled in a car. **L2**

Targeted Resources
❑ Transparency: Figure 3: Distance: Displacements Along a Line
❑ GRSW Section 11.1
❑ NSTA *sci*$_{LINKS}$ Comparing frames of reference

---

3 ASSESS

Reteach
Use Figure 4 to reteach the difference between displacement and distance traveled. **L1**

Evaluate Understanding
Ask students to write a paragraph describing a situation in which the same motion appears differently from different frames of reference. **L2**

Targeted Resources
❑ **PHSchool.com** Online Section 11.1 Assessment
❑ iText Section 11.1

Transparencies

152 **Chapter 11 Pretest**

1. How many meters are in 28 km?

2. Convert 35 km/h to a speed in m/s.

3. Rearrange the following equation to solve for d: $v = \frac{d}{t}$.

4. Rearrange the following equation to solve for v_f: $a = (v_f - v_i)/t$

5. What are the SI units for distance and time?

6. Which of the following describes the slope of a line?

   a. rise × run

   b. run/rise

   c. run − rise

   d. rise/run

Transparencies

153 **Chapter 11 Pretest** *(continued)*

7. If a graph uses units of meters on the vertical axis and units of seconds on the horizontal axis, what would be the units of the slope of a line on the graph?

8. Which of the following is true about a curved line on a graph?

   a. The slope is the same at every point.

   b. The slope of the line may be different at every point.

   c. The line has no slope.

   d. The slope of the line is zero.

Transparencies

154 **Section 11.1 Interest Grabber**

Describing Motion

Accurately describing the motion of an object using only words can be difficult.

1. Choose a destination near your home, such as school, a particular store, or a friend's house. Write out a set of directions describing how someone would get from your home to the location.

2. Draw a map illustrating the directions you wrote out in Step 1.

3. Was it easier to write out the description or to draw the map? Which method is easier to use to find the location? Explain your answers.

Transparencies

155 **Section 11.1 Reading Strategy**

Predicting

Frame of reference probably means	Frame of reference actually means
a. ?	b. ?

Program Resources

Transparencies

Figure 3 Distance: Displacements Along a Line

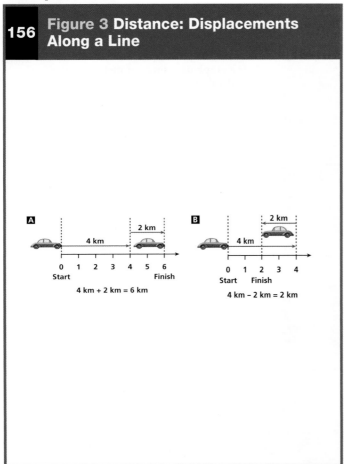

A

4 km

2 km

| 0 | 1 | 2 | 3 | 4 | 5 | 6 |

Start   Finish

4 km + 2 km = 6 km

B

2 km

4 km

| 0 | 1 | 2 | 3 | 4 |

Start   Finish

4 km − 2 km = 2 km

Guided Reading and Study Workbook

Name _____ Class _____ Date _____

Chapter 11   Motion

Section 11.1 Distance and Displacement
(pages 328–331)

This section defines distance and displacement. Methods of describing motion are presented. Vector addition and subtraction are introduced.

Reading Strategy (page 328)

Predicting Write a definition for *frame of reference* in your own words in the left column of the table. After you read the section, compare your definition to the scientific definition and explain why a frame of reference is important. For more information on this Reading Strategy, see the **Reading and Study Skills** in the **Skills and Reference Handbook** at the end of your textbook.

Frame of Reference	
Frame of reference probably means	**Frame of reference actually means**
Sample answer: The range of distances or area that you are considering in a problem	A system of objects that are not moving with respect to one another

1. What two things must you know to describe the motion of an object? You must know the direction the object is moving and how fast the object is moving.

Choosing a Frame of Reference (pages 328–329)

2. Is the following sentence true or false? A frame of reference is not necessary to describe motion accurately and completely. _____ false

3. What is a frame of reference? It is a system of objects that are not moving relative to one another.

4. Movement in relation to a frame of reference is called _____ relative motion.

5. Imagine that you are a passenger in a car. Circle the letter of the best frame of reference you could use to determine how fast the car is moving relative to the ground.

   a. the people sitting next to you in the backseat

   b. the driver of the car

   c. a van traveling in the lane next to your car

   (d.) a sign post on the side of the road

Measuring Distance (page 329)

6. Distance is the length of a path between two points.

7. Circle the letter of the SI unit best suited for measuring the length of a room in your home.

   a. kilometers   (b.) meters

   c. centimeters   d. millimeters

Guided Reading and Study Workbook

Name _____ Class _____ Date _____

Chapter 11   Motion

Measuring Displacements (page 330)

8. Is the following sentence true or false? Five blocks south is an example of a displacement. _____ true

9. Compare and contrast distance and displacement. Distance is the length of a path between two points, whereas displacement is the direction from a starting point and the length of a straight line from the starting point to the ending point.

10. What would your total displacement be if you walked from your front door, around the block, and then stopped when you reached your front door again?

   a. one block   b. two blocks

   c. the entire distance of your trip   (d.) zero

Combining Displacements (pages 330–331)

11. A vector is a quantity that has both _____ magnitude _____ and _____ direction.

12. Circle the letter of each answer that could describe the magnitude of a vector.

   (a.) length   b. direction

   (c.) amount   (d.) size

13. To combine two displacements that are in opposite directions, the magnitudes _____ subtract _____ from one another.

For questions 14 and 15, refer to the figure below.

3 km

7 km

| 0 | 1 | 2 | 3 | 4 | 5 | 6 | 7 |

Start   Finish

14. The magnitudes of the two displacement vectors are _____ 7 km _____ and _____ 3 km.

15. Because the two displacements are in opposite directions, the magnitude of the total displacement is _____ 4 km.

16. Circle the letter that answers the question. What is the displacement of a cyclist who travels 1 mile north, then 1 mile east, and finally 1 mile south?

   a. 3 miles east   b. 1 mile north

   c. 3 miles south   (d.) 1 mile east

17. The vector sum of two or more other vectors is called the _____ resultant vector.

LESSON PLAN 11.2

Speed and Velocity

Time
2 periods
1 block

Section Objectives

- **11.2.1 Identify** appropriate SI units for measuring speed.
- **11.2.2 Compare** and **contrast** average speed and instantaneous speed.
- **11.2.3 Interpret** distance-time graphs.
- **11.2.4 Calculate** the speed of an object using slopes.
- **11.2.5 Describe** how velocities combine.

Vocabulary speed • average speed • instantaneous speed • velocity

Local Standards

1 FOCUS

Build Vocabulary: Venn Diagram
Have students draw a Venn diagram to show how the key terms of the section are related to each other. **L2**

Targeted Resources
❏ Transparency: Interest Grabber 11.2
❏ Transparency: Reading Strategy 11.2

2 INSTRUCT

Build Reading Literacy: Compare and Contrast
Have students compare and contrast speed and velocity. Ask how speed and velocity are similar and different. Ask if velocity is more like distance or displacement and why? **L1**

Use Visuals: Figure 10
Use Figure 10 to show students how to find the magnitude of resultant vectors. **L1**

Build Science Skills:
Forming Operational Definitions
Ask students for operational definitions of speed for a skater on a circular track and for a person walking down the street. **L2**

Use Community Resources
Have students contact their local or state department of transportation to find out about laws or guidelines for the assignments of speed limits. Have them prepare questions ahead of time. **L2**

Teacher Demo: Ticker Tape Car
With masking tape, attach a toy car to a ticker timer with ticker tape threaded through it. Push the car at varying speeds. Students will observe a technique that visually records motion. **L2**

For Enrichment
Have students use the library or the Internet to research how speeds are measured on ships, airplanes, or spacecraft. Have them write a paragraph explaining their findings. **L3**

Targeted Resources
❏ Transparency: Math Skills: Calculating Average Speed
❏ Transparency: Figure 7: Distance-Time Graphs for Motion of Three Cars
❏ GRSW Section 11.2
❏ **NSTA** *sci*$_{INKS}$ Motion

3 ASSESS

Reteach
Use the graphs in Figure 7 to reteach the concepts in the section. **L1**

Evaluate Understanding
Ask students to write a paragraph describing how they could measure the average speed of a racecar on a racetrack. Also have them draw the velocity vectors at several locations for a racecar traveling at a constant speed around a circular track. **L2**

Targeted Resources
❏ **PHSchool.com** Online Section 11.2 Assessment
❏ iText Section 11.2

Transparencies

157 **Section 11.2 Interest Grabber**

Distance-Time Graphs

The distance traveled by an object in a period of time often is expressed using a line graph. A line graph visually conveys information using sets of data points.

1. Copy the blank graph below on your paper. Complete the graph by plotting the given data points on the graph. Each set of data points represents (time, distance). Note that time is measured in seconds and distance is measured in meters. Connect the plotted points with a straight line.

   Data points: (0, 0), (2, 40), (4, 80), (6, 120), (8, 160), (10, 200)

2. Describe the motion shown on the graph.

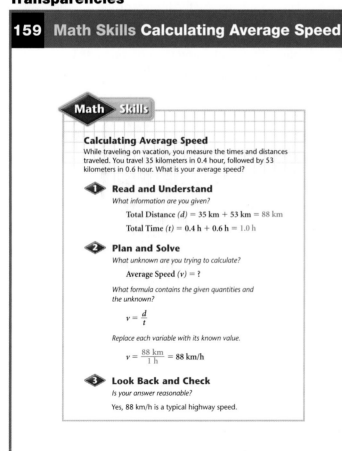

Distance vs. Time

Transparencies

158 **Section 11.2 Reading Strategy**

Monitoring Your Understanding

What Is Relevant	Why It Is Relevant
a. ?	b. ?
c. ?	d. ?
e. ?	f. ?

Transparencies

159 **Math Skills Calculating Average Speed**

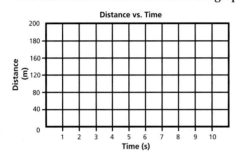 **Math Skills**

Calculating Average Speed

While traveling on vacation, you measure the times and distances traveled. You travel 35 kilometers in 0.4 hour, followed by 53 kilometers in 0.6 hour. What is your average speed?

1 **Read and Understand**

What information are you given?

  Total Distance (d) = 35 km + 53 km = 88 km

  Total Time (t) = 0.4 h + 0.6 h = 1.0 h

2 **Plan and Solve**

What unknown are you trying to calculate?

  Average Speed (v) = ?

What formula contains the given quantities and the unknown?

  $v = \dfrac{d}{t}$

Replace each variable with its known value.

  $v = \dfrac{88 \text{ km}}{1 \text{ h}} = 88$ km/h

3 **Look Back and Check**

Is your answer reasonable?

Yes, 88 km/h is a typical highway speed.

Transparencies

160 **Figure 7 Distance-Time Graphs for Motion of Three Cars**

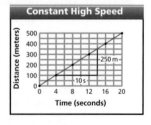

Constant High Speed

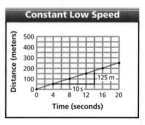

Constant Low Speed

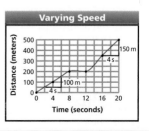

Varying Speed

Name _____ Class _____ Date _____

Chapter 11   Motion

Section 11.2 Speed and Velocity
(pages 332–337)

This section defines and compares speed and velocity. It also describes how to calculate average speed.

Reading Strategy (page 332)

Monitoring Your Understanding After you read this section, identify several things you have learned that are relevant to your life. Explain why they are relevant to you. For more information on this Reading Strategy, see the **Reading and Study Skills** in the **Skills and Reference Handbook** at the end of your textbook.

Facts About Speed and Velocity Sample answers shown below.	
What Is Important	**Why It Is Important**
Average speed is distance divided by time.	I could use this to calculate various speeds, like the average speed at which I travel getting to school.
Instantaneous speed is different from average speed.	You can't use a single speedometer reading to determine how long a trip will take.
Velocity is not the same as speed.	This could be useful in giving directions or in describing the path that you take on a walk.

Speed (pages 332–334)

1. Define speed. Speed is the ratio of the distance an object moves to the amount of time it moves.

2. The SI units for speed are _____ meters per second (m/s) _____.

3. How is instantaneous speed different from average speed? Instantaneous speed is measured at a particular instant, while average speed is computed for the entire duration of a trip.

4. The equation used for calculating average speed is _____ $\bar{v} = d/v$ _____.

5. Is the following sentence true or false? You can determine how fast you were going at the midpoint of a trip by calculating average speed for the entire trip. _____ false _____

6. A student walked 1.5 km in 25 minutes, and then, realizing he was late, ran the remaining 0.5 km in 5 minutes. Calculate his average speed on the way to school. $\bar{v}$ = Total distance/Total time = (1.5 km + 0.5 km)/(25 min + 5 min) = 2.0 km/30 min = 2.0 km/0.5 h = 4.0 km/h

7. What type of speed does an automobile's speedometer display? A speedometer displays instantaneous speed.

Graphing Motion (page 334)

8. The slope of a line on a distance-time graph represents _____ speed _____.

Name _____ Class _____ Date _____

Chapter 11   Motion

For questions 9 through 11, refer to the graph below.

Distance-Time Graph

9. Draw a point on the graph that represents 200 m traveled in 4 seconds. Draw a line connecting this point with the origin (0,0). Label this as line A.

10. Draw a point on the graph that represents 100 m traveled in 10 seconds. Draw a line connecting this point with the origin (0,0). Label this as line B.

11. Calculate the average speed (slope) of lines A and B. Be sure to include units. A: $\bar{v}$ = 200 m/4 s = 50 m/s; B: $\bar{v}$ = 100 m/10 s = 10 m/s

Velocity (page 336)

12. How do speed and velocity differ? Speed indicates distance traveled over a given amount of time; velocity describes both speed and direction of motion.

13. Circle the letter of each sentence that describes a change in velocity.
    ⓐ A moving object gains speed.
    ⓑ A moving object changes direction.
    c. A moving object moves in a straight line at a constant speed.
    ⓓ A moving object slows down.

14. Is the following sentence true or false? If a car travels around a gentle curve on a highway at 60 km/h, the velocity does not change. _____ false _____

Combining Velocities (page 337)

15. How do velocities combine? _____ Velocities combine by vector addition. _____

16. A river flows at a velocity of 3 km/h relative to the riverbank. A boat moves upstream at a velocity of 15 km/h relative to the river. What is the velocity of the boat relative to the riverbank?
    a. 18 km/h downstream
    b. 15 km/h upstream
    ⓒ 12 km/h upstream
    d. 12 km/h downstream

227

LESSON PLAN 11.3

Acceleration

Section Objectives

Local Standards

- **11.3.1 Identify** changes in motion that produce acceleration.
- **11.3.2 Describe** examples of constant acceleration.
- **11.3.3 Calculate** the acceleration of an object.
- **11.3.4 Interpret** speed-time and distance-time graphs.
- **11.3.5 Classify** acceleration as positive or negative.
- **11.3.6 Describe** instantaneous acceleration.

Vocabulary acceleration • free fall • constant acceleration
• linear graph • nonlinear graph

1 FOCUS

Build Vocabulary: Word Forms

Point out other forms of the terms or parts of the terms. For example, explain that *linear* contains the word *line* and means, "in a straight line" or "having to do with lines." **L2**

Targeted Resources

❏ Transparency: Interest Grabber 11.3
❏ Transparency: Reading Strategy 11.3

2 INSTRUCT

Build Reading Literacy: Outline

Have students create an outline of the section. Then, ask students to name two types of changes associated with acceleration and two types of graphs that can be used to represent acceleration. **L1**

Teacher Demo: Pendulum Accelerometer

Use a turntable and a pendulum to show students how the displacement of a pendulum can be used as evidence of acceleration, and how a pendulum can show that acceleration is taking place during uniform circular motion. **L2**

Build Science Skills: Calculating

Return to Figure 12 on page 343. Apply the equation for acceleration to calculate the magnitude of the stone's acceleration in the first time interval. Then, have students use the equation to calculate the acceleration of the stone for other time intervals. **L2**

Build Math Skills: Finding Slope on a Graph

Have students calculate the slope of the line on the graph in Figure 16. Tell them to include the units in their calculation. Have them calculate the slope of the line between 10 and 20 seconds on the graph in Figure 17.

Targeted Resources

❏ Transparency: Math Skills: Measuring Acceleration
❏ Transparency: Figures 16 and 17: Speed-Time Graphs
❏ Transparency: Figure 18: Distance-Time Graph of Accelerated Motion
❏ GRSW Section 11.3
❏ **NSTA** *sci*$_{LINKS}$ Acceleration

3 ASSESS

Reteach

Use the graphs on page 347 to reteach the concepts in the section. Ask students to identify which kind of acceleration cannot be shown on the graphs. **L1**

Evaluate Understanding

Ask students to sketch a speed-time graph of a car starting from rest, accelerating up to the speed limit, maintaining that speed, then slowing again to a stop. **L2**

Targeted Resources

❏ **PHSchool.com** Online Section 11.3 Assessment
❏ iText Section 11.3

Transparencies

161 Section 11.3 **Interest Grabber**

Speed-Time Graphs

The speed an object travels in a period of time can be expressed on a graph. This type of graph can give useful information about the object's motion. The speed-time graph of the object in Transparency 157 is shown below.

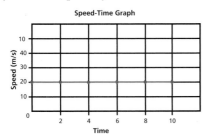

Speed-Time Graph

1. Describe the speed of the object shown on the graph.

2. The slope of the line on a distance-time graph represents the change in distance (m) per the change in time(s). Thus, the slope of a distance-time graph gives speed (m/s). What information does the slope of a speed-time graph give you?

3. What is the slope of the line on the speed-time graph?

Transparencies

162 Section 11.3 **Reading Strategy**

Summarizing

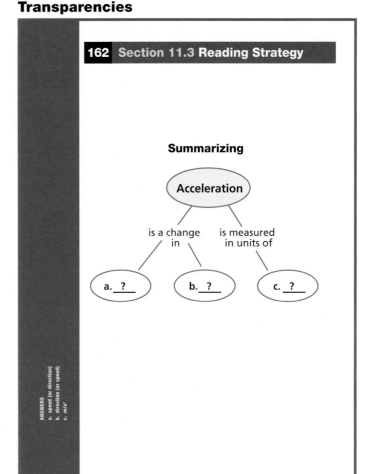

Acceleration

is a change in   is measured in units of

a. ?   b. ?   c. ?

Transparencies

163 Math Skills **Measuring Acceleration**

Calculating Acceleration
A ball rolls down a ramp, starting from rest. After 2 seconds, its velocity is 6 meters per second. What is the acceleration of the ball?

 Read and Understand

What information are you given?

    Time $= 2$ s

    Starting velocity $= 0$ m/s

    Ending velocity $= 6$ m/s

2 **Plan and Solve**

What unknown are you trying to calculate?

    Acceleration $= ?$

What formula contains the given quantities and the unknown?

$$a = \frac{(v_f - v_i)}{t}$$

Transparencies

164 Math Skills **Measuring Acceleration**
(continued)

Replace each variable with its known value.

$$\text{Acceleration} = \frac{(6 \text{ m/s} - 0 \text{ m/s})}{2 \text{ s}}$$

$$= 3 \text{ m/s}^2 \text{ down the ramp}$$

3 **Look Back and Check**

Is your answer reasonable?

Objects in free fall accelerate at a rate of 9.8 m/s². The ramp is not very steep. An acceleration of 3 m/s² seems reasonable.

Transparencies

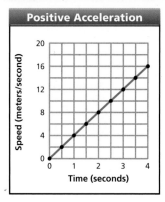

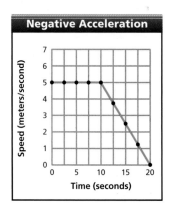

Transparencies

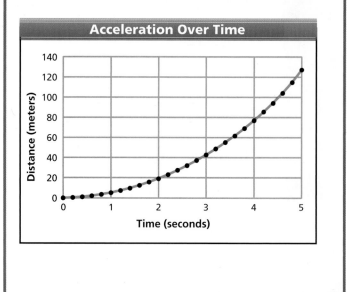

Guided Reading and Study Workbook

Name _____ Class _____ Date _____

Chapter 11   Motion

Section 11.3 Acceleration
(pages 342–348)

This section describes the relationships among speed, velocity, and acceleration. Examples of these concepts are discussed. Sample calculations of acceleration and graphs representing accelerated motion are presented.

Reading Strategy (page 342)

Summarizing Read the section on acceleration. Then complete the concept map to organize what you know about acceleration. For more information on this Reading Strategy, see the **Reading and Study Skills** in the **Skills and Reference Handbook** at the end of your textbook.

What Is Acceleration? (pages 342–345)

1. The rate at which velocity changes is called ___acceleration___

2. In terms of speed and direction, in what ways can an object accelerate? It can change its speed, its direction, or both its speed and direction.

3. Because acceleration is a quantity that has both magnitude and direction, it is a(n) ___vector___.

4. Is the following sentence true or false? Acceleration is the result of increases or decreases in speed. ___true___

5. Ignoring air resistance, a rock in free fall will have a velocity of ___39.2 m/s___ after 4.0 seconds.

6. A horse on a carousel that is moving at a constant speed is accelerating because ___its direction is constantly changing___.

7. Describe constant acceleration. Constant acceleration is a steady change in velocity.

Calculating Acceleration (pages 345–346)

8. Write the equation used to calculate the acceleration of an object.
___Acceleration = Change in velocity/ Total time___

Guided Reading and Study Workbook

Name _____ Class _____ Date _____

Chapter 11   Motion

9. Is the following sentence true or false? When the final velocity is less than the initial velocity of an object, the acceleration is negative. ___true___

10. A skateboarder begins down a ramp at a speed of 1.0 m/s. After 3 seconds, her speed has increased to 4.0 m/s. Calculate her acceleration.
   (a.) 1.0 m/s²   b. 3.0 m/s²
   c. 5.0 m/s²   d. 9.8 m/s²

Graphs of Accelerated Motion (pages 346–348)

11. A speed-time graph in which the displayed data forms a straight line is an example of a(n) ___linear graph___.

For questions 12 through 15, refer to the graphs below.

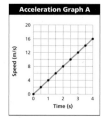 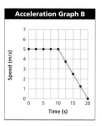

12. Graph A represents the motion of a downhill skier. How fast was the skier moving after traveling down the hill for 2.5 seconds? ___10 m/s___

13. In which graph does an object move at constant speed during the first 4 seconds? ___Graph B___

14. Graph B represents the motion of a mountain biker. What is the biker's speed at times of 10 s and 20 s? ___5 m/s (at 10 s); 0 m/s (at 20 s)___

15. Determine the acceleration of the mountain biker during the 10 second to 20 second time period. Show your work.
$a = v_f - v_i/t = (0 \text{ m/s} - 5 \text{ m/s})/10 \text{ s} = -0.5 \text{ m/s}^2$

16. The plotted data points representing acceleration in a distance-time graph form a(n) ___curve___

Instantaneous Acceleration (page 348)

17. The measure of how fast a velocity is changing at a specific instant is known as ___instantaneous acceleration___.

Guided Reading and Study Workbook

Name _____ Class _____ Date _____

Chapter 11   Motion

WordWise

Complete the sentences by using one of the scrambled vocabulary words below.

vrlaeeit oinotm	mefar fo ecrneeefr	gvaeera dspee
levotciy	nerlia	centidsa
esdep	erfe lafl	aulsettrn crovet
atnicoelecar	rotcev	nnilraeon

An equation for _____acceleration_____ is $(v_f - v_i)/t$.

A quantity that has both magnitude and direction is called a(n) _____vector_____.

The total distance traveled divided by the total time is _____average speed_____.

A speed-time graph in which data points form a straight line is an example of a(n) _____linear_____ graph.

Common units for _____speed_____ include meters per second (m/s).

In order to accurately and completely describe the motion of an object, a(n) _____frame of reference_____ is necessary.

You can determine _____distance_____ by measuring the length of the actual path between two points in space.

Two or more vectors combine to form a(n) _____resultant vector_____.

Objects in _____free fall_____ accelerate at 9.8 m/s².

A curve often connects data points on a(n) _____nonlinear_____ graph.

Together, the speed and direction in which an object is moving are called _____velocity_____.

Movement in relation to a frame of reference is _____relative motion_____.

Guided Reading and Study Workbook

Name _____ Class _____ Date _____

Chapter 11   Motion

Interpreting a Distance-Time Graph

The distance-time graph below illustrates the motion of a car whose speed varied with time during a trip. Calculate the average speed of the car during the first 8 seconds of the trip. Give your answer in km/h.

Math Skill:
Line Graphs and Conversion Factors

You may want to read more about this Math Skill in the Skills and Reference Handbook at the end of your textbook.

Varying Speed

1. **Read and Understand**
   What information are you given?
   A graph of distance versus time.

2. **Plan and Solve**
   How will you determine speed for the time interval referenced in the question?
   1. To determine the distance traveled in 8 s, move your finger up from the 8 s mark on the time axis to the plotted line.
   2. Now move your finger horizontally to the left to the distance axis. Read the value from the axis. (200 m)
   3. Calculate the average speed using the formula
      Speed = Distance/Time = 200 m/8 s = 25 m/s
   4. Convert from m/s to km/h:
      (25 m/s)(3600 s/h)(1 km/1000 m) = 90 km/h

3. **Look Back and Check**
   Is your answer reasonable?
   A quick calculation from the interval of constant speed shows that the car traveled 100 meters in 4 seconds—an average speed of 25 m/s.

Math Practice

On a separate sheet of paper, solve the following problems.

1. How long did it take the car to travel a distance of 350 m? _____16 s_____

2. Determine the speed of the car in km/h during the interval 0 s to 12 s.
   Speed = 200 m/12 s = 16.7 m/s; (16.7 m/s)(3600 s/h)(1 km/1000 m) = 60 km/h

---

Student Edition Lab Worksheet

Name _____ Class _____ Date _____

Chapter 11   Motion

Exploration Lab

Investigating the Velocity of a Sinking Marble

In this lab, you will graph the motion of a marble falling through shampoo.

See page 349 in the Teacher's Edition for more information

Problem What does a distance-time graph look like for a marble falling through shampoo?

Materials

- clear shampoo
- 100-mL graduated cylinder
- 2 small marbles
- stopwatch
- forceps
- masking tape
- metric ruler
- 10-mL graduated cylinder
- long glass stirring rod
- dropper pipet
- graph paper

Skills Measuring, Observing, Using Tables and Graphs

Procedure

1. Wrap a small amount of masking tape around the tips of the forceps. This will allow you to grip the marble with it.
2. Measure the distance between the 10-mL gradations on the 100-mL graduated cylinder. Record the new distance in the first row of the data table.

DATA TABLE

Distance (mm)	First Marble Time (s)	Second Marble Time (s)

3. Multiply this distance by 2 and write the result in the second row of the data table. For the third row, multiply the distance by 3. Continue until you have written distances in 10 rows.
4. Slowly pour 100 mL of clear shampoo into the 100-mL graduated cylinder.
5. Be ready to observe the marble as it falls through the shampoo. Grasp the marble with the forceps and hold the marble just above the shampoo-filled graduated cylinder.

Student Edition Lab Worksheet

Name _____ Class _____ Date _____

6. Say "Go!" as you drop the marble into the shampoo. At the same moment, your partner should start the stopwatch.
7. Each time the lower edge of the marble reaches a 10-mL mark on the cylinder, say "Now." Your partner should note and record the time on the stopwatch.
8. Continue calling out "Now" each time the marble reaches a 10-mL mark until it comes to rest on the bottom of the cylinder. Say "Stop!"
9. Use the 10-mL graduated cylinder to add about 8 mL of water to the 100-mL graduated cylinder. Use the glass stirring rod to mix the water and shampoo gently but thoroughly.
10. With the dropper pipet, remove enough liquid from the graduated cylinder to decrease the volume to 100 mL.
11. Repeat Steps 5 through 8, using another marble.
12. Wash all supplies as instructed by your teacher.

Analyze and Conclude

1. **Using Tables and Graphs** Use the data you collected to make a distance-time graph for each of the two marbles.

   The graph should be a nearly straight line for both marbles. The graph for the second marble will be steeper.

2. **Observing** Explain the motion of the marbles as they fell through the shampoo. How did you show this motion on your graph?

   At first, the marbles fell at a nearly constant velocity, which is shown as a straight line on the distance-time graph. The second marble fell faster than the first marble. As the marbles approached the bottom of the cylinder, the viscosity of the shampoo caused them to slow down.

3. **Inferring** Based on your graph, were the marbles accelerating? Explain your answers.

   Answers will depend on the viscosity of the shampoo. In most cases, the marbles did not accelerate because of the resistance from the viscous shampoo.

4. **Calculating** Use the data table to calculate the average speed of each marble.

   The speeds will depend on the type of shampoo used. Typical speeds are 2.5 mm/s and 6.0 mm/s for marbles falling in shampoo and diluted shampoo, respectively.

Lab Manual

Name _____ Class _____ Date _____

Chapter 11 Motion   Investigation 11A

Measuring Distance and Displacement

Refer students to pages 328–331 in their textbooks for a general discussion of vectors, distance, and displacement. **SKILLS FOCUS:** Measuring, Calculating **TIME REQUIRED:** 45 minutes

Background Information

Vectors have many uses. For example, you can use vectors to describe the distance an object travels and the displacement that results from an object's movement. Before you can make use of vectors, you must first select a frame of reference.

To use vectors to describe an object's position or movement on a flat surface, you must first define a frame of reference that includes the origin—a specific point that does not move. Two imaginary lines, or axes, that pass through the origin at right angles are then chosen, as shown in Figure 1. These two lines are the x-axis and the y-axis. Using the axes, you can describe the position of an object in terms of its x- and y-coordinates, for example, the point (4, 8) on a graph. Note that the coordinates of the origin are (0, 0).

Figure 1 shows that you can also define a vector to describe an object's position by drawing an arrow from the origin to the object's position. The object's coordinates (7, 2) determine the length and direction of the vector. Figure 2 shows that any vector in the frame of reference can be broken down into x- and y-components. Therefore, any vector is also the **resultant vector** of its own x- and y-components. Resultant vectors are also used to represent the result of vector addition.

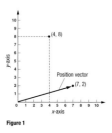

Figure 1

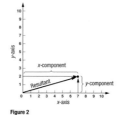

Figure 2

Lab Manual

Name _____ Class _____ Date _____

You can use a similar method to define a vector describing an object's displacement. To do this, draw a vector from the object's starting point to its ending point. Figure 3 shows the x- and y-coordinates of an object's starting and ending points. Note that the x- and y-components of the displacement vector are simply the difference between the x- and y-coordinates of the starting and ending points.

In this investigation, you will compare two methods of determining the length of a displacement vector.

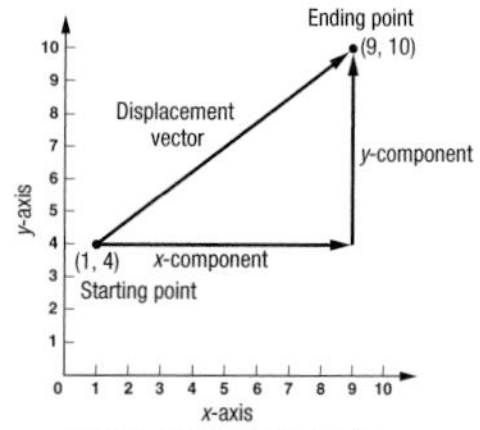

Problem

How can vectors be used to determine displacement?

Components of displacement vector:
$x = x_{\text{ending point}} - x_{\text{starting point}} = 9 - 1 = 8$
$y = y_{\text{ending point}} - y_{\text{starting point}} = 10 - 4 = 6$

Figure 3

Pre-Lab Discussion

Read the entire investigation. Then, work with a partner to answer the following questions.

1. How will you determine the x- and y-coordinates of each position?

By measuring the distance along each axis from the origin to the position

2. How will you determine the x- and y-components of the displacement vector?

By subtracting the x- and y-coordinates of the starting point from the corresponding coordinates of the ending point

3. How will you calculate the length of the displacement vector?

By taking the square root of the sum of the squares of the x- and y-components of the displacement vector

4. How will you measure the length of the displacement vector?

By using string and a meter stick to measure the straight-line distance from the starting point to the ending point

Lab Manual

Name _____ Class _____ Date _____

Materials *(per group)*

masking tape
meter stick
calculator
string

Safety 🥽 ✕

Put on safety goggles. Use caution to avoid bumping into people or objects when moving around the room. Note all safety alert symbols next to the steps in the Procedure and review the meaning of each symbol by referring to the Safety Symbols on page xiii.

Procedure

You may wish to conduct this investigation in a large, open room, such as a gymnasium, or outdoors on a paved surface.

1. Work with a classmate. Mark a dot on a small piece of masking tape. Mark the origin of your frame of reference by sticking a piece of masking tape on the floor, away from furniture and other obstacles.

2. Use the width of the classroom as the x-direction and the length of the classroom as the y-direction. Attach a 2-meter strip of tape to the floor, running from the origin in the x direction. This is the x-axis. Attach a second 2-meter strip of tape to the floor, running from the origin in the y direction. This is the y-axis. Note that the x- and y-axes should be at right angles to each other.

You may need to show students which directions should be considered the width and length of the classroom.

3. Select a point 1 to 4 meters from the origin as your starting point. Mark this point by sticking a piece of masking tape on the floor and marking a dot on it. Label this piece of tape *Start*.

You may wish to adjust the distances from the origin, depending on the size of the room and the number of students participating in the investigation.

4. Walk from the starting point to another point 1 to 4 meters from the origin. Mark this point by sticking a piece of masking tape on the floor and marking a dot on it. Label this piece of tape *End*.

5. Use a meter stick to measure the x-coordinate of the starting point to the nearest centimeter, as shown in Figure 4. Be careful to measure parallel to the x-axis. Record your measurement in the data table.

6. Repeat Step 5, measuring parallel to the y-axis, to determine the y-coordinate of the starting point. Record your measurement in the data table.

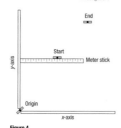

Figure 4

Lab Manual

Name _____ Class _____ Date _____

7. Measure and record the x- and y-coordinates of the ending point in the same way that you determined the coordinates of the starting point.

8. Determine the x-component of the displacement vector by subtracting the x-coordinate of the starting point from the x-coordinate of the ending point. Record this value in the data table as the vector component in the x-direction.

9. Repeat Step 8 with the y-coordinates of the starting and ending points to calculate the y-component of the displacement vector. Record this value in the data table as the vector component in the y-direction.

10. Calculate and record the square of the vector component in the x-direction. Calculate and record the square of the vector component in the y-direction.

11. Use the following formula to calculate the length of the displacement vector

$$L = \sqrt{x^2 + y^2}$$

where L is the length of the displacement vector, and x and y are the x- and y-components of the displacement vector. Record this value in the data table as the vector length of the displacement vector.

12. Working with your partner, stretch a string from the starting point to the ending point. While holding the string in this position, mark the string at both points. Use a meter stick to measure the distance between the two marks on the string. Record this measurement in the data table as the measured vector length of the displacement vector.

Observations   Sample data are shown.

DATA TABLE

			Displacement Vector			
Direction	**Coordinates of Starting Point (cm)**	**Coordinates of Ending Point (cm)**	**Vector Component (cm)**	**Square of Vector Component**	**Vector Length (cm)**	
					Calculated	**Measured**
x	46	158	112	12544		
y	171	92	79	6241	137	135

Lab Manual

Name _____ Class _____ Date _____

Analysis and Conclusions

1. Measuring What tool can you use to measure the distance moved by an object?

A meter stick or any other type of ruler

2. Measuring How can you measure the distance an object has moved?

By measuring its vector components

3. Measuring How can you measure the magnitude of the displacement of an object?

By measuring the length of a straight line from the starting point to the ending point of the path

the object has traveled

4. Calculating How can you calculate the displacement of an object?

First, determine the components of the displacement vector between the two points. Then,

use the Pythagorean formula $c^2 = a^2 + b^2$, where a is the value of $x_2 - x_1$ and b is the value of

$y_2 - y_1$. The magnitude of the displacement vector is then calculated by taking the square root

of the sum $(a^2 + b^2)$.

5. Controlling Variables How could using a large book as the displaced object produce significant error in your results?

Not measuring to the exact same location on the book would result in errors in describing

the position of the book.

6. Comparing and Contrasting How did the calculated length of the displacement vector compare with the measured length of the displacement vector?

The calculated length and the measured length were approximately equal.

Lab Manual

Name _____ Class _____ Date _____

7. Inferring Describe a condition in which it would be impossible to actually measure a displacement.

When there is an obstruction between the starting point and the final position of the object

8. Comparing and Contrasting How does the distance moved by an object between its starting point and ending point compare to the displacement vector between the same points?

Unless the object moved in a straight line, the distance moved will be greater than the

displacement.

Go Further

In this investigation, you determined the distance between two points by measuring and calculating the displacement vector. How could you determine displacement by using a graph? Write a procedure you would follow to answer this question. Have your teacher approve your procedure before you carry out the investigation. How does the displacement determined by this graphing method compare with the actual measurement of the displacement?

If drawn carefully, the displacement should be essentially the same whether it is measured or determined from a graph.

Lab Manual

Name _____ Class _____ Date _____

Chapter 11   Motion

🔍 **Investigation 11B**

Investigating Free Fall

Refer students to pages 332–348 in their textbooks for a general discussion of velocity and acceleration. **SKILLS FOCUS:** Observing, Measuring **CLASS TIME:** 45 minutes

Background Information

Free fall is the movement of an object toward Earth because of gravity. An object that is in free fall experiences acceleration. **Acceleration** is the rate at which velocity changes. Acceleration occurs when there is a change in speed, change in direction, or both. During free fall, speed increases at a constant rate. But what happens when an object also moves horizontally as it falls? The curved path that results is known as projectile motion—a topic you will cover in more detail in Chapter 12. Do you think an object's horizontal motion will affect its fall?

In this investigation, you will compare the fall of two identical objects from the same height. The first object will fall straight down. The second object will be given an initial horizontal velocity at the start of its fall. You will determine how the horizontal motion of the second object affects the time it takes to fall.

Problem

What effect does horizontal motion have on the time an object takes to fall?

Pre-Lab Discussion

Read the entire investigation. Then, work with a partner to answer the following questions.

1. Controlling Variables Identify the manipulated, responding, and controlled variables in this investigation.

a. Manipulated variable

Horizontal motion

b. Responding variable

Time for the spheres to reach the floor

c. Controlled variables

Mass and volume of spheres, distance the spheres fall

2. Formulating Hypotheses State a hypothesis about the effect of horizontal motion on the time an object takes to fall.

Horizontal motion does not affect the time an object takes to fall.

Lab Manual

Name _____ Class _____ Date _____

3. Predicting Make a prediction about the result of this investigation. Will one object fall more quickly than the other, or will both objects hit the floor at the same time?

The objects will fall at the same rate and hit the floor at the same time.

4. Controlling Variables Why are you told to let one object fall through a hole in the box, instead of rolling the object off the edge of the table?

Rolling the object off the edge of the table would give the object a horizontal velocity.

5. Calculating How will you determine the average time for the five trials?

Sum the five trial times and then divide the total by 5.

6. Measuring Why do you think you will need a stopwatch that can measure tenths of a second?

The spheres will take less than 1 second to fall to the floor.

Materials *(per group)*

2 small spherical objects Provide steel ball bearings, plastic marbles, or golf balls.
stopwatch (that can measure tenths of a second)
meter stick
masking tape

Safety 🥽🧤

Put on safety goggles. Keep your hands and feet out of the path of falling objects. Note all safety alert symbols next to the steps in the Procedure and review the meaning of each symbol by referring to the Safety Symbols on page xiii.

Lab Manual

Name _____ Class _____ Date _____

Procedure
Part A: Timing Free Fall

🔧 1. Work with a classmate. Hold the object over the floor so that its bottom is in line with the top of the table, as shown in Figure 1. Have your classmate check that the object is being held at the correct height.

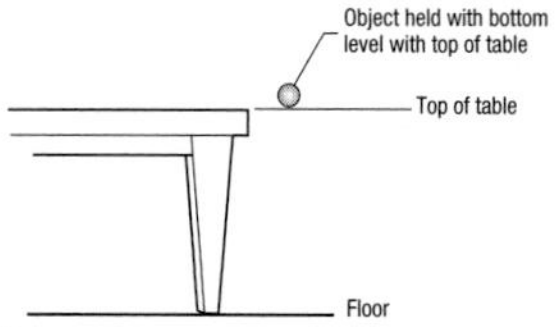

Object held with bottom level with top of table

Top of table

Floor

Figure 1

👁 2. Position your classmate so that he or she can have a clear view of the object and the floor below. Have your classmate be prepared to start the stopwatch.

3. Count down from five and release the object when you reach zero. Have your classmate begin the stopwatch as soon as he or she sees you release the object. Your classmate will use the stopwatch to measure the time it takes the object to hit the floor. Record this time in the data table.

4. Repeat Step 3 four more times. To calculate the average time that the sphere takes to reach the floor, add all five times together, then divide the total by 5. Record this value in the data table.

5. Using the meter stick, measure and place a piece of masking tape on the floor 1 meter from the point directly under the edge of the tabletop, as shown in Figure 2.

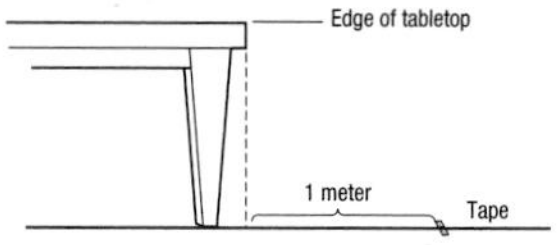

Edge of tabletop

1 meter   Tape

Figure 2

Lab Manual

Name _____ Class _____ Date _____

6. Place the object to be dropped near the edge of the tabletop. Push the object off the table with just enough force so that it lands on or close to the tape. **CAUTION:** *To avoid hurting anyone, be careful not to push the object too hard.* Practice pushing the object off the table until you can make it land on or close to the tape nearly every time.

7. Repeat Step 6 one more time and have your classmate use the stopwatch to measure the time the object takes to fall to the floor. Record this time in the data table.

8. Repeat Step 7 four more times. To calculate the average time that the object takes to fall to the floor, add all five times together and then divide the total by 5. Record this value in the data table.

Part B: Comparing Free Fall

9. Hold one of the objects above the floor and in line with the top of the table, as in Step 1. Have your classmate roll a second object toward the edge of the table. When you see the rolling object fall off the edge of the table, release the object you are holding. Watch and listen to observe whether one object hits the floor before the other.

10. Repeat Step 9 four more times. Record your observations in the space provided for results of Part B below the data table.

Observations   Sample data are shown.

DATA TABLE

Trial	Vertical Fall Time (seconds)	Fall With Horizontal Motion Time (seconds)
1	0.4	0.5
2	0.3	0.3
3	0.5	0.3
4	0.4	0.4
5	0.4	0.5
TOTAL	2.0	2.0
Average	0.4	0.4

Results of Part B

Both objects hit the floor at approximately the same time.

Lab Manual

Name _____ Class _____ Date _____

Analysis and Conclusions

1. **Calculating** What was the average time required for the object dropped straight down to hit the floor?

   0.4 second (The value will depend on the height of the table.)

2. **Calculating** What was the average time the object with the initial horizontal velocity took to hit the floor?

   0.4 second (The value will depend on the height of the table.)

3. **Observing** In Part B, did one sphere hit the floor before the other or did both spheres land at the same time?

   Both spheres hit the floor at approximately the same time.

4. **Evaluating and Revising** Did your data support or contradict your hypothesis? Explain your answer.

   Both spheres fell at the same rate. These data support the hypothesis that objects fall at the same rate, regardless of their horizontal velocity.

Go Further

The greater an object's mass, the stronger is the force of gravity on the object. Does this mean that more massive objects fall more quickly than less massive objects? Design an experiment to answer this question. Write a detailed plan for your experiment. Describe the procedures you will use and identify all the variables involved. Show your plan to your teacher. If your teacher approves, carry out your experiment.

When air resistance is minimal, the force of gravity causes all falling objects to accelerate at the same rate regardless of their masses.

Chapter Test A

Name _____ Class _____ Date _____

Chapter 11   Motion   **Chapter Test A**

Multiple Choice

Write the letter that best answers the question or completes the statement on the line provided.

_____ 1. A passenger in the rear seat of a car moving at a steady speed is at rest relative to
    a. the side of the road.
    b. a pedestrian on the corner ahead.
    c. the front seat of the car.
    d. the wheels of the car.

_____ 2. Which distance can be most accurately measured with a ruler?
    a. the length of a river
    b. the width of a book
    c. the distance between two cities
    d. the size of an object under a microscope

_____ 3. A person drives north 3 blocks, then turns east and drives 3 blocks. The driver then turns south and drives 3 blocks. How could the driver have made the distance shorter while maintaining the same displacement?
    a. by driving east 3 blocks from the starting point
    b. by driving north 1 block and east 4 blocks
    c. by driving west 3 blocks from the starting point
    d. by driving back to the starting point by the same route

_____ 4. Displacement vectors of 1 km south, 3 km north, 6 km south, and 2 km north combine to a total displacement of
    a. 12 km.   **b.** 6 km.   **c.** 4 km.   **d.** 2 km.

_____ 5. Speed is the ratio of the distance an object moves to
    a. the amount of time needed to travel the distance.
    b. the direction the object moves.
    c. the displacement of the object.
    d. the motion of the object.

_____ 6. A car traveled 88 km in 1 hour, 90 km in the next 2 hours, and then 76 km in 1 hour before reaching its destination. What was the car's average speed?
    a. 254 km/h   **b.** 63.5 km/h
    c. 209 km/h   **d.** 74.5 km/h

_____ 7. A horizontal line on a distance-time graph means the object is
    a. moving at a constant speed.
    b. moving faster.
    c. slowing down.
    d. at rest.

Chapter Test A

Name _____ Class _____ Date _____

8. A distance-time graph indicates that an object moves 100 m in 4 s and then remains at rest for 1 s. What is the average speed of the object?
   a. 50 m/s   **b.** 25 m/s   **c.** 20 m/s   **d.** 100 m/s

_____ **9.** Vector addition is used when motion involves
   a. more than one direction.   **b.** more than one velocity.
   c. more than one speed.   **d.** all of the above

_____ **10.** Which example identifies a change in motion that produces acceleration?
   a. a speed skater moving at a constant speed on a straight track
   b. a ball moving at a constant speed around a circular track
   c. a particle moving in a vacuum at constant velocity
   d. a vehicle moving down the street at a steady speed

_____ **11.** Which example describes constant acceleration due ONLY to a change in direction?
   a. increasing speed while traveling around a curve
   b. an object at rest
   c. traveling around a circular track
   d. an object in free fall

_____ **12.** An object moving at 30 m/s takes 5 s to come to a stop. What is the object's acceleration?
   a. 30 m/s^2 **b.** –30 m/s^2 **c.** –6 m/s^2 **d.** 6 m/s^2

_____ **13.** A speed-time graph shows that a car moves at 10 m/s for 10 s. The car's speed then steadily decreases until it comes to a stop at 30 s. Which of the following describes the slope of the speed-time graph from 10 s to 30 s?
   a. linear, horizontal
   b. curved, upward
   c. linear, sloping downward
   d. linear, sloping upward

_____ **14.** A train approaching a crossing changes speed from 25 m/s to 10 m/s in 240 s. How can the train's acceleration be described?
   a. The train's acceleration is positive.
   b. The train is not accelerating.
   c. The train will come to rest in 6 minutes.
   d. The train's acceleration is negative.

_____ **15.** Which of the following statements is true?
   a. An object that is accelerating is always changing direction.
   b. An object has an instantaneous acceleration, even if the acceleration vector is zero.
   c. An object at rest has an instantaneous acceleration of zero.
   d. Instantaneous acceleration is always changing.

Chapter Test A

Name _____ Class _____ Date _____

Completion
Complete each statement on the line provided.

1. Displacement and velocity are examples of _____ because they have both magnitude and direction.

2. $\overline{V} = \dfrac{d}{t}$ is the equation that defines _____.

3. A constant slope on a distance-time graph indicates _____ speed.

4. A car that increases its speed from 20 km/h to 100 km/h undergoes _____ acceleration.

5. _____ is how fast a velocity is changing at a specific instant.

Short Answer
In complete sentences, write the answers to the questions on the lines provided.

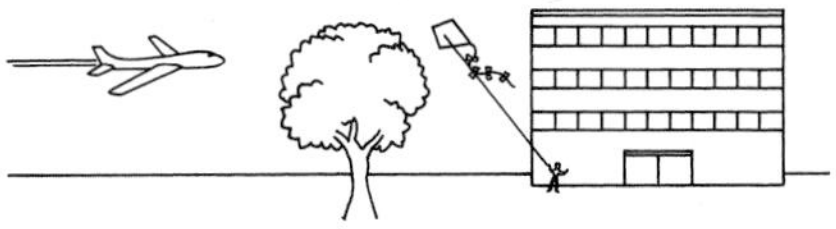

Figure 11-1

1. From which frame of reference in Figure 11-1 does the tree appear to be in motion?

_____

_____

2. What is the SI unit best suited for measuring the height of a building?

_____

_____

3. A child rolls a ball 4 m across a room. The ball hits the wall and rolls halfway back toward the child. Using vector addition, calculate the ball's displacement.

_____

_____

_____

Chapter Test A

Name _____ Class _____ Date _____

4. Which is the most suitable SI unit for expressing the speed of a race car?

_____

_____

5. Bus A travels 300 m in 12 s. Bus B travels 200 m in 12 s. Both vehicles travel at constant speed. How do the distance-time graphs for these two speeds differ?

_____

_____

_____

6. What types of changes in motion cause acceleration?

_____

_____

_____

Using Science Skills
Use the diagram to answer each question. Write the answers on a separate sheet of paper.

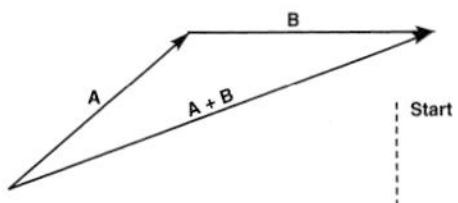

Figure 11-2

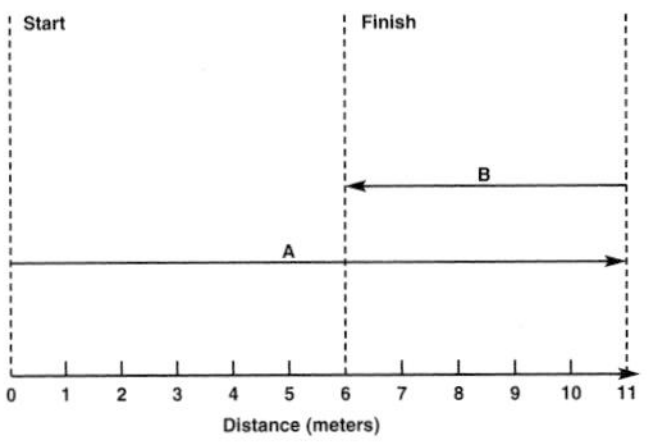

1. Interpreting Graphics Figure 11-2B illustrates the displacement of an object moving in a plane. Explain what information is provided by arrows A and B.

2. Calculating Using vector addition, calculate the distance traveled by the object and the displacement of the object represented by Figure 11-2B.

Chapter Test A

Name _____ Class _____ Date _____

3. Using Models Arrows A and B in Figure 11-3A represent velocities. Describe the motion modeled by the vectors.

4. Predicting Suppose vector B in Figure 11-3B had a length of 12 m (instead of 5 m). What would be the distance the object moved? What would be the magnitude of the object's displacement?

5. Applying Concepts Vectors A and B in Figure 11-3A represent the path walked by a student from home to school. What does the resultant vector A + B represent?

Problem
Write the answers to each question on a separate sheet of paper.

1. During a race, a runner runs at a speed of 6 m/s. Four seconds later, she is running at a speed of 10 m/s. What is the runner's acceleration? Show your work.

2. If you ride your bike at an average speed of 2 km/h and need to travel a total distance of 20 km, how long will it take you to reach your destination? Show your work.

Essay
Write the answers to each question on a separate sheet of paper.

1. Explain how velocity is different from speed.

2. Picture a ball traveling at a constant speed around the inside of a circular structure. Is the ball accelerating? Explain your answer.

3. A girl walks from her home to a friend's home 3 blocks north. She then walks east 2 blocks to the post office, 1 block north to the library, and 1 block east to the park. From the park, she walks 2 blocks west to the movie theater. After the movie, she walks 4 blocks south to the pet store. What is the girl's displacement from her starting point to the pet store? Where is the location of the pet store in relation to her home? Calculate the distance she walked in blocks.

Chapter Test B

Name _____ Class _____ Date _____

Chapter 11   Motion   **Chapter Test B**

Multiple Choice

Write the letter that best answers the question or completes the statement on the line provided.

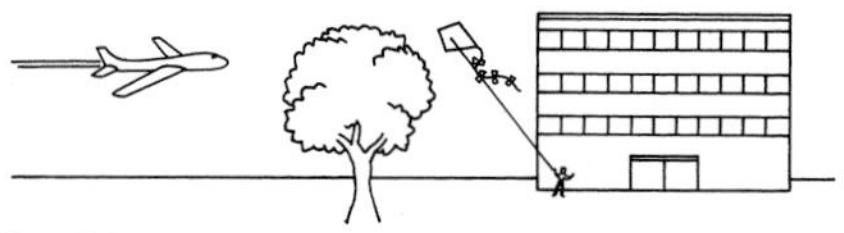

Figure 11-1

_____ **1.** Examine Figure 11-1. If you were standing under the tree, which object would appear to be moving?
   a. the tree   **b.** the airplane
   c. the boy   **d.** the building

_____ **2.** One kilometer equals 1000 meters. What does the prefix kilo- mean?
   a. 1   **b.** 10   **c.** 100   **d.** 1000

_____ **3.** A person walks 1 mile every day for exercise, leaving her front porch at 9:00 AM. and returning to her front porch at 9:25 AM. What is the total displacement of her daily walk?
   a. 1 mile   **b.** 0
   c. 25 minutes   **d.** none of the above

_____ **4.** A ball is rolled uphill a distance of 3 meters before it slows, stops, and begins to roll back. The ball rolls downhill 6 meters before coming to rest against a tree. What is the magnitude of the ball's displacement?
   a. 3 meters   **b.** 6 meters
   c. 9 meter   **d.** 18 meters

_____ **5.** What is the most appropriate SI unit to express the speed of a cyclist in the last leg of a 10-km race?
   a. km/s   **b.** km/h
   c. m/s   **d.** cm/h

_____ **6.** Instantaneous speed is measured
   a. at the starting point.
   b. when the object reaches its destination.
   c. at a particular instant.
   d. over the duration of the trip.

_____ **7.** The slope of a line on a distance-time graph is
   a. distance.   **b.** time.
   c. speed.   **d.** displacement.

Chapter Test B

Name _____ Class _____ Date _____

_____ **8.** What is the speed of a bobsled whose distance-time graph indicates that it traveled 100 m in 25 s?
   a. 4 m/s   **b.** 250 m/s
   c. 0.25 mph   **d.** 100 m/s

_____ **9.** A river current has a velocity of 5 km/h relative to the shore, and a boat moves in the same direction as the current at 5 km/h relative to the river. How can the velocity of the boat relative to the shore be calculated?
   a. by subtracting the river current vector from the boat's velocity vector
   b. by dividing the river current vector by the boat's velocity vector
   c. by multiplying the vectors
   d. by adding the vectors

_____ **10.** The rate at which velocity changes is called
   a. speed.   **b.** vectors.
   c. acceleration.   **d.** motion.

_____ **11.** Objects in free fall near the surface of the Earth experience
   a. constant speed.   **b.** constant velocity.
   c. constant acceleration. **d.** constant distance.

_____ **12.** Suppose you increase your walking speed from 1 m/s to 3 m/s in a period of 2 s. What is your acceleration?
   a. 1 m/s^2 **b.** 2 m/s^2
   c. 4 m/s^2 **d.** 6 m/s^2

_____ **13.** The slope of a speed-time graph indicates
   a. direction.   **b.** acceleration.
   c. velocity.   **d.** speed.

_____ **14.** An object that is accelerating may be
   a. slowing down.   **b.** gaining speed.
   c. changing direction   **d.** all of the above

_____ **15.** What is instantaneous acceleration?
   a. how fast a speed is changing at a specific instant
   b. how fast a velocity is changing at a specific instant
   c. how fast a direction is changing at a specific instant
   d. all of the above

Completion

Complete each statement on the line provided.

1. The motion of an object looks different to observers in different _____.

2. The SI unit for measuring _____ is the meter.

Chapter Test B

Name _____ Class _____ Date _____

3. The direction and length of a straight line from the starting point to the ending point of an object's motion is _____.

4. The sum of two or more vectors is called the_____.

5. Speed is measured in units of _____.

6. A car's speedometer measures _____.

7. The difference between speed and velocity is that velocity indicates the _____ of motion and speed does not.

8. Because its _____ is always changing, an object moving in a circular path experiences a constant change in velocity.

9. A moving object does not _____ if its velocity remains constant.

10. Freely falling objects accelerate at 9.8 m/s^2 because the force of _____ acts on them.

11. The acceleration of a moving object is calculated by dividing the change in _____ by the time over which the change occurs.

Short Answer

In complete sentences, write the answers to the questions on the lines provided.

1. Distance is a measure of length. What information does displacement give in addition to distance?

_____
_____
_____

2. What are two types of speed that can be used to describe the motion of a car driving on the highway?

_____
_____
_____
_____

3. What is the significance of the slope in a distance-time graph?

_____
_____
_____
_____

Chapter Test B

Name _____ Class _____ Date _____

4. What information does the slope of a speed-time graph provide?

_____
_____
_____

5. The slope of the curve at a single point on a distance-time graph of accelerated motion gives what information?

_____
_____
_____
_____

Using Science Skills

Use the diagram to answer each question. Write the answers on a separate sheet of paper.

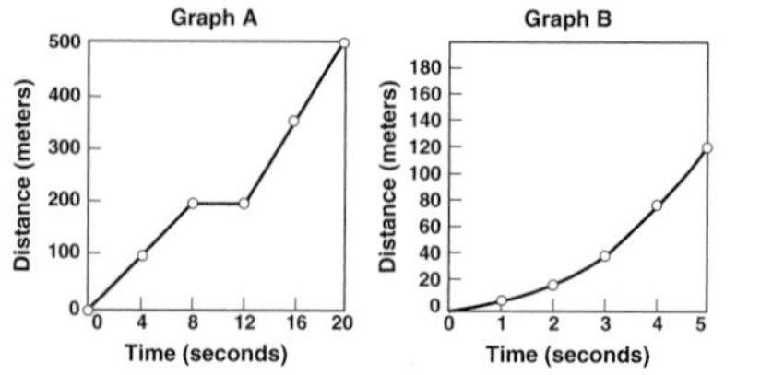

Figure 11-2

1. **Using Tables and Graphs** Which graph in Figure 11-2 shows periods of constant speed? Explain your answer.

2. **Interpreting Graphics** Look at Figure 11-2. Describe the motion of the object in Graph A.

3. **Using Models** Which graph in Figure 11-2 shows acceleration? How do you know?

4. **Calculating** Using Graph A in Figure 11-2, calculate the average speed of the object in motion from 12 s to 20 s. Explain your calculation.

5. **Comparing and Contrasting** Compare Graphs A and B in Figure 11-2. At a time of 2 seconds, which graph shows a greater velocity? How do you know?

Chapter 11 Test A Answers

Multiple Choice

1. c **2.** b **3.** a **4.** d **5.** a **6.** b
7. d **8.** c **9.** d **10.** b **11.** c **12.** c
13. c **14.** d **15.** c

Completion

1. vectors **2.** average speed **3.** constant **4.** positive
5. Instantaneous acceleration

Short Answer

1. the airplane **2.** the meter **3.** 4 m + (–2 m) = 2 m **4.** km/h
5. The slope of the line representing Bus A is steeper than the slope of the line representing Bus B. **6.** changes in speed, direction, or both

Using Science Skills

1. Arrows A and B are vectors with magnitude (distance) and direction. **2.** The object moved a total distance of 11 m + 5 m = 16 m. The object's displacement is 11 m – 5 m = 6 m to the right.
3. Figure 11-3A models an object subject to two relative velocities. Vector A + B represents velocity of the object. **4.** The distance would be 11 m + 12 m = 23 m. The displacement magnitude would be 11 m + (–12 m) = –1 m, or 1 m to the left.
5. the displacement

Problem

1. $a = \dfrac{V_f - V_i}{t}$ $\dfrac{10 m/s - 6 m/s}{4s}$ = $\dfrac{4 m/s}{4s}$ = $1\ m/s^2$

2. $\bar{V} = \dfrac{d}{t}$ $t\bar{v} = d$ $t = d/\bar{v}$ $t = 20\ km/2\ km/h = 10$

Essay

1. Speed is equal to the distance traveled divided by the time required to cover the distance. Velocity describes both speed and the direction of motion. **2.** Acceleration can be described as changes in speed, direction, or both. The ball is moving at a constant speed, but its direction is changing constantly. Because its direction is changing, the ball is experiencing constant acceleration. **3.** The girl's displacement from home is 1 block east. The pet store is located 1 block east of her home. The girl walked a total distance of 13 blocks.

Chapter 11 Test B Answers

Multiple Choice

1. b **2.** d **3.** b **4.** a **5.** b **6.** c
7. c **8.** a **9.** d **10.** c **11.** c **12.** a
13. b **14.** d **15.** b

Completion

1. frames of reference **2.** distance; length **3.** displacement
4. resultant vector **5.** meters per second **6.** instantaneous speed
7. direction **8.** direction **9.** accelerate **10.** gravity
11. speed; velocity

Short Answer

1. direction **2.** average speed and instantaneous speed
3. The slope is the change in distance divided by the change in time, which gives speed. **4.** acceleration
5. instantaneous acceleration

Using Science Skills

1. Graph A shows periods of constant speed (0–8 s, 8–12 s, 12–20 s). **2.** The object moves at constant speed for 8 seconds, is at rest for the next 4 seconds, and then moves at constant speed for the next 8 seconds. **3.** Graph B shows acceleration. The upward slope of the line indicates that an increasing distance is covered each second. **4.** The object moved a distance of 300 m in 8 s. The object's average speed is 37.5 m/s. $\bar{v} = 300\ m/8\ s = 37.5\ m/s$
5. Graph A; the slope is steeper.

Chapter 12 Forces and Motion

Planning Guide

Use these planning tools
Easy Planner
Resource Pro
Online Lesson Planner

SECTION OBJECTIVES	STANDARDS		ACTIVITIES and LABS
	NATIONAL (See p. T18.)	**STATE**	
12.1 Forces, pp. 356–362 🕐 1 block or 2 periods **12.1.1 Describe** examples of force and **identify** appropriate SI units used to measure force. **12.1.2 Explain** how the motion of an object is affected when balanced and unbalanced forces act on it. **12.1.3 Compare** and **contrast** the four kinds of friction. **12.1.4 Describe** how Earth's gravity and air resistance affect falling objects. **12.1.5 Describe** the path of a projectile and **identify** the forces that produce projectile motion.	A-1, A-2, B-4, G-1		**SE** Inquiry Activity: What Starts an Object Moving? p. 355 L2 **SE** Quick Lab: Observing the Effects of Friction, p. 360 L2 **TE** Build Science Skills: Measuring, p. 357 L2
12.2 Newton's First and Second Laws of Motion, pp. 363–369 🕐 1 block or 2 periods **12.2.1 Describe** Newton's first law of motion and its relation to inertia. **12.2.2 Describe** Newton's second law of motion and use it to **calculate** acceleration, force, and mass values. **12.2.3 Relate** the mass of an object to its weight.	A-1, A-2, B-4, F-1, G-1, G-2, G-3		**SE** Quick Lab: Investigating Inertia, p. 365 L2 **TE** Teacher Demo: Force and Acceleration, p. 365 L2 **TE** Teacher Demo: Newton's Second Law of Motion, p. 367 L2 **LM** Investigation 12A: Investigating Gravitational Acceleration and Fluid Resistance L2 **LM** Investigation 12B: Testing Galileo's Hypothesis L1
12.3 Newton's Third Law of Motion and Momentum, pp. 372–377 🕐 1 block or 2 periods **12.3.1 Explain** how action and reaction forces are related according to Newton's third law of motion. **12.3.2 Calculate** the momentum of an object and **describe** what happens when momentum is conserved during a collision.	B-4, G-1, G-2, G-3		**SE** Exploration Lab: Investigating a Balloon Jet, p. 383 L2 **TE** Build Science Skills: Predicting, p. 373 L2 **TE** Teacher Demo: Momentum, p. 374 L2
12.4 Universal Forces, pp. 378–382 🕐 1 block or 2 periods **12.4.1 Identify** the forms of electromagnetic force that can both attract and repel. **12.4.2 Identify** and **describe** the universal forces acting within the nucleus. **12.4.3 Define** Newton's law of universal gravitation and **describe** the factors affecting gravitational force. **12.4.4 Describe** centripetal force and the type of motion it produces.	A-1, A-2, B-1, B-4, E-2, G-1, G-2, G-3		**SE** Quick Lab: Investigating Force and Distance, p. 380 L2 **TE** Teacher Demo: Nuclear Forces, p. 379 L2

Ability Levels

L1 For students who need additional help
L2 For all students
L3 For students who need to be challenged

Components

SE	Student Edition
TE	Teacher's Edition
LM	Laboratory Manual
PLM	Probeware Lab Manual
GRSW	Guided Reading & Study Workbook With Math Support
CUT	Chapter and Unit Tests
CTB	Computer Test Bank
TP	Test Prep Resources
iT	iText
DC	Discovery Channel Videotapes
T	Transparencies
P	Presentation Pro CD-ROM
GO	Internet Resources

RESOURCES PRINT and TECHNOLOGY

GRSW Section 12.1 — **L1**
T Chapter 12 Pretest — **L2**
Section 12.1 — **L2**
P Chapter 12 Pretest — **L2**
Section 12.1 — **L2**
SCLINKS GO Forces — **L2**

GRSW Section 12.2 — **L1**
GRSW Math Skill — **L2**
DC Air Forces — **L2**
T Section 12.2 — **L2**
P Section 12.2 — **L2**
SCLINKS GO Mass — **L2**

PLM Lab 4: Investigating a Balloon Jet — **L2**
GRSW Section 12.3 — **L1**
T Section 12.3 — **L2**
P Section 12.3 — **L2**
SCLINKS GO Newton's laws — **L2**

GRSW Section 12.4 — **L1**
T Section 12.4 — **L2**
P Section 12.4 — **L2**
SCLINKS GO Gravity — **L2**

SECTION ASSESSMENT

SE Section 12.1 Assessment, p. 362
iT Section 12.1

SE Section 12.2 Assessment, p. 369
iT Section 12.2

SE Section 12.3 Assessment, p. 377
iT Section 12.3

SE Section 12.4 Assessment, p. 382
iT Section 12.4

Go Online

Go online for these Internet resources.

PHSchool.com
Web Code: cca-2120

NSTA SCLINKS
Web Code: ccn-2121
Web Code: ccn-2122
Web Code: ccn-2123
Web Code: ccn-2124

Materials for Activities and Labs

Quantities for each group

STUDENT EDITION

Inquiry Activity, p. 355
5 pennies

Quick Lab, p. 360
2 rubber erasers, sticky notes, scissors, metric ruler

Quick Lab, p. 364
index card, coin

Quick Lab, p. 380
balloon, bubble solution, bubble wand

Exploration Lab, p. 383
string (3 m in length), drinking straw, 4 long balloons, masking tape, stopwatch, meter stick, 2 threaded nuts, 2 chairs

TEACHER'S EDITION

Build Science Skills, p. 357
5-N spring scale, centimeter ruler, book, string, 5 objects (such as books) weighing from 1 to 5 newtons

Teacher Demo, p. 365
2 identical toy cars (or dynamics carts), 2 student volunteers, identical floor surface for each car

Teacher Demo, p. 367
wind-up toy car, 3 metal washers, tape

Build Science Skills, p. 370
sheet of paper, stopwatch, auditorium stage

Build Science Skills, p. 373
soccer ball, several heavy books

Teacher Demo, p. 374
water-filled balloons, pillow

Teacher Demo, p. 379
2 magnetic toy train cars or any 2 magnets, wide adhesive tape on a roll (or rubber band)

Chapter Assessment

CHAPTER ASSESSMENT

SE Chapter Assessment, pp. 385–386
CUT Chapter 12 Test A, B
CTB Chapter 12
iT Chapter 12
PHSchool.com GO
Web Code: cca-2120

STANDARDIZED TEST PREP

SE Chapter 12, p. 387
TP Diagnose and Prescribe

iText—interactive textbook with assessment at PHSchool.com

Forces and Motion 354B

Name_____ Class_____ Date_____ M T W T F

LESSON PLAN 12.1

Forces

Section Objectives

■ **12.1.1 Describe** examples of force and **identify** appropriate SI units used to measure force.

■ **12.1.2 Explain** how the motion of an object is affected when balanced and unbalanced forces act on it.

■ **12.1.3 Compare** and **contrast** the four kinds of friction.

■ **12.1.4 Describe** how Earth's gravity and air resistance affect falling objects.

■ **12.1.5 Describe** the path of a projectile and **identify** the forces that produce projectile motion.

Vocabulary force • newton • net force • friction • static friction • sliding friction • rolling friction • fluid friction • air resistance • gravity • terminal velocity • projectile motion

Local Standards

1 FOCUS

Build Vocabulary: LINCS
Have students use the LINCS strategy to learn and review the terms *force, friction, air resistance,* and *gravity.* **L2**

Targeted Resources
❏ Transparency: Chapter 12 Pretest
❏ Transparency: Interest Grabber 12.1
❏ Transparency: Reading Strategy 12.1

2 INSTRUCT

Use Visuals: Figure 1
Ask students in what ways the force of the wind can alter the man's motion. Ask students if these changes cause the man to accelerate. **L1**

Build Reading Literacy: Identify Main Ideas/Details
Ask students to explain the main concept in the first two paragraphs of Combining Forces on page 357. **L1**

Integrate Health
Ask students to hypothesize why a person with normal blood pressure and a normal body weight is at lower risk for heart disease. **L2**

Use Community Resources
Ask a civil engineer to visit your class and talk about the effects of friction between road surfaces and the tires of a moving car. **L2**

Quick Lab: Observing the Effects of Friction
Use two erasers, one with a sticky note attached to the bottom, to show students the effect of friction on motion. **L2**

For Enrichment
Have students use a spring scale to pull a mass across various surfaces in order to observe the difference between the forces required to overcome static and sliding friction. **L3**

Targeted Resources
❏ Transparency: Figure 4: Combining Forces Acting on an Object
❏ GRSW Section 12.1
❏ **NSTA** *sci*$_{LINKS}$ Forces

3 ASSESS

Reteach
Have students use Figure 4 to summarize the concepts of balanced and unbalanced forces. Use Figures 5 and 8 to review friction, gravity, and air resistance. **L1**

Evaluate Understanding
Have students write a review question and its answer for each objective at the beginning of this section. **L2**

Targeted Resources
❏ **PHSchool.com** Online Section 12.1 Assessment
❏ iText Section 12.1

Transparencies

167 **Chapter 12 Pretest**

1. What is relative motion?

2. What is the difference between distance and displacement?

3. How is average speed calculated?

4. On a distance-time graph, what does the slope represent?

5. What is velocity?

6. How is acceleration related to velocity?

ANSWERS
1. Relative motion is movement in relation to a frame of reference.
2. Distance is the length of a path between two points. Displacement is the direction from the starting point and the length of a straight line from the starting point to the ending point.
3. Total distance is divided by total time.
4. The slope represents the speed.
5. Velocity is speed with direction.
6. Acceleration is change in velocity, that is, any change in speed, direction, or both.

Transparencies

168 **Chapter 12 Pretest** *(continued)*

7. A backpack falls out of an open window. The backpack starts from rest and hits the ground 1.0 second later with a velocity of 9.8 m/s. What is the average acceleration of the backpack?

a. 9.8 m/s

b. 9.8 m

c. 9.8 m/s^2

d. all of the above

8. How are mass and weight different?

ANSWERS
7. c
8. Mass is a measure of inertia; weight is the measure of the force of gravity acting on an object.

Transparencies

169 **Section 12.1 Interest Grabber**

Objects in Free Fall

What factors affect a falling object? Perform the following simple activity to begin learning about the forces that act on falling objects.

1. Stand beside your desk. Hold a sheet of notebook paper level at eye level. Release the sheet of paper and watch it fall. Describe the motion of the paper.

2. Hold a sheet of notebook paper that has been crumpled into a tight ball at eye level. Release the crumpled paper and watch it fall. Describe the motion of the paper.

3. How do the motions of the flat sheet of paper and the crumbled ball of paper compare? What forces do you think are acting on each sheet of paper?

ANSWERS
1. The paper flutters slowly to the ground.
2. The crumpled sheet of paper falls straight to the ground.
3. The flat sheet of paper fluttered slowly to the ground whereas the crumpled ball of paper fell more quickly to the ground and followed a straight-line path. Do not assess students on correctly identifying the two opposing forces on the paper, but accept any reasonable response. The two opposing forces are gravity and air resistance.

Transparencies

170 **Section 12.1 Reading Strategy**

Relating Text and Visuals

Figure	Is Net Force 0?	Effect on Motion
2A	a. _____?_____	b. _____?_____
2B	c. _____?_____	d. _____?_____
3	e. _____?_____	f. _____?_____
5A	g. _____?_____	h. _____?_____
5B	i. _____?_____	j. _____?_____

ANSWERS
a. No motion
b. Yes
c. No motion
d. Yes
e. No
f. No motion
g. No
h. No motion
i. Yes
j. Potted plant accelerates.

Transparencies

Figure 4 Combining Forces Acting on an Object

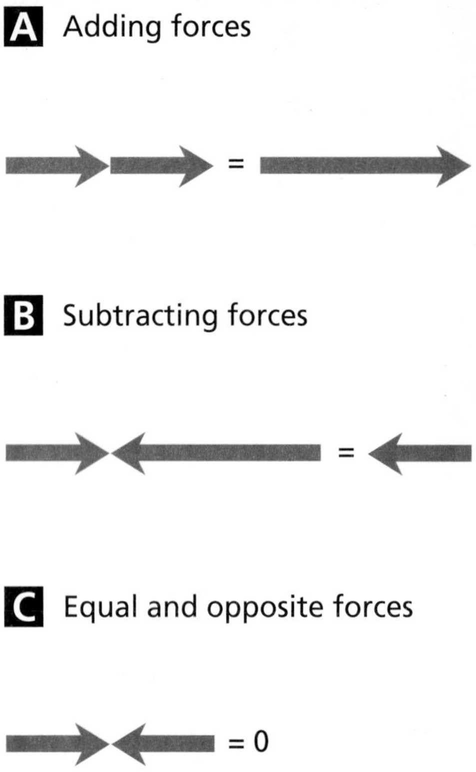

A Adding forces

$$\Longrightarrow \Longrightarrow = \Longrightarrow$$

B Subtracting forces

$$\Longrightarrow \Longleftarrow = \Longleftarrow$$

C Equal and opposite forces

$$\Longrightarrow \Longleftarrow = 0$$

Guided Reading and Study Workbook

Name _____ Class _____ Date _____

Chapter 12   Forces and Motion

Section 12.1 Forces
(pages 356–362)

This section describes what forces are and explains how forces affect the motion of various objects.

Reading Strategy (page 356)

Relating Text and Visuals As you read about forces, look carefully at Figures 2, 3, and 5 in your textbook. Then complete the table by describing the forces and motion shown in each figure. For more information on this Reading Strategy, see the **Reading and Study Skills** in the **Skills and Reference Handbook** at the end of your textbook.

Forces and Motion		
Figure	Is Net Force 0?	Effect on Motion
2A	Yes	None
2B	Yes	None
3	Yes	None
5A	Yes	None
5B	No	Potted plant accelerates

What is a Force? (pages 356–357)

1. A force is defined as a(n) _____push_____ or a(n) _____pull_____ that acts on an object.

2. Is the following sentence true or false? A force can act to cause an object at rest to move or it can accelerate an object that is already moving. _____true_____

3. How can a force change the motion of an object that is already moving?
   A force can accelerate a moving object by changing its speed, its direction, or both.

4. Circle the letter of the best answer. What force causes a 1-kg mass to accelerate at a rate of 1 meter per second each second?
   a. $1 \text{ kg/m} \cdot \text{s}^2$ b. 1 kg/s
   c. $1 \text{ kg} \cdot \text{m}$ (d.) 1 newton

Combining Forces (pages 357–358)

5. The overall force acting on an object after all the forces are combined is the _____net force_____.

6. How do balanced and unbalanced forces affect the motion of an object?
   When balanced forces act on an object, there is no change in the object's motion because the net
   force is zero. When unbalanced forces act on an object, the net force is not zero, so the object
   accelerates.

Guided Reading and Study Workbook

Name _____ Class _____ Date _____

Chapter 12   Forces and Motion

Friction (pages 359–360)

7. Is the following sentence true or false? Friction is a force that helps objects that are touching move past each other more easily. _____false_____

8. Circle the letters that identify types of friction.
   (a.) rolling   b. gravity
   (c.) static   (d.) sliding

9. The friction force that acts on objects that are at rest is _____static friction_____.

10. Why is less force needed to keep an object moving than to start the object in motion? Sliding friction, which opposes a moving object, is less than the static
    friction that acts on an object at rest, so less force is needed to keep an object moving.

11. Complete the table below about friction forces.

Types of Friction Forces	
Friction Force	Example
Static	Walking
Sliding	Pushing a book along your desk
Rolling	In-line skates

12. Is the following sentence true or false? Fluid friction is a force that opposes the motion of an object through a fluid such as water. _____true_____

Gravity (page 361)

13. Gravity is a(n) _____attractive_____ force that pulls objects together.

14. Is the following sentence true or false? Earth's gravity acts downward toward the center of Earth. _____true_____

15. Describe how gravity and air resistance affect the motion of a falling object. Gravity causes an object to accelerate downward, whereas air resistance acts
    opposite the direction of motion to reduce acceleration.

16. Is the following sentence true or false? Terminal velocity is the constant velocity of a falling object when the force of air resistance equals the force of gravity. _____true_____

Projectile Motion (page 362)

17. The curved path caused by the combination of an initial forward velocity and the downward force of gravity is known as _____projectile_____ motion.

LESSON PLAN 12.2

Newton's First and Second Laws of Motion

Time
2 periods
1 block

Section Objectives

Local Standards

- **12.2.1 Describe** Newton's first law of motion and its relation to inertia.
- **12.2.2 Describe** Newton's second law of motion and use it to **calculate** acceleration, force, and mass values.
- **12.2.3 Relate** the mass of an object to its weight.

Vocabulary inertia • mass • weight

1 FOCUS

Build Vocabulary: Vocabulary Rating Chart
Using the vocabulary terms, have students make a four-column chart with the headings Term, Can Define or Use It, Heard or Seen It, and Don't Know. **L2**

Targeted Resources
❏ Transparency: Interest Grabber 12.2
❏ Transparency: Reading Strategy 12.2

2 INSTRUCT

Use Visuals: Figures 12A and 12B
Ask students what the effect of inertia is on the car and on the dummy in Figures 12A and 12B. Ask how the mass of passenger is related to the passenger's inertia. **L1**

Build Science Skills: Inferring
Ask students what would have happened to the test dummy in Figure 12 if the air bag had not deployed and the dummy had not been wearing a seatbelt. **L2**

Quick Lab: Investigating Inertia
Using an index card and a coin, students will use the concept of inertia to explain the movement of objects. **L2**

Teacher Demo: Force and Acceleration
Use toy cars to show students that acceleration is directly proportional to force applied. **L2**

Teacher Demo: Newton's Second Law of Motion
Use a wind-up toy car and metal washers (as weights) to show students that acceleration is inversely proportional to mass. **L2**

For Enrichment
Have students research the methods used by the National Highway Traffic Safety Administration to test a vehicle's crash worthiness and its likelihood of rolling over. **L3**

Targeted Resources
❏ Transparency: Math Skills: Newton's Second Law
❏ Transparency: Figure 13: Effect of a Force on Acceleration
❏ GRSW Section 12.2
❏ 🅝🅢🅣🅐 *sci*$_{INKS}$ Mass

3 ASSESS

Reteach
Use Figures 12, 13, and 14 to review inertia and its relationship to Newton's first law of motion; Newton's second law of motion; and how Newton's second law is related to the weight formula. **L1**

Evaluate Understanding
Have students work in pairs to write three math problems (with solutions) based on Newton's second law and the weight equation. **L2**

Targeted Resources
❏ **PHSchool.com** Online Section 12.2 Assessment
❏ iText Section 12.2

Transparencies

172 Section 12.2 Interest Grabber

Describing Motion

Imagine you are carrying a bowl of soup on a food tray as you walk toward your favorite table. Suddenly, someone walks in front of you. You stop abruptly to avoid a collision.

1. Describe the motion of the soup in the bowl immediately after your abrupt stop.

2. Explain why you think the soup in the bowl behaved the way it did.

ANSWERS
1. The soup in the bowl continues forward and spills over the bowl's front edge onto the food tray.

2. Students should not be assessed on this response. Accept all reasonable responses. The soup's motion is explained by inertia—the momentum of the soup keeps it moving forward after the forward motion of the food tray has been halted.

Transparencies

173 Section 12.2 Reading Strategy

Building Vocabulary

Vocabulary	Definition
Inertia	a. ___?___
b. ___?___	c. ___?___
d. ___?___	e. ___?___

ANSWERS
a. Student answers should state that inertia is the tendency of an object to resist a change in its motion.
b. Mass
c. Student definition should state that mass is the amount of matter an object contains as measured by its inertia.
d. Weight
e. Students' answers should state that weight is the force of gravity acting on an object.

Transparencies

174 Math Skills Newton's Second Law

Math Skills

Newton's Second Law
An automobile with a mass of 1000 kilograms accelerates when the traffic light turns green. If the net force on the car is 4000 newtons, what is the car's acceleration?

1 Read and Understand
What information are you given?

Mass, $m = 1000$ kg

Force, $F = 4000$ N (in the forward direction)

2 Plan and Solve
What unknown are you trying to calculate?

Acceleration, $a = ?$

What formula contains the given quantities and the unknown?

$$\text{Acceleration} = \frac{\text{Net force}}{\text{Mass}}, a = \frac{F}{m}$$

Replace each variable with its known value and solve.

$$a = \frac{4000 \text{ N}}{1000 \text{ kg}} = 4\frac{\text{N}}{\text{kg}} = 4\frac{\frac{\text{kg} \cdot \text{m}}{\text{s}^2}}{\text{kg}} = 4 \text{ m/s}^2$$

$a = 4$ m/s^2 in the forward direction

3 Look Back and Check
Is your answer reasonable?

Powerful sports cars can accelerate at 6 m/s^2 or more. Thus, a smaller acceleration of 4 m/s^2 seems reasonable.

Transparencies

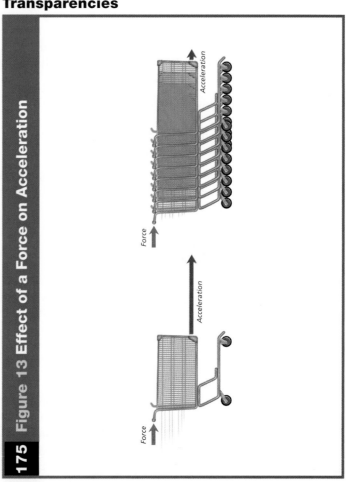

175 Figure 13 Effect of a Force on Acceleration

Name _____ Class _____ Date _____

Chapter 12   Forces and Motion

Section 12.2 Newton's First and Second Laws of Motion
(pages 363–369)

This section discusses how force and mass affect acceleration. The acceleration due to gravity is defined, and mass and weight are compared.

Reading Strategy (page 363)

Building Vocabulary As you read this section, write a definition in the table for each vocabulary word you encounter. Use your own words in the definitions. For more information on this Reading Strategy, see the **Reading and Study Skills** in the **Skills and Reference Handbook** at the end of your textbook.

Matter and Motion	
Vocabulary	**Definition**
Inertia	Inertia is the tendency of an object to resist a change in its motion.
Mass	Mass is the amount of matter an object contains as measured by its inertia.
Weight	Weight is the force of gravity acting on an object.

Aristotle, Galileo, and Newton (pages 363–364)

Match each scientist with his accomplishment.

Accomplishment	Scientist
_b_ **1.** Italian scientist who did experiments that helped correct misconceptions about force and motion	a. Aristotle
_c_ **2.** Scientist who studied in England and introduced several laws describing force and motion	b. Galileo
_a_ **3.** An ancient Greek philosopher who made many scientific discoveries through observation and logical reasoning	c. Newton

Newton's First Law of Motion (pages 364–365)

4. Is the following sentence true or false? According to Newton's first law of motion, an object's state of motion does not change as long as the net force acting on it is zero. _____true_____

5. What is inertia? Inertia is the tendency of an object to resist changes in its motion.

Name _____ Class _____ Date _____

Chapter 12   Forces and Motion

6. Is the following sentence true or false? The law of inertia states that an object in motion will eventually slow down and come to a complete stop if it travels far enough in the same direction. _____false_____

Newton's Second Law of Motion (pages 365–368)

7. According to Newton's second law of motion, acceleration of an object depends upon the _____mass_____ of the object and the _____net force_____ acting on it.

Match each term with its description.

Description	Term
_a_ **8.** A measure of the inertia of an object	a. mass
_c_ **9.** Net force/Mass	b. net force
_b_ **10.** Causes an object's velocity to change	c. acceleration

11. Is the following sentence true or false? The acceleration of an object is always in the same direction as the net force acting on the object. _____true_____

12. Is the following sentence true or false? If the same force acts upon two objects with different masses, the acceleration will be greater for the object with greater mass. _____false_____

Weight and Mass (pages 368–369)

13. What is weight? Weight is the force of gravity acting on an object.

14. Write the formula used to calculate the weight of an object.
Weight = Mass × Acceleration due to gravity

15. Is the following sentence true or false? Because the weight formula shows that mass and weight are proportional, doubling the mass of an object will not affect its weight. _____false_____

16. Complete the table below by describing the difference between mass and weight.

Mass and Weight	
Mass	**Weight**
Measure of the inertia of an object	Measure of the force of gravity acting on an object

17. On the moon, the acceleration due to gravity is only about one sixth that on Earth. Thus, an object will weigh _____less_____ on the moon than it weighs on Earth.

Name_____ Class_____ Date_____ M T W T F

Newton's Third Law of Motion and Momentum

Time
2 periods
1 block

Section Objectives

Local Standards

- **12.3.1 Explain** how action and reaction forces are related according to Newton's third law of motion.
- **12.3.2 Calculate** the momentum of an object and **describe** what happens when momentum is conserved during a collision.

Vocabulary momentum • law of conservation of momentum

1 FOCUS

Build Vocabulary: Paraphrase
Have students work with a partner to write an explanation in their own words for the law of conservation of momentum. **L2**

Targeted Resources
❏ Transparency: Interest Grabber 12.3
❏ Transparency: Reading Strategy 12.3

2 INSTRUCT

Build Reading Literacy: Relate Text and Visuals
Point out Figure 15 and ask students to describe the forces created when the bumper car strikes another car. **L1**

Build Math Skills: Equations and Formulas
Have students read Momentum and ask them to use the description from the text to write the momentum equation. **L1**

Build Science Skills: Predicting
Have students use Newton's third law of motion to predict the effect of objects that hit against one another. **L2**

Teacher Demo: Momentum
Drop a water-filled balloon on pavement and then on a pillow to show students that force is related to time during which an object's momentum changes. **L2**

Science and History: Amusement Park Rides
Have students read about the amusement park inventors shown in the timeline. Then, ask them what other science-related events they would add to the timeline. **L2**

Targeted Resources
❏ Transparency: Figure 17A and 17B: Conservation of Momentum
❏ Transparency: Figure 17C: Conservation of Momentum
❏ GRSW Section 12.3
❏ **NSTA** *sci*$_{LINKS}$ Newton's laws

3 ASSESS

Reteach
Demonstrate a force acting on an object and ask students to identify the action and reaction forces. Use Figure 17 to review momentum. **L1**

Evaluate Understanding
Ask students to write their own examples illustrating the key concepts of Newton's third law of motion, momentum, and conservation of momentum. **L2**

Targeted Resources
❏ **PHSchool.com** Online Section 12.3 Assessment
❏ iText Section 12.3

Transparencies

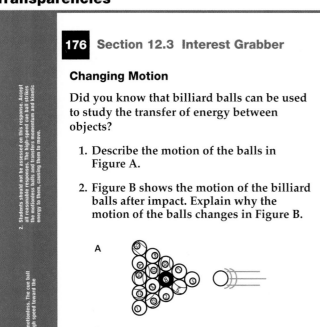

176 Section 12.3 **Interest Grabber**

Changing Motion

Did you know that billiard balls can be used to study the transfer of energy between objects?

1. Describe the motion of the balls in Figure A.

2. Figure B shows the motion of the billiard balls after impact. Explain why the motion of the balls changes in Figure B.

A

B

ANSWERS
1. The racked balls in Figure A are motionless. The cue ball moves in a straight line and at high speed toward the racked balls.

2. Students should not be assessed on this response. Accept all reasonable responses. The high-speed cue ball strikes the motionless balls and transfers momentum and kinetic energy to them, causing them to move.

Transparencies

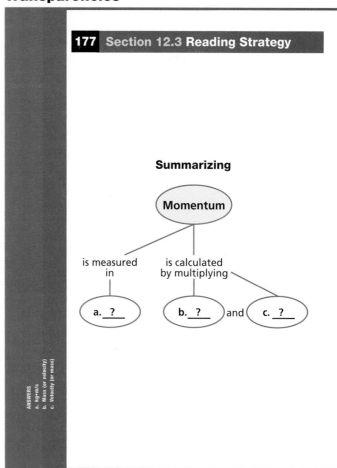

177 Section 12.3 **Reading Strategy**

Summarizing

Momentum

is measured in   is calculated by multiplying

a. ?   b. ?   and   c. ?

ANSWERS
a. kg·m/s
b. Mass (or velocity)
c. Velocity (or mass)

Transparencies

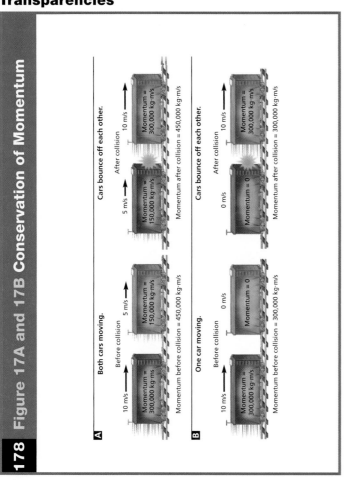

178 Figure 17A and 17B Conservation of Momentum

Transparencies

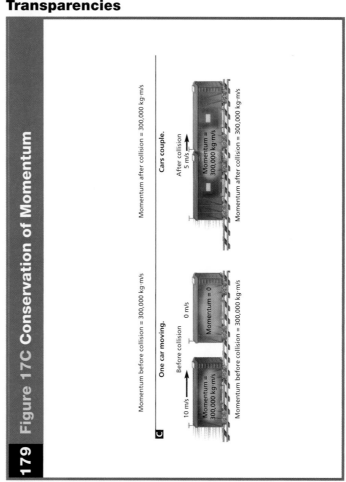

179 Figure 17C Conservation of Momentum

Name _____ Class _____ Date _____

Chapter 12   Forces and Motion

Section 12.3 Newton's Third Law of Motion and Momentum
(pages 372–377)

This section describes action-reaction forces and how the momentum of objects is determined.

Reading Strategy (page 372)

Summarizing As you read about momentum in this section, complete the concept map to organize what you learn. For more information on this Reading Strategy, see the **Reading and Study Skills** in the **Skills and Reference Handbook** at the end of your textbook.

```
                    ( Momentum )
           is measured            is calculated by
              in                    multiplying
          ( kg•m/s )         ( Mass )    ( Velocity )
```

Newton's Third Law (page 373)

1. According to Newton's third law of motion, what happens whenever one object exerts a force on a second object? The second object exerts an equal and opposite force on the first object.

2. The equal and opposite forces described by Newton's third law are called _____action_____ and _____reaction_____ forces.

3. Circle the letters that identify each sentence that is true about action-reaction forces.

   a. Newton's second law describes action-reaction forces.

   b. Forces always exist in pairs.

   c. Action-reaction forces never cancel.

   d. All action-reaction forces produce motion.

4. Is the following statement true or false? Action-reaction forces do not cancel each other because the action force is always greater than the reaction force. _____false_____

Momentum (pages 374–375)

5. Circle the letter of each factor that affects the momentum of a moving object.

   a. mass   b. volume   c. shape   d. velocity

6. If two identical objects are moving at different velocities, the object that is moving faster will have _____greater_____ momentum.

Name _____ Class _____ Date _____

Chapter 12   Forces and Motion

7. Your in-line skates are sitting in a box on a shelf in the closet. What is their momentum? _____zero_____

8. Is the following sentence true or false? An object with a small mass can have a large momentum if the object is traveling at a high speed. _____true_____

9. Write the momentum formula, including the correct units.
   Momentum (kg•m/s) = Mass (kg) × Velocity (m/s)

10. Circle the letter of the object that has the greatest momentum.

    a. a 700-gram bird flying at a velocity of 2.5 m/s

    b. a 1000-kilogram car traveling at 5 m/s

    c. a 40-kilogram shopping cart rolling along at 0.5 m/s

    d. a 300-kilogram roller coaster car traveling at 25 m/s

Conservation of Momentum (pages 376–377)

11. What does conservation of momentum mean? Momentum does not increase or decrease.

12. Is the following sentence true or false? Objects within a closed system can exert forces on one another, but other objects and forces cannot leave or enter the system. _____true_____

13. According to the law of conservation of momentum, what happens to the total momentum of a system if no net force acts on the system? The total momentum does not change.

14. Is the following sentence true or false? In a closed system with two objects, the loss of momentum of one object equals the gain in momentum of the other object. _____true_____

For questions 15 and 16, refer to the graph below.

Momentum of a 0.25-kg Ball

15. The momentum of the ball at one second is _____2.5 kg•m/s_____.

16. What is the speed of the ball at 0.5 seconds? Show your calculation. *Hint:* Solve the momentum formula for velocity.
    Momentum = Mass × Velocity; 1.25 kg•m/s = 0.25 kg × Velocity; Velocity = $\frac{1.25\ \text{kg•m/s}}{0.25\ \text{kg}}$ = 5 m/s

LESSON PLAN 12.4

Universal Forces

Section Objectives

- **12.4.1 Identify** the forms of electromagnetic force that can both attract and repel.

- **12.4.2 Identify** and **describe** the universal forces acting within the nucleus.

- **12.4.3 Define** Newton's law of universal gravitation and **describe** the factors affecting gravitation forces.

- **12.4.4 Describe** centripetal force and the type of motion it produces.

Vocabulary electromagnetic force • strong nuclear force • weak nuclear force • gravitational force • centripetal force

Local Standards

---

1 FOCUS

Build Vocabulary: Compare-Contrast Table
Have students each make a table similar to the table on page 378. Have students use *electromagnetic force, nuclear forces*, and *gravitational force* as the entries under the heading Force. **L2**

Targeted Resources
❑ Transparency: Interest Grabber 12.4
❑ Transparency: Reading Strategy 12.4

---

2 INSTRUCT

Build Reading Literacy: Relate Cause and Effect
Have students make a list of cause-and-effect relationships as they read about electromagnetic forces. **L1**

Teacher Demo: Nuclear Forces
Use toy train cars or magnets to show students that like poles repel. Students will observe forces representing the strong force in an atom's nucleus and the electrical force between protons. **L2**

Build Science Skills: Observing
Outdoors, ask a student to twirl an eraser tied to a string over his or her head in a circular motion. Ask students what force keeps the eraser moving in a circular orbit. **L2**

Targeted Resources
❑ Transparency: Figure 21: Gravitational Forces Acting on Masses at Different Distances
❑ Transparency: Figure 22: Forces Acting on the Moon
❑ GRSW Section 12.4
❑ **NSTA** *sci*$_{LINKS}$ Gravity

---

3 ASSESS

Reteach
Ask students to list all examples of electromagnetic, nuclear, and gravitational forces they can think of, both from the text and from everyday examples. Have them explain the action of each of the forces they list. **L1**

Evaluate Understanding
Have students make a poster with information about electromagnetic forces, nuclear forces, and gravitational force. Students should include examples of each type of force along with sketches or diagrams that illustrate the main concepts. **L2**

Targeted Resources
❑ **PHSchool.com** Online Section 12.4 Assessment
❑ iText Section 12.4

Transparencies

180 Section 12.4 **Interest Grabber**

Comparing Forces

No matter where you are in the universe, certain types of forces are present. You are already familiar with two of these forces—electric force and magnetic force.

1. Describe the behavior of two bar magnets that are positioned so that their north and south poles are nearly touching.

2. Describe a common behavior of clothes when they are removed from a clothes dryer.

3. How are these two forces the same? How are they different?

Transparencies

181 Section 12.4 **Reading Strategy**

Comparing and Contrasting

Force	Acts on Which Particles?	Acts Over What Distance?	Relative Strength
Strong nuclear	a. ?	b. ?	c. ?
Weak nuclear	d. ?	e. ?	f. ?

Transparencies

182 **Figure 21 Gravitational Forces Acting on Masses at Different Distances**

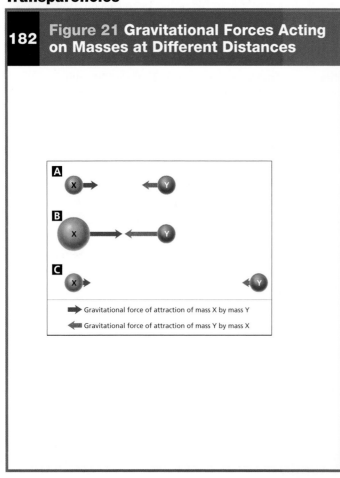

Transparencies

183 **Figure 22 Forces Acting on the Moon**

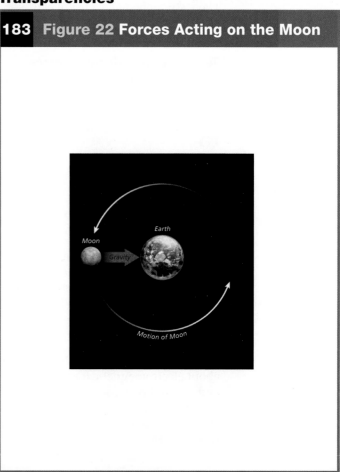

Name _____ Class _____ Date _____

Chapter 12 Forces and Motion

Section 12.4 Universal Forces
(pages 378–382)

This section defines four forces that exist throughout the universe. Each force is described and its significance is discussed.

Reading Strategy (page 378)

Comparing and Contrasting As you read this section, compare two universal forces by completing the table. For more information on this Reading Strategy, see the **Reading and Study Skills** in the **Skills and Reference Handbook** at the end of your textbook.

Universal Nuclear Forces			
Force	Acts on Which Particles?	Acts Over What Distance?	Relative Strength
Strong nuclear	Neutrons and protons	Very short	Very strong (100 times stronger than electrical force)
Weak nuclear	All particles	Short	Weaker than the strong force

1. What are the four universal forces?

a. _____Electromagnetic_____ b. _____Strong nuclear_____

c. _____Weak nuclear_____ d. _____Gravitational_____

Electromagnetic Forces (pages 378–379)

2. Is the following sentence true or false? Electromagnetic force is associated with charged particles. _____true_____

3. Name the only two forces that can both attract and repel. _Electric and magnetic forces can both attract and repel._

4. Objects with like charges ____repel____ one another, and objects with opposite charges ____attract____ one another.

5. Circle the letters of the sentences that correctly describe magnets or magnetic forces.
(a.) Magnetic forces act on certain metals.
(b.) Magnets have two poles, north and south.
c. Two poles that are alike attract each other.
(d.) Magnetic forces can both attract and repel.

Nuclear Forces (pages 379–380)

6. The force that holds particles in the nucleus together is the _____strong nuclear force_____.

7. What evidence suggests that nuclear forces have a powerful force of attraction? _These forces are strong enough to overcome the electric force of repulsion that acts among the positively charged protons in the nucleus._

Name _____ Class _____ Date _____

Chapter 12 Forces and Motion

8. Circle the letter of the best answer. Over extremely short distances, approximately how many times stronger is the strong nuclear force than the electric force of repulsion?
a. 10   (b.) 100   c. 1000   d. 10,000

9. Compare and contrast the strong and weak nuclear forces. _Both forces act within the nucleus of an atom to hold it together. The strong nuclear force affects only the neutrons and protons in the nucleus and acts over extremely short distances. The weak nuclear force acts over an even shorter distance but affects all particles, not just protons and neutrons._

Gravitational Force (pages 380–382)

10. State Newton's law of universal gravitation. _Every object in the universe attracts every other object._

11. Circle the letter of each sentence that is true about gravitational force.
a. The closer two objects are to one another, the weaker the gravitational force.
(b.) The farther apart two objects are, the weaker the gravitational force.
(c.) The greater the mass of an object, the stronger its gravitational force.
d. Earth's gravitational force is stronger than the gravitational force of the sun.

12. The gravitational force of attraction between two objects depends on ____mass____ and ____distance____.

13. Is the following sentence true or false? Gravity is the weakest universal force, but it is the most effective force over long distances. _____true_____

14. The sun's mass is much greater than the mass of Earth, so the sun's gravitational force is much ____stronger____ than that of Earth.

15. Why does the moon orbit Earth in a nearly circular path? _The moon's inertia and centripetal force from Earth produce the nearly circular path._

16. Is the following sentence true or false? The gravitational pull of the moon is the primary cause of Earth's ocean tides. ____true____

17. Is the following sentence true or false? The pull of Earth's gravity can slow an artificial satellite, causing it to lose altitude and fall from the sky. ____false____

18. List four uses of artificial satellites. _Students' answers should include four of the following: Satellites monitor Earth's weather, create detailed radar maps of Earth's surface, use telescopes to gaze into space, study Earth's climate, receive and transmit radio and microwave signals, receive and transmit cell phone and satellite television signals._

Name _____ Class _____ Date _____

Chapter 12 Forces and Motion

WordWise

Complete the sentences using one of the scrambled words below.

nicofirt	vtiyagr	aecmleorntcgeti corfe
ssma	raeeaclnocit	hwgeti
ten eofrc	lirnetcptae refco	swonten
lfudi tnfcriio	kewa cnuarel	teianri
mtnnmoemu		

A measure of an object's inertia is its _____mass_____.

The ____weak nuclear____ force affects all particles in a nucleus and acts only over a short range.

A sky diver experiences ____fluid friction____, which opposes the force of gravity.

A change in an object's speed or direction of motion is called ____acceleration____.

The product of an object's mass and its velocity is ____momentum____.

A measure of the force of gravity acting on an object is its ____weight____.

A center-directed ____centripetal force____ continuously changes the direction of an object to make it move in a circle.

A force associated with charged particles is ____electromagnetic force____.

Mass is the measure of the ____inertia____ of an object.

A force that opposes the motion of objects that touch as they move past each other is called ____friction____.

The universal force that causes every object to attract every other object is ____gravity____.

A person's weight on Mars, measured in ____newtons____, is 0.38 times the weight on Earth.

Acceleration equals ____net force____ divided by mass.

Name _____ Class _____ Date _____

Chapter 12 Forces and Motion

Calculating Acceleration

A car with a mass of 1300 kg accelerates as it leaves a parking lot. If the net force on the car is 3900 newtons, what is the car's *acceleration*?

Math Skill: Formulas and Equations

You may want to read more about this **Math Skill** in the **Skills and Reference Handbook** at the end of your textbook.

1. Read and Understand

What information are you given?

Mass , m = 1300 kg

Force, F = 3900 N (in the forward direction)

2. Plan and Solve

What unknown are you trying to calculate?

Acceleration, a = ?

What formula contains the given quantities and the unknown?

$$a = \frac{F}{m}$$

Replace each variable with its known value and solve.

$$a = \frac{3900 \text{ N}}{1300 \text{ kg}} = 3 \frac{\text{N}}{\text{kg}} = 3 \frac{\text{kg} \cdot \text{m/s}^2}{\text{kg}} = 3 \text{ m/s}^2$$

$a = 3 \text{ m/s}^2$ in the forward direction

3. Look Back and Check

Is your answer reasonable?

Powerful sports cars can accelerate at 6 m/s², so a smaller acceleration of 3 m/s² seems reasonable.

Math Practice

On a separate sheet of paper, solve the following problems.

1. A construction worker pushes a wheelbarrow with a total mass of 50.0 kg. What is the acceleration of the wheelbarrow if the net force on it is 75 N?

$$a = \frac{F}{m}; a = \frac{75 \text{ N}}{50.0 \text{ kg}} = 1.5 \text{ N/kg} = \frac{(1.5 \text{ kg} \cdot \text{m/s}^2)}{\text{kg}} = 1.5 \text{ m/s}^2, \text{ in the forward direction}$$

2. A van with a mass of 1500 kg accelerates at a rate of 3.5 m/s² in the forward direction. What is the net force acting on the van? (*Hint:* Solve the acceleration formula for force.)

$$a = \frac{F}{m}; F = ma = (3.5 \text{ m/s}^2)(1500 \text{ kg}) = 5250 \text{ kg} \cdot \text{m/s}^2 = 5300 \text{ N}$$

3. A 6.0×10^3 N force accelerates a truck entering a highway at 2.5 m/s². What is the mass of the truck? (*Hint:* Solve the acceleration formula for mass.)

$$a = \frac{F}{m}; m = \frac{F}{a} = \frac{6.0 \times 10^3 \text{ kg} \cdot \text{m/s}^2}{2.5 \text{ m/s}^2} = 2400 \text{ kg}$$

Student Edition Lab Worksheet

Name _____ Class _____ Date _____

Investigating a Balloon Jet

See page 383 in the Teacher's Edition for more information.

In this lab, you will examine the relationships among force, mass, and motion.

Problem   How does a jet-powered device move?

Materials
- string, 3 m in length
- drinking straw
- 4 long balloons
- masking tape
- stopwatch
- meter stick
- 2 threaded nuts
- 2 chairs

Skills   Applying Concepts

Procedure
1. Insert the string through the straw and tie each end of the string to the back of a separate chair. Pull the chairs apart until the string is tight and horizontal.
2. Blow up the balloon and then hold the balloon's opening closed. In the data table, record the length of the balloon. Have a classmate attach the balloon lengthwise to the straw, using tape.
3. While continuing to hold the balloon's opening closed, slide the balloon jet to the end of the string.
4. Release the balloon. Measure the time during which the balloon jet moves. Measure the distance that the balloon jet travels along the string. Record the distance and time values in the data table for 0 Nuts Used, Trial 1.

DATA TABLE

Number of Nuts Used	Trial Number	Time (seconds)	Distance (centimeters)	Average Velocity (cm/s)
0	1			
0	2			
2	1			
2	2			
Length of inflated balloon (centimeters)				

Student Edition Lab Worksheet

Name _____ Class _____ Date _____

5. Repeat Steps 2 through 4 with a new balloon. Make sure to inflate the balloon to the same size as in Step 2. Record your results in the data table for 0 Nuts Used, Trial 2.
6. Repeat Steps 2 through 5 twice more with a new balloon. This time, tape two nuts to the balloon before releasing it. Record your results in the data table for 2 Nuts Used, Trials 1 and 2.
7. Calculate and record the average velocity for each trial. The average velocity is equal to the distance divided by the time.

Analyze and Conclude

1. **Applying Concepts**   Use Newton's second and third laws to explain the motion of the balloon jet.

A balloon jet's movement depends on Newton's third law of motion. The pressurized air inside the

sealed balloon pushes outward in all directions, but as long as the air can't go anywhere,

neither can the balloon. As soon as the air inside the balloon is allowed to escape, the force

of the air on the opened end of the balloon no longer balances the force of air on the opposite

end. The reaction to this action is the movement of the balloon in the opposite direction.

Newton's second law of motion predicts that the balloon will accelerate at a rate that is

directly proportional to the force of the compressed air and inversely proportional to the

balloon's mass.

_____

_____

_____

_____

_____

2. **Analyzing Data**   How did adding mass (nuts) to the balloon jet affect its motion?

Adding nuts increased the mass of the balloon jet, which reduced its acceleration.

_____

_____

_____

_____

_____

Lab Manual

Name _____ Class _____ Date _____

Using a Pendulum to Measure the Acceleration Due to Force of Gravity

Refer students to pages 361 and 362 in their textbooks for a discussion of gravitational force. **SKILLS FOCUS:** Measuring, Calculating, Designing Experiments **CLASS TIME:** Part A, 20 minutes; Part B, 40 minutes

Background Information

A freely falling object accelerates at a rate that depends on the force of gravity. Near the surface of Earth, acceleration due to gravity (g) is equal to approximately 9.8 m/s^2. There are several ways to measure acceleration due to gravity. In this investigation, you will use a method that makes use of a pendulum. A pendulum consists of a weight, also known as a bob, that swings back and forth from a rope or string. Because the fixed end of the string is tied in place, it exerts a centripetal force that pulls the falling weight into a circular path. The time required for a pendulum to complete a back-and-forth swing is called the period of the pendulum. In Part A of this investigation, you will determine whether the period of a pendulum depends on the angle from which the bob is released.

Because the friction forces acting on the pendulum are negligible, it can be assumed that the pendulum is acted on by a single force—the force of gravity. A simple equation relating the acceleration due to gravity, the length of the pendulum, and the period of the pendulum can be written. In Part B of this investigation, you will design and carry out an experiment in which you will use a pendulum and this equation to determine the value of g.

Problem

How can you use a pendulum to determine the acceleration due to gravity?

Pre-Lab Discussion

Read the entire investigation. Then, work with a partner to answer the following questions.

1. **Designing Experiments**   In Part A of this investigation, how will you determine the period of the pendulum?

By measuring the time required for the pendulum to complete 20 back-and-forth swings and then

dividing that time by 20

_____

_____

2. **Predicting**   In Part A of this investigation, how will the angle from which the pendulum is released affect the period of the pendulum?

The angle from which the pendulum is released will have no effect on the period of the pendulum.

_____

_____

Lab Manual

Name _____ Class _____ Date _____

3. **Formulating Hypotheses**   State a hypothesis that you could test in Part B of this investigation.

Student hypotheses should be specific and subject to test by an experiment that students can

perform. Possible answers include the hypotheses that the value of g is 9.8 m/s^2 and that

the length of the pendulum will have no effect on the calculated value of g.

4. **Designing Experiments**   Describe an experiment that you could perform to test your hypothesis.

Students should describe a procedure that allows them to determine the period of a pendulum.

They can then use the period and the length of the pendulum to calculate g. They may want to

change the length of the pendulum and repeat the procedure to verify that the calculated value

of g is constant.

5. **Controlling Variables**   Identify the manipulated, responding, and controlled variables in the experiment described in Question 4.

Answers will depend on student experiments, but may include the length of the pendulum as a

manipulated variable, the period of the pendulum and calculated value of g as responding

variables, and the position from which the pendulum is released as a controlled variable.

6. **Evaluating**   What experimental result would support your hypothesis? What result would contradict your hypothesis?

Answers will depend on student hypotheses and experiments, but should follow logically from the

experiment described in the answer to Question 4. The answers should clearly support or contradict

the hypothesis described in the answer to Question 3. For example, suppose that the hypothesis

is that the length of the pendulum will have no effect on the calculated value of g. This hypothesis

will be supported if the same value for g is calculated for different pendulum lengths. The hypothesis

will be contradicted if different values for g are calculated for different pendulum lengths.

_____

Materials *(per group)*

ring stand	meter stick
2 books	100-g mass
clamp	protractor
metal rod, approximately 30 cm long	stopwatch
2-m fishing line You can substitute fine, flexible wire for the fishing line.	graph paper

Ask your teacher to provide you with any additional materials that you will need to carry out Part B of this investigation.

Lab Manual

Name _____ Class _____ Date _____

Safety 🥽⚠️

Wear safety goggles when performing this investigation. Note all safety alert symbols next to the steps in the Procedure and review the meaning of each symbol by referring to the Safety Symbols on page xiii.

Procedure

Part A: Determining If the Angle of Release Affects the Period of a Pendulum

🥽 1. Place the ring stand near the edge of a table, as shown in Figure 1. Place two textbooks on the base of the ring stand to prevent it from falling over. Use the clamp to attach the metal rod to the ring stand so that it extends beyond the edge of the table.

2. Tie one end of the fishing line to the portion of the metal rod that extends over the table. Tie the 100-g mass to the other end of the fishing line so that the center of the mass is 1.0 m below the metal rod, as shown in Figure 1.

3. Using the protractor to measure the angle, position the mass at an angle of 10 degrees. **Note:** *When the mass hangs straight down, the angle is 0 degrees.* Hold the mass in this position so that the fishing line is straight and extended. Have a group member start the stopwatch at the instant that you release the mass. Measure the time that the pendulum takes to make 20 complete back-and-forth swings. Record this time in Data Table 1. Also make note of the speed with which the pendulum swings back and forth.

4. Repeat Step 3 two more times, first releasing the mass at a 20-degree angle and then a 30-degree angle. For each trial, record in Data Table 1 the time the pendulum takes to complete 20 back-and-forth swings.

5. Calculate the period of the pendulum by dividing the time the pendulum takes to make 20 complete swings from each of the three positions by 20. Record these values in the appropriate places in Data Table 1.

6. Make a graph of your data. Plot the angle (10, 20, and 30 degrees) on the horizontal axis (x-axis) and the period of the pendulum on the vertical axis (y-axis). Draw a straight line through the data points.

Figure 1 labels: Clamp, Metal rod, Books, Ring stand, 1.0 m, Fishing line, 100-g mass, **Figure 1**

Lab Manual

Name _____ Class _____ Date _____

Part B: Design Your Own Investigation

⚠️ 7. Plan an experiment that will make use of a pendulum to determine the acceleration due to gravity (g). The acceleration due to gravity of the pendulum bob can be calculated by dividing the length of the pendulum (L) by the period of the pendulum (T) squared.

$$g = \frac{39.5L}{T^2}$$

Record the hypothesis that you will test.

Possible hypotheses: The value of g is 9.8 m/s²; the length of the pendulum will have no effect on the calculated value of g.

8. Identify the manipulated, responding, and controlled variables in your experiment.

   a. Manipulated variable

   _____

   b. Responding variable

   _____

   c. Controlled variables

   _____

9. Write out a detailed step-by-step procedure that you will use. Your procedure should produce data that will test your hypothesis. As you plan your experiment, think about what equipment you will need, what measurements you will make, and how you will record and display your data (tables, graphs). Include any safety precautions that you need to take. Construct Data Table 2 in which to record your observations in the space provided on page 127.

   Possible Procedure: Use the pendulum setup from Part A.

   1. Using the protractor to measure the angle, position the mass at an angle of 20 degrees. Have a group member start the stopwatch at the instant you release the mass. Measure the time the pendulum takes to complete 20 back-and-forth-swings. Record this time in Data Table 2.

   2. Use scissors to cut the mass from the fishing line. Retie the mass so that its center is 0.8 m below the metal rod.

   3. Repeat Step 1 for a pendulum length of 0.8 m.

   4. Repeat Step 2 and reduce the pendulum length to 0.5 m. Then, repeat Step 1.

   5. Calculate the period for each pendulum length by dividing the time required to complete 20 back-and-forth swings of the pendulum by 20. Use the equation shown in Part B, Step 7 to calculate the acceleration due to gravity for each pendulum length. Record these values in Data Table 2.

   6. Make a graph of your data. Plot the pendulum length on the horizontal axis and the calculated value of g on the vertical axis. Draw a straight line as close as possible to all three data points.

Lab Manual

Name _____ Class _____ Date _____

Safety Precautions

Students need to wear safety goggles when working with pendulums. Students should be careful when using scissors.

_____

_____

_____

10. Submit your written experimental plan to your teacher. When your teacher has approved your plan, carry out your experiment and record your observations in Data Table 2. Check student plans for practicality and safety before approving them.

Observations Sample data are shown.

DATA TABLE 1

Starting Position (degrees)	Time for 20 Swings (seconds)	Period (seconds)
10	50.1	2.5
20	48.7	2.4
30	52.4	2.6

DATA TABLE 2

If you need more space, attach additional sheets of paper.

Length of pendulum (m)	1.0	0.8	0.5
Time for 20 swings (seconds)	38	36	30
Period (seconds)	1.9	1.8	1.5
Calculated value of g (m/s²)	10.9	9.8	8.8
Reference value of g (m/s²)	9.8	9.8	9.8
Experimental error (%)	11	0	10

Lab Manual

Name _____ Class _____ Date _____

Analysis and Conclusions

1. **Observing** In Part A of this investigation, how did the angle from which you released the pendulum affect the maximum speed of the pendulum's motion?

   The pendulum's maximum speed was greater when the angle of release was larger.

2. **Analyzing Data** What did your results in Part A indicate about the relationship between the period of the pendulum and the position from which you released the pendulum?

   The angle from which the pendulum was released had no effect on the period of the pendulum.

3. **Evaluating and Revising** Did your results in Part B support or contradict your hypothesis? Explain your answer.

   Students should describe their data and explain its consequences for their hypotheses. The sample data show that reducing the length of a pendulum shortens the period of the pendulum. The sample data agree roughly with the prediction that the measured values of g will be near the accepted value of 9.8 m/s².

4. **Evaluating and Revising** Use the equation below to determine the experimental error for each of the calculated values for g. Record these error values in Data Table 2.

   $$\text{Experimental error} = \left(\frac{\text{Experimental value} - \text{Accepted value}}{\text{Accepted value}} \right) \times 100\%$$

   Why might your calculated values of g differ from the accepted value?

   The length of string and time may not have been measured accurately. Friction between the fishing line and the metal rod may have interfered with the experiment.

Go Further

Predict how the mass of a pendulum affects the period of the pendulum and the calculated value of g. Design an experiment to test your predictions. Show your teacher a detailed description of your experimental plan. When your teacher approves, carry out your experiment and report your results.

Because mass does not appear in the equation in Step 7, it has no effect on the period of a pendulum or on the calculated value of g.

Lab Manual

Chapter 12   Forces and Motion   🔍 Investigation 12B

Testing Galileo's Hypothesis

Refer students to pages 361, 362, and 365–369 in their textbooks for a discussion of the force of gravity and how it accelerates falling objects.
SKILLS FOCUS: Measuring, Calculating CLASS
TIME: 45 minutes

Background Information

In 1638, Galileo Galilei published a book that described the motion of freely falling objects. In this book, Galileo hypothesized that freely falling objects accelerate at a constant rate. However, Galileo could not test his hypothesis directly because the precise and accurate instruments needed to measure time and distance did not exist. To solve this problem, he designed an experiment to test his hypothesis indirectly by carefully measuring the time and distance of balls rolling down ramps. When a ball rolls down a ramp with a small incline, it accelerates more slowly than it does during free fall.

In this investigation, you will determine whether a steel ball accelerates at a constant rate as it rolls down ramps of varying lengths. Then, you will determine how the steepness of a ramp affects the acceleration of the ball.

Problem

How do the length and steepness of a ramp affect the rate of acceleration of an object rolling down the ramp?

Pre-Lab Discussion

Read the entire investigation. Then, work with a partner to answer the following questions.

1. **Formulating Hypotheses** State a hypothesis about whether the gravitational force on an object changes as it rolls down a ramp.

   The force of gravity remains constant as the object rolls down the ramp.

2. **Predicting** Based on your hypothesis, predict how the ball will accelerate as it rolls down the ramp. Explain your answer.

   The force of gravity on the ball is constant, and Newton's second law of motion states that a

   constant force produces a constant acceleration. As a result, the acceleration of the ball should

   be constant.

3. **Controlling Variables** Identify the manipulated, responding, and controlled variables in this experiment.

   a. Manipulated variables Distance, steepness of ramp

   b. Responding variable Time for the ball to reach the bottom of the ramp

   c. Controlled variable Mass of ball

4. **Predicting** How do you expect the steepness of the ramp to affect the acceleration of the ball?

   A steeper ramp will increase the acceleration of the ball.

Physical Science Lab Manual • Investigation 12B **129**

Lab Manual

Materials *(per group)*

1.5-m board	steel ball, approximately 4 cm in diameter
2 books	stopwatch Sand and inspect the boards to make sure that they are
meter stick	calculator smooth and free of splinters. You may want to glue or nail a strip of molding onto the board to guide the steel ball's path.

Safety 🥽 ✋

Wear safety goggles. Handle the board carefully to avoid splinters. Note all safety alert symbols next to the steps in the Procedure and review the meaning of each symbol by referring to the Safety Symbols on page xiii.

Procedure

Part A: Determining Acceleration

🥽✋ 1. Work with a partner. Put one of the books on the floor. Place one end of the board on the book to form a ramp. Then, place the meter stick on the board with its zero end at the bottom of the ramp, as shown in Figure 1. Mark a line at distances of 0.5 m and 1.0 m from the end of the board. Move the meter stick so that its zero is aligned at the 1.0 m mark you just made on the board and mark a line at a distance of 1.5 m from the end of the board. Refer to Data Table 1, which you will use to compile data obtained in Steps 2 and 8 of Part A.

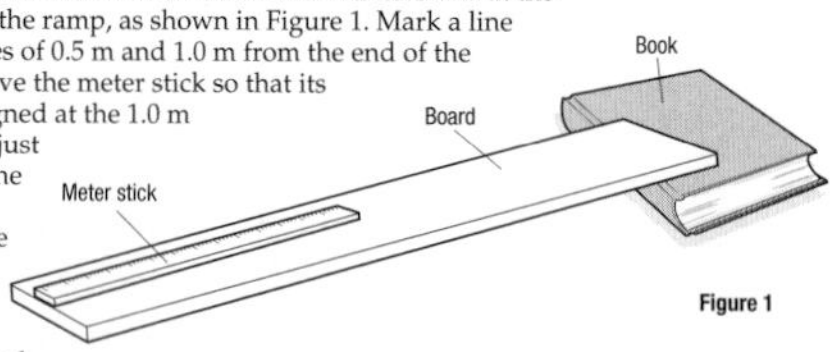

Figure 1

2. Position the steel ball at the mark located 1.5 m from the bottom of the ramp. Have your partner start the stopwatch at the instant you release the ball. Have your partner stop the stopwatch when the ball reaches the bottom of the ramp. **CAUTION:** *Stop the ball when it reaches the bottom of the ramp.* Record the time of Trial 1 for a distance of 1.5 m in the data table.

3. Repeat Step 2 four more times. Record the times of Trials 2 to 5 for a distance of 1.5 m.

4. Position the steel ball at the mark located 1.0 m from the bottom of the ramp. Release the ball and time the ball as it rolls down the ramp, as in Step 2. Record the time of Trial 1 for a distance of 1.0 m.

5. Repeat Step 4 four more times. Record the times of Trials 2 to 5 for a distance of 1.0 m.

6. Position the steel ball at the mark located 0.5 m from the bottom of the ramp. Release the ball and time its roll down the ramp as before. Record the time of Trial 1 for a distance of 0.5 m.

130 *Physical Science* Lab Manual • Investigation 12B

Lab Manual

7. Repeat Step 6 four more times. Record the times of Trials 2 to 5 for a distance of 0.5 m.

8. Calculate and record the average time for each distance. To do this, add the five times together and divide the total by 5.

Part B: Determining If the Steepness of the Ramp Affects the Ball's Acceleration

9. Place another book under the elevated end of the board to make the ramp steeper.

10. Repeat Steps 2 through 8. Record your measurements and calculations in Data Table 2.

11. It can be shown that for an object starting from rest and accelerating at a constant rate, the acceleration is equal to $2D/T^2$, where D is the distance and T is the time of travel. Use the values of D and T in Data Tables 1 and 2 to calculate the acceleration of the ball for each distance and ramp height. Record the results in Data Table 3.

Observations

Sample data are shown. Actual results will depend on the thickness of the books and the amount of friction between the ball and the ramp.

DATA TABLE 1

	Ramp Supported by One Book		
Trial	Distance = 1.5 m Time (s)	Distance = 1.0 m Time (s)	Distance = 0.5 m Time (s)
1	3.5	3.1	2.0
2	3.6	3.1	2.1
3	3.6	3.0	2.2
4	3.5	3.2	2.0
5	3.6	3.2	2.2
TOTAL	17.8	15.6	10.5
Average	3.6	3.1	2.1

DATA TABLE 2

	Ramp Supported by Two Books		
Trial	Distance = 1.5 m Time (s)	Distance = 1.0 m Time (s)	Distance = 0.5 m Time (s)
1	2.5	2.0	1.6
2	2.7	2.1	1.5
3	2.8	2.2	1.6
4	2.7	2.1	1.5
5	2.7	2.0	1.6
TOTAL	13.4	10.4	7.8
Average	2.7	2.1	1.6

Physical Science Lab Manual • Investigation 12B **131**

Lab Manual

DATA TABLE 3

Height of Ramp	Distance = 1.5 m	Distance = 1.0 m	Distance = 0.5 m
	Acceleration (m/s²) = 2D/T²		
1 book	0.23	0.21	0.23
2 books	0.41	0.45	0.39

Analysis and Conclusions

1. **Analyzing Data** Compare the accelerations that you calculated for the three distances in Part A. Did your data agree with your prediction? Explain your answer.

   There may be some variation in the calculated acceleration, but acceleration did not change as

   a result of changing the distance the ball rolled. The sample data supported the prediction that

   the ball will accelerate at a constant rate.

2. **Evaluating and Revising** Did your data support your hypothesis? Explain your answer.

   Although there was some experimental error, the sample data supported the hypothesis that

   the gravitational force and acceleration are constant as a ball rolls down a ramp.

3. **Analyzing Data** How did the steepness of the ramp affect the rate of acceleration?

   The steeper the ramp was, the greater was the rate of acceleration.

4. **Inferring** Why would it be much more difficult to perform this experiment with a very steep ramp or with a freely falling object?

   The ball would roll down the ramp or fall so quickly that it would be difficult to time accurately.

5. **Evaluating and Revising** How could this experiment be improved to produce more accurate data?

   A more precise and accurate method of timing would produce more accurate data.

Go Further

How would changing the mass of the steel ball rolling down the ramp affect the results of this experiment? Design an experiment to answer this question. Write a detailed plan for your experiment. Your plan should state the hypothesis to be tested, identify variables, and describe the procedures and safety precautions you will take. Show your plan to your teacher. When your teacher approves your plan, carry out your experiment and report your results.

Well-designed experimental plans should include detailed procedures that will test a clearly stated hypothesis. An example of an acceptable hypothesis is that increasing the mass of the ball will (or will not) increase its rate of acceleration. In the absence of friction, changing the mass of the ball should not affect the rate of acceleration. Frictional forces may cause a small change in the rate of acceleration.

132 *Physical Science* Lab Manual • Investigation 12B

Chapter Test A

Name _____ Class _____ Date _____

Chapter 12   Forces and Motion   Chapter Test A

Multiple Choice

Write the letter that best answers the question or completes the statement on the line provided.

_____ 1. Which of the following relationships is correct?
   a. 1 N = 1 kg   **b.** 1 N = 1 kg•m
   c. 1 N = 1 kg•m/s   **d.** 1 N = 1 kg•m/s^2

_____ 2. When a pair of balanced forces acts on an object, the net force that results is
   a. greater in size than both forces combined.
   b. greater in size than one of the forces.
   c. equal in size to one of the forces.
   d. equal to zero.

_____ 3. As you push a cereal box across a tabletop, the sliding friction acting on the cereal box
   a. acts in the direction of motion.
   b. equals the weight of the box
   c. is usually greater than static friction.
   d. acts in the direction opposite of motion.

_____ 4. An open parachute increases air resistance of a falling sky diver by
   a. decreasing the weight of the diver
   b. increasing surface area.
   c. increasing the terminal velocity.
   d. reducing fluid friction.

_____ 5. Projectile motion is caused by
   a. the downward force of gravity.
   b. an initial forward velocity.
   c. a final vertical velocity.
   d. the downward force of gravity and an initial forward velocity.

_____ 6. An orange might roll off your cafeteria tray when you stop suddenly because of
   a. the balanced forces acting on the orange.
   b. the centripetal force acting on the orange.
   c. the friction forces acting on the orange.
   d. the orange's inertia.

_____ 7. If a force of 10 N is applied to an object with a mass of 1 kg, the object will accelerate at
   a. 0.1 m/s^2.   **b.** 9 m/s^2.
   c. 10 m/s^2.   **d.** 11 m/s^2.

Chapter Test A

Name _____ Class _____ Date _____

_____ 8. The acceleration due to gravity on the surface of Mars is about one-third the acceleration due to gravity on Earth's surface. The weight of a space probe on the surface of Mars is about
   a. nine times greater than its weight on Earth's surface.
   b. three times greater than its weight on Earth's surface.
   c. one-third its weight on Earth's surface.
   d. the same as its weight on Earth's surface.

_____ 9. In which of the following are action and reaction forces involved?
   a. when a tennis racket strikes a tennis ball
   b. when stepping from a curb
   c. when rowing a boat
   d. all of the above

_____ 10. What is the momentum of a 50-kilogram ice skater gliding across the ice at a speed of 2 m/s?
   a. 25 $\frac{kg}{m/s}$ **b.** 48 kg•m/s   **c.** 50 kg   **d.** 100 kg•m/s

_____ 11. When opposite poles of two magnets are brought together, the poles
   a. attract each other.   **b.** repel each other.
   c. cancel each other.   **d.** cause a net force of zero.

_____ 12. With which of the following is the weak nuclear force associated?
   a. lightning   **b.** nuclear decay
   c. ocean tides   **d.** static cling

_____ 13. The gravitational force between two objects increases as mass
   a. decreases or distance decreases.
   b. decreases or distance increases.
   c. increases or distance decreases.
   d. increases or distance increases.

_____ 14. The centripetal force acting on a satellite in orbit
   a acts as an unbalanced force on the satellite.
   b. changes the direction of the satellite.
   c. is a center-directed force.
   d. all of the above

Completion

Complete each statement on the line provided.

1. The type of force measured by a grocery store spring scale is _____.

Chapter Test A

Name _____ Class _____ Date _____

2. If the forces acting on an object produce a net force of zero, the forces are called _____.

3. It usually takes more force to start an object sliding than it does to keep an object sliding because static friction is usually _____ than sliding friction.

4. The universal force that is most effective over the longest distances is _____.

5. The centripetal force acting on the moon continuously changes the _____ of the moon's motion.

Short Answer

In complete sentences, write the answers to the questions on the lines provided.

1. How can an arrow be used to represent the size and direction of a force?

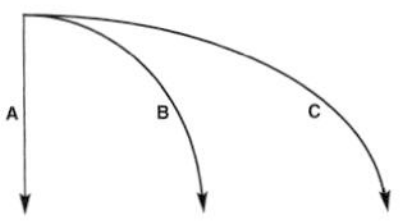

_____

_____

_____

_____

_____

Figure 12-1

2. Figure 12-1 shows the paths followed by three balls. Each ball started moving at the same time. Ball A was dropped and balls B and C were thrown sideways. Compare the times for each ball to reach the ground.

_____

_____

_____

_____

_____

_____

Chapter Test A

Name _____ Class _____ Date _____

3. During a collision, a seat belt slows the speed of a crash-test dummy. What is the direction of the net force exerted by the seat belt compared to the direction of the dummy's motion?

_____

_____

_____

4. A billiard ball with a momentum of 20 kg•m/s strikes a second ball at rest and comes to a complete stop. What is the change in momentum of the second ball?

_____

_____

_____

5. Compare the speed of a moving golf ball with the speed of a moving bowling ball if both balls have the same amount of momentum.

_____

_____

_____

Using Science Skills

Use the diagram to answer each question. Write the answers on a separate sheet of paper.

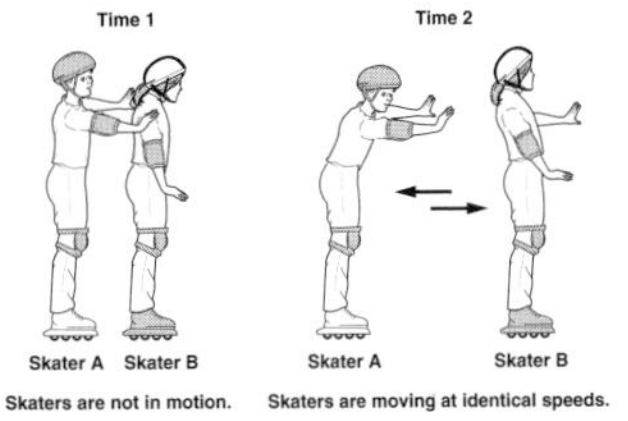

Time 1   Time 2

Skater A Skater B   Skater A Skater B
Skaters are not in motion.   Skaters are moving at identical speeds.

Figure 12-2

1. **Interpreting Graphics** In Figure 12-2, what is the momentum of each skater at Time 1?

Chapter Test A

Name _____ Class _____ Date _____

2. **Comparing and Contrasting** In Figure 12-2, compare the size and direction of the momentums of both skaters immediately after the push shown at Time 2.
3. **Interpreting Graphics** In Figure 12-2, describe the motion of Skater B after Skater A pushes her.
4. **Applying Concepts** In Figure 12-2, if Skater A is pushing Skater B, why does Skater A move?
5. **Applying Concepts** Suppose that the skaters repeat the demonstration in Figure 12-2 again. This time Skater B is holding a 10-kilogram mass. If Skater A pushes exactly as he did the first time, will Skater A's motion be different this time? Explain your answer.

Problem

Write the answers to each question on a separate sheet of paper.

1. A crane exerts a net force of 900 N upward on a 750-kilogram car as the crane starts to lift the car from the deck of a cargo ship. What is the acceleration of the car during this time? Show your work.
2. The mass of a newborn baby is 4.2 kilograms. What is the baby's weight? (The acceleration due to gravity at Earth's surface is 9.8 m/s².) Show your work.
3. A small 32-kilogram canoe broke free of its dock and is now floating downriver at a speed of 2.5 m/s. What is the canoe's momentum? Show your work.
4. A small engine causes a 0.20-kg model airplane to accelerate at a rate of 12 m/s². What is the net force on the model airplane? Show your work.

Essay

Write the answers to each question on a separate sheet of paper.

1. Why does a biker have to pedal harder to travel at a constant speed into the wind on a windy day compared to traveling on the same road at the same speed on a calm day?

Chapter Test B

Name _____ Class _____ Date _____

Chapter 12   Forces and Motion   **Chapter Test B**

Multiple Choice

Write the letter that best answers the question or completes the statement on the line provided.

_____ 1. The SI unit of force is the
a. joule.   b. kilogram.   c. meter.   d. newton.

_____ 2. When an unbalanced force acts on an object,
a. the object's motion does not change.
b. the object accelerates.
c. the weight of the object decreases.
d. the inertia of the object increases.

_____ 3. What kind of friction occurs as a fish swims through water?
a. fluid   b. rolling   c. sliding   d. static

_____ 4. The forces acting on a falling leaf are
a. air resistance and fluid friction.
b. gravity and air resistance.
c. gravity and static friction.
d. weight and rolling friction.

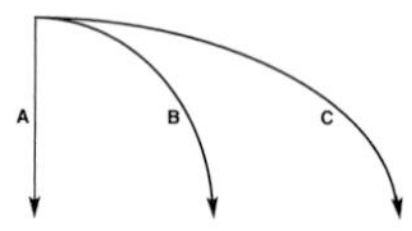

Figure 12-1

_____ 5. Figure 12-1 shows the motion of three balls. The curved paths followed by balls B and C are examples of
a. centripetal motion.   b. constant motion.
c. linear motion.   d. projectile motion.

_____ 6. The property of matter that resists changes in motion is called
a. friction.   b. gravity.   c. inertia.   d. weight.

_____ 7. According to Newton's second law of motion, the acceleration of an object equals the net force acting on the object divided by the object's
a. mass.   b. momentum.
c. velocity.   d. weight.

_____ 8. Your weight equals your
a. mass.
b. mass divided by the net force acting on you.
c. mass times the acceleration due to gravity.
d. mass times your speed.

Chapter Test B

Name _____ Class _____ Date _____

_____ 9. Newton's third law of motion describes
a. action and reaction forces.
b. balanced forces.
c. centripetal forces.
d. net force.

_____ 10. The product of an object's mass and velocity is its
a. centripetal force.   b. momentum.
c. net force.   d. weight.

_____ 11. What is conserved when two objects collide in a closed system?
a. acceleration   b. momentum
c. speed   d. velocity

_____ 12. What force is responsible for the repulsion between two positively-charged particles?
a. centripetal   b. electric
c. gravitational   d. nuclear

_____ 13. Which universal force acts only on the protons and neutrons in a nucleus?
a. electric   b. gravitational
c. magnetic   d. strong nuclear

_____ 14. Which of the following universal forces is the most effective over long distances?
a. electric   b. gravitational
c. magnetic   d. strong nuclear

_____ 15. As an astronaut travels far away from Earth, her weight
a. decreases because gravity decreases.
b. decreases because her mass decreases.
c. increases because gravity increases.
d. remains the same because her mass remains the same.

_____ 16. The force that keeps an object moving in a circle is called
a. centripetal force.   b. fluid friction.
c. inertia.   d. momentum.

Completion

Complete each statement on the line provided.

1. A push or pull is an example of a(an) _____.
2. The sum of all the forces acting on an object is called the _____.
3. The force that opposes the motion of objects that touch as they move pass each other is called _____.

Chapter Test B

Name _____ Class _____ Date _____

4. The two forces acting on a falling object are gravity and _____.
5. The path of motion of a thrown javelin is an example of _____ motion.
6. The tendency of an object to resist any change in its motion is called _____.
7. The acceleration of an object is equal to the net _____ acting on the object divided by the object's _____.
8. The force of gravity acting on an object is the object's _____.
9. If a golf ball and bowling ball are rolling at the same speed, the _____ ball has greater momentum.
10. In a closed system, the loss of momentum of one object _____ the gain in momentum of another object.

Short Answer

In complete sentences, write the answers to the questions on the lines provided.

1. What happens to the magnitude of the fluid friction acting on a submarine as the submarine's speed increases?

_____
_____
_____
_____

2. What is the direction of the net force on a falling sky diver before she reaches terminal velocity? After she is falling at terminal velocity?

_____
_____
_____
_____

3. How can you double the acceleration of an object if you cannot alter the object's mass?

_____
_____
_____

Chapter Test B

Name _____ Class _____ Date _____

4. Which of the universal forces acts only on protons and neutrons in the nucleus of an atom?

_____

_____

_____

_____

5. What is the primary cause of Earth's ocean tides?

_____

_____

_____

_____

Using Science Skills

Use the diagram to answer each question. Write the answers on a separate sheet of paper.

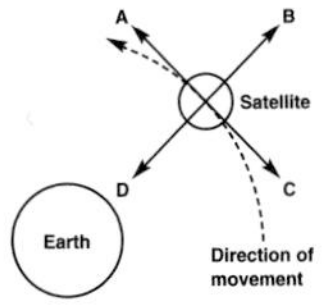

Figure 12-2

1. **Interpreting Graphics** In Figure 12-2, what is the direction of the centripetal force acting on the satellite at this location in its orbit?
2. **Predicting** What happens to the size of the centripetal force due to gravity acting on the satellite in Figure 12-2 if the satellite moves farther from Earth?
3. **Applying Concepts** The centripetal force acting on the satellite in Figure 12-2 is one of a pair of action-reaction forces. On what object is the other force in the pair acting?
4. **Interpreting Graphics** In Figure 12-2, what property of the satellite tends to keep it moving along through its orbit?
5. **Inferring** As shown in Figure 12-2, what is the direction of the fluid friction acting on the satellite as it moves through the outer layer of Earth's atmosphere?

Chapter 12 Test A Answers

Multiple Choice

1. d   **2.** d   **3.** d   **4.** b   **5.** d   **6.** d
7. c   **8.** c   **9.** d   **10.** d   **11.** a   **12.** b
13. c   **14.** d

Completion

1. weight   **2.** balanced forces; balanced   **3.** greater; larger
4. gravity   **5.** direction

Short Answer

1. The length of the arrow represents the size of the force, and the direction of the arrow represents the direction of the force.
2. Each ball will reach the ground in the same amount of time.
3. The direction of the net force is opposite the direction of the dummy's motion. **4.** 20 kg•m/s **5.** The speed of the golf ball is much greater than the speed of the bowling ball.

Using Science Skills

1. 0 kg•m/s **2.** The momentums of both skaters are equal in size but opposite in direction. **3.** The push on Skater B by Skater A accelerates Skater B forward. **4.** According to Newton's third law of motion, as Skater A pushes on Skater B, an equal and opposite force pushes back on Skater A. The unbalanced force causes Skater B to accelerate backward. **5.** No; Skater A is exerting the same force on Skater B as before and so Skater B is exerting the same force on Skater A as before. The result is that Skater's A motion will be the same.

Problem

1. $\text{Acceleration} = \dfrac{\text{Net force}}{\text{Mass}}$, $a = \dfrac{F}{m}$

$$a = \frac{900\,\text{N}}{750\,\text{kg}} = \frac{1.2\,\text{N}}{\text{kg}} = \frac{1.2\,\frac{\text{kg}\bullet\text{m}}{\text{s}^2}}{\text{kg}} = 1.2\,\text{m/s}^2$$

$a = 1/2\,\text{m/s}^2$, upward

2. Weight = Mass × Acceleration due to gravity
$W = mg$; $W = 4.2\,\text{kg} \times 9.8\,\text{m/s}^2$; $W = 41\,\text{kg}\bullet\text{m/s}^2 = 41\text{N}$
3. Momentum = Mass × Velocity
Momentum = 32 kg × 2.5 m/s = 80 kg•m/s, downriver
4. $a = \dfrac{F}{m}$ $F = ma = 0.20\,\text{kg} \times 12\,\text{m/s}^2 = 2.4\,\text{kg}\bullet\text{m/s}^2 = 2.4\,\text{N}$

Essay

1. On both the calm and windy days, the net force on the biker is zero because the biker is traveling at constant speed. On a calm day, the biker must pedal so that the forward-directed force applied to the bike balances the forces of friction opposing the forward motion. The friction forces primarily take the form rolling friction and fluid friction. On a windy day, the fluid friction force is much greater, so the rider must pedal harder to maintain the same constant speed.

Chapter 12 Test B Answers

Multiple Choice

1. d   **2.** b   **3.** a   **4.** b   **5.** d   **6.** c
7. a   **8.** c   **9.** a   **10.** b   **11.** b   **12.** b
13. d   **14.** b   **15.** a   **16.** a

Completion

1. force **2.** net force **3.** friction **4.** air resistance; drag
5. projectile **6.** inertia **7.** force, mass **8.** weight **9.** bowling
10. equals

Short Answer

1. It increases. **2.** Down; there is no net force on the sky diver.
3. Double the net force acting on the object.
4. strong nuclear force **5.** the gravitational pull of the moon

Using Science Skills

1. D **2.** The centripetal force will become less. **3.** Earth
4. inertia **5.** c

Chapter 13 Forces in Fluids

CHAPTER 13

Planning Guide

Use these planning tools
Easy Planner
Resource Pro
Online Lesson Planner

SECTION OBJECTIVES	STANDARDS		ACTIVITIES and LABS
	NATIONAL (See p. T18.)	STATE	
13.1 Fluid Pressure, pp. 390–393 🕐 1 block or 2 periods **13.1.1 Describe** and **calculate** pressure. **13.1.2 Identify** appropriate SI units for measuring pressure. **13.1.3 Describe** the relationship between water depth and the pressure it exerts. **13.1.4 Describe** how forces from pressure are distributed at a given level in a fluid. **13.1.5 Explain** how altitude affects air pressure.	A-1, B-4, G-1, G-2, G-3		**SE** Inquiry Activity: What Makes Something Sink or Float? p. 389 **L2** **TE** Teacher Demo: Relating Cause and Effect, p. 391 **L2**
13.2 Forces and Pressure in Fluids, pp. 394–397 🕐 1 block or 2 periods **13.2.1 Describe** how pressure is transmitted in a fluid according to Pascal's principle. **13.2.2 Explain** how a hydraulic system works to change a force. **13.2.3 Explain** how the speed and pressure of a fluid are related according to Pascal's principle.	B-4, G-1, G-2, G-3		**TE** Teacher Demo: Pascal's Principle, p. 394 **L2** **LM** Investigation 13B: Investigating Siphons **L1**
13.3 Buoyancy, pp. 400–404 🕐 1 block or 2 periods **13.3.1 Explain** the effect of buoyancy on the apparent weight of an object. **13.3.2 Explain** the relationship between the volume of fluid displaced by an object and buoyant force acting on the object according to Archimedes' principle. **13.3.3 Describe** the relationship among object density, fluid density, and whether an object sinks or floats in a fluid. **13.3.4 Describe** the relationship among object weight, buoyant force, and whether an object sinks or floats in a fluid.	A-1, A-2, B-4, E-2, G-1, G-2, G-3		**SE** Quick Lab: Changing Buoyancy, p. 401 **L2** **SE** Exploration Lab: Determining Buoyant Force, p. 405 **L2** **TE** Teacher Demo: Volume Measurement, p. 403 **L2** **LM** Investigation 13A: Investigating Sinking and Floating **L2**

Ability Levels

L1	For students who need additional help
L2	For all students
L3	For students who need to be challenged

Components

SE	Student Edition
TE	Teacher's Edition
LM	Laboratory Manual
PLM	Probeware Lab Manual
GRSW	Guided Reading & Study Workbook With Math Support
CUT	Chapter and Unit Tests
CTB	Computer Test Bank
TP	Test Prep Resources
iT	iText
DC	Discovery Channel Videotapes
T	Transparencies
P	Presentation Pro CD-ROM
GO	Internet Resources

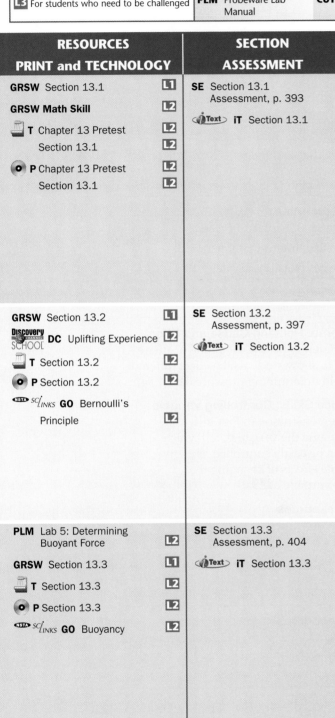

RESOURCES PRINT and TECHNOLOGY		SECTION ASSESSMENT
GRSW Section 13.1	L1	SE Section 13.1 Assessment, p. 393
GRSW Math Skill	L2	iT Section 13.1
T Chapter 13 Pretest	L2	
Section 13.1	L2	
P Chapter 13 Pretest	L2	
Section 13.1	L2	
GRSW Section 13.2	L1	SE Section 13.2 Assessment, p. 397
DC Uplifting Experience	L2	iT Section 13.2
T Section 13.2	L2	
P Section 13.2	L2	
GO Bernoulli's Principle	L2	
PLM Lab 5: Determining Buoyant Force	L2	SE Section 13.3 Assessment, p. 404
GRSW Section 13.3	L1	iT Section 13.3
T Section 13.3	L2	
P Section 13.3	L2	
GO Buoyancy	L2	

Go Online

Go online for these Internet resources.

PHSchool.com
Web Code: cca-2130

NSTA SCiLINKS
Web Code: ccn-2132
Web Code: ccn-2133

Materials for Activities and Labs

Quantities for each group

STUDENT EDITION

Inquiry Activity, p. 389
small, plastic bowl; wooden toothpick; piece of modeling clay; paper towel; water

Quick Lab, p. 401
clear plastic bottle with screw cap, dropper pipet, water

Exploration Lab, p. 405
string, rock, spring scale, can, plastic tub, sponge, paper towels, 100-g standard mass, wooden block tied to a fishing weight, 250-mL graduated cylinder

TEACHER'S EDITION

Teacher Demo, p. 391
1 shoe with large-area heel, 1 shoe with small-area heel (both shoes must fit the same student), 1 square of vinyl tile

Teacher Demo, p. 394
2 syringes (10 cc and 60 cc), 20 cm clear plastic tubing (4.8 mm ID), food coloring, water, 150-mL beaker, stirring rod

Build Science Skills, p. 399
clear straw, 1000-mL beaker or jar, several drops of dark food coloring, water

Teacher Demo, p. 403
small steel ball or irregularly shaped object, 500-mL beaker, 100-mL beaker, water

Chapter Assessment

CHAPTER ASSESSMENT

SE	Chapter Assessment, pp. 407–408
CUT	Chapter 13 Test A, B
CTB	Chapter 13
iT	Chapter 13
PHSchool.com GO	
Web Code: cca-2130	

STANDARDIZED TEST PREP

SE Chapter 13, p. 409
TP Diagnose and Prescribe

iText—interactive textbook with assessment at PHSchool.com

Name_____ Class_____ Date_____ M T W T F

LESSON PLAN 13.1

Fluid Pressure

Section Objectives   **Local Standards**

- **13.1.1 Describe** and **calculate** pressure.

- **13.1.2 Identify** appropriate SI units for measuring pressure.

- **13.1.3 Describe** the relationship between water depth and the pressure it exerts.

- **13.1.4 Describe** how forces from pressure are distributed at a given level in fluid.

- **13.1.5 Describe** how altitude affects air pressure.

Vocabulary pressure • pascal • fluid

1 FOCUS

Build Vocabulary: LINCS
Have students use the LINCS strategy to learn and review the vocabulary terms for this section. **L2**

Targeted Resources
❑ Transparency: Chapter 13 Pretest
❑ Transparency: Interest Grabber 13.1
❑ Transparency: Reading Strategy 13.1

2 INSTRUCT

Use Visuals: Figure 1
Examine Figure 1 and ask students why the pressure is not the same if the weight is the same in both cases. **L1**

Build Math Skills: Data Tables and Line Graphs
Have students create a data table and line graphs with values for water pressure, area, and force. **L1**

Build Reading Literacy: Anticipation Guide
Before students read the text, have them predict the answers to several true/false questions about the section. After students have read the section, revisit the questions. **L2**

Teacher Demo: Relating Cause and Effect
Use two differently heeled shoes and a square of vinyl tile to show students the effect different areas make in determining pressure. **L2**

Build Science Skills: Controlling Variables
Using the demonstration in Figure 4, ask students to name the variables, tell which variables can be easily controlled, and give some possible effects of changing the controllable variables. **L2**

Targeted Resources
❑ GRSW Section 13.1

3 ASSESS

Reteach
Review the definitions of a fluid and pressure. Use Figure 3 to discuss how pressure in fluids is affected by depth and altitude. **L1**

Evaluate Understanding
Have students work in pairs to write three math problems (with solutions) based on the pressure equation used in this section. **L2**

Targeted Resources
❑ **PHSchool.com** Online Section 13.1 Assessment
❑ iText Section 13.1

Transparencies

184 **Chapter 13 Pretest**

1. If two forces act in opposite directions on an object, how do you determine the net force on the object?

2. What effect do balanced forces have on the motion of an object?

3. What effect do unbalanced forces have on the motion of an object?

4. Which units could you use to describe the area of a chalkboard?

   a. meters (m)

   b. square meters (m^2)

   c. cubic meters (m^3)

5. Which of the following defines weight?

   a. the amount of matter in an object

   b. the force due to gravity acting on an object

   c. the same as mass

ANSWERS
1. Subtract the smaller force from the larger force.
2. The forces cause no change in the object's motion.
3. The object's speed increases in the direction of the greater force.

4. b
5. b

Transparencies

185 **Chapter 13 Pretest** *(continued)*

6. A tennis ball has a volume of 125 cm^3 and a mass of 57 g. What is the ball's average density? *(Hint: density = mass/volume)*

7. The distance between a home and school is 6.35 km. What is this distance in meters?

8. Which of Newton's laws describes action-reaction forces?

Answers
6. 0.46 g/cm³
7. 6350 m
8. Newton's third law

Transparencies

186 **Section 13.1 Interest Grabber**

Pressure of an Object

What happens when the same force is applied to two areas of different size? To find out, perform this simple activity. Grab a heavy book at its spine using one hand. Make sure to wrap your entire hand around the book. Hold the book several centimeters above your desktop for 20 seconds. Next, repeat the process using only your thumb and forefinger. Again hold the book for 20 seconds.

1. What difference do you notice in the two methods of holding the book?

2. Does the weight of the book change? Does the area over which you apply the force needed to hold the book change?

ANSWERS
1. It is much harder to hold the book for 20 seconds when you use only two fingers.

2. The weight of the book does not change. The area over which the force is applied does change. The area is much larger when the book is hold using the entire hand wrapped around the spine.

Transparencies

187 **Section 13.1 Reading Strategy**

Using Prior Knowledge

Meanings of *Pressure*	
Common definition	a._____?_____
Scientific definition	b._____?_____

ANSWERS
a. Definitions will vary and may involve the scientific or the nonscientific definition of pressure.
b. Pressure is the amount of force per unit area. Students should contrast the scientific definition with the common definition.

Guided Reading and Study Workbook

Section 13.1 **Program Resources**

Name _____ Class _____ Date _____

Chapter 13   Forces in Fluids

Section 13.1 Fluid Pressure
(pages 390–393)

This section defines pressure and describes factors that determine fluid pressure. The atmosphere as a fluid is discussed, including how air pressure changes with altitude.

Reading Strategy (page 390)

Using Prior Knowledge Before reading the section, write a common definition of the word *pressure*. After you have read the section, write the scientific definition of *pressure* and contrast it to your original definition. For more information on this Reading Strategy, see the **Reading and Study Skills** in the **Skills and Reference Handbook** at the end of your textbook.

Meanings of *Pressure*	
Common definition	Definitions will vary and may involve the scientific or the nonscientific definition of pressure.
Scientific definition	Pressure is the amount of force per unit area. Students should contrast this definition with their original definition given above.

Pressure (pages 390–391)

1. Pressure is the result of a(n) _____force_____ distributed over a(n) _____area_____ .

2. The same force is exerted by each of the following. Which exerts the most pressure?
   a. a foot   b. a large book
   c. a fingertip   (d.) the tip of a ball-point pen

3. How is pressure calculated? Divide the force acting on an object by the area over which the force acts; Pressure = Force/Area

4. A wooden crate that measures 2.0 m long and 0.40 m wide rests on the floor. If the crate has a weight of 600.0 N, what pressure does it exert on the floor?
   a. 0.80 m²   b. 480 Pa
   c. 3.0 × 10³ N/m²   (d.) 750 Pa

Pressure in Fluids (pages 391–392)

5. A substance that assumes the shape of its container is called a(n) _____fluid_____ .

6. List four examples of fluids. Answers should include gases and liquids such as:
   a. _____Air_____   b. _____Oil_____
   c. _____Oxygen_____   d. _____Water_____

Name _____ Class _____ Date _____

Chapter 13   Forces in Fluids

7. Circle the letter of each sentence that is true about fluid pressure.
   a. Water pressure decreases as depth decreases.
   b. Fluid pressure is exerted only at the base of the container holding the fluid.
   (c.) The pressure in a fluid at any given depth is constant, and it is exerted equally in all directions.
   (d.) The two factors that determine the pressure a fluid exerts are type of the fluid and its depth.

8. Is the following sentence true or false? The pressure at a depth of 2 feet in a large lake is greater than the pressure at the same depth in a swimming pool. _____false_____

Air Pressure and the Atmosphere (pages 392–393)

9. Instead of referring to their depth in the atmosphere, people refer to their _____altitude_____ above sea level.

For questions 10 through 13, refer to the air pressure table below.

Changes in Air Pressure with Altitude		
Altitude Above Sea Level (m)	Air Pressure (bars)	Air Pressure (kPa)
0	1.000	101.3
200	0.9971	98.97
400	0.9545	96.68
600	0.9322	94.42
800	0.9103	92.21
1000	0.8888	90.03
1200	0.8677	87.89

10. Complete the air pressure columns in the table by converting between units of air pressure. *Hint:* 1 bar = 101.3 kPa.

11. How does air pressure change as a function of altitude?
    Air pressure decreases with increasing altitude.

12. Suppose a hiker is on a mountain ridge 1200 meters above sea level. Approximately what air pressure will she experience?
    87.89 kPa or 0.8677 bars

13. By how much does the air pressure decrease, in bars, from sea level to an altitude of 1200 meters? _____0.1323 bars_____

14. Is the following sentence true or false? Air exerts a force of more than 1000 N on top of your head. _____true_____

15. What keeps a person from being crushed by air pressure? The pressure inside a person's body balances the air pressure outside, resulting in a net force of zero.

LESSON PLAN 13.2

Forces and Pressure in Fluids

Time
2 periods
1 block

Section Objectives

- **13.2.1 Describe** how pressure is transmitted in a fluid according to Pascal's principle.
- **13.2.2 Explain** how a hydraulic system works to change a force.
- **13.2.3 Explain** how the speed and pressure of a fluid are related according to Pascal's principle.

Vocabulary hydraulic system • lift

Local Standards

1 FOCUS

Build Vocabulary: Word-Part Analysis
Ask students what words they know that have the key word parts *hydro-* or *hydr-*. **L2**

Targeted Resources
❑ Transparency: Interest Grabber 13.2
❑ Transparency: Reading Strategy 13.2

2 INSTRUCT

Use Visuals: Figure 7
Ask students to use Figure 7 to explain how the truck's hydraulic system increases force. Ask approximately how many times larger the output force is than the input force. **L1**

Build Reading Literacy: Relate Cause and Effect
Ask students to create a flowchart beginning with the input force of the small piston and ending with the output force of the large piston. **L1**

Teacher Demo: Pascal's Principle
Use two syringes and plastic tubing to create a system that will show students the effects of Pascal's principle. **L2**

Address Misconceptions
Have students release a tennis ball from the bottom of a beaker of water. The ball will quickly move to the top of the water because the force of the water pushes up, not down, on it. **L2**

Build Science Skills: Applying Concepts
Divide the class into groups and have them discuss how Bernoulli's principle applies to various situations. **L2**

Targeted Resources
❑ Transparency: Figure 6: Illustrating Pascal's Principle
❑ Transparency: Figure 9: A Hose-end Sprayer
❑ GRSW Section 13.2
❑ **NSTA** *sciLINKS* Bernoulli's principle

3 ASSESS

Reteach
Use Figures 7 and 8 to review Pascal's principle and to summarize Bernoulli's principle. **L1**

Evaluate Understanding
Ask students to use either Bernoulli's principle or Pascal's principle to explain the operation of the following: sprayer (atomizer), airplane lift, and hydraulic jack. **L2**

Targeted Resources
❑ **PHSchool.com** Online Section 13.2 Assessment
❑ iText Section 13.2

Transparencies

188 Section 13.2 Interest Grabber

Using Pressure Differences to Move Objects

What do you think will happen when high-speed air is blown between two strips of paper? To find out, hold two strips of paper facing one another, about 10 centimeters apart, as shown below.

Blow gently between the strips of paper and observe what happens. Then repeat the process, but blow forcefully between the paper strips.

1. What happens when gentle, low-speed air is blown between the strips of paper?

2. What happens when high-speed air is blown between the strips of paper?

3. Based on your observations, try to infer how the speed of the air affects the air pressure acting on the inside and outside faces of the strips of paper.

ANSWERS
1. The gentle, low-speed air causes little or no movement in the paper strips.
2. The high-speed air causes the paper strips to move toward each other.
3. Do not assess student responses to this question. Accept any plausible explanation. The paper strips move toward each other because the air pressure within the high-speed air moving between the paper strips is lower than the slower- or non-moving air surrounding the strips. The pressure difference pushes the paper strips together.

Transparencies

189 Section 13.2 Reading Strategy

Predicting

Prediction	a._____?_____
Reason for prediction	b._____?_____

ANSWERS
a. Students will most likely predict that the foam balls will be blown apart from one another. Check that students provide reasons for their prediction.
b. Reasons will likely include the force the air exerts on the foam balls as it blows past them.

Transparencies

190 Figure 6 **Illustrating Pascal's Principle**

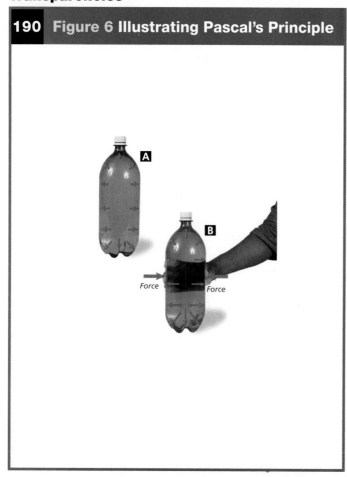

Transparencies

191 Figure 9 **A Hose-end Sprayer**

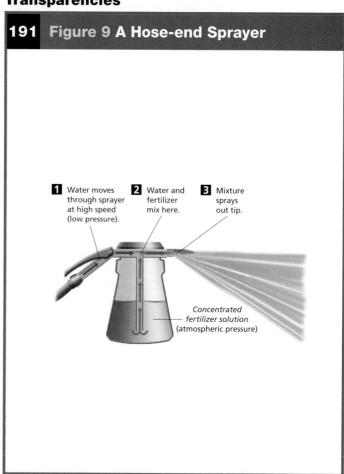

1 Water moves through sprayer at high speed (low pressure).

2 Water and fertilizer mix here.

3 Mixture sprays out tip.

Concentrated fertilizer solution (atmospheric pressure)

Name _____ Class _____ Date _____

Chapter 13   Forces in Fluids

Section 13.2 Forces and Pressure in Fluids
(pages 394–397)

This section presents Pascal's and Bernoulli's principles. Examples of each principle from nature and industry are discussed.

Reading Strategy (pages 394)

Predicting Imagine two small foam balls hanging from strings at the same height with about three centimeters of space between them. Before you read the section, write a prediction about what will happen to the balls when you blow air through the space between them. Identify your reasons. After you have read the section, check the accuracy of your prediction. For more information on this Reading Strategy, see the **Reading and Study Skills** in the **Skills and Reference Handbook** at the end of your textbook.

Predicting Forces and Pressure in Fluids	
Prediction	Students will most likely predict that the foam balls will be blown apart from one another.
Reason for Prediction	Reasons will likely include the force the air exerts on the foam balls as it blows past them.

Transmitting Pressure in a Fluid (pages 394–395)

1. In a fluid-filled container, why is the pressure greater at the base of the container? _Because the pressure exerted by a fluid increases with depth._

2. Is the following sentence true or false? If you squeeze a container filled with fluid, the pressure within the fluid increases equally throughout the fluid. ____true____

3. According to Pascal's principle, what happens when there is a change in pressure at any point in a fluid? _The change in pressure is transmitted equally and unchanged in all directions throughout the fluid._

4. The science of applying Pascal's principle is called ____hydraulics____.

5. In a hydraulic lift system, an increased output force is produced because constant ____fluid pressure____ is exerted on the larger area of the output piston.

6. Is the following sentence true or false? In a hydraulic system, the output force is greater than the input force because the pressure acting on the output piston is greater than the pressure acting on the input piston. ____false____

Name _____ Class _____ Date _____

Chapter 13   Forces in Fluids

Bernoulli's Principle (pages 396–397)

7. Circle the letter of the sentence that correctly states Bernoulli's principle.
   a. As the speed of a fluid decreases, the pressure within the fluid decreases.
   b. As the speed of a fluid increases, the pressure within the fluid increases.
   c. As the speed of a fluid increases, the pressure within the fluid decreases.
   d. Fluid motion has no effect on pressure within the fluid.

8. Because the air traveling over the top of an airplane wing moves faster than the air passing underneath the wing, the pressure above the wings is ____less____ than the pressure below the wing.

9. What is lift, and how does it relate to an airplane's flight? _Lift is an upward force created by the pressure difference between the top and the bottom of a plane's wing. This upward force keeps the airplane aloft._

10. What is a spoiler on a racecar designed to do? _It creates a downward force that improves traction._

For questions 11 through 14, refer to the figure below. Place the correct letter after each phrase.

Spray Bottle with Fertilizer

Concentrated fertilizer solution (atmospheric pressure)

11. Location where the water and fertilizer solution mix. ____B____
12. Location where water enters the sprayer at high speed. ____A____
13. Location where the water-fertilizer mixture exits the sprayer. ____C____
14. Use Bernoulli's principle to explain why the fertilizer solution moves up the tube. _The fast-moving water creates a low-pressure area above the tube reaching into the solution chamber. The pressure difference between the solution chamber and the top of the tube forces the fertilizer solution up the tube._

Name_____ Class_____ Date_____ M T W T F

LESSON PLAN 13.3

Buoyancy

Time
2 periods
1 block

Section Objectives

Local Standards

- **13.3.1 Explain** the effect of buoyancy on the apparent weight of an object.

- **13.3.2 Explain** the relationship between the volume of fluid displaced by an object and buoyant force acting on the object according to Archimedes' principle.

- **13.3.3 Describe** the relationship among object density, fluid density, and whether an object sinks or floats in a fluid.

- **13.3.4 Describe** the relationship among object weight, buoyant force, and whether an object sinks or floats in a fluid.

Vocabulary buoyancy • buoyant force • Archimedes' principle

1 FOCUS

Build Vocabulary: Word Forms
Have students find the meaning of root word *buoy* and build on it as they read page 400. **L2**

Targeted Resources
❑ Transparency: Interest Grabber 13.3
❑ Transparency: Reading Strategy 13.3

2 INSTRUCT

Build Reading Literacy: Visualize
Encourage students to visualize the concepts of objects suspended or sinking in water. **L1**

Teacher Demo: Volume Measurement
Use water displacement to show students an easy way to measure the volume of a solid object. **L2**

Build Science Skills: Inferring
Have students consider the explanation of floating and ask them how the shape of a hull could cause greater displacement of water. **L2**

Integrate Social Studies
Ask students to use the Internet to research ship museums. Have students write a paragraph about the restoration of a particular ship at one of the museums. **L2**

Use Community Resources
Arrange for a submarine or ship crew member or a commercial diver to visit your class to discuss experiences related to buoyancy. Encourage students to write questions in advance. **L2**

For Enrichment
Students may design and construct a simple model submarine and present it to the class as an illustration of Archimedes' principle. **L3**

Targeted Resources
❑ Transparency: Figure 10: Buoyant Force
❑ Transparency: Figure 11: Weight and the Buoyant Force
❑ GRSW Section 13.3
❑ **NSTA** *sci*₍ᵢₙₖₛ₎ Buoyancy

3 ASSESS

Reteach
Use Figure 11 and How It Works illustrations to review buoyancy, Archimedes' principle, and the way a submarine dives and rises. **L1**

Evaluate Understanding
Ask students to explain the relationship among buoyant force, weight of fluid displaced, and the apparent weight of floating objects. **L2**

Targeted Resources
❑ **PHSchool.com** Online Section 13.3 Assessment
❑ iText Section 13.3

192 Section 13.3 Interest Grabber

What Makes Objects Float and Sink?

Do heavy objects always sink when placed in water? Consider a dime and a large cruise ship. When placed in water the dime quickly sinks, while the cruise ship floats.

1. Which object is heavier, the cruise ship or the dime?

2. What evidence do you have that weight is not the only factor that determines whether an object floats or sinks?

3. Knowing that weight acts downward, what can you infer about other forces acting on a floating object?

193 Section 13.3 Reading Strategy

Summarizing

Section 13.3 Buoyancy
Buoyant Force Buoyant force is the apparent loss of weight of an object submerged in a fluid.
a._____?_____
b._____?_____

194 Figure 10 **Buoyant Force**

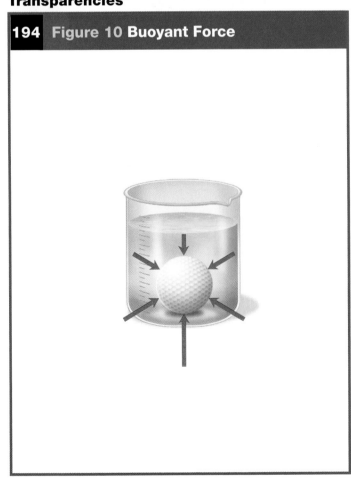

195 Figure 11 **Weight and the Buoyant Force**

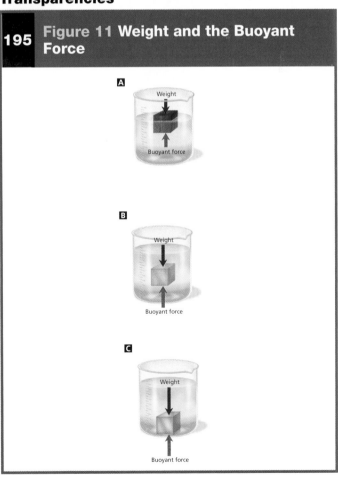

Guided Reading and Study Workbook

Name _____ Class _____ Date _____

Chapter 13   Forces in Fluids

Section 13.3 Buoyancy
(pages 400–404)

This section discusses buoyancy and Archimedes' principle of factors that determine whether an object will sink or float in a fluid.

Reading Strategy (page 400)

Summarizing As you read about buoyancy, write a brief summary of the text following each green heading. Your summary should include only the most important information. For more information on this Reading Strategy, see the **Reading and Study Skills** in the **Skills and Reference Handbook** at the end of your textbook.

Buoyant Force	Buoyant force is the apparent loss of weight of an object submerged in a fluid.
Archimedes' Principle	The buoyant force on an object is equal to the weight of fluid it displaces.
Density and Buoyancy	Objects less dense than the fluid they are in, float. Objects denser than the fluid they are in, sink. When the buoyant force is equal to the weight, the object floats or is suspended. When the buoyant force is less than the weight, the object sinks.

Buoyant Force (page 400)

1. What is buoyancy? _Buoyancy is the ability of a fluid to exert an upward force on an object within it._

2. Circle the letter of the correct answer. In which direction does a buoyant force act?
   a. in the direction of gravity   b. perpendicular to gravity
   (c.) in the direction opposite of gravity   d. from above the fluid

3. Is the following sentence true or false? The greater a fluid's density, the greater its buoyant force. _____true_____

4. Buoyancy causes an apparent _____loss_____ of weight of an object immersed in a fluid.

5. Circle the letter of each sentence that is true about buoyancy.
   (a.) Forces pushing up on a submerged object are greater than the forces pushing down on it.
   (b.) Forces acting on the sides of a submerged object cancel each other out.
   c. Gravitational forces work together with buoyant forces.
   d. The net buoyant force is non-vertical.

Physical Science Guided Reading and Study Workbook • Chapter 13 **117**

Guided Reading and Study Workbook

Name _____ Class _____ Date _____

Chapter 13   Forces in Fluids

Archimedes' Principle (page 401)

6. According to Archimedes' principle, the weight of fluid displaced by a floating object is equal to the _____buoyant force_____ acting on that object.

7. Is the following sentence true or false? When an object floats partially submerged in a fluid, it displaces a volume of fluid equal to its own volume. _____false_____

Density and Buoyancy (pages 401–404)

Match each description with the correct property. Properties may be used more than once.

	Description	Property
_c_	8. This property is the ratio of an object's mass to its volume, often expressed in g/cm³.	a. weight
_a_	9. This force is equal to the force of gravity that acts on a floating object.	b. buoyant force
_c_	10. When this property is greater for an object than for the fluid it is in, the object sinks.	c. density
_a; b_	11. These two forces act on every object in a fluid.	
_a_	12. An object will either float or be suspended when the buoyant force is equal to this.	

13. Use what you know about density and buoyancy to predict whether each of the substances listed in the table will float or sink in water. The density of water is 1.0 g/cm³.

Will It Float or Sink?		
Substance	Density (g/cm³)	Float or Sink?
Gold	19.3	Sink
Balsa Wood	0.15	Float
Ice	0.92	Float
Brick	1.84	Sink
Milk	1.03	Sink
Gasoline	0.70	Float

14. How is a heavy steel ship able to float?
   a. Because the density of steel is 7.8 g/cm³.
   (b.) The ship's shape enables it to displace a large volume of water.
   c. Because the density of water is 1 g/cm³.
   d. The ship's effective density is greater than that of water.

118 *Physical Science Guided Reading and Study Workbook • Chapter 13*

Guided Reading and Study Workbook

Name _____ Class _____ Date _____

Chapter 13   Forces in Fluids

WordWise

Solve the clues to determine which vocabulary words from Chapter 13 are hidden in the puzzle. Then find and circle the terms in the puzzle. The terms may occur vertically, horizontally, or diagonally.

h	y	d	r	a	u	l	i	c	s	y	s	t	e	m
v	a	h	u	s	p	i	a	c	f	r	h	y	e	b
s	r	q	a	z	f	f	r	e	r	f	v	d	c	q
p	c	i	u	y	t	t	p	r	e	s	s	u	r	e
t	h	d	f	r	g	s	f	l	u	t	m	a	o	e
k	i	u	b	p	l	o	e	k	j	h	t	u	f	z
k	m	t	y	u	i	r	f	l	u	i	d	l	t	d
v	e	k	p	o	o	p	f	v	b	n	m	i	n	m
o	d	k	a	r	p	y	o	i	m	q	c	c	a	f
p	e	g	s	y	h	z	a	v	b	n	h	s	y	b
p	s	e	c	u	h	n	j	n	m	l	o	m	o	q
l	r	i	a	j	u	e	r	t	c	v	f	d	u	a
p	o	i	l	m	j	g	b	h	f	y	u	j	b	o

Clues   **Hidden Words**

Mathematician who discovered that the buoyant force on an object equals the weight of the fluid displaced by the object   _Archimedes_

The result of a force distributed over an area   _pressure_

Type of substance that assumes the shape of its container   _fluid_

Ability of a fluid to exert an upward force on an object within it   _buoyancy_

SI-unit of measure used to express pressure   _pascal_

Upward force that keeps an aircraft aloft   _lift_

Device that uses pressurized fluids acting on pistons of different sizes to change a force   _hydraulic system_

Force that opposes the weight of an object floating in a fluid   _buoyant force_

Physical Science Guided Reading and Study Workbook • Chapter 13 **119**

Guided Reading and Study Workbook

Name _____ Class _____ Date _____

Chapter 13   Forces in Fluids

Calculating Pressure

Each tile on the bottom of a swimming pool has an area of 0.50 m². The water above each tile exerts a force of 11,000 N on each tile. How much pressure does the water exert on each tile?

Math Skill:
Formulas and Equations

You may want to read more about this **Math Skill** in the **Skills and Reference Handbook** at the end of your textbook.

1. Read and Understand

What information are you given?
Force = 11,000 N

Area = 0.50 m²

2. Plan and Solve

What formula contains the given quantities and the unknown?
$$\text{Pressure} = \frac{\text{Force}}{\text{Area}}$$
Replace each variable with its known value and solve.
$$\text{Pressure} = \frac{11,000 \text{ N}}{0.50 \text{ m}^2} = 22,000 \text{ N/m}^2 = 22,000 \text{ Pa} = 22 \text{ kPa}$$

3. Look Back and Check

Is your answer reasonable?
Because the area of each tile is a half square meter and pressure is defined as force per square meter, the pressure exerted will be double the magnitude of the force. Thus, an 11,000 N force will produce 22,000 Pa of pressure on the tiles. The calculation verifies this result.

Math Practice

On a separate sheet of paper, answer the following questions.

1. The weight of the gasoline in a 55-gallon drum creates a force of 1456 newtons. The area of the bottom of the drum is 0.80 m². How much pressure does the gasoline exert on the bottom of the drum?

   Pressure = Force/Area = 1456 N/0.80 m² = 1820 Pa = 1.8 kPa

2. The weight of a gallon of milk is about 38 N. If you pour 3.0 gallons of milk into a container whose bottom has an area of 0.60 m², how much pressure will the milk exert on the bottom of the container?

   Force = (3.0 gallons)(38 N/gallon) = 114 N;
   Pressure = Force/Area = 114 N/0.60 m² = 190 Pa = 0.19 kPa

3. A company makes garden statues by pouring concrete into a mold. The amount of concrete used to make a statue of a deer weighs 3600 N. If the base of the deer statue is 0.60 meters long and 0.40 meters wide, how much pressure will the statue exert on the ground? (*Hint:* Area is equal to length times width.)

   Area = 0.60 m × 0.40 m = 0.24 m²; Pressure = Force/Area = 3600 N/0.24 m² = 15,000 Pa = 15 kPa

120 *Physical Science Guided Reading and Study Workbook • Chapter 13*

Student Edition Lab Worksheet

Name _____ Class _____ Date _____

Chapter 13   Forces in Fluids   Exploration Lab

Determining Buoyant Force
See page 405 in the Teacher's Edition for more information.

In this lab, you will analyze recorded data to determine the buoyant forces acting on objects.

Problem How does the buoyant force determine whether an object sinks?

Materials
- string
- rock
- spring scale
- can
- plastic tub
- sponge
- paper towels
- 100-g standard mass
- wooden block tied to a fishing weight
- 250-mL graduated cylinder

Skills Measuring, Calculating

Procedure 🔒 🔬
1. Tie one end of the string around the rock. Tie the other end to the spring scale. Suspend the rock from the spring scale and measure and record its weight in air in the data table.

DATA TABLE Sample data are shown.

Object	Weight in Air (N)	Apparent Weight in Water (N)	Buoyant Force (weight in air – apparent weight in water, N)	Volume of Displaced Water (mL)	Weight of Displaced Water (N)
Rock	0.3	0.2	0.1	5.0	0.049
100-g standard mass	1.0	0.75	0.25	10.0	0.098
Wood block with fishing weight	1.8	1.5	0.3	25.0	0.24

2. Place the can in an upright position in the plastic tub. Completely fill the can with water. Wipe up any water that has spilled into the tub. **CAUTION:** *Wipe up any water that spills on the floor to avoid slips and falls.*
3. Lower the rock into the water until it is completely submerged. Record in the data table the apparent weight in water of the submerged rock. Remove the rock from the can.
4. Without spilling any water, carefully remove the can from the tub. Pour the water from the tub into the graduated cylinder. Record in the data table the volume of displaced water .
5. Repeat Steps 1 through 4, first with the 100-g standard mass and then with the wooden block that is tied to a fishing weight.
6. To determine the buoyant force on each object, subtract its apparent weight in water from its weight in air. In the data table, record these values.

Physical Science Lab Manual • Chapter 13 Exploration Lab **313**

Student Edition Lab Worksheet

Name _____ Class _____ Date _____

7. Calculate the weight of the water that each object displaces. (*Hint:* 1.0 mL of water has a weight of 0.0098 N.) In the data table, record these weights.

Analyze and Conclude
1. **Observing** What force is responsible for the difference between the weight of each object in the air and its apparent weight in water?

   The difference is equal to the buoyant force that the water exerts on the object.
   _____
   _____

2. **Analyzing Data** How is the buoyant force related to the weight of water displaced?

   They are equal.
   _____
   _____
   _____

3. **Forming Operational Definitions** Define buoyant force and describe two ways you can measure it or calculate it.

   Buoyant force is an upward force exerted on an object by water when the object is
   submerged in water. The buoyant force on an object is equal to the difference between
   its weight in air and its apparent weight in water. It is also equal to the weight of the water
   the object displaces.
   _____
   _____

4. **Drawing Conclusions** Explain what causes an object to sink or to float, using the terms *buoyancy, weight, force, density,* and *gravity.*

   An object will float when the upward force of buoyancy is greater than or equal to the downward
   force of gravity (the weight of the object). For the buoyant force to counteract the gravitational
   force, the object must weigh as much as or less than the volume of water it displaces. For this
   reason, floating objects have low densities.
   _____
   _____
   _____
   _____
   _____
   _____

314 *Physical Science* Lab Manual • Chapter 13 Exploration Lab

Lab Manual

Name _____ Class _____ Date _____

Chapter 13   Forces in Fluids   Investigation 13A

Investigating Sinking and Floating

Background Information
Refer students to pages 400–404 in their textbooks for a discussion of buoyancy. **SKILLS FOCUS:** Predicting, Evaluating and Revising **TIME REQUIRED:** 45 minutes

When an object is placed in a fluid, the force of gravity causes part or all of the object to sink below the upper surface of the fluid. At the same time, the fluid exerts an upward push, or **buoyant force,** on the object. The part of the object below the surface displaces the fluid. The size of the buoyant force is equal to the weight of the fluid that the object displaces. Fluids exert a buoyant force on all objects, regardless of whether the objects sink or float.

Consider an object submerged in a fluid. If the object has the same density as the fluid, then the weight of the object will be equal to the weight of an equal volume of fluid. In that case, the buoyant force will be equal to the weight of the object. As a result, the object will remain at any depth where it is placed. If the object is less dense than the fluid, the buoyant force on the object will be greater than the weight of the object. In this case, the object will rise to the surface and float. If the object is more dense than the fluid, the buoyant force on the object will be less than the weight of the object, and the object will sink.

This principle explains why a grain of sand sinks in water, whereas a basketball that has a much greater weight can float. Sand is denser than water. Therefore, the weight of the sand grain is greater than the buoyant force it receives from the water. The buoyant force acting on the basketball is greater than the weight of the basketball. As a result, the basketball floats.

In this investigation, you will predict which objects will float in water. Then, you will perform experiments to test your predictions.

Problem
What happens to the ability of an object to float as its mass and volume change?

Pre-Lab Discussion
Read the entire investigation. Then, work with a partner to answer the following questions.

1. **Controlling Variables** Identify the manipulated, responding, and controlled variables in this investigation.
   a. Manipulated variables

   Mass (number of BBs), volume of the floating container (canister or bottle)
   _____

   b. Responding variables

   Level of water, level of the canister in the water
   _____

Physical Science Lab Manual • Investigation 13A **133**

Lab Manual

Name _____ Class _____ Date _____

   c. Controlled variables

   Floating container (canister), fluid (water), diameter of container for fluid (beaker)
   _____

2. **Predicting** Predict how adding BBs to the canister will affect the following variables.
   a. The level of the canister in the water

   The canister will float at a lower level (more deeply) in the water.
   _____
   _____

   b. The level of the water in the beaker

   The level of the water will rise.
   _____
   _____

3. **Predicting** The bottle you will use in Steps 10 through 13 is larger than the canister. Which container do you predict will float at a lower level (more deeply) in the water? Explain your answer.

   The canister will float at a lower level (more deeply) than the bottle because the masses of the two
   containers will be equal, but the bottle has a greater volume. Therefore, the average density of the
   bottle is less dense and will float higher in the water.
   _____

4. **Applying Concepts** What factors determine whether an object sinks or floats in water?

   The density of an object determines whether it sinks or floats. It will float if its density is less than
   that of water. It will sink if its density is greater than that of water. Students may also express this
   concept in terms of weight and buoyant force.
   _____

Materials *(per group)*

film canister	BBs	Provide approximately 100 BBs per lab group in a nonglass container.
masking tape	paper towels	
metric ruler	triple-beam balance	
250-mL beaker	plastic bottle	Use a bottle with a larger diameter than the film canister, but small enough to fit in the beaker.

The canister and plastic bottle must have straight sides; tapered containers will not work well in this investigation. A plastic medicine bottle or similar container can be used if a film canister is not available.

134 *Physical Science* Lab Manual • Investigation 13A

Lab Manual

Name _____ Class _____ Date _____

Safety 🥽 🧤 ⚡

Put on safety goggles. Be careful to avoid breakage when working with glassware. Wipe up any spilled water immediately to avoid slips and falls. Note all safety alert symbols next to the steps in the Procedure and review the meaning of each symbol by referring to the Safety Symbols on page xiii.

Procedure

1. Attach a strip of masking tape to the side of the film canister, extending from the bottom to the top of the canister. Starting from the bottom of the canister, use the metric ruler and a pencil to accurately mark 0.5-cm intervals on the side of the canister, as shown in Figure 1.

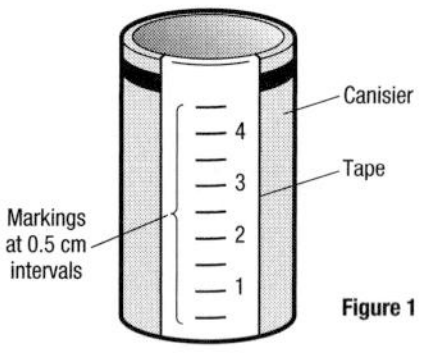

2. Repeat Step 1, using the plastic bottle.

3. Fill the beaker approximately three-fourths full with water. Place 20 BBs in the canister. Place the canister in the beaker with its open end pointed upward. Add or remove BBs from the canister, one at a time, until approximately half of the canister floats below the surface of the water. **Note:** *To remove BBs, take the canister out of the beaker. To add BBs, leave the canister in the beaker while carefully placing the BBs in the canister.* Count the BBs as you add or remove them from the canister. In the first row of Data Table 1, record the number of BBs in the canister. Remember to include the first 20 BBs that you added.

4. Use the metric ruler to measure the level of the water in the beaker from the tabletop to the surface of the water. Record this measurement in Data Table 1. Also determine the level of the canister in the water and record this measurement in Data Table 1.

5. Predict how the level of the canister in the water and the level of the water in the beaker will change if you remove 10 BBs from the canister. Record your prediction as Prediction 1 in Data Table 1.

6. Now test your prediction. Take the canister out of the beaker, first tapping it gently against the inside of the beaker to minimize any water loss from the beaker. Remove 10 BBs from the canister and carefully place the canister back in the beaker. In Data Table 1, record the number of BBs in the canister, the level of the canister in the water, and the level of the water in the beaker.

7. Replace the 10 BBs that you removed from the canister. Predict how the level of the canister and the level of the water will change if you add 10 more BBs to the canister. Record your prediction as Prediction 2 in Data Table 1.

Markings at 0.5 cm intervals

Canister

Tape

Figure 1

Lab Manual

Name _____ Class _____ Date _____

8. Test your prediction by carefully adding 10 BBs to the canister. In Data Table 1, record the number of BBs in the canister, the level of the canister in the water, and the level of the water in the beaker.

9. Carefully remove the canister of BBs from the beaker, while minimizing any water loss from the beaker. Use paper towels to dry the outside of the canister. Use the triple-beam balance to determine the mass of the canister and BBs. Record this mass in Data Table 2. Without changing the positions of the riders on the balance, remove the canister and set it aside.

10. Place the plastic bottle on the balance. Add BBs to the bottle until its mass is equal to the mass of the canister and the BBs it contains. Record this mass in Data Table 2.

11. Predict which container will float more deeply in the water by placing a check mark in the appropriate row below Prediction 3 in Data Table 2. Also predict which container will cause the greater rise of the water level in the beaker by placing a check mark in the appropriate row below Prediction 4 in Data Table 2.

12. Test your predictions by placing the canister into the beaker. In Data Table 2, record the number of BBs in the canister, the level of the canister, and the level of the water. Carefully remove the canister.

13. Repeat Step 12, using the plastic bottle.

Observations   Sample data are shown.

DATA TABLE 1

Action	Number of BBs	Level of Canister in Water (cm)	Level of Water in Beaker (cm)
Float canister halfway below surface of water	50	3.0	6.7
Remove 10 BBs	40	2.5	6.6
Add 10 BBs	60	3.5	6.8

Prediction 1 _____

Prediction 2 _____

Lab Manual

Name _____ Class _____ Date _____

DATA TABLE 2

Container	Mass of Container and BBs (g)	Prediction 3 (Identify the container that will float more deeply in water.)	Level of Container in Water (cm)	Prediction 4 (Identify which container will cause the greater rise of the water level in the beaker.)	Level of Water in Beaker (cm)
Canister			3.0		6.7
Bottle			1.5		6.7

Analysis and Conclusions

1. **Analyzing Data** How did the number of BBs in the canister affect the level at which the canister floated in the water?

   The greater the number of BBs (and mass), the deeper the canister floated in water.

2. **Evaluating and Revising** Did your observations support your predictions of how the number of BBs in the canister would affect the level of the canister in the water and the level of the water in the beaker? Explain your answer.

   The observations supported the predictions that adding BBs to the canister would cause the canister to float more deeply in the water and cause the water level to rise. This result occurred because adding BBs to the canister increased its weight and effective density. As a result, the canister sank farther into the water.

3. **Comparing and Contrasting** Compare the volume of the canister containing the BBs to the volume of water that the canister displaced. Which was greater?

   The total volume of the canister was greater than the volume of water it displaced.

4. **Predicting** Assume that the canister is made of a material that is less dense than water. What would happen if you filled the canister with water and then placed it in the beaker of water? Explain your answer.

   The canister would float because it is less dense than the water.

Lab Manual

Name _____ Class _____ Date _____

5. **Drawing Conclusions** Explain why the canister and the bottle floated at different levels in the water.

   The bottle has a larger cross-sectional area than the canister. Therefore, when displaced in water, the bottle does not have to sink as deeply in order to displace the volume of water needed to generate the buoyant force required to keep the bottle afloat.

6. **Comparing and Contrasting** Compare the water level when the canister was floating in the beaker to the water level when the plastic bottle was floating in the beaker in Steps 12 and 13. Explain your result.

   The water level was approximately the same in each case. The mass of the canister with its BBs was equal to the mass of the plastic bottle with its BBs. Because both displaced the same volume of water when floating, the water level in the beaker was also the same.

7. **Applying Concepts** Suppose a boat is in a swimming pool. You are sitting in the boat and holding a rock. You drop the rock into the pool. The rock sinks to the bottom without splashing any water out of the pool. Using what you learned in this investigation, explain whether the water level in the pool will be higher, lower, or the same after you drop the rock into the pool.

   The water level will be lower. When the rock is in the boat, it displaces a volume of water that has a weight equal to its own weight. Because the rock is denser than water, it cannot displace sufficient water on its own to float. When the rock is sitting at the bottom of the pool, it displaces only its own volume. Therefore, the rock displaces more water when it is in the boat than when it is in the water. As a result, the pool's water level is lower when the rock is in the water.

Go Further

Use your knowledge of forces and buoyancy to predict the result of the experiment described below. Then, with your teacher's approval and supervision, carry out the experiment to test your prediction.

A beaker of water is sitting on a balance. The balance indicates the mass of the beaker of water. Taking great care not to touch the sides of the beaker, you dip your finger into the water. Does the reading on the balance change? If it does, will it increase or decrease?

Supervise students closely as they perform the experiment. Students should wear safety goggles and lab aprons, and use caution to avoid breaking the glass beaker. The reading on the scale will increase. When a finger is inserted into the water, it experiences an upward buoyant force equal to the weight of the water it displaces. Newton's third law of motion requires that the finger exert a downward reaction force on the water. The water and the beaker transmit this force to the balance. The reading on the balance reflects this downward force as though it were additional weight.

Lab Manual

Name _____ Class _____ Date _____

Chapter 13   Forces in Fluids

🔍 **Investigation 13B**

Investigating Siphons

Refer students to page 390–397 for a discussion of pressure in fluids. **SKILLS FOCUS:** Observing, Predicting, Drawing Conclusions **TIME REQUIRED:** 45 minutes

Background Information

A siphon is a tube filled with liquid that connects two containers. Liquid can flow through the siphon from one container to the other. The direction of this flow depends on forces that act on the liquid. One of these forces is gravity. If one of the containers is higher than the other, the force of gravity will cause liquid to flow down through the siphon from the higher container into the lower one.

Fluid pressure due to fluid depth also affects the flow through a siphon. **Pressure** is the amount of force per unit area. All liquids exert pressure against their containers. The deeper a liquid is, the greater the pressure it can exert. The pressure exerted on the bottom of a beaker is due to the weight of the fluid above it. Therefore, fluid pressure due to fluid depth is also related to the force of gravity. If two containers have different levels of liquid, the liquid will flow through the siphon from the container with greater fluid depth (and pressure) to the container with less fluid depth (and pressure).

In this investigation, you will predict how water will flow through a siphon. Then, you will perform an experiment to test your prediction.

Problem

How does water flow through a siphon?

Pre-Lab Discussion

Read the entire investigation. Then, work with a partner to answer the following questions.

1. **Formulating Hypotheses** State a hypothesis about how water flows through a siphon.

   Water flows through a siphon from a container at a higher elevation to a container at a

   lower elevation. Water also flows from a container at higher pressure to one at lower pressure.

   As a result, if two containers are on the same level surface, water will flow from the container

   where the water is deeper and exerts greater pressure to the one where the water is shallower.

2. **Predicting** Based on your hypothesis, predict how the water will flow through a siphon that connects each of the following pairs of identical beakers.

   a. Both beakers contain equal volumes of water, but one beaker is at a higher elevation than the other.

   Water will flow from the higher beaker to the lower one.

Physical Science Lab Manual • Investigation 13B **139**

Lab Manual

Name _____ Class _____ Date _____

   b. Both beakers are at the same height, but one beaker contains more water than the other.

   Water will flow from the beaker that contains more water to the one that contains less.

   c. Both beakers are at the same height and contain equal volumes of water.

   Water will not flow between the beakers.

3. **Controlling Variables** Identify the manipulated, responding, and controlled variables in this investigation.

   a. Manipulated variables

   Elevation of each beaker, volume of water in each beaker

   b. Responding variables

   Movement of water through the siphon connecting the beakers

   c. Controlled variables

   Size of beakers, dimensions of tubing

Materials *(per group)*

2 600-mL beakers Use graduated beakers.	utility clamp
ring stand	40 cm flexible tubing Use tubing with an inside diameter of 0.5 to 1.0 cm.
iron ring	clock or watch
wire gauze	

Safety 🥽 🧤 🔥

Put on safety goggles and a lab apron. Be careful to avoid breakage when working with glassware. Wipe up any spilled water immediately to avoid slips and falls. Note all safety alert symbols next to the steps in the Procedure and review the meaning of each symbol by referring to the Safety Symbols on page xiii.

Procedure

🔥 1. Add approximately 275 mL of water to each beaker.

2. Position an iron ring and a wire gauze low on the ring stand, as shown in Figure 1. Use a utility clamp to secure one of the beakers on the wire gauze, as shown. Place the second beaker next to the ring stand.

140 *Physical Science Lab Manual • Investigation 13B*

Lab Manual

Name _____ Class _____ Date _____

3. In the data table, record your prediction of what will happen to the water in the beakers when a siphon is used to connect the beakers. Predict whether you expect water to flow through the siphon. If you predict that water will flow through the siphon, which direction do you expect the water to flow?

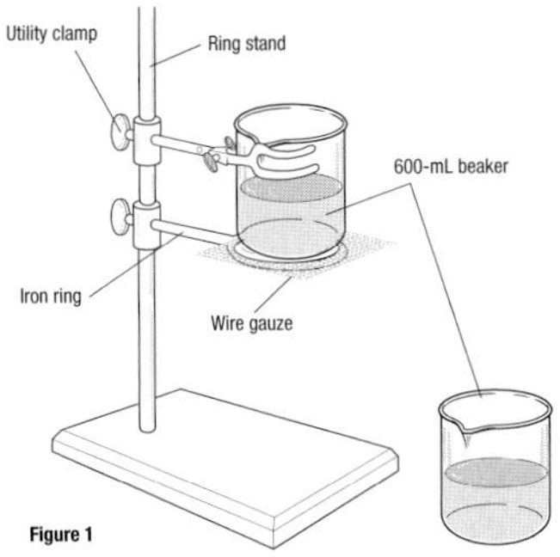

4. Place the flexible tubing in the sink. Hold one end of the tubing under the faucet and allow water to run through the tubing. When water begins to flow out the lower end of the tubing, use your finger to block the lower end. When the entire length of the tubing has filled with water, use another finger to cover the upper end. Be sure that no air remains in the tubing. Do not allow the water to flow out of the tubing.

5. Keeping the ends of the tubing covered, place one end of the tubing in the bottom of each beaker. Remove your finger from the ends of the tube only after both ends of the tube are submerged. Observe the beakers for 1 minute. Note any changes in the water level in the beakers. Record your observations in the data table.

6. Remove the elevated beaker from the ring stand. Add or remove water from each beaker so that one beaker contains 400 mL of water and the other contains 100 mL of water. Place both beakers on the tabletop. Repeat Steps 3 through 5.

7. Add or remove water from each beaker so that each beaker contains 300 mL of water. Place both beakers on the tabletop. Repeat Steps 3 through 5.

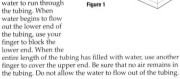

Utility clamp — Ring stand — 600-mL beaker — Iron ring — Wire gauze

Figure 1

Physical Science Lab Manual • Investigation 13B **141**

Lab Manual

Name _____ Class _____ Date _____

Observations Sample data are shown.

DATA TABLE

Positions of Beakers	Volume of Water in Beakers (mL)	Predictions	Observations
One beaker at a higher elevation than the other	275 mL in each		Water flowed from the elevated beaker to the lower beaker.
Both beakers on table	400 mL and 100 mL in the other		Water flowed from the beaker with 400 mL water to the beaker with 100 mL water.
Both beakers on table	300 mL in each		No movement of water

Analysis and Conclusions

1. **Evaluating** Did your observations support your hypothesis?

   The observations should support the hypothesis that water flows through a siphon from an

   elevated container to a lower one and from a container at higher pressure to one at lower

   pressure.

2. **Inferring** What force was responsible for the result you observed in Step 5?

   Gravity was responsible for the result observed in Step 5.

3. **Inferring** What was responsible for the result you observed in Step 6?

   The difference in pressure between the two beakers was responsible for the result observed

   in Step 6.

4. **Predicting** Explain what you would have to do in order to move the water from the lower beaker to the upper beaker in the setup you used in Step 5.

   Only gravity and pressure cause water to flow through a siphon. As a result, it would be necessary

   to increase the pressure in the lower beaker or reduce the pressure in the upper beaker. This could

   be done by connecting one of the beakers to an air pump.

5. **Predicting** Suppose two beakers sitting side by side are filled to the same depth, but one beaker is wider than the other. What would you expect to observe when the beakers are connected by a siphon? Explain your answer.

   The water will not flow between the beakers. Water flows through a siphon when the

   two containers are filled to different depths, not when they contain different volumes.

142 *Physical Science Lab Manual • Investigation 13B*

Lab Manual

Name _____ Class _____ Date _____

Go Further

How do you think the diameter of the tubing you used in this investigation affected the rate at which water flowed between the beakers? Design an experiment to answer this question. Write a detailed plan for your experiment. Your plan should state the hypothesis to be tested, identify the manipulated, responding, and controlled variables, and describe the procedures and safety precautions you will use. You will need to find a way to measure the rate at which water flows through a siphon. Show your plan to your teacher. When your teacher approves your plan, carry out your experiment, and report your results and conclusions.

Check student plans for safety, practicality, and sound experimental design. Well-designed experimental plans should include detailed procedures that will test a clearly stated hypothesis. An example of an acceptable hypothesis is that increasing the diameter of the tubing will increase the rate at which water flows between the containers. Students may wish to use a stopwatch to record the time it takes a certain volume of water to move from one container to another. Replacing the beakers with graduated cylinders will allow students to measure the volumes more accurately.

Physical Science Lab Manual • Investigation 13B   **143**

Chapter Test A

Name _____ Class _____ Date _____

Chapter 13   Forces in Fluids   **Chapter Test A**

Multiple Choice

Write the letter that best answers the question or completes the statement on the line provided.

_____ 1. If the air inside a balloon exerts a force of 1 N on an area of 0.5 m², what is the pressure inside the balloon?
   a. 0.5 N/m²   **b.** 1 N/m²
   c. 1.5 N/m²   **d.** 2 N/m²

_____ 2. A pressure of 10 N/m² equals
   a. 1 Pa.   **b.** 10 Pa.
   c. 100 Pa.   **d.** 1000 Pa.

_____ 3. Which of the following is NOT possible?
   a. compressing 10 liters of oxygen gas into a 1 liter volume
   b. compressing 2 liters of water into a 1 liter volume
   c. filling a balloon using helium gas from a pressurized tank
   d. allowing 5 liters of compressed air to expand to a volume of 100 liters

_____ 4. Two identical test tubes are filled with equal volumes of water and mercury. Which of the following statements is true?
   a. The weight of each liquid is the same.
   b. The bottom area of each test tube is the same.
   c. The pressure at the bottom of each test tube is the same.
   d. all of the above

_____ 5. The pressure of air at sea level is approximately
   a. 0 kPa   **b.** 10 kPa.
   c. 101 kPa.   **d.** 1000 kPa.

_____ 6. Where will the greatest increase in pressure occur if you squeeze the middle of an upright, closed soft-drink bottle?
   a. The greatest increase in pressure will occur at the top of the bottle.
   b. The greatest increase in pressure will occur in the middle of the bottle.
   c. The greatest increase in pressure will occur on the bottom of the bottle.
   d. The pressure will increase equally everywhere within the bottle.

Physical Science • Chapter 13 Test A   **133**

Chapter Test A

Name _____ Class _____ Date _____

Piston
(Surface Area of Piston 2 = 900 cm²)

Piston
(Surface Area of Piston 1 = 100 cm²)

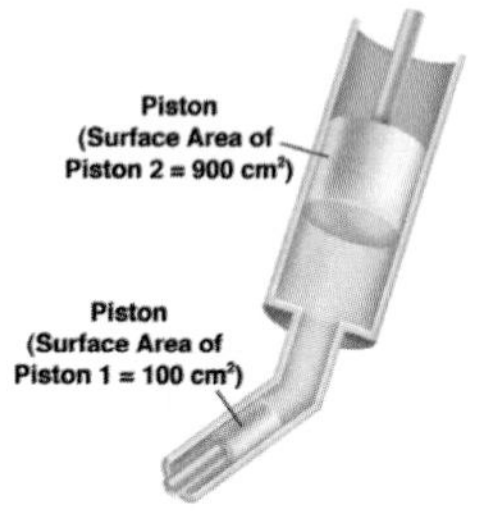

Figure 13-1

_____ 7. In Figure 13-1, Piston 1 exerts a pressure of 10 Pa on the fluid in the hydraulic lift. What is the fluid pressure on Piston 2?
   a. 1 Pa   **b.** 5 Pa
   c. 30 Pa   **d.** 90 Pa

_____ 8. Which of the following states Bernoulli's principle?
   a. As the speed of a fluid decreases, the pressure within the fluid decreases.
   b. As the speed of a fluid increases, the pressure within the fluid decreases.
   c. As the speed of a fluid changes, the pressure of the fluid remains constant.
   d. none of the above

_____ 9. Which of the following statements is true about an airplane wing during flight?
   a. Air above the wing travels faster than air below the wing.
   b. Air below the wing travels faster than air above the wing.
   c. The wing exerts pressure equally in all directions.
   d. The lift acting on the wing reduces the weight of the wing.

_____ 10. A brick weighs 21 N. Measured underwater, it weighs 12 N. What is the size of the buoyant force exerted by the water on the brick?
   a. 33 N   **b.** 21 N
   c. 12 N   **d.** 9 N

134   *Physical Science* • Chapter 13 Test A

_____11. The strength of the buoyant force acting on an object in a fluid depends on the object's
  a. mass.
  b. surface area.
  c. volume.
  d. weight.

_____12. The buoyant force on an object in a fluid is equal to the weight of the
  a. fluid.
  b. fluid surrounding the object.
  c. fluid displaced by the object.
  d. object.

_____13. A ball is floating partially submerged in a liquid. The buoyant force acting on the ball equals the
  a. volume of the ball below the surface.
  b. volume of the ball above the surface.
  c. mass of the ball.
  d. weight of the ball.

_____14. A cork is floating in salty water. As more salt is added to the water to increase its density, the cork will
  a. float at a higher level in the water.
  b. float at a lower level in the water.
  c. sink.
  d. float at the same level in the water.

_____15. Two identical corks float in separate beakers. One beaker contains water. The other contains very salty water. Which of the following statements is true?
  a. The corks both float at the same level in the liquid.
  b. The cork in the very salty water floats at a lower level than the other cork.
  c. The corks will eventually sink.
  d. Both corks are subject to the same buoyant force.

Completion
Complete each statement on the line provided.

1. A pascal, the SI unit of pressure, is equal to 1 newton per _____.

2. As a liquid is added to a beaker, the pressure exerted by the liquid on the bottom of the beaker _____.

3. The pressure exerted by a fluid at any given depth is exerted _____ in all directions.

4. As you climb a high mountain, the buoyant force exerted on you by the atmosphere_____.

5. The weight of an object that sinks in a fluid is _____ than the buoyant force acting on it.

Short Answer
In complete sentences, write the answers to the questions on the lines provided.

1. If you know the air pressure exerted on a tabletop, how can you calculate the force exerted on the tabletop?
   _____
   _____

2. Rank the following measurements in order of increasing pressure: 2 kPa, 10 N/m², 300 N/m², 0.1 Pa
   _____
   _____

3. Why aren't organisms that live on the seafloor crushed by water pressure?
   _____
   _____
   _____
   _____

4. Why does a partially inflated weather balloon expand as it rises?
   _____
   _____
   _____

5. A ball of clay sinks when placed in water. The same piece of clay floats if it is made into the shape of a boat. Compare the volume of water displaced by the ball with the volume displaced by the boat shape.
   _____
   _____
   _____
   _____
   _____
   _____

---

6. How are density and buoyancy related?
   _____
   _____
   _____
   _____
   _____

7. If you use a spring scale to measure the weight of a submerged object that has neutral buoyancy, what will the scale read?
   _____
   _____

Using Science Skills
Use the diagram to answer each question. Write the answers on a separate sheet of paper.

Figure 13-2A   **Figure 13-2B**

1. **Observing** How did the position of the spoon in Figure 13-2 change after the faucet was turned on?

2. **Inferring** On which side of the spoon in Figure 13-2B is the pressure of the air greater?

3. **Applying Concepts** According to Bernoulli's principle, is the spoon shown in Figure 13-2B pulled toward the stream of water or pushed toward the stream of water? Explain your answer.

4. **Drawing Conclusion** In Figure 13-2B, what effect does the stream of water have on the motion of the air around it?

5. **Predicting** What will happen to the spoon in Figure 13-2B if the water from the faucet is allowed to flow at a faster rate?

Problem
Write the answers to each question on a separate sheet of paper.

1. The dimensions of a brick that weighs 21 N are 0.19 m × 0.090 m × 0.055 m. What pressure does the brick exert on the ground if it is resting on its largest face? Show your work.

2. Express a pressure of 2500 N/m² in kilopascals.

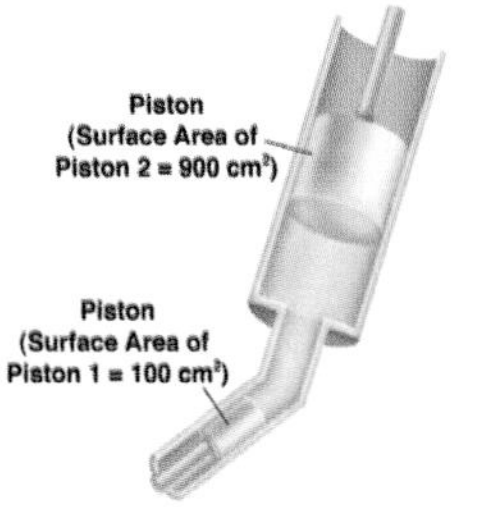

Piston
(Surface Area of
Piston 2 = 900 cm²)

Piston
(Surface Area of
Piston 1 = 100 cm²)

Figure 13-3

3. In Figure 13-3, a force of 1000 N is exerted on Piston 1 of the hydraulic lift shown. What force will be exerted on Piston 2? Show your work.

Essay
Write the answers to each question on a separate sheet of paper.

1. To prevent a window from exploding outward during a strong windstorm, it is left slightly open. Explain why a slightly open window might not blow out.

2. A cube of wood displaces half its volume when floating in water. When a 0.5-N washer is added to the cube, it floats just at the point where it is completely submerged in the water. What is the buoyant force acting on the cube when the washer is removed?

Chapter Test B

Name _____ Class _____ Date _____

Chapter 13   Forces in Fluids   Chapter Test B

Multiple Choice

Write the letter that best answers the question or completes the statement on the line provided.

_____ 1. In order to calculate pressure exerted on a surface, what quantity is divided by the surface area?
a. altitude   b. force
c. mass   d. volume

_____ 2. What is the SI unit of pressure?
a. g/cm^3 b. m/s^2
c. a newton   d. a pascal

_____ 3. Where is fluid pressure greatest?
a. 30 centimeters below the surface of a swimming pool
b. 1 meter below the surface of a swimming pool
c. 2 meters below the surface of a swimming pool
d. The pressure is the same in all parts of a swimming pool.

_____ 4. Which of the following materials is NOT a fluid?
a. air   b. cork
c. gasoline   d. water

_____ 5. The pressure of a fluid at a specific depth
a. depends only on the type of fluid.
b. is exerted only in the downward direction.
c. varies with the total volume of the fluid.
d. all of the above

_____ 6. Atmospheric pressure is caused by
a. air currents.
b. the weight of the atmosphere above a particular location.
c. clouds.
d. the altitude above sea level.

_____ 7. Which principle states that a change in the pressure at any point in a fluid in a closed container is transmitted equally and unchanged in all directions throughout the fluid?
a. Archimedes' principle b. Bernoulli's principle
c. Newton's principle   d. Pascal's principle

_____ 8. The operation of a hydraulic lift system is explained by
a. Archimedes' principle. b. Bernoulli's principle.
c. Newton's principle.   d. Pascal's principle.

_____ 9. The hydraulic system of a dump truck is designed to multiply
a. distance.   b. force.
c. pressure.   d. speed.

Chapter Test B

Name _____ Class _____ Date _____

_____ 10. The upward force acting on the wing of an airplane in flight is called
a. drag.   b. lift.
c. thrust.   d. weight.

_____ 11. The upward force acting on an object submerged in a fluid is called
a. buoyant force.   b. drag.
c. pressure.   d. weight.

_____ 12. The relationship between buoyant force and weight of a displaced fluid was first stated by
a. Archimedes.   b. Bernoulli.
c. Newton.   d. Pascal.

_____ 13. Which of the following substances will float in corn syrup? (The density of corn syrup is 1.38 g/cm^3.)
a. aluminum (2.7 g/cm^3)
b. magnesium (1.75 g/cm^3)
c. mercury (13.6 g/cm^3)
d. rubber (1.23 g/cm^3)

_____ 14. Which of the following materials will sink in water? (The density of water 1.00 g/cm^3.)
a. balsa wood (0.12 g/cm^3)
b. cooking oil (0.82 g/cm^3)
c. ethanol (0.798 g/cm^3)
d. steel (7.18 g/cm^3)

_____ 15. Why does a hot-air balloon float?
a. The shape of the balloon provides lift.
b. The volume of the air displaced by the balloon is less than the volume of the balloon.
c. The weight of the air displaced is less than the volume of the balloon.
d. The weight of the balloon is less than the weight of the air displaced by the balloon.

Completion

Complete each statement on the line provided.

1. Pressure is the result of force distributed over a(an) _____.

2. The formula, $\dfrac{\text{Force}}{\text{Area}}$, is used to calculate _____.

3. The SI unit of pressure is the _____.

4. A substance that flows and assumes the shape of its container is a(an) _____.

Chapter Test B

Name _____ Class _____ Date _____

5. A device that uses pressurized fluids acting on pistons of different sizes to change a force is called a(an) _____.

6. As the speed of a fluid increases, the _____ within the fluid decreases.

7. In a hydraulic lift system, the fluid pressure exerted throughout the system is _____.

8. The apparent loss of weight of an object in a fluid is called _____.

9. The direction of the buoyant force on an object placed in a fluid is _____.

10. A submerged submarine alters its _____ to rise or fall in the water.

Short Answer

In complete sentences, write the answers to the questions on the lines provided.

1. Which exerts greater pressure on the floor—standing flat-footed or standing on tiptoes?

_____
_____

2. For a fluid that is not moving, what are the two factors that determine the pressure that the fluid exerts?

_____
_____
_____

3. How do the particles of a liquid exert pressure on a container?

_____
_____
_____

Chapter Test B

Name _____ Class _____ Date _____

4. How is the weight of water displaced by a floating cork related to the buoyant force?

_____
_____
_____

5. Compare the weight of an object to the buoyant force acting on it if the object sinks in the fluid.

_____
_____
_____

Using Science Skills

Use the diagram to answer each question. Write the answers on a separate sheet of paper.

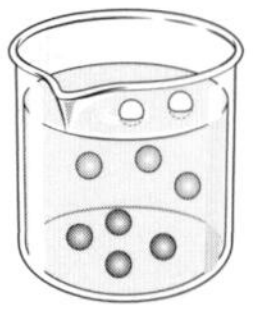

Figure 13-1

1. **Comparing and Contrasting** How does the fluid pressure exerted on the black spheres shown in Figure 13-1 compare with the pressure exerted on the gray spheres.

2. **Inferring** In Figure 13-1, spheres of which color have the greatest density?

3. **Applying Concepts** In Figure 13-1, on how many spheres is the buoyant force less than the weight of the sphere?

4. **Applying Concepts** In Figure 13-1, on how many spheres is the buoyant force equal to the weight of the sphere?

5. **Applying Concepts** In Figure 13-1, how many spheres have neutral buoyancy?

Chapter 13 Test A Answers

Multiple Choice

1. d   **2.** b   **3.** b   **4.** b   **5.** c   **6.** d
7. c   **8.** b   **9.** a   **10.** d   **11.** c   **12.** c
13. d   **14.** a   **15.** d

Completion

1. square meter; m^2 **2.** increases **3.** equally **4.** decreases; becomes smaller **5.** greater; more

Short Answer

1. Multiply the air pressure by the area of the tabletop.
2. 0.1 Pa, 10 N/m^2, 300 N/m^2, 2 kPa **3.** The pressure within the organisms' bodies balances water pressure. As a result, the net force on their bodies is zero. **4.** Air pressure that is pushing in on the balloon decreases as the balloon rises. **5.** The boat shape displaced a greater volume of water. **6.** When an object is less dense than the fluid it is in, the object will float in the fluid. When an object is more dense than the fluid it is in, the object will sink in the fluid. **7.** 0 N or zero

Using Science Skills

1. The spoon moved toward the stream of running water.
2. on the side opposite the stream of water
3. The spoon is pushed toward the stream of water; the pressure of the air on the side of the spoon opposite the stream of water is greater than the pressure of the air on the side of the spoon next to the stream of water. **4.** The stream of water causes the nearby air to move. **5.** The spoon would move closer to the stream of water.

Problem

1. Pressure = $\dfrac{\text{Force}}{\text{Area}}$ = $\dfrac{\text{Force}}{\text{Length} \times \text{Width}}$ = $\dfrac{21\text{N}}{0.19 \text{ m} \times 0.090 \text{ m}}$

Pressure = $\dfrac{21\text{N}}{0.017 \text{ m}^2}$ = 1200 N/m^2

2. 2500N/m^2 = 2500Pa $\times$ $\dfrac{1\text{kPa}}{1000\text{Pa}}$ = 2.5kPa

3. A hydraulic lift multiples force by a factor equal to the area of the large piston divided by the small piston.

$\dfrac{\text{Surface area of Piston 2}}{\text{Surface are of Piston 1}}$ = $\dfrac{900 \text{ cm}^2}{100 \text{ cm}^2}$ = 9

The hydraulic lift will multiply the force by a factor of 9.
100N $\times$ 9 = 900N
The force exerted on Piston 2 is 900 N.

Essay

1. A window may explode outward during a windstorm because the outside pressure is much less than the pressure inside the house. By opening the window, the difference in pressures is reduced. **2.** 0.5 N; because the 0.5-N washer and the cube floating on its own both displace the same volume, the 0.5-N force equals the buoyant force acting on the cube.

Chapter 13 Test B Answers

Multiple Choice

1. b   **2.** d   **3.** c   **4.** b   **5.** a   **6.** b
7. d   **8.** d   **9.** b   **10.** b   **11.** a   **12.** a
13. d   **14.** d   **15.** d

Completion

1. area **2.** pressure **3.** pascal **4.** fluid **5.** hydraulic system
6. pressure **7.** constant **8.** buoyancy **9.** upward **10.** density

Short Answer

1. standing on tiptoes **2.** depth and type of fluid
3. by coming into contact with the container
4. They are equal. **5.** The buoyant force is less than the weight.

Using Science Skills

1. The fluid pressure exerted on the black spheres is greater (about twice as great). **2.** black **3.** four spheres **4.** five spheres
5. three spheres

Chapter 14 Work, Power, and Machines

Planning Guide

Use these planning tools
Easy Planner
Resource Pro
Online Lesson Planner

SECTION OBJECTIVES	STANDARDS		ACTIVITIES and LABS
	NATIONAL (See p. T18.)	STATE	
14.1 Work and Power, pp. 412–416 🕐 1 block or 2 periods **14.1.1 Describe** the conditions that must exist for a force to do work on an object. **14.1.2 Calculate** the work done on an object. **14.1.3 Describe** and **calculate** power. **14.1.4 Compare** the units of watts and horsepower as they relate to power.	A-1, A-2, B-4, G-1, G-2, G-3		**SE** Inquiry Activity: How Do Ramps Help You Raise Objects? p. 411 **L2** **TE** Teacher Demo: Work, p. 413 **L2**
14.2 Work and Machines, pp. 417–420 🕐 1 block or 2 periods **14.2.1 Describe** what a machine is and how it makes work easier to do. **14.2.2 Relate** the work input to a machine to the work output of the machine.			
14.3 Mechanical Advantage and Efficiency, pp. 421–426 🕐 1 block or 2 periods **14.3.1 Compare** a machine's actual mechanical advantage to its ideal mechanical advantage. **14.3.2 Calculate** the ideal and actual mechanical advantages of various machines. **14.3.3 Explain** why the efficiency of a machine is always less than 100%. **14.3.4 Calculate** a machine's efficiency.	A-1, A-2, G-1, G-2, G-3		**SE** Quick Lab: Using Friction to Change Mechanical Advantage, p. 424 **L2** **SE** Consumer Lab: Determining Mechanical Advantage, pp. 438–439 **L2** **TE** Teacher Demo: Mechanical Advantage, p. 423 **L2**
14.4 Simple Machines, pp. 427–435 🕐 1 block or 2 periods **14.4.1 Name, describe,** and **give an example** of each of the six types of simple machines. **14.4.2 Describe** how to determine the ideal mechanical advantage of each type of simple machine. **14.4.3 Define** and **identify** compound machines.	A-1, A-2		**SE** Quick Lab: Comparing Lever Arms, p. 429 **L2** **TE** Teacher Demo: Inclined Planes, p. 430 **L2** **LM** Investigation 14A: Comparing the Mechanical Advantage of Levers **L2** **LM** Investigation 14B: Comparing Pulleys **L1**

410A Chapter 14

Ability Levels

L1	For students who need additional help
L2	For all students
L3	For students who need to be challenged

Components

SE	Student Edition	**GRSW**	Guided Reading	**CTB**	Computer Test Bank	**T**	Transparencies
TE	Teacher's Edition		& Study Workbook	**TP**	Test Prep Resources	**P**	Presentation Pro
LM	Laboratory Manual		With Math Support	**iT**	iText		CD-ROM
PLM	Probeware Lab	**CUT**	Chapter and Unit	**DC**	Discovery Channel	**GO**	Internet Resources
	Manual		Tests		Videotapes		

RESOURCES
PRINT and TECHNOLOGY

SECTION
ASSESSMENT

GRSW Section 14.1 **L1**

GRSW Math Skill **L2**

T Chapter 14 Pretest **L2**
Section 14.1 **L2**

P Chapter 14 Pretest **L2**
Section 14.1 **L2**

SCiLINKS **GO** Work **L2**

SE Section 14.1
Assessment, p. 416

iT Section 14.1

GRSW Section 14.2 **L1**

T Section 14.2 **L2**

P Section 14.2 **L2**

SCiLINKS **GO** Machines **L2**

SE Section 14.2
Assessment, p. 420

iT Section 14.2

GRSW Section 14.3 **L1**

T Section 14.3 **L2**

P Section 14.3 **L2**

SCiLINKS **GO** Mechanical **L2**
advantage

PHSchool.com GO Data Sharing **L2**

SE Section 14.3
Assessment, p. 426

iT Section 14.3

GRSW Section 14.4 **L1**

Discovery SCHOOL **DC** Pedal Power **L2**

T Section 14.4 **L2**

P Section 14.4 **L2**

SCiLINKS **GO** Simple machines **L2**

SE Section 14.4
Assessment, p. 435

iT Section 14.4

Go Online

Go online for these Internet resources.

PHSchool.com
Web Code: ccd-2140
Web Code: cca-2140

NSTA *SCiLINKS*
Web Code: ccn-2141
Web Code: ccn-2142
Web Code: ccn-2143
Web Code: ccn-2144

Materials for Activities and Labs

Quantities for each group

STUDENT EDITION

Inquiry Activity, p. 411
6 textbooks, 2 boards (1 long,
1 short), meter stick, spring
scale, lab cart

Quick Lab, p. 424
6 books, board, 3 different
kinds of shoes, 1-kg mass,
spring scale

Quick Lab, p. 429
pencil, masking tape, spring
scale, 500-g mass, meter stick

Consumer Lab, pp. 438–439
board with 2 nails, 4 thread
spools (3 with different
diameters), rubber band,
masking tape, multispeed
bicycle (1 or more per class),
meter stick, thick leather glove

TEACHER'S EDITION

Teacher Demo, p. 413
a rigid object

Teacher Demo, p. 423
1 pulley, 10-N spring scale,
500-g mass, string

Teacher Demo, p. 430
long board, heavy box, small
stepladder, spring scale

Build Science Skills, p. 437
1 bicycle with gears similar to
that shown on pp. 436–437

Chapter Assessment

CHAPTER ASSESSMENT

SE Chapter Assessment,
pp. 441–442
CUT Chapter 14 Test A, B
CTB Chapter 14
iT Chapter 14
PHSchool.com GO
Web Code: cca-2140

STANDARDIZED TEST PREP

SE Chapter 14, p. 443
TP Diagnose and Prescribe

iText—interactive textbook with
assessment at PHSchool.com

Name_____ Class_____ Date_____ M T W T F

LESSON PLAN 14.1

Work and Power

Time
2 periods
1 block

Section Objectives
Local Standards

- **14.1.1 Describe** the conditions that must exist for a force to do work on an object.
- **14.1.2 Calculate** the work done on an object.
- **14.1.3 Describe** and **calculate** power.
- **14.1.4 Compare** the units of watts and horsepower as they relate to power.

Vocabulary work • power • horsepower • joule • watt

1 FOCUS

Build Vocabulary: Table
Have students make a table to help them remember the definitions of work and power. The table should include the terms, the corresponding units, and the definitions. **L2**

Targeted Resources
❑ Transparency: Chapter 14 Pretest
❑ Transparency: Interest Grabber 14.1
❑ Transparency: Reading Strategy 14.1

2 INSTRUCT

Build Reading Literacy: Think Aloud
Encourage student volunteers to read Using the Work Formula while quietly verbalizing their thought processes. **L1**

Use Visuals: Figure 4
Have students refer to Figure 4 to compare the power of a 4 hp engine and the power of 4 work horses. **L1**

Address Misconceptions
Help students understand that not all forces acting on an object do work on that object. **L2**

Teacher Demo: Calculating Work
While moving a rigid object in different ways, students observe how work requires movement of an object in the direction of the applied force. **L2**

Build Science Skills: Applying Concepts
Review with students the equations for both work and power, and ask questions that help students use each equation. **L2**

Address Misconceptions
Explain to students that power is not the same as force. **L2**

Targeted Resources
❑ Transparency: Math Skills: Calculating Power
❑ GRSW Section 14.1
❑ **NSTA** *scLINKS* Work

3 ASSESS

Reteach
Use Figure 2 and its caption to summarize the key concepts related to work. **L1**

Evaluate Understanding
Have pairs of students write out two questions and answers about work and power, and then form groups of four to quiz one another. **L2**

Targeted Resources
❑ **PHSchool.com** Online Section 14.1 Assessment
❑ iText Section 14.1

Transparencies

196 Chapter 14 Pretest

1. According to Newton's first law, if no net force acts on an object, the object continues in motion with constant

   _____ .

   a. velocity

   b. force

   c. acceleration

2. A horizontal force on an object can be broken down into these components: 5 N north and 5 N east. If no other forces act on the object, in what direction will the object move?

3. Newton's second law states that the net force acting on an object equals the product of what two variables?

4. A machine produces an output force of 12.3 N when an input of 8.6 N is applied. What is the ratio of the machine's output force to its input force?

ANSWERS
1. a
2. northeast
3. mass and acceleration
4. 1.4

Transparencies

197 Chapter 14 Pretest (continued)

5. A person exerts 22 N on a box. If a frictional force of 3 N opposes this force, what is the net force acting on the box?

6. A machine has an output force of 57.3 N when a force of 32.6 N is used to operate the machine. What is the percentage increase of the force?

7. A small wheel has a radius of 32 cm, and a large wheel has a diameter of 128 cm. What is the ratio of the diameters of the large wheel to the small wheel?

   a. 4

   b. 2

   c. 0.25

   d. 0.5

ANSWERS
5. 19 N
6. 176%
7. b

Transparencies

198 Section 14.1 Interest Grabber

Work

Work is the product of force and distance. Work is done when a force acts on an object in the direction the object moves. If a force acts on an object but the object does not move, no work is done.

1. A man pushes a grocery cart at constant speed from one end of an aisle to the other. Identify the force, the distance, and the work.

2. Describe two examples of work you do on a typical day.

ANSWERS
1. The man supplies the force by pushing on the cart. The length of the aisle is the distance. The work done is the product of the force and the distance.
2. Answers will vary. Sample answers: lifting a heavy school bag; pushing or pulling a door open. Make sure students correctly identify the force, distance, and work done.

Transparencies

199 Section 14.1 Reading Strategy

Relating Text and Visuals

Figure	Direction of Force	Direction of Motion	Is Work Done?
1	a. ?	b. ?	c. ?
2A	d. ?	e. ?	f. ?
2B	g. ?	h. ?	i. ?
2C	j. ?	k. ?	l. ?

ANSWERS
a. up
b. none
c. no
d. horizontal
e. horizontal
f. yes
g. diagonal
h. horizontal
i. yes
j. up
k. horizontal
l. no

Program Resources Section 14.1

285

Transparencies

200 Math Skills Calculating Power

Math Skills

Calculating Power

You exert a vertical force of 72 newtons to lift a box to a height of 1.0 meter in a time of 2.0 seconds. How much power is used to lift the box?

1 Read and Understand

What information are you given?

Force = 72 N   Distance = 1.0 m

Time = 2.0 s

2 Plan and Solve

What formula contains the given quantities and the unknown?

$$\text{Power} = \frac{\text{Work}}{\text{Time}} = \frac{\text{Force} \times \text{Distance}}{\text{Time}}$$

Replace each variable with its known value and solve.

$$\text{Power} = \frac{72 \text{ N} \times 1.0 \text{ m}}{2.0 \text{ s}} = 36 \text{ J/s} = 36 \text{ W}$$

3 Look Back and Check

Is your answer reasonable?

36 watts is not a lot of power, which seems reasonable considering the box was lifted slowly, through a height of only 1 meter.

Guided Reading and Study Workbook

Name _____ Class _____ Date _____

Chapter 14   Work, Power, and Machines

Section 14.1 Work and Power
(pages 412–416)

This section defines work and power, describes how they are related, and explains how to calculate their values.

Reading Strategy (page 412)

Relating Text and Visuals As you read, look carefully at Figures 1 and 2 and read their captions. Complete the table by describing the work shown in each figure. For more information on this Reading Strategy, see the **Reading and Study Skills** in the **Skills and Reference Handbook** at the end of your textbook.

Figure	Direction of Force	Direction of Motion	Is Work Done?
1	Up	None	No
2A	Horizontal	Horizontal	Yes
2B	Diagonal	Horizontal	Yes
2C	Up	Horizontal	No

What Is Work? (pages 412–413)

1. In science, work is done when a(n) _____force_____ acts on an object in the direction the object moves.

2. Why isn't work being done on a barbell when a weight lifter is holding the barbell over his head? Because in order for work to be done on an object, the object must be moving.

3. Describe what conditions of force and motion result in maximum work done on an object. Work is maximized when force is applied in the same direction that the object is moving.

4. Is the following sentence true or false? A vertical force does work on an object that is moving in a horizontal direction. _____false_____

Calculating Work (pages 413–414)

5. In science, work that is done on an object can be described as the force acting on the object multiplied by the _____distance_____ the object moves.

6. Circle the letter of the correct form of the work equation to use when determining the distance an object moves as a result of a force applied to it.

a. Distance = Force × Work   b. Distance = $\frac{\text{Force}}{\text{Work}}$

c. Distance = (Force)²   (d.) Distance = $\frac{\text{Work}}{\text{Force}}$

Guided Reading and Study Workbook

Name _____ Class _____ Date _____

Chapter 14   Work, Power, and Machines

7. The SI unit of work is the _____joule_____.

8. Circle the letter of the amount of work done when a 1 newton force moves an object 1 meter.

a. 1 newton per second   (b.) 1 joule

c. 1 watt   d. 1 newton per meter

What Is Power? (pages 414)

9. Is the following sentence true or false? Power is the rate of doing work. _____true_____

10. In order to do work faster, more _____power_____ is required.

11. Circle the letter of each sentence that is true about power.

a. Power and work are always equal.

(b.) You can increase power by doing a given amount of work in a shorter period of time.

c. When you decrease the force acting on an object, the power increases.

(d.) When you do less work in a given time period, the power decreases.

Calculating Power (pages 415)

12. Write a word equation describing how to calculate power. Power equals work divided by time.

13. The SI unit of power is the _____watt_____.

14. Circle the letter of the expression that is equivalent to one watt.

a. one newton per meter

b. one joule per meter

c. one newton per second

(d.) one joule per second

15. How much work does a 100-watt light bulb do when it is lit for 30 seconds? (100 J/s)(30 s) = 3000 J

James Watt and Horsepower (page 416)

16. Circle the letter of the quantity that is approximately equal to one horsepower.

a. 746 J   (b.) 746 W

c. 7460 N/m   d. 7460 J

17. Why did James Watt use the power output of a horse to compare the power outputs of steam engines he designed? Horses were a logical choice for comparison as they were the most commonly used source of power in the 1700s.

LESSON PLAN 14.2

Work and Machines

Time
2 periods
1 block

Section Objectives

- **14.2.1 Describe** what a machine is and how it makes work easier to do.
- **14.2.2 Relate** the work input to a machine to the work output of the machine.

Vocabulary machine • input distance • output force • work output • input force • work input • output distance

Local Standards

1 FOCUS

Build Vocabulary: Paraphrase
Encourage students to make a three-column table that includes all of the vocabulary terms, paraphrased meanings for each term, and the textbook definitions. **L2**

Targeted Resources
❑ Transparency: Interest Grabber 14.2
❑ Transparency: Reading Strategy 14.2

2 INSTRUCT

Build Reading Literacy: Relate Cause and Effect
Use Figure 6 to help students identify the cause-and-effect relationship between work done on and work done by a machine. **L1**

Address Misconceptions
Explain to students that not all objects have a certain amount of force within them, and that some objects need an input force in order to perform work. **L2**

Build Science Skills: Calculating
After observing Figure 7, have students calculate input force when given values for output force, output distance, and input distance. **L2**

Targeted Resources
❑ Transparency: Figure 7: Forces and Work
❑ GRSW Section 14.2
❑ **NSTA** sci*LINKS* Machines

3 ASSESS

Reteach
Use Figure 7 to emphasize the relationship between input force, distance, and work and output force, distance, and work. **L1**

Evaluate Understanding
Show students a simple mechanical device and ask them to identify the input force, distance, and work and the output force, distance, and work. **L2**

Targeted Resources
❑ **PHSchool.com** Online Section 14.2 Assessment
❑ iText Section 14.2

Transparencies

201 Section 14.2 **Interest Grabber**

What Is a Machine?

Look around you. Do you see any machines? Some machines, like a lawn mower or a washing machine, are complicated devices with many parts. Other machines are very simple. You can tell a device is a machine if it makes work easier to do.

Identify the machines in the following list of items. If the item is a machine, describe how it makes work easier to do.

1. doorknob   4. desk

2. scissors   5. ice pick

3. chair   6. bottle opener

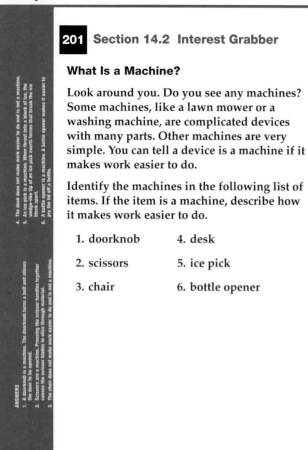

ANSWERS
1. A doorknob is a machine. The doorknob turns a bolt and allows the door to be opened.
2. Scissors are a machine. Pressing the scissor handles together causes the scissor blades to slice through material.
3. The chair does not make work easier to do and is not a machine.
4. The desk does not make work easier to do and is not a machine.
5. An ice pick is a machine. When thrust into a block of ice, the wedge-like tip of an ice pick exerts forces that break the ice block apart.
6. A bottle opener is a machine. A bottle opener makes it easier to pry the lid off a bottle.

Transparencies

202 Section 14.2 **Reading Strategy**

Summarizing

Machine	Increases or Decreases Input Force	Increases or Decreases Input Distance
Tire jack	a. ?	b. ?
Lug wrench	c. ?	d. ?
Rowing oar	e. ?	f. ?
Summary:	g. ?	

ANSWERS
a. decreases
b. increases
c. decreases
d. increases
e. increases
f. decreases
g. Machines can work easier by changing the size of the force or the direction of the force.

Transparencies

203 Figure 7 **Forces and Work**

Input distance

Output force

Input force

Output distance

Boat moves in this direction.

Name _____ Class _____ Date _____

Chapter 14   Work, Power, and Machines

Section 14.2 Work and Machines
(pages 417–420)

This section describes how machines change forces to make work easier to do. Input forces exerted on and output forces exerted by machines are identified and input work and output work are discussed.

Reading Strategy (page 417)

Summarizing As you read, complete the table for each machine. After you read, write a sentence summarizing the idea that your table illustrates. For more information on this Reading Strategy, see the **Reading and Study Skills** in the **Skills and Reference Handbook** at the end of your textbook.

Machine	Increases or Decreases Input Force	Increases or Decreases Input Distance
Tire jack	Decreases	Increases
Lug wrench	Decreases	Increases
Rowing oar	Increases	Decreases
Summary: As input force decreases, the input distance increases.		

Machines Do Work (pages 417–418)

1. Describe what a machine is able to do. A machine makes work easier to do by changing a force.

2. Is the following sentence true or false? A machine can make work easier to do by changing the size of the force needed, the direction of a force, or the distance over which a force acts. true

3. Consider the equation Work = Force × Distance. If a machine increases the distance over which a force is exerted, the force required to do a given amount of work decreases.

4. Give an example of a machine that changes the direction of an applied force. Sample answers may include oars used in rowing.

5. When you make several trips to unload a few heavy items from a car instead of moving them all at once, the total distance over which you exert yourself increases.

Work Input and Work Output (pages 419–420)

6. The work done by a machine is always less than the work done on a machine because of friction.

Name _____ Class _____ Date _____

Chapter 14   Work, Power, and Machines

7. Circle the letter of the definition for input force.
   a. the amount of force exerted by a machine
   b. the amount of friction slowing the speed of a machine
   c. the amount of work done by a machine
   d. the amount of force exerted on a machine

8. Write a word equation that describes work input.
   Work input equals the input force multiplied by the input distance.

9. Is the following sentence true or false? Every machine uses some of its work input to overcome friction. true

10. The force exerted by a machine is called the output force.

11. Circle the letter of the expression that equals the work output of a machine.
    a. $\dfrac{\text{Input distance}}{\text{Output distance}}$ b. Output distance × Input distance
    c. $\dfrac{\text{Output distance}}{\text{friction}}$ d. Output distance × Output force

12. Is the following sentence true or false? Output work always is less than input work. true

For questions 13 through 15, refer to the figure below.

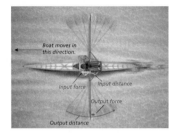

13. Which arrow represents the input force? Label it on the figure.

14. Which arrow represents the input distance? Label it on the figure.

15. Which arrow represents the output force? Label it on the figure.

16. How can you increase a machine's work output? The only way to increase work output is to increase the amount of work put into a machine.

LESSON PLAN 14.3

Mechanical Advantage and Efficiency

Time
2 periods
1 block

Section Objectives   **Local Standards**

- **14.3.1 Compare** a machine's actual mechanical advantage to its ideal mechanical advantage.

- **14.3.2 Calculate** the ideal and actual mechanical advantages of various machines.

- **14.3.3 Explain** why the efficiency of a machine is always less than 100%.

- **14.3.4 Calculate** a machine's efficiency.

Vocabulary mechanical advantage • actual mechanical advantage • ideal mechanical advantage • efficiency

1 FOCUS

Build Vocabulary: Vocabulary Knowledge Rating Chart

Have students rate their knowledge of each vocabulary term, before and after reading the section, by filling in charts with the headings Term, Can Define/Use It, Heard/Seen It, and Don't Know. **L2**

Targeted Resources

❑ Transparency: Interest Grabber 14.3

❑ Transparency: Reading Strategy 14.3

2 INSTRUCT

Use Visuals: Figure 9

Have students refer to Figure 9 and identify where the input force and the output force are for each position of a nutcracker. **L1**

Build Math Skills: Ratios and Proportions

Use the efficiency equation on page 425 to help students understand that no machine can be 100% efficient. **L1**

Teacher Demo: Mechanical Advantage

Use a scale and a pulley to demonstrate mechanical advantage for students. **L2**

Quick Lab: Using Friction to Change Mechanical Advantage

Students use a spring scale to pull a mass up a ramp in order to determine the effect of friction on mechanical advantage. **L2**

Address Misconceptions

Emphasize to students that friction causes the work output of a machine to always be less than work input. **L2**

Targeted Resources

❑ Transparency: Math Skills: Calculating IMA

❑ GRSW Section 14.3

❑ **NSTA** *sci*$_{LINKS}$ Mechanical advantage

3 ASSESS

Reteach

Use a nutcracker to demonstrate to students the concept of mechanical advantage. **L1**

Evaluate Understanding

Ask students to write a paragraph explaining ideal and actual mechanical advantage and how they are related to efficiency. **L2**

Targeted Resources

❑ **PHSchool.com** Online Section 14.3 Assessment

❑ iText Section 14.3

Transparencies

204 | **Section 14.3** Interest Grabber

How Does Input Force Location Affect a Machine?

A nutcracker is a machine used to make cracking nuts easier. As shown below, use a nutcracker to crack three nuts, each time squeezing the nutcracker's handles at a different location.

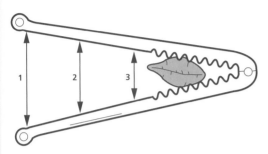

1. Applying force at which handle location resulted in the nutcracker cracking the nuts the easiest?

2. What is the relationship between the distance between the nutcracker's pivot point and where the force is applied and the nutcracker's ability to crack nuts?

ANSWERS
1. The nutcracker worked best when force was applied at location 1.
2. The greater the distance between the pivot and the force, the better the nutcracker was at breaking nuts.

Transparencies

205 | **Section 14.3** Reading Strategy

Building Vocabulary

Vocabulary	Definition
Mechanical advantage	a. _____?_____
b. ___?___	c. _____?_____
d. ___?___	e. _____?_____
f. ___?___	g. _____?_____

e. the mechanical advantage of a machine if there were no friction
f. efficiency
g. percentage of work input that becomes work output

ANSWERS
a. the number of times a machine increases force
b. actual mechanical advantage
c. ratio of output force to input force
d. ideal mechanical advantage

Transparencies

206 | Math Skills **Calculating IMA**

Math Skills

Calculating IMA

A woman drives her car up onto wheel ramps to perform some repairs. If she drives a distance of 1.8 meters along the ramp to raise the car 0.3 meter, what is the ideal mechanical advantage (IMA) of the wheel ramps?

1 **Read and Understand**
What information are you given?

Input distance = 1.8 m

Output distance = 0.3 m

2 **Plan and Solve**
What unknown are you trying to calculate?

IMA = ?

What formula contains the given quantities and the unknown?

$$IMA = \frac{Input\ distance}{Output\ distance}$$

Replace each variable with its known value and solve.

$$IMA = \frac{1.8\ \cancel{m}}{0.3\ \cancel{m}} = 6$$

3 **Look Back and Check**
Is your answer reasonable?

The IMA must be greater than 1 because the input distance is greater than the output distance. The calculated IMA of 6 seems reasonable.

Name _____ Class _____ Date _____

Chapter 14   Work, Power, and Machines

Section 14.3 Mechanical Advantage and Efficiency
(pages 421–426)

This section describes mechanical advantage and efficiency and how to calculate these values. Ways to maximize mechanical advantage and efficiency are discussed.

Reading Strategy (page 421)

Building Vocabulary As you read the section, write a definition in the table for each vocabulary term in your own words. For more information on this Reading Strategy, see the **Reading and Study Skills** in the **Skills and Reference Handbook** at the end of your textbook.

Mechanical Advantage	
Vocabulary	**Definition**
Mechanical advantage	The number of times a machine increases force
Actual mechanical advantage	Ratio of output force to input force
Ideal mechanical advantage	The mechanical advantage of a machine if there were no friction
Efficiency	Percentage of work input that become work output

Mechanical Advantage (pages 421–423)

1. The number of times that a machine increases an input force is the ___mechanical advantage___ of the machine.

2. For a given input force, what affects the output force that a nutcracker can exert on a nut? The position of the nut in the nutcracker affects the nutcracker's output force.

3. Mechanical advantage describes the relationship between input force and ___output___ force.

4. How is the actual mechanical advantage of a machine determined? It is the ratio of the output force to the input force.

5. Greater input force is required to move an object along a ramp with a rough surface, compared to a ramp with a smooth surface, because a greater force is needed to overcome ___friction___.

6. Is the following sentence true or false? A loading ramp with a rough surface has a greater mechanical advantage than one with a smooth surface. ___false___

Name _____ Class _____ Date _____

Chapter 14   Work, Power, and Machines

7. Because friction is always present, the actual mechanical advantage of a machine is never ___greater___ than its ideal mechanical advantage (IMA).

8. A machine's ___ideal mechanical advantage___ is the mechanical advantage in the absence of friction.

9. What type of materials do engineers use to increase the mechanical advantage of a machine? They use low-friction materials and lubricants.

Calculating Mechanical Advantage (pages 424–425)

10. Is the following sentence true or false? To calculate ideal mechanical advantage, divide input distance by output distance, and then divide the result by the force of friction. ___false___

11. Is the following sentence true or false? An inclined plane is an example of a machine. ___true___

12. Calculate the IMA of a ramp for the distances given in the table.

Ideal Mechanical Advantages of Ramps		
Horizontal Distance	**Vertical Rise**	**IMA**
1.5 meters	0.5 meters	3
12 meters	1.5 meters	8
3.6 meters	0.3 meters	12

13. Is the following sentence true or false? If the input distance of a machine is greater than the output distance, then the IMA for that machine is greater than one. ___true___

Efficiency (pages 425–426)

14. Why is the efficiency of a machine always less than 100 percent? Because there is always friction that must be overcome.

15. Is the following sentence true or false? To calculate the efficiency of a machine, divide the work output by work input, and then multiply by 100. ___true___

16. What is a significant factor affecting a car's fuel efficiency? air resistance

17. Calculate the efficiency of a machine with a work output of 120 J and a work input of 500 J. ___(120 J / 500 J) × 100 = 24%___

18. Circle the letter of the work input for a machine with a work output of 240 J and an efficiency of 80 percent.
    a. 300 J   b. 200 J
    c. 320 J   d. 200 W

19. Reducing friction ___increases___ the efficiency of a machine.

Name_____ Class_____ Date_____ M T W T F

LESSON PLAN 14.4

Simple Machines

Time
2 periods
1 block

Section Objectives

■ **14.4.1 Name, describe,** and **give an example** of each of the six types of simple machines.

■ **14.4.2 Describe** how to determine the ideal mechanical advantage of each type of simple machine.

■ **14.4.3 Define** and **identify** compound machines.

Vocabulary lever • fulcrum • input arm • output arm • wheel and axle • inclined plane • wedge • screw • pulley • compound machine

Local Standards

1 FOCUS

Build Vocabulary: Concept Maps

Have students expand on the concept maps used in the Reading Strategy by adding definitions for *fulcrum, IMA, input arm,* and *output arm.* **L2**

Targeted Resources

❑ Transparency: Interest Grabber 14.4

❑ Transparency: Reading Strategy 14.4

2 INSTRUCT

Build Reading Literacy: Use Prior Knowledge

Engage students in a discussion, relating the content about wedges and screws to students' prior experiences. **L1**

Quick Lab: Comparing Lever Arms

Students lift a mass with a spring scale in order to describe the relationship between the input arm length and the MA of a lever. **L2**

Build Science Skills: Observing

Have students name some mechanical devices they have observed that use the wheel-and-axle principle. **L2**

Teacher Demo: Inclined Planes

Use a spring scale to pull a heavy box up an inclined plane. Students gain appreciation for inclined-plane MA. **L2**

For Enrichment

Have students determine and compare the IMA of several tools that involve levers. **L3**

For Enrichment

Ask students to research new developments in various types of elevators and give presentations to the class. **L3**

Targeted Resources

❑ Transparency: Figure 13: Three Classes of Levers

❑ Transparency: Figure 19: Three Types of Pulleys

❑ GRSW Section 14.4

❑ **NSTA** *sci*$_{LINKS}$ Motion

3 ASSESS

Reteach

Ask students to identify each type of simple machine as used in their everyday lives. **L1**

Evaluate Understanding

Show students examples of each type of simple machine and demonstrate how to use each one. Then, ask students to identify the input and output forces for each machine. **L2**

Targeted Resources

❑ **PHSchool.com** Online Section 14.4 Assessment

❑ iText Section 14.4

Transparencies

207 Section 14.4 Interest Grabber

The Wheel and Axle

The wheel and axle is a simple machine that you probably see everyday. It uses two discs or cylinders, each one with a different radius. Look at the examples below. Can you identify each wheel and axle?

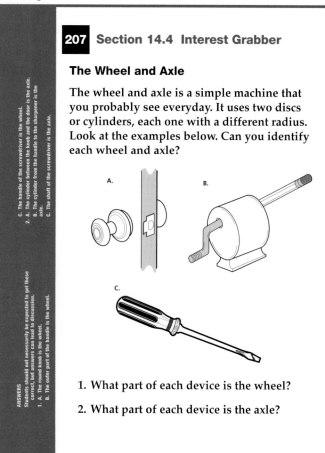

A.

B.

C.

1. What part of each device is the wheel?

2. What part of each device is the axle?

ANSWERS
Students should not necessarily be expected to get these correct, but answers can lead to discussion.
1. A. The round knob is the wheel.
   B. The outer part of the handle is the wheel.
   C. The handle of the screwdriver is the wheel.
2. A. The cylinder between the knob and the door is the axle.
   B. The cylinder from the handle to the sharpener is the axle.
   C. The shaft of the screwdriver is the axle.

Transparencies

208 Section 14.4 Reading Strategy

Summarizing

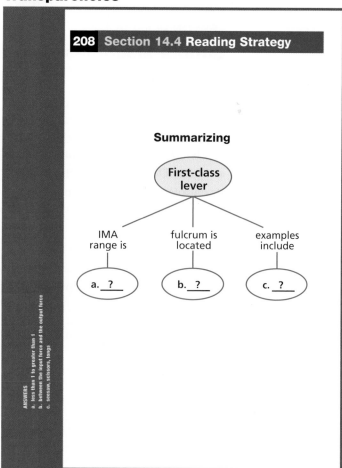

First-class lever

IMA range is

a. ?

fulcrum is located

b. ?

examples include

c. ?

ANSWERS
a. less than 1 to greater than 1
b. between the input force and the output force
c. seesaw, scissors, tongs

Transparencies

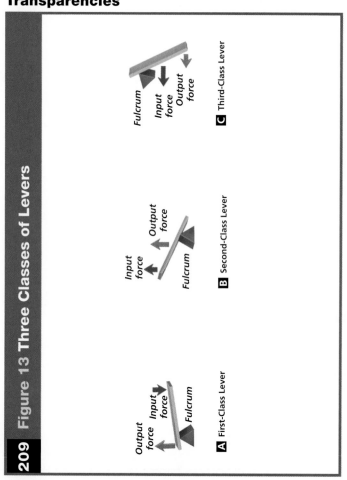

Figure 13 Three Classes of Levers

Fulcrum

Input force

Output force

C Third-Class Lever

Input force

Output force

Fulcrum

B Second-Class Lever

Output force   Input force

Fulcrum

A First-Class Lever

209

Transparencies

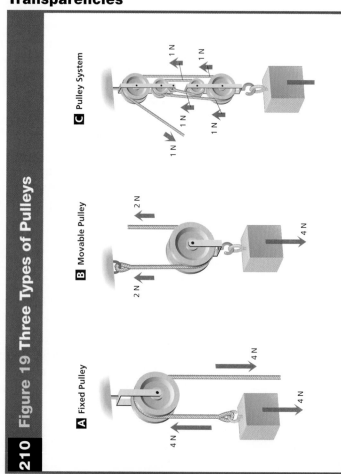

Figure 19 Three Types of Pulleys

C Pulley System

1 N 1 N 1 N 1 N

B Movable Pulley

2 N

2 N

4 N

A Fixed Pulley

4 N

4 N

4 N

210

Name _____ Class _____ Date _____

Chapter 14   Work, Power, and Machines

Section 14.4 Simple Machines
(pages 427–435)

This section presents the six types of simple machines. A discussion of how each type works and how to determine its mechanical advantage is given. Common uses of simple machines are also described.

Reading Strategy (page 427)

Summarizing After reading the section on levers, complete the concept map to organize what you know about first-class levers. On a separate sheet of paper, construct and complete similar concept maps for second- and third-class levers. For more information on this Reading Strategy, see the **Reading and Study Skills** in the **Skills and Reference Handbook** at the end of your textbook.

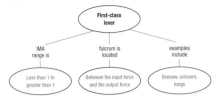

1. List the six types of simple machines.
   a. _____Lever_____   b. _____Wheel and axle_____
   c. _____Inclined plane_____ d. _____Wedge_____
   e. _____Screw_____   f. _____Pulley_____

Levers (pages 428–429)

2. A screwdriver used to pry the lid off a paint can is an example of a(n) _____lever_____.

3. The fixed point that a lever rotates around is called the _____fulcrum_____.

4. To calculate the ideal mechanical advantage of any lever, divide the input arm by the _____output arm_____.

5. What characteristics distinguish levers as first-class, second-class, or third-class?
   Levers are classified by the relative positions of the fulcrum, input force, and output force.

6. Is the following sentence true or false? First-class levers always have a mechanical advantage that is greater than one. _____false_____

Name _____ Class _____ Date _____

Chapter 14   Work, Power, and Machines

7. Is the following sentence true or false? All second-class levers have a mechanical advantage greater than one because the input arm is longer than the output arm. _____true_____

Wheel and Axle (page 430)

8. Describe a wheel and axle. A wheel and axle is a simple machine that consists of two disks or cylinders, each one with a different radius.

9. Circle the letter of the sentence that describes how to calculate the IMA of a wheel and axle.
   a. Multiply the area of the wheel by the area of the axle.
   b. Divide input force by output force.
   c. Divide the diameter where input force is exerted by the diameter where output force is exerted.
   d. Divide the radius of the wheel by the force exerted on it.

Inclined Planes (page 430–431)

10. A slanted surface along which a force moves an object to a different elevation is called a(n) _____inclined plane_____.

11. Is the following sentence true or false? The ideal mechanical advantage of an inclined plane is the distance along the incline plane divided by its change in height. _____true_____

Wedges and Screws (page 431)

12. A thin wedge of a given length has a(n) _____greater_____ mechanical advantage than a thick wedge of the same length.

13. Screws with threads that are close together have a greater _____ideal mechanical advantage_____.

Pulleys (pages 432–433)

14. A simple machine consisting of a rope fitted into a groove in a wheel is a(n) _____pulley_____.

15. What determines the ideal mechanical advantage of a pulley or pulley system?
    It is equal to the number of rope sections supporting the load being lifted.

Compound Machines (page 435)

16. Is the following sentence true or false? A compound machine is a combination of two or more simple machines that operate together. _____true_____

17. Circle each letter that identifies a compound machine.
    a. a car   b. a handheld screwdriver
    c. a washing machine   d. a watch

Name _____ Class _____ Date _____

Chapter 14   Work, Power, and Machines

WordWise

Answer the question or identify the clue by writing the correct vocabulary term in the blanks. Use the circled letter(s) in each term to find the hidden vocabulary word. Then, write a definition for the hidden word.

Clues	Vocabulary Terms
$\dfrac{\text{Work output}}{\text{Work input}} \times 100$	e f f **i** c i e n c y
A mechanical watch is an example of this.	c o m p o u **n** d m a c h i n e
One way to determine this is to divide output work by output force.	o u t **p** u t d i s t a n c e
This is the SI unit of work.	j o **u** l e
On a lever, it is the distance between the fulcrum and the input force.	i n p u **t** a r m
The IMA of this machine increases as its thickness decreases relative to its length.	w e **d** g e
This is exerted on a jack handle to lift a car.	**i** n p u t f o r c e
This unit equals about 746 joules.	h o r **s** e p o w e r
This is the distance between the output force and the fulcrum.	o u **t** p u t a r m
This SI unit of power is used to describe light bulbs.	w **a** t t
The IMA of this machine is the distance along its surface divided by the change in height.	i n c l i **n** e d p l a n e
A device that can change the size of the force required to do work.	m a **c** h i n e
This quantity is equal to Work/Time.	p o w **e** r

Hidden words: i n p u t d i s t a n c e

Definition: The distance the input force acts through.

Name _____ Class _____ Date _____

Chapter 14   Work, Power, and Machines

Calculating Work and Power

Calculate the power of a machine that exerts a force of 800.0 N over a distance of 6.0 m in 2.0 s.

Math Skill: Formulas and Equations

You may want to read more about this **Math Skill** in the **Skills and Reference Handbook** at the end of your textbook.

1. **Read and Understand**
   What information are you given?
   Force = 800.0 N
   Distance = 6.0 m
   Time = 2.0 s

2. **Plan and Solve**
   What variable are you trying to determine?
   Power =?

   What formula contains the given quantities and the unknown?
   $$\text{Power} = \frac{\text{Work}}{\text{Time}} = \frac{\text{Force} \times \text{Distance}}{\text{Time}}$$

   $$\text{Power} = \frac{800.0 \text{ N} \times 6.0 \text{ m}}{2.0 \text{ s}}$$

   $$\text{Power} = \frac{4800 \text{ J}}{2.0 \text{ s}} = 2400 \text{ J/s} = 2400 \text{ W}$$

3. **Look Back and Check**
   Is your answer reasonable?
   Work = (2400 J/s) × 2.0 s = 4800 J

   This is a reasonable answer. Substituting power and time back into the power equation yields the original value for work.

Math Practice

On a separate sheet of paper, solve the following problems.

1. Suppose 900.0 J of work are done by a light bulb in 15.0 s. What is the power of the light bulb?
   Power = Work/Time = 900.0 J/15.0 s = 60.0 J/s = 60.0 W

2. What is the power of a machine if an output force of 500.0 N is exerted over an output distance of 8.0 m in 4.0 s?
   Power = (Force)(Distance)/Time = (500.0 N × 8.0 m)/4.0 s = 1000 J/s = 1000 W

3. The power of a machine is 6.0×10^3 J/s. This machine is scheduled for design improvements. What would its power be if the same work could be done in half the time?
   Power = Work/Time = $(6.0 \times 10^3$ J/s$)/0.5$ s = 1.2×10^4 J

Student Edition Lab Worksheet

Name _____ Class _____ Date _____

Chapter 14   Machines   Consumer Lab

Determining Mechanical Advantage
See pages 438 and 439 in the Teacher's Edition for more information.

Many complex machines have an adjustable mechanical advantage. In this lab, you will learn how adjusting the mechanical advantage of a bicycle affects the bicycle's performance.

Problem How does mechanical advantage affect the performance of a bicycle?

Materials
• board with 2 nails
• 4 thread spools, 3 with different diameters
• rubber band
• masking tape
• multispeed bicycle (one or more per class)
• meter stick
• thick leather glove

Skills Measuring, Calculating

Procedure
Part A: Modeling the Mechanical Advantage of a Bicycle
1. Use a piece of masking tape to label each nail on the board. Label one nail *Pedals* and the other nail *Wheel*. To model the pedals and rear wheel of a bicycle, place a spool on each nail in the board and join the spools with a rubber band, as shown in Figure 1.

Figure 1

2. Use a pencil to make a reference mark on the edge of each spool. These marks will help you observe the motion of the spools as they turn.
3. **Measuring** Use a ruler to measure the radius of each spool in your model. Record these measurements in the data table for Part A.

Student Edition Lab Worksheet

Name _____ Class _____ Date _____

DATA TABLE: PART A

Pedal Spool Radius (cm)	Revolutions of Pedal Spool	Wheel Spool Radius (cm)	Revolutions of Wheel Spool	IMA
	5			
	5			
	5			

4. The pedal spool represents the pedals and the gears attached to them. The wheel spool represents the rear wheel and its gears. Using the reference marks, observe the wheel spool as you turn the pedal spool through five complete revolutions. In the data table, record the number of revolutions of the wheel spool.
5. Replace the wheel spool with a spool of a different diameter. Repeat Steps 2 through 4 for each diameter of wheel spool.
6. **Calculating** The ideal mechanical advantage (IMA) of a bicycle is equal to the distance the pedals move divided by the distance the rear wheel moves. For your model,

$$IMA = \frac{5 \times Pedal\ radius}{(Revolutions\ of\ wheel) \times (Wheel\ radius)}$$

Calculate the mechanical advantage of each spool combination that you used. Record these values in the data table.

Part B: Analyzing Bicycle Gears
7. **Measuring** Work in groups of three. Use a meter stick to measure the radius of the pedals and the rear wheel, as shown in Figure 2. Record these measurements in the data table for Part B.

DATA TABLE: PART B

Size of Pedal Gear	Smallest	Smallest	Largest
Size of Rear Wheel Gear	Largest	Medium	Smallest
Pedal Radius (cm)			
Revolutions of Pedal	5	5	5
Rear Wheel Radius (cm)			
Revolutions of Rear Wheel			
IMA	The mechanical advantage of a typical multispeed bicycle gear train can vary from approximately 0.7 to 4.0.		

Student Edition Lab Worksheet

Name _____ Class _____ Date _____

8. One person should hold the bicycle with its rear wheel slightly off the floor. While a second person turns the pedals, a third person should use the bicycle's gear shifters to place the chain on the smallest pedal gear and the largest rear wheel gear. **CAUTION:** *Keep your hands out of the spokes, chain, and gears.*
9. One person should put on a heavy leather glove, while a second person holds the bicycle with its rear wheel slightly off the floor.

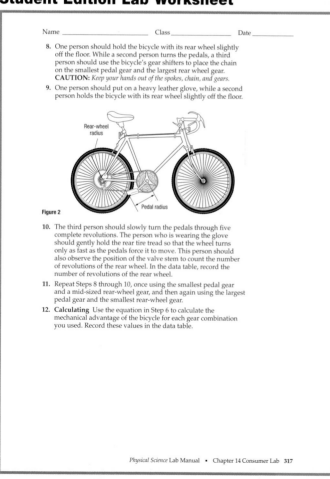

Figure 2

Rear-wheel radius

Pedal radius

10. The third person should slowly turn the pedals through five complete revolutions. The person who is wearing the glove should gently hold the rear tire tread so that the wheel turns only as fast as the pedals force it to move. This person should also observe the position of the valve stem to count the number of revolutions of the rear wheel. In the data table, record the number of revolutions of the rear wheel.
11. Repeat Steps 8 through 10, once using the smallest pedal gear and a mid-sized rear-wheel gear, and then again using the largest pedal gear and the smallest rear-wheel gear.
12. **Calculating** Use the equation in Step 6 to calculate the mechanical advantage of the bicycle for each gear combination you used. Record these values in the data table.

Student Edition Lab Worksheet

Name _____ Class _____ Date _____

Analyze and Conclude
1. **Analyzing Data** Which combination of pedal and rear-wheel gears provided the greatest mechanical advantage? The least mechanical advantage?

The largest pedal gear and the smallest rear-wheel gear provided the greatest mechanical

advantage. The smallest pedal gear and the largest rear-wheel gear provided the least

mechanical advantage.

2. **Applying Concepts** To ride quickly on a level road, would you select a gear combination with a large mechanical advantage or a small one? Explain your answer.

A large mechanical advantage would be best for riding quickly on a level road because it

would produce the greatest number of turns of the rear wheel for each turn of the pedals.

3. **Drawing Conclusions** To decrease the force needed to ride a bicycle up a steep hill, would you select a gear combination with a large mechanical advantage or a small one? What size rear-wheel gear would you use to race on a flat road? Explain.

A gear combination with a large mechanical advantage would be best for riding up a steep

hill because it would exert the greatest force on the rear wheel. A small rear-wheel gear would

be best for racing on a flat road because it would cause the rear wheel to turn fastest and

therefore cause the bicycle to move fastest. A large rear-wheel gear would be best for uphill

mountain biking because it would exert the greatest force on the rear wheel.

Lab Manual

Name _____ Class _____ Date _____

Chapter 14   Work, Power, and Machines

Investigation 14A

Comparing the Mechanical Advantage of Levers

Refer students to pages 417–429 in their textbooks for a discussion of actual mechanical advantage and levers.
SKILLS FOCUS: Measuring, Calculating, Designing Experiments **CLASS TIME:** 45 minutes

Background Information

A **lever** consists of a rigid bar that is free to rotate around a fixed point. The fixed point on the bar rotates around the **fulcrum.** Like all machines, a lever changes the size of a force that is applied to it, the direction of a force applied to it, or both. The force exerted on a lever is the **input force.** The distance between the fulcrum and the point where the input force acts is the **input arm.** The force that the lever exerts on the load is the **output force.** The distance between the fulcrum and the output force is the **output arm.** Note that the output force may be larger or smaller than the input force, depending on the type of lever.

There are three types of levers, called first-class, second-class, and third-class levers. The three classes differ in the relative positions of the fulcrum and the input and output forces. A first-class lever, such as a seesaw, has its fulcrum between the input and output forces. In a second-class lever, such as a wheelbarrow, the output force, is between the input force and the fulcrum. A third-class lever, such as a broom, has its input force between the fulcrum and the output force.

The **mechanical advantage** of any machine is the number of times that the machine multiplies the input force. The **actual mechanical advantage** (AMA) of a lever is equal to the output force divided by the input force.

$$AMA = \frac{\text{Output force}}{\text{Input force}}$$

In this investigation, you will determine and compare the actual mechanical advantage of first-class and second-class levers. Then, you will design and carry out an investigation to determine the mechanical advantage of a third-class lever.

Problem

How do the mechanical advantages of first-class, second-class, and third-class levers differ?

Pre-Lab Discussion

Read the entire investigation. Then, work with a partner to answer the following questions.

1. **Designing Experiments** Why are you told in Step 1 to record the weight of the 500-g mass as the output force for every first-class and second-class lever that you will use in this investigation?

   The 500-g mass is the load that each lever will lift. Therefore, the output force of each lever is the

   force needed to lift the mass. This force is equal in size to the weight of the mass.

Lab Manual

Name _____ Class _____ Date _____

2. **Calculating** How will you calculate the actual mechanical advantage (AMA) of the levers in this investigation?

   The actual mechanical advantage of each lever will be calculated by dividing the output force by

   the input force.

3. **Predicting** What factors do you predict will affect the actual mechanical advantage of the levers in this investigation?

   The relative lengths of the input and output arms and the efficiency of the levers will determine the

   actual mechanical advantage of the levers.

4. **Controlling Variables** Identify the manipulated, responding, and controlled variables in this investigation.

   a. Manipulated variables

      Class of lever (positions of forces and fulcrum), lengths of lever arms

   b. Responding variables

      Input force, mechanical advantage

   c. Controlled variable

      Load (output force)

5. **Predicting** Which class of levers do you expect to have the greatest actual mechanical advantage? Explain your answer.

   The greatest actual mechanical advantages will be found in second-class levers because the

   input arms of these levers are always longer than their output arms. As a result, the actual mechanical

   advantage of any second-class lever is greater than 1. A first-class lever can have an actual

   mechanical advantage that is greater or less than 1 because its arms can be of any length. All

   third-class levers have an actual mechanical advantage that is less than 1 because their output

   arms are always longer than their input arms.

6. **Formulating Hypotheses** State a hypothesis that you could test in Part C of this investigation.

   An example of an acceptable hypothesis is that the actual mechanical advantage of all

   third-class levers is less than 1.

Materials *(per group)*

500-g mass with hook
spring scale *Use spring scales with a capacity of 10–20 N.*
wedge-shaped block of wood, about 10 cm high
meter stick
string
scissors
loop of wire *Prepare short loops from 10 to 15-cm lengths of wire.*

Lab Manual

Name _____ Class _____ Date _____

Safety

Put on safety goggles. To prevent injury from falling objects, do not wear sandals or open-toed shoes. Wear only closed-toed shoes in the laboratory. Note all safety alert symbols next to the steps in the Procedure and review the meaning of each symbol by referring to the Safety Symbols on page xiii.

Procedure

Part A: Determining the AMA of First-Class Levers

1. Work with a classmate. Hang the 500-g mass from the spring scale. Read the weight of the mass on the spring scale. Record this weight as the output force in each row of Data Table 1.

2. To make a first-class lever, place the wedge-shaped block of wood on the table to serve as a fulcrum. Place the 50-cm mark of the meter stick on the fulcrum so that the 100-cm end of the meter stick extends beyond the edge of the table, as shown in Figure 1. Use string to tie the 500-g mass to the meter stick at the 10-cm mark. This mass serves as the load that the lever will lift.

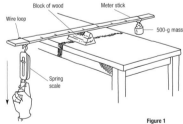

Block of wood   Meter stick
Wire loop
500-g mass
Spring scale

Figure 1

3. Place the wire loop around the meter stick at the 90-cm mark, 40 cm away from the fulcrum. Hang the spring scale from the wire loop.

4. In the first row of Data Table 1, record the distance from the fulcrum to the spring scale as the input arm. Record the distance from the fulcrum to the mass as the output arm.

5. Pull the spring scale down slowly and steadily to lift the mass. When the meter stick is horizontal, read the input force on the spring scale. Record this value in Data Table 1.

6. Leaving the mass and the spring scale at the same positions, move the fulcrum to the 30-cm mark. Record the lengths of the new input and output arms in Data Table 1.

7. Repeat Step 5.

8. Repeat Steps 6 and 7, but this time, move the fulcrum to the 20-cm mark.

9. Calculate the mechanical advantage of the first-class lever in all the positions you tested. Record these values in Data Table 1.

Lab Manual

Name _____ Class _____ Date _____

Part B: Determining the AMA of Second-Class Levers

10. To make a second-class lever, place the 10-cm mark of the meter stick on the fulcrum as shown in Figure 2. Tie the mass to the meter stick at the 50-cm mark.

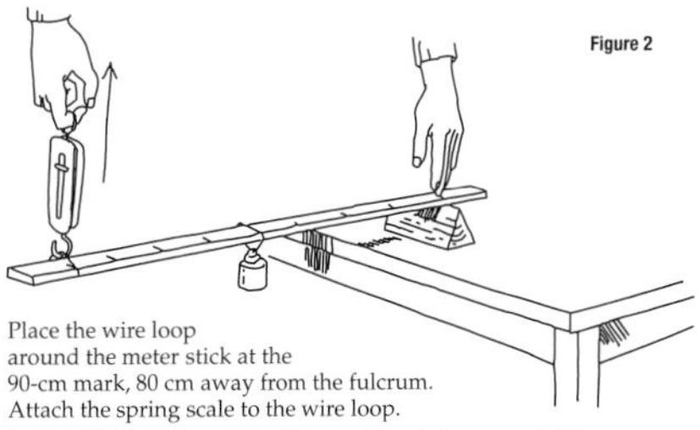

Figure 2

11. Place the wire loop around the meter stick at the 90-cm mark, 80 cm away from the fulcrum. Attach the spring scale to the wire loop.

12. In Data Table 1, record the distance from the fulcrum to the spring scale as the input arm. Record the distance from the fulcrum to the mass as the output arm.

13. Have your partner hold the meter stick down on the fulcrum so that the meter stick does not slide or rise up off of the fulcrum. Pull the spring scale up slowly and steadily to lift the mass. When the meter stick is horizontal, read the input force on the spring scale. Record this value in Data Table 1.

14. Leaving the fulcrum and the spring scale at the same positions, move the mass to the 30-cm mark. Record the lengths of the new input and output arms in Data Table 1.

15. Repeat Step 13.

16. Repeat Steps 14 and 15, but this time, move the mass to the 20-cm mark.

17. Calculate the actual mechanical advantage of the second-class lever in all the positions you tested. Record these values in Data Table 1.

Part C: Design Your Own Investigation

18. Design an investigation to determine the actual mechanical advantage of a third-class lever. Record the hypothesis that you will test.

    Hypothesis

    An example of an acceptable hypothesis is that the actual mechanical advantage of a third-class

    lever is less than 1, but increases as the input arm is made longer.

Lab Manual

Name _____   Class _____   Date _____

19. In the lines below, write a detailed plan of how you will carry out your investigation. You may choose to base your investigation on the method of determining the actual mechanical advantage of a lever that you used in Parts A and B. Construct Data Table 2 in which to record your observations in the space provided on page 150.

> 1. To make a third-class lever, place the mass on the table and tie the mass to the meter
>   stick at the 10-cm mark.
> 2. Place the wire loop around the meter stick at the 50-cm mark. Attach the spring scale to
>   the wire loop.
> 3. Place the 90-cm mark of the meter stick on the fulcrum, 40 cm away from the spring scale and
>   80 cm away from the mass.
> 4. In Data Table 2, record the distance from the fulcrum to the spring scale as the input arm.
>   Record the distance from the fulcrum to the mass as the output arm.
> 5. Have your partner hold the meter stick down on the fulcrum so that the meter stick does not
>   slide or rise up off of the fulcrum. Pull the spring scale up slowly and steadily to lift the mass.
>   Read the input force on the spring scale. Record this value in Data Table 2.
> 6. Leaving the fulcrum and the mass at the same positions, move the spring scale to the
>   30-cm mark. Record the lengths of the new input and output arms in Data Table 2.
> 7. Repeat Step 5.
> 8. Repeat Steps 6 and 7, but this time, move the spring scale to the 20-cm mark.
> 9. Calculate the actual mechanical advantage of the third-class lever in all the positions you tested.
>   Record these values in Data Table 2.

20. What are the manipulated, responding, and controlled variables in your investigation?
    a. Manipulated variable
       The lengths of one or both lever arms
    b. Responding variable
       The input force
    c. Controlled variables
       The output force, the length of one lever arm

21. What safety precautions will you need to take in your investigation?
    Students need to wear safety goggles and to take care when handling the 500-g mass.

Lab Manual

Name _____   Class _____   Date _____

22. List the possible results of your investigation. State whether each possible result would support or contradict your hypothesis.

    An example of an acceptable response is that the actual mechanical advantage of a third-class
    lever is less than 1, and the actual mechanical advantage may increase or decrease as the input
    arm is made longer. If the actual mechanical advantage is always less than 1, but increases as the
    input arm is made longer, then the sample hypothesis cited in Step 18 will be supported. Any other
    result would contradict this hypothesis.

23. Show your plan to your teacher. When your teacher approves your plan, carry out your investigation and record your observations in your data table.

Observations   Sample data are shown.

DATA TABLE 1: Parts A and B

Fulcrum Position (cm)	Output Arm (cm)	Input Arm (cm)	Output Force (N)	Input Force (N)	Actual Mechanical Advantage
First-Class Lever					
50	40	40	5	5	1
30	20	60	5	2	2.5
20	10	70	5	1	5
Second-Class Lever					
10	40	80	5	3	1.7
10	20	80	5	2	2.5
10	10	80	5	1	5

DATA TABLE 2: Part C
If you need more space, attach additional sheets of paper.

Fulcrum Position (cm)	Output Arm (cm)	Input Arm (cm)	Output Force (N)	Input Force (N)	Actual Mechanical Advantage
Third-Class Lever					
90	80	40	5	10	0.5
90	80	60	5	7	0.7
90	80	70	5	6	0.8

Lab Manual

Name _____   Class _____   Date _____

Analysis and Conclusions

1. **Analyzing Data** How did moving the fulcrum of the first-class lever closer to the output force affect the actual mechanical advantage?
   The actual mechanical advantage became greater.

2. **Comparing and Contrasting** Did changing the lengths of the input and output arms affect the actual mechanical advantage of all three classes of levers in the same way? Explain your answer.
   Yes, increasing the input arm or decreasing the output arm increases the actual mechanical
   advantage of any lever.

3. **Evaluating and Revising** In Part C of this investigation, did your data support or contradict your hypothesis? Explain your answer.
   Answers will depend on student data, but should be justified by reference to the hypothesis
   and the data. The actual mechanical advantage of a third-class lever is less than 1, but increases as
   the input arm is made longer.

4. **Drawing Conclusions** Based on the mechanical advantages that you calculated for each class of lever, how do third-class levers differ from the other two types? How could a third-class lever be useful?
   The actual mechanical advantage of a third-class lever is always less than 1. As a result, third-class
   levers produce an output force that is less than the input force. Third-class levers are useful for
   increasing the distance that a load moves because their output forces always move farther than
   their input forces.

5. **Drawing Conclusions** What could you do to any lever to increase its actual mechanical advantage?
   Make the input arm as long as possible and the output arm as short as possible.

Go Further

Suppose you need to use a nutcracker to crack an especially tough nut. You have the choice of two similar nutcrackers that each have two handles connected at one end. One nutcracker has longer handles than the other one. Which class of lever are the nutcrackers? How can you tell? Which nutcracker would you use? Where would you place the nut relative to the arms? Explain your answer in terms of actual mechanical advantage.
The nutcrackers are second-class levers because the load (nut) is between the input
force (user's hand) and the fulcrum (hinge of the nutcracker). The longer nutcracker
should be used, with the nut as close as possible to the fulcrum. This increases actual
mechanical advantage by increasing the input arm and decreasing the output arm.

Lab Manual

Name _____   Class _____   Date _____

Chapter 14   Work, Power, and Machines   **Investigation 14B**

Comparing Pulleys

Refer students to pages 417–426, 432, and 433 in their textbooks for a discussion of actual mechanical advantage and simple machines. **SKILLS FOCUS:** Measuring, Calculating **TIME REQUIRED:** 45 minutes

Background Information

One of the most common uses of machines is to increase a force. The force that you exert on a machine is the **input force.** The force that the machine exerts is the **output force.** You can compare the ability of machines to increase input force by determining their actual mechanical advantages. Actual mechanical advantage (AMA) is calculated by dividing the output force by the input force.

$$AMA = \frac{Output\ force}{Input\ force}$$

Pulleys are simple machines that are used to lift objects. A pulley consists of a rope wrapped around a wheel. The simplest kind of pulley is a grooved wheel around which a rope is pulled. Pulleys can be used to change the direction of an input force. For example, a pulley attached, or fixed, to the top of a flagpole allows you to raise the flag up by pulling down.

A combination of fixed and movable pulleys is called a pulley system, or block-and-tackle. A pulley system is used to multiply input force so that heavy objects can be lifted. Pulley systems are commonly seen around construction sites.

In this investigation, you will determine the actual mechanical advantage of several different pulleys and pulley systems.

Problem

How do pulleys help to raise objects?

Pre-Lab Discussion

Read the entire investigation. Then, work with a partner to answer the following questions.

1. **Observing** What is the output force in this investigation?
   The output force is the force needed to lift the 1-kg mass.

2. **Inferring** Why will you record the same output force for all the pulleys in this investigation?
   All the pulleys will be used to lift the same mass, so the weight of the 1-kg mass is equal to
   the output force of all the pulleys.

3. **Calculating** How will you calculate the actual mechanical advantage of the pulleys in this investigation?
   The actual mechanical advantage will be calculated by dividing the output force by the input force.

Name _____ Class _____ Date _____

4. Predicting How do you expect the actual mechanical advantage to change as more pulleys are added to the pulley system?

The actual mechanical advantage will increase as more pulleys are added to the system.

Materials (per group)

2 single pulleys
2 double pulleys
1-m nylon fishing line
ring stand

iron ring
10-N spring scale
1-kg mass

Safety 🥽

Put on safety goggles. Do not wear open-toed shoes or sandals in the laboratory. Note all safety alert symbols next to the steps in the Procedure and review the meaning of each symbol by referring to the Safety Symbols on page xiii.

Procedure

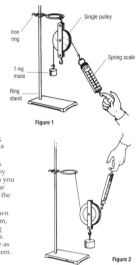

Iron ring

Single pulley

1-kg mass

Spring scale

Ring stand

Figure 1

Figure 2

🥽 1 Find the weight of the 1-kg mass by hanging it from the spring scale. Record this weight in the data table as the output force for all of the pulley arrangements.

2. Set up a single fixed pulley, as shown in Figure 1. **CAUTION:** *Make sure that the ring is over the base of the ring stand to reduce the chance that the equipment will tip over.* Pull down on the spring scale to lift the mass. As you do this, observe the reading on the spring scale. Record this value in the data table as the input force.

3. Set up a single movable pulley, as shown in Figure 2. Lift the mass by pulling up on the spring scale. As you do this, observe the reading on the spring scale. Record this value in the data table as the input force.

4. Set up the pulley systems, as shown in Figure 3. For each pulley system, observe the reading on the spring scale as you pull it to lift the mass. Record the value in the data table as the input force for the pulley system.

Name _____ Class _____ Date _____

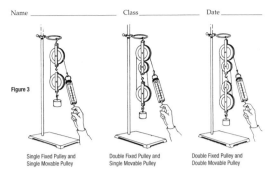

Figure 3

Single Fixed Pulley and Single Movable Pulley

Double Fixed Pulley and Single Movable Pulley

Double Fixed Pulley and Double Movable Pulley

5. Calculate the actual mechanical advantage for each pulley system. To do this, divide the output force by the input force. Record the actual mechanical advantage of each pulley system in the data table.

Observations

Sample data are shown. The weight of a 1-kg mass is approximately 10 N.

DATA TABLE

Pulleys	Output Force (newtons)	Input Force (newtons)	Actual Mechanical Advantage
Single fixed	10	10	1
Single movable	10	5	2
Single fixed and single movable	10	5	2
Double fixed and single movable	10	3.3	3
Double fixed and double movable	10	2.5	4

Name _____ Class _____ Date _____

Analysis and Conclusions

1. Analyzing Data As you added pulleys to the system, what happened to the amount of effort force needed to raise the mass?

Less effort force was needed as more pulleys were added.

2. Drawing Conclusions How did the number of pulleys in the pulley system affect the actual mechanical advantage of the system? Did this result agree with your prediction?

The sample data supported the prediction that adding pulleys to the pulley system will

increase the actual mechanical advantage.

3. Analyzing Data What type of pulley produced an output force equal in size to the input force?

A single fixed pulley

4. Inferring What is the practical use of a pulley that does not change the size of the input force?

The pulley changes the direction in which the force is applied.

5. Inferring When using any simple machine, you never "get something for nothing." Although a pulley system reduces the amount of input force needed to lift a mass, it does so at a cost. What must be increased as the amount of input force is decreased?

The distance that the rope must be pulled to lift the mass is increased.

Go Further

In this investigation, you calculated actual mechanical advantage by dividing the output force by the input force. How could you use distances moved by the output and input forces to calculate actual mechanical advantage? Design an experiment to answer this question. Write a detailed plan for your experiment. Your plan should state the hypothesis to be tested, identify the manipulated, responding, and controlled variables, and describe the procedures and safety precautions that you will use. Show your plan to your teacher. When your teacher approves your plan, carry out your experiment and report your results and conclusions. Compare your data with the data you obtained in this investigation. Is one method better for determining mechanical advantage?

Check student plans for safety, practicality, and sound experimental design. Well-designed experimental plans should include detailed procedures that will test a clearly stated hypothesis. An example of an acceptable hypothesis is that measurements of force and distance will produce the same values for mechanical advantage.

In this investigation, students measured the input and output forces to determine the actual mechanical advantage of the pulley systems. Students can compare the distances moved by the input and output forces to determine the ideal mechanical advantage, which neglects the role of friction. If the input force and the output force move the same distance, the pulley system will have an ideal mechanical advantage of 1. If the input force moves a greater distance than the output force moves, the pulley system will have an ideal mechanical advantage greater than 1.

Chapter Test A

Name _____ Class _____ Date _____

Chapter 14   Work, Power, and Machines   Chapter Test A

Multiple Choice

Write the letter that best answers the question or completes the statement on the line provided.

_____ 1. A force acting on an object does no work if
   a. a machine is used to move the object.
   b. the force is not in the direction of the object's motion.
   c. the force is greater than the force of friction.
   d. the object accelerates.

_____ 2. If you exert a force of 10.0 N to lift a box a distance of 0.75 m, how much work do you do?
   a. 0.075 J   b. 7.5 J
   c. 10.75 J   d. 75 J

_____ 3. If you perform 30 joules of work lifting a 20-N box from the floor to a shelf, how high is the shelf?
   a. 0.5 m   b. 0.6 m
   c. 1.5 m   d. 2 m

_____ 4. If you exert a force of 500 N to walk 4 m up a flight of stairs in 4 s, how much power do you use?
   a. 31 W   b. 500 W
   c. 2000 W   d. 8000 W

_____ 5. Which of the following statements is true?
   a. To increase power, you can decrease the amount of work you do in a given amount of time, or you can do a given amount of work in less time.
   b. To increase power, you can decrease the amount of work you do in a given amount of time, or you can do a given amount of work in more time.
   c. To increase power, you can increase the amount of work you do in a given amount of time, or you can do a given amount of work in less time.
   d. To increase power, you can increase the amount of work you do in a given amount of time, or you can do a given amount of work in more time.

_____ 6. A 750-W motor might also be rated as a
   a. 0.5-horsepower motor.   b. 1-horsepower motor.
   c. 2-horsepower motor.   d. 10-horsepower motor.

_____ 7. When a machine does work, it can do all of the following EXCEPT
   a. change the direction of a force.
   b. increase a force and change the distance a force moves.
   c. increase the distance a force moves and change the direction of a force.
   d. increase a force and increase the distance a force moves.

Chapter Test A

Name _____ Class _____ Date _____

_____ 8. How can you make the work output of a machine greater than the work input?
   a. by decreasing friction
   b. by increasing the input force
   c. by increasing the output distance
   d. none of the above

_____ 9. If you know the input distance and output distance of a machine, which of the following can you calculate?
   a. work   b. actual mechanical advantage
   c. efficiency   d. ideal mechanical advantage

_____ 10. A 100-m long ski lift carries skiers from a station at the foot of a slope to a second station 40 m above. What is the IMA of the lift?
   a. 0.4   b. 2.5
   c. 40   d. 140

_____ 11. The efficiency of a machine is always less than 100 percent because
   a. a machine cannot have an IMA greater than 1.
   b. some work input is lost to friction.
   c. the work input is too small.
   d. the work output is too great.

_____ 12. A motor with an efficiency rating of 80 percent must supply 300 J of useful work. What amount of work must be supplied to the motor?
   a. 80 J   b. 240 J
   c. 375 J   d. 540 J

_____ 13. Which of the following is an example of a wheel and axle?
   a. a doorknob   b. an automobile steering wheel
   c. a jar lid   d. a pencil

_____ 14. A machine is classified as a compound machine if it
   a. has moving parts.
   b. has an IMA greater than 1.
   c. is made up of two or more simple machines that operate together.
   d. is very efficient.

Completion

Complete each statement on the line provided.

1. Any part of a force that does not act in the direction of an object's motion does no _____ on an object.

2. You calculate work by multiplying the force acting in the direction of _____ by the distance the object moves.

Chapter Test A

Name _____ Class _____ Date _____

3. The watt and the horsepower are both units of _____.

4. As the thickness of a wedge of given length increases, its IMA _____.

5. A watch consists of a complex systems of gears. Each gear acts as a continuous _____.

Short Answer

In complete sentences, write the answers to the questions on the lines provided.

1. If two swimmers compete in race, does the faster swimmer develop more power?

2. Why is the work output of a machine never equal to the work input?

3. If a simple machine could be frictionless, how would its IMA and AMA compare?

4. Compare the effects of a fixed pulley and a movable pulley on the size and direction of the input force.

5. In a compound machine made up of two simple machines, how is the work output of the first simple machine related to the work input of the second simple machine?

Chapter Test A

Name _____ Class _____ Date _____

Using Science Skills

Use the diagram to answer each question. Write the answers on a separate sheet of paper.

1. **Applying Concepts** Look at Figure 14-2. If Machine A moves through an input distance of 4.0 m, what is the output distance of Machine B?

2. **Classifying** What type of simple machine is Machine A in Figure 14-2?

3. **Interpreting Graphics** What is the IMA of Machine B in Figure 14-2?

4. **Interpreting Graphics** As shown in Figure 14-2, Machines A and B operate together as what type of machine?

5. **Comparing and Contrasting** In Figure 14-2, how does the work input of Machine B compare with the work output of Machine A?

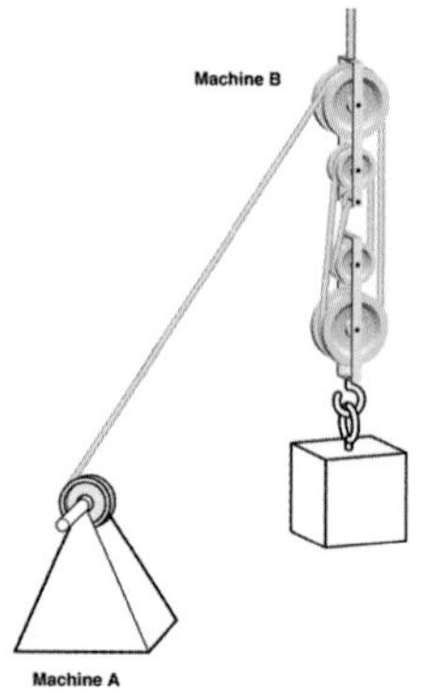

Machine B

Machine A

Figure 14-2

Problem

Write the answers to each question on a separate sheet of paper.

1. A worker uses a cart to move a load of bricks weighing 680 N a distance of 10 m across a parking lot. If he pushes the cart with a constant force of 220 N, what amount of work does he do? Show your work.

2. A girl lifts a 100-N load a height of 2.0 m in a time of 0.5 s. What power does the girl produce? Show your work.

3. The input force of a pulley system must move 6.0 m to lift a 3000-N engine a distance of 0.50 m. What is the IMA of the system? Show your work.

4. A 16-N force applied to the handle of a door produces a 30-N output force. What is the AMA of the handle? Show your work.

5. A force of 12 N is applied to the handle of a screwdriver being used to pry off the lid of a paint can. As the force moves through a distance 0.3 m, the screwdriver does 32 J of work on the lid. What is the efficiency of the screwdriver? Show your work.

Chapter Test B

Name ______________________ Class ________________ Date ___________

Chapter 14 Work, Power, and Machines — Chapter Test B

Multiple Choice

Write the letter that best answers the question or completes the statement on the line provided.

____ **1.** In which of the following is no work done?
a. climbing stairs
b. lifting a book
c. pushing a shopping cart
d. none of the above

____ **2.** What is the unit of work?
a. joule **b.** newton/meter
c. watt **d.** all of the above

____ **3.** The SI unit of power is the
a. joule. **b.** newton.
c. newton-meter. **d.** watt.

____ **4.** The power of a machine measures
a. its rate of doing work. **b.** its strength.
c. the force it produces. **d.** the work it does.

____ **5.** About 746 watts equals how many horsepower?
a. one **b.** two
c. four **d.** six

____ **6.** A machine is a device that can multiply
a. force. **b.** power.
c. work. **d.** all of the above

____ **7.** How can a machine make work easier for you?
a. by decreasing the amount of work you do
b. by changing the direction of your force
c. by increasing the work done by the machine
d. none of the above

____ **8.** The actual mechanical advantage of a machine
a. cannot be less than 1.
b. decreases as the input distance increases.
c. increases with greater friction.
d. is less than the ideal mechanical advantage of the machine.

____ **9.** If you have to apply 30 N of force on a crowbar to lift an rock that weights 330 N, what is the actual mechanical advantage of the crowbar?
a. 0.09 **b.** 11
c. 300 **d.** 9900

Physical Science • Chapter 14 Test B 147

Chapter Test B

Name ______________________ Class ________________ Date ___________

____ **10.** Reducing friction in a machine
a. decreases its actual mechanical advantage.
b. decreases the work output.
c. increases its efficiency.
d. increases its ideal mechanical advantage.

____ **11.** A mechanical device requires 400 J of work to do 340 J of work in lifting a crate. What is the efficiency of the device?
a. 0.9% **b.** 60%
c. 85% **d.** 118%

____ **12.** An inclined plane reduces the effort force by
a. increasing the distance through which the force is applied.
b. increasing the work.
c. reducing the effort distance.
d. reducing the work.

____ **13.** An ax is an example of a(an)
a. inclined plane. **b.** lever.
c. wedge. **d.** wheel and axle.

____ **14.** The ideal mechanical advantage of a pulley system is equal to the
a. distance the load has to move.
b. length of the rope.
c. number of rope segments supporting the load.
d. weight of the object being lifted.

____ **15.** The ideal mechanical advantage of a wheel and axle is found by
a. multiplying the circumference of the wheel by the radius of the axle.
b. dividing the radius of the wheel by the radius of the axle.
c. dividing the radius of the axle by the radius of the wheel.
d. multiplying the radius of the wheel by the radius of the axle.

____ **16.** An example of a compound machine is a
a. crowbar. **b.** bicycle.
c. ramp. **d.** seesaw.

Completion

Complete each statement on the line provided.

1. For work to be done on an object, the object has to ________________.
2. The SI unit of work is the ________________.
3. The rate at which work is done is called ________________.

148 *Physical Science* • Chapter 14 Test B

Chapter Test B

Name ______________________ Class ________________ Date ___________

4. The SI unit of power is the ________________.
5. A machine is a device that changes a(an) ________________.
6. The force that is exerted on a machine is called the ________________ force.
7. The ________________ of a machine is the number of times that the machine increases the input force.
8. A(An) ________________ can be described as an inclined plane wrapped around a cylinder.
9. The ideal mechanical advantage of a third-class lever is always ________________ than 1.
10. Two or more simple machines working together make up a(an) ________________ machine.

Short Answer

In complete sentences, write the answers to the questions on the lines provided.

1. How is work done when you lift a book?

2. Why don't you do work as you hold a book motionless over your head?

3. If a simple machine provides an increased output force, what happens to the output distance?

4. Which has the greater IMA—a screw with closely spaced threads or a screw with threads spaced farther apart?

Physical Science • Chapter 14 Test B 149

Chapter Test B

Name ______________________ Class ________________ Date ___________

5. How is a pair of scissors a compound machine? Explain your answer.

Using Science Skills

Use the diagram to answer each question. Write the answers on a separate sheet of paper.

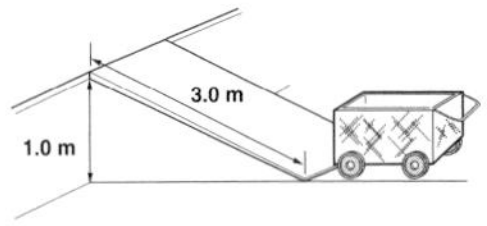

Figure 14-2

1. **Calculating** What is the IMA of the ramp in Figure 14-2? Show your work.
2. **Applying Concepts** If the ramp shown in Figure 14-2 was coated with a smoother surface, how would the AMA of the ramp change?
3. **Applying Concepts** If the ramp shown in Figure 14-2 was coated with a smoother surface, how would the ramp's efficiency change? Explain your answer.
4. **Classifying** What type of simple machine is the ramp shown in Figure 14-2?
5. **Comparing and Contrasting** In a post office, a 3-m long ramp is used to move carts onto a dock that is higher than 1 m. How does the IMA of this ramp compare with the IMA of the ramp shown in Figure 14-2?

150 *Physical Science* • Chapter 14 Test B

Chapter 14 Test A Answers

Multiple Choice

1. b	**2.** b	**3.** c	**4.** b	**5.** c	**6.** b
7. d	**8.** d	**9.** d	**10.** b	**11.** b	**12.** c
13. b	**14.** c				

Completion

1. work **2.** motion **3.** power **4.** decreases **5.** lever

Short Answer

1. The swimmer that swims faster develops more power only if both swimmers do the same amount of work. **2.** Some of work input is used to overcome friction. **3.** They would be equal. **4.** A fixed pulley changes only the direction of the input force. A movable pulley changes both the direction of the input force and its size. **5.** The work output of the first simple machine is the work input of the second simple machine.

Using Science Skills

1. 1.0 m **2.** wheel and axle **3.** 4 **4.** a compound machine **5.** The work out of Machine B equals the work output of Machine A.

Problem

1. Work = Force × Distance = 220N × 10m = 220N•m = 2200J; Work = 2200J

2. $\text{Power} = \dfrac{\text{Work}}{\text{Time}} = \dfrac{\text{Force} \times \text{Distance}}{\text{Time}} = \dfrac{100\text{N} \times 2.0\text{m}}{1\text{s}} = 200\ \dfrac{\text{J}}{\text{s}} = 200\text{W};$ Power = 200W

3. $\text{IMA} = \dfrac{\text{Input distance}}{\text{Output distance}} = \dfrac{6.0\text{m}}{0.50\text{m}} = 12;$ IMA = 12

4. $\text{AMA} = \dfrac{\text{Output force}}{\text{Input force}} = \dfrac{30\text{N}}{16\text{N}} = 1.9;$ AMA = 1.9

5. $\text{Efficiency} = \dfrac{\text{Work output}}{\text{Work input}} \times 100\% = \dfrac{\text{Work output}}{\text{Input force} \times \text{Input distance}} \times 100\%$

$\text{Efficiency} = \dfrac{32\text{J}}{12\text{N} \times 0.3\text{m}} \times 100\% = \dfrac{32\text{J}}{36\text{N•m}} \times 100\% = \dfrac{32\text{J}}{36\text{J}} \times 100\% = 89\%;$ Efficiency = 89%

Chapter 14 Test B Answers

Multiple Choice

1. d	**2.** a	**3.** a	**4.** a	**5.** a	**6.** a
7. b	**8.** d	**9.** b	**10.** c	**11.** c	**12.** a
13. c	**14.** c	**15.** b	**16.** b		

Completion

1. move **2.** joule **3.** power **4.** watt **5.** force **6.** input **7.** mechanical advantage **8.** screw **9.** less **10.** compound

Short Answer

1. Work is done because a force is applied in the direction in which the book moves. **2.** There is no movement, so no work is done. **3.** The simple machine reduces the output distance. **4.** the screw with closely spaced threads **5.** A pair of scissors contains two simple machines working together. Each arm is a first-class lever with a wedge, which is the blade, at one end.

Using Science Skills

1. $\text{Ideal mechanical advantage} = \dfrac{\text{Input distance}}{\text{Output distance}} = \dfrac{3\text{m}}{1\text{m}} = 3$

2. The ramp's AMA would increase. **3.** Its efficiency would increase; friction would decrease. **4.** an inclined plane **5.** It is less.

Chapter 15 Energy

Planning Guide

Use these planning tools
Easy Planner
Resource Pro
Online Lesson Planner

SECTION OBJECTIVES	STANDARDS		ACTIVITIES and LABS
	NATIONAL (See p. T18.)	**STATE**	
15.1 Energy and Its Forms, pp. 446–452 ⏱ 1 block or 2 periods **15.1.1 Describe** the relationship between work and energy. **15.1.2 Relate** kinetic energy to mass and speed and **calculate** these quantities. **15.1.3 Analyze** how potential energy is related to an object's position and **give examples** of gravitational and elastic potential energy. **15.1.4 Solve equations** that relate an object's gravitational potential energy to its mass and height. **15.1.5 Give examples** of the major forms of energy and **explain** how each is produced.	A-1, A-2, B-1, B-3, B-4, B-5, B-6		**SE** Inquiry Activity: How Can Energy Change Form? p. 445 L2 **SE** Quick Lab: Investigating Elastic Potential Energy, p. 450 L2 **TE** Teacher Demo: Burning a Peanut, p. 451 L2 **LM** Investigation 15A: Determining the Effect of Mass on Kinetic Energy L2
15.2 Energy Conversion and Conservation, pp. 453–459 ⏱ 1 block or 2 periods **15.2.1 Describe** conversions of energy from one form to another. **15.2.2 State** and **apply** the law of conservation of energy. **15.2.3 Analyze** how energy is conserved in conversions between kinetic energy and potential energy and **solve equations** that equate initial energy to final energy. **15.2.4 Describe** the relationship between energy and mass and **calculate** how much energy is equivalent to a given mass.	A-1, A-2, B-5, G-1, G-2, G-3		**SE** Quick Lab: Exploring Energy Conversion, p. 454 L2 **SE** Application Lab: Investigating a Spring Clip, p. 467 L2 **TE** Teacher Demo: Energy in a Pendulum, p. 456 L2 **LM** Investigation 15B: Determining the Kinetic Energy of a Pendulum L1
15.3 Energy Resources, pp. 462–466 ⏱ 1 block or 2 periods **15.3.1 Classify** energy resources as renewable or nonrenewable. **15.3.2 Evaluate** benefits and drawbacks of different energy sources. **15.3.3 Describe** ways to conserve energy resources.	A-1, A-2, B-5, D-1, F-2, F-3, F-4		**TE** Teacher Demo: Simple Solar Cell, p. 464 L2

Ability Levels

L1 For students who need additional help
L2 For all students
L3 For students who need to be challenged

Components

SE Student Edition
TE Teacher's Edition
LM Laboratory Manual
PLM Probeware Lab Manual

GRSW Guided Reading & Study Workbook With Math Support
CUT Chapter and Unit Tests

CTB Computer Test Bank
TP Test Prep Resources
iT iText
DC Discovery Channel Videotapes

T Transparencies
P Presentation Pro CD-ROM
GO Internet Resources

RESOURCES PRINT and TECHNOLOGY	SECTION ASSESSMENT
GRSW Section 15.1 **L1**	**SE** Section 15.1 Assessment, p. 452
GRSW Math Skill **L2**	
T Chapter 15 Pretest **L2**	**iText** **iT** Section 15.1
Section 15.1 **L2**	
P Chapter 15 Pretest **L2**	
Section 15.1 **L2**	
NSTA *sci*LINKS **GO** Potential and kinetic energy **L2**	
PLM Lab 6: Investigating a Spring Clip **L2**	**SE** Section 15.2 Assessment, p. 459
GRSW Section 15.2 **L1**	**iText** **iT** Section 15.2
Discovery SCHOOL **DC** Physics of Fun **L2**	
T Section 15.2 **L2**	
P Section 15.2 **L2**	
NSTA *sci*LINKS **GO** Energy **L2**	
PHSchool.com **GO** Data sharing **L2**	
GRSW Section 15.3 **L1**	**SE** Section 15.3 Assessment, p. 466
T Section 15.3 **L2**	**iText** **iT** Section 15.3
P Section 15.3 **L2**	
SCIENCE NEWS **GO** Energy and energy resources **L2**	

Go Online

Go online for these Internet resources.

PHSchool.com
Web Code: ccd-2150
Web Code: cca-2150

SCIENCE NEWS
Web Code: cce-2153

NSTA *SCI*LINKS
Web Code: ccn-2151
Web Code: ccn-2152

Materials for Activities and Labs

Quantities for each group

STUDENT EDITION

Inquiry Activity, p. 445
flashlight, solar calculator, wind-up toy; other items may be substituted if the three listed in the Procedure are not available. Alternatives include a wind-up alarm clock, electric alarm clock, jack-in-the-box, radio, or CD player.

Quick Lab, p. 450
basketball, tennis ball, meter stick

Quick Lab, p. 454
small steel ball of known mass, box lined with soft modeling clay, meter stick, graph paper

Application Lab, p. 467
clamp, spring clip, masking tape, metric ruler, 50-newton spring scale, graph paper

TEACHER'S EDITION

Teacher Demo, p. 451
peanut, paper clip, pliers, pan of water, matches, safety goggles

Teacher Demo, p. 456
pendulum bob and string, hook at top of board, chalk (or marker), level

Build Science Skills, p. 461
flexible track (like the bendable tracks used for toy cars), steel balls, books or wooden supports

Teacher Demo, p. 464
small solar array, small motor with fan, direct sunlight or bright light source

Chapter Assessment

CHAPTER ASSESSMENT

SE Chapter Assessment, pp. 469–470
CUT Chapter 15 Test A
Chapter 15 Test B
CTB Chapter 15
iT Chapter 15
PHSchool.com GO
Web Code: cca-2150

STANDARDIZED TEST PREP

SE Chapter 15, p. 471
TP Diagnose and Prescribe

iText

iText—interactive textbook with assessment at PHSchool.com

Energy **444B**

Section 15.1 Lesson Plan

LESSON PLAN 15.1

Energy and Its Forms

Time
2 periods
1 block

Section Objectives

Local Standards

- **15.1.1 Describe** the relationship between work and energy.
- **15.1.2 Relate** kinetic energy to mass and speed and **calculate** these quantities.
- **15.1.3 Analyze** how potential energy is related to an object's position and **give examples** of gravitational and elastic potential energy.
- **15.1.4 Solve equations** that relate an object's gravitational potential energy to its mass and height.
- **15.1.5 Give examples** of the major forms of energy and **explain** how each is produced.

Vocabulary energy • kinetic energy • potential energy • gravitational potential energy • elastic potential energy • mechanical energy • thermal energy • chemical energy • electrical energy • electromagnetic energy • nuclear energy

1 FOCUS

Build Vocabulary: Separating Compound Terms

Have students list the word or words modifying *energy* in each vocabulary term, and then state or guess the meaning of each modifier. Ask students to check the meanings after they have read the section. **L2**

Targeted Resources

- ❑ Transparency: Chapter 15 Pretest
- ❑ Transparency: Interest Grabber 15.1
- ❑ Transparency: Reading Strategy 15.1

2 INSTRUCT

Build Reading Literacy: Outline

Have students create an outline of pages 446–452, following the head structure used in the section. **L1**

Address Misconceptions

Remind students that, while a stationary object has no kinetic energy, it can have potential energy if there are forces acting on it. **L2**

Quick Lab: Investigating Elastic Potential Energy

Students drop a basketball and a tennis ball—first separately, then together—and record their observations. **L2**

Teacher Demo: Burning a Peanut

Burn a peanut to show students that food contains chemical energy. **L2**

For Enrichment

Have students research the slingshot effect and how this effect uses the gravitational potential energy of space probes. **L3**

Targeted Resources

- ❑ Transparency: Math Skills: Calculating Kinetic Energy
- ❑ GRSW Section 15.1
- ❑ **NSTA** *sci*$_{LINKS}$ Potential and kinetic energy

3 ASSESS

Reteach

Discuss the types of energy that Figures 3–8 illustrate. **L1**

Evaluate Understanding

Give students various examples and ask them to list at least two kinds of energy in the objects. **L2**

Targeted Resources

- ❑ **PHSchool.com** Online Section 15.1 Assessment
- ❑ iText Section 15.1

211 Chapter 15 Pretest

1. How much work is done when a weightlifter holds a barbell motionless over his head?

2. Calculate the work done on a 2-N mass when it is lifted to a height of 2 m.

3. Calculate the average speed of a bicycle that travels 100 m in 20 s.

4. Is weight a force? What is the formula for calculating weight?

5. How does the temperature of an object change when it is acted on by friction?

6. True or False: In a closed system, the loss of momentum of one object equals the gain in momentum of another object.

ANSWERS
1. No work is done.
2. 4 J
3. 5 m/s
4. Yes. $W = mg$.
5. the temperature increases
6. True

212 Chapter 15 Pretest (continued)

7. How is power related to work?

8. True or False: The amount of work done on a machine (work in) always equals the amount of work done by the machine (work out).

7. Power is the rate at which work is done.
8. False

213 Section 15.1 Interest Grabber

How Is Energy Related to Work?

Energy is defined as the ability to do work. Recall that work is the product of force and distance. If a force acts through a greater distance, it has done more work. You can use work to measure changes in energy.

Place two identical books on a table so there is a gap of about 8 cm between the books. Place a sheet of notebook paper on the books so it covers the gap as shown. Now drop a penny from a height of 10 cm onto the paper above the gap. Note what happens. Next, drop the penny from a height of 30 cm and observe the results.

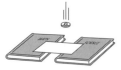

1. How did the height of the penny affect the distance the paper moved?

2. How did lifting the penny affect the work it did on the paper?

3. How did lifting the penny affect its energy?

ANSWERS
1. The paper moved farther when the penny was dropped from a greater height.
2. Lifting the penny allowed it to do more work on the paper.
3. Lifting the penny increased the penny's energy.

214 Section 15.1 Reading Strategy

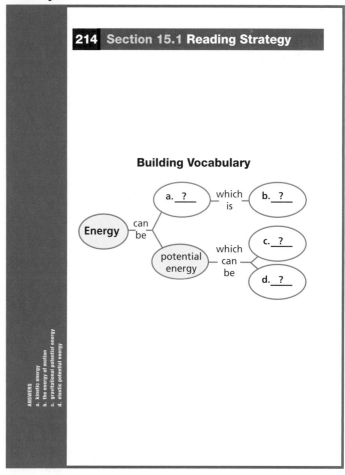

Building Vocabulary

ANSWERS
a. kinetic energy
b. the energy of motion
c. gravitational potential energy
d. elastic potential energy

Transparencies

Math Skills

Calculating Kinetic Energy

A 0.10-kilogram bird is flying at a constant speed of 8.0 m/s. What is the bird's kinetic energy?

1 Read and Understand

What information are you given?

Mass, $m = 0.10$ kg   Speed, $v = 8.0$ m/s

What unknown are you trying to calculate?

Kinetic energy of the bird, KE

2 Plan and Solve

What equation contains the given quantities and the unknown?

$$KE = \frac{1}{2}mv^2$$

Substitute the known values in the formula for KE.

$$KE = \frac{1}{2}(0.10 \text{ kg})(8.0 \text{ m/s})^2$$

$$= 3.2 \text{ kg·m}^2/\text{s}^2 = 3.2 \text{ J}$$

3 Look Back and Check

Is your answer reasonable?

It seems reasonable because the bird has a low mass, so it would not have much kinetic energy.

Guided Reading and Study Workbook

Name _____ Class _____ Date _____

Chapter 15   Energy

Section 15.1 Energy and Its Forms
(pages 446–452)

This section describes how energy and work are related. Kinetic energy and potential energy are defined, and examples are shown for calculating these forms of energy. Examples of various types of energy are discussed.

Reading Strategy (page 446)

Building Vocabulary As you read, complete the concept map with vocabulary terms and definitions from this section. For more information on this Reading Strategy, see the **Reading and Study Skills** in the **Skills and Reference Handbook** at the end of your textbook.

Energy and Work (page 447)

1. What is energy? Energy is the ability to do work.
2. When work is done on an object, _____energy_____ is transferred to that object.
3. Circle the letter of each sentence that is true about work and energy.
   (a.) Energy in food is converted into muscle movement.
   (b.) Energy is transferred when work is done.
   (c.) Both work and energy are usually measured in joules.
   d. One joule equals one meter per newton.

Kinetic Energy (pages 447–448)

4. The energy of motion is called _____kinetic energy_____.
5. Is the following sentence true or false? You can determine the kinetic energy of an object if you know its mass and its volume. ____false____
6. Write the formula used to calculate an object's kinetic energy.
   Kinetic energy = 1/2 mv²
7. Calculate the kinetic energy of a 0.25-kg toy car traveling at a constant velocity of 2 m/s.
   KE = 1/2 mv² = 1/2 (0.25 kg)(2.0 m/s)² = 0.5 kg·m²/s² = 0.5 J

Guided Reading and Study Workbook

Name _____ Class _____ Date _____

Chapter 15   Energy

Potential Energy (pages 448–450)

8. What is potential energy? It is energy that is stored as a result of position or shape.

9. Is the following sentence true or false? The work done by a rock climber going up a cliff decreases her potential energy. ____false____

10. An object's gravitational potential energy depends on its ____mass____, its ____height____, and the acceleration due to gravity.

11. Is the following sentence true or false? Gravitational potential energy of an object increases as its height increases. ____true____

12. The potential energy of an object that is stretched or compressed is known as ____elastic potential energy____

13. Complete the table about potential energy.

Potential Energy		
Type	**Description**	**Example**
Gravitational	Objects raised to heights relative to a reference level	Diver on a platform high above the water
Elastic	Stretched or compressed objects	A guitar string stretched to one side

Forms of Energy (pages 450–452)

For numbers 14 through 19, write the letter of the form of energy that best matches the description.

Descriptions	Forms of Energy
__b__ 14. Energy stored in gasoline, coal, and wood	a. mechanical energy
__a__ 15. The sum of an object's potential energy and kinetic energy, excluding atomic-scale movements	b. chemical energy
	c. electrical energy
__e__ 16. Produces the sun's heat and light	d. thermal energy
__f__ 17. Travels through space in the form of waves	e. nuclear energy
__c__ 18. Produces lightning bolts	f. electromagnetic energy
__d__ 19. Increases as atoms within an object move faster	

Name_____ Class_____ Date_____ M T W T F

LESSON PLAN 15.2

Energy Conversion and Conservation

Time
2 periods
1 block

Section Objectives

- **15.2.1 Describe** conversions of energy from one form to another.
- **15.2.2 State** and **apply** the law of conservation of energy.
- **15.2.3 Analyze** how energy is conserved in conversions between kinetic energy and potential energy and **solve equations** that equate initial energy to final energy.
- **15.2.4 Describe** the relationship between energy and mass and **calculate** how much energy is equivalent to a given mass.

Vocabulary energy conversion

Local Standards

1 FOCUS

Build Vocabulary: Paraphrasing
Ask students to describe situations where conversions take place, identifying the previous form or state and the new form or state. **L2**

Targeted Resources
❏ Transparency: Interest Grabber 15.2
❏ Transparency: Reading Strategy 15.2

2 INSTRUCT

Use Visuals: Figure 14
Use Figure 14 to ask students about the various types of energy illustrated. **L1**

Quick Lab: Exploring Energy Conversion
Have students drop a small steel ball into a box of clay; measure and record the diameter of the craters that the ball formed; and graph their data. **L2**

Teacher Demo: Energy in a Pendulum
Swing a pendulum, and have students use the law of conservation of energy to predict and explain the motion of the pendulum. **L2**

Address Misconceptions
Have students rub their hands together rapidly for a few seconds in order to demonstrate how kinetic energy is converted into thermal energy and sound. **L2**

Build Science Skills: Calculating
Have students use Einstein's mass-energy equation to calculate the energy equivalence of an electron and of their own body. **L2**

Targeted Resources
❏ Transparency: Math Skills: Conservation of Energy
❏ GRSW Section 15.2
❏ **NSTA** sc*i*_{LINKS} Energy

3 ASSESS

Reteach
Discuss the energy conversions that are taking place in Figures 10–14. **L1**

Evaluate Understanding
Ask students to describe systems or situations in which energy conversions are taking place. **L2**

Targeted Resources
❏ **PHSchool.com** Online Section 15.2 Assessment
❏ iText Section 15.2

Transparencies

216 **Section 15.2 Interest Grabber**

How Can Energy Change Forms?

Have you even seen a Rube Goldberg device? Goldberg was an award-winning cartoonist who drew complex series of devices that performed relatively simple acts. The devices were arranged so that the output of one device would act as the input of the next. Goldberg became so well known for his drawings that people all over the world hold contests to see who can build the most complicated device. Study the Rube Goldberg cartoon below and answer the questions.

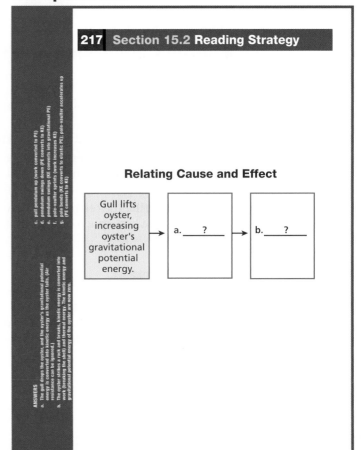

Rube Goldberg, Inc.

1. List at least three kinds of energy in the device.

2. Describe one change, in which energy from one form is converted into energy of another form.

ANSWERS
1. There is kinetic energy, chemical energy, and gravitational potential energy.
2. The chemical energy of the cannon is converted into the kinetic energy of the peanut.

Transparencies

217 **Section 15.2 Reading Strategy**

Relating Cause and Effect

| Gull lifts oyster, increasing oyster's gravitational potential energy. | → | a. ___?___ | → | b. ___?___ |

ANSWERS
c. pull pendulum up (work converted to PE)
d. pendulum swings down (PE converts to KE)
d. pendulum swings (KE converts into gravitational PE)
f. pole-vaulter sprints (work increases KE)
g. pole bends (KE converts to elastic PE); pole-vaulter accelerates up (PE converts to KE)

ANSWERS
a. The gull drops the oyster, and the oyster's gravitational potential energy is converted into kinetic energy as the oyster falls. (Air resistance can be ignored.)
b. The oyster strikes a rock and breaks, kinetic energy is converted into work (breaking the shell) and thermal energy. The kinetic energy and gravitational potential energy of the oyster are now zero.

Transparencies

218 **Math Skills Conservation of Energy**

Conservation of Mechanical Energy

At a construction site, a 1.50-kg brick is dropped from rest and hits the ground at a speed of 26.0 m/s. Assuming air resistance can be ignored, calculate the gravitational potential energy of the brick before it was dropped.

 Read and Understand

What information are you given?

Mass, $m = 1.50$ kg   Final speed, $v = 26.0$ m/s

What unknown are you trying to calculate?

Gravitational potential energy of the brick before it was dropped, PE

 Plan and Solve

What equations or formulas contain the given quantities and the unknown?

Because the brick falls without air resistance, the conservation of mechanical energy equation can be used.

$$(KE + PE)_{beginning} = (KE + PE)_{end}$$

Transparencies

219 **Math Skills Conservation of Energy** *(continued)*

You will also need to use the formula for kinetic energy (KE).

$$KE = \frac{1}{2}mv^2$$

Note that the KE at the beginning is zero because the brick has not yet begun to fall. Also, when the brick hits the ground, its potential energy is zero. Substitute these values into the conservation of energy formula.

$$(PE)_{beginning} = (KE)_{end}$$

Substitute the formula for KE.

$$PE = KE = \frac{1}{2}mv^2$$

Substitute the known values and calculate the PE.

$$PE = \frac{1}{2}(1.50\,kg)(26.0\,m/s)^2 = 507\,kg\cdot m^2/s^2 = 507\,J$$

3 **Look Back and Check**

Is your answer reasonable?

Check the answer by finding the initial height of the brick, using PE = 507 J = mgh. Substituting in m and g gives $h = 34.5$ m. This is a reasonable height for an object in free fall to reach a speed of 26.0 m/s.

Name _____ Class _____ Date _____

Chapter 15   Energy

Section 15.2 Energy Conversion and Conservation
(pages 453–459)

This section describes how energy is converted from one form to another. The law of conservation of energy also is presented.

Reading Strategy (page 453)

Relating Cause and Effect As you read, complete the flowchart to explain an energy conversion used by some gulls to obtain food. For more information on this Reading Strategy, see the **Reading and Study Skills** in the **Skills and Reference Handbook** at the end of your textbook.

How Gulls Use Energy Conversions

| Gull lifts oyster, increasing oyster's gravitational potential energy. | → | The gull drops the oyster, and the oyster's gravitational potential energy is converted into kinetic energy as the oyster falls. (Air resistance can be ignored.) | → | The oyster strikes a rock and breaks, kinetic energy is converted into thermal energy. The kinetic energy and gravitational potential energy of the oyster are now zero. |

Energy Conversion (page 454)

1. Is the following sentence true or false? Energy can be converted from one form to another. _____true_____

2. When a wind-up toy is set in motion, elastic potential energy that was stored in a compressed spring is converted into the _____kinetic energy_____ of the toy's moving parts.

3. Is the following sentence true or false? The action of striking a match shows that stored chemical energy in the match can be converted into thermal energy and electromagnetic energy of the flame in a single step. _____false_____

Conservation of Energy (page 455)

4. What does the law of conservation of energy state? _Energy cannot be created or destroyed._

5. Is the following sentence true or false? When an object slows down because of frictional force acting on it, an amount of energy is destroyed that is equivalent to the decrease in kinetic energy of the object. _____false_____

6. A moving object slows down because friction causes a continual conversion of kinetic energy into _____thermal energy_____.

Name _____ Class _____ Date _____

Chapter 15   Energy

Energy Conversions (pages 456–458)

7. As an object falls, the gravitational potential energy of the object is converted into _____kinetic energy_____.

8. Circle the letter of each sentence that is true about pendulums.
   a. A pendulum consists of a weight suspended from a string that swings back and forth.
   b. The weight at the end of a pendulum reaches maximum kinetic energy at the highest point in the pendulum's swing.
   c. Potential energy and kinetic energy undergo constant conversion as a pendulum swings.
   d. Frictional forces enable a pendulum to continue swinging without slowing down.

9. At what point during a pole-vaulter's jump is his gravitational potential energy the greatest? _It is greatest at the highest point of the jump._

10. Circle the letter of the type of energy that increases as the pole bends before it propels a pole-vaulter up into the air.
    a. kinetic energy
    b. mechanical energy
    c. frictional force
    d. elastic potential energy

11. Is the following sentence true or false? For a mechanical change in an isolated system, the mechanical energy at the beginning equals the mechanical energy at the end of the process, as long as friction is negligible. _____true_____

12. Tell whether the following situations illustrate *kinetic energy, potential energy,* or *both.*

What Type of Energy Is It?	
Situation	**Form of Energy**
A stationary wind-up toy with a compressed spring	Potential energy
A descending roller coaster car	Both
A skier poised to take off at the top of a hill	Potential energy
A car driving on a flat road	Kinetic energy
A vibrating guitar string	Both

Energy and Mass (page 459)

13. What does Einstein's equation imply about mass and energy? _Mass and energy are equivalent, and mass and energy can be converted into each other._

14. Is the following sentence true or false? Einstein's equation, $E = mc^2$, suggests that mass and energy together are conserved. _____true_____

Name_____ Class_____ Date_____ M T W T F

LESSON PLAN 15.3

Energy Resources

Time
2 periods
1 block

Section Objectives

- **15.3.1 Classify** energy resources as renewable or nonrenewable.
- **15.3.2 Evaluate** benefits and drawbacks of different energy sources.
- **15.3.3 Describe** ways to conserve energy resources.

Vocabulary nonrenewable energy resources • fossil fuels • renewable energy resources • hydroelectric energy • solar energy • geothermal energy • biomass energy • hydrogen fuel cell • energy conservation

Local Standards

---

1 FOCUS

Build Vocabulary: Word-Part Analysis
Ask students what words they know that contain the key word parts *geo-* and *bio-*. **L2**

Targeted Resources
❏ Transparency: Interest Grabber 15.3
❏ Transparency: Reading Strategy 15.3

---

2 INSTRUCT

Build Reading Literacy: Compare and Contrast
Have students compare and contrast renewable energy resources. **L1**

Teacher Demo: Simple Solar Cell
Place a solar array (attached to a motor) in direct sunlight in order to demonstrate energy conversions and renewable resources. **L2**

Use Community Resources
Have students contact the local electric company and ask what kind of power plant(s) it uses and if the company uses any renewable energy resources. **L2**

Build Science Skills: Analyzing Data
Have students examine a monthly electricity bill to find the energy usage. Ask students to convert the usage from kilowatt-hours to joules. **L2**

For Enrichment
Have students research large offshore wind farms currently in use or in development. Ask students to include their findings in a written report or a class presentation. **L3**

Targeted Resources
❏ Transparency: How It Works: Wind Turbines
❏ GRSW Section 15.3

---

3 ASSESS

Reteach
Have each student review an energy resource. Have them work in pairs and discuss the pros and cons of the resource that they reviewed. **L1**

Evaluate Understanding
Ask students to state the fundamental difference between renewable and nonrenewable energy resources and list examples of each. **L2**

Targeted Resources
❏ **PHSchool.com** Online Section 15.3 Assessment
❏ iText Section 15.3

---

220 Section 15.3 Interest Grabber

Using Wind and Water

Wind and water are two useful sources of energy found in nature.

You can demonstrate how these energy sources are converted into kinetic energy by making a model of a windmill or a water wheel. Tape a pencil to an index card. Hold the pencil loosely at both ends. Blow onto one side of the index card and observe what happens. Next, hold the index card above a bucket. Have a classmate pour water from a pitcher onto one side of the index card.

1. What happened when you blew into the card? What happened when you held the card under running water?

2. How do you think people used the kinetic energy of a water wheel or a windmill to grind corn or other kinds of grain?

ANSWERS
1. The moving air and water caused the card and pencil to rotate.
2. Accept any reasonable answers. The kinetic energy of the windmill or water wheel probably turned gears, which caused a mill stone to turn.

221 Section 15.3 Reading Strategy

Identifying Main Ideas

Heading	Main Idea
Nonrenewable energy resources	a. _____?_____
Renewable energy resources	b. _____?_____
Conserving energy resources	c. _____?_____

ANSWERS
a. Nonrenewable energy resources include oil, natural gas and coal. They exist in limited quantities.
b. Renewable energy resources include hydroelectric, solar, geothermal, wind, biomass, and nuclear fusion.
c. Energy resources can be conserved by reducing energy needs and by increasing the efficiency of energy use.

222 How It Works Wind Turbine

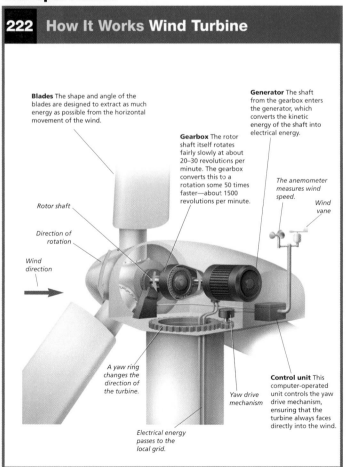

Blades The shape and angle of the blades are designed to extract as much energy as possible from the horizontal movement of the wind.

Gearbox The rotor shaft itself rotates fairly slowly at about 20–30 revolutions per minute. The gearbox converts this to a rotation some 50 times faster—about 1500 revolutions per minute.

Generator The shaft from the gearbox enters the generator, which converts the kinetic energy of the shaft into electrical energy.

The anemometer measures wind speed.

Wind vane

Rotor shaft

Direction of rotation

Wind direction

A yaw ring changes the direction of the turbine.

Yaw drive mechanism

Control unit This computer-operated unit controls the yaw drive mechanism, ensuring that the turbine always faces directly into the wind.

Electrical energy passes to the local grid.

Guided Reading and Study Workbook

Name _____ Class _____ Date _____

Chapter 15   Energy

Section 15.3 Energy Resources
(pages 462–466)
This section describes types of energy resources and ways to conserve them.

Reading Strategy (page 462)
Identifying Main Ideas As you read the section, write the main idea for each heading in the table. For more information on this Reading Strategy, see the **Reading and Study Skills** in the **Skills and Reference Handbook** at the end of your textbook.

Heading	Main Idea
Nonrenewable energy resources	Nonrenewable energy resources include oil, natural gas, and coal. They exist in limited quantities.
Renewable energy resources	Renewable energy resources include hydroelectric, solar, geothermal, wind, biomass, and nuclear fusion.
Conserving energy resources	Energy resources can be conserved by reducing energy needs and by increasing the efficiency of energy use.

Nonrenewable Energy Resources (page 462)
1. What are nonrenewable energy resources? They are resources that exist in limited quantities and, once used, cannot be replaced except over the course of millions of years.

2. List four examples of nonrenewable energy resources.
a. Oil   b. Natural gas
c. Coal   d. Uranium

3. Circle the letter of each resource that is considered to be a fossil fuel.
a. tree
b. uranium
c. oil
d. coal

4. Is the following sentence true or false? Although fossil fuels are evenly distributed throughout Earth, they only represent ten percent of total energy consumed. false

5. What are some advantages and disadvantages of using fossil fuels as a source of energy? Fossil fuels are relatively inexpensive and are usually readily available, but their use creates pollution.

Renewable Energy Resources (pages 463–464)
6. An energy resource that can be replaced in a reasonably short period of time is called a(n) renewable resource.

Physical Science Guided Reading and Study Workbook • Chapter 15 **135**

Guided Reading and Study Workbook

Name _____ Class _____ Date _____

Chapter 15   Energy

7. Circle the letter of each sentence that is true about renewable energy resources.
a. Wind and solar energy are both renewable energy resources.
b. Renewable energy resources are always more efficient than nonrenewable resources.
c. Renewable energy resources can be used to generate electricity and to heat homes.
d. Magma generates most renewable energy, either directly or indirectly.

8. Describe one energy conversion that takes place during the generation of hydroelectric power. Potential energy of water behind a dam is converted to kinetic energy upon release of the water.

9. Is the following sentence true or false? One disadvantage of hydroelectric power is that it is among the most expensive energy sources. false

For numbers 10 through 15, match the letter of each renewable energy source to its description.

Description	Renewable Energy Sources
c **10.** Water pumped below ground is converted to steam.	a. hydroelectric
f **11.** The most likely raw material is hydrogen.	b. solar
b **12.** Mirrors concentrate sunlight to produce electricity.	c. geothermal
d **13.** Kinetic energy of moving air is converted into rotational energy of a turbine.	d. wind
a **14.** Energy is obtained from flowing water.	e. biomass
e **15.** Chemical energy stored in wood, peat, and agricultural waste can be converted into thermal energy.	f. nuclear fusion

16. Is the following sentence true or false? Hydrogen fuel cells generate electricity by combining hydrogen with oxygen. true

Conserving Energy Resources (page 466)
17. What are two ways that energy resources can be conserved? Energy resources can be conserved by reducing energy needs and by increasing the efficiency of energy use.

18. Name two practical ways in which people can conserve energy. Accept reasonable responses, such as carpooling, walking or biking on short trips, using more efficient appliances, developing and driving more fuel-efficient cars.

136 *Physical Science* Guided Reading and Study Workbook • Chapter 15

Guided Reading and Study Workbook

Name _____ Class _____ Date _____

Chapter 15   Energy

WordWise
Complete the sentences by using one of the scrambled vocabulary words below.

absoism reegny	ynrege vnsnoorctaie	slisfo sluef
rslao eeyngr	neegyr seonoscvri	caurnle rygnee
mrelhta eeryng	loptnieat nygeer	gyreen
mcelhaci reeyng	ctniiek yenrge	rvtnatgialoai

When an object is raised to a higher level, its gravitational potential energy increases.

The motion of microscopic particles in matter partly determines the amount of thermal energy within it.

As a pole-vaulter springs higher into the air, her kinetic energy decreases as her gravitational potential energy increases. This is an example of energy conversion.

Atomic fission and fusion produce nuclear energy.

When your muscles move, chemical energy from the cereal you ate for breakfast is converted into kinetic energy.

The potential energy of a 100-kg boulder perched high on a cliff is greater than that of a 50-kg boulder at the same height.

You can recognize energy by the changes it causes, such as motion and sound.

Formed from the remains of once-living organisms, fossil fuels are nonrenewable energy resources.

Photovoltaic cells convert solar energy into electrical energy.

Methods of energy conservation include ways to reduce energy needs.

When you sit around a campfire, you are enjoying energy stored in wood—a type of biomass energy.

Physical Science Guided Reading and Study Workbook • Chapter 15 **137**

Guided Reading and Study Workbook

Name _____ Class _____ Date _____

Chapter 15   Energy

Calculating Potential Energy

Math Skill: Percents and Decimals

You may want to read more about this **Math Skill** in the **Skills and Reference Handbook** at the end of your textbook.

A 60.0-kg person is standing on the edge of a pier that is 2.5 m above the surface of a lake. How much higher would the pier have to be to raise the gravitational potential energy of this person by 10 percent?

1. Read and Understand
What information are you given?
Mass of person = m = 60.0 kg
Height above lake level = h = 2.5 m
Acceleration due to gravity = g = 9.8 m/s^2

2. Plan and Solve
What variable are you trying to determine?
Gravitational potential energy = ?

What formula contains the given variables?
Gravitational potential energy (PE) = mgh
Initial PE = (60.0 kg)(9.8 m/s^2)(2.5 m) = 1500 J

Determine the 10-percent increase of PE.
(1500 J)(0.10) = 150 J
Final PE = 1500 J + 150 J = 1650 J

Rearrange the equation to determine the final height.
h = PE/mg = 1650 J/(60.0 kg)(9.8 m/s^2) = 2.8 m
The height increase for the pier would be 2.8 m − 2.5 m = 0.3 m.

3. Look Back and Check
Is your answer reasonable?
This is a reasonable answer because 0.3 m is about 10 percent of 2.5 m. A 10-percent increase in h should result in a 10-percent increase in the gravitational PE.

Math Practice
On a separate sheet of paper, solve the following problems.

1. A 300-gram toy car and a 500-gram toy car are sitting on a shelf that is 2 meters higher than the floor. By what percent is the PE of the 500-g car greater than the PE of the 300-g car?
The percent increase in mass is (0.5 − 0.3)/0.3 = 67 percent. The percent increase in PE is therefore also 67 percent.

2. An 80-kg rock climber is standing on a cliff so that his gravitational PE = 10,000 J. What percent increase in height is required to raise his PE by 3500 J?
35 percent. The percent increase in PE is directly proportional to the percent increase in height.

138 *Physical Science* Guided Reading and Study Workbook • Chapter 15

Student Edition Lab Worksheet

Name _____ Class _____ Date _____

Chapter 15   Energy   **Application Lab**

Investigating a Spring Clip

See page 467 in the Teacher's Edition for more information.

There are many ways to use potential energy. A spring clip is a device used to hold weights on a barbell. The spring clip stores energy when you compress it. In this lab, you will determine how the distance you compress a spring clip is related to the force you apply and to the spring's potential energy.

Problem How does the force you apply to a spring clip affect its elastic potential energy?

Materials
- clamp
- spring clip
- masking tape
- metric ruler
- 50-newton spring scale
- graph paper

Skills Measuring, Using Tables and Graphs

Procedure
1. Using the clamp, firmly attach one handle of the spring clip to a tabletop, with the other handle facing up and away from the table, as shown. **CAUTION:** *Be careful not to pinch your fingers with the clamp or spring clip.*

2. Remove the plastic cover from the upper handle of the spring clip. Hook the spring scale to the spring clip handle, as shown, and use masking tape to secure it. Have your teacher check your setup for safety before proceeding.

3. Have a classmate hold the ruler next to the spring clip, as shown. Record the starting position of the handle. (The reading on the spring scale should be zero.)

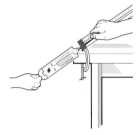

4. Slowly pull the spring scale down at a right angle to the upper handle until the handle moves 0.1 cm. In the data table, record the force and the position of the upper handle. Slowly release the scale back to the starting position.

Student Edition Lab Worksheet

Name _____ Class _____ Date _____

DATA TABLE Sample data are shown.

Force (N)	Position of Upper Handle (cm)	Total Distance Moved (cm)
3.5	6.5	0.1
5.0	6.4	0.2
7.0	6.3	0.3
9.0	6.2	0.4
12.0	6.1	0.5

5. Repeat Step 4, this time pulling the handle 0.2 cm from the starting position.

6. Repeat Step 4 a few more times, pulling the handle 0.1 cm farther each time. Continue until the spring scale reaches its maximum force.

7. Calculate the distance the handle moved each time you pulled it and record these values in the data table. Graph your data. Place the distance the handle moved on the vertical axis and the force that was applied on the horizontal axis.

Analyze and Conclude

1. **Using Graphs** What is the approximate relationship between the total distance you compressed the spring clip and the force you applied to it?

   As the distance increased, the force increased. The relationship between force and distance is directly proportional.

2. **Classifying** What type of energy transfer did you use to compress the spring clip? What type of energy did the spring clip gain when it was compressed?

   Students did work to compress the spring clip. This action increased the elastic potential energy of the spring clip.

3. **Drawing Conclusions** What relationship exists between the distance the spring clip was compressed and its potential energy? (*Hint:* The elastic potential energy of the spring clip equals the work done on it.)

   The greater the distance the spring clip was compressed, the greater was its elastic potential energy.

Lab Manual

Name _____ Class _____ Date _____

Chapter 15   Energy   🔍 **Investigation 15A**

Determining the Effect of Mass on Kinetic Energy

Refer students to pages 446–458 in their textbooks for a discussion of the relationship between kinetic energy and mass and the conversion of potential energy into kinetic energy. **SKILLS FOCUS:** Measuring, Using Tables and Graphs **CLASS TIME:** 45 minutes

Background Information

You wouldn't be afraid to stop a marble rolling down an incline, but if a bowling ball was rolling down the same incline, you'd probably move out of the way. Both objects are rolling because of Earth's gravity, yet the bowling ball has much more energy. The **potential energy** (PE) of an object being pulled by gravity is the product of its mass (*m*), the acceleration due to gravity (*g*), and its height (*h*).

$$PE = mgh$$

Think of a marble and a bowling ball rolling down the same slope from the same starting point. In the absence of friction, they move at the same speed, but they have different amounts of energy. It is a lot easier to see this difference when the potential energy is converted into **kinetic energy** as the object begins to move. As the marble and the bowling ball accelerate to the same speed (*v*) under the force of gravity, the only difference in their kinetic energies (KE) is due to mass.

$$KE = \frac{1}{2}mv^2$$

In this investigation, you will accelerate four different masses to the same speed. Then, you will compare their kinetic energies.

Problem

How is the energy of a moving object influenced by its mass?

Pre-Lab Discussion

Read the entire investigation. Then, work with a partner to answer the following questions.

1. **Controlling Variables** Identify the manipulated, responding, and controlled variables in this investigation.

   a. Manipulated variable

      Mass of bottle

   b. Responding variable

      Distance that the cup moves

   c. Controlled variables

      Length and steepness of ramp, mass and starting point of cup, starting height of bottle

---

Lab Manual

Name _____ Class _____ Date _____

2. **Applying Concepts** How will the mass of the rolling bottle affect its speed when it collides with the plastic cup? (*Hint:* The bottle accelerates much like a falling body.)

   Assuming there is only a small amount of friction acting on the rolling bottle, its speed should not be significantly affected by a change in mass.

3. **Predicting** How do you expect the mass of the bottle to affect the distance the cup moves?

   Increasing the mass of the bottle will increase the distance that the cup is moved.

4. **Applying Concepts** How is work related to the distance that the cup moves?

   Work done on the cup moves it along the floor, against the opposing frictional force. If more work is done on the cup, it moves a greater distance.

5. **Formulating Hypotheses** State a hypothesis about how the kinetic energy of the rolling bottle affects the amount of work done on the cup and the distance the cup moves.

   Increasing the kinetic energy of the rolling bottle will increase the amount of work done on the cup and the distance that it moves.

Materials *(per group)*

2 textbooks
flat board
masking tape
250-mL beaker
balance
plastic bottle that holds about 500–600 mL, with screw cap
plastic cup or margarine container
paper towel
meter stick

The floor should be smooth. The plastic cup should be lightweight and stable so that it will remain upright and slide along the floor. An empty plastic margarine container is suitable.

Lab Manual

Name _____ Class _____ Date _____

Safety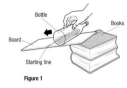

Put on safety goggles. Handle the board carefully to avoid splinters. Note all safety alert symbols next to the steps in the Procedure and review the meaning of each symbol by referring to the Safety Symbols on page xiii.

Procedure

1. Stack the two textbooks. Place one end of the board on the stack of books to form a ramp, as shown in Figure 1. Tape the ramp in place so it cannot move.

2. Attach a piece of masking tape across the ramp 15 cm from the bottom of the ramp. Use a pencil to mark the starting point on the masking tape. The bottle will be released from this point in each trial.

[Figure 1: diagram showing Bottle, Books, Board, Starting line]

3. Using the beaker, carefully pour 100 mL of water into the bottle. Close the bottle tightly and dry the outside of the bottle with the paper towel. Wipe up any spills immediately.

4. Using the balance, measure the total mass of the bottle of water and record it in the data table.

5. Place a small piece of masking tape on the floor in line with the center of the ramp at a distance of 20 cm from the base of the ramp. This is the starting position for the cup in each trial.

6. Place the empty cup at its starting point, with its closest point to the ramp touching the piece of masking tape.

7. Hold the bottle of water lying across the ramp at the starting point, as shown in Figure 1. Allow it to roll down the ramp and collide with the cup. When both the bottle and the cup have stopped moving, use the meter stick to measure the distance the cup moved from its starting point. Record the result (to the nearest centimeter) in the appropriate place in the data table.

8. Repeat Steps 6 and 7 until you have made and recorded five measurements.

9. Using the beaker, add 100 mL of water to the bottle and close it tightly. Measure and record the new mass of the bottle.

10. Repeat Steps 6 and 7 to make five measurements using the new mass.

11. Again, add 100 mL of water to the bottle and close it tightly. Measure and record the new mass.

12. Repeat Steps 6 and 7 to make five additional measurements.

If students make an obvious error in a measurement or if the bottle slides on release, have them discard that measurement and continue until they have made five satisfactory measurements for each bottle mass.

Lab Manual

Name _____ Class _____ Date _____

13. Add 100 mL of water to the bottle as before (for a total of 400 mL) and close it tightly. Measure and record the new mass.

14. Repeat Steps 6 and 7 to make five additional measurements.

15. Calculate the average distance that the cup moved for each bottle mass by adding the five distances and dividing by 5. Record your results to the nearest centimeter in the data table.

16. On the grid provided, construct a graph of your data with the mass of the bottle on the horizontal axis and the average distance the cup moved on the vertical axis. Draw a straight line as close as possible to the data points.

Observations *Sample data are shown.*

DATA TABLE

	Volume of Water			
	100 mL	200 mL	300 mL	400 mL
	Mass of Bottle and Water (g)			
	130	230	330	430
Distance Moved by Cup (cm)				
Trial 1				
Trial 2				
Trial 3				
Trial 4				
Trial 5				
Total Distance (cm)				
Average Distance (cm)	23 cm	41 cm	58 cm	73 cm

Lab Manual

Name _____ Class _____ Date _____

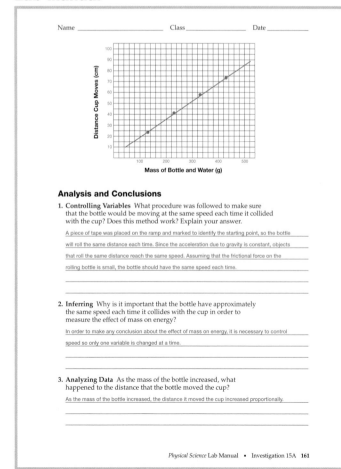

Graph: vertical axis "Distance Cup Moves (cm)" marked 10–100; horizontal axis "Mass of Bottle and Water (g)" marked 100–500.

Analysis and Conclusions

1. **Controlling Variables** What procedure was followed to make sure that the bottle would be moving at the same speed each time it collided with the cup? Does this method work? Explain your answer.

   A piece of tape was placed on the ramp and marked to identify the starting point, so the bottle will roll the same distance each time. Since the acceleration due to gravity is constant, objects that roll the same distance reach the same speed. Assuming that the frictional force on the rolling bottle is small, the bottle should have the same speed each time.

2. **Inferring** Why is it important that the bottle have approximately the same speed each time it collides with the cup in order to measure the effect of mass on energy?

   In order to make any conclusion about the effect of mass on energy, it is necessary to control speed so only one variable is changed at a time.

3. **Analyzing Data** As the mass of the bottle increased, what happened to the distance that the bottle moved the cup?

   As the mass of the bottle increased, the distance it moved the cup increased proportionally.

Lab Manual

Name _____ Class _____ Date _____

4. **Relating Cause and Effect** Why did the cup eventually come to a complete stop?

   The cup sliding along the floor experienced more friction than the rolling bottle did. The friction stopped the motion of the cup and the bottle.

5. **Forming Operational Definitions** How was the distance that the cup moved related to the bottle's kinetic energy?

   It takes energy or work to move the cup. Kinetic energy is transferred from the rolling bottle to do work on the cup. Work = Force × Distance. Because the force of friction on the cup is constant after the initial impact, the distance the cup moves is approximately proportional to the energy it receives from the bottle.

6. **Evaluating and Revising** Did your experimental results agree with your hypothesis about how the kinetic energy of the bottle affects the amount of work done on the cup? Explain your answer.

   The sample data supported the hypothesis that increasing the mass and kinetic energy of the rolling bottle will increase the amount of work done on the cup. Because of experimental error, the data points will not form a perfectly straight line.

7. **Applying Concepts** This investigation assumes that the rolling bottle experiences only a small frictional force. How accurate is this assumption? Could this assumption affect the results of the investigation? Explain your answer.

   The assumption is fairly accurate because rolling objects experience less friction than sliding objects do. However, the rolling bottle experiences some friction, which could introduce experimental error and cause the graph to be a curve instead of a straight line.

Go Further

In this investigation, you examined the relationship between the mass of a rolling bottle and its kinetic energy. Design a procedure to measure how the height of a ramp affects the kinetic energy of a bottle rolling down the ramp. Have your teacher approve your procedure before you carry out the investigation. Propose an explanation for what you find.

Check student plans for safety, practicality, and sound experimental design. Well-designed experimental plans should include detailed procedures that will test a clearly stated hypothesis. An example of an acceptable hypothesis is that a higher ramp will give the bottle more kinetic energy. Students may propose an experimental plan similar to this investigation, except that the height of the ramp would be changed by adding or removing textbooks, while keeping the mass of the bottle constant.

Lab Manual

Name _____ Class _____ Date _____

Chapter 15 Energy

Refer students to pages 447–458 in their textbooks for a discussion of kinetic and potential energy.

Investigation 15B

Determining the Kinetic Energy of a Pendulum

SKILLS FOCUS: Measuring
CLASS TIME: 45 minutes

Introduction

Energy of motion is called **kinetic energy** (KE). An object's kinetic energy depends on its mass (m) and speed (v).

$$KE = \frac{1}{2}mv^2$$

Energy of position is potential energy (PE), and it depends on mass, the acceleration due to gravity (g), and the height (h) of the object.

$$PE = mgh$$

The sum of an object's kinetic and potential energies is called its **mechanical energy.**

If you have seen a grandfather clock, you are probably familiar with a pendulum, which consists of a weight that swings back and forth on a rope or string. As the weight, or bob, moves through its arc, its mechanical energy is constantly converted between potential energy and kinetic energy. The kinetic energy increases as the potential energy decreases, and vice versa. If there were no friction, the mechanical energy of the pendulum would remain constant, and the pendulum would continue to swing back and forth, reaching the same height each time. Friction causes the height of a pendulum's swing to slowly decrease until the pendulum eventually stops.

In this investigation, you will perform an experiment to determine when a swinging pendulum has the largest amount of kinetic energy.

Problem

When does a swinging pendulum have the most kinetic energy?

Pre-Lab Discussion

Read the entire investigation. Then, work with a partner to answer the following questions.

1. **Controlling Variables** Identify the manipulated, responding, and controlled variables in this investigation.

   a. Manipulated variable

   Height of the bob at impact with the block

   b. Responding variable

   Distance the block moves along the board

   c. Controlled variables

   Size and mass of block, mass of bob, length of string, height from which bob is released,
   surface on which block moves

Physical Science Lab Manual • Investigation 15B **163**

Lab Manual

Name _____ Class _____ Date _____

2. **Predicting** At what point in its arc do you expect the bob to have the most kinetic energy? At what point will it have the least kinetic energy? Explain your answers.

   The bob will have the most KE at the bottom of its arc, where it moves fastest. The bob will have the
   least KE at the top, where its motion stops for an instant.

3. **Predicting** At what point in its arc do you expect the bob to have the most potential energy? At what point will it have the least potential energy? Explain your answers.

   The bob has the most PE at the top of its arc and the least at the bottom because an object's PE
   is proportional to its height above a reference point.

4. **Predicting** Will the block be moved farthest when the bob has the greatest potential energy or the greatest kinetic energy? Explain your answer.

   The block will move farthest when the bob has the greatest kinetic energy because at this point, the
   bob is moving with maximum speed, so it transfers the most energy to the block.

5. **Formulating Hypotheses** State a hypothesis that this investigation can be used to test.

   An example of an acceptable response is that the kinetic energy of a pendulum is greatest at
   the bottom of its swing.

Materials (per group)

1-m string
fishing weight
flat, smooth board

4 identical bricks,
approximately 8 cm in height
masking tape

lightweight wooden block
meter stick

The fishing weight should have enough mass to move the block at least a few centimeters in each trial.

Safety

Put on safety goggles. Be careful to stay out of the way of the swinging pendulum bob. Note all safety alert symbols next to the steps in the Procedure and review the meaning of each symbol by referring to the Safety Symbols on page xiii.

Procedure

1. Work with a classmate. Make a pendulum by tying the piece of string to the fishing weight. Hang the pendulum over the edge of a desk or table so that the weight, or bob, just clears a board placed on the floor beneath it. Tape the upper end of the string to the top of the desk or table, as shown in Figure 1.

2. Pull the bob slightly to the side and place a wooden block on the edge of the board, as shown, directly in the path of the pendulum's swing. Hold the bob in place next to the block while your lab partner measures the height of the bob above the floor. Record this value in the data table as the height of the bob at impact.

164 *Physical Science* Lab Manual • Investigation 15B

Lab Manual

Name _____ Class _____ Date _____

3. Pull the bob up and to the side until it reaches a height of 30 cm above the floor. Release the bob, allowing it to swing down and strike the wooden block. In the data table, measure and record the distance that the block moved along the board.

4. Replace the block on the edge of the board and repeat Step 3 two more times, releasing the bob from the same point as in the first trial.

5. Place a brick beneath each end of the board. Move the board and bricks sideways so that the bob, when released, will just clear the near end of the board.

6. Place the block on the end of the board as before. Place the bob next to the block and have your partner measure its height above the floor. In the data table, record this as the height of the bob at impact.

7. Raise the bob 30 cm off the floor, as you did in Step 3. Release the bob and again measure and record in the data table the distance that the block moved along the board after impact.

8. Replace the block and repeat Step 7 two more times, releasing the bob from the same point as before.

9. Repeat Steps 5 through 8, this time adding a second brick under each end of the board and moving the board still closer to the release point.

10. Calculate the average distance that the block moved from each position. To do this, add the three distances you recorded and divide the total by 3. In the data table, record the average distances.

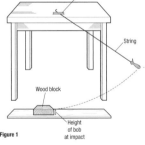

Masking tape

String

Wood block

Height of bob at impact

Figure 1

Observations

Sample data are shown. Results will depend on the size and mass of the block, the mass of the bob, and the friction between the block and the board.

DATA TABLE

Number of Bricks Supporting the Board	Height of Bob at Impact (cm)	Distance Block Moved Along Board (cm)			
		Trial 1	Trial 2	Trial 3	Average
0	4				35
2	12				24
4	20				15

Physical Science Lab Manual • Investigation 15B **165**

Lab Manual

Analysis and Conclusions

1. **Analyzing Data** How did the height of the bob at impact affect the distance that the block moved along the board?

   The lower the height of the bob at impact, the farther the block moved along the board.

2. **Drawing Conclusions** Based on your data, at what point in its swing do you think a pendulum has the greatest kinetic energy? Explain your answer.

   A pendulum has the greatest kinetic energy at the bottom of its arc. The block moved farthest when
   the bob struck it closest to the bottom of its arc. This result indicated that the bob's kinetic energy
   was greatest near the bottom of its arc because at this point it transferred the most energy to the
   block.

3. **Evaluating and Revising** Did your data support or contradict your hypothesis? Explain your answer.

   Results should support the hypothesis that the kinetic energy of a pendulum is greatest at the
   bottom of its swing.

4. **Applying Concepts** Because of weathering, a rock on the edge of a cliff may become loose and fall. In terms of kinetic and potential energy, how is the rock at the edge of the cliff similar to a pendulum at the top of its arc?

   In both cases, PE is at a maximum and KE is initially zero.

Go Further

Draw five pictures, in sequence, showing a ball that has been thrown straight upward. Draw it going up (two pictures), at its highest point (one picture), and coming down (two pictures). In each picture, indicate which quantity, KE or PE, is greater. Also, indicate for each picture whether each kind of energy is in the process of increasing, decreasing, or staying the same.

Possible answer: In pictures 1 and 5, KE is high and PE is low. In pictures 2 and 4, KE is low and PE is high. In picture 3, KE is zero and PE is at a maximum. In pictures 1 and 2, KE is decreasing and PE is increasing. In pictures 4 and 5, KE is increasing and PE is decreasing.

166 *Physical Science* Lab Manual • Investigation 15B

Chapter Test A

Name _____ Class _____ Date _____

Chapter 15   Energy   **Chapter Test A**

Multiple Choice

Write the letter that best answers the question or completes the statement on the line provided.

_____ 1. What is transferred by a force moving an object through a distance?
   a. force   **b.** mass
   c. motion   **d.** energy

_____ 2. A small 30-kilogram canoe is floating downriver at a speed of 2 m/s. What is the canoe's kinetic energy?
   a. 32 J   **b.** 60 J
   c. 120 J   **d.** 900 J

_____ 3. A 12-kg sled is moving at a speed of 3.0 m/s. At which of the following speeds will the sled have twice as much kinetic energy?
   a. 1.5 m/s   **b.** 4.2 m/s
   c. 6.0 m/s   **d.** 9.0 m/s

_____ 4. Why is the gravitational potential energy of an object 1 meter above the moon's surface less than its potential energy 1 meter above Earth's surface?
   a. The object's mass is less on the moon.
   b. The object's weight is more on the moon.
   c. The moon's acceleration due to gravity is less.
   d. both a and c

_____ 5. The gravitational potential energy of an object is always measured relative to the
   a. location where the object's kinetic energy is zero.
   b. position of maximum mechanical energy.
   c. reference level from which the height is measured.
   d. surface of Earth.

_____ 6. The total potential and kinetic energy of all the microscopic particles in an object make up its
   a. chemical energy.   **b.** electric energy.
   c. nuclear energy.   **d.** thermal energy.

_____ 7. Walking converts what type of energy into mechanical energy?
   a. chemical   **b.** electromagnetic
   c. nuclear   **d.** thermal

_____ 8. Solar cells convert what type of energy into electrical energy?
   a. chemical   **b.** electromagnetic
   c. nuclear   **d.** thermal

Chapter Test A

Name _____ Class _____ Date _____

_____ 9. If no friction acts on a diver during a dive, then which of the following statements is true?
   a. The total mechanical energy of the system increases.
   b. Potential energy can be converted into kinetic energy but not vice versa.
   c. $(KE + PE)_{beginning} = (KE + PE)_{end}$
   d. all of the above

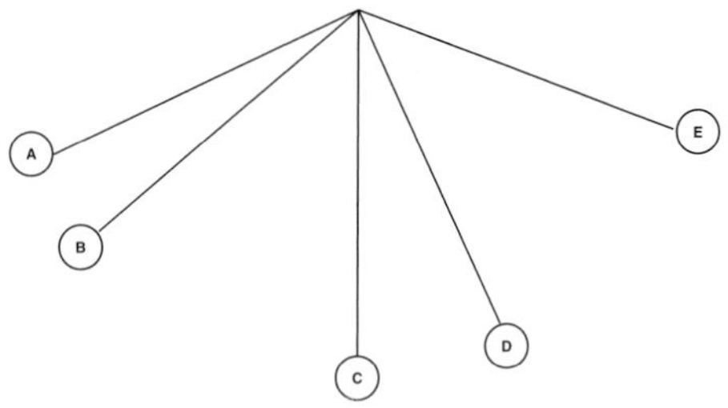

Figure 15-1

_____ 10. The kinetic energy of the pendulum bob in Figure 15-1 increases the most between locations
   a. A and B.   **b.** A and C.
   c. B and D.   **d.** C and D.

_____ 11. Which of the following statements is a consequence of the equation $E = mc^2$?
   a. Energy is released when matter is destroyed.
   b. Mass and energy are equivalent.
   c. The law of conservation of energy must be modified to state that mass and energy are conserved in any process.
   d. all of the above

_____ 12. Nonrenewable energy resources include all of the following EXCEPT
   a. coal.   **b.** hydrogen fuel cells.
   c. oil.   **d.** uranium.

_____ 13. Fossil fuels currently account for the majority of the world's energy use because they are
   a. distributed evenly throughout the world.
   b. nonpolluting.
   c. relatively inexpensive and readily available.
   d. renewable energy resources.

Chapter Test A

Name _____ Class _____ Date _____

_____ 14. A benefit of a hydrogen fuel cell is that its byproduct is
   a. carbon dioxide. **b.** oxygen.
   c. water.   **d.** uranium.

_____ 15. Based on your knowledge of energy conservation, which of the following statements is true?
   a. Manufacturers can increase a light bulb's energy efficiency by using technology that increases the amount of electromagnetic energy the bulb converts from a given amount of electrical energy.
   b. Energy can be conserved by turning off lights when they are not in use.
   c. both a and b
   d. neither a nor b

Completion

Complete each statement on the line provided.

1. Energy and work are measured in the SI unit called the _____.

2. The kinetic energy of an object is proportional to the square of its _____.

3. When a pole-vaulter flexes the pole, the pole-vaulter increases the pole's _____ potential energy.

4. Flat collector plates through which water flows are found in _____ solar energy systems.

5. Turning off unused lights or appliances is an example of energy _____.

Short Answer

In complete sentences, write the answers to the questions on the lines provided.

1. Show that the unit "kg•m²/s²," calculated from the kinetic energy equation, is equivalent to a joule.
   _____
   _____

2. Sled A (with its riders) has twice the mass of Sled B (with its riders). If both sleds have the same kinetic energy, which sled is moving faster? Explain your answer.
   _____
   _____
   _____

Chapter Test A

Name _____ Class _____ Date _____

3. In what two ways can you increase the elastic potential energy of a spring?
   _____
   _____
   _____
   _____

4. Why can you model the thermal energy of an object as the "mechanical energy" of the particles that make it up?
   _____
   _____
   _____
   _____

5. Describe one energy conversion that takes place in a hydroelectric power plant.
   _____
   _____
   _____
   _____

6. What energy conversion takes place as an arrow is shot from a bow?
   _____
   _____
   _____
   _____

7. Explain how biomass energy depends on the sun.
   _____
   _____
   _____
   _____

Chapter Test A

Name _____ Class _____ Date _____

Using Science Skills

Use the diagram to answer each question. Write the answers on a separate sheet of paper.

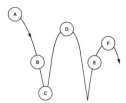

Figure 15-2

1. **Interpreting Graphics** At what location in Figure 15-2 does the ball have the least gravitational potential energy?
2. **Comparing and Contrasting** Compare the gravitational potential energy of the ball at locations B and E shown in Figure 15-2. Explain your answer.
3. **Applying Concepts** In Figure 15-2, does the total mechanical energy of the ball between locations A and F ever equal zero? Explain your answer.
4. **Inferring** In Figure 15-2, is the total mechanical energy of the ball conserved as the ball bounces? Explain your answer.
5. **Applying Concepts** Compare the kinetic energy of the ball in Figure 15-2 as it strikes the floor just before the second bounce with the first bounce (location C).

Problem

Write the answers to each question on a separate sheet of paper.

1. What is the kinetic energy of a 74.0-kg sky diver falling at a terminal velocity of 52.0 m/s? Show your work.
2. A 0.49-kg squirrel jumps from a tree branch that is 3.6 m high to the top of a bird feeder that is 1.5 m high. What is the change in gravitational potential energy of the squirrel? (The acceleration due to gravity is 9.8 m/s^2.) Show your work.
3. A small dog is trained to jump straight up a distance of 1.1 m. How much kinetic energy does the 7.7-kg dog need to jump this high? (The acceleration due to gravity is 9.8 m/s^2.) Show your work.

Chapter Test A

Name _____ Class _____ Date _____

4. In a nuclear reaction, an amount of matter having a mass of 1.0×10^{-14} kg is converted into energy, which is released. How much energy is released? (The speed of light is 3.0×10^8 m/s.) Show your work.

Essay

Write the answer to the question on a separate sheet of paper.

1. Compare and contrast biomass energy with the energy from fossil fuels.

Chapter Test B

Name _____ Class _____ Date _____

Chapter 15   Energy   **Chapter Test B**

Multiple Choice

Write the letter that best answers the question or completes the statement on the line provided.

_____ 1. Work is a transfer of
    a. energy.   **b.** force.
    c. mass.   **d.** motion.

_____ 2. The energy of motion is called
    a. kinetic energy.   **b.** potential energy.
    c. thermal energy.   **d.** work.

_____ 3. An object's gravitational potential energy is directly related to all of the following EXCEPT
    a. its height relative to a reference level.
    b. its mass.
    c. its speed.
    d. the acceleration due to gravity.

_____ 4. Which of the following is an example of an object with elastic potential energy?
    a. a wind-up toy that has been wound up
    b. a compressed basketball
    c. a stretched rubber band
    d. all of the above

_____ 5. A 4-kilogram cat is resting on top of a bookshelf that is 2 meters high. What is the cat's gravitational potential energy relative to the floor if the acceleration due to gravity is 9.8 m/s^2?
    a. 6 J   **b.** 8 J
    c. 20 J   **d.** 78 J

_____ 6. Which of the following increases when an object becomes warmer?
    a. chemical energy
    b. elastic potential energy
    c. nuclear energy
    d. thermal energy

_____ 7. The energy stored in gasoline is
    a. chemical energy.
    b. electromagnetic energy.
    c. mechanical energy.
    d. nuclear energy.

_____ 8. Nuclear power plants are designed to convert nuclear energy into what type of energy?
    a. chemical   **b.** electrical
    c. geothermal   **d.** mechanical

Chapter Test B

Name _____ Class _____ Date _____

_____ 9. Which of the following statements is true according to the law of conservation of energy?
    a. Energy cannot be created.
    b. Energy cannot be destroyed.
    c. Energy can be converted from one form to another.
    d. all of the above

_____ 10. The mechanical energy of an object equals its
    a. chemical energy plus its nuclear energy.
    b. kinetic energy plus its potential energy.
    c. nuclear energy.
    d. thermal energy.

_____ 11. The equation $E = mc^2$ relates energy and
    a. force.   **b.** gravity.
    c. mass.   **d.** work.

_____ 12. In which of the following does Einstein's famous equation apply?
    a. chemical reactions
    b. collisions between objects
    c. electromagnetic energy conversions
    d. nuclear fission and fusion reactions

_____ 13. What is biomass energy?
    a. the chemical energy stored in living things
    b. the electromagnetic energy stored in living things
    c. the nuclear energy stored in living things
    d. the thermal energy stored in living things

_____ 14. A drawback of solar energy is that it
    a. cannot be converted directly into electrical energy.
    b. depends on the climate.
    c. produces water pollution.
    d. is not a renewable resource.

_____ 15. Which of the following types of transportation is NOT mass transportation?
    a. bus   **b.** car
    c. streetcar   **d.** train

Completion

Complete each statement on the line provided.

1. Energy of an object increases when _____ is done on the object.
2. If the _____ of an object doubles, its kinetic energy doubles.

Chapter Test B

Name _____ Class _____ Date _____

3. Energy that is stored due to position or shape is called
   _____ energy.

4. Mechanical energy does not include kinetic energy or
   _____ energy

5. The sum of the kinetic energy and potential energy of an object is
   called its _____ energy.

6. Wind turbines convert _____ energy into electrical
   energy.

7. The process of changing energy from one form to another is called
   energy _____.

8. "Energy cannot be created or destroyed" is a statement of the law
   of _____.

9. In the equation $E = mc^2$, c is the speed of _____.

10. Energy resources that exist in limited amounts and, once used,
    cannot be replaced except over the course of millions of years are
    called _____ energy resources.

11. Geothermal energy, in addition to being renewable, offers the
    benefit of being _____.

Short Answer

*In complete sentences, write the answers to the questions on
the lines provided.*

1. What evidence is there that energy is transferred as a golf club
   does work on a golf ball?

   _____

   _____

   _____

   _____

2. What are the two general types of energy that can be used to
   classify many forms of energy?

   _____

   _____

   _____

   _____

3. What is the most familiar form of electromagnetic energy?

   _____

   _____

   _____

   _____

Chapter Test B

Chapter Test B

Name _____ Class _____ Date _____

4. What is a characteristic of a renewable energy resource?

   _____

   _____

   _____

5. Why might a consumer buy a more energy-efficient refrigerator
   even though it may cost more than a conventional refrigerator?

   _____

   _____

   _____

   _____

Using Science Skills

*Use the diagram to answer each question.
Write the answers on a separate sheet of paper.*

1. **Applying Concepts** In Figure 15-1,
   the block in C has 5 J of kinetic energy.
   How much work did the compressed
   spring do on the block? Explain your
   answer.

2. **Classifying** What form of energy
   does the compressed spring have in
   Figure 15-1?

3. **Inferring** In Figure 15-1, what has
   happened to the stored energy of the
   spring between A and B?

4. **Applying Concepts** In Figure 15-1,
   how would the kinetic energy of the
   block in C be different if the tabletop
   was not frictionless? Explain your
   answer.

5. **Interpreting Graphics** In Figure 15-1,
   how has the kinetic energy of the
   block changed between A and B?

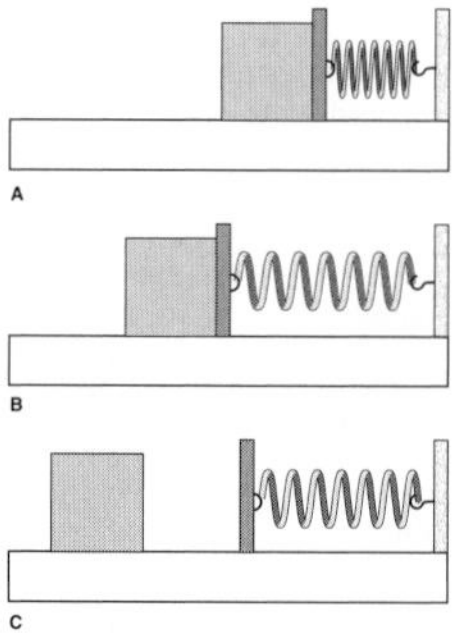

Figure 15-1

Chapter 15 Test A Answers

Multiple Choice

1. d **2.** b **3.** b **4.** c **5.** c **6.** d
7. a **8.** b **9.** c **10.** c **11.** d **12.** b
13. c **14.** c **15.** c

Completion

1. joule **2.** speed **3.** elastic **4.** active **5.** conservation

Short Answer

1. $kg \cdot m^2/s^2 = (kgm/s^2) \cdot m = N \cdot m = J$ **2.** Sled B; it has less mass.
3. Stretch it or compress it. **4.** because the thermal energy of an object is the kinetic and potential energy of its particles **5.** Accept either of the following: The potential energy of stored water is converted into kinetic energy as the water falls; as the falling water does work on the turbine, it moves the turbine's blades (KE). The KE of the rotating blades is converted into electrical energy by the generator. **6.** The elastic potential energy of the bent bow and string is converted into kinetic energy of the arrow. **7.** Biomass energy is the chemical energy stored in living things. The chemical energy is produced as plants convert sunlight in the form of electromagnetic energy into chemical energy.

Using Science Skills

1. C **2.** The gravitational potential energy of the ball is the same at both locations; the height is the same. **3.** No; since the ball is always moving to the right between locations A and F, at every point between A and F, the ball has kinetic energy. Because the ball has kinetic energy at each point, it has some mechanical energy at each point. **4.** No; because the ball does not reach the same height each time it bounces, its maximum gravitational potential energy is decreasing from one bounce to the next. Because its gravitational potential energy decreases and its maximum kinetic energy does not increase, the total mechanical energy must be decreasing. **5.** The kinetic energy is less before the second bounce. Since its gravitational potential energy is zero each time it strikes the floor, its kinetic energy equals its total mechanical energy. Because the total mechanical energy has decreased with the first bounce, its kinetic energy has decreased as it strikes the floor just before the second bounce.

Problem

1. $KE = \frac{1}{2}mv^2 = \frac{1}{2}(74.0kg)(52.0m/s)^2$

$= \frac{1}{2}(74kg)(2704m^2/s^2) = 1000,000J$

2. $PE = mgh = (0.49kg)(9.8m/s^2)(3.6m - 1.5m) = 10J$ decreased by 10J

3. $(KE)_{beginning} = (PE)_{end}$ $KE = mgh = (7.7kg)(9.8m/s^2)(1.1m) = 83J$
4. $E = mc^2 = (1.0 \times 10^{-14}kg)(3.0 \times 10^8 m/s)^2 = 9.0 \times 10^2 J$

Essay

1. Biomass energy is energy that is available immediately from the chemical energy stored in living organisms. Biomass is classified as a renewable energy resource. Fossil fuels also contain chemical energy but were formed over a long period of time from once-living organisms. Fossil fuels are classified as nonrenewable energy resources.

Chapter 15 Test B Answers

Multiple Choice

1. a **2.** a **3.** c **4.** d **5.** d **6.** d
7. a **8.** b **9.** d **10.** b **11.** c **12.** d
13. a **14.** b **15.** b

Completion

1. work **2.** mass **3.** potential **4.** chemical **5.** mechanical
6. kinetic; mechanical **7.** conversion **8.** conservation of energy
9. light **10.** nonrenewable **11.** nonpolluting

Short Answer

1. The kinetic energy of the golf ball suddenly increases as the club strikes it. **2.** kinetic energy and potential energy **3.** visible light **4.** Accept either of the following: The resource can be replaced in a relatively short period of time. The resource originates either directly or indirectly from the sun. **5.** The refrigerator uses less energy due to its efficiency, so over time, the total cost may be lower.

Using Science Skills

1. 5 J; because the block gained 5 joules of energy, the spring had to do 5 joules of work on the block. **2.** elastic potential energy
3. The elastic potential energy of the spring has decreased.
4. The block's kinetic energy would be less. Some of the elastic potential energy of the compressed spring would be converted into thermal energy due to friction. As a result, less of the spring's elastic potential energy would be converted into kinetic energy of the block. **5.** The block's kinetic energy has increased.

Chapter 16 Thermal Energy and Heat

CHAPTER 16 Planning Guide

Use these planning tools
Easy Planner
Resource Pro
Online Lesson Planner

SECTION OBJECTIVES	STANDARDS NATIONAL (See p. T18.)	STANDARDS STATE	ACTIVITIES and LABS
16.1 Thermal Energy and Matter, pp. 474–478 1 block or 2 periods **16.1.1** **Explain** how heat and work transfer energy. **16.1.2** **Relate** thermal energy to the motion of particles that make up a material. **16.1.3** **Relate** temperature to thermal energy and to thermal expansion. **16.1.4** **Calculate** thermal energy, temperature change, or mass using the specific heat equation. **16.1.5** **Describe** how a calorimeter operates and **calculate** thermal energy changes or specific heat using calorimetry measurements.	A-1, A-2, B-2, B-5, G-1, G-2, G-3		**SE** Inquiry Activity: What Happens When Hot and Cold Liquids Mix? p. 473 L2 **SE** Quick Lab: Cooling Air, p. 476 L2 **SE** Design Your Own Lab: Using Specific Heat to Analyze Metals, p. 493 L2 **TE** Teacher Demo: Calorimetry, p. 478 L2
16.2 Heat and Thermodynamics, pp. 479–483 1 block or 2 periods **16.2.1** **Describe** conduction, convection, and radiation and **identify** which of these is occurring in a given situation. **16.2.2** **Classify** materials as thermal conductors or thermal insulators. **16.2.3** **Apply** the law of conservation of energy to conversions between thermal energy and other forms of energy. **16.2.4** **Apply** the second law of thermodynamics in situations where thermal energy moves from cooler to warmer objects. **16.2.5** **State** the third law of thermodynamics.	A-1, A-2, B-2, B-5, B-6, D-1, G-1, G-2, G-3		**SE** Quick Lab: Observing Convection, p. 481 L2 **TE** Teacher Demo: Conductors and Insulators, p. 480 L2 **TE** Build Science Skills: Applying Concepts, p. 482 L2 **LM** Investigation 16A: Determining the Effect of Surface Area on Heat Transfer L2 **LM** Investigation 16B: Explaining How a Flame Can Boil Water in a Paper Cup L1
16.3 Using Heat, pp. 486–492 1 block or 2 periods **16.3.1** **Describe** heat engines and **explain** how heat engines convert thermal energy into mechanical energy. **16.3.2** **Describe** how the different types of heating systems operate. **16.3.3** **Describe** how cooling systems, such as refrigerators and air conditioners, operate. **16.3.4** **Evaluate** benefits and drawbacks of different heating and cooling systems.	A-1, B-3, B-5, F-4, G-1, G-2, G-3		**TE** Teacher Demo: Cooling by Evaporation, p. 490 L2

Ability Levels

L1	For students who need additional help
L2	For all students
L3	For students who need to be challenged

Components

SE	Student Edition	**GRSW**	Guided Reading & Study Workbook With Math Support	**CTB**	Computer Test Bank
TE	Teacher's Edition			**TP**	Test Prep Resources
LM	Laboratory Manual			**iT**	iText
PLM	Probeware Lab Manual	**CUT**	Chapter and Unit Tests	**DC**	Discovery Channel Videotapes

T	Transparencies
P	Presentation Pro CD-ROM
GO	Internet Resources

RESOURCES
PRINT and TECHNOLOGY

PLM Lab 7: Using Specific Heat to Analyze Metals	L2
GRSW Section 16.1	L1
GRSW Math Skill	L2
T Chapter 16 Pretest	L2
Section 16.1	L2
P Chapter 16 Pretest	L2
Section 16.1	L2
SCiLINKS **GO** Specific heat	L2

GRSW Section 16.2	L1
DC Powered by the Sun	L2
T Section 16.2	L2
P Section 16.2	L2
SCiLINKS **GO** Thermodynamics	L2

GRSW Section 16.3	L1
T Section 16.3	L2
P Section 16.3	L2
SCIENCE NEWS **GO** Heat	L2

SECTION ASSESSMENT

SE Section 16.1 Assessment, p. 478

iText **iT** Section 16.1

SE Section 16.2 Assessment, p. 483

iText **iT** Section 16.2

SE Section 16.3 Assessment, p. 492

iText **iT** Section 16.3

Go Online

Go online for these Internet resources.

PHSchool.com
Web Code: cca-2160

SCIENCE NEWS
Web Code: cce-2163

NSTA *SCiLINKS*
Web Code: ccn-2161
Web Code: ccn-2162

Materials for Activities and Labs

Quantities for each group

STUDENT EDITION

Inquiry Activity, p. 473
2 plastic foam cups, glass stirring rod, thermometer, 2 100-mL graduated cylinders

Quick Lab, p. 476
round balloon, 2-L plastic bottle, metric tape measure, plastic bucket, ice

Quick Lab, p. 481
100-mL beaker, cold water, dropper pipet, hot water, food coloring, paper towel

Design Your Own Lab, p. 493
10 steel bolts, balance, 50-cm length of string, clamp, ring stand, boiling water bath (shared with class), thermometer, 500-mL graduated cylinder, ice water, foam cup with lid, aluminum nails, crushed can

TEACHER'S EDITION

Teacher Demo, p. 478
plastic foam cup with lid, thermometer, water, iron bolt (~75 g)

Teacher Demo, p. 480
a block of wood, an aluminum pie plate, a metal spoon, a plastic spoon, a silk or cotton handkerchief, a metal screwdriver

Build Science Skills, p. 482
putty (enough to make 1 golf ball-sized ball per student), table or desktop

Build Science Skills, p. 484
a box with black interior, a box with white interior, clear plastic wrap, 2 beakers, 2 thermometers

Teacher Demo, p. 490
paper towels, water, tape, hand-held or electric fan, thermometer

Chapter Assessment

CHAPTER ASSESSMENT

SE	Chapter Assessment, pp. 495–496
CUT	Chapter 16 Test A, B
CTB	Chapter 16
iT	Chapter 16

PHSchool.com GO
Web Code: cca-2160

STANDARDIZED TEST PREP

SE	Chapter 16, p. 497
TP	Diagnose and Prescribe

iText—interactive textbook with assessment at PHSchool.com

Name_____ Class_____ Date_____ M T W T F

LESSON PLAN 16.1

Thermal Energy and Matter

Time
2 periods
1 block

Section Objectives

- **16.1.1 Explain** how heat and work transfer energy.
- **16.1.2 Relate** thermal energy to the motion of particles that make up a material.
- **16.1.3 Relate** temperature to thermal energy and to thermal expansion.
- **16.1.4 Calculate** thermal energy, temperature change, or mass using the specific heat equation.
- **16.1.5 Describe** how a calorimeter operates and **calculate** thermal energy changes or specific heat using calorimetry measurements.

Vocabulary heat • temperature • thermal expansion • specific heat • calorimeter

Local Standards

1 FOCUS

Build Vocabulary: Concept Map
Have students construct a concept map of the vocabulary terms in this section, placing the main concept (Thermal Energy and Matter) at the top. **L2**

Targeted Resources
❏ Transparency: Chapter 16 Pretest
❏ Transparency: Interest Grabber 16.1
❏ Transparency: Reading Strategy 16.1

2 INSTRUCT

Use Visuals: Figure 2
Ask students in what ways a water molecule can move. **L1**

Build Math Skills: Formulas and Equations
Have students rearrange the formula for heat ($Q = m \times c \times \Delta T$) in order to calculate specific heat, mass, and temperature. **L1**

Address Misconceptions
Explain to students that heat is a flow, or transfer, of thermal energy from one object or material to another. **L2**

Quick Lab: Cooling Air
Students measure an inflated balloon at two different temperatures, in order to describe the effect of temperature on the volume of a gas. **L2**

Teacher Demo: Calorimetry
Use a cup of water and a cold iron bolt to help students observe a calorimeter measuring changes in thermal energy. **L2**

Targeted Resources
❏ Transparency: Figure 3: Specific Heat
❏ Transparency: Figure 4: A Calorimeter
❏ Transparency: Math Skills: Specific Heat
❏ GRSW Section 16.1
❏ **NSTA** *sci*$_{LINKS}$ Specific heat

3 ASSESS

Reteach
Use Figure 2 to summarize key concepts about thermal energy. **L1**

Evaluate Understanding
Ask students to write a paragraph relating thermal energy, temperature, and heat. **L2**

Targeted Resources
❏ **PHSchool.com** Online Section 16.1 Assessment
❏ iText Section 16.1

223 **Chapter 16 Pretest**

1. True or False: Degrees Celsius and kelvins are units of temperature.

2. What kind of energy is released when bonds between atoms are broken?

3. True or False: Thermal energy is the total potential and kinetic energy of the microscopic particles in an object.

4. The change of state from liquid to gas is called ——————————— .

5. Which of the following is the energy of a moving object?
   a. mechanical energy
   b. chemical energy
   c. potential energy
   d. kinetic energy

ANSWERS
1. True
2. chemical energy
3. True
4. vaporization
5. d

224 **Chapter 16 Pretest** *(continued)*

6. The principle that energy cannot be created or destroyed is known as the law of ——————————— .

7. Work is a ——————————— .

8. If the input work for a simple machine is 21.0 J, and the output work is 7.0 J, the efficiency of the engine is ——————————— .
   a. 3.0%
   b. 0.33%
   c. 33%
   d. 30%

ANSWERS
6. conservation of energy
7. transfer of energy
8. c

225 **Section 16.1 Interest Grabber**

Heat Transfer

Rub sandpaper on a metal bolt. **CAUTION:** *Stop rubbing before the bolt becomes too hot to handle.* Dip the bolt in a cup of cool water. Note how this affects the bolt's temperature.

1. Describe the work that you did to add energy to the bolt.

2. What type of energy did this work produce in the bolt?

3. What happened to the temperature of the bolt after it was dipped in water?

4. What do you think would happen to the water temperature if you repeated the procedure many times?

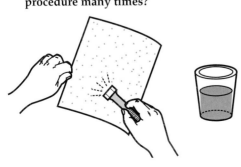

ANSWERS
1. Energy was added to the bolt by doing work to move the sandpaper back and forth.
2. thermal energy
3. The temperature of the bolt decreased.
4. The water should heat up because thermal energy from the bolt is transferred to the water.

226 **Section 16.1 Reading Strategy**

Previewing

Questions About Thermal Energy and Matter	Answers
Which has more thermal energy, a cup of tea or a pitcher of juice?	a. ___?___
b. ___?___	c. ___?___
d. ___?___	e. ___?___

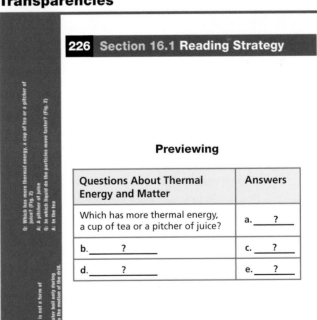

ANSWERS
Sample answers:
Q: Which has more thermal energy, a cup of tea or a pitcher of juice? (Fig. 2)
A: A pitcher of juice
Q: In which liquid do the particles move faster? (Fig. 2)
A: In the tea

Transparencies

Specific Heats of Selected Materials

Material (at 100 kPa)	Specific Heat (J/g•°C)
Water	4.18
Plastic (polypropylene)	1.84–2.09
Air	1.01
Iron	0.449
Silver	0.235

Transparencies

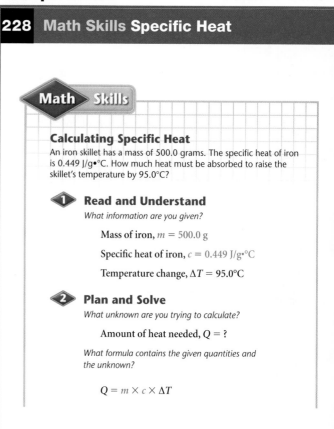

Calculating Specific Heat

An iron skillet has a mass of 500.0 grams. The specific heat of iron is 0.449 J/g•°C. How much heat must be absorbed to raise the skillet's temperature by 95.0°C?

1 Read and Understand

What information are you given?

Mass of iron, $m = 500.0$ g

Specific heat of iron, $c = 0.449$ J/g•°C

Temperature change, $\Delta T = 95.0$°C

2 Plan and Solve

What unknown are you trying to calculate?

Amount of heat needed, $Q = ?$

What formula contains the given quantities and the unknown?

$$Q = m \times c \times \Delta T$$

Transparencies

Replace each variable with its known value.

$$Q = 500.0 \text{ g} \times 0.449 \text{ J/g•°C} \times 95.0°C$$

$$= 21,375 \text{ J} = 21.4 \text{ kJ}$$

3 Look Back and Check

Is your answer reasonable?

Round off the data to give a quick estimate.

$Q = 500 \text{ g} \times 0.5 \text{ J/g•°C} \times 100°C = 25 \text{ kJ}$

This is close to 21.4 kJ, so the answer is reasonable.

Transparencies

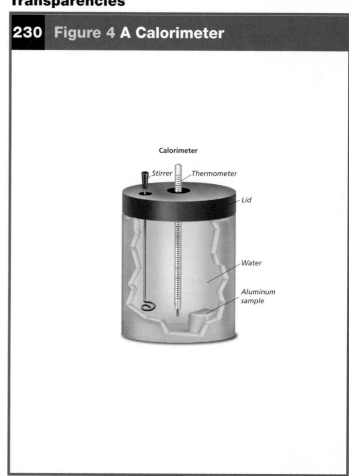

Calorimeter

Stirrer — Thermometer

Lid

Water

Aluminum sample

Name _____ Class _____ Date _____

Chapter 16   Thermal Energy and Heat

Section 16.1 Thermal Energy and Matter
(pages 474–478)

This section defines heat and describes how work, temperature, and thermal energy are related to heat. Thermal expansion and contraction of materials is discussed, and uses of a calorimeter are explained.

Reading Strategy (page 474)

Previewing Before you read, preview the figures in this section and add two more questions in the table. As you read, write answers to your questions. For more information on this Reading Strategy, see the **Reading and Study Skills** in the **Skills and Reference Handbook** at the end of your textbook.

Thermal Energy and Matter	
Questions About Thermal Energy and Matter	**Answers**
Which has more thermal energy, a cup of tea or a pitcher of juice?	A pitcher of juice
Why did Rumford conclude that heat is not a form of matter? (Fig. 1)	The brass was hot enough to make water boil only during drilling, so the heat must be related to the motion of the drill.
How is specific heat related to temperature? (Fig. 3)	The lower a material's specific heat, the more its temperature rises when a given amount of energy is absorbed by a given mass.

Work and Heat (page 474)

1. Heat is the transfer of thermal energy from one object to another as the result of a difference in _____temperature_____.

2. Circle the letter of each sentence that is true about heat.
   a. Heat is a fluid that flows between particles of matter.
   (b.) Heat flows spontaneously from hot objects to cold objects.
   (c.) Friction produces heat.
   (d.) The transfer of thermal energy from one object to another is heat.

Temperature (page 475)

3. What is temperature? Temperature is a measure of how hot or cold an object is compared to a reference point.

4. Is the following sentence true or false? On the Celsius scale, the reference points for temperature are the freezing and boiling points of water. _____true_____

Name _____ Class _____ Date _____

Chapter 16   Thermal Energy and Heat

5. Circle the letter of each sentence that explains what happens when an object heats up.
   (a.) Its particles move faster, on average.
   b. The average kinetic energy of its particles decreases.
   c. Its mass increases.
   (d.) Its temperature increases.

Thermal Energy (page 475)

6. What is thermal energy? Thermal energy is the total potential and kinetic energy of all the particles in an object.

7. Thermal energy depends upon the _____mass_____, _____temperature_____, and _____phase_____ of an object.

8. Is the following sentence true or false? Two substances can be the same temperature and have different thermal energies. _____true_____

Thermal Expansion and Contraction (page 476)

9. Is the following sentence true or false? Thermal contraction occurs when matter is heated, because particles of matter tend to move closer together as temperature increases. _____false_____

10. Describe thermal expansion and contraction by completing the table below.

Thermal Expansion and Contraction			
Condition	**Temperature**	**Space Between Particles**	**Volume**
Thermal expansion	Increases	Increases	Increases
Thermal contraction	Decreases	Decreases	Decreases

Specific Heat (pages 476–477)

11. The amount of heat needed to raise the temperature of one gram of material by one degree Celsius is called _____specific heat_____.

12. Why are you more likely to burn yourself on a metal toy than on a plastic toy if both have been sitting in the sun? The specific heats of metals tend to be lower than the specific heats of plastics. If equal masses of metal and plastic absorb the same thermal energy, the metal's temperature rises more.

Measuring Heat Changes (page 478)

13. What device is used to measure changes in thermal energy? a calorimeter

14. Is the following sentence true or false? A calorimeter uses the principle that heat flows from a hotter object to a colder object until both reach the same temperature. _____true_____

Section 16.2 Lesson Plan

LESSON PLAN 16.2

Heat and Thermodynamics

Time
2 periods
1 block

Section Objectives

- **16.2.1 Describe** conduction, convection, and radiation and **identify** which of these is occurring in a given situation.
- **16.2.2 Classify** materials as thermal conductors or thermal insulators.
- **16.2.3 Apply** the law of conservation of energy to conversions between thermal energy and other forms of energy.
- **16.2.4 Apply** the second law of thermodynamics in situations where thermal energy moves from cooler to warmer objects.
- **16.2.5 State** the third law of thermodynamics.

Vocabulary conduction • thermal conductor • thermal insulator • convection • convection current • radiation • thermodynamics • heat engine • waste heat

Local Standards

1 FOCUS

Build Vocabulary: Word-Part Analysis
Ask students what words they know that have the key word parts *therm, con, duct,* and *radia.* Then, give a definition of each word part and give additional examples. **L2**

Targeted Resources
❑ Transparency: Interest Grabber 16.2
❑ Transparency: Reading Strategy 16.2

2 INSTRUCT

Build Reading Literacy: Sequence
Have students describe the convection of warm air as a sequence of events, starting with "air heated by sunlight." **L1**

Use Visuals: Figure 5
Using Figure 5, ask students how the balls could be arranged to demonstrate conduction in a gas. **L1**

Quick Lab: Observing Convection
Have students put hot colored water into a beaker of cold water, and use the concept of convection to describe fluid motion. **L2**

Teacher Demo: Conductors and Insulators
Have students handle various objects that have been lying in sunlight or shade. Students will observe the differences between types of thermal conductors and insulators. **L2**

Address Misconceptions
Help students understand the similarities and differences between the term *radiation* as it is used in this section and the term *nuclear radiation.* **L2**

Targeted Resources
❑ GRSW Section 16.2
❑ NSTA *sc*LINKS Thermodynamics

3 ASSESS

Reteach
Use Figures 5–8 to review heat transfer, emphasizing how thermal energy is changed in each case. **L1**

Evaluate Understanding
Ask students to list examples of conduction, convection, and radiation, explaining how energy is transferred and conserved in each example. **L2**

Targeted Resources
❑ **PHSchool.com** Online Section 16.2 Assessment
❑ iText Section 16.2

Transparencies

231 Section 16.2 Interest Grabber

Temperature and Air Pressure

Blow up a balloon and tie off the end. Fill half a bucket with ice water. Dip the balloon into the ice water and hold it there for several minutes. Observe what happens. Remove the balloon from the bucket and let it sit for several minutes. Observe what happens.

1. What happened when you dipped the balloon into the ice water? Why?

2. What happened after the balloon was removed from the ice water? Why?

ANSWERS
1. The balloon contracted because the lower temperature decreased the air pressure inside the balloon.
2. The balloon expands back to its original shape because the temperature has risen, causing the air pressure to increase.

Transparencies

232 Section 16.2 Reading Strategy

Building Vocabulary

Definitions	Examples
Conduction: transfer of thermal energy without transfer of matter	Frying pan handle heats up.
Convection: a. ___?___	b. ___?___
Radiation: c. ___?___	d. ___?___

ANSWERS
a. the transfer of thermal energy by the movement of particles in a fluid
b. Hot air circulates in an oven
c. the transfer of thermal energy by waves moving through space
d. Heating coil of an electric stove glows

Guided Reading and Study Workbook

Name _____ Class _____ Date _____

Chapter 16   Thermal Energy and Heat

Section 16.2 Heat and Thermodynamics
(pages 479–483)

This section discusses three kinds of thermal energy transfer and introduces the first, second, and third laws of thermodynamics.

Reading Strategy (page 479)

Build Vocabulary As you read this section, add definitions and examples to complete the table. For more information on this Reading Strategy, see the **Reading and Study Skills** in the **Skills and Reference Handbook** at the end of your textbook.

Transfer of Thermal Energy	
Definitions	**Examples**
Conduction: transfer of thermal energy with no net transfer of matter	Frying pan handle heats up
Convection: transfer of thermal energy when particles of a fluid move from one place to another	Hot air circulating in an oven
Radiation: transfer of energy by waves moving through space	Heating coil of a stove glows

Conduction (pages 479–480)

1. The transfer of thermal energy with no overall transfer of matter is called _____conduction_____.

2. Why is conduction slower in gases than in liquids and solids? In conduction, thermal energy is transferred by collisions between particles, and there are fewer collisions among particles in a gas than in a liquid or a solid.

3. Is the following sentence true or false? Conduction is faster in metals than in other solids because metals have free electrons that transfer thermal energy. _____true_____

4. Circle the letter of each sentence that is true about conduction.
   a. Thermal energy is transferred without transfer of matter.
   b. Matter is transferred great distances during conduction.
   c. Conduction can occur between materials that are not touching.
   d. In most solids, conduction takes place as particles vibrate in place.

5. Complete the table about conduction.

Conduction		
Type of Material	**Quality of Conduction**	**Two Examples**
Thermal conductor	Conducts thermal energy well	Copper; aluminum
Thermal insulator	Conducts thermal energy poorly	Wood; air

Guided Reading and Study Workbook

Name _____ Class _____ Date _____

Chapter 16   Thermal Energy and Heat

Convection (pages 480–481)

6. The transfer of thermal energy when particles of a fluid move from one place to another is called _____convection_____.

7. Why is temperature higher at the bottom of an oven? When air at the bottom of the oven heats up, it expands, becomes less dense, and cools as it rises. Cooler, denser air sinks and is heated again at the bottom of the oven.

8. When a fluid circulates in a loop as it alternately heats up and cools down, a(n) _____convection current_____ occurs.

9. Give three examples of convection currents in nature. Ocean currents, weather systems, and movement of hot rock in Earth's interior are examples of convection currents.

Radiation (page 481)

10. The transfer of energy by waves moving through space is called _____radiation_____.

11. Circle the letter of each sentence that is true about radiation.
    a. Energy is transferred by waves.
    b. All objects radiate energy.
    c. The amount of energy radiated from an object decreases as its temperature increases.
    d. The farther away you are from a radiating object, the less radiation you receive.

Thermodynamics (pages 482–483)

12. Thermodynamics is the study of conversions between _____thermal energy_____ and other forms of energy.

13. Is the following sentence true or false? Energy cannot be created or destroyed, but it can be converted into different forms. _____true_____

14. Thermal energy flows spontaneously from _____hotter_____ objects to _____colder_____ ones.

15. According to the second law of thermodynamics, what must happen for thermal energy to flow from a colder object to a hotter object? Work must be done on the system.

16. Thermal energy that is not converted into work is called _____waste heat_____.

17. Is the following sentence true or false? Scientists have created a heat engine with 100 percent efficiency by reducing the temperature of the outside environment to absolute zero. _____false_____

18. Is the following sentence true or false? Matter can be cooled to absolute zero. _____false_____

Section 16.3 **Lesson Plan**

LESSON PLAN 16.3

Using Heat

Section Objectives

- **16.3.1 Describe** heat engines and **explain** how heat engines convert thermal energy into mechanical energy.

- **16.3.2 Describe** how the different types of heating systems operate.

- **16.3.3 Describe** how cooling systems, such as refrigerators and air conditioners, operate.

- **16.3.4 Evaluate** benefits and drawbacks of different heating and cooling systems.

Vocabulary external combustion engine • internal combustion engine • central heating system • heat pump • refrigerant

Local Standards

1 FOCUS

Build Vocabulary: LINCS
Have students use the LINCS strategy to learn and review the vocabulary terms. **L2**

Targeted Resources
❑ Transparency: Interest Grabber 16.3
❑ Transparency: Reading Strategy 16.3

2 INSTRUCT

Build Reading Literacy: Relate Cause and Effect
Have students read the paragraphs about the external combustion engine and study Figure 11, and then ask what causes the piston in the cylinder to do work. Ask students to describe the effect of the movement of the slide valve. **L1**

Use Community Resources
Suggest that students learn more about internal combustion engines by visiting an auto repair shop and talking with a mechanic. **L2**

Teacher Demo: Cooling by Evaporation
Use a fan and a wet paper towel wrapped around the bulb of a thermometer to help students observe how evaporation of a liquid can cool its surroundings. **L2**

Address Misconceptions
Remind students that the energy required to operate a heating system exceeds the amount of thermal energy distributed by the system. **L2**

For Enrichment
After doing research, interested students can make a multimedia presentation for the class explaining the hybrid automobile. **L3**

Targeted Resources
❑ Transparency: Figure 11: An External Combustion Engine
❑ Transparency: Figure 12: An Internal Combustion Engine
❑ Transparency: Figure 13: A Hot-Water Heating System
❑ Transparency: Figure 14: A Forced-Air Heating System
❑ Transparency: Figure 16: An Air Conditioner
❑ GRSW Section 16.3
❑ **NSTA** *sci*$_{INKS}$ Heat

3 ASSESS

Reteach
Use Figure 12 to review how an internal combustion engine operates . **L1**

Evaluate Understanding
Ask students to write two questions each about heating systems and cooling systems. Then, have students form groups to ask each other their questions. **L2**

Targeted Resources
❑ **PHSchool.com** Online Section 16.3 Assessment
❑ iText Section 16.3

Transparencies

233 Section 16.3 **Interest Grabber**

Cooling by Evaporation

When you step out of a swimming pool, you often feel very cool, even on a warm day. The evaporating water transfers thermal energy from your skin to the surrounding environment. Evaporation cools you down while it warms up your surroundings.

You can feel this by holding your index finger close to your mouth and blowing on it gently. Then, wet your finger and blow on it again.

1. How does wetting your finger change the way it feels when your blow on it?

2. Is there really a difference in the temperature of a wet and a dry finger when your blow on it? Explain.

ANSWERS
1. A wet finger feels cooler than a dry finger when you blow on it.
2. Yes, a wet finger is cooler when your blow on it because the evaporation of the water transfers thermal energy away from your finger.

Transparencies

234 Section 16.3 **Reading Strategy**

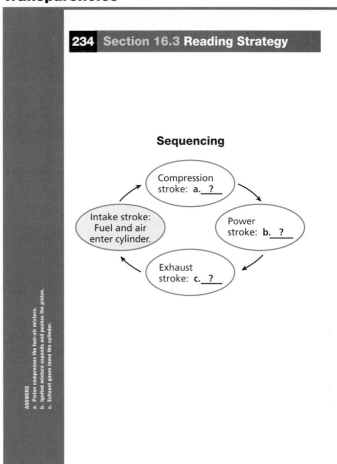

Sequencing

ANSWERS
a. Piston compresses the fuel-air mixture.
b. Ignited mixture expands and pushes the piston.
c. Exhaust gases leave the cylinder.

Transparencies

235 **Figure 11 An External Combustion Engine**

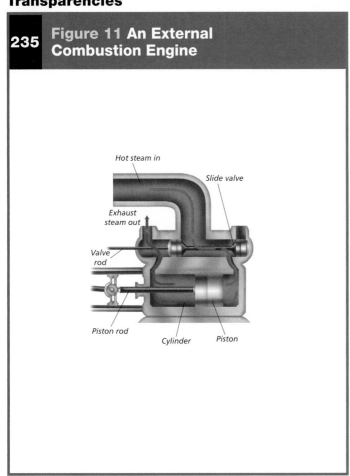

Transparencies

236 Figure 12 An Internal Combustion Engine

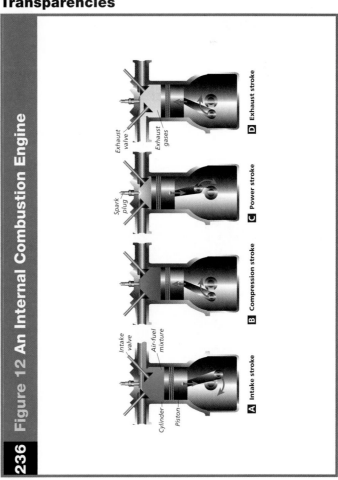

Transparencies

237 | Figure 13 **A Hot-Water Heating System**

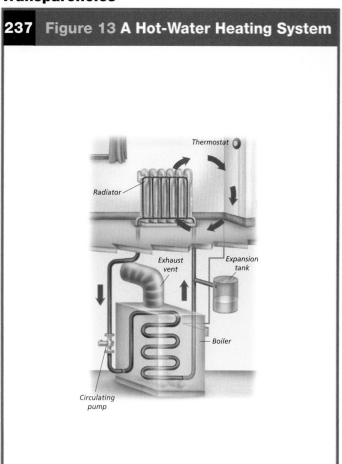

Transparencies

238 | Figure 14 **A Forced-Air Heating System**

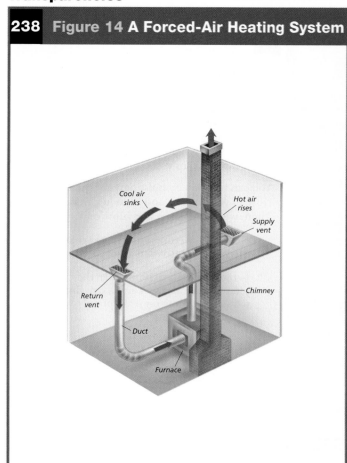

Transparencies

239 | Figure 16 **An Air Conditioner**

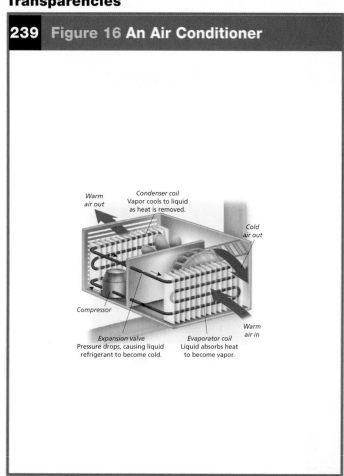

Guided Reading and Study Workbook

Name _____ Class _____ Date _____

Chapter 16   Thermal Energy and Heat

Section 16.3 Using Heat
(pages 486–492)

This section describes ways in which humans benefit from heat engines, heating systems, and cooling systems. It also discusses how each of these systems works.

Reading Strategy (page 486)

Sequencing As you read, complete the cycle diagram to show the sequence of events in a gasoline engine. For more information on this Reading Strategy, see the **Reading and Study Skills** in the **Skills and Reference Handbook** at the end of your textbook.

Sequence of Events in a Gasoline Engine

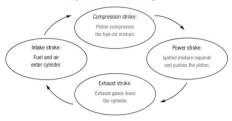

Compression stroke:
Piston compresses the fuel-air mixture.

Intake stroke:
Fuel and air enter cylinder.

Power stroke:
Ignited mixture expands and pushes the piston.

Exhaust stroke:
Exhaust gases leave the cylinder.

Heat Engines (pages 486–487)

1. The two main types of heat engines are the __external combustion engine__ and the __internal combustion engine__.

2. A steam engine is an external combustion engine because it burns fuel __outside__ the engine.

3. Who developed the first practical steam engine?
   a. James Prescott Joule
   (b.) Thomas Newcomen
   c. James Watt
   d. Benjamin Thompson

4. How is heat converted into work in a steam engine? __Expanding steam pushes against a piston.__

5. A heat engine used by most cars in which fuel burns inside the engine is called a(n) __internal combustion engine__.

6. Each upward or downward motion of a piston in an internal combustion engine is called a(n) __stroke__.

Physical Science Guided Reading and Study Workbook • Chapter 16   **143**

Guided Reading and Study Workbook

Name _____ Class _____ Date _____

Chapter 16   Thermal Energy and Heat

7. Is the following sentence true or false? In a typical car, the crankshaft produces a linear motion that turns the wheels. __false__

8. Why is it important for an internal combustion engine to have a cooling system? __Waste energy produced when the engine does work is transferred to the atmosphere by the cooling system. Without it, the engine would be damaged by thermal expansion.__

9. Is the following sentence true or false? Gasoline engines operate very efficiently in converting fuel energy to work. __false__

Heating Systems (pages 489–490)

10. What is a central heating system? __It is a system that is used to heat many rooms from one location.__

11. List four energy sources used for central heating systems.
   a. __Natural gas__   b. __Coal__
   c. __Oil__   d. __Electrical energy__

12. Is the following sentence true or false? In most heating systems, conduction is used to distribute most of the thermal energy. __false__

Match each description with the heating system it describes.

	Description	**Heating System**
a 13.	Water heated by a boiler circulates through radiators in each room, transferring thermal energy.	a. hot-water heating
d 14.	Fans are used to circulate warm air through ducts to the rooms in a building.	b. steam heating
c 15.	A hot coil heats air by conduction and radiation.	c. electric baseboard heating
b 16.	This system is often used in older buildings or to heat many buildings from a single location.	d. forced-air heating

Cooling Systems (pages 490–492)

17. Is the following sentence true or false? Most cooling systems, such as air conditioners and refrigerators, are heat pumps. __true__

18. A fluid that vaporizes and condenses inside the tubing of a heat pump is called a(n) __refrigerant__.

19. How does a heat pump reverse the normal flow of thermal energy? __A heat pump must do work on a refrigerant to remove heat from a cold area, such as the inside of a refrigerator.__

144   *Physical Science* Guided Reading and Study Workbook • Chapter 16

Guided Reading and Study Workbook

Name _____ Class _____ Date _____

Chapter 16   Thermal Energy and Heat

WordWise

Answer the questions by writing the correct vocabulary term in the blanks. Use the circled letter(s) in each term to find the hidden vocabulary word. Then, write a definition for the hidden word.

Clues	Vocabulary Terms
This flows spontaneously from hot objects to cold objects.	h e a (t)
Any device that converts heat into work	(h) (e) a t e n g i n e
A heat pump does work on this so you can keep your veggies cold.	r e f (r) i g e r a n t
The Kelvin scale is used to measure this.	t e (m) p e r a t u r e
A device used to determine the specific heat of a material	c (a) l o r i m e t e r
The transfer of thermal energy when particles of a fluid move from place to place	c o n v e c t (i) o (n)
The amount of heat needed to raise the temperature of one gram of a material by one degree Celsius	(s) p e c i f i c h e a t
The transfer of thermal energy with no overall transfer of matter	c o n d (u) c t i o n
The total potential and kinetic energy of all the particles in an object	t h e r m a (l) e n e r g y
The transfer of energy by waves moving through space	r (a) d i a (t) i (o) n
According to the first law of thermodynamics, this is conserved.	e n e (r) g y

Hidden words: __t h e r m a l   i n s u l a t o r__

Definition: __A material that conducts thermal energy poorly__

Physical Science Guided Reading and Study Workbook • Chapter 16   **145**

Guided Reading and Study Workbook

Name _____ Class _____ Date _____

Chapter 16   Thermal Energy and Heat

Calculating with Specific Heat

How much heat is required to raise the temperature of a gold earring from 25.0°C to 30.0°C? The earring weighs 25 grams, and the specific heat of gold is 0.128 J/g•°C.

Math Skill: Formulas and Equations

You may want to read more about this Math Skill in the **Skills and Reference Handbook** at the end of your textbook.

1. Read and Understand

What information are you given?

Specific heat = c = 0.128 J/g•°C

Mass = m = 25.0 grams

Change in Temperature = ΔT = (30.0°C − 25.0°C) = 5.0°C

2. Plan and Solve

What unknown are you trying to calculate?

Amount of heat needed = Q = ?

What formula contains the given quantities and the unknown?

Q = Mass × Specific heat × Change in Temperature

$Q = m \times c \times \Delta T$

Replace each variable with its known value.

Q = 25.0 g × 0.128 J/g•°C × 5.0°C = 16 J

3. Look Back and Check

Is your answer reasonable?

$$\frac{\text{Heat absorbed}}{(m \times c)} = 16 \text{ J}/(25.0 \text{ g} \times 0.128 \text{ J/g•°C}) = 5.0°C$$

This is a reasonable answer for the heat required to raise the temperature of the earring.

Math Practice

On a separate sheet of paper, solve the following problems.

1. How much heat is required to raise the temperature of 25 grams of water from 25.0°C to 30.0°C? The specific heat of water is 4.18 J/g•°C.
   $Q = m \times c \times \Delta T$ Q = 25 g × 4.18 J/g•°C × 5.0°C = 520 J
   Heat absorbed by the water = Q = 520 J

2. Determine the mass of a sample of silver if 705 J of heat are required to raise its temperature from 25°C to 35°C. The specific heat of silver is 0.235 J/g•°C.
   $m = Q / (c \times \Delta T)$ m = 705 J / (0.235 J/g•°C × 10°C)
   m = 300 g

3. An iron skillet has a mass of 500.0 g. The specific heat of iron is 0.449 J/g•°C. The pan is heated by adding 19,082.5 J of heat. How much does the temperature of the pan increase?
   $\Delta T = Q / (m \times c)$ 19,082.5 J = 500.0g × 0.449 J/g•°C × ΔT
   19,082.5 J /(500.0 g × 0.449 J/g•°C) = ΔT
   ΔT = 85.0°C

146   *Physical Science* Guided Reading and Study Workbook • Chapter 16

Student Edition Lab Worksheet

Name _____ Class _____ Date _____

Chapter 16   Thermal Energy and Heat   **Design Your Own Lab**

Using Specific Heat to Analyze Metals

In this lab, you will determine the specific heat of steel and aluminum. Then, you will use specific heat to analyze the composition of a metal can.

See page 493 in the Teacher's Edition for more information.

Problem How can you use specific heat to determine the composition of a metal can?

Materials

- 10 steel bolts
- balance
- 50-cm length of string
- clamp
- ring stand
- boiling water bath (shared with class)
- thermometer
- 500-mL graduated cylinder
- ice water
- foam cup with lid
- aluminum nails
- crushed can

Skills Calculating, Designing Experiments

Procedure ⬛ 🛠 🧪 ⚠

Part A: Determining Specific Heat

1. Measure and record the mass of 10 steel bolts.

Ten bolts with a mass of 100 g will raise the temperature of 200 mL of water by about 5°C. The same mass of aluminum nails will raise the temperature by about 9°C.

DATA TABLE

	Water	Steel Bolts	Aluminum Nails
Mass (g)			
Initial temperature (°C)			
Final temperature (°C)			
Specific heat (J/g • °C)	4.18		

2. Tie the bolts to the string. Use a clamp and ring stand to suspend the bolts in the boiling water bath. **CAUTION:** *Be careful not to splash boiling water.* After a few minutes, record in the data table the water temperature as the initial temperature of the bolts.

3. Use a graduated cylinder to pour 200 mL of ice water (without ice) into the foam cup. Record the mass and temperature of the ice water. (*Hint:* The density of water is 1 g/mL.)

4. Use the clamp to move the bolts into the cup of ice water. Cover the cup and insert the thermometer through the hole in the cover.

5. Gently swirl the water in the cup. Record the highest temperature as the final temperature for both the water and the steel bolts.

6. Calculate and record the specific heat of steel. (*Hint:* Use the equation $Q = m \times c \times \Delta T$ to calculate the energy the water absorbs.)

7. Repeat Steps 2 through 6 with aluminum nails to determine the specific heat of aluminum. Use a mass of aluminum that is close to the mass you used for the steel bolts.

Student Edition Lab Worksheet

Name _____ Class _____ Date _____

Part B: Design Your Own Experiment

8. **Designing Experiments** Design an experiment that uses specific heat to identify the metals a can might be made of.

9. In the space below, construct a data table in which to record your observations. After your teacher approves your plan, perform your experiment.

Analyze and Conclude

1. **Comparing and Contrasting** Which metal has a higher specific heat—aluminum or steel?

   The specific heat of aluminum (about 0.90 J/g°C) is higher than the specific heat of steel (about 0.45 J/g°C).

2. **Drawing Conclusions** Was the specific heat of the can closer to the specific heat of steel or of aluminum? What can you conclude about the material in the can?

   The specific heat of the can was very close to the specific heat of steel. This is evidence that the can is not made of aluminum and may be made of steel.

3. **Evaluating** Did your observations prove what the can was made of? If not, what other information would you need to be sure?

   The observations support the idea that the can is made of steel, but do not prove it; other metals may have similar specific heats. A list of the specific heats of various metals for comparison would be helpful, as would other kinds of evidence, such as the densities and chemical properties of the metals.

4. **Inferring** The can you used is often called a tin can. The specific heat of tin is 0.23 J/g°C. Did your data support the idea that the can was made mostly of tin? Explain your answer.

   The specific heat of the can is close to that of steel, not tin. This suggests that the can is not made primarily of tin.

Lab Manual

Name _____ Class _____ Date _____

Chapter 16   Thermal Energy and Heat   🔍 **Investigation 16A**

Thermal Conduction and Surface Area

Background Information

Refer students to pages 475–480 in their textbooks for a discussion of thermal energy, calorimetry, and conduction. **SKILLS FOCUS:** Predicting, Controlling Variables, Using Tables and Graphs **CLASS TIME:** 45 minutes

The quantity of energy transferred by heat from a body depends on a number of physical properties of the body and its surroundings. For a given substance, the rate at which thermal energy is transferred by conduction depends on temperature difference, cross-sectional area, and a thermal conductivity constant that is unique to the substance. By choosing one of these properties as a manipulated variable and making the other properties controlled variables, the effect of the manipulated variable on thermal conduction can be determined experimentally.

In this investigation, you will study the rates of cooling of three containers of water of equal volume but different surface area.

Problem

How does heat loss depend on surface area?

Pre-Lab Discussion

Read the entire investigation. Then, work with a partner to answer the following questions.

1. **Formulating Hypotheses** How would you expect the rate of thermal energy transfer from the water to depend on the water's surface area? What is your reason for this expectation?

   The water with the greatest surface area will lose thermal energy fastest and so will cool fastest. This happens because there are more particles of hot water in contact with cool air when the water's surface area is greater, and so more energy is transferred to the air over a given time.

2. **Controlling Variables** Identify the manipulated, responding, and controlled variables in this investigation.

   a. Manipulated variable

   The surface area of the water

   b. Responding variable

   The rate of temperature change

   c. Controlled variables

   The volume of the water, the initial temperature of the water, the room temperature, the material the containers are made of

---

Lab Manual

Name _____ Class _____ Date _____

3. **Designing Experiments** Why should plastic containers be used for holding the hot water during the experiment? Why should the containers and the graduated cylinder be warmed first with hot water?

   The containers should all be made of a good insulating plastic so that nearly all of the thermal energy lost from the water is through the water's surface. By warming the containers and graduated cylinder, the temperature of the water used for the measurements is kept more nearly constant, thus allowing the water in each container to be at nearly the same starting temperature.

4. **Using Tables and Graphs** How can you tell which graph indicates the greatest rate of thermal energy transfer?

   A steeper negative slope of the line indicates that the water's temperature declines more rapidly with time. The greater the rate at which temperature drops, the greater is the rate of energy transfer.

Materials *(per group)*

3 cylindrical plastic containers with different surface diameters

metric ruler

hot tap water

3 Celsius thermometers

100-mL graduated cylinder

grease pencil

clock or watch

graph paper

3 colored pencils

1000-mL beaker (optional)

hot plate (optional)

The hot water used should be roughly between 50°C and 60°C. If hot tap water is not available or if the tap water is cooler than 50°C, provide hot water stored in thermos bottles or use hot plates to heat water.

Safety ⬛ 🛠 🧪 💧 ⚠ 🔥

Put on safety goggles and a lab apron. Be careful to avoid breakage when working with glassware. Use extreme care when working with heated equipment or materials to avoid burns. Observe proper laboratory procedures when using electrical equipment. Note all safety alert symbols next to the steps in the Procedure and review the meaning of each symbol by referring to the Safety Symbols on page xiii.

Procedure

1. Label the plastic containers *A, B,* and *C,* using the grease pencil. Label the container with the smallest diameter *A* and the one with the largest diameter *C*.

Lab Manual

Name _____ Class _____ Date _____

2. Use the ruler to measure the diameter of each container and record this information in Data Table 1. Calculate the cross-sectional surface area, using the formula $Area = (Diameter/2)^2\pi$. Record these values in Data Table 1.

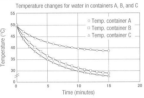 3. Run hot tap water until the water temperature reaches a constant value, about 50°C. Test the water temperature by holding a thermometer bulb in the stream of water. If you do not have a source of hot water, heat 600 mL of water in a beaker on a hot plate. Let the water reach a temperature of 50°C. **CAUTION:** *Use heat-resistant gloves. Be careful not to burn yourself or to break the thermometer or beaker. If using a hot plate, be careful to avoid burns and electrical shock. Wipe up any spilled water immediately.*

4. Warm the labeled containers by filling each of them with about 50 mL of hot water. Also fill the graduated cylinder to warm it. After a few minutes, pour out the water in the containers and the graduated cylinder. Refill the warm graduated cylinder with 100 mL of hot water. Quickly pour the water into container A. Repeat this process, pouring 100 mL of hot water into each of the other two containers.

5. Use the three thermometers to immediately measure the temperature of the water in the containers. Record the maximum temperature values in the second, third, and fourth columns of Data Table 2. The three beginning temperatures should be very similar. Look at a clock or watch and make a note of the time. Record the time in the "Time" column of Data Table 2. **CAUTION:** *Take care not to hit the thermometers against the sides of the containers.*

6. After 1 minute, record the time and the water temperature in each container. Continue to record the temperatures every minute for 15 minutes. Do not stir the water.

7. On a sheet of graph paper, make a graph of the information in Data Table 2. Plot the number of minutes from the start of the experiment on the horizontal axis (x-axis) and water temperature on the vertical axis (y-axis). Use a different-colored pencil for the data for each container. Draw curved lines to connect the data points for each container.

Use this graph to check student graphs.

Temperature changes for water in containers A, B, and C

○ Temp. container A
□ Temp. container B
△ Temp. container C

Lab Manual

Name _____ Class _____ Date _____

Observations Sample data are shown.

DATA TABLE 1

	Diameter (cm)	Surface area (cm²)
Container A	10.0	78.5
Container B	15.0	177
Container C	20.0	314

DATA TABLE 2

Time (min)	Temperature of Water in Container A (°C)	Temperature of Water in Container B (°C)	Temperature of Water in Container C (°C)
0	Specific responses will depend on the actual sizes of the containers, the initial temperature of the water, and the temperature of the room. However, for all three samples, temperature values should decrease rapidly at first and then level off. The values for container C should decrease most rapidly.		
1			
2			
3			
4			
5			
6			
7			
8			
9			
10			
11			
12			
13			
14			
15			

Lab Manual

Name _____ Class _____ Date _____

Analysis and Conclusions

1. **Observing** In general, what happened to the temperature of the water in the containers? Describe the three curves on your graph.

   The temperature decreases for all three samples. The three curves have a similar shape.

   The curves are not linear; the slope changes.

2. **Observing** From which container of water was thermal energy transferred the fastest? On what evidence do you base your answer?

   Thermal energy was transferred most quickly from container C. Container C cooled the fastest and

   produced the steepest temperature-time curve.

3. **Applying Concepts** What happened to the thermal energy that was in the water? Where did it go?

   Most of the energy was transferred to the cooler air above the water.

4. **Predicting** What would have happened, in terms of thermal energy transfer, if the water temperature had originally been 10.0°C? Explain your reasoning.

   Thermal energy would have been transferred from the warmer air to the cooler water, and

   the temperature of the water would have increased. This would have happened because the

   particles in the air would have a greater thermal energy and so would transfer that energy

   to the lower-energy water molecules.

Lab Manual

Name _____ Class _____ Date _____

5. **Drawing Conclusions** Based on your findings in this investigation, make a general statement relating thermal energy transfer to surface area. How does this statement compare to the hypothesis you made before the investigation?

   Assuming all other factors are equal, the larger the surface area is, the faster that thermal

   conduction occurs, and the faster temperature decreases. But there seems to be a limit to this

   effect because the cooling curves for containers B and C are very similar.

6. **Making Generalizations** Two lakes have exactly the same amount of water in them. The surrounding environment is at the same temperature. You can presume the ground beneath each lake is a thermal insulator. Which lake would lose thermal energy at a faster rate—one that was large and shallow or one that was small and deep? Explain your answer.

   The large, shallow lake would lose thermal energy at a faster rate because it has a greater

   surface area.

Go Further

Plan an investigation to determine how containers made of different materials affect heat loss. Indicate how the containers would differ from the containers used in the current experiment. Show your plan to your teacher. When your teacher approves your plan, carry out your experiment and report your results.

Students may suggest adding lids to containers so that the thermal conductivity of the container, and not of air, is tested. A controlled variable in the new investigation would now be surface area, which should be identical for all containers being used. In this way, the change in temperature with time would depend on the thermal properties of the container rather than differences in surface area.

Lab Manual

Name _____ Class _____ Date _____

Chapter 16   Thermal Energy and Heat   Investigation 16B

Boiling Water in a Paper Cup

Background Information

When a paper cup of water is heated over a flame, the transfer of the thermal energy occurs in three ways—conduction, convection, and radiation. Conduction occurs when there is contact between two materials. In the case of a paper cup containing water, conduction occurs from the paper cup to the water, and through the water itself. Convection occurs when a volume of heated liquid or gas moves from one place to another. When heating water in a paper cup, convection takes place in the air between the burner flame and the bottom of the paper cup, and in the water inside the cup. Radiation conveys energy by electromagnetic waves from a body at a temperature greater than that of its surroundings. In this investigation, the flame transfers thermal energy by radiation.

Because water has a high specific heat, a small amount of water can absorb a fairly large amount of energy without undergoing a large temperature change. An even greater amount of energy must be absorbed by water for it to undergo the phase change from liquid to gas. The temperature at which water boils at sea level is 100°C, and it remains at this temperature until all of the liquid water has boiled. The paper cup would start to burn if the temperature reached 233°C.

In this investigation, you will attempt to boil water in a paper cup over the flame of a Bunsen burner.

Refer students to pages 479–481 in their textbooks for a discussion of the methods of thermal energy transfer. Pages 476 and 477 introduce the concept of specific heat, which will be useful for this activity.

SKILLS FOCUS: Observing, Predicting
CLASS TIME: 30 minutes

Problem

Will the water in a paper cup boil before the cup ignites?

Pre-Lab Discussion

Read the entire investigation. Then, work with a partner to answer the following questions.

1. **Predicting** Predict the result of boiling water through a paper cup. Explain why you believe your prediction is true.

   Many students will predict that the cup will burn. However, the water will boil away, while the paper
   cup will remain unburned. During the transfer of energy to the water, the thin paper cup remains
   at the same temperature as the water it contains. Therefore, the temperature of the paper cup
   remains well below the temperature at which paper ignites and burns.

*Physical Science Lab Manual • Investigation 16B **173***

Lab Manual

Name _____ Class _____ Date _____

2. **Applying Concepts** When water boils, its temperature remains constant. Why doesn't this contradict the law of conservation of energy?

   During the phase change from liquid to gas, all of the energy added to the water breaks the
   bonds between the water molecules, so the average kinetic energy of the molecules does
   not increase. Because temperature is a measure of average kinetic energy, the temperature of
   the water does not increase during the phase change. Energy is still conserved, but it is used
   in a process that does not increase temperature.

3. **Designing Experiments** Why do you want to be sure that the paper cup does not have a wax coating?

   Wax may melt at temperatures below 100°C. The melted wax could get smoky or ignite, which would
   be hazardous.

4. **Making Generalizations** Use your prediction to explain why wet wood does not burn.

   The energy added to the wet wood is used to vaporize water rather than to ignite the wood.
   Only when the water has vaporized and the wood is dry can its temperature increase to the
   necessary temperature for burning.

Materials *(per group)*

paper cup (without wax coating)
ring stand
support ring
wire gauze
thermometer

DO NOT use plastic or polystyrene cups.

thermometer clamp
metal pie tin
Bunsen burner
matches

Safety 🥽 🧤 🔥 ⚠️ 🔦

Put on safety goggles and a lab apron. Tie back loose hair and clothing when working with flames. Do not reach over an open flame. Be careful when using matches. Use extreme care when working with heated equipment or materials to avoid burns. Make sure that fire suppressant equipment is available. Note all safety alert symbols next to the steps in the Procedure and review the meaning of each symbol by referring to the Safety Symbols on page xiii.

Procedure

1. Set up the equipment as shown in Figure 1. There should be approximately 15 cm between the top of the Bunsen burner and the bottom of the wire gauze.

174 *Physical Science Lab Manual • Investigation 16B*

Lab Manual

Name _____ Class _____ Date _____

2. Remove the paper cup. Fill three-fourths of the cup with water and carefully place it back on the center of the wire gauze. Use a thermometer clamp to make sure that the thermometer is suspended in the water so that it does not touch the bottom of the cup.

3. In the data table, record the initial temperature of the water.

4. Light the Bunsen burner and adjust the flame so that it does not touch the bottom of the wire gauze. **CAUTION:** *Be sure that the flame never touches the wire gauze directly.*

5. Observe the experiment from the time you start heating the cup of water. What happens before the water boils? What happens to the cup as the water boils? Record your observations next to the data table. **CAUTION:** *Be careful when working with boiling water.*

6. In the data table, record the water temperature every 2 minutes.

7. When the water occupies about one-fourth of the cup's volume, turn off the burner and let the water and the cup cool. **CAUTION:** *Do not handle equipment until it has cooled.*

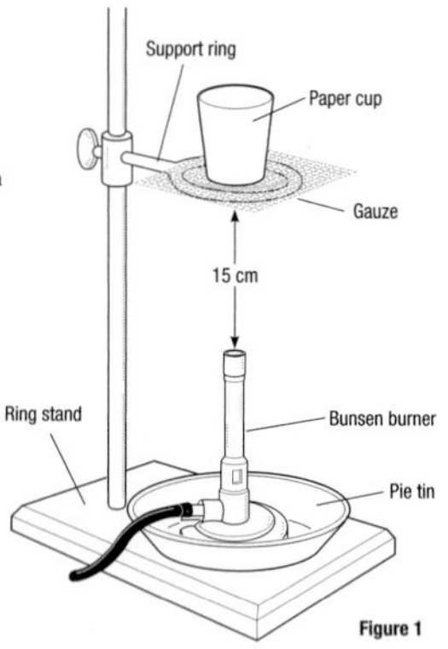

Figure 1

Observations

DATA TABLE Sample data are shown.

Time (minutes)	Water Temperature (°C)
0	21.3
2	28.0
4	36.5
6	49
8	62.5
10	77
12	89.5
14	98.9
16	98.9
18	95
20	78

Shortly after the burner is lit, small bubbles form in the water. After a few minutes, larger bubbles rise to the water's surface, and the water begins to boil. During this time, the cup remains intact.

Temperature increases with heating time. There may not be a consistent difference between readings as the liquid is heated. Temperature readings may decrease as the water level, reduced through evaporation, falls near and below the thermometer bulb.

*Physical Science Lab Manual • Investigation 16B **175***

Lab Manual

Name _____ Class _____ Date _____

Analysis and Conclusions

1. **Analyzing Data** What happened to the temperature of the water in the paper cup?

   As a result of thermal energy transfer, the water temperature increased until the water began
   to boil. Then, the temperature remained constant.

2. **Observing** What happened to the paper cup?

   The paper cup appeared unchanged although its temperature probably increased to equal that of
   the water inside it. Water boils at well below the ignition temperature of paper, so the paper cup
   did not burn. Convection within the water and conduction between the cup and water kept the
   temperature of the water and cup fairly uniform.

3. **Inferring** What determines the temperature of the paper cup?

   The water kept the cup at nearly the same temperature as the water itself. The cup's
   temperature would not rise above the boiling point of water until all of the water boils.

4. **Drawing Conclusions** Did your observations support or contradict your prediction? Explain your answer.

   Students should describe what they observed. Assuming that students predicted that the cup would
   be undamaged during the boiling of the water, then, if the cup remained intact while the water
   boiled, the prediction was supported. Students should offer explanations for any observations
   that contradict the prediction, such as if there is direct contact between the flame and the bottom
   of the paper cup.

Go Further

For an additional investigation, determine whether the wire gauze between the flame and the cup prevented the cup from igniting.
As long as the flame does not come in contact with the bottom of the paper cup, then the experimental observations will be the same as before. If the flame was to touch the bottom of the cup, the rate of heating of the bottom of the cup would be fast enough to cause the cup to ignite.

176 *Physical Science Lab Manual • Investigation 16B*

Chapter Test A

Name _____ Class _____ Date _____

Chapter 16   Thermal Energy and Heat   **Chapter Test A**

Multiple Choice

Write the letter that best answers the question or completes the statement on the line provided.

_____ 1. From his observations of cannon drilling, Count Rumford concluded that heat could NOT be a form of
    a. kinetic energy.   **b.** potential energy.
    c. matter.   **d.** radiation.

_____ 2. Heat is the transfer of thermal energy from one object to another because of a difference in
    a. specific heat.   **b.** phase.
    c. temperature.   **d.** waste heat.

_____ 3. As the temperature of an object rises, so does the
    a. kinetic energy of the object.
    b. mass of the object.
    c. thermal energy of the object.
    d. potential energy of the object.

_____ 4. Thermal energy depends on an object's
    a. mass.   **b.** phase (sold, liquid, or gas).
    c. temperature.   **d.** all of the above

_____ 5. How do you know that a sealed calorimeter is a closed system?
    a. because temperature is conserved
    b. because the masses of the sample and water are equal
    c. because thermal energy is not transferred to the environment
    d. because work is done on the test sample

_____ 6. Matter is needed to transfer thermal energy by
    a. conduction **b.** convection. **c.** radiation. **d.** both a and b

_____ 7. The vacuum inside the thermos bottle shown in Figure 16-1 stops which type of thermal energy transfer to keep the liquid hot?
    a. convection   **b.** conduction
    c. radiation   **d.** both a and b

Rubber stopper
Outside plastic case
Outer glass layer
Vacuum
Silvered inner glass layer
Hot beverage

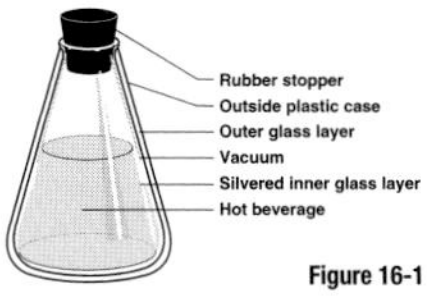

Figure 16-1

_____ 8. According to the first law of thermodynamics, the amount of work done by a heat engine equals the amount of
    a. work done on the engine.
    b. waste heat it produces.
    c. thermal energy added to the engine minus the waste heat.
    d. thermal energy added to the engine plus the waste heat.

Name _____ Class _____ Date _____

_____ 9. Disorder in the universe increases because
    a. spontaneous changes produce more order in a system.
    b. work produces disorder in a system.
    c. work produces waste heat, which leaves a system.
    d. all of the above

_____ 10. One consequence of the third law of thermodynamics is that
    a. heat engines have efficiencies less than 100 percent.
    b. in some energy conversions, energy is not conserved.
    c. engines cannot discharge waste heat.
    d. the work a heat engine produces is less than the waste heat it produces.

_____ 11. In most four-stroke internal combustion engines, when does the piston move downward?
    a. during the compression stroke only
    b. during the compression and exhaust strokes
    c. during the intake and exhaust strokes
    d. during the power and intake strokes

_____ 12. In forced-air heating systems, where are warm-air vents usually located?
    a. above windows   **b.** near the floor
    c. next to cold-air ducts **d.** under radiators

_____ 13. Which of the following happens in a heat pump?
    a. The compressor increases the pressure and temperature of the refrigerant.
    b. The compressor blows cold refrigerant into the room.
    c. The compressor absorbs heat from the refrigerant.
    d. none of the above

_____ 14. Which of the following describes an advantage of radiant heaters?
    a. They are portable.
    b. They can easily be turned on or off.
    c. They direct warm air to where it is needed.
    d. all of the above

Completion

Complete each statement on the line provided.

1. Heat is the transfer of thermal energy because of a _____ difference.

2. If the temperature change of an aluminum nail is negative, thermal energy is transferred _____ the nail _____ the surroundings.

3. In a calorimeter, the increase in the thermal energy of the water and the decrease in the thermal energy of the sample are _____.

Chapter Test A

Name _____ Class _____ Date _____

4. As the fluid in a heat pump evaporates, _____ is transferred from the surroundings to the fluid.

5. Having air cleaned as it passes through _____ near the furnace is an advantage of a(n) _____ heating system.

Short Answer

In complete sentences, write the answers to the questions on the lines provided.

1. Why does a rubber band become warm when you stretch it repeatedly?

2. What role do free electrons have in conduction in metals?

3. Explain how energy is conserved in a heat pump.

4. You add several drops of red food coloring to the water in a beaker without stirring. After a short time, the water has a red color throughout. Was the system of the food coloring and water more organized before or after you added the food coloring to the water? Which law of thermodynamics explains the change in order?

5. As what type of combustion engine would you classify steam turbines used in power plants? Why?

Name _____ Class _____ Date _____

Using Science Skills

Use the diagram to answer each question. Write the answers on a separate sheet of paper.

1. **Interpreting Data** Compare the average kinetic energy of the water molecules in the three beakers in Figure 16-2.

2. **Applying Concepts** Compare the thermal energy of the water in the three beakers in Figure 16-2.

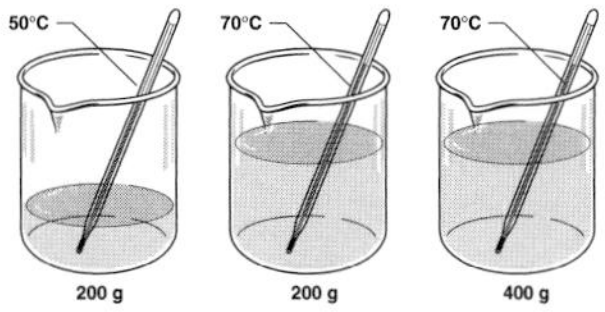

50°C   70°C   70°C

200 g   200 g   400 g

Figure 16-2

3. **Applying Concepts** Equal amounts of thermal energy are transferred to the water in each container shown in Figure 16-2. Explain why the water in B has the highest final temperature.

4. **Predicting** In Figure 16-2, what will be the final temperature of the water in each container after 200 g of 70°C water is added? Assume no heat is transferred to the environment.

5. **Drawing Conclusions** The water in the three containers shown in Figure 16-2 is combined with no heat transfer to the environment. Explain whether the temperature of the mixture will be closer to 50°C or 70°C.

Problem

Write the answers to each question on a separate sheet of paper.

1. How many kilojoules of heat must be transferred to a 420-g aluminum pizza pan to raise its temperature from 22°C to 232°C? The specific heat of aluminum in this temperature range is 0.96 J/g•°C. Show your work.

2. As 315 g of hot milk cools in a mug, it transfers 31,000 J of heat to the environment. What is the temperature change of the milk? The specific heat of milk is 3.9 J/g•°C. Show your work.

3. A 410-g cylinder of brass is heated to 95.0°C and placed in a calorimeter containing 335 g of water at 25.0°C. The water is stirred, and its highest temperature is recorded as 32.0°C. From the thermal energy gained by the water, determine the specific heat of brass. The specific heat of water is 4.18 J/g•°C. Show your work.

Essay

Write the answers to each question on a separate sheet of paper.

1. How do convection currents form in air?

2. How can a heat pump warm a house by causing a refrigerant to evaporate and condense?

Chapter Test B

Name _____ Class _____ Date _____

Chapter 16 Thermal Energy and Heat   Chapter Test B

Multiple Choice

Write the letter that best answers the question or completes the statement on the line provided.

_____ 1. Which of the following is a unit of temperature?
  a. Celsius degree   b. joule
  c. kilogram   d. calorie

_____ 2. What property of an object is related to the average kinetic energy of the particles in that object?
  a. specific heat   b. mass
  c. conductivity   d. temperature

_____ 3. Which of the following devices is based on the property of thermal expansion?
  a. balance   b. calorimeter
  c. convection oven   d. thermometer

_____ 4. In the formula $Q = m \times c \times \Delta T$, which quantity represents the specific heat?
  a. c b. m c. Q d. ΔT

_____ 5. The specific heat of copper is 0.385 J/g·°C. Which equation would you use to calculate correctly the amount of heat needed to raise the temperature of 0.75 g of copper from 10°C to 25°C?
  a. $Q = 0.385 \text{ J/g·°C} \times (25°C - 10°C)$
  b. $Q = 0.75 \text{ g} \times 0.385 \text{ J/g·°C} \times 25°C$
  c. $Q = 0.75 \text{ g} \times 0.385 \text{ J/g·°C} \times 15°C$
  d. $Q = 0.75 \text{ g} \times 0.385 \text{ J/g·°C} \times 10°C$

_____ 6. In the formula $Q = m \times c \times \Delta T$, which quantity is measured in units of J/g·°C?
  a. c b. m c. Q d. ΔT

_____ 7. What does a calorimeter directly measure?
  a. change in temperature
  b. kinetic energy
  c. specific heat
  d. radiation

_____ 8. Energy from the sun reaches Earth mostly by
  a. conduction.   b. convection.
  c. radiation.   d. thermal expansion.

_____ 9. Which of the following materials conducts heat well?
  a. glass   b. plastic   c. metal   d. wood

Chapter Test B

Name _____ Class _____ Date _____

_____ 10. To which of the following does the first law of thermodynamics apply?
  a. heating objects
  b. transferring thermal energy
  c. doing work on a system
  d. all of the above

_____ 11. The second law of thermodynamics states that thermal energy can flow from colder objects to hotter objects
  a. by convection.
  b. only if work is done on the system.
  c. spontaneously.
  d. when thermal expansion takes place.

_____ 12. Which of the following states that absolute zero cannot be reached?
  a. the first law of thermodynamics
  b. the second law of thermodynamics
  c. the third law of thermodynamics
  d. the second and third laws of thermodynamics

_____ 13. Which of the following happens in a steam engine?
  a. Fuel is burned outside the engine
  b. Heat is converted into work
  c. Hot steam pushes a piston.
  d. all of the above

_____ 14. Which central heating system involves a furnace and a blower?
  a. electric baseboard   b. forced-air
  c. hot-water   d. steam

_____ 15. A fluid that vaporizes and condenses inside the tubing of a heat pump is called the
  a. compressor. b. fuel. c. refrigerant. d. condenser.

_____ 16. Which type of central heating system is often used when heating many buildings from a central location?
  a. electric baseboard   b. forced-air
  c. hot-water   d. steam

Completion

Complete each statement on the line provided.

1. A measure of how hot or cold an object is compared to a reference point can be measured in units of _____ or _____.

2. A hot dinner plate has _____ thermal energy than a similar dinner plate at room temperature.

Chapter Test B

Name _____ Class _____ Date _____

3. The decrease in volume of a material due to a temperature increase is called _____.

4. The transfer of thermal energy with no overall transfer of matter is called _____.

5. The transfer of energy as waves moving through space is called _____.

6. The thermos bottle in Figure 16-1 has two insulators—the glass layers and the vacuum. The _____ is the better thermal insulator.

7. A material that conducts thermal energy well is called a thermal _____.

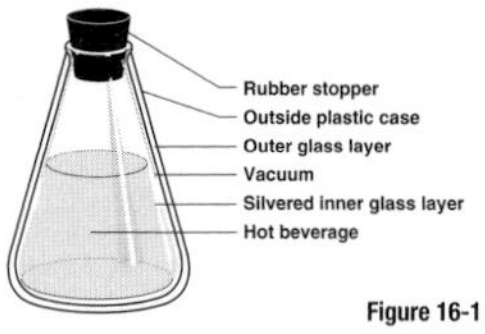

8. The study of the conversion between heat and other forms of energy is called _____.

9. Thermal energy that is not converted into work by a heat engine is called _____.

10. In most automobile engines, the linear motion of the strokes is turned into _____ motion by the crankshaft.

11. A steam-heating system is most similar to a(an) _____ heating system.

Rubber stopper
Outside plastic case
Outer glass layer
Vacuum
Silvered inner glass layer
Hot beverage

Figure 16-1

Short Answer

In complete sentences, write the answers to the questions on the lines provided.

1. Describe the spontaneous flow of heat between objects at different temperatures.

2. In general, what is the order of increasing thermal expansion among solids, liquids, and gases when a given amount of thermal energy is added?

3. How does placing the lid of a jar under hot water help loosen it?

Chapter Test B

Name _____ Class _____ Date _____

4. Explain what happens to the surrounding air when a refrigerant condenses and why this happens.

5. How has keeping foods refrigerated helped society?

Using Science Skills

Use the diagram to answer each question. Write the answers on a separate sheet of paper.

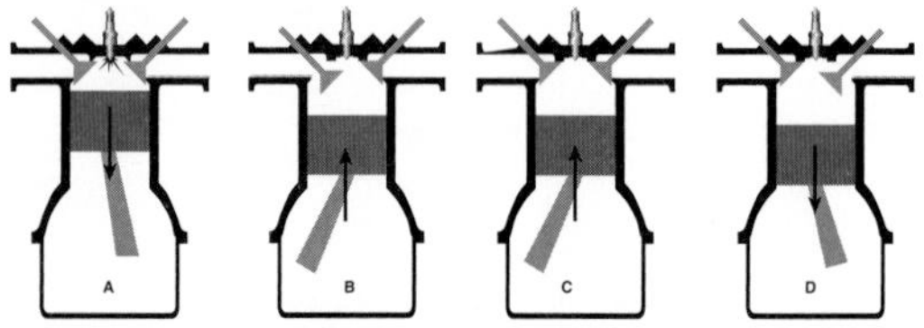

Figure 16-2

1. **Inferring** In Figure 16-2, is the temperature of the material within the cylinder greatest during the intake stroke, compression stroke, power stroke, or exhaust stroke?

2. **Interpreting Visuals** Sequence the four strokes of the engine shown in Figure 16-2 in the following order: intake stroke, compression stroke, power stroke, and exhaust stroke.

3. **Applying Concepts** What is the engine in Figure 16-2 designed to do?

4. **Applying Concepts** According to the second law of thermodynamics, why can't the engine in Figure 16-2 have an efficiency of 100 percent?

5. **Classifying** What type of combustion engine is shown in Figure 16-2?

Chapter 16 Test A Answers

Multiple Choice

1. c	2. c	3. c	4. d	5. c	6. d	7. d
8. c	9. c	10. a	11. d	12. b	13. a	14. d

Completion

1. temperature 2. from, to 3. equal; the same 4. thermal energy
5. filters, forced-air

Short Answer

1. Some of the work you do in stretching the rubber band increases the average kinetic energy of the particles in the rubber band, causing its temperature to rise. 2. Free electrons collide with each other and with atoms or ions to transfer thermal energy. 3. Energy is conserved in a heat pump because the amount of work done on the pump and the amount of thermal energy it transfers from the cold environment equals the amount of thermal energy it releases to the hotter environment. 4. more organized before; the second law of thermodynamics 5. external combustion engine; because the steam, which runs the turbine, is produced by fuel, which is burned outside the engine

Using Science Skills

1. The average kinetic energy of the water molecules in B equals the average kinetic energy of the molecules in C but is greater than the average kinetic energy of the molecules in A. 2. The thermal energy of the water in C is greater than the thermal energy of the water in B, which is greater than the thermal energy of the water in A. 3. B's water has less mass than C's water has, so B's water has a greater temperature change, making B's final water temperature higher. Even though the temperature change for A and B is the same since they have the same mass, B's final water temperature is higher because B's water had a higher beginning temperature. 4. Temperature$_A$ = 60ºC (The thermal energy transferred from the hotter water equals the thermal energy transferred to the warm water.) Because equal masses of water combine, the temperature drop of the hotter water equals the temperature rise of the warm water. The result is that the final temperature of each lies halfway between 50ºC and 70ºC, which is 60ºC. Temperature$_B$ = Temperature$_C$ = 70º (There is no transfer of heat between materials at the same temperature.) 5. Heat transferred from the hotter water equals heat transferred to the warm water. Since there are 600 g of hotter water and 200 g of warm water, the temperature change (drop) of the hotter water will be less than the temperature change (rise) of the warm water. As a result, the final temperature of the mixture will be closer to 70ºC than to 50ºC.

Problem

1. $Q = m \times c \times \Delta T = 420g \times 0.96J/g \bullet ºC \times (232ºC - 22ºC)$
$Q = 420g \times 0.96J/g \bullet ºC \times 210ºC = 85,000J = 85kJ$

2. $Q = m \times c \times \Delta T$
$\Delta T = \dfrac{Q}{m \times c} = \dfrac{31,000J}{315g \times 3.9J/g \bullet ºC} = 25ºC$

3. $Q_{water} = m_{water} \times c_{water} \times \Delta T_{water} = 335g \times 4.18J \bullet g/ºC$
$\times (32.0ºC - 25.0ºC)$ $Q_{water} = 335g \times 4.18J/g \bullet ºC \times 7.0ºC = 7000J$
The heat transferred *from* the brass equals the heat transferred *to* the water.

$Q_{brass} = Q_{water} = m_{brass} \times c_{brass} \times DT_{brass} = Q_{water}$

$c_{brass} = \dfrac{Q_{water}}{m_{brass} \times \Delta T_{brass}} = \dfrac{9800J}{410g \times (95.0ºC - 32.0ºC)}$

$c_{brass} = \dfrac{9800J}{410g \times 63.0ºC} = 0.38J/g \bullet ºC$

Essay

1. When the air near a heat source is heated, it expands, causing its density to decrease. This less dense, warmer air is buoyed up by the colder air that pushes around and under it. As the warm air is pushed upward, it cools, becomes more dense, and then sinks. It now moves in beneath the air that is being warmed by the heat source and pushes it upward. As parts of the fluid alternately heat and cool, loops of moving fluid form within the fluid itself. These loops are called convection currents. 2. If the pump causes a refrigerant to condense inside the house, the process will release thermal energy to the inside air and warm the air. If the pump releases the cooled refrigerant outside the house, the refrigerant will absorb thermal energy from the warmer surrounding air as the refrigerant evaporates. The absorbed thermal energy can then be used to warm the air inside the house.

Chapter 16 Test B Answers

Multiple Choice

1. a	2. d	3. d	4. a	5. c	6. a
7. a	8. c	9. c	10. d	11. b	12. c
13. d	14. b	15. c	16. d		

Completion

1. kelvins, degrees Celsius 2. greater 3. thermal contraction
4. conduction 5. radiation 6. vacuum 7. conductor
8. thermodynamics 9. waste heat 10. rotary 11. hot-water

Short Answer

1. Heat flows spontaneously from hot objects to cold objects.
2. solids, liquids, gases 3. When heated, the metal lid expands at a greater rate than the glass jar. The expanded lid is easier to loosen. 4. The surrounding air is warmed. The refrigerant cools and loses thermal energy as it turns from a gas to a liquid.
5. Keeping foods refrigerated keeps them from spoiling quickly. Since there is less spoilage, there is less chance of diseases from eating spoiled foods.

Using Science Skills

1. power stroke 2. D, C, A, B 3. convert heat into work
4. The efficiency of a heat engine would be 100 percent if the engine could exhaust waste heat (thermal energy) to an outside environment that had a temperature of absolute zero (0 K). However, according the third law of thermodynamics, a temperature of absolute zero cannot be reached.
5. internal combustion engine

Chapter 17 Mechanical Waves and Sound

Planning Guide

Use these planning tools
Easy Planner
Resource Pro
Online Lesson Planner

SECTION OBJECTIVES	STANDARDS		ACTIVITIES and LABS
	NATIONAL (See p. T18.)	STATE	
17.1 Mechanical Waves, pp. 500–503 🕐 1 block or 2 periods **17.1.1 Define** mechanical waves and **relate** waves to energy. **17.1.2 Describe** transverse, longitudinal, and surface waves and **discuss** how they are produced. **17.1.3 Identify** examples of transverse and longitudinal waves. **17.1.4 Analyze** the motion of a medium as each kind of mechanical wave passes through it.	A-1, A-2, B-6		**SE** Inquiry Activity: How Does a Disturbance Produce Waves? p. 499 L2 **SE** Quick Lab: Observing Waves in a Medium, p. 502 L2 **TE** Teacher Demo: Wave Dance, p. 501 L2
17.2 Properties of Mechanical Waves, pp. 504–507 🕐 1 block or 2 periods **17.2.1 Define** frequency, period, wavelength, and wave speed and **describe** these properties for different kinds of waves. **17.2.2 Solve equations** relating wave speed to wavelength and frequency or period. **17.2.3 Describe** how to measure amplitude and **relate** amplitude to the energy of a wave.	A-1, A-2, B-6		**SE** Quick Lab: Comparing Frequency and Wave Speed, p. 505 L2
17.3 Behavior of Waves, pp. 508–512 🕐 1 block or 2 periods **17.3.1 Describe** how reflection, refraction, diffraction, and interference affect waves. **17.3.2 State a rule** that explains refraction of a wave as it passes from one medium to another. **17.3.3 Identify** factors that affect the amount of refraction, diffraction, or interference. **17.3.4 Distinguish** between constructive and destructive interference and **explain** how standing waves form.	B-6		**TE** Teacher Demo: Water-Wave Reflections, p. 508 L2 **TE** Teacher Demo: Standing Waves, p. 512 L2
17.4 Sound and Hearing, pp. 514–521 🕐 1 block or 2 periods **17.4.1 Describe** the properties of sound waves and **explain** how sound is produced and reproduced. **17.4.2 Describe** how sound waves behave in applications such as ultrasound and music. **17.4.3 Explain** how relative motion determines the frequency of sound an observer hears. **17.4.4 Analyze** the functions of the main regions of the human ear.	A-1, A-2, B-6, C-6, E-2, F-1, F-2 F-5, G-1		**SE** Exploration Lab: Investigating Sound Waves, pp. 524–525 L2 **TE** Build Science Skills: Observing, p. 515 L2 **LM** Investigation 17A: Comparing the Speed of Sound L2 **LM** Investigation 17B: Comparing Sound Conduction L1

Ability Levels

L1 For students who need additional help
L2 For all students
L3 For students who need to be challenged

Components

SE	Student Edition
TE	Teacher's Edition
LM	Laboratory Manual
PLM	Probeware Lab Manual
GRSW	Guided Reading & Study Workbook With Math Support
CUT	Chapter and Unit Tests
CTB	Computer Test Bank
TP	Test Prep Resources
iT	iText
DC	Discovery Channel Videotapes
T	Transparencies
P	Presentation Pro CD-ROM
GO	Internet Resources

RESOURCES PRINT and TECHNOLOGY / SECTION ASSESSMENT

GRSW Section 17.1 **L1**
T Chapter 17 Pretest **L2**
Section 17.1 **L2**
P Chapter 17 Pretest **L2**
Section 17.1 **L2**
SCLINKS **GO** Vibrations and waves **L2**

SE Section 17.1 Assessment, p. 503
iT iT Section 17.1

GRSW Section 17.2 **L1**
GRSW Math Skill **L2**
T Section 17.2 **L2**
P Section 17.2 **L2**
SCLINKS **GO** Wave properties **L2**

SE Section 17.2 Assessment, p. 507
iT iT Section 17.2

GRSW Section 17.3 **L1**
T Section 17.3 **L2**
P Section 17.3 **L2**
SCLINKS **GO** Diffraction and interference **L2**

SE Section 17.3 Assessment, p. 512
iT iT Section 17.3

GRSW Section 17.4 **L1**
DC Noise! **L2**
T 17.4 **L2**
P Section 17.4 **L2**
SCIENCE NEWS GO Sound **L2**

SE Section 17.4 Assessment, p. 521
iT iT Section 17.4

Go Online

Go online for these Internet resources.

PHSchool.com
Web Code: cch-2173
Web Code: cca-2170

SCIENCE NEWS
Web Code: cce-2174

NSTA *SCLINKS*
Web Code: ccn-2171
Web Code: ccn-2172
Web Code: ccn-2173

Materials for Activities and Labs

Quantities for each group

STUDENT EDITION

Inquiry Activity, p. 499
dropper pipet; wide, flat-bottomed container; meter stick

Quick Lab, p. 502
large, clear container; food coloring; ruler; droppers (optional)

Quick Lab, p. 505
3-m rope, tape measure, stopwatch

Exploration Lab, pp. 524–525
meter stick, 2 cardboard tubes, scissors or scalpel, 2 rubber bands, wax paper, balloon, small mirror, transparent tape, flashlight

TEACHER'S EDITION

Teacher Demo, p. 501
10 chairs, 10 students, space to move around

Teacher Demo, p. 508
clear bowl, water, overhead projector

Teacher Demo, p. 512
long, soft, heavy rope, such as a jump rope

Build Science Skills, p. 515
set of tuning forks of similar construction

Build Science Skills, p. 522
tuning fork hammer, 2 tuning forks with the same frequency (about 400 Hz), stethoscope

Chapter Assessment

CHAPTER ASSESSMENT

SE	Chapter Assessment, pp. 527–528
CUT	Chapter 17 Test A, B
CTB	Chapter 17
iT	Chapter 17
PHSchool.com GO	

Web Code: cca-2170

STANDARDIZED TEST PREP

SE	Chapter 17, p. 529
TP	Diagnose and Prescribe

iText—interactive textbook with assessment at PHSchool.com

Mechanical Waves and Sound   498B

Name_____ Class_____ Date_____ M T W T F

Mechanical Waves

Time
2 periods
1 block

Section Objectives

Local Standards

- **17.1.1 Define** mechanical waves and **relate** waves to energy.
- **17.1.2 Describe** transverse, longitudinal, and surface waves and **discuss** how they are produced.
- **17.1.3 Identify** examples of transverse and longitudinal waves.
- **17.1.4 Analyze** the motion of a medium as each kind of mechanical wave passes through it.

Vocabulary mechanical wave • medium • crest • trough • transverse wave • compression • rarefaction • longitudinal wave • surface wave

1 FOCUS

Build Vocabulary: Paraphrase
Have students paraphrase the vocabulary terms using words they know. **L2**

Targeted Resources
❑ Transparency: Chapter 17 Pretest
❑ Transparency: Interest Grabber 17.1
❑ Transparency: Reading Strategy 17.1

2 INSTRUCT

Build Reading Literacy: Summarize
Have students construct a table to summarize what they have learned about mechanical waves. **L1**

Teacher Demo: Wave Dance
Students will simulate transverse waves and longitudinal waves. **L2**

Quick Lab: Observing Waves in a Medium
Students make waves with food coloring in water, and observe a mechanical wave as a passage of energy through a medium, with no net movement of the medium. **L2**

For Enrichment
Using bits of cork in various depths of water, students will generate waves and observe the motion of the cork bits. **L3**

Targeted Resources
❑ Transparency: Figure 2: Transverse Waves
❑ Transparency: Figure 3: Longitudinal Waves
❑ Transparency: Figure 4: Surface Waves
❑ GRSW Section 17.1
❑ **NSTA** *sci*$_{LINKS}$ Vibrations and waves

3 ASSESS

Reteach
Use Figures 2 and 3 to summarize the similarities and differences between transverse and longitudinal waves. **L1**

Evaluate Understanding
Have students write a paragraph summarizing the content of this section. **L2**

Targeted Resources
❑ **PHSchool.com** Online Section 17.1 Assessment
❑ iText Section 17.1

Transparencies

240 **Chapter 17 Pretest**

1. What is energy?

2. What is mechanical energy?

3. True or False: Displacements in opposite directions add together.

4. How is speed calculated?

5. What are the standard units of distance and time?

6. Which is longer, 0.25 m or 25 m?

7. What happens to the spacing of the particles within a solid or liquid as the temperature increases?

ANSWERS
1. ability to do work
2. energy due to the motion or position of an object
3. False; Displacement in opposite directions subtract.
4. distance/time
5. meters and seconds
6. 25 m
7. The particles move farther apart.

Transparencies

241 **Chapter 17 Pretest** *(continued)*

8. What happens to the speed of the particles in a solid, liquid, or gas as the temperature is increased?

9. If a car takes 2 hrs to travel 100 km, what is its average speed?

a. 25 km/h

b. 50 km/h

c. 75 km/h

d. 100 km/h

ANSWERS
8. The particles move faster.
9. b

Transparencies

242 **Section 17.1 Interest Grabber**

Vibrations

A wave is a vibration that carries energy from one place to another. But not all vibrations are waves.

Hold a pen lightly between your thumb and index finger. Shake your hand back and forth to make the pen seem to bend like it's made of rubber. Next, hold a length of string (about 1 meter long) at one end. Shake the end of the string back and forth. Observe the vibrations.

1. Describe the motion of the pen and the motion of the string.

2. In which case did the vibration move from one place to another? In which case did the vibration stay in one place?

ANSWERS
1. The pen's motion blurred as it vibrated back and forth. The string had a series of S-shaped curves that traveled along the string.
2. The pen vibrated in place. The vibrations moved along the string from one end to the other.

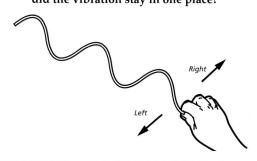
Right

Left

Transparencies

243 **Section 17.1 Reading Strategy**

ANSWERS
Longitudinal wave: compressions rarefactions, rest position, direction. Surface wave: circular motion that returns to same position, direction of wave.

a. Troughs
b. Rest position

Previewing

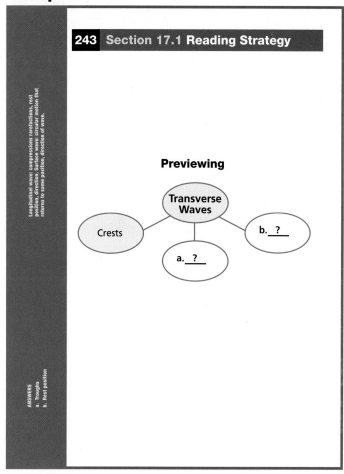

Transverse Waves

Crests

a. ?

b. ?

Transparencies

244 Figure 2 **Transverse Waves**

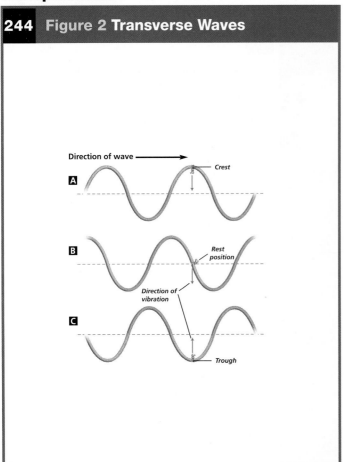

Transparencies

245 Figure 3 **Longitudinal Waves**

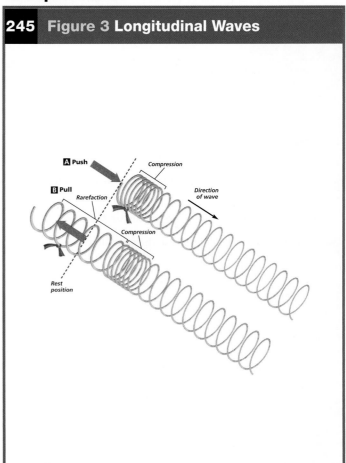

Transparencies

246 Figure 4 **Surface Waves**

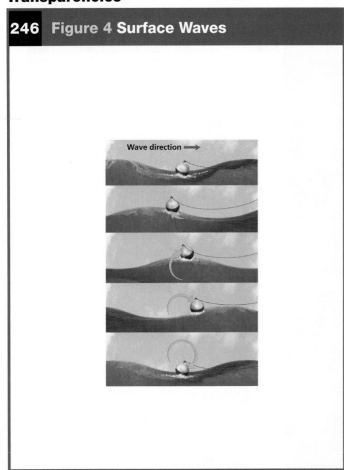

Guided Reading and Study Workbook

Section 17.1 Mechanical Waves
(pages 500–503)

This section explains what mechanical waves are, how they form, and how they travel. Three main types of mechanical waves—transverse, longitudinal, and surface waves—are discussed and examples are given for each type.

Reading Strategy (page 500)

Previewing As you read this section, use Figure 2 on page 501 to complete the web diagram. Then use Figures 3 and 4 to make similar diagrams for longitudinal waves and surface waves on a separate sheet of paper. For more information on this Reading Strategy, see the **Reading and Study Skills** in the **Skills and Reference Handbook** at the end of your textbook.

What Are Mechanical Waves? (page 500)

1. A disturbance in matter that carries energy from one place to another is called a(n) __mechanical wave__ .

2. Is the following sentence true or false? Mechanical waves can travel through empty space. __false__

3. The material through which a wave travels is called a(n) __medium__ .

4. Is the following sentence true or false? Solids, liquids, and gases all can act as mediums for waves. __true__

5. What creates a mechanical wave? __An energy source causes a vibration to travel__ __through a medium.__

Types of Mechanical Waves (pages 501–503)

6. Is the following sentence true or false? The three main types of mechanical waves are water waves, longitudinal waves, and surface waves. __false__

7. Circle the letter of the characteristic used to classify a mechanical wave.
   a. the height of its crest
   b. the depth of its trough
   c.(the way it travels through a medium
   d. the type of medium through which it travels

Guided Reading and Study Workbook

8. The highest point of a wave above the rest position is the __crest__ and the lowest point below the rest position is the __trough__ .

9. What is a transverse wave? __It is a wave that causes the medium to vibrate at right angles__ __to the direction in which the wave travels.__

10. Look at the figure below. Label the missing aspects of the wave in the rope.

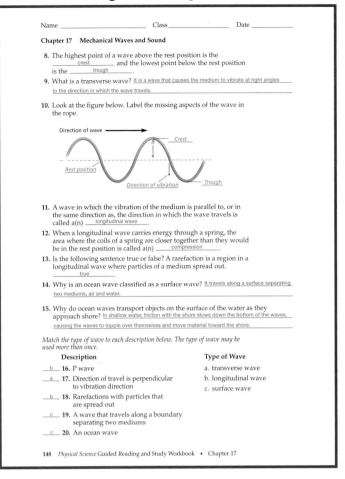

11. A wave in which the vibration of the medium is parallel to, or in the same direction as, the direction in which the wave travels is called a(n) __longitudinal wave__ .

12. When a longitudinal wave carries energy through a spring, the area where the coils of a spring are closer together than they would be in the rest position is called a(n) __compression__ .

13. Is the following sentence true or false? A rarefaction is a region in a longitudinal wave where particles of a medium spread out. __true__

14. Why is an ocean wave classified as a surface wave? __It travels along a surface separating__ __two mediums, air and water.__

15. Why do ocean waves transport objects on the surface of the water as they approach shore? __In shallow water, friction with the shore slows down the bottom of the waves,__ __causing the waves to topple over themselves and move material toward the shore.__

Match the type of wave to each description below. The type of wave may be used more than once.

	Description		Type of Wave
_b_	**16.** P wave		a. transverse wave
_a_	**17.** Direction of travel is perpendicular to vibration direction		b. longitudinal wave
_b_	**18.** Rarefactions with particles that are spread out		c. surface wave
_c_	**19.** A wave that travels along a boundary separating two mediums		
_c_	**20.** An ocean wave		

Name_____ Class_____ Date_____ M T W T F

Properties of Mechanical Waves

Time
2 periods
1 block

Section Objectives

- **17.2.1 Define** frequency, period, wavelength, and wave speed and **describe** these properties for different kinds of waves.
- **17.2.2 Solve equations** relating wave speed to wavelength and frequency or period.
- **17.2.3 Describe** how to measure amplitude and **relate** amplitude to the energy of a wave.

Vocabulary periodic motion • period • frequency • hertz • wavelength • amplitude

Local Standards

1 FOCUS

Build Vocabulary: Word Forms

Have students think of words that contain the root *ampl-*. Ask students what these words have in common. **L2**

Targeted Resources

❏ Transparency: Interest Grabber 17.2

❏ Transparency: Reading Strategy 17.2

2 INSTRUCT

Build Reading Literacy: Outline

Have students outline the section, leaving room for notes. Then, they should scan through each heading and try to find the main idea. **L1**

Build Science Skills: Measuring

Have students use a small ruler to measure the wavelength of each wave in Figure 6 and verify that the wavelength measured does not depend on which two corresponding points are used. **L2**

Quick Lab: Comparing Frequency and Wave Speed

Students will make waves by shaking a rope tied to a chair. They will record time and distance, in order to distinguish between wave frequency and wave speed. **L2**

Build Science Skills: Inferring

Ask students what happens to wavelength if the speed of a wave decreases, but the frequency stays the same. **L2**

Address Misconceptions

Emphasize that, in many mediums, mechanical waves move at approximately the same speed for a wide range of frequencies. **L2**

For Enrichment

Students can time the speed of waves in various other solid media, and attempt to determine the properties of materials that affect the speed of wave transmission. **L3**

Targeted Resources

❏ Transparency: Transparency: Figures 5 and 6: Frequency and Wavelength of Transverse Waves

❏ Transparency: Math Skills: Speed of Mechanical Waves

❏ Transparency: Figure 7: Amplitude of Transverse Waves

❏ GRSW Section 17.2

❏ **NSTA** *scLINKS* Wave properties

3 ASSESS

Reteach

Use Figure 7 to review the section's key concepts. Ask students to describe the frequency and wavelength of the waves. **L1**

Evaluate Understanding

Have students create cards of vocabulary terms and definitions, and then work in pairs to match them. **L2**

Targeted Resources

❏ **PHSchool.com** Online Section 17.2 Assessment

❏ iText Section 17.2

Transparencies

247 Section 17.2 Interest Grabber

Waves Carry Energy

When a wave travel through a medium, the wave carries energy, not particles, from one place to another. You can measure the speed of a wave by how fast energy moves from one place to another.

To model a wave's energy transfer, stand in a line with your classmates. The first person in the line should slowly pass a book to the second person. The second person should pass it to the third person, and so on down the line. Repeat the activity, but this time pass the book quickly.

1. What did the book represent?

2. How would you describe the speed of the wave in each case?

ANSWERS
1. The book represented energy being transferred by a wave. Some students may answer that the book represents a crest of the wave.
2. The energy (or crests) moved faster when the books were passed faster.

Transparencies

248 Section 17.2 Reading Strategy

d. The maximum displacement of a medium from its rest position

Building Vocabulary

Vocabulary Term	Definition
Period	a. ___?___
Frequency	b. ___?___
Wavelength	c. ___?___
Amplitude	d. ___?___

ANSWERS
a. The time required for one cycle.
b. The number of complete cycles in a given time.
c. The distance between a point on a wave and the same point on the next cycle of the wave.

Transparencies

249 Figures 5 and 6 **Frequency and Wavelength of Transverse Waves**

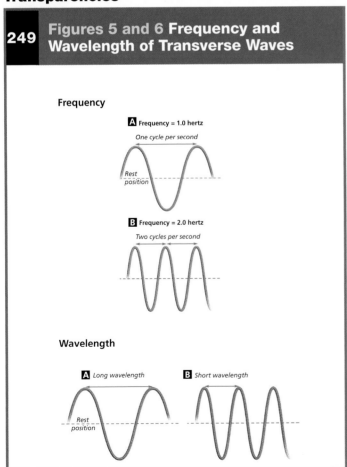

Frequency

A Frequency = 1.0 hertz

One cycle per second

Rest position

B Frequency = 2.0 hertz

Two cycles per second

Wavelength

A *Long wavelength*   **B** *Short wavelength*

Rest position

Transparencies

250 Math Skills **Speed of Mechanical Waves**

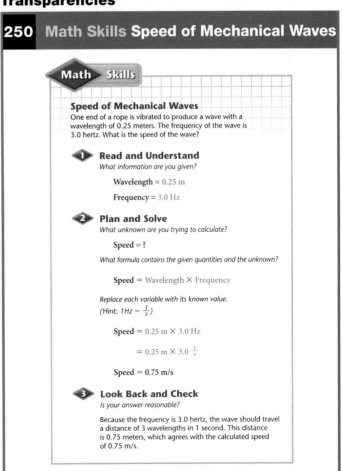

Math Skills

Speed of Mechanical Waves
One end of a rope is vibrated to produce a wave with a wavelength of 0.25 meters. The frequency of the wave is 3.0 hertz. What is the speed of the wave?

1 **Read and Understand**
What information are you given?

   Wavelength = 0.25 m

   Frequency = 3.0 Hz

2 **Plan and Solve**
What unknown are you trying to calculate?

   Speed = ?

What formula contains the given quantities and the unknown?

   Speed = Wavelength × Frequency

Replace each variable with its known value.
(Hint: $1 Hz = \frac{1}{s}$)

   Speed = 0.25 m × 3.0 Hz

   $= 0.25 \text{ m} \times 3.0 \frac{1}{s}$

   Speed = 0.75 m/s

3 **Look Back and Check**
Is your answer reasonable?

Because the frequency is 3.0 hertz, the wave should travel a distance of 3 wavelengths in 1 second. This distance is 0.75 meters, which agrees with the calculated speed of 0.75 m/s.

Transparencies

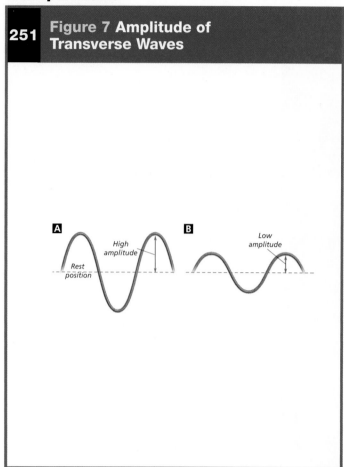

251 **Figure 7 Amplitude of Transverse Waves**

A

High amplitude

Rest position

B

Low amplitude

Guided Reading and Study Workbook

Name _____ Class _____ Date _____

Chapter 17   Mechanical Waves and Sound

Section 17.2 Properties of Mechanical Waves
(pages 504–507)

This section introduces measurable properties used to describe mechanical waves, including frequency, period, wavelength, speed, and amplitude.

Reading Strategy (page 504)

Build Vocabulary As you read, write a definition in your own words for each term in the table below. For more information on this Reading Strategy, see the **Reading and Study Skills** in the **Skills and Reference Handbook** at the end of your textbook.

Properties of Waves	
Vocabulary Term	**Definition**
Period	The time required for one cycle
Frequency	The number of complete cycles in a given time
Wavelength	The distance between a point on a wave and the same point on the next cycle of the wave
Amplitude	The maximum displacement of a medium from its rest position

Frequency and Period (page 504)

1. Is the following sentence true or false? A periodic motion repeats at regular time intervals. _____true_____
2. The time required for one cycle, a complete motion that returns to its starting point, is called the _____period_____.
3. The number of complete cycles in a given period of time is the _____frequency_____ of a periodic motion.
4. Circle the letter of each sentence that is true about frequency.
   a. Frequency is measured in cycles per second, or hertz.
   b. A wave's frequency equals the frequency of the vibrating source producing it.
   c. Five cycles per minute is a frequency of five hertz.
   d. Any periodic motion has a frequency.

Wavelength (page 505)

5. The distance between a point on one wave and the same point on the next cycle of the wave is called _____wavelength_____.
6. How is wavelength determined for a longitudinal wave?
   For a longitudinal wave, wavelength is the distance between adjacent compressions or rarefactions.

Physical Science Guided Reading and Study Workbook • Chapter 17 **149**

Guided Reading and Study Workbook

Name _____ Class _____ Date _____

Chapter 17   Mechanical Waves and Sound

Wave Speed (pages 505–506)

7. Write a formula you can use to determine the speed of a wave.
   Speed = Wavelength × Frequency
8. Is the following sentence true or false? The speed of a wave equals its wavelength divided by its period. _____true_____
9. What variables can cause the speed of a wave to change? The speed of a wave can change if it enters a new medium or if variables such as temperature and pressure change.
10. Circle the letter of the sentence that tells how wavelength is related to frequency for a wave traveling at a constant speed.
    a. Wavelength is equal to frequency.
    b. Wavelength is directly proportional to frequency.
    c. Wavelength is inversely proportional to frequency.
    d. A wave with a higher frequency will have a longer wavelength.

Amplitude (page 507)

11. What is the amplitude of a wave? Amplitude is the maximum displacement of a medium from its rest position.
12. It takes more energy to produce a wave with higher crests and deeper troughs, so the more energy a wave has, the _____greater_____ its amplitude.

Questions 13 through 17 refer to the figure below.

A

Amplitude

Rest position

B

1 wavelength

Amplitude

Rest position

13. The type of waves shown are _____transverse waves_____.
14. Label the rest position for waves A and B.
15. Add arrows to the figure to indicate the amplitude of each wave. Which wave has the greater amplitude? _____wave A_____
16. Which wave shown has more energy? _____wave A_____
17. Add an arrow to indicate one wavelength on wave B.

150 *Physical Science* Guided Reading and Study Workbook • Chapter 17

LESSON PLAN 17.3

Behavior of Waves

Time
2 periods
1 block

Section Objectives

- **17.3.1 Describe** how reflection, refraction, diffraction, and interference affect waves.
- **17.3.2 State a rule** that explains refraction of a wave as it passes from one medium to another.
- **17.3.3 Identify** factors that affect the amount of refraction, diffraction, or interference.
- **17.3.4 Distinguish** between constructive and destructive interference and **explain** how standing waves form.

Vocabulary reflection • refraction • diffraction • interference • constructive interference • destructive interference • standing wave • node • antinode

Local Standards

1 FOCUS

Build Vocabulary: Concept Map
Have students build a concept map using the terms in this section, with Behavior of Waves in an oval at the top. **L2**

Targeted Resources
❑ Transparency: Interest Grabber 17.3
❑ Transparency: Reading Strategy 17.3

2 INSTRUCT

Build Reading Literacy: Active Comprehension
Read the introductory paragraph on p. 508, and ask students what more they would like to know about wave behavior or how waves interact. After students read the section, make sure that all students' topics are addressed. **L1**

Use Visuals: Figure 11
Point out the similarities between the two images, and ask students what the diffraction pattern would look like if one of the barriers were removed in Figure 11A. **L1**

Teacher Demo: Water-Wave Reflections
Place a bowl of water on an overhead projector, making gentle waves, so that students can observe surface wave reflections. **L2**

Build Science Skills: Posing Questions
Using Figure 10, ask students how they could test the assertion that water waves move more slowly in more shallow water. **L2**

Address Misconceptions
Explain to students that, although refraction is always accompanied by a change in wavelength and speed, the direction of a wave does not always change. **L2**

Targeted Resources
❑ Transparency: Figure 12: Constructive vs. Destructive Interference of Waves
❑ GRSW Section 17.3
❑ **NSTA** *sci*_{LINKS} Diffraction and interference

3 ASSESS

Reteach
Use Figures 9–13 as examples that illustrate the key concepts of the section. **L1**

Evaluate Understanding
Have students write three review questions for this section. **L2**

Targeted Resources
❑ **PHSchool.com** Online Section 17.3 Assessment
❑ iText Section 17.3

Transparencies

252 Section 17.3 Interest Grabber

Reflected Waves

What happens when a wave hits a wall or some other fixed object? To find out, tie a rope to the back of a chair. Gently shake the rope up and down once to send a single pulse along the rope as shown. Observe what happens when the pulse hits the chair.

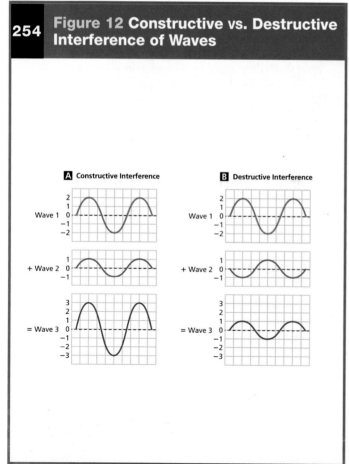

1. What happened to the direction of the pulse when it hit the chair?

2. How did the orientation of the reflected pulse compare to the original pulse?

ANSWERS
1. The pulse bounced off the chair; it reversed direction as it traveled back along the rope.
2. The pulse was turned upside down by the reflection.

Transparencies

253 Section 17.3 Reading Strategy

Identifying Main Ideas

Topic	Main Idea
Reflection	a. _____?_____
Refraction	b. _____?_____
Diffraction	c. _____?_____
Interference	d. _____?_____
Standing waves	e. _____?_____

ANSWERS
a. If reflection occurs at a fixed boundary, the reflected wave will be upside down compared to the original wave.
b. Refraction occurs when a wave enters a new medium at an angle because one side of a wave front moves more slowly than the other side.
c. The larger the wavelength is compared to the size of an opening or obstacle, the more a wave diffracts.
d. The types of interference are constructive and destructive interference.
e. A standing wave forms only if a multiple of one half wavelength fits exactly into the length of the vibrating object.

Transparencies

254 Figure 12 Constructive vs. Destructive Interference of Waves

A Constructive Interference

Wave 1

+ Wave 2

= Wave 3

B Destructive Interference

Wave 1

+ Wave 2

= Wave 3

Name _____ Class _____ Date _____

Chapter 17   Mechanical Waves and Sound

Section 17.3 Behavior of Waves
(pages 508–512)

This section describes different interactions that can occur when a mechanical wave encounters an obstacle, a change in medium, or another wave. These interactions include reflection, refraction, diffraction, and interference.

Reading Strategy (page 508)

Identifying Main Ideas Complete the table below. As you read, write the main idea of each topic. For more information on this Reading Strategy, see the **Reading and Study Skills** in the **Skills and Reference Handbook** at the end of your textbook.

Wave Interactions	
Topic	**Main Idea**
Reflection	A wave reflected at a fixed boundary will be flipped upside down.
Refraction	Refraction occurs when a wave enters a new medium at an angle because one side of a wave front moves more slowly than the other side.
Diffraction	The larger the wavelength is compared to the size of an opening or obstacle, the more a wave diffracts.
Interference	The types of interference are constructive and destructive interference.
Standing waves	A standing wave forms only if a multiple of one half wavelength fits exactly into the length of the vibrating object.

Reflection (page 508)

1. Is the following sentence true or false? Reflection occurs when a wave bounces off a surface that it cannot pass through. _____true_____

2. Circle the letter of the results that occur when a wave reflects off a fixed boundary.
   a. The reflected wave will be turned upside down.
   b. The amplitude will double as it strikes the surface.
   c. The speed of the wave will decrease.
   d. The frequency of the wave will decrease.

Refraction (page 509)

3. Why does refraction occur when a wave enters a new medium at an angle? Refraction occurs because one side of the wave moves more slowly than the other side.

4. Is the following sentence true or false? Refraction always involves a change in the speed and direction of a wave. _____true_____

Name _____ Class _____ Date _____

Chapter 17   Mechanical Waves and Sound

Diffraction (page 510)

5. What is required in order for diffraction to occur? Waves diffract when they encounter an obstacle or pass through a narrow opening.

6. Is the following sentence true or false? A wave diffracts more if its wavelength is small compared to the size of an opening or obstacle. _____false_____

Interference (pages 510–511)

7. What causes wave interference? Wave interference occurs when two or more waves overlap and combine.

8. Complete the table about interference.

Interference		
Type	**Alignment**	**Displacement Change**
Constructive	Crests align with crests; troughs align with troughs	Displacements combine to produce an increased amplitude.
Destructive	Crests align with troughs	Displacements combine to produce a reduced amplitude.

9. Is the following sentence true or false? Destructive interference can result in wave displacements that are above the rest position. _____true_____

10. How can an increased depth of a trough be considered constructive interference? When constructive interference occurs, two or more waves combine and their displacements add together, resulting in a wave with greater amplitude.

Standing Waves (page 512)

11. At certain frequencies, interference between a wave and its reflection can produce a(n) _____standing wave_____.

12. Circle each letter of a sentence that is true about standing waves.
    a. A node is a point that has no displacement from the rest position.
    b. Standing waves appear to move through a medium, such as a string.
    c. Complete destructive interference occurs at antinodes.
    d. A standing wave will form for any wavelength, as long as two ends of a rope or string are stretched tightly between two points.

13. Is the following sentence true or false? If a standing wave occurs in a medium at a given frequency, another standing wave will occur if this frequency is doubled. _____true_____

14. Give an example of a common standing wave. The vibrations you can see when plucking a stringed instrument are examples of standing waves.

Name_____ Class_____ Date_____ M T W T F

LESSON PLAN 17.4

Sound and Hearing

Time
2 periods
1 block

Section Objectives
Local Standards

- **17.4.1 Describe** the properties of sound waves and **explain** how sound is produced and reproduced.

- **17.4.2 Describe** how sound waves behave in applications such as ultrasound and music.

- **17.4.3 Explain** how relative motion determines the frequency of sound an observer hears.

- **17.4.4 Analyze** the functions of the main regions of the human ear.

Vocabulary sound waves • intensity • decibel • loudness • pitch • sonar • Doppler effect • resonance

1 FOCUS

Build Vocabulary: Paraphrase
Have students create a definition in their own words for any difficult vocabulary terms. **L2**

Targeted Resources
❑ Transparency: Interest Grabber 17.4
❑ Transparency: Reading Strategy 17.4

2 INSTRUCT

Build Reading Literacy: SQ3R
Using the study skill SQ3R, have students list the headings of this section, and write one question for each heading. Then, have students write answers to the questions as they read the section. **L1**

Use Community Resources
Invite members of a band or orchestra to demonstrate musical instruments for the class, and allow students to pose questions. **L2**

Build Science Skills: Observing
Have students model vibrations and sound waves by striking several different tuning forks and comparing their pitches. **L2**

Science and History: Sound Recording
Have students gently touch the surface of a loudspeaker grille as music is being played. Ask students to explain what is causing the vibrations. **L2**

For Enrichment
Interested students can research the origin of plucked and struck stringed instruments. **L3**

Targeted Resources
❑ Transparency: Figure 14: The Speed of Sound In Different Mediums
❑ Transparency: Figure 18: The Doppler Effect
❑ Transparency: Figure 19: The Anatomy of the Ear
❑ GRSW Section 17.4

3 ASSESS

Reteach
Have students define the vocabulary terms in their own words. **L1**

Evaluate Understanding
Have students outline and summarize the section. Then, divide the class into groups and have students edit each other's outlines. **L2**

Targeted Resources
❑ **PHSchool.com** Online Section 17.4 Assessment
❑ iText Section 17.4

Transparencies

255 Section 17.4 Interest Grabber

Can You Hear Through Your Desk?

Sound waves travel through a medium as energy is passed from particle to particle. If the particles are close together, as in a solid, the sound generally travels faster and less energy is lost.

Listen carefully to the sound as you knock on your desk. Note how far your ear is from your hand when you make the sound. Without changing this distance, place your ear against your desk and knock again.

1. In each case, how did the sound travel to your ears?

2. What was the difference in the sound when you held your ear against the desk?

ANSWERS
1. At first, the sound had to travel through air to reach your ears. When you held your ear to the desk, the sound traveled to your ear through the solid desk.
2. The sound is louder when heard through the solid material.

Transparencies

256 Section 17.4 Reading Strategy

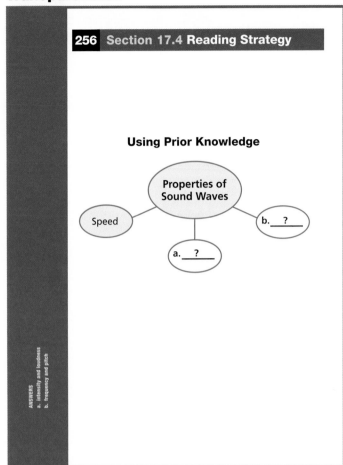

Using Prior Knowledge

Properties of Sound Waves

Speed

a. ___?___

b. ___?___

ANSWERS
a. intensity and loudness
b. frequency and pitch

Transparencies

257 Figure 14 The Speed of Sound in Different Mediums

Speed of Sound	
Medium (at 1 atm)	Speed (m/s)
Dry air, 0°C	331
Dry air, 20°C	342
Fresh water, 0°C	1401
Fresh water, 30°C	1509
Salt water, 0°C	1449
Salt water, 30°C	1546
Lead, 25°C	1210
Cast iron, 25°C	4480
Aluminum, 25°C	5000
Borosilicate glass, 25°C	5170

Transparencies

258 Figure 18 The Doppler Effect

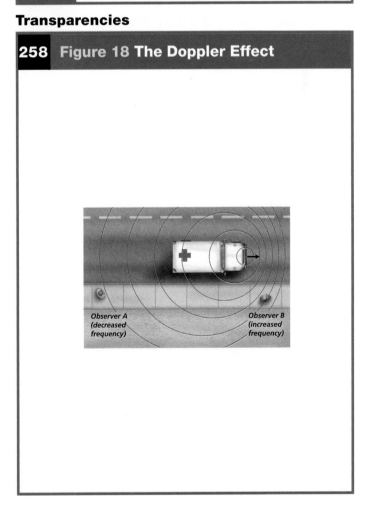

Observer A (decreased frequency)   Observer B (increased frequency)

Transparencies

259 Figure 19 The Anatomy of the Ear

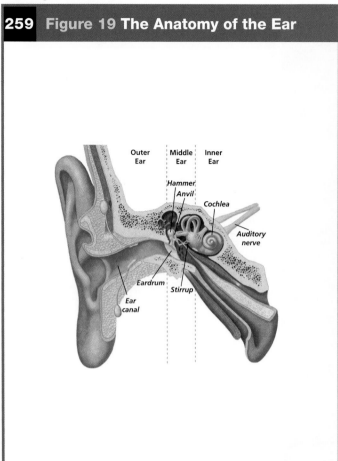

Outer Ear Middle Ear Inner Ear

Hammer
Anvil
Cochlea
Auditory nerve
Eardrum Stirrup
Ear canal

Guided Reading and Study Workbook

Name _____ Class _____ Date _____

Chapter 17   Mechanical Waves and Sound

Section 17.4 Sound and Hearing
(pages 514–521)

This section discusses properties of sound waves, how they are produced, and how the ear perceives sound. A description of how music is produced and recorded also is presented.

Reading Strategy (page 514)

Using Prior Knowledge Before you read, add properties you already know about sound waves to the diagram below. Then add details about each property as you read the section. For more information on this Reading Strategy, see the **Reading and Study Skills** in the **Skills and Reference Handbook** at the end of your textbook.

Properties of Sound Waves

Speed

Frequency and pitch

Intensity and loudness

Properties of Sound Waves (pages 514–515)

1. Circle the letter of each sentence that is true about sound.
   a. Many behaviors of sound can be explained using a few properties.
   b. Sound waves are compressions and rarefactions that travel through a medium.
   c. Sound waves usually travel more slowly in solids than in gases.
   d. The speed of sound in air is about 30 meters per second.

Match each description with one or more sound properties.

	Description	Property
c	2. This property is measured in units called decibels.	a. loudness
b, d	3. These properties are affected by the length of tubing in a musical instrument.	b. pitch
b	4. This property is the frequency of a sound as your ears perceive it.	c. intensity
a, b	5. These properties depend on factors such as your age and the health of your ears.	d. frequency
a	6. This property is a physical response to the intensity of sound.	

Guided Reading and Study Workbook

Name _____ Class _____ Date _____

Chapter 17   Mechanical Waves and Sound

Ultrasound (page 516)

7. Is the following sentence true or false? Ultrasound is sound at frequencies that are lower than most people are capable of hearing. _____false_____

8. Describe some applications of ultrasound. Ultrasound imaging is an important medical technique; sonar is used to determine the distance to an object under water.

The Doppler Effect (page 516)

9. Is the following sentence true or false? The Doppler effect is a change in sound frequency caused by motion of the sound source, motion of the listener, or both. _____true_____

10. For a stationary observer, as a moving sound source approaches, the observer will first hear a(n) _____higher_____ frequency of sound and then a(n) _____lower_____ frequency as the source moves away.

Hearing and the Ear (page 517)

Match each description with the appropriate region(s) of the ear.

	Description	Region
a	11. Sound is gathered and focused here.	a. outer ear
c	12. Nerve endings send signals to the brain.	b. middle ear
a, b	13. The eardrum is located at the boundary between these two regions of the ear.	c. inner ear
b	14. Hammer, anvil, and stirrup are located here.	
b	15. Sound vibrations are amplified.	

How Sound Is Reproduced (pages 518–519)

16. How is sound recorded? Sound waves are converted to electronic signals that can be processed and stored in different ways.

17. Sound is reproduced by converting _____electronic signals_____ back into sound waves.

Music (page 521)

18. Is the following sentence true or false? Many musical instruments vary pitch by changing the frequency of standing waves. _____true_____

19. Theaters are designed to prevent "dead spots" where the volume is reduced by _____destructive interference_____ of reflected sound waves.

20. The response of a standing wave to another wave of the same frequency is called _____resonance_____.

Guided Reading and Study Workbook

Name _____ Class _____ Date _____

Chapter 17   Mechanical Waves and Sound

WordWise

Test your knowledge of vocabulary terms from Chapter 17 by completing this crossword puzzle.

Clues across:

1. Maximum displacement of a wave
3. The time required for one complete wave cycle
6. An apparent change in frequency of a sound source that moves relative to an observer
8. A point of no displacement in a standing wave
9. Area where particles in a medium are spread out as a longitudinal wave travels through it
10. Distance from one point to the next identical point on a wave

Clues down:

2. Type of mechanical wave whose direction of vibration is perpendicular to its direction of travel
4. A unit used to compare sound intensity levels
5. Occurs when waves overlap
6. Occurs when a wave encounters an object or opening that is close in size to its wavelength
7. Lowest point of a wave below the rest position

1. A M P L I T U D E
3. P E R I O D
6. D O P P L E R E F F E C T
8. N O D E
9. R A R E F A C T I O N
10. W A V E L E N G T H

(down words: TRANSVERSE, DECIBEL, INTERFERENCE, DIFFRACTION, TROUGH)

Guided Reading and Study Workbook

Name _____ Class _____ Date _____

Chapter 17   Mechanical Waves and Sound

Calculating Wave Properties

A transverse wave in a rope is traveling at a speed of 3.0 m/s. The period of this mechanical wave is 0.25 s. What is the wavelength?

Math Skill: Formulas and Equations

You may want to read more about this **Math Skill** in the **Skills and Reference Handbook** at the end of your textbook.

1. Read and Understand

What information are you given?

Speed = 3.0 m/s

Period = 0.25 s

2. Plan and Solve

What unknown are you trying to calculate?

Wavelength = ?

What formula contains the given quantities and the unknown?

$$\text{Speed} = \text{Wavelength} \times \text{Frequency} = \frac{\text{Wavelength}}{\text{Period}}$$

Wavelength = Period × Speed

Replace each variable with its known value.

Speed = 3.0 m/s

Period = 0.25 s

Wavelength = 0.25 s × 3.0 m/s = 0.75 m

3. Look Back and Check

Is your answer reasonable?

$$\text{Speed} = \text{Wavelength} \times \text{Frequency} = \text{Wavelength} \times \frac{1}{\text{Period}}$$

$$\text{Speed} = 0.75 \text{ m} \times \frac{1}{0.25 \text{ s}} = 3.0 \text{ m/s.}$$

Substituting the calculated wavelength into the equation yields the original speed of 3.0 m/s.

Math Practice

On a separate sheet of paper, solve the following problems.

1. What is the speed, in m/s, of a wave on a cord if it has a wavelength of 4 m and a period of 0.5 s?
Speed = Wavelength/Period = 4 m × 0.5 s = 8 m/s

2. What is the period of a wave traveling 5 m/s if its wavelength is 20 m?
Period = Wavelength/Speed = (20 m)/(5 m/s) = 4 s

3. Calculate the frequency, in Hz, of a wave in a string traveling 1.25 m/s, with a wavelength of 0.50 m.
Frequency = Speed/Wavelength = (1.25 m/s)/0.50 m = 2.5 Hz

Student Edition Lab Worksheet

Name _____ Class _____ Date _____

Chapter 17   Mechanical Waves and Sound   **Exploration Lab**

Investigating Sound Waves

Sound is produced when a vibrating source causes a medium to vibrate. In this lab, you will investigate how the vibrating source affects characteristics of the sound produced.

See pages 524 and 525 in the Teacher's Edition for more information.

Problem   What determines the frequency and amplitude of the sound produced by a vibrating object?

Materials
- meter stick
- 2 cardboard tubes
- scissors or scalpel
- 2 rubber bands
- wax paper
- balloon
- small mirror
- transparent tape
- flashlight

Skills   Observing, Inferring, Drawing Conclusions, Controlling Variables

Procedure

Part A: Investigating How Length Affects Pitch

1. Hold one end of a meter stick down firmly on a table so that 20 centimeters of the meter stick extends past the edge of the table. Pluck the end of the meter stick that extends past the table to produce a vibration and a sound. Observe the vibration and sound of the meter stick.

2. Repeat Step 1, but this time allow 40 centimeters of the meter stick to extend past the edge of the table. Observe and record how the length of the vibrating part of the meter stick affects the pitch.

   Increasing the length of the overhang lowers the pitch.
   _____
   _____

3. Repeat Step 1, but this time allow 60 centimeters of the meter stick to extend past the edge of the table. Record your observations.

   Increasing the length of the overhang to 60 cm lowers the pitch even further.
   _____
   _____

Student Edition Lab Worksheet

Name _____ Class _____ Date _____

4. Investigate the relationship between length and frequency for a vibrating column of air, as you did with the vibrating meter stick. Make a kazoo by cutting a hole in the middle of one of the cardboard tubes. Make the hole approximately 1 centimeter in diameter. Use a rubber band to fasten the piece of wax paper over one end of the tube. **CAUTION:** *Be careful when cutting with sharp instruments; always cut away from yourself and away from nearby people.*

5. Make a second kazoo by cutting the second tube 10 centimeters shorter than the first tube. Using the short tube, repeat Step 4.

6. Hold the shorter kazoo in front of your mouth and hum into the open end, keeping your pitch steady. Repeat this action with the longer kazoo, making sure to hum exactly as you did before. Observe and record how the length of the kazoo affects the pitch of the sound.

   The longer kazoo makes a lower-pitch sound.
   _____
   _____
   _____
   _____
   _____

Part B: Investigating How Frequency Affects Pitch and How Amplitude Affects Loudness

7. Cut the neck off of the balloon. Replace the wax paper on the longer kazoo with the cut-open balloon. Wrap the rubber band several times around the end of the cardboard tube. The rubber band should hold the balloon tightly stretched over the end of the tube. Use tape to attach the small mirror onto the balloon on the end of the tube.

8. Have a classmate shine a flashlight on the mirror, as shown, while you hum into the kazoo. Your classmate should position the flashlight so that a spot of light is reflected on the wall. It may be necessary to darken the room. Observe how the spot of light moves when you hum into the kazoo. Make a note of your position and the position and angle of the kazoo and the flashlight.

   Students should make a sketch or carefully describe their position and the position and angle
   of the kazoo and flashlight.
   _____
   _____
   _____

Student Edition Lab Worksheet

Name _____ Class _____ Date _____

9. Without changing how loudly you hum, use your voice to raise the pitch of your humming. Observe and record how the movement of the spot of light differs from your observations in Step 8. Make sure you do not change your distance from the wall or the angle at which the light from the flashlight strikes the mirror attached to the kazoo.

   The spot will vibrate more rapidly when the pitch increases.
   _____
   _____
   _____

10. Repeat Step 9, but this time hum at a lower pitch than you did in Step 8.

    The spot will vibrate more slowly when the pitch decreases.
    _____
    _____

11. Repeat Steps 9 and 10, but this time vary the loudness of your humming while keeping the pitch constant.

    The amplitude of vibration of the spot decreases when volume decreases, and it increases
    when volume increases.
    _____

Student Edition Lab Worksheet

Name _____ Class _____ Date _____

Analyze and Conclude

1. Observing What happened to the frequency of the meter stick's vibration when you made the overhanging part longer?

The frequency was reduced.

_____

_____

2. Inferring How did the frequency of the meter stick's vibration affect the pitch of its sound?

The pitch became lower as the frequency was reduced.

_____

_____

3. Inferring How did the kazoo's length affect its pitch?

The longer kazoo had the lower pitch.

_____

_____

4. Analyzing Data When you changed the pitch of your humming, how did it affect the frequency of vibration of the mirror?

Humming at a higher pitch increased the frequency of the mirror's vibration.

_____

_____

_____

5. Analyzing Data How is the amplitude of the kazoo's vibration related to its loudness?

Increasing the loudness increased the amplitude of the kazoo's vibration.

_____

_____

6. Controlling Variables Explain why it was important to keep loudness constant when you changed the pitch of your humming in Step 9.

Keeping the loudness constant ensured that any change in the frequency of the mirror's vibration

was caused by the change in pitch.

_____

_____

_____

Lab Manual

Name _____ Class _____ Date _____

Investigation 17A

Measuring the Speed of Sound
Refer students to pages 505 and 506 and 514 and 515 in their textbooks for a discussion of the speed and transmission of sound waves. **SKILLS FOCUS:** Predicting, Measuring, Controlling Variables, Calculating **CLASS TIME:** Part A, 20 minutes; Part B, 20 minutes

Background Information
An echo is reflected sound that can be heard separately from the original sound that produced it. The original sound is heard for about 0.10 second. You will hear an echo clearly if you are far enough away so that it takes more than 0.10 second for the sound to travel to the reflecting surface and back to you. To calculate the speed of sound, you must find your distance from the reflecting surface when you are just far enough away so that you do not hear an echo. It will take 0.10 second for the sound to travel this distance and back.

Sound travels at different speeds through different materials. Temperature also affects how rapidly sound is transmitted. Sound will travel faster in warm air than in cold air. However, the speed of sound in air does not depend upon the frequency of the sound. If it did, you would not be able to listen to music because the high-pitched sounds would arrive at your ear at a different time than the low-pitched sounds would.

The speed of light is much greater than the speed of sound. You will use this principle to calculate the speed of sound. You will perform an experiment similar to one performed by French scientists in 1738. They set up a cannon on a hill and timed the interval between the flash and the sound. Since they knew the distance and the time, they could calculate the speed of sound.

In Part A of this investigation, you will create echoes and measure the distance between you and a reflecting surface in order to determine the speed of sound. Then, in Part B, you will calculate the speed of sound in air by measuring the time between seeing an event and hearing the event.

Problem
What is the speed of sound in air?

Pre-Lab Discussion
Read the entire investigation. Then, work with a partner to answer the following questions.

1. Comparing and Contrasting Which method for measuring the speed of sound in air do you think will produce more accurate results—the method used in Part A or the method in Part B? Explain your answer.

The method in Part B should be more accurate. The time that sound travels is measured with

reasonable accuracy in Part B. In Part A, the time of travel is based on when the echo is no longer

heard, which may vary a great deal with the hearing of each observer.

Lab Manual

Name _____ Class _____ Date _____

2. Controlling Variables Identify the manipulated and responding variables for both Parts A and B.

For Part A, the manipulated variable is the distance between the observer and the wall, and the

responding variable is the condition when the echo is no longer heard. In Part B, the manipulated

variable is the distance between the observer and the drum, and the responding variable is the time

interval between the time that the striking of the drum is seen and the time that the sound is heard.

_____

3. Evaluating The speed of sound in dry air at a temperature of 20°C is 342 m/s. What sources of error might account for obtaining a different value than this?

The temperature of the air may not be 20°C when the investigation is made. Shorter or longer

response times on the part of the observer will introduce error in the time values and will affect the

calculation of the speed of sound. Wind can also increase or decrease the speed at which sound

travels. Limits in the precision of measuring instruments will also affect the result.

_____

4. Controlling Variables How can the variables that introduce error in the results be controlled?

While the air temperature cannot be restricted to 20°C, its actual temperature can be kept uniform by

performing the experiment within a fairly short time. Because different observers may not hear the

echoes at different spots or may start the clock sooner or later after seeing the drum struck, the

results can be made more consistent with multiple trials, using different observers. By reversing the

positions of the drum and the observers, the effects of wind on the speed of sound would be

cancelled. Taking several measurements and averaging them will improve the precision of the

measurements.

_____

5. Designing Experiments How might you vary the design of the investigation in Part B to test if the speed of sound in air is independent of frequency?

Two drums of very different sizes would produce sounds with very different frequencies. By repeating

the experiment with each drum, the effect of frequency on the speed of sound could be determined.

_____

Lab Manual

Name _____ Class _____ Date _____

Materials *(per group)*
2 wooden blocks, each about 20 cm long
metric tape measure or meter stick
drum
stopwatch (that can measure hundredths of a second)
measuring rope, marked off in meters, or a bicycle with a metric odometer

If you carry out the investigation indoors, a room that is at least 25 m on a side, such as a gymnasium, will be necessary. If you work outdoors, students should stand at least 25 m from a high, hard, smooth surface, such as the side of a school building.

Be sure to make arrangements to perform Part B of this investigation outdoors in a very large open area.

Safety 🥽 ✂️ ⚠️
Be careful when handling sharp instruments such as a tape measure. Note all safety alert symbols next to the steps in the Procedure and review the meaning of each symbol by referring to the Safety Symbols on page xiii.

Procedure
Part A: Estimating the Speed of Sound from Echoes

✂️ **1.** In an auditorium or outdoors near a high wall, use a metric tape measure or meter stick to measure a distance of 25 meters from the wall.

2. Stand facing the wall and clap the two wooden blocks together. Listen for an echo. If you can hear one, move closer to the wall by about 1 meter, and repeat. Keep moving closer, 1 meter at a time, until you can no longer hear a separate echo.

3. Measure and record the distance between you and the wall.

Part B: Determining the Speed of Sound From the Delay Between Seeing and Hearing an Event

4. This experiment must be conducted outdoors. Select an area such as an open field or a long, lightly traveled road. Record your observations of the weather conditions.

5. With the measuring rope (or a bicycle equipped with a metric odometer), measure a distance of 100 meters in a straight line.

6. One student should stand at each end of this measured distance, as shown in Figure 1.

7. One student should create a loud, short noise by striking the drum.

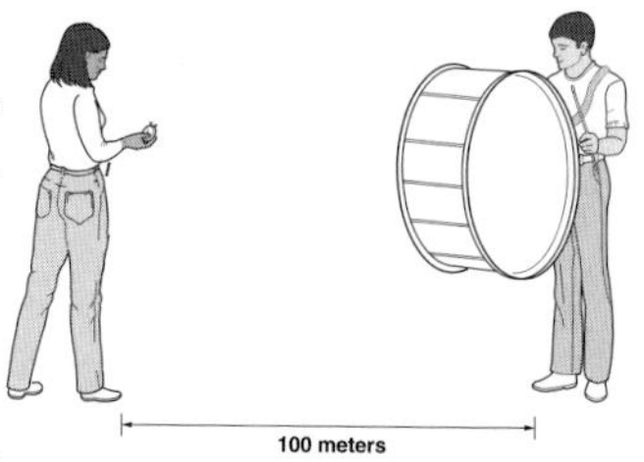

Figure 1 100 meters

8. The other student should start the stopwatch precisely when he or she sees the drum being struck. The student should stop the watch precisely when he or she hears the noise.

9. Repeat Steps 8 and 9 three more times. Record the times to a hundredth of a second in the data table.

10. The two students should change places with each other and repeat the experiment. This will help to eliminate any effect the wind might have on the speed at which the sound waves travel. Record your results in the data table.

Observations

Part A

1. What did you observe when you made the sound at a distance of 25 meters from the reflecting surface?

An echo could be heard.

2. At what distance were you no longer able to hear an echo?

The distance should be approximately 17 meters.

Part B

DATA TABLE Sample data are shown.

Trial	Time (first student with stopwatch) (s)	Time (second student with stopwatch) (s)
1	0.25 s	0.30 s
2	0.28 s	0.29 s
3	0.30 s	0.32 s
4	0.31 s	0.25 s

Analysis and Conclusions

1. **Calculating** For Part A, calculate the total distance the sound traveled from you to the reflecting surface and back again.

Approximately 17 m × 2 = 34 m

2. **Calculating** Divide the total round-trip distance by the time, 0.10 s, needed for you to hear the echo and the original clapping sound as just one sound. Express your answer in the correct units.

Approximately 34 m/0.10 s = 340 m/s

3. **Inferring** What type of surface would not have reflected sound back to you? Why?

Irregular soft surfaces, such as curtains, would not reflect sound well. Any soft material would have absorbed most of the sound energy instead of reflecting it back.

4. **Controlling Variables** For Part B, what were the weather conditions in which you measured the speed of sound? Do you think the speed would have been different under different conditions?

The conditions could include observation of temperature, clouds, and whether it feels muggy or dry. Changes in any of these may result in different speeds of sound. (For example, sound travels slightly faster in warm air than in cool air and very slightly slower at high pressure than at low pressure.)

5. **Calculating** Average the eight time values in the data table. Calculate the speed of sound by dividing the distance by the average time.

The average time will be approximately 0.29 s. The calculated speed of sound will therefore be 100 m ÷ 0.29 s = 340 m/s.

6. **Analyzing Data** What factors might have caused variations in the results of your eight trials?

Answers should take into account wind conditions and the observers' response times for starting and stopping the watches.

7. **Comparing and Contrasting** Compare the values for the speed of sound in air calculated in Part A and in Part B. Account for both the differences and similarities in the results.

At 20°C, the two answers should be close to 340 m/s. Differences may be caused by the observers' ability to detect echoes, measurements in distance, response times for observers operating stopwatches, and the presence of wind. The results will probably be very close because of limits on the precision of the measurements, which will restrict the answers to two significant figures.

8. **Applying Concepts** Explain how you can determine the distance from you that lightning strikes if you know the speed of sound and have a stopwatch.

You can determine the length of time between seeing the flash of lightning and hearing the thunder. Sound travels in dry air about 342 m/s. Using this value, you can calculate how far away the lightning struck.

9. **Applying Concepts** When fireworks burst in the sky, will you hear the explosion or see the color first? Explain your answer.

You will see the color first because light travels faster then sound.

10. **Applying Concepts** Sound usually travels faster in liquids than in gases, and faster in some solids than in liquids. Explain why a worker who puts one ear against a long steel pipe would hear two sounds if another worker struck the pipe only once at some distance away.

The listener would first hear the sound transmitted through the iron and then hear the sound transmitted through the air.

Go Further

Suspend an alarm clock inside a bell jar from which air can be evacuated by a vacuum pump. Observe what happens to the sound of the bell or alarm as the air is sucked out. Observe the speed of sound through other materials such as water or iron. Before conducting any experiments, submit your procedure to your teacher for approval. Students should describe how the sound of the alarm is greatly reduced when the air is removed from the bell jar. Although the reason for this is more complicated than simply the absence of a medium for transmitting sound, students should be aware that the ability to transmit the mechanical energy of the sound has been greatly reduced by creating the vacuum. Similarly, students should explain the faster transmission of sound through liquids and solids as relating to the distance between the particles that make up the liquid or solid and other factors such as the elasticity of the medium.

Chapter 17   Mechanical Waves and Sound   **Investigation 17B**

Sounds in Solids

Refer students to pages 502 and 514–525 in their textbooks for a discussion of longitudinal waves and sound. **SKILLS FOCUS:** Predicting, Comparing and Contrasting, Applying Concepts **CLASS TIME:** 40 minutes

Background Information

Sound is a **longitudinal wave.** As sound travels through a substance, the particles vibrate back and forth parallel to the movement of the sound wave. When the particles vibrate, regions form where they are close together (**compression**) and where they are far apart (**rarefaction**). The sound wave consists of compressions and rarefactions spreading through a substance.

Sound must travel through a **medium.** Sound cannot travel through a vacuum because there are no particles to transmit the pattern of compressions and rarefactions. To transmit sound, the medium must vibrate. The term *vibrate* implies back-and-forth movement. If the particles move forth without moving back again, there is no vibration. Once particles begin forward motion, their inertia would continue to carry them forward unless some force brought them back again. A medium that has strong forces of attraction between the particles tends to be **elastic** because the particles spring back to their original positions after a sound wave passes.

A medium in which the particles are close together so that the vibration in one particle could easily pass to its neighboring particles tends to have greater elasticity than a medium in which the particles are far apart. The particles in metals are arranged very close together in an orderly pattern. This makes the metal rigid. It is very difficult to force the particles closer together. Therefore, a metal is not easily compressed or deformed. A piece of plastic, such as a plastic straw, bends easily. A material is elastic if it is rigid and hard to deform. Metal tends to be more elastic than plastic.

In this investigation, you will compare wood, cardboard, and metal for elasticity to discover how well each transmits sound.

Problem

How well do various materials transmit sound?

Pre-Lab Discussion

Read the entire investigation. Then, work with a partner to answer the following questions.

1. **Comparing and Contrasting** A spring is placed on a tabletop, and one end is held in a fixed position. Two strings are tied to the spring on coils about 1 cm apart, as shown in Figure 1. Then, the spring is given a shove at the left end, causing a wave to travel through it toward the right.

   a. Describe the movement of either string as the wave passes by.

   The string moves forward and then backward and then returns to its original position.

Lab Manual

Name _____ Class _____ Date _____

b. What happens to the distance between the two strings as the wave travels along the spring? Explain your answer.

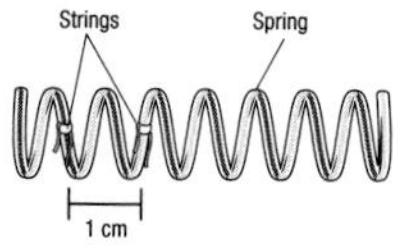

Strings   Spring

Figure 1
1 cm

As the string on the left moves to the right, the two

strings move closer together. Then, the first string

moves back to its original position, and the second

string begins to move toward the right, moving the

strings apart. Finally, the second string returns to its original position so that the distance

between the strings is the same as it was originally.

2. Using Models How is the behavior of the spring in Question 1 similar to that of a sound wave?

The motion in the spring is a longitudinal wave. The behavior of the spring is similar to that of a sound

wave because the displacement of the strings is parallel to the movement of the wave.

3. Using Models Suppose that you made a coil out of cotton and tried to send a wave down the cotton coil in the same way as described in Question 1 with a spring. What would happen? Explain your answer. Use the word *elastic* or *elasticity* in your explanation.

The wave would not spread down the cotton coil because cotton is not elastic. Instead, only part

of the cotton coil would move, and its shape would be deformed.

4. Inferring Which substance is probably the most elastic—wood, cardboard, or metal? Which is probably the least elastic? How would you test your prediction?

Metal is probably the most elastic. Cardboard is probably the least elastic. This can be tested by

applying the same force to objects composed of each material and observing whether the objects

are easily deformed (less elastic) or resist change in shape (more elastic).

5. Predicting Rank wood, cardboard, and metal from highest to lowest for their ability to conduct sound. Explain your answer.

Metal, wood, cardboard; This ranking is the same as and is based on the materials'

ranking for elasticity.

Materials *(per group)*

clock or watch with second hand (either should produce a ticking sound)
wooden meter stick
metal rod, 1 m long, (iron, steel, or aluminum)
cardboard sheet, 1 m long   Cut a strip from a corrugated cardboard box.

Lab Manual

Name _____ Class _____ Date _____

Safety

Put on safety goggles. Be careful when handling sharp instruments. Note all safety alert symbols next to the steps in the Procedure and review the meaning of each symbol by referring to the Safety Symbols on page xiii.

Procedure

1. Work with a partner. Check the elasticity of a meter stick by laying it flat on your lab table with about a third of its length hanging over the edge. One student holds the meter stick down on the lab table, and the other flicks the free end to see how easily it bends and how much it vibrates.

2. Repeat Step 1 with a metal rod and a piece of cardboard. Based on your observations, rank the three objects from the most elastic to the least elastic. The harder an object is to bend and the more vigorously it snaps back to its original shape, the more elastic the material is. In the data table, use the numbers 1 to 3 to rank elasticity, with 1 being the most elastic.

3. Hold a ticking watch or clock to your ear. Note the ticking.

4. Hold a wooden meter stick so that one end is pressed gently against your ear. Have your partner hold the watch against the far end of the meter stick. Note whether you can hear any ticking. **CAUTION:** *Use great care when placing the meter sticks and rods near the ear. Pushing these objects against the ear could result in injury.*

Figure 2

5. Repeat Step 5, substituting the metal rod for the meter stick. Note any observations.

6. Repeat Step 5, substituting a piece of cardboard for the meter stick. Note any observations.

7. Change roles with your partner and repeat Steps 3 through 7. Discuss your observations with your partner and record them, again using the numbers 1 (best) to 3 (poorest) to rank how well each medium conducts sound.

Observations   Sample data are shown.

DATA TABLE

Medium	Elasticity (1 = most elastic)	Sound Conduction (1 = best conductor)
Meter stick	2	2
Metal rod	1	1
Cardboard	3	3

Lab Manual

Name _____ Class _____ Date _____

Analysis and Conclusions

1. Forming Operational Definitions What property of sound did you observe to determine if the medium was a good conductor?

Loudness

2. Comparing and Contrasting Compare wood, metal, and cardboard as sound transmitters, based on your observations. How do these compare with your prediction?

The correct rank is metal (best), wood, cardboard (poorest). Comparisons will depend on the

initial predictions.

3. Making Generalizations Based on your observations, what is the relationship between elasticity and the ability to conduct sound?

As elasticity increases, so does the ability to conduct sound.

4. Applying Concepts Suppose that you are floating outside a spacecraft with another astronaut. You wish to say something to your fellow astronaut, but your two-way radio is not working. How could you transmit a Morse code message by using sound waves?

To be heard, you should use a medium that could be placed in contact with the two helmets.

For example, you could place the helmets together or hold both helmets against the metal body

of the spacecraft.

Go Further

Does elasticity affect the speed of a wave as well as the loudness (intensity) of the sound? Design an experiment to answer this question. Be sure to describe the responding and manipulated variables. Show your plan to your teacher. When your teacher approves your plan, carry out your experiment and report your results and conclusions.

Compare how sound travels through a metal and a wooden fence—both speed and loudness of sound. A student might have a friend tap on a portion of the metal fence, starting a stopwatch as he or she taps. The student would place an ear against the fence a measured distance away, signaling the friend when he or she hears the sound of the tap. Upon the signal, the friend would stop the stopwatch. This procedure could be repeated with a wooden fence. Metal is less compressible (more elastic) than wood, so the sound should travel faster through the metal fence than through the wooden one.

Chapter 17 Mechanical Waves and Sound   Chapter Test A

Multiple Choice

Write the letter that best answers the question or completes the statement on the line provided.

_____ 1. A mechanical wave generally does NOT
   a. move the medium from one place to another
   b. move through a medium.
   c. move through solids.
   d. disturb the medium.

_____ 2. Transverse and longitudinal waves both
   a. have compressions and rarefactions.
   b. transfer energy through a medium.
   c. move at right angles to the vibration of the medium.
   d. are capable of moving the medium a long distance.

_____ 3. A disturbance sends ripples across water in a tub. These ripples are an example of a
   a. rarefaction.   b. longitudinal wave.
   c. compression.   d. surface wave.

_____ 4. In an earthquake, a P wave is a longitudinal wave. It moves through soil and rock as a
   a. wavy line.
   b. series of faults.
   c. series of compressions and rarefactions.
   d. series of crests and troughs.

_____ 5. A period is the length of time it takes for
   a. a disturbance to start a wave.
   b. two complete wavelengths to pass a fixed point.
   c. a wave to travel the length of a rope.
   d. one complete wavelength to pass a fixed point.

_____ 6. A wave has a wavelength of 15 mm and a frequency of 4.0 hertz. What is its speed?
   a. 60 mm/s   b. 60 hertz/s
   c. 3.8 mm/s   d. 0.27 mm/s

_____ 7. To what is amplitude related?
   a. the amount of energy carried by the wave
   b. the maximum displacement from the rest position
   c. neither A nor B
   d. both A and B

_____ 8. How does reflection differ from refraction and diffraction?
   a. Reflection is the only property in which the wave does not continue moving forward.
   b. Reflection is the only property that involves a change in the wave.
   c. Reflection affects all types of mechanical waves, but refraction and diffraction do not.
   d. Reflection is the only property that changes the direction of a wave.

_____ 9. For refraction to occur in a wave, the wave must
   a. strike an obstacle larger than the wavelength.
   b. change direction within a medium.
   c. enter a new medium at an angle.
   d. enter a new medium head-on.

_____ 10. Which wave will probably be diffracted the most?
   a. a longitudinal wave
   b. the wave with the highest amplitude
   c. the wave with the longest wavelength
   d. the wave that strikes a solid barrier with the slowest speed

_____ 11. The formation of a standing wave requires
   a. the traveling of a wave for a long distance.
   b. constructive interference between two waves of slightly different frequencies.
   c. that refraction and diffraction occur at the same time in a wave.
   d. interference between incoming and reflected waves.

_____ 12. In which medium does sound travel the fastest?
   a. salt water   b. fresh wat
   c. air   d. cast iron

_____ 13. A piano, violin, or guitar uses the resonance of a wooden soundboard to
   a. amplify the sound.   b. dampen the sound.
   c. raise the pitch.   d. limit standing waves.

_____ 14. When a sound source approaches you, the pitch you hear is
   a. lower than when the source is stationary.
   b. higher than when the source is stationary.
   c. the same as when the source is stationary.
   d. first higher and then lower than the pitch of the source when stationary.

_____ 15. The part of the ear that sends coded nerve signals to the brain is
   a. the outer ear.   b. the inner ear.
   c. the middle ear.   d. the eardrum.

Completion

Complete each statement on the line provided.

1. The crest of a transverse wave is most similar to a(an) _____ in a longitudinal wave.

2. Waves in a rope are transverse waves because the medium's vibration is _____ to the direction in which the wave travels.

3. A pebble drops straight down into a tub of water, setting off _____ waves that travel between the water and air.

4. On a piano, striking strings with the hammers sets up _____ between the strings and the soundboard.

5. When a train streaks by blowing its whistle, the changing pitch you hear is due to the _____.

Short Answer

In complete sentences, write the answers to the questions on the lines provided.

1. Why is a mechanical wave not always produced when a source vibrates?
   _____
   _____
   _____

2. Consider the properties of a wave—wave speed, amplitude, wavelength, period, and frequency. Which two properties could you determine the numerical values of by using only the information given in Figure 17-1?
   _____
   _____

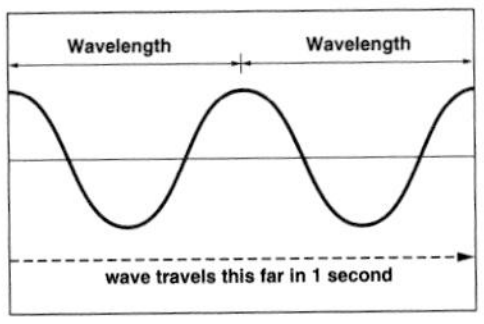

Figure 17-1

3. How can you change the wavelength of a wave in a rope without changing the amplitude?
   _____
   _____
   _____
   _____

4. How could you compare the energy carried in two different longitudinal waves?
   _____
   _____
   _____

5. Describe how a wave must enter a new medium in order for refraction to occur.
   _____
   _____
   _____

6. What sounds can damage hearing?
   _____
   _____
   _____
   _____

Chapter Test A

Using Science Skills

Use the diagram to answer each question. Write the answers on a separate sheet of paper.

1. **Analyzing Data** What is the difference between wave A and wave B in Figure 17-2?

2. **Inferring** In Figure 17-2, both wave A and wave B were started by the same type of force—an up-and-down motion. What conclusion can you make about the energy of these two wave-starting forces?

3. **Predicting** Suppose you add the following panel E to the diagram: a wave pattern with a frequency of four waves per second. How will wavelength in this panel compare with the wavelength in panel D? How will it compare with the wavelength in panel C? Assume all the waves travel at the same speed.

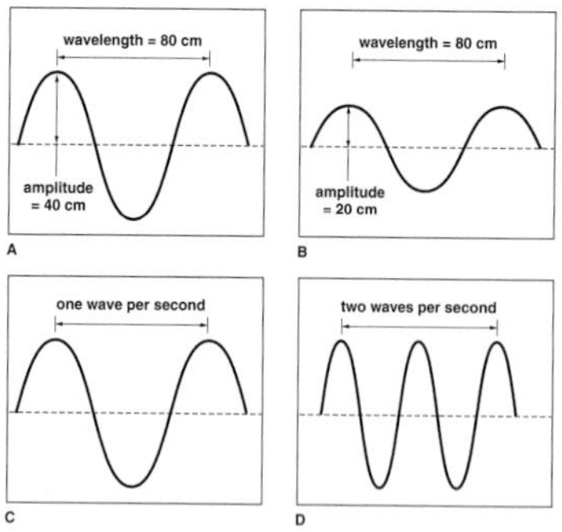

4. **Analyzing Data** What is the difference between wave C and wave D in Figure 17-2?

5. **Drawing Conclusions** Consider both frequency and wavelength in Figure 17-2. How does each variable change between wave C and wave D? What is the relationship between the change? Assume the waves travel at the same speed.

Figure 17-2

Essay

Write the answers to each question on a separate sheet of paper.

1. In a large cave, you can hear an echo a few seconds after you speak. Explain how this happens in terms of wave properties.

2. Explain the difference between reflection and refraction.

3. Sound waves have relatively long wavelengths. We can hear people around a corner before we can see them. Which wave behavior does this illustrate? Explain how wavelength relates to this behavior.

Chapter Test A

4. While practicing on the trumpet, you notice that every time you play a particular note, a window in the room rattles. How can you explain this rattling in terms of wave behaviors?

5. Compare the visible part of the ear to a satellite dish in terms of form and function.

Chapter Test B

Chapter 17   Mechanical Waves and Sound   **Chapter Test B**

Multiple Choice

Write the letter that best answers the question or completes the statement on the line provided.

_____ 1. A mechanical wave moves through a medium, which can be
a. a liquid.   b. a solid.
c. a gas.   d. all of the above

_____ 2. Which type of mechanical wave needs a source of energy to produce it?
a. a transverse wave   b. a longitudinal wave
c. a surface wave   d. all of the above

_____ 3. Which wave causes the medium to vibrate only in a direction parallel to the wave's motion?
a. a transverse wave   b. a surface wave
c. a longitudinal wave   d. none of the above

_____ 4. When a surfer rides an ocean wave on her surfboard, she is actually riding on
a. a crest that is toppling over.
b. a trough of the wave.
c. the rest position of the wave.
d. a region of rarefaction.

_____ 5. Figure 17-1 shows a wave movement during 1 second. What is the frequency of this wave?
a. 2 hertz
b. 2 meters/second
c. 0.5 second
d. 1 hertz

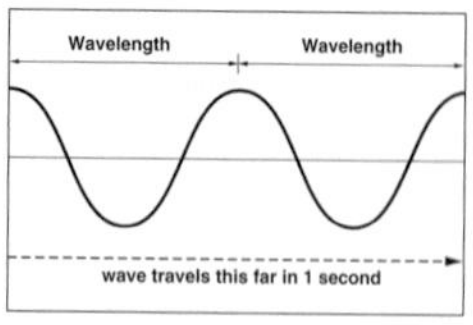

Figure 17-1

_____ 6. To determine the speed of a wave, you would use which of the following formulas?
a. speed = frequency × amplitude
b. speed = wavelength × frequency
c. speed = wavelength × amplitude
d. speed = wavelength × period

_____ 7. To find amplitude, measure
a. from a trough to the rest position.
b. from a crest to the rest position.
c. neither A nor B
d. either A or B

Chapter Test B

_____ 8. When a wave strikes a solid barrier, it behaves like a basketball hitting a backboard. This wave behavior is called
a. constructive interference.
b. diffraction.
c. refraction.
d. reflection.

_____ 9. In refraction, when two parts of a wave travel through different mediums, the parts move
a. at different speeds.
b. in step.
c. always in the same direction.
d. in opposite directions.

_____ 10. What is one property of a wave that determines how much it will diffract when it encounters an obstacle?
a. frequency   b. amplitude
c. period   d. wavelength

_____ 11. Suppose two waves collide and the temporary combined wave that results is smaller than the original waves. What term best describes this interaction?
a. diffraction
b. destructive interference
c. standing wave formation
d. constructive interference

_____ 12. A sound wave is an example of a
a. transverse wave.   b. longitudinal wave.
c. standing wave.   d. surface wave.

_____ 13. Sonar equipment sends sound waves into deep water and measures
a. refraction of the transmitted wave.
b. only the direction of the reflected wave.
c. the time delay of the returning echoes.
d. interference of the transmitted and reflected waves.

_____ 14. An ambulance siren sounds different as it approaches you than when it moves away from you. What scientific term would you use to explain how this happens?
a. ultrasound   b. diffraction
c. rarefaction   d. the Doppler effect

_____ 15. Which part of the ear amplifies the vibrations from sound waves?
a. outer ear   b. inner ear
c. middle ear   d. both a and b

Name _____ Class _____ Date _____

Completion

Complete each statement on the line provided.

1. You can make a wave in a rope by adding _____ at one end of the rope.

2. Instead of crests and troughs, as in an ocean wave, a longitudinal wave has compressions and _____.

3. A wave in a rope is a transverse wave, but a sound wave is a(n) _____ wave.

4. To determine the speed of a wave, you must know the wave's wavelength and _____.

5. Amplitude measures the greatest displacement of a wave from the _____.

6. Ocean waves will not bend if they approach the shore _____.

7. At the _____ of a standing wave, there is no displacement from the rest position.

8. The standard measure used to compare sound intensities is the _____.

9. When a person plucks a guitar string, the number of half wavelengths that fit into the length of the string determines the _____ of the sound produced.

10. The part of the ear that collects sound waves and focuses them inward is the _____ ear.

Short Answer

In complete sentences, write the answers to the questions on the lines provided.

1. What is a medium?

_____

_____

2. What type of mechanical wave is produced by pushing sharply on the end of a spring toy?

_____

_____

3. When you shake the end of a rope to make a wave, how can you increase the amplitude of the wave?

_____

_____

_____

Name _____ Class _____ Date _____

4. How do the frequencies of ultrasound compare to the frequencies that people normally hear?

_____

_____

_____

5. What is the Doppler effect?

_____

_____

_____

Using Science Skills

Use the diagram to answer each question. Write the answers on a separate sheet of paper.

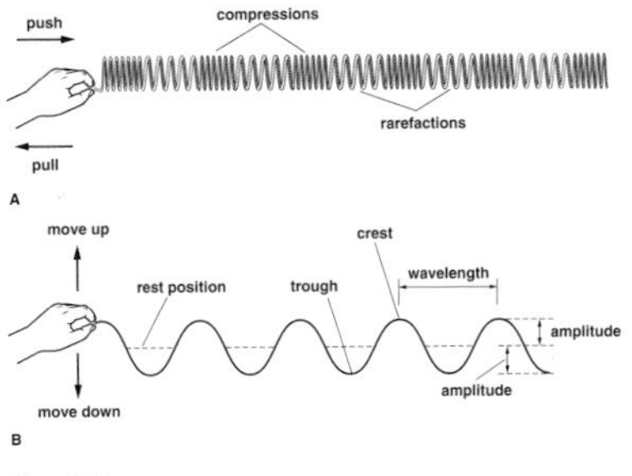

1. **Interpreting Illustrations** What kind of wave does A in Figure 17-2 represent? What kind of wave does B represent?

2. **Comparing and Contrasting** Figure 17-2 shows how someone starts the waves. How are these ways of starting waves alike? How are they different?

Figure 17-2

3. **Inferring** Compare the two waves in Figure 17-2. To what in wave B do the compressions of wave A correspond? To what in wave B do the rarefactions correspond?

4. **Inferring** What represents one wavelength in wave A of Figure 17-2? Define and describe the portion of the wave.

5. **Using Analogies** In Figure 17-2, wave A is produced by a spring toy, representing the concept of a sound wave in air. In sound, what is being squeezed together in the compressions, and what is being released in the rare factions?

Chapter 17 Test A Answers

Multiple Choice

1. a **2.** b **3.** d **4.** c **5.** d **6.** a
7. d **8.** a **9.** c **10.** c **11.** d **12.** d
13. a **14.** b **15.** b

Completion

1. compression **2.** at right angles; perpendicular **3.** surface
4. standing waves; resonance **5.** Doppler effect

Short Answer

1. The vibration has to carry energy through a medium. **2.** period and frequency **3.** Shake the rope faster or slower while using the same force as before. **4.** The wave with greater compressions has more energy. **5.** The wave must enter the new medium at an angle. **6.** sounds greater than 90 decibels, such as a jet plane or rock concert

Using Science Skills

1. Wave B has an amplitude that is one-half the amplitude of wave A. **2.** The force that caused wave A added more energy to the wave than the force that caused wave B. **3.** The wavelength in E will be one-half that of the wavelength in D; it will be one-fourth that of the wavelength in C. **4.** Wave D has a frequency twice that of wave C. Also, the wavelength in wave D is about one-half that of wave C. **5.** Between wave C and wave D, frequency doubles, but wavelength is halved. Wavelength is inversely proportional to frequency.

Essay

1. Sound waves, like other kinds of waves, reflect, or bounce back, when they strike a solid barrier. It takes time for the echo to return, traveling at the speed of sound, so there is a delay. **2.** In reflection, a wave hits a solid barrier that it cannot penetrate, so it reflects, or bounces back, in roughly the same direction from which it came. In refraction, a wave hits a change in the medium, but instead of reflecting (bouncing back), it continues on into the new medium, bending as its speed changes. **3.** Diffraction; a wave diffracts more if its wavelength is large compared to the size of the obstacle (the corner people are walking around). Because sound waves have relatively long wavelengths, we hear sound around the corner as the waves diffract, or spread out. **4.** The window must have the same natural frequency as that particular note played on the trumpet. When the note is played, resonance causes the window to rattle in much the same way as a soundboard on a musical instrument vibrates as the instrument is played. **5.** Both structures are shaped like a funnel to collect waves and focus them into an opening where they can be channeled to a specific location for processing. In the case of the ear, waves are funneled into the middle and inner ear, and then on to the brain. In the case of a satellite dish, waves are funneled into digital circuitry where they can be processed into cable television programs.

Chapter 17 Test B Answers

Multiple Choice

1. d **2.** d **3.** c **4.** a **5.** a **6.** b
7. d **8.** d **9.** a **10.** d **11.** b **12.** b
13. c **14.** d **15.** c

Completion

1. energy **2.** rarefactions **3.** longitudinal **4.** frequency **5.** rest position **6.** head-on **7.** node; nodes **8.** decibel **9.** frequency; pitch **10.** outer

Short Answer

1. A medium is the material through which a mechanical wave travels. **2.** a longitudinal wave **3.** Shake the rope with more force. **4.** Ultrasound frequencies are higher than the sounds that people normally hear. **5.** As the source of a sound approaches, you hear a higher frequency, and as the source moves away from you, you hear a lower frequency.

Using Science Skills

1. a longitudinal wave; a transverse wave **2.** Both waves are started by application of a force. However, wave A, the longitudinal wave, is started by a back-and-forth, or push-and-pull, movement in the same direction as the resulting wave movement, while wave B, the transverse wave, is started by an up-and down movement that is at right angles to the resulting direction in which the wave travels. **3.** Compressions in wave A correspond to crests in wave B. Rare factions in wave A correspond to troughs in wave B. Each of these conditions represents an extreme in which the coil is being displaced from its rest position. **4.** In wave A, one wavelength equals the distance between center of a compression in the spring toy and the corresponding location in the next compression. Wavelength is the distance between a point on one wave and the same point on the next cycle of waves. **5.** In a sound wave in air, the compressions consist of regions of bunched-up air, while the rare factions consist of regions in which the molecules are more spread out.

Chapter 18 The Electromagnetic Spectrum and Light

CHAPTER 18

Planning Guide

Use these planning tools
Easy Planner
Resource Pro
Online Lesson Planner

SECTION OBJECTIVES	STANDARDS NATIONAL (See p. T18.)	STANDARDS STATE	ACTIVITIES and LABS
18.1 Electromagnetic Waves, pp. 532–538 1 block or 2 periods **18.1.1** **Describe** the characteristics of electromagnetic waves in a vacuum and how Michelson measured the speed of light. **18.1.2** **Calculate** the wavelength and frequency of an electromagnetic wave given its speed. **18.1.3** **Describe** the evidence for the dual nature of electromagnetic radiation. **18.1.4** **Describe** how the intensity of light changes with distance from a light source.	A-1, B-5, B-6, G-1, G-2, G-3		**SE** Inquiry Activity: How Do Color Filters Work? p. 531 L2 **TE** Teacher Demo: The Photoelectric Effect, p. 537 L2 **TE** Build Science Skills: Observing, p. 538 L2
18.2 The Electromagnetic Spectrum, pp. 539–545 1 block or 2 periods **18.2.1** **Rank** and **classify** electromagnetic waves based on their frequencies and wavelengths. **18.2.2** **Describe** the uses for different waves of the electromagnetic spectrum.	A-1, A-2, B-5, B-6, E-1, E-2, F-1, F-5, G-1, G-2, G-3		**SE** Quick Lab: Evaluating Sunscreen, p. 544 L2 **TE** Teacher Demo: Radio Reception, p. 541 L2
18.3 Behavior of Light, pp. 546–549 1 block or 2 periods **18.3.1** **Classify** materials as transparent, translucent, or opaque to visible light. **18.3.2** **Describe** what happens when light is reflected, refracted, polarized, or scattered.	A-1, A-2, B-5, B-6		**TE** Teacher Demo: Reflected Light and Vision, p. 547 L2 **TE** Build Science Skills: Observing, p. 548 L2 **LM** Investigation 18B: Using Polarized Light to Measure Sugar Concentration L1
18.4 Color, pp. 550–557 1 block or 2 periods **18.4.1** **Explain** how a prism disperses white light into different colors. **18.4.2** **Analyze** factors that determine the color of an object. **18.4.3** **Distinguish** among primary, secondary, and complementary colors of light and of pigments.	A-1, B-5, B-6, E-1, E-2, G-1, G-2, G-3		**SE** Exploration Lab: Mixing Colored Lights, p. 563 L2 **TE** Teacher Demo: Overlapping Filters, p. 553 L2 **LM** Investigation 18A: Predicting Spectra L2
18.5 Sources of Light, pp. 558–562 1 block or 2 periods **18.5.1** **Explain** how light is produced by common sources of light. **18.5.2** **Describe** the uses of different light sources. **18.5.3** **Distinguish** lasers from other light sources.	A-1, A-2, B-5, B-6, C-6, E-1, E-2, F-1, F-5, F-6, G-1, G-2, G-3		**SE** Quick Lab: Comparing Fluorescent and Incandescent Light, p. 559 L2 **TE** Build Science Skills: Inferring, p. 561 L2

Ability Levels

L1 For students who need additional help
L2 For all students
L3 For students who need to be challenged

Components

SE	Student Edition	**GRSW**	Guided Reading & Study Workbook With Math Support	**CTB**	Computer Test Bank
TE	Teacher's Edition			**TP**	Test Prep Resources
LM	Laboratory Manual			**iT**	iText
PLM	Probeware Lab Manual	**CUT**	Chapter and Unit Tests	**DC**	Discovery Channel Videotapes
				T	Transparencies
				P	Presentation Pro CD-ROM
				GO	Internet Resources

RESOURCES
PRINT and TECHNOLOGY

	SECTION ASSESSMENT
GRSW Section 18.1 **L1**	**SE** Section 18.1 Assessment, p. 538
GRSW Math Skill **L2**	
T Chapter 18 Pretest **L2**	**iT** Section 18.1
Section 18.1 **L2**	
P Chapter 18 Pretest **L2**	
Section 18.1 **L2**	
scLINKS **GO** Waves **L2**	
GRSW Section 18.2 **L1**	**SE** Section 18.2 Assessment, p. 545
T Section 18.2 **L2**	
P Section 18.2 **L2**	**iT** Section 18.2
scLINKS **GO** Electromagnetic spectrum **L2**	
GRSW Section 18.3 **L1**	**SE** Section 18.3 Assessment, p. 549
T Section 18.3 **L2**	
P Section 18.3 **L2**	**iT** Section 18.3
GRSW Section 18.4 **L1**	**SE** Section 18.4 Assessment, p. 553
DC Finding the Fakes **L2**	
T Section 18.4 **L2**	**iT** Section 18.4
P Section 18.4 **L2**	
scLINKS **GO** Color **L2**	
GRSW Section 18.5 **L1**	**SE** Section 18.5 Assessment, p. 562
T Section 18.5 **L2**	
P Section 18.5 **L2**	**iT** Section 18.5
SCIENCE NEWS **GO** Light and optics **L2**	

Go Online

Go online for these Internet resources.

PHSchool.com
Web Code: cca-2180

SCIENCE NEWS
Web Code: cce-2185

NSTA *scLINKS*
Web Code: ccn-2181
Web Code: ccn-2182
Web Code: ccn-2184

Materials for Activities and Labs

Quantities for each group

STUDENT EDITION

Inquiry Activity, p. 531
cardboard with slit, light source, prism, white paper, filters (red, green, blue), colored markers

Quick Lab, p. 544
2 black paper strips, 2 petri dishes, 12 ultraviolet-detecting beads, sunscreen, clock/watch with second hand

Quick Lab, p. 559
spectroscope, clear incandescent bulb, fluorescent bulb, colored pencils

Exploration Lab, p. 563
light source (red, blue, green), tape, large sheet of white paper

TEACHER'S EDITION

Teacher Demo, p. 537
electroscope, zinc strip, rubber rod, wool, incandescent and UV light sources

Build Science Skills, p. 538
low-wattage bulb, light source

Teacher Demo, p. 541
portable radio with antenna, cardboard or wooden box, chicken wire

Teacher Demo, p. 547
wooden or cardboard box with removable top, white paper

Build Science Skills, p. 548
2 polarizing filters, light source

Teacher Demo, p. 553
2 overhead projectors; red, green, and blue acetate filters

Build Science Skills, p. 556
paints (acrylic, watercolor, oil), artist brushes, watercolor paper, hand lens, flat, wooden sticks

Build Science Skills, p. 561
spectroscope, neon lights

Chapter Assessment

CHAPTER ASSESSMENT

SE	Chapter Assessment, pp. 565–566
CUT	Chapter 18 Test A, B
CTB	Chapter 18
iT	Chapter 18
PHSchool.com GO	
	Web Code: cca-2180

STANDARDIZED TEST PREP

SE	Chapter 18, p. 567
TP	Diagnose and Prescribe

iText—interactive textbook with assessment at PHSchool.com

The Electromagnetic Spectrum and Light 530B

Name_____ Class_____ Date_____ M T W T F

LESSON PLAN 18.1

Electromagnetic Waves

Time
2 periods
1 block

Section Objectives

- **18.1.1 Describe** the characteristics of electromagnetic waves in a vacuum and how the speed of light was measured.
- **18.1.2 Calculate** the wavelength and frequency of an electromagnetic wave, given its speed.
- **18.1.3 Describe** the evidence for the dual nature of electromagnetic radiation.

Vocabulary electromagnetic waves • electric field • magnetic field • electromagnetic radiation • photoelectric effect • photons • intensity

Local Standards

1 FOCUS

Build Vocabulary: Word-Part Analysis
Ask students what words they know that have the key word parts *electro*, *magnet*, and *photo*. Relate these word parts to the new vocabulary terms. **L2**

Targeted Resources
- ❑ Transparency: Chapter 18 Pretest
- ❑ Transparency: Reading Strategy 18.1
- ❑ Transparency: Interest Grabber 18.1

2 INSTRUCT

Build Reading Literacy: Sequence
Have students sequence the path light traveled in Michelson's experiment. **L1**

Build Math Skills: Equations and Formulas
Have students practice solving for each unknown in the frequency-wavelength formula. **L1**

Teacher Demo: The Photoelectric Effect
Shine different light sources on a strip of charged zinc attached to an electroscope. Students indirectly observe the photoelectric effect. **L2**

Build Science Skills: Inferring
After observing Figure 6, have students describe the photoelectric effect. **L2**

Build Science Skills: Observing
Students observe light intensity. **L3**

Targeted Resources
- ❑ Transparency: Figure 2: Electromagnetic Wave
- ❑ Transparency: Math Skills: Calculating Wave Speed
- ❑ Transparency: Figure 4: Light –Wave Model
- ❑ Transparency: Figure 6: Light –Particle Model
- ❑ GRSW Section 18.1
- ❑ GRSW Math Skill: Exponents
- ❑ **NSTA** *sci*_{LINKS} Waves

3 ASSESS

Reteach
Use Figure 2 to summarize the key features of an electromagnetic wave. **L1**

Evaluate Understanding
Have students write three math problems (with solutions) based on the frequency-wavelength formula. **L2**

Targeted Resources
- ❑ **PHSchool.com** Online Section 18.1 Assessment
- ❑ iText Section 18.1

Transparencies

260 **Chapter 18 Pretest**

1. How are electric and magnetic forces related?

2. Can a mechanical wave move through a vacuum? Explain.

3. What is the equation that relates wave speed, wavelength, and frequency?

4. If 3.0×10^7 people share a tax refund of 2.0×10^6 dollars, how much money does each person get?

5. True or False: An object radiates more energy at higher temperatures.

6. If intensity equals x at 10 meters from an ambulance siren, what is the intensity at 20 meters from an ambulance siren?

   a. $4x$

   b. $0.25x$

   c. $2x$

   d. $0.5x$

ANSWERS
1. They are two aspects of the same force.
2. No, a mechanical wave is transmitted by matter.
3. Wave speed = Wavelength × Frequency
4. $0.07 per person
5. True
6. b

Transparencies

261 **Chapter 18 Pretest** *(continued)*

7. A refracted wave can do which of the following?
   a. slow down

   b. speed up

   c. bend

   d. all of the above

8. Electromagnetic energy can be converted into which of the following?
   a. chemical energy

   b. mechanical energy

   c. thermal energy

   d. all of the above

ANSWERS
7. d
8. d

Transparencies

262 **Section 18.1 Interest Grabber**

How Can Waves Differ?

Light is like a mechanical wave, but there are important differences. Light travels much faster than mechanical waves, and light can travel through a vacuum, or empty space.

Work in small teams to brainstorm examples of light moving through a vacuum. Here is one example to start with: An astronaut sees Earth from the space shuttle.

1. Could an astronaut on a space walk hear the engines of the Space Shuttle through the vacuum of outer space? Explain your answer.

2. List at least three objects that you have seen through the vacuum of outer space.

ANSWERS
1. No; sound waves are mechanical waves, so they cannot travel through a vacuum.
2. The sun, the moon, and stars are all seen through the vacuum of outer space.

Transparencies

263 **Section 18.1 Reading Strategy**

Comparing and Contrasting

Travels through vacuum	E
Travels through medium	a. ___?___
Fits wave model	B
Fits particle model	b. ___?___
Transverse wave	c. ___?___
Longitudinal wave	d. ___?___

ANSWERS
a. B (both)
b. E (electromagnetic waves)
c. B (both)
d. M (mechanical waves)

Transparencies

264 | **Figure 2 Electromagnetic Waves**

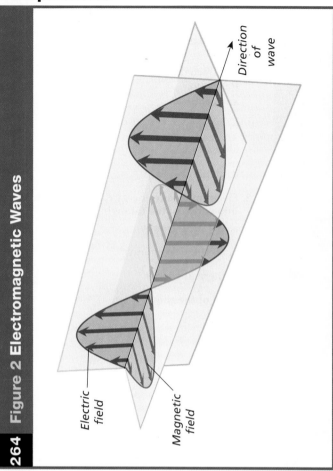

Direction of wave

Electric field

Magnetic field

Transparencies

Math Skills

Calculating Wave Speed

A radio station broadcasts a radio wave with a wavelength of 3.0 meters. What is the frequency of the wave?

1 Read and Understand

What information are you given?

Speed $= c = 3.00 \times 10^8$ m/s

Wavelength $= 3.0$ m

2 Plan and Solve

What unknown are you trying to calculate?

Frequency $= ?$

What formula contains the given quantities and the unknown?

Speed = Wavelength $\times$ Frequency

or, Frequency $= \dfrac{\text{Speed}}{\text{Wavelength}}$

Replace each variable with its known value.

Frequency $= \dfrac{3.00 \times 10^8 \text{ m/s}}{3.0 \text{ m}}$

$= 1.0 \times 10^8$ Hz

3 Look Back and Check

Is your answer reasonable?

Check that product of wavelength and frequency gives a speed of 3.0×10^8 m/s.

Speed $= 3.0$ m $\times (1.0 \times 10^8$ Hz$) = 3.0 \times 10^8$ m/s

Transparencies

266 | **Figure 5 Interference (Wave Model of Light)**

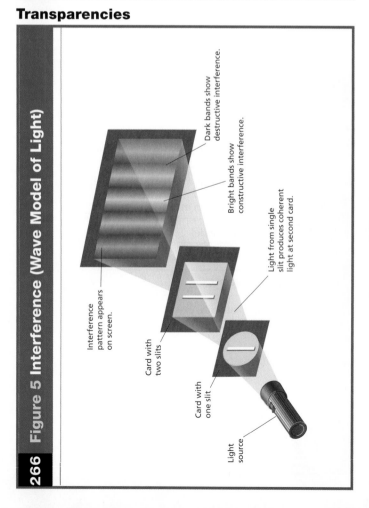

Dark bands show destructive interference.

Bright bands show constructive interference.

Light from single slit produces coherent light at second card.

Interference pattern appears on screen.

Card with two slits

Card with one slit

Light source

Transparencies

267 | **Figure 6 Photoelectric Effect (Particle Model of Light)**

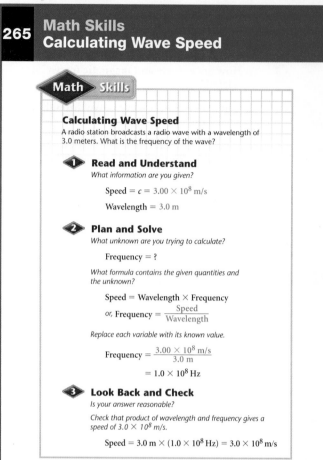

B Electrons are emitted.

Dim blue light or ultraviolet rays

Metal plate

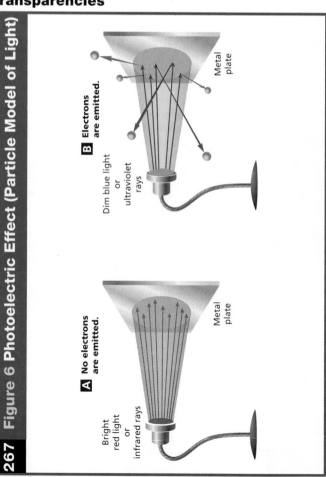

A No electrons are emitted.

Bright red light or infrared rays

Metal plate

Name _____ Class _____ Date _____

Section 18.1 Electromagnetic Waves
(pages 532–538)

This section describes the characteristics of electromagnetic waves.

Reading Strategy (page 532)

Comparing and Contrasting As you read about electromagnetic waves, fill in the table below. If the characteristic listed in the table describes electromagnetic waves, write E in the column for Wave Type. Write M for mechanical waves and B for both. For more information on this Reading Strategy, see the **Reading and Study Skills** in the **Skills and Reference Handbook** at the end of your textbook.

Electromagnetic and Mechanical Waves	
Travels through a vacuum	E
Travels though medium	B
Fits wave model	B
Fits particle model	E
Transverse wave	B
Longitudinal wave	M

What Are Electromagnetic Waves? (page 533)

1. What are electromagnetic waves? They are transverse waves that consist of changing electric fields and changing magnetic fields.

2. Electric fields are produced by electrically charged particles and by changing ___magnetic fields___.

3. Magnetic fields are produced by magnets, by changing ___electric fields___, and by vibrating charges.

4. Electromagnetic waves are produced when a(n) ___electric charge___ vibrates or accelerates.

5. Circle the letter of each sentence that is true about electric and magnetic fields.

   (a.) An electromagnetic wave occurs when electric and magnetic fields vibrate at right angles to each other.

   b. A magnetic field is surrounded by an electric current.

   (c.) Changing electric and magnetic fields regenerate each other.

   (d.) Electromagnetic waves are produced when an electric charge vibrates.

6. Is the following sentence true or false? Electromagnetic waves need a medium to travel through. ___false___

7. The transfer of energy by electromagnetic waves traveling through matter or across space is called ___electromagnetic radiation___.

Name _____ Class _____ Date _____

The Speed of Electromagnetic Waves (page 534)

8. As a thunderstorm approaches, you see the lightning before you hear the thunder, because light travels ___faster___ than sound.

9. Is the following sentence true or false? All electromagnetic waves travel at the same speed through a vacuum. ___true___

10. Circle the letter that gives the correct speed of light in a vacuum.

    a. 3.00×10^8 kilometers per second

    b. 3.00×10^8 meters per hour

    (c.) 3.00×10^8 meters per second

    d. 3.00×10^8 kilometers per hour

Wavelength and Frequency (page 535)

11. Circle the letter of each sentence that is true about electromagnetic waves.

    (a.) Different electromagnetic waves can have different frequencies.

    b. Wavelength is directly proportional to frequency.

    c. Electromagnetic waves always travel at the speed of light.

    (d.) All electromagnetic waves travel at the same speed in a vacuum.

12. As the wavelengths of electromagnetic waves increase, the frequencies ___decrease___, for waves moving in a(n) ___vacuum___.

Wave or Particle? (pages 536–537)

13. Electromagnetic radiation behaves sometimes like a(n) ___wave___ and sometimes like a stream of ___particles___.

14. Interference only occurs when two or more waves overlap, so ___Young's___ experiment showed that light behaves like a ___wave___.

15. The emission of electrons from a metal caused by light striking the metal is called the ___photoelectric___ effect.

16. Blue light has a higher frequency than red light, so photons of blue light have ___more___ energy than photons of red light.

Intensity (page 538)

17. The closer you get to a source of light, the ___brighter___ the light appears.

18. Intensity is the ___rate___ at which a wave's energy flows through a given unit of area.

19. As photons travel farther from the source, the ___intensity___ of light decreases.

Name_____ Class_____ Date_____ M T W T F

LESSON PLAN 18.2

The Electromagnetic Spectrum

Time
2 periods
1 block

Section Objectives

Local Standards

- **18.2.1 Rank** and **classify** electromagnetic waves based on their frequencies and wavelengths.

- **18.2.2 Describe** the uses for different waves of the electromagnetic spectrum.

Vocabulary electromagnetic spectrum • amplitude modulation • frequency modulation • thermograms

1 FOCUS

Build Vocabulary: LINCS
Have students use LINCS to remember vocabulary terms. **L2**

Targeted Resources
❑ Transparency: Interest Grabber 18.2
❑ Transparency: Reading Strategy 18.2

2 INSTRUCT

Build Reading Literacy: Outline
Have students outline section 18.2. **L1**

For Extra Help
Discuss the basic features of a line graph. **L1**

Teacher Demo: Radio Reception
Place a radio with extended antenna inside a cardboard box and a metal wire enclosure. Students observe factors that affect radio signal reception. **L2**

Address Misconceptions
Discuss with students that light has different speeds in different materials. **L2**

Build Science Skills: Observing
Have students assess the quality of AM and FM radio signals. **L3**

Targeted Resources
❑ Transparency: Figure 9: The Electromagnetic Spectrum
❑ Transparency: Figure 13: The Visible Spectrum
❑ GRSW Section 18.2
❑ **NSTA** *sci*$_{LINKS}$ The electromagnetic spectrum

3 ASSESS

Reteach
Use Figure 9 to review the section's key concepts. **L1**

Evaluate Understanding
Ask students to list the general properties and application for each electromagnetic wave type in the section. **L2**

Targeted Resources
❑ **PHSchool.com** Online Section 18.2 Assessment
❑ iText Section 18.2

Transparencies

268 **Section 18.2 Interest Grabber**

The Colors of Waves

Electromagnetic waves exist in a spectrum of wavelengths. Most of the spectrum is invisible. You can't see microwaves or radio waves, for example. But you can see the spectrum of visible light by looking at the surface of a CD. Hold the CD near a light source so the light reflects off its surface. Move the CD slightly and notice how the colors change.

1. What did you see when you looked at the light reflecting off the CD surface?

2. Copy the picture below. Use markers or colored pencils to color the spectrum of light as you saw it on your CD.

3. How were the colors similar to the colors of a rainbow?

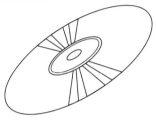

ANSWERS
1. Students saw a spectrum of colors that change with the CD's movement.
2. Student diagrams should show the correct order of colors of the rainbow: red, orange, yellow, green, blue, and violet.
3. The colors were in the same order as the colors of a rainbow, from red to violet.

Transparencies

269 **Section 18.2 Reading Strategy**

Summarizing

Type of Waves	Uses	
Radio Waves	Communications	a. ?
Infrared Rays	b. ?	Keeping food warm

ANSWERS
a. Cooking and radar detection systems
b. Detecting heat differences
Additional rows:
visible light: aids in vision and communication; Ultraviolet rays: health (kill microorganisms in heating and cooling systems), agriculture, (energy source to promote plant growth); X-rays: medicine, transportation (inspection tool); Gamma rays: medicine (kill cancer cells, form images of the brain), industry (inspection tool)

Transparencies

270 **Figure 9 The Electromagnetic Spectrum**

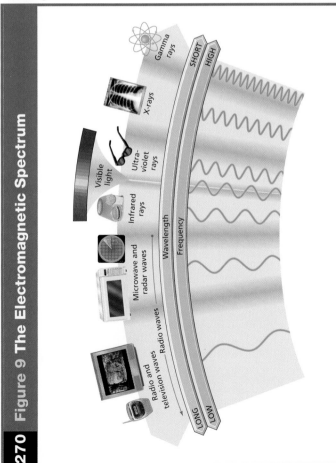

Transparencies

271 **Figure 13 The Visible Spectrum**

The Visible Spectrum		
Color	Wavelength (nm)	Frequency (× 10^{14} Hz)
Red	610–750	4.9–4.0
Orange	590–610	5.1–4.9
Yellow	570–590	5.3–5.1
Green	500–570	6.0–5.3
Blue	450–500	6.7–6.0
Violet	400–450	7.5–6.7

Name _____ Class _____ Date _____

Chapter 18   The Electromagnetic Spectrum and Light

Section 18.2 The Electromagnetic Spectrum
(pages 539–545)

This section identifies the waves in the electromagnetic spectrum and describes their uses.

Reading Strategy (page 539)

Summarizing Complete the table for the electromagnetic spectrum. List at least two uses for each kind of wave. For more information on this Reading Strategy, see the **Reading and Study Skills** in the **Skills and Reference Handbook** at the end of your textbook.

The Electromagnetic Spectrum		
Type of Waves	Uses Sample answers:	
Radio Waves	Communications	Cooking and radar detection systems
Infrared Rays	Detecting heat differences	Keeping food warm
Visible Light	Aids in vision	Communication and signaling
Ultraviolet Rays	Health (kill microorganisms in heating and cooling systems)	Agriculture (energy source to promote plant growth), Medicine
X-rays	Medicine	Transportation industry
Gamma Rays	Medicine (kill cancer cells, form images of the brain)	Industry (inspection tool)

The Waves of the Spectrum (pages 539–540)

1. Is the following sentence true or false? William Herschel determined that the temperature of colors of light was higher at the blue end and lower at the red end. _____false_____
2. Herschel's curiosity led him to conclude there must be invisible _____radiation_____ beyond the red end of the color band.
3. Is the following sentence true or false? The full range of frequencies of electromagnetic radiation is called the electromagnetic spectrum. _____true_____
4. Name each kind of wave in the electromagnetic spectrum, from the longest to shortest wavelength.

   a. ____Radio waves____   b. ____Infrared rays____

   c. ____Visible light____   d. ____Ultraviolet rays____

   e. _____X-rays_____   f. ____Gamma rays____

Name _____ Class _____ Date _____

Chapter 18   The Electromagnetic Spectrum and Light

Radio Waves (pages 540–542)

5. Circle the letter of each way that radio waves might be used.

   a. x-ray machines   (b.) microwave ovens

   (c.) radio technology   (d.) television technology

6. What is the difference between amplitude modulation (AM) and frequency modulation (FM)? In amplitude modulation, the amplitude of the wave is varied and the frequency remains the same. In frequency modulation, the frequency of the wave is varied and the amplitude remains the same.

7. How far do microwaves generally penetrate food? Microwaves penetrate food a few centimeters.

8. How is the Doppler effect used to detect the speed of a vehicle? Radio waves are sent from a stationary source toward a moving car. The faster a car is moving toward the source, the higher the frequency of the radio waves returning to the source.

Infrared Rays (page 543)

9. Circle the letter of each way infrared rays are used.

   a. source of light   (b.) to discover areas of heat differences

   (c.) source of heat   d. to discover areas of depth differences

10. Thermograms show variations in ____temperature____ and are used to find places where a building loses heat to the environment.

Visible Light (page 543)

11. Is the following sentence true or false? One use for visible light is to help people communicate with one another. _____true_____

Ultraviolet Rays (page 544)

12. Ultraviolet radiation has applications in ___health and medicine___ and ____agriculture____.

13. Is the following sentence true or false? Ultraviolet radiation helps your skin produce vitamin D. _____true_____

X-rays (page 544)

14. Is the following sentence true or false? X-rays have higher frequencies than ultraviolet rays. _____true_____

15. Why are X-rays helpful? They are used in medicine, industry, and transportation to make pictures of the inside of solid objects.

Gamma Rays (page 545)

16. Gamma rays have the highest ____frequencies____ and therefore the most ____energy____ and the greatest penetrating ability of all the electromagnetic waves.

17. How is gamma radiation used in medicine? Gamma radiation is used to kill cancer cells and to make pictures of the brain.

Name_____ Class_____ Date_____ M T W T F

LESSON PLAN 18.3

Behavior of Light

Time
2 periods
1 block

Section Objectives

- **18.3.1 Classify** materials as transparent, translucent, or opaque to visible light.
- **18.3.2 Describe** what happens when light is reflected, refracted, polarized, or scattered.

Vocabulary transparent • translucent • opaque • image • regular reflection • diffuse reflection • mirage • polarized light • scattering

Local Standards

1 FOCUS

Build Vocabulary: Concept Map
Have students construct a concept map of the vocabulary terms used in this section. **L2**

Targeted Resources
❑ Transparency: Interest Grabber 18.3
❑ Transparency: Reading Strategy 18.3

2 INSTRUCT

Build Reading Literacy: Anticipation Guide
Ask students which of three statements about the behavior of light are true. **L1**

Address Misconceptions
Relate to students that ordinary objects reflect light. **L2**

Teacher Demo: Reflected Light and Vision
Have students look through a small hole in the side of a closed box that has a white interior. Students observe the role of reflected light in vision perception. **L2**

Build Science Skills: Observing
Students observe the effect of polarizing filters by holding the filters up to light coming through the window. **L2**

Targeted Resources
❑ Transparency: Figure 20: Polarization
❑ GRSW Section 18.3

3 ASSESS

Reteach
Use Figures 16 to 21 as examples that illustrate key concepts of the section. **L1**

Evaluate Understanding
Have students identify and explain examples of transparency, translucency, opaqueness, regular reflection, and diffuse reflection. **L2**

Targeted Resources
❑ **PHSchool.com** Online Section 18.3 Assessment
❑ iText Section 18.3

Transparencies

272 Section 18.3 Interest Grabber

What Can You See Through?

Just by looking around, you know that light can travel through air. A transparent material, such as air, transmits light. An opaque material, such as metal, blocks light. Look around your classroom. What are some transparent and opaque materials that you see?

Can an object block light and also allow some light to pass through it? Hold a book up toward a light. Put your hand between the light and the book. Can you see your hand through the book? Now hold a piece of white paper up toward the light, and put your hand between them. Can you see your hand through the paper?

1. Could light pass through the book?

2. Was light able to pass through the paper?

3. List some transparent and opaque objects that you saw in the classroom.

Transparencies

273 Section 18.3 **Reading Strategy**

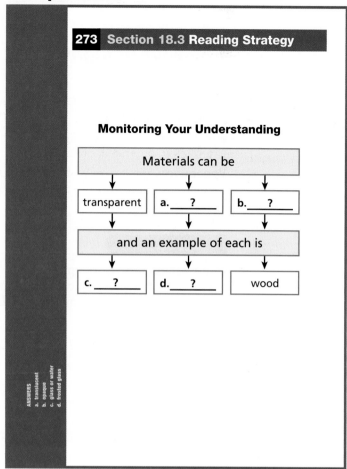

Monitoring Your Understanding

Materials can be

transparent	a. ?	b. ?

and an example of each is

c. ?	d. ?	wood

Transparencies

274 **Figure 20 Polarization**

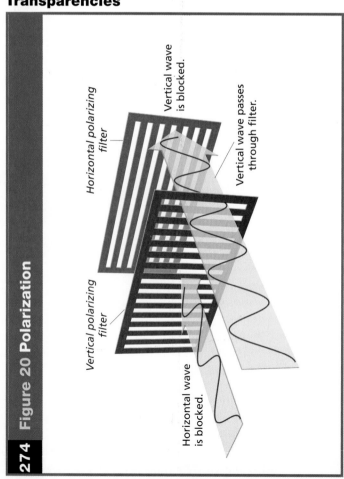

Horizontal polarizing filter

Vertical wave is blocked.

Vertical wave passes through filter.

Vertical polarizing filter

Horizontal wave is blocked.

Guided Reading and Study Workbook

Name _____ Class _____ Date _____

Section 18.3 Behavior of Light
(pages 546-549)

This section discusses the behavior of light when it strikes different types of materials.

Reading Strategy (page 546)

Monitoring Your Understanding As you read, complete the flowchart to show how different materials affect light. For more information on this Reading Strategy, see the **Reading and Study Skills** in the **Skills and Reference Handbook** at the end of your textbook.

Light and Materials

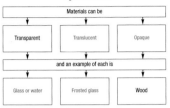

Materials can be

| Transparent | Translucent | Opaque |

and an example of each is

| Glass or water | Frosted glass | Wood |

Light and Materials (pages 546–547)

1. Is the following sentence true or false? Without light, nothing is visible. _____true_____

Match each term to its definition.

	Term		Definition
b	**2.** transparent		a. Material that absorbs or reflects all of the light that strikes it
a	**3.** opaque		b. Material that transmits light
c	**4.** translucent		c. Material that scatters light

Interactions of Light (pages 547–549)

5. Is the following sentence true or false? Just as light can affect matter, matter can affect light. _____true_____

6. When light strikes a new medium, it can be _____reflected_____, _____absorbed_____, or _____transmitted_____.

Guided Reading and Study Workbook

Name _____ Class _____ Date _____

7. When light is transmitted, it can be refracted, polarized, or _____scattered_____.

8. A copy of an object formed by reflected or refracted light waves is known as a(n) _____image_____.

9. When parallel light waves strike an uneven surface and reflect off it in the same direction, _____regular_____ reflection occurs.

10. When parallel light waves strike a rough, uneven surface and reflect in many different directions, _____diffuse_____ reflection occurs.

11. Light bends, or _____refracts_____, when it passes at an angle from one type of medium into another.

12. Explain why a mirage occurs. Light travels faster in hot air than in cooler, denser air. On a hot day, light is gradually refracted as it moves into layers of hotter and hotter air. This refraction causes some of the light to follow a curved path to the ground.

13. Is the following sentence true or false? Light with waves that vibrate in only one plane is polarized light. _____true_____

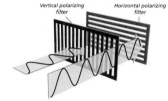

Vertical polarizing filter   *Horizontal polarizing filter*

14. Refer to the drawing and complete the table on polarizing filters.

Polarizing Filters		
Direction of Light Vibration	**Filter Type**	**Action**
Horizontal wave	Vertically polarizing filter	Light is blocked.
Vertical wave	Vertically polarizing filter	Light passes through.

15. How do sunglasses block glare? The vertically polarized filters of the sunglasses block the horizontally polarized light being reflected.

16. The effect when light is redirected as it passes through a medium is called _____scattering_____.

17. Explain why the sun looks red at sunset and sunrise. Small particles in the atmosphere scatter shorter-wavelength blue light more than light of longer wavelengths. Longer wavelengths of orange and red light reach the eyes.

Name_____   Class_____   Date_____   M T W T F

LESSON PLAN 18.4

Color

Time
2 periods
1 block

Section Objectives

- **18.4.1 Explain** how a prism disperses white light into different colors.
- **18.4.2 Analyze** factors that determine the color of an object.
- **18.4.3 Distinguish** among primary, secondary, and complementary colors of light and of pigments.

Vocabulary dispersion • primary colors • secondary colors • complementary colors of light • pigment • complementary colors of pigment

Local Standards

1 FOCUS

Build Vocabulary: Vocabulary Knowledge Rating Chart
Have students construct a four-column chart and share their knowledge of vocabulary terms. **L2**

Targeted Resources
❑ Transparency: Interest Grabber 18.4
❑ Transparency: Reading Strategy 18.4

2 INSTRUCT

Use Visuals: Figure 23
Review refraction with students. **L1**

Build Reading Literacy: Compare and Contrast
Students can study similarities and differences in Figures 25 and 26 to avoid confusing light and pigments. **L1**

Build Science Skills: Controlling Variables
Help students see the importance of changing one variable at a time. **L2**

Address Misconceptions
Explain to students that when two beams of differently colored light overlap, colors are added. **L2**

Teacher Demo: Overlapping Filters
On an overhead projector, overlap red, green, and blue acetate filters. Students investigate how colors combine by addition and subtraction. **L2**

Targeted Resources
❑ GRSW Section 18.4
❑ **NSTA** *sci*$_{LINKS}$ Color

3 ASSESS

Reteach
Compare Figures 25 and 26 to review how colors of light are different from colors of pigment. **L1**

Evaluate Understanding
Have students invent stage-lighting scenarios. **L2**

Targeted Resources
❑ **PHSchool.com** Online Section 18.4 Assessment
❑ iText Section 18.4

Transparencies

275 **Section 18.4 Interest Grabber**

What Makes a Red Marker Red?

Different objects have different colors. Have you ever wondered why a green object looks green while a red object looks red?

In a darkened room, place a piece of white paper flat on your desk. Rest a flashlight on the desk so it's light beam passes over the paper. Hold a red marker just above the paper. Observe the color change of the paper near the marker. Next, replace the red marker with a green marker so that it is just above the paper. Observe the color of the paper near it.

1. What color was the paper near each marker?

2. Do you think the colors you saw resulted from light reflected or absorbed by the markers? Explain your answer.

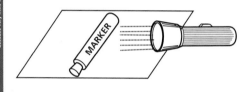

ANSWERS
1. The paper was red near the red marker and green near the green marker.
2. It must be reflected light from the marker, because no other colored light is striking the paper. The color can be seen because very little white light strikes the paper.

Transparencies

276 **Section 18.4 Reading Strategy**

Venn Diagram

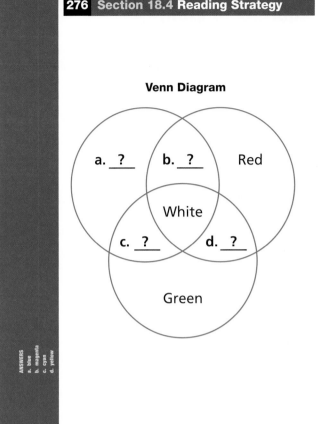

a. ?   b. ?   Red

White

c. ?   d. ?

Green

ANSWERS
a. blue
b. magenta
c. cyan
d. yellow

Guided Reading and Study Workbook

Name _____ Class _____ Date _____

Chapter 18   The Electromagnetic Spectrum and Light

Section 18.4 Color
(pages 550–553)

This section explains how a prism separates white light. It also discusses factors that influence the various properties of color.

Reading Strategy (page 550)

Venn Diagram As you read, label the Venn diagram for mixing primary colors of light. For more information on this Reading Strategy, see the **Reading and Study Skills** in the **Skills and Reference Handbook** at the end of your textbook.

Mixing Colors of Light

Magenta

Blue   Red

White

Cyan   Yellow

Green

Separating White Light Into Colors (page 551)

1. What did Isaac Newton's experiments with a prism in 1666 show? They showed that white sunlight is made up of all the colors of the visible spectrum.

2. What happens when white light passes through a prism? Shorter wavelengths refract more than longer wavelengths, and the colors separate.

3. Circle the letter of the process in which white light is separated into the colors of the rainbow.
   a. reflection   (b.) dispersion
   c. absorption   d. polarization

4. How does a rainbow form? Water droplets act like prisms and separate sunlight into the spectrum.

Guided Reading and Study Workbook

Name _____ Class _____ Date _____

Chapter 18   The Electromagnetic Spectrum and Light

The Colors of Objects (pages 551–552)

5. List two factors that determine the color of an object seen by reflected light.
   a. What the object is made of
   b. The color of light that strikes the object

6. Is the following sentence true or false? I see a red car in sunlight because the color of light reaching my eyes is mostly red light. true

Mixing Colors of Light (page 552)

Match the colors of light with the correct type of color.

Type of Color	Colors of Light
c **7.** primary colors	a. Cyan, yellow, and magenta
a **8.** secondary colors	b. Blue and yellow
b **9.** complementary colors	c. Red, green and blue

Match each color of light to its definition.

Type of Color	Definition
b **10.** primary colors	a. Formed when two primary colors combine
a **11.** secondary colors	b. Combine in varying amounts to form all possible colors
c **12.** complementary colors	c. Combine to form white light

Mixing Pigments (page 553)

13. What is a pigment? A pigment is a material that absorbs some colors of light and reflects other colors.

14. List four natural sources of pigments.
    a. Metal oxide compounds   b. Minerals
    c. Plants   d. Animals

15. The primary colors of pigments are cyan, yellow, and magenta.

Match the primary colors of pigment to the color they produce when combined.

Primary Colors	Color Produced
c **16.** Cyan and magenta	a. green
a **17.** Cyan and yellow	b. red
b **18.** Yellow and magenta	c. blue

19. Any two colors of pigments that combine to make black pigment are complementary colors of pigments.

Name_____ Class_____ Date_____ M T W T F

LESSON PLAN 18.5
Sources of Light

Time
2 periods
1 block

Section Objectives

- **18.5.1 Explain** how light is produced by common sources of light.
- **18.5.2 Describe** the uses of different light sources.
- **18.5.3 Distinguish** lasers from other light sources.

Vocabulary luminous • incandescent • fluorescence • phosphor • laser • coherent light

Local Standards

1 FOCUS

Build Vocabulary: Word-Part Analysis
Ask students what words they know other than those in the vocabulary list that have the vocabulary key word parts. **L2**

Targeted Resources
❏ Transparency: Interest Grabber 18.5
❏ Transparency: Reading Strategy 18.5

2 INSTRUCT

Use Visuals: Figure 27
Have students carefully examine the photograph and answer questions. **L1**

Quick Lab: Comparing Fluorescent and Incandescent Light
Students view incandescent light and fluorescent light through a spectroscope, in order to explain the difference in spectra of incandescent and fluorescent lights. **L2**

Address Misconceptions
Use observations in the Quick Lab activity to help students understand that all white light is not similar. **L2**

Build Reading Literacy: SQ3R
Teach the study skill SQ3R to help students understand the concepts in this section. **L2**

Build Science Skills: Inferring
Ask, Why do sodium-vapor light have less glare than incandescent lights? **L2**

For Enrichment
Interested students can make a multimedia presentation for the class explaining an application such as CD players, fiber optic networks, and laser eye surgery. **L3**

Build Science Skills: Inferring
Students observe and compare the spectra of different neon lights. **L3**

Targeted Resources
❏ GRSW Section 18.5

3 ASSESS

Reteach
Make a flow chart showing how each light source emits light. **L1**

Evaluate Understanding
Invite students to write quiz questions with answers. **L2**

Targeted Resources
❏ **PHSchool.com** Online Section 18.5 Assessment
❏ iText Section 18.5

277 Section 18.5 Interest Grabber

Energy From Light Bulbs

When you turn on a lamp, you expect the room to suddenly become brighter. You know that incandescent light bulbs give off light. But is that all they give off?

Observe a lamp that has been turned off for a while. Look at the light bulb. What do you see? Place your hand a few centimeters from the light bulb. What do you feel? Next, turn the lamp on. Without looking directly at the bulb, note what you see. Again, place your hand a few centimeters from the lamp and note what you feel. **CAUTION:** *Do not touch the bulb.*

1. Compare your observations when the lamp was off with your observations after the lamp was on.

2. What are two types of energy that are given off by an incandescent light bulb?

ANSWERS
1. The light bulb gave off light when it was on. The bulb was much warmer when the lamp was on.
2. The incandescent bulb gave off light energy and thermal energy.

278 Section 18.5 Reading Strategy

Sequencing

Incandescent Bulb

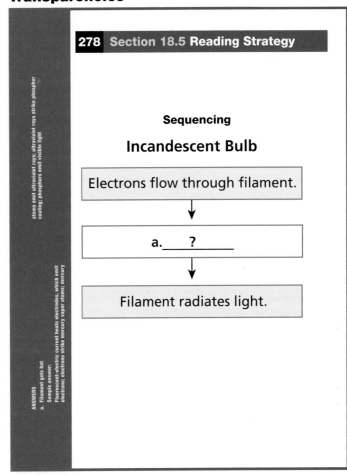

Electrons flow through filament.

↓

a. _____?_____

↓

Filament radiates light.

atoms emit ultraviolet rays; ultraviolet rays strike phosphor coating; phosphors emit visible light

ANSWERS
a. Filament gets hot
Sample answer:
Fluorescent–electric current heats electrodes, which emit electrons; electrons strike mercury vapor atoms; mercury

---

Guided Reading and Study Workbook

Name _____ Class _____ Date _____

Chapter 18   The Electromagnetic Spectrum and Light

Section 18.5 Sources of Light
(pages 558–562)
This section discusses the major sources of light and their uses.

Reading Strategy (page 558)

Flowchart Complete the incandescent bulb flowchart. For more information on this Reading Strategy, see the **Reading and Study Skills** in the **Skills and Reference Handbook** at the end of your textbook.

Incandescent Bulb

Electrons flow through filament.
↓
Filament gets hot.
↓
Filament radiates light.

1. Objects that give off their own light are ___luminous___.

2. List six common sources of light.
   a. ___Incandescent bulbs___   b. ___Fluorescent bulbs___
   c. ___Laser___   d. ___Neon___
   e. ___Tungsten-halogen bulbs___   f. ___Sodium-vapor bulbs___

Incandescent Light (page 558)

3. The light produced when an object gets hot enough to glow is ___incandescent___.

4. As electrons flow through an incandescent light bulb, the ___filament___ heats up.

5. Is the following sentence true or false? To increase the life of the filament, incandescent light bulbs contain oxygen at very low pressure. ___false___

6. Most of the energy given off by incandescent bulbs is in the form of ___heat___.

Fluorescent Light (page 559)

7. What happens in the process of fluorescence? ___A material absorbs light at one wavelength and then emits light at a longer wavelength.___

8. A solid material that can emit light by fluorescence is called a(n) ___phosphor___.

9. Fluorescent bulbs emit most of their energy in the form of ___photons___.

10. Is the following sentence true or false? Incandescent bulbs are more energy efficient than fluorescent bulbs. ___false___

Guided Reading and Study Workbook

Name _____ Class _____ Date _____

Chapter 18   The Electromagnetic Spectrum and Light

Laser Light (page 560)

11. A laser is a device that generates ___a beam of coherent light___.

12. The letters in the word *laser* stand for
    l ___light___
    a ___amplification___
    s ___stimulated___
    e ___emission___
    r ___radiation___

13. What is coherent light? ___Coherent light is light in which waves have the same wavelength, and the crests and troughs are lined up.___

14. Why does coherent light have a relatively constant intensity? ___Coherent light doesn't spread out significantly from its source.___

Neon Light (page 561)

15. How is neon light emitted? ___Neon light is emitted when electrons move through a gas or a mixture of gases inside glass tubing.___

16. List three gases used to produce neon light.
    a. ___Helium___
    b. ___Argon___
    c. ___Krypton___

17. Why do different types of neon light glow in different colors? ___Each kind of gas emits photons of different energies and color. The different photons combine to give each glowing gas a distinctive color. The color of the glass tube also affects the color of the light.___

Sodium-Vapor Light (page 562)

18. Sodium-vapor lights contain a mixture of ___neon and argon gases___ and a small amount of solid ___sodium___.

19. Explain what happens when an electric current passes through a sodium-vapor bulb. ___The electric current ionizes the gas mixture, which warms up. The heat causes the sodium to change from a solid into a gas.___

Tungsten-Halogen Light (page 562)

20. Explain how a tungsten-halogen light bulb works. ___The bulb is filled with a halogen gas. Electrons flow through a tungsten filament. The filament gets hot and emits light.___

Chapter 18 **Program Resources**

Guided Reading and Study Workbook

Name _____ Class _____ Date _____

Chapter 18   The Electromagnetic Spectrum and Light

WordWise

Complete the sentences using one of the scrambled words below.

nrcteleos	tarfes	qucreynef
treclefs	rigehh	kabcl
mefailnt	riotrafecn	ratenemypocml
yrecurm	snohpot	dairo
sifdel	culstantren	otehccrn

Electromagnetic waves consist of changing electric and changing magnetic ____fields____.

You hear thunder from a distant lightning bolt a few seconds after you see the lightning because light travels much ____faster____ than sound.

If you know the wavelength of an electromagnetic wave in a vacuum, you can calculate its ____frequency____.

Although light behaves as a wave, the photoelectric effect shows that light also consists of bundles of energy called ____photons____.

Antennas use ____radio____ waves to send signals to television receivers.

Ultraviolet rays have a ____higher____ frequency than waves of violet light.

If you can look through a material but what you see is not clear or distinct, then the material is said to be ____translucent____.

When a beam of light enters a new medium at an angle, it changes direction, and ____refraction____ occurs.

A truck appears red in the sunlight because its paint ____reflects____ mainly red light.

A color of light mixed equally with its ____complementary____ color of light yields white light.

Complementary colors of pigments combine to form ____black____ pigment.

An incandescent bulb produces light by using an electric current to heat a(n) ____filament____.

Inside a fluorescent bulb, an electric current passes through ____mercury____ vapor and produces ultraviolet light.

Light that consists of a single wavelength of light with its crests and troughs lined up is called ____coherent____ light.

Neon lights emit light when ____electrons____ flow through gas in a tube.

Physical Science Guided Reading and Study Workbook • Chapter 18 **167**

Guided Reading and Study Workbook

Name _____ Class _____ Date _____

Chapter 18   The Electromagnetic Spectrum and Light

Calculating Wavelength and Frequency

A particular AM radio station broadcasts at a frequency of 1030 MHz. What is the wavelength of the transmitted radio wave assuming it travels in a vacuum?

Math Skill: Multiplication and Division of Exponents

You may want to read more about this Math Skill in the **Skills and Reference Handbook** at the end of your textbook.

1. Read and Understand

What information are you given?

Speed = c = 3.00×10^8 m/s

Frequency = 1030 kHz = 1030×10^3 Hz

2. Plan and Solve

What unknown are you trying to calculate?

Wavelength = ?

What formula contains the given quantities and the unknown?

Speed = Wavelength × Frequency

Wavelength = $\dfrac{\text{Speed}}{\text{Frequency}}$

Replace each variable with its known value.

Wavelength = $\dfrac{3.00 \times 10^8 \text{ m/s}}{1030 \text{ Hz} \times 10^8 \text{ Hz}}$

$= \dfrac{3.00 \times 10^8 \text{ m/s}}{1.030 \times 10^6 \text{ 1/s}} = 291$ m

3. Look Back and Check

Is your answer reasonable?

Radio waves have frequencies greater that 1 mm, so 291 m is a reasonable wavelength for a radio wave.

Math Practice

On a separate sheet of paper, solve the following problems.

1. In a vacuum, the wavelength of light from a laser is 630 nm (630×10^{-9} m). What is the frequency of the light?

Frequency = $\dfrac{\text{Speed}}{\text{Wavelength}}$ = $\dfrac{3.0 \times 10^8 \text{ m/s}}{630 \times 10^{-9} \text{ m}}$ = 4.8×10^{14} Hz

2. If a radio wave vibrates at 80.0 MHz, what is its wavelength?

Wavelength = $\dfrac{\text{Speed}}{\text{Frequency}}$ = $\dfrac{3.0 \times 10^8 \text{ m/s}}{80.0 \times 10^6 \text{ Hz}}$ = 3.8 m

3. A radio station broadcasts at 780 kHz. The wavelength of its radio waves is 385 m. Verify that the radio wave travels at the speed of light.

Speed = Wavelength × Frequency = 385 m × (780 × 10^3 Hz) = 3.0×10^8 m/s

168 *Physical Science* Guided Reading and Study Workbook • Chapter 18

Student Edition Lab Worksheet

Name _____ Class _____ Date _____

Chapter 18   The Electromagnetic Spectrum and Light   **Exploration Lab**

Mixing Colored Lights

See page 563 in the Teacher's Edition for more information.

What is color? How many different colors can be formed from a combination of only three colors? In this exploration, you will examine what happens when lights of three different colors are mixed.

Problem How can you produce a range of colors from three lights of different colors?

Materials
- sources of red, blue, and green light
- tape
- large sheet of white paper

Skills Observing

Procedure 🖐 📋

1. Tape a large sheet of white paper to the wall.
2. Dim the room lights. Turn on the red light source and shine it on the large sheet of white paper. In the data table, record the colors you observe on the paper. **CAUTION:** *Do not touch lamps when they are on. They may be hot.*

DATA TABLE

Light Sources	Colors of Lights	Colors of Shadows
Red only		
Blue only		
Green only		
Red and blue		
Red and green		
Blue and green		
Red, blue, and green		

3. Place your hand between the light source and the paper. Record the color of your hand's shadow.
4. Repeat Steps 2 and 3 with the blue and then with the green light source.

Physical Science Lab Manual • Chapter 18 Exploration Lab **327**

Student Edition Lab Worksheet

Name _____ Class _____ Date _____

5. Now turn on the red and blue light sources and allow their beams to overlap. Record your observations in the data table.
6. Place your hand in the overlapping beams of light. Note the colors of any shadows that your hand makes. Record your observations in the data table.
7. Repeat Steps 5 and 6 with the red and green light sources. Then repeat Steps 5 and 6 with the blue and green light sources.
8. Turn on all three light sources and allow their beams to overlap. Record your observations in the data table.
9. Place your hand in the overlapping red, green, and blue beams. Note the colors of any shadows that your hand makes on the white paper. Record your observations in the data table.

Analyze and Conclude

1. **Observing** What happened when two colored lights overlapped?

Two colors combined to make a new color.

2. **Analyzing Data** How did the combination of two colored lights produce the shadows you observed?

Because there were two light sources, there were two overlapping shadows. In areas on the paper where the hand blocked only one beam of light, the other area was lit by the other beam of light. Therefore, each shadow was the color of one beam of light.

3. **Applying Concepts** Explain how combining three colored lights produced the colors you observed.

Overlapping two beams of primary-colored light produced secondary colors. Combining all three primary colors in equal intensity produced white light.

4. **Drawing Conclusions** From the shadows you observed when using three colored lights, what can you conclude about how colors of light combine? Explain your answer.

The colors of the shadows show how colors of light combine. In areas where the hand blocked one beam, the shadow was lit by the two other lights. Therefore, these areas were secondary colors of light. For example, where the hand blocked only the blue beam, the shadow was lit by red and green light, producing a yellow shadow. Similarly, red and blue light combined to produce a magenta shadow, and blue and green light combined to produce a cyan shadow.

_____

_____

_____

328 *Physical Science* Lab Manual • Chapter 18 Exploration Lab

384

Name _____ Class _____ Date _____

Chapter 18   The Electromagnetic Spectrum and Light   🔍 **Investigation 18A**

Predicting Spectra

Refer students to pages 546, 547, and 550–553 in their textbooks for a discussion of transparency and color. **SKILL FOCUS:** Predicting, Observing, Drawing Conclusions **CLASS TIME:** 30 minutes

Background Information

Some materials are **transparent** to nearly all frequencies of visible light. This means that these materials transmit most of the light that strikes them. For example, window glass is transparent to nearly all frequencies of visible light. Most materials, however, transmit some frequencies and absorb others. These materials can appear colored.

If you observe the spectrum of light before and after it passes through a material, you can determine which frequencies the material absorbs. You can view the spectrum of light through a prism or an instrument known as a spectroscope. These instruments separate white light into its colors, a process called **dispersion.**

In this investigation, you will predict and observe how the spectrum of white light changes as the light passes through several solutions of different colors. Then, you will use your observations to explain how the color of a material is related to the wavelengths of light that it absorbs.

Problem

How is the color of a solution related to the wavelengths of light that it absorbs?

Pre-Lab Discussion

Read the entire investigation. Then, work with a partner to answer the following questions.

1. **Predicting** Imagine observing a white light through a piece of blue glass.

    a. What color would the light appear to be?

    Blue _____

    b. What color of light would the glass transmit?

    Blue _____

    c. What colors of light would the glass absorb?

    Red, orange, yellow, green, and violet _____

2. **Predicting** Describe the spectrum you would see if you passed white light through a piece of blue glass.

    The spectrum would include only blue light. _____

    _____

Name _____ Class _____ Date _____

3. **Controlling Variables** Identify the manipulated, responding, and controlled variables in this investigation.

    a. Manipulated variable   colored solutions

    b. Responding variable   appearance of spectrum

    c. Controlled variables   light source, spectroscope

4. **Formulating Hypotheses** State a hypothesis about how the spectrum of white light changes as the light passes through a colored solution.

    Passing white light through a colored solution removes one or more colors.

Materials *(per group)*

lamp and incandescent bulb
spectroscope
colored pencils
stoppered test tube of chlorophyll solution
stoppered test tube of phenolphthalein-sodium hydroxide solution
stoppered test tube of potassium permanganate solution

Safety 🥽🧤🔲🔥☣️⚠️

Put on safety goggles, a lab apron, and plastic gloves. Be careful to avoid breakage when working with glassware. Observe proper laboratory procedures when using electrical equipment. Never touch or taste any chemical unless instructed to do so. The chemicals used in this investigation are toxic and corrosive. Do not open any of the test tubes. Note all safety alert symbols next to the steps in the Procedure and review the meaning of each symbol by referring to the Safety Symbols on page xiii.

Procedure

1. With the room darkened, turn on the incandescent lamp. Observe the light from the bulb. In the data table, draw the spectrum that you expect to see when you view the bulb through the spectroscope. If necessary, use colored pencils to draw the spectrum.

2. Now, use the spectroscope to observe the spectrum of the light from the incandescent bulb. In the data table, draw and describe the spectrum that you observed.

3. Examine the test tube of the chlorophyll solution. Observe the light from the incandescent bulb through this test tube. Record in the data table the color that you see.

4. In the data table, draw the spectrum that you expect to see when you view the chlorophyll solution through the spectroscope.

Do not allow students to prepare solutions. To prepare the chlorophyll solution, heat 300 mL isopropyl alcohol to 60°C on a hot plate in a fume hood. Do not heat the alcohol to a temperature greater than 60°C. Place four or five dark green plant leaves in the alcohol. Add more leaves if necessary until the alcohol becomes deep green. Allow the solution to cool before removing the leaves and dispensing the solution into test tubes. To prepare the phenolphthalein-sodium hydroxide solution, dissolve 1.2 g sodium hydroxide in 300 mL water and add 1% alcoholic phenolphthalein solution one drop at a time until a deep pink color is attained. To prepare the potassium permanganate solution, dissolve 0.3 g potassium permanganate (KMnO₄) in 300 mL water. **CAUTION:** *Potassium permanganate is a skin irritant and can explode on sudden heating. Alcohol vapors are flammable and can be explosive. Wear safety goggles, a lab apron, and plastic gloves when preparing all solutions. Review the safety information in the MSDS on hazardous chemicals with students before performing this investigation.*

Dim the lights in the classroom by closing window shades or turning off the classroom lights.

Show students how to use the spectroscopes.

CAUTION: *Do not touch heated bulbs as they can burn skin.*

Name _____ Class _____ Date _____

5. Hold the test tube of chlorophyll solution against the far end of the spectroscope so that the light from the bulb passes through the solution before entering the spectroscope. In the data table, draw the spectrum of the chlorophyll solution. Record any differences between this spectrum and the one you observed in Step 2. You may note gaps or differences in the brightness of some colors.

    CAUTION: *Handle glass test tubes carefully to avoid breakage and exposure to hazardous chemicals*

6. Repeat Steps 3 through 5 with the test tube of phenolphthalein-sodium hydroxide solution.

7. Repeat Steps 3 through 5 with the test tube of potassium permanganate solution.

8. Return the test tubes to your teacher. Wash your hands thoroughly after carrying out this investigation.

Observations   Sample data are shown.

DATA TABLE

Solution	Color	Drawing of Predicted Spectrum	Drawing of Observed Spectrum	Description of Observed Spectrum
None	None			Continuous spectrum of red, orange, yellow, green, blue, and violet
Chlorophyll	Green			Green and yellow are predominant; other colors are nearly absent.
Phenolphthalein-sodium hydroxide	Pink			Green and yellow are absent; violet, orange and red are predominant.
Potassium permanganate	Purple			Green and yellow are absent; blue and red are predominant.

Analysis and Conclusions

1. **Analyzing Data** Did passing white light through the colored solutions add colors to the light or remove colors from the light?

    Passing white light through colored solutions removed colors from the light.

    _____

    _____

Name _____ Class _____ Date _____

2. **Formulating Hypotheses** What happened to the colors of light that did not pass through the solutions? Explain your answer.

    The solutions absorbed the colors of light that did not pass through the solutions. The energy of

    this light was then converted to thermal energy, or heat.

3. **Inferring** Which colors of light were absorbed in the spectrum of each of the following solutions?

    a. Chlorophyll solution

    Red, orange, blue and violet light were absorbed.

    b. Phenolphthalein-sodium hydroxide solution

    Green and yellow light were absorbed.

    c. Potassium permanganate solution

    Green and yellow light were absorbed.

4. **Drawing Conclusions** What is the relationship between the color of a solution and the colors of light that the solution absorbs?

    A solution that is a primary color of light (green) must absorb at least the other two primary colors

    (red and blue). A solution that is a secondary color of light (magenta) at a minimum must absorb its

    complementary color (green).

5. **Drawing Conclusions** What is the relationship between the color of a solution and the colors of light that the solution transmits?

    Light of the same color as the solution passes through the solution.

    _____

6. **Applying Concepts** If you shine a red light through a block of red gelatin, the red beam of light is clearly visible in the gelatin. However, if you shine a red light through a block of blue gelatin, the light is not visible in the gelatin. Explain these observations.

    The red light is visible in the red gelatin because the red gelatin transmits red light and absorbs blue

    and green light. Blue gelatin absorbs red light and transmits blue light. The red light would therefore

    be absorbed by the blue gelatin and would not be seen.

Lab Manual

Name _____ Class _____ Date _____

Go Further

The spectroscope that you used in this investigation enabled you to see whether there were any gaps in the spectrum of the light you observed and to judge whether some parts of the spectrum were brighter than others. A more precise instrument called a spectrophotometer enables you to measure the percentage of the light falling on a sample of a solution that the solution absorbs or transmits. The spectrophotometer can make this measurement at any visible wavelength.

Ask your teacher to show you how to use the spectrophotometer. Then, design an experiment to determine whether it is possible to use the spectrophotometer to measure the concentration of a light-absorbing substance in a solution. Write a detailed plan of your experiment. Your plan should state the hypothesis to be tested, identify the manipulated, responding, and controlled variables, and describe the procedures and safety precautions that you will use. Show your plan to your teacher. When your teacher approves your plan, carry out your experiment and report your results and conclusions.

Examine students' plans for sound experimental design and safety. An example of an acceptable hypothesis is that the percentage of the light falling on a solution that is absorbed is proportional to the concentration of the solution. Have students practice using the spectrophotometer to measure the light absorption of a solution of the substance at a range of wavelengths. Then, have students plot the results against wavelength to obtain an absorption spectrum. Students can use this spectrum to select the wavelength at which the substance absorbs the most light. At this wavelength, the percentage of absorption should be proportional to the concentration of the substance. Students can use a set of solutions of known concentrations to calibrate the spectrophotometer to estimate the concentration of the light-absorbing substance.

Lab Manual

Name _____ Class _____ Date _____

Using Polarized Light
Refer students to pages 548 and 549 in their textbooks for a discussion of polarized light. **SKILL FOCUS:** *Measuring, Using Graphs and Tables* **CLASS TIME:** *45 minutes*

Background Information

Some substances change the direction in which polarized light waves vibrate. These substances are said to be optically active. Sucrose, or table sugar, is optically active. When polarized light passes through a solution of sucrose dissolved in water, the polarization of the light changes—the light waves begin to vibrate in a different direction.

To measure this change, a device called a polarimeter is used. A polarimeter contains two polarizing filters. A container between the two filters holds a sample to be tested for optical activity. If the filters are at right angles to each other, no light can pass through the polarimeter. However, if you place an optically active sample between the filters, it will change the polarization of the light. As a result, some light will pass through the second filter. To measure the optical activity of a sample, you would look through the polarimeter and rotate the second filter until no light is able to pass though the filter. The angle that you rotate the second filter depends on the sample's optical activity.

In this investigation, you will use a polarimeter to determine how the optical activity of a sugar solution is related to the concentration of the solution.

Problem

How is the concentration of a sugar solution related to its optical activity?

Pre-Lab Discussion

Read the entire investigation. Then, work with a partner to answer the following questions.

1. **Inferring** Explain how two polarizing filters can completely block a beam of light.

   The first filter polarizes the light. If the second filter is placed at right angles to the first,

   the second filter will completely block the polarized light that reaches it from the first filter.

2. **Designing Experiments** Why will you need to be able to change the angle between the polarizing filters in the polarimeter?

   The sugar solution will change the direction in which the polarized light vibrates. The second

   filter must be able to rotate because the distance that the second filter must be rotated to block

   the light measures the optical activity of the solution.

Lab Manual

Name _____ Class _____ Date _____

3. **Applying Concepts** Could you determine the optical activity of a solution if the light passed through the sample before it passed through the two polarizing filters? Explain your answer.

   No, the optical activity could not be measured in this way because the light would not be polarized

   when it passed through the sample. As a result, the sample would not affect the polarization of the

   light or how much light passed through the filters.

4. **Controlling Variables** Identify the manipulated, responding, and controlled variables in this investigation.
   a. Manipulated variable
      Sugar concentration

   b. Responding variable
      Direction of polarization of light

   c. Controlled variables
      Starting position of the filters; distance that light passes through each sample; optical activity
      of pure water

5. **Controlling Variables** Why will you need to measure the optical activity of water in Step 9?
   The water serves as a control. Any optical activity of the water should be subtracted from the

   optical activity of the sugar solutions to determine the optical activity of the sugar in the solutions.

Materials *(per group)*

2 cardboard tubes	bright light source
scissors	red pencil
transparent tape	paper towels
metric ruler	10 mL 20% sugar solution
glass vial with cap	10 mL 30% sugar solution
2 square polarizing filters,	10 mL 40% sugar solution
approximately 2 cm × 2 cm	unknown sugar solution
duct tape	
graph paper with millimeter	
rulings	

CAUTION: *Do not permit students to look directly at the sun.*

Polarizing film can be ordered from a scientific supply house or cut from inexpensive polarizing clip-on sunglasses. Use toilet paper rolls for the cardboard tubes. To prepare 20%, 30%, and 40% sugar solutions, dissolve 20 g, 30 g, and 40 g, respectively, of sucrose in 80 mL, 70 mL, and 60 mL water. Make the unknown sugar solution by dissolving 35 g sucrose in 65 mL water.

Safety

Put on a lab apron. Be careful to avoid breakage when working with glassware. Be careful when handling sharp instruments. Never look directly at the sun. Note all safety alert symbols next to the steps in the Procedure and review the meaning of each symbol by referring to the Safety Symbols on page xiii.

Lab Manual

Name _____ Class _____ Date _____

Procedure
Part A: Building a Polarimeter

1. Use scissors to cut a cardboard tube open lengthwise. Then, overlap the cut edges to make a slightly smaller tube that just fits inside the second cardboard tube, as shown in Figure 1. Use transparent tape to hold the cut edges of the smaller tube together. **CAUTION:** *Be careful not to puncture or cut skin when using scissors.*

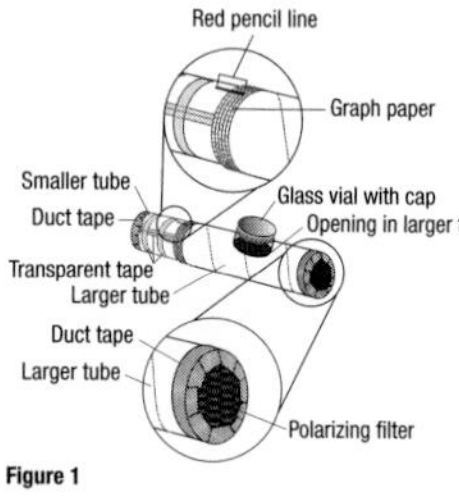

2. Using a metric ruler to measure, make a pencil mark on the side of the larger tube 4 cm from one end of the tube. Hold the glass vial with the center of its base on this mark. Use a pencil to trace the outline of the base of the vial on the tube.

3. Cut out the circle that you traced on the tube in Step 2. The resulting opening in the tube should be just large enough to allow the vial to fit snugly inside the tube, as shown in Figure 1.

4. Use small pieces of duct tape to carefully mount a polarizing filter over one end of the larger tube. Place tape only on the edges of the filter. To avoid getting any dirt or fingerprints on the polarizing filter, handle the filter only by its edges. If necessary, use small pieces of duct tape to cover any gaps between the edges of the filter and the tube. To hold the pieces of duct tape in place, wrap a piece of duct tape around the end of the tube, as shown in Figure 1.

5. Repeat Step 4 with the second polarizing filter and the smaller tube.

6. Cut a strip of graph paper that is 12 cm long and 1 cm wide. Wrap this strip around the open end of the larger tube, as shown in Figure 1. Use transparent tape to attach the strip of graph paper to the tube.

7. Insert the vial into the hole that you made in Step 3. Then, gently insert the smaller tube into the larger tube as far as the smaller tube will go.

8. Hold the polarimeter in one hand. Use your other hand to cover the vial to prevent it from falling out of the larger tube. Then, look at the bright light source through the polarimeter. As you look at the light through the polarimeter, rotate the smaller tube to make the light as dim as possible. Have a member of your group mark a short red pencil line on the strip of graph paper. Extend this line onto the smaller tube, as shown in Figure 1. **CAUTION:** *Do not aim the polarimeter at the sun.*

Figure 1

Labels in Figure 1: Red pencil line; Graph paper; Smaller tube; Glass vial with cap; Duct tape; Opening in larger tube; Transparent tape; Larger tube; Duct tape; Larger tube; Polarizing filter

Lab Manual

Name _____ Class _____ Date _____

Part B: Measuring Optical Activity

9. Remove the vial from the polarimeter. Fill the vial with water and place the cap tightly on the vial. Use a paper towel to remove any water on the outside of the vial. Hold the polarimeter with the opening on top. Carefully put the vial back into the opening. Line up the red lines on both tubes. Look at the bright light source through the polarimeter. Rotate the smaller tube clockwise if necessary until the light is as dim as possible. **CAUTION:** *Immediately wipe up any spilled water. Make sure the vial does not slip out of the polarimeter.*

10. Observe the red pencil lines on the graph paper strip and on the smaller tube. Note that the rulings on the graph paper strip are 1 mm apart. In the data table, record the distance between the two red pencil lines. If the red pencil lines are precisely end to end, record this distance as zero.

11. Carefully remove the vial from the polarimeter. Discard the water in the sink. Rinse out the vial with water and use a paper towel to dry the vial.

12. Repeat Steps 9 through 11 with the 20%, 30%, and 40% sugar solutions. Then, repeat Steps 9 through 11 with the unknown sugar solutions.

13. Make a graph of the data from your observations of the water and the 20%, 30%, and 40% sugar solutions. Plot sugar concentration and optical activity on the vertical axis. Draw a straight line as close as possible to all four data points.

14. Find the point on the vertical axis of your graph that corresponds to the optical activity of the unknown sugar solution. Draw a horizontal dotted line from this point to the solid line. Then, draw a vertical dotted line from the point where the two lines meet down to the horizontal axis. The point where the vertical dotted line meets the horizontal axis marks the concentration of the unknown solution. Record this concentration in the data table.

Observations   Sample data are shown.

DATA TABLE

Sugar Concentration (percent)	Optical Activity (mm)
0 (water)	0.0
20	2.1
30	3.0
40	4.2
Unknown 35	3.5

Lab Manual

Name _____ Class _____ Date _____

Analysis and Conclusions

1. **Analyzing Data** What was the relationship between the concentration of the sugar solutions and their optical activities?

   The optical activities were directly proportional to the concentration of sugar.

2. **Using Graphs** Was it reasonable to use your graph to determine the concentration of sugar in the unknown solution? Explain your answer.

   Yes, because the unknown value was between two known values, it was reasonable to expect that the relationship between sugar concentration and optical activity did not change in this range.

3. **Evaluating and Revising** When would it be unreasonable to use your graph to determine the concentration of an unknown sugar solution? Explain your answer.

   If the optical activity of the unknown solution was very different from the range of known values, it would be unreasonable to assume that the relationship between sugar concentration and optical activity is the same for the known and unknown solutions.

4. **Predicting** How do you think the distance that light passes through the sample affects the observed optical activity?

   The observed optical activity is directly proportional to the distance that light passes through the sample.

Go Further

Design an experiment to use your polarimeter to determine the concentration of sugar in liquids such as fruit juices or syrups. Write a detailed plan of your experiment. Your plan should state the hypothesis to be tested, identify the manipulated, responding, and controlled variables, and describe the procedures and safety precautions that you will use. If the liquids you choose to test contain sugar other than sucrose, you will need to make solutions of known concentrations. After your teacher approves your plan, carry out your experiment and report your results and conclusions.

Examine student plans for sound experimental design and safety. Many foods are sweetened with corn syrup, which consists of a 70% solution of glucose in water. Students will need to measure the optical activity of various concentrations of corn syrup. High fructose corn syrup (HFCS) is used to sweeten many foods, especially soft drinks. You can make a solution with the approximate composition of HFCS by dissolving 31.3 g fructose and 43.3 g glucose in 30 mL water. Students can use this solution as a standard for calibrating a polarimeter to measure the concentration of HFCS.

Chapter Test A

Name _____ Class _____ Date _____

Chapter 18   The Electromagnetic Spectrum and Light   **Chapter Test A**

Multiple Choice

Write the letter that best answers the question or completes the statement on the line provided.

_____ 1. Electromagnetic waves vary in
   a. the speed they travel in a vacuum.
   b. wavelength and frequency.
   c. the way they reflect.
   d. their direction.

_____ 2. An electromagnetic wave in a vacuum has a wavelength of 0.032 m. What is its frequency?
   a. $f = 3.00 \times 10^8$ m/s   b. $f = 9.38 \times 10^9$ m/s
   c. $f = 3.00 \times 10^9$ m/s   d. $f = 9.38 \times 10^8$ m/s

_____ 3. Because light travels in a straight line and casts a shadow, Isaac Newton hypothesized that light is
   a. radiation.   b. a stream of particles.
   c. a wave.   d. heat.

_____ 4. Which of the following occurs as light travels farther from its source?
   a. Far from the source, photons spread through a small area.
   b. The intensity of light increases as photons move away from the source.
   c. The source gives off less light as photons move away from it.
   d. Farther from the source, photons spread over a larger area.

_____ 5. The full range of frequencies of electromagnetic radiation is called
   a. visible light.
   b. radio waves.
   c. the electromagnetic spectrum.
   d. invisible radiation.

_____ 6. The visible light spectrum ranges between
   a. radar waves and X-rays.
   b. television waves and infrared rays.
   c. infrared rays and ultraviolet rays.
   d. ultraviolet rays and gamma rays.

_____ 7. X-ray photographs show softer tissue
   a. as invisible.
   b. as dark, highly exposed areas.
   c. the same as dense bones.
   d. as bright white areas.

Chapter Test A

Name _____ Class _____ Date _____

_____ 8. In order of the light-transmitting capabilities of materials from none to all, which is the correct sequence?
   a. transparent → opaque → translucent
   b. opaque → transparent → translucent
   c. opaque → translucent → transparent
   d. translucent → transparent → opaque

_____ 9. Polarized sunglasses work by
   a. blocking light waves that vibrate in one plane.
   b. gradually refracting light as it passes through the lenses
   c. bending light as it passes from air into the lenses.
   d. reflecting most of the light that strikes the sunglasses.

_____ 10. When droplets of water in the atmosphere act like prisms, the colors in sunlight undergo
   a. interference.   b. absorption.
   c. polarization.   d. dispersion.

_____ 11. Blue light and yellow light combine to produce white light because
   a. they absorb each other's wavelengths.
   b. blue, yellow, and white are primary colors.
   c. they are complementary colors of light.
   d. they are both primary colors of light.

_____ 12. The primary colors of pigments
   a. are cyan, yellow, and magenta.
   b. are the same as the secondary colors of light.
   c. combine in equal amounts to produce black.
   d. all of the above

_____ 13. Which of the following is NOT true regarding neon lights?
   a. Light is emitted as electrons move through a gas in a tube.
   b. All neon lights are colored by the color of the tubing.
   c. Neon lights may contain other gases, such as helium or krypton.
   d. Each kind of gas produces its own distinctive color.

_____ 14. Light whose waves all have the same wavelength, direction, and coincidental peaks is called
   a. coherent light.   b. incandescent light.
   c. fluorescent light.   d. neon light.

_____ 15. Which kind of light is used to carry information through optical fibers?
   a. incandescent   b. fluorescent
   c. sodium-vapor light d. laser

Chapter Test A

Name _____ Class _____ Date _____

Completion

Complete each statement on the line provided.

1. A transparent object _____ almost all of the light that strikes it.

2. An ultraviolet light wave has a wavelength of 300 nm and a frequency of 7.0×10^{14} Hz. The ultraviolet light is NOT traveling through a(an) _____.

3. In microwave cooking, the food is heated _____ in the areas near the surface of the food than in the center.

4. Light amplification by stimulated emission of radiation is known as _____ light.

5. The following electromagnetic waves are arranged in order of increasing frequency: infrared, _____, ultraviolet.

Short Answer

In complete sentences, write the answers to the questions on the lines provided.

1. What is a basic difference between electromagnetic waves and sound waves?

_____
_____
_____
_____
_____
_____

2. What is the photoelectric effect?

_____
_____
_____
_____
_____

Chapter Test A

Name _____ Class _____ Date _____

3. Describe what happens to photons as they travel away from a light source.

_____
_____
_____

4. Both gamma rays and X-rays are used to see inside the body. Which one is used to make images of bones? How are the other rays used?

_____
_____
_____
_____

5. What two factors influence the color of an object?

_____
_____
_____

6. What is common to all light sources including incandescent, fluorescent, neon, halogen, laser, and sodium-vapor devices?

_____
_____
_____
_____

Chapter Test A

Name _____ Class _____ Date _____

Using Science Skills

Use the diagram to answer each question. Write the answers on a separate sheet of paper.

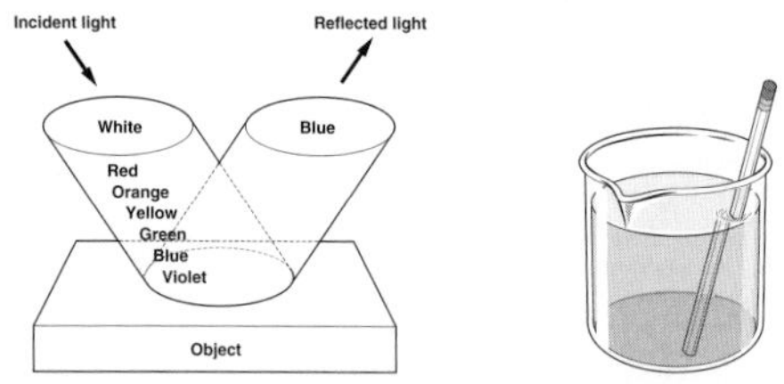

Figure 18-1

1. **Classifying** Examine Figure 18-1, which represents a pencil in a glass container of a liquid. Is the liquid transparent, translucent, or opaque to visible light? Explain.

2. **Applying Concepts** Explain why the pencil in Figure 18-1 appears to be broken.

3. **Interpreting Graphics** Figure 18-1 represents white light striking an object. Explain why the beam of white light is also labeled with colors.

4. **Drawing Conclusions** What color is the object in Figure 18-1? Explain your answer.

5. **Applying Concepts** Suppose the light striking the object in Figure 18-1 was a combination of red and green. What color would the object be when viewed in this light? Explain your answer.

Problem

Write the answer to the question on a separate sheet of paper.

1. A communications satellite transmits a radio wave at a frequency of 9.4×10^9 Hz. What is the signal's wavelength? Assume the wave travels in a vacuum. Show your work.

Chapter Test A

Name _____ Class _____ Date _____

Essay

Write the answers to each question on a separate sheet of paper.

1. Is light a particle or a wave? Briefly explain your answer and give examples.

2. What is the electromagnetic spectrum? Give examples of each kind of wave and relate each example to its relative position in the spectrum.

3. What is polarized light? What is unpolarized light? Name at least one familiar kind of polarizing filter and explain how it works.

4. Describe the economic advantage of using sodium-vapor lights and a disadvantage of the color it produces.

Name _____ Class _____ Date _____

Chapter 18   The Electromagnetic Spectrum and Light   Chapter Test B

Multiple Choice

Write the letter that best answers the question or completes the statement on the line provided.

_____ 1. In 1926, Michelson was able to measure the speed of
 light using
 a. lanterns.   b. stars.
 c. mirrors.   d. sunlight.

_____ 2. To calculate the frequency of an electromagnetic wave, you
 need to know the speed of the wave and its
 a. wavelength.   b. intensity.
 c. refraction.   d. amplitude.

_____ 3. Light acts like
 a. a wav.
 b. a particle.
 c. both a wave and a particle.
 d. neither a wave nor a particle.

_____ 4. Photons travel outward from a light source in
 a. a single straight line.   b. increasing intensity.
 c. a small, dense area.   d. all directions.

_____ 5. Infrared rays have a shorter wavelength than
 a. ultraviolet rays.   b. X-rays.
 c. radar waves.   d. gamma rays.

_____ 6. The waves with the longest wavelengths in the
 electromagnetic spectrum are
 a. infrared rays.   b. radio waves.
 c. gamma rays.   d. X-rays.

_____ 7. Cellular telephones utilize
 a. radar waves.
 b. very high frequency waves.
 c. very low frequency waves.
 d. microwaves.

_____ 8. A translucent material
 a. scatters some light.   b. transmits all light.
 c. absorbs all light.   d. reflects all light.

_____ 9. Which of the following occurs as a light wave bends when it
 passes from one medium into another?
 a. constructive interference
 b. refraction
 c. destructive interference
 d. reflection

Name _____ Class _____ Date _____

_____ 10. Newton's prism experiments showed that white sunlight is
 made up of
 a. the full electromagnetic spectrum.
 b. only blue light when separated by a prism.
 c. all the colors of the visible spectrum.
 d. only the longest wavelengths.

_____ 11. What an object is made of and the color of light that strikes
 it determines the
 a. color of the object.   b. transparency of the object.
 c. opacity of the object.   d. translucence of the object.

_____ 12. The primary colors of light are
 a. green, blue, and black.
 b. cyan, magenta, and yellow.
 c. red, yellow, and blue.
 d. blue, green, and red.

_____ 13. An incandescent light bulb produces light when electrons
 flow through the
 a. air.   b. glass.
 c. filament.   d. vacuum.

_____ 14. Many streets and parking lots are illuminated with
 a. laser lights.   b. tungsten-halogen lights.
 c. sodium-vapor lights.   d. fluorescent lights.

_____ 15. A fluorescent light bulb usually contains
 a. a vacuum.   b. oxygen.
 c. mercury vapor.   d. fluorescent powder.

Completion

Complete each statement on the line provided.

1. Electromagnetic waves are _____ waves consisting
 of changing electric and magnetic fields.
2. Warm objects give off more _____ radiation than
 cool objects give off.
3. The speed of light in a vacuum is _____ m/s.
4. The farther away you are from a light source, the
 _____ intense it is.
5. Objects that scatter some of the light that is transmitted through
 them are _____.
6. When viewed in red light, an object that reflects all the colors of
 light will appear _____.
7. Combining equal amounts of the three primary pigments
 produces _____.

Name _____ Class _____ Date _____

8. Electromagnetic waves can travel through a(an)
 _____.
9. Light is produced when _____ change energy
 levels in an atom.
10. Visible light waves have a shorter _____ than
 infrared waves have.
11. The electromagnetic waves with the shortest wavelengths are
 _____ rays.
12. To form white light from the combination of only two colors of
 light, the colors must be _____.

Short Answer

*In complete sentences, write the answers to the questions on
the lines provided.*

1. In which medium does light travel faster, air or glass?

 _____
 _____

2. Which type of electromagnetic wave has the longest wavelength
 and lowest frequency?

 _____
 _____

3. Which waves have wavelengths longer than those of visible light?
 Give an example of how each kind of wave is used.

 _____
 _____
 _____
 _____

4. Magenta is a secondary color of light. What type of color is
 magenta when it is a pigment?

 _____
 _____
 _____

5. What distinguishes a laser from other common light sources?

 _____
 _____
 _____
 _____

Name _____ Class _____ Date _____

Using Science Skills

*Use the diagram to answer each question. Write the answers on a separate
sheet of paper.*

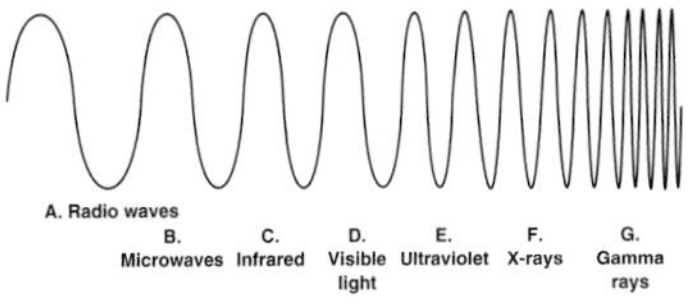

A. Radio waves
B. Microwaves
C. Infrared
D. Visible light
E. Ultraviolet
F. X-rays
G. Gamma rays

Figure 18-1

1. **Comparing and Contrasting** Which waves in Figure 18-1 carry
 AM and FM signals? How do the frequencies of AM and FM
 signals compare?
2. **Analyzing Data** How does photon energy change with increasing
 frequency? Use Figure 18-1 to answer this question.
3. **Interpreting Graphics** Which waves in Figure 18-1 are used to
 expose heat-sensitive film? Where are these waves located in the
 electromagnetic spectrum?
4. **Classifying** In Figure 18-1, which waves can be separated into
 different wavelengths of colored light?
5. **Inferring** Look at Figure 18-1. Without knowing the specific
 frequencies and wavelengths of the colors of the visible spectrum,
 at which end of the visible spectrum would you place red? At
 which end would you place violet? *Hint:* Use the names of the
 waves outside the visible spectrum to help you.

Chapter 18 Test A Answers

Multiple Choice

1. b   **2.** b   **3.** b   **4.** d   **5.** c   **6.** c
7. b   **8.** c   **9.** a   **10.** d   **11.** c   **12.** d
13. b   **14.** a   **15.** d

Completion

1. transmits **2.** vacuum **3.** more **4.** laser **5.** visible light

Short Answer

1. Electromagnetic waves can travel through a vacuum; sound waves cannot. Also, electromagnetic waves are transverse waves, whereas sound waves are longitudinal waves. **2.** the emission of electrons from metal caused by light striking the metal **3.** Light intensity decreases as distance from the source increases.
4. X-rays are used to make images of bones. Gamma rays are used to make images of the brain and to kill cancer cells. **5.** what the object is made of and the color of light striking the object
6. excited atoms emitting electrons

Using Science Skills

1. The liquid is transparent because the submerged portion of the pencil can be seen clearly regardless of the apparent break caused by refraction. **2.** Because the light bends as it moves from one medium into another, the image you see appears bent as well.
3. White light is made up of all the frequencies that produce colored light. **4.** The object is blue. All colors are absorbed except blue. **5.** The object would appear black because there is no blue incident light to reflect.

Problem

1. wavelength $= \dfrac{\text{speed}}{\text{frequency}} = \dfrac{3.00 \times 10^8 \text{m/s}}{9.4 \times 10^9 \text{Hz}} = 0.032\text{m}$

Essay

1. According to modern theory, light is both a particle and a wave. In 1801, Thomas Young proved that light behaves like a wave by showing that light produces interference patterns like a wave. A century later, Albert Einstein proposed that light consists of discrete particles called photons and demonstrated the effects of light striking metal—the photoelectric effect. **2.** The full range of wave frequencies of electromagnetic radiation is called the electromagnetic spectrum. In order of increasing frequency, the electromagnetic spectrum includes radio waves (radio, television, microwave ovens, radar), infrared rays (heat lamps), visible light (communication), ultraviolet rays (kill microorganisms), X-rays (medical imaging), and gamma rays (kill cancer cells). Visible light is the only part of the spectrum that we can see, and it is a very small part. **3.** Polarized light is light with waves that vibrate in only one plane. Unpolarized light vibrates in all directions. A vertical polarizing filter, such as polarized sunglasses, do not transmit light waves that vibrate in a horizontal plane, thus blocking some glaring light. **4.** Sodium-vapor lights are efficient. Where many lights are needed, such as in streets and parking lots, they can be economical to use. They give off a very bright, yellow light. The yellow light can alter the color of the objects it illuminates, which can be a disadvantage.

Chapter 18 Test B Answers

Multiple Choice

1. c   **2.** a   **3.** c   **4.** d   **5.** c   **6.** b
7. d   **8.** a   **9.** b   **10.** c   **11.** a   **12.** d
13. c   **14.** c   **15.** c

Completion

1. transverse **2.** infrared **3.** 3.00×10^8, 300,000,000 **4.** less
5. translucent **6.** red **7.** black **8.** vacuum **9.** electrons
10. wavelength **11.** gamma **12.** complementary

Short Answer

1. air **2.** radio waves **3.** radio waves (radio and television signals); microwaves and radar waves (microwave ovens); infrared rays (heat lamps) **4.** Magenta is one of the primary colors of pigments.
5. A laser emits a straight, narrow, intense beam of coherent light; other light sources produce light that spreads out in all directions as it moves away from the source.

Using Science Skills

1. Radio waves; FM signals usually have higher frequencies than AM signals have. **2.** High frequency waves such as X-rays and gamma rays have higher energy photons than lower frequency waves such as radio waves and infrared rays. **3.** Infrared rays are located between visible light and microwaves. **4.** visible light
5. Red would be at the end of the visible spectrum with the lowest frequency and longest wavelength of all the colors, just above the infrared range. *Infra* means "under," so *infrared* means "under red." In the same way, *ultra* means "beyond," so *ultraviolet* means "beyond violet." Violet would be at the end of the visible spectrum with the shortest wavelength and the highest frequency.

Chapter 19 Optics

CHAPTER

19

Planning Guide

Use these planning tools
Easy Planner
Resource Pro
Online Lesson Planner

SECTION OBJECTIVES	STANDARDS		ACTIVITIES and LABS
	NATIONAL (See p. T18.)	STATE	
19.1 Mirrors, pp. 570–573 🕐 1 block or 2 periods **19.1.1 Describe** the law of reflection. **19.1.2 Describe** how a plane mirror produces an image. **19.1.3 Describe** real and virtual images and relate them to converging and diverging light rays. **19.1.4 Describe** the physical characteristics of plane, concave, and convex mirrors and **distinguish** between the types of images they form.	A-1, A-2, C-6		**SE** Inquiry Activity: How Can You Make Glass Disappear? p. 569 [L2] **SE** Quick Lab: Measuring the Height of Your Mirror Image, p. 571 [L2] **SE** Consumer Lab: Selecting Mirrors, p. 593 [L2] **TE** Build Science Skills: Observing, p. 570 [L2] **TE** Teacher Demo: Flashlight Mirrors, p. 572 [L2]
19.2 Lenses, pp. 574–578 🕐 1 block or 2 periods **19.2.1 Explain** what causes light to refract. **19.2.2 Define** index of refraction. **19.2.3 Describe** the physical characteristics of concave and convex lenses and **distinguish** between the types of images they form. **19.2.4 Describe** total internal reflection and **explain** its relationship to the critical angle.	A-1, B-6		**TE** Teacher Demo: Combining Lenses, p. 576 [L2] **TE** Build Science Skills: Observing, p. 577 [L2] **LM** Investigation 19A: Investigating Reflection and Refraction [L2]
19.3 Optical Instruments, pp. 580–585 🕐 1 block or 2 periods **19.3.1 Distinguish** between how reflecting and refracting telescopes form images. **19.3.2 Explain** how cameras regulate and focus light to form images. **19.3.3 Describe** how light travels in a compound microscope to produce an enlarged image.	A-1, A-2, B-6, C-6, E-2, F-1, G-1, G-2, G-3		**SE** Quick Lab: Building a Pinhole Viewer, p. 585 [L2] **TE** Teacher Demo: Making a Telescope, p. 581 [L2] **TE** Teacher Demo: Two Types of Microscopes, p. 584 [L2] **LM** Investigation 19B: Testing a Solar Furnace [L1]
19.4 The Eye and Vision, pp. 588–592 🕐 1 block or 2 periods **19.4.1 Name** the main parts of the eye and **describe** their functions. **19.4.2 Name** common vision problems, **identify** their causes, and **explain** how they can be corrected.	B-6, C-6, E-2, F-1, G-3		

Ability Levels

L1	For students who need additional help
L2	For all students
L3	For students who need to be challenged

Components

SE	Student Edition	**GRSW**	Guided Reading & Study Workbook With Math Support	**CTB**	Computer Test Bank
TE	Teacher's Edition			**TP**	Test Prep Resources
LM	Laboratory Manual			**iT**	iText
PLM	Probeware Lab Manual	**CUT**	Chapter and Unit Tests	**DC**	Discovery Channel Videotapes

T	Transparencies
P	Presentation Pro CD-ROM
GO	Internet Resources

RESOURCES PRINT and TECHNOLOGY		SECTION ASSESSMENT
GRSW Section 19.1	**L1**	**SE** Section 19.1 Assessment, p. 573
T Chapter 19 Pretest	**L2**	**iText iT** Section 19.1
Section 19.1	**L2**	
P Chapter 19 Pretest	**L2**	
Section 19.1	**L2**	
SC_LINKS_ **GO** Mirrors	**L2**	
GRSW Section 19.2	**L1**	**SE** Section 19.2 Assessment, p. 578
GRSW Math Skill	**L2**	**iText iT** Section 19.2
T Section 19.2	**L2**	
P Section 19.2	**L2**	
GRSW Section 19.3	**L1**	**SE** Section 19.3 Assessment, p. 585
DC Traveling Light	**L2**	**iText iT** Section 19.3
T Section 19.3	**L2**	
P Section 19.3	**L2**	
SCIENCE NEWS GO Light and optics	**L2**	
GRSW Section 19.4	**L1**	**SE** Section 19.4 Assessment, p. 592
T Section 19.4	**L2**	**iText iT** Section 19.4
P Section 19.4	**L2**	

Go Online

Go online for these Internet resources.

PHSchool.com
Web Code: cch-2193
Web Code: cca-2190

NSTA **SC**_LINKS_
Web Code: ccn-2191

SCIENCE NEWS
Web Code: cce-2193

Materials for Activities and Labs

Quantities for each group

STUDENT EDITION

Inquiry Activity, p. 569
vegetable oil, water, 2 clear plastic or glass containers, 2 equal lengths of borosilicate glass tubing

Quick Lab, p. 571
plane mirror, meter stick, newspaper, masking tape

Quick Lab, p. 585
aluminum foil, black construction paper, cardboard tube, pin, wax paper, 4 rubber bands

Consumer Lab, p. 593
plane, convex, and concave mirrors; 2 metric rulers; roll of string; protractor

TEACHER'S EDITION

Build Science Skills, p. 570
graph paper, metric ruler, pencil, plane mirror

Teacher Demo, p. 572
flashlight with a beam that can be focused

Teacher Demo, p. 576
modeling clay, 2 convex lenses, 2 concave lenses, 2 index cards

Build Science Skills, p. 577
5-cm diameter double-convex lens, pencil

Teacher Demo, p. 581
2 convex lenses (one with a focal length of 10 cm and the other with a focal length of 30 cm), 1 stick of modeling clay

Teacher Demo, p. 584
compound microscope, stereo microscope

Build Science Skills, p. 587
flashlight, fiber optic bundle

Chapter Assessment

CHAPTER ASSESSMENT

SE	Chapter Assessment, pp. 595–596
CUT	Chapter 19 Test A, B
CTB	Chapter 19
iT	Chapter 19
PHSchool.com GO	
Web Code: cca-2190	

STANDARDIZED TEST PREP

SE	Chapter 19, p. 597
TP	Diagnose and Prescribe

iText—interactive textbook with assessment at PHSchool.com

Optics   568B

Name_____ Class_____ Date_____ M T W T F

LESSON PLAN 19.1

Mirrors

Section Objectives

■ **19.1.1 Describe** the law of reflection.

■ **19.1.2 Describe** how a plane mirror produces an image.

■ **19.1.3 Describe** real and virtual images and relate them to converging and diverging light rays.

■ **19.1.4 Describe** the physical characteristics of plane, concave, and convex mirrors and **distinguish** between the types of images they form.

Vocabulary ray diagram • angle of incidence • angle of reflection • plane mirror • virtual image • concave mirror • focal point • real image • convex mirror

Local Standards

1 FOCUS

Build Vocabulary: Vocabulary Knowledge Rating Chart

Have students use the vocabulary terms and construct a chart with four columns: Term, Can Define or Use It, Have Heard or Seen It, Don't Know. **L2**

Targeted Resources

❏ Transparency: Chapter 19 Pretest

❏ Transparency: Interest Grabber 19.1

❏ Transparency: Reading Strategy 19.1

2 INSTRUCT

Build Reading Literacy: Use Prior Knowledge

Ask students to think about times they have looked in a store's convex mirror. Ask them to explain the advantages and disadvantages a convex mirror has over a plane mirror. **L1**

Build Science Skills: Observing

Using a plane mirror mounted vertically to a sheet of graph paper, students compare object and image distance. **L2**

Teacher Demo: Flashlight Mirrors

Use a flashlight to show students how a small flashlight can focus a beam. **L2**

Address Misconceptions

Explain that rays must converge to form a real image, and that a real image produced by a mirror is always inverted. **L2**

Targeted Resources

❏ Transparency: Figure 1: The Law of Reflection

❏ Transparency: Figure 3: Concave Mirror

❏ Transparency: Figure 4: Convex Mirror

❏ GRSW Section 19.1

❏ **NSTA** *sci*$_{LINKS}$ Mirrors

3 ASSESS

Reteach

Have students make a chart summarizing how different types of images can be made with each mirror. **L1**

Evaluate Understanding

Have students roll a ball at an angle toward a wall. Encourage them to explain the angle of incidence and the angle of reflection of the ball's path. **L2**

Targeted Resources

❏ **PHSchool.com** Online Section 19.1 Assessment

❏ iText Section 19.1

Transparencies

279 **Chapter 19 Pretest**

1. What five things can happen to light that strikes a new medium?

2. Define *image*.

3. Which of the following makes an underwater object appear closer and larger than it really is?
   a. reflection

   b. absorption

   c. refraction

4. True or False: Parallel light rays reflect in many different directions off a smooth surface.

5. Which of the following types of material transmits almost all of the light that strikes it?
   a. translucent

   b. opaque

   c. transparent

   d. mirror

Transparencies

280 **Chapter 19 Pretest** (continued)

6. Which of the following occurs to a light ray when it passes from one transparent medium into another at an angle other than 90°?
   a. bent

   b. changed speed

   c. refracted

   d. all of these

7. True or False: It is impossible to see unless light enters the eye.

Transparencies

281 **Section 19.1 Interest Grabber**

Why Can You See Your Reflection in a Mirror?

You see your reflection in a mirror because light reflects off you. This reflected light travels to the mirror, reflects off the mirror, and travels back to your eyes. Without light and without a smooth, reflecting mirror surface, you could not see a clear image in a mirror.

Try the following activity. Tear a flat, unwrinkled sheet of aluminum foil from a roll. In a dimly lit room with only one primary light source, position yourself with your back to the light. Observe your image in the foil. Next, turn so you are facing the light and try to again observe your image in the foil. Now crumple the foil and repeat the previous two observations.

1. Why can you see your image more easily when you face the light than when your back is to the light?

2. Why can't you see your reflection in the crumpled foil?

Transparencies

282 **Section 19.1 Reading Strategy**

Comparing and Contrasting

Mirror	Shape of Surface	Image (virtual, real, or both)
Plane	Flat	Virtual
Concave	a. _____?_____	b. _____?_____
Convex	c. _____?_____	d. _____?_____

283 **Figure 1 The Law of Reflection**

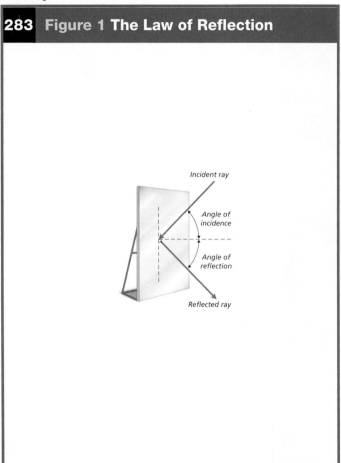

284 Figure 3 Concave Mirror

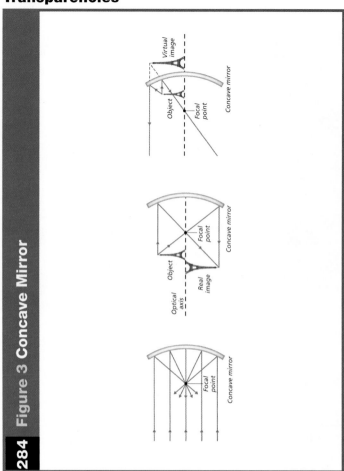

285 Figure 4 Convex Mirror

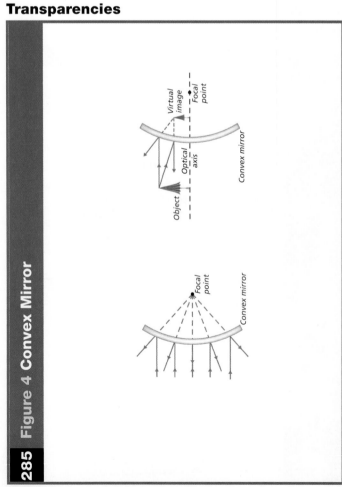

Name _____ Class _____ Date _____

Chapter 19   Optics

Section 19.1 Mirrors
(pages 570–573)

This section describes the law of reflection and explains how images are formed by plane, concave, and convex mirrors. Uses of mirrors are also described.

Reading Strategy (page 570)

Comparing and Contrasting After reading this section, compare mirror types by completing the table. For more information on this Reading Strategy, see the **Reading and Study Skills** in the **Skills and Reference Handbook** at the end of your textbook.

Mirror Types		
Mirror	Shape of Surface	Image (virtual, real, or both)
Plane	Flat	Virtual
Concave	Inside curved surface	Both
Convex	Outside curved surface	Virtual

The Law of Reflection (pages 570–571)

1. A ray diagram shows how rays ____change direction____ when they strike mirrors and pass through lenses.

2. Is the following sentence true or false? On a ray diagram, the angle of incidence is the angle that a reflected ray makes with a line drawn perpendicular to the surface of a mirror. ____false____

3. Circle the letter of the sentence that best answers the following question. What does a ray diagram of the law of reflection show?
   a. The angle of incidence is greater than the angle of reflection.
   b. The angle of reflection is greater than the angle of incidence.
   c. The angle of incidence is equal to the angle of reflection.
   d. The angle of incidence increases as the angle of reflection decreases.

Plane Mirrors (page 571)

4. A mirror with a flat surface is known as a(n) ____plane mirror____.

5. Circle the letter of each sentence that is true about plane mirrors.
   a. Plane mirrors always produce virtual images.
   b. Plane mirrors produce right-left reversed images of objects.
   c. Light rays reflect from a mirror at an angle that is twice as large as the angle of incidence.
   d. Your image appears to be the same distance behind a mirror as you are in front of it.

Physical Science Guided Reading and Study Workbook • Chapter 19 **169**

Name _____ Class _____ Date _____

Chapter 19   Optics

6. What type of image is a copy of an object formed at the location from which the light rays appear to come?
   a. reversed image
   b. virtual image
   c. real image
   d. reflected image

Concave and Convex Mirrors (pages 572–573)

7. Circle the letter of the object that is most like the shape of a concave mirror.
   a. the inside of a shallow bowl
   b. the bottom of a bucket
   c. the outside surface of a ball
   d. a glass window pane

8. What is the focal point? ____When a concave mirror reflects light rays that are parallel to the optical axis, the curved reflecting surface causes the light rays to come together at the focal point.____

9. Is the following sentence true or false? A real image is a copy of an object formed at the point where light rays actually meet. ____true____

For questions 10 through 12, refer to the diagrams below.

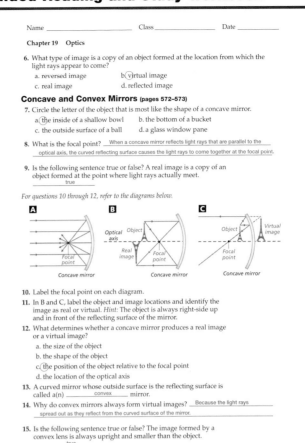

Concave mirror   Concave mirror   Concave mirror

10. Label the focal point on each diagram.

11. In B and C, label the object and image locations and identify the image as real or virtual. *Hint:* The object is always right-side up and in front of the reflecting surface of the mirror.

12. What determines whether a concave mirror produces a real image or a virtual image?
    a. the size of the object
    b. the shape of the object
    c. the position of the object relative to the focal point
    d. the location of the optical axis

13. A curved mirror whose outside surface is the reflecting surface is called a(n) ____convex____ mirror.

14. Why do convex mirrors always form virtual images? ____Because the light rays spread out as they reflect from the curved surface of the mirror.____

15. Is the following sentence true or false? The image formed by a convex lens is always upright and smaller than the object. ____true____

170 *Physical Science* Guided Reading and Study Workbook • Chapter 19

Name_____ Class_____ Date_____ M T W T F

LESSON PLAN 19.2

Lenses

Time
2 periods
1 block

Section Objectives

- **19.2.1 Explain** what causes light to refract.
- **19.2.2 Define** index of refraction.
- **19.2.3 Describe** the physical characteristics of concave and convex lenses and **distinguish** between the types of images they form.
- **19.2.4 Describe** total internal reflection and **explain** its relationship to the critical angle.

Vocabulary index of refraction • lens • concave lens • convex lens • critical angle • total internal reflection

Local Standards

1 FOCUS

Build Vocabulary: Concept Maps
Have students create concept maps that include the following topics: lens shape, images formed, applications, diverging rays, and converging rays. **L2**

Targeted Resources
❑ Transparency: Interest Grabber 19.2
❑ Transparency: Reading Strategy 19.2

2 INSTRUCT

Build Reading Literacy: Outline
Have students create an outline of the section. Ask them to define index of refraction and total internal reflection, based on their outlines. **L1**

Use Visuals: Figure 6
Using Figure 6, have students use a small ruler to compare the directions of the incoming light ray and the outgoing light ray. Have students compare the change from air into water with glass into air. **L1**

Use Community Resources
Invite a person who repairs cameras to come to your class and demonstrate how a camera operates and forms images. Encourage students to prepare questions to ask. **L2**

Address Misconceptions
Use a convex lens and a lamp to demonstrate to students that blocking part of the surface of a convex lens will not always block the corresponding part of the image. **L2**

Teacher Demo: Combining Lenses
Set up two pictures behind convex lenses and concave lenses, so that students can see the effects of combining lenses. **L2**

Integrate Social Studies
Have students research early scientists (other than Alhazen) who studied optics, such as Archimedes, Galileo, and Kepler. **L2**

Targeted Resources
❑ Transparency: Figure 7: Concave Lens
❑ Transparency: Figure 9: Convex Lens
❑ Transparency: Figure 11: Fiber Optics
❑ GRSW Section 19.2

3 ASSESS

Reteach
Have students draw sketches of the different types of image formation by lenses. **L1**

Evaluate Understanding
Ask students to list the general properties of a convex or concave lens, and name at least one application for the lens. **L2**

Targeted Resources
❑ **PHSchool.com** Online Section 19.2 Assessment
❑ iText Section 19.2

Transparencies

Transparencies

287 Section 19.2 Reading Strategy

Building Vocabulary

Vocabulary Term	Definition
Index of refraction	a. _____?_____
Critical angle of refraction	b. _____?_____
Total internal reflection	c. _____?_____

ANSWERS
a. Ratio of the speed of light in a vacuum to the speed of light in the material.
b. Angle of incidence that produces an angle of refraction of 90 degrees.
c. The complete reflection of a light ray back into its original medium.

Transparencies

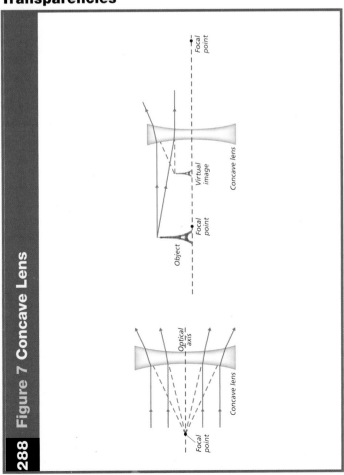

Figure 7 Concave Lens

288

Transparencies

289 **Figure 9 Convex Lens**

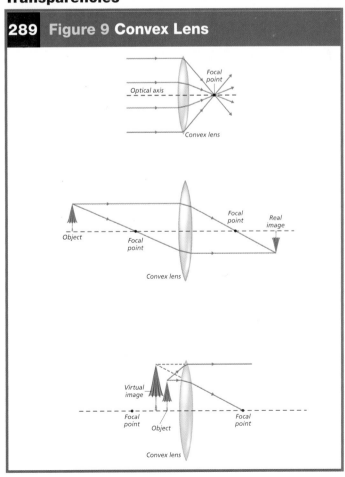

399

Transparencies

290 **Figure 11 Fiber Optics**

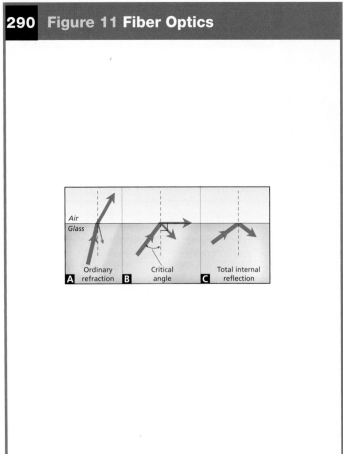

Air
Glass

A Ordinary refraction B Critical angle C Total internal reflection

---

Guided Reading and Study Workbook

Name _____ Class _____ Date _____

Chapter 19 Optics

Section 19.2 Lenses
(pages 574–578)

This section defines index of refraction and discusses how it is related to the way light behaves upon entering different materials. Image formation in concave and convex lenses are presented.

Reading Strategy (page 574)

Building Vocabulary As you read the section, define in your own words each vocabulary word listed in the table. For more information on this Reading Strategy, see the **Reading and Study Skills** in the **Skills and Reference Handbook** at the end of your textbook.

Refraction and Reflection	
Vocabulary Term	**Definition**
Index of refraction	Ratio of the speed of light in a vacuum to the speed of light in the material
Critical angle	Angle of incidence that produces an angle of refraction of 90 degrees
Total internal reflection	The complete reflection of a light ray back into its original medium

Index of Refraction of Light (pages 574–575)

1. Circle the letter of the sentence about the speed of light through media that is true.
   a. Once light passes from a vacuum into any medium, it speeds up.
   (b.) Compared to other media, air slows the speed of light only slightly.
   c. The speed of light is greater in water than in air.
   d. The speed of light in a new medium depends on the size of the new medium.

2. What determines how much a light ray bends when it passes from one medium to another? The amount of refraction depends upon the difference between the speeds of light in the two media.

3. The ratio of the speed of light in a vacuum to the speed of light in a particular material is known as the ____index of refraction____ of that material.

Concave and Convex Lenses (pages 576–577)

4. An object made of transparent material that has one or two curved surfaces that can refract light is called a(n) ____lens____.

5. Two properties of a lens that affect the way it refracts light are ____curvature____ and ____thickness____.

6. A lens that is curved inward at the center and is thickest at the outside edges is called a(n) ____concave____ lens.

Guided Reading and Study Workbook

Name _____ Class _____ Date _____

Chapter 19 Optics

7. Concave lenses always cause light rays to ____spread out or diverge____.

8. Circle the letter of each sentence that is true about convex lenses.
   a. Convex lenses are diverging lenses.
   (b.) Fly eyes have many facets shaped like the surface of convex lenses.
   (c.) Convex lenses can form either real or virtual images.
   d. Convex lenses are shaped somewhat like the inside of a bowl.

9. What determines whether a convex lens will form a real image or a virtual image? The type of image depends upon the position of the object with respect to the focal point and the lens.

For questions 10 and 11, refer to the diagrams below.

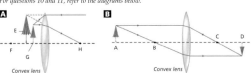

A

E

F   G   H

Convex lens

B

A   B   C   D

Convex lens

10. In each diagram identify the labeled items as the object, focal point, or image. Also, identify the image as virtual or real.
    A. ____Object____   B. ____Focal point____
    C. ____Focal point____   D. ____Real image____
    E. ____Virtual image____   F. ____Focal point____
    G. ____Object____   H. ____Focal point____

11. Which diagram shows the formation of a virtual image? ____Diagram A____

Total Internal Reflection (page 578)

12. Circle each letter of a sentence that is true about the critical angle.
    (a.) At the critical angle, light refracts along the surface between two media.
    b. All the light is reflected back into the first medium at the critical angle.
    c. Only concave lenses have critical angles.
    (d.) All the light is reflected back into the second, denser medium when the critical angle is exceeded.

13. Is the following sentence true or false? Materials that have small critical angles, such as the glass used in fiber optics, cause most of the light entering them to be totally internally reflected. ____true____

LESSON PLAN 19.3

Optical Instruments

Section Objectives

- **19.3.1 Distinguish** between how reflecting and refracting telescopes form images.

- **19.3.2 Explain** how cameras regulate and focus light to form images.

- **19.3.3 Describe** how light travels in a compound microscope to produce an enlarged image.

Vocabulary telescope • reflecting telescope • refracting telescope • camera • microscope

Local Standards

1 FOCUS

Build Vocabulary: Flowchart
As students read about reflecting telescopes, have them make a flowchart showing the steps in the image formation process. **L2**

Targeted Resources
❑ Transparency: Interest Grabber 19.3
❑ Transparency: Reading Strategy 19.3

2 INSTRUCT

Build Reading Literacy: Using Context Clues
As students read the section, have them look for unfamiliar words. Encourage them to use surrounding sentences and figures to help them understand the word. **L1**

Use Community Resources
Invite a member of the local astronomical society to discuss how different types of telescopes form images and demonstrate their use. **L2**

Teacher Demo: Making a Telescope
Help students observe the basic requirements for a telescope by making a telescope out of two convex lenses. **L2**

Build Science Skills: Comparing and Contrasting
Have students examine the first camera and the modern digital camera. Students should compare and contrast the features of the cameras. **L2**

Science and History
Assign to groups of students dates from the time line on p. 583. Have each group discuss how the events they're investigating helped spread the use of photography. **L2**

Quick Lab: Building a Pinhole Viewer
Students will construct a pinhole viewer, in order to describe the formation of an inverted image by a pinhole camera. **L2**

Targeted Resources
❑ Transparency: Figure 13: Reflecting and Refracting Telescopes
❑ Transparency: Figure 14: A Modern Film Camera
❑ GRSW Section 19.3

3 ASSESS

Reteach
Have students write several sentences that briefly explain how telescopes, cameras, and microscopes form images. **L1**

Evaluate Understanding
Ask students to name some optical instruments they use, and describe what kind of lens or mirror they think is used in each device. **L2**

Targeted Resources
❑ **PHSchool.com** Online Section 19.3 Assessment
❑ iText Section 19.3

Transparencies

291 Section 19.3 Interest Grabber

What's Inside Binoculars?

Many instruments use mirrors and lenses to bend and reflect light. Binoculars are used to make distant objects look larger.

Look through the eyepieces of a pair of binoculars. Notice how the image appears larger. Turn the binoculars around and look through the opposite end. Note the image you observe.

1. How does the image change when you look through the opposite end of the binoculars?

2. Look carefully at the shape of the binoculars. Do the binoculars you are using contain mirrors and lenses, lenses only, or mirrors only? Offer an explanation for your answer.

ANSWERS
1. When looked through from the opposite end, the images in the binoculars are greatly reduced in size.

2. Binoculars generally use lenses and mirrors. This can be inferred from their shape because the place where you view images is not in line with the place where light enters the binoculars.

Transparencies

292 Section 19.3 Reading Strategy

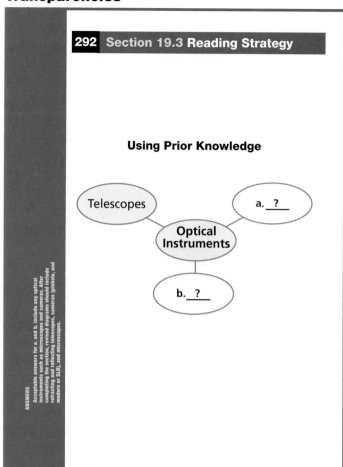

Using Prior Knowledge

ANSWERS
Acceptable answers for a. and b. include any optical instruments such as microscopes and cameras. After completing the section, revised diagrams should include refracting and reflecting telescopes, cameras (pinhole, and modern or SLR), and microscopes.

Transparencies

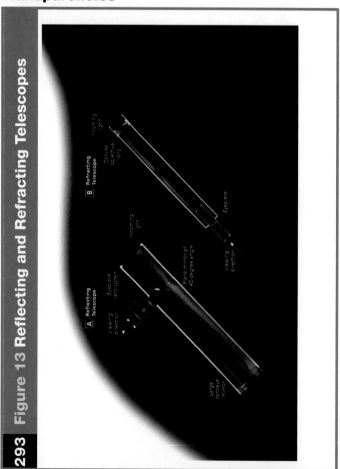

293 Figure 13 **Reflecting and Refracting Telescopes**

Transparencies

294 Figure 14 **A Modern Film Camera**

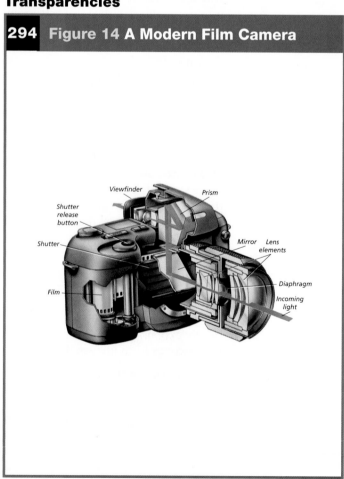

Name _____ Class _____ Date _____

Chapter 19   Optics

Section 19.3 Optical Instruments
(pages 580–585)

This section describes optical instruments, including telescopes, cameras, and microscopes. The basic principles of image formation by these instruments are explained.

Reading Strategy (page 580)

Using Prior Knowledge Add the names and descriptions of other optical instruments you know to the diagram. Revise the diagram after you read the section. For more information on this Reading Strategy, see the **Reading and Study Skills** in the **Skills and Reference Handbook** at the end of your textbook.

Note: Acceptable answers for the two ovals before reading the section include any optical instruments such as microscopes and cameras. After completing the section, revised diagrams should include refracting and reflecting telescopes, cameras (pinhole, and modern or SLR), and microscopes

Telescopes (pages 580–581)

1. Circle the letter that best describes the amount of time it takes light from the most distant stars to reach Earth.

   a. seconds   b. hours

   c. millions of years   (d.) billions of years

2. An instrument that uses lenses or mirrors to collect and focus light from distant objects is called a(n) _____telescope_____.

3. Complete the table about telescopes.

Telescopes		
Type	**Parts That Collect and Focus Light**	**Description of How Image Is Formed**
Reflecting telescope	Mirrors and convex lenses	A concave mirror focuses light from a distant object, and this light is reflected by an angled mirror to form a real image; the convex lens of the eyepiece enlarges the image.
Refracting telescope	Convex lenses	Light from a distant object passes through a convex lens, which forms a real image inside the telescope; another convex lens in the eyepiece forms an upside down virtual image of the real image.

Name _____ Class _____ Date _____

Chapter 19   Optics

Cameras (pages 582–584)

4. Describe what a camera does. A camera is an optical instrument that records an image of an object.

5. Circle the letter of each sentence that describes how cameras form or record images.

   (a.) An image is recorded on film or by a sensor.

   b. Light rays are focused to form virtual images.

   (c.) Light rays enter through an opening.

   (d.) Light rays are focused by the opening or lens.

6. Is the following sentence true or false? In a simple pinhole camera made from a box, an upside-down, real image is formed on the back wall of the box. _____true_____

7. What is the purpose of the lens elements in a film camera? They focus incoming rays of light.

8. The device that controls the amount of light passing through a camera is the _____diaphragm_____.

9. Describe what happens when you push the shutter release button on a modern film camera. The mirror flips up and the shutter briefly opens to let the focused light rays strike the film.

10. How is the position of the lens of a modern film camera used to bring an object into focus? The lens is moved toward or away from the film.

Microscopes (page 584)

11. An optical instrument that uses two convex lenses to magnify small objects is called a(n) _____compound microscope_____.

12. Circle the letter that describes the path light rays follow through a compound microscope.

   a. Light rays from the objective lens pass through the object and then pass through the light source.

   b. Light rays from above pass up through the object and then pass through the objective lens.

   (c.) Light rays from below pass up through the object, the objective lens, and the eyepiece lens.

   d. Light rays from below pass up through the object, the concave lens, and the objective lens.

13. Is the following sentence true or false? When you look through the eyepiece of a compound microscope you see an enlarged, virtual image of the object. _____true_____

Section 19.4 Lesson Plan

LESSON PLAN 19.4

The Eye and Vision

Time
2 periods
1 block

Section Objectives

■ **19.4.1 Name** the main parts of the eye and **describe** their functions.

■ **19.4.2 Name** common vision problems, **identify** their causes, and **explain** how they can be corrected.

Vocabulary cornea • pupil • iris • retina • rods • cones • nearsightedness • farsightedness • astigmatism

Local Standards

1 FOCUS

Build Vocabulary: Word-Part Analysis
Have students give each word part for the terms *nearsightedness* and *farsightedness*. Then, have students tell what the words mean based on their word parts. **L2**

Targeted Resources
❏ Transparency: Interest Grabber 19.4
❏ Transparency: Reading Strategy 19.4

2 INSTRUCT

Build Reading Literacy:
Relate Cause and Effect
Ask students why it may take a few minutes before your eye fully adjusts to the low light conditions when entering a dark theatre from bright sunlight. **L1**

Address Misconceptions
Explain to students that light is focused most by the cornea because light entering the eye encounters the greatest difference in optical density when it passes from the air to the cornea. **L2**

Build Science Skills: Observing
Have students use an index card marked with an X and a dot to detect their blind spot. Ask them to explain why the dot disappeared. **L2**

Integrate Health
Have students research and describe methods of treatment used by ophthalmologists for eye diseases, and any means of preventing the diseases. **L2**

For Enrichment
Have interested students interview a physician who performs laser eye surgery or a person who has undergone the procedure, and present their findings in a class report. **L3**

Targeted Resources
❏ Transparency: Figure 17: The Eye
❏ Transparency: Figure 18: Nearsightedness
❏ Transparency: Figure 19: Farsightedness
❏ GRSW Section 19.4

3 ASSESS

Reteach
After reviewing the structure of the eye in Figure 17, have students use Figures 18 and 19 to discuss how the shape of the eyeball affects the eye's ability to focus. **L1**

Evaluate Understanding
Quiz students about the parts of the eye and their function. Have students draw diagrams showing vision correction for nearsightedness and farsightedness. **L2**

Targeted Resources
❏ **PHSchool.com** Online Section 19.4 Assessment
❏ iText Section 19.4

Transparencies

295 **Section 19.4 Interest Grabber**

Why Do Some People Need Glasses?

Two common vision problems are **farsightedness** and **nearsightedness**. A farsighted person cannot focus on nearby objects because the image focuses beyond the retina. A nearsighted person cannot focus on far away objects because the image focuses too close to the lens. Both of these conditions are caused by the image not forming on the retina. If the image forms in front of or beyond the retina, it will be blurry.

Look at each diagram below. Notice where the light rays come together. This is where the image has focused.

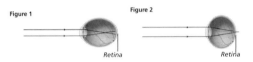

Figure 1   Figure 2

Retina   Retina

1. Is Figure 1 an example of farsightedness or nearsightedness? Why?

2. Is Figure 2 an example of farsightedness or nearsightedness? Why?

ANSWERS
1. Nearsightedness. The image focused in front of the retina.
2. Farsightedness. The image focused beyond the retina.

Transparencies

296 **Section 19.4 Reading Strategy**

Outlining

I. The Eye and Vision
  A. Structure of the Eye
    1. _____
    2. _____
       and so on . . .
  B. _____
       and so on . . .

B. Correcting Vision Problems
1. Nearsightedness
2. Farsightedness
3. Astigmatism

ANSWERS
I. The Eye and Vision
  A. Structure of the Eye
    1. Cornea
    2. Pupil and Iris
    3. Lens
    4. Retina
    5. Rods and Cones

Transparencies

297 **Figure 17 The Eye**

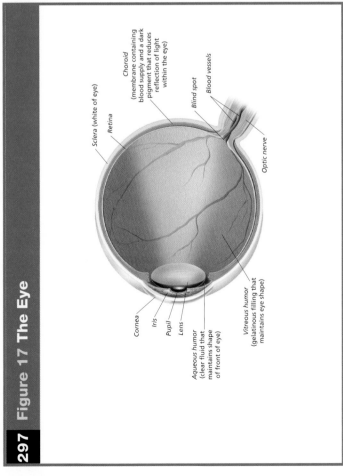

Choroid (membrane containing blood supply and a dark pigment that reduces reflection of light within the eye)

Sclera (white of eye)

Retina

Blind spot

Blood vessels

Optic nerve

Cornea

Iris

Pupil

Lens

Aqueous humor (clear fluid that maintains shape of front of eye)

Vitreous humor (gelatinous filling that maintains eye shape)

Transparencies

298 **Figure 18 Nearsightedness**

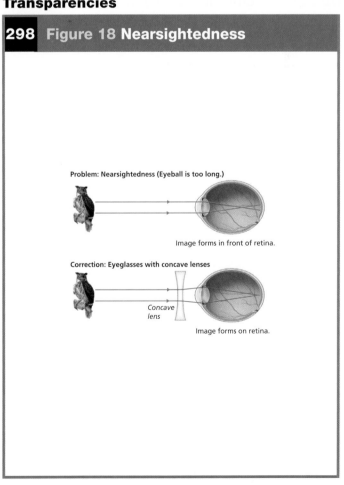

Problem: Nearsightedness (Eyeball is too long.)

Image forms in front of retina.

Correction: Eyeglasses with concave lenses

Concave lens

Image forms on retina.

Transparencies

299 | Figure 19 Farsightedness

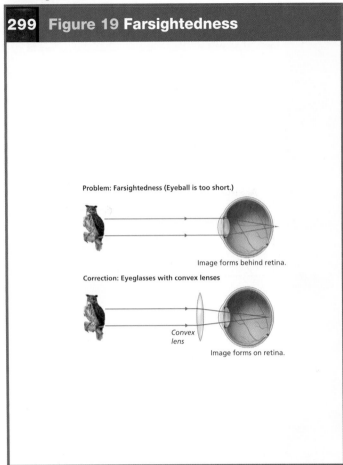

Problem: Farsightedness (Eyeball is too short.)

Image forms behind retina.

Correction: Eyeglasses with convex lenses

Convex lens

Image forms on retina.

Guided Reading and Study Workbook

Name _____ Class _____ Date _____

Chapter 19   Optics

Section 19.4 The Eye and Vision
(pages 588–592)

This section describes the eye as an optical instrument. Parts of the eye and their functions are defined. Vision problems and how they can be corrected are also described.

Reading Strategy (page 588)

Outlining As you read, make an outline of the important ideas in this section. Use the green headings as the main topics and the blue headings as subtopics. For more information on this Reading Strategy, see the **Reading and Study Skills** in the **Skills and Reference Handbook** at the end of your textbook.

Section 19.4 Outline
I. The Eye and Vision
A. Structure of the Eye
1. Cornea
2. Pupil and Iris
3. Lens
4. Retina
5. Rods and Cones
B. Correcting Vision Problems
1. Nearsightedness
2. Farsightedness
3. Astigmatism

Structure of the Eye (pages 588–590)

Write the letter of the part of the eye that best matches each description.

Description	Part of Eye
___c___ **1.** Its curved surface helps to focus light entering the eye.	a. pupil
___e___ **2.** It focuses light onto sensor cells at the back of the eye.	b. retina
___a___ **3.** This opening allows light to pass through the eye.	c. cornea
___d___ **4.** This expands and contracts to control the amount of light entering the eye.	d. iris
___c___ **5.** This is the transparent outer coating of the eye.	e. lens
___b___ **6.** Its surface has rods and cones.	

Guided Reading and Study Workbook

Name _____ Class _____ Date _____

Chapter 19   Optics

7. Is the following sentence true or false? Nerve endings called rods and cones convert light into electrical signals that are sent to the brain through the optic nerve. _____true_____

8. Where on the retina does a blind spot occur? A blind spot occurs in the area of the retina where the nerve endings come together to form the optic nerve.

Correcting Vision Problems (pages 590–592)

For questions 9 and 10, refer to the figures below.

Problem: Nearsightedness (Eyeball is too long.)

Correction:

9. Circle the letter of the location where the image forms when nearsightedness occurs.

a. on the retina   b. behind the retina
c. before it reaches the retina   d. on the lens

10. Nearsightedness can be corrected by placing a(n) ____diverging concave____ lens in front of the eye.

Match each type of vision problem to its definition.

Vision Problem	Definition
___b___ **11.** astigmatism	a. A condition that causes distant objects to appear blurry because the cornea is too curved or the eyeball is too long
___c___ **12.** farsightedness	b. A condition that causes objects at any distance to appear blurry because the cornea or lens is misshapen
___a___ **13.** nearsightedness	c. A condition that causes nearby objects to appear blurry because the cornea is not curved enough or the eyeball is too short

Name _____ Class _____ Date _____

Chapter 19   Optics

WordWise

Use the clues below to identify vocabulary terms from Chapter 19. Write the terms below, putting one letter in each blank. When you finish, the term enclosed in the diagonal will reveal a term that is important in the study of optics.

Clues

1. Shows how the paths of light rays change when they strike mirrors or pass through lenses
2. Transparent material with one or two curved surfaces that can refract light
3. A mirror with a flat surface
4. An instrument that uses lenses or mirrors to collect and focus light from distant objects
5. Expands and contracts to control the amount of light entering the eye
6. An optical instrument that records an image of an object
7. Transparent outer layer of the eye
8. When the cornea is misshapen, this vision problem can result.
9. Type of lens that causes light rays to diverge

1. r a y   d i a g r a m

2. l e n s

3. p l a n e   m i r r o r

4. t e l e s c o p e

5. i r i s

6. c a m e r a

7. c o r n e a

8. a s t i g m a t i s m

9. c o n c a v e   l e n s

Hidden Word: r e a l   i m a g e

Definition: A copy of an object that forms where light rays converge

Name _____ Class _____ Date _____

Chapter 19   Optics

Calculating Index of Refraction

**Math Skill:
Ratios and
Proportions**

You may want to read more about this **Math Skill** in the **Skills and Reference Handbook** at the end of your textbook.

The speed of light in the mineral halite, NaCl, is approximately 1.95×10^8 m/s. Calculate the index of refraction for halite. (Recall that the speed of light in a vacuum is 3.00×10^8 m/s.)

1. Read and Understand

What information are you given?

Speed of light in halite = 1.95×10^8 m/s

Speed of light in vacuum = 3.00×10^8 m/s

2. Plan and Solve

What variable are you trying to determine?

Index of refraction = ?

What formulas contain the given variables?

$$\text{Index of refraction} = \frac{\text{Speed of light}_{vacuum}}{\text{Speed of light}_{material}} = \frac{(3.00 \times 10^8 \text{ m/s})}{(1.95 \times 10^8 \text{ m/s})} = 1.54$$

3. Look Back and Check

Is your answer reasonable?

Speed of light in vacuum = $(1.95 \times 10^8 \text{ m/s})(1.54) = 3.00 \times 10^8$ m/s

Yes, the answer is reasonable. Substituting the calculated index of refraction for halite back into the equation yields the value of the speed of light in a vacuum.

Math Practice

On a separate sheet of paper, solve the following problems.

1. The mineral uvarovite has an index of refraction of 1.86. Calculate the speed of light in this sample of uvarovite.

   Speed of light $_{uvarovite}$ = $(3.00 \times 10^8$m/s)/(1.86) = 1.61×10^8 m/s

2. What is the index of refraction of a sample of opal, if the speed of light passing through it is 2.05×10^8 m/s?

   Index of refraction = $(3.00 \times 10^8$m/s)/(2.05×10^8 m/s) = 1.46

3. Because its atomic structure varies with direction, a sample of the mineral calcite has an index of refraction of 1.486 along one direction in the crystal, while another direction has an index of refraction of 1.658. Which index represents the faster speed of light through the calcite? Explain your answer.

   1.486; The lower the index of refraction, the greater the speed of light moving through the calcite, as indicated by the reciprocal relationship between the index of refraction and the speed of light.

Name _____ Class _____ Date _____

Chapter 19   Optics   **Consumer Lab**

Selecting Mirrors

See page 593 in the Teacher's Edition for more information.

In this lab, you will compare several mirrors and select the type that is best for a specific use.

Problem What mirror shape is best for magnifying images? For providing a wide view?

Materials

- plane, convex, and concave mirrors
- 2 metric rulers
- roll of string
- protractor

Skills Observing, Measuring

Procedure

Part A: Comparing Magnification

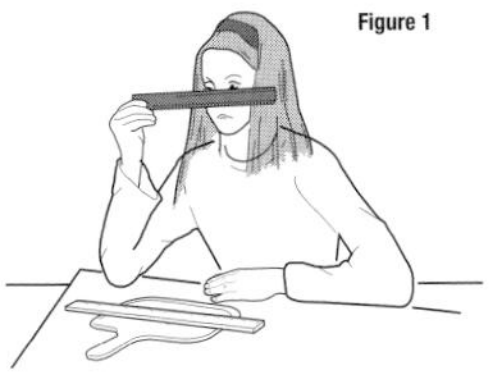

1. Place the plane mirror on a tabletop with its mirror side facing up. Position a metric ruler horizontally across the center of the mirror.

2. Hold the other metric ruler horizontally against your nose, just below your eyes, as shown below. Make sure the ruler's markings face away from you. Look down at the mirror.

3. Use the ruler resting on the mirror to measure the actual length of the image of a 3-cm-long portion of the ruler you are holding. In the data table, record the size of the image.

Figure 1

DATA TABLE

Mirror	Size of Image	Magnification	Field of View
Plane	A typical concave hand mirror magnifies by a factor of 2 to 3, and a plane mirror produces an image that is reduced by approximately one-third. Typical fields of view for concave, plane, and		
Concave	convex mirrors are 70°, 80° and 140°, respectively.		
Convex			

4. Repeat Steps 1 through 3, using concave and convex mirrors. Observe each image from the same distance.

5. Divide each image size you measured by 3 cm to determine its magnification. Record the magnification in the data table.

Name _____ Class _____ Date _____

Part B: Comparing Fields of View

6. Tie a string to a ruler. Hold the protractor, mirror, and free end of the string. Have a classmate hold the ruler vertically off to one side of the mirror. Position a third classmate (the observer) directly in front of and about 2 meters away from the mirror, as shown in Figure 2.

7. Have the classmate holding the ruler slowly move toward the observer while keeping the string tight. The observer should look directly into the mirror and say "Stop!" as soon as the reflection of the ruler can be seen.

8. Measure the angle the string makes with the protractor. Multiply this angle by 2 and record it as the field of view in the data table.

9. Repeat Steps 6 through 8, using concave and convex mirrors. Observe each mirror from the same distance.

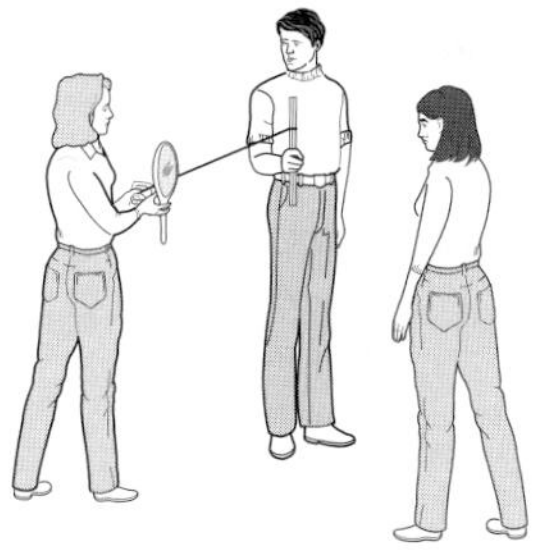

Figure 2

Analyze and Conclude

1. **Observing** Which mirror provided the greatest magnification? The widest view?

   The concave mirror provided the greatest magnification, and the convex mirror produced the widest field of view.

2. **Applying Concepts** Which mirror shape would work best for a dentist who needs to see a slightly magnified image of a tooth? Explain your answer.

   A concave mirror is best for a dentist because it magnifies the most.

3. **Drawing Conclusions** Could one of the mirrors be used both to view a wide area and to magnify? Explain your answer.

   None of these mirrors could be used to observe both a wide area and a magnified view of small details because increasing the magnification reduces the width of the field of view, and increasing the width of the field of view reduces the magnification.

Lab Manual

Name _____ Class _____ Date _____

Refraction and Reflection

Refer students to pages 570–575 in their textbooks for a discussion of reflection and refraction. **SKILLS FOCUS:** Inferring, Analyzing Data, Interpreting Diagrams/Photographs **CLASS TIME:** Part A, 25 minutes; Part B, 25 minutes

Background Information

In a vacuum, light travels in a straight line at 3.0×10^8 m/s. The situation is different, however, when light is not in a vacuum. Light can change direction when it passes through, bounces off, or is absorbed by substances. When light rays enter a substance, they change speed and may change direction. This behavior is called **refraction.** When light rays bounce off a surface, or undergo **reflection,** they also change direction. The angle between an incoming ray of light and a line perpendicular to the surface—called the normal line—is the **angle of incidence.** The angle between the reflected ray of light and the normal to the reflecting surface is the **angle of reflection.** If the light enters the substance and is refracted, the angle between the refracted light and the normal is the **angle of refraction.**

In this investigation, you will examine how the direction of light changes during refraction and reflection.

Problem

How do reflection and refraction change the direction of light?

Pre-Lab Discussion

Read the entire investigation. Then, work with a partner to answer the following questions.

1. **Inferring** In what direction will the tennis ball bounce if it is thrown directly at a wall? In what direction will the tennis ball bounce when it hits the wall at an angle? How is the direction influenced by the size of the angle?

   The ball bounces straight back along the same path. When thrown at an angle, the ball's angle of

   incidence equals the angle of reflection. As the angle of incidence increases, so does the angle of

   reflection.

2. **Using Analogies** Think of a photon of light as if it were a tennis ball and a mirror as if it were a wall. Use this analogy to describe what happens when light is reflected from a mirror's surface.

   A light ray that approaches a mirror straight on is reflected straight back along its path. When a light

   ray approaches a mirror at an angle, the angle of incidence will always equal the angle of reflection.

Lab Manual

Name _____ Class _____ Date _____

3. **Inferring** Consider the tractor shown in Figure 1. The tractor goes straight as long as both belts are going the same speed.

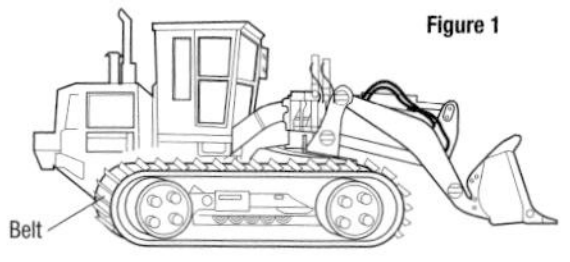

   Figure 1

   a. Suppose the tractor exits a road and enters a field such that both belts enter the field at the same time. If the field slows the speed of the belts, how are the speed and direction of motion of the tractor affected as it enters the field?

      Both belts slow down equally, and the tractor continues to move in a straight line at

      a slower speed.

4. **Inferring** Suppose the tractor exits the road and enters the field at an angle such that one belt enters the field before the other.

   a. Describe how the speeds of the belts and the direction of motion are affected as the tractor enters the field at an angle.

      The belt entering the field first slows down before the other belt does. This results in a speed

      difference between the belts that causes the tractor to change direction.

   b. Suppose that the tractor continues through the field in its new direction until it reaches a road parallel to the first. How will the tractor's final direction on the new road compare to its original direction on the first road? Explain your answer.

      The new direction will be parallel to the original direction. As the tractor reenters the road, the

      opposite speed difference between the belts occurs, turning the tractor back to

      its original direction.

5. **Using Analogies** Think of a photon of light as if it were a tractor with belts on each side. Think of the medium that light is traveling through as if it were the surface on which the tractor is traveling. Light moving through air into glass is therefore similar to the tractor moving from the road to the field. Use this analogy to describe what happens when light moves from one medium to another.

   As light moves from one medium to another, its speed changes. If the light directly approaches

   the boundary between the mediums, its speed changes uniformly and it continues straight ahead. If

   the light approaches the boundary at an angle, the change in speed is not uniform, and the light

   bends from its original path.

Lab Manual

Name _____ Class _____ Date _____

Materials *(per group)*

cardboard (approximately 30 cm × 30 cm)

30-cm ruler

4 straight pins

protractor

unlined paper

small mirror

support for mirror (wood block and glue, tape, or rubber band)

transparent container with a square base (7 cm × 7 cm)

Safety

Be careful when handling sharp instruments. Note all safety alert symbols next to the steps in the Procedure and review the meaning of each symbol by referring to the Safety Symbols on page xiii.

Procedure

Part A: Observing Reflection

1. Place the paper on the cardboard. Stand the mirror in the center of the paper. Support the mirror by gluing, taping, or tying it with a rubber band to a small wooden block. Draw a line along the edge of the mirror. Stick a pin in the paper and cardboard about 4 cm in front of the center of the mirror. Draw a small circle around the pin position and label it *Object*, as shown in Figure 2. **CAUTION:** *Pinpoints can cut or puncture skin, so handle pins carefully.*

   Figure 2
   (Not to scale)

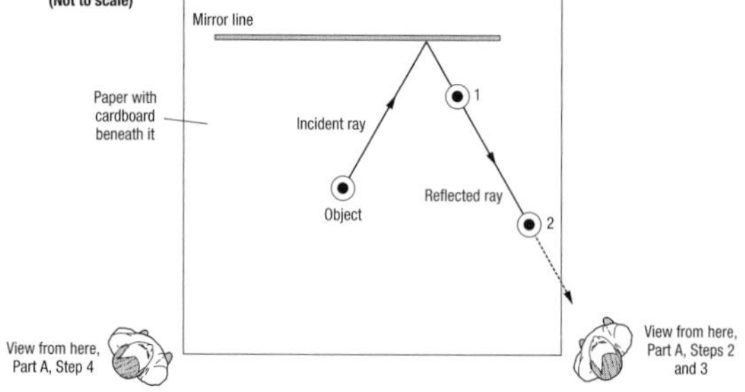

2. Refer to Figure 2. Position your head near the lower-right corner of the paper. Look at the mirror with one eye closed and observe the reflection of the pin. Do not look at the real pin. Insert a pin in the paper near the mirror so that it hides the reflection of the Object pin. Draw a small circle around the pin position and label it *1*.

Lab Manual

Name _____ Class _____ Date _____

3. Refer to Figure 2. From the same viewing position, place a second pin in the paper near the mirror so that it hides the pin you placed in position 1 and the reflection of the Object pin. Draw a small circle around the pin position and label it *2*.

4. Remove the pins from positions 1 and 2. Use them to repeat Steps 2 and 3 from the lower-left corner of the paper. Draw circles around these pin positions and label them *3* and *4*.

5. Remove the mirror and all the pins. Using the ruler, draw a solid line through pin positions 1 and 2 and extend it as far as the mirror line. This line is a reflected ray. Draw a line from the Object pin position to the point where the reflected ray leaves the mirror. This line is the incident ray. Label each ray and draw an arrow on the ray to show its direction.

6. Repeat Step 5 for pin positions 3 and 4.

7. Draw two lines perpendicular to the mirror line at the two points where the incident rays and the reflected rays touch. These lines are the normal lines. Label and measure the angles of incidence and reflection for the rays coming from the left and right corners of the paper, as shown in Figure 3. Record your measurements in Data Table 1.

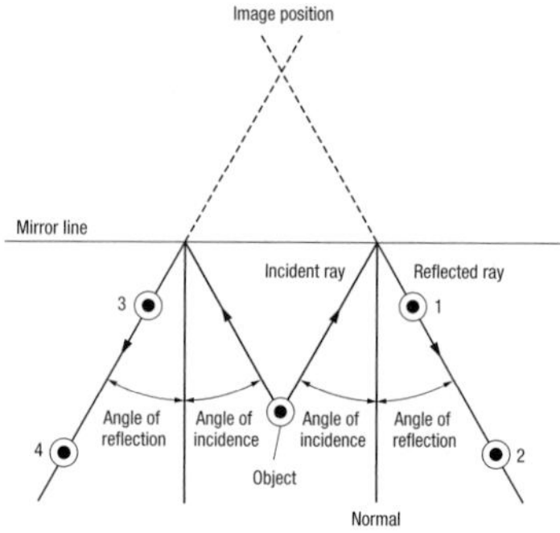

   Figure 3
   (Not to scale)

8. Using the ruler, draw two dashed lines extending from the two reflected rays beyond the mirror line. Continue these dashed lines just beyond the point where they cross. This point is the position of the Object pin's image in the mirror. Label this point *Image*.

Name _____ Class _____ Date _____

Part B: Observing Refraction

9. Fill a transparent square-based container with tap water. Place a piece of unlined paper on a piece of cardboard. Place the container in the center of the paper and trace a line around the edges.

10. Using the ruler, draw a line on your paper at an angle to one edge of the container. Do not draw this line perpendicular to the edge of the container.

11. Place two pins on the line about 3 cm apart from each other. Draw circles around the base of the pins and label the circles *Pin 1* and *Pin 2*, as shown in Figure 4. Look through the bottom edge of the container until you see Pins 1 and 2 positioned exactly behind each other. (They will look like only one pin.)

12. Place two more pins on the lower part of your paper so that they also seem to line up with Pins 1 and 2. (All four pins should appear to be one pin.) Draw circles around the base of these pins and label them *Pin 3* and *Pin 4*.

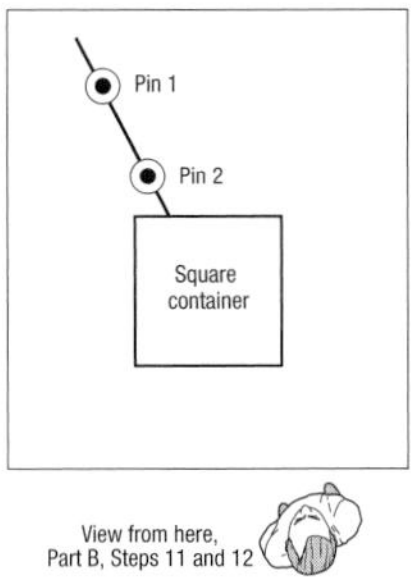

13. Remove the pins and the container. Using a ruler, draw a line through the positions of Pins 3 and 4 just to where they meet the line made by the container.

14. The line through Pins 1 and 2 represents a ray of light entering the container and is called the incident ray. Label this ray and draw arrows on it to show its direction.

15. The line through Pins 3 and 4 represents a ray of light leaving the container and going to your eye. It is called the emergent ray. Label this ray and draw arrows on it to show its direction.

16. Using the ruler, connect the incident ray and the emergent ray through the container. This line is called the refracted ray. Label this ray and draw arrows on it to show its direction.

17. Using the protractor, construct normal lines (lines perpendicular to the edge of the container) at the points where the incident and emergent rays touch the container. Extend the normal lines into the container area. You should have formed two angles on each side of the container.

18. Two angles are formed with the normal lines as the incident ray touches the side of the container and as the refracted ray touches the opposite side of the container. These two angles are called angles of incidence. Label these two angles *I*.

19. Two angles are formed with the normal lines as the refracted ray enters the container and again as the emergent ray leaves the opposite side of the container. These two angles are called angles of refraction. Label these two angles *R*.

● Pin 1

● Pin 2

Square container

View from here, Part B, Steps 11 and 12

Figure 4
(Not to scale)

Name _____ Class _____ Date _____

20. Measure the angles of incidence and the angles of refraction and record your measurements in Data Table 2.

21. Using the ruler and a dashed line, extend the emergent ray backward through the container and beyond it.

Observations Sample data are shown.

DATA TABLE 1

Side	Angle	
	Incidence	Reflection
Left	Answers will vary.	Answers should be the same or close to the angle of incidence.
Right	Answers will vary.	Answers should be the same or close to the angle of incidence.

DATA TABLE 2

Pins	Angle	
	Incidence (I)	Reflection (R)
1 and 2	Answers will vary.	Answers will vary.
3 and 4	Answers will vary, but should be the same or close to the angle of refraction for light entering the container.	Answers will vary, but should be the same or close to the angle of incidence for light entering the container.

Analysis and Conclusions

1. **Analyzing Data** In Part A, how do the distances of the object and image from the mirror compare?

They are approximately the same.

2. **Analyzing Data** How do the angles of incidence and the angles of reflection in Part A compare in size?

They are approximately the same.

Name _____ Class _____ Date _____

3. **Interpreting Diagrams** Follow the path of one of the incident rays to the mirror and the path of its reflected ray. Repeat for the other incident ray and reflected ray. How does the direction of the incident ray compare to the direction of the reflected ray? As a result, how is the image oriented with respect to the object?

The directions of the incident and reflected rays are opposite. As a result, the image is oriented

opposite (reversed left to right) the object.

4. **Inferring** The image you see in a mirror is formed from many incident and reflected rays. How would the image be affected if there were no relationship between the angles of the incident and reflected rays?

No clear image would be formed.

5. **Relating Cause and Effect** When you look in a plane mirror, the image seems to be "inside" or "behind" the mirror, even though no light rays can pass through the mirror. What kind of image (real or virtual) exists where there are no actual light rays? Explain how the image appears in a place from which no actual light rays are coming.

It is a virtual image. The image appears to be behind the mirror because the reflected rays follow

the same path as light rays coming from an object in that position would.

6. **Analyzing Data** In Part B, as the incident ray enters the container of water, how does it bend with respect to the normal line? As the emergent ray leaves the glass, how does it bend with respect to the normal line?

The refracted ray bends toward the normal line. The emergent ray bends away from the

normal line.

7. **Analyzing Data** In Part B, How does the angle of incidence of the incident ray compare with the angle of refraction for the emerging ray? How does the angle of refraction for the incident ray compare with the angle of incidence for the emerging ray?

They are the same. They are the same.

Name _____ Class _____ Date _____

8. **Analyzing Data** How do the directions of the emergent ray and the incident ray compare?

They are parallel.

9. **Applying Concepts** Why does a light ray bend as it passes from air to a container of water or from the container of water to air at an angle?

Light changes speed as it goes from one medium to another. When light approaches the

boundary between mediums at an angle, the change in speed is not uniform and the light bends.

Go Further

Some substances refract light more than others do. Diamond bends light so much that light approaching at even a small angle reflects inside the diamond instead of passing through. This process is called total internal reflection. It is responsible for diamond's characteristic sparkle.

When the pathway of light is disrupted in this way, it can produce some interesting illusions. Try the following experiments:

1. Put a penny on a flat surface and place an empty, transparent cup directly over the penny. Observe the penny through the side of the cup.

2. Completely fill the cup with water and observe the penny through the side of the cup.

3. Carefully remove the cup and use an eyedropper to put several drops of water on the penny.

4. Put the cup containing the water back on the penny. Observe the penny through the side of the cup.

5. What did you observe in each case? How can your observations be explained.

The penny is visible through the cup when it is empty. It is not visible when viewed through the water except when water is placed directly on the penny. In the first example there is no refraction as the light passes basically from air to air. In the second example light from the penny passes from air to water and is refracted at such a large angle that it never reaches the eyes. This makes the penny invisible. Putting water on the penny makes the light rays pass from water to water, resulting in minimum refraction.

Lab Manual

Name _____ Class _____ Date _____

Harnessing Solar Energy

Refer students to pages 570–573 in their textbooks for a discussion of mirrors and reflection. **SKILLS FOCUS:** Applying Concepts, Inferring, Interpreting Diagrams/Photographs **CLASS TIME:** 45 minutes

Background Information

The sun radiates a tremendous amount of energy. Even from a great distance away, sunlight warms Earth. As the cost of fossil fuels rises, solar energy becomes a more attractive alternative energy source. Some people install solar panels on the roofs of their houses. These devices are often used to heat water that is then used as a hot-water source or to heat the house.

In order to make the greatest use of energy from the sun, it is necessary to focus the sun's rays. This can be accomplished by using a curved, or concave, mirrored surface or a magnifying lens.

In this investigation, you will use a mirror to focus the sun's rays and measure the effect it has on the temperature of a sample of water.

Problem

What happens to the thermal energy of a substance when light rays from the sun are focused on it?

Pre-Lab Discussion

Read the entire investigation. Then, work with a partner to answer the following questions.

1. **Applying Concepts** Suppose parallel rays of light strike a plane mirror at an angle. How will the directions of the reflected rays compare with the directions of the incident rays?

   The rays will still be parallel. Because the light rays are parallel, they all have the same angle

   of incidence, and upon reflection, they all have the same angle of reflection.

2. **Interpreting Diagrams** Two plane mirrors are joined at an angle of 120° and oriented toward two parallel incident rays of light, as shown in Figure 1. Construct the normal lines for each plane mirror, measure the angles of incidence, and draw the reflected rays as dashed lines with arrowheads to show their directions. Are the reflected rays parallel to each other? Explain.

   Although the two plane mirrors are symmetrically oriented

   to the incoming parallel light rays, the mirrors are not

   parallel to each other. Therefore, when the parallel light

   rays each strike one of the mirrors, they reflect at the same angle, but are reflected

   in different directions.

Incident ray   Incident ray

120°   **Figure 1**

Lab Manual

Name _____ Class _____ Date _____

3. **Interpreting Diagrams** A spherical concave mirror is shown in Figure 2. Draw dashed lines to represent the reflected rays and use arrowheads to indicate direction. Label the point at which the rays cross as the Focus. How is this concave mirror similar to the V-shaped mirror in Question 2? How does the concave mirror affect the direction of the incident rays?

   Both mirrors have surfaces that are not parallel to

   each other. The parallel incident rays are reflected

   toward each other so that they cross at a common

   point called the focus.

Incident ray (×5)

Concave mirror   **Figure 2**

4. **Inferring** How does the amount of light energy at the focus compare to the amount of energy at any other location near the mirror? Explain.

   There is more light energy at the focus than at any other location because all of the incident

   light energy converges there.

5. **Predicting** Two water-filled test tubes are set up so the sun is shining on them. One of the test tubes is positioned to be at the focus of a concave mirror. How would you expect the temperature of the water in the two test tubes to compare after they have each had sun shining on them for an hour? Explain.

   The test tube positioned at the focus of the mirror will be warmer because more light rays

   are incident upon it.

Materials *(per group)*

compass	2 thermometers
protractor	2 test tubes
reflector from a large flashlight	2 test-tube clamps
ring stand	triangular file
graduated cylinder	tape

Safety 🥽🔪🧤

Put on safety goggles. Be careful to avoid breakage when working with glassware. Be careful when handling sharp instruments. Note all safety alert symbols next to the steps in the Procedure and review the meaning of each symbol by referring to the Safety Symbols on page xiii.

Lab Manual

Name _____ Class _____ Date _____

Procedure

1. Insert one of the test tubes through the hole in the center of a flashlight reflector so that it extends about 1 cm below the bottom of the reflector. The test tube should fit snugly. If the hole is too small, enlarge it with a triangular file. If the test tube is loose, secure it with some tape.

2. Set up a ring stand with two test-tube clamps. Secure the test tube in the reflector and the second test tube in the test-tube clamps, as shown in Figure 3. Place a thermometer into each test tube.

3. Using a graduated cylinder, add 5 mL of water to each test tube. Wait a few minutes. In the data table, record the initial temperature in each test tube.

4. Place the test setup in bright sunlight and position the reflector toward the sun. Tilt the reflector in such a way that a bright spot appears in the water of the test tube. Adjust the position of the other test tube so that it is tilted the same way as the test tube in the reflector.

5. Expose the test tubes to the sun for 5 minutes. Observe the temperatures of the water in each test tube and record the values in the data table.

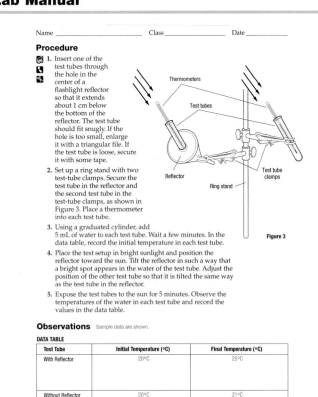

Thermometers

Test tubes

Reflector

Ring stand

Test tube clamps

Figure 3

Observations Sample data are shown.

DATA TABLE

Test Tube	Initial Temperature (°C)	Final Temperature (°C)
With Reflector	20°C	25°C
Without Reflector	20°C	21°C

Lab Manual

Name _____ Class _____ Date _____

Analysis and Conclusions

1. **Comparing and Contrasting** How did the temperature in the two test tubes compare? What caused the difference in temperature? How did this result compare to your earlier prediction?

   The temperature in the test tube with the reflector was higher. This occurred because the

   reflector focuses more light onto the test tube. This result agrees with the earlier prediction.

2. **Controlling Variables** Why did you need to set up two test tubes with the same amount of water in each?

   Two test tubes are needed for comparison because sunlight will heat the water with or

   without the mirror. The amount of the temperature rise depends on the amount of incident

   light and the volume of water. By making the volume of water equal in both test tubes, this

   variable was eliminated as a factor in the results.

3. **Relating Cause and Effect** How did the concave mirror heat the water? What observations support your explanation?

   The concave mirror focuses the incoming light energy on the contents of the test tube. This focused

   light was visible as a bright spot in the test tube.

4. **Applying Concepts** Explain how an apparatus similar to the one you constructed could be used to change the sun's radiant energy into mechanical energy.

   Many answers are possible. One example is to have the sun's rays heat water to run a steam

   engine or turbine.

Go Further

With adult supervision, construct a device to heat water by using a magnifying lens. Use a similar apparatus to the one you used in the investigation. Use two test tubes so that you can evaluate the effect of the lens. Attempt to position the lens in such a way that a large amount of sunlight is focused in a small volume of water. Compare the results of your experiment with the results from this investigation. **CAUTION:** *Focused light from the lens can produce very high temperatures.*

The temperature of the water in the test tube under the magnifying lens will probably be comparable to the temperature of the water in the test tube within the concave mirror.

Name _____ Class _____ Date _____

Chapter 19 Optics

Multiple Choice

Write the letter that best answers the question or completes the statement on the line provided.

_____ **1.** What is the angle of incidence?
   a. the angle that the reflected ray makes with a line drawn perpendicular to the reflecting surface
   b. the angle that the incident ray makes with a line drawn perpendicular to the reflecting surface
   c. the angle the reflecting surface makes with the ground
   d. the angle that is parallel to the reflection angle

_____ **2.** In a plane mirror, the light rays appear to come from
   a. in front of the mirror.
   b. an angle above the mirror.
   c. a distance behind the observer.
   d. behind the mirror.

_____ **3.** What is the point called at which the reflected rays intersect in Figure 19-1?
   a. virtual image
   b. plane image
   c. focal point
   d. illumination point

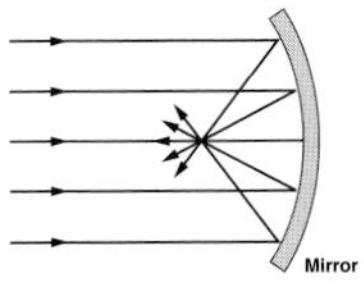

Figure 19-1

_____ **4.** Why do plane mirrors and convex mirrors form only virtual images?
   a. because they both cause light rays to spread out
   b. because reflected rays appear to come from behind the mirror
   c. because the focal point is in front of the mirror
   d. because they both show a wide angle of view

_____ **5.** Suppose a light ray traveling in air passes sideways through a glass of water and comes out the other side. How many times will the light ray refract?
   a. one time; through the water
   b. two times; through the glass and the water
   c. three times; through glass, water, and glass again
   d. four times; through glass, water, glass, and air

_____ **6.** The speed of light in water is 2.25×10^8 m/s. What is correct about the index of refraction of water?
   a. It is 0.   **b.** It is <1.
   c. It is equal to 1.   **d.** It is >1.

_____ **7.** Which index of refraction represents the most optically dense material?
   a. 1.77   **b.** 2.42   **c.** 1.33   **d.** 1.00

Name _____ Class _____ Date _____

_____ **8.** An object located between a convex lens and its focal point forms a(an)
   a. reduced virtual image.   **b.** enlarged virtual image.
   c. reduced real image.   **d.** enlarged real image.

_____ **9.** Total internal reflection occurs when the angle of incidence
   a. is zero.
   b. is less than the critical angle.
   c. exceeds the critical angle.
   d. equals the angle of reflection.

_____ **10.** Which statement is correct regarding a refracting telescope?
   a. It produces an enlarged real image.
   b. It produces an enlarged virtual image.
   c. It produces a reduced-size image.
   d. It produces a small, upside-down image.

_____ **11.** Which statement best explains how a compound microscope produces the image you see?
   a. The objective lens produces an image that becomes the "object" for the eyepiece lens.
   b. The glass slide enlarges the object placed over the light.
   c. The objective lens magnifies an image, and the eyepiece lens is used to focus the image.
   d. The eyepiece magnifies the object on the slide.

_____ **12.** Which of the following correctly describes the path that light takes when it enters the eye?
   a. cornea, pupil, lens, retina
   b. pupil, cornea, lens, retina
   c. lens, cornea, pupil, retina
   d. retina, lens, cornea, pupil

_____ **13.** How is the iris of an eye similar to the diaphragm of a film camera?
   a. They both control the amount of light passing through.
   b. They both focus light rays.
   c. They both produce an upside-down image.
   d. They both control the movement of the lens.

_____ **14.** Farsightedness can be corrected by using eyeglass lenses that are
   a. concave in shape and cause light rays entering the eyes to converge.
   b. convex.
   c. concave in shape and cause light rays entering the eyes to diverge.
   d. convex in shape and cause light rays entering the eyes to converge.

Name _____ Class _____ Date _____

Completion

Complete each statement on the line provided.

1. The angles of incidence and reflection are the angles that rays make relative to a line drawn _____ to the surface of a mirror.

2. The image that appears to be behind a plane mirror is a(an) _____ image.

3. The type of image that can be projected on a screen is a(an) _____ image.

4. Nerve endings in the retina that are most sensitive to low-intensity light are called _____.

5. Nerves on the retina that are sensitive to color are called _____.

Short Answer

In complete sentences, write the answers to the questions on the lines provided.

1. List two facts about the blind spot in the human eye.

2. Describe how you could focus the light from a bulb into a beam.

3. What is the principle that makes fiber optics able to transmit data in the form of light pulses over long distances with little loss in signal strength?

4. What is the purpose of the diaphragm in a film camera?

5. Why must a microscope slide be made of a transparent material like glass if the glass does not magnify the image?

Name _____ Class _____ Date _____

Using Science Skills

Use the diagram to answer each question. Write the answers on a separate sheet of paper.

1. Predicting Figure 19-2 shows the lens of an eye that is focused on a nearby object at point Z. If the eye refocuses on a far object, what happens to the shape of the lens? How?

2. Applying Concepts Locate and name the part of the eye in Figure 19-2 that first refracts light. Why does light refract there?

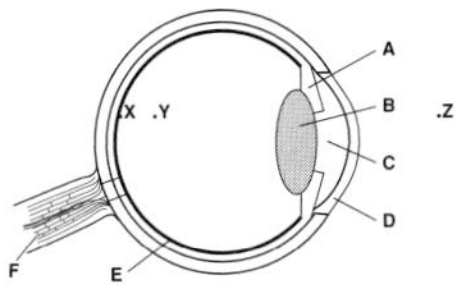

3. Inferring In Figure 19-2, a real image is formed at point X. What part of the eye is located at point X? How does the brain interpret the image formed at point X?

Figure 19-2

4. Using Models Examine Figure 19-2. List the structures labeled A–F, and state the function of each structure.

5. Applying Concepts Find the location of label Y in Figure 19-2. In an eye exam, the doctor finds that your eyes form images at point Y. What is her diagnosis, and how will she most likely treat it?

Essay

Write the answers to each question on a separate sheet of paper.

1. An incident ray of light strikes a plane mirror at an angle of 45 degrees with the surface of the mirror. What is the angle of reflection? Explain your answer. It may help to sketch a ray diagram.

2. What is refraction? Compare the refraction of light in water with light in diamond.

3. Suppose a beam of light passes straight up through water toward a water-air boundary. Then, the beam is gradually rotated so the angle of incidence becomes larger and larger. What will be observed about the reflection and refraction of the beam of light?

4. Infer why it is necessary, after focusing the image, to control the amount of light that enters a film camera when taking a photograph.

5. Explain the difference between rods and cones in the retina of the human eye. Also, explain the effectiveness of rods and cones in varying light levels.

Chapter Test B

Chapter 19   Optics   Chapter Test B

Multiple Choice

Write the letter that best answers the question or completes the statement on the line provided.

_____ 1. For reflection off a plane mirror, the angle of incidence
a. is greater than the angle of reflection.
b. is less than the angle of reflection.
c. equals the angle of reflection.
d. changes the angle of reflection.

_____ 2. The law of reflection states that if the angle of incidence is 45 degrees, the angle of reflection is
a. 90 degrees.   b. 20.25 degrees.
c. 45 degrees.   d. 180 degrees.

_____ 3. A mirror with a flat surface is a
a. plane mirror.   b. convex mirror.
c. concave mirror.   d. virtual mirror.

_____ 4. Unlike a virtual image, a real image
a. forms at the curvature of a reflecting surface.
b. can be viewed on a screen.
c. cannot be viewed on a screen.
d. is always upright.

_____ 5. A concave mirror can form
a. only virtual images.
b. only real images.
c. both virtual and real images.
d. none of the above

_____ 6. Light refracts when it
a. bounces off a surface.
b. changes speed.
c. comes from a laser.
d. spreads out from its source.

_____ 7. Because air causes light to slow only slightly, air's index of refraction is
a. low.   b. high.
c. moderate.   d. nonexistent.

_____ 8. A concave lens can only form a
a. real image.   b. reversed image.
c. virtual image.   d. magnified image.

_____ 9. Light can be transmitted through long fiber optic strands because of total
a. refraction.   b. external diffraction.
c. internal reflection. d. interference.

Chapter Test B

_____ 10. Which optical instrument uses a large concave mirror, a plane mirror, and a convex lens to gather light, focus, and enlarge an image?
a. refracting telescope   b. microscope
c. reflecting telescope   d. film camera

_____ 11. What must be done to a film camera to bring an object into focus on the film?
a. The lens must be moved toward or away from the film.
b. The diaphragm must be closed.
c. The film must be coated with a light-sensitive chemical.
d. The film must be developed and printed.

_____ 12. What is the function of a diaphragm in a film camera?
a. It directs the image to the viewfinder.
b. It focuses incoming light rays.
c. It opens the shutter.
d. It controls the amount of light passing through the film camera.

_____ 13. Which part of a film camera focuses incoming light rays?
a. diaphragm   b. lens
c. shutter   d. viewfinder

_____ 14. A compound microscope uses
a. a mirror to reflect an image of a small object.
b. two convex lenses to magnify a small object.
c. a convex mirror and a lens to enlarge an image.
d. a mirror that flips up to let light through the lens.

_____ 15. The lens of the human eye focuses light by
a. changing its index of refraction.
b. controlling the amount of light entering the eye.
c. changing color.
d. changing shape.

_____ 16. A vision problem that results in seeing blurry images at all distances is called
a. nearsightedness.   b. farsightedness.
c. astigmatism.   d. a blind spot.

Completion

Complete each statement on the lin

1. The law of reflection states that the angle of reflection is equal to the angle of _____.

Chapter Test B

2. The mirror in Figure 19-1 is a(an) _____ mirror.

3. Mirrors that curve outward and away from the center are called _____ mirrors.

4. When light exits a vacuum and enters any other medium, it _____.

5. Light rays passing through a convex lens converge at the _____ point on the other side of the lens.

Figure 19-1

6. Light rays are generally unable to _____ through the sides of curving fiber optic strands.

7. Like a human eye, a film camera has a convex _____ that forms an upside-down image.

8. The iris controls the amount of light entering the eye by adjusting the size of the _____.

9. Nearsightedness results when light rays from distant objects focus in front of the _____.

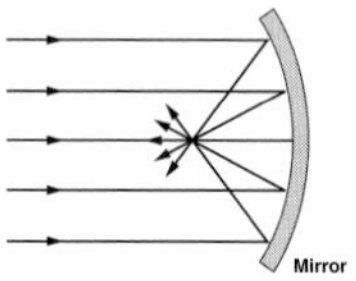

Short Answer

In complete sentences, write the answers to the questions on the lines provided.

1. What is the usual method of graphically analyzing how light rays behave when they strike mirrors or pass through lenses?
_____
_____

2. If you are standing 1 meter in front of a plane mirror, how far does your image appear to be behind the mirror?
_____
_____

3. What determines the type of image produced in a concave mirror?
_____
_____

4. What controls the movement of the iris of the human eye?
_____
_____
_____
_____
_____

Chapter Test B

5. What are two causes of farsightedness?
_____
_____
_____
_____
_____
_____

Using Science Skills

Use the diagram to answer each question. Write the answers on a separate sheet of paper.

1. **Comparing and Contrasting** Compare A, B, and C in Figure 19-2. Which best illustrates the law of reflection? Explain your answer.

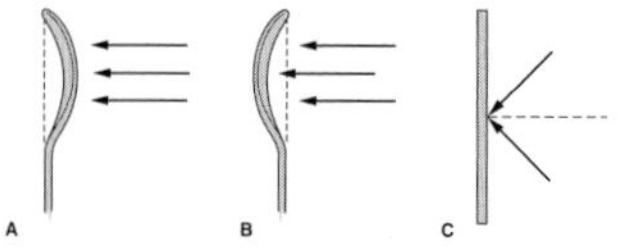

Figure 19-2

2. **Interpreting Graphics** What kind of mirror is C in Figure 19-2? What kind of image does it produce?

3. **Applying Concepts** What type of mirrors are represented by A, B, and C in Figure 19-2? How does each mirror affect parallel light rays that strike it?

4. **Interpreting Graphics** What kind of image does A in Figure 19-2 produce?

5. **Applying Concepts** In an experiment, the three mirrors shown in A, B, and C in Figure 19-2 are placed the same distance from an object so that each mirror produces the same type of image. What type of image do the three mirrors form, and how do the sizes of the images compare? (Assume that the shapes of mirror A and B are similar.)

Chapter 19 Test A Answers

Multiple Choice

1. b **2.** d **3.** c **4.** b **5.** d **6.** d
7. b **8.** a **9.** c **10.** b **11.** a **12.** a
13. a **14.** d

Completion

1. perpendicular; at right angles **2.** virtual **3.** real **4.** rods **5.** cones

Short Answer

1. Student answers may include the following: located on the retina, has no rods or cones, cannot sense light, location where the nerve endings come together to form the optic nerve. **2.** When the bulb is placed at the focal point of a concave mirror, the reflected light rays will be parallel. **3.** total internal reflection of light rays **4.** The diaphragm controls the amount of light passing into the film camera. **5.** to allow light to pass from the source below the slide up through the lenses of the microscope

Using Science Skills

1. The lens becomes longer and thinner. The muscles that control the shape of the lens relax. **2.** Light first enters the eye at D, the cornea, and refracts because the index of refraction in the cornea is different from the index of refraction in air. **3.** Point X is the retina. The brain interprets the image right-side-up. **4.** A, iris; controls the amount of light entering the eye; B, lens; focuses incoming light; C, pupil; opening that allows light rays to enter the eye D, cornea; outer coating of the eye that helps focus light; E, retina; back of the eye, which has light-sensitive cells that send image messages to the optic nerve; F, optic nerve; carries image messages to the brain **5.** nearsightedness; eyeglasses with diverging lenses to reposition the image on the retina

Essay

1. The angle of incidence is 45 degrees because the angle is measured between the incident ray and a line perpendicular to the mirror (not the ray and the mirror). The angle of reflection is equal to the angle of incidence of 45 degrees. **2.** Refraction is the bending of the light rays as they enter a new medium at an angle. Because it has a greater index of refraction, a light ray would bend more entering diamond than it would entering air. **3.** As the beam rotates and the angle of incidence increases, the amount of light reflected increases and the amount of light refracted decreases. Eventually, the angle of incidence reaches the critical angle, and the light undergoes total internal reflection. **4.** The focused light reacts with a light-sensitive chemical coating on the film. In dim light, more light needs to strike the film to record the image. In very bright light, less light is required to keep from overexposing the film. The diaphragm is the part of the film camera that controls light exposure. **5.** Rods are nerve endings that are sensitive to low light levels and are more effective at sensing objects at night. They help distinguish black, white, and shades of gray. Cones are sensitive to color, but are not as sensitive as rods in low light. In low light, it is more difficult to distinguish colors.

Chapter 19 Test B Answers

Multiple Choice

1. c **2.** a **3.** c **4.** b **5.** c **6.** b
7. a **8.** c **9.** c **10.** c **11.** a **12.** d
13. b **14.** b **15.** d **16.** c

Completion

1. incidence **2.** concave **3.** concave **4.** slows down **5.** focal
6. exit **7.** lens **8.** pupil **9.** retina

Short Answer

1. ray diagrams **2.** 1 meter **3.** the location of the object relative to the focal point **4.** The brain, by responding to the sensed light level in the eye, controls the amount of light in the eye by expanding and contracting the iris. **5.** a cornea that is not curved enough and an eyeball that is too short

Using Science Skills

1. C; the ray diagram shows that the angle of incidence is equal to the angle of reflection. **2.** a plane mirror; a virtual image
3. Possible answers: A: convex mirror; a convex mirror causes light rays that are parallel to its optical axis to spread out after reflection.; B: concave mirror; a concave mirror causes light rays that are parallel to its optical axis to come together after reflection.; C: plane mirror; a plane mirror causes parallel light to remain parallel after reflection. **4.** a virtual image **5.** Each image is a virtual image. The image formed by A is reduced, the image formed by B is enlarged, and the image formed by C is the same size as the object.

Chapter 20 Electricity

CHAPTER 20

Planning Guide

Use these planning tools
Easy Planner
Resource Pro
Online Lesson Planner

SECTION OBJECTIVES	STANDARDS		ACTIVITIES and LABS
	NATIONAL (See p. T18.)	STATE	
20.1 Electric Charge and Static Electricity, pp. 600–603 🕐 1 block or 2 periods **20.1.1 Analyze** factors that affect the strength and direction of electric forces and fields. **20.1.2 Describe** how electric forces and fields affect electric charges. **20.1.3 Describe** how electric charges are transferred and **explain** why electric discharges occur.	A-1, B-4, B-6, G-1, G-3		**SE** Inquiry Activity: How Can You Reverse the Battery Direction in a Flashlight? p. 599 · L2 **TE** Teacher Demo: Electric Attraction and Repulsion, p. 601 · L2 **LM** Investigation 20B: Investigating Static Charge · L1
20.2 Electric Current and Ohm's Law, pp. 604–607 🕐 1 block or 2 periods **20.2.1 Describe** electric current and **identify** the two types of current. **20.2.2 Describe** conduction and **classify** materials as good electrical conductors or good electrical insulators. **20.2.3 Describe** the factors that affect resistance. **20.2.4 Explain** how voltage produces electric current. **20.2.5 Calculate** voltage, current, and resistance using Ohm's law.	A-1, A-2, B-4, B-5, B-6, F-6, G-3		**SE** Quick Lab: Modeling Resistance in a Wire, p. 606 · L2 **LM** Investigation 20A: Investigating the Telephone · L2
20.3 Electric Circuits, pp. 609–613 🕐 1 block or 2 periods **20.3.1 Analyze** circuit diagrams for series circuits and parallel circuits. **20.3.2 Solve equations** that relate electric power to current, voltage, and electrical energy. **20.3.3 Describe** devices and procedures for maintaining electrical safety.	A-1, A-2, B-4, E-2, F-1, G-3		**SE** Quick Lab: Modeling a Fuse, p. 612 · L2 **SE** Forensics Lab: Evaluating Electrical Safety, p. 623 · L2 **TE** Teacher Demo: Series and Parallel Circuits, p. 610 · L2
20.4 Electronic Devices, pp. 618–622 🕐 1 block or 2 periods **20.4.1 Explain** how electronics conveys information with analog or digital signals. **20.4.2 Describe** electronic devices used to control electron flow. **20.4.3 Illustrate** how semiconductors are used to make three kinds of solid-state components. **20.4.4 Describe** how solid-state components are used in electronic devices.	A-1, A-2, B-4, B-6, E-2, F-1, G-3		**TE** Teacher Demo: Semiconductors and Current, p. 621 · L2

Ability Levels

L1 For students who need additional help
L2 For all students
L3 For students who need to be challenged

Components

SE	Student Edition	**GRSW**	Guided Reading & Study Workbook With Math Support	**CTB**	Computer Test Bank
TE	Teacher's Edition			**TP**	Test Prep Resources
LM	Laboratory Manual			**iT**	iText
PLM	Probeware Lab Manual	**CUT**	Chapter and Unit Tests	**DC**	Discovery Channel Videotapes

T	Transparencies
P	Presentation Pro CD-ROM
GO	Internet Resources

RESOURCES PRINT and TECHNOLOGY / SECTION ASSESSMENT

GRSW Section 20.1 **L1**
T Chapter 20 Pretest **L2**
Section 20.1 **L2**
P Chapter 20 Pretest **L2**
Section 20.1 **L2**

SE Section 20.1 Assessment, p. 603
iT Section 20.1

GRSW Section 20.2 **L1**
T Section 20.2 **L2**
P Section 20.2 **L2**
SCiLINKS GO Conductors and insulators **L2**

SE Section 20.2 Assessment, p. 607
iT Section 20.2

PLM Lab 8: Evaluating Electrical Safety **L2**
GRSW Section 20.3 **L1**
GRSW Math Skill **L2**
DC Current Computers **L2**
T Section 20.3 **L2**
P Section 20.3 **L2**
SCiLINKS GO Electric circuits **L2**

SE Section 20.3 Assessment, p. 613
iT Section 20.3

GRSW Section 20.4 **L1**
T Section 20.4 **L2**
P Section 20.4 **L2**

SE Section 20.4 Assessment, p. 622
iT Section 20.4

Go Online

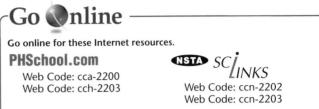

Go online for these Internet resources.

PHSchool.com
Web Code: cca-2200
Web Code: cch-2203

NSTA SCiLINKS
Web Code: ccn-2202
Web Code: ccn-2203

Materials for Activities and Labs

Quantities for each group

STUDENT EDITION

Inquiry Activity, p. 599
flashlight (uses 2 D batteries), 2 D batteries

Quick Lab, p. 606
white paper, metric ruler, number 2 pencil, multimeter

Quick Lab, p. 612
6-volt battery, 2 wires with stripped ends, strip of aluminum foil, scissors, wooden block, unpainted thumbtacks

Forensics Lab, p. 623
9-volt battery, battery clip, multimeter, 3 alligator clips, 4 resistors: 1-ohm, 10-ohm, 100-ohm, 1000-ohm

TEACHER'S EDITION

Teacher Demo, p. 601
pith ball, thread, rubber or ebonite rod, fur

Teacher Demo, p. 610
a 6-volt battery, 3 small light bulbs with sockets, 2 long strands of wire (12 cm), 4 short strands of wire (6 cm)

Build Science Skills, p. 616
several discarded computers, each having its top removed

Teacher Demo, p. 621
a light-emitting diode (LED), an ohmmeter, a DC power source, wires, alligator clips

Chapter Assessment

CHAPTER ASSESSMENT

SE Chapter Assessment, pp. 625–626
CUT Chapter 20 Test A, B
CTB Chapter 20
iT Chapter 20
PHSchool.com GO
Web Code: cca-2200

STANDARDIZED TEST PREP

SE Chapter 20, p. 627
TP Diagnose and Prescribe

iText—interactive textbook with assessment at PHSchool.com

Electricity   598B

Name_____ Class_____ Date_____ M T W T F

LESSON PLAN 20.1

Electric Charge and Static Electricity

Time
2 periods
1 block

Section Objectives

■ **20.1.1 Analyze** factors that affect the strength and direction of electric forces and fields.

■ **20.1.2 Describe** how electric forces and fields affect electric charges.

■ **20.1.3 Describe** how electric charges are transferred and **explain** why electric discharges occur.

Vocabulary electric charge • electric force • electric field • static electricity • law of conservation of charge • induction

Local Standards

---

1 FOCUS

Build Vocabulary: Word-Part Analysis
Ask students what they can infer from the fact that the root word for *electricity* comes from the Greek word for "amber," a substance that is easily charged. **L2**

Targeted Resources
❏ Transparency: Chapter 20 Pretest
❏ Transparency: Interest Grabber 20.1
❏ Transparency: Reading Strategy 20.1

---

2 INSTRUCT

Build Reading Literacy: Outline
Have students create an outline of the section, following the head structure used in the section. Then, ask them to list three ways static electric charges are transferred. **L1**

Use Visuals: Figure 5
Ask students what would happen if electrons were conveyed by contact to an object with a positive charge. Ask what would happen if the positive and negative charges were equal. **L1**

Build Science Skills: Using Models
Have students apply what they know about force and mass to explain why negative charges are more mobile than positive charges. **L2**

Teacher Demo: Electric Attraction and Repulsion
Use a pith ball, fur, and a rubber rod to show students that attractive forces exist between unlike charges, and repelling forces exist between like charges. **L2**

Address Misconceptions
Emphasize to students that only a small fraction of the atoms or molecules in a substance give up electrons. **L2**

Build Science Skills: Relating Cause and Effect
Have students write a short paragraph describing lightning, and have them suggest a reason why excess electrons in a cloud induce a positive charge in the ground. **L2**

Targeted Resources
❏ Transparency: Figure 4: Fields of Positive and Negative Charges
❏ GRSW Section 20.1

---

3 ASSESS

Reteach
Have students use Figure 3 to summarize the way electric forces act between charges. **L1**

Evaluate Understanding
Ask students to write a paragraph describing interactions between charges, indicating the two kinds of charges, the forces between the charges, and the ways that charges are transferred to and from surfaces. **L2**

Targeted Resources
❏ **PHSchool.com** Online Section 20.1 Assessment
❏ iText Section 20.1

Transparencies

300 **Chapter 20 Pretest**

1. Which particles move freely through metals, speeding the transfer of thermal energy?

   a. atoms

   b. electrons

   c. protons

   d. molecules

2. Electric forces act between
   _____ .

3. True of False: Objects with opposite charges repel one another.

4. How will doubling the distance between two masses affect the strength of the gravitational force between them?

5. Energy that is stored and can later be used to move an object is called
   _____ .

ANSWERS
1. b
2. charged objects or particles
3. False
4. The force of gravity will be only one fourth as strong.
5. potential energy

Transparencies

301 **Chapter 20 Pretest** *(continued)*

6. What happens to the kinetic energy of the particles in an object when the thermal energy of the object is increased?

7. True or False: Power is measured in units of joules.

8. If 2.0×10^4 J of energy are produced in 5 s, how much power is generated?

   a. 4×10^3 W

   b. 1×10^5 W

   c. 1×10^4 W

   d. 4×10^4 W

ANSWERS
6. The kinetic energy of the particles increases.
7. False
8. a

Transparencies

302 **Section 20.1 Interest Grabber**

Attract or Repel?

If you have ever seen clothes stick together when they come out of the dryer, you have seen electric forces attract. But did you know that electric forces can also be repulsive?

Rub a balloon on your hair while a classmate blow bubbles. Bring the balloon near the bubbles and observe what happens.

Now try this with a double bubble—two bubbles that are attached. Bring the balloon very close to a double bubble so that one of the bubbles pops. Then observe what happens when you bring the balloon near the remaining bubble.

1. What happens when you bring the balloon near a single bubble?

2. What happens when you bring the balloon near a bubble that was part of a double bubble?

3. Describe the forces you are observing.

ANSWERS
1. The balloon attracts the bubble.
2. The balloon repels the bubble.
3. This shows that electric forces can be attractive or repulsive.

Transparencies

303 **Section 20.1 Reading Strategy**

Identifying Main Ideas

Topic	Main Idea
Electric Charge	An excess or shortage of electrons produces a net electric charge.
Electric Forces	b._____
Electric Fields	c._____
Static Electricity	d._____

ANSWERS
b. The attraction or repulsion between electrically charged objects.
c. Field strength depends on the net charge and distance from the charge.
d. Charge can be transferred by friction, contact, or induction.

Transparencies

Figure 4 Fields of Positive and Negative Charges

Field of a positive charge

Field of a negative charge

Guided Reading and Study Workbook

Name _____ Class _____ Date _____

Chapter 20   Electricity

Section 20.1 Electric Charge and Static Electricity
(pages 600–603)

This section explains how electric charge is created and how positive and negative charges affect each other. It also discusses the different ways that electric charge can be transferred.

Reading Strategy (page 600)

Identifying Main Ideas Copy the table on a separate sheet of paper. As you read, write the main ideas. For more information on this Reading Strategy, see the **Reading and Study Skills** in the **Skills and Reference Handbook** at the end of your textbook.

Characteristics of Electric Charge	
Topic	**Main Idea**
Electric Charge	An excess or shortage of electrons produces a net electric charge.
Electric Forces	Like charges repel and opposite charges attract.
Electric Fields	The strength of a field depends on the net charge and distance from the charge.
Static Electricity	Charge can be transferred by friction, contact, and induction.

Electric Charge (pages 600–601)

1. What are the two types of electric charge?

a. _____Positive_____   b. _____Negative_____

2. Is the following sentence true or false? In an atom, negatively charged electrons surround a positively charged nucleus. _____true_____

3. Is the following sentence true or false? If a neutral atom gains one or more electrons, it becomes a positively charged ion. _____false_____

4. What is the SI unit of electric charge? ___The coulomb___

Electric Forces (page 601)

5. Circle the letter of each sentence that is true about electric force.

a. Like charges attract and opposite charges repel.

b. Electric force is the attraction or repulsion between electrically charged objects.

c. Electric force is inversely proportional to the amount of charge.

d. Electric force is inversely proportional to the square of the distance between two charges.

Guided Reading and Study Workbook

Name _____ Class _____ Date _____

Chapter 20   Electricity

6. Which are stronger inside an atom, electric forces or gravitational forces? ___Electric forces are stronger.___

7. Is the following sentence true or false? Electric forces cause friction and other contact forces. _____true_____

Electric Fields (page 602)

8. A charge's electric field is the effect the charge has on _____other charges_____ in the space around it.

9. Circle the letters of the factors that the strength of an electric field depends on.

a. the direction of the field

b. whether the charge is positive or negative

c. the amount of charge that produces the field

d. the distance from the charge

10. Is the following sentence true or false? The field of a negative charge points away from the charge. _____false_____

Static Electricity and Charging (pages 602–603)

11. Static electricity is the study of the ___behavior of electric charges___ .

12. Is the following sentence true or false? Charge can be transferred by friction, by contact, and by induction. _____true_____

13. What is the law of conservation of charge? ___The total charge in an isolated system is constant.___

14. Rubbing a balloon on your hair is an example of charging by _____friction_____ .

15. A charge transfer between objects that touch each other is called ___charging by contact___ .

16. Circle the letter of each sentence that is true about charging.

a. When you rub a balloon on your hair, your hair loses electrons and becomes positively charged.

b. The sphere of a Van de Graaff generator transfers all of its charge to you when you touch it.

c. Induction occurs when charge is transferred without contact between materials.

d. Static charges cannot move.

Static Discharge (page 603)

17. Is the following sentence true or false? Static discharge occurs when a pathway through which charges can move forms suddenly. _____true_____

18. How does lightning occur? ___Negative charge in the lower part of a storm cloud induces a positive charge in the ground below the cloud. Eventually the air becomes charged, forming a pathway for the electrons to travel from the cloud to the ground.___

LESSON PLAN 20.2

Electric Current and Ohm's Law

Time
2 periods
1 block

Section Objectives

Local Standards

- **20.2.1 Describe** electric current and **identify** the two types of current.
- **20.2.2 Describe** conduction and **classify** materials as good electrical conductors or good electrical insulators.
- **20.2.3 Describe** the factors that affect resistance.
- **20.2.4 Explain** how voltage produces electric current.
- **20.2.5 Calculate** voltage, current, and resistance using Ohm's law.

Vocabulary electric current • direct current • alternating current • electrical conductor • electrical insulator • resistance • superconductor • potential difference • voltage • battery • Ohm's law

1 FOCUS

Build Vocabulary: LINCS
Have students apply LINCS to the vocabulary terms. **L2**

Targeted Resources
❑ Transparency: Interest Grabber 20.2
❑ Transparency: Reading Strategy 20.2

2 INSTRUCT

Build Reading Literacy: Outline
Have students create an outline of the section. Then, ask them to define index of refraction and total internal reflection. **L1**

Use Visuals: Figure 7
Ask students how the direction of current is related to the direction of the flow of electrons. Then, ask students to explain the function of the switch. **L1**

Address Misconceptions
Point out to students that many solutions containing ions are good conductors. Tell students that charges also flow freely in ionized gases. **L2**

Integrate Earth Science
Have students research the history of superconducting ceramics and report on their findings. **L2**

Quick Lab: Modeling Resistance in a Wire
Students will use a multimeter and pencil drawings to describe how the thickness of a conductor affects its resistance. **L2**

Build Science Skills: Calculating
Help students use Ohm's law to calculate voltage. Then, help students understand that current is indirectly proportional to resistance. **L2**

Targeted Resources
❑ Transparency: Figure 8: A Flashlight
❑ GRSW Section 20.2
❑ **NSTA** *sci*$_{LINKS}$ Conductors and insulators

3 ASSESS

Reteach
Have students use Figure 9 to explain how voltage increases the electrical potential of a charge. **L1**

Evaluate Understanding
Ask students to write two questions each about current, resistance, and voltage. Then, have students form groups and ask each other their questions. **L2**

Targeted Resources
❑ **PHSchool.com** Online Section 20.2 Assessment
❑ iText Section 20.2

Transparencies

305 Section 20.2 Interest Grabber

Conductors and Insulators

Test a two-battery flashlight by turning it on. Then open the flashlight and remove one battery. Insert a small square of aluminum foil on top of the remaining battery. Then reassemble the flashlight, making sure the top battery faces the same direction as before. Test the flashlight again.

Repeat this procedure by inserting different materials between the ends of the batteries. You might try thin materials such as paper, plastic food wrap, duct tape, cardboard, a penny, and a quarter.

1. Which materials allowed the flashlight to light? Which did not?

2. How would you classify materials that allow the flashlight to light?

Transparencies

306 Section 20.2 Reading Strategy

Predicting

Electric Current Probably Means	Electric Current Actually Means
a. ?	b. ?

Transparencies

307 Figure 8 **A Flashlight**

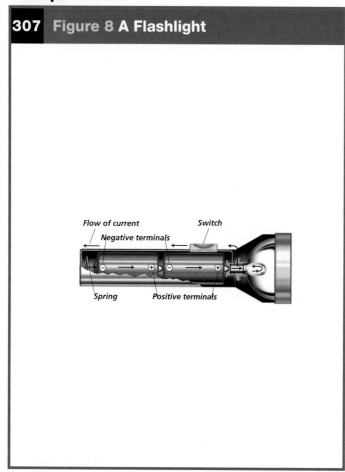

Flow of current
Switch
Negative terminals
Spring
Positive terminals

Name _____ Class _____ Date _____

Chapter 20   Electricity

Section 20.2 Electric Current and Ohm's Law
(pages 604–607)

This section discusses electric current, resistance, and voltage. It also uses Ohm's Law to explain how voltage, current, and resistance are related.

Reading Strategy (page 604)

Predicting Before you read, write a prediction of what electric current is in the table below. After you read, if your prediction was incorrect or incomplete, write what electric current actually is. For more information on this Reading Strategy, see the **Reading and Study Skills** in the **Skills and Reference Handbook** at the end of your textbook.

Electric Current	
Electric Current Probably Means	**Electric Current Actually Means**
Sample answer: Current is moving charge.	Electric current is a continuous flow of charge.

Electric Current (page 604)

1. What is electric current? Electric current is a continuous flow of charge.

2. Complete the following table about electric current.

Electric Current		
Type of Current	**How Charge Flows**	**Examples**
Direct	One direction	Flashlight
Alternating	Two directions	Home or school

3. Electrons flow in the wire from a(n) _____negative_____ terminal to a(n) _____positive_____ terminal.

Conductors and Insulators (page 605)

4. What is an electrical conductor? An electrical conductor is material through which charge can easily flow.

5. What is an electrical insulator? An electrical insulator is material through which charge cannot easily flow.

6. Is the following sentence true or false? Metals are good conductors because they do not have freely moving electrons. _____false_____

Name _____ Class _____ Date _____

Chapter 20   Electricity

Match each material to the category of a conductor or insulator.

	Material	Category
a	7. Copper	a. conductor
b	8. Plastic	b. insulator
b	9. Rubber	
a	10. Silver	
b	11. Wood	

Resistance (page 605)

12. Explain why the current is reduced as electrons move through a conductor. The electrons collide with electrons and ions. These collisions convert some kinetic energy into thermal energy, leaving less energy to move the electrons.

13. Circle the letter of each factor that affects a material's resistance.
    (a) its length   (b) its temperature
    c. its velocity   (d) its thickness

14. What is a superconductor? A superconductor is a material that has almost zero resistance when it is cooled to low temperatures.

Voltage (page 606)

Match each term to its definition.

	Definition	Term
c	15. A device that converts chemical energy to electrical energy	a. flow of charge
a	16. Requires a complete loop	b. voltage
b	17. The difference in electrical potential energy between two places in an electric field	c. battery

18. Is the following sentence true or false? Three common voltage sources are batteries, solar cells, and generators. _____true_____

Ohm's Law (page 607)

19. Is the following sentence true or false? According to Ohm's law, the voltage in a circuit equals the product of the energy and the resistance. _____false_____

20. Doubling the voltage in a circuit doubles the current if _____resistance_____ is held constant.

21. Is the following sentence true or false? Doubling the resistance in a circuit will halve the current if voltage is held constant. _____true_____

Section 20.3 Lesson Plan

LESSON PLAN 20.3

Electric Circuits

Time
2 periods
1 block

Section Objectives

- **20.3.1 Analyze** circuit diagrams for series circuits and parallel circuits.
- **20.3.2 Solve equations** that relate electric power to current, voltage, and electrical energy.
- **20.3.3 Describe** devices and procedures for maintaining electrical safety.

Vocabulary electric circuit • series circuit • parallel circuit • electric power • fuse • circuit breaker • grounding

Local Standards

1 FOCUS

Build Vocabulary: Vocabulary Knowledge Rating Chart
Have students use the vocabulary terms to construct a chart with four columns labeled Term, Can Define or Use It, Have Heard or Seen It, and Don't Know. **L2**

Targeted Resources
❏ Transparency: Interest Grabber 20.3
❏ Transparency: Reading Strategy 20.3

2 INSTRUCT

Build Reading Literacy: Summarize
Have students read the paragraphs about circuit diagrams and summarize them by restating the main idea in their own words. **L1**

Teacher Demo: Series and Parallel Circuits
Create a series circuit and a parallel circuit so that students can observe how current moves in each kind of circuit. **L2**

Address Misconceptions
Stress to students that electrical energy is conserved in electric circuits, and that power is the rate at which electrical energy is used or converted to other forms of energy. **L2**

Quick Lab: Modeling a Fuse
Students form a circuit with a strip of aluminum foil in order to describe the principle of an electric fuse. **L2**

For Enrichment
Have students repeat the Quick Lab experiment using a multimeter to measure current and voltage. Ask students to explain their observations. **L3**

Targeted Resources
❏ Transparency: Figure 12: Series and Parallel Circuits
❏ Transparency: Math Skills: Calculating Electric Power
❏ GRSW Section 20.3
❏ **NSTA** *sci*$_{INKS}$ Electric circuits

3 ASSESS

Reteach
Hold up diagrams of series circuits or parallel circuits and ask students to identify the type of circuit shown. **L1**

Evaluate Understanding
Have students write three math problems (with solutions) based on the electric power equation. Have students take turns analyzing and solving the problems. **L2**

Targeted Resources
❏ **PHSchool.com** Online Section 20.3 Assessment
❏ iText Section 20.3

Transparencies

308 Section 20.3 **Interest Grabber**

Open and Closed Circuits

A current must move in a closed path called a circuit. A closed circuit is a complete path through which charge can flow. In an open circuit, there is no current because the path is interrupted.

Try connecting the bulb and battery with a paper clip as shown. Make sure the base of the bulb touches the battery terminal. Then see if you can make the light bulb flash on and off by tapping its base against the battery terminal.

ANSWERS
1. There is a current when the light bulb is lit.
2. When the base is not touching the battery terminal, the circuit is incomplete (an open circuit). Therefore there is no current, and the light bulb is not lit.

1. How can you tell when there is a current?

2. Explain what happens when the base of the bulb is not touching the battery.

Transparencies

309 Section 20.3 **Reading Strategy**

Relating Text and Visuals

What Can Be Seen in the Circuit Diagram?
Wire bringing current from outside
a. ?
b. ?
c. ?

ANSWERS
a. Meter
b. Fuse box or circuit breaker
c. Ground

Transparencies

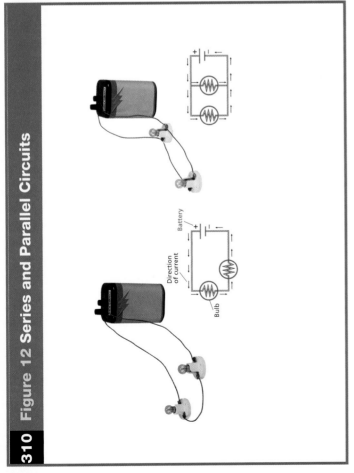

Figure 12 Series and Parallel Circuits

310

Transparencies

311 Math Skills **Calculating Electric Power**

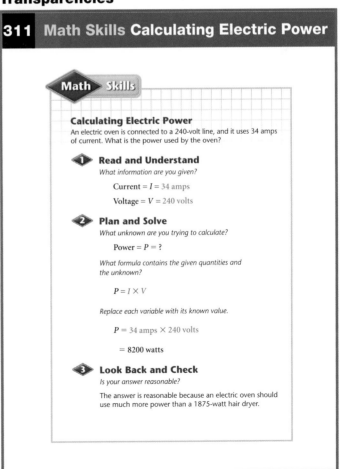

Math Skills

Calculating Electric Power

An electric oven is connected to a 240-volt line, and it uses 34 amps of current. What is the power used by the oven?

1 **Read and Understand**
What information are you given?

Current = I = 34 amps

Voltage = V = 240 volts

2 **Plan and Solve**
What unknown are you trying to calculate?

Power = P = ?

What formula contains the given quantities and the unknown?

$$P = I \times V$$

Replace each variable with its known value.

$$P = 34 \text{ amps} \times 240 \text{ volts}$$

$$= 8200 \text{ watts}$$

3 **Look Back and Check**
Is your answer reasonable?

The answer is reasonable because an electric oven should use much more power than a 1875-watt hair dryer.

Name _____ Class _____ Date _____

Chapter 20   Electricity

Section 20.3 Electric Circuits
(pages 609–613)

This section describes circuit diagrams and types of circuits. It also explains calculation of electric power and electric energy and discusses electrical safety.

Reading Strategy (page 609)

Relating Text and Visuals As you read about household circuits, complete the table by listing three things the diagram in Figure 13 helps you understand about circuits. For more information on this Reading Strategy, see the **Reading and Study Skills** in the **Skills and Reference Handbook** at the end of your textbook.

Understanding a Circuit Diagram
What Can Be Seen in the Circuit Diagram?
Wire bringing current from outside
Grounding wire
Separate circuit for the lights
Separate circuit for the dryer

Circuit Diagrams (pages 609–610)

1. Circuit diagrams use _____symbols_____ to represent parts of a circuit, including a source of electrical energy and devices that are run by the electrical energy.

Match each symbol to what it indicates on a circuit diagram.

	Symbol	What Symbol Indicates
_c_	**2.** +	a. The direction of current
_b_	**3.** –	b. A negative terminal
_a_	**4.** →	c. A positive terminal

Series Circuits (page 610)

5. Is the following sentence true or false? In a series circuit, if one element stops functioning, then none of the elements can operate. ____true____

6. Explain why the bulbs shine less brightly when more bulbs are added to a series circuit. Adding more bulbs increases the resistance, which decreases the current.

Parallel Circuits (page 610)

7. Is the following sentence true or false? Circuits in a home are rarely wired in parallel. ____false____

8. If one element stops functioning in a parallel circuit, the rest of the elements ____can still operate____.

Name _____ Class _____ Date _____

Chapter 20   Electricity

Power and Energy Calculations (pages 611–612)

9. The rate at which electrical energy is converted to another form of energy is called ____electric power____.

10. The SI unit of electric power is the joule per second, or ____watt____, which is abbreviated ____W____.

11. Is the following sentence true or false? Electric power is calculated by multiplying current times voltage. ____true____

12. Write the formula for calculating electrical energy.
____$E = P \times t$____

13. The unit of energy usually used by electric power companies is the ____kilowatt-hour____.

Electrical Safety (pages 612–613)

14. Circle the letters of what could happen if the current in a wire exceeds the circuit's safety limit.
    (a.) The wire could overheat.   b. The wire could get cooler.
    (c.) A fire could start.   (d.) A fuse could blow.

15. Explain how a fuse prevents current overload in a circuit. A wire in the center of the fuse melts, which stops the flow of charge in the circuit.

16. A switch that opens to prevent overloads when current in a circuit is too high is called a(n) ____circuit breaker____.

17. Explain why touching an electrical device with wet hands is dangerous. Your hands conduct electricity more readily when they are wet.

18. Is the following sentence true or false? A ground-fault circuit interrupter shuts down the circuit if the current flowing through the circuit and current returning to ground are equal. ____false____

19. The transfer of excess charge through a conductor to Earth is called ____grounding____.

20. Complete the following table about equipment used to prevent electrical accidents.

Equipment to Prevent Current Overload	Equipment to Protect People from Shock	Equipment to Prevent Short Circuits
a. Fuse Circuit breaker	b. Insulation c. Three-prong plug Grounding wire d. Ground-fault circuit interrupter	e. Insulation

LESSON PLAN 20.4

Electronic Devices

Section Objectives

Local Standards

- **20.4.1 Explain** how electronics conveys information with analog or digital signals.
- **20.4.2 Describe** electronic devices used to control electron flow.
- **20.4.3 Illustrate** how semiconductors are used to make three kinds of solid-state components.
- **20.4.4 Describe** how solid-state components are used in electronic devices.

Vocabulary electronics • electronic signal • analog signal • digital signal • semiconductor • diode • transistor • integrated circuit • computer

1 FOCUS

Build Vocabulary: Concept Map

Have students construct a concept map of the vocabulary terms used in this section, placing the main concept (Electronics) at the top or the center. **L2**

Targeted Resources

❑ Transparency: Interest Grabber 20.4

❑ Transparency: Reading Strategy 20.4

2 INSTRUCT

Build Reading Literacy: Anticipation Guide

Ask students if they have ever seen an old radio or television set with vacuum tubes. Ask them to think of problems that might arise from using vacuum tubes. **L1**

Build Science Skills: Comparing and Contrasting

Have students list in the ways in which digital and analog signals contrast. Then, have them write a list of the similarities of the signals. **L2**

Teacher Demo: Semiconductors and Current

Using an ohmmeter attached to an LED, have students note the resistance readings. Students can observe how a semiconductor allows and limits current. **L2**

Address Misconceptions

Tell students that the only charges that are actually moving in p-type semiconductors are electrons. **L2**

For Enrichment

Interested students can make a presentation showing a digital camera and how its images are electronically stored and manipulated. **L3**

Targeted Resources

❑ Transparency: Figure 17: Analog and Digital Signals

❑ Transparency: Figure 19: Semiconductors

❑ GRSW Section 20.4

3 ASSESS

Reteach

Have students use Figure 20 to explain how semiconductors allow electrons to flow in a preferred direction. **L1**

Evaluate Understanding

Ask students to list the general properties of either a solid-state or vacuum-tube component. Then, have students give examples of applications for these devices. **L2**

Targeted Resources

❑ **PHSchool.com** Online Section 20.4 Assessment

❑ iText Section 20.4

Transparencies

312 Section 20.4 **Interest Grabber**

Using Current to Process and Send Information

An electronic device uses current to process or send information. Signals are encoded in a pattern of changes in the current or voltage.

If you look around the room, you will probably see many devices that use electric current. A lamp uses current to produce light. A heater uses current to produce heat. But these are not electronic devices because no information is being processed or transmitted.

1. Make a list of different electronic devices you use.

2. Describe the information that is processed or transmitted by each type of device.

ANSWERS
1. Possible devices include computers, telephones, CD players, and stereos.
2. CD players and stereos or transmit information in the form of music. Computers process and transmit data such as reports, music, and graphics. Telephone systems transmit voice and data (modem) communications.

Transparencies

313 Section 20.4 **Reading Strategy**

Summarizing

Solid-State Component	Description	Uses
Diode	a. ?	b. ?
Transistor	c. ?	d. ?
Integrated circuit	e. ?	f. ?

ANSWERS
a. Two semiconductors combined, so that current moves in one direction but not the other.
b. Amplifies telephone signals
c. Three semiconductors combined, so that current can be switched on or off, or voltage can be amplified.
d. Amplifies telephone signals
e. A thin slice of silicon with many tiny solid-state components built up on it.
f. Processes and stores information in computers

Transparencies

314 **Figure 17 Analog and Digital Signals**

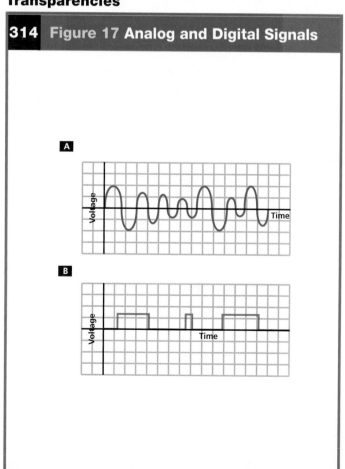

Transparencies

315 **Figures 19 and 20 Semiconductors**

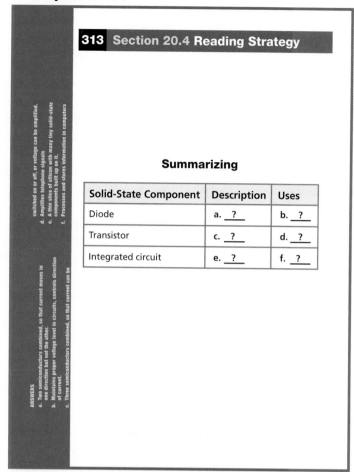

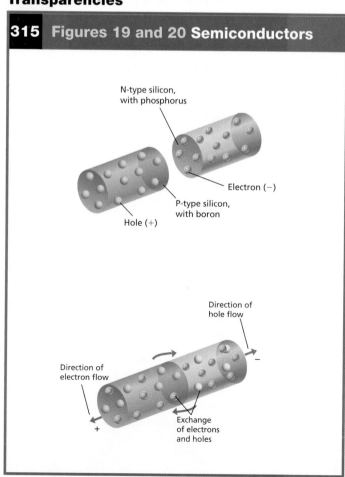

Guided Reading and Study Workbook

Name _____ Class _____ Date _____

Chapter 20   Electricity

Section 20.4 Electronic Devices
(pages 618–622)

This section discusses how various electronic devices operate and what they are used for.

Reading Strategy (page 618)

Summarizing Copy the table on a separate sheet of paper. As you read, complete the table to summarize what you learned about solid-state components. For more information on this Reading Strategy, see the **Reading and Study Skills** in the **Skills and Reference Handbook** at the end of your textbook.

Solid–State Components		
Solid–State Component	**Description**	**Uses**
Diode	Electrons flow from an n-type to a p-type semiconductor.	Change alternating current to direct current
Transistor	A small current flows through the middle layer of three layers of semiconductors, changing the resistance.	Switch, amplifier
Integrated Circuit	A thin slice of silicon that contains many solid-state components	Mobile phones, pagers, computers

Electronic Signals (pages 618–619)

Match each term to its definition.

Definition

__c__ 1. Information sent as patterns in the controlled flow of electrons through a circuit

__a__ 2. The science of using electric current to process or transmit information

__b__ 3. A smoothly varying signal produced by continuously changing the voltage or current in a circuit

__d__ 4. A signal that encodes information as a string of 1's and 0's

Term

a. electronics
b. analog signal
c. electronic signal
d. digital signal

5. Which type of signal is usually used by an AM radio station?
Analog signals are used by AM radio stations.

6. Is the following sentence true or false? Analog signals are more reliable than digital signals. __false__

Physical Science Guided Reading and Study Workbook • Chapter 20 **185**

Guided Reading and Study Workbook

Name _____ Class _____ Date _____

Chapter 20   Electricity

Vacuum Tubes (page 619)

7. Circle the letter of each item that is a true about vacuum tubes.
   (a.) can change alternating current to direct current
   b. never burn out
   (c.) can increase the strength of a signal
   (d.) can turn a current on or off

8. Is the following sentence true or false? An image is produced in a CRT when phosphors glow red, green, and blue in response to electron beams. __true__

Semiconductors (page 621)

9. What is a semiconductor? A semiconductor is a crystalline solid that conducts current only under certain conditions.

10. Name the two types of semiconductors.
    a. __P-type__   b. __N-type__

11. Circle the letter of each sentence that is true about a p-type semiconductor.
    (a.) It can be made by adding a trace amount of boron to a silicon.
    (b.) Electrons are attracted to positively charged holes at each boron atom.
    (c.) As the electrons jump from hole to hole, it looks like a flow of positive charge.
    d. Boron atoms provide weakly bound electrons that can flow.

12. Is the following sentence true or false? In an n-type semiconductor, weakly bound electrons can conduct a current. __true__

Solid-State Components (pages 621–622)

Match each term to its definition.

Term

__c__ 13. diode

__a__ 14. transistor

__b__ 15. integrated circuit

Definition

a. A solid-state component with three layers of semiconductors

b. A thin slice of silicon that contains many solid-state components

c. A solid-state component that combines an n-type and p-type semiconductor

16. A chip or microchip is another name for a(n) __integrated circuit__.

Communications Technology (page 622)

17. Why is it useful for communication devices to use microchips? Microchips make them more portable, reliable, and affordable.

18. A mobile phone can store data such as phone numbers because capacitors store electric charge

186 *Physical Science* Guided Reading and Study Workbook • Chapter 20

Guided Reading and Study Workbook

Name _____ Class _____ Date _____

Chapter 20   Electricity

WordWise

Match each definition with the correct term in the grid and then write its number under the appropriate term. When you have filled in all the boxes, add up the numbers in each column, row, and the two diagonals. What is surprising about the sums? __They all equal 34.__

Definitions

1. A property that causes subatomic particles such as protons and electrons to attract or repel other matter
2. The attraction or repulsion between electrically charged objects
3. Charge transfer without contact between materials
4. Law that total charge in an isolated system is constant
5. A continuous flow of electric charge
6. Material through which charge can easily flow
7. Material through which a charge cannot easily flow
8. The opposition to the flow of charges in a material
9. A circuit in which the charge has only one path through which it can flow
10. An electric circuit with two or more paths through which charge can flow
11. A switch that opens when current in a circuit is too high
12. Information sent as patterns in the controlled flow of electrons through a circuit
13. A smoothly varying signal produced by continuously changing the voltage or current in a circuit
14. A complete path through which a charge can flow
15. A solid-state component with three layers of semiconductors
16. A thin slice of silicon that contains many solid-state components

				Diagonal = 34
integrated circuit 16	induction 3	electric force 2	analog signal 13	= 34
electric current 5	parallel circuit 10	circuit breaker 11	resistance 8	= 34
series circuit 9	electrical conductor 6	electrical insulator 7	electronic signal 12	= 34
law of conservation of charge 4	transistor 15	electric circuit 14	electric charge 1	= 34
= 34	= 34	= 34	= 34	Diagonal = 34

Physical Science Guided Reading and Study Workbook • Chapter 20 **187**

Guided Reading and Study Workbook

Name _____ Class _____ Date _____

Chapter 20   Electricity

Power, Voltage, and Current

The power rating on an electric soldering iron is 40.0 watts. If the soldering iron is connected to a 120-volt line, how much current does it use?

Math Skill: Formulas and Equations

You may want to read more about this **Math Skill** in the **Skills and Reference Handbook** at the end of your textbook.

1. Read and Understand

What information are you given in the problem?
Power = P = 40.0 watts
Voltage = V = 120 volts

2. Plan and Solve

What unknown are you trying to calculate?
Current = I = ?

What formula contains the given quantities and the unknown?
$$P = I \times V; I = \frac{P}{V}$$

Replace each variable with its known value.
$$I = \frac{40.0 \text{ watts}}{120 \text{ volts}} = 0.33 \text{ amps}$$

3. Look Back and Check

Is your answer reasonable?
The answer is reasonable because a soldering iron needs a relatively low current to generate heat.

Math Practice

On a separate sheet of paper, solve the following problems.

1. A steam cleaner has a power rating of 1100 watts. If the cleaner is connected to a 120-volt line, what current does it use?
$P = I \times V; I = P/V = $ 1100 watts/120 volts = 9.2 amps

2. A coffee maker uses 10.0 amps of current from a 120-volt line. How much power does it use?
$P = I \times V = $ 10.0 amps × 120 volts = 1200 watts

3. A power mixer uses 3.0 amps of current and has a power rating of 360 watts. What voltage does this appliance require?
$P = I \times V; V = P/I = $ 360 watts/3.0 amps = 120 volts

188 *Physical Science* Guided Reading and Study Workbook • Chapter 20

Student Edition Lab Worksheet

Name _____ Class _____ Date _____

Chapter 20   Electricity   Forensics Lab

Evaluating Electrical Safety   See page 623 in the Teacher's Edition for more information.

Electric appliances must be safely insulated to protect users from injury. In this lab, you will play the role of a safety engineer determining whether an electric power supply is safely insulated.

Problem   How much resistance is needed in series with a known resistance to reduce the voltage by 99 percent?

Materials
- 9-volt battery
- battery clip
- multimeter
- 3 alligator clips
- 4 resistors: 1-ohm, 10-ohm, 100-ohm, 1000-ohm

Skills   Calculating, Using Tables

Procedure
1. Attach the battery clip to the battery.
   CAUTION: *The circuit may become hot.*
2. Use an alligator clip to attach one wire of the 1-ohm resistor to one of the battery clip's wires, as shown in Figure 1.
3. Clip one wire of the 1000-ohm resistor to the free end of the 1-ohm resistor. Clip the other wire of the 1000-ohm resistor to the free wire of the battery clip.
4. The 1-ohm resistor represents the current-carrying part of the appliance. The 1000-ohm resistor represents the insulation for the current-carrying part. Place one of the multimeter's electrodes on each wire of the 1-ohm resistor. Record the voltage difference.

Resistors

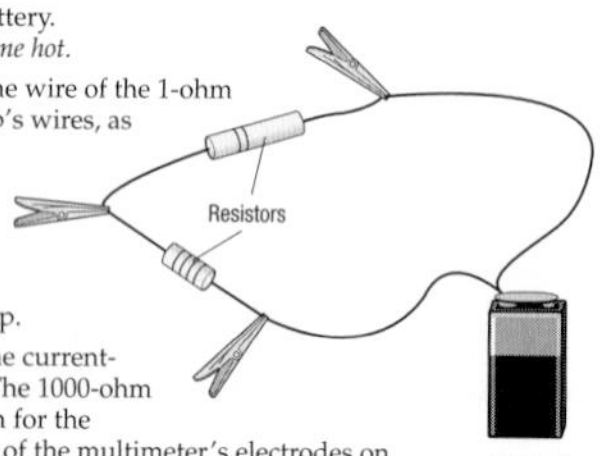

Figure 1

Data Table

Resistance (ohms)		Voltage difference (volts)	
Current-Carrying	Insulating	Current-Carrying	Insulating
1	1000	0.01	8.6
1	100	0.09	8.5
10	1000	0.09	8.5
10	100	0.9	7.7

Student Edition Lab Worksheet

Name _____ Class _____ Date _____

5. Place the multimeter's electrodes on the wires of the 1000-ohm resistor. Record the voltage difference.
6. To model a reduction in the resistance of the insulation, repeat Steps 4 and 5, replacing the 1000-ohm resistor with a 100-ohm resistor. Disconnect the resistors from the battery clip.
7. **Predicting**   Record your prediction of how increasing the resistance of the current-carrying part of the appliance will affect the voltage difference across the insulating part.

   Sample prediction: Increasing the current-carrying resistance will decrease the voltage difference
   across the insulating part.

8. To test your prediction, repeat Steps 2 through 6, using a 10-ohm resistor to represent the current-carrying part of the appliance.

Analyze and Conclude

1. **Calculating**   When the resistance of the current-carrying part was 1 ohm and the resistance of the insulating part was 100 ohms, what was the ratio of the voltage differences across the current-carrying part and the insulating part?

   The ratio of the voltage differences was 0.01 (1/100).

2. **Drawing Conclusions**   In the circuit you built, what is the voltage difference across each resistor proportional to?

   The voltage difference across each resistor was proportional to its resistance.

3. **Applying Concepts**   You know the resistance of the current-carrying part of an appliance. What should the resistance of the insulation be to reduce the voltage by 99 percent?

   The resistance of the insulation should be 100 times the resistance of the current-carrying part.

Lab Manual

Name _____ Class _____ Date _____

Chapter 20   Electricity   Investigation 20A

Constructing a Telephone   Refer students to page 498–523 in their textbooks for a discussion of mechanical waves and sound.

SKILLS FOCUS: Observing, Applying Concepts, Inferring   CLASS TIME: 20 minutes

Background Information
The operation of the telephone involves energy conversions. In the transmitter of the telephone, sound waves exert a pressure on a flexible film, or diaphragm, that conducts electricity, and which vibrates with the same frequency as the sound waves. The louder the sound waves are, the larger the vibrations of the diaphragm are. In some older telephone transmitters, finely granulated carbon was placed between the diaphragm and a conducting plate. Changes in the diaphragm's vibrations change the distance between the diaphragm and the plate, causing the electric current through the carbon grains to vary. In this way, the variations in intensity and frequency of sound are converted into changes in current. These current changes form electronic signals that travel over wires. In the receiver of the telephone, the electronic signals are converted back into sound waves by a somewhat similar process.

The first telephone conversation took place on March 10, 1876, between the inventor of the telephone, Alexander Graham Bell, and his assistant, Thomas Watson.

In this investigation, you will build a simple device that changes pressure into an electrical signal, which illustrates the operation of a transmitter in older models of telephones.

Problem
How do energy conversions take place within the transmitter of a telephone?

Pre-Lab Discussion
Read the entire investigation. Then, work with a partner to answer the following questions.

1. **Observing**   What process is this investigation meant to test?

   This investigation will test how mechanical energy is converted into electrical energy, such as
   the energy conversion that takes place within a telephone transmitter.

Lab Manual

Name _____ Class _____ Date _____

2. **Controlling Variables**   What is the manipulated variable in this investigation?

   Pressure on the copper strips

3. **Controlling Variables**   What is the responding variable in this investigation?

   The amount of electric current

4. **Predicting**   What do you predict will occur at the transmitting end of the energy conversion?

   Possible answer: Change in the pressure on the copper strips causes change in the resistance of
   the circuit, and therefore the amount of current in the circuit.

5. **Predicting**   What do you predict will occur at the receiving end of the energy conversion?

   Possible answer: Change in the current causes change in the brightness of the light bulb.

Materials (per group)
plastic cup
1.5-V lamp with socket
carbon grains
2 copper strips
2 alligator clips
1.5-V dry cell
3 connecting wires, each 30 cm long

Lab Manual

Name _____ Class _____ Date _____

Safety 🥽🧤

Put on safety goggles and a lab apron. Be careful to avoid breakage when working with glassware. Observe proper laboratory procedures when using electrical equipment. Note all safety alert symbols next to the steps in the Procedure and review the meaning of each symbol by referring to the Safety Symbols on page xiii.

Procedure

1. Place the two copper strips on opposite sides of the plastic cup. **CAUTION:** *Metal strips can be sharp and can cut skin.*

2. Half-fill the cup with carbon grains.

3. Using an alligator clip, connect one end of a wire to one of the copper strips. Connect the other end of the wire to one side of the lamp socket. **CAUTION:** *Observe proper laboratory procedures when using electrical equipment.* **CAUTION:** *Wire ends can puncture skin.*

4. Using the other alligator clip, connect another wire to the second copper strip. Connect the other end of this wire to one terminal of the dry cell, as shown in Figure 1.

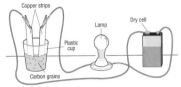

Figure 1

5. Connect a third wire to the other side of the lamp socket. Connect the other end of this wire to the other terminal of the dry cell.

6. Squeeze the lower sides of the plastic cup so that the distance between the copper strips changes. Do not bring the strips into direct contact with each other. Observe how the brightness of the light bulb varies with the pressure applied to the cup.

Observations

The main features that should be observed are as follows: As the pressure on the cup's

sides increased, the copper strips moved closer together. This reduced the resistance in the

circuit, and therefore increased the current. As the current increased, the light bulb burned brighter.

Lab Manual

Name _____ Class _____ Date _____

Analysis and Conclusions

1. **Observing** What happened when you squeezed the copper strips together?

   The light bulb became brighter.

2. **Observing** What happened when you stopped squeezing the copper strips together?

   The light bulb became dimmer.

3. **Drawing Conclusions** How did pressure on the carbon grains affect the flow of electricity?

   The greater the pressure that was applied on the carbon grains, the stronger the electric current was.

4. **Inferring** How is the process observed in this investigation comparable to the operation of a telephone transmitter?

   The pressure applied to the sides of the cup is comparable to the pressure applied to the diaphragm

   in a transmitter. The change in the distance between the copper strips is comparable to the change in

   the distance between the conducting plate and diaphragm, while the carbon grains in the cup serve

   the same role as in older transmitters. The variation in the electric current is revealed by the changes

   in the brightness of the light bulb.

Go Further

Using the Internet or the library, perform additional research about telephone transmitters. How similar were old transmitters to the apparatus in the investigation? How are they different now? What materials are currently used in transmitters? What is piezoelectricity, and how are certain crystal used to produce it? Has the basic process of energy conversion changed significantly? Use the results of your research to write a short report.

You may need to provide some guidance to students as they do their research. If possible, provide access to reference books and Internet resources, notably on subjects such as piezoelectricity and capacitors.

Lab Manual

Name _____ Class _____ Date _____

Chapter 20   Electricity   **Investigation 20B**

Charging Objects

Refer students to pages 602 and 603 in their textbook for a discussion of static electricity and charging. **SKILLS FOCUS:** Predicting; Observing; Recording Data; Inferring; Comparing and Contrasting **CLASS TIME:** 60 minutes

Background Information

An object can become charged in several different ways. When electrons are transferred between objects that are rubbed together, the objects become charged due to friction. An object can sometimes become charged simply by touching it with another charged object. In this case, the object is charged by direct contact, or conduction. An object can also be charged by an object that is already charged, without contact between them. This newly charged object is said to be charged by **induction**. The charge on an object can be detected by using a device called an electroscope.

In this investigation, you will construct an electroscope and use it to explore charging by friction, conduction, and induction.

Problem

How do electrons move when objects become charged?

Pre-Lab Discussion

Read the entire investigation. Then, work with a partner to answer the following questions.

1. **Forming Hypotheses** What hypotheses are to be tested in this investigation?

   Students may hypothesize that objects charged by friction and induction will

   have opposite charges, while objects charged by conduction will have like charges.

2. **Predicting** When the balloon is rubbed with flannel, in what manner will the balloon become charged?

   Electrons are transferred between objects that are rubbed together. The objects become charged

   by friction.

3. **Predicting** What type of electron transfer will take place when the electroscope is touched by the balloon?

   The electroscope will be temporarily charged (or electrons will be transferred) by direct contact,

   or conduction.

Lab Manual

Name _____ Class _____ Date _____

4. **Predicting** When the charged glass rod is held near the electroscope and then moved away, what type of electron transfer will occur?

   The electroscope will be temporarily charged (or electrons will be transferred) without contact,

   by induction.

5. **Drawing Conclusions** What is the purpose of this investigation?

   That electron transfer takes place between objects in several ways, always resulting in

   those objects becoming charged

Materials *(per group)*

scissors	very thin aluminum foil from a gum wrapper	string
cardboard	masking tape	glass rod
glass jar	2 balloons	silk
thick wire	wool flannel	
aluminum foil		

Safety 🥽✂️🧤

Put on safety goggles. Be careful when handling sharp instruments. Be careful to avoid breakage when working with glassware. Observe proper laboratory procedures when using electrical equipment. Note all safety alert symbols next to the steps in the Procedure and review the meaning of each symbol by referring to the Safety Symbols on page xiii.

Procedure

Allow two class periods for this investigation. In the first period (Procedure Steps 1–4), students will build and test an electroscope. In the second period (Steps 5–10), they will use the device to detect and identify charges. Carry out the investigation on a dry day.

1. To build an electroscope, cut out a circle of cardboard slightly larger than the opening of the glass jar. Use the point of the scissors to make a small hole in the center of the cardboard. **CAUTION:** *Be careful not to cut yourself when handling sharp instruments.*

2. Push the wire through the hole in the cardboard. Bend one end of the wire to form an L-shaped hook, as shown in Figure 1. Crumple the aluminum foil into a ball and push it onto the other end of the wire. **CAUTION:** *Use care when handling wire; it can cut or puncture skin.*

Lab Manual

Name _____ Class _____ Date _____

- Aluminum ball
- Cardboard circle
- Tape
- Jar
- Copper wire
- Thin foil leaves

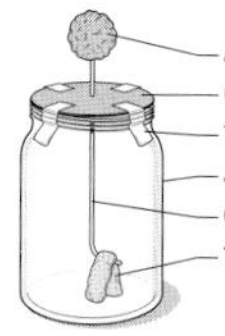

Figure 1

3. Cut a small strip of thin foil from a gum wrapper. Fold the foil strip in half and hang it over the hook so that the two leaves of foil hang down side by side. Lower the cardboard lid assembly onto the jar and tape it in place. **CAUTION:** *Be careful when handling sharp instruments.* Collect scissors from students when they are finished cutting the foil strips.

4. Inflate the two balloons and tie the ends so that the air does not escape.

5. To test your electroscope, rub one of the inflated balloons with the wool flannel. This will give the balloon a negative charge and the wool a positive charge. Gently touch the rubbed part of the balloon to the aluminum ball of your electroscope. The foil leaves should move apart. (*Hint: If they do not move, remove the lid from the jar and check that the leaves are not stuck together.*) Touch the top of the electroscope with your hand.

6. Tie a piece of string to the end of each balloon. Rub both balloons with the wool flannel. Hang both balloons by their string and bring the rubbed parts of the balloons together. Observe what happens.

7. Hold the wool flannel near one of the hanging balloons. Observe what happens.

8. Touch one of the charged balloons to the top of the electroscope. Record what happens in the data table.

9. Move the balloon away. Record what happens in the data table.

10. Touch the top of the electroscope with your hand and again record what happens in the data table.

11. Rub the glass rod with the silk. Doing this gives a positive charge to the glass and a negative charge to the silk. Touch the glass rod to the electroscope. Record what happens in the data table.

12. Move the glass rod away from the electroscope. Again, record what happens in the data table. Touch the electroscope with your hand.

13. Rub one of the balloons again with the wool. Move the balloon close to but not touching the top of the electroscope. Record what happens in the data table.

Lab Manual

Name _____ Class _____ Date _____

14. Move the balloon away from the electroscope. Record what happens in the data table.

15. Rub the glass rod again with the silk. Hold the glass close to but not touching the electroscope. Record what happens in the data table.

16. Move the glass rod away. Record what happens in the data table.

Observations Sample data are shown.

DATA TABLE

Procedure Step Number	Action	Observation of Electroscope Leaves
8	Rubbed balloon touches electroscope	Move apart
9	After touching, balloon is moved away	Stay apart
10	Hand touches electroscope	Move back together
11	Rubbed glass rod touches electroscope	Move apart
12	Rubbed glass rod is moved away	Stay apart
13	Rubbed balloon held near	Move apart
14	Rubbed balloon moved away	Move back together
15	Rubbed glass held near rod	Move apart
16	Rubbed glass rod is moved away	Move back together

Lab Manual

Name _____ Class _____ Date _____

Analysis and Conclusions

1. **Observing** After being rubbed with wool flannel, what happened to the balloons in Step 6 when they were brought near each other?

The balloons repelled from each other.

2. **Observing** What happens to an electroscope that indicates that a charged object is near?

The leaves of an electroscope separate when a charged object is near.

3. **Inferring** Recall that rubbing a balloon with flannel gives the balloon a negative charge. Does the balloon gain or lose electrons in this situation? Is this an example of charging by friction, contact, or induction?

The balloon gains electrons when rubbed with wool flannel. This is an example of charging by friction.

4. **Inferring** By what method was the electroscope charged in Step 8? Did the leaves become positively or negatively charged? What happened when the charged glass rod touched the electroscope in Step 11?

The electroscope was charged by conduction when touched by the balloon. Because electrons moved to the electroscope, the leaves became negatively charged. The electroscope lost electrons and became positively charged when touched by the glass rod.

5. **Inferring** What happened to the charged electroscope when you touched it with your hand in Step 10? Did the electroscope gain or lose electrons?

The electrons moved from the electroscope to your hand. The electroscope lost electrons.

Lab Manual

Name _____ Class _____ Date _____

6. **Inferring** Why did the electroscope leaves behave as they did when the charged balloon was brought near in Step 13? Did any electrons from the balloon move into the electroscope?

Electrons in the top of the electroscope were repelled from the negatively charged balloon. They moved to the leaves, giving the leaves a negative charge. Like charges repel, and the leaves moved apart. No electrons, however, entered the electroscope.

7. **Inferring** Why did the electroscope leaves behave as they did when the charged balloon was moved away in Step 14?

Once the balloon was moved away, the surplus electrons in the leaves moved back to the top and the leaves moved together. The net charge on the electroscope is still zero.

8. **Classifying** Explain what happened when the charged glass rod was held near and then moved away from the electroscope in Steps 15 and 16. Was the electroscope charged by friction, conduction, or induction?

Electrons in the leaves were attracted to the glass rod and moved to the top. A shortage of electrons existed in the leaves, leaving both positively charged, and they repelled. Since no contact was made and therefore no electrons entered the electroscope, this is charging by induction.

9. **Comparing and Contrasting** Compare the three methods of charging in terms of electron movement.

In charging by friction, electrons are rubbed off one object onto another. In charging by friction, electrons are rubbed off one object onto another. In charging by conduction, electrons move from one object to another when the objects are in direct contact. In charging by induction, electrons are rearranged within an object only; electrons do not transfer between objects.

Go Further

Design an experiment to compare how much different substances are charged by friction. Show your plan to your teacher. When your teacher approves your plan, carry out your experiment and report your results and conclusions.

Examine student plans for sound experimental design and safety. Students will need to place a scale on the inner wall of the electroscope to measure the amount that the leaves are separated. Then, they will have to test how the angle between the leaves varies with the distance of a charged object from the top of the electroscope. Controlled variables such as the distance between the electroscope and the charged object, and the number of times the objects are rubbed together need to be described in the experimental design.

Name _____ Class _____ Date _____

Chapter 20   Electricity   Chapter Test A

Multiple Choice

Write the letter that best answers the question or completes the statement on the line provided.

_____ 1. The strength of an electric field depends on the
   a. amount of charge that produced the field.
   b. distance from the charge.
   c. amount of charge on a test charge placed in the field.
   d. both A and B

_____ 2. What is the SI unit of electric charge?
   a. ampere   b. ohm
   c. volt   d. coulomb

_____ 3. If a neutral metal comb is held near an object with a negative charge, the comb will become charged by
   a. induction.   b. contact.
   c. friction.   d. static discharge.

_____ 4. The type of current in your school is mostly
   a. direct current.   b. alternating current.
   c. series current.   d. produced by batteries.

_____ 5. An electrical insulator has
   a. electrons that freely move.
   b. more protons than electrons.
   c. negatively charged ions.
   d. electrons tightly bound to its atoms.

_____ 6. Which of the following would reduce the resistance of a metal wire?
   a. increasing its thickness
   b. increasing its temperature
   c. increasing its length
   d. all of the above

_____ 7. Which of the following is maintained across the terminals of a battery?
   a. a potential difference   b. a voltage drop
   c. an electric charge   d. both A and B

_____ 8. The current in a clothes iron measures 5.0 amps. The resistance of the iron is 24 ohms. What is the voltage?
   a. 120 V   b. 4.8 V   c. 19 V   d. 600 V

_____ 9. How many paths through which charge can flow would be shown in a circuit diagram of a series circuit?
   a. one   b. two
   c. none   d. an unlimited number

Name _____ Class _____ Date _____

_____ 10. Most of the circuits in your home are
   a. series circuits.   b. parallel circuits.
   c. reversible circuits. d. closed circuits.

_____ 11. If you know the power rating of an appliance and the voltage of the line it is attached to, you can calculate the current the appliance uses by
   a. multiplying the voltage by the power.
   b. subtracting the power from the voltage.
   c. dividing the voltage by the power.
   d. dividing the power by the voltage.

_____ 12. A ground-fault circuit interrupter shuts down a circuit if it
   a. melts.
   b. senses an overload.
   c. senses unequal currents.
   d. senses moisture.

_____ 13. Which of the following is made from a crystalline solid that conducts a current only under certain circumstances?
   a. vacuum tube   b. cathode-ray tube
   c. analog devise   d. semiconductor

_____ 14. What do transistors do in a mobile phone?
   a. store electric charge
   b. maintain proper voltage
   c. store data
   d. amplify the phone's incoming signal

_____ 15. What solid-state component in a mobile phone maintains proper voltage levels in the circuits?
   a. transistors   b. capacitors   c. diodes   d. microchips

Completion

Complete each statement on the line provided.

1. Electric force is _____ proportional to the amount of charge and _____ proportional to the square of the distance between the charges.

2. When a pathway through which charges can move forms suddenly, _____ occurs.

3. Scientists usually define the direction of current as the direction in which _____ charges would flow.

4. A p-type semiconductor is made by adding a trace amount of boron to _____.

5. Communication devices use _____ circuits known as _____ to make them more portable, reliable, and affordable.

Name _____ Class _____ Date _____

Short Answer

In complete sentences, write the answers to the questions on the lines provided.

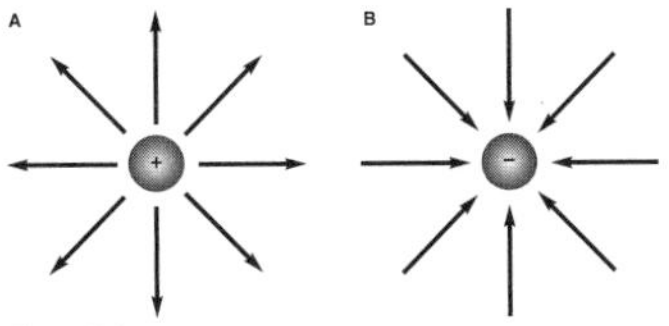

A   B

Figure 20-1

1. In Figure 20-1, where is the field of each charge the strongest?
   _____
   _____

2. What is a charge's electric field?
   _____
   _____

3. What is the law of conservation of charge?
   _____
   _____

4. Explain why metal wire coated with plastic or rubber is used in electric circuits.
   _____
   _____

5. If the voltage is 90 volts and the resistance is 30 ohms, what is the current? Explain your answer.
   _____
   _____
   _____

Name _____ Class _____ Date _____

6. How much energy does a 50-watt light bulb use compared to a 100-watt light bulb if both are shining for the same length of time? Explain your answer.
   _____
   _____
   _____

7. What are two types of electronic signals, and how is each produced?
   _____
   _____
   _____

8. What is the difference between n-type and p-type semiconductors?
   _____
   _____
   _____

9. Name three kinds of solid-state components.
   _____
   _____
   _____

Chapter Test A

Name _____ Class _____ Date _____

Using Science Skills

Use the diagram to answer each question. Write the answers on a separate sheet of paper.

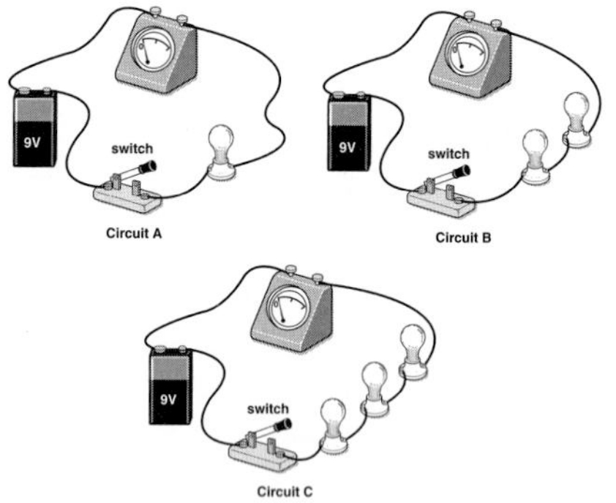

Figure 20-2

1. **Comparing and Contrasting** Compare the resistance in the three circuits shown in Figure 20-2 when the switches are closed. Explain the cause of any differences.
2. **Comparing and Contrasting** In Figure 20-2, how will the current compare in Circuits A, B, and C when the switches are closed? Explain your answer.
3. **Applying Concepts** Explain why the filaments in the light bulbs become hotter than the connecting wires in Figure 20-2.
4. **Predicting** When the switches are closed in Figure 20-2, which bulbs will be the brightest and which will be the dimmest? Assume that all of the light bulbs and batteries are identical. Explain your answer.
5. **Problem Solving** Using the same materials, how could you change the circuits in Figure 20-2 so that all the bulbs would have the same brightness? Explain your answer.

Chapter Test A

Name _____ Class _____ Date _____

Essay

Write the answers to each question on a separate sheet of paper.

1. How are friction, induction, and static discharge involved in lightning?
2. Explain why a battery causes charge to flow spontaneously when the battery is inserted in a circuit.
3. Suppose you have one light bulb in a simple circuit. If you add a second identical light bulb in series, what would happen to the brightness of the first bulb? If instead you add the second bulb in parallel, what would happen to the brightness of the first bulb? Explain your answers.
4. Why does plugging too many appliances into the same circuit cause too much current to flow through the circuit? What can happen as a result?
5. Explain the flow of electrons in p-type semiconductors and why it looks like positive charges flow.

Chapter Test B

Name _____ Class _____ Date _____

Chapter 20 Electricity   **Chapter Test B**

Multiple Choice

Write the letter that best answers the question or completes the statement on the line provided.

_____ 1. If an atom loses electrons, it becomes a
   a. negatively charged ion.
   b. positively charged ion.
   c. neutral atom.
   d. neutral ion.

_____ 2. If the two charges represented in Figure 20-1 were brought near each other, they would
   a. attract each other.
   b. repel each other.
   c. cause static discharge.
   d. have no affect on each other.

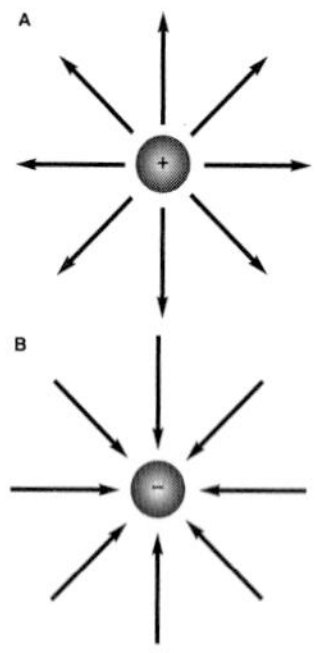

_____ 3. Walking across a carpet is an example of charge being transferred by
   a. contact.   b. induction.
   c. static electricity.   d. friction.

_____ 4. What type of current is used in a battery?
   a. parallel current   b. alternating current
   c. direct current   d. potential current

_____ 5. Which of the following materials allows charges to flow easily?
   a. glass
   b. wood
   c. an electrical conductor
   d. an electrical insulator

_____ 6. Resistance is affected by a material's
   a. thickness.   b. length.
   c. temperature.   d. all of the above

_____ 7. What is the difference in electrical potential energy between two places in an electric field?
   a. current   b. resistance
   c. potential difference d. induction

_____ 8. Which of the following represents Ohm's law?
   a. $I = V \times R$ b. $V = I \times R$
   c. $R = V \times I$ d. $V = I \times R$

_____ 9. What is the unit of electric power?
   a. ampere   b. volt
   c. watt   d. ohm

Figure 20-1

Chapter Test B

Name _____ Class _____ Date _____

_____ 10. Which of the following provides electrical safety?
   a. circuit breaker
   b. fuse
   c. ground-fault circuit interrupter
   d. all of the above

_____ 11. Information sent as patterns and codes in the controlled flow of electrons through a circuit is a(an)
   a. electronic signal.   b. digital signal.
   c. analog signal.   d. integrated signal.

_____ 12. Electronic signals that are smoothly varying signals produced by continuously changing the voltage or current in a circuit are
   a. digital signals.   b. cathode rays.
   c. diode signals.   d. analog signals.

_____ 13. A vacuum tube can be used to
   a. change alternating current into direct current.
   b. increase the strength of a signal.
   c. turn a current on or off.
   d. all of the above

_____ 14. A solid-state component with three layers of semiconductors is a(an)
   a. transistor.   b. diode.
   c. vacuum tube.   d. integrated circuit.

_____ 15. A thin slice of silicon that contains many solid-state components is a(an)
   a. transistor.   b. integrated circuit.
   c. diode.   d. cathode-ray tube.

Completion

Complete each statement on the line provided.

1. The electric field around a positive charge points _____ the charge.
2. Like charges _____ and opposite charges _____
3. The SI unit of electric current is the _____
4. Wood, plastic, and rubber are good electrical _____, and copper is a good electrical _____
5. The SI unit of resistance is the _____.
6. A complete path through which charge can flow is an electric _____

7. To calculate power, multiply voltage measured in _____ by ____ _____ measured in amps.

8. The transfer of excess charge through a conductor to Earth is called _____

9. A(An) _____ signal encodes information as a string of 1's and 0's.

10. A cathode-ray tube is a type of _____ tube.

11. A solid-state component that combines an n-type and a p-type semiconductor is a(an) _____.

12. In an electronic device, a diode can be used to change alternating current to _____ current.

Short Answer

In complete sentences, write the answers to the questions on the lines provided.

1. What are three ways that a charge can be transferred?
   _____
   _____

2. What is the difference between direct current and alternating current?
   _____
   _____
   _____
   _____

3. What are three common voltage sources?
   _____
   _____

4. What is a circuit breaker?
   _____
   _____
   _____
   _____

5. Electric current is used for different purposes. Compare the use of electric current by a computer and by a toaster.
   _____
   _____
   _____
   _____

Using Science Skills

Use the diagram to answer each question. Write the answers on a separate sheet of paper.

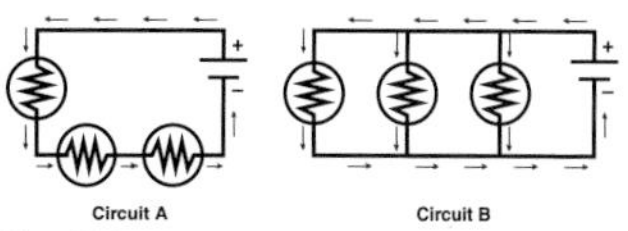

Circuit A   Circuit B

Figure 20-2

1. **Classifying** Are both circuits in Figure 20-2 series circuits? Explain your answer.

2. **Comparing and Contrasting** In which direction do the electrons move in Figure 20-2? How does this compare to the direction of the current?

3. **Interpreting Graphics** What objects and how many of each object would you need to draw if symbols were not used in Figure 20-2?

4. **Predicting** Based on the circuit diagrams in Figure 20-2, what would happen if one of the bulbs in Circuit A burned out? What would happen if one of the bulbs in Circuit B burned out? Explain your answers.

5. **Comparing and Contrasting** In Figure 20-2, what device could be added to the circuits to open the circuits? Explain how this device works. Compare this device to safety devices that stop the current in a home.

Chapter 20 Test A Answers

Multiple Choice

1. d **2.** d **3.** a **4.** b **5.** d **6.** a **7.** d
8. a **9.** a **10.** b **11.** d **12.** c **13.** d **14.** d
15. c

Completion

1. directly, inversely **2.** static discharge; electric discharge
3. positive **4.** silicon; germanium **5.** integrated, microchips

Short Answer

1. Both fields are strongest nearest the charge, where the lines representing the field are closest together. **2.** the effect an electric charge has on other charges in the space around it **3.** It is a law that states that the total charge in an isolated system is constant.
4. The wire is a conductor and carries the charges. The plastic or rubber is an insulator and does not carry the charges. The coating helps control the current and keep it where it is needed.
5. 3 amps, or amperes; because current is equal to voltage (90 volts) divided by resistance (30 ohms) **6.** A 50-watt light bulb uses half the energy that a 100-watt light bulb uses. Energy equals power (watts) multiplied by time. The time is the same, and the power of a 50-watt bulb is half as much, so the energy used by the 50-watt bulb is half as much. **7.** Analog signals are produced by continuously varying the voltage or current, and digital signals are produced by turning the current on and off. **8.** In n-type semiconductors, electrons flow, and in p-type semiconductors, positively charged "holes" flow. **9.** diodes, transistors, and integrated circuits

Using Science Skills

1. The light bulbs are sources of resistance, so Circuit A has the least resistance because the electrons pass through only one light bulb. Circuit B has more resistance than A has because Circuit B has two light bulbs. Circuit C has three light bulbs and the most resistance. Although other parts of the circuits, such as the wire, are sources of resistance, they are the same in all three circuits.
2. Circuit A will have more current flowing through it than Circuit B will, and Circuit C will have the least current flowing through it. More current can flow when there is less resistance, and, since light bulbs are a source of resistance, Circuit A has the least resistance and the most current. **3.** In the filament, which is a thin wire, the resistance is high. The electrons collide more often in the filament, so the filaments become hotter than the connecting wires. **4.** The bulb in Circuit A will be the brightest. The bulbs in Circuit C will be the dimmest. Each bulb is a source of resistance, and as resistance increases, current decreases. Bulbs shine less brightly as the current decreases. **5.** All the bulbs would have the same brightness if Circuits B and C were rewired as parallel circuits. Some wires would need to be cut in half to do this. Then, the current would have a separate path through each bulb and would not be affected by the resistance of another bulb.

Essay

1. Charges can build up in a storm cloud from friction between moving air masses. Negative charge in the lower part of the cloud induces a positive charge in the ground below the cloud. As the amount of charge in the cloud increases, the force of attraction between the charges in the cloud and charges in the ground increases. Eventually, the air becomes charged, forming a pathway for electrons to travel from the cloud to the ground. The sudden discharge that follows is lightning. **2.** The battery is a source of electrical energy. A voltage drop, or potential difference, is maintained across the negative and positive terminals of a battery. Charge flows spontaneously from a higher electrical potential energy to a lower electrical potential energy. **3.** The brightness of the first bulb decreases if a second bulb is added in series but does not change if a second bulb is added in parallel. By adding a second bulb in series, the overall current is reduced because the resistance of the circuit increases. With less current, the brightness of the first bulb decreases because $P = IV$, and I decreases, while V is unchanged. By adding a second bulb in parallel, the total current increases, but the current through the first bulb is unchanged, so its brightness is unchanged. **4.** The amount of current in a circuit can increase if the devices are connected in parallel. Each device that is turned on increases the current. If the current exceeds safety limits, the wire many overheat and start a fire unless a fuse melts or the circuit breaker switches off. **5.** A p-type semiconductor is made by adding trace amounts of boron to silicon. A space, called a hole, occurs at each boron atom. The holes are positively charged. When charge flows, electrons are attracted toward the positively charged holes in the p-semiconductor. As electrons jump from hole to hole, it looks like a flow of positive charge because the locations of the holes change.

Chapter 20 Test B Answers

Multiple Choice

1. b **2.** a **3.** d **4.** c **5.** c **6.** d
7. c **8.** b **9.** c **10.** d **11.** a **12.** d
13. d **14.** a **15.** b

Completion

1. away from **2.** repel, attract **3.** ampere; amp **4.** insulators, conductor **5.** ohm **6.** circuit **7.** volts, current **8.** grounding
9. digital **10.** vacuum **11.** diode **12.** direct

Short Answer

1. by friction, contact, and induction **2.** In direct current, the charge flows only in one direction. In alternating current, the charge regularly reverses its direction. **3.** batteries, solar cells, and generators **4.** 9 volts; because voltage is equal to the current multiplied by the resistance **5.** A computer uses electric current to process or transmit information, while a toaster uses electric current to change electrical energy into thermal energy.

Using Science Skills

1. No; only Circuit A is a series circuit. In Circuit A, the current can follow only one path through all three bulbs. Circuit B is a parallel circuit because the current can follow a separate path through each of the three bulbs. **2.** The electrons move from the negative terminal of the battery to the positive terminal of the battery. This is opposite the direction in which the current moves. **3.** For each circuit, three bulbs and a battery would need to be drawn. **4.** If a bulb in Circuit A burned out, the path for a charge is broken, and the other two light bulbs will go out. If a bulb in Circuit B burned out, the charge can still flow through the paths with the other two bulbs, and the other bulbs stay lit. **5.** A switch could be added. When the switch is open, the circuit is not a complete loop, and the current immediately stops. A person must manually open and close the switch. In a home, fuses and circuit breakers are safety devices that automatically stop the current if too much current flows through the circuit.

Chapter 21 Magnetism

Planning Guide

Use these planning tools

Easy Planner
Resource Pro
Online Lesson Planner

SECTION OBJECTIVES	STANDARDS		ACTIVITIES and LABS
	NATIONAL (See p. T18.)	**STATE**	
21.1 Magnets and Magnetic Fields, pp. 630–633	A-1, A-2, B-1, B-4		**SE** Inquiry Activity: How Do Magnets Interact With One Another? p. 629 **L2**
🕐 1 block or 2 periods			**SE** Quick Lab: Observing Magnetic Field Lines, p. 632 **L2**
21.1.1 Describe the effects of magnetic forces and magnetic fields and **explain** how magnetic poles determine the direction of magnetic force.			**TE** Build Science Skills: Inferring, p. 631 **L2**
21.1.2 Interpret diagrams of magnetic field lines around one or more bar magnets.			**LM** Investigation 21B: Investigating a Compass **L1**
21.1.3 Describe Earth's magnetic field and its effect on compasses.			
21.1.4 Explain the behavior of ferromagnetic materials in terms of magnetic domains.			
21.2 Electromagnetism, pp. 635–639	A-1, A-2, B-4, B-6, E-2, F-1, G-1, G-2, G-3		**SE** Quick Lab: Making an Electromagnet, p. 637 **L2**
🕐 1 block or 2 periods			**TE** Teacher Demo: Magnetic Field from Electric Current, p. 636 **L2**
21.2.1 Describe how a moving electric charge creates a magnetic field and **determine** the direction of the magnetic field based on the type of charge and the direction of its motion.			**TE** Teacher Demo: Electromagnetic Force, p. 638 **L2**
21.2.2 Relate the force a magnetic field exerts on a moving electric charge to the type of charge and the direction of its motion.			
21.2.3 Explain how solenoids and electromagnets are constructed and **describe** factors that affect the field strength of both.			
21.2.4 Describe how electromagnetic devices use the interaction between electric currents and magnetic fields.			
21.3 Electrical Energy Generation and Transmission, pp. 642–647	A-1, A-2, B-4, E-1, F-1, F-3, G-1, G-2, G-3		**SE** Application Lab: Investigating an Electric Generator, pp. 648–649 **L2**
🕐 1 block or 2 periods			**TE** Teacher Demo: Generating Alternating Current, p. 643 **L2**
21.3.1 Describe how electric current is generated by electromagnetic induction.			**LM** Investigation 21A: Modeling a Computer **L2**
21.3.2 Compare AC and DC generators and **explain** how they work.			
21.3.3 Analyze factors that determine the output voltage and current produced by a transformer.			
21.3.4 Summarize how electrical energy is produced, transmitted, and converted for use in the home.			

Ability Levels

L1 For students who need additional help
L2 For all students
L3 For students who need to be challenged

Components

SE	Student Edition	**GRSW**	Guided Reading & Study Workbook With Math Support	**CTB**	Computer Test Bank
TE	Teacher's Edition			**TP**	Test Prep Resources
LM	Laboratory Manual			**iT**	iText
PLM	Probeware Lab Manual	**CUT**	Chapter and Unit Tests	**DC**	Discovery Channel Videotapes

T	Transparencies
P	Presentation Pro CD-ROM
GO	Internet Resources

RESOURCES
PRINT and TECHNOLOGY

GRSW Section 21.1 **L1**

T Chapter 21 Pretest **L2**
Section 21.1 **L2**

P Chapter 21 Pretest **L2**
Section 21.1 **L2**

GRSW Section 21.2 **L1**

DC Magnetic Viewpoints **L2**

T Section 21.2 **L2**

P Section 21.2 **L2**

SC/LINKS GO Electromagnets **L2**

PLM Lab 9: Investigating an Electric Generator **L2**

GRSW Section 21.3 **L1**

GRSW Math Skill **L2**

T Section 21.3 **L2**

P Section 21.3 **L2**

SC/LINKS GO Transformers **L2**

PHSchool.com Data sharing **L2**

SECTION ASSESSMENT

SE Section 21.1 Assessment, p. 633

iT Section 21.1

SE Section 21.2 Assessment, p. 639

iT Section 21.2

SE Section 21.3 Assessment, p. 647

iT Section 21.3

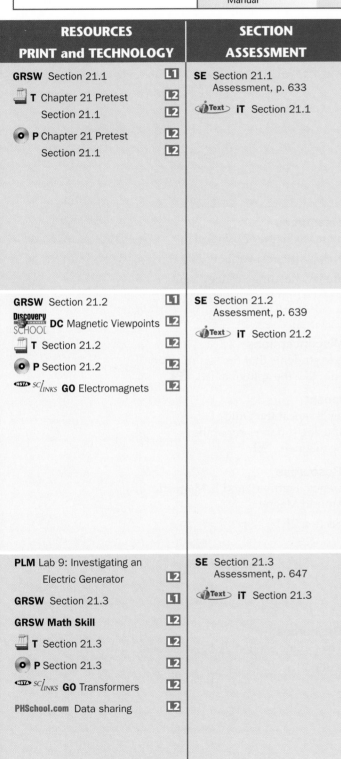

Go Online

Go online for these Internet resources.

PHSchool.com
Web Code: ccd-2210
Web Code: cca-2210

NSTA SCiLINKS
Web Code: ccn-2212
Web Code: ccn-2213

Materials for Activities and Labs

Quantities for each group

STUDENT EDITION

Inquiry Activity, p. 629
2 bar magnets

Quick Lab, p. 632
small container of iron filings, 2 bar magnets, paper, 2 textbooks, masking tape

Quick Lab, p. 637
iron nail, 20 small metal paper clips, 20-cm length and 1-m length of insulated wire with stripped ends, 6-volt battery, switch

Application Lab, pp. 648–649
cardboard tube, 5-m length of insulated wire, metric ruler, multimeter, bar magnet, graph paper

TEACHER'S EDITION

Build Science Skills, p. 631
2 bar magnets, a small magnetic compass

Teacher Demo, p. 636
insulated wire, cardboard (10 cm × 10 cm), a burner tripod, a variable DC power supply, 4–6 compasses

Teacher Demo, p. 638
insulated wire, a large horseshoe magnet, a variable DC power supply, 2 ring stands with clamps

Build Science Skills, p. 640
a short pencil (about 5 cm long), a cardboard disk (7 cm wide), a steel thumbtack, a bar magnet, paper

Teacher Demo, p. 643
a hand-operated generator, a galvanometer, insulated wire (2 strands)

Chapter Assessment

CHAPTER ASSESSMENT

SE Chapter Assessment, pp. 651–652
CUT Chapter 21 Test A, B
CTB Chapter 21
iT Chapter 21
PHSchool.com GO
Web Code: cca-2210

STANDARDIZED TEST PREP

SE Chapter 21, p. 653
TP Diagnose and Prescribe

iText—interactive textbook with assessment at PHSchool.com

Magnetism   628B

Name_____ Class_____ Date_____   M T W T F

LESSON PLAN 21.1

Magnets and Magnetic Fields

Section Objectives

- **21.1.1** **Describe** the effects of magnetic forces and magnetic fields and **explain** how magnetic poles determine the direction of magnetic force.

- **21.1.2** **Interpret diagrams** of magnetic field lines around one or more bar magnets.

- **21.1.3** **Describe** Earth's magnetic field and its effect on compasses.

- **21.1.4** **Explain** the behavior of ferromagnetic materials in terms of magnetic domains.

Vocabulary magnetic force • magnetic pole • magnetic field • magnetosphere • magnetic domain • ferromagnetic material

Local Standards

1 FOCUS

Build Vocabulary: Word-Part Analysis
Have students research the origin of the word *magnet* and write a short paragraph explaining how the word originated. **L2**

Targeted Resources
❏ Transparency: Chapter 21 Pretest
❏ Transparency: Interest Grabber 21.1
❏ Transparency: Reading Strategy 21.1

2 INSTRUCT

Build Reading Literacy: KWL
Have students create a chart that includes what they know about magnetic forces, questions they have about magnetic forces, and answers to their questions. **L1**

Build Science Skills: Inferring
Have students place a compass about 1–2 cm away from two magnets. Students will gain an understanding of the shape of the magnetic field around two bar magnets. **L2**

Quick Lab: Observing Magnetic Field Lines
Students will use two bar magnets and iron filings to recognize how the magnetic fields of two magnets combine. **L2**

Address Misconceptions
Emphasize to students that the "spin" of an electron is not like the spin of a ball. **L2**

For Enrichment
Have students repeat the Quick Lab experiment using different separations between the magnets. **L3**

Targeted Resources
❏ Transparency: Figures 2 and 3: Magnetic Fields Around Magnets
❏ GRSW Section 21.1

3 ASSESS

Reteach
Use Figure 3 to explain the shape and direction of a magnetic field around a bar magnet. **L1**

Evaluate Understanding
Ask students why a refrigerator magnet sticks to the door of a refrigerator. **L2**

Targeted Resources
❏ **PHSchool.com** Online Section 21.1 Assessment
❏ iText Section 21.1

316 **Chapter 21 Pretest**

1. True or False: Like charges exert an attractive force on each other.

2. True or False: Electric force and magnetic force are two aspects of the same force.

3. An electric field tells you
   a. force on a charge in the field.
   b. how force varies with position.
   c. direction of force on a positive charge.
   d. all of the above.

4. What is the difference between a series circuit and a parallel circuit?

ANSWERS
1. False
2. True

3. d
4. A series circuit has only one path for the electrical current to follow; a parallel circuit has more than one path.

317 **Chapter 21 Pretest** (continued)

5. What is an insulator?

6. True or False: The particle in an atom that moves around the nucleus is the electron.

7. If current in a circuit increases and power stays the same, what happens to the voltage?

8. True or False: An alternating current is one in which the charges change direction.

ANSWERS
5. a material through which charge cannot easily flow
6. True
7. It decreases.
8. True

318 **Section 21.1 Interest Grabber**

How Does a Compass Work?

A compass is a device used to determine direction. A typical compass has a thin magnetic needle that freely rotates in response to other magnets. The north end of a compass needle is marked "N." The south end is marked "S" or it is often left unmarked.

Hold a compass near a bar magnet. Watch the direction of the compass needle when you hold the compass near the end of the magnet marked "S". Move the compass near other parts of the magnet. Notice how the direction of the compass needle changes.

1. In what direction did the compass needle point when you held it near different parts of the magnet?

2. How is the behavior of the compass needle like the behavior of electric charges?

ANSWERS
1. The north end of the compass needle pointed toward the south end of the bar magnet when it was near this end. The needle did not point directly toward "S" when it was near the middle of the bar magnet. Near the north end of the bar magnet, the south end of the compass needle pointed toward the "N."

2. Students should recognize that north and south attract, just like positive and negative charges attract. Students may not yet realize that north repels north and south repels south. This is like the electric repulsion between like charges.

319 **Section 21.1 Reading Strategy**

Using Prior Knowledge

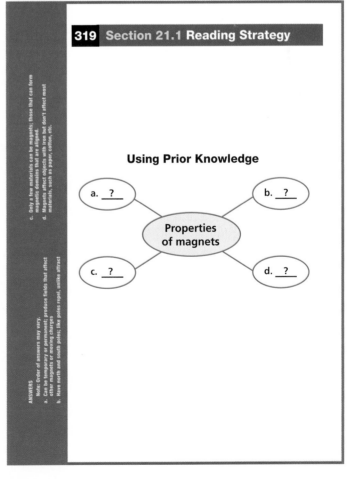

ANSWERS
Note: Order of answers may vary.
a. Can be temporary or permanent; produce fields that affect other magnets or moving charges
b. Have north and south poles; like poles repel, unlike attract
c. Only a few materials can be magnets; those that can form magnetic domains that are aligned.
d. Magnets affect objects with iron but don't affect most materials, such as paper, cotton, etc.

Transparencies

320 | **Figures 2 and 3 Magnetic Fields Around Magnets**

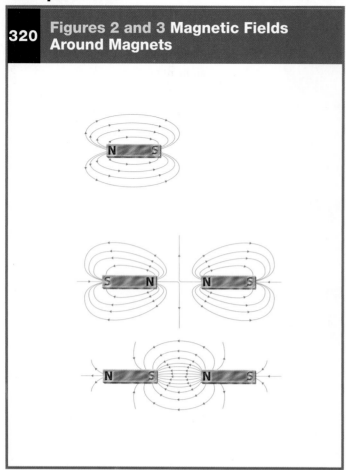

Guided Reading and Study Workbook

Name _____ Class _____ Date _____

Chapter 21   Magnetism

Section 21.1 Magnets and Magnetic Fields
(pages 630–633)

This section describes magnetic forces and magnetic fields. Characteristics of magnetic materials also are discussed.

Reading Strategy (page 630)

Using Prior Knowledge Before you read, copy the diagram below and add what you already know about magnets to the diagram. After you read, revise the diagram based on what you learned. For more information on this Reading Strategy, see the **Reading and Study Skills** in the **Skills and Reference Handbook** at the end of your textbook.

```
  Can be temporary              Have north and south
   or permanent                 poles; like poles repel,
                                  unlike attract
                  Properties
                  of Magnets
 Composed of magnetic
 domains that are aligned        Produce fields
```

1. In the year 1600, William Gilbert published a book explaining the properties of _____magnets_____ .

Magnetic Forces (page 630)

2. Is the following sentence true or false? Magnetic force can be exerted on moving charges, as well as on iron or on another magnet. _____true_____

3. What did William Gilbert discover when he used a compass to map forces around a magnetic sphere? He discovered that the force is strongest at the poles.

4. Circle the letter of each sentence that is true about magnetic force.
(a.) Two magnets that approach each other may attract or repel.
  b. Magnetic forces do not vary with distance.
  c. Opposite magnetic poles repel one another.
(d.) Magnetic forces act over a distance.

Guided Reading and Study Workbook

Name _____ Class _____ Date _____

Chapter 21   Magnetism

Magnetic Fields (pages 631–632)

For questions 5 and 6, refer to the figure below.

5. Where is the magnetic field the strongest? The field in the gap between the magnets is very strong, where field lines are close together.

6. Based on this figure, what would you expect to happen when the north pole of one magnet faces the south pole of another magnet? Opposite poles will attract.

7. Circle the letter of each sentence that is true about magnetic fields.
(a.) Magnetic fields surround a magnet and can exert a magnetic force.
  b. Field lines begin near the south pole of a magnet and extend toward the north pole.
(c.) Iron filings are most attracted to areas where the field is strongest.
(d.) A magnetic field is strongest near the north and south poles of a magnet.

8. The area that is influenced by the magnetic field surrounding Earth is called the _____magnetosphere_____ .

Magnetic Materials (pages 632–633)

Match each term with its description.

Description	Term
_a_ **9.** Can be magnetized because it has many domains	a. ferromagnetic material
_c_ **10.** Has randomly oriented domains	b. magnetic domain
_b_ **11.** Region that has many atoms with aligned magnetic fields	c. nonmagnetized material

12. What can cause the realignment of magnetic domains in a material? Heat, a jarring impact, or moving a material relative to a magnet can cause realignment of magnetic domains.

LESSON PLAN 21.2

Electromagnetism

Time
2 periods
1 block

Section Objectives

Local Standards

- **21.2.1 Describe** how a moving electric charge creates a magnetic field and **determine** the direction of the magnetic field based on the type of charge and the direction of its motion.
- **21.2.2 Relate** the force a magnetic field exerts on a moving electric charge to the type of charge and the direction of its motion.
- **21.2.3 Explain** how solenoids and electromagnets are constructed and **describe** factors that affect the field strength of both.
- **21.2.4 Describe** how electromagnetic devices use the interaction between electric currents and magnetic fields.

Vocabulary electromagnetic force • solenoid • electromagnet • galvanometer • electric motor

1 FOCUS

Build Vocabulary: Concept Map
Have students make a concept map comparing the devices in the vocabulary list. **L2**

Targeted Resources
❏ Transparency: Interest Grabber 21.2
❏ Transparency: Reading Strategy 21.2

2 INSTRUCT

Build Reading Literacy: Predict
Have students read the first two paragraphs on p. 635. Ask them to predict what Oersted discovered about the relationship between electricity and magnetism. **L1**

Use Visuals: Figure 8
Ask students how they could use their hand to determine the deflection of an electron moving through the magnetic poles. **L1**

Teacher Demo: Magnetic Field from Electric Current
Connect insulated wire to a power supply, and place compasses around the wire. Increase the current so that students can observe how an electric current produces a magnetic field. **L2**

Quick Lab: Making an Electromagnet
Students will make an electromagnet using an insulated wire wrapped around an iron nail. They will predict how the number of turns of wire affects the strength of the electromagnet. **L2**

Teacher Demo: Electromagnetic Force
Use an insulated wire (connected to a power supply) and a large horseshoe magnet to demonstrate for students a magnetic force exerted on a wire carrying an electric current. **L2**

Build Science Skills: Applying Concepts
Ask students what forms of energy are shown for the electric motor in Figure 11. Then, ask what energy transformations take place when operating the motor. **L2**

Targeted Resources
❏ Transparency: Figure 11: An Electric Motor
❏ GRSW Section 21.2
❏ **NSTA** *scLINKS* Electromagnets

3 ASSESS

Reteach
Use Figures 7 and 9 to review the direction of magnetic fields produced by electric currents. **L1**

Evaluate Understanding
Ask students to list and discuss three examples of devices that use electromagnetic forces. **L2**

Targeted Resources
❏ **PHSchool.com** Online Section 21.2 Assessment
❏ iText Section 21.2

Transparencies

321 Section 21.2 Interest Grabber

What Devices Use an Electric Motor?

Have you thought about how many different devices use electric motors?

Take a look at the list below and decide which ones you think use an electric motor.

photocopier	digital camera
refrigerator	hair dryer
electric toothbrush	lamp
microwave oven	fax machine
modem	mobile phone
computer	CD player
electric wheelchair	radio

1. Classify the devices in the list based on whether you think they include an electric motor. You may need a category called "uncertain."

2. What are some of the tasks an electric motor can do?

Transparencies

322 Section 21.2 Reading Strategy

Identifying Main Ideas

Topic	Main Idea
Electricity and magnetism	a. ?
Direction of magnetic fields	b. ?
Direction of electric currents	c. ?
Solenoids and electromagnets	d. ?
Electromagnetic devices	e. ?

Transparencies

323 Figure 11 **An Electric Motor**

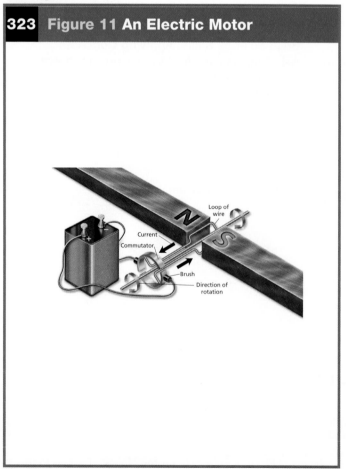

Name _____ Class _____ Date _____

Chapter 21   Magnetism

Section 21.2 Electromagnetism
(pages 635–639)

This section describes how electricity and magnetism are related. Uses of solenoids and electromagnetic devices are discussed, and a description of how these devices work is presented.

Reading Strategy (page 635)
Identifying Main Ideas Copy the table on a separate sheet of paper. As you read, write the main idea of the text that follows each topic in the table. For more information on this Reading Strategy, see the **Reading and Study Skills** in the **Skills and Reference Handbook** at the end of your textbook.

Electromagnetism	
Topic	**Main Idea**
Electricity and magnetism	Electricity and magnetism are different aspects of a single force known as the electromagnetic force.
Direction of magnetic fields	Moving charges create a magnetic field.
Direction of electric currents	A charge moving in a magnetic field will be deflected in a direction perpendicular to both the magnetic field and the velocity of the charge.
Solenoids and electromagnets	Changing the current in an electromagnet controls the strength and direction of its magnetic field.
Electromagnetic devices	Electromagnetic devices such as galvanometers, electric motors, and speakers change electrical energy into mechanical energy.

1. In 1820 Hans Oersted discovered a connection between electricity and _____ magnetism _____.

Electricity and Magnetism (pages 635–636)

2. Electricity and magnetism are different aspects of a single force known as the _____ electromagnetic _____ force.

3. Both aspects of the electromagnetic force are caused by _____ electric charges _____.

4. Is the following sentence true or false? Moving electric charges create a magnetic field. _____ true _____

5. Is the following sentence true or false? The vibrating charges that produce an electromagnetic wave also create a magnetic field. _____ true _____

6. A charge moving in a magnetic field will be deflected in a direction that is _____ perpendicular _____ to both the magnetic field and to the velocity of the charge.

Name _____ Class _____ Date _____

Chapter 21   Magnetism

Solenoids and Electromagnets (pages 637–638)

7. Is the following sentence true or false? The strength of the magnetic field through the center of a coil of current-carrying wire is calculated by adding together the fields from each turn of the coil. _____ true _____

8. A coil of current-carrying wire that produces a magnetic field is called a(n) _____ solenoid _____.

9. What is an electromagnet? _____ An electromagnet is a solenoid with a core made of ferromagnetic material. _____

10. Circle the letter of each sentence that is true about electromagnets.
    a. Placing an iron rod in a solenoid reduces the strength of its magnetic field.
    (b.) Devices that utilize electromagnets include doorbells and telephones.
    (c.) A magnetic field can be turned on and off with an electromagnet.
    (d.) An electromagnet can control the direction of a magnetic field.

11. List three factors that determine the strength of an electromagnet.
    a. _____ Type of ferromagnetic core _____
    b. _____ Number of turns in the solenoid coil _____
    c. _____ Current in the solenoid _____

12. Is the following sentence true or false? Decreasing the current in the solenoid decreases the strength of an electromagnet. _____ true _____

13. What types of solenoid cores make stronger electromagnets? _____ Cores that are easily magnetized, such as "soft" iron, make stronger electromagnets. _____

Electromagnetic Devices (pages 638–639)

14. Electromagnetic devices change _____ electrical _____ energy into _____ mechanical _____ energy.

15. Complete the following table about electromagnetic devices.

Description	Device
Uses electromagnets to convert electrical signals into sound waves	Loudspeaker
Uses a rotating electromagnet to turn an axle	Electric motor
Uses an electromagnet to measure small amounts of current	Galvanometer

LESSON PLAN 21.3

Electrical Energy Generation and Transmission

Time
2 periods
1 block

Section Objectives

- **21.3.1 Describe** how electric current is generated by electromagnetic induction.
- **21.3.2 Compare** AC and DC generators and **explain** how they work.
- **21.3.3 Analyze** factors that determine the output voltage and current produced by a transformer.
- **21.3.4 Summarize** how electrical energy is produced, transmitted, and converted for use in the home.

Vocabulary electromagnetic induction • generator • transformer • turbine

Local Standards

1 FOCUS

Build Vocabulary: Paraphrase
Have students explain what the vocabulary terms mean by writing a sentence in which the vocabulary term appears followed by the phrase *in other words*. **L2**

Targeted Resources
❏ Transparency: Interest Grabber 21.3
❏ Transparency: Reading Strategy 21.3

2 INSTRUCT

Build Reading Literacy: Reciprocal Teaching
Have students apply the strategies of summarize, question, clarify, and predict as they read the section under the heading Transformers. **L1**

Build Science Skills: Classifying
Have students recall the process of charge induction from Chapter 20. Then, ask students how electromagnetic induction is similar to electric charge induction. **L2**

Address Misconceptions
Explain to students that, while transformers do not create electrical energy, they do help to reduce the loss of electrical energy. **L2**

Use Community Resources
Suggest that students learn more about different transformers, as well as the efficiency of transformers, by contacting the Public Information Office of the local electric utility. **L2**

Targeted Resources
❏ Transparency: Figure 14: A Simple AC Generator
❏ Transparency: Figure 16: Types of Transformers
❏ GRSW Section 21.3
❏ **NSTA** *sci*$_{LINKS}$ Transformers

3 ASSESS

Reteach
Use Figure 14 to review how a generator uses electromagnetic induction to produce an alternating current. **L1**

Evaluate Understanding
Ask each student to write two questions about generating and transmitting electric power. Then, have students form groups and quiz each other using their questions. **L2**

Targeted Resources
❏ **PHSchool.com** Online Section 21.3 Assessment
❏ iText Section 21.3

Transparencies

324 Section 21.3 **Interest Grabber**

Can Magnets Produce Electric Current?

You've learned that an electric current produces a magnetic field. The reverse process is also possible: a changing magnetic field can produce an electric current.

To see this, attach a loop of wire to a galvanometer as shown in the figure. The galvanometer displays the current in the wire. By moving the magnet back and forth past the wire, a changing magnetic field is produced. This causes the galvanometer needle to swing back and forth.

1. Why was there no current when the magnet was stationary?

2. Hypothesize why the back-and-forth motion of the magnet produced an alternating current.

3. What would happen if you kept the magnet stationary and moved the wire back and forth between the poles of the magnet?

Transparencies

325 Section 21.3 **Reading Strategy**

Sequencing

| Alternating current in smaller coil | → | a. ___?___ | → | b. ___?___ |

Transparencies

326 Figure 14 **A Simple AC Generator**

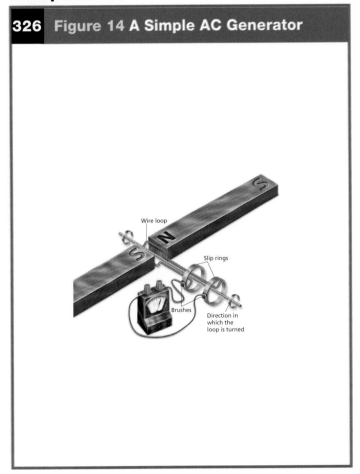

Transparencies

327 Figure 16 **Types of Transformers**

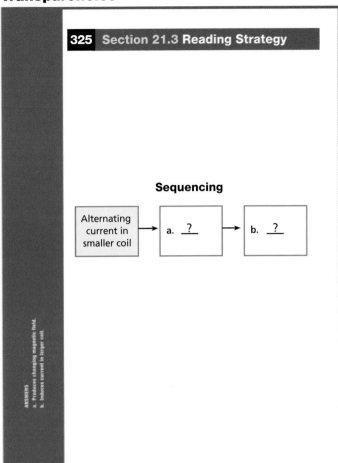

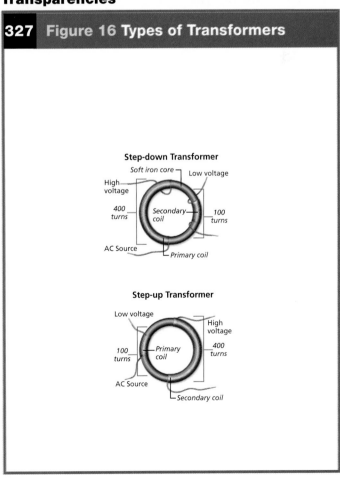

Guided Reading and Study Workbook

Name _____ Class _____ Date _____

Chapter 21 Magnetism

Section 21.3 Electrical Energy Generation and Transmission
(pages 642–647)

This section describes how electricity is generated and transmitted for human use. A description of how generators and transformers function is given.

Reading Strategy (page 642)

Sequencing As you read the section, complete the flowchart to show how a step-up transformer works. Then make a similar flowchart for a step-down transformer. For more information on this Reading Strategy, see the **Reading and Study Skills** in the **Skills and Reference Handbook** at the end of your textbook.

Step-up Transformers

Current flows through smaller coil. → Produces magnetic field → Induces current in larger coil

Generating Electric Current (pages 642–643)

1. Is the following sentence true or false? A magnetic field can be used to produce an electric current. __true__

2. Circle the letter for the name of the process of generating a current by moving an electrical conductor relative to a magnetic field.
   a. electromagnetic force
   b. electromagnetic field
   c. electromagnetic induction
   d. electromagnetic conduction

3. Electrical charges can easily flow through materials known as __conductors__

4. Why is the discovery of electromagnetic induction significant? __It opened the way for practical uses of electromagnetism.__

5. According to Faraday's law, electric current can be induced in a conductor by __a changing magnetic field__

6. Is the following sentence true or false? Moving a magnet relative to a coil of wire induces a current in the wire if the coil is part of a complete circuit. __true__

Physical Science Guided Reading and Study Workbook • Chapter 21 **193**

Guided Reading and Study Workbook

Name _____ Class _____ Date _____

Chapter 21 Magnetism

Generators (pages 643–644)

7. A generator converts __mechanical__ energy into __electrical__ energy.

8. Circle the letter that best describes how most of the electrical energy used in homes and businesses is produced.
   a. with DC generators
   b. using AC generators at large power plants
   c. with small magnets moving inside coils
   d. by rotating a magnetic field around a coil of wire

9. Is the following sentence true or false? In an alternating current produced by an AC generator, the flow direction of charges switches back and forth. __true__

10. Circle the letter of each sentence that is true about generators.
    a. Small generators can produce enough electricity for a small business.
    b. DC generators produce current that flows back and forth.
    c. Small generators are available for purchase by the public.
    d. Most modern power plants use DC generators.

Transformers (pages 644–645)

11. A device that increases or decreases voltage and current of two linked AC circuits is called a(n) __transformer__.

12. How does a transformer change voltage and current? __It induces a changing magnetic field in one coil, which then induces an AC current in a nearby coil with a different number of turns.__

13. Why are transformers necessary for home electrical service? __They are needed to transmit power at high voltage so power loss can be reduced.__

14. Is the following sentence true or false? To prevent overheating wires, voltage is decreased for long-distance transmission. __false__

15. How is voltage calculated in a transformer? __Dividing the number of turns in the secondary coil by the number of turns in the primary coil gives the ratio of the output voltage to the input voltage.__

16. Is the following sentence true or false? A step-down transformer decreases voltage and increases current. __true__

Electrical Energy for Your Home (pages 646–647)

17. Name at least three sources used to produce electrical energy in the United States. __Answers may include coal, water (hydroelectric), nuclear energy, wind, natural gas, and petroleum.__

18. A device with fanlike blades that can convert energy from various sources into electrical energy is called a(n) __turbine__.

194 *Physical Science Guided Reading and Study Workbook • Chapter 21*

Guided Reading and Study Workbook

Name _____ Class _____ Date _____

Chapter 21 Magnetism

WordWise

Solve the clues to determine which vocabulary words from Chapter 21 are hidden in the puzzle. Then find and circle the terms in the puzzle. The terms may occur vertically, horizontally, or diagonally. Some terms may be spelled backwards.

f	g	d	e	l	o	p	c	i	t	e	n	g	a	m
e	a	a	t	s	o	r	m	e	v	r	p	e	a	b
r	r	q	l	z	f	f	r	e	r	e	v	g	c	t
r	c	i	u	v	t	t	c	h	n	g	n	r	r	t
o	s	d	o	m	a	i	n	i	u	e	t	a	o	r
m	o	u	b	p	l	n	b	k	t	n	u	u	f	a
a	l	t	y	o	i	r	o	o	n	e	r	m	t	n
g	e	k	p	o	u	d	s	m	a	r	b	i	n	s
n	o	g	o	y	h	z	a	v	b	b	a	c	a	f
e	i	e	e	e	h	n	j	n	m	o	e	m	o	o
t	d	i	r	j	u	e	r	t	c	r	f	r	u	r
c	t	e	z	z	w	y	n	r	p	e	r	j	b	

Clues

Region where a magnetic field is strongest

Nickel is a(n) _____ material.

Current-carrying wire with a loop in it

Uses an electromagnet to measure small amounts of current

Device with fanlike blades that converts energy from various sources to electrical energy

Area influenced by Earth's magnetic field

Converts mechanical energy into electrical energy

Aligned magnetic fields

Step-down or step-up

Hidden Words

magnetic pole

ferromagnetic

solenoid

galvanometer

turbine

magnetosphere

generator

domain

transformer

Physical Science Guided Reading and Study Workbook • Chapter 21 **195**

Guided Reading and Study Workbook

Name _____ Class _____ Date _____

Chapter 21 Magnetism

Calculating Voltage

A step-down transformer has a primary coil with 500 turns of wire, and a secondary coil with 50 turns. If the input voltage is 120 V, what is the output voltage?

Math Skill: Ratios and Proportions

You may want to read more about this **Math Skill** in the **Skills and Reference Handbook** at the end of your textbook.

1. **Read and Understand**
   What information are you given?
   Input Voltage = 120 V
   Primary Coil: 500 turns
   Secondary Coil: 50 turns

2. **Plan and Solve**
   What unknown are you trying to calculate?
   Output Voltage = ?

   What formula contains the given quantities and the unknown?
   $$\frac{\text{Secondary Coil turns}}{\text{Primary Coil turns}} = \frac{\text{Output Voltage}}{\text{Input Voltage}}$$

   Replace each variable with its known value.
   $$\frac{50 \text{ turns}}{500 \text{ turns}} = \frac{\text{Output Voltage}}{120 \text{ V}}$$

   $$\text{Output Voltage} = \frac{50 \text{ turns}}{500 \text{ turns}} \times 120 \text{ V} = 12 \text{ V}$$

3. **Look Back and Check**
   Is your answer reasonable?
   The ratio of secondary to primary turns is 1 : 10. 12 V is one tenth of 120 V, so the answer is reasonable.

Math Practice

On a separate sheet of paper, solve the following problems.

1. What is the ratio of turns for the secondary to primary coils in a step-down transformer, if the input voltage from a substation is 7200 V, and the output voltage to a home is 240 V?
   $\frac{240 \text{ V}}{7200 \text{ V}} = 0.033$. The ratio of the secondary to primary turns is 1 : 30.

2. The input voltage from a generating plant to a transformer is 11,000 V. If the output voltage from the transformer to high-voltage transmission lines is 240,000 V, what is the ratio of secondary to primary turns in this step-up transformer?
   $\frac{240,000 \text{ V}}{11,000 \text{ V}} = 21.8$. The ratio of turns in the secondary to primary coils is about 22 : 1.

3. A step-down transformer has 200 turns of wire in its primary coil. How many turns are in the secondary coil if the input voltage is 120 V, and the output voltage is 6 V?
   $(6 \text{ V}/120 \text{ V}) \times 200 \text{ turns} = 10 \text{ turns}$

196 *Physical Science Guided Reading and Study Workbook • Chapter 21*

Student Edition Lab Worksheet

Name _____ Class _____ Date _____

Chapter 21   Magnetism

Application Lab

Investigating an Electric Generator

See pages 648 and 649 in the Teacher's Edition for more information.

All generators have two main parts—a magnet and a wire that is wrapped into a coil. The arrangement of these parts varies, depending on the size and power of the generator and whether it produces direct or alternating current. In this lab, you will determine how several variables affect the current produced by a simple generator.

Problem How do the direction in which the magnet moves and the number and direction of the turns in the coil affect the current that a generator produces?

Materials
- cardboard tube
- 5-m length of insulated wire
- metric ruler
- multimeter
- bar magnet
- graph paper

Skills Observing, Using Graphs

Procedure
Part A: Changing the Number of Turns
1. Slip the wire between your hand and the tube so that 15 cm of wire extends from the tube. Use your other hand to wrap the long end of the wire around the tube 10 times in a clockwise direction, as shown in Figure 1. Make sure all the turns are within 10 cm of the end of the tube. **CAUTION:** *Be careful not to cut yourself on the sharp ends of the wire.*

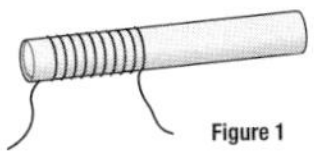

Figure 1

2. Connect both ends of the wire to the multimeter. Set the multimeter to measure current.
3. Hold the bar magnet by its south pole. Observe the multimeter as you quickly insert the bar magnet into the open end of the cardboard tube that is wrapped with the wire coil. Repeat this step if necessary as you adjust the scale of the multimeter. Record the maximum current in the data table.

DATA TABLE

Number of Turns	Direction of Turns	Pole Inserted	Current (mA)
10	Clockwise	North	
20	Clockwise	North	
30	Clockwise	North	
30	Clockwise	South	
30	Counterclockwise	South	

Student Edition Lab Worksheet

Name _____ Class _____ Date _____

4. Disconnect the multimeter from the end of the wire that is farther from the turns.
5. **Predicting** Record your prediction of how increasing the number of turns in the coil will affect the current.

   Sample prediction: Increasing the number of turns increases the current.
   _____
   _____

6. To test your prediction, wrap the wire around the end of the tube 10 more times in the same direction that you wound it previously—clockwise. You should now have a total of 20 turns. Reconnect the wire to the multimeter.
7. Repeat Step 3.
8. Again, disconnect the multimeter from the same end of the wire. Wrap the wire clockwise around the tube 10 more times for a total of 30 turns. Reconnect the wire to the multimeter.
9. Repeat Step 3 and then disconnect the multimeter from the same end of the wire.

Part B: Changing Other Properties of the Generator
10. **Predicting** Record your prediction of how reversing the direction of the magnet will affect the current.

    Sample prediction: Reversing the direction of the magnet will reverse the direction of the current.
    _____
    _____

11. To test your prediction, reconnect the wire to the multimeter exactly as you did before. Repeat Step 3, but this time, hold the magnet by its north pole.
12. **Predicting** Record your prediction of how reversing the direction of the turns in the coil will affect the current if you hold the magnet by its south pole.

    Sample prediction: Reversing the direction of the turns will reverse the direction of the current.
    _____
    _____

13. To test your prediction, remove the wire from the tube. Now wrap 30 turns of wire in the opposite direction— counterclockwise.
14. Repeat Step 3, holding the magnet by its south pole.
15. Construct a graph using the data from the first three rows in the data table. Plot the number of turns on the horizontal axis and the current on the vertical axis.

Student Edition Lab Worksheet

Name _____ Class _____ Date _____

Analyze and Conclude
1. **Inferring** What caused a current in the wire?

   A current flowed in the wire because the moving magnetic field exerted a force on the electrons
   in the wire, causing them to move.
   _____
   _____

2. **Using Graphs** Based on your graph, what is the relationship between the number of turns and the amount of current?

   The graph indicates that the number of turns are in direct proportion to the amount of current.
   _____
   _____
   _____

3. **Analyzing Data** Explain the effect that reversing the direction of the magnet or the direction of the turns had on the direction of the current.

   Reversing the direction of the magnet or the turns reversed the direction of the force of the
   magnetic field on the electrons in the wire. This change in direction caused the charges to move
   in the opposite direction.
   _____
   _____

4. **Predicting** Explain whether a generator could be built with a stationary magnet and a coil that moved.

   Yes, it is possible for such a generator to be built. It is only necessary that the magnetic field
   in the wire coils change. It does not matter which part moves to accomplish this task.
   _____
   _____
   _____
   _____
   _____

Student Edition Lab Worksheet

Name _____ Class _____ Date _____

5. **Evaluating and Revising** Did your observations support your predictions? If not, evaluate any flaws in the reasoning you used to make the predictions.

   Correct predictions should state that an increase in the number of turns in the coil increases
   the strength of the current, and that reversing the direction of the turns or the magnet will
   reverse the direction of the current. Errors in reasoning may involve assuming that the
   direction of the coil or magnet motion does not affect current direction. If a current is too
   weak to observe, students may fail to realize that the speed of the magnet's motion may
   account for a weak induced current, and that increasing the number of turns may not provide
   the right results if the change in the magnetic field is not kept fairly constant throughout the
   experiment.
   _____
   _____
   _____
   _____
   _____
   _____
   _____
   _____
   _____
   _____

Lab Manual

Name _____ Class _____ Date _____

Chapter 21 Magnetism   Investigation 21A

Studying Electromagnetic Induction

Background Information Refer students to pages 642 and 643 in their textbook for a general discussion of electromagnetic induction. **TIME REQUIRED:** 40 minutes

In 1831, Michael Faraday discovered that when a coil of wire is moved in a magnetic field, an electric current is generated, or induced, in the wire. This process is called electromagnetic induction. A current is generated only if the wire is part of a circuit. The current is induced because in the frame of reference of the wire, the magnetic field is changing.

In this investigation, you will move a bar magnet through a coil of wire to induce a current. You will use a simple galvanometer (a second coil of wire wrapped around a compass) to detect the induced current. In this galvanometer, the compass needle responds to the magnetic field produced by the induced current.

Problem

How can you measure an electric current in a a wire using a magnetic compass?

Pre-Lab Discussion

Read the entire investigation. Then, work with a partner to answer the following questions.

1. **Inferring** Why does a compass needle move?

   A compass needle moves so that it aligns with a magnetic field. If the magnetic field changes,
   the compass needle moves to realign.

2. **Inferring** Why does a moving magnet produce a changing magnetic field?

   The field lines of a stationary magnet are also stationary. Therefore, at any one point, the magnetic
   field is constant. But if the magnet moves, then at any one point, the magnetic field can change as
   a stronger or weaker part of the field crosses that point.

3. **Predicting** What will happen when the number of turns in the coil in the 3-m wire is increased? Explain your answer.

   Students may predict that the current will increase. If the current increases, then this should cause
   a greater deflection in the compass needle because a stronger current produces a stronger
   magnetic field.

Lab Manual

Name _____ Class _____ Date _____

4. **Predicting** What will happen when the magnet is moved back and forth inside the coil? Explain your answer.

   The current will move first in one direction and then the other because the force on the electrons in
   the wire is changing direction. Students may not realize this is an alternating current.

Materials *(per group)*

connecting wire with bare ends, 1 m in length
connecting wire with bare ends, 3 m in length
magnetic compass
bar magnet

Safety 🔲

Use caution when connecting wires. Note all safety alert symbols next to the steps in the Procedure and review the meaning of each symbol by referring to the Safety Symbols on page xiii.

Procedure

1. Using a piece of wire 1 m long, wrap a coil with 20 turns of wire around the compass, as shown in Figure 1.

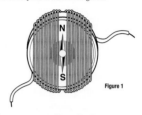

Figure 1

2. Place the compass on a table or other flat surface. Rotate the compass to align the compass needle with the wire.

3. In the middle of the 3-m length of wire, wind a coil with ten turns of wire around your finger. The coil should be large enough for the bar magnet to fit through.

🔲 4. Connect the two coils of wire by twisting the bare ends of the wires together, as shown in Figure 2. **CAUTION:** *Be careful when handling the sharp ends of wires; they can puncture skin.* The second coil should be at least 1 m away from the compass so that the magnet does not directly affect the compass needle. Hold the compass in a horizontal position so the needle moves freely.

Lab Manual

Name _____ Class _____ Date _____

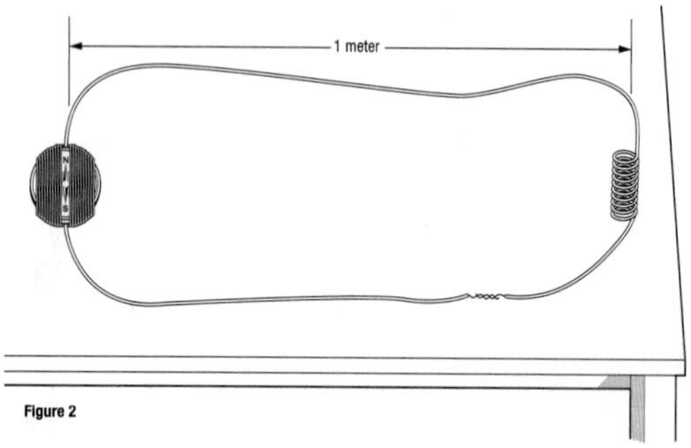

Figure 2

5. Slowly push the north pole of the bar magnet into the coil of wire. Have a partner observe what happens to the compass needle. Record your observations in the data table.

6. Have your partner observe what happens to the compass needle as you slowly pull the magnet out of the coil of wire. Record your observations in the data table.

7. Add ten more loops of wire to the coil in the 3-m wire. Then, repeat Steps 5 and 6.

8. Repeat Steps 5 and 6, but this time make the south pole of the magnet the leading edge.

9. Repeat Steps 5 and 6, but this time move the magnet quickly instead of slowly.

10. Try pushing and pulling the magnet continuously into and out of the coil. Record your observations in the data table.

Lab Manual

Name _____ Class _____ Date _____

Observations

Note that the actual directions (clockwise or counterclockwise) that students record will depend on the direction in which they wind the turns of the coil that surrounds the compass.

DATA TABLE

How Magnet Is Moved	Pole (N or S) at Leading Edge of Magnet	Number of Turns in Coil	Observations of Compass Needle
Push inward slowly	North	10	Compass needle deflects and then returns to its original position.
Pull outward slowly	North	10	Compass needle deflects in opposite direction.
Push inward slowly	North	20	Compass needle deflects by a greater amount.
Pull outward slowly	North	20	Compass needle deflects by a greater amount in opposite direction.
Push inward slowly	South	20	The deflection is reversed by using the opposite pole.
Pull outward slowly	South	20	The deflection is reversed by using the opposite pole.
Push inward quickly	South	20	The deflection is even greater.
Pull outward quickly	South	20	The deflection is even greater in the opposite direction.
Push and pull continuously	South	20	The compass needle vibrates back and forth.

Analysis and Conclusions

1. **Observing** Explain what you observed happening when you moved a magnet in a coil of wire.

   When the magnet was moved into or out of the coil of wire, the wire crossed magnetic field lines
   surrounding the magnet. This changing magnetic field caused an electric current to be induced in
   the wire, as shown by the deflection of the compass needle.

Lab Manual

Name _____ Class _____ Date _____

2. Drawing Conclusions How does the number of turns in the coil affect the current in the wire?

The more turns in the coil there are, the greater is the current in the wire.

_____

_____

3. Drawing Conclusions How did changing the pole of the magnet affect the direction of the current in the wire? How can you tell?

Changing the pole of the magnet reversed the direction of the current. The compass needle was

deflected in the opposite direction.

_____

_____

4. Predicting Would a current be induced in the wire if you did not move the magnet? Why or why not?

No, because the magnetic field lines would not be crossed if there was no motion.

_____

_____

5. Predicting Would a current be induced if you moved the coil of wire instead of the magnet? Why or why not?

Yes, because the magnetic field lines are crossed if either the magnet or the wire is moved.

_____

_____

6. Inferring What kind of current was induced in Step 10? Explain your answer.

An alternating current was induced. The compass needle continually reversed because the direction

of current continuously reversed.

_____

_____

Go Further

What do you think would happen if you made a coil of wire by first winding ten turns of wire in one direction and then winding ten turns in the opposite direction? Try it and find out.

The current may start but then suddenly stop. Depending on how the coil is wound, the magnet may move into the first part of the coil and induce a current. As soon as it is moving through both coils, however, there will be no current because the effects from the two coils will cancel.

Physical Science Lab Manual • Investigation 21A **225**

Lab Manual

Name _____ Class _____ Date _____

Chapter 21   Magnetism

Investigation 21B

Making a Compass

Refer students to pages 630–633 in their textbook for a discussion of magnet fields and magnetic materials. **SKILLS FOCUS:** Predicting, Observing, Inferring **CLASS TIME:** 25 minutes

Background Information

A compass is basically a floating magnet used to find directions. It responds to the magnetic poles of Earth. The north-seeking pole of the floating magnet points in the northern direction and is therefore called the north pole of the compass. The south-seeking pole of the floating magnet points in the southern direction and is therefore called the south pole of the compass.

The Earth's magnetic pole in the northern hemisphere is located in the Hudson Bay region of northern Canada, nearly 1800 km from the geographical North Pole. The magnetic pole in the southern hemisphere is south of Australia.

In this investigation, you will use a permanent magnet and a needle to make a floating compass. You will then test your compass by comparing it to a standard compass.

Problem

How accurate is a classroom compass that you make?

Pre-Lab Discussion

Read the entire investigation. Then, work with a partner to answer the following questions.

1. Predicting What do you expect to happen when you hold the north pole of a bar magnet near a compass needle?

The south pole of the compass needle will be attracted to the north pole of the magnet.

_____

2. Predicting In what direction do you expect the magnetized needle to point when you magnetize it with the south pole of the bar magnet? Explain your answer.

Students may predict that the needle will point north. The south pole of the bar magnet aligns

the atoms in the needle so that the tip of the needle closest to the magnet becomes a north

magnetic pole.

3. Designing Experiments Why is it important to stroke the needle with the magnet in only one direction?

By stroking in only one direction, the atoms in the needle will magnetically align in one direction.

In this way, the needle becomes magnetized.

_____

Physical Science Lab Manual • Investigation 21B **227**

Lab Manual

Name _____ Class _____ Date _____

4. Applying Concepts How do the properties of magnets make it possible to use compasses?

The poles of a magnet are attracted to the opposite magnetic poles of Earth. Because the

geographical positions of Earth's magnetic poles are known, magnets can be used in compasses

to determine direction.

_____

_____

_____

_____

5. Applying Concepts Why might the use of a compass mislead you if you were seeking geographic north?

Earth's magnetic poles are not at the geographic poles. If a compass is to be used to find

geographic north or south, an angle between the magnetic poles and the geographic poles must

be taken into account.

_____

_____

Materials *(per group)*

magnetic compass
permanent bar magnet
file
cork strip or disk, 3 cm in length or diameter
grease pencil
petri dish or other shallow dish
2 needles

Safety 🔲 🔲 🔲

Be careful to avoid breakage when working with glassware. Be careful when handling sharp instruments. Note all safety alert symbols next to the steps in the Procedure and review the meaning of each symbol by referring to the Safety Symbols on page xiii.

Procedure

🔲 1. Use the grease pencil to label one point on the side of a petri dish with the letter *N*. Label the point on the opposite side *S*. Label with an *E* the point that is to the right when the *S* is closest to you. Label with a *W* the point that is on the left of *S*. Make an intermediate marking at each of the four positions midway between the pairs of letters.

228 *Physical Science* Lab Manual • Investigation 21B

Lab Manual

Name _____ Class _____ Date _____

2. Obtain a bar magnet. If its north and south poles are not marked (with an *N* and an *S*), place one end near the north-pointing end of a magnetic compass. If the compass needle is deflected, the end of the bar magnet is its north pole. If the compass needle is attracted, the end of the bar magnet is its south pole.

🔲 3. Use the file to make a straight, shallow groove lengthwise on the cork strip or disk. **CAUTION:** *Be careful when handling sharp instruments.*

🔲 4. Hold the needle at its eye end (the end with the opening in it). Stroke the needle at least ten times along the south pole of the bar magnet. The strokes should all be in the same direction and should all start near the eye end of the needle. Do not use a back-and-forth motion. Instead, lift the needle each time you bring it back to its starting position for the next stroke.

5. Move the bar magnet at least a meter from where you are working so that it will not interfere with your observations.

6. Fill the labeled petri dish halfway with water. Float the cork groove side up in the water so that it floats freely.

7. Lay the stroked needle inside the groove in the cork. Observe what happens. Rotate the cork by 90° in either direction. Again, observe what happens.

8. Repeat Steps 4 through 7, using a different needle and stroking the needle along the bar magnet's north pole. You must stroke the new needle in exactly the same direction as in Step 4.

   If the needle is stroked by accident in the opposite direction, the opposite pole is produced.

9. To check the accuracy of your floating compass, compare its orientation with that of the standard magnetic compass. Turn the dish so that the *N* and *S* markings you made are oriented like those on the standard compass.

Observations

1. What happened when you floated the cork with the needle that was stroked along the magnet's south pole? What happened when you tried to turn the cork in other directions?

The needle and cork turned so that the tip of the needle pointed north. The cork returned to this

orientation after it was turned.

_____

_____

2. What happened when you floated the cork with the needle that was stroked along the magnet's north pole? What happened when you tried to turn the cork in other directions?

The needle and cork turned so that the tip of the needle pointed south. The cork returned to this

orientation after it was turned.

_____

Physical Science Lab Manual • Investigation 21B **229**

Lab Manual

Name _____ Class _____ Date _____

Analysis and Conclusions

1. **Observing** Which needle for the floating compass lined up in the same way as the needle of a standard magnetic compass?

The needle stroked by the south pole of the bar magnet lined up the same way.

_____

_____

_____

2. **Inferring** How could you use your floating compass to find east? To find southwest?

When the dish is turned so that the north pole of the needle points toward the *N* marked on the dish,

east will be directly to the right, and southwest will be in the direction of the mark between the *W*

and *S* markings.

_____

_____

_____

3. **Inferring** What does the magnetic polarity of your compass tell about the polarity of Earth's magnetic poles?

Earth's magnetic poles are opposite their geographical locations. Because the north magnetic pole

of the compass points north, the Earth's magnetic pole near geographical north must be a south

magnetic pole. Similarly, the pole near Earth's south geographical pole is a north magnetic pole.

_____

_____

_____

Go Further

Try to improve on the design of your compass. For example, you can find ways to reduce friction in the compass so that the needle aligns with Earth's magnetic field more easily. Think of other designs that do not require the use of liquid in a petri dish. Write a description of your improved design. When your teacher has approved your design, carry it out and test it, using all necessary safety procedures. Report your observations and conclusions.

Review student designs for appropriateness and difficulty before students begin testing. Suggestions that can help students are to reduce surface contact between the water and the needle, the use of less viscous fluids in the petri dish, or eliminating fluid resistance by devising ways of suspending a magnet in air.

Chapter Test A

Name _____ Class _____ Date _____

Chapter 21   Magnetism   **Chapter Test A**

Multiple Choice

Write the letter that best answers the question or completes the statement on the line provided.

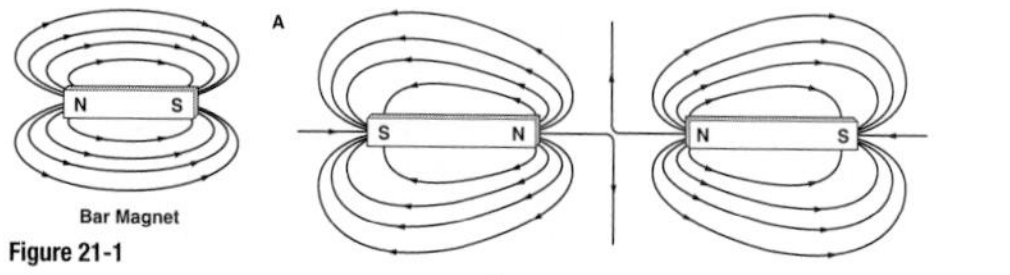

Bar Magnet

Figure 21-1

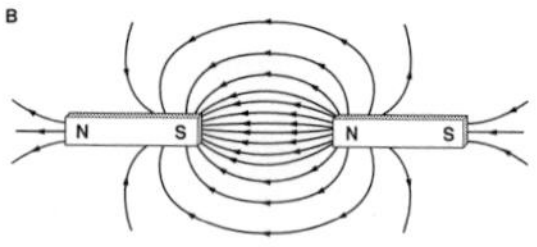

_____ 1. In Figure 21-1, what magnetic poles are shown on the two bar magnets in A and B?
   a. A: north and south; B: both north
   b. A: both south; B: both north
   c. A: both north; B: both south
   d. A: north and south; B: both south

_____ 2. Which statement describes magnetic field lines at the north pole and south pole of a bar magnet?
   a. Field lines begin near the magnet's south pole and extend toward its north pole.
   b. Field lines begin near both the magnet's north and south poles and meet in the middle.
   c. Field lines begin near the center of the magnet and extend toward the north and south poles.
   d. Field lines begin near the magnet's north pole and extend toward its south pole.

_____ 3. Which of the following statements is true about Earth's magnetic poles?
   a. They are located at Earth's geographic poles.
   b. They are the areas where Earth's magnetic field is weakest.
   c. They are the areas where Earth's magnetic field is strongest.
   d. Earth has four magnetic poles.

Chapter Test A

Name _____ Class _____ Date _____

_____ 4. Which of the following statements is true about ferromagnetic materials?
   a. All ferromagnetic materials are permanent magnets.
   b. Ferromagnetic materials that are permanent magnets have domains that are randomly oriented.
   c. Ferromagnetic materials that are permanent magnets have domains that remain aligned for long periods of time.
   d. Ferromagnetic materials do not have domains and cannot be magnetized.

_____ 5. How can a permanent magnet be demagnetized?
   a. Cut the magnet in half.
   b. Heat the magnet up.
   c. Strike the magnet with a heavy blow.
   d. both b and c

_____ 6. If the current in a wire is directed upward, what is the direction of the magnetic field produced by the current?
   a. counterclockwise in the horizontal plane
   b. clockwise in the horizontal plane
   c. in the same direction as the current
   d. in the opposite direction to the current

_____ 7. Which of the following statements is true about a current-carrying wire in a magnetic field?
   a. Reversing the current direction will cause the force deflecting the wire to be parallel to the magnetic field.
   b. Reversing the current direction will cause the force deflecting the wire to be perpendicular to the magnetic field but in the opposite direction.
   c. Reversing the current direction will cause the force deflecting the wire to be parallel to the velocity of the charge.
   d. Reversing the current direction will not affect the force deflecting the wire.

_____ 8. The electromagnet in a galvanometer
   a. increases the voltage in a circuit.
   b. moves a pointer along a numbered scale in response to a current.
   c. induces an electric current.
   d. increases the current in a circuit.

Chapter Test A

Name _____ Class _____ Date _____

_____ 9. In an electric motor, periodically changing the direction
of current in the electromagnet can cause the axle to
spin because
  a. the electromagnet loses its magnetism.
  b. mechanical energy is converted to electric energy.
  c. the moving electrons push the electromagnet in the
opposite direction.
  d. the magnetic field reverses direction.

_____ 10. How can the voltage in a coil of wire be increased in the
process of electromagnetic induction?
  a. Move the magnet inside the coil of wire more slowly.
  b. Hold the magnet stationary.
  c. Move the coil of wire slowly, and keep the magnet
stationary.
  d. Move the magnet inside the coil of wire more rapidly.

_____ 11. A DC generator is similar to an AC generator except that in
  a. DC generators, slip rings produce direct current.
  b. DC generators, commutators produce direct current.
  c. AC generators, commutators produce alternating current.
  d. AC generators, no commutators or slip rings are used.

_____ 12. A transformer has a primary coil with 500 turns and a
secondary coil with 250 turns. If the output voltage is 240
volts, what is the input voltage?
  a. 96 volts   **b.** 120 volts   **c.** 480 volts   **d.** 500 volts

_____ 13. If a step-up transformer has a primary coil with 10 turns,
how many turns would be required in the secondary coil in
order to increase the voltage from 60 volts to 120 volts?
  a. 5 turns   **b.** 20 turns
  c. 60 turns   **d.** 120 turns

_____ 14. How are step-up transformers used in the transmission of
electrical energy?
  a. They increase the voltage and the current for a home.
  b. They decrease the voltage before it leaves a power plant.
  c. They increase the voltage for efficient long-distance
transmission.
  d. all of the above

_____ 15. How are fossil fuels used to generate electrical energy?
  a. Heat from burning fuel spins magnets inside an electric
motor.
  b. Heat from burning fuel creates steam that spins a turbine.
  c. Heat from burning fuel causes an electric motor to
produce a current.
  d. Heat from burning fuel creates steam that turns a
transformer.

Chapter Test A

Name _____ Class _____ Date _____

Completion
Complete each statement on the line provided.

1. The region where a magnet's force is strongest is at the
_____.

2. The magnetic field lines of a bar magnet begin near the magnet's
_____.

3. The angle between the direction a compass points and geographic
north is called _____.

4. Transformers only work with _____ current.

5. The energy source used to produce most of the electrical energy in
the United States is _____.

Short Answer
*In complete sentences, write the answers to the questions on
the lines provided.*

1. How does magnetic declination vary?
_____
_____
_____

2. Explain why Earth's magnetic North Pole would be a south pole
of a bar magnet.
_____
_____
_____
_____

3. How does a vibrating electric charge produce an electromagnetic
wave?
_____
_____
_____
_____
_____
_____

Chapter Test A

Name _____ Class _____ Date _____

4. How does a galvanometer use a magnetic field to indicate the
strength of an electric current?
_____
_____
_____
_____
_____
_____

5. Compare generators and electric motors.
_____
_____
_____
_____
_____

Using Science Skills
*Use the diagram to answer each question. Write the answers on a separate
sheet of paper.*

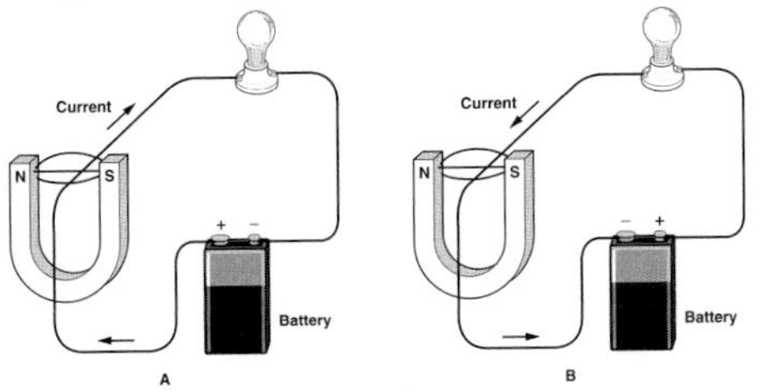

Figure 21-2

1. **Inferring** In Figure 21-2, in what direction do magnetic field lines
point in A in the area between the poles of the horseshoe magnet?

2. **Inferring** In Figure 21-2, will electrons in B be pushed in the same
direction as the wire is pushed or in the opposite direction?
Explain your answer.

3. **Using Models** Use Figure 21-2 to determine whether the current
flows toward the negative or positive connection on a battery.

Chapter Test A

Name _____ Class _____ Date _____

4. **Interpreting Graphics** In Figure 21-2, in what direction is the force
deflecting the wire in B?

5. **Interpreting Graphics** In Figure 21-2, in what direction is the force
deflecting the wire in A? How does this compare with the force
deflecting the wire in B?

Essay
Write the answers to each question on a separate sheet of paper.

1. Why does a compass point to the east or west of true north in
different locations?

2. What are solenoids and electromagnets, and how are they
constructed?

3. Describe two household devices that use electromagnets.

4. How does a transformer decrease the voltage that is transmitted
across power lines before it enters homes?

5. Explain how a step-up transformer is different from a step-down
transformer.

Chapter Test B

Name _____ Class _____ Date _____

Chapter 21   Magnetism   **Chapter Test B**

Multiple Choice

Write the letter that best answers the question or completes the statement on the line provided.

_____ 1. The force a magnet exerts on another magnet, on iron or a similar metal, or on moving charges is
  a. an electric force.
  b. a magnetic force.
  c. proportional to the charge of the magnet.
  d. proportional to the mass of the magnet.

_____ 2. Which of the following statements describes the interaction between magnetic poles?
  a. Like poles attract each other.
  b. Like poles repel each other, and opposite poles attract each other.
  c. Opposite poles repel each other.
  d. Like poles attract each other, and opposite poles repel each other.

_____ 3. How does the magnetic force exerted by a magnet change as the distance between two magnets increases?
  a. The magnetic force increases.
  b. The magnetic force stays the same.
  c. The magnetic force decreases.
  d. The magnetic force does not change with distance.

_____ 4. What is the name of the area surrounding Earth that is influenced by Earth's magnetic field?
  a. magnetosphere   b. atmosphere
  c. magnetic domain   d. magnetic declination

_____ 5. A region that has a large number of atoms whose magnetic fields are lined up parallel to a magnet's field is
  a. the magnetosphere.
  b. the magnetic declination.
  c. a magnetic domain.
  d. a ferromagnetic region.

_____ 6. A ferromagnetic material that has domains that remain aligned for a long period of time is called
  a. a neutral object.   b. nonmagnetic.
  c. a permanent magnet.   d. a temporary magnet.

_____ 7. What creates a magnetic field?
  a. charged particles that do not move
  b. moving electric charges
  c. gravity
  d. an isolated magnetic pole

Physical Science • Chapter 21 Test B   **213**

Chapter Test B

Name _____ Class _____ Date _____

_____ 8. If a current-carrying wire is in a magnetic field, in what direction will a force be exerted on the wire?
  a. perpendicular to the magnetic field and parallel to the current direction
  b. parallel to both the current direction and the magnetic field
  c. perpendicular to the current direction and parallel to the magnetic field
  d. perpendicular to both the magnetic field and the current direction

_____ 9. A coil of wire that is carrying a current and produces a magnetic field is
  a. a galvanometer.   b. a solenoid.
  c. a magnetic domain.   d. an electric motor.

_____ 10. Which of the following is the reason "soft" iron is used for the cores of electromagnets?
  a. It is difficult to magnetize.
  b. It is easily magnetized.
  c. It has no magnetic domains.
  d. It is a permanent magnet.

_____ 11. The device that measures current in a wire by using the deflections of an electromagnet in an external magnetic field is
  a. a galvanometer.   b. a solenoid.
  c. an electric motor.   d. a loudspeaker.

_____ 12. The process of generating an electric current by moving an electrical conductor relative to a magnetic field is called
  a. magnetization.
  b. electromagnetic force.
  c. electromagnetic induction.
  d. alternating current.

_____ 13. A device that changes mechanical energy to electric energy by rotating a coil of wire through a magnetic field is called a(an)
  a. transformer.   b. generator.
  c. electromagnet.   d. current meter.

_____ 14. The strength of the output voltage and current of a transformer are determined by the
  a. number of turns in the primary and secondary coils.
  b. strength of the DC current in the primary coil.
  c. ferromagnetic material of the rings connecting the coils.
  d. direction of the current in the primary coil.

214 *Physical Science* • Chapter 21 Test B

Chapter Test B

Name _____ Class _____ Date _____

_____ 15. Before electric current in power lines can be safe for your home, it must pass through a
  a. turbine.   b. step-down transformer.
  c. step-up transformer. d. generator.

Completion

Complete each statement on the line provided.

1. The region around a magnet that exerts magnetic force is called a(an) _____.

2. In most materials, the magnetic fields of _____ cancel their effects.

3. The _____ are caused by charged particles from the sun entering Earth's magnetic field.

4. In ferromagnetic materials, regions with large numbers of atoms with aligned magnetic fields are called _____.

5. A charged particle moving in a magnetic field will be deflected in a direction _____ to the magnetic field.

6. In a solenoid, there will be no magnetic field if there is no _____ in the wires of the coil.

7. Moving a magnet through a wire coil can produce a(an) _____ in the coil.

8. A(An) _____ converts mechanical energy into electric energy.

9. Large power plants in the United States currently use _____ generators.

10. _____ transformers decrease the current and increase the voltage in the output circuit.

Short Answer

In complete sentences, write the answers to the questions on the lines provided.

1. What are magnetic poles?

_____
_____
_____

2. In Figure 21-1, what do the lines around the bar magnets represent?

_____
_____
_____

Physical Science • Chapter 21 Test B   **215**

Chapter Test B

Name _____ Class _____ Date _____

3. What is a generator and how does it work?

_____
_____

4. List five energy sources that are used in the United States to produce electrical energy.

_____
_____
_____

5. How is water used to produce electric energy in a hydroelectric power plant?

_____
_____

Using Science Skills

Use the diagram to answer each question. Write the answers on a separate sheet of paper.

1. **Interpreting Graphics** In Figure 21-1, use the direction of the magnetic field lines to determine what type of magnetic pole is located at the magnetic South Pole.

2. **Predicting** Use Figure 21-1 to predict where Earth's magnetic field is strongest. Explain your answer.

3. **Inferring** Use Figure 21-1 to determine in what direction the north magnetic pole of the compass will point. What type of magnetic pole is the compass pointing toward?

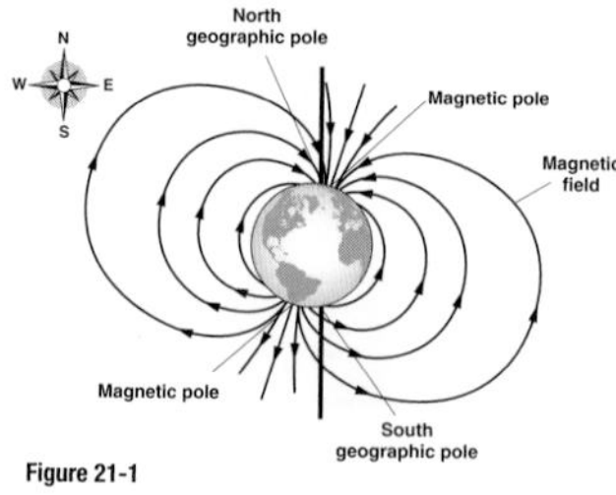

4. **Applying Skills** A scientist studying Earth's magnetic field found that at Hot Springs, Arkansas, her compass pointed 5° east of true north. In Durango, Colorado, she took another reading and found that her compass pointed 14° east of true north. Use Figure 21-1 to explain why the two readings were different.

5. **Interpreting Graphics** In Figure 21-1, where is the magnetic field the weakest?

Figure 21-1

(Diagram labels: North geographic pole, Magnetic pole, Magnetic field, Magnetic pole, South geographic pole, N W E S)

216 *Physical Science* • Chapter 21 Test B

Chapter 21 Test A Answers

Multiple Choice

1. a   **2.** d   **3.** c   **4.** c   **5.** a   **6.** a
7. b   **8.** b   **9.** d   **10.** d   **11.** b   **12.** c
13. b   **14.** c   **15.** b

Completion

1. magnetic poles; poles **2.** north pole **3.** magnetic declination
4. alternating **5.** coal

Short Answer

1. Magnetic declination varies with your location on Earth.
2. Opposite poles of magnets will attract each other, so the magnetic North Pole must be a south pole because it attracts the north pole of a compass needle. **3.** A vibrating electric charge induces a changing magnet field, which induces a changing electric field. The changing electric and magnetic fields regenerate each other, producing an electromagnetic wave. **4.** An electromagnet on a spring is placed between the poles of a permanent magnet. When there is current in the coil, the resulting magnetic field lines up with the field of the permanent magnet and indicates the strength of the current by deflecting a needle on a dial. **5.** Generators convert mechanical energy into electrical energy, while electric motors convert electrical energy into mechanical energy.

Using Science Skills

1. The magnetic field lines point from the north pole to the south pole. **2.** The same direction; the direction of current associated with the electron flow is the same as the direction of the current in the wire. **3.** The current always flows from the positive connection toward the negative connection on a battery. **4.** The force is perpendicular to the direction of the current, in an upward direction. **5.** The force is perpendicular to the direction of the current, in a downward direction. The force is in the opposite direction as it would be on the wire in B.

Essay

1. The magnetic poles of Earth are not at the same position as the geographic poles. A compass will point along field lines towards the magnetic poles, not the geographic poles. Therefore, the compass direction will vary depending on where you are. The angle between the direction to geographic north and the direction a compass points is called the magnetic declination. **2.** A solenoid is a coil of current-carrying wire that produces a magnetic field. A solenoid can be constructed by coiling a length of wire, then connecting either end to a battery. An electromagnet is a solenoid with a core of ferromagnetic material, such as an iron bar. To build an electromagnet, wrap wire around a nail and connect the ends of the wire to a battery or other source of electric current. **3.** With an electromagnet, the magnetic field can be turned on and off, which can control a diaphragm to make sounds in a loudspeaker (for example, in a telephone). The strength and direction of the magnetic field can be controlled by modifying the current. This can be used to control the speed with which a motor operates in a device such as a fan. **4.** A step-down transformer is used, which has a primary coil with a large number of turns and a secondary coil with fewer turns, so the ratio of the number of secondary coil turns to the primary coil turns is the same as the ratio of the output voltage to the input voltage. This will decrease the voltage.

5. A step-up transformer increases voltage and decreases current. A step-up transformer has a primary coil with fewer turns than in the secondary coil. A step-down transformer increases current and decreases voltage. A step-down transformer has a primary coil with more turns than the secondary coil has.

Chapter 21 Test B Answers

Multiple Choice

1. b   **2.** b   **3.** c   **4.** a   **5.** c   **6.** c
7. b   **8.** d   **9.** b   **10.** b   **11.** a   **12.** c
13. b   **14.** a   **15.** b

Completion

1. magnetic field **2.** electrons; unpaired electrons **3.** aurora
4. magnetic domains; domains **5.** perpendicular; at right angles
6. current **7.** electric current; current; voltage **8.** generator **9.** AC; alternating current **10.** Step-up

Short Answer

1. areas of a magnet where the magnetic force is strongest **2.** The force will be very weak. **3.** a generator is a device that induces an electric current by rotating a coil of wire in a magnetic field.
4. Accept any five of the following: coal, oil, natural gas, hydroelectric, nuclear, wind, solar. **5.** Falling water pushes the blades of a turbine, which turns the axle of a generator or spins magnets around coils of wire.

Using Science Skills

1. The magnetic pole near the magnetic South Pole is a north magnetic pole. **2.** Earth's magnetic field is strongest at the magnetic North Pole and at the magnetic South Pole. The field lines are closest together in these regions. **3.** The north pole of a compass will point along Earth's magnetic field lines in the general direction of the magnetic pole near the geographic North Pole. This pole is a south magnetic pole. **4.** The difference in the angle between the direction toward true north and the direction toward the magnetic pole is called magnetic declination. It varied because the two readings were taken in different locations. **5.** midway between the poles, and far from Earth's surface.

Name _____ Class _____ Date _____

Unit 2   Physics   Unit Test A

Multiple Choice

Write the letter that best answers the question or completes the statement on the line provided.

_____ 1. Which distance can be most accurately measured with a ruler?
a. the length of a river
b. the width of a book
c. the distance between two cities
d. the size of an object under a microscope

_____ 2. A horizontal line on a distance-time graph means the object is
a. moving at a constant speed.
b. moving faster.
c. slowing down.
d. at rest.

_____ 3. A train approaching a crossing changes speed from 25 m/s to 10 m/s in 240 s. How can the train's acceleration be described?
a. The train's acceleration is positive.
b. The train is not accelerating.
c. The train will come to rest in 6 minutes.
d. The train's acceleration is negative.

_____ 4. As you push a cereal box across a tabletop, the sliding friction acting on the cereal box
a. acts in the direction of motion.
b. equals the weight of the box.
c. is usually greater than static friction.
d. acts in the direction opposite of motion.

_____ 5. The acceleration due to gravity on the surface of Mars is about one-third the acceleration due to gravity on Earth's surface. The weight of a space probe on the surface of Mars is about
a. nine times greater than its weight on Earth's surface.
b. three times greater than its weight on Earth's surface.
c. one-third its weight on Earth's surface.
d. the same as its weight on Earth's surface.

_____ 6. The centripetal force acting on a satellite in orbit
a. acts as an unbalanced force on the satellite.
b. changes the direction of the satellite.
c. is a center-directed force.
d. all of the above

Name _____ Class _____ Date _____

_____ 7. If the air inside a balloon exerts a force of 1 N on an area of 0.5 m2, what is the pressure inside the balloon?
a. 0.5 N/m^2 b. 1 N/m^2 c. 1.5 N/m^2 d. 2 N/m^2

_____ 8. Where will the greatest increase in pressure occur if you squeeze the middle of an upright, closed soft-drink bottle?
a. The greatest increase in pressure will occur at the top of the bottle.
b. The greatest increase in pressure will occur in the middle of the bottle.
c. The greatest increase in pressure will occur on the bottom of the bottle.
d. The pressure will increase equally everywhere within the bottle.

_____ 9. The buoyant force on an object in a fluid is equal to the weight of the
a. fluid.
b. fluid surrounding the object.
c. fluid displaced by the object.
d. object.

_____ 10. If you exert a force of 500 N to walk 4 m up a flight of stairs in 4 s, how much power do you use?
a. 31 W   b. 500 W   c. 2000 W   d. 8000 W

_____ 11. Which of the following statements is true?
a. To increase power, you can decrease the amount of work you do in a given amount of time, or you can do a given amount of work in less time.
b. To increase power, you can decrease the amount of work you do in a given amount of time, or you can do a given amount of work in more time.
c. To increase power, you can increase the amount of work you do in a given amount of time, or you can do a given amount of work in less time.
d. To increase power, you can increase the amount of work you do in a given amount of time, or you can do a given amount of work in more time.

_____ 12. Which of the following is an example of a wheel and axle?
a. a doorknob
b. an automobile steering wheel
c. a jar lid
d. a pencil

_____ 13. A small 30-kilogram canoe is floating downriver at a speed of 2 m/s. What is the canoe's kinetic energy?
a. 32 J   b. 60 J   c. 120 J   d. 900 J

Name _____ Class _____ Date _____

_____ 14. Walking converts what type of energy into mechanical energy?
a. chemical   b. electromagnetic
c. nuclear   d. thermal

_____ 15. The kinetic energy of the pendulum bob in Figure 15-1 increases the most between locations
a. A and B.   b. A and C.
c. B and D.   d. C and D.

_____ 16. Thermal energy depends on an object's
a. mass.
b. phase (sold, liquid, or gas).
c. temperature.
d. all of the above

_____ 17. According to the first law of thermodynamics, the amount of work done by a heat engine equals the amount of
a. work done on the engine.
b. waste heat it produces.
c. thermal energy added to the engine minus the waste heat.
d. thermal energy added to the engine plus the waste heat.

_____ 18. Which of the following happens in a heat pump?
a. The compressor increases the pressure and temperature of the refrigerant.
b. The compressor blows cold refrigerant into the room.
c. The compressor absorbs heat from the refrigerant.
d. none of the above

_____ 19. A mechanical wave generally does NOT
a. move the medium from one place to another.
b. move through a medium.
c. move through solids.
d. disturb the medium.

_____ 20. A period is the length of time it takes for
a. a disturbance to start a wave.
b. two complete wavelengths to pass a fixed point.
c. a wave to travel the length of a rope.
d. one complete wavelength to pass a fixed point.

_____ 21. The formation of a standing wave requires
a. the traveling of a wave for a long distance.
b. constructive interference between two waves of slightly different frequencies.
c. that refraction and diffraction occur at the same time in a wave.
d. interference between incoming and reflected waves.

Name _____ Class _____ Date _____

_____ 22. Which of the following occurs as light travels farther from its source?
a. Far from the source, photons spread through a small area.
b. The intensity of light increases as photons move away from the source.
c. The source gives off less light as photons move away from it.
d. Farther from the source, photons spread over a larger area.

_____ 23. X-ray photographs show softer tissue
a. as invisible.
b. as dark, highly exposed areas.
c. the same as dense bones.
d. as bright white areas.

_____ 24. Which of the following is NOT true regarding neon lights?
a. Light is emitted as electrons move through a gas in a tube.
b. All neon lights are colored by the color of the tubing.
c. Neon lights may contain other gases, such as helium or krypton.
d. Each kind of gas produces its own distinctive color.

_____ 25. Why do plane mirrors and convex mirrors form only virtual images?
a. because they both cause light rays to spread out
b. because reflected rays appear to come from behind the mirror
c. because the focal point is in front of the mirror
d. because they both show a wide angle of view

_____ 26. Total internal reflection occurs when the angle of incidence
a. is zero.
b. is less than the critical angle.
c. exceeds the critical angle.
d. equals the angle of reflection.

_____ 27. Which of the following would reduce the resistance of a metal wire?
a. increasing its thickness
b. increasing its temperature
c. increasing its length
d. all of the above

_____ 28. A ground-fault circuit interrupter shuts down a circuit if it
a. melts.
b. senses an overload.
c. senses unequal currents.
d. senses moisture.

_____**29.** How can the voltage in a coil of wire be increased in the process of electromagnetic induction?
  a. Move the magnet inside the coil of wire more slowly.
  b. Hold the magnet stationary.
  c. Move the coil of wire slowly, and keep the magnet stationary.
  d. Move the magnet inside the coil of wire more rapidly.

_____**30.** A DC generator is similar to an AC generator except that in
  a. DC generators, slip rings produce direct current.
  b. DC generators, commutators produce direct current.
  c. AC generators, commutators produce alternating current.
  d. AC generators, no commutators or slip rings are used.

Completion

Complete each statement on the line provided.

1. A constant slope on a distance-time graph indicates _____ speed.

2. _____ is how fast a velocity is changing at a specific instant.

3. It usually takes more force to start an object sliding than it does to keep an object sliding because static friction is usually _____ than sliding friction.

4. The universal force that is most effective over the longest distances is _____.

5. The pressure exerted by a fluid at any given depth is exerted _____ in all directions.

6. As you climb a high mountain, the buoyant force exerted on you by the atmosphere _____.

7. As the thickness of a wedge of given length increases, its IMA _____.

8. A watch consists of a complex systems of gears. Each gear acts as a continuous _____.

9. Flat collector plates through which water flows are found in _____. solar energy systems.

10. Turning off unused lights or appliances is an example of energy _____.

11. If the temperature change of an aluminum nail is negative, thermal energy is transferred _____ the nail _____. the surroundings.

12. In a calorimeter, the increase in the thermal energy of the water and the decrease in the thermal energy of the sample are _____.

---

13. The crest of a transverse wave is most similar to a(an) _____ in a longitudinal wave.

14. Waves in a rope are transverse waves because the medium's vibration is _____ to the direction in which the wave travels.

15. An ultraviolet light wave has a wavelength of 300 nm and a frequency of 7.0×10^{14} Hz. The ultraviolet light is NOT traveling through a(an) _____.

16. In microwave cooking, the food is heated _____ in the areas near the surface of the food than in the center.

17. Nerve endings in the retina that are most sensitive to low-intensity light are called _____.

18. Communication devices use _____ circuits known as _____ to make them more portable, reliable, and affordable.

19. The angle between the direction a compass points and geographic north is called _____.

20. Transformers only work with _____ current.

Short Answer

In complete sentences, write the answers to the questions on the lines provided.

1. Which is the most suitable SI unit for expressing the speed of a race car?

2. A billiard ball with a momentum of 20 kg•m/s strikes a second ball at rest and comes to a complete stop. What is the change in momentum of the second ball?

3. Why does a partially inflated weather balloon expand as it rises?

4. Compare the effects of a fixed pulley and a movable pulley on the size and direction of the input force.

---

5. Explain how biomass energy depends on the sun.

6. What role do free electrons have in conduction in metals?

7. How could you compare the energy carried in two different longitudinal waves?

8. Why must a microscope slide be made of a transparent material like glass if the glass does not magnify the image?

9. What is the law of conservation of charge?

10. How does a vibrating electric charge produce an electromagnetic wave?

Using Science Skills

Use the diagram to answer each question. Write the answers on a separate sheet of paper.

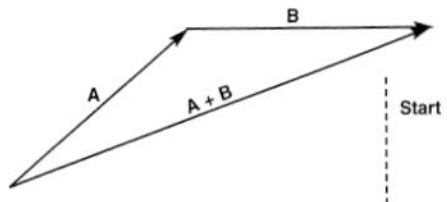

Figure 2-1A

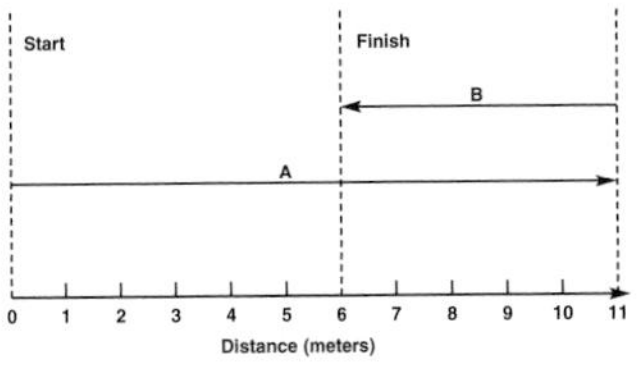

Figure 2-1B

1. **Interpreting Graphics** Figure 2-1 illustrates the displacement of an object moving in a plane. Explain what information is provided by arrows A and B.

2. **Comparing and Contrasting** In Figure 2-2, compare the size and direction of the momentums of both skaters immediately after the push shown at Time 2.

3. **Observing** How did the position of the spoon in Figure 2-3 change after the faucet was turned on?

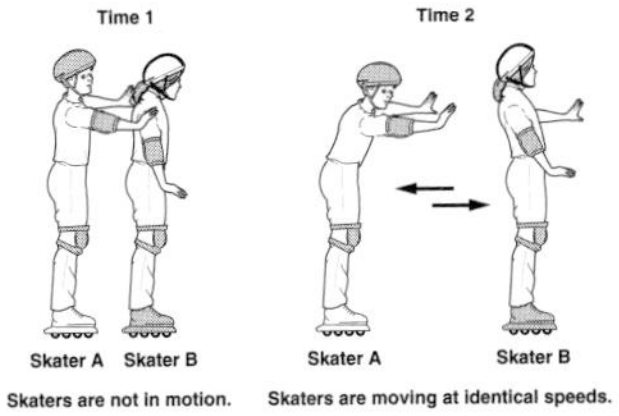

Figure 2-2

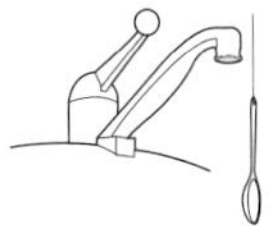

Figure 2-3A 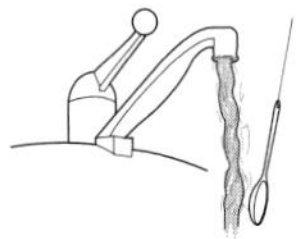   Figure 2-3B

Unit 2 Test A

Name _____ Class _____ Date _____

4. **Applying Concepts** Look at Figure 2-4. If Machine A moves through an input distance of 4.0 m, what is the output distance of Machine B?

5. **Inferring** In Figure 2-5, is the total mechanical energy of the ball conserved as the ball bounces? Explain your answer.

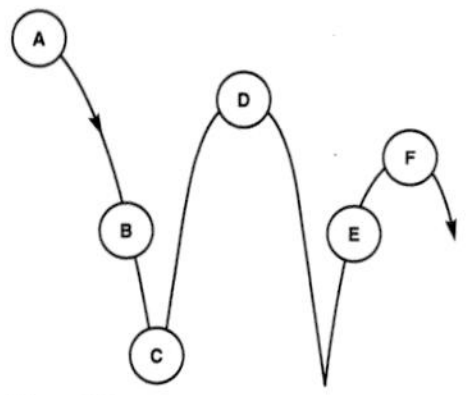

Machine B

Machine A

Figure 2-5

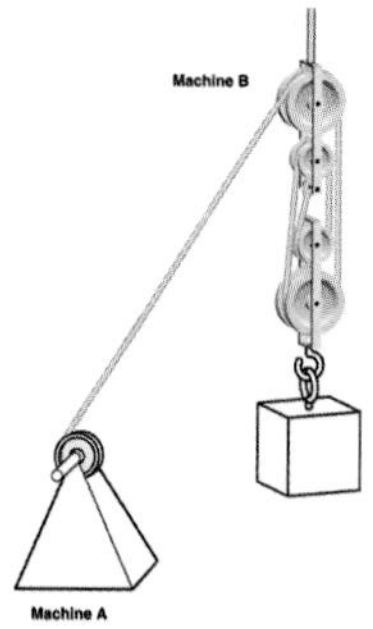

Figure 2-4

6. **Interpreting Data** Compare the average kinetic energy of the water molecules in the three beakers in Figure 2-6.

7. **Analyzing Data** What is the difference between wave A and wave B in Figure 2-7?

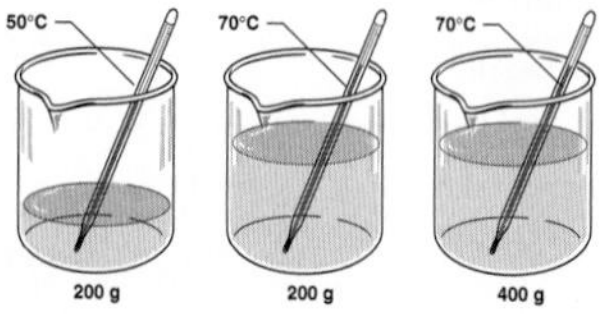

50°C   70°C   70°C

200 g   200 g   400 g

Figure 2-6

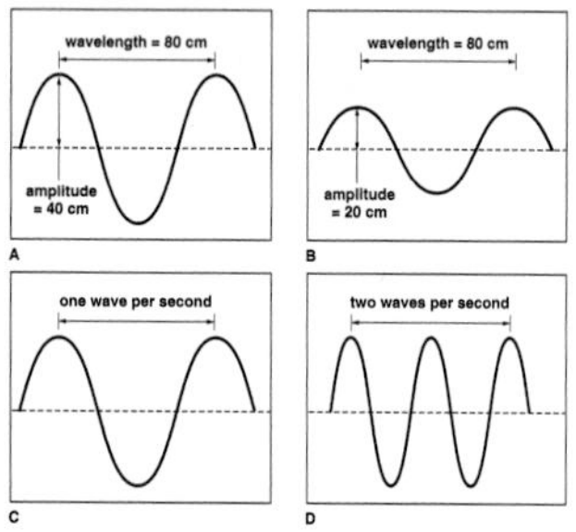

wavelength = 80 cm

amplitude = 40 cm

A

wavelength = 80 cm

amplitude = 20 cm

B

Figure 2-7

one wave per second

C

two waves per second

D

Unit 2 Test A

Name _____ Class _____ Date _____

8. **Predicting** Figure 2-8 shows the lens of an eye that is focused on a nearby object at point Z. If the eye refocuses on a far object, what happens to the shape of the lens? How?

9. **Comparing and Contrasting** Compare the resistance in the three circuits shown in Figure 2-9 when the switches are closed. Explain the cause of any differences.

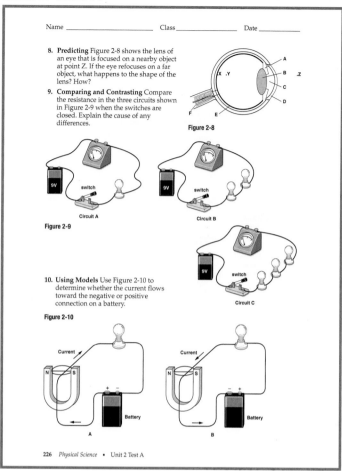

Figure 2-8

Circuit A

Circuit B

Figure 2-9

10. **Using Models** Use Figure 2-10 to determine whether the current flows toward the negative or positive connection on a battery.

Figure 2-10

Circuit C

Current

N   S

Battery

A

Current

N   S

Battery

B

Unit 2 Test A

Name _____ Class _____ Date _____

Problem

Write the answers to each question on a separate sheet of paper.

1. During a race, a runner runs at a speed of 6 m/s. Four seconds later, she is running at a speed of 10 m/s. What is the runner's acceleration? Show your work.

Essay

Write the answers to each question on a separate sheet of paper.

1. Why does a biker have to pedal harder to travel at a constant speed into the wind on a windy day compared to traveling on the same road at the same speed on a calm day?

2. A cube of wood displaces half its volume when floating in water. When a 0.5-N washer is added to the cube, it floats just at the point where it is completely submerged in the water. What is the buoyant force acting on the cube when the washer is removed?

3. Sound waves have relatively long wavelengths. We can hear people around a corner before we can see them. Which wave behavior does this illustrate? Explain how wavelength relates to this behavior.

4. How does a transformer decrease the voltage that is transmitted across power lines before it enters homes?

Name _____ Class _____ Date _____

Unit 2   Physics   Unit Test B

Multiple Choice

Write the letter that best answers the question or completes the statement on the line provided.

_____ 1. One kilometer equals 1000 meters. What does the prefix kilo- mean?
   a. 1   **b.** 10   **c.** 100   **d.** 1000

_____ 2. What is the speed of a bobsled whose distance-time graph indicates that it traveled 100 m in 25 s?
   a. 4 m/s   **b.** 250 m/s
   c. 0.25 mph   **d.** 100 m/s

_____ 3. According to Newton's second law of motion, the acceleration of an object equals the net force acting on the object divided by the object's
   a. mass.   **b.** momentum.   **c.** velocity.   **d.** weight.

_____ 4. What is the SI unit of pressure?
   a. g/cm^3 **b.** m/s^2
   c. a newton   **d.** a pascal

_____ 5. Which principle states that a change in the pressure at any point in a fluid in a closed container is transmitted equally and unchanged in all directions throughout the fluid?
   a. Archimedes' principle
   b. Bernoulli's principle
   c. Newton's principle
   d. Pascal's principle

_____ 6. The relationship between buoyant force and weight of a displaced fluid was first stated by
   a. Archimedes.   **b.** Bernoulli.   **c.** Newton.   **d.** Pascal.

_____ 7. What is the unit of work?
   a. joule   **b.** newton/meter
   c. watt   **d.** all of the above

_____ 8. How can a machine make work easier for you?
   a. by decreasing the amount of work you do
   b. by changing the direction of your force
   c. by increasing the work done by the machine
   d. none of the above

_____ 9. An inclined plane reduces the effort force by
   a. increasing the distance through which the force is applied.
   b. increasing the work.
   c. reducing the effort distance.
   d. reducing the work.

Name _____ Class _____ Date _____

_____ 10. Which of the following is an example of an object with elastic potential energy?
   a. a wind-up toy that has been wound up
   b. a compressed basketball
   c. a stretched rubber band
   d. all of the above

_____ 11. A 4-kilogram cat is resting on top of a bookshelf that is 2 meters high. What is the cat's gravitational potential energy relative to the floor if the acceleration due to gravity is 9.8 m/s^2?
   a. 6 J   **b.** 8 J   **c.** 20 J   **d.** 78 J

_____ 12. What is biomass energy?
   a. the chemical energy stored in living things
   b. the electromagnetic energy stored in living things
   c. the nuclear energy stored in living things
   d. the thermal energy stored in living things

_____ 13. Which of the following is a unit of temperature?
   a. Celsius degree   **b.** joule
   c. kilogram   **d.** calorie

_____ 14. What does a calorimeter directly measure?
   a. change in temperature
   b. kinetic energy
   c. specific heat
   d. radiation

_____ 15. Which central heating system involves a furnace and a blower?
   a. electric baseboard   **b.** forced-air
   c. hot-water   **d.** steam

_____ 16. When a surfer rides an ocean wave on her surfboard, she is actually riding on
   a. a crest that is toppling over.
   b. a trough of the wave.
   c. the rest position of the wave.
   d. a region of rarefaction.

_____ 17. To determine the speed of a wave, you would use which of the following formulas?
   a. speed = frequency × amplitude
   b. speed = wavelength × frequency
   c. speed = wavelength × amplitude
   d. speed = wavelength × period

Name _____ Class _____ Date _____

_____ 18. Sonar equipment sends sound waves into deep water and measures
   a. refraction of the transmitted wave.
   b. only the direction of the reflected wave.
   c. the time delay of the returning echoes.
   d. interference of the transmitted and reflected waves.

_____ 19. To calculate the frequency of an electromagnetic wave, you need to know the speed of the wave and its
   a. wavelength.   **b.** intensity.
   c. refraction.   **d.** amplitude.

_____ 20. Light acts like
   a. a wave.
   b. a particle.
   c. both a wave and a particle.
   d. neither a wave nor a particle.

_____ 21. Newton's prism experiments showed that white sunlight is made up of
   a. the full electromagnetic spectrum.
   b. only blue light when separated by a prism.
   c. all the colors of the visible spectrum.
   d. only the longest wavelengths.

_____ 22. A concave mirror can form
   a. only virtual images.
   b. only real images.
   c. both virtual and real images.
   d. none of the above

_____ 23. Which optical instrument uses a large concave mirror, a plane mirror, and a convex lens to gather light, focus, and enlarge an image?
   a. refracting telescope   **b.** microscope
   c. reflecting telescope   **d.** film camera

_____ 24. The lens of the human eye focuses light by
   a. changing its index of refraction.
   b. controlling the amount of light entering the eye.
   c. changing color.
   d. changing shape.

_____ 25. Walking across a carpet is an example of charge being transferred by
   a. contact.   **b.** induction.
   c. static electricity.   **d.** friction.

Name _____ Class _____ Date _____

_____ 26. What is the difference in electrical potential energy between two places in an electric field?
   a. current   **b.** resistance
   c. potential difference   **d.** induction

_____ 27. A solid-state component with three layers of semiconductors is a(an)
   a. transistor.   **b.** diode.
   c. vacuum tube.   **d.** integrated circuit.

_____ 28. The force a magnet exerts on another magnet, on iron or a similar metal, or on moving charges is
   a. an electric force.
   b. a magnetic force.
   c. proportional to the charge of the magnet.
   d. proportional to the mass of the magnet.

_____ 29. What creates a magnetic field?
   a. charged particles that do not move
   b. moving electric charges
   c. gravity
   d. an isolated magnetic pole

_____ 30. The process of generating an electric current by moving an electrical conductor relative to a magnetic field is called
   a. magnetization.
   b. electromagnetic force.
   c. electromagnetic induction.
   d. alternating current.

Completion

Complete each statement on the line provided.

1. The direction and length of a straight line from the starting point to the ending point of an object's motion is _____

2. The force that opposes the motion of objects that touch as they move pass each other is called _____

3. The two forces acting on a falling object are gravity and _____

4. In a hydraulic lift system, the fluid pressure exerted throughout the system is _____

5. A machine is a device that changes a(an) _____.

6. Mechanical energy does not include kinetic energy or _____ energy.

7. "Energy cannot be created or destroyed" is a statement of the law of _____.

Unit 2 Test B

Name _____ Class _____ Date _____

8. The transfer of thermal energy with no overall transfer of matter is called _____.

9. At the _____ of a standing wave, there is no displacement from the rest position.

10. Objects that scatter some of the light that is transmitted through them are _____.

11. Electromagnetic waves can travel through a(an) _____.

12. Light rays passing through a convex lens converge at the _____ point on the other side of the lens.

13. To calculate power, multiply voltage measured in _____ by _____ measured in amps.

14. In ferromagnetic materials, regions with large numbers of atoms with aligned magnetic fields are called _____.

15. A charged particle moving in a magnetic field will be deflected in a direction _____ to the magnetic field.

Short Answer

In complete sentences, write the answers to the questions on the lines provided.

1. What are two types of speed that can be used to describe the motion of a car driving on the highway?

2. How can you double the acceleration of an object if you cannot alter the object's mass?

3. Which of the universal forces acts only on protons and neutrons in the nucleus of an atom?

4. Compare the weight of an object to the buoyant force acting on it if the object sinks in the fluid.

Unit 2 Test B

Name _____ Class _____ Date _____

5. Which has the greater IMA—a screw with closely spaced threads or a screw with threads spaced farther apart?

6. What are the two general types of energy that can be used to classify many forms of energy?

7. What is the most familiar form of electromagnetic energy?

8. In general, what is the order of increasing thermal expansion among solids, liquids, and gases when a given amount of thermal energy is added?

9. When you shake the end of a rope to make a wave, how can you increase the amplitude of the wave?

10. Which waves have wavelengths longer than those of visible light? Give an example of how each kind of wave is used.

11. Magenta is a secondary color of light. What type of color is magenta when it is a pigment?

12. What is the usual method of graphically analyzing how light rays behave when they strike mirrors or pass through lenses?

Unit 2 Test B

Name _____ Class _____ Date _____

13. What is a circuit breaker?

14. What is a generator and how does it work?

15. List five energy sources that are used in the United States to produce electrical energy.

Using Science Skills

Use the diagram to answer each question. Write the answers on a separate sheet of paper.

1. **Interpreting Graphics** In Figure 2-1, what is the direction of the centripetal force acting on the satellite at this location in its orbit?

2. **Comparing and Contrasting** How does the fluid pressure exerted on the black spheres shown in Figure 2-2 compare with the pressure exerted on the gray spheres.

3. **Calculating** What is the IMA of the ramp in Figure 2-3? Show your work.

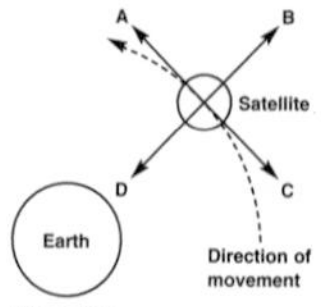

Figure 2-1

Figure 2-2

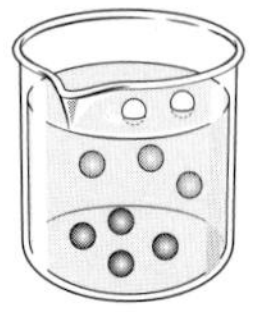

Figure 2-3

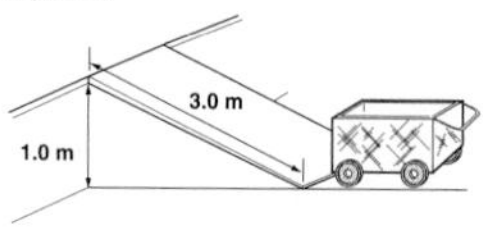

3.0 m

1.0 m

Unit 2 Test B

Name _____ Class _____ Date _____

4. **Applying Concepts** In Figure 2-4, the block in C has 5 J of kinetic energy. How much work did the compressed spring do on the block? Explain your answer.

5. **Inferring** In Figure 2-5, is the temperature of the material within the cylinder greatest during the intake stroke, compression stroke, power stroke, or exhaust stroke?

6. **Interpreting Illustrations** What kind of wave does A in Figure 2-6 represent? What kind of wave does B represent?

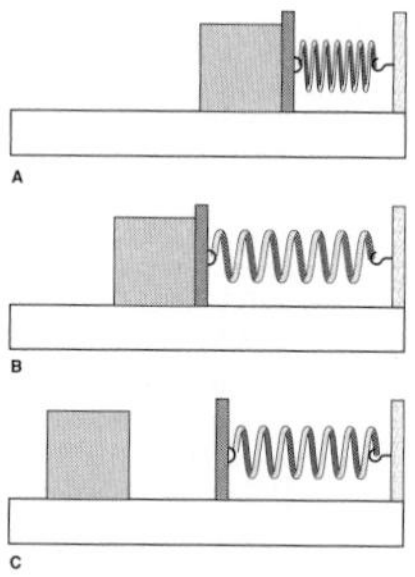

Figure 2-5

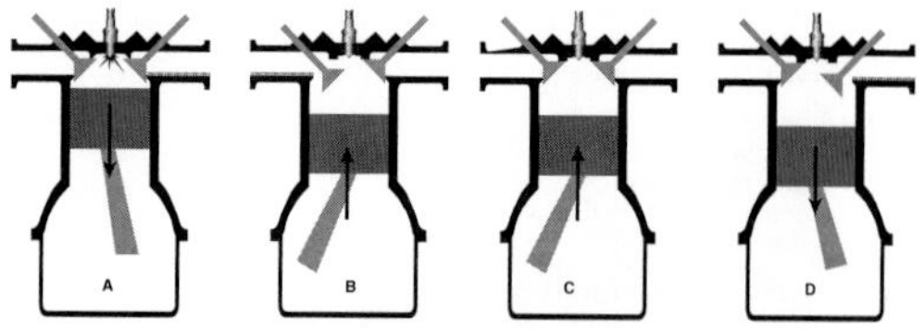

Figure 2-4

Figure 2-6

push

compressions

pull

rarefactions

A

move up

rest position   trough   crest   wavelength

amplitude

amplitude

move down

B

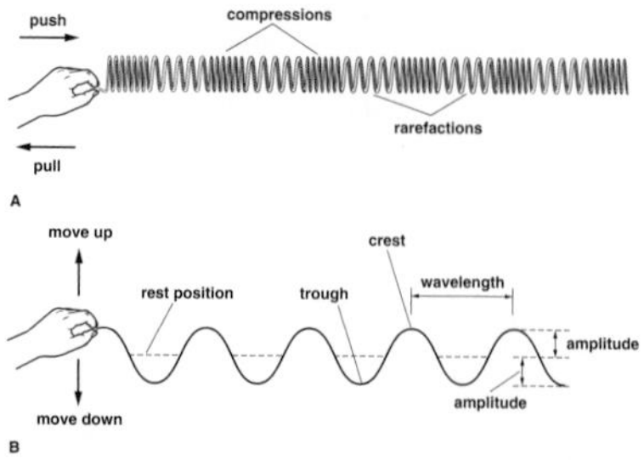

Unit 2 Test B

Name ____________________ Class ______________ Date __________

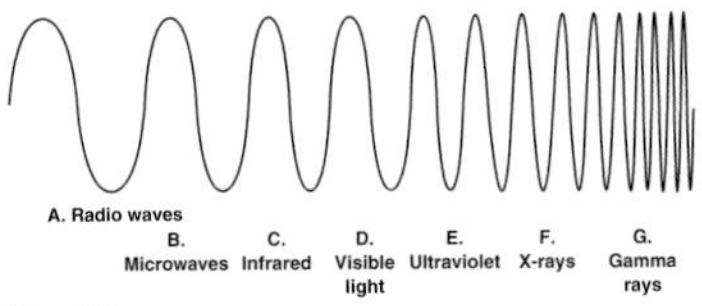

Figure 2-7

7. **Comparing and Contrasting** Which waves in Figure 2-7 carry AM and FM signals? How do the frequencies of AM and FM signals compare?

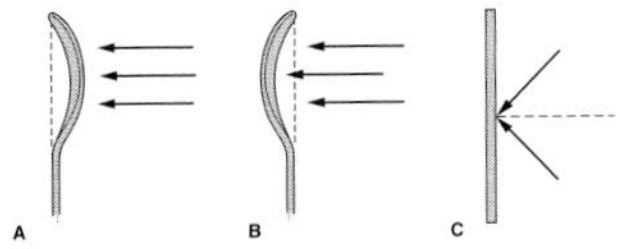

Figure 2-8

8. **Applying Concepts** What type of mirrors are represented by A, B, and C in Figure 2-8? How does each mirror affect parallel light rays that strike it?

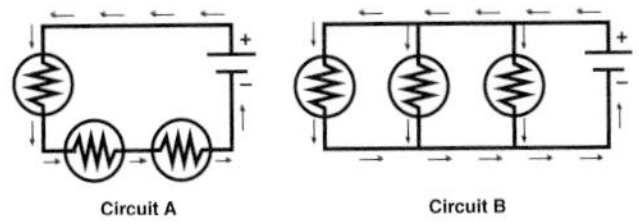

Figure 2-9

9. **Classifying** Are both circuits in Figure 2-9 series circuits? Explain your answer.

Unit 2 Test B

Name ____________________ Class ______________ Date __________

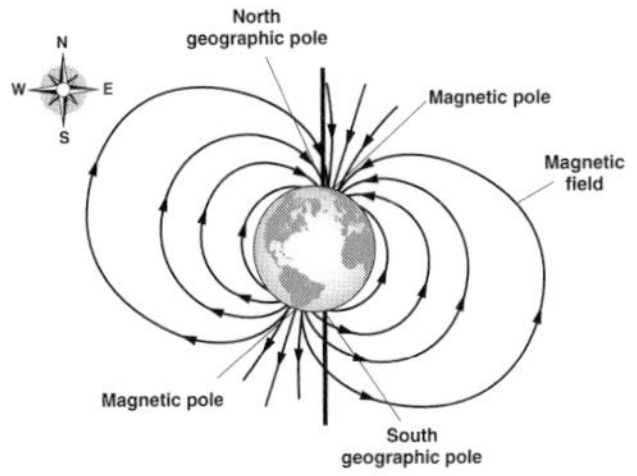

Figure 2-10

10. **Interpreting Graphics** In Figure 2-10, use the direction of the magnetic field lines to determine what type of magnetic pole is located at the magnetic South Pole.

Unit 2 Test A Answers

Multiple Choice

1. b	**2.** d	**3.** d	**4.** d	**5.** c	**6.** d
7. d	**8.** d	**9.** c	**10.** b	**11.** c	**12.** b
13. b	**14.** a	**15.** c	**16.** d	**17.** c	**18.** a
19. a	**20.** d	**21.** d	**22.** d	**23.** b	**24.** b
25. b	**26.** c	**27.** a	**28.** c	**29.** d	**30.** b

Completion

1. constant **2.** Instantaneous acceleration **3.** greater; larger **4.** gravity **5.** equally **6.** decreases; becomes smaller **7.** decreases **8.** lever **9.** active **10.** conservation **11.** from, to **12.** equal; the same **13.** compression **14.** at right angles; perpendicular **15.** vacuum **16.** more **17.** rods **18.** integrated, microchips **19.** magnetic declination **20.** alternating

Short Answer

1. km/h **2.** 20 kgm/s **3.** Air pressure that is pushing in on the balloon decreases as the balloon rises. **4.** A fixed pulley changes only the direction of the input force. A movable pulley changes both the direction of the input force and its size. **5.** Biomass energy is the chemical energy stored in living things. The chemical energy is produced as plants convert sunlight in the form of electromagnetic energy into chemical energy. **6.** Free electrons collide with each other and with atoms or ions to transfer thermal energy. **7.** The wave with greater compressions has more energy. **8.** to allow light to pass from the source below the slide up through the lenses of the microscope **9.** It is a law that states that the total charge in an isolated system is constant. **10.** A vibrating electric charge induces a changing magnet field, which induces a changing electric field. The changing electric and magnetic fields regenerate each other, producing an electromagnetic wave.

Using Science Skills

1. Arrows A and B are vectors with magnitude (distance) and direction. **2.** The momentums of both skaters are equal in size but opposite in direction. **3.** The spoon moved toward the stream of running water. **4.** 1.0 m **5.** No; because the ball does not reach the same height each time it bounces, its maximum gravitational potential energy is decreasing from one bounce to the next. Because its gravitational potential energy decreases and its maximum kinetic energy does not increase, the total mechanical energy must be decreasing. **6.** The average kinetic energy of the water molecules in B equals the average kinetic energy of the molecules in C but is greater than the average kinetic energy of the molecules in A. **7.** Wave B has an amplitude that is one-half the amplitude of wave A. **8.** to allow light to pass from the source below the slide up through the lenses of the microscope **9.** The light bulbs are sources of resistance, so Circuit A has the least resistance because the electrons pass through only one light bulb. Circuit B has more resistance than A has because Circuit B has two light bulbs. Circuit C has three light bulbs and the most resistance. Although other parts of the circuits, such as the wire, are sources of resistance, they are the same in all three circuits. **10.** The current always flows from the positive connection toward the negative connection on a battery.

Problem

1. $a = \dfrac{V_f - V_i}{t} = \dfrac{10m/s - 6m/s}{4s} = \dfrac{4m/s}{4s} = 1m/s^2$

Essay

1. On both the calm and windy days, the net force on the biker is zero because the biker is traveling at constant speed. On a calm day, the biker must pedal so that the forward-directed force applied to the bike balances the forces of friction opposing the forward motion. The friction forces primarily take the form rolling friction and fluid friction. On a windy day, the fluid friction force is much greater, so the rider must pedal harder to maintain the same constant speed. **2.** 0.5 N; because the 0.5-N washer and the cube floating on its own both displace the same volume, the 0.5-N force equals the buoyant force acting on the cube.

3. Diffraction; a wave diffracts more if its wavelength is large compared to the size of the obstacle (the corner people are walking around). Because sound waves have relatively long wavelengths, we hear sound around the corner as the waves diffract, or spread out. **4.** A step-down transformer is used, which has a primary coil with a large number of turns and a secondary coil with fewer turns, so the ratio of the number of secondary coil turns to the primary coil turns is the same as the ratio of the output voltage to the input voltage. This will decrease the voltage.

Unit 2 Test B Answers

Multiple Choice

1. d	**2.** a	**3.** a	**4.** d	**5.** d	**6.** a
7. a	**8.** b	**9.** a	**10.** d	**11.** d	**12.** a
13. a	**14.** a	**15.** b	**16.** a	**17.** b	**18.** c
19. a	**20.** c	**21.** c	**22.** c	**23.** c	**24.** d
25. d	**26.** c	**27.** a	**28.** b	**29.** b	**30.** c

Completion

1. displacement **2.** friction **3.** air resistance; drag **4.** constant **5.** force **6.** chemical **7.** conservation of energy **8.** conduction **9.** node; nodes **10.** translucent **11.** vacuum **12.** focal **13.** volts, current **14.** magnetic domains; domains **15.** perpendicular; at right angles

Short Answer

1. average speed and instantaneous speed **2.** Double the net force acting on the object. **3.** strong nuclear force **4.** The buoyant force is less than the weight. **5.** the screw with closely spaced threads **6.** kinetic energy and potential energy **7.** visible light **8.** solids, liquids, gases **9.** Shake the rope with more force. **10.** radio waves (radio and television signals); microwaves and radar waves (microwave ovens); infrared rays (heat lamps) **11.** Magenta is one of the primary colors of pigments. **12.** ray diagrams **13.** 9 volts; because voltage is equal to the current multiplied by the resistance **14.** A generator is a device that induces an electric current by rotating a coil of wire in a magnetic field. **15.** Accept any five of the following: coal, oil, natural gas, hydroelectric, nuclear, wind, solar.

Using Science Skills

1. D **2.** The fluid pressure exerted on the black spheres is greater (about twice as great). **3.** Ideal mechanical

advantage = $\dfrac{\text{Input distance}}{\text{Output distance}} = \dfrac{3\text{m}}{1\text{m}} = 3$ **4.** 5 J;

because the block gained 5 joules of energy, the spring had to do 5 joules of work on the block. **5.** power stroke **6.** a longitudinal wave; a transverse wave **7.** Radio waves; FM signals usually have higher frequencies than AM signals have. **8.** Possible answers: A: convex mirror; a convex mirror causes light rays that are parallel to its optical axis to spread out after reflection.; B: concave mirror; a concave mirror causes light rays that are parallel to its optical axis to come together after reflection.; C: plane mirror; a plane mirror causes parallel light to remain parallel after reflection. **9.** No; only Circuit A is a series circuit. In Circuit A, the current can follow only one path through all three bulbs. Circuit B is a parallel circuit because the current can follow a separate path through each of the three bulbs. **10.** The magnetic pole near the magnetic South Pole is a north magnetic pole.

Chapter 22 Earth's Interior

Planning Guide

CHAPTER 22

SECTION OBJECTIVES	STANDARDS		ACTIVITIES and LABS
	NATIONAL (See p. T18.)	STATE	
22.1 Earth's Structure, pp. 660–663 1 block or 2 periods **22.1.1 Describe** the science of geology. **22.1.2 Describe** the main layers of Earth's interior.	A-1, B-6, D-1, D-3, G-1, G-2, G-3		**SE** Inquiry Activity: How Are Rocks and Minerals Different? p. 659 **L2** **TE** Teacher Demo: Density, p. 662 **L2** **LM** Investigation 22B: Modeling Petroleum Recovery **L1**
22.2 Minerals, pp. 664–669 1 block or 2 periods **22.2.1 Distinguish** between rocks and minerals and **explain** several properties used to identify minerals.	A-1, A-2, B-2		**SE** Quick Lab: Mineral Hardness, p. 668 **L2** **TE** Build Science Skills: Design an Experiment, p. 666 **L2**
22.3 Rocks and the Rock Cycle, pp. 670–675 1 block or 2 periods **22.3.1 Classify** rocks as igneous, sedimentary, or metamorphic and **explain** how different types of rocks form. **22.3.2 Describe** the processes by which rocks continually change from one type to another in the rock cycle.	A-1, A-2, B-2, B-3, D-2		**SE** Quick Lab: Observing the Size of Crystals, p. 671 **L2** **TE** Build Science Skills: Classifying, p. 672 **L2** **LM** Investigation 22A: Identifying Rocks **L2**
22.4 Plate Tectonics, pp. 676–683 1 block or 2 periods **22.4.1 Explain** the hypothesis of continental drift. **22.4.2 Relate** how the theory of plate tectonics explains sea-floor spreading, subduction, and the formation of mountains. **22.4.3 Explain** the mechanisms of plate movement.	D-1, D-3, G-1, G-2, G-3		**TE** Teacher Demo: Convection and Plate Motion, p. 680 **L2**
22.5 Earthquakes, pp. 684–689 1 block or 2 periods **22.5.1 Describe** the causes and effects of stress in Earth's crust. **22.5.2 Explain** why earthquakes occur and how their energy is propagated as seismic waves. **22.5.3 Explain** how earthquakes are measured and how earthquake data is used to learn about Earth's interior.	A-1, A-2, B-6, D-1, D-3, F-5		**SE** Quick Lab: Modeling a Seismograph, p. 687 **L2** **SE** Exploration Lab: Using Earthquakes to Map Plate Boundaries, p. 697 **L2** **TE** Teacher Demo: Faults and Folds, p. 685 **L2** **TE** Build Science Skills: Using Models, p. 686 **L2**
22.6 Volcanoes, pp. 690–696 1 block or 2 periods **22.6.1 Describe** the internal structure of a volcano and how volcanoes form. **22.6.2 Relate** the type of volcanic eruption to the characteristics of magma. **22.6.3 Describe** the different types of volcanoes and where they are typically located. **22.6.4 Describe** several types of igneous features and how they are formed.	B-2, D-1, D-2, D-3, F-5		

Ability Levels

L1	For students who need additional help
L2	For all students
L3	For students who need to be challenged

Components

SE	Student Edition	**GRSW**	Guided Reading & Study Workbook With Math Support	**CTB**	Computer Test Bank
TE	Teacher's Edition			**TP**	Test Prep Resources
LM	Laboratory Manual	**CUT**	Chapter and Unit Tests	**iT**	iText
PLM	Probeware Lab Manual			**DC**	Discovery Channel Videotapes

T	Transparencies
P	Presentation Pro CD-ROM
GO	Internet Resources

RESOURCES PRINT and TECHNOLOGY	SECTION ASSESSMENT
GRSW Section 22.1 **L1** **T** Chapter 22 Pretest **L2** **P** and Section 22.1 **L2** SCiLINKS **GO** Earth's layers **L2**	SE Section 22.1 Assessment, p. 663 iText **iT** Section 22.1
GRSW Section 22.2 **L1** **T P** Section 22.2 **L2** SCiLINKS **GO** Minerals **L2**	SE Section 22.2 Assessment, p. 669 iText **iT** Section 22.2
GRSW Section 22.3 **L1** **T P** Section 22.3 **L2** SCiLINKS **GO** Rocks **L2**	SE Section 22.3 Assessment, p. 675 iText **iT** Section 22.3
GRSW Section 22.4 **L1** **T P** Section 22.4 **L2** SCIENCE NEWS **GO** Earthquakes, volcanoes, and plate tectonics **L2**	SE Section 22.4 Assessment, p. 683 iText **iT** Section 22.4
GRSW Section 22.5 **L1** GRSW Math Skill **L2** **T P** Section 22.5 **L2** PLANETDIARY **GO** Earthquake activity **L2**	SE Section 22.5 Assessment, p. 689 iText **iT** Section 22.5
GRSW Section 22.6 **L1** Discovery SCHOOL **DC** Mountains of Fire **L2** **T P** Section 22.6 **L2** PLANETDIARY **GO** Volcano activity **L2**	SE Section 22.6 Assessment, p. 696 iText **iT** Section 22.6

Go Online

Go online for these Internet resources.
PHSchool.com
Web Code: cca-3220

SCIENCE NEWS
Web Code: cce-3224

NSTA SCiLINKS
Web Code: ccn-3221
Web Code: ccn-3222
Web Code: ccn-3223

PLANETDIARY
Web Code: ccc-3225
Web Code: ccc-3226

Materials for Activities and Labs

STUDENT EDITION

Inquiry Activity, p. 659
4 mineral samples labeled as minerals A to D, 4 rock samples labeled as rocks A to D, newspaper, plastic bag, small hammer, hand lens

Quick Lab, p. 668
labeled samples of graphite, galena or halite, hornblende, feldspar, pyrite, and olivine; penny; iron nail; steel file

Quick Lab, p. 671
salol, plastic spoon, 2 watch glasses, tongs, hot plate, hand lens, Petri dish, ice cube, watch with second hand

Quick Lab, p. 687
pencil, roll of cash-register paper, felt-tip pen

Exploration Lab, p. 697
graph paper

TEACHER'S EDITION

Teacher Demo, p. 662
2 glass jars with lids, $\frac{1}{2}$ cup

of salt, sand, and metal filings; 100 mL of water, vegetable oil, and corn syrup

Build Science Skills, p. 666
mineral samples, beakers, graduated cylinders, balances

Build Science Skills, p. 672
10 numbered rock samples for each group of students

Teacher Demo, p. 680
Bunsen burner or hot plate, deep and wide glass container, thin tomato soup, large sponges, scissors, tongs

Teacher Demo, p. 685
several different shades of potter's clay, 6 wood blocks, hammer, large garbage bags

Build Science Skills, p. 686
1 spring toy per group

Build Science Skills, p. 694
several samples of pumice, obsidian, ropy basalt, and angular rhyolite

Chapter Assessment

CHAPTER ASSESSMENT

SE	Chapter Assessment, pp. 699–700
CUT	Chapter 22 Test A, B
CTB	Chapter 22
iT	Chapter 22

PHSCHOOL.COM GO
Web Code: cca-3220

STANDARDIZED TEST PREP

SE	Chapter 22, p. 701
TP	Diagnose and Prescribe

iText—interactive textbook with assessment at PHSchool.com

Earth's Interior   658B

Name_____ Class_____ Date_____ M T W T F

LESSON PLAN 22.1

Earth's Structure

Time
2 periods
1 block

Section Objectives

- **22.1.1 Describe** the science of geology.
- **22.1.2 Describe** the main layers of Earth's interior.

Vocabulary geologists • uniformitarianism • crust • silicates • mantle • lithosphere • asthenosphere • mesosphere • core

Local Standards

1 FOCUS

Build Vocabulary: Word-Part Analysis
Ask students to define the word *sphere* and to think of any words they know that include *sphere* as a word part. Have students use a dictionary to look up the prefixes *litho-*, *astheno-*, and *meso-*. **L2**

Targeted Resources
- ❏ Transparency: Chapter 22 Pretest
- ❏ Transparency: Interest Grabber 22.1
- ❏ Transparency: Reading Strategy 22.1

2 INSTRUCT

Build Reading Literacy: Preview
Before students read A Cross Section of Earth, have them preview the words in bold, including subheadings and vocabulary, and write down what they already know. **L1**

Use Community Resources
Ask a USGS geologist to talk to your class about all of the different types of studies and activities that a professional geologist undertakes. **L2**

Build Science Skills: Inferring
Have students work in groups to make an inference about the layering of Earth's interior, and then create a visual aid to explain their deductions. **L2**

Integrate Math
Ask students to calculate the difference between Earth's diameter at the equator and at the poles. **L2**

Teacher Demo: Density
Place various liquids in one jar and various solids in a second jar. Shake the contents of each jar so that students can see how liquids separate into layers based on density and composition. **L2**

Address Misconceptions
Point out to students that, while we perceive gravity as a "downward" force, it is more properly described as a force acting toward the center of the planet. **L2**

Targeted Resources
- ❏ Transparency: Figure 4: The Earth's Layers
- ❏ Transparency: Figure 5: The Lithosphere and the Asthenosphere
- ❏ GRSW Section 22.1
- ❏ **NSTA** *sci*_{LINKS} Earth's layers

3 ASSESS

Reteach
Use Figure 4 to review the layers of Earth. Review the main characteristics of each layer while discussing the diagram. **L1**

Evaluate Understanding
Ask students to create a compare-contrast chart with the headings Lithosphere and Asthenosphere. **L2**

Targeted Resources
- ❏ **PHSchool.com** Online Section 22.1 Assessment
- ❏ iText Section 22.1

Transparencies

328 **Chapter 22 Pretest**

1. True or False: Covalent bonds can be stronger or weaker depending on the type of atoms sharing the bond.

2. Which of these statements best describes what happens when a solution of salt water is left in the sun?

   a. The solution will change phases.

   b. Water will condense from the solution.

   c. Salt crystals will precipitate from the solution as water evaporates.

3. Which of these statements best describes mechanical waves?

   a. They travel at different speeds through different substances.

   b. They travel at the same speed in a vacuum.

   c. They are produced by vibrations in an electric field.

   d. They have properties of both particles and waves.

ANSWERS
1. True
2. c
3. a

Transparencies

329 **Chapter 22 Pretest** *(continued)*

4. Which of these statements best describes what happens when a guitar string is plucked?

   a. Kinetic energy is created.

   b. Potential energy is created.

   c. Matter is converted into kinetic energy.

   d. Potential energy is converted into kinetic energy.

ANSWERS
4. d

Transparencies

330 **Section 22.1 Interest Grabber**

Modeling Underground Features

In the following activity, you will create a model of a geologic formation using two different colors of modeling clay.

1. In a small tray or plate, choose a location for your geologic formation. Place a small piece of clay in that location and flatten it so that it covers at least a quarter of the area of the tray to a depth of at least a centimeter. Make a map of the tray that identifies the location, shape, and size of the small piece of clay. Cover the entire area inside the tray to a depth of at least 2 centimeters with a larger piece of clay that is of a different color. Flatten the clay so that an observer cannot tell the location of the original piece of clay. Exchange trays with a partner, and perform the next step using your partner's tray.

2. Holding a clear plastic straw vertically, press the end of the straw directly into the clay until it hits the bottom of the tray. Close the top end of the straw with your finger and remove the straw. Some of the clay will remain in the straw. This is a core sample that shows the layers of clay in the tray. Record the color and width of the layer(s) in the core sample. Make a map of the new tray and use it to label the location from which you took the sample. Take several core samples until you have approximated the location, shape, and size of the geologic formation that your partner made.

ANSWERS
1. Acceptable maps will show the approximate location, shape, and size of the geologic formation.
2. When students compare their maps with their partner's, they should match the map of their partner's geologic formation.

Transparencies

331 **Section 22.1 Reading Strategy**

c. Earth's rocky outer layer

Building Vocabulary

Vocabulary Term	Definition
Geologist	a. ____?____
Uniformitarianism	b. ____?____
Crust	c. ____?____

ANSWERS
a. A scientist who studies Earth and the processes that have shaped Earth over time
b. The concept that geologic processes that are occurring today also occurred in the past

Transparencies

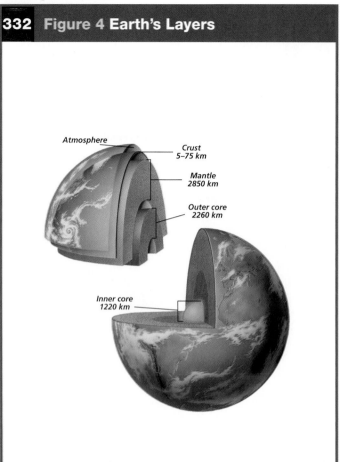

Transparencies

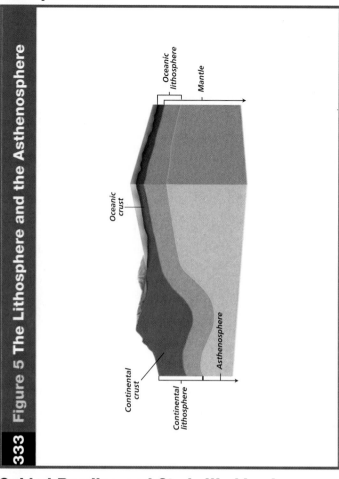

Guided Reading and Study Workbook

Name _____ Class _____ Date _____

Chapter 22   Earth's Interior

Section 22.1 Earth's Structure
(pages 660–663)

This section explains what geologists study. It describes the main layers of Earth.

Reading Strategy (page 660)

Building Vocabulary Copy the table on a separate sheet of paper and add more rows as needed. As you read the section, define each vocabulary term in your own words. For more information on this Reading Strategy, see the **Reading and Study Skills** in the **Skills and Reference Handbook** at the end of your textbook.

Earth's Structure	
Vocabulary Term	**Definition**
Geologist	A scientist who studies Earth and the processes that have shaped Earth over time
Uniformitarianism	The concept that geologic processes that are occurring today also occurred in the past
Crust	Earth's rocky outer layer

The Science of Geology (pages 660–661)

1. The study of planet Earth, including its composition and structure is called _____geology_____

2. Is the following sentence true or false? People who study Earth and the processes that have shaped Earth over time are called geologists. _____true_____

3. What is uniformitarianism? _Uniformitarianism is the idea that the geologic processes_ _that operate today also operated in the past._

A Cross Section of Earth (pages 661–663)

4. Circle the letters of the major layers of Earth's interior.
(a.) crust
b. atmosphere
(c.) mantle
(d.) core

5. Scientists divide Earth's interior into the crust, mantle, and core based on the _____materials in each layer_____

6. Much of the Earth's crust is made up of _____silicates_____.

Guided Reading and Study Workbook

Name _____ Class _____ Date _____

Chapter 22   Earth's Interior

Match each type of crust to its characteristics. Each type of crust will have more than one characteristic.

	Crust	Characteristic
a, d, e	**7.** oceanic crust	a. Averages about 7 kilometers thick
b, c, f	**8.** continental crust	b. Consists mainly of less-dense rocks
		c. Averages 40 kilometers in thickness
		d. Composed mostly of dense rocks
		e. Makes up the ocean floor
		f. Makes up the continents

9. The layer of Earth called the _____mantle_____ is found directly below the crust.

10. Circle the letters of each sentence that is true about Earth's mantle.
(a.) It is the thickest layer of Earth.
(b.) It is divided into layers based on the physical properties of rock.
c. It is less dense than the crust.
(d.) It is made mainly of silicates.

11. The lithosphere includes the uppermost part of Earth's mantle and Earth's _____crust_____.

12. Is the following sentence true or false? Rock flows slowly in the asthenosphere. _____true_____

13. The stronger, lower part of the mantle is called the _____mesosphere_____.

14. The sphere of metal inside Earth is called the _____core_____.

15. Is the following sentence true or false? The outer core of Earth is liquid. _____true_____

16. Label the main layers of Earth's interior in the diagram below.

a. Crust
b. Mantle
c. Outer core
d. Inner core

LESSON PLAN 22.2

Minerals

Section Objectives

■ **22.2.1 Distinguish** between rocks and minerals and **explain** several properties used to identify minerals.

Vocabulary rock • inorganic • streak • luster • hardness • fracture • cleavage

Local Standards

---

1 FOCUS

Build Vocabulary: Paraphrase
Use mineral samples to demonstrate each of the properties of minerals, and have students describe the property in their own words. **L2**

Targeted Resources
❑ Transparency: Interest Grabber 22.2
❑ Transparency: Reading Strategy 22.2

---

2 INSTRUCT

Use Visuals: Figure 8
Ask students what the most common mineral is in this piece of granite. Then, ask what properties they can use to identify the minerals in a piece of granite. **L1**

Build Reading Literacy: Monitor Your Understanding
Have students apply a reading technique such as outlining, summarizing, or identifying main ideas, if they have not fully understood a paragraph of Rocks and Minerals. **L2**

Build Science Skills: Design an Experiment
Have students work in groups to design an experiment to test the density of solid crystals using the materials provided. **L2**

Address Misconceptions
Have students perform a scratch test with clear quartz and glass, in order to demonstrate that any mineral that is 6 or higher on the hardness scale will scratch glass. **L2**

Quick Lab: Mineral Hardness
Students will scratch the surface of minerals with various items, in order to determine the hardness of minerals. **L2**

For Enrichment
Provide students with some unlabeled minerals and ask them to identify the minerals by determining their hardness. **L3**

Targeted Resources
❑ GRSW Section 22.2

❑ **NSTA** sc*i*LINKS Minerals

---

3 ASSESS

Reteach
Show students samples of pure quartz, feldspar, mica, hornblende, and granite. Have students use a magnifying lens to identify the mineral constituents of the granite samples. **L1**

Evaluate Understanding
Provide students with 5–10 common mineral samples to identify based on the properties covered in this section. **L2**

Targeted Resources
❑ **PHSchool.com** Online Section 22.2 Assessment
❑ iText Section 22.2

Transparencies

334 Section 22.2 Interest Grabber

Examining Crystal Shapes

1. Using a magnifying lens, examine crystals of table salt provided by your teacher. What shape do the crystals have?
2. Using a magnifying lens, examine crystals of rock salt provided by your teacher. How do the shapes of rock salt crystals compare to the shapes of table salt crystals?
3. Your friend shows you some crystals that she found. They have the following shape. Is it likely that these are salt crystals? Explain your reasoning.

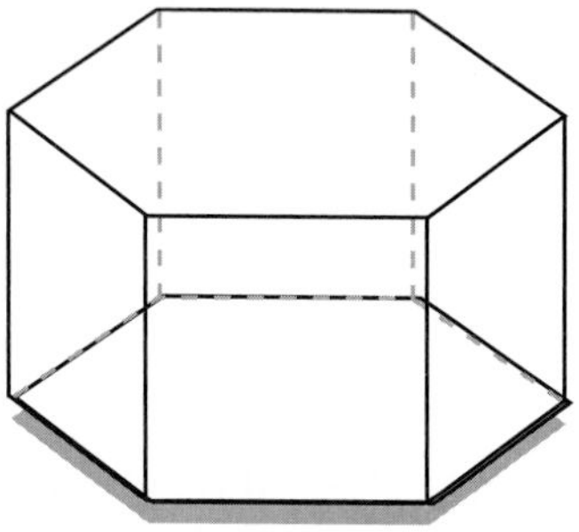

ANSWERS
1. Most of the table salt crystals have cubic shapes.
2. While the crystals are not perfect cubes, the rock salt crystals will have portions that have cubic shapes.
3. It is not likely that the crystals are salt, because they have a hexagonal shape.

Transparencies

335 Section 22.2 Reading Strategy

Outlining

Minerals

I. Minerals and Rocks
II. The Properties of Minerals
  A. Crystal Structure
  B. ________
  C. ________
  D. ________

ANSWERS
B. Color
C. Streak
D. Luster

Guided Reading and Study Workbook

Name ________ Class ________ Date ________

Chapter 22 Earth's Interior

Section 22.2 Minerals
(pages 664–669)

This section describes minerals and rocks found on Earth and their different properties.

Reading Strategy (page 664)

Outlining Copy the outline on a separate sheet of paper and add more lines as needed. Before you read, make an outline of this section. Use the green headings as main topics and the blue headings as subtopics. As you read, add supporting details. For more information on this Reading Strategy, see the **Reading and Study Skills** in the **Skills and Reference Handbook** at the end of your textbook.

Minerals

I. Minerals and Rocks
II. The Properties of Minerals
  A. Crystal Structure
  B. Color
  C. Streak
  D. Luster

Minerals and Rocks (page 665)

1. A solid combination of minerals or mineral materials is a(n) rock.
2. Is the following sentence true or false? A mineral is a naturally occurring, inorganic solid with a crystal structure and a characteristic chemical composition. true
3. A material is called inorganic if it is not produced from a living thing.
4. Circle the letters of sentences that are true about minerals.
   (a.) Within each mineral, chemical composition is nearly constant.
   b. Minerals are organic.
   c. There are about 4000 known minerals.
   (d.) Minerals are the building blocks of rocks.

The Properties of Minerals (pages 666–669)

5. Is the following sentence true or false? Minerals such as sulfur can sometimes be identified by color. true
6. What could cause two samples of the same mineral to have different colors? Slight changes in the mineral's composition could cause the two samples to have different colors.
7. Is the following sentence true or false? The color of a mineral's streak is not always the same color as the mineral. true

Physical Science Guided Reading and Study Workbook ▪ Chapter 22 199

Guided Reading and Study Workbook

Name ________ Class ________ Date ________

Chapter 22 Earth's Interior

8. How is a mineral's streak found? A mineral's streak is usually found by scraping it on a streak plate.
9. The density of a mineral depends on its chemical composition.
10. Is the following sentence true or false? The hardness of a mineral is the way in which its surface reflects light. false
11. To determine the hardness of a mineral, geologists use scratch tests.
12. Is the following sentence true or false? The fracture of a mineral is how it breaks. true
13. A type of fracture in which a mineral splits evenly is called cleavage.
14. Complete the table about the properties by which minerals can be identified.

Minerals and Properties

Property	Description
Crystal Structure	The particular geometric shape that the atoms of a mineral are arranged in
Streak	The color of a mineral's powder
Luster	The way in which a mineral's surface reflects light
Density	A mineral's mass divided by its volume
Hardness	The resistance of a mineral to scratching
Fracture	How a mineral breaks
Cleavage	A type of fracture where a mineral splits along regular, well-defined flat surfaces where the bonds are weakest

Match each mineral to its property.

Mineral	Property
e 15. calcite	a. Gives off visible light under an ultraviolet light
c 16. Iceland spar	b. Becomes electrically charged when heated
d 17. magnetite	c. Refracts light into two separate rays
b 18. tourmaline	d. Is attracted by a magnet
a 19. fluorite	e. Easily dissolved by acids

200 *Physical Science* Guided Reading and Study Workbook ▪ Chapter 22

LESSON PLAN 22.3

Rocks and the Rock Cycle

Section Objectives

- **22.3.1 Classify** rocks as igneous, sedimentary, or metamorphic and **explain** how different types of rocks form.
- **22.3.2 Describe** the processes by which rocks continually change from one type to another in the rock cycle.

Vocabulary igneous rock • magma • lava • intrusive rock • extrusive rock • sediment • sedimentary rock • clastic rocks • metamorphic rock • foliated rocks • rock cycle

Local Standards

1 FOCUS

Build Vocabulary: Concept Map
Have students build a concept map to organize the vocabulary words pertaining to the classification of rocks. **L2**

Targeted Resources
❏ Transparency: Interest Grabber 22.3
❏ Transparency: Reading Strategy 22.3

2 INSTRUCT

Build Reading Literacy: Preview
Before reading the section, have students read the bold subheads and examine Figure 21. Then, ask students to list the important concepts they will learn in the section. **L1**

Use Visuals: Figure 21
Ask students what the process is by which metamorphic rock can become sedimentary rock. Then, ask what type of rock is produced by melting and cooling. Have students name the conditions necessary for the formation of metamorphic rock. **L1**

Quick Lab: Observing the Size of Crystals
Students will heat salol and observe crystals reforming as it cools, in order to describe the effect of cooling rate on the size of crystals in igneous rocks. **L2**

Build Science Skills: Classifying
Have students work in groups to classify rock samples into the three main groups: igneous, sedimentary, or metamorphic. **L2**

Integrate Language Arts
Ask students what a *clast* is in a clastic rock. Then, have them describe the subgroups of clastic rocks based on the types of clasts they contain. **L2**

Address Misconceptions
Explain to students that, although the process often takes millions of years, rocks are continually changing from one type to another in the rock cycle. **L2**

Targeted Resources
❏ GRSW Section 22.3
❏ **NSTA** *sci*_{LINKS} Rocks

3 ASSESS

Reteach
Use Figure 21 to review the processes by which each of the three major groups of rocks are formed. **L1**

Evaluate Understanding
Ask students to classify the rocks in Figure 20 using the categories in the section. **L2**

Targeted Resources
❏ **PHSchool.com** Online Section 22.3 Assessment
❏ iText Section 22.3

Transparencies

336 **Section 22.3 Interest Grabber**

Modeling Sedimentary and Metamorphic Rock

1. Remove the paper from several crayons of different colors. Use a pencil sharpener to shave the crayons onto a sheet of wax paper. Place a second sheet of wax paper on top of the pile of crayon shavings. Place a heavy book on top of the top sheet of wax paper and carefully press down on the book. Remove the book and the top sheet of wax paper. Examine the shavings and describe your observations. What type of rock does this model?

2. Place the mass of crayon shavings onto a sheet of aluminum foil. Using tongs, carefully place the foil onto a hotplate. **CAUTION:** *The hotplate will be hot. Use caution when placing the foil on the hotplate.* After the shavings have melted, use tongs to carefully remove the foil from the hotplate. Set it aside for about five minutes to cool. Once it has cooled, remove the shavings from the foil and examine the resulting mass. Record your observations. What type of rock does this model?

ANSWERS
1. The shavings are stuck together and have packed into a flat shape with a bumpy surface. You can still see the individual colors and shapes of the shavings. This models a sedimentary rock.
2. You can still see the individual colors, but the shavings have melted together to form a shape with a smooth surface. This models a metamorphic rock.

Transparencies

337 **Section 22.3 Reading Strategy**

Comparing and Contrasting

Rock Group	Formed by	Example
Igneous	a. ___?___	b. ___?___
c. ___?___	d. ___?___	Sandstone
e. ___?___	Heat and pressure	f. ___?___

ANSWERS
a. cooling of magma or lava
b. Possible answers include granite, basalt, and gabbro.
c. Sedimentary
d. compression and cementing together of sediment
e. Metamorphic
f. Possible answers include slate, schist, and gneiss.

Guided Reading and Study Workbook

Name _____ Class _____ Date _____

Chapter 22   Earth's Interior

Section 22.3 Rocks and the Rock Cycle
(pages 670–675)

This section describes how rocks are classified. It also explains how rocks change form in the rock cycle.

Reading Strategy (page 670)
Comparing and Contrasting After you read, compare groups of rocks by completing the table. For more information on this Reading Strategy, see the **Reading and Study Skills** in the **Skills and Reference Handbook** at the end of your textbook.

Groups of Rocks		
Rock Group	**Formed by**	**Example**
Igneous	Cooling of magma or lava	Possible answers include granite, basalt, and gabbro.
Sedimentary	Compression and cementing together of sediment	Sandstone
Metamorphic	Heat and pressure	Possible answers include slate, schist, and gneiss.

Classifying Rocks (page 670)

1. Circle the letters of the major groups into which rocks are classified.
   a. sedimentary   b. igneous
   c. calcite   d. metamorphic

2. Scientists divide rocks into groups based on ___how they form___.

Igneous Rock (page 671)

3. A rock that forms from magma is called a(n) ___igneous rock___.

4. A mixture of molten rock and gases that forms underground is called ___magma___.

5. What is lava? Lava is magma that flows onto the surface.

6. Is the following sentence true or false? Igneous rock is formed when molten material cools and solidifies either inside Earth or at the surface. ___true___

Match each type of igneous rock to its characteristics. Each type of crust will have more than one characteristic.

	Igneous Rock	**Characteristic**
a, d, f	7. intrusive rock	a. Forms underground
b, c, e	8. extrusive rock	b. Forms at Earth's surface
		c. Has a fine-grained texture
		d. Has a coarse-grained texture
		e. Cools quickly
		f. Cools slowly

Guided Reading and Study Workbook

Name _____ Class _____ Date _____

Chapter 22   Earth's Interior

Sedimentary Rock (pages 672–673)

9. The process of ___weathering___ breaks down rock at Earth's surface.

10. When sediment is squeezed and cemented together, ___sedimentary___ rocks are formed.

11. Circle the groups into which geologists classify sedimentary rocks.
    a. clastic rocks
    b. foliated rocks
    c. organic rocks
    d. chemical rocks

12. Sedimentary rocks formed from broken fragments of other rocks are called ___clastic___ rocks.

13. Is the following sentence true or false? Clastic rocks are classified mainly based on the number of fragments they have. ___false___

14. Minerals that precipitate out of solution form ___chemical sedimentary rocks___.

Metamorphic Rock (page 674)

15. Circle the ways a rock can be transformed into a metamorphic rock.
    a. by heat
    b. by precipitation
    c. by pressure
    d. by chemical reaction

16. Where do most metamorphic rocks form? Most metamorphic rocks form deep underground.

17. Is the following sentence true or false? Metamorphism can change the mineral content and texture of a rock. ___true___

18. Metamorphic rocks with crystals arranged in parallel bands or layers are called ___foliated___ rocks.

The Rock Cycle (pages 674–675)

19. Circle the letters of the sentences that are true about the rock cycle.
    a. A metamorphic rock that melts and cools to form a new rock becomes an igneous rock.
    b. Forces within Earth and at the surface cause rocks to change form in the rock cycle.
    c. In the rock cycle, rocks may wear away, undergo metamorphism, or melt and form new igneous rock.
    d. The rock cycle is a series of processes in which rocks change from one type to another continuously.

LESSON PLAN 22.4

Plate Tectonics

Time
2 periods
1 block

Section Objectives
Local Standards

- **22.4.1 Explain** the hypothesis of continental drift.
- **22.4.2 Relate** how the theory of plate tectonics explains sea-floor spreading, subduction, and the formation of mountains.
- **22.4.3** Explain the mechanisms of plate movement.

Vocabulary plate tectonics • Pangaea • continental drift • mid-ocean ridge • sea-floor spreading • subduction • trench • divergent boundary • convergent boundary • transform boundary

1 FOCUS

Build Vocabulary: Word Forms
Have students look up the meanings of *convergent* and *divergent* and find other related word forms. **L2**

Targeted Resources
❏ Transparency: Interest Grabber 22.4
❏ Transparency: Reading Strategy 22.4

2 INSTRUCT

Use Visuals: Figure 29
Ask students what type of boundary exists between the Arabian plate and the Eurasian plate. **L1**

Address Misconceptions
Explain to students that plate movement occurs on the order of 0.1–10 cm/yr, and that during the course of millions of years, continents can move great distances. **L2**

Build Science Skills: Using Models
Have students use a geologic globe to learn about sea-floor spreading and plate tectonics. **L2**

Build Reading Literacy: Sequence
Have students create a flowchart describing the process of ocean floor subduction. **L2**

Integrate Social Studies
Ask students how the collection of data on the magnetic field of the ocean floor helped advance the theory of plate tectonics. **L2**

Teacher Demo: Convection and Plate Motion
Place sponges (cut into rough plate shapes) on top of heating tomato soup, so that students can observe how convection cells can move crustal masses. **L2**

Targeted Resources
❏ Transparency: Figure 24: Earth's Moving Continents
❏ Transparency: Figure 26: Subduction
❏ GRSW Section 22.4

3 ASSESS

Reteach
Use Figure 26 to discuss how oceanic crust is created and destroyed. **L1**

Evaluate Understanding
Refer to Figure 29 and ask students to create index cards for each type of boundary, including the name of the boundary type and a description of the geologic features nearby. **L2**

Targeted Resources
❏ **PHSchool.com** Online Section 22.4 Assessment
❏ iText Section 22.4

Transparencies

Modeling Continental Drift

1. Cut a large photograph out of an old magazine. The photo should be at least 10 cm by 10 cm. Make a puzzle by cutting the photo into five pieces with different shapes. Mix up the pieces, and exchange the puzzle with a partner. Put together the puzzle that your partner made. Record any methods you used to solve the puzzle.

2. How might solving a puzzle made out of a plain sheet of paper be more difficult to solve?

3. How might solving a puzzle with pieces that are all the same shape and size be more difficult to solve?

Transparencies

Previewing

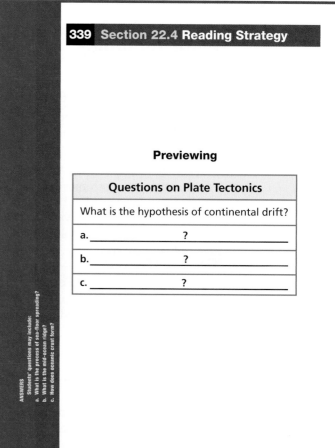

Questions on Plate Tectonics
What is the hypothesis of continental drift?
a. _____ ?
b. _____ ?
c. _____ ?

Transparencies

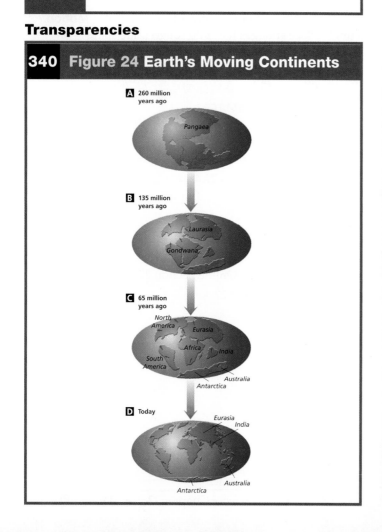

Transparencies

Figure 26 Subduction **341**

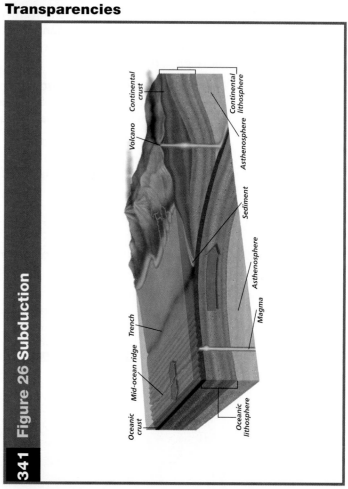

476

Name _____ Class _____ Date _____

Chapter 22   Earth's Interior

Section 22.4 Plate Tectonics
(pages 676–683)

This section describes the theory of plate tectonics. It also examines sea-floor spreading, plate boundaries, and mountain building.

Reading Strategy (page 676)

Previewing Before you read this section, rewrite the headings as how, why, and what questions about plate tectonics. As you read, write answers to the questions. For more information on this Reading Strategy, see the **Reading and Study Skills** in the **Skills and Reference Handbook** at the end of your textbook.

Plate Tectonics	
Questions on Plate Tectonics	
What is the hypothesis of continental drift?	Students' questions may include:
What is the process of sea-floor spreading?	
What is the mid-ocean ridge?	
How does oceanic crust form?	

1. Is the following sentence true or false? According to the theory of plate tectonics, Earth's plates move about quickly on top of the crust. _____false_____

2. What does the theory of plate tectonics explain about Earth's plates? _It explains their formation and movement._

Continental Drift (page 677)

3. Explain Alfred Wegener's hypothesis about the continents. _The continents were once joined in a single supercontinent, which then broke into pieces that moved apart._

4. The process by which the continents move slowly across Earth's surface is called _____continental drift_____.

Sea-floor Spreading (pages 678–679)

5. The world's longest mountain chain is the underwater chain called the _____mid-ocean ridge_____.

6. Is the following sentence true or false? The theory of sea-floor spreading explains why rocks of the ocean floor are youngest near the mid-ocean ridge. _____true_____

7. Is the following sentence true or false? Old oceanic plates sink into the mantle at mid-ocean ridges in a process called subduction. _____false_____

8. A depression in the ocean floor where subduction takes place is called a(n) _____trench_____.

Name _____ Class _____ Date _____

Chapter 22   Earth's Interior

9. Circle the letter that completes the sentence. Sea-floor spreading _____ new oceanic crust at mid-ocean ridges.
   a. creates   b. destroys

10. The process called _____subduction_____ destroys old oceanic crust at subduction zones.

The Theory of Plate Tectonics (pages 679–680)

11. Is the following sentence true or false? The concept of sea-floor spreading supports the theory of plate tectonics by providing a way for the pieces of Earth's crust to move. _____true_____

12. Heat from Earth's interior causes convection currents in Earth's _____mantle_____.

13. Circle the sentences that are true about the theory of plate tectonics.
    a. The ocean floor sinks back into the mantle at subduction zones.
    b. The heat that drives convection currents comes from solar energy.
    c. Hot rock rises at mid-ocean ridges, cools and spreads out as ocean sea floor.
    d. Plate motions are the surface portion of mantle convection.

14. Describe the two sources of the heat in Earth's mantle.
    a. _Earth was very hot when it formed and some of the heat is from its gradual cooling._
    b. _As radioactive isotopes decay in the mantle and crust, they produce heat._

Plate Boundaries (pages 681–682)

15. Identify each type of plate boundary.

a. _____Divergent boundary_____   b. _____Convergent boundary_____   c. _____Transform boundary_____

Mountain Building (page 683)

16. Is the following sentence true or false? Most mountains form along plate boundaries. _____true_____

17. Describe how the Himalayan Mountains were formed. _The Indo-Eurasian plate and the Eurasian plate collided and buckled to form the Himalayan Mountains._

Name_____ Class_____ Date_____ M T W T F

LESSON PLAN 22.5

Earthquakes

Time
2 periods
1 block

Section Objectives

■ **22.5.1 Describe** the causes and effects of stress in Earth's crust.

■ **22.5.2 Explain** why earthquakes occur and how their energy is propagated as seismic waves.

■ **22.5.3 Explain** how earthquakes are measured and how earthquake data is used to learn about Earth's interior.

Vocabulary earthquake • seismic waves • stress • fault • fold • focus • epicenter • P waves • S waves • surface waves • seismograph

Local Standards

1 FOCUS

Build Vocabulary: Concept Map
Have students build a concept map using all of the vocabulary terms, beginning with the main concept (Earthquakes). **L2**

Targeted Resources
❏ Transparency: Interest Grabber 22.5
❏ Transparency: Reading Strategy 22.5

2 INSTRUCT

Build Reading Literacy: Use Prior Knowledge
Have students read the key concept on p. 689. Then, ask why faults and earthquakes are concentrated along plate boundaries. **L1**

Address Misconceptions
Inform students that, in some rare cases, crevasses may open up during a quake, but they would be too small to swallow buildings, much less entire cities. **L2**

Teacher Demo: Faults and Folds
Demonstrate the compressional force of a continental collision by applying horizontal force to model clay crusts. Students observe a model of the creation of faults and folds in Earth's crust. **L2**

Quick Lab: Modeling a Seismograph
Students will make a seismograph using cash register paper rolled around a pencil. As the free end of the paper is pulled, another student will hold a felt-tip pen so that it marks a line on the paper. **L2**

For Enrichment
Repeat the Quick Lab experiment using two paper-strip seismographs. Have students compare the two ink lines to determine the direction of the shaking **L3**

For Enrichment
Have interested students research the locations of recent earthquakes in their region, or in the United States. Ask students to present their findings in class. **L3**

Targeted Resources
❏ Transparency: Figure 37: Propagation of Seismic Waves
❏ GRSW Section 22.5

3 ASSESS

Reteach
Use Figure 35 to review the focus, epicenter, and propagation of seismic waves. **L1**

Evaluate Understanding
Ask students to create a visual showing each of the three kinds of seismic waves. **L2**

Targeted Resources
❏ **PHSchool.com** Online Section 22.5 Assessment
❏ iText Section 22.5

Transparencies

342 Section 22.5 Interest Grabber

Modeling Faults and Folds

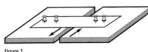

Figure 1

1. Place two pieces of foam-core board flat on your desk, side by side so that their longest edges are aligned. Using four thumb tacks, attach a 1-cm-wide strip of paper to both boards so that the strip lies perpendicular to the board edges, as shown in the diagram above. **CAUTION:** *Thumb tacks have sharp points. Be careful when handling them.* Slowly slide the boards as shown by the arrows in the diagram. Record your observations.

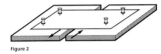

Figure 2

2. Reposition the boards so that there is a 2-3 cm space between them. Attach a larger sheet of paper to the boards as shown in the second diagram. Slowly slide the boards as shown by the arrows in the diagram. Record your observations.

3. Does Figure 1 model a fault or a fold? What about Figure 2?

ANSWERS
1. The strip of paper breaks.
2. The paper bends and bulges upward.
3. Figure 1 models a fault and Figure 2 models a fold.

Transparencies

343 Section 22.5 Reading Strategy

c. A force within Earth that either squeezes rocks together, pulls them apart, or pushes them in different directions

Building Vocabulary

Vocabulary Term	Definition
Earthquake	a. _____?_____
Seismic waves	b. _____?_____
Stress	c. _____?_____

ANSWERS
a. A movement of the lithosphere that occurs when rocks in the lithosphere suddenly shift, releasing energy
b. Vibrations caused by an earthquake that carry the earthquake's energy away

Transparencies

344 **Figure 37 Propagation of Seismic Waves**

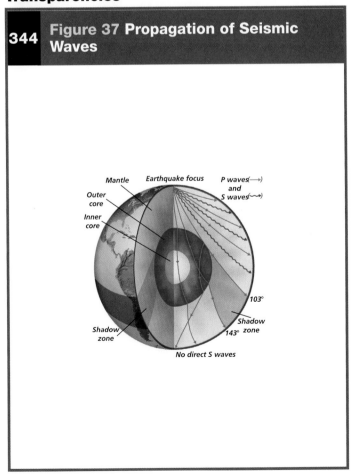

479

Section 22.5   Program Resources

Name _____ Class _____ Date _____

Chapter 22   Earth's Interior

Section 22.5 Earthquakes
(pages 684–689)

This section explains what earthquakes are, what causes them, and their effects.

Reading Strategy (page 684)

Building Vocabulary Copy the table on a separate sheet of paper and add more rows as needed. As you read, define each term for this section in your own words. For more information on this Reading Strategy, see the **Reading and Study Skills** in the **Skills and Reference Handbook** at the end of your textbook.

Earthquake Terms	
Vocabulary Terms	**Definitions**
Earthquake	A movement of Earth's lithosphere that occurs when rocks in the lithosphere suddenly shift, releasing energy
Seismic waves	Vibrations caused by an earthquake that carry the earthquake's energy away
Stress	A force within Earth that either squeezes rocks together, pulls them apart, or pushes them in different directions

1. An earthquake releases ___stored (or potential)___ energy that is carried by vibrations called ___seismic waves___.

Stress in Earth's Crust (page 685)

2. Name three ways that stress can affect rocks.

   a. It can squeeze them together.

   b. It can stretch or pull them apart.

   c. It can push them in different directions.

3. Is the following sentence true or false? Stress from moving tectonic plates produces faults and folds in Earth's crust. ___true___

Match each result of stress to its characteristics. Each result will have more than one characteristic.

	Result of Stress	Characteristic
_b,c_	**4.** fault	a. A bend in layers of rock
_a,d_	**5.** fold	b. Many occur along plate boundaries
		c. A break in a mass of rock where movement happens
		d. Forms where rocks are squeezed but do not break

6. Is the following sentence true or false? Rocks tend to fold instead of break under low temperature or pressure. ___false___

Name _____ Class _____ Date _____

Chapter 22   Earth's Interior

Earthquakes and Seismic Waves (pages 686–687)

7. Why do earthquakes occur? ___They happen because underground stress forces have exceeded the strength of rock.___

8. Is the following sentence true or false? The location underground where an earthquake begins is called the focus. ___true___

9. The location on Earth's surface directly above the focus of an earthquake is called the ___epicenter___.

10. Circle the sentences that are true about the physics of earthquakes.

    (a.) Stress builds in areas where rocks along fault lines snag and remain locked.

    (b.) In an earthquake, rocks break and grind past each other, releasing energy.

    (c.) Potential energy is transformed into kinetic energy in the form of seismic waves.

    d. Potential energy increases as rocks break and move.

Match each type of seismic wave to its characteristic.

	Seismic Waves	Characteristic
_c_	**11.** P waves	a. Transverse waves that cannot travel through liquids
_a_	**12.** S waves	b. Slowest moving type of wave that develops when seismic waves reach Earth's surface
_b_	**13.** surface waves	c. Longitudinal waves similar to sound waves that cause particles in the material to vibrate in the direction of the waves' motion

14. Typically, the first seismic waves to be detected at a distance are ___P___ waves.

Measuring Earthquakes (page 687)

15. What devices do geologists use to record seismic waves? ___They use a seismograph.___

Seismographic Data (page 689)

16. Most earthquakes are concentrated along ___plate boundaries___.

17. Is the following sentence true or false? Some earthquakes will occur in the interior of plates. ___true___

18. Is the following statement true or false? When seismic waves interact with boundaries between different kinds of rock within Earth, they can be reflected, refracted, or diffracted. ___true___

LESSON PLAN 22.6

Volcanoes

Section Objectives

- **22.6.1 Describe** the internal structure of a volcano and how volcanoes form.
- **22.6.2 Relate** the type of volcanic eruption to the characteristics of magma.
- **22.6.3 Describe** the different types of volcanoes and where they are typically located.
- **22.6.4 Describe** several types of igneous features and how they are formed.

Vocabulary volcano • magma chamber • pipe • vent • crater • caldera • hot spot • shield volcano • cinder cone • composite volcano • batholith • sill • dike • volcanic neck

Local Standards

1 FOCUS

Build Vocabulary: Venn Diagram
Have students build a Venn diagram to compare the similarities and differences between *composite volcanoes, shield volcanoes,* and *cinder cones.* **L2**

Targeted Resources
❏ Transparency: Interest Grabber 22.6
❏ Transparency: Reading Strategy 22.6

2 INSTRUCT

Build Reading Literacy: Identify Main Idea/Details
Have students read Quiet and Explosive Eruptions, and then find the details that support the key concept. **L1**

Use Visuals: Figure 42
Ask students which volcanoes are formed from melting slabs of subducting oceanic crust. Then, ask where volcanoes are located in the United States. **L1**

Build Science Skills: Inferring
After reading the Concepts in Action feature, have students work in groups to study the characteristics of volcanic rock samples. **L2**

Address Misconceptions
After students read Other Igneous Features, have them work in groups to create a visual describing ways igneous rocks can form. **L2**

Going Further
Have interested students research volcanoes on other planets or moons and present photos to the class. **L3**

Targeted Resources
❏ Transparency: Figure 39: The Structure of a Volcano
❏ GRSW Section 22.6

3 ASSESS

Reteach
Use Figure 39 to explain the main features of a volcano. **L1**

Evaluate Understanding
Using Figure 41, ask students what type of volcano most likely produced this type of lava. **L2**

Targeted Resources
❏ **PHSchool.com** Online Section 22.6 Assessment
❏ iText Section 22.6

Transparencies

345 Section 22.6 Interest Grabber

Modeling a Hot Spot

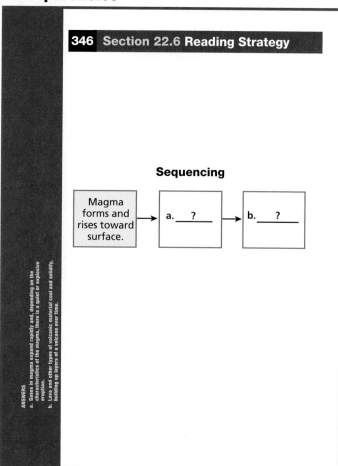

1. Using a pen, poke a 1-cm hole in a corner of a piece of foam-core board as shown in diagram A. Using a thumb tack, attach a paper towel (roughly the same size as the board) to the opposite corner of the board, as shown in diagram B. Insert a felt-tip marker into the hole from underneath the board, and make a mark that is absorbed by the paper towel. This mark represents a volcano that has formed from hot rock coming up through Earth's surface. If the paper towel represents an oceanic plate, what type of geologic formation does the volcano make?

2. Rotate the paper towel about the thumb tack, as shown by the arrow in diagram B. Every few centimeters of rotation, make a mark with the marker from underneath the paper towel. What type of design forms on the paper towel?

ANSWERS
1. a volcanic island
2. An arc of dots (representing an island chain) forms.

Transparencies

346 Section 22.6 Reading Strategy

Sequencing

Magma forms and rises toward surface. → a. _____?_____ → b. _____?_____

ANSWERS
a. Gases in magma expand rapidly and, depending on the characteristics of the magma, there is a quiet or explosive eruption.
b. Lava and other types of volcanic material cool and solidify, building up layers of a volcano over time.

Transparencies

347 **Figure 39 The Structure of a Volcano**

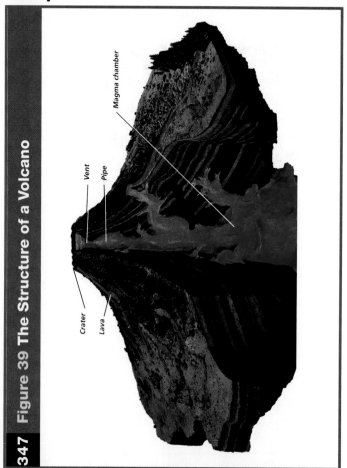

Magma chamber

Vent

Pipe

Crater

Lava

Guided Reading and Study Workbook

Name _____ Class _____ Date _____

Chapter 22   Earth's Interior

Section 22.6 Volcanoes
(pages 690–696)

This section describes volcanoes, how they form, and the different ways they erupt. It also describes the different types of volcanoes and other features created by magma.

Reading Strategy (page 690)

Sequencing As you read, complete the flowchart to show how a volcano forms. For more information on this Reading Strategy, see the **Reading and Study Skills** in the **Skills and Reference Handbook** at the end of your textbook.

Formation of a Volcano

| Magma forms and rises toward surface. | → | Gases in magma expand rapidly and, depending on the characteristics of the magma, there is a quiet or explosive eruption. | → | Lava and other types of volcanic material cool and solidify, building up layers of a volcano over time. |

1. A mountain that forms when magma reaches the surface is called a(n) ___volcano___ .

Formation of a Volcano (page 691)

2. Is the following sentence true or false? Liquid magma is formed when small amounts of mantle rock melt. ___true___

3. Describe how a volcano forms. ___Liquid magma rises upward through the crust and erupts at the surface as a volcano.___

4. Describe how a volcano erupts. ___When the expanding gases in magma bubble out through a crack in the crust, magma is propelled to the surface.___

5. Magma collects in a pocket called the ___magma chamber___ before a volcanic eruption.

Match each feature of a volcano to its correct description.

	Feature	Description
_a_	6. pipe	a. A narrow, vertical channel where magma rises to the surface
_b_	7. vent	b. An opening in the ground where magma escapes to the surface
_d_	8. crater	c. A huge depression created if the shell of the magma chamber collapses
_e_	9. magma chamber	d. A bowl-shaped pit at the top of a volcano
_c_	10. caldera	e. A pocket where the magma collects

Physical Science Guided Reading and Study Workbook • Chapter 22 **207**

Guided Reading and Study Workbook

Name _____ Class _____ Date _____

Chapter 22   Earth's Interior

Quiet and Explosive Eruptions (page 692)

11. Is the following sentence true or false? How easily magma flows depends on its viscosity. ___true___

12. List three factors that determine the viscosity of magma.
    a. ___Temperature___
    b. ___Water content___
    c. ___Silica content___

13. Is the following sentence true or false? Magma with higher temperatures has higher viscosity. ___false___

14. Hot, fast-moving lava is called ___pahoehoe___ and cooler, slow-moving lava is called ___aa___ .

Location and Types of Volcanoes (page 693)

15. Where do most volcanoes occur? ___Most volcanoes occur along plate boundaries or at hot spots in Earth's crust.___

16. Is the following sentence true or false? A region where hot rock extends from deep within the core to the surface is called a hot spot. ___false___

17. Is the following sentence true or false? A composite volcano is produced by a quiet eruption of low-viscosity lava. ___false___

18. An eruption of ash and cinders will produce a volcano called a(n) ___cinder cone___ .

19. Is the following sentence true or false? A composite volcano is formed from an explosive eruption of lava and ash. ___true___

Other Igneous Features (page 696)

20. Circle the letters of the igneous features that are formed by magma.
    (a.) dikes
    (b.) sills
    (c.) volcanic necks
    (d.) batholiths

21. The largest type of intrusive igneous rock mass is called a(n) ___batholith___ .

22. Is the following sentence true or false? A crack that has been filled in by magma and hardens parallel to existing rock layers is called a dike. ___false___

208 *Physical Science* Guided Reading and Study Workbook • Chapter 22

Guided Reading and Study Workbook

Name _____ Class _____ Date _____

Chapter 22   Earth's Interior

WordWise

Use the clues below to identify vocabulary terms from Chapter 22. Write the terms below, putting one letter in each blank. When you finish, the term enclosed in the diagonal will reveal an important process on Earth.

Clues

1. A solid combination of minerals or mineral materials
2. The central layer of Earth
3. A type of fracture in which a mineral tends to split along regular, well-defined planes
4. A movement of Earth's lithosphere that occurs when rocks shift suddenly, releasing stored energy
5. A region where plates collide
6. The type of rock that forms when small pieces of sediment are squeezed together
7. A mountain that forms when magma reaches the surface
8. A bend in layers of rock
9. Wegener's hypothesis in which continents move slowly across Earth's surface

Vocabulary Terms

1. r o c k
2. c o r e
3. c l e a v a g e
4. e a r t h q u a k e
5. c o n v e r g e n t   b o u n d a r y
6. s e d i m e n t a r y   r o c k
7. v o l c a n o
8. f o l d
9. c o n t i n e n t a l   d r i f t

Hidden Word: r o c k   c y c l e

Definition: A series of processes in which rocks continuously change from one type to another

Physical Science Guided Reading and Study Workbook • Chapter 22 **209**

Guided Reading and Study Workbook

Name _____ Class _____ Date _____

Chapter 22   Earth's Interior

Calculating Wavelength and Frequency

Math Skill:
Line Graphs

An earthquake occurs 1000 km from seismograph station B. What is the difference in time between the arrivals of the first P wave and the first S wave at station B?

You may want to read more about this **Math Skill** *in the* **Skills and Reference Handbook** *at the end of your textbook.*

1. **Read and Understand**

   What information are you given in the problem?
   Station B is 1000 km from where an earthquake occurred.

2. **Plan and Solve**

   What does the question ask you to find?
   The difference in time between the arrivals of the first P wave and the first S wave at station B

   Find the amount of time it took the first P wave to reach station B by following the 1000-km line up to where it meets the P wave curve.
   2 minutes

   Find the amount of time it took the first S wave to reach station B by following the 1000-km line up to where it meets the S wave curve.
   4 minutes

   Subtract the amount of time it took the P wave to travel to station B from the amount of time it took the S wave to travel to station B.
   4 minutes − 2 minutes = 2 minutes

3. **Look Back and Check**

   Is your answer reasonable? Yes, because S waves move slower than P waves.

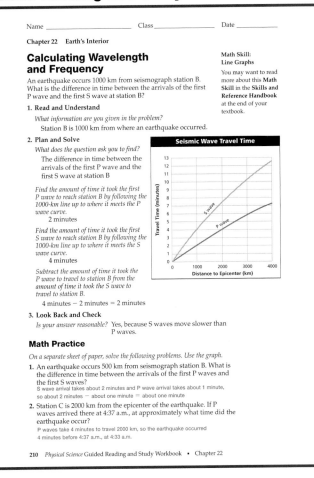

Seismic Wave Travel Time

(Travel Time (minutes) vs. Distance to Epicenter (km))

Math Practice

On a separate sheet of paper, solve the following problems. Use the graph.

1. An earthquake occurs 500 km from seismograph station B. What is the difference in time between the arrivals of the first P waves and the first S waves?
   S wave arrival takes about 2 minutes and P wave arrival takes about 1 minute, so about 2 minutes − about 1 minute = about one minute

2. Station C is 2000 km from the epicenter of the earthquake. If P waves arrived there at 4:37 a.m., at approximately what time did the earthquake occur?
   P waves take 4 minutes to travel 2000 km, so the earthquake occurred 4 minutes before 4:37 a.m., at 4:33 a.m.

210 *Physical Science* Guided Reading and Study Workbook • Chapter 22

Student Edition Lab Worksheet

Name _____ Class _____ Date _____

Chapter 22   Earth's Interior   Exploration Lab

Using Earthquakes to Map Plate Boundaries
See page 697 in the Teacher's Edition for more information.

In this lab, you will analyze data from several earthquakes to determine how the plates in the northwestern United States are moving.

Problem   How can you use earthquake data to infer the movement of tectonic plates?

Materials
• graph paper

Skills   Inferring, Analyzing Data

Procedure
1. Examine the map of Oregon and Washington states. Earthquakes occur in the western parts of these states as a result of the movements of two plates—the Juan de Fuca Plate, which lies under the Pacific Ocean, and the North American plate.

2. Examine the table of earthquake data. Record any patterns that you observe.

_____

DATA TABLE

Year	Location of Epicenter	Distance From Coast (km)	Depth of Focus (km)
1949	Olympia	116	53
1965	Seattle-Tacoma	141	63
1999	Satsop	58	41
2001	Nisqually	108	52
2001	Matlock	60	41

3. Draw a diagram showing how the edges of the Juan de Fuca and North American plates would move if they formed a convergent boundary. Use Figure 30 on page 682 of your textbook to help you draw this diagram.

Student Edition Lab Worksheet

Name _____ Class _____ Date _____

4. Draw a diagram showing how the edges of the two plates would move if they formed a transform boundary. Use Figure 30 again to help you draw this diagram.

5. Use the information in the data table to construct a graph showing the location and depth of earthquakes. Plot the distance from the coast on the horizontal axis and the depth of the focus on the vertical axis. Label the vertical axis with zero at the top and maximum depth at the bottom.

6. Draw a curve as close as possible to all the points you plotted on your graph. The curve shows the shape and position of the boundary between the Juan de Fuca and North American plates. Compare your graph to the two diagrams you drew in Steps 3 and 4.

Analyze and Conclude

1. **Using Graphs**   What kind of boundary do the Juan de Fuca and North American plates form? Explain how your graph supports your answer.

   The curve slopes down to the right, indicating that the border between the two plates slopes down

   to the East under the North American Plate as a convergent boundary.

2. **Inferring**   What does your graph suggest about the direction in which the Juan de Fuca and North American plates are moving?

   The graph suggests that the North American Plate is moving west, over the Juan de Fuca Plate.

3. **Predicting**   In California, the Pacific plate and the North American plate meet along a transform boundary called the San Andreas fault. Would you expect to observe a similar curve in a graph of the earthquake data from the San Andreas fault? Explain your answer.

   No, in a transform boundary, the plates form a vertical boundary that would appear as a vertical

   line on the graph.

4. **Drawing Conclusions**   Based on your data, how is earthquake depth related to distance from a convergent plate boundary? Explain your answer.

   The depth of the earthquakes increases with distance from the boundary because the earthquake

   foci are located along the upper surface of the subducting plate.

Lab Manual

Name _____ Class _____ Date _____

Chapter 22   Earth's Interior   Investigation 22A

Identifying Rocks
Refer students to pages 670–675 in their textbooks for a general discussion of rocks. **SKILLS:** Observing, Classifying, Using Tables and Graphs **CLASS TIME:** 45 minutes

Background Information

A rock is a solid combination of one or more minerals or other materials. Geologists classify rocks into three major groups (igneous, sedimentary, and metamorphic) based on how the rocks form. To identify rocks, geologists observe a rock's texture—the size, shape, and arrangement of the crystals and other particles that make up the rock.

Igneous rock forms from magma that cools either underground (intrusive rock) or on Earth's surface (extrusive rock). Intrusive rocks cool slowly, allowing crystals to grow larger and giving the rock a coarse-grained texture. Extrusive rocks cool quickly and have a fine-grained, or even glassy, texture.

Sedimentary rock forms from sediment that is squeezed and cemented together. Sedimentary rocks that form from the broken fragments of other rocks are called clastic rocks. The fragments might be fairly large, such as pebbles, somewhat smaller, such as grains of sand, or very small, such as grains of clay. Other kinds of sedimentary rock include chemical rocks, which form when minerals precipitate out of solution, and organic rocks, which form when the shells and skeletons of marine animals become compacted and cemented together over time.

Metamorphic rock forms from rock that has been changed by temperature, pressure, or chemical reactions. Metamorphic rocks may be foliated, in which the particles are arranged in parallel bands, or nonfoliated, in which the particles are not arranged in bands.

In this investigation, you will learn how to identify the three major types of rocks as well as some rock types within each major category.

Problem

What are the identifying properties of rocks?

Pre-Lab Discussion

Read the entire investigation. Then, work with a partner to answer the following questions.

1. **Inferring**   What is the purpose of this investigation?

   The purpose of this investigation is to categorize and identify the major types of rocks.

   _____
   _____
   _____
   _____

Lab Manual

Name _____ Class _____ Date _____

2. **Observing**   What property distinguishes the two main types of igneous rock? Explain your answer.

   Grain size distinguishes intrusive igneous rock from extrusive igneous rock. Intrusive rocks

   have larger grains than do extrusive rocks.

   _____
   _____

3. **Drawing Conclusions**   Chalk is made of tiny fragments of marine animals. What kind of rock is chalk?

   Chalk is an organic sedimentary rock.

   _____
   _____

4. **Drawing Conclusions**   If you have a rock that has parallel bands in it, what kind of rock might you have? Might it be another type of rock? Explain your answer.

   It might be a foliated metamorphic rock. However, it might be a sedimentary rock, which

   also sometimes has bands. Other observations would have to be made to identify the rock.

   _____
   _____
   _____

Materials *(per group)*

igneous rocks	Hand lens
sedimentary rocks	Dropper bottle of dilute
metamorphic rocks	hydrochloric acid (HCl)
	Paper towels

Safety

Put on safety goggles and wear plastic disposable gloves when handling chemicals, as they may irritate the skin or stain skin or clothing. Never touch or taste a chemical unless instructed to do so. Note all safety alert symbols next to the steps in the Procedure and review the meaning of each symbol by referring to the Safety Symbols on page xiii.

Provide students with a variety of rock specimens from all three major types. Examples: igneous—basalt, granite, and obsidian; sedimentary—limestone, sandstone, and shale; metamorphic—marble, slate, and schist. Choose specimens so that at least most of them will be identifiable by using the key in Figure 1. You may have to help students identify the specimens that are more difficult.

If so, discuss the properties of that specimen or the subtleties that make identification difficult. Identify each specimen with a letter either by using masking tape and a marker or by painting a small solid white circle on the rock and marking the circle. Prepare a 1M solution of HCl by slowly adding 82 mL of concentrated (12M) HCl to 500 mL of distilled water in a flask. Then fill the flask with distilled water to the 1000 mL mark.

Lab Manual

Name _____ Class _____ Date _____

Procedure

1. Choose one of the rock samples provided by your teacher. Observe its texture, color, and other properties.

2. Use the key in Figure 1 to identify the sample. Begin by reading the first question. Answer yes or no based on your observations.

3. After Yes or No, you will find a phrase telling you to proceed to another question. Continue working through the key in this way until you come to a phrase that identifies your rock sample. In the data table, record the route that you take through the key, using the numbers of the questions. Then, record the type of rock you have identified.

4. Work through the key for each of your samples to identify them.

5. Check your identifications with the true identifications from your teacher.

Figure 1   Key to Identification of Some Rocks

1. Does the rock contain visible interlocking crystals?	Yes: Go to Step 2.
	No: Go to Step 4.
2. Are all of the crystals the same color and shape?	Yes: nonfoliated metamorphic (possibly marble or quartzite)
	No: Go to Step 3.
3. Are all of the crystals in a mixed "salt-and-pepper" pattern?	Yes: intrusive igneous (possibly granite or diorite)
	No: foliated metamorphic (possibly schist or gneiss)
4. Does the rock contain many small holes or have a uniform dark appearance?	Yes: extrusive igneous (possibly pumice or basalt)
	No: Go to Step 5.
5. Is the rock glassy, like broken black or brown glass?	Yes: extrusive igneous (obsidian)
	No: Go to Step 6.
6. Is the rock made of strong, flat sheets that can be split in layers?	Yes: foliated metamorphic (slate)
	No: Go to Step 7.
7. Does the rock contain pebbles, sand, or smaller particles cemented together?	Yes: clastic sedimentary (possibly conglomerate or sandstone)
	No: Go to Step 8.
8. Does the rock fizz when dilute HCl is added to it?	Yes: chemical or organic sedimentary (limestone or chalk)
	No: Ask your teacher for help.

Note: Answer Question 8 by placing the rock on a paper towel, then placing a single drop of HCl on the rock. **CAUTION:** *Wear safety goggles and disposable gloves when using the HCl.*

Lab Manual

Name _____ Class _____ Date _____

Observations   Data will vary depending on samples chosen.

Letter of Sample	Route Taken	Identity of Rock Sample

Lab Manual

Name _____ Class _____ Date _____

Analysis and Conclusions

1. **Evaluating and Revising** How difficult was it to use the key to identify your rock samples? What problems did you encounter?

   Answers will depend partly on how clearly the samples represent the rock type. Students

   may encounter difficulty if samples appear to exhibit properties of more than one rock type or

   have subtle properties.

2. **Evaluating and Revising** For each sample that you incorrectly identified, retrace the route you took through the key. Do you need to correct your route? If so, write it below. If not, why might you have incorrectly identified the sample?

   If the route was correct, yet the rock is incorrectly identified, it might be because the key does

   not provide enough information for identification of that sample.

3. **Generalizing** How helpful is a rock's color in identifying the rock? Explain your answer.

   Color is not very helpful for identification. Often, more than one kind of rock has the same color.

   Also, a particular kind of rock often has more than one color.

Lab Manual

Name _____ Class _____ Date _____

4. **Comparing and Contrasting** Which two of the rock samples were the easiest to identify? What properties made them easy to identify?

   Answers may include rocks that have distinguishing properties such as the glassy

   texture of obsidian, the fizzing of HCl in contact with limestone, or the bands or layers

   of a foliated metamorphic rock.

Go Further

Collect several rock samples from the area around your home or school and attempt to identify them by using the key in this investigation.

Students should be able to find a variety of rocks. Suggest that they look in different places to get the greatest variety, such as road sides, along a creek, in a field, and so on.

Lab Manual

Name _____ Class _____ Date _____

Chapter 22 Earth's Interior

🔍 **Investigation 22B**

Recovering Oil

Refer students to pages 267 and 667 in their textbooks for general discussions of petroleum and density. **SKILLS FOCUS:** Predicting, Inferring, Comparing and Contrasting

CLASS TIME: 45 minutes

Background Information

Crude oil, or petroleum, is usually found beneath nonporous rock in underground deposits. The petroleum can be recovered by a well pipe lowered to the deposit through a drilled hole. In some cases, the petroleum is automatically pushed up by the pressure of underground water. In other cases, however, pressure must be applied by methods involving pumping water into the petroleum deposit. This method works because petroleum is less dense than water and so will float on top of it.

In this investigation, you will use various methods to recover the maximum amount of oil from a pump bottle.

Problem

How does water affect the recovery of oil from a petroleum deposit?

Pre-Lab Discussion

Read the entire investigation. Then, work with a partner to answer the following questions.

1. **Predicting** What do you expect to happen when you add water to the bottle after the first attempt to remove the oil has been made? Do you expect more oil to be brought up after adding cold water or hot water? Explain your answer.

   Additional oil will be brought up along with the added water. Hot water will make the oil more fluid,

   so more oil should be brought up after adding hot water.

2. **Applying Concepts** Would you expect more oil to be removed by using hot water or cold water? Explain your answer.

   Hot water should remove more water. The higher temperature of the water will increase the

   temperature of the oil, making it flow more easily and so removing it from small places between

   the rocks.

3. **Applying Concepts** How does adding water increase pressure within a petroleum deposit?

   By adding water to the oil in the deposit, the total amount of fluid within the deposit increases.

   Because the volume of the deposit does not expand, this added material will cause an increase

   in pressure.

Lab Manual

Name _____ Class _____ Date _____

4. **Inferring** What properties of oil makes water the preferred substance for pushing oil up to Earth's surface?

   Oil is less dense than water and so will float on the water. The oil will therefore be pushed to the

   top levels of the deposit.

5. **Controlling Variables** Why must the investigation be repeated with hot water after it has been performed with cold water?

   By performing the investigation first with cold water and again with hot water, all variables

   except water temperature will be controlled. Therefore, the effect of water temperature can be more

   clearly observed.

Materials *(per group)* Collect the oil to reuse in the next class.

plastic bottle with spray pump
plastic tubing to fit the pump nozzle
pebbles (enough to half-fill the plastic bottle)
2 graduated cylinders
200 mL of vegetable or mineral oil

4 250-mL beakers
cold tap water
hot tap water
paper towels
clock or watch

Safety 🧤 🥽 🔥 🧷

Be careful to avoid breakage when working with glassware. Use extreme care when working with hot water to avoid burns. Wash your hands thoroughly after carrying out this investigation. Note all safety alert symbols next to the steps in the Procedure and review the meaning of each symbol by referring to the Safety Symbols on page xiii.

Procedure

🧷 1. Build a model of an oil pump, as shown in Figure 1. Remove the spray pump top of the spray bottle and half-fill the spray bottle with clean pebbles.

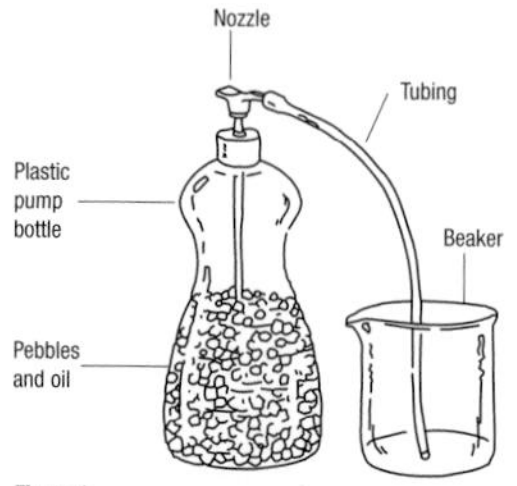

Figure 1

Lab Manual

Name _____ Class _____ Date _____

2. Use a graduated cylinder to measure 100 mL of vegetable or mineral oil and pour the oil into the bottle. **CAUTION:** *Be careful to avoid breakage when working with glassware. Be careful not to spill any oil onto your clothing. Immediately wipe up any spilled water or oil.*

3. Place the spray-pump top back onto the bottle while working its tube down through the pebbles. Attach the plastic tubing to the nozzle and place the other end of the tubing into a 250-mL beaker.

4. Use the spray pump to remove as much oil as you can from the bottle within 5 minutes. Use the graduated cylinder to measure the amount of oil removed. Record this information in the data table.

5. Measure 80 mL of cold tap water in the second graduated cylinder and add this water to the spray bottle. Attempt to pump as much liquid as possible into the second beaker within 5 minutes. Let the mixture stand for 1 or 2 minutes so that the oil and water separate. Carefully pour into the first graduated cylinder the oil layer that is on top of the water in the beaker. Record in the data table how much oil you collected.

🧤 6. Rinse the bottle and pebbles with hot water to remove any excess oil and wipe them dry with paper towels. Place the used oil in a container designated by your teacher. Clean the first graduated cylinder and add 100 mL of fresh oil.

🔥 7. Repeat Steps 1 through 5, but in Step 5, use 80 mL of hot tap water instead of cold water. Record in the data table the amount of oil collected. Place the used oil in a container designated by your teacher. The water with traces of oil can be poured down the sink. **CAUTION:** *Use extreme care when working with hot water to avoid burns. Wash your hands thoroughly after carrying out this investigation.*

Observations Sample data are shown.

DATA TABLE

	Oil Added to Bottle (mL)	Oil Removed Before Adding Water (mL)	Oil Removed After Adding Water (mL)
Cold water	99.0–101.0	50.0–65.0	15.0–20.0
Hot water	99.0–101.0	50.0–65.0	25.0–30.0

Lab Manual

Name _____ Class _____ Date _____

Analysis and Conclusions

1. **Analyzing Data** How did your results compare with your prediction?

   The prediction that hot water would remove more oil than cold water was confirmed by the results.

2. **Observing** Why were you unable to remove all the oil from the bottle when you pumped it in Step 4?

   Some of the oil clung to the pebbles.

3. **Applying Concepts** Explain the effect of adding cold water.

   Cold water removed some of the oil that was around the pebbles, allowing more oil to be pumped.

4. **Applying Concepts** Explain the effect of adding hot water.

   As well as removing oil around the pebbles, hot water rendered the oil more fluid and more easily

   separated and pumped.

Go Further

Repeat the investigation, using different kinds of oil to determine how the density and thickness, or viscosity, of the oil affects recovery. Show your plan to your teacher. When your teacher approves your plan, carry out your experiment and report your results.

Review student designs for appropriateness and difficulty before students begin testing. If samples of motor oil are used, be sure that the investigation is performed under your supervision and that all oil is collected and taken to a garage for proper disposal.

Chapter Test A

Name _____ Class _____ Date _____

Chapter 22 Earth's Interior

Multiple Choice

Write the letter that best answers the question or completes the statement on the line provided.

_____ 1. Forces that shape Earth's surface can be divided into
a. constructive and physical.
b. constructive and destructive.
c. chemical and destructive.
d. chemical and physical.

_____ 2. The two layers that make up the lithosphere are the
a. upper mantle and lower mantle.
b. oceanic crust and continental crust.
c. inner core and outer core.
d. crust and upper mantle.

_____ 3. What is a mineral's cleavage?
a. the resistance of a mineral to scratching
b. a type of fracture in which a mineral breaks along regular, well-defined planes c. the color of a mineral's powder
d. a type of fracture in which a mineral breaks along a curved surface

_____ 4. Intense heat, intense pressure, or reactions with hot water can modify a pre-existing rock to form a(an)
a. metamorphic rock.   b. sedimentary rock.
c. igneous rock.   d. organic rock.

_____ 5. What changes are involved when mud from a lake bottom turns into a sedimentary rock, then into a metamorphic rock?
a. compaction and cementation, then melting
b. heat and pressure, then weathering
c. compaction and cementation, then heat and pressure
d. melting, then compaction and cementation

_____ 6. Why was Wegener's hypothesis of continental drift originally rejected by geologists?
a. Wegener did not have any data to support his hypothesis.
b. The continents of South America and Africa do not fit well together.
c. Wegener could not explain how the continents could move through the ocean floor.
d. Wegener's data was incorrect.

_____ 7. A subducting oceanic plate
a. is less dense than the plate it moves under.
b. is pushed up and over the continental crust.
c. sinks into the mantle, forming a trench.
d. moves horizontally in the opposite direction past the other plate.

Chapter Test A

Name _____ Class _____ Date _____

_____ 8. The heat that drives mantle convection comes from the cooling of Earth's interior and
a. the sun.
b. the decay of radioactive isotopes.
c. sea-floor spreading.
d. trenches.

_____ 9. Stress in Earth's crust is caused by
a. folds.   b. plate movements.   c. earthquakes.   d. faults.

_____ 10. P waves
a. cause Earth to vibrate in the direction of the wave's motion.
b. cause Earth to vibrate at right angles to the direction the wave moves.
c. travel along Earth's surface.
d. move in a rolling motion similar to ocean waves.

_____ 11. Geologists have inferred that Earth's outer core is liquid because
a. P waves cannot pass through the outer core.
b. S waves speed up in the outer core.
c. S waves are bent downward as they travel through the outer core.
d. S waves cannot pass through the outer core.

_____ 12. What causes the magna inside a volcano to rise towards the surface?
a. It is a thick liquid, denser than the surrounding rock.
b. It does not contain dissolved gases.
c. It is less dense than the surrounding rock.
d. It is cooler than the surrounding rock.

_____ 13. What causes the magna inside a volcano to rise towards the surface?
a. It is a thick liquid, denser than the surrounding rock.
b. It does not contain dissolved gases.
c. It is less dense than the surrounding rock.
d. It is cooler than the surrounding rock.

_____ 14. A steep-sided volcano formed entirely of ash and cinders is a
a. shield volcano.   b. composite volcano.
c. cinder cone.   d. hot spot.

_____ 15. A sequence of rock layers consists of horizontal layers of sandstone, granite, and limestone. What type of intrusive igneous feature does the granite layer represent?
a. a sill   b. a dike
c. a batholith   d. a volcanic neck

Chapter Test A

Name _____ Class _____ Date _____

Completion

Complete each statement on the line provided.

1. The type of sedimentary rock that forms when fragments of pre-existing rocks are cemented together is called a(an) _____ rock.

2. Alfred Wegener proposed that a continent was formed by continental drift. This supercontinent was called _____.

3. Due to sea-floor spreading, the youngest rocks in the ocean floor are found near a(an) _____.

4. The seismic waves that compress and expand the ground are called _____ waves.

5. The mineral pyrite has a metallic _____.

Short Answer

In complete sentences, write the answers to the questions on the lines provided.

1. How is the streak of a mineral obtained?

_____
_____

2. Describe the physical properties of the three layers of the mantle.

_____
_____
_____

3. What is the difference between how an intrusive rock and an extrusive rock forms?

_____
_____
_____

4. Why did most geologists initially reject Alfred Wegener's hypothesis of continental drift?

_____
_____
_____
_____

Chapter Test A

Name _____ Class _____ Date _____

5. Use Figure 22-1 to determine when the P waves and S waves reached a seismograph station located 40 km from the earthquake epicenter.

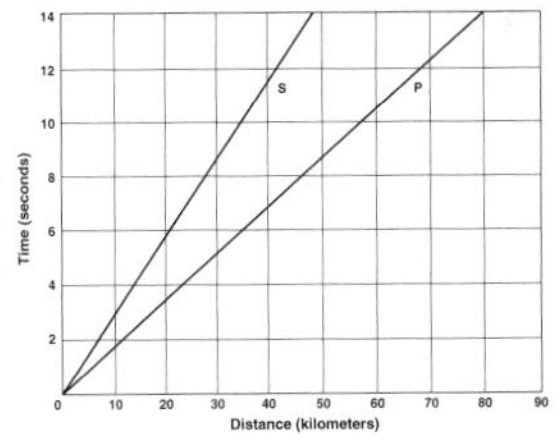

_____
_____
_____

Figure 22-1

Using Science Skills

Use the diagram to answer each question. Write the answers on a separate sheet of paper.

1. **Interpreting Graphics** In Figure 22-2, what process is occurring in the area labeled D, and what feature will result at C?

2. **Interpreting Graphics** In Figure 22-2, what is occurring at A?

3. **Interpreting Graphics** In Figure 22-2, what is occurring at the feature labeled B?

4. **Using Models** Use Figure 22-2 to identify where new crust is being created and where it is being destroyed. Give the letter on the diagram and the terms used to describe these areas.

Figure 22-2

5. **Classifying** In Figure 22-4, what type of plate boundary is illustrated at E?

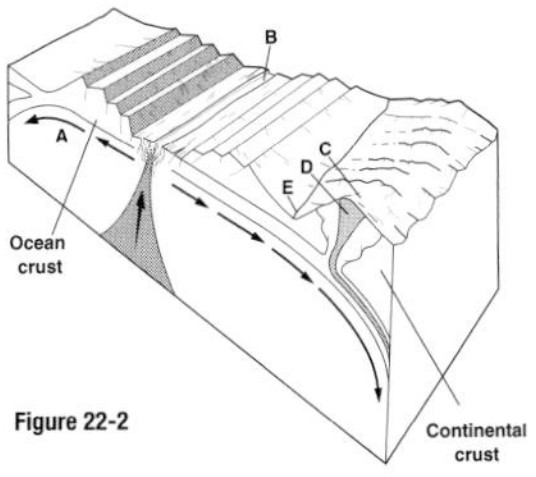

Essay

Write the answers to each question on a separate sheet of paper.

1. How does the subduction of an oceanic plate result in the formation of a volcano?
2. Describe the rock cycle.
3. Use plate tectonics to explain where mountains form.
4. How can earthquakes be used to map the location of a plate boundary?
5. Your teacher provides you with two white mineral samples. One is quartz and one is calcite. Describe the tests you could use to identify the samples.

Chapter Test B

Name _____ Class _____ Date _____

Chapter 22   Earth's Interior   Chapter Test B

Multiple Choice

Write the letter that best answers the question or completes the statement on the line provided.

_____ 1. The study of Earth's composition, structure, and history is called
   a. seismology.   **b.** physics.
   c. chemistry.   **d.** geology.

_____ 2. The three main layers of Earth's interior are the
   a. crust, core, and lithosphere.
   b. crust, mantle, and core.
   c. mantle, inner core, and outer core.
   d. crust, mantle, and aesthenosphere.

_____ 3. A naturally occurring, inorganic solid with a crystal structure and a characteristic chemical composition is a
   a. rock.   **b.** fossil.
   c. mineral.   **d.** piece of granite.

_____ 4. Rocks are classified as
   a. sandstone, limestone, or granite.
   b. organic, intrusive, or clastic.
   c. igneous, metamorphic, or sedimentary.
   d. sedimentary, intrusive, or metamorphic.

_____ 5. A series of processes in which rocks are continuously changed from one type to another is called
   a. a volcanic eruption.   **b.** the rock cycle.
   c. geology.   **d.** melting.

_____ 6. The hypothesis that the continents move slowly over Earth's surface and once were joined into one supercontinent is called
   a. plate tectonics.   **b.** continental drift.
   c. sea-floor spreading.   **d.** subduction.

_____ 7. New ocean crust is formed along
   a. mid-ocean ridges.   **b.** subduction zones.
   c. mountain belts.   **d.** trenches.

_____ 8. Plates slide pass each other, and crust is neither created nor destroyed at a
   a. convergent boundary.   **b.** divergent boundary.
   c. mid-ocean ridge.   **d.** transform boundary.

_____ 9. What is a break in a rock mass along which movement occurs?
   a. fold   **b.** earthquake
   c. fault   **d.** epicenter

Chapter Test B

Name _____ Class _____ Date _____

_____ 10. What is the name of the location within Earth where an earthquake begins?
   a. fold   **b.** focus   **c.** epicenter   **d.** core

_____ 11. The amount of energy released by an earthquake is measured on the
   a. Richter scale.
   b. moment magnitude scale.
   c. modified Mercalli scale.
   d. seismic scale.

_____ 12. The area where magma collects inside a volcano before an eruption is called
   a. the crater.   **b.** a caldera.
   c. a vent.   **d.** the magma chamber.

_____ 13. What determines whether a volcano erupts quietly or explosively?
   a. the size of the volcano
   b. the age of the volcano
   c. the characteristics of the magma
   d. the magnitude of nearby earthquakes

_____ 14. Shield volcanoes are produced by
   a. explosive eruptions of lava and ash.
   b. quiet eruptions of lava.
   c. explosive eruptions of ash and cinders.
   d. quiet eruptions that alternate with explosive eruptions.

_____ 15. The largest type of intrusive igneous feature is a
   a. sill.   **b.** dike.   **c.** volcanic neck.   **d.** batholith.

Completion

Complete each statement on the line provided.

1. The study of the composition, structure, and the history of Earth is called _____.

2. The crust and upper mantle together form the _____.

3. The color of the powder a mineral leaves on an unglazed porcelain tile is called the mineral's _____.

4. Igneous rocks that form at Earth's surface are called _____ rocks.

5. The process by which oceanic plates sink into the mantle through a trench is called _____.

6. The sinking of dense slabs of lithosphere and _____ from within Earth drive the mantle convection current.

Chapter Test B

Name _____ Class _____ Date _____

7. In Figure 22-1, the P wave will reach a seismograph located 40 kilometers from the earthquake epicenter in _____ seconds.

8. A(an) _____ is a device that is used to detect and record seismic waves.

9. A(an) _____ is the bowl-shaped pit at the top of a volcano.

10. A(an) _____ volcano is created by alternating lava flows and explosive eruptions.

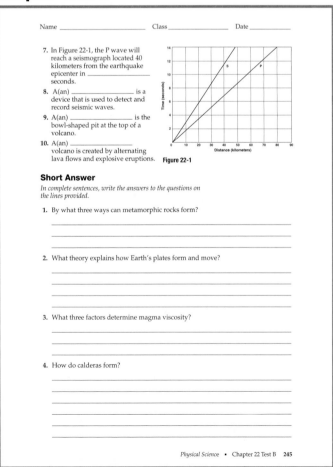

Figure 22-1

Short Answer

In complete sentences, write the answers to the questions on the lines provided.

1. By what three ways can metamorphic rocks form?
   _____
   _____
   _____

2. What theory explains how Earth's plates form and move?
   _____
   _____
   _____

3. What three factors determine magma viscosity?
   _____
   _____
   _____

4. How do calderas form?
   _____
   _____
   _____
   _____

Chapter Test B

Name _____ Class _____ Date _____

5. In what two types of locations do most volcanoes occur?
   _____
   _____
   _____
   _____

Using Science Skills

Use the diagram to answer each question. Write the answers on a separate sheet of paper.

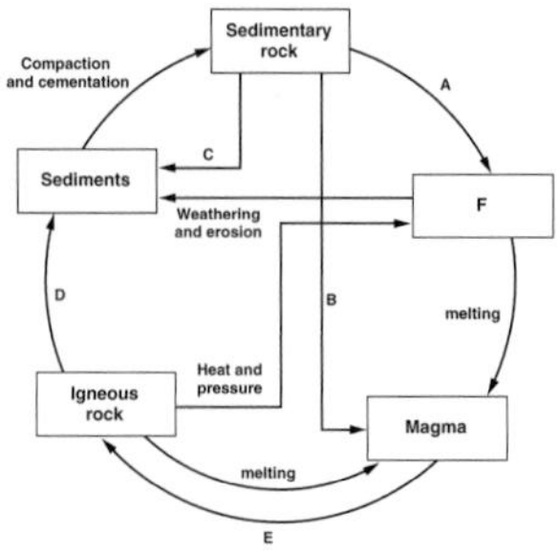

Figure 22-2

1. **Classifying** What type of rock would fit into Figure 22-2 at the location shown by the letter F?

2. **Interpreting Graphics** In Figure 22-2, what processes are represented by the arrow labeled A?

3. **Interpreting Graphics** In Figure 22-2, what process is represented by the arrow labeled E?

4. **Drawing Conclusions** Use Figure 22-2 to describe how an igneous rock could turn into a sedimentary rock and then into a metamorphic rock.

5. **Using Models** Use Figure 22-2 to describe the process involved in the formation of a sedimentary rock.

Chapter 22 Test A Answers

Multiple Choice

1. d 2. d 3. b 4. a 5. c 6. c
7. c 8. b 9. b 10. a 11. d 12. c
13. c 14. c 15. a

Completion

1. clastic 2. Pangaea 3. mid-ocean ridge 4. P 5. luster

Short Answer

1. by scraping the mineral on a piece of unglazed porcelain called a streak plate 2. The lithosphere is cool and rigid; the aesthenosphere is a layer of soft, weak rock that can flow slowly; and the mesosphere is the strong, lowest layer. 3. An intrusive rock cools from magma inside Earth, and an extrusive rock cools from lava at Earth's surface. 4. Wegener could not explain how the continents could move through the solid rock of the ocean floor or what force could move entire continents. 5. The P wave arrived in about 7 seconds, and the S wave arrived in about 11.9 seconds.

Using Science Skills

1. melting; volcanoes 2. An ocean plate is being subducted beneath a continental plate. 3. New ocean crust is being added as sea-floor spreading is occurring. 4. New crust is being created at B, at a mid-ocean ridge. Crust is being destroyed at A and E in subduction zones. 5. a convergent boundary

Essay

1. As the oceanic plate sinks into the mantle in the subduction zone, the plate causes melting. Magma forms and rises to the surface, where it erupts and forms volcanoes. 2. The rock cycle is a series of processes in which rocks continuously change from one type to another. These processes include erosion, weathering, melting, cooling, heat and pressure, and compaction and cementation. 3. Some mountains form at convergent plate boundaries where two plates collide. Other mountains form at divergent plate boundaries along the mid-ocean ridge systems. 4. Earthquake epicenters can occur anywhere, but most earthquakes occur at plate boundaries. Earthquake epicenters commonly follow along a plate boundary and can be used to map the location of the boundary. 5. You could use the hardness test. Quartz would scratch glass, but calcite would not. Calcite also reacts with dilute hydrochloric acid. Place a drop of acid on both samples. The sample that bubbles is calcite.

Chapter 22 Test B Answers

Multiple Choice

1. d 2. b 3. c 4. c 5. b 6. b
7. a 8. d 9. c 10. b 11. b 12. d
13. c 14. b 15. d

Completion

1. geology 2. lithosphere 3. streak 4. extrusive 5. subduction
6. heat 7. 7 8. seismograph 9. crater 10. composite

Short Answer

1. by heat, pressure, or reactions with hot water 2. the theory of plate tectonics 3. water content, silica content, and temperature 4. After an eruption, the empty magma chamber or main vent of a volcano may collapse, forming a large depression at the top of the volcano. 5. at plate boundaries and at hot spots

Using Science Skills

1. metamorphic rock 2. heat and pressure 3. cooling 4. An igneous rock would undergo weathering and erosion to form sediment. The sediment would undergo compaction and cementation to form a sedimentary rock. Heat and pressure would change the sedimentary rock to a metamorphic rock.
5. Weathering and erosion form sediment, which piles up. Over time, this sediment is squeezed and cemented together to form sedimentary rock.

Chapter 23 Earth's Surface

CHAPTER 23

Planning Guide

Use these planning tools
Easy Planner
Resource Pro
Online Lesson Planner

SECTION OBJECTIVES	STANDARDS		ACTIVITIES and LABS
	NATIONAL (See p. T18.)	STATE	
23.1 Fresh Water, pp. 704–708 🕐 1 block or 2 periods **23.1.1 Describe** the processes that make up the water cycle. **23.1.2 Identify** the sources of fresh water on Earth.	A-1, A-2, D-1, D-2		**SE** Inquiry Activity: How Do Freezing and Thawing Affect Rocks? p. 703 **L2** **SE** Quick Lab: Modeling the Water Cycle, p. 705 **L2** **TE** Build Science Skills: Using Models, p. 706 **L2**
23.2 Weathering and Mass Movement, pp. 709–712 🕐 1 block or 2 periods **23.2.1 Describe** the processes by which erosion wears down and carries away rock. **23.2.2 Distinguish** between chemical and mechanical weathering and **describe** the factors that affect the rate of weathering. **23.2.3 Explain** how the force of gravity contributes to erosion by mass movement.	B-3, D-2, D-3, F-5		**TE** Teacher Demo: Chemical Weathering, p. 710 **L2**
23.3 Water Shapes the Land, pp. 713–717 🕐 1 block or 2 periods **23.3.1 Explain** how running water erodes the land. **23.3.2 Identify** features formed by erosion and deposition due to running water. **23.3.3 Describe** how caves and sinkholes are formed by groundwater erosion.	A-1, A-2, D-2, D-3		**SE** Quick Lab: Forming Sedimentary Layers, p. 714 **L2** **SE** Exploration Lab: Modeling Erosion, p. 739 **L2** **LM** Investigation 23B: Modeling Beach Erosion **L1**
23.4 Glaciers and Wind, pp. 719–724 🕐 1 block or 2 periods **23.4.1 Describe** the formation and movement of glaciers and **identify** features formed by glacial erosion and deposition. **23.4.2 Explain** the mechanisms and effects of wind erosion and deposition.	D-2, D-3		**TE** Teacher Demo: Glacial Erosion and Deposition, p. 720 **L2** **LM** Investigation 23A: Constructing a Relief Map **L2**
23.5 The Restless Oceans, pp. 725–729 🕐 1 block or 2 periods **23.5.1 Explain** how the properties of ocean water change with depth. **23.5.2 Distinguish** between surface currents, deep currents, and upwelling. **23.5.3 Explain** the processes by which waves and currents cause erosion and deposition.	D-1, D-2, D-3, E-2, F-1		**TE** Teacher Demo: Salinity of Ocean Water, p. 726 **L2**
23.6 Earth's History, pp. 732–738 🕐 1 block or 2 periods **23.6.1 Distinguish** between the relative and absolute dating of rocks. **23.6.2 Describe** the geologic time scale and what happened during the major divisions of geologic time.	A-1, A-2, B-1, C-3, D-3		

702A   Chapter 23

Ability Levels

L1	For students who need additional help
L2	For all students
L3	For students who need to be challenged

Components

SE	Student Edition
TE	Teacher's Edition
LM	Laboratory Manual
PLM	Probeware Lab Manual
GRSW	Guided Reading & Study Workbook With Math Support
CUT	Chapter and Unit Tests
CTB	Computer Test Bank
TP	Test Prep Resources
iT	iText
DC	Discovery Channel Videotapes
T	Transparencies
P	Presentation Pro CD-ROM
GO	Internet Resources

RESOURCES PRINT and TECHNOLOGY		SECTION ASSESSMENT
GRSW Section 23.1	**L1**	**SE** Section 23.1 Assessment, p. 708
T Chapter 23 Pretest and Section 23.1	**L2**	**iText iT** Section 23.1
P		
SCIENCE NEWS GO Earth's waters	**L2**	
GRSW Section 23.2	**L1**	**SE** Section 23.2 Assessment, p. 712
T Section 23.2	**L2**	**iText iT** Section 23.2
P Section 23.2	**L2**	
SCILINKS GO Weathering	**L2**	
GRSW Section 23.3	**L1**	**SE** Section 23.3 Assessment, p. 717
T Section 23.3	**L2**	**iText iT** Section 23.3
P Section 23.3	**L2**	
SCIENCE NEWS GO Earth's surface	**L2**	
GRSW Section 23.4	**L1**	**SE** Section 23.4 Assessment, p. 724
T Section 23.4	**L2**	**iText iT** Section 23.4
P Section 23.4	**L2**	
SCILINKS GO Glaciers and landforms	**L2**	
GRSW Section 23.5	**L1**	**SE** Section 23.5 Assessment, p. 729
DC Under the Sea	**L2**	**iText iT** Section 23.5
T Section 23.5	**L2**	
P Section 23.5	**L2**	
GRSW Section 23.6	**L1**	**SE** Section 23.6 Assessment, p. 738
GRSW Math Skill	**L2**	**iText iT** Section 23.6
T Section 23.6	**L2**	
P Section 23.6	**L2**	
SCIENCE NEWS GO Earth's history	**L2**	

Go Online

Go online for these Internet resources.

PHSchool.com
Web Code: cca-3230
Web Code: cch-3233

SCIENCE NEWS
Web Code: cce-3231
Web Code: cce-3233
Web Code: cce-3236

NSTA SCILINKS
Web Code: ccn-3232
Web Code: ccn-3234

Materials for Activities and Labs

Quantities for each group

STUDENT EDITION

Inquiry Activity, p. 703
5 pieces of pumice, waterproof marker, 5 plastic freezer bags

Quick Lab, p. 705
100-mL graduated cylinder, 250-mL beaker, evaporating dish or large watch glass, hot plate, ice

Quick Lab, p. 714
clay; gravel; sand; small dish; tall, narrow jar with cover; tablespoon; clock or watch

Exploration Lab, p. 739
metric ruler, large sheet of cardboard, plastic wrap, newspaper, soil, blocks, pencil, paper cup, scissors, drinking straw, modeling clay, paper towels, small rocks

TEACHER'S EDITION

Build Science Skills, p. 706
USGS Topographic Quadrangle for your area, state and/or U.S. topographic map (if your watershed extends beyond your quadrangle), tracing paper, markers

Teacher Demo, p. 710
calcite, 1M HCl, dropper

Teacher Demo, p. 720
a block of ice, approximately 15×25×12 cm; clay, sand, gravel, and pebbles to fill a 25×30-cm baking pan 3–5 cm deep; flat metal or plastic surface such as an old cutting board or cookie sheet; freezer; sink

Teacher Demo, p. 726
1-L beaker, 100-mL beaker, mass balance, salt, water

Build Science Skills, p. 730
large sheets of paper connected to make a 1.5-m square, metric ruler, markers

Chapter Assessment

CHAPTER ASSESSMENT

SE Chapter Assessment, pp. 741–742
CUT Chapter 23 Test A, B
CTB Chapter 23
iT Chapter 23
PHSchool.com GO Web Code: cca-3230

STANDARDIZED TEST PREP

SE Chapter 23, p. 743
TP Diagnose and Prescribe

iText—interactive textbook with assessment at PHSchool.com

Earth's Surface 702B

493

Name_____ Class_____ Date_____ M T W T F

LESSON PLAN 23.1

Fresh Water

Time
2 periods
1 block

Section Objectives

- **23.1.1 Describe** the processes that make up the water cycle.
- **23.1.2 Identify** the sources of fresh water on Earth.

Vocabulary groundwater • water cycle • transpiration • glacier • runoff • tributaries • watershed • saturated zone • water table • permeable • aquifer • impermeable

Local Standards

---

1 FOCUS

Build Vocabulary: Word-Part Analysis

Have students discuss the meanings of the word parts of *permeable* and *impermeable*, and ask them to define the prefix *im-*. **L2**

Targeted Resources

❑ Transparency: Chapter 23 Pretest

❑ Transparency: Interest Grabber 23.1

❑ Transparency: Reading Strategy 23.1

---

2 INSTRUCT

Build Reading Literacy: Preview

Before reading Fresh Water, have students preview all of the bold subheads, and ask them to list the major sources of fresh water on Earth. **L1**

Quick Lab: Modeling the Water Cycle

Students observe a covered beaker of water on a hot plate. Students use a model water cycle to test ideas about Earth's water cycle. **L2**

Build Science Skills: Using Models

Students will model their own watershed by creating a map of the creeks, streams, and land area that contributes runoff to their watershed. **L2**

Address Misconceptions

Explain to students that groundwater often exists in the pore spaces of rock, like water in a sponge. Have students create a Venn diagram comparing and contrasting ground and surface water. **L2**

Targeted Resources

❑ Transparency: Figure 2: The Water Cycle

❑ Transparency: Figure 5: Groundwater

❑ GRSW Section 23.1

---

3 ASSESS

Reteach

Use Figure 2 to review the processes by which water moves from one reservoir to another in the water cycle. **L1**

Evaluate Understanding

Have students create a mnemonic device to remember all of the sources of fresh water on Earth. **L2**

Targeted Resources

❑ **PHSchool.com** Online Section 23.1 Assessment

❑ iText Section 23.1

Transparencies

348 **Chapter 23 Pretest**

1. What type of phase change is described by the word *sublimation?*

2. An acid is a substance that has
   a. more H^+ than OH^-.
   b. more OH^- than H^+.
   c. the same amount of H^+ and OH^-.

3. Which of these processes causes iron to rust?
   a. radiation
   b. oxidation
   c. dissolution
   d. evaporation

4. What is the equation that describes the relationship between kinetic energy, mass, and velocity?

ANSWERS
1. from a solid directly to a gas
2. a
3. b
4. $KE=\frac{1}{2}mv^2$

Transparencies

349 **Chapter 23 Pretest** *(continued)*

5. Which of the following best describes isotopes?
   a. atoms with the same number of protons, but different number of electrons
   b. atoms with the same number of electrons, but different number of protons
   c. atoms with the same number of protons, but different number of neutrons
   d. atoms with the same number of neutrons, but different number of protons

5. c

Transparencies

350 **Section 23.1 Interest Grabber**

Determining Permeability

1. Cut off the top half of an empty plastic water bottle. Remove the cap from the mouth of the bottle. Using a rubber band, secure a small piece of cotton cloth over the mouth of the bottle, as shown above. Invert the bottle so that the open end is upwards. Pour 100 mL of water into the open end and time how long it takes the water to drain into a bucket.

2. With the cloth still in place over the mouth of the bottle, place about 100 mL of gravel in the open end of the bottle. Pour 100 mL of water over the gravel and time how long it takes to drain out into a bucket.

3. Remove the gravel from the bottle. With the cloth still in place over the mouth of the bottle, place about 100 mL of clay in the open end of the bottle. Press the clay into the closed end of the bottle. Pour 100 mL of water over the clay and time how long it takes to drain out into a bucket.

ANSWERS
1. The time it takes for the water to drain will depend on the type of cotton cloth used, but the water should drain fairly quickly.
2. The time it takes for the water to drain will depend on the type of gravel used. Some types of gravel will not affect the rate at which the water drains. Finer gravels should slow the rate at which the water drains. (Gravel is permeable.)
3. The water should not drain out. (Clay is not very permeable.)

Transparencies

351 **Section 23.1 Reading Strategy**

Building Vocabulary

Vocabulary Term	Definition
Groundwater	a. _____?_____
Water cycle	b. _____?_____
Transpiration	c. _____?_____

ANSWERS
a. fresh water found underground among particles of rock and soil
b. the continuous movement of water among the oceans, atmosphere, and land
c. the process by which water evaporates from the leaves of plants and enters the atmosphere

Transparencies

352 Figure 2 The Water Cycle

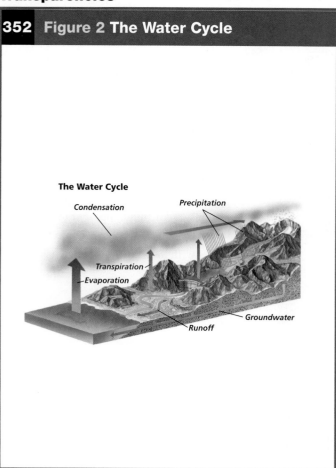

The Water Cycle

Condensation

Precipitation

Transpiration

Evaporation

Runoff

Groundwater

Transparencies

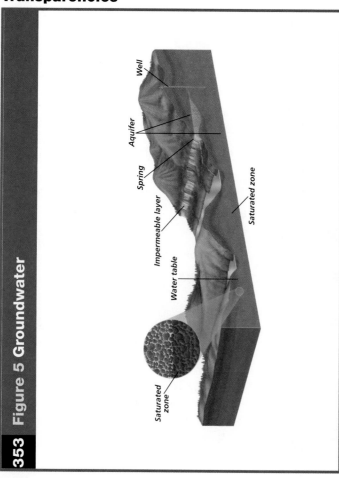

353 Figure 5 Groundwater

Well

Aquifer

Spring

Impermeable layer

Water table

Saturated zone

Saturated zone

Guided Reading and Study Workbook

Name _____ Class _____ Date _____

Chapter 23   Earth's Surface

Section 23.1 Fresh Water
(pages 704–708)

This section describes where water is found on Earth. It also explains the water cycle.

Reading Strategy (page 704)
Build Vocabulary Copy the table on a separate sheet of paper. As you read, add terms and definitions from this section to the table. For more information on this Reading Strategy, see the **Reading and Study Skills** in the **Skills and Reference Handbook** at the end of your textbook.

Earth's Fresh Water	
Vocabulary Term	**Definition**
Groundwater	Fresh water found underground among particles of rock and soil
Water cycle	The continuous movement of water among the oceans, atmosphere, and land
Transpiration	The process by which water evaporates from the leaves of trees and other plants and enters the atmosphere

1. Water found underground in soil and within cracks in rocks is called _____groundwater_____.

The Water Cycle (pages 705–706)

2. Name five major processes of the water cycle.

a. _____Evaporation_____

b. _____Condensation_____

c. ___Return of flowing water to oceans___

d. _____Transpiration_____

e. _____Precipitation_____

Match each process with its correct description.

Description	Process
_d_ **3.** When water droplets or ice crystals fall to the ground	a. evaporation
_a_ **4.** The process through which a liquid changes into a gas	b. transpiration
_c_ **5.** The process that forms clouds	c. condensation
_b_ **6.** When water is released from a plant's leaves	d. precipitation

7. What is a glacier? _A glacier is a large mass of moving ice and snow._

Guided Reading and Study Workbook

Name _____ Class _____ Date _____

Chapter 23   Earth's Surface

Fresh Water (pages 706–708)

8. Circle the letters of the places where portions of Earth's fresh water are located.
   (a.) in streams   (b.) in the atmosphere
   c. in the oceans   (d.) in lakes

9. Most of Earth's fresh water is located in _____groundwater_____ and _____glaciers_____.

10. What is runoff? _Runoff is water that flows over Earth's surface._

11. A smaller stream that flows into a river is called a(n) _____tributary_____.

12. Circle the letters of the sentences that are true about watersheds.
   (a.) Watersheds are areas of land that contribute water to a river system.
   (b.) Watersheds can be large or small.
   (c.) The Mississippi River watershed drains most of the central United States.
   (d.) Watersheds are also called drainage basins.

13. Where do lakes and ponds form? _Lakes and ponds form in depressions in the land._

14. Is the following sentence true or false? Ponds usually form in large, deep depressions, but lakes form in smaller depressions. _____false_____

15. An area underground where the pore spaces are entirely filled with water is called the _____saturated zone_____.

16. Is the following sentence true or false? The water table is found at the bottom of the saturated zone. _____false_____

17. Water cannot pass through _____impermeable_____ rocks.

18. Circle the letters of the sentences that are true about aquifers.
   (a.) They are permeable rock layers that are saturated with water.
   (b.) They are recharged or refilled as rainwater seeps into them.
   c. They are often made of shale and unbroken granite.
   (d.) Many people rely on aquifers for drinking water.

19. Where do glaciers form? _Glaciers form in areas where more snow falls than melts each year._

20. Circle the letter of each word that describes how ice is removed from a glacier.
   (a.) melting   (b.) sublimation
   c. precipitation   (d.) formation of icebergs

21. A large piece of ice that breaks off when a glacier reaches the ocean is called a(n) _____iceberg_____.

LESSON PLAN 23.2

Weathering and Mass Movement

Time
2 periods
1 block

Section Objectives

- **23.2.1 Describe** the processes by which erosion wears down and carries away rock.
- **23.2.2 Distinguish** between chemical and mechanical weathering and **describe** the factors that affect the rate of weathering.
- **23.2.3 Explain** how the force of gravity contributes to erosion by mass movement.

Vocabulary erosion • weathering • mechanical weathering • abrasion • chemical weathering • mass movement

Local Standards

1 FOCUS

Build Vocabulary: Venn Diagram
Have students construct a Venn diagram to compare chemical and mechanical weathering. **L2**

Targeted Resources
❏ Transparency: Interest Grabber 23.2
❏ Transparency: Reading Strategy 23.2

2 INSTRUCT

Build Reading Literacy: Predict
Before reading Erosion, tell students to examine Figure 7 and make a prediction about how this landscape was formed. **L1**

Build Reading Literacy: Identify Main Ideas/Details
Have students read the main topic sentence of Rates of Weathering. Then, ask them to name the selection's main ideas. **L1**

Teacher Demo: Chemical Weathering
Drip hydrochloric acid on calcite so that students can observe how rock can be broken down by a chemical reaction. **L2**

Address Misconceptions
Explain to students that soil has not always existed in its present form, but is a product of weathering and decaying organic matter. **L2**

Build Science Skills: Relating Cause and Effect
Have students work in groups to create a poster showing the cause and effect of each type of mass movement described on p. 712. **L2**

Targeted Resources
❏ Transparency: Figure 11: Creep and Slumping
❏ GRSW Section 23.2
❏ **NSTA** *sci*$_{LINKS}$ Weathering

3 ASSESS

Reteach
Use Figures 8 and 9 to review the differences between chemical and mechanical weathering. **L1**

Evaluate Understanding
Have students create flowcharts describing the processes that produced the formations in Figure 7. **L2**

Targeted Resources
❏ **PHSchool.com** Online Section 23.2 Assessment
❏ iText Section 23.2

Transparencies

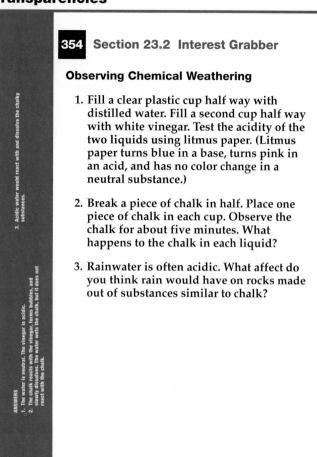

354 Section 23.2 Interest Grabber

Observing Chemical Weathering

1. Fill a clear plastic cup half way with distilled water. Fill a second cup half way with white vinegar. Test the acidity of the two liquids using litmus paper. (Litmus paper turns blue in a base, turns pink in an acid, and has no color change in a neutral substance.)

2. Break a piece of chalk in half. Place one piece of chalk in each cup. Observe the chalk for about five minutes. What happens to the chalk in each liquid?

3. Rainwater is often acidic. What affect do you think rain would have on rocks made out of substances similar to chalk?

ANSWERS
1. The water is neutral. The vinegar is acidic.
2. The chalk reacts with the vinegar, forms bubbles, and slowly dissolves. The water wets the chalk, but it does not react with the chalk.
3. Acidic water would react with and dissolve the chalky substances.

Transparencies

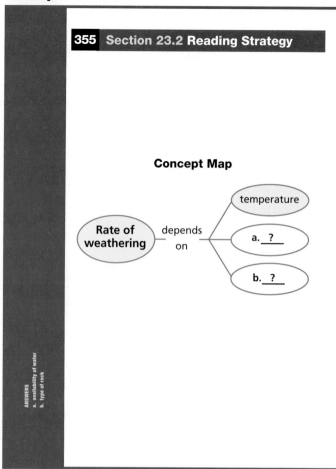

355 Section 23.2 Reading Strategy

Concept Map

Rate of weathering — depends on — temperature

a. ___?___

b. ___?___

ANSWERS
a. availability of water
b. type of rock

Transparencies

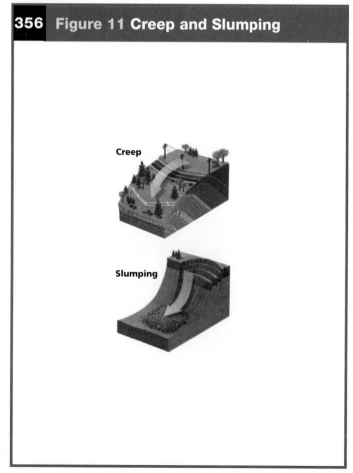

356 **Figure 11 Creep and Slumping**

Creep

Slumping

Name _____ Class _____ Date _____

Chapter 23   Earth's Surface

Section 23.2 Weathering and Mass Movement
(pages 709–712)

This section describes how land is changed by weathering and erosion. It also discusses mass movement.

Reading Strategy (page 709)

Concept Map As you read, complete the concept map showing the key factors which affect the rate of weathering. For more information on this Reading Strategy, see the **Reading and Study Skills** in the **Skills and Reference Handbook** at the end of your textbook.

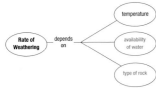

Erosion (page 709)

1. The process that wears down and carries away rock and soil is called _____erosion_____ .

2. Circle the letters of the sentences that are true about erosion.
   a. It acts through hoodoos.
   (b.) It acts through weathering.
   (c.) It acts through the force of gravity.
   (d.) It acts through the movement of glaciers, wind, or waves.

3. Is the following sentence true or false? The end product of erosion is sediment. _____true_____

Weathering (pages 710–711)

4. The process by which rocks are chemically changed or physically broken into fragments is called _____weathering_____ .

5. Circle the letters of the sentences that are true about weathering.
   (a.) It can be mechanical.
   (b.) It can be chemical.
   c. It only breaks down soft rocks.
   (d.) It can break down rocks into fragments.

Name _____ Class _____ Date _____

Chapter 23   Earth's Surface

6. Circle the letters of the sentences that are true about mechanical weathering.
   (a.) It occurs through frost wedging.
   b. It occurs from acidic rain.
   c. It occurs through rusting.
   (d.) It occurs through abrasion.

7. Is the following sentence true or false? Abrasion happens when rocks scrape against each other. _____true_____

8. In the process of chemical weathering, rock is broken down by _____chemical reactions_____ .

9. Circle the letters of the sentences that are true about chemical weathering.
   (a.) Chemical weathering occurs because rain is slightly acidic.
   (b.) Rocks are broken down by chemical reactions.
   (c.) Water is the main agent of chemical weathering.
   d. Chemical weathering involves abrasion and frost wedging.

10. What happens to the minerals found in rocks during the process of chemical weathering? _____They are changed into new minerals._____

Rates of Weathering (page 711)

11. What factors determine the rate at which mechanical and chemical weathering take place?
    a. _____Temperature_____   b. _____The availability of water_____
    c. _____The type of rock_____

12. The kind of weathering that most likely occurs in places where temperature conditions alternate between freezing and thawing is _____mechanical_____ weathering.

Mass Movement (page 712)

13. In mass movement, rocks and soil move downhill because of _____gravity_____ .

Match each type of mass movement with its correct description.

Description	Mass Movement
____c____ 14. Rapid mass movement of soil and other sediment mixed with water	a. creep
	b. slumping
____d____ 15. The rapid movement of large amounts of rock and soil	c. mudflow
	d. landslide
____b____ 16. Weak layers of soil or rock suddenly moving down a slope as a single unit	
____a____ 17. Soil gradually moving down a slope	

Name_____ Class_____ Date_____ M T W T F

LESSON PLAN 23.3

Water Shapes the Land

Section Objectives

- **23.3.1 Explain** how running water erodes the land.
- **23.3.2 Identify** features formed by erosion and deposition due to running water.
- **23.3.3 Describe** how caves and sinkholes are formed by groundwater erosion.

Vocabulary deposition • saltation • flood plain • meander • oxbow lake • alluvial fan • delta • stalactite • stalagmite • sinkhole

Local Standards

---

1 FOCUS

Build Vocabulary: Compare/Contrast Table
Have students use the vocabulary terms to make compare/contrast tables with the headings Features Formed by Erosion and Features Formed by Deposition. **L2**

Targeted Resources
❏ Transparency: Interest Grabber 23.3
❏ Transparency: Reading Strategy 23.3

---

2 INSTRUCT

Build Reading Literacy: Visualize
Read Flood Plains aloud to the students, and have them close their eyes and form mental images of the processes described. **L1**

Quick Lab: Forming Sedimentary Layers
Students observe clay, gravel, and sand in a jar of water, in order to describe the formation of sedimentary layers under water. **L2**

Address Misconceptions
Explain to students that erosion is a slow, constant process that wears down old landforms, and that new landforms are created through erosion and deposition, often over thousands of years. **L2**

Build Science Skills: Inferring
Have groups of students examine a variety of river rocks, make inferences about the geologic history of the rocks, and create a flowchart for each rock's history. **L2**

Use Community Resources
Ask a park ranger or geologist to present a slide show to the class that includes pictures of caves in your region. **L2**

For Enrichment
Collect a core sample of sediment from a riverbed or the bottom of a lake. Have students examine the particle sizes in each layer and determine their distribution. **L3**

Targeted Resources
❏ GRSW Section 23.3

❏ **NSTA** sc*i*LINKS Glaciers and landforms

---

3 ASSESS

Reteach
Use Figure 14 to explain the features formed by water erosion. **L1**

Evaluate Understanding
Have students create a flowchart that explains how an oxbow lake like the one in Figure 15 formed. **L2**

Targeted Resources
❏ **PHSchool.com** Online Section 23.3 Assessment
❏ iText Section 23.3

---

357 Section 23.3 Interest Grabber

Modeling River Erosion

1. Use three balls of clay of different colors. Press each ball of clay into a 10 cm by 10 cm by 1 cm shape. Stack the pieces of clay so that you make one block of clay that is 3 cm high, as shown in Step 1 below. Using colored pencils, draw the top view of the block of clay.

2. Using a plastic knife, make a scratch in the surface of the top layer of clay down the center of the block, as shown in Step 2 below. Scrape along the scratch and remove small amounts of clay. Continue scraping away clay until you have made a ditch that is about 2.5 cm deep, as shown in Step 3 below. Using colored pencils, draw the top view of the altered block of clay.

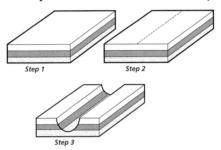

Step 1   Step 2

Step 3

ANSWERS
1. The drawing should be of a solid colored square.
2. The drawing should be of a square with colored stripes down the center. The outer stripes should be one color, the middle stripes should be a second color, and the center stripe should be a third color. For example:

358 Section 23.3 Reading Strategy

Concept Map

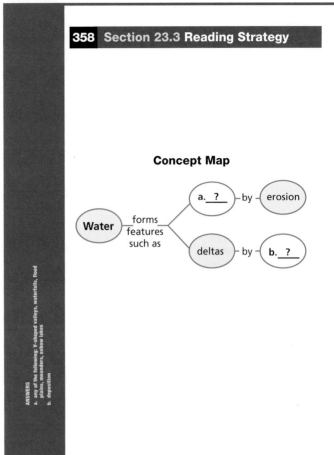

Water — forms features such as

a. __?__ — by — erosion

deltas — by — b. __?__

ANSWERS
a. any of the following: V-shaped valleys, waterfalls, flood plains, meanders, oxbow lakes
b. deposition

Guided Reading and Study Workbook

Chapter 23   Earth's Surface

Section 23.3 Water Shapes the Land
(pages 713–717)

This section describes how water erodes the land. It also describes features created by water erosion and water deposition.

Reading Strategy (page 713)

Concept Map As you read, complete the concept map showing how moving water shapes the land. For more information on this Reading Strategy, see the **Reading and Study Skills** in the **Skills and Reference Handbook** at the end of your textbook.

Water — forms features such as

V-shaped valleys — by — erosion

deltas — by — deposition

Answers may also include other features formed by erosion such as waterfalls, flood plains, meanders, or oxbow lakes.

1. The process through which sediment is laid down in new locations is called _____deposition_____.

Running Water Erodes the Land (pages 714–715)

Match each method that sediment is transported in streams with its correct description.

Description	Method of Transportation
_b_ **2.** Dissolved sediment is carried this way	a. in suspension
_d_ **3.** Large boulders can be moved this way during floods	b. in solution
_a_ **4.** Tiny sediment grains move along with the water in a stream	c. by saltation
_c_ **5.** Large particles bounce along the bottom of a stream	d. pushed or rolled

6. What does a stream's ability to erode mainly depend on? It depends mainly on the stream's speed.

Features Formed by Water Erosion (pages 715–716)

7. A(n) _____V-shaped_____ valley is formed by a fast-moving stream.

8. Is the following sentence true or false? A waterfall may develop where a stream crosses layers of rock that differ in hardness. _____true_____

Guided Reading and Study Workbook

Chapter 23   Earth's Surface

9. A flat area alongside a stream or river that is covered by water only during times of flood is called a(n) _____flood plain_____.

10. A loop-like bend in a river is called a(n) _____meander_____.

11. Is the following sentence true or false? Oxbow lakes form when an old meander is cut off from the rest of a river. _____true_____

12. Circle the letters of features that are formed by water erosion.
   (a.) oxbow lakes   (b.) V-shaped valleys
   (c.) meanders   (d.) waterfalls

Features Formed by Water Deposition (page 716)

13. Name two main features that are formed by deposits made by flowing water.
   a. _____Alluvial fans_____   b. _____Deltas_____

14. A fan-shaped deposit of sediment found on land is called a(n) _____alluvial fan_____

15. Is the following sentence true or false? Deltas are masses of sediment that form where rivers enter large bodies of water. _____true_____

Groundwater Erosion (page 717)

16. What type of weathering causes groundwater erosion?
   chemical weathering

17. Name two features that are formed by groundwater erosion.
   a. _____Caves_____   b. _____Sinkholes_____

a.

b.

18. Identify the two types of cavern formations shown in the figure above.
   a. _____Stalactite_____   b. _____Stalagmite_____

Name_____ Class_____ Date_____   M T W T F

LESSON PLAN 23.4

Glaciers and Wind

Time
2 periods
1 block

Section Objectives

- **23.4.1 Describe** the formation and movement of glaciers and **identify** features formed by glacial erosion and deposition.

- **23.4.2 Explain** the mechanisms and effects of wind erosion and deposition.

Vocabulary continental glacier • valley glacier • plucking • cirques • till • moraines • deflation • dunes • loess

Local Standards

---

1 FOCUS

Build Vocabulary: Compare/Contrast Table
Have students use the vocabulary terms to make compare/contrast tables with the headings Features Formed by Glacial Erosion and Features Formed by Glacial Deposition. **L2**

Targeted Resources
❑ Transparency: Interest Grabber 23.4
❑ Transparency: Reading Strategy 23.4

---

2 INSTRUCT

Build Reading Literacy: Using Context Clues
Have students read the first paragraph of How Glaciers Form and Move, and ask them to use clues from the selection to infer the meaning of the term *sublimate*. **L1**

Teacher Demo: Glacial Erosion and Deposition
Use ice, clay, sand, gravel, and pebbles to model glacial erosion and deposition. Students will observe how glaciers can move boulders and create depositional features. **L2**

Address Misconceptions
Use Figure 18 to help students understand that glaciers are not formed by one sudden action, but form and change over long periods of time. **L2**

Build Science Skills: Inferring
Have students examine photographs and make deductions about which landscapes were formed by glacial activity. **L2**

Build Science Skills: Comparing and Contrasting
Have students work in groups to make a presentation comparing the processes of wind and water erosion. **L2**

For Enrichment
Have students research the extent of the glacial advances during the most recent ice age, and create a map showing the location of the glacial activity and prominent glacial features. **L3**

Targeted Resources
❑ Transparency: Figure 22: Movement of Particles by Wind
❑ GRSW Section 23.4
❑ **NSTA** sc*L_INKS* Landforms

---

3 ASSESS

Reteach
Use the How It Works feature on p. 722 to discuss the ways that a continental glacier affects the landscape by erosion and deposition. **L1**

Evaluate Understanding
Have students make flashcards of features caused by erosion and deposition from glaciers and wind. **L2**

Targeted Resources
❑ **PHSchool.com** Online Section 23.4 Assessment
❑ iText Section 23.4

Transparencies

359 Section 23.4 Interest Grabber

Modeling Glacial Erosion

Use a sandy ice cube that was made by sprinkling sand in an ice cube tray, filling the tray with water, and freezing the ice cubes.

1. The sandy ice cube is a small model of a glacier. Using a towel, grasp the ice cube and rub the sandy side against a soft rock, such as limestone. Record your observations.

2. If the mini-glacier were to form in a cold climate and travel to a warmer climate, what would happen to the sand it contains?

ANSWERS
1. The sandy ice cube will scratch the surface of the rock (cause abrasions).
2. The sand would be moved from the cold climate and deposited in the warmer climate when the glacier melted.

Transparencies

360 Section 23.4 Reading Strategy

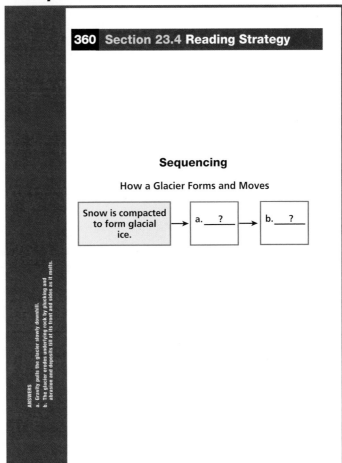

Sequencing

How a Glacier Forms and Moves

Snow is compacted to form glacial ice. → a. ___?___ → b. ___?___

ANSWERS
a. Gravity pulls the glacier slowly downhill.
b. The glacier erodes underlying rock by plucking and abrasion and deposits till at its front and sides as it melts.

Transparencies

361 Figure 22 **Movement of Particles by Wind**

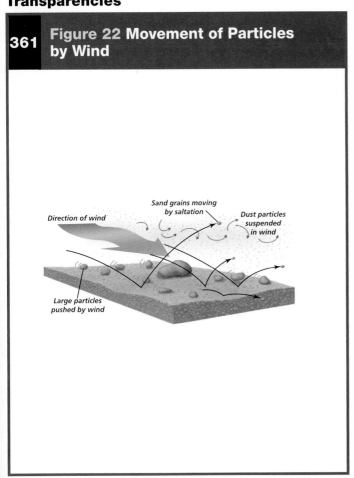

Direction of wind

Sand grains moving by saltation

Dust particles suspended in wind

Large particles pushed by wind

Guided Reading and Study Workbook

Name _____ Class _____ Date _____

Chapter 23   Earth's Surface

Section 23.4 Glaciers and Wind
(pages 719–724)

This section describes how glaciers form and how landscape features are created. It also describes wind erosion and deposition.

Reading Strategy (page 719)

Sequencing As you read, complete the flowchart to show how a glacier forms and moves, and how it erodes and deposits sediment. For more information on this Reading Strategy, see the **Reading and Study Skills** in the **Skills and Reference Handbook** at the end of your textbook.

| Snow is compacted to form glacial ice. | → | Gravity pulls the glaciers slowly downhill. | → | The glacier erodes underlying rock through plucking and abrasion and deposits till at its front and sides as it melts. |

How Glaciers Form and Move (page 719)

1. Glaciers form in places where snow melts ____faster____ than it falls.

Match the type of glacier to its description.

	Description	Glacier Type
a	**2.** Found in high mountain valleys	a. valley glacier
b	**3.** Covers a continent or large island	b. continental glacier

Glacial Erosion and Deposition (page 720–722)

4. What are the two ways through which glaciers erode rock?
   a. ____Abrasion____   b. ____Plucking____

5. Circle the letters of the sentences that are true about glacial erosion.
   (a.) Glacial ice widens cracks in bedrock beneath a glacier.
   b. Pieces of loosened rock stick to the top of a glacier.
   (c.) Rocks stuck to the bottoms and sides of a glacier act like sandpaper, scraping rock and soil.
   d. As a glacier moves, it gently brushes the rocks and soil underneath it.

6. What are four distinctive features caused by glacial erosion?
   a. ____Cirques____
   b. ____Horns or ridges____
   c. ____U-shaped valleys____
   d. ____Glacial lakes____

Guided Reading and Study Workbook

Name _____ Class _____ Date _____

Chapter 23   Earth's Surface

7. Large bowl-shaped valleys carved high on a mountainside are called ____cirques____.

8. How does a U-shaped valley form? ____It forms when a glacier flows through and erodes a V-shaped valley.____

9. Is the following sentence true or false? Continental glaciers fill depressions in the surface with water, where they create cirques. ____false____

10. How does a glacier create landforms? ____As it moves, it transports rock and soil, and when it melts, it deposits this load of sediment.____

11. Mounds of sediment at the downhill end of a glacier are called ____moraines____.

Match each feature formed by glacial deposition to its correct description.

	Description	Feature Formed
d	**12.** Long teardrop-shaped mounds of till	a. outwash plain
a	**13.** A flat plain made of particles of rock that were deposited from glacial streams	b. erratics
		c. eskers
e	**14.** A lake formed where large blocks of glacial ice become buried and melt	d. drumlins
		e. kettle lake
c	**15.** Ridges made from sand and gravel that were deposited in the bed of a glacial stream	
b	**16.** Boulders that a glacier has carried away from their place of origin	

Wind Erosion and Deposition (pages 723–724)

17. Name two ways that wind erodes the land.
    a. ____Deflation____   b. ____Abrasion____

18. Is the following sentence true or false? Deflation happens when the wind picks up and carries away loose surface material. ____true____

19. Circle the letters of the features deposited by wind.
    a. cirques   b. glacial lakes
    (c.) sand dunes   (d.) loess deposits

20. Is the following sentence true or false? Deposits formed from windblown dust are called loess deposits. ____true____

LESSON PLAN 23.5

The Restless Oceans

Time
2 periods
1 block

Section Objectives

Local Standards

- **23.5.1 Explain** how the properties of ocean water change with depth.
- **23.5.2 Distinguish** between surface currents, deep currents, and upwelling.
- **23.5.3 Explain** the processes by which waves and currents cause erosion and deposition.

Vocabulary salinity • continental shelf • surface current • density currents • upwelling • hydraulic action • longshore drift

1 FOCUS

Build Vocabulary: Paraphrase
Have students come up with a definition of each vocabulary term in their own words, and create an index card for each term with the definition. **L2**

Targeted Resources
❏ Transparency: Interest Grabber 23.5
❏ Transparency: Reading Strategy 23.5

2 INSTRUCT

Build Reading Literacy: Summarize
Have students work in groups to summarize the information in Ocean Currents. **L1**

Integrate Biology
Ask students what physical factors would be most challenging for organisms that live in the deep sea. **L2**

Address Misconceptions
Show students a globe so that they can observe that the ocean basins of the four major oceans are not the same size. **L2**

Teacher Demo: Salinity of Ocean Water
Add 35 g of salt to 1 L of water so that students can observe the ratio of salt to water in the ocean. **L2**

Build Science Skills: Interpreting Photographs
Have students examine Figure 30, then work in groups to explain the processes of erosion or deposition that formed each feature. **L2**

Targeted Resources
❏ Transparency: Figure 27: Surface Currents
❏ GRSW Section 23.5

3 ASSESS

Reteach
Use Figure 27 to review how surface currents are formed, and how they circulate water around the world's oceans. **L1**

Evaluate Understanding
Have students create a simple cross-sectional diagram describing how physical factors change with depth in the ocean. **L2**

Targeted Resources
❏ **PHSchool.com** Online Section 23.5 Assessment
❏ iText Section 23.5

Transparencies

362 Section 23.5 Interest Grabber

Observing the Density of Saltwater

1. Fill a jar half way with tap water. Gently place a hard-boiled egg in the jar. Does the egg float or sink in the water?

2. Remove the egg from the jar. Add several tablespoons of salt to the water and stir to dissolve the salt. Continue adding salt and stirring until no more will dissolve. Gently place the hard-boiled egg in the jar. Does the egg float or sink in the saltwater?

3. An object will float in a liquid if it is less dense than the liquid. What can you conclude about the relative densities of water and saltwater based on your observations?

ANSWERS
1. The egg sinks in tap water.
2. The egg floats in saltwater.
3. The egg is denser than tap water, but less dense than saltwater. Thus, saltwater must be denser than tap water.

Transparencies

363 Section 23.5 Reading Strategy

Relating Cause and Effect

Movement Type	Causes	Effects
Surface current	a. ___?___	b. ___?___
Density current	c. ___?___	d. ___?___
Upwelling	e. ___?___	f. ___?___
Longshore drift	g. ___?___	h. ___?___

ANSWERS
a. Winds
b. Warm water generally flows away from the equator along the east side of continents; cold water generally flows away from polar regions along the west side of continents.
c. Differences in ocean water density
d. Responsible for slow mixing of water between the surface and deep ocean.
e. Warm water is blown aside by winds and currents, allowing colder water to rise from the deep ocean.
f. Nutrients are brought up from the deep ocean, providing a food source for algae, which serve in turn as food for fish.
g. Waves carrying sediment approach a beach at an angle.
h. Sand can be moved great distances along a beach.

Transparencies

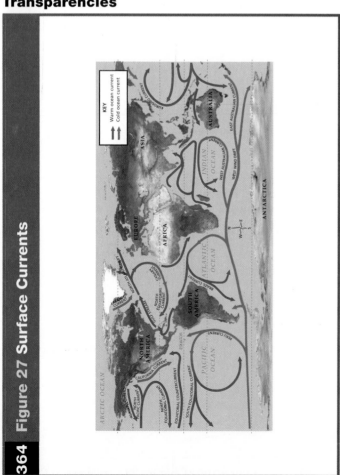

364 Figure 27 Surface Currents

Name _____ Class _____ Date _____

Chapter 23   Earth's Surface

Section 23.5 The Restless Oceans
(pages 725–729)

This section describes the oceans and ocean currents. It also describes water erosion and deposition in the oceans.

Reading Strategy (page 725)

Relating Cause and Effect Copy the table on a separate sheet of paper. After you read, complete the table to compare ways that ocean water can move. For more information on this Reading Strategy, see the **Reading and Study Skills** in the **Skills and Reference Handbook** at the end of your textbook.

Ways Ocean Water Moves		
Movement Type	**Causes**	**Effects**
Surface current	Winds	Warm water generally flows away from the equator along the east side of continents; cold water generally flows away from polar regions along the west side of continents.
Density current	Differences in ocean water density	Responsible for slow mixing of water between the surface and deep ocean
Upwelling	Warm water is blown aside by winds and currents, allowing colder water to rise from the deep ocean.	Nutrients are brought up from the deep ocean, providing a food source for algae, which serve, in turn, as food for fish.
Longshore drift	Waves carrying sediment approach a beach at an angle.	Sand can be moved great distances along a beach.

Exploring the Ocean (pages 725–726)

1. The proportion of dissolved salts in water is called ___salinity___.
2. Is the following sentence true or false? Salt is removed from the ocean by animals and plants and through deposition as sediment. ___true___
3. Circle the letters of the conditions that decrease with the ocean's depth.
   a. pressure
   (b.) light
   (c.) temperature
   d. salinity
4. What is the continental shelf? The continental shelf is the gentle sloping plain that forms an apron of shallow water around most continents.

Name _____ Class _____ Date _____

Chapter 23   Earth's Surface

Ocean Currents (pages 726–728)

Match each type of ocean current with its correct description.

Description	Ocean Current
__b__ 5. A current responsible for a slow mixing of water between the surface and deeper ocean	a. surface current
__c__ 6. Movement of water from the deep ocean to the surface	b. density current
__a__ 7. A large stream of ocean water that moves continuously in about the same path near the surface	c. upwelling

8. What causes the continuous flow of surface currents? Winds blowing across the surface of the ocean cause the continuous flow of surface currents.
9. Winds blow warm surface water aside, allowing cold water to rise, in the process of ___upwelling___.
10. What does each letter in the diagram below represent?

a. ___Cold water upwelling___   b. ___Warm surface water___   c. ___Surface wind___

Wave Erosion and Deposition (pages 728–729)

11. What are two hydraulic processes that can be responsible for wave erosion?
   a. ___Hydraulic action___   b. ___Abrasion___
12. Circle the letters of the sentences that are true about hydraulic action.
   (a.) A wave fills a crack with water.
   b. Hydraulic action causes no changes to earth's coastlines.
   (c.) Waves compress air as they slam into cracked rocks.
   (d.) Pressure from waves causes cracks in rocks to get bigger.
13. Is the following sentence true or false? The process that moves sand along a shore is called hydraulic action. ___false___

Name_____ Class_____ Date_____ M T W T F

LESSON PLAN 23.6

Earth's History

Time
2 periods
1 block

Section Objectives

Local Standards

- **23.6.1 Distinguish** between the relative and absolute dating of rocks.

- **23.6.2 Describe** the geologic time scale and what happened during the major divisions of geologic time.

Vocabulary fossils • relative age • law of superposition • extinct • index fossils • absolute age • era • periods • mass extinction

1 FOCUS

Build Vocabulary: Compare/Contrast Table

Have students make a simple T-Chart with the headings Relative Age and Absolute Age, and include an explanation of how the relative and absolute ages of rocks are determined. **L2**

Targeted Resources

❑ Transparency: Interest Grabber 23.6

❑ Transparency: Reading Strategy 23.6

2 INSTRUCT

Build Reading Literacy: Identify Main Idea/Details

While reading A Brief History of Earth, have students record the main details of each of the four geologic eras on separate index cards. **L1**

Build Science Skills: Inferring

Using Figures 32 and 33, have students work in groups to create a relative timeline describing the evolution of the Grand Canyon. **L2**

Use Visuals: Figure 34

Ask students how long Precambrian time lasted. Ask them how long the current period has lasted. Then, ask when the Jurassic Period occurred. **L2**

Integrate Chemistry

Ask students to give the approximate age of pottery if three-quarters of the carbon-14 in the pottery had decayed into daughter isotopes. Then, ask why carbon-14 would not be useful for dating rocks. **L2**

Build Science Skills: Using Models

After examining Figures 34 and 36, have students work in groups to create their own model to describe geologic time. **L2**

Address Misconceptions

Point out to students that all remaining dinosaurs were killed in a mass extinction 65 million years ago, and that modern humans did not evolve until approximately 100,000 years ago. **L2**

Targeted Resources

❑ Transparency: Figure 36: Earth's History

❑ GRSW Section 23.6

3 ASSESS

Reteach

Use Figure 36 to discuss the main events that occurred in each era of geological time. **L1**

Evaluate Understanding

Ask students to write a quiz question on the topic of geologic history, then work in groups to quiz each other. **L2**

Targeted Resources

❑ **PHSchool.com** Online Section 23.6 Assessment

❑ iText Section 23.6

Transparencies

365 Section 23.6 **Interest Grabber**

Understanding Superposition

A sculptor carves a sculpture out of a different kind of stone every month. For example, in January, she carved a sculpture out of gray granite, and in February, she carved a sculpture out of pink granite. After she finishes her work, she sweeps away the dust and rock chips that fall to the ground at the end of every day. Over time, the rock chips collect and form a large pile near the side of her workshop. The diagram below shows a cross section of this pile.

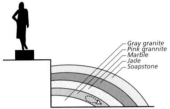

Gray granite
Pink grannite
Marble
Jade
Soapstone

1. What was her most recent sculpture made out of?

2. In what month did she make a sculpture out of jade?

3. The sculptor has been missing a necklace for some time. In what month do you think she lost it? Explain your reasoning.

ANSWERS
1. soapstone
2. April
3. February; the necklace is buried in the layer of pink granite, which collected during February.

Transparencies

366 Section 23.6 **Reading Strategy**

Previewing

Questions on Geologic Time
a. _____?_____
b. _____?_____

ANSWERS
Students' questions may include:
a. What events mark the beginning and end of each geologic era?
b. When did the dinosaurs live?

Transparencies

367 Figure 36 Earth's History

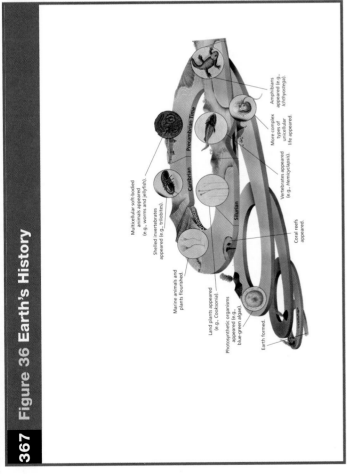

Transparencies

368 Figure 36 Earth's History (continued)

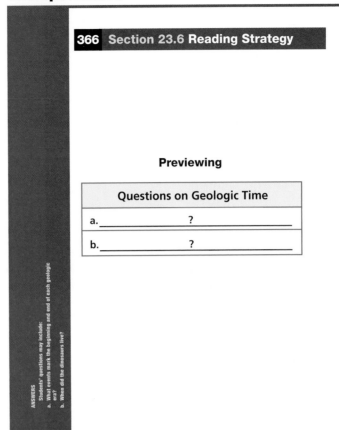

Guided Reading and Study Workbook

Name _____ Class _____ Date _____

Chapter 23   Earth's Surface

Section 23.6 Earth's History
(pages 732–738)

This section explains how scientists determine the age of rocks and how they use these methods to develop a time line for the history of Earth. It also describes the four major divisions of Earth history.

Reading Strategy (page 732)
Previewing Before you read, examine Figures 34 and 36 to help you understand geologic time. Write at least two questions about them in the table. As you read, write answers to your questions. For more information on this Reading Strategy, see the **Reading and Study Skills** in the **Skills and Reference Handbook** at the end of your textbook.

Questions on Geologic Time
Students' questions may include: What events mark the beginning and end of each geologic era?
When did the dinosaurs live?

1. What are fossils? _Fossils are preserved traces of once living things._

Determining the Age of Rocks (pages 732–734)

2. Is the following sentence true or false? The relative age of a rock is its age compared to the ages of rocks above or below it. _____true_____

3. Circle the letter that identifies the direction in which layers of sedimentary rocks form.
   a. vertically
   (b.) horizontally
   c. diagonally
   d. randomly

4. Circle the letter of the sentence that is true about the law of superposition.
   (a.) Younger rocks lie above older rocks if the layers are undisturbed.
   b. Older rocks lie above younger rocks if the layers are undisturbed.
   c. Rock layers are never disturbed.
   d. The youngest rock layers are typically at the bottom.

5. How do geologists use the law of superposition to determine the relative age of rocks?
   a. _From the sequence of rock layers_
   b. _From the fossils within each layer_

Guided Reading and Study Workbook

Name _____ Class _____ Date _____

Chapter 23   Earth's Surface

6. Organize and write the letters of the layers of rock in the diagram from oldest to youngest. If two rock layers are the same age, write them as a pair. _____D, C, B and E, A and F, G_____

7. Circle the letters of the sentences that are true about index fossils.
   (a.) They can be easily identified.
   (b.) They help to determine the relative ages of rocks.
   (c.) The organisms that formed them occurred over a large area.
   (d.) The organisms that formed them lived during a well-defined time period.

8. Geologists use radioactive dating to determine the _____absolute age_____ of rocks.

A Brief History of Earth (pages 734–738)

9. What is the geologic time scale based on?
   a. _Relative ages of rock layers_   b. _Absolute ages of rock_

10. What is a mass extinction? _A mass extinction is when many different kinds of organisms become extinct in a relatively short time._

Match each division of Earth's history to its correct description.

Description	Time
_b_ **11.** Dinosaurs appeared.	a. Precambrian time
_d_ **12.** Fishes and other animals first developed in the oceans.	b. Mesozoic Era
_c_ **13.** Humans first appeared in Africa.	c. Cenozoic Era
_a_ **14.** Earth was formed.	d. Paleozoic Era

Guided Reading and Study Workbook

Name _____ Class _____ Date _____

Chapter 23   Earth's Surface

WordWise

Solve the clues to determine which vocabulary terms from Chapter 23 are hidden in the puzzle. Then find and circle the terms in the puzzle. The terms may occur vertically, horizontally, or diagonally.

```
t a v f n o l k w e f r z h
g b i m e t l o e s s k d r
s i y b r w f a d u o l u
b a x a s d q t w i d m j
p r l l c n p t h r p e p d
s j e i n s g i e a q p y e
u a k p n p j p r u n o f f
p x l v c i b x i a b s c l
w g i t q r t c n s f i p a
e z e f a z y g q a t t i
l n b o r t x f o s s i l l
l f p j g i i o p d f o g o
i d a n b o l o e m k n c n
n z g d e n r q n i g f s d
g l j q c i s o n a z l x j
m a s s m o v e m e n t n a
```

Clues	Hidden Words
When water is released from the leaves of plants	transpiration
Water that flows over Earth's surface	runoff
The process by which rocks are broken down into fragments	weathering
The downward movement of rock and soil due to gravity	mass movement
The process through which sediment is laid down in new locations	deposition
The process wherein pieces of sediment bounce and skip	saltation
When wind picks up and carries away loose surface material	deflation
Deposits formed from windblown dust	loess
The proportion of dissolved salts in water	salinity
The movement of water from the deep ocean to the surface	upwelling
A preserved remain or trace of a once living thing	fossil
A smaller unit of an era	period

Guided Reading and Study Workbook

Name _____ Class _____ Date _____

Chapter 23   Earth's Surface

Exploring Radioactive Dating

A fossil contains 100.0 milligrams of Thorium-232, which has a half-life of 14.0 billion years. How much Thorium-232 will remain after three half-lives?

Math Skill:
Fractions
You may want to read more about this **Math Skill** in the **Skills and Reference Handbook** at the end of your textbook.

1. Read and Understand

How many milligrams of Thorium-232 does the fossil contain?
   100.0 milligrams

What is the half-life of Thorium-232?   14.0 billion years

What are you asked to find?   the amount of Thorium-232 that will remain in the fossil after three half-lives

2. Plan and Solve

During a half-life, one half of the original amount of a radioisotope decays. To find the amount of Thorium-232 left in the fossil after three half-lives, begin by multiplying $\frac{1}{2}$ by the number of half-lives.

$$\frac{1}{2} \times \frac{1}{2} \times \frac{1}{2} = \frac{1}{8}$$

This is the fraction of Thorium-232 that will be left in the fossil after three half-lives. Multiply this fraction by the original amount of Thorium-232 to find the amount of Thorium-232 that will remain.

$$100.0 \text{ milligrams} \times \frac{1}{8} = 12.5 \text{ milligrams}$$

3. Look Back and Check

Is your answer reasonable?

To check your answer, divide the number of milligrams in the fossil after three half-lives by the fraction of Thorium-232 left after three half-lives. Your answer should equal the original amount of Thorium-232 in the fossil.   100.0 milligrams

Math Practice

On a separate sheet of paper, solve the following problems.

1. A fossil contains 40.0 milligrams of Uranium-238, which has a half-life of 4.5 billion years. How much Uranium-238 will remain after two half-lives?
   $40.0 \text{ milligrams} \times \frac{1}{4} = 10.0 \text{ milligrams}$

2. How long will it take for 50.0 milligrams of Thorium-232 in a rock to decay to 25.0 milligrams?
   $\frac{25.0 \text{ milligrams}}{50.0 \text{ milligrams}} = .50$; A half-life of Thorium-232 = 14.0 billion years

3. How long will it take for the amount of Rubidium-87 (which has a half-life of 48.8 billion years) in a rock to decay from 80.0 milligrams to 10.0 milligrams?
   $\frac{10 \text{ billion years}}{80 \text{ billion years}} = \frac{1}{8}$; Three half-lives = 146.4 billion years

Student Edition Lab Worksheet

Name _____ Class _____ Date _____

Chapter 23   Earth's Surface   Exploration Lab

Modeling Erosion

See page 739 in the Teacher's Edition for more information.

Moving water is the major cause of erosion on Earth. In this lab, you will investigate some factors that affect the rate of erosion by moving water.

Problem What are some of the factors that affect the rate of water erosion?

Materials
- metric ruler
- large sheet of cardboard
- plastic wrap
- newspaper
- soil
- blocks
- pencil
- paper cup
- scissors
- drinking straw
- modeling clay
- paper towels
- small rocks

Skills Using Models, Inferring

Procedure
1. Measure and record the length of the cardboard in centimeters. Wrap the cardboard with plastic wrap to keep it dry.
2. Put several sheets of newspaper on a flat surface. Place cardboard on the newspaper and spread a thin layer of soil over the cardboard.
3. To model a hillside, raise one end of the cardboard about 5 cm from the flat surface by placing blocks under one end.
4. Using a pencil, make a hole in a paper cup 1 cm from the bottom.
5. Cut the straw in half with the scissors and insert the end of one of the halves 2 cm into the hole in the cup.
6. Use modeling clay to seal the hole around the straw. Make sure that the clay forms a tight seal around the straw.
7. Place the cup in the middle of the raised end of the cardboard so that the straw is pointing downhill, as shown.
8. Place your finger over the straw's opening as another student fills the cup with water.
9. Remove your finger. Record your observations in the data table.

Physical Science Lab Manual • Chapter 23 Exploration Lab **339**

Student Edition Lab Worksheet

Name _____ Class _____ Date _____

DATA TABLE

Elevation of Cardboard	Slope of Cardboard	Rocks	Observations

10. Clean the cardboard with paper towels and cover it again with soil. Put used soil in the trash.
11. Now use blocks to raise the end of the cardboard 15 cm above the flat surface. Repeat Steps 7 through 10.
12. Lower the end of the cardboard to 5 cm above the flat surface. Repeat Steps 7 through 10 again, but this time place a small rock on the cardboard directly in front of the straw. In the data table, record your observations about how water moves around the rock.
13. Repeat Step 12, but this time place a pile of several small rocks on the cardboard directly in front of the straw. In the data table, record your observations about how water moves around the rocks.

Analyze and Conclude
1. **Observing** Does water erosion create smooth curves or sharp angles?

   Water erosion produces smooth curves.

2. **Analyzing Data** How did increasing the elevation of the cardboard affect the speed of the water?

   Increasing the elevation of the cardboard increased the speed of the water.

3. **Calculating** The slope of a hillside is equal to its height divided by the horizontal distance it covers. Using the length of the table under the cardboard and the height it was raised, calculate and record the slope of the model hillside in each row of the data table.

   The slope equals the height the cardboard is raised divided by the length of the table under the
   cardboard. If the table under the cardboard is 100 cm long, the slope is 0.05. Note that the length
   of the table under the cardboard decreases slightly as the elevation of the cardboard is increased.

4. **Inferring** What is the relationship between the slope of a hillside and the rate of erosion?

   The steeper the hillside, the greater is the rate of erosion.

5. **Analyzing Data** Compare the movement of the water with one rock and several rocks in front of the straw. Explain any differences you observed.

   Increasing the number of rocks caused the stream of water to spread out more widely and to move
   more quickly than was the case with one rock.

340 *Physical Science* Lab Manual • Chapter 23 Exploration Lab

---

Lab Manual

Name _____ Class _____ Date _____

Chapter 23   Earth's Surface   Investigation 23A

Using a Contour Map to Create a Landform

Refer students to pages 706–708 and 713–717 in their textbooks for a discussion of fresh water motion, deposition, and erosion. **SKILLS FOCUS:** Measuring, Inferring, Using Models, Interpreting Diagrams/Photographs **CLASS TIME:** 60 minutes

Background Information

Water is responsible for shaping much of Earth. For example, the southeastern part of the United States is part of a coastal plain that was deposited by water. The coastal plain is a flat, fertile plain that gently slopes down to the coast from the mountains farther inland. Much of the coastal plain is underlain with limestone and other water-deposited rocks. The surface soil tends to be chiefly sand or clay. These conditions produce a somewhat flat landscape except where interrupted by unusual rock formations, tectonic uplift, or depressions such as **sinkholes.**

One of the tools that scientists use to study the landscape and its history is a contour map. Contour maps are also called topographic maps. The high and low elevations created by mountains, hills, and valleys cannot be observed on a typical map. Contour maps show differences in elevation, or height above sea level, and outline the shapes, or contours, of the landscape by using contour lines. A contour line connects the points on a map that have the same elevation. The contour interval is the difference in elevation between one contour line and the next contour line.

In this investigation, you will interpret the contour lines of a topographic map and use them to create a three-dimensional model, or landform, of the region shown on the map.

Problem

How can you use a contour map to create a landform?

Pre-Lab Discussion

Read the entire investigation. Then, work with a partner to answer the following questions.

1. **Using Models** What is the advantage of creating a landform from a topographic map?

   A landform makes it easier to visualize elevation and, therefore, to interpret the form of the land
   in three dimensions.

Physical Science Lab Manual • Investigation 23A **241**

Lab Manual

Name _____ Class _____ Date _____

2. **Applying Concepts** Why does the land vary so much throughout the United States?

   The processes of erosion and deposition, as well as the interactions between tectonic plates,
   have had different effects on the land in various parts of United States. These processes have
   resulted in the great geographical variety observed.

3. **Applying Concepts** How does a topographic map illustrate the elevation of the land?

   Contour maps show differences in elevation through the use of contour lines. A contour line
   connects points on a map that have the same elevation.

4. **Applying Concepts** What do all contour intervals on a single topographic map have in common? Why is this done?

   Contour intervals indicate the change in elevation between contour lines on a given topographic map.
   In this way, the scale for elevation can be made constant for a given map, just as the distance scale
   for the other two dimensions is constant.

5. **Using Models** What do narrow contour intervals indicate? What do wide contour intervals indicate? Explain your answers.

   A narrow contour interval indicates a relatively steep change in elevation. This is because the
   change in elevation indicated by the contour interval occurs over a small lateral distance. A wide
   contour interval indicates a relatively small change in elevation. This is because the change in
   elevation indicated by the contour interval occurs over a large lateral distance.

242 *Physical Science* Lab Manual • Investigation 23A

Program Resources Chapter 23

511

Lab Manual

Name _____ Class _____ Date _____

Materials (per group)

transparent plastic box with lid
nonpermanent marking pen
enlarged photocopy of a regional contour map
modeling clay
meter ruler

Make an enlarged photocopy of either the Northeast, Southeast, or Midwest contour map shown in Figure 3 for each group of students. The copy should be slightly smaller than the box lid used in the Procedure.

Procedure

1. Place the contour map provided by your teacher inside the lid of the plastic box so that the map can be seen through the top side of the lid. Secure the map to the lid by using small pieces of masking tape near the corners. Using a nonpermanent marking pen, trace the contour map onto the box lid. Then, remove the contour map from the lid.

2. Using the marking pen and a ruler, make a centimeter scale on one of the vertical sides of the transparent box. Start by making a mark at the bottom edge of the box. Then, continue to make marks at centimeter intervals upward along the side of the box until you reach the top of the box, as in Figure 1.

3. Find the lowest elevation on the regional contour map. Write this elevation next to the bottom edge of the box.

4. Find the contour interval for your regional map. Each centimeter mark on the side of the box will represent the same vertical distance as the contour interval. Next to each cm mark, write the elevation in meters.

5. Using modeling clay, construct the first layer of the landform shown in your regional contour map. Start at the lowest elevation and work your way up to the next contour interval.

6. When you have finished the first layer of the landform, check it for accuracy. Do this by placing the lid with the contour map on top of the box. Looking down through the lid, compare the landform with the corresponding contour lines shown on the map, as in Figure 2.

7. Repeat Steps 5 and 6 for each layer of the landform until all of the contour lines of the map have a corresponding level on the landform.

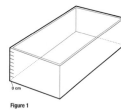
0 cm
Figure 1

258 m
252 m
246 m
240 m
Figure 2

Physical Science Lab Manual • Investigation 23A **243**

Lab Manual

Name _____ Class _____ Date _____

Observations

1. Describe the shape of the landform you made.

   Answers will vary depending on the accuracy of student models and the map used,
   but they should resemble one or two low mounds.

2. How many meters above sea level is the base of the landform?

   Answers will vary depending on the map used. The base for the Southeast map is at 24 m,
   the Northeast map is 730 m, and the Midwest map is 240 m.

3. What is the contour interval of the contour map you used to make the landform?

   Answers will vary depending on the map used. The contour interval for the Southeast map is 3 m,
   the Northeast map is 30 m, and the Midwest map is 6 m.

Analysis and Conclusions

1. **Analyzing Data** What does your landform indicate about the region modeled?

   Answers will vary depending on the map used. The Southeast and Midwest maps indicate fairly
   flat topography with gradual changes in elevation. The regions modeled are fairly flat plains. The
   map of the Northeast indicates a much steeper landform. The region modeled is hilly.

2. **Drawing Conclusions** What might you conclude about the type of region that you modeled? Explain your answer.

   Answers will vary depending on the map used. The Southeast and Midwest maps indicate gently
   sloping land, which is typical of floodplains. The Northeast map indicates a hilly region, which
   could be formed from material that has not been affected by weathering or erosion or
   or could be associated with tectonic uplift throughout the region.

244 *Physical Science* Lab Manual • Investigation 23A

Lab Manual

Name _____ Class _____ Date _____

3. **Using Models** Look at the contour maps in Figure 3. How does the feature in the map for the Southwest differ from the features depicted in the other maps?

   The map for the Southwest shows a feature that is higher at the edges and drops in elevation
   toward the center. This is a map of a canyon or gorge. The other maps indicate hills or rising
   areas of plains.

4. **Inferring** Compare the contour map for the Southeast with the contour map for the Southwest. Do you think the feature in the map for the Southwest was also formed by water? Explain your answer.

   Students should note that the Grand Canyon was also formed by water but the processes were
   different—deposition versus erosion.

Go Further

Repeat the investigation, using one of the two other maps shown in Figure 3 or find a contour map of a different region and model it with a landform. Be sure to choose a region that does not cover too large an area or does not have too great an elevation change so that your landform will still be reasonably accurate. First, show your selected map to your teacher. When your teacher approves your plan, carry out the investigation.

Be sure that students choose a small enough area to construct an accurate model. Have them avoid regions with extreme and irregular changes in elevation. Be sure that the map is enlarged sufficiently so that the contour intervals can be easily seen and measured.

Physical Science Lab Manual • Investigation 23A **245**

Lab Manual

Name _____ Class _____ Date _____

Southwest—Grand Canyon, Arizona
Contour interval: 50 meters

River
1250
1000
750
750
1000
1250
0   1 km

Northeast—Vermont
Contour interval: 30 meters

820
730
0   1 km

N
W   E
S

Southeast—Florida
Contour interval: 3 meters

27
33
30
0   1 km

Midwest—Wisconsin
Contour interval: 6 meters

240
0   1 km

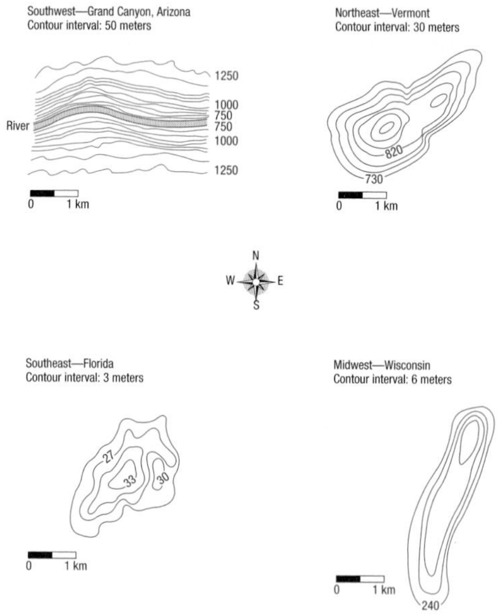

Figure 3

246 *Physical Science* Lab Manual • Investigation 23A

Lab Manual

Name _____ Class _____ Date _____

Beach Erosion

Refer students to pages 728 and 729 in their textbooks for a discussion of wave erosion and deposition. SKILLS FOCUS: Observing, Inferring, Using Models CLASS TIME: 40 minutes

Background Information

Ocean waves are examples of kinetic energy transferred through the medium of water. If ocean waves hit a beach at an angle, some of their kinetic energy is transferred to sand and pebbles, causing them to move. Some of the energy is reflected back through the water at right angles to the incoming waves, and some energy is dissipated by heat because of friction.

The kinetic energy transferred to the rocks and sand on the shore causes them to move not in the direction of either the incoming or reflected waves, but in a direction perpendicular to the shore. This is part of the process called **longshore drift**. Sand and small rocks move away from the shore at right angles to the shore as they obtain kinetic energy from the waves. Eventually, the sand and rocks are far from the shore, and so the incoming waves they encounter simply push them along in the direction of the wave. This direction is back toward the shore, but further along than where the rocks and sand originally were. Once they reach a new location on the shore, the rocks and sand once again move away from the shore at right angles. This cycle is repeated so that over time, the sand and small rocks on a beach can move long distances along the shore.

In this investigation, you will create a shoreline model with a beach and rocks. By simulating ocean waves, you will observe how the sand and rocks are moved by the energy from the waves.

Problem

How does the energy in ocean waves affect the material on the shore?

Pre-Lab Discussion

Read the entire investigation. Then, work with a partner to answer the following questions.

1. **Applying Concepts** What happens to the kinetic energy of a wave as the wave comes ashore?

   Some of the kinetic energy is transferred to sand and pebbles, causing them to move. Some of
   the energy is dissipated by heat. The remainder of the kinetic energy is reflected back through
   the water at right angles to the incoming waves.

2. **Inferring** From your answer to Question 1, what can you infer about the amount of kinetic energy of the waves reflected from the shore compared to the amount of kinetic energy of the incoming waves?

   The reflected waves will have less kinetic energy than the incoming waves will have.

Lab Manual

Name _____ Class _____ Date _____

3. **Controlling Variables** What are the manipulated and responding variables in this investigation?

   The number of waves or length of time that the waves strike the shore is the manipulated variable.
   The motion of the sand and rocks is the responding variable.

4. **Controlling Variables** What variables must be kept constant in this investigation so that the results will be meaningful?

   The intensity and angle of the waves should be kept as constant as possible so that changes on
   the simulated shoreline are the result of the number of waves, rather than the incoming angle or
   intensity of the waves.

5. **Predicting** If you perform this investigation long enough, what do you expect will happen?

   Much of the sand at one end of the simulated beach will undergo longshore drift and gradually
   will move to the other end of the pan.

Materials *(per group)*

large rectangular aluminum baking dish   water
fine sand   ruler or flat stick 10–12 cm long
5 very small pebbles, each about 1 cm in diameter   newspaper
clock or watch

Safety

Put on safety goggles and a lab apron. Note all safety alert symbols next to the steps in the Procedure and review the meaning of each symbol by referring to the Safety Symbols on page xiii.

Procedure

1. Mix the sand with a little water so that it will hold its shape. Use the sand to create a shoreline along one side of the baking dish. Make the sand deeper along the edge of the pan and taper it, as shown in the side view in Figure 1.

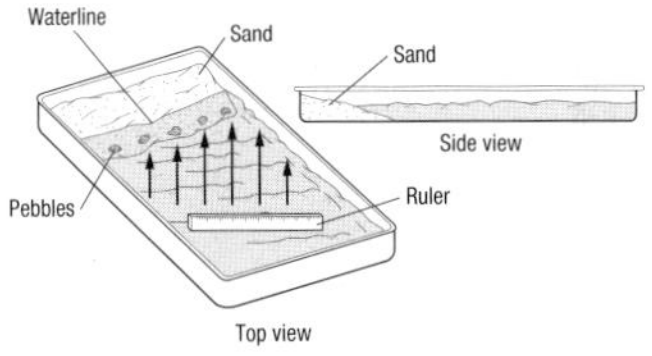

Figure 1

Lab Manual

Name _____ Class _____ Date _____

2. Place the dish on a sheet of newspaper so that any water that is spilled over the sides will be absorbed. Add water to the dish very slowly so that you do not disturb the sand. Leave 4 or 5 cm of beach above the water line. **CAUTION:** *Wipe up any spilled liquids immediately to avoid slips and falls.*

3. Place a small pebble every few centimeters along the simulated beach.

4. Set the ruler on edge in the water, as shown in Figure 1. Gently rock the top edge of the ruler back and forth to create waves. Try to keep the intensity with which you rock the ruler steady and uniform so that the waves are nearly the same throughout the investigation. Observe the movement of the sand and pebbles. Record your observations.

5. Restore the pebbles and sand to their original positions. Repeat Step 4 for three minutes.

Observations

Answers will vary, depending on how vigorous the waves are and how long the investigation
is performed. Assuming that the waves are directed along the length and slightly to the right side
of the dish, over time sand should be seen to drift away from the shore toward the water
and then back toward the shore and to the right of its original location. Stronger waves should
move the pebbles slightly in the same manner, though not as far.

Analysis and Conclusions

1. **Observing** In what direction did the reflected waves move with respect to the incoming waves? How did the intensity of the reflected waves compare to the intensity of the incoming waves?

   The reflected waves were at right angles to the incoming wave, and they were less intense.

Lab Manual

Name _____ Class _____ Date _____

2. **Interpreting Diagrams** The diagram in Figure 2 shows how a pebble on the shore moves as an incoming wave strikes the beach at an angle. Draw the path that the pebble will take as the next three waves hit the beach.

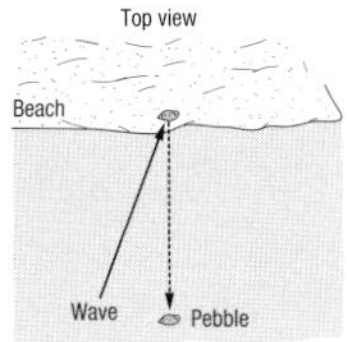

Figure 2

Student art should show the pebble moved toward the shore in the same direction as the next incoming wave. If after this wave the pebble is on the shore, the next wave will move the pebble away from the shore in a perpendicular direction as shown in the diagram. The third wave will move the pebble toward the shore in the same direction as the wave. If the pebble is not shown on the shore after the first wave, the second wave will move it toward the shore in the same direction as the wave.

3. **Drawing Conclusions** Based on your investigation, in what direction will beach erosion occur?

   Beach erosion will occur in the direction of the wave component that moves along the shore. In
   this investigation, this was toward the right side of the dish.

Go Further

Plan an experiment to show how the angle and intensity of the incoming waves affect longshore drift. Vary the procedure of this investigation accordingly, making sure to account for all controlled, manipulated, and responding variables. Show your plan to your teacher. When your teacher approves your plan, carry out your experiment and report your results.

Student plans for observing drift dependence on incoming wave angle should indicate that wave angle changes while wave intensity and time of observation are kept as constant as possible. Students should make observations for at least four different wave angles. For observing drift dependence on wave intensity, wave angle and time of observation should be kept constant. Observations should be made for at least four levels of wave intensity.

Chapter Test A

Name ______________________ Class ________________ Date ____________

Chapter 23 Earth's Surface — Chapter Test A

Multiple Choice

Write the letter that best answers the question or completes the statement on the line provided.

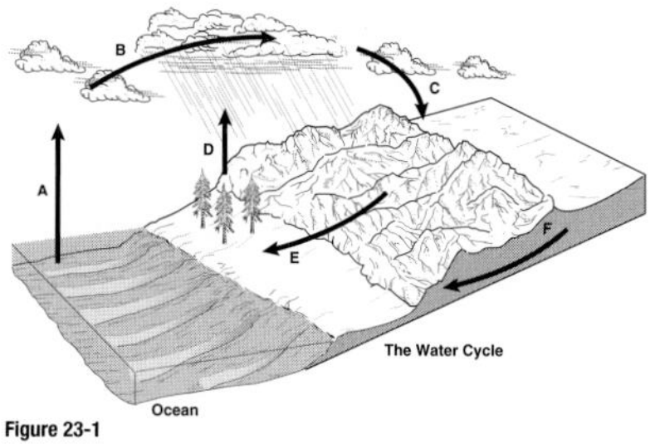

Figure 23-1

____ 1. In Figure 23-1, what process does the arrow labeled A represent?
a. transpiration b. condensation
c. evaporation d. precipitation

____ 2. Which processes are involved in erosion?
a. precipitation, evaporation, and condensation
b. weathering, runoff, and transpiration
c. weathering, evaporation, and runoff
d. weathering, the force of gravity, and wind

____ 3. Which of the following rock types and conditions would result in the highest rate of chemical weathering?
a. granite in a cold and dry area
b. limestone in a hot and rainy area
c. slate in a hot and rainy area
d. granite in a hot and dry area

____ 4. Tilted telephone poles and fences curving in a downward direction on a hillside are evidence of
a. a landslide. b. a mudflow. c. a slump. d. creep.

____ 5. Meanders, V-shaped valleys, and oxbow lakes are all features formed by
a. glaciers. b. water erosion.
c. water deposition. d. groundwater erosion.

Physical Science ▪ Chapter 23 Test A 247

Chapter Test A

Name ______________________ Class ________________ Date ____________

____ 6. The portion of a stream that flows through gently sloping flood plains is often characterized by
a. V-shaped valleys and waterfalls.
b. steep valleys and rapids.
c. meanders and oxbow lakes.
d. meanders and waterfalls.

____ 7. Groundwater forms caves and sinkholes by the process of
a. chemical weathering. b. physical weathering.
c. condensation. d. mineral deposition.

____ 8. What pyramid-shaped glacial formation is a combination of several connected ridges?
a. a horn b. a U-shaped valley
c. a moraine d. a cirque

____ 9. Why do most ocean organisms live above a water depth of 500 meters?
a. Pressure below that depth is too great.
b. Temperature below that depth is too high.
c. Pressure below that depth is too low.
d. Light below that depth is too bright.

____10. What type of ocean current brings cold water from the deep ocean to the surface?
a. a density current b. upwelling
c. a surface current d. a current caused by wind

____11. Which of the following is an example of a feature caused by wave erosion?
a. a delta b. an alluvial fan c. a sea stack d. a spit

____12. Geologists could use which of the following to compare the age of sedimentary rock layers in Bryce Canyon with sedimentary rock layers in the Grand Canyon?
a. radioactive isotopes b. index fossils
c. relative dating d. all of the above

____13. When did the first land plants and animals appear in the fossil record?
a. in the Mesozoic Era
b. in the Paleozoic Era
c. during the Triassic period
d. during the Carboniferous period

Completion

Complete each statement on the line provided.

1. When a stream flows out of a mountain range onto a flat area of land, it deposits sediments in a(an) ________________.

248 *Physical Science* ▪ Chapter 23 Test A

Chapter Test A

Name ______________________ Class ________________ Date ____________

2. The carbonic acid that is involved in the formation of caves is formed when rainwater combines with ________________ in the air.
3. The ________________ is a gently sloping plain covered with shallow water along the edges of continents.
4. In mountainous areas, valley glaciers cut ________________ valleys.
5. Wave erosion is caused by abrasion and the ________________ of waves.

Short Answer

In complete sentences, write the answers to the questions on the lines provided.

1. What are the processes that make up the water cycle?

2. Compare and contrast weathering and erosion.

3. How are landslides and mudflows alike?

4. Describe three ways that wind erosion moves sediment.

Physical Science ▪ Chapter 23 Test A 249

Chapter Test A

Name ______________________ Class ________________ Date ____________

5. Describe how a glacier erodes the land.

Using Science Skills

Use the diagram to answer each question. Write the answers on a separate sheet of paper.

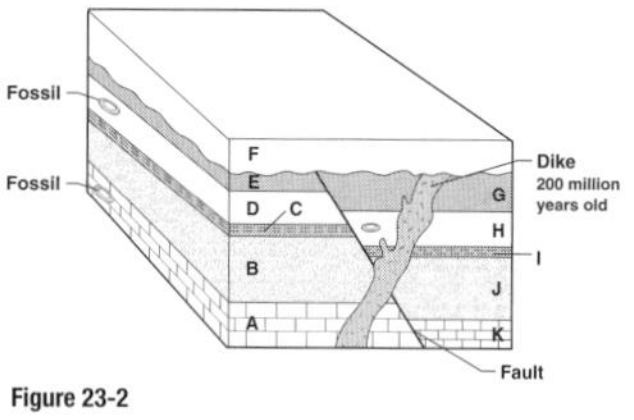

Figure 23-2

1. **Inferring** Which rock layer is the youngest layer shown in Figure 23-2?
2. **Analyzing Data** In Figure 23-2, would a fossil in layer D be younger or older than fossils found in layer B?
3. **Analyzing Data** In Figure 23-2, is the fault older or younger than the dike? Explain.
4. **Interpreting Graphics** In Figure 23-2, on either side of the fault, which rock layers were a single layer before the faulting?
5. **Drawing Conclusions** In Figure 23-2, what can be concluded about the relative ages of the rock layers below layer F? What can be concluded about the absolute ages of these layers?

Essay

Write the answers to each question on a separate sheet of paper.

1. Describe the two types of glaciers.
2. Explain how a stream transports sediment of various sizes.
3. Describe the journey of a water molecule through the water cycle.
4. Describe and discuss what causes surface currents and deep currents in the ocean.
5. In order to be useful, an index fossil must be easy to identify, have been widespread, and lived during a short, well-defined period of time. Explain why each of these three factors is important to the usefulness of index fossils in the relative dating of sedimentary rocks.

250 *Physical Science* ▪ Chapter 23 Test A

Chapter Test B

Name _____ Class _____ Date _____

Chapter 23   Earth's Surface   Chapter Test B

Multiple Choice

Write the letter that best answers the question or completes the statement on the line provided.

_____ 1. In the water cycle, the process that changes a liquid into a
gas is called
   a. transpiration.   b. evaporation.
   c. condensation.   d. precipitation.

_____ 2. Most of Earth's liquid fresh water is found in
   a. groundwater.   b. lakes and streams.
   c. reservoirs.   d. glaciers.

_____ 3. A permeable layer of rock that is saturated with water is
called a(an)
   a. water table.   b. lake.   c. watershed.   d. aquifer.

_____ 4. Which of the following is an example of erosion?
   a. to wear down and carry away rock and soil through
      the force of gravity
   b. to wear down and carry away rock and soil through
      the action of wind
   c. to wear down and carry away rock and soil through the
      action of water
   d. all of the above

_____ 5. Which of the following is NOT an agent of chemical
weathering?
   a. rainwater   b. oxidation
   c. frost wedging   d. carbonic acid

_____ 6. A rapid mass movement of large amounts of rock and soil
down a slope is called a
   a. landslide.   b. slump.   c. creep.   d. mudflow.

_____ 7. A stream's ability to erode depends mainly on
   a. its temperature.
   b. the size of the sediment in the stream.
   c. its speed.
   d. the shape of its valley.

_____ 8. A sediment deposit formed when a stream flows into a lake
or the ocean is called a(an)
   a. alluvial fan.   b. delta.   c. meander.   d. natural levee.

_____ 9. Caves are formed by erosion from
   a. glaciers.   b. streams.   c. wind.   d. groundwater.

_____ 10. Unsorted sediment deposited by a glacier is called
   a. a cirque.   b. till.   c. a horn.   d. an erratic.

Chapter Test B

Name _____ Class _____ Date _____

_____ 11. Wind erodes the land by
   a. deflation and oxidation.
   b. abrasion and chemical weathering.
   c. deflation and plucking.
   d. deflation and abrasion.

_____ 12. Deposits formed from windblown dust are called
   a. moraines.   b. dunes.   c. loess.   d. cirques.

_____ 13. Which of the following describes the changing conditions in
the ocean as depth increases?
   a. pressure increases, light decreases, and temperature
      decreases
   b. pressure decreases, light decreases, and temperature
      decreases
   c. pressure increases, light increases, and temperature
      decreases
   d. pressure increases, light increases, and temperature
      increases

_____ 14. Surface currents in the ocean are caused by
   a. deep upwelling.
   b. salinity changes with depth.
   c. density differences of ocean water.
   d. wind blowing across the ocean surface.

_____ 15. What is the process that moves sand along a shore?
   a. abrasion   b. hydraulic action
   c. a spit   d. longshore drift

_____ 16. The absolute age of an igneous rock found on a beach can be
determined by using
   a. radioactive isotopes.
   b. fossils.
   c. the law of superposition.
   d. relative dating.

_____ 17. The Triassic, Jurassic, and Cretaceous periods are
divisions of
   a. Precambrian time.   b. the Cenozoic Era.
   c. the Paleozoic Era.   d. the Mesozoic Era.

Completion

Complete each statement on the line provided.

1. A rock that allows water to flow through it is said to be
   _____

Chapter Test B

Name _____ Class _____ Date _____

2. Fresh water on Earth occurs in lakes, ponds, rivers, streams, in
   groundwater, in the atmosphere as water vapor, and in
   _____.

3. _____ is the process by which rocks are chemically
   altered or physically broken down into fragments at or near
   Earth's surface.

4. The main agent of chemical weathering is _____.

5. Slumping, landslides, mudflows, and _____ are all
   forms of mass movement.

6. _____ is the process in which particles move in a
   stream by bouncing along the bottom.

7. A(An) _____ glacier is a thick sheet of ice that
   covers large areas of land.

8. Deposits of windblown dust are called _____.

9. The process by which sand is moved along a shore is called
   _____.

10. Humans evolved during the _____ Era.

Short Answer

*In complete sentences, write the answers to the questions on
the lines provided.*

1. What are three common features of fast-moving streams in
   mountainous areas?
   _____
   _____
   _____

2. What are two features formed by deposition that are often found
   in caves?
   _____
   _____

3. Describe the changes in amount of light, temperature, and
   pressure as depth in the ocean increases.
   _____
   _____
   _____
   _____
   _____
   _____
   _____

Chapter Test B

Name _____ Class _____ Date _____

4. List at least four agents of erosion.
   _____
   _____
   _____
   _____

5. What are the four largest divisions of the geologic time scale?
   _____
   _____
   _____
   _____

Using Science Skills

*Use the diagram to answer each question. Write the answers on a separate
sheet of paper.*

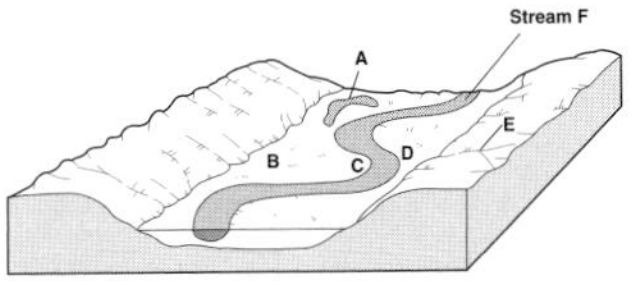

Figure 23-1

1. **Inferring** In Figure 23-1, is the stream flow moving faster at point
   C or at point D? Explain your answer.

2. **Interpreting Graphics** What is the feature labeled A in
   Figure 23-1?

3. **Inferring** In Figure 23-1, what process is occurring at C? What
   process is occurring at D?

4. **Interpreting Graphics** Use Figure 23-1 to describe the area that
   forms the floodplain for stream F.

5. **Inferring** In Figure 23-1, what are the smaller streams, which
   are labeled E, called?

Chapter 23 Test A Answers

Multiple Choice

1. c   **2.** d   **3.** b   **4.** d   **5.** b   **6.** c
7. a   **8.** a   **9.** a   **10.** b   **11.** c   **12.** d
13. b

Completion

1. alluvial fan **2.** carbon dioxide **3.** continental shelf **4.** U-shaped
5. hydraulic action

Short Answer

1. precipitation, evaporation, condensation, transpiration, and the return of water to the ocean via runoff or groundwater flow
2. Weathering breaks down or chemically alters rocks, while erosion wears down and carries away rock and soil. Weathering contributes to erosion. **3.** Both occur rapidly on steep slopes.
4. Fine particles are suspended in the air and blown about by the wind. Larger particles bounce along the ground by saltation. The largest particles are pushed along the ground by the wind. **5.** As the glacier moves, it grinds and scrapes the bedrock and soil at its base and sides.

Using Science Skills

1. Layer F **2.** younger **3.** The fault is older than the dike. The fault must be older than the dike because the fault is cut by the dike.
4. layers A and K, layers B and J, layers C and I, layers D and H, and layers E and G **5.** The layers are older than layer F, with layer A–K being the oldest, and E–G the youngest. All of the layers are older than 200 million years because they are cut by the dike, which is 200 million years old.

Essay

1. The two types of glaciers are continental glaciers and valley glaciers. A continental glacier is a thick sheet of ice that covers a very large area. A valley glacier occurs high in a mountain valley. Valley glaciers are much smaller than continental glaciers. **2.** Fine sediment is carried in suspension. Some material is carried in solution by the water. Larger particles slide or are pushed along the bottom. Some medium-sized particles move by bouncing along the bottom. This process is called saltation. **3.** Possible answer: A molecule of water falls as precipitation; it flows as runoff along the surface; it then soaks into the soil to become groundwater. The groundwater flows toward the coast, where the water molecule flows into the ocean. It then evaporates and travels up into the atmosphere. As it travels up, it cools and condenses. It is joined by other water molecules and then falls back to the surface as precipitation. **4.** Surface currents are large streams of ocean water that move continuously over the ocean surface in about the same path. Surface currents are caused by wind blowing across the ocean's surface. Deep currents are caused by differences in the density of ocean water. These density differences can be caused by differences in water temperature or salinity. Cold temperatures or high salinity cause water to become denser. **5.** The fossil must be easy to identify so it can be identified by geologists who are not experts in that particular fossil group. In order to date rock layers over large distances, the index fossil must have occurred in a widespread area. If the fossil occurred only in a small, restricted area it will not be useful for matching up or relatively dating rock layers over large regions. If the fossil lived for a long period of time, it would not be very useful in narrowing down the relative age of a rock layer.

Chapter 23 Test B Answers

Multiple Choice

1. b   **2.** a   **3.** d   **4.** d   **5.** c   **6.** a
7. c   **8.** b   **9.** d   **10.** b   **11.** d   **12.** c
13. a   **14.** d   **15.** d   **16.** a   **17.** d

Completion

1. permeable **2.** glaciers **3.** Weathering **4.** water **5.** creep
6. Saltation **7.** continental **8.** loess **9.** longshore drift
10. Cenozoic

Short Answer

1. waterfalls, rapids, and V-shaped valleys **2.** stalactites and stalagm **3.** The amount of light decreases, temperature decreases, and pressure increases. **4.** Accept any four of the following: wind, glaciers, gravity, groundwater, waves, streams, weathering.
5. Precambrian time, Paleozoic Era, Mesozoic Era, and Cenozoic Era

Using Science Skills

1. At point D; the stream flow is faster because water moves faster on the outside of the curve in a meander. **2.** an oxbow lake
3. deposition; erosion **4.** The flat area around stream F, between the steeper walls of the main valley, is the floodplain. **5.** tributaries

Chapter 24 Weather and Climate

Planning Guide

Use these planning tools
Easy Planner
Resource Pro
Online Lesson Planner

SECTION OBJECTIVES	STANDARDS		ACTIVITIES and LABS
	NATIONAL (See p. T18.)	STATE	
🕐 1 block or 2 periods for each of the following sections. **24.1 The Atmosphere, pp. 746–751** **24.1.1 Describe** Earth's atmosphere and **explain** how it is essential to life. **24.1.2 Describe** the layers of the atmosphere and their properties.	A-1, A-2, C-1, C-5, D-1, F-1, F-5, G-1		**SE** Inquiry Activity: Why Do Cold Surfaces Become Wet? p. 745 **L2** **SE** Quick Lab: Demonstrating the Effect of Air Pressure, p. 749 **L2** **TE** Teacher Demo: Air Pressure, p. 748 **L2**
24.2 The Sun and the Seasons, pp. 752–754 **24.2.1 Describe** how Earth moves through space and **explain** how seasons are caused by the tilt of Earth's axis. **24.2.2 Explain** why different latitude zones have different average temperatures.	D-1		**TE** Teacher Demo: Solar Energy and the Seasons, p. 753 **L2**
24.3 Solar Energy and Winds, pp. 755–759 **24.3.1 Describe** the processes by which solar energy heats the troposphere. **24.3.2 Identify** local and global winds and **explain** how they are produced.	B-5, D-1		**TE** Teacher Demo: Wind Creation, p. 757 **L2** **TE** Teacher Demo: Convection Cells, p. 758 **L2**
24.4 Water in the Atmosphere, pp. 760–764 **24.4.1 Explain** condensation in the atmosphere and **describe** the formation and characteristics of basic cloud forms. **24.4.2 Identify** the common types of precipitation and **explain** how they form.	D-1, D-2, G-1, G-2, G-3		**SE** Exploration Lab: Determining Relative Humidity, p. 783 **L2** **LM** Investigation 24A: Modeling Cloud Formation **L2**
24.5 Weather Patterns, pp. 765–771 **24.5.1 Explain** how air masses form and how they are classified. **24.5.2 Describe** the four types of fronts, and the weather associated with each. **24.5.3 Describe** cyclones and anticyclones. **24.5.4 Describe** the major types of storms and how they are formed.	A-1, A-2, B-4, D-1, F-5		**SE** Quick Lab: Modeling Air Masses, p. 766 **L2**
24.6 Predicting the Weather, pp. 774–777 **24.6.1 Interpret** weather map features and **describe** the technology used to forecast weather.	A-1, E-2		
24.7 Climate, pp. 778–782 **24.7.1 Distinguish** between weather and climate and **describe** the main factors that affect a region's climate. **24.7.2 Compare** climate variations due to natural and human causes.	A-1, A-2, D-1, F-1, F-2, F-4, F-5		**LM** Investigation 24B: Modeling Global Warming **L1**

Ability Levels

L1 For students who need additional help
L2 For all students
L3 For students who need to be challenged

Components

SE	Student Edition	GRSW	Guided Reading & Study Workbook With Math Support	CTB	Computer Test Bank
TE	Teacher's Edition			TP	Test Prep Resources
LM	Laboratory Manual			iT	iText
PLM	Probeware Lab Manual	CUT	Chapter and Unit Tests	DC	Discovery Channel Videotapes

T	Transparencies
P	Presentation Pro CD-ROM
GO	Internet Resources

RESOURCES — PRINT and TECHNOLOGY / SECTION ASSESSMENT

GRSW Section 24.1 — **L1**
GRSW Math Skill — **L2**
T ⊙ P Chapter 24 Pretest — **L2**
Section 24.1 — **L2**
PLANETDIARY **GO** Atmosphere — **L2**

SE Section 24.1 Assessment, p. 751
iText **iT** Section 24.1

GRSW Section 24.2 — **L1**
T ⊙ P Section 24.2 — **L2**

SE Section 24.2 Assessment, p. 754
iText **iT** Section 24.2

GRSW Section 24.3 — **L1**
T ⊙ P Section 24.3 — **L2**
NSTA SC*LINKS* **GO** Winds — **L2**

SE Section 24.3 Assessment, p. 759
iText **iT** Section 24.3

PLM Lab 10: Determining Relative Humidity — **L2**
GRSW Section 24.4 — **L1**
T ⊙ P Section 24.4 — **L2**
NSTA SC*LINKS* **GO** Clouds and fog — **L2**
PHSchool.com **GO** Data sharing — **L2**

SE Section 24.4 Assessment, p. 764
iText **iT** Section 24.4

GRSW Section 24.5 — **L1**
Discovery SCHOOL **DC** Wild Weather — **L2**
T ⊙ P Section 24.5 — **L2**
PLANETDIARY **GO** Storms — **L2**

SE Section 24.5 Assessment, p. 771
iText **iT** Section 24.5

GRSW Section 24.6 — **L1**
T ⊙ P Section 24.6 — **L2**
SCIENCE NEWS **GO** Weather — **L2**

SE Section 24.6 Assessment, p. 777
iText **iT** Section 24.6

GRSW Section 24.7 — **L1**
T ⊙ P Section 24.7 — **L2**
PLANETDIARY **GO** Drought — **L2**
PHSchool.com **GO** Data sharing — **L2**

SE Section 24.7 Assessment, p. 782
iText **iT** Section 24.7

Go Online

Go online for these Internet resources.

PHSchool.com
Web Code: ccd-3240
Web Code: cca-3240

SCIENCE NEWS
Web Code: cce-3246

NSTA SC*LINKS*
Web Code: ccn-3243
Web Code: ccn-3244

PLANETDIARY
Web Code: ccc-3241
Web Code: ccc-3245
Web Code: ccc-3247

Materials for Activities and Labs

Quantities for each group

STUDENT EDITION

Inquiry Activity, p. 745
metal pitcher, thermometer, crushed ice, long-handled spoon, paper towels, 100-mL beaker

Quick Lab, p. 749
plastic cup, index card, plastic tub

Quick Lab, p. 766
shallow, clear 3–4-L tank; plastic or cardboard divider; 1-L beaker of cold sugar solution; 1-L beaker of warm, colored, sugar solution

Exploration Lab, p. 783
sling psychrometer, relative humidity chart from Appendix G, clock or watch with second hand

TEACHER'S EDITION

Teacher Demo, p. 748
2 large sheets of newspaper, ruler

Teacher Demo, p. 753
large-face flashlight, globe with stand

Teacher Demo, p. 757
clear plastic tank, plastic wrap, 2 1-L beakers, water, hot plate or Bunsen burner, ice, wood splint (smoker), matches

Teacher Demo, p. 758
1-L beaker, water, hot plate or Bunsen burner, 5–10 drops of food coloring

Build Science Skills, p. 772
colored pencils, hurricane-tracking map (This can be downloaded from the NOAA Web site or made by superimposing a map of North America on graph paper. Label 5° intervals of latitude and longitude.)

Chapter Assessment

CHAPTER ASSESSMENT

SE Chapter Assessment, pp. 785–786
CUT Chapter 24 Test A, B
CTB Chapter 24
iT Chapter 24
PHSchool.com GO
Web Code: cca-3240

STANDARDIZED TEST PREP

SE Chapter 24, p. 787
TP Diagnose and Prescribe

iText—interactive textbook with assessment at PHSchool.com

Weather and Climate 744B

LESSON PLAN 24.1

The Atmosphere

Section Objectives

- **24.1.1 Describe** Earth's atmosphere and **explain** how it is essential to life.
- **24.1.2 Describe** the layers of the atmosphere and their properties.

Vocabulary atmosphere • air pressure • barometer • troposphere • weather • stratosphere • ozone layer • mesosphere • thermosphere • ionosphere • aurora

Local Standards

1 FOCUS

Build Vocabulary: Word-Part Analysis
Have students guess what some of the prefixes used with *sphere* might mean. Have students look up the definitions of all of the prefixes used with *sphere* in this section. **L2**

Targeted Resources
❑ Transparency: Chapter 24 Pretest
❑ Transparency: Interest Grabber 24.1
❑ Transparency: Reading Strategy 24.1

2 INSTRUCT

**Build Reading Literacy:
Active Comprehension**
Ask students what they would like to know about how the atmosphere protects Earth. Have students address each question after they finish reading Earth's Protective Layer. **L1**

Use Visuals: Figure 3
Have students examine Figure 3 and ask them questions about what various components of the figure represent. **L1**

Address Misconceptions
Help students understand that water does not disappear or disintegrate into hydrogen and oxygen as it enters the gaseous phase. **L2**

Teacher Demo: Air Pressure
Use a ruler and 2 sheets of newspaper to help students observe the presence of air pressure. **L2**

**Quick Lab: Demonstrating the
Effect of Air Pressure**
Students place an index card on top of a cup filled with water, and then invert the cup. Students use the concept of air pressure to explain how water can be held inside an inverted container. **L2**

Build Science Skills: Using Tables
Have students create a table to organize the key information about each layer of the atmosphere. **L2**

Targeted Resources
❑ Transparency: Figure 5: The Layers of the Atmosphere
❑ GRSW Section 24.1

3 ASSESS

Reteach
Use Figure 3 to review the relationship between air pressure, density of gas molecules, and altitude. **L1**

Evaluate Understanding
Ask students to create flashcards showing the ways in which the atmosphere protects Earth and provides conditions suitable for life. **L2**

Targeted Resources
❑ **PHSchool.com** Online Section 24.1 Assessment
❑ iText Section 24.1

Transparencies

369 Chapter 24 Pretest

1. What does density measure?

2. Which of these changes is most likely to occur when the temperature of a gas increases?

   a. density increases

   b. energy decreases

   c. volume increases

   d. pressure decreases

3. What is the gas law equation that relates temperature, pressure, and volume?

4. Which type of heat transfer requires the physical movement of matter?

   a. conduction

   b. convection

   c. radiation

Transparencies

370 Chapter 24 Pretest *(continued)*

5. Which of these phase changes is most likely to occur with a decrease in temperature?

   a. evaporation

   b. sublimation

   c. condensation

6. Briefly explain the Doppler effect.

Transparencies

371 Section 24.1 Interest Grabber

Altitude and Air Pressure

Think about the relationship between altitude and air pressure. As altitude increases, air pressure decreases.

1. How would a baseball hit in Denver, Colorado travel differently than a baseball hit the exact same way in Washington, D.C.?

2. Why?

Transparencies

372 Section 24.1 Reading Strategy

Relating Text and Diagrams

Layer	Altitude Range	Temperature Change
Troposphere	a. ___?___	b. ___?___
c. ___?___	12–50 km	d. ___?___
e. ___?___	f. ___?___	Decreases as altitude increases
Thermosphere	g. ___?___	h. ___?___

Transparencies

373 Figure 5 The Layers of the Atmosphere

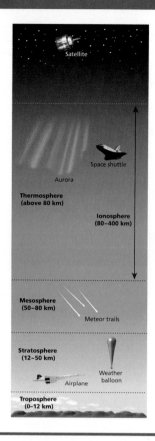

Satellite

Space shuttle

Aurora

Thermosphere
(above 80 km)

Ionosphere
(80–400 km)

Mesosphere
(50–80 km)

Meteor trails

Stratosphere
(12–50 km)

Weather
balloon

Airplane

Troposphere
(0–12 km)

Guided Reading and Study Workbook

Name _____ Class _____ Date _____

Chapter 24   Weather and Climate

Section 24.1 The Atmosphere
(pages 746–751)

This section describes Earth's atmosphere, its composition, and its different layers. It also explains air pressure and the effects of altitude on air pressure.

Reading Strategy (page 746)

Relating Text and Diagrams As you read, refer to Figure 5 and the text to complete the table on the layers of the atmosphere. For more information on this Reading Strategy, see the **Reading and Study Skills** in the **Skills and Reference Handbook** at the end of your textbook.

Layers of the Atmosphere		
Layer	Altitude Range	Temperature Change
Troposphere	0–12 km	Temperature decreases as altitude increases.
Stratosphere	12–50 km	Temperature remains nearly constant to 20 km, then increases with altitude.
Mesosphere	50–80 km	Temperature decreases as altitude increases.
Thermosphere	above 80 km	Temperature increases rapidly with altitude.

Earth's Protective Layer (page 747)

1. Is the following sentence true or false? The layer of gases that surrounds Earth is called the atmosphere. _____ true

2. How does the atmosphere make Earth's temperatures suitable for life? The atmosphere forms a protective layer between Earth and space.

3. Name two gases in the atmosphere that are essential for life.
   a. _____ Carbon dioxide _____ b. _____ Oxygen _____

Composition of the Atmosphere (page 747)

4. Is the following sentence true or false? The composition of the atmosphere changes every few kilometers as you move away from Earth. _____ false

5. Earth's atmosphere is a mixture of nitrogen, oxygen, water vapor, and many other gases

6. What two gases together make up about 99% of Earth's atmosphere? a. _____ Nitrogen _____ b. _____ Oxygen _____

7. Is the following sentence true or false? Both water droplets and solid particles are suspended in the atmosphere. _____ true

Air Pressure (page 748)

8. What is air pressure? Air pressure is the force exerted by the weight of a column of air on a surface.

9. As altitude increases, air pressure and density _____ decrease _____.

Guided Reading and Study Workbook

Name _____ Class _____ Date _____

Chapter 24   Weather and Climate

10. Circle the letter of the instrument used to measure air pressure.
   a. a thermometer
   (b.) a barometer
   c. a psychrometer
   d. Doppler radar

Layers of the Atmosphere (pages 749–751)

11. Scientists divide the atmosphere into layers based on variations in _____ temperature _____.

12. List the four layers of the atmosphere.
   a. _____ Troposphere _____ b. _____ Stratosphere _____
   c. _____ Mesosphere _____ d. _____ Thermosphere _____

13. Is the following sentence true or false? Weather is the average condition of the atmosphere in a particular place over a period of many years. _____ false

14. What is the ozone layer? The ozone layer is a region of high ozone concentration in the stratosphere.

15. How is ozone formed? An oxygen atom (O) collides with a molecule of oxygen (O_2).

16. Is the following sentence true or false? Infrared radiation in sunlight is absorbed by ozone before it reaches Earth. _____ false

17. The layer above the stratosphere is the _____ mesosphere _____.

18. Is the following sentence true or false? The temperature of the outer thermosphere is quite high. _____ true

Match the layer of the atmosphere with a characteristic that would best describe it.

Layer of the Atmosphere	Characteristic
_d_ **19.** troposphere	a. Contains the ozone layer
_a_ **20.** stratosphere	b. The outermost layer of the atmosphere
_c_ **21.** mesosphere	c. The layer where most meteoroids burn up
_b_ **22.** thermosphere	d. The layer where most weather occurs

23. What is the ionosphere? The ionosphere is a region of charged particles, called ions, that overlaps the lower thermosphere.

24. When charged particles from the sun are attracted to Earth's magnetic poles, a(n) _____ aurora _____ may appear.

Name_____ Class_____ Date_____ M T W T F

LESSON PLAN 24.2

The Sun and the Seasons

Time
2 periods
1 block

Section Objectives

- **24.2.1 Describe** how Earth moves through space and **explain** how seasons are caused by the tilt of Earth's axis.
- **24.2.2 Explain** why different latitude zones have different average temperatures.

Vocabulary rotation • revolution • tropic zone • temperate zones • polar zones • solstice • equinox

Local Standards

1 FOCUS

Build Vocabulary: LINCS
Use the LINCS strategy to help students review vocabulary terms that sound like other words they may be familiar with. **L2**

Targeted Resources
❑ Transparency: Interest Grabber 24.2
❑ Transparency: Reading Strategy 24.2

2 INSTRUCT

Build Reading Literacy: Use Prior Knowledge
Before reading The Seasons, have students work in groups to brainstorm lists of things they know about the seasons and the cause of the seasons. **L1**

Build Science Skills: Using Models
Draw Earth and the sun on the board in order to represent how solar radiation is distributed on Earth. **L2**

Teacher Demo: Solar Energy and the Seasons
Use a globe and a flashlight to help students observe how the angle of incoming solar radiation affects how regions of Earth are heated. **L2**

Address Misconceptions
Have students prepare presentations to help them understand that the seasons are not caused by the changing distance from Earth to the sun throughout the year. **L2**

Targeted Resources
❑ Transparency: Figure 7: Earth's Rotation and Revolution
❑ Transparency: Figure 10: The Seasons
❑ GRSW Section 24.2

3 ASSESS

Reteach
Use Figure 8 to reinforce the concept that parts of Earth experience summer when hit by more direct sunlight. **L1**

Evaluate Understanding
Have students explain the cause of local (Northern Hemisphere) seasons. **L2**

Targeted Resources
❑ **PHSchool.com** Online Section 24.2 Assessment
❑ iText Section 24.2

Transparencies

The Earth's Movements

Study the diagram of Earth's movements. Answer the questions using the diagram.

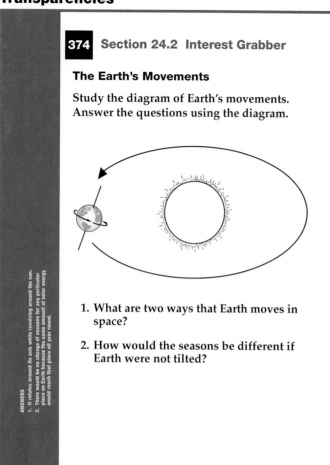

1. What are two ways that Earth moves in space?

2. How would the seasons be different if Earth were not tilted?

ANSWERS
1. It rotates around its axis while revolving around the sun.
2. There would be no change of seasons for any particular place on Earth because the same amount of solar energy would reach that place all year round.

Transparencies

Building Vocabulary

Vocabulary Term	Definition
Rotation	a. _____?_____
Revolution	b. _____?_____

ANSWERS
a. The spinning of Earth on its axis
b. The movement of one body in space around another

Transparencies

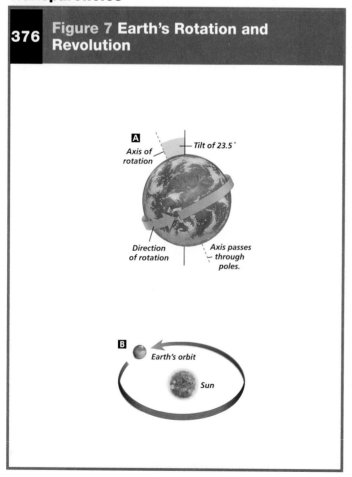

Transparencies

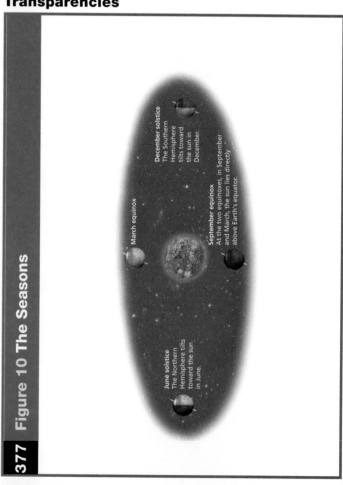

Name _____ Class _____ Date _____

Chapter 24   Weather and Climate

Section 24.2 The Sun and the Seasons
(pages 752–754)

This section describes the two major ways Earth moves. It also explains what causes the seasons.

Reading Strategy (page 752)

Building Vocabulary Copy the table on a separate sheet of paper. As you read, complete it by defining each vocabulary term from the section. For more information on this Reading Strategy, see the **Reading and Study Skills** in the **Skills and Reference Handbook** at the end of your textbook.

Vocabulary Term	Definition
Rotation	The spinning of Earth on its axis
Revolution	The movement of one body in space around another

1. What are the two major ways Earth moves?

a. _____Rotation_____

b. _____Revolution_____

2. The spinning of Earth on its axis, called _____rotation_____, causes day and night.

3. Is the following sentence true or false? It takes Earth one year to complete one rotation. _____false_____

4. The movement of one body in space around another is called _____revolution_____.

5. Earth completes a full revolution around the sun in _____one year, about 365 ¼ days_____.

6. The path Earth takes around the sun is called its _____orbit_____.

Earth's Latitude Zones (pages 752–753)

7. What is latitude? Latitude measures distance in degrees north or south of the equator.

8. Circle the letter that identifies the latitude of the North Pole.

a. 70° north

b. 80° south

c.) 90° north

d. 100° south

Name _____ Class _____ Date _____

Chapter 24   Weather and Climate

9. The part of Earth that receives the most direct sunlight is near the _____equator_____.

10. Is the following sentence true or false? Scientists use lines of latitude to mark out three different types of regions on Earth. _____true_____

Match each type of region to its latitude.

Region	Latitude
_c_ **11.** temperate zone	a. Falls between latitudes of 23.5° south and 23.5° north
_a_ **12.** tropic zone	b. From 66.5° north to the North Pole, and 66.5° south to the South Pole
_b_ **13.** polar zone	c. From 23.5° north to 66.5° north, and 23.5° south to 66.5° south

The Seasons (pages 753–754)

14. In which type of region is most of the United States located? _____the temperate zone_____

15. Is the following sentence true or false? Earth's axis of rotation is tilted at an angle of about 25.3°. _____false_____

16. The north end of Earth's axis points to _____the North Star_____.

17. The _____seasons_____ are caused by the tilt of Earth's axis as it moves around the sun.

18. Circle the letter of each sentence that is true about a solstice.

a. A solstice occurs when the sun is directly above the North Pole.

b. A solstice occurs when the sun is directly above the South Pole.

c.) A solstice occurs when the sun is directly above the latitude 23.5° north or 23.5° south.

d. A solstice occurs when the sun is directly above the latitude 66.5° north or 66.5° south.

19. Is the following sentence true or false? When the winter solstice begins in the Northern Hemisphere, the Southern Hemisphere is tilted toward the sun. _____true_____

20. Is the following sentence true or false? Earth is closer to the sun when it is summer than when it is winter in the Northern Hemisphere. _____false_____

21. Circle the letter that identifies the season that begins with the vernal equinox.

a. summer   b.) spring

c. autumn   d. winter

LESSON PLAN 24.3

Solar Energy and Winds

Time
2 periods
1 block

Section Objectives

Local Standards

- **24.3.1 Describe** the processes by which solar energy heats the troposphere.
- **24.3.2 Identify** local and global winds and **explain** how they are produced.

Vocabulary greenhouse effect • wind • local wind • sea breeze • land breeze • global winds • Coriolis effect • monsoon • jet stream

1 FOCUS

Build Vocabulary: Concept Map
Have students construct a concept map connecting the main topic of Wind to *local winds* and *global winds*, then include *sea breeze*, *land breeze*, *monsoon*, and *jet stream*. **L2**

Targeted Resources
❏ Transparency: Interest Grabber 24.3
❏ Transparency: Reading Strategy 24.3

2 INSTRUCT

Build Reading Literacy: Summarize
Have students summarize pp. 755–756, presenting verbal, written or pictorial summaries. **L1**

Address Misconceptions
Help students understand that the greenhouse effect is not always bad by having students write a paragraph describing what Earth would be like without the greenhouse effect. **L2**

Integrate Physics
Ask students why only 20% of incoming solar energy is absorbed by the atmosphere. Then, ask which has more energy, infrared or ultraviolet radiation. **L2**

Build Science Skills: Designing Experiments
Have groups of students design an experiment to test whether a breeze over a lake is produced by the same process described on p. 757. **L2**

Teacher Demo: Convection Cells
Use food coloring in heated water to help students observe a convection cell produced in water. **L2**

For Enrichment
Students can research the specific wavelengths of infrared radiation that are absorbed by each of the major gases in the atmosphere. **L3**

Targeted Resources
❏ Transparency: Figure 12: Sea Breezes and Land Breezes
❏ Transparency: Figure 13: Earth's Global Wind Belts
❏ GRSW Section 24.3
❏ NSTA *sci*LINKS Winds

3 ASSESS

Reteach
Use Figure 13 to explain convection cells and the Coriolis effect. **L1**

Evaluate Understanding
Ask students to create a flowchart describing how local winds are created. **L2**

Targeted Resources
❏ **PHSchool.com** Online Section 24.3 Assessment
❏ iText Section 24.3

378 Section 24.3 Interest Grabber

Coriolis Effect

Study the figure below. Notice the different belts of global winds on the Earth's surface.

1. Why do you think that the global winds curve?

2. If a rocket left Earth at the North Pole, what direction would it travel over the Earth's surface as it approached the equator?

ANSWERS
1. Global winds curve because Earth rotates.
2. The rocket would curve to the right due to the rotation of Earth on its axis.

379 Section 24.3 Reading Strategy

Comparing and Contrasting

Type of Wind	Day or Night?	Direction of Air Movement
Sea breeze	a. ___?___	b. ___?___
Land breeze	c. ___?___	d. ___?___

ANSWERS
a. day
b. toward land
c. night
d. toward the water

380 Figure 12 **Sea Breezes and Land Breezes**

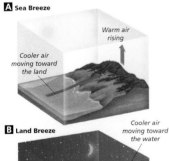

A Sea Breeze

Warm air rising

Cooler air moving toward the land

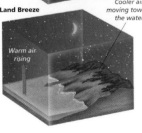

B Land Breeze

Cooler air moving toward the water

Warm air rising

381 Figure 13 **Earth's Global Wind Belts**

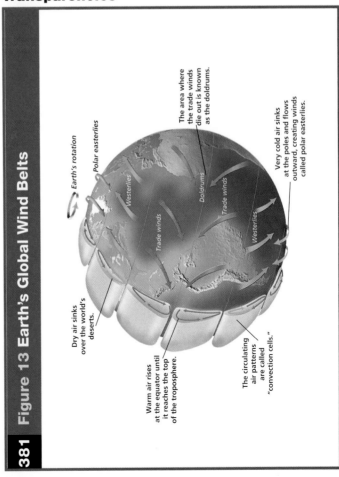

Earth's rotation

Polar easterlies

Westerlies

The area where the trade winds die out is known as the doldrums.

Very cold air sinks at the poles and flows outward, creating winds called polar easterlies.

Dry air sinks over the world's deserts.

Westerlies

Doldrums

Trade winds

Trade winds

Warm air rises at the equator until it reaches the top of the troposphere.

The circulating air patterns are called "convection cells."

527

Name _____ Class _____ Date _____

Chapter 24 Weather and Climate

Section 24.3 Solar Energy and Winds
(pages 755–759)

This section explains what happens to solar energy that reaches Earth's atmosphere and how it is transferred within the troposphere. It also describes the different winds on Earth and what causes them.

Reading Strategy (page 755)

Comparing and Contrasting After you read, complete the table to compare and contrast sea and land breezes. For more information on this Reading Strategy, see the **Reading and Study Skills** in the **Skills and Reference Handbook** at the end of your textbook.

Sea and Land Breezes		
	Day or Night?	**Direction of Air Movement**
Sea breeze	Day	Cool air moves toward land.
Land breeze	Night	Cool air moves toward water.

Energy in the Atmosphere (page 755)

1. What happens to the solar energy that reaches Earth's atmosphere?
   a. It is reflected back into space.   b. The atmosphere absorbs it.
   c. Earth's surface absorbs it.

2. Is the following sentence true or false? The atmosphere is heated mainly by energy that is reradiated by Earth's surface. _____true_____

3. The process where certain gases in the atmosphere radiate absorbed energy back to Earth's surface, warming the lower atmosphere, is called the ____greenhouse effect____.

4. Circle the letter of each way energy can be transferred within the troposphere.
   a. convection   b. radiation
   c. precipitation   d. conduction

5. Name the type of energy transfer in the troposphere that each type of arrow on the diagram represents.
   a. ___Conduction/radiation___   b. ___Convection___   c. ___Radiation___

Name _____ Class _____ Date _____

Chapter 24 Weather and Climate

6. Is the following sentence true or false? The air that directly contacts Earth's surface is heated by conduction. _____true_____

7. Heat is circulated through the troposphere by ___convection___

Wind (page 757)

8. Is the following sentence true or false? Air flows from areas of high pressure to areas of low pressure. _____true_____

9. What causes winds? _Winds are caused by differences in air pressure._

10. Is the following sentence true or false? The equal heating of Earth's surface causes differences in air pressure. _____false_____

11. What happens to air as it warms, expands, and becomes less dense? ___It rises.___

Local Winds (page 757)

12. Is the following sentence true or false? A local wind blows over a long distance. _____false_____

13. Circle the letter of each example of a local wind.
   a. a sea breeze   b. a trade wind
   c. a jet stream   d. a land breeze

14. Would you expect to find a land breeze on the beach during the day or during the night? ___during the night___

Global Winds (pages 758–759)

15. Is the following sentence true or false? Winds that blow over short distances from a specific direction are global winds. _____false_____

16. Global winds move in a series of circulating air patterns called ___convection cells___.

Match the global winds to their locations.

	Global Winds	Location
c	17. polar easterlies	a. Just north and south of the equator
a	18. tradewinds	b. Between 30° and 60° latitude in both hemispheres
b	19. westerlies	c. From 60° latitude to the poles in both hemispheres

20. The curving effect that Earth's rotation has on global winds is called the ___Coriolis effect___.

21. A wind system characterized by seasonal reversals of direction is called a(n) ___monsoon___.

22. Is the following sentence true or false? A jet-stream is a belt of high-speed wind in the upper troposphere. _____true_____

LESSON PLAN 24.4

Water in the Atmosphere

Time
2 periods
1 block

Section Objectives

- **24.4.1 Explain** condensation in the atmosphere and **describe** the formation and characteristics of basic cloud forms.
- **24.4.2 Identify** the common types of precipitation and **explain** how they form.

Vocabulary humidity • relative humidity • dew point • cloud • fog • stratus clouds • cumulus clouds • cirrus clouds

Local Standards

1 FOCUS

Build Vocabulary: Concept Map
Have students create a concept map with the topic Clouds, connecting *stratus clouds*, *cumulus clouds*, and *cirrus clouds*. **L2**

Targeted Resources
❏ Transparency: Interest Grabber 24.4
❏ Transparency: Reading Strategy 24.4

2 INSTRUCT

Use Visuals: Cloud Photos
Ask students questions about the types of clouds pictured. Discuss such topics as identifying features, precipitation, altitude, and thunderstorms. **L1**

Build Reading Literacy: Compare and Contrast
Have students verbally compare and contrast cloud types, using features such as sky coverage, precipitation, and altitude. **L1**

Address Misconceptions
Reiterate to students that condensation consists of water droplets, and that water vapor is only one component of air. **L2**

Build Science Skills: Observing
Have students keep a log of cloud and weather observations for at least one month, and analyze patterns based on their observations. **L2**

Targeted Resources
❏ GRSW Section 24.4
❏ **NSTA** *sci*$_{LINKS}$ Clouds and fog

3 ASSESS

Reteach
Use the flowchart students completed for the Reading Strategy activity on p. 760 to review cloud formation, and have students extend the flowchart to include various forms of precipitation. **L1**

Evaluate Understanding
Ask students to create a table describing what type of weather they would expect to experience with each of the cloud types shown on pages 762 and 763. **L2**

Targeted Resources
❏ **PHSchool.com** Online Section 24.4 Assessment
❏ iText Section 24.4

Transparencies

382 Section 24.4 Interest Grabber

Water Vapor and Temperature

Hold a small mirror that has been refrigerated for about an hour in front of your mouth and exhale onto its surface.

1. What happens when you do this? Why does this happen?

2. How is this experiment similar to being able to "see your breath" when you go outside when the temperature is below freezing?

(sidebar, rotated text)
As the air cools on the mirror it can no longer hold as much water vapor, so the water condenses and forms the fog on the mirror.
2. The experiment models the same concept. As the breath cools, water vapor condenses and is seen as a cloud.

ANSWERS
1. The mirror gets foggy. Student answers to the second part of the question may vary. The mirror gets foggy because air that leaves the body contains water vapor. Its temperature is approximately 98° F, warmer than the temperature of the mirror. Warm air can hold more water vapor than cooler air.

Transparencies

383 Section 24.4 Reading Strategy

Sequencing

Cloud Formation

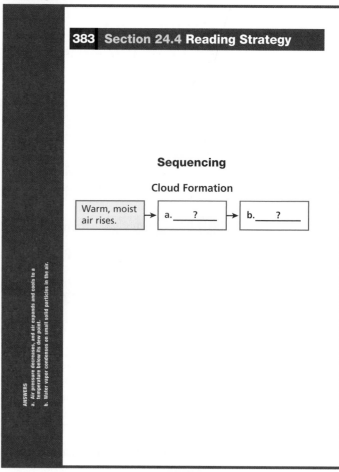

| Warm, moist air rises. | → | a. ____?____ | → | b. ____?____ |

(sidebar, rotated text)
ANSWERS
a. Air pressure decreases, and air expands and cools to a temperature below its dew point.
b. Water vapor condenses on small solid particles in the air.

Guided Reading and Study Workbook

Name _____ Class _____ Date _____

Chapter 24 Weather and Climate

Section 24.4 Water in the Atmosphere
(pages 760–764)

This section discusses the water in the atmosphere. It explains the effect water has on processes in the atmosphere such as cloud formation and precipitation.

Reading Strategy (page 760)

Sequencing As you read, complete the flowchart to show how a cloud forms. For more information on this Reading Strategy, see the **Reading and Study Skills** in the **Skills and Reference Handbook** at the end of your textbook.

Cloud Formation

| Warm, moist air rises. | → | Air pressure decreases. | → | Air expands and cools to a temperature below its dew point. | → | Water vapor condenses on small solid particles in the air. |

Humidity (pages 760–761)

1. The amount of ____water vapor____ in the air is called humidity.

2. Is the following sentence true or false? The ratio of the amount of water vapor in the air to the amount of water vapor the air can hold at that temperature is relative humidity. ____true____

3. What is the dew point? ____The dew point is the temperature at which air becomes saturated.____

4. Name what water vapor may condense into.
   a. ____Dew____ b. ____Frost____
   c. ____Clouds____ d. ____Fog____

5. When water vapor in air changes directly from a gas to a solid, ____frost____ forms.

Cloud Formation (page 761)

6. What is a cloud? ____A cloud is a dense, visible mass of tiny water droplets or ice crystals that are suspended in the atmosphere.____

7. Is the following sentence true or false? Clouds are formed when cool, dry air rises and water vapor condenses. ____false____

8. Clouds may form when moist air rises and the temperature cools below the ____dew point____.

9. Besides water vapor, what must be present for a cloud to form? ____Solid particles such as dust and salt must be in the air for a cloud to form.____

Classifying Clouds (pages 762–763)

10. Scientists classify clouds based on their form and ____height____.

Student Edition Lab Worksheet

Name _____ Class _____ Date _____

Chapter 24 Weather and Climate

11. What are the three basic cloud forms?
    a. ____Stratus____ b. ____Cumulus____ c. ____Cirrus____

12. A cloud that is near or touching the ground is called ____fog____.

13. Is the following sentence true or false? Flat layers of clouds that cover much of the sky are stratus clouds. ____true____

14. The letters ____nimbo- or –nimbus____ are added to a cloud's name to mean that the cloud produces precipitation.

15. Is the following sentence true or false? Altostratus clouds are low-level clouds similar to fog. ____false____

16. Circle the letter of the cloud form that looks like puffy, white clouds with flat bottoms.
    a. fog b. stratus
    c. altostratus (d.) cumulus

17. What do cirrus clouds look like? ____Cirrus clouds are thin, white, wispy clouds that often have a feathery appearance.____

18. Circle the letter of each type of cloud you often see on sunny days.
    a. cumulonimbus (b.) cumulus
    c. altostratus (d.) cirrus

Match each cloud to its description.

Cloud	Description
_b_ **19.** cumulus	a. Thin, high-altitude clouds that generally produce no rain
_a_ **20.** cirrus	b. "Fair-weather clouds" that look like piles of cotton balls
_d_ **21.** altostratus	c. Clouds that produce heavy precipitation and are sometimes called thunderheads
_c_ **22.** cumulonimbus	d. Middle-level clouds that can produce light rain

Forms of Precipitation (page 764)

23. What are the five most common types of precipitation?
    a. ____Rain____ b. ____Snow____
    c. ____Hail____ d. ____Sleet____
    e. ____Freezing rain____

24. Is the following sentence true or false? Snow is precipitation in the form of ice crystals. ____true____

25. How does hail form? ____Small pellets of ice are tossed up and down by rising and falling air. They collide and combine with water droplets that then freeze and fall to the ground.____

26. Rain that freezes as it falls is called ____sleet____.

LESSON PLAN 24.5

Weather Patterns

Time
2 periods
1 block

Section Objectives

Local Standards

- **24.5.1 Explain** how air masses form and how they are classified.
- **24.5.2 Describe** the four types of fronts, and the weather associated with each.
- **24.5.3 Describe** cyclones and anticyclones.
- **24.5.4 Describe** the major types of storms and how they are formed.

Vocabulary air mass • front • cold front • warm front • stationary front • occluded front • cyclone • anticyclone • thunderstorm • lightning • thunder • tornado • hurricane

1 FOCUS

Build Vocabulary: : Compare/Contrast Table
Have students create a compare/contrast table with the headings Cyclone and Anticyclone. **L2**

Targeted Resources
❑ Transparency: Interest Grabber 24.5
❑ Transparency: Reading Strategy 24.5

2 INSTRUCT

Build Reading Literacy: Predict
Before reading Fronts, have student look at Figure 20 and predict what will happen when one of the warm air masses meets one of the cold air masses. **L1**

Quick Lab: Modeling Air Masses
Students will observe warm colored sugar solution and cold sugar solution in a tank, and describe how the effect of temperature on the density of a fluid can cause water or air masses to move relative to one another. **L2**

Build Science Skills: Relating Cause and Effect
Have students work in groups to design a graphic that explains why there is often precipitation at the edge of a front. **L2**

Address Misconceptions
Point out to students that the term cyclone has two distinct meanings in weather—a hurricane and a low-pressure system. **L2**

Integrate Physics
Have students work in groups to create a poster that shows light and sound moving away from a lightning strike. **L2**

Targeted Resources
❑ Transparency: Figure 20: North American Air Masses
❑ Transparency: Figures 21 and 22: Cold Fronts and Warm Fronts
❑ GRSW Section 24.5

3 ASSESS

Reteach
Use Figures 21 and 22 to help students distinguish between cold fronts and warm fronts. **L1**

Evaluate Understanding
Ask students to create a study guide to help them remember what types of weather occur with each of the four types of fronts. **L2**

Targeted Resources
❑ **PHSchool.com** Online Section 24.5 Assessment
❑ iText Section 24.5

Transparencies

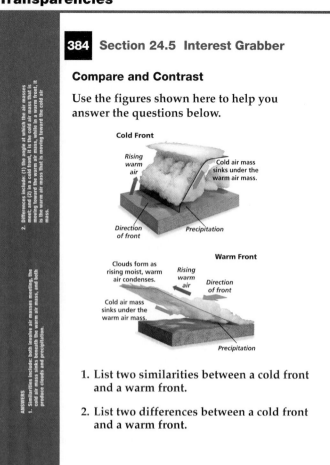

384 Section 24.5 Interest Grabber

Compare and Contrast

Use the figures shown here to help you answer the questions below.

Cold Front

Rising warm air

Cold air mass sinks under the warm air mass.

Direction of front

Precipitation

Warm Front

Clouds form as rising moist, warm air condenses.

Rising warm air

Direction of front

Cold air mass sinks under the warm air mass.

Precipitation

1. List two similarities between a cold front and a warm front.

2. List two differences between a cold front and a warm front.

Transparencies

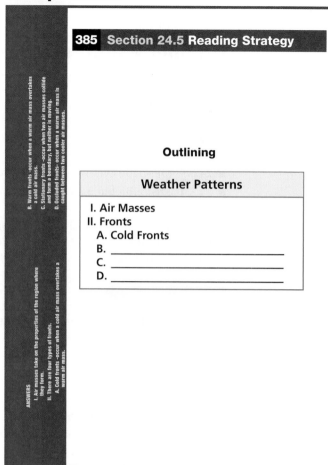

385 Section 24.5 Reading Strategy

Outlining

Weather Patterns
I. Air Masses
II. Fronts
A. Cold Fronts
B. _____
C. _____
D. _____

Transparencies

386 Figure 24.5 North American Air Masses

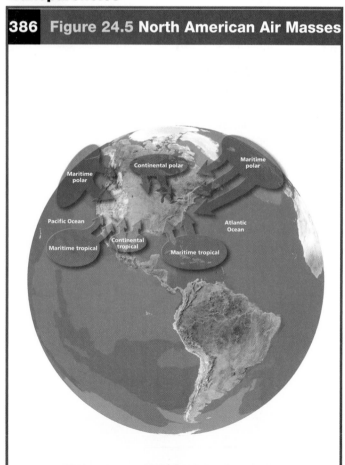

Transparencies

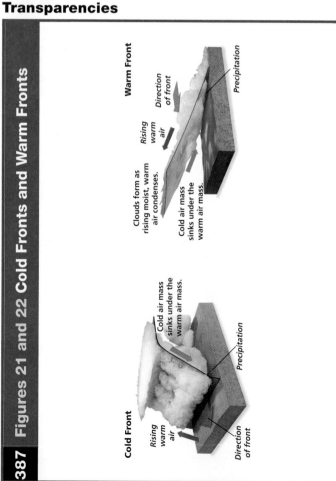

Name _____ Class _____ Date _____

Chapter 24   Weather and Climate

Section 24.5 Weather Patterns
(pages 765–771)

This section describes the weather patterns on Earth. It explains how air masses form and create fronts, low and high-pressure systems, and storms.

Reading Strategy (page 765)

Outlining Complete the outline with information from the section. Use the green headings as the main topics and the blue headings as subtopics. As you read, add supporting details to the subheadings. For more information on this Reading Strategy, see the **Reading and Study Skills** in the **Skills and Reference Handbook** at the end of your textbook.

Weather Patterns
I. Air Masses
II. Fronts
A. Cold fronts occur when a cold air mass overtakes a warm air mass.
B. Warm fronts occur when a warm air mass overtakes a cold air mass.
C. Stationary fronts occur when two air masses collide and form a boundary but neither is moving.
D. Occluded fronts occur when a warm air mass is caught between two cooler air masses.

Air Masses (pages 765–766)

1. A large body of air that has fairly uniform physical properties such as temperature and moisture content at any given altitude is a(n) _____air mass_____.

2. When do air masses form? _Air masses form when a large body of air becomes fairly stationary over a region of Earth's surface or when air moves over a large uniform region like an ocean._

Match the classifications of air masses to where they form.

	Classification of Air Mass	Where They Form
_b_	3. maritime	a. Originates where it is very warm
_a_	4. tropical	b. Forms over water transpiration
_d_	5. polar	c. Forms over land
_c_	6. continental	d. Originates where it is very cold

Fronts (pages 767–768)

7. When a continental polar air mass collides with a maritime tropical air mass, a(n) _____front_____ forms.

8. Circle the letters of the weather conditions often associated with cold fronts.
   (a.) large amounts of precipitation   b. clear skies
   (c.) severe thunderstorms   (d.) strong winds

Name _____ Class _____ Date _____

Chapter 24   Weather and Climate

Match each front to the way it forms.

	Front	How It Forms
_c_	9. cold front	a. Occurs when a warm air mass is caught between two cooler air masses
_b_	10. warm front	b. Occurs when a warm air mass overtakes a cold air mass
_d_	11. stationary front	c. Occurs when a cold air mass overtakes a warm air mass
_a_	12. occluded front	d. Occurs when two unlike air masses have formed a boundary and neither is moving

Low- and High-Pressure Systems (page 769)

13. A weather system around a center of low pressure is called a(n) _____cyclone_____.

14. Circle the letter of each weather condition associated with cyclones.
    (a.) precipitation   (b.) clouds
    (c.) stormy weather   d. clear skies

15. Is the following sentence true or false? An anticyclone is a weather system with a swirling center of low pressure. _____false_____

16. What kind of weather conditions are associated with an anticyclone? _Clear skies, little precipitation, and generally calm conditions are associated with anticyclones._

Storms (pages 770–771)

17. Is the following sentence true or false? A thunderstorm is a small weather system with thunder and lightning. _____true_____

18. Circle the letter of each characteristic of a thunderstorm.
    (a.) strong winds and heavy rain or hail
    b. only occurs on cool days
    (c.) forms when columns of air rise within a cumulonimbus cloud
    (d.) thunder and lightning

19. Is the following sentence true or false? A tornado is a small, intense windstorm in the shape of a rotating column that touches the ground. _____true_____

20. How does a tornado form? _A tornado forms when a vertical cylinder of rotating air develops in a thunderstorm._

21. A hurricane is a large tropical _____cyclone_____ with winds of at least 119 kilometers per hour.

Name_____ Class_____ Date_____   M T W T F

LESSON PLAN 24.6

Predicting the Weather

Time
2 periods
1 block

Section Objectives

■ **24.6.1 Interpret** weather map features and **describe** the technology used to forecast weather.

Vocabulary meteorologists • isotherm • isobar

Local Standards

---

1 FOCUS

Build Vocabulary: Word-Part Analysis
Have students look up the words *isotherm* and *isobar*. Ask them to infer the meaning of the prefix *iso-*, and ask if they know any other words with this prefix. **L2**

Targeted Resources
❑ Transparency: Interest Grabber 24.6
❑ Transparency: Reading Strategy 24.6

---

2 INSTRUCT

Build Reading Literacy: Use Prior Knowledge
Have students work in groups to make lists of the information they already know about weather forecasting, then read the section and add any new knowledge to their lists. **L1**

Use Community Resources
Ask a meteorologist from the NWS to talk to the class about advances in weather forecasting technology. **L2**

Address Misconceptions
Use Figure 29 or other weather maps to help students interpret the meanings of the symbols used. **L2**

Build Science Skills: Using Models
Have students practice plotting isotherms in order to help them understand the weather map as a model of weather over a large region. **L2**

Targeted Resources
❑ Transparency: Figure 29: Weather Map with Key
❑ GRSW Section 24.6

---

3 ASSESS

Reteach
Use Figure 29 to review all of the features of a weather map. **L1**

Evaluate Understanding
Show students a weather map, and ask them to identify all of the fronts, isotherms, and high- and low-pressure regions. **L2**

Targeted Resources
❑ **PHSchool.com** Online Section 24.6 Assessment
❑ iText Section 24.6

---

388 Section 24.6 **Interest Grabber**

A Weather Forecast

Think about the daily weather report you see on TV, read in the newspaper, or hear on the radio.

1. What types of information are given in the weather report?

2. What kinds of instruments do meteorologists use to measure current weather conditions and to forecast the weather?

389 Section 24.6 **Reading Strategy**

Identifying the Main Idea

Heading	Main Idea
Weather forecasting	a. _____?_____
Weather maps	b. _____?_____

390 Figure 29 **Weather Map with Key**

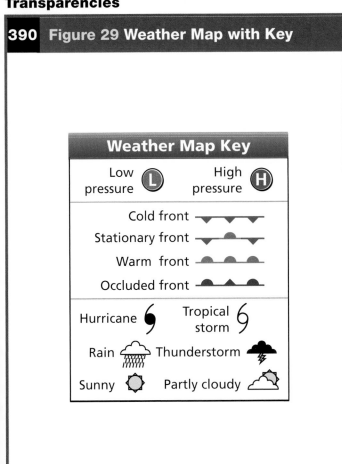

391 Figure 29 **Weather Map with Key**
(continued)

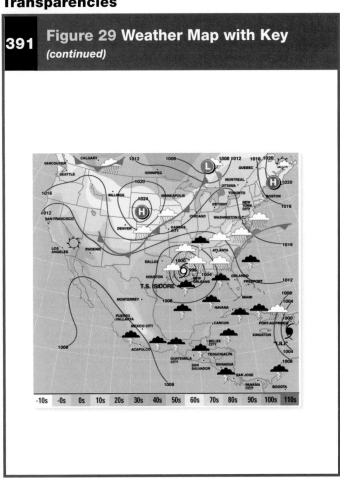

Name _____ Class _____ Date _____

Chapter 24   Weather and Climate

Section 24.6 Predicting the Weather
(pages 774–777)

This section explains some of the technology meteorologists use to predict the weather. It also explains some of the symbols found on weather maps.

Reading Strategy (page 774)

Identifying the Main Idea As you read the text, write the main idea for each heading of this section in the table. For more information on this Reading Strategy, see the **Reading and Study Skills** in the **Skills and Reference Handbook** at the end of your textbook.

Heading	Main Idea
Weather forecasting	Meteorologists use a variety of technologies to help forecast the weather.
Weather maps	Weather maps include a variety of symbols that help to illustrate the weather patterns across a certain region.

Weather Forecasting (pages 774–776)

1. What is meteorology? _Meteorology is the study of Earth's atmosphere._

2. Is the following sentence true or false? Scientists who study weather are called weatherologists. _____false_____

3. What are four technologies that help meteorologists predict the weather?

   a. _____Doppler radar_____   b. _____Automated weather stations_____

   c. _____Weather satellites_____   d. _____High-speed computers_____

4. With Doppler radar, _____radio_____ waves are bounced off particles of precipitation in moving storms.

5. Scientists can calculate a storm's _____speed_____ by calculating how much the frequency of Doppler radar waves changes.

6. The types of weather data that can be collected by a typical weather station include _____temperature, precipitation, wind speed, and direction_____

7. Meteorologists use high-speed computers to analyze data and create short- and long-term _____weather forecasts_____

8. Meteorologists can accurately forecast the movement of large weather systems for a period of _____3 to 7_____ days.

9. Why is it difficult for meteorologists to predict the weather beyond a week? _There are too many variables regarding the movement of weather systems for meteorologists to forecast reliably._

Weather Maps (pages 776–777)

10. What does a weather map show? _A weather map shows weather patterns of different regions._

Name _____ Class _____ Date _____

Chapter 24   Weather and Climate

11. Circle the letter of each type of information that a typical weather map shows.
    a. temperatures   b. mountain altitudes
    c. symbols for cloud cover   d. areas of precipitation

12. Is the following sentence true or false? Weather maps often include symbols for fronts and areas of high and low pressure. _____true_____

Look at the weather map and the key to answer questions 13–15.

13. What type of front is shown near Calgary, Canada?
    _____cold front_____

14. What are the weather conditions in Los Angeles?
    _____sunny_____

15. What is the highest air pressure shown on the map?
    _____1024 mb_____

16. A line on a map that connects points of equal air temperatures is called a(n) _____isotherm_____.

17. How is a map with isotherms helpful to meteorologists? _Meteorologists can quickly see temperature patterns on a map with isotherms._

18. Is the following sentence true or false? An isobar is a line that connects points of unequal air pressure. _____false_____

19. Circle the letter of each type of weather information that isobars help meteorologists to identify.
    a. areas of cloud cover   b. centers of low-pressure systems
    c. locations of fronts   d. centers of high-pressure systems

Name_____ Class_____ Date_____ M T W T F

LESSON PLAN 24.7

Climate

Time
2 periods
1 block

Section Objectives

■ **24.7.1 Distinguish** between weather and climate and **describe** the main factors that affect a region's climate.

■ **24.7.2 Compare** climate variations due to natural and human causes.

Vocabulary climate • desert • ice ages • El Niño • global warming

Local Standards

1 FOCUS

Build Vocabulary: Paraphrase
Working in groups of five, have students explain one of the section vocabulary terms in his or her own words. **L2**

Targeted Resources
❏ Transparency: Interest Grabber 24.7
❏ Transparency: Reading Strategy 24.7

2 INSTRUCT

Build Reading Literacy: Predict
Before reading Factors Affecting Precipitation, have groups of students brainstorm a list of factors that they think would affect the amount of precipitation a region gets. **L1**

Address Misconceptions
Point out to students that, in science, the terms "weather" and "climate" have different meanings. **L2**

Build Science Skills: Relating Cause and Effect
Using Figure 2 and their prior knowledge of global convection cells, have students discuss why arid climates are typically found at 30° N and 30° S. **L2**

Use Community Resources
Invite a local farmer, gardener, or landscaper to talk about the resources he or she uses to make seasonal climate predictions. **L2**

Targeted Resources
❏ Transparency: Figure 32: Climate Map with Key
❏ GRSW Section 24.7

3 ASSESS

Reteach
Use Figure 32 to review the major climate subtypes, some regions where they are located, and why they occur in those locations. **L1**

Evaluate Understanding
Ask students to discuss their local climate subtype, including naming factors that affect local temperature and precipitation. **L2**

Targeted Resources
❏ **PHSchool.com** Online Section 24.7 Assessment
❏ iText Section 24.7

Transparencies

392 **Section 24.7 Interest Grabber**

What Climate Do You Live In?

Use the figure shown here to help you answer the questions below.

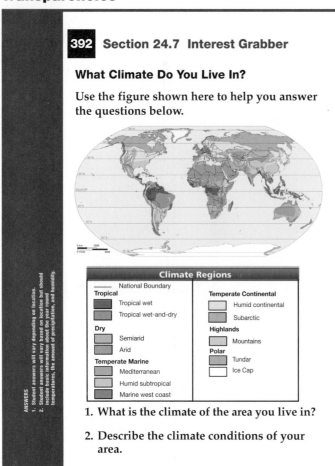

1. What is the climate of the area you live in?

2. Describe the climate conditions of your area.

Transparencies

393 **Section 24.7 Reading Strategy**

Building Vocabulary

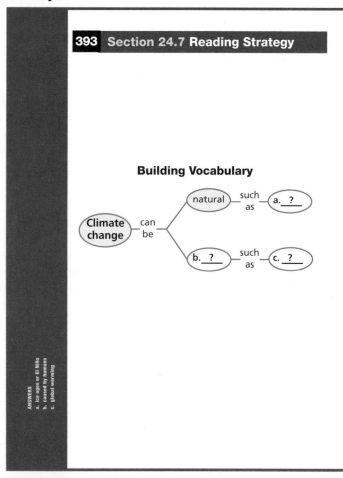

Transparencies

Figure 32 Climate Map with Key

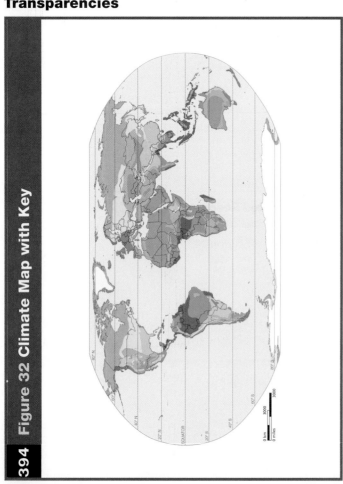

394

Transparencies

395 **Figure 32 Climate Map with Key**
(continued)

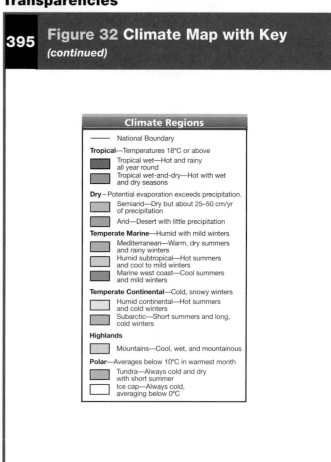

Guided Reading and Study Workbook

Name _____ Class _____ Date _____

Chapter 24   Weather and Climate

Section 24.7 Predicting the Weather
(pages 778–782)

This section describes climate and climate changes. It also describes factors that affect the patterns of temperature and precipitation of a region.

Reading Strategy (page 778)

Building Vocabulary As you read, complete the concept map with terms from this section. For more information on this Reading Strategy, see the **Reading and Study Skills** in the **Skills and Reference Handbook** at the end of your textbook.

Climate change — can be → natural — such as → Ice ages or El Niño
Climate change — can be → caused by humans — such as → global warming

1. What is climate? Climate is the long-term weather conditions of a place or region.

Classifying Climates (pages 778–779)

2. What are the six major climate groups?
   a. Tropical rainy   b. Temperate continental
   c. Dry   d. Temperate marine
   e. Polar   f. Highlands

3. Circle the letters of the two main factors that determine a region's climate.
   a. elevation   (b.) temperature
   (c.) precipitation   d. winds

Factors Affecting Temperature (pages 779–780)

4. What are four factors that affect a region's temperature?
   a. Latitude   b. Distance from large bodies of water
   c. Ocean currents   d. Altitude

5. What factors influence the temperature of coastal regions? The temperature of coastal regions is influenced by large bodies of water and ocean currents.

6. Is the following sentence true or false? As altitude increases, temperature generally increases. ___false___

Factors Affecting Precipitation (page 780)

7. Circle the letter of each factor that can affect a region's precipitation.
   (a.) the existence of a mountain barrier   (b.) distribution of air pressure systems
   (c.) distribution of global winds   (d.) latitude

8. Precipitation is generally higher near the ___equator___ than the poles.

Physical Science Guided Reading and Study Workbook • Chapter 24 **237**

Guided Reading and Study Workbook

Name _____ Class _____ Date _____

Chapter 24   Weather and Climate

Use the diagram below to answer the questions that follow.

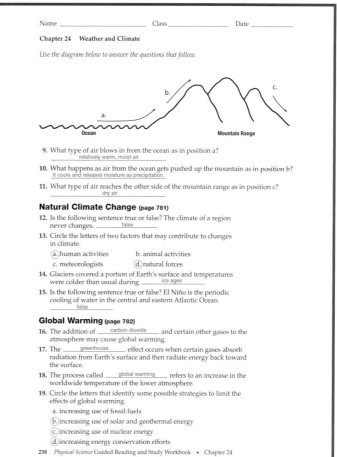

9. What type of air blows in from the ocean as in position a? relatively warm, moist air

10. What happens as air from the ocean gets pushed up the mountain as in position b? It cools and releases moisture as precipitation.

11. What type of air reaches the other side of the mountain range as in position c? dry air

Natural Climate Change (page 781)

12. Is the following sentence true or false? The climate of a region never changes. ___false___

13. Circle the letters of two factors that may contribute to changes in climate.
   (a.) human activities   b. animal activities
   c. meteorologists   (d.) natural forces

14. Glaciers covered a portion of Earth's surface and temperatures were colder than usual during ___ice ages___.

15. Is the following sentence true or false? El Niño is the periodic cooling of water in the central and eastern Atlantic Ocean. ___false___

Global Warming (page 782)

16. The addition of ___carbon dioxide___ and certain other gases to the atmosphere may cause global warming.

17. The ___greenhouse___ effect occurs when certain gases absorb radiation from Earth's surface and then radiate energy back toward the surface.

18. The process called ___global warming___ refers to an increase in the worldwide temperature of the lower atmosphere.

19. Circle the letters that identify some possible strategies to limit the effects of global warming.
   a. increasing use of fossil fuels
   (b.) increasing use of solar and geothermal energy
   (c.) increasing use of nuclear energy
   (d.) increasing energy conservation efforts

238 *Physical Science* Guided Reading and Study Workbook • Chapter 24

Guided Reading and Study Workbook

Name _____ Class _____ Date _____

Chapter 24   Weather and Climate

WordWise

Complete the sentences by using one of the scrambled vocabulary terms from Chapter 24.

mertpoheas   ria superers   prehopotres
trainoot   quieoxn   hoeusegren tefefc
ase zebere   rilocosi ceteff   wed tinpo
rai sams   dunterh   mosthrei
emailtc

The lower-most layer of the atmosphere is called the ___troposphere___

A description of the pattern of weather over many years in a place or region is its ___climate___

A time when neither hemisphere is tilted toward the sun and lengths of daylight and sunlight are approximately equal is called a(n) ___equinox___

A large body of air that has fairly uniform physical properties such as temperature and moisture content at any given altitude is a(n) ___air mass___

The process by which gases in the atmosphere radiate absorbed energy back to Earth's surface, warming the atmosphere is known as the ___greenhouse effect___

The layer of gases that surrounds Earth is called the ___atmosphere___

The spinning of Earth on its axis is called its ___rotation___

A local wind that blows from sea to land is a(n) ___sea breeze___

The curving effect that Earth's rotation has on all free-moving objects is the ___Coriolis effect___

A line on a map that connects points of equal air temperature is called a(n) ___isotherm___

The force exerted by the weight of a column of air on a surface is called ___air pressure___

The temperature at which air becomes saturated is its ___dew point___

The sound produced by rapidly expanding air along the path of a lightning discharge is called ___thunder___

Physical Science Guided Reading and Study Workbook • Chapter 24 **239**

Guided Reading and Study Workbook

Name _____ Class _____ Date _____

Chapter 24   Weather and Climate

Calculating Volume of Gases

About 78% of the volume of dry air is composed of nitrogen. About how much nitrogen would there be in a 500 m^3 volume of dry air?

1. Read and Understand

What information are you given in the problem?

Dry air = 78% nitrogen

2. Plan and Solve

What unknown are you trying to calculate?

500 m^3 volume of dry air contains ___?___ m^3 of nitrogen

Convert the percent of nitrogen in dry air (78%) to a decimal.

Move the decimal point in 78% two places to the left and drop the percent sign. = 0.78

To find the amount of nitrogen in a 500 m^3 volume of dry air, multiply 500 by the decimal conversion of 78%. 0.78 × 500 m^3 = 390 m^3

About how much nitrogen will a 500 m^3 volume of dry air have?

500 m^3 volume of dry air contains about 390 m^3 nitrogen

3. Look Back and Check

To check your answer, find what percent of 500 m^3 your answer is. To do this, first divide your answer by 500.

$$\frac{390 \ m^3}{500 \ m^3} = 0.78$$

Then, convert the decimal to a percent by moving the decimal point two places to the right and placing a percent symbol after the number. If the percent is the same as the percentage of nitrogen found in dry air, your answer is correct. 0.78 becomes 78%

Math Practice

On a separate sheet of paper, solve the following problems.

1. Helium makes up 0.00052% of dry air. About how much helium would there be in a 10,000 m^3 volume of dry air?
   0.00052% = 0.0000052 = 5.2 × 10^{-6}; 10,000 m^3 = 10^4 m^3
   5.2 × 10^{-6} × 10^4 m^3 = 5.2 × 10^{-2} m^3 = 0.052 m^3

2. A 500 m^3 volume of dry air contains 0.185 m^3 of carbon dioxide. What percent of this sample of air is made up of carbon dioxide?
   $\frac{0.185 \ m^3}{500 \ m^3}$ = $\frac{1.85 \times 10^{-1} \ m^3}{5 \times 10^2 \ m^3}$ = 0.37 × 10^{-3} = 0.00037 = 0.037%

3. Oxygen makes up 20.946% of dry air. Argon makes up 0.934% of dry air. About much more oxygen than argon would you find in a 1000-m^3 volume of dry air?
   20.946% = 0.20946; 0.20946 × 1000 m^3 = 209.46 m^3 .934% = 0.00934;
   0.00934 × 1000 m^3 = 9.34 m^3; 209.46 m^3 − 9.34 m^3 = about 200.12 m^3 more oxygen than argon

Math Skill:
Percents and Decimals

You may want to read more about this Math Skill in the Skills and Reference Handbook at the end of your textbook.

240 *Physical Science* Guided Reading and Study Workbook • Chapter 24

Student Edition Lab Worksheet

Name _____ Class _____ Date _____

Chapter 24   Weather and Climate   Exploration Lab

Determining Relative Humidity
See page 783 in the Teacher's Edition for more information.

To measure relative humidity, you can use a sling psychrometer. This device contains two thermometers. An absorbent wick keeps the bulb of one thermometer wet. As you spin the psychrometer, air flows over the wet bulb, increasing the rate of evaporation. In this lab, you will discover how a sling psychrometer measures the relative humidity of the surrounding air.

Problem   How can you measure the relative humidity of the air?

Materials
- sling psychrometer
- relative humidity chart from Appendix G
- clock or watch with second hand

Skills   Using Tables, Formulating Hypotheses

Procedure 🔲 🔧 🔋 ✋ 🔲

1. Wet the cotton wick of the sling psychrometer with water.
2. Observe the temperature of the wet-bulb thermometer. Then, spin the psychrometer for 30 seconds. **CAUTION:** *Take care not to spin the psychrometer near anyone or anything.*
3. Repeat Step 2 until the temperature of the wet-bulb thermometer remains constant. Then, in the data table, record the temperature of both thermometers.

DATA TABLE

Location	Dry Bulb Temp. (°C)	Wet Bulb Temp. (°C)	Relative Humidity (%)
Classroom	Typical data could consist of a dry-bulb reading of 21°C, a wet-bulb reading of 15°C, and a relative humidity of 53%. Data will depend on local conditions. In any case, the wet-bulb reading will be less than or equal to the dry bulb reading.		

4. Calculate the difference between your dry-bulb and wet-bulb temperatures.
5. In the relative humidity chart, find the row and column that list the dry-bulb temperature and the difference in temperature that you calculated. The number located where this row and column meet is the relative humidity of the classroom. Record the relative humidity in the data table.

Student Edition Lab Worksheet

Name _____ Class _____ Date _____

6. Place the psychrometer on a flat surface. Observe the temperature of the wet-bulb thermometer every 30 seconds until it remains constant. Then, repeat Steps 2 through 5 at a location your teacher indicates.

Analyze and Conclude

1. **Analyzing Data**   Why did the two thermometers have different temperatures?

   The temperature of the wet-bulb thermometer is usually lower than the temperature of the dry-bulb
   thermometer because evaporation of water from the wet bulb absorbed energy from the
   thermometer, which cooled it.
   _____
   _____

2. **Formulating Hypotheses**   Explain how the relative humidity of the air affected the difference between the temperatures of the two thermometers.

   The difference in temperature between the two thermometers depends on the degree to which
   evaporation cools the wet bulb. The lower the relative humidity, the greater is the rate at which water
   evaporates, cooling the wet bulb. Relative humidity does not affect the temperature of the dry-bulb
   thermometer. Therefore, the lower the relative humidity, the cooler the wet bulb will be, and the
   greater the difference in temperature between the two thermometers will be.
   _____

3. **Drawing Conclusions**   What do you think caused the difference in relative humidity between the two locations?

   Factors that are likely to affect the relative humidity in various locations include sources of water,
   especially warm water, and variation in the effectiveness of heating and cooling throughout the
   school building.
   _____

4. **Predicting**   How would the relative humidity change if you cooled the air in the classroom?

   Cooling the room would increase the relative humidity. The maximum concentration of water vapor
   in air is reduced at lower temperatures. Therefore, as the air in the room is cooled, the same
   concentration of water vapor becomes a higher percentage of the maximum concentration, or a
   higher relative humidity.
   _____
   _____

Lab Manual

Name _____ Class _____ Date _____

Chapter 24   Weather and Climate   🔍 **Investigation 24A**

Recipe for a Cloud

Refer students to pages 761–763 in their textbooks for a discussion of cloud formation and cloud classification.

SKILLS FOCUS: Predicting; Measuring; Observing; Inferring; Controlling Variables; Using Models **CLASS TIME:** 30 minutes

Background Information

The scientific study of clouds was begun in 1803 by Luke Howard, a British meteorologist. However, it was not until the late 1800s that clouds were classified according to their different forms.

Clouds consist of tiny water droplets or ice crystals. These droplets or crystals form when water vapor in the atmosphere condenses. Condensation occurs when air pressure decreases so that the water vapor in the air expands and cools. Therefore, factors such as atmospheric pressure and the relative humidity of the air determine when clouds form and what form they take.

For a cloud to form, there must be a surface of some kind for water vapor to condense on, and so form the small water droplets or (if it is cold enough) ice crystals that make up the cloud. In most cases, small particles of dust provide the surfaces for such condensation. By artificially adding small particles, such as salt or dry ice crystals, to clouds at certain temperatures, condensation can be stimulated, causing rain. Such a process is called cloud seeding.

In this investigation, you will examine how the temperature and humidity of air, as well as the presence or absence of tiny particles in the air, affects the formation of cloud droplets.

Problem

Under what basic conditions do clouds form?

Pre-Lab Discussion

Read the entire investigation. Then, work with a partner to answer the following questions.

1. **Formulating Hypotheses**   Write a hypothesis about how you expect pressure, humidity, and the presence of tiny particles in the air to affect cloud formation.

   For clouds to form, there must be enough water vapor in the air (high humidity), low enough
   temperatures (reduced air pressure), and some particles upon which condensation can occur.
   _____

2. **Designing Experiments**   Why is it important to this investigation to use a container in which the pressure can be easily and significantly changed?

   The pressure must be changed significantly so that the water vapor in the air will expand and cool
   significantly. This will allow the vapor to condense on any small particles that are in the air.
   _____

Lab Manual

Name _____ Class _____ Date _____

3. **Controlled Variables**   For the first half of the investigation, in which cold water is used, what are the manipulated and controlled variables?

   Air pressure is the manipulated variable, and humidity and the absence of particles are the
   controlled variables. Then, particles are introduced in the investigation as a controlled variable,
   humidity is still kept controlled, and pressure is again the manipulated variable.
   _____
   _____

4. **Controlled Variables**   What controlled variable is changed in the second half of the investigation, in which hot water is used?

   The temperature of the water changes the humidity, which is a controlled variable throughout
   the second half of the investigation.
   _____

5. **Predicting**   Do you expect to observe cloud formation before or after smoke is added to the container? Explain your answer.

   Students may think that cloud formation may occur without smoke added to the container
   because the temperature may drop sufficiently to cause condensation or because there
   may be unidentified particles in the air that can promote condensation. Cloud formation will
   occur because the change in temperature will allow water vapor to condense, and the smoke
   particles will provide surfaces on which condensation can occur.
   _____
   _____

Materials *(per group)*
graduated cylinder
gallon glass pickle jar
plastic freezer storage bag (26 cm × 26 cm)
rubber band (15 cm circumference; 0.5 cm width)
cold tap water
hot tap water
safety matches

Safety 🔲 🔋 ⚠️ 🔥

Put on safety goggles. Be careful to avoid breakage when working with glassware. Be careful when using matches. Do not reach over an open flame. Tie back loose hair and clothing when working with flames. Note all safety alert symbols next to the steps in the Procedure and review the meaning of each symbol by referring to the Safety Symbols on page xiii.

Lab Manual

Name _____ Class _____ Date _____

Procedure

1. Use the graduated cylinder to measure 40 mL of cold water.
   Pour the water into the jar. Place the plastic bag into the jar so that the top edges of the bag lie just outside the rim of the jar, as shown in Figure 1. **CAUTION:** *Wipe up any spilled liquids immediately to avoid slips and falls.*

1-gallon pickle jar
Plastic freezer bag
Water

Figure 1

2. Secure the top of the bag to the outer rim of the jar using the rubber band, as shown in Figure 2.

Top edge of plastic bag — Rubber band

Figure 2

3. Place your hand inside the bag, grab the bag's bottom edge, and rapidly pull the bag out of the jar. Observe the inside of the jar while pulling the bag out. Record your observations in the data table provided on the following page.
4. Remove the rubber band and plastic bag. Light a match, allow it to burn for about 3 seconds, then drop the match into the jar. Quickly place the plastic bag inside the jar, again securing its top edge around the rim of the jar with the rubber band.
5. Repeat Step 3. Again, observe the inside of the jar as you pull the bag rapidly out of the jar. Record your observations in the data table.
6. Remove the plastic bag and rinse out the bottle. Throw away the burnt match as directed by your teacher.
7. Repeat Steps 1 through 6, this time using 40 mL of hot tap water. **CAUTION:** *Be careful not to burn yourself when using hot water.*

Lab Manual

Name _____ Class _____ Date _____

Observations Sample data are shown.

DATA TABLE

Water Type	Smoke	Cloud Formation
Cold	Absent	No
Cold	Present	Yes
Hot	Absent	No
Hot	Present	Yes

If clouds formed under more than one set of conditions, did you observe any difference between the clouds?

Answers will depend on whether or not clouds formed in the absence of smoke. The most common result is that, in the presence of smoke particles, the hot water will produce a somewhat denser cloud than the cold water.

Analysis and Conclusions

1. **Inferring** What effect did pulling the plastic bag out of the jar have on the water vapor inside the jar?

   It reduced the air pressure so that the water vapor rapidly expanded. As it did so, the water vapor's temperature decreased temporarily, and it was able to condense on particles in the air in those cases where particles of smoke were added to the container.

Lab Manual

Name _____ Class _____ Date _____

2. **Drawing Conclusions** What conditions proved most important for forming clouds?

   The most important condition was the presence of smoke particles for water to condense on. Cloud formation was slightly better for hot water than for cold water, but both provided sufficient humidity for clouds to form in the presence of smoke.

3. **Drawing Conclusions** Did your results support or contradict your hypothesis? Explain your answer.

   Results of the investigation showed that a small quantity of water and a rapid decrease in pressure can produce the necessary humidity and temperature decrease needed to form clouds, provided there are some particles on which the water vapor can condense. These results confirmed the hypothesis.

4. **Designing Experiments** What improvements could you make to the apparatus to provide quantitative information?

   One improvement may consist of a thermometer attached to the inner wall of the jar. While one student pulls on the plastic bag and reduces pressure, the other student can observe the thermometer to determine the minimum temperature reached within the jar when the pressure is reduced. Another improvement might consist of replacing the plastic bag with a lid that can be screwed in place and which has an opening through which a known quantity of smoke can be added. The pressure within the jar could be steadily lowered by a vacuum pump so that the exact pressure at which condensation occurs could be measured.

5. **Using Models** Relate each ingredient in your cloud-making procedure to the process of making clouds in nature.

   The decrease in pressure and temperature in the bottle correspond to such decreases when air rises and expands. The high humidity and subsequent condensation in the bottle correspond to the humidity needed to cause condensation at a given temperature in the atmosphere. The particles of smoke correspond to small particles in the atmosphere around which water vapor can condense.

Lab Manual

Name _____ Class _____ Date _____

6. **Making Generalizations** A topic of discussion in astronomy is terraforming, the process by which other planets can be modified so that their climates are like those on Earth. One important feature of terraforming is starting and maintaining a water cycle in the planet's atmosphere. What conditions would be necessary for rain to be stimulated and maintained on a terraformed planet?

   Features that should be included in answers are 1) enough water on the planet's surface so that it can evaporate and enter the atmosphere, 2) sufficient changes in the atmospheric pressure so that water vapor can condense to form rain, 3) particles in the atmosphere so that condensation can take place when humidity and temperature are satisfactory.

Go Further

Plan an investigation to determine the way that different changes in pressure and different particles sources may affect cloud formation. You can plan your design, using the same equipment used in the investigation or using some or all of the improvements listed in your answer to Question 4 of Analysis and Conclusions. Identify which variables are to be manipulated and which are to be controlled throughout the investigation. Show your plan to your teacher. When your teacher approves your plan, carry out your experiment and report your results and conclusions.

Student designs may include a number of features to make the investigation more quantifiable. A spray bottle, for example, may be used to introduce a known quantity of water mist or smoke into the jar. A thermometer may be used to estimate the minimum temperature reached when pressure is lowered. Substances such as chalk dust or talcum powder might be used to induce cloud formation. Be sure that the manipulated and controlled variables are clearly defined in the plan and that all aspects of the plan are safe to perform.

Lab Manual

Name _____ Class _____ Date _____

Chapter 24   Weather and Climate   🔍 **Investigation 24B**

Modeling Global Warming
Refer students to pages 779–782 in their textbook for a discussion of factors affecting climate and global warming.
SKILLS FOCUS: Observing; Inferring; Comparing and Contrasting
CLASS TIME: 50 minutes

Background Information
Some atmospheric gases keep Earth much warmer than it would be otherwise. Energy from the sun is transferred to Earth through radiation and is absorbed by the surface of Earth. Then, some of this energy is transferred back toward space through the process of radiation. Carbon dioxide, water vapor, and other gases in the atmosphere absorb some of this radiated energy, making the atmosphere warmer. The warm atmosphere re-radiates this energy, some of which is directed back toward Earth's surface. This entire process is called the greenhouse effect.

In this investigation, you will describe how carbon dioxide affects the temperature of the atmosphere. You will also understand more about the process that results in the greenhouse effect.

Problem
Does carbon dioxide really affect the atmosphere's temperature?

Pre-Lab Discussion
Read the entire investigation. Then, work with a partner to answer the following questions.

1. **Posing Questions** Write a question that summarizes the purpose of this investigation.

   How does carbon dioxide affect the temperature of the atmosphere?
   _____
   _____

2. **Controlling Variables** What is the manipulated variable in this investigation?

   The presence or absence of carbon dioxide, which in turn is dependent on the presence
   or absence of baking soda
   _____

3. **Controlling Variables** What are the controlled variables in this investigation?

   The amount of light shone on the two bottles and the size of the bottles
   _____
   _____
   _____

Physical Science Lab Manual • Investigation 24B   **257**

Lab Manual

Name _____ Class _____ Date _____

4. **Controlling Variables** What is the responding variable in this investigation?

   The temperature in the bottle
   _____
   _____
   _____

5. **Predicting** Predict the outcome of this investigation.

   The bottle of carbon dioxide will undergo a larger temperature increase than the bottle of air
   during the same period of time.
   _____
   _____
   _____

Materials *(per group)*
2 clear 2-L plastic bottles
2 one-hole rubber stoppers with a Celsius non-mercury
    thermometer inserted into each   Wrap each thermometer in a thick towel for your protection when gently inserting it in the stopper.
funnel
plastic spoon
baking soda
vinegar
25-mL graduated cylinder
bright incandescent lamp or flood lamp

Safety 🥽 🧤 🔌 🔥 🧯
Put on safety goggles and a lab apron. Be careful to avoid breakage when working with glassware. Use extreme care when working with heated equipment or materials to avoid burns. Observe proper laboratory procedures when using electrical equipment. Note all safety alert symbols next to the steps in the Procedure and review the meaning of each symbol by referring to the Safety Symbols on page xiii.

Procedure
🥽🔥 1. Fill a bottle with carbon dioxide by adding baking soda and vinegar to the bottle. **CAUTION:** *Leave the bottle open until the bubbling stops.* Show students how to fill a bottle with carbon dioxide in Step 1. They must insert a funnel in the bottle and put one spoonful of baking soda into the funnel. Then, they should pour 20 mL of vinegar into the funnel and remove the funnel.

258   *Physical Science* Lab Manual • Investigation 24B

Lab Manual

Name _____ Class _____ Date _____

🔌 2. Put a one-hole stopper containing a thermometer in the bottle of carbon dioxide. Put the other stopper with its thermometer in the bottle of air. In the data table, record the initial temperature for each bottle.

🔌🔥 3. Shine a lamp on both bottles at the same angle from a distance of 30 cm. In the data table, record the temperature of each bottle every two minutes for 20 minutes. **CAUTION:** *Lamps can get very hot. Be sure not to come too close to the lamps when they are in use.*

Observations
DATA TABLE

Elapsed Time (minutes)	Temperature in Bottle With Air (°C)	Temperature in Bottle With Carbon Dioxide (°C)
0		
2		
4		
6		
8		
10		
12		
14		
16		
18		
20		

Physical Science Lab Manual • Investigation 24B   **259**

Lab Manual

Name _____ Class _____ Date _____

Analysis and Conclusions

1. **Comparing and Contrasting** What was the difference in the temperatures of the two bottles at the end of the experiment?

   Results will vary, but the temperature of the bottle of carbon dioxide will be higher than the
   temperature of the bottle of air.
   _____

2. **Inferring** What can you infer about how carbon dioxide affects air temperature?

   Carbon dioxide in the air causes the air temperature to rise more quickly when the air is illuminated.
   _____
   _____

3. **Drawing Conclusions** What do your observations suggest about the effect of carbon dioxide on global warming?

   The bottle of carbon dioxide became warmer than the bottle of air. This observation supports the
   idea that the presence of carbon dioxide in air helps to warm the atmosphere.
   _____
   _____

4. **Applying Concepts** How do you think your conclusions for this investigation could be applied to situations that you observe in your everyday life?

   Further research into the ways that the greenhouse effect influences climate would help
   understand changes in climate and suggest ways to limit those changes.
   _____
   _____

Go Further
Conduct this investigation on a larger scale. Set up terrariums next to sunlit windows in two large, clear, wide-mouth bottles. Place plants in only one of the terrariums. Record the temperature of each terrarium at the same time of day over several days. Write a report of your observations and your conclusions based on your analysis of the data. Remind students that plants consume carbon dioxide. Have students consider this when they explain their observations. The greenhouse effect will be more pronounced in the terrarium without plants. Plants absorb carbon dioxide, which in turn reduces the temperature of the terrarium.

260   *Physical Science* Lab Manual • Investigation 24B

Name _____ Class _____ Date _____

Chapter 24 Weather and Climate   Chapter Test A

Multiple Choice

Write the letter that best answers the question or completes the statement on the line provided.

_____ 1. As altitude increases,
   a. air pressure decreases and density increases.
   b. air pressure increases and density decreases.
   c. air pressure and density increase.
   d. air pressure and density decrease.

_____ 2. The ozone layer is located in the
   a. lower troposphere.   b. lower thermosphere.
   c. upper ionosphere.   d. upper stratosphere.

_____ 3. As Earth completes one orbit around the sun, it has completed one
   a. rotation.   b. year.   c. revolution.   d. both b and c

_____ 4. Which of the following lists all the zones in the correct order, starting at the North Pole and ending at the South Pole?
   a. polar, temperate, tropic, polar
   b. polar, temperate, tropic, temperate, polar
   c. polar, tropic, temperate, polar
   d. polar, tropic, temperate, tropic, polar

_____ 5. Earth's atmosphere is heated mainly by
   a. heat that travels directly from the sun.
   b. visible light as it passes through the air.
   c. reflected sunlight.
   d. energy reradiated by Earth's surface.

_____ 6. The daily breezes that occur in a city that is located near a large body of water are examples of
   a. local winds.   b. monsoons.
   c. global winds.   d. westerlies.

_____ 7. Low, flat layers of clouds that often cover much of the sky and produce steady and widespread rain are
   a. cumulonimbus clouds.   b. cirrus clouds.
   c. nimbostratus clouds.   d. altostratus clouds.

_____ 8. Round, solid pieces of ice more than 5 millimeters in diameter fall as
   a. hail.   b. sleet.   c. snow.   d. freezing rain.

_____ 9. Which of the following air masses forms over land north of 50° north latitude?
   a. maritime polar   b. temperate continental
   c. continental polar   d. continental tropical

Physical Science • Chapter 24 Test A   **255**

Name _____ Class _____ Date _____

_____ 10. A cold front forms when a cold air mass
   a. collides with a warm air mass and pushes the warm air up.
   b. collides with a warm air mass and slides over the warm air.
   c. collides with another cold air mass.
   d. stops moving over a particular area.

_____ 11. Which of the following is a characteristic of an anticyclone?
   a. has a center of high pressure
   b. has clockwise winds in the Northern Hemisphere
   c. is generally associated with clear weather
   d. all of the above

_____ 12. A small, intense storm formed when a vertical cylinder of rotating air develops is a
   a. thunderstorm.   b. tornado.   c. monsoon.   d. hurricane.

_____ 13. Lines on a weather map that connect points that have the same air temperature are called
   a. millibars.   b. isobars.   c. isotherms.   d. front lines.

_____ 14. Which of the following factors affect a region's temperature?
   a. latitude and altitude
   b. distance from large bodies of water
   c. ocean currents
   d. all of the above

_____ 15. Which of the following climate changes may be affected by human activities?
   a. ice age   b. El Niño   c. global warming   d. monsoon

Completion

Complete each statement on the line provided.

1. Plants need _____ from the air for photosynthesis, and many animals need _____ from the air to breathe.

2. Of the four layers of the atmosphere, the _____ has the hottest temperatures.

3. On the two days each year when the sun is directly overhead at noon at latitude 23.5° north or 23.5° south, a _____ occurs.

4. Air spirals in toward the center of a cyclone but flows away from the center of a(an) _____.

5. _____ is a short-term variation in climate that is caused by a change in the normal direction of winds, which causes ocean currents to shift direction.

256 *Physical Science* • Chapter 24 Test A

Name _____ Class _____ Date _____

Short Answer

In complete sentences, write the answers to the questions on the lines provided.

1. Describe what the temperatures on Earth would be like during the day and at night if the atmosphere did not exist.

_____

_____

_____

_____

2. What is the difference between sleet and freezing rain?

_____

_____

_____

3. How does a thunderstorm form?

_____

_____

_____

Figure 24-1

4. What is the name of each type of front represented by the symbols in Figure 24-1?

_____

_____

_____

5. What are three factors that affect a region's pattern of precipitation?

_____

_____

_____

Physical Science • Chapter 24 Test A   **257**

Name _____ Class _____ Date _____

Using Science Skills

Use the diagram to answer each question. Write the answers on a separate sheet of paper.

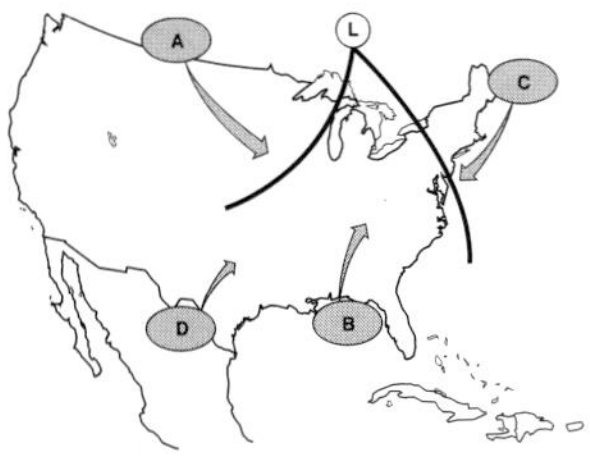

Figure 24-2

1. **Inferring** What factors are used to classify the air masses in Figure 24-2?

2. **Classifying** Based on their locations in Figure 24-2, name the types of air masses represented by A and D and describe the characteristics of each.

3. **Comparing and Contrasting** Based on their locations in Figure 24-2, name the types of air masses represented by B and C. How are they similar, and how are they different?

4. **Predicting** Based on Figure 24-2, what would you expect weather conditions to be like in the southeastern section of the United States at the time this map was drawn? Explain your answer.

5. **Applying Concepts** What does the symbol L represent in 24-2, and what type of weather system is it the center of? What are the characteristics of this weather system?

Essay

Write the answers to each question on a separate sheet of paper.

1. Explain why temperate zones in the Northern Hemisphere and the Southern Hemisphere have the same seasons but are six months apart.

2. What are trade winds and what causes them? How are trade winds in the Northern Hemisphere different from those in the Southern Hemisphere?

3. What are humidity, relative humidity, and dew point? Explain what happens to each if the temperature of the air decreases.

4. Compare the weather that might occur in an area as a warm front passes through, after the warm front has passed through, as a cold front passes through, and after the cold front has passed through.

5. What information can meteorologists obtain from Doppler radar, automated weather stations, and weather satellites? How do high-speed computers help meteorologists?

258 *Physical Science* • Chapter 24 Test A

Chapter Test B

Name _____   Class _____   Date _____

Chapter 24   Weather and Climate   Chapter Test B

Multiple Choice

Write the letter that best answers the question or completes the statement on the line provided.

_____ 1. What gas makes up about 78 percent of dry air?
    a. oxygen   b. nitrogen
    c. hydrogen   d. carbon dioxide

_____ 2. Most weather takes place in the
    a. stratosphere.   b. thermosphere.
    c. troposphere.   d. mesosphere.

_____ 3. Day and night are caused by Earth's
    a. rotation.   b. revolution.   c. orbit.   d. tilt.

_____ 4. Which region usually has temperatures cooler than temperatures near the equator?
    a. tropic zone   b. polar zone
    c. temperate zone   d. both b and c

_____ 5. About how much of the solar energy that reaches Earth passes through the atmosphere and is absorbed by the surface of Earth?
    a. 20 percent   b. 30 percent
    c. 50 percent   d. 80 percent

_____ 6. Which of the following is NOT an example of a global wind?
    a. westerlies   b. trade winds
    c. polar easterlies   d. sea breezes

_____ 7. A cloud is a dense, visible mass of
    a. tiny water droplets.   b. ice crystals.
    c. water vapor.   d. both a and b

_____ 8. Which of the following forms of precipitation falls as a liquid?
    a. rain   b. freezing rain   c. hail   d. both a and b

_____ 9. A maritime tropical air mass that affects weather in the Unites States might form over
    a. the Gulf of Mexico.   b. Mexico.
    c. Canada.   d. the North Atlantic ocean.

_____ 10. What type of front forms when two unlike air masses form a boundary but neither is moving?
    a. warm   b. cold   c. stationary   d. occluded

_____ 11. Which of the following is a weather system with a center of low pressure?
    a. cyclone   b. anticyclone   c. warm front   d. cold front

Chapter Test B

Name _____   Class _____   Date _____

_____ 12. A tropical storm with sustained winds of at least 119 kilometers per hour is called a
    a. tornado.   b. thunderstorm.   c. monsoon.   d. hurricane.

Front A   Front B   Front C   Front D

Figure 24-1

_____ 13. Which of the symbols in Figure 24-1 represents a warm front?
    a. Front A   b. Front B   c. Front C   d. Front D

_____ 14. A description of the pattern of weather over many years is a region's
    a. weather forecast.   b. air mass.
    c. climate.   d. weather system.

_____ 15. An example of a long-term climate change that occurs naturally is
    a. an ice age.   b. an El Niño.
    c. global warming.   d. the greenhouse effect.

Completion

Complete each statement on the line provided.

1. The _____ forms a protective boundary between Earth and space and provides conditions that are suitable for life.

2. The _____ seasons are caused by the _____ of Earth's _____ as Earth moves around the sun.

3. The latitude of the equator is _____, and the latitude of the North Pole is _____.

4. Wind is air blowing from an area of _____ pressure to an area of _____ pressure.

5. The three basic cloud forms are _____, _____, and _____.

6. Rain, sleet, and snow are types of _____.

7. The sharply defined boundary that forms where two unlike air masses meet is called a(an) _____.

8. A major type of storm associated with lightning, strong winds, and heavy rain or hail is called a(an) _____.

9. _____ works by bouncing radio waves off particles of precipitation in moving storms and then measuring the frequency of the waves that return.

10. The two main factors that determine a region's climate are _____ and _____.

Chapter Test B

Name _____   Class _____   Date _____

Short Answer

In complete sentences, write the answers to the questions on the lines provided.

1. List the four layers of the atmosphere, starting with the layer closest to Earth.

_____

_____

_____

2. Why is Earth generally warmer near the equator and colder toward the poles?

_____

_____

_____

_____

3. What is the greenhouse effect?

_____

_____

_____

_____

_____

4. What weather is associated with a cyclone?

_____

_____

_____

_____

_____

5. What are some ways that people could limit the effects of global warming? Explain how these ways would help.

_____

_____

_____

_____

_____

Chapter Test B

Name _____   Class _____   Date _____

Using Science Skills

Use the diagram to answer each question. Write the answers on a separate sheet of paper.

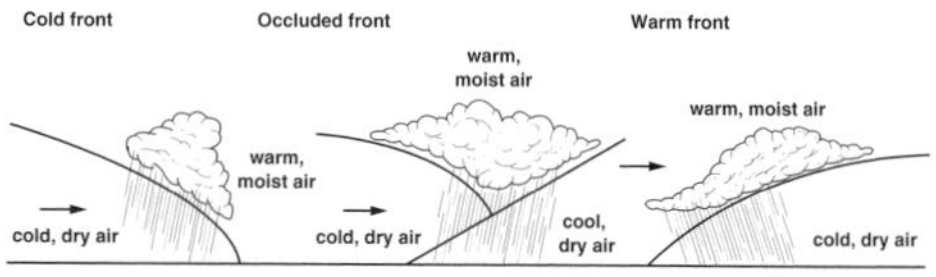

Cold front   Occluded front   Warm front

warm, moist air

warm, moist air

warm, moist air

cold, dry air   cold, dry air   cool, dry air   cold, dry air

Figure 24-2

1. **Inferring** What causes clouds to form in the three fronts in Figure 24-2?

2. **Interpreting Graphics** Explain what is happening to the two air masses in the cold front in Figure 24-2.

3. **Comparing and Contrasting** Based on your observations of Figure 24-2, how are a cold front and a warm front alike?

4. **Comparing and Contrasting** Based on your observations of Figure 24-2, how are a cold front and a warm front different?

5. **Interpreting Graphics** What has happened to the warm air mass in the occluded front in Figure 24-3?

Chapter 24 Test A Answers

Multiple Choice

1. d **2.** d **3.** d **4.** b **5.** d **6.** a
7. c **8.** a **9.** c **10.** a **11.** d **12.** b
13. c **14.** d **15.** c

Completion

1. carbon dioxide, oxygen **2.** thermosphere **3.** solstice
4. anticyclone **5.** El Niño

Short Answer

1. During the day, temperatures would be boiling hot, and at night, they would be freezing cold. **2.** Sleet is rain that freezes as it falls. Freezing rain falls as rain and freezes after hitting the surface.
3. A thunderstorm forms when columns of air rise within a cumulonimbus cloud. If the rising air is cooled to the dew point and the convection is strong enough, a thunderstorm results.
4. Front A is a cold front, Front B is a warm front, Front C is an occluded front, and Front D is a stationary front. **5.** latitude, the distribution of air pressure systems and global winds, and the existence of a mountain barrier

Using Science Skills

1. Air masses are classified by whether they form over land or over water and the latitude at which they form. **2.** A is a continental polar air mass and has cold, dry air. D is a continental tropical air mass and has warm, dry air. **3.** B is a maritime tropical air mass, and C is a maritime polar air mass. They both form over water and contain moist air. B has warm air and C has cool air. **4.** Possible answer: The weather is warm and humid because a maritime tropical air mass, which has warm, moist air, is moving into the area. **5.** L represents a center of low pressure or a low. A weather system with an area of low pressure at its center is called a cyclone. This weather system is associated with clouds, precipitation, and stormy weather.

Essay

1. As Earth revolves around the sun, the north end of Earth's axis points in the same direction, which is toward the North Star. But the orientation of the axis changes relative to the sun over the course of a year. When the north end of Earth's axis is tilted toward the sun, the south end is tilted away from the sun. At this time, the temperate zone in the Northern Hemisphere has summer, and the temperate zone in the Southern Hemisphere has winter. Six months later, Earth has reached the opposite side of its orbit, and the north end of its axis tilts away from the sun. The temperate zone in the Northern Hemisphere has winter, and the temperate zone in the Southern Hemisphere has summer. **2.** Trade winds are wind belts or convection cells just north and south of the equator. They are caused by temperature variations across Earth's surface. At the equator, temperatures tend to be warmer than at other latitudes. Warm air rises at the equator, creating a low-pressure region. This warm air is replaced by cooler air brought by global winds blowing near the surface. Higher in the atmosphere, the air blows away from the equator toward the poles. The winds curve because of the Coriolis effect caused by Earth's rotation. Trade winds in the Northern Hemisphere curve to the right and blow from the northeast to the southwest. Trade winds in the Southern Hemisphere curve to the left and blow from the southeast to the northwest.

3. Humidity is the amount of water vapor in the air. The humidity stays the same if the temperature decreases. Relative humidity is a ratio of the amount of water vapor in the air compared to the maximum amount of water vapor that can exist at that temperature. The maximum amount of water vapor that can exist in air is greater at high temperatures than at low temperatures. If the temperature decreases, the relative humidity increases even though the amount of water vapor stays the same. The temperature at which air becomes saturated, which is when the relative humidity is 100 percent, is the dew point. If the temperature decreases to the dew point, water vapor will condense. **4.** As a warm front passes through, the area might have stratus clouds, steady rain, and occasionally heavy showers or thunderstorms. After the warm front passes through, the skies are mostly clear, there may be some cumulus clouds, and temperatures rise. As a cold front passes through, the area might have cumulus or cumulonimbus clouds, strong winds, severe thunderstorms, and large amounts of precipitation, which usually lasts for only a short time. After the cold front passes through, the skies clear and temperatures drop. **5.** Meteorologists use Doppler radar to obtain information about the speed of storms and to track the path of storms. Automated weather stations gather data such as temperature, precipitation, and wind speed and direction. Weather satellites provide information such as cloud cover, humidity, temperature, and wind speed. High-speed computers help meteorologists compile and analyze the large amount of weather data and make forecasts.

Chapter 24 Test B Answers

Multiple Choice

1. b	**2.** c	**3.** a	**4.** d	**5.** c	**6.** d
7. d	**8.** d	**9.** a	**10.** c	**11.** a	**12.** d
13. b	**14.** c	**15.** a			

Completion

1. atmosphere **2.** tilt, axis **3.** 0°, 90° **4.** high, low **5.** stratus, cumulus, cirrus **6.** precipitation **7.** front **8.** thunderstorm **9.** Doppler radar **10.** temperature, precipitation

Short Answer

1. troposphere, stratosphere, mesosphere, thermosphere **2.** Regions near the equator receive more direct sunlight than regions near the poles receive. **3.** the process by which gases, including water vapor and carbon dioxide, absorb energy, radiate energy, and warm the lower atmosphere **4.** clouds, precipitation, and stormy weather **5.** Conserving energy and a greater reliance on solar, nuclear, or geothermal power could limit the effects of global warming because they would reduce the amount of carbon dioxide released.

Using Science Skills

1. Because cold, dry air is denser than warm, moist air, the cold air pushes the warm air up. As warm air rises, it cools, and water vapor in the air condenses and forms clouds. **2.** A cold, dry air mass is overtaking a warm, moist air mass, and the warm air mass is being lifted up by the cold air. **3.** Both a cold front and a warm front have a cold, dry air mass and a warm, moist air mass colliding. In both fronts, the cold air is under the warm air, and in both fronts, precipitation can occur. **4.** At a cold front, a cold air mass is overtaking a warm air mass and lifting it up. At a warm front, a warm air mass is overtaking a cold air mass and rising over the cold air. **5.** The warm air mass has been trapped between two cold air masses, which have forced it to rise, cutting it off from the ground.

Chapter 25 The Solar System

CHAPTER 25

Planning Guide

Use these planning tools

Easy Planner
Resource Pro
Online Lesson Planner

SECTION OBJECTIVES	STANDARDS		ACTIVITIES and LABS
	NATIONAL (See p. T18.)	STATE	
25.1 Exploring the Solar System, pp. 790–794 1 block or 2 periods 25.1.1 **Compare** and **contrast** the geocentric and heliocentric models of the solar system. 25.1.2 **Describe** the orbits of the planets around the sun and **explain** how gravity and inertia keep the planets in orbit. 25.1.3 **Name** the components of the solar system. 25.1.4 **Identify** different technologies used for exploring the solar system.	A-1, A-2, D-3, E-2, F-1, G-1, G-2, G-3		**SE** Inquiry Activity: Why Does the Sun Seem to Move? p. 789 **L2** **SE** Quick Lab: Modeling Orbits, p. 793 **L2** **TE** Teacher Demo: Ellipses, p. 792 **L2** **LM** Investigation 25B: Investigating Eccentric Orbits **L1**
25.2 The Earth-Moon System, pp. 796–801 1 block or 2 periods 25.2.1 **Explain** why the moon lacks an atmosphere and the effect this has on the range of temperatures on the moon. 25.2.2 **Describe** the features of the moon's surface. 25.2.3 **State** a theory about the formation of the moon. 25.2.4 **Explain** why phases of the moon, eclipses, and tides occur and **interpret diagrams** of the relative positions of the sun, moon, and Earth during these events.	D-3, F-6, G-1		**TE** Build Science Skills: Using Models, p. 796 **L2**
25.3 The Inner Solar System, pp. 803–809 1 block or 2 periods 25.3.1 **Compare** the terrestrial planets and **describe** characteristics of each. 25.3.2 **Define** asteroids and **state** alternative hypotheses about how they formed.	D-1, D-3, G-1, G-2, G-3		**TE** Build Science Skills: Designing Experiments, p. 805 **L2** **TE** Teacher Demo: Asteroids, p. 809 **L2**
25.4 The Outer Solar System, pp. 810–815 1 block or 2 periods 25.4.1 **Compare** the gas giants and **describe** characteristics of each. 25.4.2 **Distinguish** between comets and meteoroids and **describe** their characteristics. 25.4.3 **Locate** and **describe** the Kuiper belt and the Oort cloud.	D-1, D-3, G-1, G-2, G-3		**SE** Exploration Lab: Modeling the Solar System, p. 821 **L2** **TE** Teacher Demo: Rings of Uranus, p. 813 **L2** **LM** Investigation 25A: Modeling an Asteroid's Path **L2**
25.5 The Origin of the Solar System, pp. 818–820 1/2 block or 1 period 25.5.1 **State** the nebular theory. 25.5.2 **Relate** the nebular theory to the orbits of the planets and the composition and size of the planets.	A-1, A-2, D-3		**SE** Quick Lab: Forming Planets, p. 819 **L2**

Ability Levels

L1	For students who need additional help
L2	For all students
L3	For students who need to be challenged

Components

SE	Student Edition	**GRSW**	Guided Reading & Study Workbook With Math Support	**CTB**	Computer Test Bank
TE	Teacher's Edition			**TP**	Test Prep Resources
LM	Laboratory Manual			**iT**	iText
PLM	Probeware Lab Manual	**CUT**	Chapter and Unit Tests	**DC**	Discovery Channel Videotapes
				T	Transparencies
				P	Presentation Pro CD-ROM
				GO	Internet Resources

RESOURCES PRINT and TECHNOLOGY / SECTION ASSESSMENT

GRSW Section 25.1 — L1
GRSW Math Skill — L2
T Chapter 25 Pretest — L2
Section 25.1 — L2
P Chapter 25 Pretest — L2
Section 25.1 — L2
SCiLINKS **GO**
Early astronomers — L2

SE Section 25.1 Assessment, p. 794
Text iT Section 25.1

GRSW Section 25.2 — L1
T Section 25.2 — L2
P Section 25.2 — L2

SE Section 25.2 Assessment, p. 801
Text iT Section 25.2

GRSW Section 25.3 — L1
T Section 25.3 — L2
P Section 25.3 — L2
SCiLINKS **GO** The solar system — L2

SE Section 25.3 Assessment, p. 809
Text iT Section 25.3

GRSW Section 25.4 — L1
DC Lighting Up the Sky — L2
T Section 25.4 — L2
P Section 25.4 — L2
SCIENCE NEWS **GO** The solar system — L2

SE Section 25.4 Assessment, p. 815
Text iT Section 25.4

GRSW Section 25.5 — L1
T Section 25.5 — L2
P Section 25.5 — L2

SE Section 25.5 Assessment, p. 820
Text iT Section 25.5

Go Online

Go online for these Internet resources.

PHSchool.com
Web Code: cca-3250
Web Code: cch-3252

SCIENCE NEWS
Web Code: cce-3254

NSTA SCiLINKS
Web Code: ccn-3251
Web Code: ccn-3253

Materials for Activities and Labs

Quantities for each group

STUDENT EDITION

Inquiry Activity, p. 789
pencil, tape, magnetic compass

Quick Lab, p. 793
string, scissors, ball, duct tape, meter stick

Quick Lab, p. 819
2 2.5-cm by 30-cm strips of paper, tape, pencil, metric ruler

Exploration Lab, p. 821
calculator, large sheet of unlined paper, meter stick, scale models of the sun and planets

TEACHER'S EDITION

Teacher Demo, p. 792
string, 2 thumbtacks, pencil, cardboard

Build Science Skills, p. 796
clay or pens and paper

Build Science Skills, p. 805
pencils and paper

Teacher Demo, p. 809
pile of pebbles (about 5 cm high), large rock, chunk of dried plaster or foam

Teacher Demo, p. 813
penlight, window blind

Build Science Skills, p. 816
4 small fans, foam ball, strips of newspaper, thumbtacks

Chapter Assessment

CHAPTER ASSESSMENT

SE	Chapter Assessment, pp. 823–824
CUT	Chapter 25 Test A, B
CTB	Chapter 25
iT	Chapter 25
PHSchool.com GO	

Web Code: cca-3250

STANDARDIZED TEST PREP

SE	Chapter 25, p. 825
TP	Diagnose and Prescribe

iText

iText—interactive textbook with assessment at PHSchool.com

Section 25.1 **Lesson Plan**

LESSON PLAN 25.1

Exploring the Solar System

Time
2 periods
1 block

Section Objectives

■ **25.1.1 Compare** and **contrast** the geocentric and heliocentric models of the solar system.

■ **25.1.2 Describe** the orbits of the planets around the sun and **explain** how gravity and inertia keep the planets in orbit.

■ **25.1.3 Name** the components of the solar system.

■ **25.1.4 Identify** different technologies used for exploring the solar system.

Vocabulary geocentric • heliocentric • ecliptic plane • moon • astronomical unit • space probe

Local Standards

1 FOCUS

Build Vocabulary: Word-Part Analysis
Have students look up the Greek words *helio* and *centric*. Tell students to review the list of key concepts, and then infer the meaning of *geocentric model* and *heliocentric model*. **L2**

Targeted Resources
❏ Transparency: Chapter 25 Pretest
❏ Transparency: Interest Grabber 25.1
❏ Transparency: Reading Strategy 25.1

2 INSTRUCT

Use Visuals: Figure 2
Using Figure 2, ask students in which model Earth is the center. Then, ask where the sun is in the heliocentric model. **L1**

Build Reading Literacy: Identify Main Idea/Details
Have students read the text on p. 794, and ask them to identify the topic sentence of the first paragraph. Then, ask students to give details that support the main idea. **L1**

Build Science Skills: Communicating Results
Have students research the evidence gathered by early astronomers in support of the heliocentric model, then present the results of their research in written reports. **L2**

Teacher Demo: Ellipses
Using string, trace a line around two thumbtacks so that students can observe the shape of planetary orbits. **L2**

Address Misconceptions
Remind students that all objects exert gravitational forces on other objects. **L2**

Quick Lab: Modeling Orbits
Students will swing a ball above their heads in order to describe the relationship between the radius and speed of a planet's orbit. **L2**

Targeted Resources
❏ Transparency: Figure 3: The Planets' Average Distances From the Sun
❏ GRSW Section 25.1
❏ **NSTA** *sciLINKS* Early astronomers

3 ASSESS

Reteach
Have students create a time line showing the space missions discussed in this section in chronological order. **L1**

Evaluate Understanding
Have students take turns describing a fact that they have learned about one of the vocabulary words in this section. **L2**

Targeted Resources
❏ **PHSchool.com** Online Section 25.1 Assessment
❏ iText Section 25.1

396 Chapter 25 Pretest

1. What determines the strength of the gravitational attraction between two objects?
   a. mass and weight
   b. weight and distance
   c. mass and distance
   d. distance and density

2. What are the two most abundant gases in Earth's atmosphere?

3. True or False: Earth's atmosphere plays a role in regulating its surface temperature.

Transparencies

397 Chapter 25 Pretest (continued)

4. What is Newton's first law of motion?

5. Describe Earth's structure. What are the three main layers?

6. Explain the process of condensation.

Transparencies

398 Section 25.1 Interest Grabber

Training for Weightlessness

Astronauts train for weightlessness in a modified plane that dives at a steep angle. For about 20 seconds, the astronauts are in free fall. This training can be repeated about 40 times a day!

To observe how objects behave in free fall, tie together two paper clips with a thread about 20 cm long. Pull the paper clips apart so the thread is horizontal. Pull gently so there is no tension on the thread. Then drop the paper clips from a height of 1 meter. Observe the thread as the paper clips fall.

1. What did the thread's motion tell you about the relative position of two objects in free fall?

2. Imagine that you are aboard the International Space Station and you have just spilled your morning coffee. Predict what would happen to the liquid. How would you clean it up?

Transparencies

399 Section 25.1 Reading Strategy

Comparing and Contrasting

	Location of Earth	Location of Sun	Developer(s) of Theory
Geocentric System	Center of universe	a. ?	b. ?
Heliocentric System	c. ?	d. ?	Aristarchus, Copernicus

Transparencies

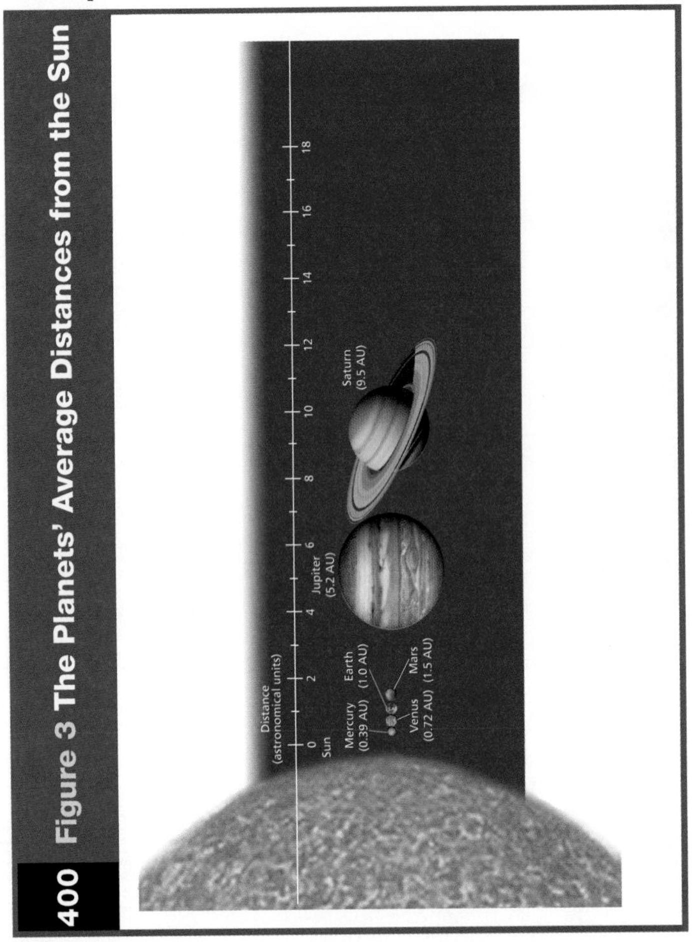

Figure 3 The Planets' Average Distances from the Sun

400

Transparencies

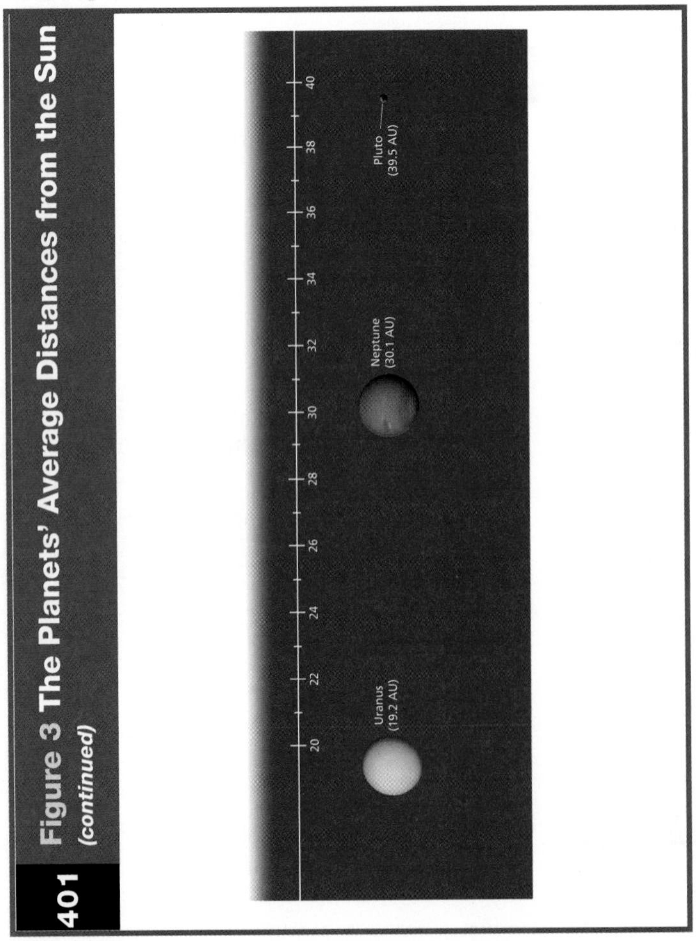

Figure 3 The Planets' Average Distances from the Sun *(continued)*

401

Guided Reading and Study Workbook

Name _____ Class _____ Date _____

Chapter 25   The Solar System

Section 25.1 Exploring the Solar System
(pages 790–794)

This section explores early models of our solar system. It describes the components of the solar system and scientific exploration of the solar system.

Reading Strategy (page 790)

Comparing and Contrasting After you read, compare the geocentric and heliocentric systems by completing the table below. For more information on this Reading Strategy, see the **Reading and Study Skills** in the **Skills and Reference Handbook** at the end of your textbook.

Solar System Models		
	Location of Earth	Location of Sun	Developer(s) of Theory
Geocentric System	Center of universe	Revolves around Earth	Ancient Greeks, Ptolemy
Heliocentric System	Revolves around sun	Center of solar system	Aristarchus, Copernicus

Models of the Solar System (pages 790–791)

1. Is the following sentence true or false? In the Northern Hemisphere, the stars appear to circle around the North Star. _____true_____

2. Name the five planets besides Earth that ancient observers could see with the unaided eye.

   a. ____Mercury____   b. ____Venus____

   c. ____Mars____   d. ____Jupiter____

   e. ____Saturn____

3. Many ancient Greeks thought ____Earth____ was the center of the universe.

4. Circle the letter of each sentence that is true about a geocentric model.

   a. Earth is stationary at the center.

   b. Objects in the sky move around Earth.

   c. The sun is the center of the solar system.

   d. The planets revolve around the sun.

5. Name the center of the solar system in a heliocentric model. ____the sun____

6. Is the following sentence true or false? The first heliocentric model was widely accepted by most ancient Greeks. ____false____

Guided Reading and Study Workbook

Name _____ Class _____ Date _____

Chapter 25   The Solar System

7. Is the following sentence true or false? The sun, moon, and stars appear to move because the Earth is rotating on its axis. ____true____

Planetary Orbits (page 792)

8. Planets move around the sun in orbits that are in the shape of a(n) ____ellipse____.

9. The plane containing Earth's orbit is called the ____ecliptic plane____.

10. Name the two factors that combine to keep the planets in orbit around the sun. ____Gravity and inertia combine to keep the planets in orbit around the sun.____

Components of the Solar System (pages 792–793)

11. Circle the letters that identify objects in our solar system.

    a. moons of the planets   b. nine planets

    c. the sun   d. the stars other than the sun

12. Name three planets that were identified after the invention of the telescope in the early 1600s.

    a. ____Uranus____   b. ____Neptune____   c. ____Pluto____

13. Is the following sentence true or false? All of the planets have moons. ____false____

14. Unlike the sun, planets and moons do not produce their own ____light____.

15. Is the following sentence true or false? The sun's mass is smaller than the combined mass of the rest of the solar system. ____false____

Exploring the Solar System (pages 793–794)

16. Name three examples of types of modern technology that scientists use to explore the solar system.

    a. ____Complex telescopes____   b. ____Piloted spacecraft____   c. ____Space probes____

17. Circle the letter that identifies the first person to walk on the moon.

    a. Alan Shepard   b. Yuri Gagarin

    c. Chuck Yeager   d. Neil Armstrong

18. An unpiloted vehicle that sends data back to Earth is called a(n) ____space probe____.

19. Describe the space shuttle. ____The space shuttle is a reusable space vehicle that is launched like a rocket but lands like an airplane.____

20. Is the following sentence true or false? The International Space Station is a permanent laboratory designed for research in space. ____true____

LESSON PLAN 25.2

The Earth-Moon System

Time
2 periods
1 block

Section Objectives

- **25.2.1 Explain** why the moon lacks an atmosphere and the effect this has on the range of temperatures on the moon.
- **25.2.2 Describe** the features of the moon's surface.
- **25.2.3 State** a theory about the formation of the moon.
- **25.2.4 Explain** why phases of the moon, eclipses, and tides occur and **interpret diagrams** of the relative positions of the sun, moon, and Earth during these events.

Vocabulary maria • crater • meteoroids • phases • eclipse • umbra • penumbra • tides • spring tide • neap tide

Local Standards

1 FOCUS

Build Vocabulary: Compare/Contrast Tables
Have students make tables that compare and contrast several groups of vocabulary words for this section. **L2**

Targeted Resources
❏ Transparency: Interest Grabber 25.2
❏ Transparency: Reading Strategy 25.2

2 INSTRUCT

Use Visuals: Figure 6
Using Figure 6, ask students to compare maria with craters. Then, ask which type of feature covers most of the moon's surface seen from Earth. **L1**

Build Reading Literacy: Relate Text and Visuals
Have students read the text on p. 798 relating to the formation of the moon. Then, ask students how Figure 7 improves their understanding of the formation of the moon. **L1**

Build Science Skills: Using Models
Students make scale models of the moon and Earth. **L2**

Use Community Resources
Arrange for students to visit a local observatory and observe lunar craters through telescopes, or invite an astronomer to discuss lunar craters with the class. **L2**

Address Misconceptions
Model the positions of the moon, the sun, and Earth during a new moon, in order to help students understand that the phases of the moon are not caused by the shadow of Earth. **L2**

Integrate Social Studies
Show students photographs of Stonehenge, and ask them if they think the alignment of the stones was accidental. **L2**

Targeted Resources
❏ Transparency: Figure 9: Solar and Lunar Eclipses
❏ GRSW Section 25.2

3 ASSESS

Reteach
Have students summarize the surface features and characteristics of the moon. **L1**

Evaluate Understanding
Have students draw diagrams showing the positions of the sun, the moon, and Earth during a solar eclipse, lunar eclipse, spring tide, and neap tide. **L2**

Targeted Resources
❏ **PHSchool.com** Online Section 25.2 Assessment
❏ iText Section 25.2

Transparencies

402 Section 25.2 Interest Grabber

Shadow Dance

Have you ever see an eclipse? This activity shows you why you don't see an eclipse every month.

Darken the classroom. One student in each group shines a flashlight (the sun) toward the wall from 1 m away. Another student holds a basketball (representing Earth) about 30 cm in front of the wall. A third student makes the tennis ball (the moon) orbit horizontally around the basketball. Observe what happens when the moon enters Earth's shadow. Then change the moon's orbit so it is not horizontal.

Wall

1. What happened when the moon entered Earth's shadow?

2. When the moon's orbit was horizontal, how often did the moon enter Earth's shadow?

3. When the moon's orbit was tilted, how did this affect how often it entered Earth's shadow?

ANSWERS
1. Light from the sun was blocked, and the moon became dark.
2. The moon entered Earth's shadow once every orbit.
3. Depending on how students tilt the orbit, they may never see an eclipse, or see an eclipse once per orbit. It depends on where in the moon's orbit the moon crosses the horizontal plane containing Earth and the sun.

Transparencies

403 Section 25.2 Reading Strategy

Building Vocabulary

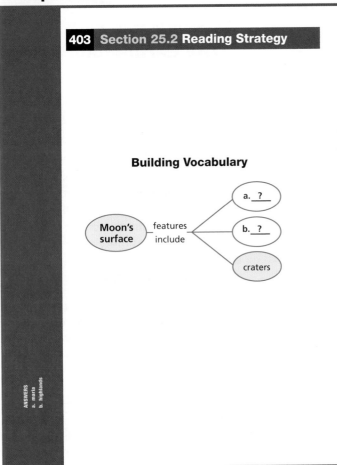

Moon's surface — features include — a. ? / b. ? / craters

ANSWERS
a. maria
b. highlands

Transparencies

404 Figure 9 Solar and Lunar Eclipses

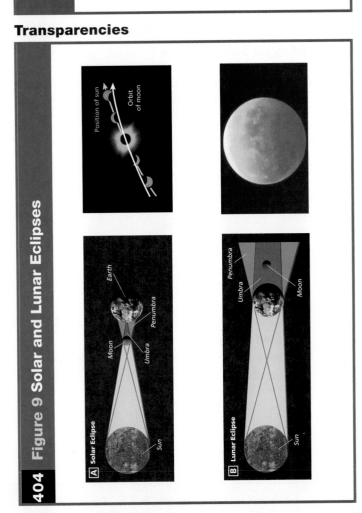

A Solar Eclipse

Position of sun

Orbit of moon

Earth

Moon

Penumbra

Umbra

Sun

B Lunar Eclipse

Penumbra

Umbra

Moon

Sun

Section 25.2 The Earth-Moon System
(pages 796–801)

This section describes Earth's moon, how it was formed, and its phases. It also explains solar and lunar eclipses and tides on Earth.

Reading Strategy (page 796)

Building Vocabulary As you read, complete the concept map with terms from this section. Make similar concept maps for eclipses and tides. For more information on this Reading Strategy, see the **Reading and Study Skills** in the **Skills and Reference Handbook** at the end of your textbook.

The Moon's Surface

```
                              ( marias )
  ( Moon's )  features
  ( surface )  include  ——   ( highlands )

                              ( craters )
```

1. What is the force of gravity on the moon's surface compared to the force of gravity on Earth's surface? The force of gravity on the moon's surface is one sixth that of the force of gravity on Earth's surface.

Earth's Moon (pages 796–797)

2. How does the moon's lack of an atmosphere affect its temperatures? The lack of atmosphere allows the moon's surface temperature to vary tremendously.

3. Evidence of ice on the moon has been found near the moon's North and South Poles.

Surface Features (page 797)

4. Circle the letter of each major surface feature of the moon.
   a. highlands
   b. maria
   c. seas
   d. craters

Match each lunar surface feature with its correct description.

Description	Surface Feature
_b_ 5. A round depression caused by a meteoroid	a. maria
_a_ 6. Low, flat plains formed by ancient lava flows	b. crater
_c_ 7. A rough, mountainous region	c. highland

Formation of the Moon (page 798)

8. Explain the leading hypothesis of how the moon formed. The moon formed after an enormous collision between the early Earth and a Mars-sized object.

Phases of the Moon (pages 798–799)

9. Circle the letter of each sentence that is true about phases of the moon.
   a. The moon's phases change according to an irregular cycle.
   b. Phases are the different shapes of the moon visible from Earth.
   c. Phases are caused by changes in the relative positions of the moon, sun, and Earth as the moon revolves around Earth.
   d. The sunlit portion of the moon always faces Earth.

10. When does a full moon occur? A full moon occurs when the moon is on the opposite side of Earth from the sun, and the whole side of the moon facing Earth is lit by the sun.

Eclipses (pages 799–800)

11. When the shadow of a planet or moon falls on another body in space, a(n) __eclipse__ occurs.

Solar Eclipse

```
   Sun         a.          Earth
              b.  c.
```

12. Look at the diagram showing a solar eclipse and label the parts.
    a. ___Moon___   b. ___Umbra___   c. ___Penumbra___

13. Circle the letter of each sentence that is true about a lunar eclipse.
    a. A lunar eclipse occurs when Earth casts a shadow on the moon.
    b. A lunar eclipse occurs when the moon casts a shadow on a portion of Earth's surface.
    c. A lunar eclipse occurs during a full moon, when Earth is between the sun and moon.
    d. A lunar eclipse occurs during a new moon, when the moon is between the sun and Earth.

Tides on Earth (page 801)

14. Describe the cause of tides. Tides are caused by differences in the moon's gravitational pull on Earth.

15. Is the following sentence true or false? A spring tide is produced when the change between daily high and low tides is the greatest. __true__

Name_____ Class_____ Date_____ M T W T F

LESSON PLAN 25.3

The Inner Solar System

Time
2 periods
1 block

Section Objectives

- **25.3.1 Compare** the terrestrial planets and **describe** characteristics of each.
- **25.3.2 Define** asteroids and **state** alternative hypotheses about how they formed.

Vocabulary terrestrial planets • asteroids • asteroid belt

Local Standards

---

1 FOCUS

Build Vocabulary: Concept Maps
Have students construct three concept maps using the vocabulary words from this section. **L2**

Targeted Resources
❑ Transparency: Interest Grabber 25.3
❑ Transparency: Reading Strategy 25.3

---

2 INSTRUCT

Build Reading Literacy: Use Prior Knowledge
Have students recall what they learned about Earth's greenhouse effect and global warming, then predict what surface temperatures might be like on a planet whose atmosphere is mainly CO_2. **L1**

Use Visuals: Figure 16
Have students compare and contrast the photos of Mars to the photo of Earth on p. 805. **L1**

Integrate Language Arts
Have students research which mythical figure each planet was named for, then write a brief statement describing why they think the name is appropriate. **L2**

Build Science Skills: Designing Experiments
Students design an experiment demonstrating the effects of erosion on Earth's surface. **L2**

Science and History: Exploring the Solar System
Have students compare this time line to those in other chapters, and lead them in a discussion on the future of space exploration. **L2**

Teacher Demo: Asteroids
Drop a large rock on a pile of pebbles so that students can observe the structure of asteroids. **L2**

Targeted Resources
❑ Transparency: Figure 12: The Inner Planets
❑ GRSW Section 25.3
❑ **NSTA** sc_{INKS} The solar system

---

3 ASSESS

Reteach
Make a table on the board similar to the one in Figure 12 that lists characteristics of the inner planets. Describe additional characteristics, such as surface features. **L1**

Evaluate Understanding
Have students review the role water plays or may have played on Earth, Venus, and Mars. **L2**

Targeted Resources
❑ **PHSchool.com** Online Section 25.3 Assessment
❑ iText Section 25.3

Transparencies

Transparencies

405 Section 25.3 **Interest Grabber**

Earth vs. Mars

Use the information in the table shown here to help you answer the questions below.

Characteristic	Earth	Mars
Diameter	12,700 km	6,800 km
Period of Rotation on Axis	24 hrs	24.5 hrs
Period of Revolution Around the Sun	365 days	678 Earth days
Water at Surface	71% coverage	0% (at present time)

1. How are Earth and Mars similar?

2. How are Earth and Mars different?

3. What characteristic of Mars in the table prohibits life (as we know it on Earth) from existing there?

406 Section 25.3 **Reading Strategy**

Summarizing

I. The Terrestrial Planets
  • Four planets closest to the sun
  • Small, dense, with rocky surfaces
II. Mercury
  a. _____
III. Venus
  b. _____

Transparencies

407 **Figure 12 The Inner Planets**

Planet		Equatorial Diameter (kilometers)	Average Distance to Sun (AU)	Period of Rotation (Earth days)	Period of Revolution (Earth years)	Number of Moons
		The Inner Planets				
Mercury		4,880	0.39	59	0.24	0
Venus		12,104	0.72	243	0.62	0
Earth		12,756	1.00	1.00	1.00	1
Mars		6,794	1.52	1.03	1.88	2

Section 25.3 Program Resources

Name _____ Class _____ Date _____

Section 25.3 The Inner Solar System
(pages 803–809)

This section describes the terrestrial planets found in the inner solar system.

Reading Strategy (page 803)

Summarizing Copy the table on a separate sheet of paper. Write all the headings for the section in the table. Write a brief summary of the text for each heading. For more information on this Reading Strategy, see the **Reading and Study Skills** in the **Skills and Reference Handbook** at the end of your textbook.

Answers may include:

The Terrestrial Planets

I. The Terrestrial Planets
- Four planets closest to the sun
- Small, dense, with rocky surfaces

II. Mercury
   a. Smallest terrestrial planet, closest planet to the sun, fastest moving planet, extreme temperatures

III. Venus
   b. Thick atmosphere, very hot surface, many volcanoes

The Terrestrial Planets (pages 803–804)

1. Identify the four terrestrial planets.
   a. ____Mercury____   b. ____Venus____
   c. ____Earth____   d. ____Mars____

2. Circle the letter of each sentence that is true about the terrestrial planets.
   (a.) They all are relatively small and dense.
   (b.) They all have rocky surfaces.
   c. They all have thick atmospheres.
   (d.) They all have a crust, mantle, and iron core.

Mercury (pages 804–805)

3. Circle the letter of each sentence that is true about Mercury.
   (a.) It is the closest planet to the sun.
   (b.) It is the smallest of the terrestrial planets.
   (c.) It is geologically dead.
   d. It is the slowest-moving planet.

4. Is the following sentence true or false? Mercury has a large number of craters, suggesting that the surface has been largely unchanged for billions of years. ____true____

Name _____ Class _____ Date _____

Venus (page 805)

5. Circle the letter of each sentence that is true about Venus.
   (a.) It rotates in the direction opposite to which it revolves.
   (b.) It is the brightest object in Earth's night sky besides the moon.
   c. It rotates once every 24 hours.
   d. Its rotation rate is very fast.

6. Describe the effect that carbon dioxide in Venus's atmosphere has on its temperature. ____The carbon dioxide traps heat and raises the planet's temperature.____

Earth (pages 805–806)

7. Circle the letter of each sentence that is true about Earth.
   a. Its atmosphere is very thin and composed mostly of carbon dioxide.
   (b.) It supports millions of different species of living things.
   (c.) It has a suitable atmosphere and temperature for liquid water to exist.
   d. Its core has cooled down to the point where it is geologically dead.

8. Why does Earth's surface continue to change? ____Earth has retained its internal heat because it is large and has not had a chance to cool down much. Also, it still has moving tectonic plates.____

Mars (pages 807–808)

9. Circle the letter of each sentence that is true about Mars.
   (a.) The largest volcano in the solar system is on Mars.
   (b.) Iron-rich rocks on Mars's surface give it a reddish color.
   c. It has a thick atmosphere that keeps the planet warm.
   (d.) The surface of Mars is colder than Earth's surface.

10. Is the following sentence true or false? Mars shows evidence of once having liquid surface water. ____true____

Asteroids (page 809)

11. Small, rocky bodies in space are called ____asteroids____.

12. Circle the letter of each sentence that is true about asteroids.
   (a.) Most small asteroids have irregular forms.
   b. The asteroid belt formed when a giant planet was shattered by a collision with a meteoroid.
   c. Most asteroids are found in the asteroid belt between Earth and Mars.
   (d.) Most asteroids are less than 1 kilometer in diameter.

13. What do scientists hypothesize about how the asteroids formed? ____The asteroids are remnants of the early solar system that never came together to form a planet.____

LESSON PLAN 25.4

The Outer Solar System

Section Objectives

- **25.4.1 Compare** the gas giants and **describe** characteristics of each.
- **25.4.2 Distinguish** between comets and meteoroids and **describe** their characteristics.
- **25.4.3 Locate** and **describe** the Kuiper belt and the Oort cloud.

Vocabulary gas giants • ring • Kuiper belt • Oort cloud

Local Standards

1 FOCUS

Build Vocabulary: Venn Diagram
Have students construct two Venn diagrams—one comparing and contrasting the gas giants, and the other comparing and contrasting the Kuiper belt and the Oort cloud. **L2**

Targeted Resources
❏ Transparency: Interest Grabber 25.4
❏ Transparency: Reading Strategy 25.4

2 INSTRUCT

Build Reading Literacy: Outline
Have students create an outline with heads and subheads from the section, filling in details as they read. **L1**

Use Visuals: Figure 22
Ask students why the surface of Europa appears so smooth. **L1**

Address Misconceptions
Use Figure 20 to point out to students the vast distances between planets. **L2**

Teacher Demo: Rings of Uranus
Pass a penlight across window blinds so that students can observe how astronomers discovered the rings of Uranus. **L2**

Build Science Skills: Comparing and Contrasting
Have students compare and contrast Pluto to the other planets, and explain why Pluto is considered an "oddball" planet in some ways. **L2**

Build Math Skills: Conversion Factors
Have students convert 100 AU (the approximate edge of the Kuiper belt) and 50,000 AU (the approximate size of the Oort cloud) to kilometers. **L2**

Targeted Resources
❏ Transparency: Figure 20: The Outer Planets
❏ Transparency: Figure 24: Uranus's Orbit
❏ GRSW Section 25.4

3 ASSESS

Reteach
Use Figure 20 to summarize physical properties of the outer planets. **L1**

Evaluate Understanding
State aloud facts about the outer planets, and have students identify the outer planet that matches each fact. **L2**

Targeted Resources
❏ **PHSchool.com** Online Section 25.4 Assessment
❏ iText Section 25.4

Transparencies

408 Section 25.4 **Interest Grabber**

Gravity on Other Planets

The gravitational force on the surface of other planets can be calculated relative to the force of gravity at Earth's surface. The gravitational force on Earth is designated as 1 G. Your weight on Earth is a result of the force of gravity acting on your mass. You can calculate your weight on other planets using the surface gravity of these planets, listed below.

Jupiter = 2.36 G
Saturn = 0.916 G
Uranus = 0.889 G
Neptune = 1.12 G
Pluto = 0.059 G

1. Calculate what your weight would be on the planets listed above by multiplying your weight by the numbers given for each planet.

2. Assume you could reach these planets and be on the surface in a protected space suit. How would the differences in gravity affect your actions?

ANSWERS
1. Student answers will vary depending on their weight. Their greatest weight would be on Jupiter. The lowest weight would be on Pluto.
2. On Saturn and Uranus, students would feel lighter and it would be easier to move around and jump higher. Students would feel heavier on Neptune and it would be harder to move around. On Jupiter, students would have difficulty moving or may not be able to move at all. On Pluto, students could jump very high and throw an object very far.

Transparencies

409 Section 25.4 **Reading Strategy**

Summarizing

Outer Planets	Characteristics
Jupiter	largest; most mass; most moons; Great Red Spot
a. ____?____	b. ____?____
c. ____?____	d. ____?____

ANSWERS
Sample answer for Saturn and Uranus:
a. Saturn
b. second largest planet; largest rings; more than 30 moons
c. Uranus
d. colder; methane gives blue-green color; tilted axis

Transparencies

410 Figure 20 **The Outer Planets**

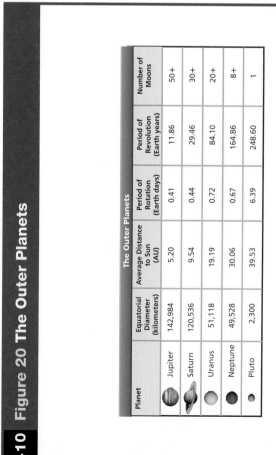

The Outer Planets

Planet	Equatorial Diameter (kilometers)	Average Distance to Sun (AU)	Period of Rotation (Earth days)	Period of Revolution (Earth years)	Number of Moons
Jupiter	142,984	5.20	0.41	11.86	50+
Saturn	120,536	9.54	0.44	29.46	30+
Uranus	51,118	19.19	0.72	84.10	20+
Neptune	49,528	30.06	0.67	164.86	8+
Pluto	2,300	39.53	6.39	248.60	1

Transparencies

411 Figure 24 **Uranus's Orbit**

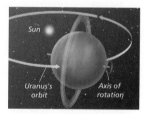

Sun

Uranus's orbit

Axis of rotation

Name _____ Class _____ Date _____

Chapter 25 The Solar System

Section 25.4 The Outer Solar System
(pages 810–815)

This section describes the planets in the outer solar system. It also describes comets and meteoroids and the edge of the solar system.

Reading Strategy (page 810)

Summarizing Copy the table on a separate sheet of paper. Fill in the table as you read to summarize the characteristics of the outer planets. For more information on this Reading Strategy, see the **Reading and Study Skills** in the **Skills and Reference Handbook** at the end of your textbook.

The Outer Planets	
Outer Planets	**Characteristics** Answers may include the following:
Jupiter	Largest; most mass; most moons; Great Red Spot
Saturn	Second largest; largest and most visible rings; at least 30 moons
Uranus	Axis tilted more than 90°; immense storms

Gas Giants (page 811)

1. Circle the letter of each sentence that is true about Jupiter, Saturn, Uranus, and Neptune compared to the terrestrial planets.
   a. Their years are shorter than the terrestrial planets.
   b. They are colder than the terrestrial planets.
   c. They are further from the sun than the terrestrial planets.
   d. They are much larger than the terrestrial planets.

2. Why are the outer planets called the gas giants? They are made mostly of hydrogen and helium.

3. Describe the cores of the gas giants. The cores are small and dense.

Jupiter (pages 811–812)

4. The _____Great Red Spot_____ is a huge storm on Jupiter.

5. Circle the letter of each sentence that is true about Jupiter's moons.
   a. Callisto and Ganymede are Jupiter's largest moons.
   b. Scientists hypothesize that Europa could support life.
   c. Ganymede has a metal core and rocky mantle.
   d. Io is covered with ice.

Name _____ Class _____ Date _____

Chapter 25 The Solar System

Saturn (pages 812–813)

6. Saturn has the largest and most visible _____rings_____ in the solar system.

7. Is the following sentence true or false? Saturn has the largest atmosphere and the lowest average density of all the planets in the solar system. _____true_____

Uranus (page 813)

8. Is the following sentence true or false? Uranus gets its distinctive blue-green appearance from large amounts of methane in its atmosphere. _____true_____

9. Uranus's _____axis of rotation_____ is tilted more than 90°.

Neptune (page 814)

10. Circle the letter of each sentence that is true about Neptune.
    a. It has visible cloud patterns in its atmosphere.
    b. It has only five known moons.
    c. It has large storms in its atmosphere.
    d. It has no rings.

11. The _____methane_____ in Neptune's atmosphere causes its bluish color.

Pluto (page 814)

12. Is the following sentence true or false? Pluto is both larger and denser than the other outer planets. _____false_____

13. Describe Pluto's probable composition. Pluto may be a mixture of ice and rock.

Comets and Meteoroids (page 815)

14. A(n) _____comet_____ is made of ice and rock that partially vaporizes when it passes near the sun.

15. Chunks of rock, usually less than a few hundred meters in size, that travel through the solar system are called _____meteoroids_____.

16. The radioactive dating of ancient meteoroids has allowed scientists to establish that the age of the solar system is _____4.6 billion years_____

The Edge of the Solar System (page 815)

17. The _____Kuiper Belt_____ contains tens of thousands of objects made of ice, dust, and rock that orbit the sun beyond Pluto.

18. The thick sphere of comets encircling the solar system out to a distance of about 50,000 AU is called the _____Oort cloud_____

LESSON PLAN 25.5

The Origin of the Solar System

Time
1 period
1/2 block

Section Objectives

- **25.5.1** **State** the nebular theory.
- **25.5.2** **Relate** the nebular theory to the orbits of the planets and the composition and size of the planets.

Vocabulary solar nebula • protoplanetary disk • planetesimals • accretion

Local Standards

---

1 FOCUS

Build Vocabulary: Paraphrase
Explain the meaning of the vocabulary words by using terms that are familiar to students. **L2**

Targeted Resources
❑ Transparency: Interest Grabber 25.5
❑ Transparency: Reading Strategy 25.5

---

2 INSTRUCT

Use Visuals: Figure 28
Have students examine Figure 28. Then, ask how the shape of the nebula changed. **L1**

Build Reading Literacy: Relate Cause and Effect
After students have read about the composition and size of the planets, ask if low density is a cause or an effect. **L1**

Address Misconceptions
Explain to students that scientific laws are generalizations about principles or processes that occur in nature, and can only be confirmed, not proven. **L2**

Quick Lab: Forming Planets
Students spin a paper sphere on a pencil and explain the shape of the protoplanetary disk. **L2**

Build Science Skills: Communicating Results
Have groups of students conduct research about extrasolar planets and display their results with multimedia presentations. **L2**

For Enrichment
Have students examine Figure 3 on pp. 792 and 793 for evidence for an alternative theory to the nebular theory. **L3**

Targeted Resources
❑ GRSW Section 25.5

---

3 ASSESS

Reteach
Explain to students that any rotating object, such as a nebula or an ice skater, will spin faster if its mass is redistributed closer to its axis of rotation. **L1**

Evaluate Understanding
Have students identify any concepts they find unclear. Have student volunteers explain the concepts. **L2**

Targeted Resources
❑ **PHSchool.com** Online Section 25.5 Assessment
❑ iText Section 25.5

Transparencies

412 Section 25.5 Interest Grabber

Why Are the Terrestrial Planets Dense?

The solar system formed from a spinning cloud of gas and dust called the solar nebula. In this activity, you will model how materials settled in the solar nebula.

Remove the lid from a clear plastic jar. Fill the jar halfway with water. Drop a spoonful of sand into the jar. Firmly reattach the lid so water cannot leak out. Turn the jar upside down and swirl it to set the water spinning inside. Stop swirling and observe the sand in the jar.

1. Which is denser, water or sand? *HINT: What happened to the sand when you first added it to the water?*

2. Where does the sand end up after the water stops spinning?

3. Hypothesize why the terrestrial planets are denser than the gas giants.

ANSWERS
NOTE: This activity requires a plastic jar with a clear bottom and a screw-on lid. An empty peanut-butter jar will work well.
1. Sand is denser.
2. The sand ends up in the center of the lid.
3. Hypothesis: Terrestrial planets are denser because in a spinning cloud, denser materials tend to move toward the center.

Transparencies

413 Section 25.5 Reading Strategy

Identifying Main Ideas

Topic	Main Idea
The Nebular Theory	a. _____?_____
Formation of the Protoplanetary Disk	b. _____?_____
Planetesimals and Protoplanets	c. _____?_____
Composition and Size of the Planets	d. _____?_____

ANSWERS
a. The solar system formed from a large rotating cloud of dust and gas.
b. As the solar nebula rotated, it began to flatten out and form a protoplanetary disk.
c. Dust grains within the protoplanetary disk combined and grew larger. Eventually, these combined to form planetesimals and later protoplanets.
d. The temperatures in the early solar system were very high near the sun and much lower in the outer system. These temperatures affected which materials condensed to form the planets.

Guided Reading and Study Workbook

Name _____ Class _____ Date _____

Chapter 25 The Solar System

Section 25.5 The Origin of the Solar System
(pages 818–820)

This section explains a theory of how the solar system originated. It also describes how this theory explains the composition and size of the planets.

Reading Strategy (page 818)

Identifying Main Ideas As you read, write the main idea for each topic. For more information on this Reading Strategy, see the **Reading and Study Skills** in the **Skills and Reference Handbook** at the end of your textbook.

Theories on the Origin of the Solar System	
Topic	**Main Idea**
The Nebular Theory	The solar system formed from a large rotating cloud of dust and gas.
Formation of the protoplanetary disk	As the solar nebula rotated, it began to flatten out and form a protoplanetary disk.
Planetesimals and protoplanets	Dust grains within the protoplanetary combined and grew larger. Eventually, these combined to form planetesimals and later protoplanets.
Composition and size of the planets	The temperatures in the early solar system were very high near the sun and much lower in the outer system. These temperatures affected which materials condensed to form planets.

The Nebular Theory (pages 818–819)

1. The generally accepted explanation for the formation of the solar system is called the ___nebular theory___.

2. Circle the letter of each sentence that is true about the nebular theory.
   a. The solar nebula formed from the remnants of previous stars.
   b. The explosion of a nearby star likely caused the solar nebula to start to contract.
   c. As the solar nebula contracted, it began to spin more slowly.
   d. The solar system formed from a rotating cloud of dust and gas.

3. Describe a solar nebula. A solar nebula is a large, thin cloud of dust and gas.
_____

4. A large, spherical cloud of dust and gas in space is called a(n) ___protoplanetary disk___.

5. Is the following sentence true or false? Most planets and moons are revolving now in the direction that the protoplanetary disk was spinning. ___true___

Guided Reading and Study Workbook

Name _____ Class _____ Date _____

Chapter 25 The Solar System

6. Circle the letter of each sentence that is true about the formation of the protoplanetary disk.
   a. The disk was densest in the center and thinner toward the edges.
   b. At the center of the disk, nuclear reactions fused hydrogen and helium and the sun was formed.
   c. The temperature at the center of the disk was extremely low.
   d. Nearly all of the mass of the solar nebula became concentrated near the outer edge of the disk.

7. Asteroid-like bodies that combined to form planets were called ___planetesimals___.

8. The process by which planetesimals grew is called ___accretion___.

9. Put the following events about the formation of planetesimals and protoplanets in correct order. Number the events 1–5 in the order that they occurred.
   __1__ Balls of gas and dust collided and grew larger.
   __3__ Planetesimals became large enough to exert gravity on nearby objects.
   __2__ Planetesimals grew by accretion.
   __5__ Protoplanets joined to form the current planets in a series of collisions.
   __4__ Planetesimals grew into protoplanets.

Composition and Size of the Planets (page 820)

10. At ___low___ pressures, such as those found in space, cooling materials can change from a gas directly into a solid.

11. Ice-forming materials ___vaporize___ at temperatures between 500 K and 1200 K.

12. Why are the terrestrial planets relatively small and rocky? They are relatively small and rocky because the inner solar system was too hot when they formed for ice-forming compounds to solidify.

13. Circle the letter of each sentence that is true about the formation of the gas giants.
   a. The gravity of the gas giants decreased as they grew larger.
   b. Ice-forming material could condense in the outer solar system.
   c. The planets grew large and were able to capture hydrogen and helium from nearby space.
   d. Less material was available for the gas giants to form than was available for the terrestrial planets.

14. Is the following sentence true or false? Scientists have found planets in orbit around distant stars that provide support for the nebular theory. ___true___

Guided Reading and Study Workbook

Name _____ Class _____ Date _____

WordWise

Test your knowledge of vocabulary words from Chapter 25 by completing this crossword puzzle.

Clues across:

3. A model where Earth is stationary while objects in the sky move around it
4. A small natural body in space that revolves around a planet
6. Asteroid-like bodies that eventually combined to form planets
9. The regular rise and fall of ocean waters
10. A chunk of rock that moves through the solar system

Clues down:

1. The event that occurs when the shadow of one body in space falls on another
2. Dusty pieces of ice and rock that partially vaporize when they pass near the sun
5. Small, rocky bodies that travel through the solar system
7. Low, flat plains on the moon
8. A disk made of many small particles of rock and ice in orbit around a planet

(crossword puzzle)

Across: 3. GEOCENTRIC 4. MOON 6. PLANETESIMALS 9. TIDES 10. METEOROID
Down: 1. ECLIPSE 2. COMET 5. ASTEROIDS 7. MARIA 8. RINGS

Guided Reading and Study Workbook

Name _____ Class _____ Date _____

Calculating Distances Between Objects in Space

Jupiter is, on average, 5.2 astronomical units (AU) from the sun. About how many kilometers is Jupiter from the sun?

Math Skill:
Conversion Factors

You may want to read more about this **Math Skill** in the **Skills and Reference Handbook** at the end of your textbook.

1. **Read and Understand**

   What information are you given?
   Jupiter's distance = 5.2 AU from the sun

2. **Plan and Solve**

   What are you asked to find?
   Jupiter's distance = ? kilometers from the sun

   How many kilometers are in one AU?
   149,598,000 kilometers

   Write a conversion factor that can be used to change AU to kilometers.

   $$\frac{149{,}598{,}000 \text{ km}}{1 \text{ AU}}$$

   Multiply the distance from the sun to Jupiter in AU by the conversion factor.

   $$5.2 \text{ AU} \times \frac{149{,}598{,}000 \text{ km}}{1 \text{ AU}} = 780 \text{ million km}$$

   Jupiter's distance = 780 million km from the sun

3. **Look Back and Check**

   Is your answer reasonable?
   To check your answer, convert the distance between the sun and Jupiter in kilometers back to AU.

   $$\frac{780{,}000{,}000 \text{ km}}{149{,}598{,}000 \text{ km/AU}} = 5.2 \text{ AU}$$

Math Practice

On a separate sheet of paper, solve the following problems.

1. Pluto is an average distance of 39.5 AU from the sun. How many kilometers from the sun is Pluto?

   $39.5 \text{ AU} \times \frac{149{,}598{,}000 \text{ km}}{1 \text{ AU}} = 5{,}910{,}000{,}000 \text{ km} = 5.91 \times 10^9 \text{ km}$

2. Mercury is 58.3×10^6 km from the sun on average. How many AU is Mercury from the sun?

   $(58.3 \times 10^6 \text{ km}) \times \frac{1 \text{ AU}}{1.4958 \times 10^8 \text{ km}} = 0.392 \text{ AU}$

3. Mars is 1.52 AU from the sun on average. Saturn is 9.54 AU. About how far apart, in kilometers, are Mars and Saturn when they are closest to each other?

   $9.54 \text{ AU} - 1.52 \text{ AU} = 8.02 \text{ AU}; 8.02 \text{ AU} \times 1.4958 \times 10^8 \text{ km/AU} = 1.20 \times 10^9 \text{ km}$

Student Edition Lab Worksheet

Name _____ Class _____ Date _____

Exploration Lab

Modeling the Solar System

See page 821 in the Teacher's Edition for more information.

You may have seen models and illustrations that compare the sizes of the planets, but do not accurately show their relative distances from the sun. In this lab, you will compare the sizes of the planets to their distances from the sun.

Problem How can you model both the relative sizes and distances of the planets in the solar system?

Materials
• calculator
• large sheet of unlined paper
• meter stick
• scale models of the sun and planets

Skills Calculating, Using Models

Procedure

1. To model the relative sizes of the planets' orbits, convert the distances of the planets from the sun in astronomical units to kilometers, using Figure 3 on pages 792 and 793 of your textbook. Record these distances in scientific notation.

Mercury: 5.8×10^7 km	Mars: 2.2×10^8 km	Uranus: 2.87×10^9 km
Venus: 1.1×10^8 km	Jupiter: 7.8×10^8 km	Neptune: 4.50×10^9 km
Earth: 1.5×10^8 km	Saturn: 1.4×10^9 km	Pluto: 5.91×10^9 km

2. Use the meter stick to draw a straight line down the entire length of the large sheet of unlined paper. Measure and record the length of this line in centimeters.

   Sample answer: 42 cm

3. Label one end of the line *sun* and the other end *Pluto*.

4. To calculate the scale of your model, divide the length of the line in centimeters by Pluto's average distance from the sun in kilometers.

   The answer will depend on the length given in Step 2. If the line is 42 cm long, the scale is
   7.1×10^{-9} cm/km.

5. To determine Neptune's position, multiply Neptune's average distance from the sun by the scale of your model. Mark Neptune's position on the line in your model.

6. Repeat Step 5 for each of the remaining planets in the solar system.

Student Edition Lab Worksheet

Name _____ Class _____ Date _____

7. Your teacher will provide a set of scale models of the sun and planets. Use a meter stick to measure and record the diameter of the model of Jupiter.

   If a ball 17.5 cm in diameter is used for the sun, Jupiter would be about 2.3 cm in diameter.

8. To determine the scale of the planet models, divide the diameter of the model of Jupiter in centimeters by the actual diameter of Jupiter, which can be found in Figure 20 on page 811 of your textbook.

   If the Jupiter model is 2.3 cm in diameter, the scale is 2.3 cm/143,000 km = 1.6×10^{-5} cm/km

9. To determine the size of the solar system at the scale of the planet models, multiply the actual distance from Pluto to the sun by the scale of the planet models. Convert the result from centimeters to meters and record this distance.

   At the scale of the planet models provided in the answer to Step 7, the solar system model
   would be approximately 983 m long.

Analyze and Conclude

1. **Using Models** How big would a model of the solar system be at the scale of the planet models you used? Explain your answer.

   Answers should be twice the distance from Pluto to the sun given as an answer to Step 9,
   which represents about half the major axis of Pluto's orbit.

2. **Analyzing Data** What difficulty would you have including the relative sizes of the planets on the paper model you made in Steps 1 through 6?

   The orbits of the inner planets would be too small to draw or observe.

3. **Drawing Conclusions** Explain why it is difficult to model the sizes and distances of the planets at the same scale.

   The distances among the planets and between the planets and the sun are many times greater
   than the sizes of the planets.

Lab Manual

Name _____ Class _____ Date _____

Chapter 25   The Solar System

Investigation 25A

Deflecting an Asteroid

Refer students to page 809 in their textbooks for a discussion of asteroids. **SKILLS FOCUS:** Predicting, Observing, Making Analogies, Controlling Variables, Using Models **CLASS TIME:** 45 minutes

Background Information

Although asteroids and comets often have well-defined orbits, these orbits can be disturbed by the gravitational forces of massive bodies that the asteroids or comets encounter. Such gravitational disturbances, or perturbations, cause the asteroid or comet to change direction and follow a new orbital path.

The perturbation of an asteroid or comet depends on its speed and how close it approaches the more massive body. Sometimes the perturbations are strong enough that the asteroid or comet is captured by the more massive body. In these cases, the asteroid or comet orbits or collides with the larger object.

In this investigation, you will simulate the perturbation of an asteroid's motion by observing how a magnet deflects a steel ball bearing from its path.

Problem

How does the amount an object is deflected from its path depend on its speed and its distance from a perturbing force?

Pre-Lab Discussion

Read the entire investigation. Then, work with a partner to answer the following questions.

1. **Formulating Hypotheses** Write a hypothesis about how you expect the speed of the ball bearing and the distance of the magnet from the ball bearing's path to affect the deflection of the ball bearing.

   For a given magnet distance, the faster the ball bearing moves, the less it will be deflected. For a
   given ball bearing speed, the closer the magnet is to the ball bearing's path, the greater the ball
   bearing will be deflected.

2. **Using Models** What force is being modeled in this investigation by the magnet?

   The gravitational force exerted by a massive body on an asteroid is the force being modeled.

Physical Science Lab Manual • Investigation 25A **261**

Lab Manual

Name _____ Class _____ Date _____

3. **Controlling Variables** What are the manipulated and controlled variables in this investigation?

   For the first part of the investigation, the height of the tube and thus the speed of the ball bearing are
   the manipulated variables. The distance between the ball bearing and the magnet is the controlled
   variable. For the second part of the investigation, the distance of the magnet from the ball bearing's
   path is the manipulated variable, and the tube height (ball bearing speed) is the controlled variable.

4. **Controlling Variables** What is the responding variable in this investigation?

   The responding variable is the deflection of the ball bearing from the target.

5. **Predicting** Assuming that all other conditions are the same, how would placing the magnet near the target produce different results from placing it near the end of the tube? Explain your answer.

   The deflection of the ball bearing will be greater when the magnet is placed near the end of the
   tube than if it is placed near the target. Assuming the angle of deflection is the same in both cases,
   the ball bearing travels farther to the side as it travels farther forward.

Materials *(per group)*

cardboard tube, 30 cm long
steel ball bearing, 1.5 cm in diameter
magnet (preferably a strong alnico or rare-earth type)
3 books, each about 3 cm thick
wooden block, at least 6 cm long on each side
meter stick
paper strip, 60 cm × 4 cm
masking tape
pencil

262 *Physical Science* Lab Manual • Investigation 25A

Lab Manual

Name _____ Class _____ Date _____

Procedure

1. Set up the materials, as shown in Figure 1. Center the block (target) in the middle of the paper strip and tape the edges of the strip to the table surface.

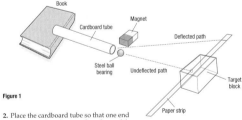

Figure 1

2. Place the cardboard tube so that one end is supported on the top edge of one of the books and the other end is on the table. The target block should be in a direct line with the tube so that a ball bearing rolled down the tube will strike the center of the block, as shown by the undeflected path in Figure 1.

3. The distance from the end of the cardboard tube to the target block should be between 50 and 75 cm. Measure the actual distance and record the value in the data table.

4. Measure the height of the tube above the table (that is, the thickness of the book). Record the value in the data table.

5. Place the magnet 6 cm to the side of the lower end of the cardboard tube. Roll the ball bearing down the tube and observe how it deviates from the straight path it followed before the magnet was introduced. Adjust the position of the magnet so that the ball bearing is deflected enough to miss the target. (*Hint:* Depending on how strong the magnet is, you may have to try positioning the magnet farther or closer to the side of the tube so as to keep the ball bearing from attaching itself to the magnet or from not causing any deflection at all).

6. Repeat the trial, marking on the paper strip the point where the ball bearing crosses the strip. Measure the distance from the center of the block to the mark and record it in the data table.

7. Place a second book on top of the first book, measure the tube height, and record the value in the data table. Repeat Step 6 and record your observations in the data table.

8. Place a third book on top of the first two books, measure the tube height, and record the value in the data table. Repeat Step 6 and record your observations in the data table.

Physical Science Lab Manual • Investigation 25A **263**

Lab Manual

Name _____ Class _____ Date _____

9. Repeat Steps 6 through 8, after halving the distance between the magnet and the end of the tube. Record your observations in the data table.

10. Repeat Steps 6 through 8, placing the magnet against the end of the tube. Record your observations in the data table.

Observations   Sample data are shown.

DATA TABLE

Distance of Magnet From Tube (cm)	Tube Height (cm)	Distance Between Tube and Target (cm)	Deflection Distance (cm)
6.0	3.5	55.0	2.3
6.0	7.0	55.0	1.5
6.0	10.5	55.0	0.75
3.0	3.5	55.0	4.5
3.0	7.0	55.0	3.0
3.0	10.5	55.0	1.5
0.0	3.5	55.0	9.0
0.0	7.0	55.0	6.0
0.0	10.5	55.0	3.0

264 *Physical Science* Lab Manual • Investigation 25A

Lab Manual

Name _____ Class _____ Date _____

Analysis and Conclusions

1. Observing What effect did raising the height of the tube have on the deflection of the ball bearing?

It caused the ball bearing to move faster and so reduced the amount that the ball bearing

was deflected.

2. Applying Concepts How does the speed of the ball bearing relate to the amount of deflection? Explain your answer.

The faster the ball bearing moves, the farther it goes forward in a given time. During that same

time, the force causing the deflection accelerates the ball bearing, causing it to travel a certain

distance sideways. The greater the forward speed of the ball bearing, the shorter is the time for

deflection and the smaller is the distance of deflection.

3. Observing What effect did moving the magnet closer to the opening of the tube have on the deflection of the ball bearing?

It caused the deflection of the ball bearing to increase.

4. Drawing Conclusions Did your results support or contradict your hypothesis? Explain your answer.

The results confirmed that, for a given magnet distance, the faster the ball bearing moves, the less

it will be deflected. The results also confirmed that, for a given ball bearing speed, the closer the

magnet is to the ball bearing's path, the greater the ball bearing is deflected.

5. Designing Experiments How might you redesign the experiment so that the deflecting force was provided by gravity instead of by magnetism?

A direct means of using gravity for deflection would be to design a test surface that tilts

to one side or the other of the undeflected path. As the ball bearing rolls forward, it also rolls

down the plane to the side, and thus is deflected by gravity. The greater the tilt of the plane,

the greater is the deflection. Students may also suggest using a bowl rather than a flat surface.

Lab Manual

Name _____ Class _____ Date _____

6. Designing Experiments How would the design improvement you have suggested in Question 5 allow you to test spherical objects with different masses?

The use of magnetism for deflection limits the spheres to ferromagnetic materials. By

designing a deflection method that uses gravity, any material can be used. This provides a

wider range of densities for the rolling spheres so that spheres of the same size but much

different mass can be tested. Note, however, that friction may vary for different materials,

so this variable would need to be controlled.

7. Inferring From you observations, infer why a small gravitational force could cause an asteroid to travel far off course as it moves through the solar system.

A small force might pull an asteroid only a short distance in one direction, but as

the asteroid continued to travel, it would move farther from its original path.

8. Inferring A concern about asteroids is that they might collide with Earth, causing tremendous destruction. Why is this concern greater for asteroids moving at high speeds than for those moving at lowers speeds?

Asteroids that move at higher speeds have greater kinetic energies than those moving at lower

speeds. This energy is given up during impact, and so the collision is more destructive. Also, it

would be more difficult to deflect a fast-moving asteroid by human intervention, as any

force acting on the asteroid will deflect it less than if the asteroid was moving at a slower speed.

Go Further

Design an experiment to determine how the mass of an asteroid affects the deflection by a given force. Your plan can use the same materials used in this investigation or some or all of the improvements you suggested in Question 5. Specify which variables are to be manipulated and which need to be controlled throughout the experiment. Submit your procedure and design to your teacher for approval before conducting your experiment. Record your observations and report your results.
Check to be sure that the manipulated and controlled variables are clearly defined in the plan and that all aspects of the plan will produce measurable results. Be sure that the experimental design is safe to perform.

Lab Manual

Name _____ Class _____ Date _____

Chapter 25   The Solar System   **Investigation 25B**

Exploring Orbits

Refer students to pages 790–795 in their textbooks for a discussion of planetary orbits. **SKILLS FOCUS:** Measuring, Inferring, Comparing and Contrasting **CLASS TIME:** 45 minutes

Background Information

All bodies that move in closed orbits around the sun follow a path described by an **ellipse**. An ellipse is an oval-shaped figure that is characterized by two quantities. The first of these quantities is the width of the ellipse, which is called the major axis.

Along the major axis and on either side of the center of the ellipse are two points called the foci. For elliptical orbits, the sun is at one focus. The distance between the foci is called the focal length of the ellipse, as shown below. This distance determines the eccentricity of the ellipse. Eccentricity is an indicator of how elongated an ellipse is. Ellipses can be very elongated, or they can be nearly circular. The planets of the solar system have orbits with different major axes and eccentricities.

In this investigation, you will draw some elliptical shapes, calculate the eccentricity of these ellipses, and compare them to the orbital eccentricities of Earth and other planets in the solar system.

Major axis — Focus — Focal length — Sun (at focus)

Problem

What do the elliptical orbits of the planets look like?

Pre-Lab Discussion

Read the entire investigation. Then, work with a partner to answer the following questions.

1. Predicting Predict the shapes of the planets' orbits (more circular or more flattened).

Many students may predict that the planets' orbits are flattened ellipses.

2. Applying Concepts What is the one thing that the elliptical orbits of all planets, asteroids, and most comets have in common?

The sun is at one focus of all these elliptical orbits.

3. Controlling Variables What is the manipulated variable for the various ellipses drawn?

The focal length is the manipulated variable.

Lab Manual

Name _____ Class _____ Date _____

4. Controlling Variables What are the responding variables for the various ellipses drawn?

The eccentricity and the major axis are responding variables.

5. Designing Experiments What purpose do the two pushpins serve in this investigation?

The pushpins mark the foci of the ellipses.

Materials *(per group)*

3 sheets of paper	string, 30 cm in length
heavy corrugated cardboard	colored pencils
2 pushpins	tape
metric ruler	calculator

Safety 🔲

Be careful when handling sharp instruments. Note all safety alert symbols next to the steps in the Procedure and review the meaning of each symbol by referring to the Safety Symbols on page xiii.

Procedure

🔲 **1.** Fold a sheet of paper in half lengthwise. Flatten it out again.

2. Place the paper on the cardboard and push the two pins on the crease so that they are centered on the page and are 10.0 cm apart. **CAUTION:** *Be careful when handling pins; they can puncture skin.* (*Hint:* As the focal length for ellipses in this investigation becomes smaller, you may have to tape additional sheets of paper above and below to show the entire ellipse).

3. Label one of the pushpins as the sun.

4. Take the string, tie it in a loop, and place it around the pins. Using one of the colored pencils, gently pull the string taut. Keep the string taut without pulling the pins out of the cardboard and carefully drag the pencil around the pins to draw an ellipse, as shown in Figure 1.

5. Remove the pin that is not labeled as the sun. In its place, draw a noticeable dot the same color as the ellipse.

6. Use the metric ruler to measure the length of the major axis and focal length. Record these values in the data table.

Figure 1

7. Reposition the second pin so that it is now 8.0 cm from the other pin. Repeat Steps 4 through 6, using a different colored pencil.

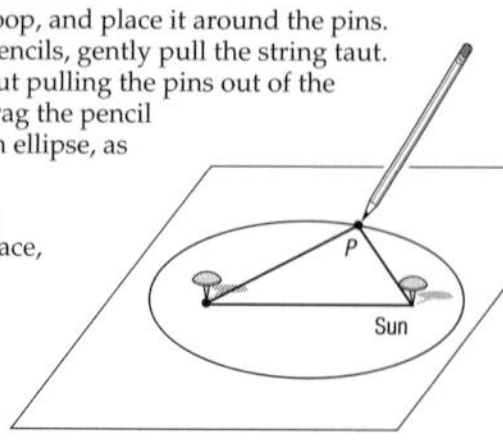

Lab Manual

Name _____ Class _____ Date _____

8. Repeat Step 7, using distances of 6.0 cm, 4.0 cm, and 2.0 cm between the pins.
9. The eccentricity for each ellipse is calculated by dividing the focal length by the length of the major axis:

$$\text{Eccentricity} = \frac{\text{Focal length}}{\text{Major axis}}$$

Calculate the eccentricity for each ellipse and record the values in the data table.
10. Label each ellipse on your diagram with its matching eccentricity.

Observations Sample data are shown.

DATA TABLE

Ellipse (color)	Major Axis (cm)	Focal Length (cm)	Eccentricity
Black	20.0	10.0	0.500
Red	22.0	8.0	0.36
Blue	24.0	6.0	0.25
Green	26.0	4.0	0.15
Purple	28.0	2.0	0.071

Lab Manual

Name _____ Class _____ Date _____

Analysis and Conclusions

1. **Drawing Conclusions** Did the investigation results confirm your prediction? Explain why or why not.

If students predicted the orbits to be flattened ellipses, they will not find the prediction to be

confirmed. Even the orbits of Mars and Mercury are only slightly flattened.

2. **Compare and Contrast** Compare the following values for planetary eccentricities to those you calculated for your ellipses. What can you state about the orbits of the various planets?

Planet	Eccentricity
Mercury	0.206
Venus	0.007
Earth	0.017
Mars	0.093
Jupiter	0.048
Saturn	0.056
Uranus	0.047
Neptune	0.009
Pluto	0.250

Most planets have nearly circular orbits. The planets with greater eccentricities have more elongated

orbits. The most elongated orbits are for Pluto and Mercury. Venus and Neptune have the least

elongated orbits.

Go Further

Research the orbits of various smaller bodies in the solar system, such as asteroids or comets. Use the materials from this investigation and researched values for the major axis and eccentricity to produce drawings of these objects' orbits. Include in your report all values used and your drawings.
Review student information before students begin drawing the orbits to be sure that eccentricities are not too small (not much less than 0.10) nor too large (greater than 0.90).

Chapter Test A

Name _____ Class _____ Date _____

Chapter 25 The Solar System   **Chapter Test A**

Multiple Choice

Write the letter that best answers the question or completes the statement on the line provided.

_____ 1. Which of the following is the most likely reason that ancient observers believed that Earth was the center of the universe?
   a. The Earth seemed to move on its axis.
   b. Earth's motions are only recently known because of high-powered telescopes.
   c. Objects in the sky appear to circle around Earth.
   d. Ancient observers believed the universe was stationary.

_____ 2. Which of the following helps explain why the planets remain in motion around the sun?
   a. density b. gravity c. inertia d. both b and c

_____ 3. What led to the discovery of three more planets than those that the ancient observers knew about?
   a. the invention of the telescope in 1600
   b. the Hubble telescope launched in 1990
   c. space missions in the Apollo program
   d. observations by *Sputnik 1* in 1957

_____ 4. Which of the following are currently operating the space station?
   a. Soviet cosmonauts
   b. a cooperative team of scientists from 16 countries
   c. American astronauts
   d. a cooperative team of scientists from Russia and the United States

_____ 5. How might a nitrogen-oxygen atmosphere on the moon affect the range of temperatures on the moon?
   a. An atmosphere might hold heat in, making the moon very hot.
   b. An atmosphere might block heat radiating from the sun, making the moon very cold.
   c. An atmosphere might moderate temperatures, making them more even, such as on Earth.
   d. An atmosphere would have no effect on the range of temperatures on the moon.

_____ 6. What is meant by the statement "The moon is geologically dead"?
   a. The moon has little erosion and no plate movement.
   b. The moon is devoid of living things.
   c. The moon has no atmosphere.
   d. The moon has no air currents or weather patterns.

Chapter Test A

Name _____ Class _____ Date _____

_____ 7. Soon after the collision with Earth, the materials that eventually formed the moon
   a. orbited Earth in a large, irregular clump.
   b. were bits of Earth's mantle encircling Earth.
   c. were mostly broken pieces of the object that hit Earth.
   d. none of the above

_____ 8. Study Figure 25-1. Suppose you are an astronaut on the side of the moon facing Earth during a total lunar eclipse. Which would you see as you look toward Earth?

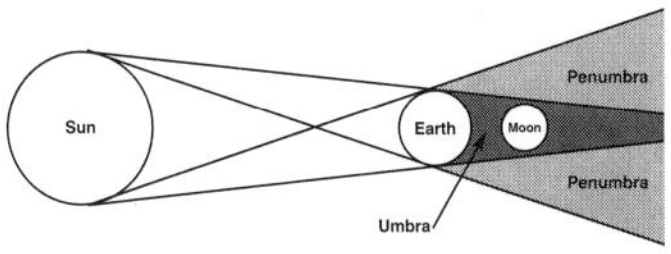

Figure 25-1   NOT TO SCALE

   a. Nothing; there would be total darkness.
   b. The normal view; there is always reflected light from the moon's surface.
   c. You could not see the sun because Earth blocks its light.
   d. The light from the sun behind Earth would be blinding.

_____ 9. Which characteristic of the inner planets increases with increasing distance from the sun?
   a. equatorial diameter   b. period of rotation
   c. average temperature   d. period of revolution

_____ 10. What evidence suggests that asteroids are like rubble heaps and not solid like rock?
   a. They are held together by weak gravity.
   b. They have not shattered on impact with other objects.
   c. They mostly have irregular shapes.
   d. They are remnants of a shattered planet.

_____ 11. Which characteristic of the gas giants decreases with increasing distance from the sun?
   a. equatorial diameter   b. period of rotation
   c. number of moons   d. both a and c

_____ 12. What is the difference between a meteoroid and a meteorite?
   a. A meteoroid is made of metal; a meteorite is made of rock.
   b. A meteoroid is larger than a meteorite.
   c. A meteoroid is located in space; it becomes a meteorite when it hits Earth.
   d. A meteoroid has a tail like a comet; a meteorite burns up in Earth's atmosphere.

Chapter Test A

_____ **13.** In astronomical units (AU), what is the approximate distance of the outer edge of the Oort cloud from the outer edge of the Kuiper belt?
  a. 100 AU   **b.** 20,000 AU
  c. 30,000 AU   **d.** more than 49,000 AU

_____ **14.** In the formation of our solar system, nearly all of the mass of the solar nebula became
  a. the terrestrial planets. **b.** the gas giants.
  c. the sun.   **d.** the Oort cloud.

_____ **15.** Which evidence provides support for the nebular theory?
  a. Scientists have observed the formation of a distant solar system.
  b. The nebular theory has been proven mathematically.
  c. Astronomers have observed protoplanetary disks around distant newborn stars.
  d. none of the above

Completion
Complete each statement on the line provided.

1. Because Earth's orbit around the sun is an ellipse, and Earth is not always the same distance from the sun, one AU is defined as the _____ distance from Earth to the sun.

2. All of the planets in our solar system have _____ with the exception of Mercury and Venus.

3. A person weighing 600 newtons (about 120 pounds) on Earth would weigh about _____ newtons on the moon.

4. The _____ belt contains perhaps tens of thousands of objects orbiting within about 100 AU of the sun.

5. The difference in the composition of the terrestrial planets and the gas giants can be explained by the different condensation _____ in the regions near and far from the sun during the formation of the solar system.

Short Answer
In complete sentences, write the answers to the questions on the lines provided.

1. What is the fundamental difference between Ptolemy's view of the universe and that of Aristarchus?

2. What is the ecliptic plane?

Chapter Test A

3. What is the difference between a full moon and a new moon?

4. Explain why Mars is called the most Earthlike of all the other planets.

5. Explain the odd and irregular shapes of most asteroids.

6. Explain why the gas giants are many times larger than Earth.

Using Science Skills
Use the diagram to answer each question. Write the answers on a separate sheet of paper.

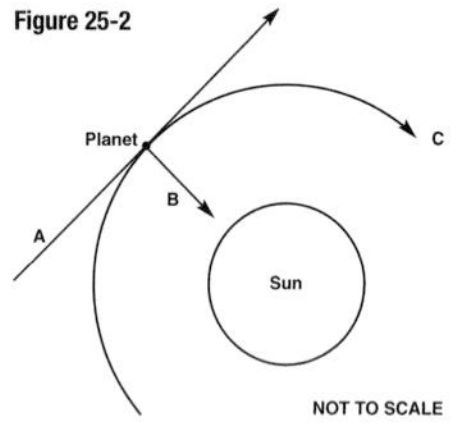

1. **Applying Concepts** If a planet is orbiting along path C in Figure 25-2, explain why it stays in orbit. Refer to Figure 25-2 in your explanation.

2. **Inferring** Based on Figure 25-2, describe the path that the planet would follow if the sun did not exist. Why would this happen?

3. **Formulating Hypotheses** In Figure 25-2, why would you expect B to lie in the planet's orbital plane?

4. **Drawing Conclusions** Saturn is the least dense of all the planets. Why does Saturn remain in orbit instead of drifting away in space or crashing into the sun?

5. **Applying Concepts** The period of revolution of the planet shown in Figure 25-2 is 1.88 Earth years. What planet is it? How does the period of an asteroid in the asteroid belt compare with the period of the planet shown?

Figure 25-2

Planet *A B C* *Sun*

NOT TO SCALE

Chapter Test A

Essay
Write the answers to each question on a separate sheet of paper.

1. Describe two kinds of technology in use today for the exploration of space.

2. Explain why Earth is currently in little danger of being hit by a Mars-sized object.

3. Compare the four largest moons of Jupiter.

4. Describe the tails of a comet.

5. What three criteria must any theory of the origin of the solar system satisfy? What theory satisfies all three?

Chapter Test B

Name _____ Class _____ Date _____

Chapter 25   The Solar System   Chapter Test B

Multiple Choice
Write the letter that best answers the question or completes the statement on the line provided.

_____ **1.** In a diagram depicting the solar system as heliocentric, what is located at the center?
a. Earth   **b.** the sun   **c.** the moon   **d.** Mars

_____ **2.** The orbit of a planet around the sun is a(an)
a. ellipse.   **b.** straight line.   **c.** circle.   **d.** parabola.

_____ **3.** Which of the following objects does NOT orbit directly around the sun?
a. planets   **b.** comets   **c.** moons   **d.** all of the above

_____ **4.** Who was the first American in space?
a. Yuri Gargarin   **b.** Alan Shepard
c. Chuck Yeager   **d.** Neil Armstrong

_____ **5.** Why does Earth's moon have no atmosphere?
a. The average temperature is too high.
b. There are no plants to release oxygen.
c. The moon is too far from Earth.
d. The moon's gravity is too weak to hold onto gas molecules.

_____ **6.** On the moon, maria are
a. meteoroid craters.   **b.** low, flat plains.
c. rough mountains.   **d.** lunar seas filled with water.

_____ **7.** The moon most likely formed
a. from a collision with a Mars-sized object.
b. in another region of space and drifted toward Earth
c. from material in the solar system that came together.
d. in the same way as Earth was formed

_____ **8.** Ocean tides are the result of
a. the rotation of the Earth.
b. the sun's gravitational pull on Earth.
c. changes in Earth's orbital position around the sun.
d. differences in both the sun's and moon's gravitational pull on Earth.

_____ **9.** The four terrestrial planets are so called because they
a. are the nearest planets to Earth.
b. were all once part of Earth.
c. are similar in structure to Earth.
d. can all be seen from Earth without a telescope.

Chapter Test B

Name _____ Class _____ Date _____

_____ **10.** Asteroids are mainly found
a. in the asteroid belt beyond Mars.
b. in orbit around Jupiter.
c. throughout the solar system.
d. beyond the farthest known planet.

_____ **11.** Which of the gas giants has the largest diameter?
a. Jupiter   **b.** Uranus   **c.** Saturn   **d.** Neptune

_____ **12.** Comets are made mostly of
a. iron.   **b.** ice and rock.
c. hydrogen and helium.   **d.** methane.

_____ **13.** Which of the following is a sparse sphere of comets that surrounds the sun and planets?
a. the asteroid belt   **b.** the Kuiper belt
c. the Oort cloud   **d.** none of the above

_____ **14.** According to the nebula theory, the solar system formed from
a. accretion of protoplanets.
b. a large, thin cloud of dust and gas.
c. colliding planetesimals.
d. all of the above

_____ **15.** Which of the following statements explains why the terrestrial planets are small and rocky instead of large and less dense like the gas giants?
a. The inner planets were exposed to much higher temperatures.
b. Ice-forming compounds vaporize at high temperatures.
c. Rock-forming materials can condense at high temperatures.
d. all of the above

Completion
Complete each statement on the line provided.

1. The force of gravity that the sun exerts on a planet is directed _____.

2. The beginning of the "space race" occurred when the _____ launched the first artificial satellite in 1957.

3. Because there is no _____ on the moon, any liquid water would have evaporated long ago.

4. The model of the universe in which Earth is stationary is the _____ model.

Chapter Test B

Name _____ Class _____ Date _____

5. The total lunar eclipse shown in Figure 25-1 is occurring during the _____ phase of the moon.

6. The length of a planet's day is determined by its _____.

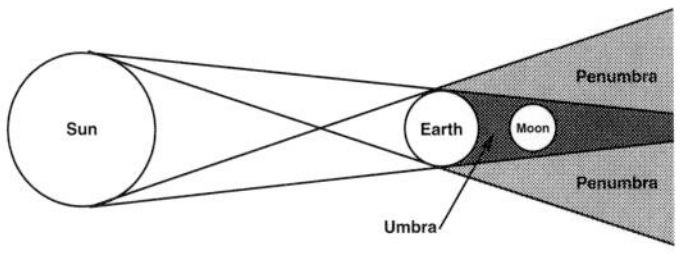

Figure 25-1

Sun   Earth   Moon   Penumbra   Penumbra   Umbra   NOT TO SCALE

7. The large, irregular objects mostly located between Mars and Jupiter are _____.

8. Icy objects that mostly travel in long, elliptical orbits around the sun are _____.

9. The great reservoir of comets beyond the Kuiper belt is called the _____.

10. The material that formed our solar system originated from a solar _____.

Short Answer
In complete sentences, write the answers to the questions on the lines provided.

1. What are the components of our solar system?
_____
_____
_____

2. Who was the first human to step onto the moon?
_____

3. What caused most craters on the moon?
_____
_____

4. What is the composition of the Kuiper belt?
_____
_____

5. What is the theoretical source of the solar nebula from which our solar system formed?
_____
_____

Chapter Test B

Name _____ Class _____ Date _____

Using Science Skills
Use the diagram to answer each question. Write the answers on a separate sheet of paper.

1. Interpreting Graphics Is the model in Figure 25-2 geocentric or heliocentric? Explain how you know.

2. Classifying In Figure 25-2, which components of the solar system are indicated by orbits 1– 9? Name each component in order from the sun, and classify each according to type.

3. Using Models Look at Figure 25-2. Where would you mark the position of the asteroid belt?

4. Applying Concepts During the time the solar system was forming, which region had sufficiently cool temperatures for ice crystals to form? Use Figure 25-2 to indicate the location.

5. Drawing Conclusions Given that Pluto is about 39.5 AU from the sun, where would you locate the Kuiper belt on Figure 25-2? What would be the location of the Oort cloud?

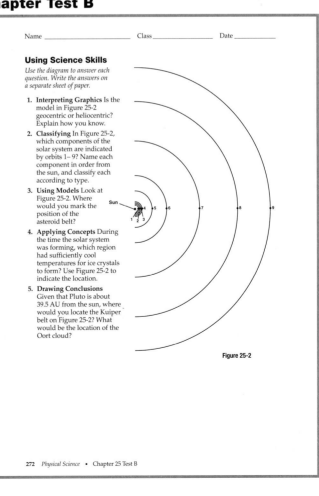

Sun   1 2 3   4   5   6   7   8   9

Figure 25-2

Chapter 25 Test A Answers

Multiple Choice

1. c	**2.** d	**3.** a	**4.** b	**5.** c	**6.** a
7. b	**8.** c	**9.** d	**10.** b	**11.** d	**12.** c
13. d	**14.** c	**15.** c			

Completion

1. average **2.** moons **3.** 100 **4.** Kuiper **5.** temperatures

Short Answer

1. Ptolemy's view was geocentric. Aristarchus' view was heliocentric. **2.** the plane of Earth's orbit **3.** A full moon occurs when the side of the moon facing Earth is fully lit by the sun, and Earth is between the sun and the moon. A new moon occurs when the moon is between the sun and Earth, and the moon's dark side faces Earth. **4.** Mars is most similar to Earth of all the planets in size, mass, and density. It has distinct seasons and shows evidence of once having a great deal of water. **5.** The weak gravity of small asteroids and impacts with other objects caused these shapes. **6.** Planetesimals grew larger because more gas condensed in the outer solar system. The gravity of these larger planetesimals could attract and capture hydrogen and helium, which were abundant.

Using Science Skills

1. Newton's first law of motion states that an object in motion will continue to move in a straight line unless acted upon by a force. A planet in orbit C would move approximately along path A if another force—gravity—was not acting on it. The planet has inertia, which carries it in direction A, but force B pulls the planet in a curved path C. The planet stays in orbit because of the balance between inertia and the gravitational pull of the sun. **2.** The planet's inertia would carry it forward in a straight-line path, such as A. Because there would be no gravitational force on the planet from the sun, the net force on the planet would be zero. As a result, there would be no change in the planet's speed or direction. **3.** Arrow B represents the gravitational force between the planet and the sun. The force acts between the center of the planet and the center of the sun, and both the center of the planet and the center of the sun lie in the orbital plane. Therefore, the force of attraction between the centers must also lie in the same plane. **4.** Saturn is not dense, but it still has mass, so inertia and gravity balance to keep Saturn in orbit. **5.** Mars; the period of the asteroid would be greater than 1.88 years because the asteroid belt is beyond the orbit of Mars, and orbital periods increase as distance from the sun increases.

Essay

1. Possible answers: Space probes, or unpiloted vehicles, are being used to photograph and measure parameters of the planets, moons, and other objects, and then transmit information back to Earth. The Hubble telescope in orbit around Earth and others telescopes provide views and information about the solar system and beyond. The space shuttle is a reusable vehicle that sends humans into orbit around Earth to do scientific research. The International Space Station is a permanent laboratory designed for research in space. **2.** Most of that material of this mass has already joined a solar-system component, such as a planet, or is already in orbit. **3.** Two moons, Ganymede and Callisto, are about the size of Mercury. Io and Europa are about the size of Earth's moon. Unlike Jupiter, Ganymede, Io, and Europa have metal cores and rocky mantles. Io is the most volcanically active body in the solar system. Europa has an icy crust that appears to rest on a liquid-water ocean. Ganymede and Callisto are covered with ice.

4. Comets are dusty pieces of ice and rock that have no tails in the regions of space far from the sun. Comets travel in highly elliptical orbits around the sun. A comet develops two tails as it approaches the sun. The bluish tail is an ion tail comprised of charged gas particles pushed away from the comet by the solar wind. The dust tail is white and is produced by dust that is pushed away from the sun by photons. The ion tail of a comet can be millions of kilometers long and always faces away from the sun. **5.** Any theory must explain the following: 1) why the planets lie in a single plane, 2) why all the planets orbit the sun in a single direction, and 3) the difference in size and composition between the terrestrial planets and the gas giants. The nebular theory satisfies all three criteria.

Chapter 25 Test B Answers

Multiple Choice

1. b	**2.** a	**3.** c	**4.** b	**5.** d	**6.** b
7. a	**8.** d	**9.** c	**10.** a	**11.** a	**12.** b
13. c	**14.** d	**15.** d			

Completion

1. toward the sun **2.** Soviet Union **3.** atmosphere **4.** geocentric **5.** full moon **6.** period of rotation **7.** asteroids **8.** comets **9.** Oort cloud **10.** nebula

Short Answer

1. the sun, planets and their moons, and a variety of smaller objects, such as asteroids, meteoroids, and comets **2.** Neil Armstrong **3.** the impact of high speed meteoroids **4.** tens of thousands of objects, mostly made of ice, dust, and rock **5.** remnants of previous stars

Using Science Skills

1. Heliocentric; the sun is shown at the center, and other bodies are indicated in orbit around the sun. **2.** Planets; 1. Mercury, terrestrial; 2. Venus, terrestrial; 3. Earth, terrestrial; 4. Mars, terrestrial; 5. Jupiter, gas giant; 6. Saturn, gas giant; 7. Uranus, gas giant; 8. Neptune, gas giant; 9. Pluto, neither (can't be classified as either terrestrial or gas giant) **3.** The asteroid belt lies mostly between Mars and Jupiter, so the diagram could be marked anywhere between 4 and 5. **4.** Sufficiently cool temperatures for ice-forming compounds to condense must occur beyond Mars (4). Mars is the last terrestrial planet before the first of the gas giants, Jupiter. Cool temperatures had to exist in this region for the gas giants to form. **5.** The Kuiper belt would have to be drawn extending from Pluto (9) to a little more than twice the distance of Pluto from the sun. The Oort cloud could not be drawn on this scale because it extends out to 50,000 AU.

Chapter 26 Exploring the Universe

CHAPTER

26

Planning Guide

Use these planning tools

Easy Planner
Resource Pro
Online Lesson Planner

SECTION OBJECTIVES	STANDARDS		ACTIVITIES and LABS
	NATIONAL (See p. T18.)	STATE	
26.1 The Sun, pp. 828–833 1 block or 2 periods **26.1.1 Describe** how the sun produces energy. **26.1.2 Explain** why the sun remains stable over time. **26.1.3 Diagram** and **describe** the interior structure and atmospheric features of the sun.	A-1, A-2, B-1, B-5, B-6, D-1, D-3, G-1, G-2, G-3		**SE** Inquiry Activity: Can You Tell How Bright a Light Really Is? p. 827 L2 **SE** Quick Lab: Calculating the Sun's Power, p. 832 L2 **TE** Teacher Demo: Balanced Forces, p. 829 L2 **TE** Build Science Skills: Observing, p. 831 L2 **TE** Teacher Demo: Sunspot Model, p. 833 L2 **LM** Investigation 26A: Measuring the Sun L2
26.2 Stars, pp. 834–839 1 block or 2 periods **26.2.1 Demonstrate** how distance to a star is measured. **26.2.2 Classify** stars according to chemical and physical properties. **26.2.3 Interpret** the H-R diagram.	A-1, A-2, B-4, B-5, B-6, D-4, E-2, G-1, G-2, G-3		**SE** Exploration Lab: Investigating Parallax, pp. 856–857 L2
26.3 Life Cycles of Stars, pp. 840–844 1 block or 2 periods **26.3.1 Describe** how stars form. **26.3.2 Estimate** how long a star remains on the main sequence. **26.3.3 Predict** what happens to a star when it runs out of fuel.	B-6, D-4, G-2, G-3		**TE** Teacher Demo: Brown Dwarfs, p. 843 L2 **LM** Investigation 26B: Modeling a Neutron Star L1
26.4 Groups of Stars, pp. 846–849 1 block or 2 periods **26.4.1 Explain** how stars are distributed in space. **26.4.2 Identify** basic types of star clusters. **26.4.3 Classify** galaxies based on their appearance and composition and **describe** the four main types of galaxies.	D-3, D-4, E-2, G-1, G-2, G-3		
26.5 The Expanding Universe, pp. 852–855 1 block or 2 periods **26.5.1 Relate** Hubble's Law to red shifts and to the expansion of the universe. **26.5.2 Apply** the big bang theory to observations of the present-day universe. **26.5.3 Describe** how dark matter can be detected and **explain** the importance of its effects on the expanding universe.	A-1, A-2, B-6, D-3, D-4, G-1, G-2, G-3		**SE** Quick Lab: Modeling Expansion of the Universe, p. 855 L2

Ability Levels

L1	For students who need additional help
L2	For all students
L3	For students who need to be challenged

Components

SE	Student Edition	**GRSW**	Guided Reading	**CTB**	Computer Test Bank
TE	Teacher's Edition		& Study Workbook	**TP**	Test Prep Resources
LM	Laboratory Manual		With Math Support	**iT**	iText
PLM	Probeware Lab	**CUT**	Chapter and Unit	**DC**	Discovery Channel
	Manual		Tests		Videotapes

T	Transparencies
P	Presentation Pro
	CD-ROM
GO	Internet Resources

RESOURCES PRINT and TECHNOLOGY / SECTION ASSESSMENT

RESOURCES PRINT and TECHNOLOGY		SECTION ASSESSMENT
GRSW Section 26.1	L1	**SE** Section 26.1 Assessment, p. 833
T Chapter 26 Pretest	L2	
Section 26.1	L2	(iText) **iT** Section 26.1
P Chapter 26 Pretest	L2	
Section 26.1	L2	
SCiLINKS **GO** The sun	L2	
GRSW Section 26.2	L1	**SE** Section 26.2 Assessment, p. 839
GRSW Math Skill	L2	
T Section 26.2	L2	(iText) **iT** Section 26.2
P Section 26.2	L2	
PLANETDIARY GO Astronomy	L2	
GRSW Section 26.3	L1	**SE** Section 26.3 Assessment, p. 844
T Section 26.3	L2	
P Section 26.3	L2	(iText) **iT** Section 26.3
SCIENCE NEWS GO Stars, galaxies, and the universe	L2	
GRSW Section 26.4	L1	**SE** Section 26.4 Assessment, p. 849
DC Measuring Up to Space	L2	(iText) **iT** Section 26.4
T Section 26.4	L2	
P Section 26.4	L2	
GRSW Section 26.5	L1	**SE** Section 26.5 Assessment, p. 855
T Section 26.5	L2	
P Section 26.5	L2	(iText) **iT** Section 26.5

Go Online

Go online for these Internet resources.

PHSchool.com
Web Code: cca-3260

SCIENCE NEWS
Web Code: cce-3263

NSTA *SCiLINKS*
Web Code: ccn-3261

PLANETDIARY
Web Code: ccc-3262

Materials for Activities and Labs

Quantities for each group

STUDENT EDITION

Inquiry Activity, p. 827
2 flashlights of different brightnesses

Quick Lab, p. 832
portable socket with clear light bulb, paraffin-block photometer, meter stick, calculator

Quick Lab, p. 855
large, wide rubber band that has been cut open; pen; meter stick

Exploration Lab, pp. 856–857
unlined paper, tape, marker, pencil, meter stick, index card, graph paper

TEACHER'S EDITION

Teacher Demo, p. 829
2 identical rubber balls with hollow centers, small nail

Build Science Skills, p. 831
telescope or pair of binoculars, 25-cm by 25-cm piece of cardboard

Teacher Demo, p. 833
iron filings, horseshoe magnet, paper plate

Teacher Demo, p. 843
dark clay, pencil, string, aluminum foil, flashlight

Build Science Skills, p. 850
modeling clay, metric ruler

Chapter Assessment

CHAPTER ASSESSMENT

SE Chapter Assessment, pp. 859–860
CUT Chapter 26 Test A, B
CTB Chapter 26
iT Chapter 26
PHSchool.com GO
Web Code: cca-3260

STANDARDIZED TEST PREP

SE Chapter 26, p. 861
TP Diagnose and Prescribe

iText

iText—interactive textbook with assessment at PHSchool.com

Name_____ Class_____ Date_____ M T W T F

LESSON PLAN 26.1

The Sun

Time
2 periods
1 block

Section Objectives

■ **26.1.1 Describe** how the sun produces energy.

■ **26.1.2 Explain** why the sun remains stable over time.

■ **26.1.3 Diagram** and **describe** the interior structure and atmospheric features of the sun.

Vocabulary core • radiation zone • convection zone • photosphere • chromosphere • corona • solar wind • sunspots • prominences • solar flare

Local Standards

1 FOCUS

Build Vocabulary: Word Forms
Ask students questions to help them relate familiar meanings of vocabulary terms to the section content. **L2**

Targeted Resources
❑ Transparency: Chapter 26 Pretest
❑ Transparency: Interest Grabber 26.1
❑ Transparency: Reading Strategy 26.1

2 INSTRUCT

Use Visuals: Figure 2
Write equations on the board to help students visualize nuclear fusion. Ask students to explain the process in their own words. **L1**

Build Reading Literacy: Think Aloud
Verbalize your thoughts as you read aloud the text on p. 830. This will help students to recognize the cognitive and metacognitive strategies used to promote comprehension. **L1**

Quick Lab: Calculating the Sun's Power
Students use a photometer to find the power of a light bulb, then use the known power of the light bulb to estimate the sun's power. **L2**

Address Misconceptions
Have students study Figures 6 and 7 so that they can see and describe the visible features of the sun's surface. **L2**

Teacher Demo: Sunspot Model
Use iron filings and a magnet to help students observe the association between sunspots and solar magnetic fields. **L2**

For Enrichment
Students can design an experiment using bulbs of various powers and the photometer to determine the relationship between apparent brightness and distance. **L3**

Targeted Resources
❑ Transparency: Figure 3: Pressure vs. Gravity in the Sun
❑ Transparency: Figure 4: The Layers of the Sun
❑ GRSW Section 26.1
❑ **NSTA** *sci*$_{LINKS}$ The sun

3 ASSESS

Reteach
Using Figure 4 as a guide, draw the interior structure and atmosphere of the sun on the board. As you draw each layer, orally summarize its characteristics. **L1**

Evaluate Understanding
Have students take turns describing a fact that they have learned about one of the vocabulary words in this section. **L2**

Targeted Resources
❑ **PHSchool.com** Online Section 26.1 Assessment
❑ iText Section 26.1

Transparencies

414 **Chapter 26 Pretest**

1. Describe the process of nuclear fusion.

2. True or False: Plasmas are ionized, electrically charged gases.

3. How does the intensity of light change with distance from the source?
   a. stays the same
   b. increases
   c. decreases
   d. doubles

4. How did the solar system form?

5. Which type of electromagnetic wave has the longest wavelength? The shortest?

ANSWERS
1. Less massive nuclei combine to form more massive nuclei.
2. True
3. c
4. The solar system formed from a large, thin cloud of dust and gas called a solar nebula.
5. radio waves; gamma rays

Transparencies

415 **Chapter 26 Pretest** (continued)

6. How fast does light move in a vacuum?

7. The mass of the sun is 1.99×10^{30} kg. The mass of the star Achernar is 1.29×10^{31} kg. Achernar is how many times more massive than the sun?

8. True or False: In a fluid acted on by gravity, such as the ocean, pressure increases with depth.

9. As a source of sound recedes, the frequency of sound _____

ANSWERS
6. 3×10^8 m/s
7. 6.5
8. True
9. decreases

Transparencies

416 **Section 26.1 Interest Grabber**

Is the Sun a Star?

A star is a large, glowing ball of gas in space that generates energy through nuclear fusion reactions such as the conversion of hydrogen into helium. In this section, you will learn that the sun is composed mostly of hydrogen and helium gas.

1. Based on the information above, do you think the sun is a star? Explain your reasoning.

2. If the sun is a star, why is it so much brighter than the stars you see at night?

ANSWERS
1. Students should conclude that the sun is a star because it is large, it gives off energy (light and heat), and it has the raw materials needed for fusion. Some students may suggest that more information is needed because you cannot tell just from the sun's appearance how far away it is (and therefore how large it is). It is also possible that the sun has the fuel needed for fusion but is not producing its energy from fusion.
2. The sun is much brighter because it is much closer to Earth than the stars seen at night.

Transparencies

417 **Section 26.1 Reading Strategy**

Building Vocabulary

Vocabulary Term	Definition
Core	a. ?
Radiation zone	b. ?
Convection zone	c. ?

ANSWERS
a. The central region of the sun where fusion occurs
b. A region of highly compressed gas where energy is transferred mainly by radiation
c. The outer layer of the sun's interior, where energy is transferred mainly by convection

Transparencies

418 Figure 3 Pressure vs. Gravity in the Sun

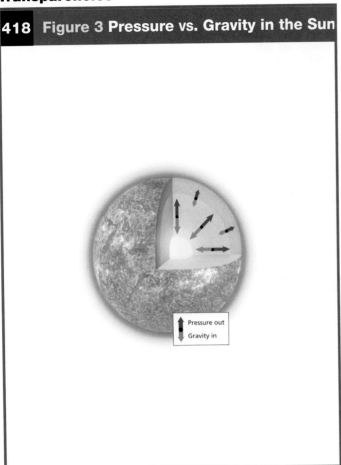

Pressure out
Gravity in

Transparencies

419 Figure 4 The Layers of the Sun

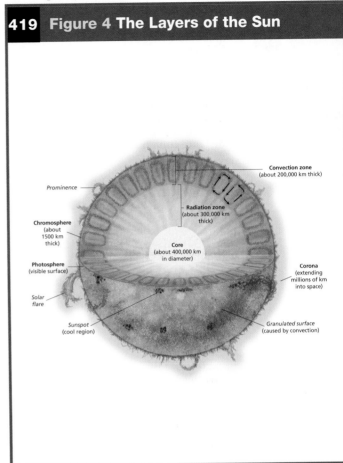

Convection zone
(about 200,000 km thick)

Prominence

Radiation zone
(about 300,000 km thick)

Chromosphere
(about 1500 km thick)

Core
(about 400,000 km in diameter)

Photosphere
(visible surface)

Corona
(extending millions of km into space)

Solar flare

Sunspot
(cool region)

Granulated surface
(caused by convection)

Guided Reading and Study Workbook

Name _____ Class _____ Date _____

Chapter 26 Exploring the Universe

Section 26.1 The Sun
(pages 828–833)

This section describes how the sun produces energy. It also describes the sun's interior and atmosphere.

Reading Strategy (page 828)

Build Vocabulary Copy the table on a separate sheet of paper and add more lines as needed. As you read, write a definition of each vocabulary term in your own words. For more information on this Reading Strategy, see the **Reading and Study Skills** in the **Skills and Reference Handbook** at the end of your textbook.

The Sun	
Vocabulary Term	**Definition**
Core	The central region of the sun where fusion occurs
Radiation zone	A region of highly compressed gas where energy is transferred mainly by radiation
Convection zone	The outer layer of the sun's interior, where energy is transferred mainly by convection

Energy from the Sun (pages 828–829)

1. The sun gives off a large amount of energy in the form of ____electromagnetic____ radiation.

2. Circle the letter of each sentence that is true about nuclear fusion in the sun.
   - a. Less massive nuclei combine into more massive nuclei.
   - b. The end product of fusion is hydrogen.
   - c. Fusion is a type of chemical reaction.
   - d. Hydrogen nuclei fuse into helium nuclei.

Forces in Balance (page 829)

3. For the sun to be stable, inward and outward forces within it must be in ____equilibrium or balance____.

4. Is the following sentence true or false? The sun remains stable because the inward pull of gravity balances the outward push of thermal pressure from nuclear fission. ____false____

The Sun's Interior (pages 830–831)

5. Circle the letter of each layer of the sun's interior.
   - a. the radiation zone
   - b. the photosphere
   - c. the convection zone
   - d. the core

Guided Reading and Study Workbook

Name _____ Class _____ Date _____

Chapter 26 Exploring the Universe

6. Circle the letter of each way that energy moves through the sun.
   - a. gravity
   - b. convection
   - c. radiation
   - d. nuclear fusion

7. List the layers of the sun's interior shown on the diagram.

a. (about 200,000 km thick)
b. (about 300,000 km thick)
c. (about 400,000 km in diameter)

a. ____Convection zone____
b. ____Radiation zone____
c. ____Core____

The Sun's Atmosphere (page 831)

8. Circle the letter of each layer of the sun's atmosphere.
   - a. photosphere
   - b. chromosphere
   - c. corona
   - d. core

9. When can the corona be seen? ____The corona is usually seen only during a total solar eclipse.____

Features of the Sun's Atmosphere (pages 832–833)

Match each description to a feature of the sun's atmosphere.

Description	Feature of Sun's Atmosphere
__b__ 10. Spectacular features of the sun's atmosphere that occur near sunspots	a. solar flares
__c__ 11. Areas of gas in the atmosphere that are cooler than surrounding areas	b. prominences
__a__ 12. Sudden releases of energy that produce X-rays and hurl charged particles into space	c. sunspots

LESSON PLAN 26.2

Stars

Section Objectives

- **26.2.1 Demonstrate** how distance to a star is measured.
- **26.2.2 Classify** stars according to chemical and physical properties.
- **26.2.3 Interpret** the H-R diagram.

Vocabulary star • light-year • parallax • apparent brightness • absolute brightness • absorption lines • H-R diagram • main sequence • supergiants • giants • white dwarf

Local Standards

---

1 FOCUS

Build Vocabulary: : Compare/Contrast Tables

Have students make tables comparing and contrasting groups of vocabulary terms for this section. **L2**

Targeted Resources
- ❏ Transparency: Interest Grabber 26.2
- ❏ Transparency: Reading Strategy 26.2

---

2 INSTRUCT

Build Reading Literacy: Predict

Ask students to predict which color indicates the hottest star, then read the text to see if their predictions were correct. **L1**

Build Math Skills: Conversion Factors

Have students convert the surface temperatures of various stars from kelvins to degrees Celsius. **L1**

Address Misconceptions

Have students read The Light-Year on p. 834 to help them understand that a light-year is a unit of measure, rather than a unit of time. **L2**

Build Science Skills: Communicating Results

Have students research and write brief reports about how scientists use the Stefan-Boltzmann Law. **L2**

Integrate Chemistry

Ask students how it is possible that two stars can have a similar composition, but radiate different spectra. **L2**

Use Community Resources

Invite a local astronomer to discuss spectral types with the class. **L2**

Targeted Resources
- ❏ Transparency: Figure 9: Parallax
- ❏ Transparency: Figure 13: H-R Diagram
- ❏ GRSW Section 26.2

---

3 ASSESS

Reteach

Use graphics to emphasize how the absolute brightness of a star depends on its surface temperature and its size. **L1**

Evaluate Understanding

Provide students with the temperature, color, absolute brightness, and star type for a set of stars. Then, have students construct their own H-R diagrams. **L2**

Targeted Resources
- ❏ **PHSchool.com** Online Section 26.2 Assessment
- ❏ iText Section 26.2

Section 26.2 Program Resources

Transparencies

420 **Section 26.2 Interest Grabber**

Classification of Stars

Have you ever looked at the stars and realized that not all stars are white? Stars can be red, orange, yellow, white, or blue. Stars are classified according to their surface temperature, which determines each star's color. Use the data in the table to help you answer the questions below.

Surface Temperature (K)	Color
25,000 and greater	Blue
11,000–25,000	Blue-white
7500–11,000	White
6000–7500	Yellow-white
5000–6000	Yellow
3500–5000	Orange
3000–3500	Red

1. In the last section, you learned that the surface temperature of the sun is 5800 K. What color is the sun?

2. Sirius, the brightest star in the night sky as seen from Earth, has a surface temperature of approximately 10,000 K. What color would you expect Sirius to be?

3. Another star, Betelgeuse, is red in color. Estimate the surface temperature of Betelgeuse.

ANSWERS
1. The sun is yellow.
2. Sirius is white.
3. The surface temperature of Betelgeuse is between 3000 K and 3500 K.

Transparencies

421 **Section 26.2 Reading Strategy**

Using Prior Knowledge

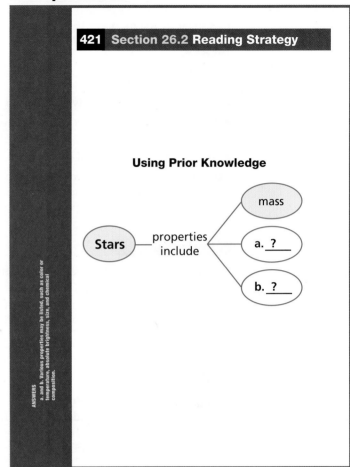

ANSWERS
a. and b. Various properties may be listed, such as color or temperature, absolute brightness, size, and chemical composition.

Transparencies

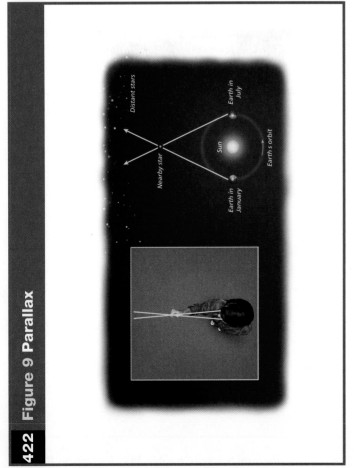

422 **Figure 9 Parallax**

Transparencies

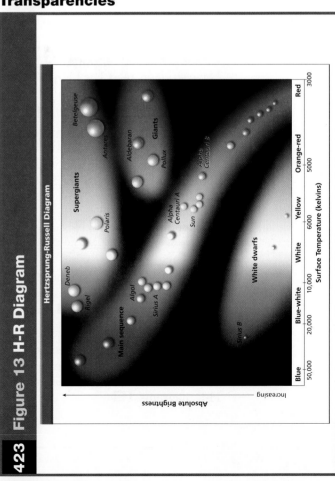

423 **Figure 13 H-R Diagram**

578

Name _____ Class _____ Date _____

Chapter 26   Exploring the Universe

Section 26.2 Stars
(pages 834–839)

This section discusses how scientists classify stars. It also describes other important properties of stars.

Reading Strategy (page 834)

Using Prior Knowledge Add what you already know about stars to the concept map. After you read, complete your concept map, adding more ovals as needed. For more information on this Reading Strategy, see the **Reading and Study Skills** in the **Skills and Reference Handbook** at the end of your textbook.

Distances to the Stars (pages 834–836)

1. Circle the letter of each sentence that is true about a light-year.
   a. It is a typical unit of measure for distances on Earth.
   (b.) It is a distance of about 9.5 trillion kilometers.
   (c.) It is the distance that light travels in a vacuum in a year.
   d. It is a unit of time.

2. Is the following sentence true or false? Parallax is the apparent change in position of an object with respect to a distant background. _____true_____

3. Astronomers measure the parallax of a nearby star to determine its _____distance_____.

Properties of Stars (pages 836–837)

4. Circle the letter of each property that astronomers use to classify stars.
   (a.) brightness   b. distance
   (c.) color   (d.) size

5. Is the following sentence true or false? The brightness of a star as it appears from Earth is called its absolute brightness. _____false_____

6. A star's _____absorption lines_____ can be used to identify different elements in the star.

Name _____ Class _____ Date _____

Chapter 26   Exploring the Universe

7. Describe the chemical makeup of most stars. Hydrogen and helium combine to make up 96 to 99.9 percent of the mass of most stars.

The Hertzprung-Russell Diagram (pages 838–839)

8. Circle the letter of each way that Hertzprung-Russell (H-R) diagrams might be used.
   (a.) to study sizes of stars
   b. to study distant planets
   (c.) to determine a star's absolute brightness
   (d.) to determine a star's surface temperature or color

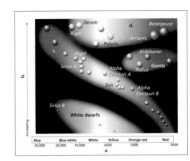

9. Provide labels for each of the letters shown on the H-R diagram above.
   a. ____Surface temperature or color____   b. ____Absolute brightness____
   c. ____Main sequence____   d. ____Supergiants____

10. Circle the letter of each sentence that is true about supergiants.
    (a.) They are found at the upper right of the H-R diagram.
    (b.) They are much brighter than main sequence stars of the same temperature.
    (c.) They are 100 to 1000 times the diameter of the sun.
    d. They are smaller and fainter than giants.

11. How does the brightness of white dwarfs compare to the brightness of main sequence stars? White dwarfs are dimmer than main sequence stars of the same temperature.

LESSON PLAN 26.3

Life Cycles of Stars

Time
2 periods
1 block

Section Objectives

- **26.3.1 Describe** how stars form.
- **26.3.2 Estimate** how long a star remains on the main sequence.
- **26.3.3 Predict** what happens to a star when it runs out of fuel.

Vocabulary nebula • protostar • planetary nebula • supernova • neutron star • pulsar • black hole

Local Standards

---

1 FOCUS

Build Vocabulary: Latin Plural Forms
Have students look up the plural forms of the vocabulary words *nebula* and *nova*. **L2**

Targeted Resources
❏ Transparency: Interest Grabber 26.3
❏ Transparency: Reading Strategy 26.3

---

2 INSTRUCT

Build Reading Literacy: KWL
Have students make and fill in a chart with columns labeled What I Know, What I Want to Know, and What I Learned. **L1**

Use Visuals: Figure 19
Have students examine Figure 19, then ask from where the beams of radiation originate. Ask students why we detect pulses on Earth. **L1**

Address Misconceptions
Tell students that stars do not last forever, and that all star's eventually die. **L2**

Build Science Skills: Classifying
Have students locate on the periodic table the most abundant elements found in stars, and then discuss what these elements have in common. **L2**

Integrate Physics
Have students work in groups to diagram the processes of fission and fusion. **L2**

Teacher Demo: Brown Dwarfs
Shine a flashlight on a model of a star and brown dwarf so that students can observe how astronomers detect a brown dwarf by observing the effect it has on a star's moon. **L2**

Targeted Resources
❏ Transparency: Figure 17: Stellar Evolution
❏ GRSW Section 26.3

---

3 ASSESS

Reteach
Use spectra to illustrate the different temperatures and compositions of high-mass and low-mass stars. **L1**

Evaluate Understanding
Have students diagram the life cycle of a massive star, using captions to explain the stages of stellar evolution. **L2**

Targeted Resources
❏ **PHSchool.com** Online Section 26.3 Assessment
❏ iText Section 26.3

424 Section 26.3 Interest Grabber

When Stars Run Out of Hydrogen Fuel

What happens when a star uses up its hydrogen fuel? The star shrinks because the force of gravity is now greater than the outward pressure in the star. As the star collapses, pressure increases. The star stops collapsing when the outward pressure once again balances the inward force of gravity.

The collapse of a star is similar to the shrinking of a balloon when the balloon is cooled. Use the figure to answer the questions below.

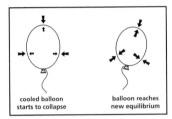

cooled balloon starts to collapse

balloon reaches new equilibrium

1. In the diagram on the left, pressure inside the balloon decreased because the balloon was cooled. Explain why the balloon started collapsing.

2. Explain why the balloon stopped collapsing in the diagram on the right.

ANSWERS
1. Pressure inside the balloon was less than the outside pressure, so there was a net inward force that caused the balloon to start collapsing.
2. The inside and outside pressures were equal, so there was no net force, and the balloon stopped collapsing.

425 Section 26.3 Reading Strategy

Sequencing

Evolution of a Low-Mass Star

Main sequence → a. _?_ → b. _?_

ANSWERS
a. Red giant
b. Planetary nebula, white dwarf, black dwarf

Program Resources Section 26.3

Figure 17 Stellar Evolution

426

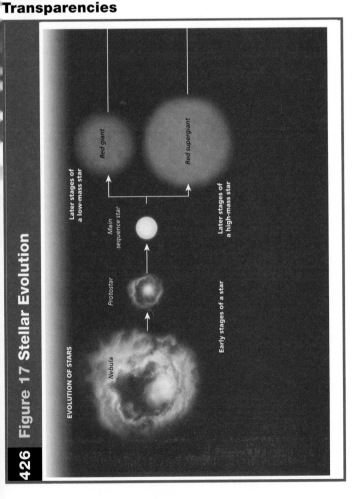

EVOLUTION OF STARS

Nebula

Protostar

Main sequence star

Later stages of a low-mass star

Red giant

Red supergiant

Later stages of a high-mass star

Early stages of a star

Figure 17 Stellar Evolution (continued)

427

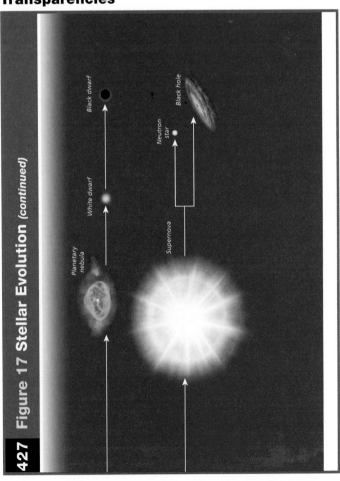

Planetary nebula

White dwarf

Black dwarf

Supernova

Neutron star

Black hole

Guided Reading and Study Workbook

Name _____ Class _____ Date _____

Chapter 26   Exploring the Universe

Section 26.3 Life Cycles of Stars
(pages 840–844)

This section explains how stars form, their adult stages, and how they die.

Reading Strategy (page 840)

Sequencing Copy the flowchart on a separate sheet of paper. As you read, extend and complete it to show how a low-mass star evolves. For more information on this Reading Strategy, see the **Reading and Study Skills** in the **Skills and Reference Handbook** at the end of your textbook.

Evolution of a Low-Mass Star

Main sequence	→	Red giant	→	Planetary nebula

Extended answers include white dwarf and black dwarf

How Stars Form (pages 840–841)

1. A large cloud of dust and gas spread out over a large volume of space is called a(n) _____nebula_____.

2. Circle the letter of each sentence that is true about a protostar.
   a. Nuclear fusion is taking place within it.
   b. It has enough mass to form a star.
   c. Its internal pressure and temperature continue to rise as it contracts.
   d. It is a contracting cloud of dust and gas.

3. Describe how a star is formed. A star is formed when a contracting cloud of gas and dust becomes so dense and hot that nuclear fusion begins.

Adult Stars (page 841)

4. A star's _____mass_____ determines the star's place on the main sequence and how long it will stay there.

5. Circle the letter of each true sentence about adult main-sequence stars.
   a. High-mass stars become the bluest and brightest main-sequence stars.
   b. Low-mass stars are usually short-lived.
   c. Yellow stars like the sun are in the middle of the main sequence.
   d. Red stars are the hottest and brightest of all visible stars.

The Death of a Star (pages 842–844)

6. The core of a star starts to shrink when the core begins to run out of _____hydrogen (or fuel)_____.

Physical Science Guided Reading and Study Workbook • Chapter 26 **257**

Guided Reading and Study Workbook

Name _____ Class _____ Date _____

Chapter 26   Exploring the Universe

7. Name three possible end stages of a star.
   a. _White dwarf or black dwarf_ b. _Neutron star_ c. _Black hole_

8. Is the following sentence true or false? The final stages of a star's life depend on its mass. _____true_____

9. Circle the letter of each sentence that is true about the death of low-mass and medium-mass stars.
   a. The dying stars are called planetary nebulas.
   b. They remain in the giant stage until their supplies of helium and hydrogen are gone and there are no other elements to fuse.
   c. The energy coming from the stars' interiors decreases and the stars eventually collapse.
   d. The cores of the stars shrink and only their atmospheres remain.

10. The glowing cloud of gas that surrounds a dying low- or medium-mass star is called a(n) _____planetary nebula_____.

11. List the stages in the evolution of a low-mass star shown in the diagram below.

a. _____Nebula_____	b. _____Protostar_____
c. _Main sequence star_	d. _Planetary nebula_
e. _____White dwarf_____	f. _____Black dwarf_____

12. Is the following sentence true or false? A high-mass star dies quickly because it consumes fuel rapidly. _____true_____

13. An explosion so brilliant that a dying high-mass star becomes more brilliant than an entire galaxy is called a(n) _____supernova_____.

Match each final stage of a high-mass star to its correct description.

	Description	Final Stage of a High-Mass Star
_b_	14. Surface gravity is so great that nothing can escape from it	a. pulsar
_a_	15. A spinning neutron star that gives off strong pulses of radio waves	b. black hole
_a or c_	16. The remnant of a high-mass star that has exploded as a supernova, which begins to spin more and more rapidly as it contracts	c. neutron star

258 *Physical Science* Guided Reading and Study Workbook • Chapter 26

LESSON PLAN 26.4

Groups of Stars

Time
2 periods
1 block

Section Objectives

- **26.4.1 Explain** how stars are distributed in space.
- **26.4.2 Identify** basic types of star clusters.
- **26.4.3 Classify** galaxies based on their appearance and composition and **describe** the four main types of galaxies.

Vocabulary constellation • star system • binary star • globular cluster • galaxy • spiral galaxies • barred-spiral galaxies • elliptical galaxies • irregular galaxies • quasars

Local Standards

1 FOCUS

Build Vocabulary: Concept Maps

Have students construct two concept maps—one showing the relationships among star clusters, and the other showing the relationships among galaxies. **L2**

Targeted Resources

❑ Transparency: Interest Grabber 26.4
❑ Transparency: Reading Strategy 26.4

2 INSTRUCT

Build Reading Literacy: Active Comprehension

Read aloud the first paragraph under the heading Star Clusters. Ask what more students would like to know about young star clusters. **L1**

Use Visuals: Figure 22

Ask students how a barred-spiral galaxy differs from a spiral galaxy. Then, ask how an elliptical galaxy differs from an irregular galaxy. **L1**

Address Misconceptions

Emphasize to students that not all stars are found alone in space. Ask what percentage of stars would be members of groups of two or more stars if all of the stars in the sky were visible. **L2**

Build Science Skills: Using Models

Have students work in pairs to devise models of star clusters. **L2**

Build Science Skills: Predicting

Ask students why they think that ancient Population II stars contain much lower levels of heavy elements than do young Population I stars. **L2**

Targeted Resources

❑ Transparency: Figure 23: The Milky Way
❑ GRSW Section 26.4

3 ASSESS

Reteach

Use the list of vocabulary words to summarize the characteristics of star systems, star clusters, and galaxies. **L1**

Evaluate Understanding

Have each student write a quiz question on a slip of paper. Have students take turns choosing one of the slips of paper from a box and answering the question. **L2**

Targeted Resources

❑ **PHSchool.com** Online Section 26.4 Assessment
❑ iText Section 26.4

Transparencies

428 **Section 26.4 Interest Grabber**

Constellations

Constellations are groups of stars that appear to form a pattern when seen from Earth. The ancient Greeks named 48 constellations, many of them after mythological characters or creatures. Today there are 88 named constellations that cover the entire sky. Most of the additional constellations cover Southern Hemisphere stars that could not be seen by the Greeks because they were never above the horizon in Greece.

Draco

1. The constellation Draco, or the dragon, appears low in north in the early evening sky during the winter months in the Northern Hemisphere. Other constellations are only visible at certain times of the year. Why do the positions of constellations change throughout the year and in the course of a single night?

2. List some other constellations you are familiar with.

Transparencies

429 **Section 26.4 Reading Strategy**

Comparing and Contrasting

Cluster Type	Appearance	Age and Type of Stars
Open cluster	a. ___?___	b. ___?___
c. ___?___	d. ___?___	Bright, young stars
e. ___?___	Spherical, densely packed	f. ___?___

Transparencies

430 **Figure 23 The Milky Way**

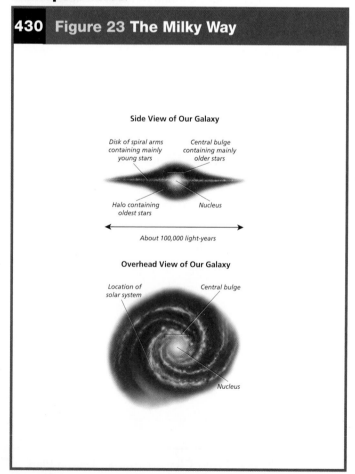

Side View of Our Galaxy

Disk of spiral arms containing mainly young stars

Central bulge containing mainly older stars

Halo containing oldest stars

Nucleus

About 100,000 light-years

Overhead View of Our Galaxy

Location of solar system

Central bulge

Nucleus

Name _____ Class _____ Date _____

Section 26.4 Groups of Stars
(pages 846–849)

This section describes star systems, star clusters, and galaxies.

Reading Strategy (page 846)

Comparing and Contrasting After you read, compare types of star clusters by completing the table. For more information on this Reading Strategy, see the **Reading and Study Skills** in the **Skills and Reference Handbook** at the end of your textbook.

Types of Star Clusters		
Cluster Type	Appearance	Age and Type of Stars
Open cluster	Disorganized, loose appearance	Bright supergiants and other young stars, also gas and dust clouds
Associations	Larger and more spread out than an open cluster	Bright, young stars
Globular cluster	Spherical, densely packed	Older stars, generally no bright blue stars

1. A group of stars that seems to form a pattern as seen from Earth is called a(n) ____constellation____ .

2. Is the following sentence true or false? Constellations are important to astronomy because they help to form a map of the sky. ____true____

Star Systems (pages 846–847)

3. A group of two or more stars that are held together by gravity is called a(n) ____star system____ .

4. Is the following sentence true or false? Astronomers have concluded that more than half of all stars are members of groups of two or more stars. ____true____

5. A star system with two stars is called a(n) ____binary star____ .

Star Clusters (page 847)

Match each basic kind of star cluster to its description.

Description	Star Cluster
__b__ 6. A loose grouping of no more than a few thousand stars that are well spread out	a. globular cluster
__c__ 7. Loose groupings of bright, young stars	b. open cluster
__a__ 8. A large group of older stars	c. associations

Name _____ Class _____ Date _____

9. Is the following sentence true or false? Astronomers estimate that the oldest globular clusters are at least 20 billion years old. ____false____

Galaxies (pages 848–849)

10. A huge group of individual stars, star systems, star clusters, dust, and gas bound together by gravity is called a(n) ____galaxy____ .

11. Our galaxy is called the ____Milky Way____ .

12. Galaxies that have a bulge of stars at the center with arms extending outward like a pinwheel are called ____spiral galaxies____ .

13. Is the following sentence true or false? The arms of spiral galaxies contain very little gas and dust. ____false____

14. A spiral galaxy that has a bar through the center with the arms extending outward from the bar on either side is called a(n) ____barred-spiral galaxy____ .

15. Circle the letter of each sentence that is true about elliptical galaxies.
    a. They are spherical or oval shaped.
    b. They typically have lots of dust and gas.
    c. They come in a wide range of sizes.
    d. They usually contain only old stars.

16. A(n) ____irregular____ galaxy has a disorganized appearance and is typically smaller than other types of galaxies.

Match each type of galaxy to its description.

Description	Galaxy
__b__ 17. Spherical or oval, no spiral arms, and usually contains only old stars	a. barred-spiral galaxy
__c__ 18. Bulge of stars at the center with arms extending outward like a pinwheel	b. elliptical galaxy
__d__ 19. Composed of many young stars, comes in many shapes, and has a disorganized appearance	c. spiral galaxy
__a__ 20. Has a bar through the center with arms extending outward from the bar on either side	d. irregular galaxy

21. Is the following sentence true or false? The Milky Way appears as a band from Earth because we are looking at it edgewise. ____true____

22. The enormously bright centers of distant galaxies are called ____quasars____ .

Name_____ Class_____ Date_____ M T W T F

LESSON PLAN 26.5

The Expanding Universe

Time
2 periods
1 block

Section Objectives

Local Standards

- **26.5.1 Relate** Hubble's Law to red shifts and to the expansion of the universe.
- **26.5.2 Apply** the big bang theory to observations of the present-day universe.
- **26.5.3 Describe** how dark matter can be detected and **explain** the importance of its effects on the expanding universe.

Vocabulary red shift • Hubble's Law • big bang theory • dark matter

---

1 FOCUS

Build Vocabulary: Flowchart
Have students make flowcharts showing in chronological order the sequence of events that followed the big bang. **L2**

Targeted Resources
❏ Transparency: Interest Grabber 26.5
❏ Transparency: Reading Strategy 26.5

---

2 INSTRUCT

Use Visuals: Figure 24
Using Figure 24, ask students which spectrum show a galaxy that is moving toward Earth, and which spectrum shows a galaxy that is moving away from Earth. **L1**

Build Reading Literacy: Using Context Clues
Tell students that they might learn the meanings of new terms by looking for familiar words or phrases that surround the terms. **L1**

Build Science Skills: Problem Solving
Explain that Hubble's Law can be expressed by the formula $v = H_0 d$. Ask students how to find distance when given the values of recessional velocity and Hubble's constant. **L2**

Address Misconceptions
Explain to students that all galaxies are receding from one another, and that there is no center from which the universe is expanding. **L2**

Quick Lab: Modeling Expansion of the Universe
Students will stretch a rubber band with marks on it, in order to explain why galaxies that are farther away recede faster. **L2**

Targeted Resources
❏ GRSW Section 26.5

---

3 ASSESS

Reteach
Summarize how Hubble's Law relates to the expanding universe. **L1**

Evaluate Understanding
Using Figure 26 as a guide, have students make a time line from the big bang to Earth's formation. **L2**

Targeted Resources
❏ **PHSchool.com** Online Section 26.5 Assessment
❏ iText Section 26.5

---

431 Section 26.5 Interest Grabber

Cosmology

The Greek word *kosmos* means order, harmony, or the world. In the English language, the root word *cosmos* is derived from the Greek *kosmos*.

1. In astronomy, *cosmology* is the study of the origin of the universe as it relates to the present observable structure of the universe. How does the definition of cosmology relate to the meaning of its root *kosmos*?

2. List other words that are formed from the root *cosmos*. How are they related to the meaning of the root word?

432 Section 26.5 Reading Strategy

Previewing

Questions on the Evolution of the Universe
a._____?
b._____?

Name _____ Class _____ Date _____

Chapter 26 Exploring the Universe

Section 26.5 The Expanding Universe
(pages 852–855)

This section describes Hubble's Law. It also explains the big bang theory.

Reading Strategy (page 852)

Previewing Before reading, examine Figure 26 and write at least two questions to help you understand the information in it. As you read, write answers to your questions. For more information on this Reading Strategy, see the **Reading and Study Skills** in the **Skills and Reference Handbook** at the end of your textbook.

The Evolution of the Universe
Questions on the Evolution of the Universe
Students' questions may include: What was the big bang?
What happened afterwards?
What evidence supports the big bang theory?

Hubble's Law (pages 852–853)

1. Is the following sentence true or false? The apparent change in frequency and wavelength of a wave as it moves towards or away from an observer is known as the Doppler effect. _____true_____

2. How can astronomers use the Doppler effect? _The Doppler effect can be used to_ _determine how fast stars or galaxies are approaching or moving away from Earth._

3. Circle the letter of each sentence that is true about spectrums of stars or galaxies.
   a. As a star or galaxy circles the Earth, the lines in its spectrum shift toward the middle of the spectrum.
   b. As a star moves toward Earth, the lines in its spectrum are shifted toward shorter wavelengths.
   c. As a star or galaxy moves away from Earth, the lines in its spectrum are shifted toward longer wavelengths.
   d. The greater the observed shift in spectrum, the greater the speed the star or galaxy is moving.

4. The shift in the light of a galaxy toward the red wavelengths is called a(n) _____red shift_____

5. Describe Hubble's Law. _Hubble's Law says that the speed at which a galaxy is moving_ _away is proportional to its distance from us._

6. Is the following sentence true or false? The most distant galaxies that can be seen from Earth are moving away at more than 90% of the speed of light. _____true_____

Name _____ Class _____ Date _____

Chapter 26 Exploring the Universe

7. Describe what the observed red shift in the spectra of galaxies shows. _It shows that the universe is expanding._

The Big Bang Theory (page 854)

8. Astronomers theorize that the universe came into being in an event called the _____big bang_____

9. Circle the letter of each sentence that is true according to the big bang theory.
   a. The matter and energy in the universe was once concentrated in a very hot region smaller than a sentence period.
   b. The universe began billions of years ago with an enormous explosion.
   c. The universe came into existence in an instant.
   d. The matter and energy in the universe has taken billions of years to form.

10. After the big bang, it is theorized that the universe _____expanded quickly and cooled down_____.

11. How large was the universe when the sun and solar system formed? _It was about two thirds of its present size._

12. Circle the letter of each sentence that gives evidence that supports the big bang theory.
   a. The existence of cosmic microwave background radiation.
   b. The red shift in the spectra of distant galaxies.
   c. The fact that the sun is about 20 billion years old.
   d. The pulling of atoms together into gas clouds by gravity.

13. Recent measurements of the microwave background radiation have led astronomers to estimate that the universe is _____13.7 billion years old_____.

Continued Expansion (page 855)

14. Matter that does not give off radiation is known as _____dark matter_____

15. Circle the letter of each sentence that is true about dark matter.
   a. Astronomers currently don't know what it is or how it is distributed.
   b. It cannot be seen directly.
   c. It can be measured using the Doppler effect.
   d. It can be detected by observing how its gravity affects visible matter.

16. Why is it significant that the galaxies contain as much as ten times more dark matter than visible matter? _Without this amount of dark matter, there would not_ _be enough gravitational force to keep galaxies from flying apart._

Name _____ Class _____ Date _____

Chapter 26 Exploring the Universe

WordWise

Answer the questions by writing the correct vocabulary terms from the chapter in the blanks. Use the circled letter in each word to find the hidden word.

Clues	Vocabulary Terms
What is the central region of the sun?	ⓒ o r e
What is the surface layer of the sun?	p ⓗ o t o s p h e r e
What is a dramatic eruption on the sun that produces X-rays and hurls charged particles into space at nearly the speed of light?	s o l a ⓡ f l a r e
What is a contracting cloud of gas and dust with enough mass to form a star?	p r ⓞ t o s t a r
What is the diagonal band of stars on the H-R diagram?	ⓜ a i n s e q u e n c e
What is the dense remnant of a high-mass star that has exploded as a supernova?	n e u t r ⓞ n s t a r
What are the very bright stars at the upper right of the H-R diagram?	ⓢ u p e r g i a n t s
What is the apparent change in position of an object with respect to a distant background?	ⓟ a r a l l a x
What is an object whose surface gravity is so great that nothing, not even light, can escape from it?	b l a c k ⓗ o l e
What is the distance that light travels in a vacuum in a year?	l i g h t - y ⓔ a r
What is a large glowing ball of gas in space?	s t a ⓡ
What is a large cloud of gas and dust spread out over a large volume of space?	n ⓔ b u l a

Hidden Word: c h r o m o s p h e r e

Definition: _The middle layer of the sun's atmosphere, normally visible only when the brighter_ _photosphere is blocked._

Name _____ Class _____ Date _____

Chapter 26 Exploring the Universe

Calculating Distances to Stars

A star is 3.6×10^{19} kilometers from Earth. How many light-years is this?

Math Skill: Exponents

You may want to read more about this **Math Skill** in the **Skills and Reference Handbook** at the end of your textbook.

1. **Read and Understand**
   How many kilometers from Earth is the star?
   Star = 3.6×10^{19} kilometers from Earth

   What are you asked to find?
   Star = ? light-years from Earth

2. **Plan and Solve**
   Write the number of kilometers in a light-year using scientific notation.
   9.5×10^{12} kilometers

   To find the number of light-years the star is from Earth, divide its distance by the number of kilometers in a light-year. Begin by dividing 3.6 by 9.5. Round your answer to the nearest hundredth.
   0.38

   To divide numbers with exponents, subtract the exponents. What will the exponent of the answer be?
   7

   To write your answer in scientific notation, a number other than zero must be in the ones place. Move the decimal one place to the right and subtract one from the exponent. How many light-years is the star from Earth?
   3.8×10^6 light-years

3. **Look Back and Check**
   Is your answer reasonable?
   To check your answer, multiply the number of light-years away the star is by the number of kilometers in a light-year. Remember to add the exponents when you multiply. Your answer should be the distance from Earth to the star in kilometers.

   3.6×10^{19} kilometers

Math Practice

On a separate sheet of paper, solve the following problems.

1. A star is 8.6×10^{14} kilometers from Earth. How many light-years away is the star? Round your answer to the nearest tenth.
   Dividing 8.6 by 9.5 and rounding = 0.91. The exponent is 2.
   Scientific notation = 9.1×10 = 91 light-years

2. The star Proximi Centauri is about 4.3 light-years from Earth. How many kilometers from Earth is it?
   4.1×10^{13} kilometers

3. A star is 6.8×10^8 light-years from Earth. How many kilometers from Earth is the star? 6.5×10^{21} kilometers

Name _____ Class _____ Date _____

Chapter 26   Exploring the Universe

Investigating Parallax   See pages 856 and 857 in the Teacher's Edition for more information.

Exploration Lab

Astronomers use parallax to measure the distances to nearby stars. In this lab, you will investigate the effect of distance on parallax. You will observe how an object appears to move against a distant background as you look at it first through one eye, and then through the other.

Problem   How is parallax related to the distance to a star?

Materials
- unlined paper
- pencil
- index card
- tape
- meter stick
- graph paper
- marker

Skills   Measuring, Using Models

Procedure

1. Tape three sheets of unlined paper to the wall horizontally, at eye level. Use a marker to draw 11 vertical marks 5 centimeters apart on the paper, as shown in Figure 1. The marks represent a distant background against which you will view a closer star. Label the marks in multiples of five from left to right, starting with 0 and ending with 50.

2. Facing the sheets of paper, stand directly in front of the 25-cm mark. Then, use a meter stick to measure a perpendicular distance of 7 m from the mark. Move to that spot and face toward the 25-cm mark. You must remain at this position until you have finished collecting all data.

3. Have a partner hold a pencil vertically at your eye level, as shown in Figure 1. The pencil should be 1 m in front of you. Your partner should use a meter stick to measure this distance. The pencil represents a nearby star.

4. Hold an index card over your left eye and look at the pencil with your right eye. Your right eye represents Earth's position at one point in its orbit. Move your head so the pencil lines up with the mark labeled 0.

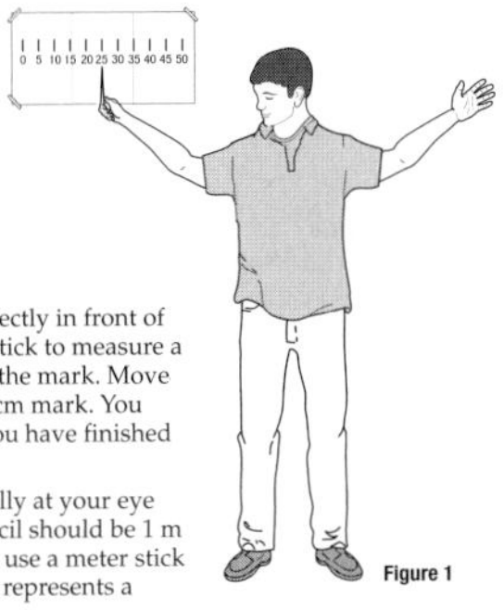

Figure 1

Name _____ Class _____ Date _____

5. Now, without moving your head, hold the index card over your right eye and look at the pencil with your left eye. Your left eye represents Earth's position at the opposite end of its orbit six months later. Note the number of the mark that lines up with the pencil. If the pencil is between two marks, estimate its position to the nearest whole number. Your partner should record this number in the appropriate place in the data table.

DATA TABLE   Sample data are shown.

Distance to Star (m)	Right Eye (cm)	Left Eye (cm)	Parallax (cm) (Difference)
1.0	0	40	40
1.5	0	15	15
2.0	0	7	7
2.5	0	5	5
3.0	0	3	3

6. To determine the parallax, subtract the right-eye measurement (zero, in this case) from the left-eye measurement. Record the parallax in the appropriate place in the data table.

7. **Predicting**   How do you and your partner think the parallax will change as your partner moves the pencil away from you? Your partner should record your prediction.

   Sample prediction: Parallax will decrease as the pencil moves.

8. Have your partner use a meter stick to move the pencil 0.5 m toward the marks. Without moving your head, cover your left eye and look at the pencil with your right eye. Your partner should record the number of the mark the pencil lines up with.

9. Without moving your head, cover your right eye and look at the pencil with your left eye. Your partner should record the number of the mark the pencil lines up with.

10. To determine the parallax, subtract the right-eye measurement from the left-eye measurement. Record the parallax in the appropriate place in the data table.

11. Repeat Steps 8 through 10 until the parallax is less than 1 cm.

12. Construct a graph of the distance to the star (pencil) against the parallax you calculated. Plot the parallax on the horizontal axis and the distance on the vertical axis.

Name _____ Class _____ Date _____

Analyze and Conclude

1. **Using Graphs**   What does your graph show is the relationship between the distance to the pencil and the pencil's parallax?

   The graph shows that as the distance increases, parallax decreases.

2. **Analyzing Data**   Was your prediction in Step 7 correct? Explain your answer.

   If students predicted that the parallax would decrease, they were correct. They should explain

   that the parallax decreases as distance increases.

3. **Drawing Conclusions**   Assume that a parallax of less than 1 cm is too small to be measured. What is the maximum distance at which the pencil would still have a parallax you can measure?

   Students should report a maximum distance of 4 to 6 m, depending on their visual acuity, the

   distance between their eyes, and the precision of their measurements.

4. **Applying Concepts**   Parallax can only be used to measure the distances to nearby stars. Why can't this method be used to find the distances to far-away stars?

   Parallax of distant stars is too small to be measured using current technology.

5. **Inferring**   Astronomers usually make two measurements of the position of a star six months apart, when Earth is at opposite sides of its orbit. How is this useful in determining the star's parallax?

   Making the measurements six months apart allows the points at which the measurements are

   made to be as far apart as possible. This allows parallax to be measured as accurately as

   possible, and thus for the greatest possible distances to be measured.

Lab Manual

Name _____ Class _____ Date _____

Chapter 26 Exploring the Universe

Investigation 26A

Measuring the Diameter of the Sun

Refer students to pages 828–833 in their textbooks for a discussion of the sun.

SKILLS FOCUS: Observing, Measuring, Calculating **CLASS TIME:** 45 minutes

Background Information

The sun is approximately 150,000,000 km from Earth. To understand how far away this is, consider the fact that light travels approximately 300,000 km/s. At this incredible speed, it takes the light from the sun a little over 8 minutes to reach Earth.

Even though the sun is very far away, it is still possible to make an accurate measurement of its size. This can be done by making two simple measurements and then setting up and solving a proportion problem. You can estimate the diameter of the sun by solving the following proportion problem.

$$\frac{\text{Diameter of sun}}{\text{Distance to sun}} = \frac{\text{Diameter of sun's image}}{\text{Distance between two cards}}$$

If you can determine three of the terms in a proportion problem, the fourth term, such as the diameter of the sun, can be solved mathematically.

In this investigation, you will construct a simple device and use it to collect data that will enable you to calculate the diameter of the sun.

Problem

What is the diameter of the sun, and how can it be determined?

Pre-Lab Discussion

Read the entire investigation. Then, work with a partner to answer the following questions.

1. **Inferring** What is the purpose of this investigation?

   The purpose is to calculate distances mathematically, using three of the four proportional terms and

   calculating for the fourth. With this method, estimation of the sun's diameter is solved

   mathematically.

2. **Calculating** To prepare for this calculation, solve for x in the following proportion problems.

   a. $\dfrac{x}{5} = \dfrac{100,000}{20}$

   $x = 25,000$

   b. $\dfrac{5}{x} = \dfrac{200,000}{50}$

   $x = 0.00125$

Physical Science Lab Manual • Investigation 26A **271**

Lab Manual

Name _____ Class _____ Date _____

3. **Inferring** Why is it important to never look directly at the sun?

   Looking directly at the sun can be very harmful to the eyes and can cause blindness because of the

   high-energy ultraviolet radiation that the sun emits.

4. **Applying Concepts** In what way is the process of proportional relationships practical for determining the diameter of the sun?

   Student answers should indicate that the image of the sun on the card is a scaled down version

   of the actual sun, so the physical relationships present in the sun are also present in the scaled

   image except that the values are smaller.

5. **Predicting** Would you expect error in the value you calculate for the sun's diameter? Explain your answer.

   All measurements will have some error.

   _____

Materials *(per group)*

2 index cards (10 cm × 15 cm)   metric ruler
drawing compass   tape
meter stick

Safety 🛡 ✂ ✋

Be careful when handling sharp instruments. Never look directly at the sun. Note all safety symbols next to the steps in the Procedure and review the meaning of each symbol by referring to the Safety Symbols on page xiii.

Procedure

Part A: Measuring Distances and Calculating Ratios

1. In Figure 1, measure the base of each of the two triangles. Record your measurements in Data Table 1.
2. Measure the altitude (distance from tip to base) of each of the two triangles. Record your measurements in Data Table 1.
3. Determine the ratio between the base of the large triangle and the base of the small triangle. Record this ratio in Data Table 1.
4. Determine the ratio between the altitude of the large triangle and the altitude of the small triangle. Record this ratio in Data Table 1.
5. Think about how these two ratios compare. In Part B of this lab, you will use a similar procedure to determine the diameter of the sun. The base of the small triangle will represent the diameter of the image of the sun on a card. The altitude of the small triangle will represent the distance between the two cards

272 *Physical Science* Lab Manual • Investigation 26A

Lab Manual

Name _____ Class _____ Date _____

in the device you will construct. The altitude of the large triangle will represent the distance from Earth to the sun. The base of the large triangle will represent the diameter of the sun, which you will determine. **CAUTION:** *Never look directly at the sun.*

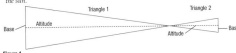

Triangle 1   Triangle 2

Base — Altitude — Altitude — Base

Figure 1

Part B: Determining the Diameter of the Sun

✂✋ 6. Using scissors, cut I-shaped slits in each card in the positions shown in Figure 2. The meter stick should be able to slide through the slits, but the slits should be small enough so that the meter stick fits snugly. **CAUTION:** *Be careful when handling sharp instruments.*

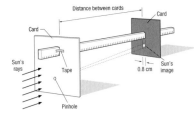

Distance between cards

Card

Card

Sun's rays

Tape

0.8 cm

Sun's image

Pinhole

Figure 2

✋ 7. With the tip of the compass, punch a pinhole in one of the cards, in the position shown in Figure 2. Tape this card to the meter stick at the 5-cm mark so that it is perpendicular to the meter stick. **CAUTION:** *Be careful when handling sharp instruments.*

8. On the other card, draw two parallel lines exactly 0.8 cm (8 mm) apart, directly above the slit, as shown in Figure 2. Slide this card onto the meter stick. Do not tape this card to the meter stick.

✋ 9. While outdoors on a sunny day, position the meter stick so that the taped card is directly facing the sun and casts a shadow over the movable card. **CAUTION:** *Never look directly at the sun.* You should be able to see a bright circle on the movable card caused by the sun's rays passing through the pinhole on the first card.

Do not attempt this investigation if it is cloudy or windy outside.

Physical Science Lab Manual • Investigation 26A **273**

Lab Manual

Name _____ Class _____ Date _____

10. The bright circle on the second card is an image of the sun. Slide the movable card until the image of the sun fits exactly between the two parallel lines you drew earlier.

11. Make sure that both cards are perpendicular to the meter stick. You will know they are perpendicular when the bright circle, the sun's image, is as close to a circle as possible. Tape the second card in place. Measure the distance between the two cards. Record all data in Data Table 2.

Observations Sample data are shown.

DATA TABLE 1

Base of small triangle (Triangle 1)	0.85 cm
Altitude of small triangle (Triangle 1)	2.90 cm
Base of large triangle (Triangle 2)	2.60 cm
Altitude of large triangle (Triangle 2)	8.90 cm
Ratio of base of large triangle to base of small triangle	3.05:1
Ratio of altitude of large triangle to altitude of small triangle	3.07:1

DATA TABLE 2

Distance between two cards (cm)	80 cm
Diameter of sun's image (cm)	0.8 cm

274 *Physical Science* Lab Manual • Investigation 26A

Name _____ Class _____ Date _____

Analysis and Conclusions

1. **Calculate** Using the formula below, calculate the diameter of the sun. Show your work.

$$\frac{\text{Diameter of sun (km)}}{\text{Distance to sun (km)}} = \frac{\text{Diameter of sun's image (cm)}}{\text{Distance between two cards (cm)}}$$

$$\frac{x \text{ km}}{150,000,000 \text{ km}} = \frac{0.8 \text{ cm}}{80 \text{ cm}}$$

$$x = 1,500,000 \text{ km}$$

2. **Calculate** The actual diameter of the sun is 1,391,000 km. Using the formula below, determine the amount of error in your calculated value for the sun's diameter. Show your work.

$$\text{Percentage of error} = \frac{\text{Difference between your value and the correct value}}{\text{Correct value}} \times 100$$

Sample answer: % error = [(1,500,000 − 1391,000)/1,391,000] × 100 = 7.8%

3. **Analyze Data** What could account for your error in calculating the sun's diameter?

Students used an average value for the distance between the sun and Earth; in fact, the

distance varies from a maximum of 152,086,000 km to a minimum of 147,097,000 km. There may

also be error involved in accurately measuring the diameter of the sun's image or the

distance between the cards.

4. **Apply Concepts** How might the technique used in this investigation be useful in making other astronomical measurements?

If the light is bright enough, the diameter of the moon could be measured. With a light-gathering

instrument such as a telescope, the diameters of planets could be measured.

5. **Relate Cause and Effect** How might clouds in the sky affect the accuracy of your measurement in this investigation?

If a cloud partially covers the sun, the image might appear smaller in diameter than it normally

would. Total cloud cover would probably make the image too faint to be seen and measured

properly.

Name _____ Class _____ Date _____

Go Further

A sunspot moves along the sun's equator. If the sunspot takes 14 days to move from one side of the sun to the other, calculate how fast the sunspot is moving. Explain why this value is also the speed at which the sun's surface is moving at the equator.

1. Using the actual value for the diameter of the sun and the formula below, calculate the circumference of the sun. The value of p (pi) is approximately 3.14.

$$\text{Circumference} = \pi \times \text{Diameter}$$

C = 3.14 × 1,391,000 km = 4,368,000 km

2. The sunspot moved only halfway around the sun, so to calculate the distance it traveled in 14 days, divide the value for the circumference by 2.

Distance C ÷ 2 = 14,368,000 km ÷ 2 = 2,184,000 km

3. To calculate the distance traveled by the sunspot in one day, divide the distance you calculated in Step 2 by 14.

Speed = distance/time = 2,184,000 km/14 days = 156,000 km/day

4. The sunspot is part of the sun's surface, so it moves as the sun moves. Therefore,

the speed of the sunspot is the same as the speed at which the sun's surface is moving

at the equator.

Name _____ Class _____ Date _____

Chapter 26   Exploring the Universe   **Investigation 26B**

Modeling Rotation of Neutron Stars

Background Information

SKILLS: Measuring, Recording Data, Observing, Calculating, Inferring

Angular momentum measures an object's tendency to continue to spin. If the mass of the spinning object is being pulled closer to the axis of the spin (shrinking in size), then the speed of the spin must increase in order to conserve momentum. For example, when a spinning skater pulls in his arms, he spins faster because his mass is less spread out.

Stars also spin on an axis. When a supergiant with 15 times the sun's mass collapses into a neutron star, much of the star's mass is lost in a supernova explosion. Although the mass decreases somewhat, the diameter of the star drastically decreases. A star that is a supergiant may have a diameter of several million kilometers and may rotate on its axis about once a month. The neutron star into which a supergiant develops may be only a few kilometers across but may rotate thousands of times per second.

In this investigation, you will use a rotating square of cardboard and weights to model the effect of mass distribution on rotation rate.

Problem

Why do neutron stars rotate so rapidly?

Pre-Lab Discussion

Read the entire investigation. Then, work with a partner to answer the following questions.

1. **Inferring** What is the purpose of this investigation?

The purpose is to answer the question of why neutron stars rotate with such great speed.

2. **Observing** After a supergiant becomes a neutron star, what is its size and mass, and what happens to its rotation speed?

The neutron star into which a supergiant develops may be only a few kilometers across but may

rotate thousands of times per second.

3. **Inferring** How will this investigation answer the question of why neutron stars rotate with such great speed?

In this investigation, a rotating square of cardboard and two weights are used to model the effect

of mass distribution on rotation rate. The rotating cardboard square and weights are a model for

the supergiant and the neutron star. The model can show the effect of mass on the speed of rotation.

Name _____ Class _____ Date _____

4. **Predicting** What would you predict would be the outcome of this investigation?

The rate of rotation will increase as the masses are placed closer to the center.

Materials *(per group)*

pencil with eraser
square of stiff cardboard, at least 35 cm wide
pushpin
masking tape
2 identical small weights
centimeter ruler
clock or watch with second hand

Provide small stones or balance weights to use as weights. As the mass of the weights increases, they may pull the pushpin out of the eraser while rotating. Students may have to experiment with which size of weights works best for their cardboard. Corrugated cardboard works best. Odd shaped weights can be difficult to tape down. A nickel weighs 5 g. Students can use multiple nickels to increase the mass of the weights.

Note that if a smaller square is used, it is more difficult to get variance in the number of spins for a given weight.

Safety 🥽 ✂️ 🔨

Put on safety goggles. Be careful when handling sharp objects. Make sure that weights stay attached and do not fly off and hit anyone. Note all safety alert symbols next to the steps in the Procedure and review the meaning of each symbol by referring to the Safety Symbols on page xiii.

Procedure

1. Draw lines along the two diagonals of the cardboard square, as shown in Figure 1. Punch a hole through the center of the cardboard with the pushpin. Then, push the pushpin into the eraser end of the pencil. Check that the cardboard is able to spin freely. If it sticks, use the pushpin to widen the hole. **CAUTION:** *Be careful when handling sharp objects.*

2. **Measure** Attach a piece of masking tape to one corner of the square. Then, attach the two weights to the cardboard so that each weight is 30 cm from the center, as shown in Figure 1. The weights should both lie along one of the two diagonals that pass through the center. The card is still balanced because the weights are equidistant from the center.

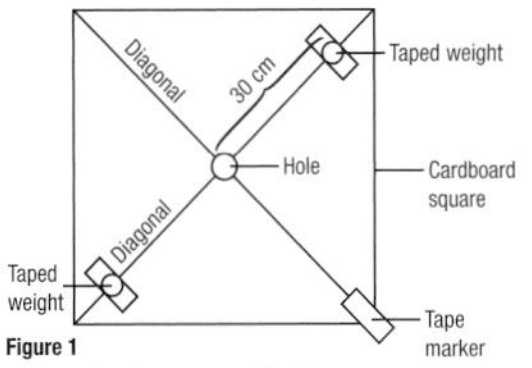

Figure 1

3. Hold the pencil in front of you and perpendicular to your body so that the square of cardboard rotates below eye level and parallel to your body. Try to give each spin of the square the same force. **CAUTION:** *Make sure that weights stay attached and do not fly off and hit anyone.*

To make sure the forces are the same, have students attach a paper clip to the free corner of the square and hook a weight to the paper clip. Be sure to cushion the floor under the weight because it will fall off as the square rotates.

Lab Manual

4. Spin the square. Watch the taped corner as it goes by and count the number of times it passes in 5 seconds. (If the square slows down during this time, adjust the pushpin so that it turns with less friction. Then, try again.) In Data Table 1, record the number of rotations.

5. Move the weights inward toward the center so that each is 20 cm from the center and tape them down. Spin and count the rotations. Make sure that you apply the same force you did before. In Data Table 1, record the number of rotations.

6. Repeat Step 5, but this time, tape the weights so that each is only 10 cm from the center. In Data Table 1, record the number of rotations.

Observations

DATA TABLE 1

Distance of Weights from Center of Square	Number of Rotations (spins)
30 cm	10 (for a 25-g weight)
20 cm	13
10 cm	22

Analysis and Conclusions

1. **Calculate** Calculate the rotation rate for each case by dividing the number of spins by 5 seconds.

Results will vary widely, but rates should increase as the radius decreases so that angular momentum is conserved. For example, angular momentum = mvr, so if the radius is halved, the speed doubles, assuming the initial angular momentum is always the same in each trial.

Lab Manual

2. **Infer** Explain why the rate of rotation of a neutron star is so great compared to that of the star from which it was formed.

A neutron star is much smaller but retains a great deal of mass. The size of the star decreases

dramatically. The effect of decreasing mass is therefore much less than the effect of decreasing size.

Both effects cause the rotation rate to increase.

3. **Infer** Suggest reasons why this model might not give accurate results.

A star is a fluid, and rotating fluids behave differently than solids. Also, a star loses mass when

it becomes a neutron star.

Go Further

What happens to the rotation rate when mass decreases? Repeat Step 5 two more times, but for the first repetition, use weights that are about one-half the mass of the initial weights used. For the second repetition, use weights that are one-fourth the mass of the initial weights used. Create a data table in which to record your results.

Students could compare the number of rotations of the cardboard square at three different masses located the same distance from the center.

The tape is sometimes difficult for students to see when the square is spinning very fast, so there may be a wide variance from the theoretical number of spins.

DATA TABLE Sample data are given.

Mass of Weights Taped at 20 cm	Number of Rotations (spins) From Center of Cardboard Square
25 g	13
15 g	22
5 g	38

Name _____ Class _____ Date _____

Chapter 26 Exploring the Universe   Chapter Test A

Multiple Choice

Write the letter that best answers the question or completes the statement on the line provided.

_____ 1. What will happen to the relative amounts of hydrogen and helium in the sun over the next few billion years?
   a. Hydrogen will increase and helium will decrease.
   b. Hydrogen will decrease and helium will increase.
   c. Both hydrogen and helium will decrease.
   d. Both hydrogen and helium will remain the same.

_____ 2. The sun remains stable over time because
   a. its supply of hydrogen is inexhaustible.
   b. the product of fusion, helium, is a stable element.
   c. the inward pull of gravity and outward push of thermal pressure are balanced.
   d. nuclear fusion is a stabilizing process.

_____ 3. The stream of electrically charged particles sent into space by the sun is called
   a. a solar flare.   b. a sunspot.
   c. a solar prominence.   d. the solar wind.

_____ 4. The parallax of a star is observed because
   a. all stars have the same apparent brightness.
   b. parallax increases with distance.
   c. stars do not move.
   d. the observer moves.

_____ 5. The apparent brightness of a star
   a. varies with the position from which it is viewed.
   b. can be calculated from its absolute brightness and mass.
   c. is greater as distance from the sun increases.
   d. is a measure of its light viewed from any position.

_____ 6. A cool, bright star would appear in which section of an H-R diagram?
   a. lower left   b. upper left
   c. upper right   d. lower right

_____ 7. Which kind of star will most likely remain on the main sequence the longest?
   a. a low-mass, red star   b. a yellow star like the sun
   c. a high-mass blue star d. a bright white star

_____ 8. What is a pulsar?
   a. the remains of a low-mass star after it explodes
   b. a spinning neutron star emitting radio waves
   c. another name for a protostar
   d. the stage before a dying star becomes a supernova

Name _____ Class _____ Date _____

_____ 9. Why is studying star clusters useful?
   a. because there is such a large diversity of stars in a cluster
   b. because they are about the same age and distance from Earth
   c. because they are all about the same size and temperature
   d. because all of them are always young, bright stars

_____ 10. Older stars are most likely found in
   a. the arms of spiral and barred-spiral galaxies.
   b. elliptical galaxies.
   c. irregular galaxies.
   d. both a and b

_____ 11. Hubble's Law states that the speed at which a galaxy is moving away is proportional to the
   a. mass of the galaxy.
   b. number of stars in the galaxy.
   c. galaxy's distance from Earth.
   d. age of the galaxy.

_____ 12. Which of the following provides support for the big bang theory?
   a. red shift
   b. cosmic microwave background radiation
   c. elliptical galaxies
   d. both a and b

_____ 13. Much of the mass of the universe may be composed of
   a. electromagnetic waves.
   b. cosmic microwaves.
   c. background radiation.
   d. dark matter.

Completion

Complete each statement on the line provided.

1. Nuclear fusion within the sun takes place within the _____.

2. The apparent change in position of an object with respect to a distant background is called _____.

3. The main sequence lifetime of a star is dependent upon the star's _____.

4. A binary system in which one star passes in front of the other, blocking some light from reaching Earth is called a(an) _____ binary.

5. The observation that cosmic microwave background radiation is detected n all directions in the universe supports the hypothesis that the universe is _____.

Name _____ Class _____ Date _____

Short Answer

In complete sentences, write the answers to the questions on the lines provided.

1. In Figure 26-1, name and describe area C and tell how it differs from area B in the way it transfers energy.

_____
_____
_____
_____
_____
_____

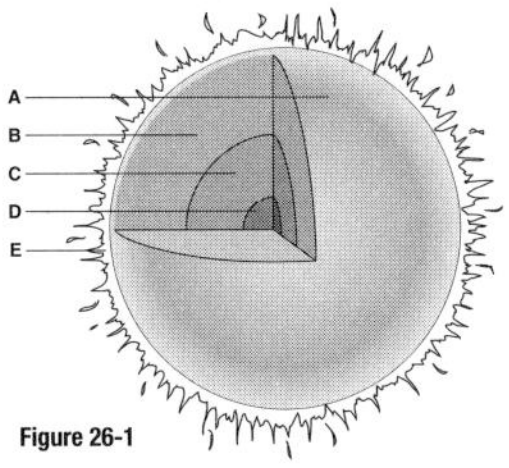

Figure 26-1

2. What characteristic of a star's spectrum do astronomers use to determine the different elements in the star?

_____
_____
_____

3. What are the very bright stars in the upper right of an H-R diagram called?

_____
_____

4. What two factors cause a nebula to develop into a star?

_____
_____

5. How are elements other than helium produced?

_____
_____
_____

6. To what do astronomers attribute the increasing rate of expansion of the universe?

_____
_____

Name _____ Class _____ Date _____

Using Science Skills

Use the diagram to answer each question. Write the answers on a separate sheet of paper.

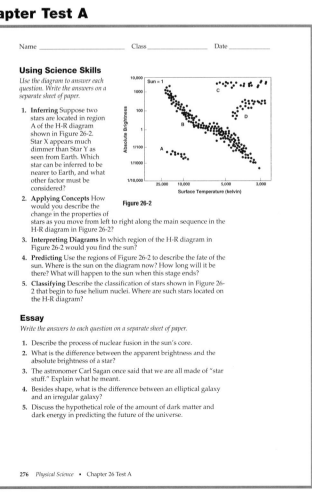

Figure 26-2

1. **Inferring** Suppose two stars are located in region A of the H-R diagram shown in Figure 26-2. Star X appears much dimmer than Star Y as seen from Earth. Which star can be inferred to be nearer to Earth, and what other factor must be considered?

2. **Applying Concepts** How would you describe the change in the properties of stars as you move from left to right along the main sequence in the H-R diagram in Figure 26-2?

3. **Interpreting Diagrams** In which region of the H-R diagram in Figure 26-2 would you find the sun?

4. **Predicting** Use the regions of Figure 26-2 to describe the fate of the sun. Where is the sun on the diagram now? How long will it be there? What will happen to the sun when this stage ends?

5. **Classifying** Describe the classification of stars shown in Figure 26-2 that begin to fuse helium nuclei. Where are such stars located on the H-R diagram?

Essay

Write the answers to each question on a separate sheet of paper.

1. Describe the process of nuclear fusion in the sun's core.

2. What is the difference between the apparent brightness and the absolute brightness of a star?

3. The astronomer Carl Sagan once said that we are all made of "star stuff." Explain what he meant.

4. Besides shape, what is the difference between an elliptical galaxy and an irregular galaxy?

5. Discuss the hypothetical role of the amount of dark matter and dark energy in predicting the future of the universe.

Chapter Test B

Chapter 26   Exploring the Universe   **Chapter Test B**

Multiple Choice

Write the letter that best answers the question or completes the statement on the line provided.

_____ **1.** The sun's energy is produced by
   a. the sun burning fuel.
   b. nuclear fission.
   c. an ordinary chemical reaction.
   d. nuclear fusion.

_____ **2.** For the sun to be stable, the inward and outward forces within the sun must be
   a. in equilibrium.
   b. part of the fusion reaction.
   c. focused in the core.
   d. balanced with temperature and density.

_____ **3.** Examine Figure 26-1. Which area is the convection zone?
   a. A
   b. B
   c. C
   d. D

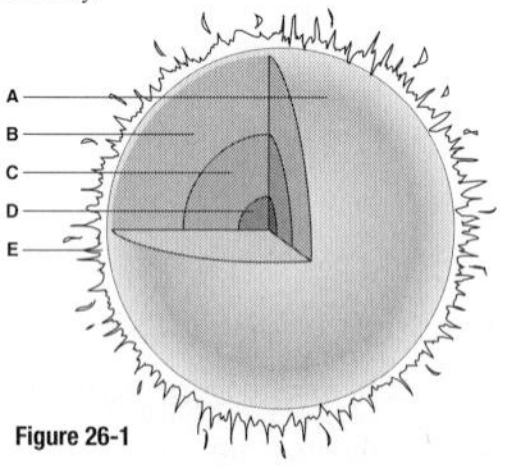

Figure 26-1

_____ **4.** The distance between stars is typically measured in
   a. light-years.
   b. kilometers.
   c. astronomical units.
   d. miles.

_____ **5.** Astronomers classify stars according to their
   a. distance from Earth.
   b. color, size, and absolute brightness.
   c. age and parallax.
   d. all of the above

_____ **6.** An H-R diagram
   a. is a map of the positions of the stars.
   b. graphs stars according to their size and distance.
   c. lists every known star.
   d. graphs a sample of stars according to surface temperature and absolute brightness.

_____ **7.** The life cycle of a star begins with a cloud of gas and dust called a
   a. protoplanet.   **b.** constellation.   **c.** nebula.   **d.** protosun.

Chapter Test B

_____ **8.** Both high-mass and low-mass adult stars are classified as
   a. main-sequence stars.   **b.** white dwarfs.
   c. supernovas.   **d.** neutron stars.

_____ **9.** All stars remain on the main sequence
   a. until they stabilize.
   b. for about 90 percent of their lifetimes.
   c. until they become protostars.
   d. for about 10 billion years.

_____ **10.** Low-mass and medium-mass stars eventually
   a. grow into supergiants.
   b. become supernovas.
   c. become neutron stars.
   d. turn into white dwarfs.

_____ **11.** Which of the following is true about more than half of all stars?
   a. They are dying red giants.
   b. They are visible to the unaided eye.
   c. They are members of a star system.
   d. They are high-mass stars.

_____ **12.** How do open star clusters differ from associations?
   a. Associations are usually larger and have fewer stars.
   b. Open clusters are organized into constellations.
   c. Associations are usually smaller and have more stars.
   d. Open clusters typically contain loose groupings of old stars.

_____ **13.** A large group of older stars would be found in which of the following star clusters?
   a. open cluster   **b.** association
   c. globular cluster   **d.** both a and b

_____ **14.** Galaxies are classified into four groups based on their
   a. shapes.   **b.** sizes.   **c.** number of stars.   **d.** brightness.

_____ **15.** When the absorption lines of a galaxy shift toward the red end of the spectrum, it means that the galaxy is
   a. moving closer to Earth.
   b. small and young.
   c. moving away from Earth.
   d. large and old.

_____ **16.** The big bang theory explains the
   a. origin of the universe.
   b. life cycle of a star.
   c. Doppler effect.
   d. arrangement of constellations.

Chapter Test B

_____ **17.** Dark matter can be detected by its
   a. cosmic microwave background radiation.
   b. red shift.
   c. gravitational effects on visible matter.
   d. velocity.

Completion

Complete each statement on the line provided.

1. The sun's major source of fuel is _____.

2. The two forces that are balanced when a star is in equilibrium are outward pressure and _____.

3. By using a spectrograph, a star's absorption lines can identify the different _____ that a star is composed of.

4. In an H-R diagram, most stars are found in a diagonal band from the upper left to the lower right, which is called the _____.

5. A contracting cloud of dust and gas with enough mass to form a star is called a(an) _____.

6. A young star forms when the pressure from _____ supports the star against the tremendous inward pull of gravity.

7. The sun will end its life as a red giant and eventually end up as a(an) _____.

8. A group of two or more stars held together by gravity is called a(an) _____.

9. A large spherical group of older stars is called a(an) _____.

10. The theory that the universe came into being in a single moment with an enormous explosion is the _____ theory.

11. Matter that does not give off any radiation is called _____.

Short Answer

In complete sentences, write the answers to the questions on the lines provided.

1. At least how much longer is the sun expected to remain a stable main sequence star?

_____
_____

2. What is the innermost layer of the sun's atmosphere called?

_____
_____

Chapter Test B

3. Why do astronomers measure the parallax of nearby stars?

_____
_____
_____

4. How can an object's red shift tell us how fast the object is moving away from Earth?

_____
_____
_____

5. How have scientists used Hubble's Law to estimate the age of the universe?

_____
_____
_____
_____

Using Science Skills

Use the diagram to answer each question. Write the answers on a separate sheet of paper.

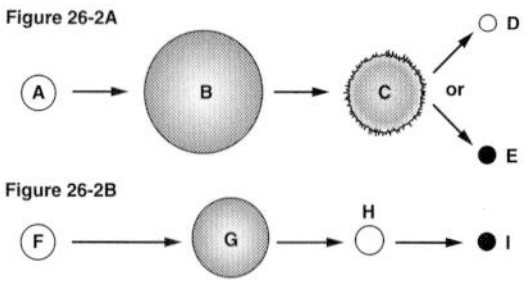

1. Applying Concepts Would you expect to find helium fusion occurring in stage F or stage G of the star shown in Figure 26-2B? Explain your answer.

2. Using Models Which figure—26-2A or 26-2B—models the evolution of a high-mass star? Explain how you know.

3. Inferring Which figure—26-2A or 26-2B—can you infer is a model of a star formed from a small nebula? Explain your answer.

4. Interpreting Graphics In Figure 26-2A, what is the event occurring at stage C? Explain why there are two possible outcomes (stage D and stage E).

5. Drawing Conclusions Relate two differences between the life cycles shown in Figure 26-2 that will allow you to conclude which star will be longer lived.

Figure 26-2A

Figure 26-2B

Figure 26-2

apter 26 Test A Answers

tiple Choice

2. c **3.** d **4.** d **5.** a **6.** c

8. b **9.** b **10.** b **11.** c **12.** d

mpletion

re 2. parallax **3.** mass **4.** eclipsing **5.** expanding

rt Answer

rea C is the radiation zone of the sun. Area B is the convection
e. The radiation zone transfers energy primarily by
tromagnetic waves. The convection zone transfers energy
marily by moving gases in convection currents. **2.** absorption
3. supergiants **4.** gravity and heat from contraction **5.** When
rogen is gone, helium fusion begins, producing carbon,
gen, and certain heavier elements. Elements heavier than iron
created in a supernova. **6.** a mysterious force called dark
rgy

g Science Skills

y the placement on the H-R diagram, we know that both stars
of roughly equal absolute brightness and surface temperature,
that both are white dwarfs. Because star X appears dimmer, it
st be farther from Earth. **2.** The hottest stars are blue and very
ht. The coolest stars are red and have a much lower absolute
htness. They are found in the lower right of the main sequence.
egion B, the main sequence, near the center (surface
perature of 5800 K) **4.** The sun is a yellow star located in about
middle of region B, the main sequence. It will remain stable
e for at least another 5 billion years. In its next stage, the sun
be classified as a red giant (region D). It will then become a
te dwarf (region A). **5.** As a star begins to fuse helium nuclei, its
r shell expands greatly. The outer shell then cools as it
ands. The star is then classified as a red giant or a supergiant,
ending on its original mass. Red giants are located in region D,
supergiants are located in region C.

ay

he sun's core has a high enough temperature and pressure for
on to take place. Less massive hydrogen nuclei combine into
re massive helium nuclei, releasing enormous amounts of
rgy. 2. The apparent brightness is how bright a star appears
varies with the distance from which the star is viewed.
solute brightness is a characteristic of the star and does not
end on how far it is from Earth. **3.** As high-mass stars evolve
he fusion of elements other than hydrogen, they create other
ments, including iron. The stars eventually run out of elements
use. Gravity overcomes the lower thermal pressure, and the
collapses, producing a violent explosion called a supernova.
heavier elements in our solar system, including the atoms in
bodies, come from a supernova that occurred billions of years
. **4.** New stars are not forming in older elliptical galaxies
cause there is little gas or dust between the stars. Irregular
axies have many young stars and large amounts of gas and
st from which to produce new stars. **5.** Dark matter seems to
ply most of the gravitational attraction that keeps the galaxies
m flying apart. The amount of dark matter in the universe will
ermine if the universe will continue to expand, stop expanding,
perhaps, increase in the rate at which it is expanding. The
ount of dark energy will determine if the universe will continue
xpand forever.

Chapter 26 Test B Answers

Multiple Choice

1. d **2.** a **3.** b **4.** a **5.** b **6.** d

7. c **8.** a **9.** b **10.** d **11.** c **12.** a

13. c **14.** a **15.** c **16.** a **17.** c

Completion

1. hydrogen **2.** gravity **3.** elements **4.** main sequence **5.** protostar
6. fusion **7.** white dwarf; black dwarf **8.** star system **9.** globular
cluster **10.** big bang **11.** dark matter

Short Answer

1. 5 billion years **2.** the photosphere **3.** to determine the stars'
distances from Earth **4.** The larger the observed shift is, the faster
is the speed. **5.** Scientists know how fast the universe is
expanding and can infer how long it has been expanding since the
big bang.

Using Science Skills

1. Helium fusion would be occurring in stage G. In stage F, the star
is a main-sequence star, and its energy is supplied by the fusion of
hydrogen. Stage G represents the star as a red giant. As the core
of the red giant collapses, it becomes hot enough to cause helium
to undergo fusion. **2.** Figure 26-2A; the subsequent stages of the
model indicate a supernova at stage C and two possible fates at
stages D and E. Low-mass stars have only one ultimate fate as a
black dwarf at stage I from the white dwarf at stage H. Also, Figure
26-2A shows a supergiant, which is not a stage for a low mass
star. **3.** Figure 26-2B; small nebulas most likely produce low-mass
to medium-mass stars because of the lower available mass in the
nebula. **4.** A high-mass star; a supernova results in one of two
fates, depending on the star's mass. It could become a neutron
star (stage D) or, for more massive stars, a black hole (stage E).
5. Figure 26-2B is a low-mass star, and Figure 26-2A represents a
high-mass star. Figure 26-2A depicts the fate of the star as either a
neutron star or a black hole. High-mass stars are shorter lived than
low-mass stars because high-mass stars burn brighter, use up
their hydrogen fuel in the core sooner, and therefore leave the main
sequence sooner.

Name _____ Class _____ Date _____

Unit 3   Earth and Space   Unit Test A

Multiple Choice

Write the letter that best answers the question or completes the statement on the line provided.

_____ 1. Forces that shape Earth's surface can be divided into
  a. constructive and physical.
  b. constructive and destructive.
  c. chemical and destructive.
  d. chemical and physical.

_____ 2. What is a mineral's cleavage?
  a. the resistance of a mineral to scratching
  b. a type of fracture in which a mineral breaks along regular, well-defined planes
  c. the color of a mineral's powder
  d. a type of fracture in which a mineral breaks along a curved surface

_____ 3. Intense heat, intense pressure, or reactions with hot water can modify a pre-existing rock to form a(an)
  a. metamorphic rock.   b. sedimentary rock.
  c. igneous rock.   d. organic rock.

_____ 4. Stress in Earth's crust is caused by
  a. folds.   b. plate movements.
  c. earthquakes.   d. faults.

_____ 5. P waves
  a. cause Earth to vibrate in the direction of the wave's motion.
  b. cause Earth to vibrate at right angles to the direction the wave moves.
  c. travel along Earth's surface.
  d. move in a rolling motion similar to ocean waves.

_____ 6. Geologists have inferred that Earth's outer core is liquid because
  a. P waves cannot pass through the outer core.
  b. S waves speed up in the outer core.
  c. S waves are bent downward as they travel through the outer core.
  d. S waves cannot pass through the outer core.

_____ 7. Which of the following rock types and conditions would result in the highest rate of chemical weathering?
  a. granite in a cold and dry area
  b. limestone in a hot and rainy area
  c. slate in a hot and rainy area
  d. granite in a hot and dry area

Physical Science • Unit 3 Test A   **281**

Name _____ Class _____ Date _____

_____ 8. Tilted telephone poles and fences curving in a downward direction on a hillside are evidence of
  a. a landslide.   b. a mudflow.
  c. a slump.   d. creep.

_____ 9. Meanders, V-shaped valleys, and oxbow lakes are all features formed by
  a. glaciers.   b. water erosion.
  c. water deposition.   d. groundwater erosion.

_____ 10. Which of the following is an example of a feature caused by wave erosion?
  a. a delta   b. an alluvial fan
  c. a sea stack   d. a spit

_____ 11. Geologists could use which of the following to compare the age of sedimentary rock layers in Bryce Canyon with sedimentary rock layers in the Grand Canyon?
  a. radioactive isotopes
  b. index fossils c. relative dating
  d. all of the above

_____ 12. When did the first land plants and animals appear in the fossil record?
  a. in the Mesozoic Era
  b. in the Paleozoic Era
  c. during the Triassic period
  d. during the Carboniferous period

_____ 13. Which of the following lists all the zones in the correct order, starting at the North Pole and ending at the South Pole?
  a. polar, temperate, tropic, polar
  b. polar, temperate, tropic, temperate, polar
  c. polar, tropic, temperate, polar
  d. polar, tropic, temperate, tropic, polar

_____ 14. Earth's atmosphere is heated mainly by
  a. heat that travels directly from the sun.
  b. visible light as it passes through the air.
  c. reflected sunlight.
  d. energy reradiated by Earth's surface.

_____ 15. The daily breezes that occur in a city that is located near a large body of water are examples of
  a. local winds.   b. monsoons.
  c. global winds.   d. westerlies.

_____ 16. A small, intense storm formed when a vertical cylinder of rotating air develops is a
  a. thunderstorm. b. tornado. c. monsoon. d. hurricane.

282   Physical Science • Unit 3 Test A

Name _____ Class _____ Date _____

_____ 17. Lines on a weather map that connect points that have the same air temperature are called
  a. millibars. b. isobars. c. isotherms. d. front lines.

_____ 18. Which of the following factors affect a region's temperature?
  a. latitude and altitude
  b. distance from large bodies of water
  c. ocean currents
  d. all of the above

_____ 19. Which of the following is the most likely reason that ancient observers believed that Earth was the center of the universe?
  a. The Earth seemed to move on its axis.
  b. Earth's motions are only recently known because of high-powered telescopes.
  c. Objects in the sky appear to circle around Earth.
  d. Ancient observers believed the universe was stationary.

_____ 20. Which of the following helps explain why the planets remain in motion around the sun?
  a. density   b. gravity
  c. inertia   d. both b and c

_____ 21. What led to the discovery of three more planets than those that the ancient observers knew about?
  a. the invention of the telescope in 1600
  b. the Hubble telescope launched in 1990
  c. space missions in the Apollo program
  d. observations by *Sputnik 1* in 1957

_____ 22. Which of the following are currently operating the space station?
  a. Soviet cosmonauts
  b. a cooperative team of scientists from 16 countries
  c. American astronauts
  d. a cooperative team of scientists from Russia and the United States

_____ 23. How might a nitrogen-oxygen atmosphere on the moon affect the range of temperatures on the moon?
  a. An atmosphere might hold heat in, making the moon very hot.
  b. An atmosphere might block heat radiating from the sun, making the moon very cold.
  c. An atmosphere might moderate temperatures, making them more even, such as on Earth.
  d. An atmosphere would have no effect on the range of temperatures on the moon.

Physical Science • Unit 3 Test A   **283**

Name _____ Class _____ Date _____

_____ 24. What is meant by the statement "The moon is geologically dead"?
  a. The moon has little erosion and no plate movement.
  b. The moon is devoid of living things.
  c. The moon has no atmosphere.
  d. The moon has no air currents or weather patterns.

_____ 25. What is a pulsar?
  a. the remains of a low-mass star after it explodes
  b. a spinning neutron star emitting radio waves
  c. another name for a protostar
  d. the stage before a dying star becomes a supernova

_____ 26. Why is studying star clusters useful?
  a. because there is such a large diversity of stars in a cluster
  b. because they are about the same age and distance from Earth
  c. because they are all about the same size and temperature
  d. because all of them are always young, bright stars

_____ 27. Older stars are most likely found in
  a. the arms of spiral and barred-spiral galaxies.
  b. elliptical galaxies.
  c. irregular galaxies.
  d. both a and b

_____ 28. Hubble's Law states that the speed at which a galaxy is moving away is proportional to the
  a. mass of the galaxy.
  b. number of stars in the galaxy.
  c. galaxy's distance from Earth.
  d. age of the galaxy.

_____ 29. Which of the following provides support for the big bang theory?
  a. red shift
  b. cosmic microwave background radiation
  c. elliptical galaxies
  d. both a and b

_____ 30. Much of the mass of the universe may be composed of
  a. electromagnetic waves.
  b. cosmic microwaves.
  c. background radiation.
  d. dark matter.

284   Physical Science • Unit 3 Test A

Name _____ Class _____ Date _____

Completion

Complete each statement on the line provided.

1. The type of sedimentary rock that forms when fragments of pre-existing rocks are cemented together is called a(an) _____ rock.

2. Alfred Wegener proposed that a continent was formed by continental drift. This supercontinent was called _____.

3. Due to sea-floor spreading, the youngest rocks in the ocean floor are found near a(an) _____.

4. The seismic waves that compress and expand the ground are called _____ waves.

5. When a stream flows out of a mountain range onto a flat area of land, it deposits sediments in a(an) _____.

6. The carbonic acid that is involved in the formation of caves is formed when rainwater combines with _____ in the air.

7. The _____ is a gently sloping plain covered with shallow water along the edges of continents.

8. In mountainous areas, valley glaciers cut _____ valleys.

9. Of the four layers of the atmosphere, the _____ has the hottest temperatures.

10. On the two days each year when the sun is directly overhead at noon at latitude 23.5° north or 23.5° south, a _____ occurs.

11. Air spirals in toward the center of a cyclone but flows away from the center of a(an) _____.

12. _____ is a short-term variation in climate that is caused by a change in the normal direction of winds, which causes ocean currents to shift direction.

13. Because Earth's orbit around the sun is an ellipse, and Earth is not always the same distance from the sun, one AU is defined as the _____ distance from Earth to the sun.

14. All of the planets in our solar system have _____ with the exception of Mercury and Venus.

15. A person weighing 600 newtons (about 120 pounds) on Earth would weigh about _____ newtons on the moon.

16. The _____ belt contains perhaps tens of thousands of objects orbiting within about 100 AU of the sun.

17. Nuclear fusion within the sun takes place within the _____.

18. The apparent change in position of an object with respect to a distant background is called _____.

Name _____ Class _____ Date _____

19. The main sequence lifetime of a star is dependent upon the star's _____.

20. A binary system in which one star passes in front of the other, blocking some light from reaching Earth is called a(an) _____ binary.

Short Answer

In complete sentences, write the answers to the questions on the lines provided.

1. How is the streak of a mineral obtained?

2. Describe the physical properties of the three layers of the mantle.

3. How are landslides and mudflows alike?

4. Describe three ways that wind erosion moves sediment.

5. What is the difference between sleet and freezing rain?

6. How does a thunderstorm form?

7. What is the ecliptic plane?

Name _____ Class _____ Date _____

8. What is the difference between a full moon and a new moon?

9. What are the very bright stars in the upper right of an H-R diagram called?

10. What two factors cause a nebula to develop into a star?

Using Science Skills

Use the diagram to answer each question. Write the answers on a separate sheet of paper.

1. **Interpreting Graphics** In Figure 3-1, what process is occurring in the area labeled D, and what feature will result at C?

2. **Interpreting Graphics** In Figure 3-1, what is occurring at A?

3. **Inferring** Which rock layer is the youngest layer shown in Figure 3-2?

4. **Analyzing Data** In Figure 3-2, would a fossil in layer D be younger or older than fossils found in layer B?

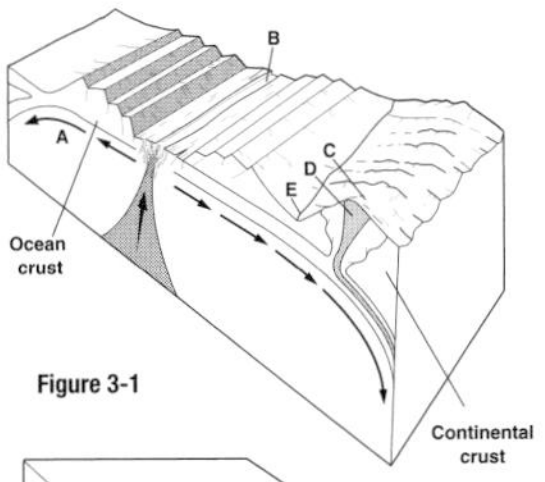

Figure 3-1

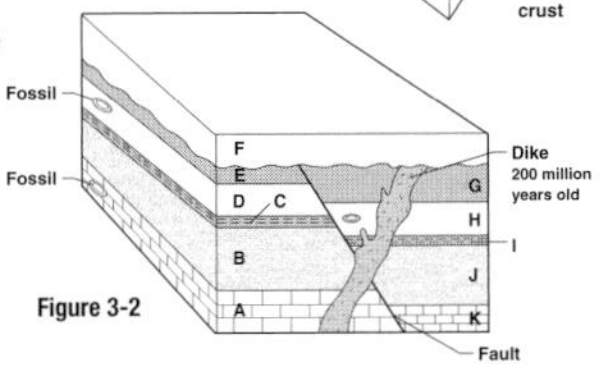

Figure 3-2

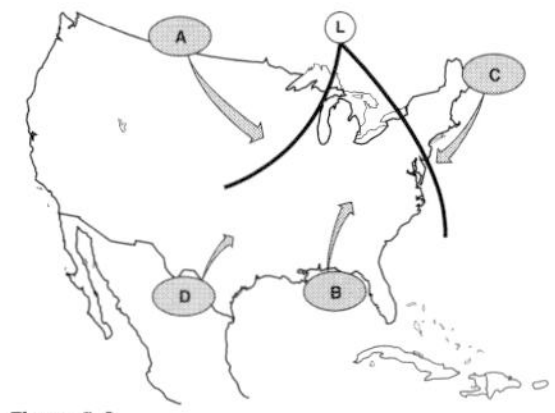

Figure 3-3

5. **Inferring** What factors are used to classify the air masses in Figure 3-3?

6. **Classifying** Based on their locations in Figure 3-3, name the types of air masses represented by A and D and describe the characteristics of each.

Name _____ Class _____ Date _____

7. **Formulating Hypotheses** In Figure 3-4, why would you expect B to lie in the planet's orbital plane?

8. **Drawing Conclusions** Saturn is the least dense of all the planets. Why does Saturn remain in orbit instead of drifting away in space or crashing into the sun?

9. **Inferring** Suppose two stars are located in region A of the H-R diagram shown in Figure 3-5. Star X appears much dimmer than Star Y as seen from Earth. Which star can be inferred to be nearer to Earth, and what other factor must be considered?

10. **Applying Concepts** How would you describe the change in the properties of stars as you move from left to right along the main sequence in the H-R diagram in Figure 3-5?

Figure 3-4

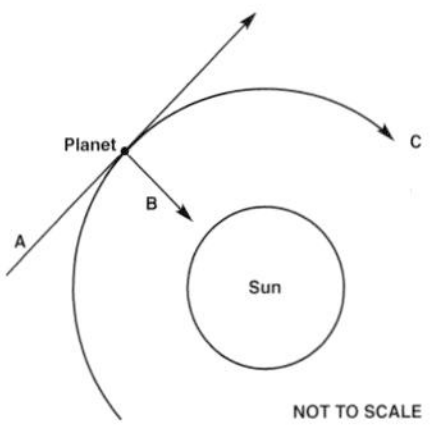

Figure 3-5

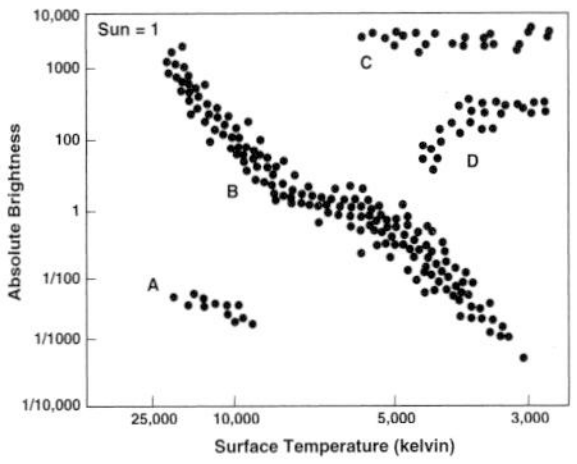

Essay

Write the answers to each question on a separate sheet of paper.

1. How does the subduction of an oceanic plate result in the formation of a volcano?

2. Describe the journey of a water molecule through the water cycle.

3. Compare the weather that might occur in an area as a warm front passes through, after the warm front has passed through, as a cold front passes through, and after the cold front has passed through.

4. What three criteria must any theory of the origin of the solar system satisfy? What theory satisfies all three?

5. The astronomer Carl Sagan once said that we are all made of "star stuff." Explain what he meant.

Unit 3 Test B

Name _____ Class _____ Date _____

Unit 3   Earth and Space   Unit Test B

Multiple Choice

Write the letter that best answers the question or completes the statement on the line provided.

_____ 1. The study of Earth's composition, structure, and history is called
  a. seismology.   b. physics.   c. chemistry.   d. geology.

_____ 2. The three main layers of Earth's interior are the
  a. crust, core, and lithosphere.
  b. crust, mantle, and core.
  c. mantle, inner core, and outer core.
  d. crust, mantle, and aesthenosphere.

_____ 3. A naturally occurring, inorganic solid with a crystal structure and a characteristic chemical composition is a
  a. rock.   b. fossil.
  c. mineral.   d. piece of granite.

_____ 4. The area where magma collects inside a volcano before an eruption is called
  a. the crater.   b. a caldera.
  c. a vent.   d. the magma chamber.

_____ 5. What determines whether a volcano erupts quietly or explosively?
  a. the size of the volcano
  b. the age of the volcano
  c. the characteristics of the magma
  d. the magnitude of nearby earthquakes

_____ 6. Shield volcanoes are produced by
  a. explosive eruptions of lava and ash.
  b. quiet eruptions of lava.
  c. explosive eruptions of ash and cinders.
  d. quiet eruptions that alternate with explosive eruptions.

_____ 7. Which of the following is NOT an agent of chemical weathering?
  a. rainwater   b. oxidation
  c. frost wedging d. carbonic acid

_____ 8. A rapid mass movement of large amounts of rock and soil down a slope is called a
  a. landslide.   b. slump.   c. creep.   d. mudflow.

_____ 9. A stream's ability to erode depends mainly on
  a. its temperature.
  b. the size of the sediment in the stream.
  c. its speed.
  d. the shape of its valley.

Physical Science • Unit 3 Test B   **289**

Unit 3 Test B

Name _____ Class _____ Date _____

_____ 10. A sediment deposit formed when a stream flows into a lake or the ocean is called a(an)
  a. alluvial fan.   b. delta.
  c. meander.   d. natural levee.

_____ 11. Caves are formed by erosion from
  a. glaciers.   b. streams.   c. wind.   d. groundwater.

_____ 12. Unsorted sediment deposited by a glacier is called
  a. a cirque.   b. till.   c. a horn.   d. an erratic.

_____ 13. Which region usually has temperatures cooler than temperatures near the equator?
  a. tropic zone   b. polar zone
  c. temperate zone d. both b and c

_____ 14. About how much of the solar energy that reaches Earth passes through the atmosphere and is absorbed by the surface of Earth?
  a. 20 percent   b. 30 percent
  c. 50 percent   d. 80 percent

_____ 15. Which of the following is NOT an example of a global wind?
  a. westerlies   b. trade winds
  c. polar easterlies d. ea breezes

_____ 16. What type of front forms when two unlike air masses form a boundary but neither is moving?
  a. warm   b. cold   c. stationary   d. occluded

_____ 17. Which of the following is a weather system with a center of low pressure?
  a. cyclone   b. anticyclone   c. warm front   d. cold front

_____ 18. A tropical storm with sustained winds of at least 119 kilometers per hour is called a
  a. tornado.   b. thunderstorm.
  c. monsoon.   d. hurricane.

_____ 19. Ocean tides are the result of
  a. the rotation of the Earth.
  b. the sun's gravitational pull on Earth.
  c. changes in Earth's orbital position around the sun.
  d. differences in both the sun's and moon's gravitational pull on Earth.

_____ 20. The four terrestrial planets are so called because they
  a. are the nearest planets to Earth.
  b. were all once part of Earth.
  c. are similar in structure to Earth.
  d. can all be seen from Earth without a telescope.

290   *Physical Science* • Unit 3 Test B

Unit 3 Test B

Name _____ Class _____ Date _____

_____ 21. Asteroids are mainly found
  a. in the asteroid belt beyond Mars.
  b. in orbit around Jupiter.   c. throughout the solar system.
  d. beyond the farthest known planet.

_____ 22. Which of the gas giants has the largest diameter?
  a. Jupiter   b. Uranus   c. Saturn   d. Neptune

_____ 23. Comets are made mostly of
  a. iron.
  b. ice and rock.
  c. hydrogen and helium.
  d. methane.

_____ 24. Which of the following is a sparse sphere of comets that surrounds the sun and planets?
  a. the asteroid belt   b. the Kuiper belt
  c. the Oort cloud   d. none of the above

_____ 25. Astronomers classify stars according to their
  a. distance from Earth.
  b. color, size, and absolute brightness.
  c. age and parallax.
  d. all of the above

_____ 26. An H-R diagram
  a. is a map of the positions of the stars.
  b. graphs stars according to their size and distance.
  c. lists every known star.
  d. graphs a sample of stars according to surface temperature and absolute brightness.

_____ 27. The life cycle of a star begins with a cloud of gas and dust called a
  a. protoplanet.   b. constellation.
  c. nebula.   d. protosun.

_____ 28. Both high-mass and low-mass adult stars are classified as
  a. main-sequence stars.   b. white dwarfs.
  c. supernovas.   d. neutron stars.

_____ 29. All stars remain on the main sequence
  a. until they stabilize.
  b. for about 90 percent of their lifetimes.
  c. until they become protostars.
  d. for about 10 billion years.

_____ 30. Low-mass and medium-mass stars eventually
  a. grow into supergiants.
  b. become supernovas.
  c. become neutron stars.
  d. turn into white dwarfs.

Physical Science • Unit 3 Test B   **291**

Unit 3 Test B

Name _____ Class _____ Date _____

Completion

Complete each statement on the line provided.

1. The study of the composition, structure, and the history of Earth is called _____.

2. The crust and upper mantle together form the _____.

3. The color of the powder a mineral leaves on an unglazed porcelain tile is called the mineral's _____.

4. A(An) _____ glacier is a thick sheet of ice that covers large areas of land.

5. Deposits of windblown dust are called _____.

6. The process by which sand is moved along a shore is called _____.

7. A major type of storm associated with lightning, strong winds, and heavy rain or hail is called a(an) _____.

8. _____ works by bouncing radio waves off particles of precipitation in moving storms and then measuring the frequency of the waves that return.

9. The two main factors that determine a region's climate are _____ and _____.

10. The force of gravity that the sun exerts on a planet is directed _____.

11. The beginning of the "space race" occurred when the _____ launched the first artificial satellite in 1957.

12. Because there is no _____ on the moon, any liquid water would have evaporated long ago.

13. In an H-R diagram, most stars are found in a diagonal band from the upper left to the lower right, which is called the _____.

14. A group of two or more stars held together by gravity is called a(an) _____.

15. The theory that the universe came into being in a single moment with an enormous explosion is the _____ theory.

Short Answer

In complete sentences, write the answers to the questions on the lines provided.

1. By what three ways can metamorphic rocks form?

_____

_____

_____

292   *Physical Science* • Unit 3 Test B

Unit 3 Test B

Name _____ Class _____ Date _____

2. What theory explains how Earth's plates form and move?
_____

3. What three factors determine magma viscosity?
_____

4. Describe the changes in amount of light, temperature, and pressure as depth in the ocean increases.
_____
_____
_____

5. List at least four agents of erosion.
_____
_____
_____

6. What are the four largest divisions of the geologic time scale?
_____
_____

7. Why is Earth generally warmer near the equator and colder toward the poles?
_____
_____
_____

8. What is the greenhouse effect?
_____
_____

9. What weather is associated with a cyclone?
_____
_____

Unit 3 Test B

Name _____ Class _____ Date _____

10. Who was the first human to step onto the moon?
_____

11. What caused most craters on the moon?
_____

12. What is the composition of the Kuiper belt?
_____

13. Why do astronomers measure the parallax of nearby stars?
_____

14. How can an object's red shift tell us how fast the object is moving away from Earth?
_____

15. How have scientists used Hubble's Law to estimate the age of the universe?
_____

Using Science Skills

Use the diagram to answer each question. Write the answers on a separate sheet of paper.

1. **Classifying** What type of rock would fit into Figure 3-1 at the location shown by the letter F?
2. **Interpreting Graphics** In Figure 3-1, what processes are represented by the arrow labeled A?

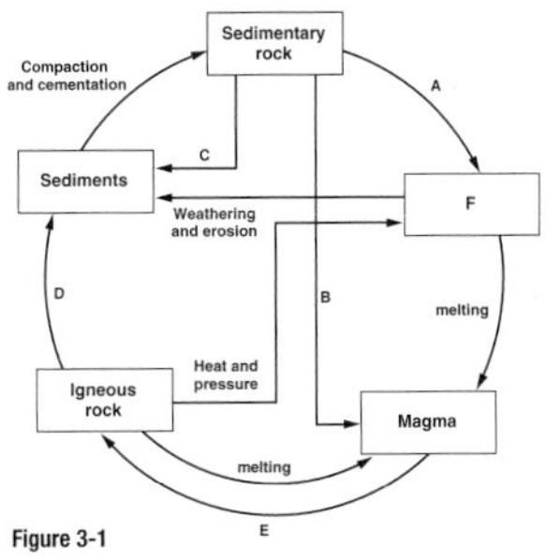

Figure 3-1

Unit 3 Test B

Name _____ Class _____ Date _____

3. **Inferring** In Figure 3-2, is the stream flow moving faster at point C or at point D? Explain your answer.
4. **Interpreting Graphics** What is the feature labeled A in Figure 3-2?
5. **Interpreting Graphics** Explain what is happening to the two air masses in the cold front in Figure 3-3.
6. **Comparing and Contrasting** Based on your observations of Figure 3-3, how are a cold front and a warm front alike?

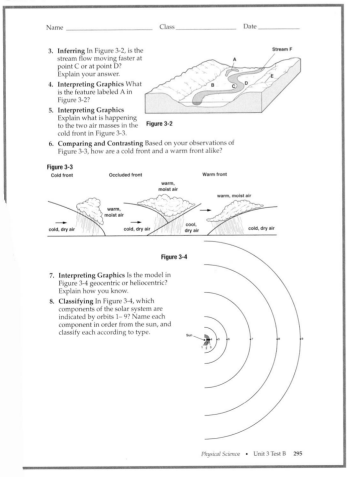

Figure 3-2

Figure 3-3

7. **Interpreting Graphics** Is the model in Figure 3-4 geocentric or heliocentric? Explain how you know.
8. **Classifying** In Figure 3-4, which components of the solar system are indicated by orbits 1– 9? Name each component in order from the sun, and classify each according to type.

Figure 3-4

Unit 3 Test B

Name _____ Class _____ Date _____

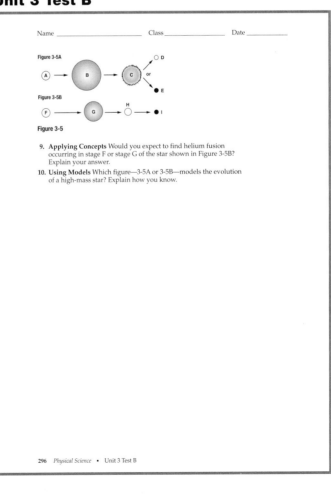

Figure 3-5A

Figure 3-5B

Figure 3-5

9. **Applying Concepts** Would you expect to find helium fusion occurring in stage F or stage G of the star shown in Figure 3-5B? Explain your answer.
10. **Using Models** Which figure—3-5A or 3-5B—models the evolution of a high-mass star? Explain how you know.

Unit 3 Test A Answers

Multiple Choice

1. d	**2.** b	**3.** a	**4.** b	**5.** a	**6.** d
7. b	**8.** a	**9.** b	**10.** c	**11.** d	**12.** b
13. b	**14.** d	**15.** a	**16.** b	**17.** c	**18.** d
19. c	**20.** d	**21.** a	**22.** b	**23.** c	**24.** a
25. b	**26.** b	**27.** b	**28.** c	**29.** d	**30.** d

Completion

1. clastic **2.** Pangaea **3.** mid-ocean ridge **4.** P **5.** alluvial fan
6. carbon dioxide **7.** continental shelf **8.** U-shaped
9. thermosphere **10.** solstice **11.** anticyclone **12.** El Niño
13. average **14.** moons **15.** 100 **16.** Kuiper **17.** core **18.** parallax
19. mass **20.** eclipsing

Short Answer

1. by scraping the mineral on a piece of unglazed porcelain called a streak plate **2.** The lithosphere is cool and rigid; the aesthenosphere is a layer of soft, weak rock that can flow slowly; and the mesosphere is the strong, lowest layer. **3.** Both occur rapidly on steep slopes. **4.** Fine particles are suspended in the air and blown about by the wind. Larger particles bounce along the ground by saltation. The largest particles are pushed along the ground by the wind. **5.** Sleet is rain that freezes as it falls. Freezing rain falls as rain and freezes after hitting the surface. **6.** A thunderstorm forms when columns of air rise within a cumulonimbus cloud. If the rising air is cooled to the dew point and the convection is strong enough, a thunderstorm results.
7. the plane of Earth's orbit **8.** A full moon occurs when the side of the moon facing Earth is fully lit by the sun, and Earth is between the sun and the moon. A new moon occurs when the moon is between the sun and Earth, and the moon's dark side faces Earth.
9. supergiants **10.** gravity and heat from contraction

Using Science Skills

1. melting; volcanoes **2.** An ocean plate is being subducted beneath a continental plate. **3.** Layer F **4.** younger **5.** Air masses are classified by whether they form over land or over water and the latitude at which they form. **6.** A is a continental polar air mass and has cold, dry air. D is a continental tropical air **7.** Arrow B represents the gravitational force between the planet and the sun. The force acts between the center of the planet and the center of the sun, and both the center of the planet and the center of the sun lie in the orbital plane. Therefore, the force of attraction between the centers must also lie in the same plane. **8.** Saturn is not dense, but it still has mass, so inertia and gravity balance to keep Saturn in orbit. **9.** By the placement on the H-R diagram, we know that both stars are of roughly equal absolute brightness and surface temperature, and that both are white dwarfs. Because star X appears dimmer, it must be farther from Earth. **10.** The hottest stars are blue and very bright. The coolest stars are red and have a much lower absolute brightness. They are found in the lower right of the main sequence.

Essay

1. As the oceanic plate sinks into the mantle in the subduction zone, the plate causes melting. Magma forms and rises to the surface, where it erupts and forms volcanoes. **2.** Possible answer: A molecule of water falls as precipitation; it flows as runoff along the surface; it then soaks into the soil to become groundwater. The groundwater flows toward the coast, where the water molecule flows into the ocean. It then evaporates and travels up into the atmosphere. As it travels up, it cools and condenses. It is joined by other water molecules and then falls back to the surface as precipitation. **3.** As a warm front passes through, the area might have stratus clouds, steady rain, and occasionally heavy showers or thunderstorms. After the warm front passes through, the skies are mostly clear, there may be some cumulus clouds, and temperatures rise. As a cold front passes through, the area might have cumulus or cumulonimbus clouds, strong winds, severe thunderstorms, and large amounts of precipitation, which usually lasts for only a short time. After the cold front passes through, the skies clear and temperatures drop. **4.** Mars; the period of the asteroid would be greater than 1.88 years because the asteroid belt is beyond the orbit of Mars, and orbital periods increase as distance from the sun increases. **5.** As high-mass stars evolve to the fusion of elements other than hydrogen, they create other elements, including iron. The stars eventually run out of elements to fuse. Gravity overcomes the lower thermal pressure, and the star collapses, producing a violent explosion called a supernova. The heavier elements in our solar system, including the atoms in our bodies, come from a supernova that occurred billions of years ago.

Unit 3 Test B Answers

Multiple Choice

1. d **2.** b **3.** c **4.** d **5.** c **6.** b
7. c **8.** a **9.** c **10.** b **11.** d **12.** b
13. d **14.** c **15.** d **16.** c **17.** a **18.** d
19. d **20.** c **21.** a **22.** a **23.** b **24.** c
25. b **26.** d **27.** c **28.** a **29.** b **30.** d

Completion

1. geology **2.** lithosphere **3.** streak **4.** continental **5.** loess
6. longshore drift **7.** thunderstorm **8.** Doppler radar
9. temperature, precipitation **10.** toward the sun **11.** Soviet Union
12. atmosphere **13.** main sequence **14.** star system **15.** big bang

Short Answer

1. by heat, pressure, or reactions with hot water **2.** the theory of plate tectonics **3.** water content, silica content, and temperature **4.** The amount of light decreases, temperature decreases, and pressure increases. **5.** Accept any four of the following: wind, glaciers, gravity, groundwater, waves, streams, weathering. **6.** Precambrian time, Paleozoic Era, Mesozoic Era, and Cenozoic Era **7.** Regions near the equator receive more direct sunlight than regions near the poles receive. **8.** the process by which gases, including water vapor and carbon dioxide, absorb energy, radiate energy, and warm the lower atmosphere **9.** clouds, precipitation, and stormy weather **10.** Neil Armstrong **11.** the impact of high speed meteoroids **12.** tens of thousands of objects, mostly made of ice, dust, and rock **13.** to determine the stars' distances from Earth **14.** The larger the observed shift is, the faster is the speed. **15.** Scientists know how fast the universe is expanding and can infer how long it has been expanding since the big bang.

Using Science Skills

1. metamorphic rock **2.** heat and pressure **3.** At point D; the stream flow is faster because water moves faster on the outside of the curve in a meander. **4.** an oxbow lake **5.** A cold, dry air mass is overtaking a warm, moist air mass, and the warm air mass is being lifted up by the cold air. **6.** Both a cold front and a warm front have a cold, dry air mass and a warm, moist air mass colliding. In both fronts, the cold air is under the warm air, and in both fronts, precipitation can occur. **7.** Heliocentric; the sun is shown at the center, and other bodies are indicated in orbit around the sun. **8.** Planets; 1. Mercury, terrestrial; 2. Venus, terrestrial; 3. Earth, terrestrial; 4. Mars, terrestrial; 5. Jupiter, gas giant; 6. Saturn, gas giant; 7. Uranus, gas giant; 8. Neptune, gas giant; 9. Pluto, neither (can't be classified as either terrestrial or gas giant) **9.** Helium fusion would be occurring in stage G. In stage F, the star is a main-sequence star, and its energy is supplied by the fusion of hydrogen. Stage G represents the star as a red giant. As the core of the red giant collapses, it becomes hot enough to cause helium to undergo fusion. **10.** Figure 26-2A; the subsequent stages of the model indicate a supernova at stage C and two possible fates at stages D and E. Low-mass stars have only one ultimate fate as a black dwarf at stage I from the white dwarf at stage H. Also, Figure 26-2A shows a supergiant, which is not a stage for a low mass star.